YEARBOOK
COMMERCIAL ARBITRATION

KLUWER LAW INTERNATIONAL
The Hague/London/Boston

INTERNATIONAL COUNCIL
FOR COMMERCIAL ARBITRATION

YEARBOOK

COMMERCIAL ARBITRATION

VOLUME XXIVa - 1999

GENERAL EDITOR
ALBERT JAN VAN DEN BERG

with the assistance of
International Bureau of the
Permanent Court of Arbitration
The Hague

A C.I.P. Catalogue record for this book is available from the Library of Congress

ISBN (set)	90 411 1327 4
ISBN (a)	90 411 1313 4
ISBN (b)	90 411 1314 2
ISSN	0169-0981

Published by Kluwer Law International
P.O. Box 85889, 2508 CN The Hague, The Netherlands
sales@kli.wkap.nl
Http://www.kluwerlaw.com

Sold and distributed in North, Central and South America and Canada by
Kluwer Law International
675 Massachusetts Avenue, Cambridge, MA 02139, USA

Sold and distributed in all other countries by Kluwer Law International
Distribution Centre, P.O. Box 322, 3300 AH Dordrecht, The Netherlands

Printed on acid-free paper

INTRODUCTION

The twenty-fourth Volume of the Yearbook, published only few several months before the millennium, is marked by a sign of the times, the issuance of an Arbitration CD-Rom by our publisher Kluwer Law International. This CD-Rom contains the full text of the twenty-three previous Volumes of the Yearbook and the present Volume will soon follow on a future release of the CD-Rom.

ICCA publications presently comprise the major portion of the CD-Rom which also reproduces all of the *International Handbook on Commercial Arbitration* and ICCA's Congress Series nos. 3 (New York) and 8 (Bahrain). It is ICCA's policy that all of its publications will be released in electronic form shortly after the "paper publication".

Apart from two other Kluwer journals, "Arbitration Journal" and "Journal of International Arbitration", the CD-Rom includes "Revue de l'arbitrage" and a Bibliography compiled and regularly updated by the Chamber of National and International Arbitration of Milan. More information on this CD-Rom may be found in the announcement in the Bibliography of this Volume at pp. 987-988 under the new category "6. Electronic Publications".

Part I of the Yearbook as usual reproduces the Table of Contents of the *International Handbook on Commercial Arbitration*, emphasizing the historic link between the Yearbook, which formerly included National Reports on Arbitration Law and Practice in this Part and the text of new arbitration legislation in Part IV. The increased use of arbitration throughout the world and the proliferation of new arbitration legislation led to the creation of the loose-leaf Handbook which could better accommodate this ever-increasing quantity of new information and materials. Part IV of the Yearbook now announces and briefly summarizes new arbitration legislation and refers the reader to the Handbook where the new Acts will be published in full.

Arbitral institutions also respond to the rapid pace of change and continue to update their rules to meet new demands and to bring them in conformity with new national legislation. This year, the Yearbook in Part III – A reproduces new Rules from the American Arbitration Association, the Stockholm Chamber of Commerce and the China International and Economic Trade Arbitration Commission, as well as the newly revised International Bar Association Rules on the Taking of Evidence in International Commercial Arbitration with an Introduction by David Rivkin.

Arbitral awards are reported in Part II – A as well as in Part III – B on the Iran-US Claims Tribunal. For the first time, the Yearbook reports on an ad hoc arbitration under the UNCITRAL Rules constituted under NAFTA. In the NAFTA arbitral tribunal's Decision on Jurisdiction, as well as in two ICSID Decisions on Jurisdiction, also reported in this Volume, the arbitral tribunals examined the definition of "investment" under the respective treaties. A broad selection of ICC awards examine familiar issues such as jurisdiction, applicable law, breach of contract, liability for termination of contract and calculation of damages. Further awards from the Hamburg Friendly Arbitration, the Italian Arbitration Association, the Chamber of National and International Arbitration of Milan, the Tokyo Maritime Arbitration Commission at the Japan Shipping Exchange and the Chamber of Commerce and Industry of the Russian Federation address an even wider selection of issues such as the consequences of a settlement by the parties, the application of the 1980 UN Sales Convention and the UNIDROIT Principles, as well as the determination of the statute of limitation and its effects on an action.

The Award of the Full Tribunal of the Iran-US Claims Tribunal in Case A27 is reported both in Part III – B which reports on this year's developments at the Tribunal as well as in Part V – A in the reporting on the 1958 New York Convention as it deals with the question of whether Tribunal awards can be reviewed by national courts under the New York Convention.

Leading court decisions of general interest are reported in Part II – B, this year from courts in Egypt, the European Court of Justice, France, Germany, India, Sweden, United Kingdom and the United States. It is becoming increasingly difficult to limit the number of decisions reported in this Part. In the cases selected, the courts have decided on important issues relating to grounds for setting aside, the role of the 1968 Brussels Convention and its successors in arbitration matters, interim measures, truncated tribunals, the responsibilities of arbitral institutions, the distinction between procedural orders and awards, confidentiality, the enforceability of arbitral awards upholding illegal contracts and ICC arbitral clauses in consumer contracts.

Part V of this Volume includes decisions on the New York, European and Panama Conventions. The emphasis lies with the New York Convention where 42 decisions from fifteen jurisdictions are reported, including for the first time, the Court of Justice of the European Union and the Full Tribunal of the Iran-US Claims Tribunal.

A Consolidated Commentary on the New York Convention court decisions reported in Volumes XXII (1997) through XXIV (1999) will be published in several months Volume XXIVb. Please note the enclosed card for ordering this Volume. Subscribers to the Yearbook will receive this Volume as part of their subscription.

It goes beyond the scope of this brief Introduction to enumerate the variety of issues which arise under these Conventions. It is interesting to note however, that the issue of enforcement abroad of awards set aside in the country of origin continues to be addressed, this time in Austria where the Oberster Gerichtshof [Supreme Court] granted enforcement under the European Convention of an award which had been set aside in Croatia (Austria No. E3, pp. 919-927) and in the United States where the United States Court of Appeals for the Second Circuit refused enforcement of two awards which had been set aside in Nigeria (US no. 288, pp. 909-913).

A publication of the size and scope of the Yearbook requires the willing cooperation of many correspondents, as well as a dedicated staff. It is the latter group whom I would like especially to thank here:

- Ms. Ellen Meijkamp, my secretary, who provides a vital link between my practice in Amsterdam and the editorial staff in their offices in the Peace Palace;
- Ms. Elisabeth Spencer who gave essential last minute assistance, particularly in compiling the Bibliography;
- Ms. Hilmara Requena who in producing the CRCs with unfailing accuracy assures that the Yearbook is presented in a reliable and consistent form;
- D.ssa Silvia Borelli, former researcher at the Sanders Institute at the Erasmus University, Rotterdam, and presently employed by the Permanent Court of Arbitration as a member of the editorial staff, for her linguistic and analytic input in the preparation of translations and excerpts of arbitral awards and court decisions;
- Ms. Judy Freedberg who quite simply makes sure it all happens as and when it should.

ICCA would also like to add a special additional word of thanks to Mr. Hans Jonkman who retired in May 1999 as Secretary-General of the Permanent Court of Arbitration for his kindness and hospitality to the ICCA publications and the Editorial Staff. We would also like to welcome his successor, Mr. Tjaco T. van den Hout, and to express our wish for many future years of fruitful cooperation.

In all of its publications, ICCA is advised by ICCA's Editorial Board composed of members and advisory members as follows: Prof. Giorgio Bernini, in his capacity as past President of ICCA; Prof. Karl-Heinz Böckstiegel (Germany); Mr. Robert Coulson (USA); Me Yves Derains (France); Dr. Mauro Ferrante (Italy); Me Michel Gaudet (France); Prof. Gerold Herrmann (Austria);

Prof. Pierre Lalive (Switzerland); DDr. Werner Melis (Austria); Mr. Fali Nariman, President of ICCA (India); Dr. Jan Paulsson (France and as General Editor of the *International Handbook on Commercial Arbitration*); Prof. Tudor R. Popescu (Romania); Prof. José Luis Siqueiros (Mexico); Prof. Iván Szász (Hungary); Prof. Yasuhei Taniguchi (Japan); Prof. Pieter Sanders (Netherlands) and the undersigned as General Editor of the ICCA publications.

The readers of the Yearbook throughout the world are also a major source of the materials which it contains. Therefore, may I call on you, as reader and user of the Yearbook, to submit texts concerning:

- recent changes in arbitration legislation
- newly enacted arbitration rules
- arbitral awards (the confidentiality of which is ensured)
- court decisions of general interest and, in particular, court decisions applying the UNCITRAL Model Law or the New York, European, Washington or Panama Conventions.

The names of the readers who have provided materials for this Volume are acknowledged in the appropriate Parts.

Amsterdam
October 1999

Albert Jan van den Berg
General Editor

Materials for the Yearbook are to be addressed to the General Editor or to the ICCA editorial staff at their new address at the International Bureau of the Permanent Court of Arbitration as indicated below.

ICCA Publications
c/o International Bureau of the
Permanent Court of Arbitration
Carnegieplein 2
2517 KJ The Hague, The Netherlands
E-mail: icca@pca-cpa.org

Prof. Dr. Albert Jan van den Berg
c/o Freshfields
Coengebouw, 6th floor
Kabelweg 37
1014 BA Amsterdam
and as of 1 February 2000:
Gebouw Minerva
Appollolaan 151
1077 AR Amsterdam
The Netherlands
E-mail: ajvandenberg@freshfields.com

TABLE OF CONTENTS

VOLUME XXIVa - 1999

PREFACE

Fali S. Nariman, President ICCA

This latest YEARBOOK is also the last before the next millennium. As we slide into the year 2000 AD we cannot help but reflect on the impact of fast-moving modern technology: and the increasing influence of computers in our daily lives. At present our most advanced computers are simpler than the human brain. But experts predict this will not remain for long. Computers doubled in speed every two years in the 1950s and 1960s: they are now doubling in speed every twelve months! And we are reliably assured that the trend will continue; with computers achieving the memory-capacity and speed of the human brain by around 2020! But all is not lost. Computers, howsoever sophisticated, cannot (and hopefully, will not) match the flexibility of human intelligence. Our emotions are hard wired into our very being: and the brain gives *feelings* priority over *thoughts*. The working relationship of the emotional brain and the thinking brain (a recently discovered phenomenon) is known as "emotional intelligence". It is one of the more important ideas to hit the modern commercial world. Daniel Goleman, now acclaimed as a management guru, has influenced much thinking in the development of the multiple intelligence theory. His book *Working with Emotional Intelligence* (1998) argues that workplace competencies based on emotional intelligence play a far greater role in star performances than do mere intellect and skill; it is superior emotional capacity which throws up "leaders" – in every field. The odds are that in the decades ahead the human brain will still outwit the computer. And that, I believe, is a sign of hope, for the millennium.

Last year in the month of May some of us met in Paris to felicitate Michel Gaudet, Honorary Chairman of the International Court of Arbitration of the ICC, at a one day Seminar. The theme was: "Improving International Arbitration". There were exciting prospects revealed, and new paths shown for dispute resolution, with use of new technology; and use of new means of communication was recommended in aid of accelerating the pace of international arbitration. Michel Gaudet responded to all this with words of distilled wisdom:

> ".... We are going towards another world and we are trying to make it a better world.... We are discovering that this new world perhaps needs speed. Globalization may indeed need speed, provided it remains in

> connection with our basic aims of justice and community spirit. If we want speed we need to have trust.... I think it is one of my great discoveries for myself that you can't have speed if you don't have trust between those who are partners in whatever is happening."

The important thing then is not to get too impressed with the prospect of new inventions, new ideas and new machines confidently predicted for the next century. Let us certainly improve arbitration, its methods and its delivery system with new technology, but let not technological change sweep us off our "arbitral feet". They must remain firmly rooted in trust and justice. For arbitration to continue to prosper it is vital that the quality of justice, which it is seen to dispense, remains impeccable – and this quality is dependent not on machines, but on the impartiality and independence of individual arbitrators, and the competence and excellence of arbitral institutions.

What I should like to see in the millennium is a determination by all Nation-States to proclaim arbitral freedom as a guaranteed human right. Without it the first letter in the acronym ADR has little meaning. I welcome the recent ICSID decision (December 1998) which gives transcendental importance to the arbitration clause in bilateral treaties between States: it overrides stipulations in the individual contracts between parties (from each of those States) that their disputes would be resolved only by the courts of the defendant State.

In India, as in France, arbitration though increasingly encouraged, is still an exception to State justice, not an alternative to it. No one having full legal capacity and enjoying full possession of his civil rights should be prevented from coming to an agreement with another person having the same capacity and right, to submit disputes, consensually, to an arbitral tribunal of their choice. And arbitral institutions around the world must work to this end. If you will recall, this was one of the suggestions made by Jean-Louis Delvolvé on September 1993, at the centenary celebrations of the LCIA – but nothing has come of it, because justice remains the sovereign function of the State – a function not to be shared with private parties: This view of justice being a solely sovereign function may require some modification early in the next millennium – with more institutional privatisation of the justice-system in Nation-States around the world.

But till then we will have to live with the same "Never Ending Story": the interaction of international commercial arbitration with national courts. That is the theme of the ICCA 2000 Conference to be held in New Delhi from 2 March to 4 March 2000. ICCA last met in New Delhi in January 1975. Since then we have peregrinated the globe, meeting in Conferences and Congresses: in Vienna (1976), in Mexico City (1978), in Warsaw (1980), in Hamburg (1982), in Lausanne (1984), in New York (1986), in Tokyo (1988), in Stockholm (1990), in Bahrain (1993), in Vienna again (1994), in Seoul (1996), in Paris (1998) – and now back in New Delhi. Much has happened since January 1975 – international arbitration – like international aviation – has gained in speed and repute. But problems with "ground-handling" remain. It is to sort out some of them that we meet once more in a country with a new arbitration statute (based on the UNCITRAL Model Law) where the ghosts of our old law (The Arbitration Act 1940) have not yet been laid!

The Conference, which will be inaugurated by the President of India, deals with a series of familiar subjects: approached from the standpoint of the parties: as to how parties may act *at each stage so as to achieve judicial support of their expectation*. There are four working sessions slated over two days (Friday 3 and Saturday 4 March 2000), followed by a Judicial Colloquium on Sunday 5 March to be inaugurated by the Chief Justice of India. The subjects of each of the four sessions are:

(i) The Contract: What Causes Courts to Disregard Agreements to Arbitrate, and How Can Such Agreements Be Improved to Avoid That Fate?;
(ii) Interim Relief: How Can It Be Obtained Without Harming the Arbitral Process?;
(iii) The Proceedings: How to Avoid Judicial Interruptions; and
(iv) Looking to Enforcement: Awards That Pass Judicial Scrutiny.

The Conference (like Delhi's weather in March) promises to be invigorating. You will be able to hear the talk with leading players in the world of international arbitration, as also with Judges, from India and abroad. You may not learn much more than you already know: but new ideas, not thought of before, get forged at Conferences like these, and many old ideas and impressions also get swept away!

On behalf of ICCA I extend to you all a warm welcome to New Delhi – with a traditional NAMASTE.

Part I
National Reports

Note General Editor. For the last decade, since Volume XIII (1988) of the Yearbook, it has been the policy to publish National Reports on arbitration law and practice in the *International Handbook on Commercial Arbitration*, the companion publication to the Yearbook (now under the general editorship of Dr. Jan Paulsson). Part I of the Yearbook has been reserved for selective new National Reports. No new National Reports are, however, included in this Volume. Recent developments in arbitration law and practice are reported in summary form in Part IV of the Yearbook. These summaries refer to National Reports and related legal texts which are published in ICCA's *International Handbook on Commercial Arbitration.*

The Table of Contents of the Handbook as of Supplement 28, January 1999, is reproduced below. **Bold face** type is used in the Table of Contents to highlight the changes that have occurred since Yearbook XXIII (1998).

TABLE OF CONTENTS

BINDER I

BINDER II

BINDER III

POLISH PEOPLE'S REPUBLIC: Dr. habil. Tadeusz Szurski and Dr. Andrzej W. Wiśniewski

ANNEX I: Code of Civil Procedure, Part One, Book Three, Arbitral Tribunal

ANNEX II: Code of Civil Procedure, Other Provisions

PORTUGAL: Prof. Fernando Cruz and Dr. Dário Moura Vicente

ANNEX I: Law No. 31/86 of 29 August, in force 29 November 1986, Voluntary Arbitration

ANNEX II: Code of Civil Procedure Book III, Title IV, Chapter XII, Review of Foreign Arbitral Awards

ROMANIA: Prof. Octavian Capatina

ANNEX I: Book IV, Code of Civil Procedure, On Arbitration, Articles 340-370, as amended by Law No. 59 of 23 July 1993

ANNEX II: Law on the Settlement of Private International Law Relations, Law No. 105 of 22 September 1992, Chapter XII, Section 4 (Articles 165/178) and Section 6 (Articles 180-181)

ANNEX III: Law on the Settlement of Private International Law Relations, Law No. 105 of 22 September 1992, Chapter VIII, Section 1 (Articles 73-85)

RUSSIAN FEDERATION: Note General Editor

ANNEX I: Law of the Russian Federation on International Commercial Arbitration (14 August 1993)

SAUDI ARABIA: Nancy B. Turck

ANNEX I: Arbitration Regulation of Saudi Arabia, 25 April 1983

ANNEX II: Rules for the Implementation of the Saudi Arabian Arbitration Regulation, 27 May 1985

ANNEX III: Convention of the Arab League on the Enforcement of Judgments and Arbitral Awards, 14 September 1952

SCOTLAND: The Honourable Lord Dervaird

ANNEX I: Arbitration (Scotland) Act, 1894

ANNEX II: Administration of Justice (Scotland) Act 1972

ANNEX III: Law Reform (Miscellaneous Provisions) (Scotland) Act 1990, Section 66 and Schedule 7 (excerpts)

SINGAPORE: Lawrence G.S. Boo

ANNEX I: International Arbitration Act, No. 23 of 1994

ANNEX II: Arbitration Act 1953 (1985 Edition)

ANNEX III: Schedules to the Arbitration Act

ANNEX IV: Reciprocal Enforcement of Commonwealth Judgments Act 1921

ANNEX V: Reciprocal Enforcement of Foreign Judgments Act 1959

SOUTH AFRICA: Patrick M.M. Lane SC

ANNEX I: Arbitration Act 1965, No. 42 of 1965, Date of Commencement: 14 April 1965

ANNEX II: Recognition and Enforcement of Foreign Arbitral Awards Act 1977, No. 40 of 1977, Date of Commencement: 13 April 1977

ANNEX III: Protection of Business Act 1978, Act to restrict the enforcement in the Republic of certain foreign judgments, orders, directions, arbitration awards and letters of request;...

SPAIN: Prof. Bernardo Cremades

ANNEX I: Law 36/1988 on Arbitration of 5 December 1988

ANNEX II: Code of Civil Procedure, Second Section, Judgments Handed Down by Foreign Tribunals, Articles 951-958

ANNEX III: Royal Decree 1094/1981 Concerning Implementation through the Superior Council of the Official Chamber of Commerce of International Commercial Arbitration

SRI LANKA: Note General Editor

ANNEX I: Arbitration Act, No. 11 of 1995, in force 30 June 1995

SWEDEN: Dr. Ulf Holmbäck and Justice Nils Mangård

ANNEX I: The Arbitration Act of 1929, No. 145

ANNEX II: The Act of 1929 concerning Foreign Arbitration Agreements and Awards, No. 147

SWITZERLAND: Dr. Robert Briner

ANNEX I: Intercantonal Arbitration Convention, 27 March/29 August 1969

ANNEX II: Chapter 12 of the Federal Act on Private International Law of 18 December 1987, and selected Articles

BINDER IV

THAILAND: Prof. Saowanee Asawaroj

ANNEX I: Arbitration Act BE 2530 (AD 1987)

ANNEX II: Code of Civil Procedure BE 2477 (AD 1934), Challenge of Judges

TUNISIA: Habib Malouche

ANNEX I: Arbitration Code, Law No. 93-42 of 26 April 1993

TURKEY: Prof. Rabi Koral

ANNEX I: Code of Civil Procedure, Title 8 (18 June 1927)

ANNEX II: International Private and Procedural Law (20 May 1980)

UKRAINE: Prof. Igor G. Pobirchenko

ANNEX I: Ukrainian Law on International Commercial Arbitration

UNCITRAL

Model Law on International Commercial Arbitration, 21 June 1985

UNCITRAL, COMMENTARY ON THE UNCITRAL MODEL LAW: Dr. Aron Broches

UNCITRAL ARBITRATION RULES

UNCITRAL Arbitration Rules, adopted 28 April 1976

Part II

A. Arbitral Awards

Note General Editor. It is the long-standing policy of the Yearbook to respect the confidentiality of arbitral awards. Therefore, in many of the excerpts of arbitral awards published in the Yearbook, all data which might reveal the identity of the parties is omitted. In certain circumstances, however, the award or the identity of the parties may become a matter of public record, if, for example, the award has been published in full elsewhere or has given rise to court proceedings. In such cases, strict confidentiality is no longer required and the extract in the Yearbook may report the names of the parties.

The arbitral awards are presented in a uniform style for the convenience of the reader. To achieve this result, headings may have been altered or added and minor editorial changes have been made which in no way affect the substance of the award. Once again, a number of the arbitral awards have been translated into English by D.ssa Silvia Borelli, whose linguistic talents are always greatly appreciated.

An "Index of Arbitral Awards" containing a subject index of the arbitral awards appearing in Part II – A of this Volume is included at the end of this Part. Arbitral awards in earlier volumes have been indexed as follows:

- Index of Arbitral Awards Volumes I (1975) – XV (1990) published in *Yearbook Key 1990*
- Index of Arbitral Awards Volumes XVI (1991) – XX (1995) published in Volume XX (1995)
- Index of Arbitral Awards Volume XXI published in Volume XXI (1996)
- Index of Arbitral Awards Volume XXII published in Volume XXII (1997)
- Index of Arbitral Awards Volume XXIII published in Volume XXIII (1998).

The full text of all of the arbitral awards published in Volumes I-XXIII (1976-1998) of the Yearbook have been included in Kluwer Law International's *Arbitration CD-Rom, Resources on International Commercial Arbitration* where they can be accessed on the basis of key words and full text. For further information on this CD-Rom, see Bibliography, pp. 987-988.

GERMANY

HAMBURG FRIENDLY ARBITRATION

Final award of 29 December 1998

Parties:	Claimant: Buyer (nationality not indicated) Defendant: Seller (Czech Republic)
Place of arbitration:	Hamburg, Germany
Published in:	Rechtsprechung Kaufmännischer Schiedsgerichte, Vol. 6 (in preparation), E 5a no. 68
Subject matters:	- termination of contract for delivery of goods by instalments - UN Sales Convention 1980

Facts

On 21 January 1998, the buyer and the Czech seller agreed on the sale of 300 tonnes of cheese at US$ 2,520 per tonne, to be delivered in 15 instalments. The buyer was to pay for each instalment by cable within five days of taking delivery. The order was confirmed by the buyer on the same day. The sales confirmation contained a clause reading: "Payment: 5 days after taking delivery - Special Conditions: Hamburg Friendly Arbitration".

On 10 February 1998, broker M informed the buyer that the first instalment would be delivered on 13 February 1998 and that the seller requested that "for the first two truckloads the payment be made at the latest one day before taking delivery". M consequently asked the buyer to pay US$ 50,400 for the first instalment by 12 February, which the buyer did. The first instalment of cheese was delivered on 13 February. On 16 February, the buyer made an advance payment of US$ 50,400 for the second delivery. However, while a truck was already on its way to the Czech Republic, the buyer was informed by telephone that the second instalment would not be delivered.

Negotiations proved unsuccessful and the buyer commenced arbitration in Hamburg as provided for in the sales confirmation. The Czech seller did not appear in the arbitration.

Applying the United Nations Vienna Convention on Contracts for the International Sale of Goods 1980 (CISG), the arbitrators found that the buyer had validly terminated the contract and was entitled to restitution of the advance payment.

Excerpt

[1] "The buyer claims restitution of the advance payment and explicit termination of the contract, maintaining that the seller has refused to perform under the contract in a serious and final manner, in that it has unilaterally made delivery dependent on conditions which had not been agreed upon.

[2] "The seller has not appeared in the arbitration. It has neither made a request nor submitted a statement on the merits. The seller was sent the statement of claim by courier on 21 August, the notice of appointment and of the time limit [to appoint an arbitrator] by registered mail on 24 August, the summons of 9 October for the oral hearing by registered mail with notice of receipt on 14 October and again by courier on 23 November. Further, the seller has confirmed in a telephone conversation with the arbitral tribunal on 7 December that it will neither appear nor make a statement in the arbitral proceedings.

(....)

[3] "The jurisdiction of the arbitral tribunal ensues from the arbitration agreement for 'Hamburg Friendly Arbitration' concluded in writing by the parties (Sects. 1025 et seq., 1029, 1031(1)-(2) and 1040 [German Code of Civil Procedure (ZPO)] as in force since 1998 (*new*), Arts. I and II [1958] New York Convention, Art. I European Convention [of 1961]; see Court of Appeal of Bavaria, 17 September 1998, ZSch 1/1998, RiW 1998, 965, RKS A 1 No. 95).[1]

[4] "The Hamburg Friendly Arbitration follows Sect. 20 of the Hamburg Local Trade Usages. According to these rules, the buyer validly commenced the arbitration by appointing an arbitrator for the dispute it defined and by requesting the seller to appoint an arbitrator (Sect. 1044 ZPO *new*).[2] The latter

---

1. Published in this volume of the Yearbook, pp. 645-647 as Germany no. 48.
2. Sect. 1044 of the German Code of Civil Procedure (ZPO) *new* reads:

"Unless otherwise agreed by the parties, the arbitral proceedings in respect of a particular dispute commence on the date on which a request for that dispute to be referred to arbitration

was appointed by the Chamber of Commerce of Hamburg on 10 July 1998 after expiry of an adequate period of time (Sect. 20 no. 2 Local Usages). Hamburg Friendly Arbitration takes place in Hamburg (Sect. 20 no. 5 Local Usages, Sect. 1043 ZPO *new*).[3] This choice of the arbitration seat leads, in the absence of an agreement to the contrary, to the application of German procedural law (Sect. 1025(1) ZPO *new*,[4] Art. V(1)(*d*) New York Convention).

[5] "Independent of the unjustified default of the seller, the arbitral tribunal must decide on the claim at issue on the evidence before it (Sect. 1048 ZPO *new*),[5] since the seller has been duly informed of the arbitration and has not made use of the attention given to it (Art. V(1)(*b*) New York Convention, Art. IX(1)(b) European Convention). Before the seller affirmed that it would not participate nor make a statement, the request for arbitration, the statement of claim, a notice of time limit, the summons to the oral hearing and a

---

is received by the respondent. The request shall state the names of the parties, the subject-matter of the dispute and contain a reference to the arbitration agreement."

3. Sect. 1043 ZPO *new* reads:

"(1) The parties are free to agree on the place of arbitration. Failing such agreement, the place of arbitration shall be determined by the arbitral tribunal having regard to the circumstances of the case, including the convenience of the parties.
(2) Notwithstanding the provisions of subsection 1 of this section, the arbitral tribunal may, unless otherwise agreed by the parties, meet at any place it considers appropriate for an oral hearing, for hearing witnesses, experts or the parties, for consultation among its members or for inspection of property or documents."

4. Sect. 1025(1) ZPO *new* reads:

"The provisions of this Book apply if the place of arbitration as referred to in section 1043 subs. 1 is situated in Germany."

5. Sect. 1048 ZPO *new* reads:

"(1) If the claimant fails to communicate his statement of claim in accordance with section 1046 subs. 1, the arbitral tribunal shall terminate the proceedings.
(2) If the respondent fails to communicate his statement of defence in accordance with section 1046 subs. 1, the arbitral tribunal shall continue the proceedings without treating such failure in itself as an admission of the claimant's allegations.
(3) If any party fails to appear at an oral hearing or to produce documentary evidence within a set time limit, the arbitral tribunal may continue the proceedings and make the award on the evidence before it.
(4) Any default which has been justified to the tribunal's satisfaction will be disregarded. Apart from that, the parties may agree otherwise on the consequences of default."

supplement to the statement of claim were sent to it by courier or registered mail, although lacking a representative in Germany a communication by mail would have sufficed according to Sect. 175(1) second sentence ZPO (OLG Munich, 30 September 1997, 7 W 2520/97, RiW 1998, 969).

[6] "The law applicable to the merits is determined according to German private international law (BGH, 24 September 1995, VII ZR 248/94, NJW 1996, 54, BB 1995, 2472). According to this law, the choice of Hamburg as the seat of arbitration leads not only to [the application of] local procedural law but also, in the absence of a specific agreement, to a choice for German substantive law (Sect. 1051(1) ZPO *new*,[6] Art. 27 Application Law of the Civil Code (EGBGB),[7] Art. VII(1) European Convention; Arbitral Award, Hamburg Chamber of Commerce, 21 March 1996, NJW 1996, 3229, RiW 1996, 766, RKS E 5 b No. 84, Palandt/Heldrich, note 6 to Art. 27 EGBGB and references therein).

[7] "According to both German and Czech law, the United Nations Convention on Contracts for the International Sale of Goods (CISG) of 11 April 1980 applies to sale contracts between parties in different States. In the present case the requirements of Art. 1(1)(a)-(b) CISG are met because both the States in which the parties have their place of business are Contracting States (1(a))

---

6. Sect. 1051(1) ZPO *new* reads:

"The arbitral tribunal shall decide the dispute in accordance with such rules of law as are chosen by the parties as applicable to the substance of the dispute. Any designation of the law or legal system of a given State shall be construed, unless otherwise expressed, as directly referring to the substantive law of that State and not to its conflict of laws rules."

7. Art. 27 of the Introductory Law to the German Civil Code (EGBGB) reads:

"(1) The contract is governed by the law chosen by the parties. The choice of law must be explicit or result from the provisions of the contract or the circumstances of the case with sufficient certainty. The parties may agree on a choice of law for the whole contract or only for a part thereof.
(2) The parties may agree at any moment that the contract shall be governed by a law different from the law which applies to it on the basis of a previous choice of law or of other provisions in this sub-chapter. The formal validity of the contract according to Art. 11 and the rights of third parties are not affected by a modification of the provision concerning the applicable law, made after conclusion of the contract.
(3) If the contents [of the contract] are connected to one State only at the time of the choice of law, the choice for the law of another State may not – also where complemented by an agreement on the jurisdiction of a court of another State – affect the provisions which may not be contractually derogated from under the law of that State (mandatory provisions).
(4) Arts. 11, 12 and 29(3) and Art. 31 apply to the coming into existence and validity of the agreement of the parties on the applicable law."

and because the rules of private international law lead to the application of the law of a Contracting State (1(b)).[8] According to Art. 7(2) CISG, the national law applicable by virtue of [the rules of] private international law, i.e., German law which was chosen by the parties, applies complementarily only in so far as questions are neither provided for in the CISG nor can be settled in conformity with the CISG principles.[9]

[8] "The claim for restitution of the advance payment is grounded. The buyer can request restitution from the seller of US$ 50,400 which it paid for the failed second delivery under Art. 81(2) first sentence CISG, since [the seller] declared that it terminated the contract (for delivery of goods by instalments) with effect for all instalments not yet delivered.[10]

[9] "Sale contract no. 3297/8 of 21 January 1998 was validly entered into by the parties. According to Arts. 8, 9 and 11 CISG, [this contract] must be deemed to mean that the buyer would take delivery of 300 tonnes of cheese by separate truckloads (15-20 tonnes) in the Czech Republic at the price of US$ 2,520 per tonne. This is a contract for delivery of goods by instalments in the sense of Art. 73 CISG (Arbitral Award, Hamburg Chamber of Commerce, RKS E 5 b No. 84; *Cour d'appel*, Grenoble, 22 February 1995 (*sarl Bri Production Bonaventure v. Société Pan African Export*), Recueil Dalloz Sirey 1995, Informations Rapides 100).[11] According to Arts. 30 and 31(b) CISG, the

8. Art. 1(a) and (b) CISG reads:

"This Convention applies to contracts of sale of goods between parties whose places of business are in different States:
(a) when the States are Contracting States; or
(b) when the rules of private international law lead to the application of the law of a Contracting State."

9. Art. 7(2) CISG reads:

"Questions concerning matters governed by this Convention which are not expressly settled in it are to be settled in conformity with the general principles on which it is based or, in the absence of such principles, in conformity with the law applicable by virtue of the rules of private international law."

10. Art. 81(2) first sentence CISG reads:

"A party who has performed the contract either wholly or in part may claim restitution from the other party of whatever the first party has supplied or paid under the contract."

11. Art. 73 CISG reads:

seller had to place the goods at the disposal of the buyer at the deposit indicated by the seller.[12] This interpretation ensues from previous contracts, negotiations [of this contract] and from the first delivery made on 13 February as agreed.

[10] "As to the advance payment made [by the buyer], this is, in the sense of Art. 81(2) first sentence CISG, a performance of the contract by the buyer under Art. 53 CISG,[13] which is consistent with the size of the second instalment as expected at the time of payment on 16 February. The conditions of Art. 81(2) CISG are met already because the advance payment was made, independent of the fact that the manner of payment originally agreed on ('5

"(1) In the case of a contract for delivery of goods by instalments, if the failure of one party to perform any of his obligement constitutes a fundamental breach of contract with respect to that instalment, the other party may declare the contract avoided with respect to that instalment.

(2) If one party's failure to perform any of his obligations in respect of any instalment gives the other party good grounds to conclude that a fundamental breach of contract will occur with respect to future instalments, he may declare the contract avoided for the future, provided that he does so within a reasonable time.

(3) A buyer who declares the contract avoided in respect of any delivery may, at the same time, declare it avoided in respect of deliveries already made or of future deliveries if, by reason of their interdependence, those deliveries could not be used for the purpose contemplated by the parties at the time of the conclusion of the contract."

12. Arts. 30 and 31(b) CISG read in relevant part:

Article 30
"The seller must deliver the goods, hand over any documents relating to them and transfer the property in the goods, as required by the contract and this Convention."

Article 31
"If the seller is not bound to deliver the goods at any other particular place, his obligation to deliver consists:
(....)
(b) if, in cases not within the preceding subparagraph, the contract relates to specific goods, or unidentified goods to be drawn from a specific stock or to be manufactured or produced, and at the time of the conclusion of the contract the parties knew that the goods were at, or were to be manufactured or produced at, a particular place – in placing the goods at the buyer's disposal at that place;
(....)"

13. Art. 53 CISG reads:

"The buyer must pay the price for the goods and take delivery of them as required by the contract and this Convention."

days after taking delivery') was modified by the seller so that an advance payment was to be made in its favour as regards the two first instalments. A different use of the advance payment requested by the seller was not agreed on by the parties.

[11] "Also, according to the provisions of the CISG, the seller could not unilaterally set off and retain [the advance payment] on the basis of legal claims. The conditions for the seller being possibly entitled to claim damages (Art. 61 together with Art. 74 et seq. CISG), retain the goods (Art. 85 together with Art. 87 CISG) or sell them to avoid deterioration (Art. 85 together with Art. 88 CISG) are not met. Further, it would be necessary, for the seller to be so entitled, that the buyer had not met its obligation to pay the sales price (Art. 54 et seq. CISG) or take delivery (Art. 60 CISG). This does not appear to have happened. Also, the seller has repeatedly cancelled delivery of instalments and loading dates.

[12] "The buyer's claim for restitution of the advance payment under Art. 81(2) first sentence CISG requires that the contract has been terminated (Art. 81(1) first sentence).[14] The buyer has made a valid declaration in this sense with respect to the instalment paid for and never delivered and to further, yet to be delivered instalments. Its right to terminate the contract also ensues from Arts. 45, 47 and 49 CISG and, in so far as a contract for the delivery of goods by instalments is concerned, from Art. 73 CISG. A termination assumes that the seller did not meet its obligations (Art. 45(1)(a))[15] and that the breach of contract is a fundamental one (Art. 49(1)(a) and Art. 25 CISG),[16] or that, in

---

14. Art. 81(1) first sentence CISG reads:

"Avoidance of the contract releases both parties from their obligations under it, subject to any damages which may be due."

15. Art. 45(1)(a) CISG reads:

"If the seller fails to perform any of his obligations under the contract or this Convention, the buyer may:
(a) exercise the rights provided in articles 46 to 52;"

16. Arts. 49(1)(a) and 25 CISG reads:

Article 49
"1. The buyer may declare the contract avoided:
(a) if the failure by the seller to perform any of his obligations under the contract or this Convention amounts to a fundamental breach of contract;
(....)"

case of non-delivery, the seller, within the additional period of time fixed under Art. 47(1) CISG,[17] neither delivers the goods nor declares that it will not deliver within the period so fixed (Art. 49(1)(b) CISG)."[18] Even if no additional period of time is fixed, the buyer can only claim under its rights when the seller declares that it will not (be able) to deliver or that it will only deliver against an additional counterperformance (Arbitral Award, Hamburg Chamber of Commerce, RKS E 5 b No. 84; Hober, in von Caemmerer/ Schlechtriem, notes nos. 6 and 22 to Art. 49 CISG).

[13] "Such an unjustified breach of contract also occurs when the seller, as is the case here, makes delivery dependent on further conditions after an advance payment has been agreed on. In the absence of findings to the contrary, an agreement for advance payment is per se to be interpreted, also in international commerce (Art. 8 CISG)[19] in the sense that the counterperformance shall be

---

Article 25
"A breach of contract committed by one of the parties is fundamental if it results in such detriment to the other party as substantially to deprive him of what he is entitled to expect under the contract, unless the party in breach did not foresee and a reasonable person of the same kind in the same circumstances would not have foreseen such a result."

17. Art. 47(1) CISG reads:

"The buyer may fix an additional period of time of reasonable length for performance by the seller of his obligations."

18. Art. 49(1)(b) CISG reads:

"The buyer may declare the contract avoided:
(....)
(b) in case of non-delivery, if the seller does not deliver the goods within the additional period of time fixed by the buyer in accordance with paragraph (1) of article 47 or declares that he will not deliver within the period so fixed."

19. Art. 8 CISG reads:

"(1) For the purposes of this Convention statements made by and other conduct of a party are to be interpreted according to his intent where the other party knew or could not have been unaware what that intent was.
(2) If the preceding paragraph is not applicable, statements made by and other conduct of a party are to be interpreted according to the understanding that a reasonable person of the same kind as the other party would have had in the same circumstances.
(3) In determining the intent of a party or the understanding a reasonable person would have had, due consideration is to be given to all relevant circumstances of the case including the negotiations, any practices which the parties have established between themselves, usages and any subsequent conduct of the parties."

made without further requests (Arbitral Award, RKS E 5 b No. 84; BGH, 18 May 1995, I ZR 151/93, MDR 1995, 1017, NJW 1995, 2917). Hence, the buyer would also have had a ground for terminating the contract if the requests made by the seller had been met.

[14] "In a contract for the delivery of goods by instalments, a fundamental failure to perform under an obligation related to an instalment justifies the termination of the contract with respect to that instalment (Art. 73(1) CISG); the expectation of a failure relating to future instalments justifies the termination of the contract for the future (Art. 73(2) CISG). This also applies to a refusal to perform. Since the seller has refused not only to deliver the second instalment, which was not delivered notwithstanding the advance payment, but also to make further deliveries at the conditions agreed in the contract, the buyer could terminate the contract with respect to all future instalments under the contract.

[15] "The buyer did communicate the termination of the contract to the seller in conformity with Art. 26 CISG.[20] An informal declaration aimed at terminating the relationship suffices thereto, according to Art. 11 CISG[21] (Arbitral Award, RKS E 5 b No. 84; Leser, in von Caemmerer/Schlechtriem, note no. 8 et seq. to Art. 26 CISG). The buyer declared in its letter of 26 March that in the future it would no longer do business with the seller.

[16] "According to Art. 81(2) CISG, the termination of a contract by the buyer results in the buyer being entitled to restitution of what it has paid. The termination of a contract for delivery of goods by instalments with respect to the instalments yet to be delivered only entitles the buyer to restitution of what it has paid, in casu, restitution of the advance payment made for the second, undelivered instalment (Leser, op. cit., note no. 15 to Arts. 81-84 CISG).

[17] "Certainly it could be examined, even after the contract has been terminated, whether the seller is entitled to set-off or retain [the sum] because of counterclaims possibly based on an agreement on the cost of pallets of previous deliveries or on the payment of labels. German law would apply

---

20. Art. 26 CISG reads:

"A declaration of avoidance of the contract is effective only if made by notice to the other party."

21. Art. 11 CISG reads:

"A contract of sale need not be concluded in or evidenced by writing and is not subject to any other requirement as to form. It may be proved by any means, including witnesses."

hereto to complement UN sales law (Art. 7(2) CISG, Sects. 387, 273 Civil Code). However, the buyer has not relied on such counterclaims after the termination of the contract and in this arbitration; since counterclaims can be taken into consideration only at a party's initiative, they cannot be opposed to the buyer's present claim and can only be claimed in a new arbitration.

[18] "According to Art. 84(1) CISG, the seller must pay interest on the restitution of the advance payment from the day of payment (16 February 1998).[22] The amount of interest is determined by complementary application of domestic (in casu, German) law (Art. 7(2) CISG; Arbitral Award, RKS E 5 b No. 84 and references therein; Court of First Instance, Oldenburg, 9 November 1994, 12 O 674/93, RiW 1996, 65). Consequently, the buyer can claim legal interest at a rate of 5% under Sect. 352 Commercial Code from the day on which interest began to run (payment on 16 February 1998), and delay interest under Sects. 284 and 286 [Commercial Code] only after it requested payment again on 26 March 1993.

[19] "Although the parties have not specifically agreed on the costs of the arbitration, the arbitral tribunal must, according to Sect. 1057 ZPO,[23] decide on these costs, including defence costs (Arbitral Award, Hamburg Chamber of Commerce, 21 June 1996, RKS B 5 No. 21; NJW 1997, 613; RiW 1996, 771). In conformity with the outcome of the proceedings, the seller shall pay these costs and shall refund to the buyer the fees of the arbitrators, legal fees and other costs which the buyer has advanced and shall specify, to the exclusion of the turnover tax which the buyer can deduct as tax paid in advance."

---

22. Art. 84(1) CISG reads:

"If the seller is bound to refund the price, he must also pay interest on it, from the date on which the price was paid."

23. Sect. 1057 ZPO *new* reads:

"(1) Unless the parties agree otherwise, the arbitral tribunal shall allocate, by means of an arbitral award, the costs of the arbitration as between the parties, including those incurred by the parties necessary for the proper pursuit of their claim or defence. It shall do so at its discretion and take into consideration the circumstances of the case, in particular the outcome of the proceedings.

(2) To the extent that the costs of the arbitral proceedings have been fixed, the arbitral tribunal shall also decide on the amount to be borne by each party. If the costs have not been fixed or if they can only be fixed once the arbitral proceedings have been terminated, the decision shall be taken by means of a separate award."

INTERNATIONAL CENTRE FOR SETTLEMENT OF INVESTMENT DISPUTES

Decision of 11 July 1997 on Objections to Jurisdiction and award of 9 March 1998 in case no. ARB/96/3[1]

Arbitrators:	Francisco Orrego Vicuña (Chile) (President); Meir Heth (Israel); Roberts B. Owen (US)
Parties:	Claimant: Fedax N.V. (Neth. Antilles) Respondent: Republic of Venezuela
Place of arbitration:	Washington D.C., USA
Published in:	37 International Legal Materials (1998) pp. 1378-1398
Subject matters:	- Bilateral Investment Treaty Netherlands-Venezuela - jurisdiction of arbitral tribunal - definition of "investment" - promissory notes - legal costs

Facts

The Republic of Venezuela (Venezuela) issued six promissory notes, each in the amount of US$ 99.825, plus interest, to Industrias Metalúrgica Van Dam, C.A. as acknowledgement of its debt for the provision of services under a contract signed in 1988 with the latter. The notes were assigned by endorsement to Fedax N.V.

A dispute arose between Venezuela and Fedax regarding the repayment of the notes, and on 17 June 1996, Fedax submitted a request for ICSID arbi-

1. 9 March 1998 is the date of dispatch to the parties.

tration. At the first session of the arbitral tribunal, held in Washington, D.C., on 17-18 January 1997, Venezuela objected to the jurisdiction of the Centre and the arbitral tribunal, alleging that the promissory notes did not qualify as an investment.

In the Decision of the Tribunal on Objections to Jurisdiction of 11 July 1997, the arbitral tribunal, applying Art. 25(1) of the 1965 Washington Convention as well as the Agreement between the Kingdom of the Netherlands and the Republic of Venezuela (the Agreement), the bilateral investment treaty governing the consent to arbitration, found that the promissory notes did qualify as an investment. In particular, Art. 1(a) of the Agreement included "titles to money" under the definition of "investment". Although the identity of the investor had changed with the endorsement to Fedax, the investment remained constant.

With respect to the remaining dispute on the merits, Venezuela stated in its counter-memorial of 4 September 1997 that, on 28 May 1997, the President and the Council of Ministers of the Republic of Venezuela had authorized the payment of the capital and interest on the promissory notes in question. The counter-memorial contained a settlement offer indicating that Fedax should request payment of the promissory notes. Fedax and Venezuela subsequently agreed that the payment would be in US dollars and would include interest up to the day of payment. The arbitral tribunal decided, in its *Award of 9 March 1998*, on the remaining questions of legal costs and the date of payment, specifying 7 May 1998, the date on which the current six-month period of interest would be complete, as the date of payment and holding that each party was to pay its own legal costs.

Excerpt

Decision of 11 July 1997

(....)

[1] "In deciding on the question of jurisdiction of the Centre and its own competence in this case, the Tribunal must first consider whether there is a legal dispute between the parties as required by Art. 25(1) of the Convention.[2]

---

2. Art. 25(1) of the 1965 Washington Convention reads:

"The jurisdiction of the Centre shall extend to any legal dispute arising directly out of an investment, between a Contracting State (or any constituent subdivision or agency of a Contracting State designated to the Centre by that State) and a national of another Con-

Although the term 'legal dispute' is not defined in the Convention, its drafting history makes abundantly clear that such term refers to conflicts of rights as opposed to mere conflicts of interests: '[t]he dispute must concern the existence or scope of a legal right or obligation, or the nature or extent of the reparation to be made for breach of a legal obligation.'[3] The discussions held on the drafts leading to this provision also evidence that legal disputes were meant to exclude moral, political, economic or purely commercial claims.[4]

[2] "In the light of this background and of the evidence of the record, the Tribunal is satisfied that a dispute of a legal nature is involved in this case as it concerns the different views of the parties on questions of legal rights and obligations in connection with the existence of an investment, and the effects this may have on the issue of an obligation to honor certain debt instruments consisting of six promissory notes accompanying the request for arbitration (the promissory notes), which were issued by the Republic of Venezuela.

[3] "The Tribunal also notes that jurisdiction *ratione personae* has not been a matter of contention between the parties, nor has an objection to jurisdiction on this ground been raised. It has been properly established that the Republic of Venezuela is a Contracting State under the Convention, and the Fedax N.V. is a company established under the laws of Curaçao, Netherlands Antilles, thus having the nationality of a Contracting State other than the State party to the dispute on the date on which the parties consented to arbitration, as well as on the date on which the request was registered by the Secretary-General of the Centre.

[4] "The main jurisdictional question raised in this case concerns whether the dispute involves an 'investment' within the meaning of Art. 25(1) of the Convention. In fact, the Republic of Venezuela has objected to the jurisdiction of the Centre in the matter of its dispute with Fedax N.V., on the ground that the latter company cannot be considered to have made an investment for the purposes of the Convention, because it acquired by way of endorsement the promissory notes issued by the Republic of Venezuela in connection with the contract made with the Venezuelan corporation Industrias Metalúrgicas Van Dam C.A. The interpretation of the term 'investment' is therefore crucial in determining the scope of the Centre's jurisdiction under the Convention.

---

tracting State, which the parties to the dispute consent in writing to submit to the Centre. When the parties have given their consent, no party may withdraw its consent unilaterally."

3. "'Report of the Executive Directors on the Convention on the Settlement of Investment Disputes between States and Nationals of Other States', Doc. ICSID/2, 1 *ICSID Reports* (1993) p. 23, para. 26."

4. "ICSID, *Documents Concerning the Origin and the Formulation of the Convention* (1968) Vol. II, at pp. 54, 203. Hereinafter cited as *Convention History*."

[5] "The Republic of Venezuela has argued in this respect that Fedax N.V.'s holding of the above-mentioned promissory notes does not qualify as an 'investment' because this transaction does not amount to a direct foreign investment involving 'a long term transfer of financial resources – capital flow – from one country to another (the recipient of the investment) in order to acquire interests in a corporation, a transaction which normally entails certain risks to the potential investor.' (footnote omitted) Neither would this transaction qualify, in Venezuela's view, as a portfolio investment to acquire titles to money since in that country this occurs 'when the investor acquires shares of a corporation through the Stock Exchange – Caracas or Maracaibo – basically those known as "Global Depository Receipts" represented by GDS and ADR,' a type of investment which is 'only considered direct when the acquisition of the title is done in a primary way.' (footnote omitted) Venezuela has further argued that in the light of the rule of interpretation laid down in Art. 31.1 of the 1969 Vienna Convention on the Law of Treaties, the term 'investment' should be interpreted 'in good faith in accordance with the ordinary meaning to be given to the terms of the treaty in their context and in the light of its object and purpose.'[5] Under such an interpretation, in Venezuela's view, investment in an economic context means 'the laying out of money or property in business ventures, so that it may produce a revenue or income.'[6] Venezuela contends that this particular interpretation is necessary to accommodate the definition of investments as comprising 'every kind of asset' as that phrase appears in Art. 1(a) of the 1991 Agreement.

[6] "The Tribunal has examined with great attention the arguments put forward by the Republic of Venezuela since they express a legitimate concern about the interpretation of the Convention and the Agreement. The Tribunal has also carefully considered the jurisdictional arguments of the claimant contesting the views set out by the Republic of Venezuela. The Tribunal does of course concur with the Republic of Venezuela about the need to apply the rules of interpretation laid down in the Vienna Convention on the Law of Treaties. In order to satisfy these requirements the Tribunal shall examine the question in the light of Art. 25(1) of the Convention, Art. 1(a) and related provisions of the Agreement and other relevant considerations discussed below.

[7] "The Tribunal shall first examine the meaning of the term 'investment' under Art. 25(1) of the Convention. It is well established that numerous attempts to define investments were made during the negotiations of the

5. "Convention on the Law of Treaties, 1969, Article 31.1, International Legal Materials, Vol. 8 (1969) p. 679."

6. "Brief [Republic of Venezuela] with reference to Andrés S. Suarez et al., *Diccionario Económico de la Empresa* (1977) at p. 212."

Convention,[7] but none were generally acceptable.[8] Because of this difficulty, it was finally decided to leave any definition of the 'investment' to the consent of the parties.[9] As explained by the Report of the Executive Directors:

> 'No attempt was made to define the term "investment" given the essential requirement of consent by the parties, and the mechanism through which Contracting States can make known in advance, if they so desire, the classes of disputes which they would or would not consider submitting to the Centre (Article 25(4)).'[10]

An account on these negotiations given by Mr. A. Broches is also most pertinent:

> 'During the negotiations several definitions of "investment" were considered and rejected. It was felt in the end that a definition could be dispensed with "given the essential requirement of consent by the parties." This indicates that the requirement that the dispute must have arisen out of an "investment" may be merged into the requirement of consent to jurisdiction. Presumably, the parties' agreement that a dispute is an "investment dispute" will be given great weight in any determination of the Centre's jurisdiction, although it would not be controlling.'[11]

[8] "In light of the above, distinguished commentators of the Convention have concluded that 'a broad approach to the interpretation of this term in Art. 25 is warranted,'[12] that it 'is within the sole discretion of each Contracting State to determine the type of investment disputes that it considers

7. "Christoph Schreuer, 'Commentary on the ICSID Convention', ICSID Review – Foreign Investment Law Journal, Vol. 11 (1996) p. 316 at pp. 355-358."

8. "*Convention History*, Vol. II, at pp. 835-837."

9. "Ibid., at p. 1078; Carolyn B. Lamm and Abby Cohen Smutny, 'The Implementation of ICSID Arbitration Agreements', ICSID Review – Foreign Investment Law Journal, Vol. 11 (1996) p. 64 at p. 80."

10. "Report cit., supra fn. 3, para. 27."

11. "A. Broches, 'The Convention on The Settlement of Investment Disputes: Some Observations on Jurisdiction', Columbia Journal of Transnational Law, Vol. 5 (1966) pp. 261-280 at p. 268, footnote omitted."

12. "C.F. Amerasinghe, 'The Jurisdiction of the International Centre for the Settlement of Investment Disputes', Indian Journal of International Law, Vol. 19 (1979) pp. 166-227 at p. 181."

arbitrable in the context of ICSID.'[13] or that the parties 'thus have a large measure of discretion to determine for themselves whether their transaction constitutes an investment for the purposes of the Convention.'[14] Within this broad framework for the definition of investment under the ICSID Convention, the Tribunal also notes that a number of transactions have been identified as qualifying as investments in given circumstances. It has also been noted by commentators of the Convention, and during the history of its negotiation, that jurisdiction over loans,[15] suppliers' credits,[16] outstanding payments,[17] ownership of shares[18] and construction contracts,[19] among other aspects, was left to the discretion of the parties.[20]

[9] "It is also most relevant to note the conclusions of a distinguished author in this respect:

> 'These new types of investment, and especially those relating to the supply of services are sometimes on the borderline between investment proper and commercial transactions, which would fall outside the scope of ICSID.
>
> However, the characterization of transnational loans as "investments" has not raised difficulty. The reason is twofold. First, it has been assumed from the origin of the Convention that loans, or more precisely those of a certain duration as opposed to rapidly concluded commercial financial facilities, were included in the concept of "investment". This is evidenced by the first Draft of the Convention according to which:
>
> For the purpose of this Chapter
>
> (i) "investment" means any contribution of money or other asset of economic value for an indefinite period or, if the period be defined, for not less than five years.

13. "Georges R. Delaume, 'ICSID and the Transnational Financial Community', ICSID Review – Foreign Investment Law Journal, Vol. 1 (1986) pp. 237-256 at pp. 239-240; Ibrahim F.I. Shihata, 'Towards a Greater Depoliticization of Investment Disputes: The Roles of ICSID and MIGA', ICSID Review – Foreign Investment Law Journal, Vol. 1 (1986) p. 1 at p. 4."
14. "Lamm and Smutny, loc. cit., supra fn. 9, at p. 80."
15. "*Convention History*, Vol. II, at pp. 261, 474."
16. "Ibid., at p. 451."
17. "Ibid., at p. 542."
18. "Ibid., at p. 661."
19. "Ibid., at p. 500."
20. "Schreuer, loc. cit., supra fn. 7, at p. 357; Amerasinghe, loc. cit., supra fn. 12, at p. 181."

Although attempts at defining the notion of investment were given up by the authors of the Convention and this provision disappeared, there is no reason to doubt that loans can be considered as investments for the purposes of the Convention. Another reason why the issue of definition is not a serious one is that, in the case of loan contracts involving foreign public borrowers referring to ICSID as a means of settling loan disputes, the parties take the precaution of stipulating expressly that the loan is an investment for the purposes of the Convention.'[21]

This matter will be discussed below in connection with the promissory notes as a form of loan or credit.

[10] "In addition to the background of Art. 25(1) of the Convention, there is also a problem of textual interpretation that the Tribunal must consider. The Republic of Venezuela has made the argument that the disputed transaction is not a 'direct foreign investment' and therefore could not qualify as an investment under the Convention. However, the text of Art. 25(1) establishes that the 'jurisdiction of the Centre shall extend to any legal dispute arising directly out of an investment.' It is apparent that the term 'directly' relates in this Article to the 'dispute' and not to the 'investment'. It follows that jurisdiction can exist even in respect of investments that are not direct, so long as the dispute arises directly from such transaction. This interpretation is also consistent with the broad reach that the term 'investment' must be given in light of the negotiating history of the Convention.

[11] "Precisely because the term 'investment' has been broadly understood in the ICSID practice and decisions, as well as in scholarly writings, it has never before been a major source of contention before ICSID Tribunals.[22] This is the first ICSID case in which the jurisdiction of the Centre has been objected to on the ground that the underlying transaction does not meet the requirements of an investment under the Convention. On prior occasions ICSID Tribunals have examined on their own initiative the question whether an investment was involved,[23] and in each such case have reached the conclusion that the 'investment' requirement of the Convention has been met. In *Kaiser Bauxite v. Jamaica*,[24] as in *Alcoa Minerals of Jamaica Inc. v. Jamaica*,[25] the Tribunal established the Centre's jurisdiction both on the consent given by the parties

21. "Delaume, loc. cit., supra fn. 13, at p. 242, footnote omitted."
22. "Lamm and Smutny, loc. cit., supra fn. 9, at p. 80; Schreuer, loc. cit., supra fn. 7, at p. 360."
23. "Schreuer, loc. cit., supra fn. 7, at p. 360; Lamm and Smutny, loc. cit., supra fn. 9, at p. 80."
24. "*Kaiser Bauxite Company v. Government of Jamaica*, 1975, 1 *ICSID Reports* (1993) p. 296."
25. "*Alcoa Minerals of Jamaica Inc. v. Government of Jamaica*, 1975, *Yearbook Commercial Arbitration*, Vol. IV (1979) p. 206."

and on the fact that the case 'in which a mining company has invested substantial amounts in a foreign State in reliance upon an agreement with that State, is among those contemplated by the Convention.' Amounts paid out to develop a concession and other undertakings based on a concession agreement, were also considered to qualify as an investment under the Convention in *LETCO v. Liberia*.[26] Also in *SOABI v. Senegal* the Tribunal considered the issue of jurisdiction in respect of an operation encompassing separate agreements, but this dealt only indirectly with the existence of an investment.[27]

[12] "The issue of whether a given dispute arises directly out of an investment has been also raised in a number of cases, although such cases have not considered whether an investment was made in the first place. In *Holiday Inns v. Morocco*, for example, the Tribunal found that the Centre had jurisdiction over loan contracts that had their origin in agreements separate from the investment; although the respondent argued that these constituted different transactions, the Tribunal emphasized 'the general unity of an investment operation.'[28] In *Amco Asia et al. v. Indonesia* an *ad hoc* Committee also affirmed the Centre's jurisdiction in respect of an international tort arising from lack of protection to the claimant by the Indonesian Army and Police; the Tribunal stated that it 'does not think of "international tort" and "investment dispute" as comprising mutually exclusive categories,' and that '[t]he jurisdiction of the Tribunal is not successfully avoided by applying a different formal characterization to the operative facts of the dispute.'[29] In this same case an important distinction was made at a later stage in the following terms:

> '... the Tribunal believes that it is correct to distinguish between rights and obligations that are applicable to legal or natural persons who are within the reach of a host State's jurisdiction, as a matter of general law; and rights and obligations that are applicable to an investor as a consequence of an investment agreement entered into with that host State.

---

26. "*Liberian Eastern Timber Corporation v. Government of the Republic of Liberia*, 1984, 2 *ICSID Reports* (1994) p. 346."
27. "*Société Ouest Africaine des Bétons Industriels v. State of Senegal*, 1988, 2 *ICSID Reports* (1994) p. 165."
28. "*Holiday Inns S.A., Occidental Petroleum Corporation et al. v. Government of Morocco*, Case No. ARB/72/1; Schreuer, loc. cit., supra fn. 7, at pp. 350-351, with reference to P. Lalive, 'The First "World Bank" Arbitration (Holiday Inns v. Morocco) – Some Legal Problems', *British Year Book of International Law*, Vol. 51 (1980) p. 123."
29. "*Amco Asia Corporation, Pan American Development Limited and P.T. Amco Indonesia v. Republic of Indonesia*, 1986, 1 *ICSID Reports* (1993) p. 509 at p. 527."

Legal disputes relating to the latter will fall under Art. 25(1) of the Convention.'[30]

[13] "The Tribunal must also note that while some parallel exists between the ICSID Convention and the Convention Establishing the Multilateral Investment Guarantee Agency (MIGA),[31] in as much as investments insured under the latter would qualify as investments under Art. 25(1) of the former, the two systems ought not to be considered identical. Among other differences, it is conceivable that an investment under ICSID terms will not qualify for insurance under MIGA if it does not meet the stricter definitions of the MIGA Convention. MIGA is essentially concerned with direct foreign investment,[32] while, as discussed above, ICSID may cover investments which may not be direct if the circumstances so warrant. Even so, MIGA's coverage may eventually extend to 'any other medium or long-term form of investment,' including loans relating to investments,[33] an alternative which also broadens the scope of the MIGA Convention, and to this extent narrows the differences with the ICSID Convention.

[14] "Another aspect which the Tribunal has not overlooked is the relationship between the ICSID Convention and the Rules Governing the Additional Facility,[34] since the latter may apply, among other situations, in cases where ICSID jurisdiction is not available because the dispute does not arise directly out of an investment.[35] Here again the term 'directly' relates to the evolution of the dispute and not to the investment. In this respect it would appear that, as in the case of ICSID, the Additional Facility Rules might cover types of investment that were not direct if the circumstances so warranted. On this point, the Tribunal must also note that the comment accompanying Art. 4, Paragraph (4), of the Additional Facility Rules is somewhat restrictive, because it relates only to a situation in which a Tribunal might declare itself incompetent on the ground that it considered the underlying transaction not to be an 'investment';[36] in fact, a Tribunal might be satisfied that there is an

30. "Ibid., Resubmission, 1988, 1 *ICSID Reports* (1993) p. 543 at p. 565."

31. "Convention Establishing the Multilateral Investment Guarantee Agency, 1985, International Legal Materials, Vol. 24 (1985) p. 1605."

32. "Operational Regulations of the Multilateral Investment Guarantee Agency, 1988, as amended, ICSID Review – Foreign Investment Law Journal, Vol. 3 (1988) p. 360; Lamm and Smutny, loc. cit., supra fn. 9, at p. 80."

33. "Operational Regulations cit., supra fn. 32, p. 370; Lamm and Smutny, loc. cit., supra fn. 9, at p. 82."

34. "ICSID Additional Facility, Document ICSID/11, 1979."

35. "Rules Governing the Additional Facility, Art. 2(b)."

36. "Ibid. Art. 4(4), *Comment* (iv)."

investment, but decline jurisdiction because the dispute does not arise directly from it, and this situation could also be brought to settlement under the Additional Facility Rules. However, under both ICSID and the Additional Facility Rules the investment in question, even if indirect, should be distinguishable from an ordinary commercial transaction.[37] The Tribunal shall consider the question of distinguishing between an investment and an ordinary commercial transaction in this case further below.

[15] "The Tribunal considers that the broad scope of Art. 25(1) of the Convention and the ensuing ICSID practice and decisions are sufficient, without more, to require a finding that the Centre's jurisdiction and its own competence are well-founded. In addition, as explained above, loans qualify as an investment within ICSID's jurisdiction,[38] as does, in given circumstances, the purchase of bonds.[39] Since promissory notes are evidence of a loan and a rather typical financial and credit instrument, there is nothing to prevent their purchase from qualifying as an investment under the Convention in the circumstances of a particular case such as this. This conclusion, however, has to be examined next in the context of the specific consent of the parties and other provisions which are controlling in the matter.

[16] "The Tribunal turns now to a consideration of the relevant terms and provisions of the Agreement between the Kingdom of the Netherlands and the Republic of Venezuela, which is the specific bilateral investment treaty governing the consent to arbitration by the latter Contracting Party. Under Art. 9(1) of this Agreement, disputes between one Contracting Party and a national of the other Contracting Party 'concerning an obligation of the former under this Agreement in relation to an investment of the latter' shall be submitted to ICSID for settlement by arbitration or conciliation. In Art. 9(4) each Party 'gives its unconditional consent' to such submission of disputes.

[17] "It follows that, as contemplated by the Convention, the definition of 'investment' is controlled by consent of the Contracting Parties, and the particular definition set forth in Art. 1(a) of the Agreement is the one that governs the jurisdiction of ICSID:

> '[T]he term "investments" shall comprise every kind of asset and more particularly though not exclusively:
>
> ....

37. "Schreuer, loc. cit., supra fn. 7, at p. 368."
38. "Aron Broches, 'Choice-of-law provisions in contracts with governments', in Ibid.: *Selected Essays*, pp. 523-532 at p. 529; Delaume, loc. cit., supra fn. 13, pp. 241-242."
39. "Schreuer, loc. cit., supra fn. 7, at p. 372."

(ii) rights derived from shares, bonds, and other kinds of interests in companies and joint ventures;
(iii) titles to money, to other assets or to any performance having an economic value...'.

[18] "This definition evidences that the Contracting Parties to the Agreement intended a very broad meaning for the term 'investment'. The Tribunal notes in particular that titles to money in this definition are not in any way restricted to forms of direct foreign investment or portfolio investment, as argued by the Republic of Venezuela. Some such restrictions may perhaps apply to other types of investment listed in such definition, such as rights derived from shares or other similar types of investment, but they do not apply to the credit transactions of different categories that are embodied in the meaning of 'titles to money' as referred to in subparagraph (iii) of the definition set out above. It should be noted, moreover, that titles to money are not necessarily excluded from the concept of direct foreign investment.

[19] "The Tribunal has also undertaken a close examination of other provisions of the Agreement which are related to the definition of an investment, including Art. 5 of the Agreement, under which the Contracting Parties guarantee the transfer of payments related to an investment, including the transfer of interests (Art. 5(a)) and funds for the reimbursement of loans (Art. 5(d)). The conclusion that the definition of 'investment' and the meaning of 'titles to money' under the Agreement include loans and related credit transactions is thus reinforced. It must also be noted that the Republic of Venezuela has not exercised its right under Art. 25(4) of the ICSID Convention to notify the Centre of any class or classes of disputes it would or would not consider submitting to the jurisdiction of the Centre. This provision allows Contracting States to put investors on notice as to what class of disputes they would or would not consider consenting to within the broad meaning of investment under the Convention.

[20] "A broad definition of investment such as that included in the Agreement is not at all an exceptional situation. On the contrary, most contemporary bilateral treaties of this kind refer to 'every kind of asset' or to 'all assets', including the listing of examples that can qualify for coverage; claims to money and to any performance having a financial value are prominent features of such listings.[40] This broad approach has also become the

40. "Antonio R. Parra, 'The scope of new investment laws and international instruments', in Robert Pritchard (ed.): *Economic Development, Foreign Investment and the Law* (1996) pp. 27-44, at pp. 35-36; 'ICSID and Bilateral Investment Treaties', News from ICSID, Vol. 2, No. 1 (1985) pp. 12-20 at pp. 19-20."

standard policy of major economic groupings such as the European Communities. In providing for the protection of investments the EC have included 'all types of assets, tangible and intangible, that have an economic value, including direct or indirect contributions in cash, kind or services invested or received.' Among the transactions listed as investments are 'stocks, bonds, debentures, guarantees or other financial instruments of a company, other firm, government or, other public authority or an international organization; claims to money, goods, services or other performance having economic value.'[41] Since the Kingdom of the Netherlands is a prominent member of the European Communities, it is hardly surprising that a similar approach has been followed in its bilateral investment treaties.[42] Indeed,. only very exceptionally do bilateral investment treaties explicitly relate the definition of the assets or transactions included in this concept to questions such as the existence of a lasting economic relation,[43] or specifically associate titles to money and similar transactions strictly to a concept of investment.[44]

[21] "A similar trend can be identified in the context of major multilateral instruments. It has been rightly noted that the World Bank Guidelines on the Treatment of Foreign Direct Investment[45] are not at all restricted to 'direct' investments.[46] The explanatory Report makes clear that there are no restrictions in this context as to the nature of covered investments and that the Guidelines are applicable to 'indirect, as well as to direct, investments and to modern contractual and other forms of investment.'[47] The Energy Charter Treaty[48] and Mercosur Protocols[49] have included 'every kind of asset', the

41. "Council of the European Communities, 'Community position on investment protection principles in the ACP States', ACP-CEE 2172/92, 3 November 1992, at p. 5."
42. "See for example the Agreement between the Kingdom of the Netherlands and the Republic of Paraguay on Encouragement and Reciprocal Protection of Investments, 29 October 1992, in Alejandro A. Escobar, 'Introductory Note on Bilateral Investment Treaties Recently Concluded by Latin American States', ICSID Review – Foreign Investment Law Journal, Vol. 11 (1996) pp. 86-220 at p. 197."
43. "See, for example, the Agreement concerning the promotion and reciprocal protection of investments between Denmark and Ukraine, 23 October 1992, Art. 1, as cited in Parra, loc. cit., supra fn. 40, at p. 36."
44. "See, for example, the Agreement between the United States and Zaire of 3 August 1984, Art. 1, in News from ICSID cit., supra fn. 40, at p. 20."
45. "'World Bank Guidelines on the Treatment of Foreign Direct Investment', 1991, ICSID Review – Foreign Investment Law Journal, Vol. 7 (1992) p. 295."
46. "Parra, loc. cit., supra fn. 40, at p. 40."
47. "'Report to the Development Committee on the legal framework for the treatment of foreign investments', accompanying the Guidelines cit., supra fn. 45, at para. 13."
48. "Energy Charter Treaty, 17 December 1994, International Legal Materials, Vol. 34 (1995) p. 360, Art. 1(6), and comments by Parra, loc. cit., supra fn. 40, at pp. 40-41."
49. "MERCOSUR: Protocol on the Reciprocal Promotion and Protection of Investments in

former listing 'claims to money and claims to performance pursuant to certain contracts,' and the latter referring to 'claims to performance having an economic value.'[50] Again only exceptionally has a multilateral treaty strictly related the listing of given assets such as interests to equity investments, or excluded claims to money that arise solely from commercial contracts for the sale of goods or services.[51]

[22] "The Tribunal has also examined the practice of the Republic of Venezuela as to the various investment treaties it has made with other countries and the definition of investment therein included.[52] While this practice is varied, it is possible to conclude that every time the Republic of Venezuela has wished to exclude investments that are not manifestly direct, it has done so in unequivocal terms. Two examples are the Andean Group Regulation on Foreign Investments as amended,[53] which in essence refers to direct foreign investments, and the 1994 Mexico-Colombia-Venezuela Free Trade Agreement, which excludes money claims arising from commercial contracts for the sale of goods or services and commercial credits.[54] In other instances the language of the Agreement with the Kingdom of the Netherlands has been followed.[55]

[23] "The Tribunal being satisfied that loans and other credit facilities are within the jurisdiction of the Centre under both the terms of the Convention and the scope of the bilateral Agreement governing consent in this case, it must now examine the specific situation of the six promissory notes issued by the Republic of Venezuela. A promissory note is by definition an instrument of credit, a written recognition that a loan has been made. In this particular case the six promissory notes in question were issued by the Republic of Venezuela in order to acknowledge its debt for the provision of services under

---

Mercosur, Colonia, 17 January 1994, Art. 1(1); and Protocol for the promotion and protection of investments made by countries that do not belong to Mercosur, Buenos Aires, 5 August 1994, Art. 2; and comments by Parra, loc. cit., supra fn. 40, at pp. 40-41."

50. "Parra, loc. cit., supra fn. 40, at p. 41."

51. "North American Free Trade Agreement, 17 December 1992, International Legal Materials, Vol. 32 (1993) pp. 289, 605, Art. 1139, and comments by Parra, loc. cit., supra fn. 40, at p. 42."

52. "For recent Latin American practice and treaties, see Escobar, loc. cit., supra fn. 42."

53. "'Reglamento del régimen común de tratamiento a los capitales extranjeros y sobre marcas, patentes y regalias, aprobado por las Decisiones Nos. 291 y 292 de la Comisión del Acuerdo de Cartagena', *Gaceta Oficial de la República de Venezuela*, 25 March 1992, Art. 2.1."

54. "1994 Mexico-Colombia-Venezuela Free Trade Agreement, Art. 17-01, as cited in Schreuer, loc. cit., supra fn. 7, at p. 364."

55. "'Acuerdo entre el Gobierno de la República de Venezuela y el Gobierno de Barbados para la promoción y protección de inversiones', Art. 1(a)(iii), in Escobar, loc. cit., supra fn. 42, at p. 213."

a contract signed in 1988 with Industrias Metalúrgicas Van Dam C.A.; Venezuela had simply received a loan for the amount of the notes for the time period specified therein and with the corresponding obligation to pay interest.

[24] "The Tribunal notes first that there is nothing in the nature of the foregoing transaction, namely the provision of services in return for promissory notes, that would prevent it from qualifying as an investment under the Convention and the Agreement. Specifically, the Tribunal has raised the question whether if Fedax N.V., as a Netherlands company, had been doing business in Venezuela at the time in question and had entered into exactly the same arrangement with the Republic of Venezuela as Industrias Metalúrgicas Van Dam C.A. did, such transaction would have involved an 'investment' or whether, in Venezuela's view, the transaction would be excluded from that category. The record shows that Venezuela does not contend that such an exclusion would be appropriate. It follows that the issue for decision is focussed not in the nature of the underlying service transaction but in whether the subsequent endorsement of the notes to foreign holders somehow requires the Tribunal to treat the matter as one falling outside the concept of foreign investment.

[25] "The claimant has rightly argued that promissory notes of this kind have a legal standing of their own, separate and independent from the underlying transaction. It is not disputed in this case that the Government of Venezuela foresaw the possibility that the promissory notes would be transferred and endorsed to subsequent holders, since they explicitly allow for such a possibility. The fact that these notes were denominated in US dollars is further evidence that their eventual international circulation and availability to foreign investors was contemplated from the outset. The record also evidences that in the view of the Republic of Venezuela those promissory notes

> '... due to their nature, in accordance with the provisions of the Venezuelan Commercial Code and because it is expressly stated in their own text, are eminently negotiable instruments in the secondary market, with national or foreign financial institutions.' (footnote omitted)

[26] "In such a situation, although the identity of the investor will change with every endorsement, the investment itself will remain constant, while the issuer will enjoy a continuous credit benefit until the time the notes become due. To the extent that this credit is provided by a foreign holder of the notes, it constitutes a foreign investment which in this case is encompassed by the terms of the Convention and the Agreement. While specific issues relating to the promissory notes and their endorsements might be discussed in connection with the merits of the case, the argument made by the Republic of Venezuela

that the notes were not purchased on the Venezuelan stock exchanges does not take them out of the category of foreign investment because these instruments were intended for international circulation. Nor can the Tribunal accept the argument that, unlike the case of an investment, there is no risk involved in this transaction: the very existence of a dispute as to the payment of the principal and interest evidences the risk that the holder of the notes has taken.

[27] "Like a number of other bilateral investment treaties and multilateral arrangements,[56] the Agreement contains several references to investments made 'in the territory' of the Contracting Parties.[57] In this context the Republic of Venezuela has argued that Fedax N.V. does not qualify as an investor because it has not made any investment 'in the territory' of Venezuela. While it is true that in some kinds of investments listed under Art. 1(a) of the Agreement, such as the acquisition of interests in immovable property, companies and the like, a transfer of funds or value will be made into the territory of the host country, this does not necessarily happen in a number of other types of investments, particularly those of a financial nature. It is a standard feature of many international financial transactions that the funds involved are not physically transferred to the territory of the beneficiary, but put at its disposal elsewhere. In fact, many loans and credits do not leave the country of origin at all, but are made available to suppliers or other entities. The same is true of many important offshore financial operations relating to exports and other kinds of business. And of course, promissory notes are frequently employed in such arrangements. The important question is whether the funds made available are utilized by the beneficiary of the credit, as in the case of the Republic of Venezuela, so as to finance its various governmental needs. It is not disputed in this case that the Republic of Venezuela, by means of the promissory notes, received an amount of credit that was put to work during a period of time for its financial needs.

[28] "The nature of the transactions involved in this case, and the fact that they qualify as a foreign investment for the purposes of the Convention and the Agreement, serves to distinguish them from an ordinary commercial transaction. In this connection, however, there is one additional element that the Tribunal has to take into consideration. The promissory notes were issued by the Republic of Venezuela under the terms of the Law on Public Credit (the Law),[58] which specifically governs public credit operations aimed at raising funds and resources 'to undertake productive works, attend to the needs

56. "Parra, loc. cit., supra fn. 40, at pp. 35, 40."

57. "See, for example, Agreement, Preamble, para. 2, and Arts. 2, 4, 7."

58. "Venezuela: *Ley Orgánica de Crédito Público*, 12 August 1983, *Gaceta Oficial de la República de Venezuela*, 14 September 1983, as amended, *Gaceta Legal*, No. 594, 30 September 1983."

of national interest and cover transitory needs of the treasury.'[59] It is quite apparent that the transactions involved in this case are not ordinary commercial transactions and indeed involve a fundamental public interest. The Law specifically mentions medium and long-term bonds and obligations, short-term treasury instruments and operations, short-term credit, obtaining credit with national or foreign financial, commercial and industrial institutions, contracting for works and services, and other types of transactions as well.[60] Promissory notes are also expressly governed by the Law in connection with obtaining domestic or foreign credit and contracts for works and services.[61] Detailed authorizations and procedures are provided for the issuance of these instruments, all of which have been duly observed in respect of the promissory notes involved in this case. This Law was enacted to provide for the orderly development of public financial arrangements and has been appropriately utilized by the Republic of Venezuela in this case, as in other matters.

[29] "The status of the promissory notes under the Law of Public Credit is also important as evidence that the type of investment involved is not merely a short-term, occasional financial arrangement, such as could happen with investments that come in for quick gains and leave immediately thereafter – i.e. 'volatile capital'. The basic features of an investment have been described as involving a certain duration, a certain regularity of profit and return, assumption of risk, a substantial commitment and a significance for the host State's development.[62] The duration of the investment in this case meets the requirement of the Law as to contracts needing to extend beyond the fiscal year in which they are made.[63] The regularity of profit and return is also met by the scheduling of interest payments through a period of several years. The amount of capital committed is also relatively substantial. Risk is also involved as has been explained. And most importantly, there is clearly a significant relationship between the transaction and the development of the host State, as specifically required under the Law for issuing the pertinent financial instrument. It follows that, given the particular facts of the case, the transaction meets the basic features of an investment.

[30] "Other objections to jurisdiction were originally raised by the Republic of Venezuela, but the record before the Tribunal expressly indicates that these other matters will not be pursued, and hence that there is no need for the Tribunal to consider them further.

59. "Ibid., Art. 3."
60. "Ibid., Art. 4."
61. "Ibid., Art. 29."
62. "Schreuer, loc. cit., supra fn. 7, at p. 372."
63. "Law cit., supra fn. 59, Art. 4(c)."

[31] "For the foregoing reasons the Tribunal unanimously decides that the present dispute is within the jurisdiction of the Centre and the competence of the Tribunal. The Tribunal has, accordingly, made the necessary Order for the continuation of the procedure pursuant to Arbitration Rule 41(4)."

Award of 9 March 1998

(....)

[32] "In examining the merits of the dispute subject matter of this proceeding, the Tribunal notes that the facts alleged in the request for arbitration (which has also served as Fedax N.V.'s memorial on the merits) have not been contested by the Republic of Venezuela, and, furthermore, that the basic issues involved have been partially settled by the parties.

[33] "The Tribunal will first set forth the following statement of the facts of the dispute as it finds them. ... Fedax N.V. alleges that the Republic of Venezuela has not paid the principal of each of the six promissory notes subject matter of its claim, regular interest from 7 May 1994 on five of such promissory notes, and penal interest from the dates of maturity on all six such promissory notes. This statement has not been contested by the Republic of Venezuela. Both in the course of the proceeding on jurisdiction and [in] its counter-memorial, the Republic of Venezuela has indeed confirmed that her authorities had suspended all payments on these and other promissory notes issued on occasion of the contract entered into between the Republic of Venezuela and Industrias Metalúrgicas Van Dam C.A. The Republic of Venezuela ... has furthermore stated ... that her authorities have authorized the payment of capital and interest on the above-mentioned promissory notes, including 'the promissory notes subject to this arbitration procedure'.... In view of the above, the Tribunal finds the facts of the dispute to be those described [in the Facts].

[34] "The Tribunal will now examine the issues raised by the dispute and partially agreed upon by the parties. First and foremost, the Republic of Venezuela has agreed to the payment of the capital and interest of the promissory notes that were the object of the request for arbitration by Fedax N.V. As stated in the offer for settlement of 4 September 1997, the Republic of Venezuela has authorized such payments by means of a decision adopted at the highest level of Government, including the President of the Republic and the Council of Ministers. Instructions for the implementation of this decision have also been issued within the Venezuelan administration and the appropriate steps for budgetary appropriations have been undertaken before the Congress of Venezuela. Second, as a result of further clarifications, it has

been agreed that the payments shall be made in dollars of the United States of America, just as it is indicated in the text of the promissory notes, and that Venezuela shall pay its part in the expenses of this proceeding. Third, it has been also agreed that accrued interest will be paid until the date of payment of the principal.

[35] "Although the elements set out above are the core issues of the dispute, the parties have not specifically agreed to a few other items. These are the date of payment and the question of payment of expenses and legal costs of Fedax N.V. Because the agreement does not include all the elements relating to the dispute, the parties have not filed with the Secretary-General the full and signed text of their settlement nor requested the Tribunal to embody such settlement in the award, as provided under Rule 43(2) of the ICSID Arbitration Rules. In fact, while the Republic of Venezuela requested the discontinuance of the proceeding, Fedax N.V. on its part requested the Tribunal to embody the settlement reached in its award, but both parties did not jointly agree to one and the same option. None of these questions detract from the significance of the settlement reached on the merits, this being the basis on which the Tribunal shall render its award.

[36] "As decided in respect of jurisdiction on 11 July 1997, the Tribunal is fully satisfied that the purchase by Fedax N.V. of the promissory notes subject matter of the request for arbitration meets the requirement of an investment both under the Convention and the Agreement. It follows that the Republic of Venezuela is under the obligation to honor precisely the terms and conditions governing such investment, laid down mainly in Art. 3 of the Agreement, as well as to honor the specific payments established in the promissory notes issued, and the Tribunal so finds in the terms of Art. 9(3) of the Agreement. The payments due shall be established further below.

[37] "Besides the provisions of the Convention and the Agreement, the Tribunal finds that Venezuelan law is also relevant as the applicable law in this case. In fact, the promissory notes subject matter of the dispute are in turn governed by the provisions of the Venezuelan Commercial Code and more specifically by those of the Law on Public Credit,[64] having been issued under the terms of the latter. Both parties have pointed in their pleadings to relevant aspects of the Venezuelan legislation and the Tribunal has examined these provisions with particular attention. It is of interest to note in this respect that the various sources of the applicable law referred to in Art. 9(5) of the Agreement, including the laws of the Contracting Party, the Agreement, other

64. "República de Venezuela: *Ley Orgánica de Crédito Público*, 12 August 1983, *Gaceta Oficial de la República de Venezuela*, 14 September 1983, as amended, *Gaceta Legal*, No. 594, 30 September 1983."

special agreements connected with the investment and the general principles of international law, have all had an important and supplementary role in the considerations of this case as well as in providing the basis for the decision on jurisdiction and the award on the merits. This broad framework of the applicable law further confirms the trends discernible in the ICSID practice and decisions.[65]

[38] "The first item that the Tribunal must establish is the amount of the principal of the promissory notes. The parties have not disputed the figure since it is specifically recorded in each promissory note, and the Republic of Venezuela has agreed to its payment under the terms of the partial settlement referred to above. Such principal is established in the amount of US$ 598,950.

[39] "The Tribunal turns now to the question of accrued interest. In this respect the Tribunal is satisfied that the figures submitted by Fedax N.V. and supplemented by the Tribunal's own finding as explained above, correspond exactly to the calculation of interest established in the promissory notes.[66] The current six-month period of interest began on 7 November 1997, and is due at the latest on 7 May 1998. The amount of regular interest overdue is US$ 22,148.50. Penal interest as provided also in the promissory notes amounts to US$ 139,096.64, including the current period. Total interest is therefore in the amount of US$ 161,245.14. The total amount of principal and interest is US$ 760,195.14. These figures have not been objected to by the Republic of Venezuela and payment of interest has also been agreed in the partial settlement reached by the parties. It has been further agreed that both principal and interest shall be paid in dollars of the United States of America.

---

65. "Ibrahim F.I. Shihata and Antonia R. Parra, 'Applicable Substantive Law in Disputes Between States and Private Foreign Parties: The Case of Arbitration under the ICSID Convention', ICSID Review - Foreign Investment Law Journal, Vol. 9, No. 2 (Fall 1994) pp. 183-213 at p. 212."

66. "*Tribunal's translation of promissory notes as they relate to interest:*

This promissory note shall bear from [date] until it is due an annual interest equal to the London Interbank Offered Rate (LIBOR) for six-month deposits in US dollars, as established further below, adjustable and payable at maturity on 7 May and 7 November each year, except the last payment of interest which shall be made when this promissory note becomes due ...

The LIBOR rate shall be that established by the Union Bank of Switzerland, London, England, two working days immediately before the beginning of the corresponding period of interest ...

Calculation of interest shall be made on the basis of the number of days passed in respect of one year of 365 days ...

In case the Republic of Venezuela fails to pay this promissory note at maturity, it shall pay penalty interest on the amount of capital at the rate of interest of this note, plus 1% annually, until its total payment."

[40] "Concerning the date of payment, the Tribunal considers that the appropriate date is 7 May 1998. This date, as noted above, is when the current six-month period of interest will be completed. Moreover, such date should provide ample time for the Republic of Venezuela to finalize its budgetary arrangements for the payment of the amounts involved. Should the Republic of Venezuela pay before that date it may of course adjust the amount of interest to the number of days lapsed, a figure which can be established without difficulty in the terms of the promissory notes.

[41] "In respect of the expenses incurred in the present proceeding, including the charges for the use of the facilities of the Centre and the fees and expenses of the Tribunal, it is the decision of the Tribunal that each of the parties shall bear an equal share of such institutional expenses. Accordingly, the Republic of Venezuela shall reimburse Fedax N.V. the amount of US$ 50,150 representing one half of the charges and of the costs of the proceeding for which advance payments have been made by Fedax N.V. The Tribunal must also record that the Republic of Venezuela has agreed to the payment of its share in such expenses in the terms of the partial settlement referred to above.

[42] "The Applicant has also requested that the Republic of Venezuela pay the expenses and legal costs of counsel for Fedax N.V., an aspect which has not been agreed to by the Republic. Arguments based on Venezuelan domestic law and the Convention have been put forth by the parties in support of their respective positions. Taking into consideration these arguments and the professionalism of counsel for the parties which is commended in the following paragraph, the Tribunal decides that each party, shall bear the entirety of its own expenses and legal fees for its own counsel.

[43] "In reaching its award, the Tribunal must note with satisfaction that this is the first case decided under the Convention in which the Contracting Party, namely the Republic of Venezuela, is a prominent member of the Latin American region, a fact which in itself illustrates well the evolution that the legal treatment of foreign investments has had in this region as elsewhere in the world. Moreover, the settlement which the Republic of Venezuela has made possible is fully consistent with its good standing in the international financial community and honors a long tradition of observance of international agreements. The Tribunal also notes with appreciation that counsel for both parties have been prominent Venezuelan lawyers, who have performed their duties with outstanding professionalism and have at all times fully cooperated with the task of the Tribunal, an attitude for which they must be commended.

[44] "For the reasons stated above the Tribunal unanimously decides that:

(1) The Republic of Venezuela shall pay Fedax N.V. the amount of US$ 598,950 representing the principal of the promissory notes due.

(2) The Republic of Venezuela shall pay Fedax N.V. the amount of US$ 161,245.14 for the regular and penal interest due on the promissory notes.
(3) The Republic of Venezuela shall pay Fedax N.V. the amount of US$ 50,150 representing one half of the charges and costs of the proceeding for which advance payment was made by the Applicant.
(4) Each of the parties shall bear the entirety of its own expenses and legal fees for its own counsel.
(5) The payments referred to above shall be made at the latest on 7 May 1998. Should payments be made by the Republic of Venezuela before this date, she may adjust the calculation of interest according to the number of days lapsed."

Decision of the Tribunal on Objections to Jurisdiction, 24 May 1999

Arbitrators:	Prof. Thomas Buergenthal (President); Prof. Piero Bernardini; Prof. Andreas Bucher
Parties:	Claimant: Ceskoslovenska Obchodni Banka, A.S. (Czech Republic) Respondent: The Slovak Republic
Place of arbitration:	Washington, DC, USA
Published in:	14 ICSID Review - Foreign Investment Law Journal (1999, no. 1) pp. 250-283
Subject matters:	- nationality of another Contracting State - consent to ICSID jurisdiction - bilateral investment treaty - investor

Facts

Following the separation of the Czech and Slovak Republics, the bank, Ceskoslovenska Obchodni Banka, A.S. (CSOB), was privatised. A Consolidation Agreement was concluded which was designed to facilitate the privatization of CSOB by providing, inter alia, for the assignment by CSOB of certain non-performing loan portfolio receivables to two so-called "Collection Companies", to be established in each of the two Republics. The Consolidation Agreement also stipulated that each Collection Company was to pay CSOB for the assigned receivables. To enable them to do so, each Collection Company was to receive the necessary funds from CSOB under the terms of separate loan agreements, such loans to be paid down in accordance with a stipulated repayment schedule.

The Collection Companies were established and CSOB and the Slovak Collection Company concluded the "Loan Agreement on the Refinancing of Assigned Receivables" (Loan Agreement) effective 31 December 1993. Sect. 7 of this Agreement, entitled "Security", referred to the Consolidation Agreement and declared that pursuant to the latter agreement, "the repayment of the loan including interest thereon is secured by an obligation of the Ministry of Finance of the Slovak Republic".

Disputes arose between CSOB and the Slovak Republic regarding losses incurred by the Slovak Collection Company (Slovenska inkasni spol. s.r.o.) and on 18 April 1997, CSOB filed a Request for Arbitration with ICSID, alleging that the Slovak Republic had failed to cover the losses incurred by the Slovak Collection Company. The request was registered by the Centre on 25 April 1997.

CSOB relied on the 1965 Washington Convention to which both the Czech and Slovak Republics are parties, the Czech Republic as of 22 April 1993 and the Slovak Republic as of 26 June 1994. CSOB based the Centre's jurisdiction on three grounds. First, it contended that the Agreement between the Government of the Slovak Republic and the Government of the Czech Republic Regarding the Promotion and Reciprocal Protection of Investments (Bilateral Investment Treaty or BIT), signed on 23 November 1992 had entered into force on 1 January 1993 and that Art. 8(2) thereof conferred jurisdiction on the Centre to hear the dispute. Art. 8 of the BIT reads:

> "1. Any dispute which may arise between the investor of one Party and the other Party in relation to any investments made in the territory of such other Party, shall be subject to negotiations between the parties to the dispute.
>
> 2. If the dispute between the investor of one Party and the other Party continues after a period of three months, the investor and the Party shall have the right to submit the dispute to either:
> a) the International Centre for the Resolution of Investment-Related Disputes with special regard to the applicable provisions of the [1965 Washington Convention], provided, however, that both Parties are parties to such Treaty; or
> b) an arbitrator or an ad hoc international arbitration tribunal established in accordance with the [UNCITRAL] Arbitration Rules.... The arbitration award shall be final and binding on both parties to the dispute.
>
> 3. The dispute shall be resolved by such agency referred to in Section 2 above as was the first one to which a proposal for the resolution of the dispute was submitted."

CSOB further contended that even if the BIT had not entered into force as between the two Contracting States, it was binding on the Slovak Republic by virtue of the fact that the Slovak Foreign Ministry, in a Notice published on 22 October 1993 in the Official Gazette of the Slovak Republic, declared that the BIT had entered into force on 1 January 1993.

Finally, CSOB contended that Art. 7 of the Consolidation Agreement incorporated the BIT by reference because it provided that "this Agreement shall be governed by the laws of the Czech Republic and the [BIT] dated 23 November 1992". CSOB argued that the incorporation bound the Slovak Republic, regardless of whether the BIT itself had entered into force.

The Slovak Republic contested the jurisdiction of the Centre, contending that Art. 25(1) of the 1965 Washington Convention had not been complied with. In the view of the Slovak Republic, CSOB was merely an agent of the Czech Republic and the subsequent assignments to the Czech Republic of CSOB's interest in the receivables, which constituted the subject matter of the dispute, transformed the Czech Republic into the real party in interest in the dispute.

The Slovak Republic also contended that written consent to arbitration was lacking because: 1) the BIT had never entered into force; 2) the notice in the Official Gazette did not bring the BIT into force; 3) the clause in the BIT referring to the Consolidation Agreement did not constitute effective consent because the BIT was not in force; and 4) even if the BIT were in force, the parties had not jointly invoked Art. 8, nor was this an investment dispute.

During the proceedings leading to the decision on jurisdiction, CSOB requested a number of provisional measures seeking the suspension of bankruptcy proceedings pending against the Slovak Collection Company in Slovak courts. The Tribunal, in Procedural Order No. 4 recommended the suspension of the bankruptcy proceedings "to the extent that such proceedings might include determinations as to whether the [Slovak Collection Company] has a valid claim in the form of a right to receive funds from the Slovak Republic to cover its losses as contemplated in the Consolidation Agreement at issue in this arbitration."

The Tribunal found that it did have jurisdiction. Although it could not be shown that the BIT had entered into force, by referring to the BIT in the Consolidation Agreement, the parties had intended to incorporate Art. 8 of the BIT into it as their chosen dispute-settlement method. Further, in the view of the Tribunal, the Consolidation Agreement involved a significant contribution by CSOB to the economic development of the Slovak Republic and qualified CSOB as an investor.

Excerpt

I. IS CLAIMANT A NATIONAL OF A CONTRACTING STATE?

[1] "The first ground on which respondent challenges the jurisdiction of the Centre and the competence of the Tribunal is that claimant does not meet that requirement of Art. 25(1),[1] which provides that the dispute must be between a Contracting State and a national of another Contracting State. According to respondent, the instant dispute is between two Contracting States because: a) claimant is a state agency of the Czech Republic rather than an independent commercial entity; and b) the real party in interest to this dispute is the Czech Republic."

1. National of Another Contracting State

[2] "The language of Art. 25(1) of the Convention makes clear that the Centre does not have jurisdiction over disputes between two or more Contracting States. Instead, the dispute settlement mechanism set up by the Convention is designed to deal with disputes between Contracting States and nationals of other Contracting States. Although the concept of 'national', as that term is used in Art. 25(1), is in Art. 25(2) declared to include both natural and juridical persons, neither term is defined as such in the Convention. The

1. Art. 25 of the 1965 Washington Convention reads in relevant part:

"(1) The jurisdiction of the Centre shall extend to any legal dispute arising directly out of an investment, between a Contracting State ... and a national of another Contracting State, which the parties to the dispute consent in writing to submit to the Centre. When the parties have given their consent, no party may withdraw its consent unilaterally.
(2) 'National of another Contracting State' means:
(....)
(b) any juridical person which had the nationality of a Contracting State other than the State party to the dispute on the date on which the parties consented to submit such dispute to conciliation or arbitration and any juridical person which had the nationality of the Contracting State party to the dispute on that date and which, because of foreign control, the parties have agreed should be treated as a national of another Contracting State for the purposes of this Convention.
(....)
(4) Any Contracting State may, at the time of ratification, acceptance or approval of this Convention or at any time thereafter, notify the Centre of the class or classes of disputes which it would or would not consider submitting to the jurisdiction of the Centre. The Secretary-General shall forthwith transmit such notification to all Contracting States. Such notification shall not constitute the consent required by paragraph (1)."

legislative history of the Convention does provide some answers, however, that bear on the issues presented in this case. It indicates that the term 'juridical persons' as employed in Art. 25 and, hence, the concept of 'national', was not intended to be limited to privately-owned companies, but to embrace also wholly or partially government-owned companies. This interpretation has found general acceptance.

[3] "It follows that the question whether a company qualifies as a 'national of another Contracting State' within the meaning of Art. 25(1) does not depend upon whether or not the company is partially or wholly owned by the government. Instead, the accepted test for making this determination has been formulated as follows: '... for purposes of the Convention a mixed economy company or government-owned corporation should not be disqualified as a "national of another Contracting State" unless it is acting as an agent for the government or is discharging an essentially governmental function'. Both parties to this dispute accept this test as determinative.

[4] "The soundness of respondent's contention that claimant is not 'a national of another Contracting State' must therefore be judged by reference to this test. Standing alone, respondent's submission that more than 65% of CSOB's shares are owned in one form or another by the Czech Republic and that some 24% are owned by the Slovak Republic demonstrate that CSOB is a public sector rather than a private sector entity, does not address the here crucial issue. Neither does the submission that the Czech Republic's 65% stock ownership gives it absolute control over CSOB. For, as has been shown above, such ownership or control alone will not disqualify a company under the here relevant test from filing a claim with the Centre as 'a national of another Contracting State'.

[5] "Respondent does not, however, rest this aspect of its case solely on the above arguments. It contends further that CSOB is a government agency which has been discharging essentially governmental functions throughout its existence and, more specifically, with regard to all events pertinent to this dispute. In this regard, respondent seeks to show that since its inception CSOB has served as agent or representative of the State to the international banking and trading community, that its subsequent reorganization has not changed its status, and that, moreover, the instant dispute arises out of the functions CSOB performed in that capacity.

[6] "It cannot be denied that for much of its existence, CSOB acted on behalf of the State in facilitating or executing the international banking transactions and foreign commercial operations the State wished to support and that the State's control of CSOB required it to do the State's bidding in that regard. But in determining whether CSOB, in discharging these functions, exercised governmental functions, the focus must be on the nature of these activities and

not their purpose. While it cannot be doubted that in performing the above-mentioned activities, CSOB was promoting the governmental policies or purposes of the State, the activities themselves were essentially commercial rather than governmental in nature.

[7] "In also appears that beginning in the early 1990's and following the 1989 'Velvet Revolution', as the State began to transform its command economy into a market economy, CSOB took various steps to gradually throw off its exclusive economic dependence on the State and to adopt measures to enable it to function in this new economic environment as an independent commercial bank. By 1993, CSOB seemed to have basically achieved that purpose, although its competitive position continued to be adversely affected by the existence on its books of non-performing receivables. These receivables, which became the subject of the Consolidation Agreement and play a role in the instant dispute, grew out of CSOB's earlier lending activities during the State's non-market economy period. Although these activities were driven by State policies, as was true generally of economic activities during the country's command economy, the banking transactions themselves that implemented these policies did not thereby lose their commercial nature. They cannot therefore be characterized as governmental in nature. Moreover, even if one were to conclude that the non-performing assets derived from activities conducted by CSOB as an agent of the State, the measures taken by CSOB to remove them from its books in order to improve its balance and consolidate its financial position in accordance with the provisions of the Consolidation Agreement, must be deemed to be commercial in character.

[8] "In support of its contention that the dispute is between two Contracting States, respondent also submits that the ultimate goal of the Consolidation Agreement was the privatization of CSOB. Characterizing privatization as a State function, respondent argues that in concluding the Consolidation Agreement, CSOB was performing State functions and could therefore not claim to be a private investor. In this connection, respondent submits that

> 'The principal ingredient in the Consolidation Agreement preparing CSOB for privatization was the proposed removal of the poor-quality assets resulting from CSOB's role in financing the Czechoslovak State's foreign trade.... The whole structure of Consolidated Agreement, Loan Agreement and Collection Companies, which is central to this arbitration, was thus conceived and implemented with the express purpose of facilitating CSOB's privatization.'

[9] "It cannot be denied that a State's decision to transform itself from a command economy to a free market economy involves the exercise of govern-

mental functions. The same is no doubt true of legislative and administrative measures adopted by the State that are designed to enable or facilitate the privatization of State-owned enterprises. It does not follow, however, that a State-owned enterprise is performing State functions when it takes advantage of these State policies and proceeds to restructure itself, with or without governmental cooperation, in order to be in a position to compete in a free market economy. Nor does it follow that the measures taken by such an enterprise to achieve this objective involve the performance of State or governmental functions. In both instances, the test as to whether or not the acts are governmental or private turn on their nature.

[10] "There appears to be some disagreement between the parties to this case as to whether the conclusion of the Consolidation Agreement and the Loan Agreement was driven by or was part of the privatization process instituted by the Government or whether it was the result largely of CSOB's unrelated business decision to strengthen its financial position. The Tribunal does not believe that it matters which of these views is accepted, for whether CSOB's actions were or were not driven by the privatization process set in motion or facilitated by the State is not determinative of the issue to be decided. What is determinative is the nature of these acts.

[11] "In the instant case, the steps taken by CSOB to solidify its financial position in order to attract private capital for its restructured banking enterprise do not differ in their nature from measures a private bank might take to strengthen its financial position. It is no doubt true that CSOB's ability to negotiate the Consolidation Agreement and Loan Agreements on favorable conditions can be attributed to the interest both the Czech and Slovak Governments had in seeing CSOB survive in a free market environment and continue to provide needed banking services. But that fact does not transform the otherwise commercial or private transactions here at issue into governmental acts.

[12] "Finally, in support of its submission that the instant dispute is between two States Parties, respondent contends that all the parties to the Consolidation Agreement are State entities and they include, in addition to CSOB and the Czech and Slovak Republics, the Czech National Bank, the Czech National Property Fund and the National Bank of Slovakia. Even assuming, without deciding, that these other entities had also become parties to the Consolidation Agreement, this fact would not weaken or overcome the Tribunal's conclusions, set out in the preceding paragraphs, about the commercial character of the Consolidation Agreement or the functions CSOB performed.

[13] "The Tribunal concludes, accordingly, that respondent has failed to sustain its contention that the Centre lacks jurisdiction and the Tribunal

competence to hear this case on the ground that claimant was acting as an agent of the State or discharging essentially governmental activities as far as this dispute is concerned. This is so whether or not this determination is made by reference to the date of the conclusion of the Consolidation Agreement (19 December 1993) or the date when the Request for Arbitration was registered by the Centre (25 April 1997)."

2. *Real Party in Interest*

[14] "Respondent next points to two assignments, dated 24 April 1998 and 25 June 1998, respectively, which CSOB concluded with the Czech Ministry of Finance. These assignments, according to respondent, have transformed the Czech Republic – the assignee – into the real party in interest to the instant arbitration by relieving CSOB of the economic risk arising from the claims relating to the Slovak Collection Company receivables. Respondent argues that the assignments require the Tribunal to dismiss the case for lack of jurisdiction because claimant no longer has the requisite standing under Art. 25(1) and because the Czech Republic is disqualified under the same provision from stepping into CSOB's shoes.

[15] "In view of the fact that the first assignment has been fully superseded by the second, the Tribunal needs to focus here only on the latter. In that instrument CSOB agrees to assign to the Czech Republic on a so-called 'effective date' all claims CSOB has against the Slovak Collection Company relating to the receivables transferred to the latter under the Loan Agreement as well as the claims CSOB has against the Slovak Republic under the Consolidation Agreement. The 'effective date' is three days after the date on which the assignee receives in writing assignor's request for the delivery of the receivables and the rights attaching thereto. However, the assignee does not have the right to request the assignment prior to the completion of the instant arbitration proceedings.

[16] "The specified 'consideration' which assignee is required to pay to assignor consists of an amount equal to 90% of the nominal value of the receivables as of 31 December 2002. This payment is to be made within three days following the termination of the arbitration proceedings, but no earlier than the above mentioned date. If the arbitration should not be completed by 31 December 2002, assignee is required to increase that amount to a 'deposit' of 100% of the agreed upon nominal value of the receivables. On the other hand, if the assignor should receive any payment in settlement of the receivables, the consideration is to be reduced by 75% of the amount so received. The assignor is entitled to 25% of any amounts received by assignee

following the assignment in repayment of the assigned receivables paid after 31 December 2002, and 10% before 1 January 2003.

[17] "In assessing the effect of the 25 June 1998 assignment (and of the 24 April 1998 assignment it superseded) on the Centre's jurisdiction to hear this dispute, the Tribunal notes, in the first place, that the Request for Arbitration in the instant case was filed on 17 April 1997 and that the case was registered on 25 April 1997. Hence, at the time when these proceedings were instituted, neither of these assignments had been concluded. Second, it is generally recognized that the determination whether a party has standing in an international judicial forum for purposes of jurisdiction to institute proceedings is made by reference to the date on which such proceedings are deemed to have been instituted. Since the claimant instituted these proceedings prior to the time when the two assignments were concluded, it follows that the Tribunal has jurisdiction to hear this case regardless of the legal effect, if any, the assignments might have had on claimant's standing had they preceded the filing of the case.

[18] "In the light of what has just been said, it is not really necessary for the Tribunal to address respondent's contention that the assignments here in question transformed the Czech Republic into the real party in interest because it became, for all practical purposes, the beneficial owner of the disputed claims and because claimant, as a result, no longer has a real economic interest in the outcome of these proceedings. But even if the Tribunal, for purposes of the argument, were to accept this contention, it would not follow that this case would have to be dismissed for lack of jurisdiction. This conclusion is compelled by the consideration that absence of beneficial ownership by a claimant in a claim or the transfer of the economic risk in the outcome of a dispute should not and has not been deemed to affect the standing of a claimant in an ICSID proceeding, regardless whether or not the beneficial owner is a State Party or a private party. It must be emphasized, moveover, that the second assignment does not deprive claimant of an interest in the outcome of the case because the assignment becomes effective only after these proceedings terminate and because the assignor remains entitled to a share (either 25 or 10%) of the amount received by the assignee."

II. CONSENT TO ICSID JURISDICTION

[19] "Under the system created by the ICSID Convention, consent by both parties is an indispensable condition for the exercise of the Centre's jurisdiction under Art. 25(1). The Convention only requires that consent be in writing, leaving the parties otherwise free to choose the manner in which to

express their consent. Although the most common form of consent is an agreement recorded in a single instrument, other expressions of consent are equally valid, provided they are in writing.

[20] "In determining how to interpret agreements to arbitrate under the ICSID Convention, the Tribunal is guided by an ICSID decision which held that

> 'a convention to arbitrate is not to be construed *restrictively*, nor, as a matter of act, *broadly* or *liberally*. It is to be construed in a way which leads to find out and to respect the common will of the parties.... Moreover,... any convention, including conventions to arbitrate, should be construed in good faith, that is to say by taking into account the consequences of the commitments the parties may be considered as having reasonably and legitimately envisaged.'[2]

[21] "The question of whether the parties have effectively expressed their consent to ICSID jurisdiction is not to be answered by reference to national law. It is governed by international law as set out in Art. 25(1) of the ICSID Convention.

[22] "In the instant case, claimant invokes ICSID jurisdiction by pointing to three independent bases of consent, namely: a) the Bilateral Investment Treaty (BIT) as an international treaty in force between the two States; b) the notice published by the Ministry of Foreign Affairs of the Slovak Republic in the Official Gazette on 22 October 1993 (the Notice), announcing the entry into force of the BIT on 1 January 1993; and c) the reference to the BIT in the Consolidation Agreement."

1. *The BIT*

[23] "The question whether the BIT is in force is relevant in the instant case since Art. 8 of the BIT contains an ICSID arbitration clause. If the BIT entered into force on 1 January 1993 or on some other date, the Slovak Republic would be bound by the consent so given, because Art. 8 provides for the settlement of investment disputes at the option of the party initiating the arbitration proceedings, either under the ICSID Convention or the Arbitration Rules of the United Nations Commission on International Trade Law (UNCITRAL).

2. "*Amco Asia et al. v. Indonesia*, Decision on Jurisdiction of 25 September 1983, 23 ILM 359 (1984) [reported in Yearbook X (1995) pp 61-71]."

[24] "Since claimant by its Request for Arbitration, dated 18 April 1997, submitted the instant dispute to ICSID, claimant would be deemed to have accepted ICSID jurisdiction on that date, respondent having already unequivocally consented to it. The exchange of consents in this form would satisfy the requirement of a 'written consent' under Art. 25(1) of the ICSID Convention. This type of consent has been accepted as a valid submission to the Centre's jurisdiction in the first case brought by an investor under a bilateral investment treaty,[3] and has found acceptance in subsequent practice.[4]

[25] "The elements of proof presented by claimant and respondent on the question whether the BIT has entered into force are by no means conclusive enough to permit a definite answer. Art. 12 of the BIT provides that 'each Party shall give notice to the other Party of the completion of the constitutional formalities required for this Agreement to enter into force'. In the Tribunal's view, this language shows that the parties were aware and mutually recognized that the signature of the BIT by the two heads of government was not sufficient to bring the treaty into force and that further formalities were required under the respective constitutions. Whether or not such constitutional formalities needed to be complied with as a matter of domestic law – an issue on which the parties disagree – is relatively immaterial, considering the above-quoted stipulation included in the 'Entry into force' provision of the BIT. This provision must be deemed to have some meaning as required under the principle of effectiveness (*effet utile*). It may, consequently, not be disregarded as contemplating a mere procedural formality not affecting the coming into force of the BIT. This is so particularly when the language is read in the light of Art. 24(1) of the Vienna Convention on the Law of Treaties (the Vienna Convention), which provides that 'a treaty enters into force in such manner and upon such date as it may provide or as the negotiating States may agree'. The Tribunal notes, in this connection, that the parties agree that no such exchange of notices has taken place. The documents on file in this case indicate, moreover, that this is also the position of the Czech Republic.

[26] "In its pleadings, claimant has made reference to Art. 46 of the Vienna Convention. Under that provision a State's right to invoke the fact that its consent to be bound by a treaty violates a provision of its internal law regarding competence to conclude treaties is limited to cases in which such violation was manifest, that is, 'if it would be objectively evident to any State conducting itself in the matter in accordance with normal practice and in good

---

3. "*Asian Agricultural Products Ltd. (AAPL) v. Republic of Sri Lanka*, 4 ICSID Rep. 245, 30 ILM 577 (1991) [reported in Yearbook XVII (1992) pp. 106-152]."

4. "C. Schreuer, 'Commentary on the ICSID Convention: Article 25', 11 ICSID Rev. – Foreign Investment L.J. 441 (1996)."

faith'. However, this provision deals with the 'Invalidity of Treaties', whereas the Slovak Republic claims that the BIT never came into force due to the non-compliance with its Art. 12. The Slovak Republic does not claim that the treaty is invalid, although that assertion was made in the corrective notice published by the Slovak Ministry of Foreign Affairs in the Official Gazette on 20 November 1997.

[27] "The second sentence of Art. 12 of the BIT provides that the treaty shall come into force as of the date of the division of the two Republics. Claimant contends that this provision should prevail over the above-quoted procedural formalities calling for the exchange of notices signalling the completion of the constitutional requirement found in the first sentence of Art. 12, especially because both States knew that the division would occur on 1 January 1993. Respondent submits, on the other hand, that this provision should be interpreted to mean that once the exchange of notices contemplated by the first sentence had taken place, the treaty would be effective as of the date of division, the division being another condition for the coming into force of the BIT. In the Tribunal's view, respondent's interpretation is more consistent with the requirements of the principle of effectiveness than is claimant's submission on that subject.

(....)

[28] "The Tribunal accordingly holds that the uncertainties relating to the entry into force of the BIT prevent that instrument from providing a sound basis upon which to found the parties' consent to ICSID jurisdiction."

2. *The Notice*

[29] "ICSID practice also indicates that the exchange of written consents required for ICSID jurisdiction can be satisfied not only by the mutual acceptances of bilateral investment treaties, but also by other forms of acceptances. Many investment laws of developing countries provide for the State's acceptance of ICSID jurisdiction (or for alternative dispute resolution methods) for disputes with the investor arising out of a particular investment. Under some laws the offer is deemed to be accepted as soon as the foreign investor files an investment application pursuant to such a law, regardless of whether the application includes a reference to the arbitration provision contained in the law. The aforementioned laws differ from the present case in that the offer of consent by the Slovak State is not contained in a domestic legislative act (or an international treaty in force for that State) but, rather, in a notice of the Ministry of Foreign Affairs of the Slovak Republic, published in the Official Gazette, announcing that the BIT had entered into force on 1 January 1993. (footnote omitted)

[30] "Respondent contends that the publication of the BIT in the Official Gazette did not result in its entry into force, nor give that treaty any other legal effect under Slovak law. Claimant, on the other hand, considers the publication to constitute a sufficient basis upon which to found the Slovak Republic's consent to ICSID jurisdiction, even if the underlying legal instrument (the BIT) did not enter into force. In this connection, it should be noted that if the Notice were to be held to constitute a valid offer by the Slovak State to submit to international arbitration, the corrective notice published by the Slovak Ministry of Foreign Affairs in the Official Gazette on 20 November 1997, asserting the invalidity of the BIT, would be of no avail to respondent, since claimant accepted the offer in the Request for Arbitration filed prior to the publication of the corrective notice.

[31] "It must now be determined whether the original Notice published in the Official Gazette provides a sufficient basis for holding the Slovak State to be bound under Art. 8 of the BIT. Even if the Notice were to be characterized as a unilateral declaration by the Slovak State, it still needs to be asked whether it was 'the intention of the State making the declaration that it should become bound according to its terms', as required by the international law principles applicable to unilateral declarations.[5] Pursuant to these principles, unilateral assumption of the contractual obligations is 'not lightly to be presumed...' and requires 'a very consistent course of conduct.'[6] As noted by one authoritative source, 'while the principle applied by the [International] Court [of Justice] – that a unilateral declaration may have certain legal effects – is not new, when the declaration is not directed to a specific state or states but is expressed *erga omnes*, as here, the detection of an intention to be legally bound, and of the structure of such intention, involves very careful appreciation of the facts'.[7] Given this standard, the Tribunal considers that the Slovak Republic's intention to be bound by the treaty through the Notice has not been established. This is so particularly when it is recalled that the entry into force of the treaty appears to have been conditioned on an exchange of notices which, as we have seen did not take place. (See [25], supra).

[32] "The Tribunal must now turn to the question whether the Slovak State is estopped because of the Notice from denying that it is bound by the arbitration offer under the BIT. An essential element of estoppel is that 'there must be reliance in good faith upon the statement either to the detriment of

---

5. "Nuclear Tests Case (Australia v. France), I.C.J. Reports 1974, p. 253 at 274. See also Case Concerning Military and Paramilitary Activities in and against Nicaragua (Nicaragua v. United States of America), I.C.J. Reports 1986, p. 14 at 13 Nuclear 2."
6. "North Sea Continental Shelf Cases, I.C.J. Reports 1969, p. 4 at 25."
7. "I. Brownlie, *Public International Law* 638-639 (4th ed. 1990)."

the party so relying on the statement or to the advantage of the party making the statement'.[8] Claimant nowhere alleged that it was misled by respondent or that it relied on any allegedly misleading statements by respondent and that it was prejudiced as a consequence of such reliance. Instead, it is clear from a draft of the Consolidation Agreement, prepared by CSOB after the date of the Notice, that it relied neither on the BIT being in force nor on the fact that Art. 8 thereof had become binding on the Slovak State. In that draft, CSOB initially proposed arbitration in Prague and referred to the BIT 'after it is ratified'. (See [35] infra.)

[33] "Since the second basis for consent to ICSID jurisdiction has not been established, the Tribunal must now examine claimant's third basis for establishing such consent."

3. *The Consolidation Agreement*

[34] "The Consolidation Agreement, entered into between the parties to these proceedings (the question of identifying all parties to the Agreement being immaterial for the purposes of the present analysis), provides in the relevant part of Art. 7 that 'this Agreement shall be governed by the laws of the Czech Republic and the Treaty on the Promotion and Mutual Protection of Investments between the Czech Republic and the Slovak Republic dated 23 November 1992'. It must, therefore, be determined whether this reference to the BIT must be deemed to constitute acceptance by the Slovak Republic of ICSID jurisdiction. Specifically, the question to be resolved is whether the consent required under the ICSID Convention can be satisfied by a reference to a treaty that is not in force on the international plane.

[35] "The parties have expressed conflicting views regarding the significance of the reference to the BIT in the Consolidation Agreement. Claimant contends that it is immaterial whether the reference is characterized as a choice-of-law clause or an incorporation by reference. To claimant, the decisive question is whether the provision can be interpreted as an agreement to submit to ICSID jurisdiction. Relying on the text of the clause and its reference to the BIT, claimant contends that it constitutes an incorporation by reference of ICSID jurisdiction. Respondent submits that the reference to the BIT is made in the context of a choice-of-law provision, with both Czech law and the BIT equally governing the interpretation of the contract. Since the BIT never came into force, the reference to it should be disregarded. Respondent further contends that even if Art. 7 of the Consolidation Agreement were to be

8. "Brownlie, supra at 641. See also B. Cheng, *General Principles of Law as Applied by International Courts and Tribunals* 141 et seq. (1987)."

interpreted as an incorporation by reference, the reference itself cannot be deemed to amount to consent to arbitration. In support of this contention, respondent points, inter alia, to the UNCITRAL's Model Law on International Commercial Arbitration of 21 June 1985, whose Art. 7(2) states in part:

> 'The reference in a contract to a document containing an arbitration clause constitutes an arbitration agreement provided that the contract is in writing and the reference is such as to make that clause part of the contract.'

[36] "The negotiating history of the provision under examination offers elements permitting the Tribunal to determine the parties' common intent regarding the issue here under consideration. The documents submitted by the parties show that the Consolidation Agreement was the subject of various drafts due to changes requested by respondent. This latter circumstance provides a sufficient basis for rejecting respondent's argument that the *contra proferentem* rule should be applied against claimant by holding that the reference to the BIT in Art. 7 of the Consolidation Agreement does not embody consent to ICSID jurisdiction.

[37] "It is uncontested and fully borne out by the record that in reply to a draft of the Consolidation Agreement submitted by the Slovak Republic on or about 15 November 1993, containing neither a governing law clause nor a dispute-settlement provision, CSOB proposed various drafts in the period between 15 November-17 December 1993, including a governing law provision referring to Czech law only and an arbitration clause referring disputes to the Arbitration Tribunal of the Chamber of Commerce and Industry in Prague. The latter reference was not accepted by respondent. After further revision the parties agreed to a final draft, which included the following provision:

> 'This agreement shall be governed by the laws of the Czech Republic and the Treaty on the promotion and mutual protection of investments between the Czech Republic and the Slovak Republic after it is ratified.'

The final draft of the Consolidation Agreement makes no express reference to arbitration or to any other method of dispute settlement, but before it was signed on 17/19 December 1993, the above provision was amended by deleting the words 'after it is ratified' and by replacing it with the date of the signature of the BIT.

[38] "The parties have given different explanations for this amendment. For the purposes of the present analysis, it is relevant to note, first, that the issue of the settlement of disputes through arbitration was raised in the negotiations

leading up to the conclusion of the Consolidation Agreement; that a clause proposed by CSOB on that subject was rejected by the Slovak Republic; and that the final text as agreed by the parties contains no separate arbitration clause, although it does make reference to the BIT which provides for a dispute settlement method that permits resort either to the ICSID Convention or the UNCITRAL Arbitration Rules. Second, the reference in the final draft to the BIT 'after it is ratified' would have justified the conclusion that the acceptance of the arbitration provision was conditioned upon the BIT's coming into force at international level; however, the phrase relating to ratification was eliminated from the signed text.

[39] "The negotiating history of the clause under consideration thus indicates that the issue of the dispute settlement method had been discussed by the parties and that the proposal to resort to domestic arbitration in the Czech Republic had been rejected by the Slovak party. These considerations support claimant's contention that the parties eventually agreed on international arbitration. In the absence of a separate dispute resolution provision, the reference to the BIT satisfies the requirement that international arbitration, as specified in its Art. 8, is the agreed dispute resolution mechanism. This reference cannot be understood to mean that the contested provision was intended to deal exclusively with the governing law question, as respondent contends, if only because by eliminating the phrase relating to the BIT's ratification, the parties made the reference to the BIT and to the consent to arbitration expressed by it effective and unconditional. As a matter of fact, the elimination of the phrase may be deemed to indicate either that the parties were convinced that the BIT was already in force (the Notice announcing the BIT's status had appeared less than two months before) or, what is more likely, that they intended the reference to the BIT to be a valid expression of consent for purposes of their contract, including the provision for the settlement of disputes, independently of the BIT's entry into force on the international plane.

[40] "The Tribunal concludes, therefore, that by referring to the BIT, the parties intended to incorporate Art. 8 of the BIT by reference into the Consolidation Agreement, in order to provide for international arbitration as their chosen dispute-settlement method. The soundness of this conclusion is confirmed by the fact that the provisions of the BIT were well known to the negotiators for both parties.

[41] "Respondent also contends that even if the BIT is held to be applicable, its dispute-settlement mechanism under Art. 8 can be invoked only by means of a joint submission of the dispute by the parties either to an ICSID arbitration tribunal or to a tribunal established under the UNCITRAL Arbitration Rules. Since claimant has not sought ICSID arbitration jointly with res-

pondent, the latter submits that the requirements of Art. 8 of the BIT have not been satisfied.

[42] "Respondent's contention, which is based on its translation of the Czech and Slovak texts of Art. 8, has been convincingly refuted by expert evidence presented by claimant. The Tribunal also notes that in its last submission, respondent itself admits that the wording of Art. 8 is 'ambiguous'. Moreover, a holding that the parties must submit their dispute to arbitration jointly would amount to a finding that the terms of Art. 8 of the BIT, even if otherwise effective for purposes of ICSID jurisdiction, do not provide for binding arbitration unless the parties agree to arbitration if and when a dispute arises. As correctly pointed out by claimant, such an interpretation would leave investors without the protection afforded by international arbitration, contrary to the main objective of bilateral investment treaties. The fact that some such treaties may contain provisions for joint submission of disputes to arbitration does not compel the conclusion that provisions whose wording is at best ambiguous must be interpreted in like manner. Such a construction of the terms of a treaty would be incompatible with the applicable international rules for the interpretation of these types of agreements (Vienna Convention, Art. 31(1)).

[43] "The Tribunal notes, furthermore, that Art. 8(3) of the BIT provides that whichever of the two dispute-settlement facilities envisaged under Art. 8(2) – ICSID or the UNCITRAL Rules – first receives a dispute shall resolve it. The language of this provision makes sense only if it is predicated on the assumption that each party to a dispute has the right separately to initiate the arbitration proceedings.

[44] "For all of the above reasons, the Tribunal holds that the parties have consented in the Consolidation Agreement to ICSID jurisdiction and that the date of such Agreement is, for all relevant purposes, the date of their consent. Since each party may separately institute the arbitration proceedings, claimant was entitled to elect ICSID jurisdiction."

III. IS THERE A LEGAL DISPUTE ARISING OUT OF AN INVESTMENT?

[45] "The Tribunal must now consider the objection raised by the Slovak Republic in which it challenges the jurisdiction of the Centre and the Tribunal's competence in this case on the ground that the dispute between the parties is not a 'legal dispute arising directly out of an Investment' as required by Art. 25(1) of the Convention.

[46] "The Slovak Republic stresses the political nature of the instant dispute and its close link with the dissolution of the former Czech and Slovak Federal

Republic, but it does not question the legal nature of the dispute. CSOB's claim is based on Art. 3 of the Consolidation Agreement. The Tribunal must therefore analyze the rights and obligations set forth therein, as well as the question whether CSOB is entitled to damages due to the breach of the obligations alleged to have been committed by the Slovak Republic. CSOB does not seek a determination relating to the division of assets and liabilities between the two Republics, a subject expressly excluded from the scope of the BIT by its Art. 11. While it is true that investment disputes to which a State is a party frequently have political elements or involve governmental actions, such disputes do not lose their legal character as long as they concern legal rights or obligations or the consequences of their breach. Given these considerations, the Tribunal is satisfied that CSOB's claim is legal in character.

[47] "The Slovak Republic bases its objection to the jurisdiction of the Centre and the competence of this Tribunal on the ground that the dispute in the instant case is not related to an 'investment' and, moreover, that it does not arise 'directly' out of an investment within the meaning of Art. 25(1) of the Convention.

[48] "It is common ground that the Convention does not define the term 'investment' and that various proposals to define it during the drafting negotiations failed. This fact is reflected in the Report of the Executive Directors of the World Bank, which noted that:

> '27. No attempt was made to define the term "investment" given the essential requirements of consent by the parties, and the mechanisms through which Contracting States can make known in advance, if they so desire, the classes of disputes which they would or would not consider submitted to the Centre (Art. 25(4)).'[9]

[49] "This statement also indicates that investment as a concept should be interpreted broadly because the drafters of the Convention did not impose any restrictions on its meaning. Support for a liberal interpretation of the question whether a particular transaction constitutes an investment is also found in the first paragraph of the Preamble to the Convention, which declares that 'the Contracting States [are] considering the need for international cooperation for economic development, and the role of private international investment therein'. This language permits an inference that an international transaction which contributes to cooperation designed to promote the economic development of a Contracting State may be deemed to be an investment as that term is understood in the Convention.

9. "1 ICSID Rep. 28 (1993)."

[50] "It is worth noting, in this connection, that a Contracting State that wishes to limit the scope of the Centre's jurisdiction can do so by making the declaration provided for in Art. 25(4) of the Convention. The Slovak Republic has not made such a declaration and has, therefore, submitted itself broadly to the full scope of the subject matter jurisdiction governed by the Convention.

[51] "It follows that an important element in determining whether a dispute qualifies as an investment under the Convention in any given case is the specific consent given by the parties. The parties' acceptance of the Centre's jurisdiction with respect to the rights and obligations arising out of their agreement therefore creates a strong presumption that they considered their transaction to be an investment within the meaning of the ICSID Convention.

[52] "The Tribunal must accordingly attach considerable significance to the reference made in Art. 7 of the Consolidation Agreement to the BIT and thus to the ICSID arbitration clause contained therein (Art. 8). The parties' acceptance of the relevance and applicability of the BIT to the Consolidation Agreement expresses their view that the latter transaction relates to an investment within the meaning of the BIT. The contrary conclusion would deprive the reference to the BIT in Art. 7 of the Consolidation Agreement of its meaning or *effet utile*.

[53] "The Slovak Republic is correct in pointing out, however, that an agreement of the parties describing their transaction as an investment is not, as such, conclusive in resolving the question whether the dispute involves an investment under Art. 25(1) of the Convention. The concept of an investment as spelled out in that provision is objective in nature in that the parties may agree on a more precise or restrictive definition of their acceptance of the Centre's jurisdiction, but they may not choose to submit disputes to the Centre that are not related to an investment. A two-fold test must therefore be applied in determining whether this Tribunal has the competence to consider the merits of the claim: whether the dispute arises out of an investment within the meaning of the Convention and, if so, whether the dispute relates to an investment as defined in the parties' consent to ICSID arbitration, in their reference to the BIT and the pertinent definitions contained in Art. 1 of the BIT.

[54] "CSOB's claim is based on the allegation that the Slovak Republic breached its obligation under the Consolidation Agreement by failing and refusing to cover the losses incurred by the Slovak Collection Company. Viewed in isolation, this undertaking does not involve any spending, outlays or expenditure of resources by CSOB in the Slovak Republic. Standing alone, therefore, it does not constitute an investment.

[55] "Claimant argues, however, that the loan made to the Slovak Collection Company qualifies as an investment and that the actual dispute is therefore

within the Centre's jurisdiction and the competence of this Tribunal. The Slovak Republic rejects the view that CSOB's loan is an investment and contends that the dispute does not arise directly out of the Loan Agreement. It submits that the dispute is concerned exclusively with the purported obligation of the Slovak Republic to cover the losses of the Slovak Collection Company.

[56] "The Slovak Republic's argument calls for an analysis of the meaning of the word 'directly' as used in that part of Art. 25(1) of the Convention which reads as follows: 'The jurisdiction of the Centre shall extend to any legal dispute arising directly out of an investment,...'. Here it is relevant to note that in the *Fedax* case, the Tribunal stated:

> 'It is apparent that the term "directly" relates in this Article to the "dispute" and not to the "investment". It follows that jurisdiction can exist even in respect of investments that are not direct, so long as the dispute arises directly from such transaction. This interpretation is also consistent with the broad reach that the term "investment" must be given in the light of the negotiating history of the Convention.'[10]

[57] "The Tribunal agrees with the interpretation adopted in the *Fedax* case. An investment is frequently a rather complex operation, composed of various interrelated transactions, each element of which, standing along, might not in all cases qualify as an investment. Hence, a dispute that is brought before the Centre must be deemed to arise directly out of an investment even when it is based on a transaction which, standing alone, would not qualify as an investment under the Convention, provided that the particular transaction forms an integral part of an overall operation that qualifies as an investment.[11]

[58] "The Preamble of the Convention confirms the foregoing interpretation. Here, after 'considering the need for international cooperation for economic development, and the role of private international investment therein', the Contracting Parties bear 'in mind the possibility that from time to time disputes may arise in connection with such investment between Contracting States and nationals of other Contracting States'.

[59] "The foregoing analysis indicates that the term 'directly', as used in Art. 25(1) of the Convention, should not be interpreted restrictively to compel the conclusion that CSOB's claim is outside the Centre's jurisdiction and the

10. "*Fedax N.V. v. Republic of Venezuela*, Decision on Objections to Jurisdiction, 11 July 1997, 37 ILM 1378, at para. [10] (1998) [reported in this volume of the Yearbook, pp. 23-62]."

11. "See ibid., paras. [12] and [13], and cases cited therein."

Tribunal's competence merely because it is based on an obligation of the Slovak Republic which, standing alone, does not qualify as an investment.

[60] "Hence, in deciding whether the obligation referred to in CSOB's requested relief forms part of an investment, the Tribunal has to determine whether the purported obligation of the Slovak Republic forms an integral part of a transaction which qualifies as an investment. The Slovak Republic's undertaking to cover the losses incurred by the Slovak Collection Company is closely linked to the loan provided by CSOB pursuant to Art. 3 of the Consolidation Agreement and the provisions of the Loan Agreement. This loan was basically designed to secure the refinancing of the Collection Company up to an amount corresponding to the payment by the Company of the value of the receivables assigned by CSOB on the basis of the schedule of payments covering the years 1995 to 2003. As stated in Art. 3 of the Consolidation Agreement, it follows from the nature of the assigned receivables, which are qualified therein as 'non-performing', that the Collection Company will incur a loss resulting from the operating costs of the Company and the schedule of payments, including interests, due to CSOB and the amounts eventually recovered from those described as 'non-performing' debtors. The purpose of the Slovak Republic's obligation to cover the loss of the Collection Company is therefore to allow this Company to meet its obligation towards CSOB under the schedule of payments based on the Loan Agreement. Given this close link, the dispute arising out of the alleged breach of the Slovak Republic's obligation is closely related to the loan made by CSOB to the Slovak Collection Company.

[61] "The Slovak Republic submits that loans as such do not qualify as investments under Art. 25(1) of the Convention, nor under Art. 1 of the BIT. It contends further that the loan in the instant case is not an investment because it did not involve a transfer of resources in the territory of the Slovak Republic. As to the first point, the Tribunal considers that the broad meaning which must be given to the notion of an investment under Art. 25(1) of the Convention is opposed to the conclusion that a transaction is not an investment merely because, as a matter of law, it is a loan. This is so, if only because under certain circumstances a loan may contribute substantially to a State's economic development. In this connection, claimant correctly points out that other ICSID Tribunals have affirmed their competence to deal with the merits of claims based on loan agreements.[12]

[62] "In support of its conclusion that the CSOB loan qualifies as an investment under the BIT, claimant points to Art. 1(1), which reads in part as follows:

---

12. "See, e.g., the *Fedax* case, paras. [8] and [16], supra."

> '1. "Investment" shall mean any asset invested or obtained by an investor of one Party in the territory of the other Party in accordance with the laws of the other Party, including, without limitation:...
> c) monetary receivables or claims to any performance related to an investment;...
> e) any rights under an act or under any contract, license or permit issued under an act, including any concession to search for, cultivate or exploit natural resources.'

Although loans are not expressly mentioned in this list, terms as broad as 'assets' and 'monetary receivables or claims' clearly encompass loans extended to a Slovak entity by a national of the other Contracting Party. Loans as such are therefore not excluded from the notion of an investment under Art. 1(1) of the BIT. It does not follow therefrom, however, that any loan and, in particular, the loan granted by CSOB to the Slovak Collection Company meets the requirements of an investment under Art. 25(1) of the Convention or, for that matter, under Art. 1(1) of the BIT, which speaks of an 'asset invested or obtained by an investor of one Party in the territory of the other Party'.

[63] "The Slovak Republic contends that the CSOB loan does not constitute an investment. It defines an investment essentially as the acquisition of property or assets through the expenditure of resources by one party (the 'investor') in the territory of a foreign country (the 'host State'), which is expected to produce a benefit on both sides and to offer a return in the future, subject to the uncertainties of the risk involved. While the Slovak Republic argues that the CSOB loan does not meet any elements of the above definition, CSOB submits that its loan qualifies as an investment thereunder. The Tribunal notes, in this connection, that while it is undisputed that CSOB's loan did not cause any funds to be moved or transferred from CSOB to the Slovak Collection Company in the territory of the Slovak Republic, a transaction can qualify as an investment even in the absence of a physical transfer of funds.[13]

[64] "Claimant argues that the loan provided the Slovak Collection Company with the funds necessary to settle the purchase price of the assigned receivables, and that these funds therefore represented an asset acquired by CSOB in the territory of the Slovak Republic. An analysis of the particular circumstances of this transaction indicates, however, that while CSOB's receivables against the Slovak Collection Company had a defined value, as determined in the loan agreement and the schedule of payments agreed upon by the parties, these

13. "Ibid., at para. [28], supra."

receivables had no corresponding value for the Slovak Collection Company. Indeed, the price to be paid by the Company to CSOB, that is, the return-payment of the advances received from CSOB under the loan facility, had value far above the expected recovery from the collection of the assigned non-performing receivables. To that extent, CSOB's loan did not involve any spending or outlay of resources in the territory of the Slovak Republic.
[65] "The contractual scheme embodied in the Consolidation Agreement shows, however, that the CSOB loan to the Slovak Collection Company is closely related to and cannot be disassociated from all other transactions involving the restructuring of CSOB. As stated in the first part of Art. 1, the Consolidation Agreement was designed to provide for 'the implementation of the project of the second phase of CSOB's transformation', and further:

> 'This process shall consist primarily of a financial consolidation of CSOB in preparation for the future privatization of CSOB. The consolidation of CSOB shall involve the improvement of CSOB's balance by the disposal of non-performing assets of CSOB to such level as agreed herein.'

Those provisions of Art. 1 that deal with the objects to be achieved show that the Agreement constituted the legal framework for a 'consolidation process' consisting of several interrelated actions, as defined in the second part of Art. 1:

> 'The following actions shall be taken as part of the consolidation process:
> I. An increase in the registered capital of CSOB;
> II. Improvement of the balance of CSOB, comprising:
> (a) the coverage of a part of the Non-Performing Assets of CSOB (as defined below) out of the profit and reserves;
> (b) the establishment of Collection Companies and the transfer of the Non-Performing Assets to such Collection Companies.
> III. The privatization of CSOB.'

[66] "The assignments of a part of CSOB's non-performing receivables to the respective Collection Company to be established in each Republic was thus an integral part of the whole process. This transfer improved CSOB's balance by crediting CSOB with payments equivalent to 'the nominal value of the assigned receivables, including any interest accrued until the time of the assignment', where as the Collection Company had to suffer the loss resulting 'from the nature of the assigned receivables'. (Art. 3.)

[67] "The sole or exclusive purpose of the CSOB loan was to ensure that the refinancing by the Collection Company of CSOB. The loan facility was therefore a mere instrument in ensuring the payment by the Collection Company of the nominal value of the assigned receivables, which was part of the improvement of CSOB's balance. This close link is further evidenced by the fact that CSOB's loan to the Collection Companies is part of the Consolidation Agreement concluded between CSOB and the Republics. (Art. 3.) Similarly, the Slovak Republic's undertaking to compensate its Collection Company for the losses made as a consequence of unsuccessful recoveries of the non-performing assets was instrumental to ensuring the refinancing of CSOB and thus to covering the payment of the assigned receivables up to their nominal value. This obligation of the Slovak Republic is also included in the terms of the Consolidation Agreement (Art. 3) and referred to in Art. 7 of the Loan Agreement.

[68] "The Slovak Republic's undertaking and the CSOB loan form an integrated whole in the process defined in the Consolidation Agreement. Hence, individual transactions comprising it may still meet the requirements of an investment under the Convention, provided the overall operation for the consolidation of CSOB, to which it is closely connected, qualifies as an investment.

[69] "The basic feature of the Consolidation Agreement was not the financial consolidation of CSOB as such, but the development of the role and activities of CSOB in both Republics. When considering the implementation of the second phase of CSOB's transformation, the parties to the Agreement referred to:

> 'The special position and role of CSOB is managing the central foreign exchange source for both Republics and in performing foreign banking transactions, and the extraordinary role that CSOB plays in the economy of both Republics... (Art. 1.)'

The second phase was to render CSOB more attractive to potential new shareholders from the private sector and thus prepare for the future privatization of CSOB. The ultimate goal of this process was to enable CSOB to exercise fully its role and to develop its activities in both Republics within the framework of a market economy.

[70] "The Slovak Republic is correct in submitting that both Republics undertook to initiate this process and to ensure the capital increase of CSOB as well as the funding necessary to cover the losses of the Collection Companies and, consequently, the refinancing of CSOB. These important financial contributions to the benefit of CSOB are not investments within the meaning of the

Convention, for they do not involve investments made in a Contracting State by a national of another Contracting State. This conclusion does not, however, resolve the issue whether or not CSOB qualifies as an 'investor' under the Consolidation Agreement. To answer that question, the Tribunal must focus on CSOB's role in achieving the ultimate goal of the Agreement, irrespective of whether or not the funds required to allow CSOB to exercise this role were provided by the Republics.

[71] "The function attributed to CSOB in the Consolidation Agreement was, as stated in the heading of Art. 5, the 'Development of CSOB in the Czech Republic and the Slovak Republic'. According to the first sentence of this provision, '[t]he development of CSOB in the Czech Republic and in the Slovak Republic shall reflect the needs of the Company and the interest of the shareholders in maximizing the value of CSOB.' This development was designed to improve what Art. 1 qualifies as 'the extraordinary role that CSOB plays in the economy of both Republics'.

[72] "The drafting history of the Consolidation Agreement shows that the Slovak Republic wished to ensure that CSOB would maintain and extend its activities on its territory. This conclusion finds support in the Slovak insistence on this point during the negotiations of the Agreement:

> 'The Slovak party demands guarantees of sound development of CSOB in the Slovak Republic, and makes the compensation of the collection company's losses conditional upon the honoring of such guarantees.'[14]

[73] "The Consolidation Agreement provides basically for the development of CSOB's activities in both Republics. A particular consideration was given to CSOB's role in the Slovak Republic in two respects. First, pursuant to the last sentence of Art. 5, the Czech National Bank (CNB), in consultation with the Ministry of Finance of the Czech Republic, 'shall enable CSOB to develop business in the Slovak Republic in line with the above principle by issuing a general foreign-exchange licence'. Second, the parties provide in Art. 6 for the establishment of a CSOB subsidiary domiciled in the Slovak Republic that would take over the entire range of banking services provided by the CSOB branch network in the Slovak Republic and enable CSOB to reduce its equity interest below 50%. Although this subsidiary has not as yet been created, there can be no doubt that the parties intended to strengthen CSOB as a leading entity in the Slovak banking sector. Since the Loan Agreement was concluded by CSOB's branch in Bratislava, CSOB's accounts receivable were recorded in

14. "Minutes of Interdepartmental Discussion of the Project of CSOB's Restructuring as Part of the Preparation for CSOB's Privatization on 21 October 1993."

the accounting books of that branch. They were to be paid in Slovak currency and constituted a working asset designed to enable CSOB to engage in business activities through its Slovak branches.

[74] "In the Tribunal's view, the basic and ultimate goal of the Consolidation Agreement was to ensure a continuing and expanding activity of CSOB in both Republics. This undertaking involved a significant contribution by CSOB to the economic development of the Slovak Republic, it qualified CSOB as an investor and the entire process as an investment in the Slovak Republic within the meaning of the Convention. This is evident from the fact that CSOB's undertakings include the spending or outlays of resources in the Slovak Republic in response to the need for the development of the Republic's banking infrastructure.

[75] "The Tribunal concludes, moreover, that the requirements spelled out in Art. 1(1) of the BIT for a qualifying investment are also met in the instant case. This must have been the view of the parties when they accepted a reference to the BIT in Art. 7 of the Consolidation Agreement. The contrary conclusion would deprive this reference to the BIT of any meaning (cf. [52]). Furthermore, CSOB's activity in the Slovak Republic and its undertaking to ensure a sound banking infrastructure in that country compel the conclusion that CSOB qualifies as the holder of an 'asset invested or obtained' in the territory of the Slovak Republic within the meaning of Art. 1(1) of the BIT, including 'movable and immovable property and any other encumbrances, including any mortgages, liens, guarantees, and similar rights' (Art. 1(1)(a)) and 'monetary receivables or claims to any performance related to an investment' (Art. 1(1)(c)).

[76] "Finally, applying the definition of an investment proffered by the Slovak Republic ([63], supra), it would seem that the resources provided through CSOB's banking activities in the Slovak Republic were designed to produce a benefit and to offer CSOB a return in the future, subject to an element of risk that is implicit in most economic activities. The Tribunal notes, however, that these elements of the suggested definition, while they tend as a rule to be present in most investments, are not a formal prerequisite for the finding that a transaction constitutes an investment as that concept is understood under the Convention.

[77] "The Tribunal concludes, accordingly, that CSOB's claim and the related loan facility made available to the Slovak Collection Company are closely connected to the development of CSOB's banking activity in the Slovak Republic and that they qualify as investments within the meaning of the Convention and the BIT."

IV. CONCLUSION

[78] "For all of the above reasons, the Tribunal unanimously decides that this dispute is within the jurisdiction of the Centre and the competence of the Tribunal. Accordingly, the Tribunal will issue the necessary Order for the continuation of the proceedings on the merits."

INTERNATIONAL CHAMBER OF COMMERCE

Final award in case no. 6497 of 1994

Parties:	Claimant: Consultant (Liechtenstein) Respondent: Contractor (Germany)
Place of arbitration:	Geneva, Switzerland
Published in:	Unpublished
Subject matters:	- proof of bribery - appointment of expert - power of arbitral tribunal to draw its own conclusions from failure of party to cooperate

Facts

Over a period of approximately ten years, the parties entered into a number of consultancy agreements designated as "Basic Agreements". The main object of those agreements was to provide the services of claimant for respondent to obtain construction contracts in a number of countries including a certain Middle Eastern country (country X). In their dealings, claimant was represented by its top manager, Mr. Z, and respondent was represented by Mr. B, a special representative chosen for this purpose, and acting under the authority of Mr. A, a member of respondent's board of directors. During this ten-year period, respondent obtained a number of contracts in country X. In conformity with the Basic Agreements, claimant was to receive a percentage of 1.5% of the amounts received by respondent. However, in addition to the Basic Agreements, the parties entered into a great number of specific 'Product Agreements', providing additional remuneration as well as, in some cases, new obligations for claimant. Claimant's remuneration over this period amounted to approximately 5.5% of the amounts received by respondent. The Basic Agreements as well as each Product Agreement contained a "termination date".

A dispute arose between the parties regarding the payment of the balance of the payments with respect to certain contracts. All these contracts contained an ICC arbitration clause and arbitration was initiated in Geneva. In the Terms of Reference, the parties agreed that Swiss law was applicable to the merits of the case. Claimant sought the payment of the amount due related to a number of contracts while respondent argued that no payments were due because the real object of the agreements was to bribe officials in country X.

The arbitral tribunal first held that it is the party alleging bribery which has the burden of proof. This could under certain circumstances be reversed. The arbitral tribunal then found that although the amounts paid to claimant were very high, and the effective costs of claimant have been only a small fraction of such amount, such payment was not perceived as being "abnormal for a consultancy agreement, without any bribery nature". With respect to Product Agreement Q, however, the arbitral tribunal found that there was a high enough degree of probability that the real object of Product Agreement Q was to channel bribes to officials in country X for this to be considered a case of bribery.

Excerpt

I. BRIBERY

[1] "Respondent alleges that the real object of all agreements between the parties was to organise the 'bribing' of officials of country X, through claimant. Respondent has no direct written evidence about the bribery nature of the agreements and about the bribes in particular. However, they rely on ... 'circumstantial' written evidence and on their witnesses (in particular Mr. A).

[2] "If the bribery nature of the agreements would be demonstrated, such agreements would be null and void in Swiss law. This is not because such bribe would be prohibited by the criminal law of the country in which bribes had been paid, but because the bribes in themselves cannot be, in Swiss law, the object of a valid contract (ATF 95 II p. 37 ss = JT 1970 I p. 79 ss). This is also admitted in most legal systems. (By the way, the result of such nullity is not necessarily equitable. The enterprise having benefited from the bribes (i.e., having obtained substantial contracts thanks to the bribes) has not a better moral position than the enterprise having organised the payment of the bribes. The nullity of the agreement is generally only beneficial to the former, and thus possibly inequitable. But this is legally irrelevant.)

[3] "The demonstration of the bribery nature of the agreement has to be made by the Party alleging the existence of bribes (hereafter the 'alleging Party'). A civil court, and in particular an arbitral tribunal, has not the power to make an official inquiry and has not the duty to search independently the truth. A civil court has to hear the allegations and the proofs offered by the parties. The 'alleging Party' has the burden of the proof. If its demonstration is not convincing, the tribunal should reject its argument, even if the tribunal has some doubts about the possible bribery nature of the agreements.

[4] "The 'alleging Party' may bring some relevant evidence for its allegations, without these elements being really conclusive. In such case, the arbitral tribunal may exceptionally request the other party to bring some counter-evidence, if such task is possible and not too burdensome. If the other party does not bring such counter-evidence, the arbitral tribunal may conclude that the facts alleged are proven (Art. 8 Swiss Civil Code).[1] However, such change in the burden of the proof is only to be made in special circumstances and for very good reasons.

[5] "During the proceedings, and in particular at the last hearing, respondent admitted that claimant has effectively rendered a number of services to them, quite apart from the alleged organisation of bribery. For some specific contracts ... respondent admitted that no bribes were contemplated or paid.

[6] "The main argument put forward by respondent is the importance of claimant's remuneration as against the alleged limited costs of their organisation. On this point, the argumentation presented by claimant is vague and often contradictory. In particular, claimant has often referred to the important costs of 'subcontractors' without being able to give any details about such subcontracts and the identity of the subcontractors. In particular, although claimant has admitted that most of those subcontracts were made in writing, it has refused to produce any of them, alleging (without precision) general business secrecy or legitimate interests of third parties (cf. in particular hereunder [19]). Claimant has also alleged that their top employees were receiving very high remunerations, based on some percentages of the amounts awarded to respondent. However, here also, the indications given by claimant have been vague and often contradictory.

[7] "Respondent insists also on the fact that the structure of claimant's group is not transparent and that claimant has refused to give any precise indication

1. Art. 8 of the Swiss Civil Code reads:

"Unless otherwise provided by law, each party shall prove the facts that it has alleged in order to derive its rights from them."

on this point. Respondent concludes that the real reason for not giving more information is the fact that probably some officials of country X have a stake in some companies of the claimant group. Moreover, respondent alleges that, if the structure of the group would be better known, it would appear that such group has not many employees, but mainly people with personal relations with officials of some countries.

[8] "This argument is not conclusive for deciding which was the real object of the agreements between the parties and if bribes were paid in fact. However, the refusal of claimant to give more precisions weakens their own argumentation about the importance and the standing of their group.

[9] "Apart from these general arguments, respondent presents a number of documents containing some curious expressions. In particular, those documents are letters or telexes sent by claimant to respondent and referring to nicknames,... etc. Those documents, which are not numerous, are not conclusive evidence that *all* agreements between the parties were of a bribery nature. Many of them concern specific agreements which are not litigious in the present proceedings. Insofar as some of those documents concern agreements which are litigious, they will be considered hereunder.

[10] "In his testimony, Mr. A declared that respondent was aware of most of the names of the persons to which bribes were paid. He said that, in many instances, the names of those beneficiaries were given orally by Mr. Z, to Mr. B. In other cases, the 'beneficiaries' presented their 'request' to respondent and respondent transmitted the message to claimant. Mr. A precised that he did not know all such names, but roughly 70% of them. He thought he knew about 30 names of such beneficiaries of bribes. He did not know the amount of bribes paid to each of them. However, Mr. A refused to mention any such names, because it could be 'dangerous', as he had received some threats in this respect.

[11] "Another person who knew even better the situation than Mr. A is Mr. B. Mr. A decided that it would be unfair to request Mr. B to testify in these proceedings. He mentioned in particular that the decision to stop the payments to claimant was taken by him personally and not by Mr. B, who was no more with respondent at the time. As a consequence, Mr. B refused to come as a witness when invited by the arbitral tribunal and also by claimant.

[12] "Taking into account all circumstances summarised above, the arbitral tribunal considers that respondent has not proved conclusively that the real object of all agreements between the parties is of a bribery nature.

[13] "The most convincing argument of respondent is the relatively important remuneration of claimant, compared with their costs. Concerning those costs, the figure for the ten year period is not proven by respondent, but it is

important to note that, on this point, the allegations of claimant have been especially vague and often contradictory.

[14] "However, considering the fact that respondent has decided not to tell the many names of beneficiaries which they allegedly knew, it is not appropriate to shift the burden of the proof on claimant and to request them to demonstrate the justification of their global costs for that period of ten years. One may also mention here that it is respondent who took the decision not to call Mr. B as witness (which practically led Mr. B to refuse the invitation to come, even at the request of the arbitral tribunal). Claimant argues that Mr. B would have testified that the real object of the agreements was *not* of bribery nature. This allegation is impossible to verify, but respondent has to bear the consequences of its decision in this respect.

[15] "One can also notice that, even if the figure for the amounts paid to claimant is very high, even if it is possible that the effective costs of claimant have been only a small fraction of such amount, such amount is 'only' 5.5% of the global amount awarded to respondent. Such percentage is not perceived as being abnormal for a consultancy agreement (without any bribery nature)."

(....)

II. PRODUCT AGREEMENT Q

(....)

[16] "Respondent considered that they were entitled to receive immediately two payments from the client in country X.... Respondent signed with the client in country X the 'Memorandum of Agreement for Final Acceptance', providing for the payment of [two sums]. However those payments were not made as quickly as envisaged in the said Memorandum, but partly much later.

(....)

[17] "Product Agreement Q is very different from all other Product Agreements which were shown to the arbitral tribunal in these proceedings. It is also clear from the hearing of the witnesses that the signature of this Agreement was the very beginning of the grave difficulties between the parties. The importance of the commission paid to claimant in this case is indeed extraordinary. Even if claimant alleges that, without their assistance, respondent would have recovered nothing on those amounts, a commission of 33.33% is extremely unusual. Claimant notes that the global amount of such compensation was 'only' representing a very small percent of the total contract value. However, the services rendered here were not concerning the total value of the contract, but only the payment by the clients of two precise amounts and it

is only logical that the compensation should be calculated on those amounts, as indeed is stipulated in Product Agreement Q.

[18] "In addition to that, such Product Agreement does not describe the services to be rendered by claimant, but affirms that the commission is paid 'for the performance of extraordinary services *received in full*' by respondent. The explanations given by Mr. Z on this point were confusing and contradictory.

(....)

[19] "It is relevant to recall here the positions taken by claimant concerning the expertise envisaged and later ordered by the arbitral tribunal: Respondent requested the production by claimant of banking documents related to payments made on the basis of several agreements (in particular for Product Agreement Q), to see which was the destination of such payments. Claimant strongly objected, arguing that such production would jeopardize their legitimate business secrets and possibly secrets of third parties. At the hearing in October 1991, taking into account the objections presented by claimant, the arbitral tribunal envisaged to order an independent expertise upon the payments already made on the basis of some Product Agreements (i.e., Product Agreements P and Q). For Product Agreement Q, only five such payments were made, at only three different dates. Thus, the expert could examine all relevant documents, but abstain from reporting details and names if they were not absolutely relevant.

[20] "... [C]laimant opposed the principle of such independent expertise.... [T]he arbitral tribunal confirmed that an independent expertise would be ordered and that the envisaged expert was accounting firm 'ABCD'. A hearing was held in Geneva to discuss the principle and the modalities of the expertise. At that hearing, claimant informed the envisaged expert that an affiliated company of the group ABCD was auditing in country Y an affiliated company of claimant. They informed ABCD that if they would accept the mission of expertise in this case, this would jeopardize the relationship between the two groups in country Y. The arbitral tribunal asked claimant whether they were willing to demonstrate that there was a real conflict of interest for ABCD; claimant replied that they were not willing to argue, but just stated that such conflict existed in their opinion. Consequently, ABCD renounced to serve as expert.

[21] "By its Procedural Ordinance No. 3, the arbitral tribunal decided in particular:

> 'Requests (i) and (ii) concern subcontracts entered into in relation with Product Agreements P and Q. Claimant confirmed that some subcontracts had been entered into. However, when their counsel was asked

to say whether these subcontracts were made in writing or not, he was not sure. Claimant has not submitted any precise argument which would oppose the production by them of such subcontracts. Indeed, such production would clearly be helpful for the discussion of this case. Consequently, requests (i) and (ii) are accepted. Claimant is ordered to produce copies of all subcontracts entered into by them concerning Product Agreements P and Q and made in writing. For those subcontracts which were made orally, claimant is requested to present a written statement exposing the content of such alleged oral agreements, their scope and the identity of the subcontractor....'

By letter of their counsel, claimant refused to produce those subcontracts.
[22] "By its Procedural Ordinance No. 4, the arbitral tribunal decided:

'*Production of subcontracts*
The arbitral tribunal takes note that claimant has refused to produce such documents. The arbitral tribunal notes that the only reasons invoked by claimant in the documents cited in their letter [of their counsel], as far as the production of copies of subcontracts are concerned, is "business secrecy over matters which are not in dispute". The arbitral tribunal will draw in due time the possible consequences of claimant's position.'

[23] "By its Procedural Ordinance No. 3, with detailed motivation, the arbitral tribunal decided to order an independent expertise. The arbitral tribunal decided in particular:

'(f) At any point of time, if some particular difficulty appears (in particular, if some debits apparently corresponding to the credits had been transferred to other accounts of the claimant group), the expert will report to the arbitral tribunal. After having heard the parties, the arbitral tribunal will give to the expert the appropriate directions and possibly complete the present mission.

....

(h) Claimant is invited to confirm in writing to the arbitral tribunal..., whether they accept to co-operate in principle with the expert to be appointed. In the affirmative, the arbitral tribunal will appoint an expert. The parties will have a time-limit of ten days to present possibly their grounds for challenging such expert. In the negative, the arbitral tribunal will renounce to such expertise, taking such attitude of claimant in consideration for its final decision.'

[24] "... [C]laimant accepted to cooperate with the experts to be appointed by the arbitral tribunal. By its Procedural Ordinance No. 4, the arbitral tribunal decided to appoint as expert Mr. C. The parties were invited to present their possible requests to challenging such expert within 10 days.
[25] "... [C]laimant challenged the substance of the mission decided for the expertise in Procedural Ordinance No. 3 (although they had accepted such mission in their letter (see above [23]). Respondent commented such letter in the letter of their counsel. By letter of its Chairman (which is considered to be Procedural Ordinance No. 5 of the arbitral tribunal), the arbitral tribunal considered the following, after having summarized the situation:

> 'It is now too late for claimant to request a modification of Procedural Ordinance No. 3. In particular, the arbitral tribunal understands that, instead of allowing the expert to examine completely the account in question during a number of months as specified in the Ordinance, claimant proposes to choose themselves the debits which would allegedly correspond to the credits mentioned. This proposal is unacceptable.
>
> The arbitral tribunal considers therefore that, by their letter claimant now refuses to co-operate with the expertise, as decided in Ordinance No. 3. *Consequently, such expertise will not take place. The arbitral tribunal will take account of these circumstances in its final Award.*
>
> Claimant should be given a last possibility to accept to co-operate with the expertise as decided in Procedural Ordinance No. 3. Such a decision may be notified to the other party and to the arbitrators latest [within one week]. After such date, refusal of claimant will be deemed to be final.
>
> ....
>
> It is clear that claimant's legitimate interests of business secrecy, especially concerning third parties, could be taken into account in the way the expert's report would be drafted and distributed to the parties.'

[26] "By the letter of their counsel, claimant confirmed that they would not cooperate with the expertise as ordered in Procedural Ordinance No. 3. However, claimant proposed to produce the banking documents originally requested by respondent.... Respondent opposed such production.... The arbitral tribunal decided in principle to admit the production of those documents. A formal request was presented by claimant and was accepted by the arbitral tribunal.
[27] "As claimant produced the banking documents concerning the debits and credits corresponding to the payments made by respondent concerning Product Agreement Q, it appeared that the account in which such payments were made

was only a 'transit account', each amount credited being immediately sent by the bank to another account of the group. This demonstrates that, contrary to what claimant had alleged to begin with, such a production was not revealing any kind of business secrecy.

[28] "The arbitral tribunal notes here that, when contesting the principle of the expertise, claimant had produced three affidavits of Mr. D (describing himself as 'independent auditor for the claimant group of companies ...'). In his affidavit, Mr. D attested that, concerning the account for which the expertise was envisaged, 'the monthly entries numbered in the many thousands and the turnover per year was hundreds of millions of dollars'. As it appears now, this statement was completely untrue. Mr. D was invited to come as a witness, but he did not appear.

[29] "At the hearing of March 1994, the Chairman of the arbitral tribunal asked Mr. E (the 'internal controller' of the claimant group) to tell who had given the instruction to the bank to prepare the banking documents which were produced by claimant. Mr. E answered that the owner of the account gave those instructions, but that he did not know who was in fact the person who gave those instructions. The Chairman asked him whether he had any contact with the bank concerning the production of those documents; Mr. E answered that he had no contact at all, but refused that Mr. F, director of the bank, who had to appear later as witness, would be permitted to confirm such statement. Mr. Z confirmed that he opposed Mr. F to testify on this subject, 'as it was irrelevant'. Consequently, Mr. F could not testify on this point, being bound by his banking secrecy obligation.

[30] "Taking into account all circumstances, the arbitral tribunal considers (contrary to its decision on all other Agreements ...) that there is a high degree of probability that the real object of Product Agreement Q was to channel bribes to officials in country X who had the power to decide that both amounts mentioned in the Agreement were to be paid to respondent. Such probability is high enough for the arbitral tribunal to consider that such allegation presented by respondent is to be admitted. Claimant (rightfully) does not contest that, if such is the case, Product Agreement Q is null and void in Swiss law. Consequently, claimant's claim based on Product Agreement Q is rejected."

Final award in cases nos. 6515 and 6516 of 1994

Parties:	Claimant: Engineering company (Italy) Defendants: (1) Engineering company (Greece); (2) Producer (Greece)
Place of arbitration:	Athens, Greece
Published in:	Unpublished
Subject matters:	- applicable law to substance - jurisdiction - sovereign immunity - tax liability - economic disruption of contract - contractual requirement to negotiate in good faith - damages based on "reasonable adjustment" of contract price

Facts

Second defendant and claimant entered into a Shareholders Agreement for the purpose of forming first defendant. First defendant was to render technical services within Greece as well as elsewhere. The three parties entered a number of agreements which were intended to associate claimant with the development of a major project to be undertaken in Greece by second defendant (the Project): (1) a *Service Agreement*, between first defendant and claimant, the purpose of which was to contract to claimant services which first defendant was due to render within Greece and elsewhere; (2) a *Sub-Contract* between first defendant and claimant, the purpose of which was to sub-contract to claimant part of the services which first defendant was due to render to second defendant with respect to the Project; and (3) an *Agreement* between second defendant and claimant the purpose of which was to allow claimant to render directly to second defendant certain services in connection with the development of the Project.

Both defendants were required to compensate claimant for services rendered under the contracts. The understanding of the parties was that, because of Greek Law no. 549, passed in 1970, compensation paid by either defendant to claimant was not subject to Greek taxes. This was based on the reasoning that claimant did not have a permanent establishment in Greece, claimant's services were rendered from its Italian office and accordingly, compensation paid by either defendant was subject to Italian, not Greek taxes, by reason of the Tax Treaty between Italy and Greece.

The Greek tax authorities decided that claimant had acquired a permanent establishment in Greece. Therefore the services rendered by claimant to the defendants should be deemed services rendered through claimant's permanent establishment in Greece and accordingly compensation paid by defendants to claimant should be subject to withholding tax. This determination resulted in double taxation as claimant already bore Italian corporate income taxes in Italy on these payments. Claimant argued that the burden of these withholdings should be borne by defendants.

Claimant initiated arbitration against each of the defendants separately. Each of the parties appointed the same arbitrator in each of the two cases, and the ICC decided to join the two cases and appointed the chairman.

The arbitral tribunal held that it had jurisdiction over what it found to be a purely contractual dispute, rejecting the argument that the dispute lay within the exclusive jurisdiction of the tax authorities. The contract language provided that the parties should negotiate in good faith in case of changed circumstances. Defendants' failure to do so had damaged claimant and claimant was awarded damages amounting to 65% of the Greek tax liability.

Excerpt

I. APPLICABLE LAW

[1] "The agreements which have been attached to the Requests for Arbitration submitted by claimant to the International Chamber of Commerce contain the same Arbitration Clause.... This clause in substance reads as follows:

> 'Jurisdiction and Applicable Law
> 1. Any eventual dispute between the Parties arising herefrom should be ironed out by the Parties undertaking to make all necessary efforts for settling them amicably. However, if a dispute will finally have to be litigated, it will be by Arbitration in Athens, in accordance with the provisions of the International Chamber of Commerce.
> 2. This agreement shall be governed and interpreted in accordance with Greek Laws.'

[2] "It is clear that under Paragraph 2 of the clause, the parties have selected *one* governing law in order to settle any and all disputes arising out of the interpretation and application of their contractual relationship. *This governing law is Greek law.* Thus, it is the duty of the arbitral tribunal to resort to Greek law in order to adjudicate the present dispute – provided, of course, the arbitral tribunal has competent jurisdiction both in rem and in personam.

[3] "The arbitral tribunal therefore will apply the rules of Greek statutory law, including, namely, the rules provided for by the Greek Civil Code. In that connection the arbitral tribunal finds that the provision in Art. 1 (Sources of Law) of the Greek Civil Code is of particular relevance here. Art. 1 provides that:

> 'The rules of law are embodied in statutory and customary law.'

Thus, not only must the arbitral tribunal look into the provisions of statutory law, whenever relevant. The arbitral tribunal must also query whether there are any customs which would be of relevance here, under Greek law, or because the parties, consonant with Greek law, would have elected to make them applicable to resolution of their dispute.

[4] "The arbitral tribunal also notes that under the Terms of Reference, by subjecting themselves to ICC Arbitration, the parties also subjected themselves to the Rules of Arbitration of the International Chamber of Commerce. The arbitral tribunal therefore finds that due regard should be given to Art. 13(5) of the Rules of Arbitration, under which,

> 'in all cases, the Arbitration shall take into account the provisions of the contract and the relevant trade usages',

be they the usages of internal or international trade. Thus, it results from the combination between the provisions of the second paragraph in the arbitral clauses, of Art. 2 [rectius 1] in the Greek Civil Code and of Art. 13(5) in the Rules of Arbitration that the arbitral tribunal must primarily resort to Greek law and subsidiarily, to the relevant usages of international trade, if and when needed."

II. JURISDICTION OF THE ARBITRAL TRIBUNAL

1. *General Considerations*

[5] "The defendants have strongly argued, all throughout these present arbitral proceedings, that the arbitral tribunal had no jurisdiction over the dispute. As a consequence, the defendants have consistently urged the arbitral tribunal to dismiss the case in its entirety, for lack of jurisdiction. At the core of this position of the defendants lies the argument that the sole dispute is in essence one between claimant and the Government of Greece, a Sovereign State. What is at stake here, it is contended, is the power of the Government of Greece to exercise one of the most basic prerogatives of any Government, i.e., taxation of economic activities. In other words, the request of claimant, in and by itself, would constitute an untenable challenge to the power of the Government of Greece to tax whatever economic activities it would elect to tax in its sovereign discretion.

[6] "The defendants have further argued, as a consequence of the foregoing, that the case should be dismissed for another reason, which is that the arbitral tribunal has no jurisdiction whatsoever over the Government of Greece. The Government of Greece, again, is the Government of a Sovereign State, and, as such, the Government of Greece is not amenable before [an] arbitral tribunal, all the more since the Government of Greece never waived its immunity of jurisdiction by entering into an arbitration clause, and, as a consequence, never subjected itself to the jurisdiction of the arbitral tribunal.

[7] "The arbitral tribunal feels compelled to meet these frontal attacks against its jurisdiction. In so doing, the arbitral tribunal must pay all due respect to the prerogatives of the Government of Greece. Considerations of sovereignty are certainly not to be dismissed lightly. But the arbitral tribunal also has obligations of its own, to wit, resolve the dispute which it was the duty to finally and peacefully put at rest. This duty was vested in the arbitral tribunal by the parties, and the arbitral tribunal would be at breach if it failed to honor it.

[8] "This is not to say, however, that the arbitral tribunal is going to embark upon some balancing exercise, whereby it would weigh the sovereign interests of the Government of Greece as against the private interests of the litigants. *Quite on the contrary, the arbitral tribunal will carefully refrain from infringing upon the prerogatives of the Government of Greece, and, as a consequence, will assert jurisdiction over the instant case only and insofar as it will be fully satisfied that this assertion of jurisdiction in no way can be deemed to constitute such an infringement*. In other words, it is the firm belief of the arbitral tribunal that it should not entertain jurisdiction over the instant case, as long as there would

be the slightest scintilla of substance in the allegation that, by so doing, it would assume rights not vested with it.

[9] "One thing nevertheless remains clear, as first defendant has pointed out, which is that the 'kompetenz-kompetenz' belongs to the arbitral tribunal. This is one of the most basic principles in international commercial arbitration, not to say international arbitration. The Rules of Arbitration of the International Chamber of Commerce, to which the parties have subjected themselves, reflect that principle (see Art. 8(3) of the Rules).[1] Furthermore, the Terms of Reference, which have been agreed upon by the parties, also entrust the arbitral tribunal with the duty to delineate the boundaries of its own jurisdiction. Clearly, in discharging this duty, the arbitral tribunal must take each and every step in order to ensure that the award which it has to render will be enforceable in the forum where enforcement is going to be sought."

2. *Jurisdiction in Rem*

(....)

[10] "[T]he arbitral tribunal will start with the general proposition that it should assume jurisdiction over Joint Cases 6515 and 6516, if for no other reason that defendants have failed to make a conclusive showing to the effect that *each and every issue* raised by claimant could not be resolved through international commercial arbitration. The main question presented to the arbitral tribunal, thus, is the question to know whether it can entertain jurisdiction over the so-called 'tax issue'.

[11] ".... [W]ould an assertion of jurisdiction by the arbitral tribunal over this 'tax issue' constitute an infringement over the sovereign prerogatives of the Government of Greece? Again, this is not a question to be taken lightly. In that connection, the arbitral tribunal wishes to underscore that it is fully aware of the fact that it does not possess the status of a court of law, since its existence results from an agreement between claimant and defendants, and not from the operation of Greek law. Indeed, the arbitral tribunal perfectly understands that the Government of Greece would find it patently offensive to its sovereign rights if a private body, like the arbitral tribunal, should

---

1. Art. 8(3) of the ICC Rules of Conciliation and Arbitration (1988) reads:

"Should one of the parties raise one or more pleas concerning the existence or validity of the agreement to arbitrate, and should the Court be satisfied of the prima facie existence of such an agreement, the Court may, without prejudice to the admissibility or merits of the plea or pleas, decide that the arbitration shall proceed. In such a case any decision as to the arbitrator's jurisdiction shall be taken by the arbitrator himself."

somehow pass judgment upon the validity of Greek law, or upon the validity of the acts of the Government of Greece.

[12] "But, according to the opinion of a majority of the members of the arbitral tribunal, no question of validity of Greek law or of validity of the acts of the Government of Greece is involved here. The issue with which the arbitral tribunal is presented here is *not* one to decide whether the Government of Greece was or was not right in passing a particular piece of tax legislation; it is *not* either one to decide whether the Government of Greece was right or was not right in assessing and levying a withholding tax on income earned by the claimant. Such issues would clearly fall without the ambit of the jurisdiction of the arbitral tribunal.... The arbitral tribunal recognizes that, under the laws of Greece, there are legal procedures in order to challenge the validity of a tax, or the validity of the tax determinations made by the Government of Greece, and that arbitration is not one of these legal procedures.

[13] "The arbitral tribunal further recognizes that the Government of Greece and the Government of Italy have entered into an International Agreement for the purpose of avoiding double taxation with respect to income taxes, which International Agreement has been abundantly cited by the parties; that, under the provisions of that Tax Treaty, Greece and Italy have devised a so-called 'mutual agreement procedure', – a common feature in Tax Treaties – in order to amicably settle disputes arising from conflicting tax determinations made by the Governments of both contracting countries; and that the arbitral tribunal certainly ought not to interfere with the operation of the said 'mutual agreement procedure'.

[14] "To make things short, the arbitral tribunal therefore accepts that it should not ascertain jurisdiction over such issues in case they would be submitted to it for decision. But, again, a majority of the members of the arbitral tribunal finds itself totally unable to conclude that such issues were ever submitted to it for decision.... [T]he arbitral tribunal has come to the conclusion that the question presented here is the following: under the various contracts entered into by claimant, on the one hand, and defendants, on the other hand, who should ultimately bear the burden of the withholding tax here under consideration? In other words, did the parties, at the time they negotiated the contracts, make any provision for the purpose of allocating or re-allocating the burden of taxes, present or future, as between themselves?

[15] "This question is merely one of interpretation of the contractual documents. What did the parties intend with respect to final allocation or re-allocation of taxes? How was their intent reflected in the contractual documents? These are questions which have been often raised in international commercial arbitration, with respect to international commercial transactions. International commercial transactions are frequently negotiated in the context

of a growing economic competition. In that context, a sound financial analysis becomes more and more relevant, because it is based upon that analysis that the parties will ultimately decide whether any particular transaction is economically feasible or economically unfeasible. Taxes are an important element of a sound financial analysis. Therefore, international commercial contracts more and more often make provisions in order to reflect that analysis, namely with respect to taxes, present or future, and the allocation or re-allocation thereof between parties. The arbitral tribunal, speaking through a majority of its members, fails to see how litigation of these provisions, which have to do solely with the economics of contracts, could be deemed to be offensive to State sovereignty.

[16] "Allocation or re-allocation of taxes between contracting parties does not purport to frustrate any State interest; it merely purports to strike an economic balance between the interests of the contracting parties. As a consequence, the arbitral tribunal hereby holds that it *has jurisdiction to decide over the ultimate allocation or re-allocation of the withholding taxes here under dispute as between the parties, insofar as this question is solely one of interpretation of the contracts entered into by the said parties.*

[17] "Defendants have argued, time and again, that Greek law would not allow to contractually shift the burden of taxes from the taxpayer – in that case claimant – to a payor other than the taxpayer, i.e., to first defendant and/or to second defendant. That may well be. The arbitral tribunal however, does not think that it needs to address that question, because resolution thereof is not necessary to resolution of the dispute before the arbitral tribunal. As a majority of the members of the arbitral tribunal sees it, *the question here is not one to determine who should or who should not pay the tax; it is one to determine how the parties have handled, as between themselves, the economics of taxation.* Even if Greek law were to prohibit first defendant and/or second defendant to pay taxes in lieu of claimant, this does not mean that the contractual provisions relating to prices should not reflect the burden of the taxes borne by claimant. In that connection, the arbitral tribunal wants to make it clear that the words 'allocation or re-allocation of taxes', such as used in this arbitral award, should not be taken as synonymous with the words 'responsibility for payment of taxes'. Use of the words 'allocation or re-allocation of taxes' is a convenient way to mean that the various contracts may embody provisions dealing with the economics of taxation as between parties."

3. *Jurisdiction in Personam*

[18] "Defendants have both argued that the arbitral tribunal has no jurisdiction 'in personam' against them because of the provisions of Arts. 62 to 73

of the Greek Code of Civil Procedure.... These provisions may be summarized as follows:

> Any person – including any legal entity –, whether claimant or defendant, must have his day in the Greek Court of competent jurisdiction.
>
> Accordingly, any creditor who seeks enforcement of some legal obligation, must be permitted to appear in the Greek Court of competent jurisdiction as claimant.
>
> Conversely, any debtor against whom enforcement of that very same legal obligation is sought, must be permitted to appear before that Greek Court of competent jurisdiction as defendant.
>
> The claim, however, must be directed by the right claimant – i.e., the creditor of the legal obligation, against the right defendant – i.e., the debtor of the legal obligation. If this would not be the case, then the Greek Court should dismiss the suit, because the lack of 'active' or 'passive' jurisdiction as the case may be.

[19] "Defendants do not contend that these present arbitral proceedings are vitiated by lack of 'active' jurisdiction. In other words, they do not contend that claimant is wrong in seeking enforcement of its claim. Rather, defendants contend that these present proceedings are vitiated by lack of 'passive' jurisdiction. In other words, they contend that claimant is seeking enforcement of its claim against the wrong defendants. The argument, here again, is made in connection with the so-called 'tax issue'. The position of the defendants, in that respect, is that claimant should not try to recover from defendants the amounts of the taxes withheld, because defendants did not actually withhold any amount whatsoever; but that claimant should try to recover from the Greek Tax Office the amounts of the taxes withheld, because it is the Greek Tax Office which actually withheld these amounts.

[20] "Again, in the view of a majority of the members of the arbitral tribunal, this argument stems from a mis-conception of the issues which are being litigated. The arbitral tribunal would totally agree with defendants, if claimant was trying to obtain an award dealing with the validity of Greek tax law, or with the validity of the acts of the Greek Tax Office, and was trying to recover the amount of the withholdings from the Greek Tax Office. But this is not the case. Claimant is seeking, inter alia, an interpretation of the provisions regarding allocation or re-allocation of taxes in contracts entered into by claimant on the one hand, and by defendants, on the other hand. Thus, claimant and defendants, who were parties to these contracts, must be deemed to be the proper parties in arbitration. As a consequence, *the arbitral tribunal, through a majority of its members, hereby rejects the argument of the*

defendants, and holds that it has jurisdiction in personam over both the claimant and the defendants."

4. *Allegation of Vagueness and Indefiniteness*

[21] "It also has been contended that the arbitral tribunal should dismiss a number of claims, because of their vagueness and indefiniteness. This contention has been made by second defendant, with respect to payment of 'additional works' and payment of 'compensatory interests'. Second defendant has argued that these claims are inadmissible under Art. 118 of the Greek Code of Civil Procedure, which requires that the claim be adequately and precisely stated when litigated in the Greek Courts of competent jurisdiction.

[22] "The arbitral tribunal does not dispute that any claim before any court must be properly submitted, and that Art. 118 of the Greek Code of Civil Procedure precisely requires that. But the arbitral tribunal is satisfied that claimant did satisfy this procedural requirement.

(....)

[23] "[T]he legal basis for the claims, as well as the tentative estimation of such claims, have been known to second defendant even before this arbitral tribunal was formed. To be sure, it may be that by asserting these claims as it did, claimant was in gross error, both legally and factually; it may be that the legal basis thereof is incorrect, because claimant failed to properly characterize it; it also may be that the tentative amounts are unrealistic, because claimant, as claimants often do, may have exaggerated them. But these are clearly matters for the arbitral tribunal to decide, after having given all due weight to the arguments of the parties. Indeed, the arbitral tribunal would be in serious breach of its duty, if it failed to consider claims which were specifically submitted to it by claimants, or defenses or counter-claims which were specifically submitted to it by defendants. The arbitral tribunal will not embark upon that course – and will therefore reject the contention of second defendant. But, obviously, by rejecting this contention of second defendant, the arbitral tribunal does not imply any position on the merits of the claims – a question which will be later dealt with in the course of the present award."

5. *Allegation of Shift in Legal Grounds*

[24] "Defendants have also argued that the claim relating to the so-called 'tax issues' should be deemed unadmissible, because claimant shifted legal grounds between the time of filing of the Requests for Arbitration and the time of filing of subsequent submissions. As defendants see it, the original claims rested upon the doctrine of *factum principis*. They contend that, under the Request

for Arbitration, claimant argued (i) that the actions taken by the Greek Tax Authorities were tantamount to a *factum principis*; (ii) that this *factum principis* adversely affected the interests of defendants, not the interests of claimant; and (iii) that this *factum principis* did not excuse defendants from satisfying in full their payment obligations vis-à-vis claimant, such as these payment obligations resulted from the provisions in the contracts.

[25] "As defendants further see it, the subsequent submissions shifted legal grounds. Instead of continuing to rely upon the doctrine of *factum principis*, claimant elected to rest upon the concept that contracts ought to be re-negotiated in good faith whenever some change in circumstances causes hardship upon one of the parties. Thus claimant allegedly dequalified its original claim for re-imbursement of taxes withheld and requalified it, in its later submissions, as one for re-negotiation of contract. This shift in legal grounds, it is contented, by and in itself, ought to be found violative of Art. 224 of the Greek Code of Civil Procedure.

[26] "The arbitral tribunal sees no merit in the contention of defendants, because, in the view of a majority of its members, claimant did not shift legal grounds. At the core of the claim always lay the allegation that, *under the provisions of the contracts*, the ultimate burden of the taxes withheld was to be borne by defendants, not by claimant. This is apparent from the very wording of the two Requests of Arbitration directed respectively against first and second defendants. Both Requests referred to the Tax Clauses in the contract, and stressed that, under these tax clauses, the contract price was deemed to be '*inclusive of corporate income tax*'. And both Requests went on to say that the common sense interpretation of this type of provision, which is habitual in international commercial contracts, is that the contractor – here claimant – cannot claim extra-compensation from the co-contractor – here defendants – by reason of the 'income tax' that the contractor is obligated to pay either in the country of his domicile or in the country where the income is generated. And claimant, of course, concluded the argument by contending that the withholdings were not in the nature of an 'income tax'.

[27] "This may or may not be true, and the arbitral tribunal will discuss these arguments on their merits only if and when needed. Again, the only question which the arbitral tribunal ought to address here and now is the question whether there was any shift in legal grounds which would be violative of the command in Art. 224 of the Greek Code of Civil Procedure. A majority of the members of the arbitral tribunal feels compelled to answer this question by holding that *there was no violation of Art. 224 of the Greek Code of Civil Procedure, because there was no shift in legal grounds*. Claimant has consistently sustained, since the inception of these present arbitral proceedings, that a sound interpretation of the tax provisions in the contracts required that the ultimate

burden of the taxes withheld be borne by defendants. Claimant has invoked a number of arguments (moyens) in order to support that claim. But the claim itself has never varied."

6. *Issues Raised in Motions*

[28] "Defendants have taken two other exceptions to the continuance of these present arbitral proceedings.... First defendant filed three separate Motions with the arbitral tribunal, whereby it requested the arbitral tribunal (i) to dismiss the case for lack of jurisdiction; (ii) in the event the arbitral tribunal would not dismiss the case, to postpone any further action pending resolution of the tax issue through recourse to the mutual agreement procedure provided for by the Tax Treaty between Greece and Italy; and (iii) in the event the arbitral tribunal would not dismiss the case, to postpone any further action before asking the Government of Greece to intervene in these present arbitral proceedings.
(....)
[29] "The arbitral tribunal then turns to the substance of the three Motions.... The first Motion, whereby first defendant requested the arbitral tribunal to dismiss the case, must be summarily disposed of on the grounds stated hereinabove in paragraphs [5] to [17]. The arbitral tribunal cannot base its award upon conflicting grounds, and hold at the same time that it has and has not jurisdiction over the case.
[30] "This leaves the arbitral tribunal with Motions no. 2 and no. 3, which will be dealt with separately. Under *Motion no. 2*, first defendant has requested the arbitral tribunal to postpone any further action pending a resolution of the tax issues through resort to the mutual agreement procedures provided by the Tax Treaty. The arbitral tribunal feels compelled to reject this Motion for two reasons:
[31] "Resolution of the tax issues through resort to the mutual agreement procedure has no incidence whatsoever on the issue at stake here. The issue at stake here is one to decide who should bear the cost of the tax under the contracts. This issue is not going to be resolved through resort to the mutual agreement procedure. The Joint Committee operating under the Tax Treaty has been asked to determine whether claimant had a permanent establishment in Greece. It may find that claimant had or had not such a permanent establishment; or it may find, in the event claimant had such a permanent establishment, that under the applicable law, the tax was or was not due by claimant. But these findings have nothing to do with the issue which the arbitral tribunal has to decide, and which relates to contractual allocation or re-allocation of the taxes.

[32] "Postponement of these present proceedings, pending resolution of the tax issues through resort to the mutual agreement procedure, would therefore, in the opinion of the arbitral tribunal, be purely dilatory. The Joint Committee operating under the Tax Treaty met for the first time [six years before these proceedings]. It could not come up with any solution to the problem, and there is no indication whatsoever that it will come up any time soon with a solution to that problem. Six years is a long time for business purposes. But the arbitral tribunal would be prepared to admit that six years are not sufficient in order to resolve the issue, if such resolution were necessary for the arbitral tribunal to decide over the case which has been submitted to it by the parties; and the arbitral tribunal would readily defer to the jurisdiction of the Joint Committee, if its own Award would depend from the findings of the said Joint Committee. This is not the case, however, and the two issues – i.e. the issue to be resolved by the Joint Committee and the issue to be resolved by the arbitral tribunal – are quite independent one from the other. Furthermore, the arbitral tribunal sees no risk of conflicting decisions here. Even assuming, arguendo, that the Joint Committee, on the one hand, would ultimately find that, under the provisions of the Treaty, the tax was due by claimant, and that the arbitral tribunal, on the other hand, would hold in the meanwhile that, under the provisions the contract, such as interpreted and applied in the light of Greek law, the burden of this tax was shifted from claimant to defendant, a majority of the members of the arbitral tribunal still fails to find that the two decisions would be conflicting one with the other. Since no risk of conflicting decisions would be involved, postponement would serve no purpose, and would be purely dilatory in character.

[33] "Under *Motion no. 3*, first defendant has requested the arbitral tribunal to postpone any further action before asking the Government of Greece to intervene in these present proceedings – a request which may not be totally consistent with the contention that the arbitral tribunal has no jurisdiction whatsoever over the Government of Greece. The arbitral tribunal, through a majority of its members, feels compelled to reject this motion for two reasons:

[34] "There are no substantive grounds which would warrant intervention of the Government of Greece in these present proceedings. The arbitral tribunal is not going to pass judgment over the validity of Greek law, or to pass judgment over the validity of the actions of the Government of Greece. The arbitral tribunal is going to adjudicate a contractual dispute. By so doing, it may have to interpret and to apply Greek law. But nothing in Greek law, the arbitral tribunal understands, prevents an arbitral tribunal from interpreting and applying Greek law, consistent with the will of the parties, in order to settle their dispute. Furthermore, and even assuming, again arguendo, that the arbitral tribunal should find in favour of claimant, such a finding certainly

would adversely affect the interests of the defendants. But the arbitral tribunal, once again, fails to see how such a finding would frustrate any interest of the Government of Greece.

[35] "From the procedural standpoint, the arbitral tribunal will certainly not embark upon such a course. The Government of Greece is a sovereign Government, and as such, it enjoys privileges and immunities, among which immunity from jurisdiction. What the arbitral tribunal is asked, in essence, is to disregard the immunity from jurisdiction which the Government of Greece enjoys, as do any and all sovereign Governments. To be sure, sovereign Governments may validly waive their immunity from jurisdiction – namely in an international commercial transaction, by subjecting themselves to international commercial arbitration. It is true that the arbitral tribunal is dealing here with an international commercial transaction. But the Government of Greece is no party to this international commercial transaction, and not being a party to this international commercial transaction, certainly never agreed to subject itself to international commercial arbitration by reason of disputes arising thereof. A majority of the members of the arbitral tribunal finds that to grant the Motion would be patently offensive and even violative of the sovereign rights of the Government of Greece; and as a consequence, will not grant that Motion."

(....)

III. SUBSTANTIVE ISSUES

(....)

1. *Tax Issues*

(....)

a. *Discussion of relevant provisions in the contracts*

[36] "The question with which the arbitral tribunal is faced therefore appears to be of a purely legal nature....

i. The "Variation Clauses"

[37] "The contracts here under consideration contain a number of so-called 'Variation Clauses', the effect of which is to allow an increase in the prices which were originally agreed upon by the parties – provided, of course, certain conditions would be met in order for these clauses to be brought into play. The arbitral tribunal will not discuss these clauses for two reasons: Reason no. 1 is that neither party has relied upon these clauses in order to claim or disclaim any modification of its contractual obligations; Reason no. 2 is that

the arbitral tribunal finds that such a discussion would be irrelevant, because the 'Variation Clauses' have no bearing whatsoever on the resolution of the issues here under consideration.

[38] "As the arbitral tribunal understands it, the claimant does not ask first and second defendants to agree upon an increase in the prices which were originally agreed upon. There has never been any argument on the part of claimant to the effect that the total compensation to be paid by either first or second defendant should be increased in order to take account of the withholdings. Rather, the claim of claimant is limited to payment *in full* of the price which was originally agreed upon. Thus, the claim of claimant is not one for increase in prices, but one for allocation or re-allocation of the tax burden. As a consequence, the arbitral tribunal concludes that there is no need to take into account the so-called 'Variation Clauses' in order to resolve the tax issues here under consideration."

ii. The "Tax Clauses"

(....)

[39] "The 'Tax Clauses' in the Sub-Contract between first defendant and claimant ... and in the Agreement between second defendant and claimant ... slightly differ in their wording. Under [the Sub-Contract], the 'Lump Sum Price and the Unit Rates ... are inclusive of Corporate and Personnel Income Taxes, but are exclusive of Turnover Tax and Stamp Duties required by law, including Stamp Duties on Contract registration'. Under the Agreement, 'Contract Price and any other compensation related to this contract are inclusive [of] all Corporate and Personnel Income Taxes, but are exclusive of Turnover Taxes and Stamp Duties on Contract registration'. The arbitral tribunal, however, is of the opinion that these differences are not of such a nature as to impact on the substance of the relevant provisions. The arbitral tribunal will, therefore, abide by the statement made by first defendant to the effect that these are 'identical stipulations'.

[40] "The arbitral tribunal must, thus, decide whether the withholdings here under consideration fall within the category of 'Corporate and Personnel Income Taxes', which are included in the contract prices, or within the Category of 'Turnover Taxes and Stamp Duties', which are excluded from the contract prices. This, indeed, is a key issue. The arbitral tribunal takes these clauses to mean that, since contract prices are inclusive of Corporate and Personal Income Taxes, claimant, or its Personnel, as a matter of principle, should bear the cost of the said Taxes, whereas, since contract prices are exclusive of Turnover Taxes and Stamp Duties, first and/or second defendant as a matter of principle, should bear the cost of the said Taxes or Duties. Thus, the arbitral tribunal must decide whether, for purposes of interpretation and

application of the contract, the withholdings here under consideration ought to be considered as Taxes falling within the 'Corporate and Personnel Income Taxes' category, on the one hand, or as Taxes falling within the 'Turnover Taxes and Stamp Duties' category, on the one hand.

[41] ".... The arbitral tribunal, however, has come to the conclusion that this issue is a foregone issue, and that there is no need, for the purposes of this arbitral award, to enter into that tax thicket. Suffice it to remember that, at the time the tax authorities started to withhold the amounts in dispute, claimant, by its own admission, decided to lodge a claim with the Joint Commission provided for by Art. 24 of the Tax Treaty between Greece and Italy. In other words, claimant did make the decision, at that time, that, under Art. 24, the Joint Commission had competent jurisdiction in order to resolve, through the so-called 'mutual agreement procedure', the tax difficulty which had arisen with respect to the interpretation and application of the Treaty provisions in connection with the validity of the withholdings.

[42] "The 1965 Tax Treaty between Greece and Italy here under consideration is captioned 'For the avoidance of double taxation and prevention of fiscal evasion with respect to taxes on income'. It applies to income earned by legal entities. It provides that shall be regarded as Taxes on Income 'all taxes imposed on total income, or on elements of income' (Art. 2(2)). It further provides that these taxes shall be regarded as 'income taxes, irrespective of the manner in which they are levied'. Thus, a withholding tax imposed by the Greek Tax Office on that part of its income which claimant derived from Greek sources appears to be, prima facie, an 'Income Tax' within the meaning of the Tax Treaty. This is actually the way claimant understood it, since it elected, when the difficulty arose, to subject itself to the mutual agreement procedures of the Tax Treaty, and, by so doing, acknowledged and recognized that the withholdings were in the nature of corporate income taxes.

[43] "The arbitral tribunal, therefore, finds it unnecessary to discuss the question to know whether the withholdings are or are not in the nature of a 'Corporate Income Tax', if for no other reason that claimant did make this initial determination before resorting to the mutual agreement procedure provided for by the Tax Treaty between Greece and Italy.... The arbitral tribunal, in light of the foregoing, cannot but conclude that claimant, during the present proceedings, may not rely upon a position different from the position upon which it relied during the course of the proceedings before the Joint Commission – all the more since that shift in the positions of claimant would be at the entire expense of first and second defendants. *Non concedit venire contra factum proprium.* The arbitral tribunal thus *holds that, for the purpose of this arbitral award, the withholding here in dispute must be treated as 'Corporate Income Tax'.*

[44] "First and second defendants have suggested, time and again, that while claimant may have incurred some damage because of the imposition of the withholdings by the Greek Tax Office, the contracts nevertheless provided for an allocation of taxes which pre-empted claimant from successfully claiming redress by reason of any such damage. The arbitral tribunal does not quite agree with that position. It is true that, at the time they entered into the relevant contracts, the parties thereto made some forecast with respect to the economic viability of the deal – not an unusual step to be taken under this sort of circumstances.... But the so-called 'Tax Clauses', which have been analyzed heretofore, were negotiated as between the parties based upon the tax determinations which had been made by the said parties. If one thing is clear, it is that the parties did not anticipate, at that time, that Greek tax law would be interpreted and applied so as to impose a 20% or 25% withholding on payments made by either first or second defendant to claimant. Accordingly, the parties based their business analysis on the assumption that *no* corporate income tax was exigible and Greece, and that *no* corporate income tax would be exigible in Greece. This assumption proved wrong.

[45] "It is therefore the duty of the arbitral tribunal to decide whether disruption of the economic balance of the contracts which resulted from the imposition of the withholdings ought or ought not to be taken into consideration. A majority of the members of the arbitral tribunal thinks it does. The parties did agree upon an *initial* allocation of the taxes as between themselves, because this *initial* allocation worked out an economic balance which was satisfactory to all of them. But they never said that this initial allocation should be maintained at all costs, including the cost of disruption of the economic balance of the contracts. Indeed, as will be seen hereunder, they just said quite the opposite. The initial allocation of taxes provided by the contracts was to remain unchanged *rebus sic stantibus*. But changes in economic circumstances certainly could warrant a re-allocation of taxes as between parties. They certainly dictated that the parties make a bona fide effort in order to reach agreement with that re-allocation of taxes.

[46] "The arbitral tribunal does not harbour any doubt that the imposition of the withholdings on the compensation paid by first and/or second defendant to claimant constituted such a change in economic circumstances. As has been discussed hereinabove, the contracts were based upon an analysis of the economic profitability of the underlying transactions. That analysis led the parties to agree upon the initial allocation of taxes. Thus, this initial allocation of taxes was one of the elements which the parties took into account in order to work out their agreement. It may well be that the imposition of the withholdings did not result in any excessive hardship for claimant – a highly doubtful conclusion in light of the facts that (i) profit margins are usually low

in such a competitive environment as engineering, and that (ii) these profit margins were flattened out by double taxation. But whether the imposition of the withholdings resulted or did not result in excessive hardship within the meaning of Art. 388 of the Greek Civil Code is totally irrelevant here, since the parties had agreed that, in any case, they would enter into a bona fide attempt at settling the financial consequences thereof."

iii. The "Amendment Clauses"

(....)

[47] The "Amendment Clause" of the Service Agreement stated:

> "Whilst the parties have satisfied themselves (that) the provisions of the Agreement cover their overall relations, it may be reasonably expected that, during the execution of the Agreement and of the projects related therewith, some issues may need further arrangements and accordingly the parties undertake to effect any such additional arrangements/ amendments in writing and by mutual consent along the lines and the philosophy of the present Agreement."

The "Amendment Clauses" in the Sub-Contract and the Agreement both contained as opening sentence:

> "Should circumstances arise which call for waiver, alteration, or modification of the (contract), they may be made by mutual consent."

The Sub-Contract contained an additional sentence:

> "Proposals in this respect from one party shall be given due consideration by the other party."

[48] "Taken together, these three Amendment Clauses undoubtedly show that the parties had intended to forge as between themselves an enduring relationship. As a consequence, the parties to that enduring relationship did foresee that the contractual balance which they had defined at the inception of their relationship could be substantially modified by circumstances which were unforeseen at the time of the conclusion of the original Agreements. Very wisely, the parties thus made provisions for that type of situation, in the sense that they agreed that waivers, alterations or modifications in the said original Agreements could be made in order to take into account these circumstances. In other words, what they did was agree to open the re-negotiation of the original contracts, through '*waivers*', '*alterations*' or '*modifications*' thereof.

[49] "This re-negotiation, however, was made dependent upon a condition precedent, to wit, that the circumstances would '*call*' for waiver, alteration, or modification of the contracts. This condition, the arbitral tribunal understands, was inserted so as to prevent either party from using the Amendment Clause by reason of changes in circumstances having no impact on the balance of the contractual obligations. However, once it became clear that the change in circumstances was of such a nature as to warrant '*waiver*', '*alterations*' or '*modifications*' of the contracts, then the provision in the Amendment Clause [of the Subcontract and the Agreement] made it an obligation for either party to enter into bona fide negotiations in order to determine which waivers, alterations or modifications would be necessary in order to strike a new balance between the obligations of the parties.

[50] "This is not to say, however, that the parties had an obligation to reach agreement on the proposed waivers, alterations or modifications. The parties were left free to agree or not to agree upon such waivers, alterations or modifications. But what they could not possibly escape was the obligation to listen to the proposals which were put by one party to the other party. In short, they had the obligation, should circumstances require it, to sit and talk, and to talk in good faith. This is precisely the meaning of the second sentence of the Amendment Clause: 'proposals from one party shall be given due consideration by the other party'. It is true that this sentence is to be found solely in one contract[, the Subcontract]. But even if it were to be found in none of the contracts, the obligation to re-negotiate in good faith, which is inherent in the opening sentence of the Amendment Clause, still would be binding upon the parties. In that connection, the arbitral tribunal finds that the second sentence of the Amendment Clause is redundant, since it merely re-stated the intent of the parties, such as embodied in the opening sentence of the Amendment Clause. In so holding, the arbitral tribunal does not rest upon some freshly discovered principle of international trade law. It rests upon the very wording of Arts. 288 and 388 in the Greek Civil Code, which have been cited by the parties in their written submissions and oral presentations.

[51] "*Under Art. 288*, debtor is required to perform in *good faith*, taking into account business practices. The arbitral tribunal will not discuss here whether business practices, namely in the field of international commercial transactions, warrant or do not warrant reliance upon a general obligation to renegotiate in good faith. The arbitral tribunal is fully satisfied that the principle of performance in good faith, such as expressed in the Amendment Clauses, required that defendants renegotiate in good faith, if for no other reason that they had undertaken that obligation under the contracts.

[52] "*Under Art. 388*, changes in circumstances which the parties could not foresee at the time of conclusion of the Agreement warrant judicial modifi-

cation or even judicial termination of such Agreement. This is precisely what the arbitral tribunal has been called upon in order to decide. Claimant does argue that changes in economic circumstances prevailing at the time of conclusion of its contracts with first and/or second defendant resulted in a grave imbalance, which grave imbalance worked at the sole expense of claimant. Such an argument certainly could be made under Art. 388 of the Greek Civil Code.

[53] "As a consequence, claimant is seeking the only redress which it may seek, i.e., monetary damages, since the contracts between claimant and defendants have been fully carried out. The arbitral tribunal finds that neither Art. 288 nor Art. 388 preclude claimant from seeking such damages, since failure of first and/or second defendant to enter into re-negotiations left only that avenue open. The arbitral tribunal, by a majority decision, therefore holds that the contracts here under consideration *made it an obligation for the parties to re-negotiate their Agreements in case of change in circumstances* – an obligation which was totally consonant with Greek law, and namely Arts. 288 and 388 of the Greek Civil Code."

iv. The "Arbitration Clauses"

[54] "The Arbitration clauses ... may seem defective under a number of respects – though none of these defects, in the eyes of the arbitral tribunal, is of such gravity as to vitiate the clauses. Quite on the contrary, the clauses clearly reflect the common intent of the parties to resort to arbitration rather than to adjudication by courts of law. It is the duty of the arbitral tribunal to honour that common intent.

(....)

[55] "Paragraph 1 [cited above at [1]] clearly calls for a two steps procedure in order for the parties to settle their disputes. First step is a bona fide attempt at amicable settlement; second step is a final resolution of the dispute through international commercial arbitration. First step is a pre-requisite, in the sense that the parties cannot resort to international commercial arbitration before having made a bona fide attempt at amicable settlement. Thus, the parties must exhaust each and every possibility to amicably settle before they file a Request for Arbitration. But the arbitral tribunal notes that this obligation is not bearing upon *one* party; it is bearing upon *both* parties. In other words, whenever one of the parties lodges a claim as against the other party, then, both parties ought to make 'all necessary efforts' in order to amicably settle. This clearly means that each of the parties in dispute must make some effort, and that failure to make any effort therefore results in breach of a contractual obligation.

[56] "To be sure, this bona fide attempt at an amicable settlement is aimed at 'ironing out' any eventual dispute 'arising' out of the contracts. In that connection, first and second defendants have adamantly refused to acknowledge that the 'tax issues' here under consideration are disputes 'arising' out of the interpretation of the contracts. The arbitral tribunal has held that first and second defendants, in so doing, were clearly in error (see [10] et seq. hereinabove). The arbitral tribunal cannot but draw the consequences from that holding, and find that the 'tax issues' must be deemed to be 'disputes' within the meaning of paragraph 1 of the Clauses relating to 'Jurisdiction and Applicable Law'. The conclusion unescapably follows that, under the 'jurisdictional' clauses, first and second defendants had a duty to make 'all necessary efforts' in order to amicably settle the 'tax issues', and that failure to obey that duty resulted in a breach of their contractual obligations.

[57] "Of course, it has been argued that first and second defendants did make some efforts in order to resolve the 'tax issues', in the sense that they went to the Greek Tax Office and undertook to have the Greek Tax Authorities withdraw their decision. The arbitral tribunal does not dispute that fact – though the arbitral tribunal has not been convinced that first and second defendants used their best effort in that connection. But the arbitral tribunal finds that this is not the sort of efforts contemplated in the jurisdictional clauses. What the jurisdictional clauses contemplate is that both parties make all necessary efforts, *as between themselves*, in order to settle their dispute – and that, therefore, they make all necessary efforts in order to negotiate, as *between themselves*, an amicable settlement. The arbitral tribunal finds that the efforts which first or second defendant made *in the direction of the Greek Tax Office* do not satisfy that requirement."

b. Defendants found to be in violation of contractual obligations

[58] "Claimant has contended that failure by first and second defendants to take any action with respect to re-allocation of the tax burden as between claimant and defendants was clearly violative of their obligations. A majority of the arbitral tribunal, after having reviewed the various arguments of the parties, finds that first and second defendants are in violation of their contractual obligations, under the three following respects:

- first and second defendants, pending completion of the works, failed to take a clear and unambiguous position as to whether they would agree or would not agree to re-negotiate the contracts thereafter;
- first and second defendants, after completion of the works, failed to enter into bona fide negotiations with claimant for the purpose of determining

whether the change in economic circumstances warranted a re-allocation of the tax burden as between claimant, on the one hand, [and] first and second defendants on the other hand;

- first and second defendants, once the Greek Tax Office had started to impose the withholdings on the amounts paid to claimant, failed to enter into bona fide negotiations in order to amicably settle their differences with claimant, thereby forcing claimant into arbitration."

i. Defendants, pending completion of the works, failed to take a clear and unambiguous position as to whether they would agree or would not agree to re-negotiate the contracts

[59] "The parties do not dispute the fact that, at the time the Greek Tax Office started to impose the withholdings, claimant went to first and second defendants for the purpose of re-negotiating the contracts. However, the parties disagree as to what happened thereafter. Claimant, in that respect, contends that, once the Government of Greece had started to withhold the amounts in dispute, claimant, on the one hand, first and/or second defendant, on the other hand, did embark upon some re-negotiation of the contract price; that, during the oral phase of this re-negotiation, the parties did agree that a reasonable adjustment of the contract should take place, so that the additional burden resulting from the withholdings should be borne not only by claimant but also by first and second defendants.

[60] "Claimant points out to a number of documents in support of that contention.... While it is true that these documents and testimony do refer to some kind of an understanding between claimant, on the one hand, first and/or second defendant, on the other hand, they emanate solely from claimant, and the arbitral tribunal has been unable to find in the files any piece of evidence emanating from either first and/or second defendant, which would expressly corroborate the existence of any such understanding between the parties. Quite on the contrary, both first and second defendants have consistently denied, with the utmost vigor, the existence of that understanding. Their position is that, while claimant did try to impose upon them a re-negotiation of the contract prices, they certainly were never amenable or agreeable to such a re-negotiation.

[61] "But the argument of first and second defendants, however, cuts two ways. While it is clear that the evidence submitted to the arbitral tribunal does not warrant the conclusion that an understanding was reached between parties with regards to readjustment of contract prices, it is also clear that neither first nor second defendant expressed a firm willingness not to re-negotiate the contract prices, until the works had been completed and the payment obligations had arguably been discharged in full. By failing to express any such firm

willingness, first and second defendants indeed created an ambiguous situation which they may have found most convenient to them, because it enabled them to come out as the sole winners. Because they expressed no firm willingness not to re-negotiate, claimant had no reason not to perform under the contracts; but, because they expressed no firm willingness to renegotiate, they made it difficult for claimant to prove that some understanding had been reached with respect to readjustment of contract prices.

[62] "The arbitral tribunal also wishes to point out that, under the Amendment Clauses in the contracts, claimant could have elected, in light of the changes in economic circumstances, to negotiate a '*waiver*' of its obligation vis-à-vis first and second defendants. It chose not to go that route – a most commendable decision, since it avoided putting completion of the works into jeopardy. In that sense, claimant demonstrated a high sense of responsibility. But it also is clear that, by so doing, claimant also lost the upper hand in the negotiations with first and second defendants: once the works had been completed, claimant was very much dependent upon the good faith and good will of both first and second defendants in order to re-open negotiations. The arbitral tribunal must also take this factor into consideration when assessing the respective liabilities of the parties.

[63] "Therefore, a majority of the members of the arbitral tribunal finds that the behaviour of defendants, in and by itself, constituted a violation of their contractual obligations. First and second defendants, as has been shown hereinabove, had committed themselves to enter into re-negotiations with claimant, should changes in circumstances require it. This must have meant, at minimum, that first and second defendants should open discussions with claimant. This is not what happened. By failing to take any clear position, first and second defendants led claimant to believe that re-negotiations would take place. In light of that attitude claimant chose to complete its share of the works, with no other warranty tha[n] what it believed was an implicit commitment by first and second defendants to enter into re-negotiations.

[64] "Furthermore, a majority of the members of the arbitral tribunal finds that this behaviour, in and by itself, also constitutes a violation of the commands of the Greek Legislator, such as expressed in the Greek Civil Code. Art. 288 of the Greek Civil Code requires that contracts be performed in good faith. Performance in good faith means that no contracting party to a contract should be misled into expecting the other contracting party to do or not to do something, because of the ambiguous attitude of that other contracting party. The command of Art. 288 certainly would be violated, if the ambiguous attitude of one contracting party would mislead the other contracting party into doing or not doing something which was not provided for in the contract, or into doing or not doing something it would be excused from doing or not

doing under the contract. *Good faith excludes misleading attitudes, all the more when such misleading attitudes impact on performance.*

[65] "In light of the foregoing, a majority of the members of the arbitral tribunal finds that by failing to take a clear and unambiguous position with respect to re-negotiation of the contract while performance was still in progress, first and second defendants, be it unintentionally, or intentionally, misled claimant into believing that a re-allocation of taxes would take place once performance would be completed. Thus, the arbitral tribunal cannot but conclude that this failure on the part of first and second defendants to clearly inform claimant of their unwillingness to re-negotiate was wrongful and caused injury to claimant, if for no other reason that, due to this failure, claimant was entitled to entertain legitimate expectations with respect to the possibility of a re-allocation of taxes."

ii. Defendants, after completion of the works, failed to enter into bona fide negotiations with claimant for the purpose of determining whether the change in economic circumstances warranted a re-allocation of the tax burden between claimant, on the one hand, first and second defendants, on the other hand

[66] "As has just been stated, the ambiguous attitude of first and second defendants misled claimant into believing that first and second defendants were willing to enter into re-negotiations in order to re-allocate the tax burden as between the contracting parties. Indeed, claimant did take a number of steps in order to provoke such a negotiation. Conversations took place between claimant and defendants – at least according to claimant; letters followed letters. But apparently no real discussions ensued, since the proposals made by claimant were never clearly approved or disapproved by first and/or second defendant. Here again, the ambiguous attitude of defendants misled claimant into believing that bona fide negotiations had taken place and that these bona fide negotiations had resulted into a firm agreement between the parties as to readjustment of contracts.

[67] "Neither first or second defendant made the least effort in order to dissipate these ambiguities. The letters from claimant went unanswered, re-inforcing claimant into its belief that an agreement had been reached in respect to re-allocation of taxes."

iii. First and second defendants, after the dispute had developed, failed to enter into bona fide negotiations in order to amicably settle, thereby forcing claimant to resort to arbitration

[68] "Claimant, on the one hand, second defendant, on the other hand, had intended their relationship to develop into a long term partnership. This is

precisely the reason why first defendant was formed as between claimant and second defendant. Thus, each and every contract provided for mechanisms which would allow the parties to continue working together, even though some disputes might develop in the course of their relationship. Negotiation was an essential part of that mechanism. The parties fully understood that a process of continuing negotiation would be most useful in order to defuse conflicts which were bound to happen. Thus, they tried to incorporate that essential ingredient into the provisions of the so-called 'jurisdictional' clauses.

[69] "This, unfortunately, was of no avail. Once the dispute over the 'tax issue' had arisen, claimant did attempt to open negotiations with both first and second defendants in order to initiate an amicable settlement. At no time and in no way did first and second defendants ever respond to that attempt. They pretended that this was no dispute between parties; and that claimant was arbitrarily trying to shift the burden of the taxes withheld from claimant to first and second defendants. Indeed, not only first and second defendants [n]ever responded to the efforts of claimant, but first and second defendants, quite on the contrary, made their best efforts in order to block any direct negotiation as between claimant, on the one hand, [and] first and second defendants, on the other hand. The arbitral tribunal cannot but find that this attitude, by and in itself, constitutes a violation of the command in the so-called 'jurisdictional' clause."

c. *Measure of damages*

[70] "The arbitral tribunal, still speaking through a majority of its members, then turns to the next question, i.e., how should be measured the damages inflicted upon claimant by reason of failure by first and second defendants to enter into negotiations for the purpose of taking into account the consequences of the imposition of the withholdings on the balance of the contractual obligations.

[71] "It has been suggested that claimant suffered no injury because, notwithstanding the imposition of the withholdings, claimant was able to fully carry out its obligations. Then, and since, allegedly, claimant did not suffer any injury, the claim should be dismissed. The arbitral tribunal does not think, however, that this is true. Claimant did suffer injury, because its compensation was decreased by a significant percentage. It may be that this injury was not an irreparable injury; but, fortunately, there is no rule of law which would require that an injury be irreparable in order that the one who suffers it be allowed redress.

[72] "In that connection, the arbitral tribunal would like to point at the provision in Art. 345 of the Greek Civil Code. Art. 345 contemplates payment

of interest on the so-called 'monetary debt'. It provides that in the case of a 'monetary debt', interest shall accrue at the rate fixed by applicable legislation and/or regulations, and that debtor shall pay the corresponding amounts to creditor, even though creditor might not be able to prove that he or she suffered a *loss*. The clear implication of that provision is that Greek law does not require that creditor should always prove a loss in order to be awarded damages.

[73] "Furthermore, it ought to be remembered that claimant paid Italian corporate income taxes on the total amount of the compensation paid by first and/or second defendant to claimant. In other words, claimant paid Italian corporate income taxes on the total amount invoiced, not on the total amount received. Thus, claimant was caught in a typical double taxation situation, because its Greek source income was at the same time subject to Greek corporate income tax and Italian corporate income tax on its total amount. *Vide* the tax certificates ... which ... made it clear that claimant included in its tax statement the total amount of its 'earned billings', even though the 20% or 25% withholdings were applied by the Greek tax authorities on such 'earned billings'.

[74] Certainly, double taxation situations are highly destructive, and this is the reason why bilateral Treaties have been entered into for the purpose of avoiding such double taxation situations. It is true that the Greek-Italian Tax Treaty, which has been mentioned hereinabove, makes provision for mutual agreement procedures in order to precisely avoid that type of situations. But this does not mean that the arbitral tribunal ought not to take into consideration the destructive consequence of this double taxation situation when assessing the damage actually suffered by claimant.

[75] "Clearly, the damages *cannot be higher* than the total amount of the withholding here under consideration.... The position of claimant is that the arbitral tribunal ought to award that total amount to claimant – a position with which the arbitral tribunal finds itself unable to agree. In the eyes of the arbitral tribunal, the damages *must be somewhat lesser* than the withholdings here under consideration. In that connection, the arbitral tribunal has taken note of the fact that, at the time claimant made its first request to defendants with respect to re-allocation of the tax burden [in its letter to defendants], claimant limited its claim to 'a *reasonable readjustment* of contract price to compensate claimant *of the financial consequences suffered*' by reason of the withheld money.

[76] "What were '*the financial consequences suffered*' by reason of the withheld money? Nowhere does claimant suggest that these '*financial consequences*' were to be measured by the total amount of the money withheld. Quite differently and significantly, claimant wrote that these financial consequences were to be

measured by what they had '*suffered as a consequence of the money withheld*'. In other words, claimant suffered a damage because of the imposition of the withholdings. But this is not to say that the measure of that damage ought to be the total amount of the withholdings. Indeed, claimant's letter to defendants implied that there was a connection between the amount of the damage and the amount of the withheld money, but expressed no exact measure for that damage.

[77] "This interpretation of the arbitral tribunal is supported by the fact that claimant's letter to defendants, did not ask for a flat readjustment of the contract price which would take into account the total amount of the withheld money. Rather, the letter asked for a '*reasonable adjustment*' of the contract price, which ought to be '*discussed*' between claimant and the addressees of that letter. The concept of a 'reasonable adjustment' of the contract price, to be discussed between the parties to such contract, just means that the amount of that 'reasonable adjustment' was open to negotiation. And, indeed, if it was open to negotiation, this means that claimant was calling upon defendants in order to make a 'reasonable' offer. In short, claimant's letter cannot be read, according to the arbitral tribunal, as a firm claim for the total amount of the 'money withheld'.

[78] "The arbitral tribunal, on that basis, could have found that an even division between claimant and defendants of the total amount of the money withheld ought to be made in order to fulfill the request which claimant made at that time for a 'reasonable adjustment'. However, the arbitral tribunal also has to take into account the subsequent behaviour of defendants ... in order to assess the damages due and owing to claimant. The arbitral tribunal has found that this subsequent behaviour misled claimant into believing that a 'reasonable adjustment' of contract price would take place, thereby aggravating in the end the damage suffered by claimant, if for no other reason [than] that claimant continued to perform in good faith, before any clear understanding had been reached as between parties with respect to the 'reasonable adjustment'.

[79] "The arbitral tribunal, in order to assess the damage caused to claimant, must also take into consideration the fact that the defendants did try some efforts, if not their best efforts, in order to have the Greek authorities withdraw their decision on the withholdings. First and second defendants allege that they have made a number of attempts and gone through a number of steps in order to reach a solution to that problem. The arbitral tribunal certainly does not dispute these allegations. But whatever first and second defendants may have done in that connection should not obscure what they did not do, i.e., sit at the negotiation table with claimant, talk, and, if possible, settle. This, first and second defendants always refused, and the fact that they tried, to some extent, to mitigate the damages has no bearing on their refusal.

[80] "The arbitral tribunal, all considered, and speaking through a majority of its members, therefore holds that *the total amount of the moneys withheld should be split 35%-65%; and that 35% of the withholdings should be borne by claimant, whereas 65% of the withholdings should be borne by first and second defendants.*"

Final award in case no. 6955 of 1993

Parties:	Claimant: Trading company (Switzerland) Defendant: Manufacturer (US)
Place of arbitration:	Geneva, Switzerland
Published in:	Unpublished
Subject matters:	- non-conformity of goods - breach of warranty - timely notification of breach - acceptance of goods - revocation of acceptance of goods - re-acceptance of goods - trade usages regarding conformity of goods to standard specifications - material breach - replacement as remedy - calculation of damages

Facts

Claimant contracted to purchase from defendant a quantity of goods. The contract incorporated by way of reference various standards and specifications. Under the contract, all of the goods were to be delivered to the claimant's subcontractor where they were to undergo a further processing.

The goods were delivered to the subcontractor where they were processed and packaged. Agents of the defendant were present during these procedures and issued a report on the quality of the procedures and recommendations for improvements. When the goods were delivered to the end purchaser, they were rejected as defective due to non-conformity to specifications, lack of identifying marking, lack of waterproofing and corrosion. The end purchaser requested that claimant replace the goods. Agents of both claimant and defendant carried out various inspections both at the end purchaser and at the subcontractor. Following the inspection of the residual goods at the subcontractor, defendant wrote to claimant to explain that the results of its laboratory inspection had shown that the goods were only stained, not corroded.

Claimant initiated arbitration relying on the arbitration clause in the sale contract which provided for ICC arbitration. The contract provided that the law applicable to the dispute was the law of the State of Illinois and the application of the 1980 UN Sales Convention was excluded. Claimant sought the current replacement value of the goods as of the date of the award or alternatively, their actual replacement cost. Claimant subsequently ordered a quantity of goods from company Z, its parent company, as replacement in order to obtain the release of samples from end purchaser.

The arbitral tribunal appointed experts who were to inspect the goods. They issued two reports relative to their inspection of the residual goods at the subcontractor and to their inspection of samples of the goods that had been shipped to the end purchaser.

Applying the Uniform Commercial Code (UCC), which has been adopted by the State of Illinois, the arbitral tribunal found that claimant had accepted the goods from defendant, but that did not imply that the goods conformed to the contract. Although claimant only became aware that there was a question of non-conformity (corrosion) after the goods had been delivered to the end purchaser, and communicated this to defendant in a conditional manner, it had given defendant notice of breach within a reasonable time. The corrosion was not a non-conformity which claimant should have discovered earlier. Claimant was entitled to revoke acceptance because the corrosion had been difficult to discover and it had relied on defendant's assurances as to conformity. In spite of the indefiniteness of claimant's communications to defendant, the tribunal found that claimant had made an oral demand for replacement of the goods following the inspection at the subcontractor and had done so within a reasonable time. The tribunal also found that there was a trade usage allowing the goods to comply with the specifications as actually applied, rather than the exact wording. Further, claimant's actions concerning access for inspections and acquiring samples did not amount to a material breach relieving defendant of its duties to claimant.

Having found that the goods were not in conformity with the contract due to corrosion, the tribunal examined the available statutory and contractual remedies and found that they were not mutually exclusive. Claimant had made "cover" purchases from its parent company so that the price paid could not be shown to be a reasonable one in the marketplace. Consequently, no damages could be recovered for the difference between the cost of the cover and the contract price. Defendant was ordered to pay claimant the contractual price of the goods and claimant was ordered to return the goods in their present condition.

Excerpt

I. LACK OF CONFORMITY

1. *Applicable Law*

[1] "Illinois has adopted the UCC, a uniform act in effect in all American states except Louisiana. The pertinent articles are Art. 2, Sales, and Art. 1, General Provisions. Although variations in the application of the UCC do occur among the different states, in general it is applied uniformly. Thus it is common to cite cases from other jurisdictions, particularly when there is no local case on point, but also to reinforce local decisions. Nonetheless, in the case of conflict, local, here Illinois, judicial interpretations prevail over interpretations from other courts.

[2] "Most of the legal questions in this case are governed by UCC provisions. The UCC is not, however, a complete contract code comparable to the Civil Code. There are thus some contract questions here covered by the UCC only partially or not at all. These are governed by the common law of contracts as applied by Illinois courts."

2. *Non-conformity and Breach of Warranty*

[3] "In the UCC the term 'non-conformity' means that goods do not conform to the terms of the contract. The term 'breach of warranty' is broader, but generally encompasses non-conformity. Thus some circumstances could constitute a breach of warranty even though there is no non-conformity of the goods to the terms of the contract. But non-conformity is probably always a breach of warranty. See *Bodine Sewer, Inc. v. Eastern Illinois Precast, Inc.*, 143 Ill. App. 3d 920, 493 N.E.2d 705 (1986),... Non-conformity, not breach of warranty as such, is the basis for this award, and hence will be referred to throughout, even though the non-conformity also constitutes a breach of warranty under UCC Sect. 2-313(a) and probably (b)."

a. *Non-conformity of goods, inspection and certification, agency*

[4] "Claimant treats as separate issues the alleged non-conformity of the goods and claims that defendant violated its duties under the contract to inspect the goods properly and give accurate certificates of conformity. Claimant also asserts that in conducting inspections and certifying conformity defendant acted as claimant's agent and had fiduciary obligations to claimant. There is no question but that defendant had a duty under the contract to

inspect the goods and to certify the results of the inspections.... This right is moreover, one claimant purchased, as the price explicitly includes the cost of 'Acceptance inspection'. That the result of the inspections were to be certified is shown by the Annex which calls for a 'Certificate of Quality Control Inspection issued and signed by the Manufacturers' own system of inspecting and quality control...' as a term of the letter of credit arrangements. So too the express warranty of 5 years shelflife [starts] from the date of the Certificate of Conformance.

[5] "The fact that claimant had an optional right to be 'present during inspection' does not alter defendant's duties to inspect or provide accurate certificates. Claimant's rights to defendant inspection and certification is indeed a separate right from its rights to be supplied conforming goods. It is, however, unnecessary for the tribunal to decide whether these rights made defendant claimant's agent with fiduciary obligations, and if so, what those fiduciary obligations involved.

[6] "The only non-conformity the tribunal has found concerns corrosion (see below, II). This conclusion entails the further finding that defendant also violated its duties to inspect by failing to discover that corrosion, and by certifying the non-conforming goods. This, however, adds nothing to claimant's substantive rights nor does it raise the question of additional remedies.

[7] "Apart from claimant's assertions of non-conformities of the goods, the written record discloses no independent factual basis for finding a breach of defendant's duties to inspect and certify. Thus, the tribunal's findings that there were no non-conformities other than corrosion are also findings that defendant did not breach its duties to inspect and certify in any respect other than its failure to find corrosion. In view of the foregoing, the tribunal throughout will address non-conformities, without addressing failures to inspect and certify that could be inferred from the existence of non-conformities."

(....)

b. Acceptance of the goods; UCC Section 2-606(1)(c)

[8] "UCC Sect. 2-606 provides:

> '(1) Acceptance of goods occurs when the buyer
> ...
> (c) does any act inconsistent with the seller's ownership;...'

Defendant asserts that claimant accepted the goods. Claimant challenges this assertion. Claimant mingled the various defendant lots of goods and unpacked, processed, and repacked it in different lots, all of which are acts inconsistent with defendant's ownership. More important, the reselling of the goods to a third party, the end purchaser, is certainly a clear act inconsistent with the first seller's ownership. The tribunal therefore has no doubt that claimant accepted the goods under Sect. 2-606(1)(c)...."

c. *Effect of acceptance*

[9] "Under the UCC, the acceptance of goods has limited effects. These are set out in Sect. 2-607. The buyer must pay for the goods, Sect. 2-607(1), which claimant has done. The buyer can no longer reject the goods. Sect. 2-607(2). After acceptance, the buyer must give notice of any breach or be barred from any remedy (Sect. 2-607(3)(a)). Also, following acceptance, the buyer has the burden of proving any breach (UCC Sect. 2-607(4)) (Prior to acceptance, if buyer rejects the goods, the burden is on seller to show that the goods conformed and that buyer therefore breached the contract). Finally, UCC Sect. 2-607(2) provides that 'acceptance does not of *itself* impair any other remedy provided by this Article [2] for non-conformity' [Emphasis added].

[10] "To the extent that defendant asserts that there was acceptance, the tribunal agrees. However, the tribunal does not accept that claimant's acceptance – or at least the form it took, claimant's agent's signing of the Certificates of Quality Control Inspection – means that the goods conformed to the contract. It is evident that at the time claimant signed the Certificates it had not inspected the goods and was not expected to do so. The Certificates were sent to it in Switzerland by courier. Thus the claimant could not be found to have signaled that the goods were conforming. This could only signify that the content of the certificate itself conformed with the contract."

d. *Notice of breach: UCC Section 2-607(3)(a)*

[11] "UCC Sect. 2-607 provides:

> '(3) Where a tender has been accepted
> (a) the buyer must within a reasonable time after he discovers or should have discovered any breach notify the seller of breach or be barred from any remedy;'"

e. *Notice after actual discovery of breach*

[12] "The first written claimant communication to defendant which might be thought to constitute such notice was claimant's faxed letter to defendant of

November 1989. There were also telephone conversations around this time. This notice was given no more than four days after claimant received a telegram from the end purchaser setting out complaints about the goods. This was the first indication claimant had that the goods might be defective and that defendant might have supplied non-conforming goods. Unquestionably claimant's letter was sent within a reasonable time after claimant received end purchaser's telegram which is the earliest it could be said to have discovered a breach. But a question remains as to whether that letter constituted notification of a breach of the parties' contract.

[13] "On the date of the faxed letter, claimant's knowledge of possible breaches was limited to the information provided by end purchaser's telegram. Claimant did not then know that there was a breach, but only that there might be. This lack of knowledge was compounded by the fact that end purchaser's telegram dealt with the goods of two contracts. Claimant's letter is couched in cautious terms reflecting this uncertainty. This is hardly unusual in commercial situations, and the letter and phone conversations were in the circumstances enough to give defendant notice that the matter may be problematic.... In some circumstances notice of this kind might possibly suffice to constitute notice required by Sect. 2-607(3)(a). In this case, however, subsequent events cast more doubt on whether this fax was actual notice of breach of the contract. It is therefore necessary to consider further communications from claimant concerning breach.

[14] "... Following the faxed letter there was considerable communication between claimant and defendant respecting this matter. This culminated in a joint claimant-defendant inspection at end purchaser in February 1990.... The tribunal feels that the situation was sufficiently fluid and uncertain not to hold that claimant had knowledge of corrosion constituting a breach as of that time.... [T]he tribunal finds that defendant could reasonably have understood at the conclusion of the February inspection at the end purchaser that it had received no notice of a breach of the contract. It is also a reasonable inference that at this point claimant did not think there was a breach of the contract, although it thought there might be a breach of claimant's contract with the end purchaser respecting the processing of the goods.

[15] "In March 1990, claimant's Resident Director met with end purchaser officers to discuss alleged defects in the goods. This period appears to be the first time that claimant became fully aware of the seriousness of the end purchaser allegations of corrosion. This raises two questions. The first is whether claimant's awareness of the end purchaser's claims constituted discovery of a breach of the contract, such as to start the time running for giving notice under UCC Sect. 2-607(3)(a). It could be argued that it did not until claimant became reasonably convinced that in fact there was corrosion

at sufficient levels to breach the contract, which may have been later. The tribunal's resolution of the second question, however, makes it unnecessary to answer this first question."

f. Second question: Timely notice of breach?

[16] "The second question is whether, assuming claimant discovered the alleged corrosion breach in March 1990, it gave notice to defendant of that alleged breach within a reasonable time thereafter. In April 1990 claimant faxed defendant suggesting a second claimant-defendant inspection to be conducted at end purchaser in May. The key section relating to notice of breach is:

> 'If the second inspection results in a rejection of any or all of the processed goods, we will be required to replace the defective goods. This will require that [defendant] replace at its own costs all required processed goods in accordance with the contract specifications of the customer.'"

i. No mention of corrosion

[17] "Two aspects of this letter require consideration: first its failure to mention corrosion and second the conditional nature of its assertion of the existence of breach.

[18] "First, that the letter does not mention corrosion and appears to concern only processing defects does not make it defective under Sect. 2-607(3)(a). Comment 4 to that section states:

> 'The content of the notification need merely be sufficient to let the seller know that the transaction is still troublesome and must be watched. There is no reason to require that the notification which saves the buyer's rights under this section must include a clear statement of all the objections that will be relied on by the buyer, as under the section covering statements of defects upon rejection (Sect. 2-605).'

When the UCC is enacted by a particular state it is normal practice to include these comments with the published statute and this was done in Illinois. They do not constitute positive enacted law as to the UCC sections. Nonetheless, they typically carry a great deal of weight with the courts in interpreting and applying the UCC. As a leading textbook says: 'Besides the text itself, the Official Comments ... are by far the most useful aids to interpretation and construction.' (James J. White & Robert S. Summers, *Uniform Commercial Code*, p. 12 (3d ed. 1988) (hereafter, White & Summers). Accordingly, the tribunal finds that claimant's letter of April 1990 meets the first aspect of the notice requirements under UCC Sect. 607(3)(a).

(....)

[19] "The unexplained failure of claimant promptly to tell defendant of the end purchaser claims relative to corrosion is the cause of this present uncertainty. Nonetheless, in light of Comment 4, the tribunal does not believe claimant was required to mention corrosion in order to comply with UCC Sect. 2-607(3)(a).

[20] "Defendant suggests that the foregoing failure constituted a breach of claimant's duty of good faith under UCC Sect. 2-103. The measure of good faith under that section is 'honesty in fact and the observation of reasonable commercial standards of fair dealing in the trade'. Although claimant's failure to mention corrosion to defendant in its letter of April 1990 is both unexplained and now, with the benefit of hindsight properly viewed as unfortunate, the tribunal does not believe that it has been shown to amount to a violation of this standard."

ii. Conditional nature of assertion

[21] "The second aspect of claimant's letter of April 1990 is the conditional nature of its assertion of breach. Claimant does not clearly say that there has been a breach. Rather it couches its concerns in terms of further inspection aimed at determining if there has been a breach. This is not surprising, because apart from its omission of reference to corrosion, already discussed, claimant's letter provided defendant with all of claimant's information, which was that the end purchaser was asserting claims of breach of contract, and which, if correct, would constitute a breach of the contract. The tribunal finds that, in these circumstances, such a conditional assertion of potential breach meets the test of Sect. 2-607(3)(a). In fact, a strictly literal reading of that section would render it quite nugatory. In countless cases a buyer will discover facts it believes to be a breach, but until a court or arbitrator has held that this is a breach it cannot be said that the buyer has discovered a breach. Allowing a buyer in such circumstances to escape giving any notice at all except bringing a lawsuit or commencing an arbitration at its leisure would destroy Sect. 2-607(3)(a). So too, in circumstances like these, where the buyer with good reason seriously believes that there may be a breach, but cannot be sure even in its own mind that there is, a notice so stating complies with the section. This is such a case and claimant's letter of April is 'sufficient to let the seller know that the transaction is still troublesome and must be watched'."

(....)

g. *Should claimant have discovered the breach earlier?*

[22] "The foregoing findings concern only the question of the timeliness of the notice of breach after claimant actually discovered the alleged breach. They thus do not dispose of the question of Sect. 2-607(3)(a) notice. The claimant's notice of breach must also have been made within a reasonable time after claimant should have discovered the breach. Defendant argues that claimant should have discovered the allegedly incorrect specifications when it signed the Certificates of Quality Control Inspection respecting certain of the goods. It argues that claimant should have discovered the alleged breaches respecting the identifying marks, waterproofing, and corrosion when the goods were opened at the subcontractors and the processing undertaken. For the purpose of analysis only it may be assumed that if these contentions are correct, claimant's letter of April 1990 was not made 'within a reasonable time' under Sect. 2-607(3)(a).

[23] "The tribunal finds that claimant should have discovered the allegedly incorrect specifications for the certain product when its agent signed the Certificates of Quality Control Inspection in March 1989. The 'A' specification appears clearly on the cover page signed by its agent. He should have observed that the specification as so stated did not comply with the contract requirement of a 'B' specification. Pursuant to UCC Sect. 2-607(3)(a), notification of such an alleged breach should have been given within a reasonable time thereafter. There appears to have been no notice of alleged breach until claimant's Request for Arbitration in August 1990, which is not within a reasonable time. Thus the tribunal concludes that if there had been a breach respecting the specifications claimant would have lost its remedy therefore.

[24] "The foregoing conclusion gives rise to the question whether claimant's failure to comply with Sect. 2-607(3)(a) respecting one breach bars it from any remedy for all breaches. Read literally UCC Sect. 607(3)(a) might seem to have that effect. This would, however, have the absurd result of barring a buyer who discovers or should discover some minor breach and fails to advise seller from any remedy for serious breaches neither discovered nor reasonably discoverable until much later. The tribunal concludes UCC Sect. 2-607(3)(a) was not intended to bar remedies for non-conformities which buyer did not and need not have discovered simply because of others that should have been discovered but were not. Thus the bar posed by Sect. 2-607(3)(a) to claimant's failure to notify of the incorrect specification has no effect on claimant's remedies respecting other breaches.

[25] "... [T]he tribunal addresses the issue of notice of breach respecting only corrosion, which is the only breach it has found to have occurred. For several reasons the tribunal finds that the corrosion it has held to be a non-conformity

is not a condition that claimant 'should have discovered' at the subcontractors within the meaning of UCC Sect. 2-607(3)(a). *First*, whether or not a given unit is corroded so as to constitute a defect under the applicable Standards can be, and in this dispute was and is, a complicated and difficult question. The presence of corrosion at the low, but nonetheless non-conforming, levels occurring in this case is not something which necessarily leaps to the eye. Thus the tribunal's finding as a fact that there was such corrosion does not carry with it a necessary implication that the claimant should have discovered that corrosion at the subcontractors, even assuming the goods were in the same condition in 1989 that they were in 1992 and 1993.

[26] "*Second*, even if claimant had observed corrosion constituting non-conforming defects on particular goods that would not by itself have meant that the contract had been breached. The contract would only have been breached if there were enough such defects so that a lot sample would fail to meet the Standards. Thus, unless claimant was under an initial obligation to engage in such formal sampling procedures, its simply observing some corroded samples would not have been a breach claimant 'should have discovered'. Only if there were enough so that a reasonable person would have investigated further can it be said that a buyer in such circumstances 'should have discovered' the breach. This is a closer question, as there are substantially more corroded goods than the Acceptable Quality Level permits. Given these quantities, if the corrosion had been more highly visible than it was claimant might have had a duty to go further. Given the actual levels the tribunal finds that it did not.

[27] "*Third*, under the contract defendant was required to inspect pursuant to its 'own system of Inspection and quality control'. Defendant had done so, and had issued the pertinent Certificates of Quality Control Inspection. Claimant was entitled to rely on these certificates, perhaps not in the face of blatent non-conformities, but the corrosion was not blatant.

[28] "*Fourth*, other than subcontractor personnel, claimant apparently had no resident representative at the subcontractor during the processing....

[29] "In sum, the tribunal finds that, except with respect to the allegedly incorrect specifications, claimant complied with UCC Sect. 2-607(3)(a)."

3. *Revocation of Acceptance: UCC Section 2-608*

a. *Right to revoke: The law summarized*

[30] "The law governing the question of revocation of acceptance is UCC Sect. 2-608, the pertinent parts of which provide:

> '(1) The buyer may revoke his acceptance of a lot or commercial unit whose non-conformity substantially impairs its value to him if he has accepted it
> (a) ...
> (b) without discovery of such non-conformity if his acceptance was reasonably induced either by the difficulty of discovery before acceptance or by the seller's assurances.
> (2) Revocation of acceptance must occur within a reasonable time after the buyer discovers or should have discovered the ground for it and before any substantial change in the condition of the goods which is not caused by their own defects. It is not effective until the buyer notifies the seller of it.
> (3) A buyer who so revokes has the same rights and duties with regard to the goods involved as if he had rejected them.'"

(....)

b. Right to revoke: the law applied

[31] "UCC Sect. 2-608 Comment 2 states respecting impairment of value to the buyer:

> 'Revocation of acceptance is possible only where the non-conformity substantially impairs the value of the goods to the buyer. For this purpose the question is whether the non-conformity is such as will in fact cause a substantial impairment of value to the buyer though the seller had no advance knowledge of the buyer's particular circumstances.'

In claimant's role as intermediary, impairment of value of the goods turns on the rights of its customer, the end purchaser, and the reaction of the customer to any failures of the goods to conform to the contract between claimant and defendant. Since both contract[s] ... required the goods to be manufactured to [certain] specifications a non-conformity under one of the contracts is also a non-conformity under the claimant-end purchaser contract....

[32] "Defendant argues that the alleged non-conformities did not substantially impair the value of the goods to claimant, because of an absence of a showing that the non-conformities led to the end purchaser's rejection of the goods. The argument is repeated respecting damages and in terms of causation [by] defendant. This position is, however, belied by the evidence....

[33] "In [8] the tribunal concluded that acceptance of the of the goods took place at the latest when claimant transferred ownership of the goods to the end

purchaser.... [T]he tribunal [also] concluded that the earliest claimant discovered the existence of non-conforming corrosion was at the claimant-end purchaser meeting in March 1990, which was long after the acceptance.... Thus the tribunal concludes that claimant's acceptance was 'without discovery' of the corrosion, as required by UCC Sect. 2-608(1)(b). For claimant to have a right of revocation, it is not enough that it accepted without prior discovery of the corrosion. It must also show that its failure to discover was induced by either one of two things: (1) difficulty of discovery before acceptance; or (2) by defendant's assurances.

[34] "If 'difficulty of discovery' of the corrosion reasonably induced the acceptance then claimant is not barred from revocation. [T]he tribunal [has] concluded that the corrosion was not a condition claimant 'should have discovered' at subcontractor's within the meaning of UCC Sect. 2-607(3)(a). Two of the factors leading to that conclusion are applicable here. First is the difficulty of deciding in a case like this what is and what is not corrosion of a given item. Second is the need for a full audit with proper sampling techniques to determine whether there is enough of what is seen. The latter is no small undertaking. Nothing in the case suggests that either defendant or claimant ever anticipated that claimant would undertake such inspections. In fact the contract itself contemplated that claimant would satisfy its curiosity on that score, if at all, by attending defendant's inspections, not by conducting its own. In the tribunal's view the need for fullscale sampling and inspection to ascertain whether there was a breach respecting corrosion constituted 'difficulty of discovery' within the meaning of UCC Sect. 2-608(1)(b).

[35] "Claimant's failure to discover the corrosion is also excused under UCC Sect. 2-608(1)(b) if it was induced by defendant's assurances. No one does or could question that defendant gave assurances that there was no non-conforming corrosion.... The only question is whether those assurances induced claimant's nondiscovery of the corrosion. The tribunal concludes that it did, for the same reasons that it concluded that claimant was entitled to rely on defendant's Certificates of Quality Control Inspection respecting the giving of notice under UCC Sect. 2-607(3)(a)."

c. *Right to revoke: Did claimant exercise its right to revoke?*

[36] "UCC Sect. 2-608 is silent on what constitutes an exercise of the right to revoke an acceptance, except that Sect. 2-608(2) clearly requires notification of the seller. Both comments and case law, however, fill out this omission. Comment 5 provides:

> 'The content of the notice under subsection (2) is to be determined in this case as in others by considerations of good faith, prevention of surprise, and reasonable adjustment. More will generally be necessary than the mere notification of breach required under the preceding section. [UCC Sect. 2-607(3)(a)].... The fact that quick notification of trouble is desirable affords good ground for being slow to bind a buyer by his first statement.' (Id.).

Thus notification is required, but it must be more than mere notification of breach (White & Summers, p. 374). The notification must 'also inform the seller that the buyer does not wish to keep the goods' (Id.). White & Summers go on to state that: 'If the buyer equivocates in word or deed, his purported revocation will very likely be invalid'

[37] "We will now examine claimant's communications to defendant to determine which, if any, constituted such notification.

(....)

[38] "The next communication which needs to be considered is claimant's faxed letter of April 1990. In [11]-[21] above the tribunal found that this letter constituted a notice of breach complying with UCC Sect. 2-607(3)(a). The language pertinent to revocation of acceptance is the same as that respecting notice of breach:

> 'If the second inspection results in a rejection of any or all of the processed goods, we will be required to replace the defective goods. This will require that defendant replace at its own costs all required processed goods in accordance with the contract specifications of the customer.'

While this language was found (with some difficulty) to constitute notice of breach it does not state that claimant was revoking its acceptance of the goods. The most it can be argued to do is to imply the claimant will do so if a second inspection shows non-conformity with the contract. It is not an unequivocal statement that claimant does not wish to keep the goods.

(....)

[39] "Given the indefiniteness of [the] testimony on that score the tribunal is not disposed to find that the claimant ever gave defendant a written demand for replacement of the goods prior to its Request for Arbitration in August 1990. On the other hand, while there is confusion in Mr. X's testimony concerning defendant's response to an alleged oral demand for replacement, Mr. X was definite that such a demand had been made. As mentioned earlier, nothing in UCC Sect. 2-608 requires notice of revocation of acceptance to be in writing. The tribunal has no reason to disbelieve Mr. X's testimony that an

oral demand was made for replacement of the goods, and nothing occurring in the relations between the parties after [events at the subcontractors], makes such a demand seem unlikely. Accordingly, the tribunal finds that claimant made an oral demand for replacement of the goods sometime not long after the inspection at the subcontractors.

[40] "A question remains whether a buyer's demand for replacement sufficiently notifies the seller that the buyer intends to return the original goods, a requirement for revocation of acceptance. As a matter of ordinary commercial understanding such a demand would normally imply that the buyer expects to give up the original goods when they are replaced.

(....)

[41] "Although the tribunal has held that a notice of revocation of acceptance need not be in writing, it may be noted that claimant's first written demand for replacement of the ammunition which has been satisfactorily established is in its Request for Arbitration in August 1990. This too is silent respecting claimant's intention to return the original goods, and hence to revoke its acceptance of the goods. Such an intention can, however, be inferred for the reasons stated above.

[42] "An aspect of revocation of acceptance is that the buyer inform the seller that the buyer does not wish to keep the goods. Underlying this proposition is the basic idea that the seller is reacquiring its ownership interest in the goods, subject to any security interest the buyer may have in them for repayment of the price and various expenses. Thus a mere notice of intention to revoke the acceptance may be ineffective if, for one reason or another, actions of the buyer have made it impossible for the seller to reacquire ownership. A question concerning this aspect arises in this case because of the resale to the end purchaser. This question is best considered in detail in connection with language of UCC Sect. 2-608(2) discussed [below] relating to changes in the condition of the goods.

[43] "UCC Sect. 2-608(2) requires that

> 'Revocation of acceptance must occur within a reasonable time after the buyer discovers or should have discovered the grounds for it *and* before any substantial change in the condition of the goods which is not caused by their own defects.' [Emphasis added]

(....)

[44] "[T]he latter part of March – is the starting point for determining whether claimant's notice of an intention to evoke its acceptance was timely, apart from the question of the change of condition of the goods. The tribunal has found that claimant gave an oral notice of an intention to revoke

acceptance not long after the inspections at the subcontractors in June. It has also found that its Request for Arbitration, in August 1990 constituted a written notice of such intention (Id.). The tribunal believes that either of these times can be considered to be within a reasonable time after the latter part of March for claimant to give notice of revocation of acceptance.

[45] "In general the spirit of the UCC is that of going forward with contracts rather than undoing them.... In contrast to this, the remedy of revocation of acceptance is a drastic action for a party to take since it undoes the contract the parties made. Thus, unlike prompt notice under UCC Sect. 2-607(3)(a), which is to be encouraged, parties should not, in the absence of prejudice to the seller, be put under pressure to revoke hastily in order to avoid losing the right to have this particular remedy.

(....)

[46] "The oral demand for replacement of the goods was made shortly after the inspections at the subcontractor in June 1990 and in close proximity to the communications to end purchaser in which claimant told the end purchaser it would replace the goods. The tribunal finds that defendant was not prejudiced by claimant's wait for the outcome of the inspections at the subcontractors and defendant's response to them to make their demand."

d. Right to revoke: Change of condition of goods

[47] "The second requirement of UCC Sect. 2-608(2) is that the revocation must occur 'before any substantial change in condition of the goods which is not caused by their own defects'. This provision is possibly pertinent because of the processing of the goods and because of the resale to the end purchaser, both of which occurred long before claimant's revocation of acceptance.

[48] "It may be true that the processing of the goods has changed its condition within the literal meaning of UCC Sect. 2-608(2). A literal reading, however, is not a sound reading. Comment 6 describes the policy of the subsection as that of

> 'seeking substantial justice in regard to the condition of goods restored to the seller. Thus the buyer may not revoke his acceptance if the goods have materially deteriorated except by reason of their own defects.'

Examples of such deterioration, [are] provided by White & Summers.... They go on, however, to say that 'reasonable changes due to good faith efforts by the buyer to make the goods usable do not bar revocation' (Id. p. 374).

[49] "The tribunal finds that the processing constituted the latter type of change. Loose goods of this kind and in these quantities must be either

processed or put into containers to be usable. Assuming the processing was done properly – at the end of the day, after much dispute, this appears to be the case – it adds to the value of the goods. There is thus no deterioration either physical or economic due to the processing. The processed goods defendant will receive back are more valuable than if they had not been processed, and hence the policy of Sect. 2-608(2) will be achieved by allowing revocation insofar as processing is concerned.

(....)

[50] "Resale, and the fact that the goods were still in the hands of and under the control of the end purchaser as of the final hearings poses the greatest problem to claimant's successful revocation of acceptance. As White & Summers state, a resale of the goods without recalling them constitutes a change in the condition of the goods within the meaning of UCC Sect. 2-608(2) (White & Summers, p. 374). The question thus arises whether claimant has recalled the goods.... The tribunal finds that the claimant's insistence with the end purchaser that the goods be returned to the United States when replacement goods [were] supplied was sufficient for claimant to avoid falling afoul of the change of condition limitation of UCC Sect. 2-608(2).

(....)

[51] "[T]o the extent it is unable to return the full quantity claimant's revocation is necessarily ineffective. No evidence was produced that any goods have been scrapped or otherwise disposed of because of corrosion, except perhaps a literal handful which have taken apart or subjected to destructive testing. To the extent that it is unable to do so its recovery of the price under the contract should be reduced proportionally.

[52] "The general idea underlying revocation of acceptance under UCC Sect. 2-608 is that the buyer ceases to be the beneficiary of ownership of the goods and that the goods remain or become again goods belonging to the seller. Thus, it is not enough simply that there be a revocation of acceptance, but the buyer must not thereafter re-accept the goods by any further 'act inconsistent with the seller's ownership' (UCC Sect. 2-606(1)(c) see also White & Summers, p. 375). Typically this involves continued use of the goods....

[53] "In the present case claimant no longer has possession or ownership of the goods and it might at first glance seem that re-acceptance is not possible. Claimant has, however, the price of the goods paid to it by end purchaser. It's retention of that price coupled with its acquiescence at any point in the end purchaser retaining the goods would be a 'resale without recall' and hence would constitute an acceptance precluding further revocation.

[54] "Thus far nothing on the record suggests that claimant has withdrawn its insistence that the end purchaser return the goods to the United States contemporaneously with delivery of the replacement goods. Hence nothing

suggests that claimant has thus far re-accepted the goods by reasons of the existence of a 'resale without recall'. If, however, claimant wants to keep its revocation of acceptance intact, it must avoid such a re-acceptance by in fact recalling the goods from end purchaser and at the appropriate time making it available to defendant....

[55] "Claimant properly notes that under UCC Sect. 2-608(3)

> 'A buyer who so revokes has the same rights and duties with regard to the goods involved as if he had rejected them.'

Claimant goes on to argue that a buyer rejecting goods has no duty to return them, and hence claimant has no duty to return the goods."

[56] Claimant cited two Illinois cases for this proposition but the arbitral tribunal found that they were not on point. It concluded: "The major part of the claimant quotation, including the words emphasized by the court, is simply statutory language from UCC Sect. 2-602(2). It is most important respecting this case to note that claimant substituted an ellipsis in its quotation where the court included subsection (a) of UCC Sect. 2-602(2):

> '(a) after rejection any exercise of ownership by the buyer with respect to any commercial unit is wrongful as against the seller.'

It would be an exercise of ownership were claimant, particularly while retaining the purchase price it received from the end purchaser, to allow the end purchaser to keep the goods permanently. Not only would it be wrongful while claimant maintains that it has revoked acceptance, but it would also constitute a re-acceptance.

[57] "[The termination article] of the contract provides:

> '... should the Seller hereto fail to perform or observe any of the obligations or conditions on his part to be performed or observed here under this Contract, or fail to meet the delivery schedule and fail to remedy the breach within 90 days after written notice to remedy the same, the Buyer should be entitled, in addition to and without prejudice to any other remedy available, forthwith to terminate the contract.'

This provision appears to confer a right on claimant comparable to the right to revocation of acceptance under UCC Sect. 2-608, but without all of the Sect. 2-608 limitations...."

(....)

4. Compliance with Contractual Specifications

[58] "The question arises as to just what it means for the goods to be in compliance with or to meet the criteria of a particular specification. At least two related, but nonetheless different meanings are possible here. One is that the goods must comply with the exact wording of the specification irrespective of how that specification is applied in the trade. This is the position urged by claimant throughout its brief. Another is that the language means that the goods must comply with the specification as actually applied by the specifying organization in plants supplying such goods to it. This is the position urged by defendant. For two reasons the tribunal believes that the second of these meanings is that intended by defendant and claimant in entering this contract. The first concerns additional language in the contract; the second concerns trade usage at specifier's goods plants." The tribunal concluded that additional contract language and trade usages supported this interpretation.
(....)

a. General requirements for establishing a usage of trade

[59] "UCC Sect. 1-205(2) provides:

> 'A usage of trade is any practice or method of dealing having such regularity of observance in a place, vocation or trade as to justify an expectation that it will be observed with respect to the transaction in question. The existence and scope of such a usage are to be proved as facts....'

[60] "Before dealing with the elements of usage of trade, it should be noted that usage of trade must not be confused with course of dealing, which concerns prior dealings between the parties (UCC Sect. 1-205(1)).... Usage of trade on the other hand concerns usages of a place, vocation, or trade, and its proof does not depend upon anything going on between the parties other than their participation in trading at the place, in the vocation, or in the trade in question. There are three elements in the UCC formulation of usage of trade: (1) regularity of observance, (2) in a place, vocation or trade, (3) justifying the expectation that the usage will be observed in the transaction. For a trade usage to be used in a case there is a fourth requirement: proof of the usage as a fact.

[61] "*Regularity of observance.* Prior to enactment of the UCC, and to a considerable extent still respecting non-UCC law, usage of trade – or custom as it was more commonly called – was often said to have to be '"ancient and

immemorial", "universal" or the like', to quote UCC Sect. 1-205, Comment 5. (These were ancient English tests). Comment 5 states that the ancient English tests are abandoned. It states that UCC Sect. 1-205 provides for full recognition 'for new usages and for usages currently observed by the great majority of decent dealers'. As examination of UCC Sect. 1-205(2) shows, the test now is related to whether there is such regularity of observance as to justify an expectation that it will be observed in the transaction in question. Thus whether there is sufficient regularity of observance is largely determined by the third element, discussed below.

[62] "*Place, vocation or trade.* This language raises the question whether the usage of the specifying organization and defendant at approved goods plants is that of a place, vocation, or trade. Ordinarily one would expect to find more than two identifiable parties establishing a trade usage. But that is because ordinarily more than two identifiable parties are involved in business at a particular place, in a particular vocation, or in a particular trade. In this instance, however, the evidence (undisputed) is that [the] goods are made in only two places, in both of which the dominant party is the specifying organization, and a second permanent party is the defendant. Other customers are undoubtedly part of the 'trade', but the content of the usages are those established by the specifying organization with the acquiescence of defendant and its other customers who necessarily have to go along with them if they want defendant to make the goods. In this respect it may be noted that UCC Sect. 1-205 Comment 7 states that the usage 'may be either general to trade or particular to a special branch of trade'.

(....)

[63] "*Justifying the expectation that the usage will be observed in the transaction.* The preceding elements – regularity of occurrence and place, vocation, or trade – are to be tested by whether they justify the expectation that the usage will be observed in the transaction. Under the UCC (and indeed under older law), this does not require that both (or indeed, perhaps either) parties actually have such an expectation. UCC Sect. 1-205(3) provides that 'any usage of trade in the vocation or trade in which [the parties] are engaged or of which they are or should be aware give particular meaning to and supplement or qualify terms of the agreement.' Thus the standard is an objective one; by engaging in the trade claimant is assumed to have the expectations generated by (proven) trade usages of that trade.

[64] "*Proof of trade usage as facts.* The final requirement is that the usage be adequately proven as a fact. The trade usage pertinent to this case is the practice of the specifying organization to modify its specifications or standards. Defendant has proved as a fact to the satisfaction of the tribunal that the

specifying agency has done this respecting identifying marking, waterproofing, and corrosion....

[65] "The question remains whether these three examples are sufficient to establish as a fact that a trade usage exists meeting the requirements of UCC Sect. 1-205(2). The tribunal concludes that they are. This is in part because the trade usage harmonizes with the interpretation the tribunal otherwise places on the contract language. Thus the Illinois authorities cited by claimant refusing to find trade usages where they were in substantial conflict with the contract language or made substantial changes in the content of the contract are not persuasive. The trade usage is pertinent here because it confirms the contract, not because it modifies or contradicts the contract. The tribunal is also influenced by the experience of its members that practices such as those described are common to bureaucracies governed by extremely intricate rules which otherwise are too rigid for practical operation.

[66] "Although the specific modifications can be stated as only three, one of them – the corrosion standard – affects all the goods defendant manufactures. They are thus more prevalent than may at first appear. The tribunal concludes that their existence justifies the parties' expectations that the usage would be observed in the contract.... [C]laimant need not actually have such an expectation, only that it would have had it been aware of these facts, as it should have been as a trader in this market."

b. Trade usage: Explanation/supplementation not contradiction

[67] "UCC Sect. 2-202(a) provides:

> 'Terms ... which are ... set forth in a writing intended by the parties as a final expression of their agreement with respect to such terms as are included therein may not be contradicted by evidence of any prior agreement or ... but may be explained or supplemented
> (a) by a usage of trade (Section 1-205);'

It is often excruciatingly difficult to distinguish between explanation or supplementation on the one hand and contradiction on the other.... This common difficulty does not, however, create a problem here, because as noted above, the usage of trade pertinent here supports the interpretation the tribunal has put on the contract. Thus this usage explains or supplements the language of the contract, it does not contradict it."

(....)

5. *Claimant's Alleged Failure to Provide Access to Records and Facilities*

[68] "Defendant argues that claimant was guilty of a material breach of contract by reason of defendant's not being given access to records and facilities to investigate the cause of the alleged defects. Defendant appears to argue that this material breach bars claimant from all remedies. Defendant bases this argument on two grounds, the first being a provision in the Annex to the contract providing:

> 'Seller shall be given full access to records and facilities to investigate the cause of the alleged defect.'

The other basis is UCC Sect. 2-515(a), which provides:

> 'In furtherance of the adjustment of any claim or dispute
> (a) either party on reasonable notification to the other and for the purpose of ascertaining the facts and preserving evidence has the right to inspect, test and sample the goods including such of them as may be in the possession or control of the other;'

[69] "The tribunal holds that the contract provision should be understood as binding claimant only insofar as it had control over the facilities and records. Since this is clear respecting UCC Sect. 2-515 the effect of the provision in the Annex is to expand defendant's right respecting access beyond the goods themselves to include records and facilities. The tribunal thinks it would be unreasonable to read the Annex as going further and imposing an absolute duty to supply access even though claimant had no control and was unable to supply it. Thus the fact alone that defendant was unable to inspect the goods in the hands of the end purchaser constitutes a breach of neither the Annex nor of UCC Sect. 2-515. Such failure to provide access would be a breach only if claimant had some control and failed to exercise it upon defendant's request. (....)

[70] "It is unnecessary for the tribunal to make a firm decision respecting the difficult questions whether the delays respecting inspection of the goods constituted a breach of claimant's duties under the Annex, because only if the breach were material breach might it have the effect defendant desires, which is to bar claimant from the remedies it seeks. As will be seen the tribunal holds that claimant's conduct did not constitute a material breach."

6. *Material Breach*

[71] "A great deal of time and energy was expended throughout the arbitration by both parties respecting claimant's and defendant's participation and non-participation in various inspections, with each party alleging various breaches by the other giving rise to various rights, including the one addressed here. It is necessary to resolve the factual disputes on these points here only if what claimant did or did not do was a material breach. That is, only if claimant's alleged derelictions were ones which would relieve defendant of all of its duties under the contract, as distinct from a breach merely giving rise to any damages defendant could prove. Defendant argues that claimant's conduct constituted not only a breach, but a material breach relieving it of all of its duties to claimant. The tribunal rejects this argument for two related reasons. It concludes that, assuming claimant's actions or inactions were a breach, they were not a material breach.

[72] "A material breach is one which may relieve the other party of its obligations under a contract. Under Illinois law whether a breach is material is a question of fact (*Sahadi v. Continental Illinois National Bank*, 706 F.2d 193 (7th Cir. 1983); *F.E. Holmes & Son Construction Co. v. Gualdoni Electric Service Inc.*, 105 Ill. App.3d 1135, 435 N.E.2d 724 (5th Dist. 1982). Nonetheless principles have emerged in Illinois (and in American law generally) describing what kinds of facts are pertinent. These were described in *Trapkus v. Edstroms, Inc.*, 140 Ill. App.3d 720, 489 N.E.2d 340, 345 (3d Dist. 1986) where the court quotes with approval an Alabama case:

> '... the circumstances attending the breach, the intention with which it was committed, and its effect on the other party and on the general object sought to be accomplished by the contract, must be considered in determining whether the breach will operate as a discharge; that if the circumstances are such as manifest an intention on the part of the party in default to abandon the contract, or not to comply with its terms in the future, or if by reason of the breach, the object sought to be effected is rendered impossible of accomplishment according to the original design of the parties, the breach will operate as a discharge of the whole contract unless waived; and that the right to claim a discharge of the whole contract depends, not on whether the act constituting the breach was inconsistent with the terms of the contract, but whether it was inconsistent with an intention to be further bound by its terms or whether the breach was such as to defeat the purpose of the contract.'

Illinois cases also lay down the principle that materiality of breach is to be determined by 'the inherent justice of the matter' (*Susman v. Cypress Venture*, 187 Ill. App.3d 312, 543 N.E.2d 184 (1st Dist. 1989); *Niemoth v. Kohls*, 177 Ill. App.3d 54, 524 N.E.2d 1085 (1st Dist. 1988).

[73] "Prior to the commencement of the arbitration claimant's response to defendant's informal request for inspection in June 1990 was that it would be difficult. Defendant did not press its request pending the inspection at the subcontractor (Id.). Certainly at this point none of the *Trapkus* tests for a material breach are met, nor would 'the inherent justice of the matter' call for holding claimant's breach, if any, to be material. Defendant's next request in October 1990, was a formal one made after the arbitration had commenced. Claimant's response two weeks later was negative but subject to possible discovery in arbitration. If communication had stopped here the tribunal would have had to decide whether, in the context of the parties being now locked in the adversary process of arbitration, this met the *Trapkus* tests or led to an inherently unjust situation. But communication did not stop. Defendant tried again a week later. Claimant replied three weeks later expressing claimant's willingness to request the end purchaser to 'provide a reasonable number of lot samples' on a number of conditions. If this was a breach it was one not meeting the *Trapkus* tests for a material breach. Nor in the context of the dispute having been submitted to arbitration did it lead to an inherently unjust situation. It was, indeed, a situation the arbitrators and parties were able to remedy through the return of a quantity of goods to a laboratory, albeit after extensive delays. While the delays undoubtedly caused defendant (as well as claimant) some problems they were not such as would create an inherently unjust situation.

[74] "A final and independently conclusive reason why any claimant failures to supply access are not breaches relieving defendant of all of its duties lies in the nature of the warranty article and the Annex. Defendant appears to argue that they confer independent rights on defendant to have access to records and goods sold. Thus, if material, a breach of these rights would relieve defendant of its duties generally under the contract and bar claimant from all remedies. Defendant, given its proper concern to avoid damage to its reputation as a leading quality producer of goods, might well desire such independent rights. They are not, however, to be inferred in an ordinary commercial contract..., and would require to be spelled out clearly. That has not been done or even attempted in the contract. The warranty article and the Annex do not confer independent rights on defendant to 'be given full access to records and facilities to investigate the cause of the alleged defect'. These words are in provisions conferring remedial rights on claimant for breaches by defendant. In that context such access in the contract is no more than a condition to claimant's

entitlement to remedies under the warranty article and the Annex. Thus, the only effect failure of that condition can have is to bar claimant's remedies under the warranty article and the Annex."

II. CONFORMITY OF GOODS

[75] The tribunal determined that the goods were properly marked, and adequately waterproofed. However, it found that the existence of corrosion on the goods meant that the whole order was contaminated.

III. REMEDIES SOUGHT

[76] "The following discussion is founded on the tribunal's finding that defendant breached the contract by supplying goods that were non-conforming in that the goods had an excessive number of corroded units."
(....)

1. Bases for Replacement Remedy

[77] "There are two possible bases for a replacement remedy. One is the general law governing specific performance found in UCC Sect. 2-716. Because claimant has abandoned its claim to specific replacement of the goods, it is unnecessary to consider whether its original claim to such right met the requirements of UCC Sect. 2-716 for that remedy. The other is in the specific provisions contained in the contract.
[78] "Because claimant has abandoned its claim to specific replacement of the goods, it is as well unnecessary to consider the provisions in the contract relating to replacement respecting specific relief. It is, nonetheless, necessary to set out those provisions briefly because they affect one issue still alive in the case: defendant's argument that these provisions constitute an exclusive remedy and that claimant has waived that remedy. Related to this is claimant's contention that defendant breached its duties under these provisions to replace the goods as argued by claimant....
[79] "The contract contains two clauses pertaining directly to this subject, one, the 'non-conformity article' and the 'warranty article'. The *non-conformity article*,... provides:

> 'In case any item/items are rejected by the Buyer for non-conformity with specifications and modifications agreed upon, as per conditions of

> Contract, then all expenses incurred by the Buyer resulting from the return movement of rejected items to the Seller must be borne by the Seller. The Seller must arrange for replacement of rejected items returned to him free of charge (including the freight and insurance charges) as per the specifications and modifications.'

The tribunal finds that this provision confers explicit rights on claimant to replacement of non-conforming goods, along with reimbursement for expenses incidental to their return.

(....)

[80] "Finally, the *warranty article* states: 'Details of the warranty are given in the Annex.' The Annex 'guarantees' against defects 'in material or manufacture' for 5 years, and provides that the guarantee 'shall cover the replacement and repair of defective materials'.

[81] "The tribunal finds that the warranty article repeats claimant's rights to replacement of goods not conforming to the contract specifications. The non-conformity article and the warranty article (with the Annex) go beyond the UCC by providing the buyer with a specific replacement remedy apparently without the necessity of meeting the requirements of UCC Sect. 2-716 for specific performance. It is thus an 'additional remedy' within the meaning of UCC Sect. 2-719(1)(a) which permits the parties to agree to additional remedies. The tribunal has little doubt that these provisions are valid provisions under the UCC.

(....)

[82] "Defendant has raised the warranty article, in particular the Annex, as a defense against claimant's claims. This in turns raises, inter alia, questions of defendant's alleged breach of the provisions. We turn now to this defensive aspect of the provisions."

a. Exclusivity of remedial provisions in contract

[83] "UCC Sect. 2-719(1)(a) provides:

> '[T]he agreement may provide for remedies in addition or in substitution for those provided in this Article and may *limit* or alter the measure of damages recoverable under this Article, *as by limiting* the buyer's remedies to return of the goods and repayment of the price or *to repair and replacement of non-conforming goods or parts*;' [Emphasis added]

Comment 1 to Sect. 2-719 states that

> 'Under this section parties are left *free* to shape their remedies to their particular requirements and reasonable agreements limiting or modifying remedies are to be given effect.' [Emphasis added]

Under these tests there is little doubt of the validity of the Annex even if it does limit claimant's remedies to replacement pursuant to the Annex. The question to which we now turn is, however, whether it does so."

b. Did the parties limit the remedy to replacement?

[84] "UCC Sect. 2-719(1)(b) provides that

> '[R]esort to a remedy as provided is *optional unless* the remedy is *expressly agreed* to be exclusive, in which case it is the sole remedy.' [Emphasis added]

Comment 2 to Sect. 2-719 states that

> 'Subsection (1)(b) creates a *presumption* that clauses prescribing remedies are cumulative rather than exclusive. If the parties intend the term to describe the sole remedy under the contract, this must be clearly expressed.' [Emphasis added]

[85] "Defendant asserts that the Annex (incorporated by the warranty article) is an exclusive remedy. The key language in the Annex supporting this assertion is the following:

> 'The above stated warranty and remedies are exclusive and in lieu of any other warranties or remedies whether express or implied including any warranty of merchantability or fitness for a particular purpose.'

If the warranty article and the Annex were the only provisions in the contract dealing with remedies, this assertion would be sound. This is not the case, however. Both the non-conformity article and remedy article are separate remedial provisions. The non-conformity article deals with remedies for 'non-conformity with specifications and modifications'. There is no language in the non-conformity article making it an exclusive remedy, nor any language referring to its terms being limited by the warranty article and the Annex. Thus the non-conformity article is in its own language unquestionably not itself an exclusive remedy under UCC Sect. 2-719(1)(b).

[86] "The question remains, however, whether the Annex limits the non-conformity article. In other words, does the Annex, which limits remedies for breach of warranties, also limit the remedies in the non-conformity article for non-conformity to specifications? Although the difference between breach by non-conformity and breach of warranty may often be difficult to see, it is a distinction made not only by this contract, but also by the UCC. UCC Sect. 2-714(1) sets out buyer's damages for 'non-conformity of tender', and UCC Sect. 2-714(2) sets out a different approach to buyer's damages for 'breach of warranty'.

[87] "The key language in the exclusionary language of the Annex starts with the words: 'The above stated warranty and remedies are exclusive...'. This language clearly limits the exclusion to the warranties and their remedies specified in the Annex and leaves the non-conformity remedy of the non-conformity article unaffected. The sentence goes on 'and in lieu of any other warranties or *remedies* whether express or implied including any warranty of merchantability or fitness for a particular purpose'. [Emphasis added] This language *could* be read as superseding the non-conformity article. To do so, however, requires ignoring the language in the warranty article incorporating the Annex into the contract: 'Details of the *warranty* are given in the Annex.' [Emphasis added] If the phrase 'or remedies' is read as governing non-conformity remedies as well as warranties, the Annex goes beyond its incorporating language. Moreover, in context, 'or remedies' is in both a provision and a sentence dealing exclusively with warranties and not with non-conformity to specifications. Common principles of contract interpretation suggest that the phrase is limited to remedies relating to warranties. And finally, if 'or remedies' is interpreted as superseding the non-conformity article, the non-conformity article is surplusage, and contracts are generally read to avoid surplusage. The tribunal finds that the non-conformity article remedies are not superseded by the warranty article and the Annex.

[88] "Consideration must also be given to the remedy article, which provides:

> 'Notwithstanding anything contained in ... Articles ... hereof [penalty for late delivery and force majeure respectively] should the Seller hereto fail to perform or observe any of the obligation or conditions on his part to be performed or observed here under this Contract or fail to meet the delivery schedule and fail to remedy the breach within 90 days after written notice the Buyer to remedy the same, the Buyer shall be entitled, in addition to and without prejudice to any other remedy available, forthwith to terminate the contract.'

This is unquestionably a remedial provision and expressly non-exclusive. To read the phrase 'or remedies' in the Annex as making the warranty article and the Annex claimant's sole and exclusive remedy would read this important provision right out of the contract.

[89] "In light of the non-conformity and remedy articles it cannot be said that the remedy provided in the warranty article and the Annex is 'expressly agreed to be exclusive' as required by UCC Sect. 2-719(1)(b). Under that section it is thus an optional remedy. Claimant's waiving it or otherwise failing to use it does not bar any other remedy it has under the express terms of the contract. Nor do the three articles together constitute a contractual set of remedies which collectively have been 'expressly agreed to be exclusive'. If there were any doubt of this, the express non-exclusivity of one of them would set that doubt to rest. Thus claimant is entitled to whatever rights and remedies it would otherwise have under the UCC for non-conformity of the goods."

(....)

2. *Remedies*

a. *Recovery of price*

[90] "UCC Sect. 2-711 provides:

> '(1) Where the ... buyer ... *justifiably revokes acceptance* then with respect to any goods involved, and with respect to the whole if the breach goes to the whole contract ..., the buyer may cancel and whether or not he has done so may in addition *to recovering so much of the price as has been paid* ...'. [Emphasis added]

The tribunal has found that claimant justifiably revoked its acceptance of the goods. The tribunal has also found, however, that the revocation remains conditional in that claimant must avoid reaccepting the goods if it wishes to keep its revocation of acceptance intact. The tribunal finds that keeping its revocation of acceptance intact is essential to a recovery of the price. To do that claimant must recall the goods from the end producer and return it to defendant when defendant tenders payment of the purchase price under the contract.

[91] "The breach affected all of the goods and therefore went to the whole contract, not just to some of the goods. That being the case, claimant is, provided it meets the foregoing conditions, entitled under this provision to recover the price it paid defendant for the goods.

[92] "The tribunal believes that the foregoing is a sound analysis of the issues relating to revocation of acceptance, repayment of the purchase price, and return of the goods in a situation like this where the goods are in the hands of a further buyer. The tribunal would, however, reach the same result to achieve justice under its powers of 'amiable composition'. The tribunal believes it would be unjust either for defendant to avoid repayment of the purchase price simply because the goods had been resold especially where they can be recovered and returned to defendant, or for claimant to recover the full purchase price of the goods without tendering them to defendant.
[93] "The tribunal pointed out that it was likely that the full quantity of undamaged goods no longer still existed to be returned to defendant.... UCC Sect. 2-711 is sufficiently flexible to deal with this circumstance. It provides that 'Where the ... buyer ... justifiably revokes acceptance then with respect to any goods involved' the buyer may recover so much of the price as has been paid. The tribunal reads this to mean recover so much of the price as had been paid for the goods for which the acceptance has been revoked. Thus, if claimant is unable to return the full quantity of the goods, the return of the purchase price should be prorated accordingly.... Furthermore, since the contract provided for 'EX WORKS' prices, claimant should bear the costs of tendering the goods to defendant."

b. Damages

[94] "Following the language quoted above, UCC Sect. 2-711 continues

> '(a) "cover" and have damages under the next section as to all goods affected ...'.

The 'next section', Sect. 2-712, provides

> '(1) After a breach within the preceding section the buyer may "cover" by making in good faith and without unreasonable delay any reasonable purchase or contract to purchase goods in substitution for those due from the seller.
> (2) The buyer may recover from the seller as damages the difference between the cost of cover and the contract price ...'.

Claimant urges that its purchase of replacement goods from company Z meets the tests of subsection (1). Defendant challenges this on several grounds."
(....)

[95] The cover purchases were paid for in pounds sterling. The arbitrators noted: "The independence of international arbitrators vis-à-vis States means that no currency is foreign for them and, a contrario, that the notion of local currency has no special significance to them (see the comments in Clunet 1976, p. 978, on ICC Case No 2375, 1975). This is now a well established principle in international arbitration: damages must be compensated for in the currency in which they were incurred. The tribunal accepts this approach which has the merits of eliminating exchange rate distortions which can otherwise prevent the full compensation for a loss actually suffered. Accordingly, were the tribunal to award damages based on the contract between claimant and its company Z, the very amounts in pounds sterling would be used.

[96] "The question before the tribunal is whether the contract between claimant and company Z constituted a 'reasonable purchase or contract to purchase' made 'in good faith and without unreasonable delay'. Taking the last of these first, the tribunal has no difficulty in finding that claimant acted without unreasonable delay in making these purchases, and does not understand defendant to contend otherwise....

[97] "Respecting good faith, the tribunal has no reason to question claimant's 'honesty in fact' in making this purchase. Under UCC 2-103(b), however, 'good faith' ... also requires the 'observance of reasonable commercial standards of fair dealing in the trade'. No showing has been made that a subsidiary's buying from a parent violates any 'reasonable commercial standards of fair dealing' in this or any other trade.

[98] "There remains the question whether the arrangement with company Z was a 'reasonable purchase or contract to purchase' for the purpose of using the price to calculate a recovery under UCC Sect. 2-712(2). The tribunal finds that it is not. Company Z is the parent company holding 100% interest in subsidiary A which in turn is the holding company holding 100% interest in claimant. The tribunal would not go so far as to say that no transaction between parent and wholly owned subsidiary can ever constitute a reasonable purchase for the purposes of using the price under Sect. 2-712(2). See, for example, White & Summers, p. 250, discussing what the authors call 'internal cover' where the buyer has been allowed to recover its costs of manufacturing the goods in question. In a sense, claimant's purchase from the parent company may be considered internal cover. That a purchase from an affiliate may in some circumstances be used to establish cover does not, however, mean that it can be here. To make a purchase from an affiliate a 'reasonable purchase' to prove cover would seem to require either a showing that the purchase would have been a reasonable one in the marketplace or that the price charged was no more than the reasonable costs of the parent in producing the product. Neither has been shown here.

(....)

[99] "Following the language quoted above, UCC Sect. 2-711 continues:

> '(b) recover damages for non-delivery as provided in this Article' (Section 2-713).

UCC Sect. 2-713 provides:

> '(1) Subject to the provisions of this Article with respect to proof of market price (Section 2-723), the measure of damages for non-delivery ... by the seller is the difference between the market price at the time when the buyer learned of the breach and the contract price....'

.... There are only two significant items of evidence bearing on the question of 'the market price at the time when the buyer learned of the breach'. One is the price claimant paid defendant in the contract; the other is the price claimant has contracted with company Z. The price in the contract is useless to claimant because if applied as the appropriate measure of market price it would yield zero damages under Sect. 2-713. The price in company Z's contract is inadequate to show market price for the same reasons it was inadequate to constitute cover, namely the fact that claimant is an affiliate of the parent company. Without a usable figure for market price it is not possible to apply the formula in UCC Sect. 2-713. In light of the foregoing, the tribunal finds that claimant has failed to show damages under the market price-contract price formula in UCC Sect. 2-713."

(....)

c. *Incidental and consequential damages*

[100] "Both UCC Sect. 2-712 and Sect. 2-713 contain identical language relating to incidental and consequential damages following the setting out of their respective market-oriented formulae:

> 'together with any incidental or consequential damages as hereinafter defined (Section 2-715), but less expenses saved in consequence of the seller's breach.'

UCC Sect. 2-715 in turn provides:

> '(1) Incidental damages resulting from the seller's breach include expenses reasonably incurred in inspection, receipt, transportation and care and

custody of goods rightfully rejected, any commercially reasonable charges, expenses or commissions in connection with effecting cover and any other reasonable expense incident to the delay or other breach.
(2) Consequential damages resulting from the seller's breach include (a) any loss resulting from the general or particular requirements and needs of which the seller at the time of contracting had reason to know and which could not reasonably be prevented by cover or otherwise;...'

[101] "Claimant has claimed three items of damages which it might be argued come within the language of UCC Sect. 2-715: (1) costs of cover; (2) costs relating to testing of samples in the arbitration; (3) possible liability under penalty bonds.

[102] "UCC Sect. 2-715 allows the buyer to recover 'any commercially reasonable charges, expenses or commissions in connection with effecting cover'. This does not, of course, include the price of the covering goods themselves, which is provided for in the formula in Sect. 2-712. The reasons given above for denying claimant recovery under that formula do not apply to any 'commercially reasonable' costs incurred with non-affiliates that were incidental to that transaction. Claimant has produced in its Submission of Costs evidence of such costs as they relate to the transportation of the replacement goods to country X.... The tribunal sees no reason to question this amount. Accordingly, the tribunal holds that claimant is entitled to recover the costs of cover under UCC Sect. 2-715; such costs are to be granted in the currency in which claimant incurred the expenses for the reasons set forth above.

[103] "Claimant claims the costs associated with the inspection of the rejected goods during the arbitration, including the costs of obtaining the samples by the tribunal's experts. It might be argued that these constitute 'expenses reasonably incurred in inspection, receipt, *transportation and care and custody of goods* rightfully rejected'. However, the tribunal is of the opinion that almost all such costs were incurred for the purposes of this arbitration and in particular for the defense by claimant of its interests and as such, will be dealt with at the same time as the costs of arbitration....

[104] "Claimant's expenses relating to what it calls the first inspection at end purchaser, the second inspection at end purchaser, and the third inspection at subcontractor's would be covered by this language. These three inspections occurred as part of claimant's process of deciding whether the goods could be 'rightfully rejected', – in this case by revoking an acceptance – and hence their costs, if commercially reasonable, are recoverable under UCC Sect. 2-715(1). Claimant has submitted evidence of such costs ... which the tribunal will allow claimant to recover from defendant.

[105] "... [T]he tribunal has decided that the costs of the arbitration should lie with each party as it incurred them. The tribunal understands UCC Sect. 2-715 to be limited to costs of inspections conducted in the course of the buyer's determining to its own satisfaction whether the goods can be 'rightfully rejected'. This excludes from its coverage inspections after such rightful rejection, in this instance inspections conducted as part of an arbitral proceeding. Thus the tribunal finds that claimant is not entitled under UCC Sect. 2-715 to recover the costs of the inspection conducted during the arbitration.

[106] "Claimant has claimed 'any penalties paid by claimant by reason of unreasonable delivery of the goods to the end purchaser'. It refers to two performance bonds given the end purchaser.... Some or all the actual imposition of liability by the end purchaser on claimant under the bond pertaining to the contract goods might or might not be such consequential damages. Defendant would be entitled to raise many factual issues respecting such a claim, as well as legal issues such as the effect of the enforcement against buyer of a penalty bond which may be invalid under Illinois law. Both claimant's claim and any possible defendant defenses are highly speculative. Furthermore, claimant advised the tribunal that the bonds had not been called and gave no indication as to whether they might be or not. Accordingly, the tribunal finds that no element of damages is allowable concerning either of the two bonds.

[107] "Claimant makes no claim for the payment of interest. This is appropriate since claimant presumably was paid for the goods by the end purchaser. Nor has claimant produced evidence that it has yet paid company Z for the replacement goods. Even if it had, the same questions concerning cover with an affiliate would affect any claim for interest."

(....)

IV. COSTS

[108] ".... The tribunal is reluctant to award costs in favor of either party. Not only has the claimant in this case not fully succeeded, but the dispute in this instance is one that could have been handled in a more commercially effective manner and although the tribunal has found for the claimant on the merits with respect to the issue of product corrosion, it must be borne in mind that the gravamen of the claimant's case against defendant only came to the defendant's attention and awareness upon the commencement of arbitral proceedings and during the course of same. Neither party has contributed in any way to lessening the number or complexity of the issues to be resolved by the tribunal on the contrary, each has contributed to inflate this arbitration in particular by raising numerous procedural matters. Therefore, the tribunal has

no difficulty in deciding that each party shall bear an equal share of the costs of the arbitration, including all the costs relating to the sampling and the testing of samples in this arbitration; likewise, each party shall bear the legal costs, including lawyers' fees that it has incurred in its defense."

V. DECISION

[109] "For these reasons the arbitral tribunal decides that (1) defendant must pay to the claimant [contractual price of the goods], without interest. (2) Claimant must return, to defendant ... at claimant's costs, all of the goods it purchased from defendant under the contract between them in their present condition. (3) The award in (1) above shall be pro-rated ... for any amount of the goods claimant cannot or fails to return under (2) above...."

Partial award in case no. 7319 of 1992

Parties:	Claimant: Manufacturer (France) Defendant: Distributor (Ireland)
Place of arbitration:	Paris, France
Published in:	5 The ICC International Court of Arbitration Bulletin (1994, no. 2) pp. 56-59
Subject matters:	- jurisdiction - applicable law - insufficient indication of choice of lex mercatoria - cumulative application of rules of conflict - closest connection with contract - 1980 Rome Convention represents general principles of conflict of laws - scope of arbitration agreement

Facts

Parties entered into a Distribution Agreement (Agreement I) whereby distributor was granted an exclusive distributorship right to sell manufacturers products in the Republic of Eire (Ireland) and a non-exclusive distribution right to sell them in Northern Ireland. Agreement I was replaced with a new Distribution Agreement (Agreement II). Both Agreements contained an arbitral clause providing for ICC arbitration.

A dispute arose between the parties and the manufacturer initiated arbitration. Pursuant to the Terms of Reference, the sole arbitrator should first determine the law applicable to the Distributorship Agreement(s) and whether the arbitral clause conferred jurisdiction in respect of the claims relating to unfair competition. Using both the cumulative application of different rules of conflict and generally recognized principles of conflict of laws as embodied in the 1980 Rome Convention, the sole arbitrator held that Irish law applied. Furthermore, the arbitral clause was found to encompass the unfair competition claims.

Excerpt

I. APPLICABLE LAW

[1] "The applicable law paragraph of the arbitral clause in Agreement II which provides for ICC arbitration states as follows:

> 'This Agreement shall be construded (sic) in accordance with and governed by laws and regulations applying to members of the European Economic Community.'

[2] "Claimant argues that Irish law has been excluded by the parties, that the applicable law paragraph of the arbitral clause of Agreement II applies and that the Agreement is governed by the common principles applied in the twelve member states of the EEC.... According to claimant, the first draft 'Distribution Agreement' was submitted by defendant providing – in contrast to the versions of Agreement I and II signed by the parties – for Irish arbitration, for Dublin as place of arbitration, for Irish attorneys as arbitrators and for the agreement to be construed in accordance with and governed by Irish law or, where applicable, the laws and regulations applying to members of the European Economic Community. Therefore, it was clear that the parties, by agreeing on the arbitral clause of Agreement II which was identical to the clause in Agreement I, decided to eliminate all references to Irish law, Irish jurisdiction, Irish attorneys acting as arbitrators and to Dublin as the place of the arbitration. Furthermore, the parties, according to claimant, intended also to exclude French law.

[3] "Instead, the parties intended, according to claimant, not to choose any particular national law but to refer to an international system of law, similar at least in principle, to 'lex mercatoria' or, for example, to Art. 68 of the Channel Tunnel Contract. To state that the governing law should be Irish law would clearly defeat the intent of the parties. Therefore, even if the sole arbitrator were to find the paragraph of Agreement II regarding applicable law to be meaningless, he would be obliged to treat the contract as 'anational' and to apply anational rules. The references in Agreement II to certain Irish rules and regulations, according to claimant, are irrelevant to the choice of the applicable law.

[4] "Defendant argues that sentence 3 [on applicable law] of the arbitral clause of Agreement II is without meaning and, therefore, necessarily invalid as a purported expression of an agreed choice of applicable law. Consequently, the proper law falls to be determined by the application by the sole arbitrator of those conflict rules which he deems appropriate. Both the French and the

Irish conflict rules are the only ones having a direct relation to the dispute and to the parties in question and, if applied, would result in the law of Ireland being the proper law governing the contract....

[5] "Defendant denies that the first draft contract was submitted by defendant. Rather, according to defendant, the first draft was submitted by claimant and was the standard Distribution Agreement providing for the French law as the law governing the contract. Defendant, however, rejected the law of France. Since neither party accepted the national law of the other party, the applicable law clause of Agreement II was a compromise, leaving the problem of the interpretation of the agreed wording unanswered.

[6] "The wording of the applicable law clause of Agreement II, according to defendant, however, is meaningless insofar as it is not capable of fulfilling the functions of the 'proper law' governing the Agreement. The only meaning that could be given to said clause is that the terms of the Agreement are to be governed by European Community laws as such. By contrast, the clause cannot be deemed to refer to a system of law derived by extracting the common elements of the twelve different national laws of the EEC member states. Consequently, the law governing the Agreement, according to defendant, must be determined by applying the appropriate rules of conflict. Whether one applies the French or the Irish rules of conflict, the relevant criteria clearly indicate Irish law to be the applicable law.

[7] "Pursuant to Art. 13(3) of the Rules of Conciliation and Arbitration of the ICC (the Rules):

> '[T]he parties shall be free to determine the law to be applied by the arbitrator to the merits of the dispute. In the absence of any indication by the parties as to the applicable law, the arbitrator shall apply the law designated as the proper law by the rule of conflicts which he deems appropriate.'

[8] "As a general observation, the sole arbitrator notes the undisputed fact that neither of the parties accepted the national law of the other party. As a result, the parties agreed on wording according to which 'the agreement shall be construded (sic) in accordance with and governed by Laws and Regulations applying to members of the European Economic Community'. The first question, therefore, is whether this wording is to be considered as the parties' determination of the substantive law applicable to the Agreement, within the meaning of Art. 13(3) of the Rules.

[9] "On this issue, the sole arbitrator finds firstly that the above wording was initially only part of a clause on the applicable law contained in a draft agreement submitted to claimant by defendant. Indeed, said clause provided for

the Agreement to 'be construded (sic) in accordance with and governed by *Irish law or, where applicable, the* Laws and Regulations applying to members of the European Economic Community' (my emphasis). Later in the negotiations, the words 'Irish law or, where applicable, the' were deleted, so that only the present wording remained. It therefore appears to the sole arbitrator that the present wording, at least initially, was not intended as being, in itself, the determination of the substantive law governing the Agreement. Rather, the remaining wording was obviously meant as supplementary to the applicable national Irish law, then rejected by claimant.

[10] "On the basis of the foregoing, the sole arbitrator does not find the remaining wording to be totally meaningless, as argued in first instance by defendant. Rather, the sole arbitrator considers the wording as being a reference to European Community law, where applicable, including the European Treaties and the secondary body of Community legislation. This interpretation is meaningful even if one is of the view that it was not necessary in the Agreement to refer to European Community Law because of the fact that European Community law, where applicable, is mandatory because it forms part of the national laws of each member state.

[11] "Nevertheless, the sole arbitrator does not consider the remaining wording as having a meaning going beyond what was stated above. In particular, the wording does not support claimant's view that it means a reference to international legal or trade principles, such as 'lex mercatoria', or the common principles of the twelve member states of the European Community. If this had been the intention of the parties, they could have chosen and agreed on wording expressly indicating such a reference, as for example in Art. 68 of the Channel Tunnel Contract, or by specifically referring to 'lex mercatoria'. This, however, was not the case, since the parties did not replace the deleted reference to a particular national law – the Irish or the French respectively – by any specific reference to such anational rules.

[12] "Claimant further appears to be arguing that, by eliminating a particular national law, the parties implicitly expressed their intention to refer to anational rules and to exclude any national law. As far as this argument is concerned, the sole arbitrator considers that the parties, rather than eliminating by mutual agreement the Irish and French national law, were unable to agree on a particular national law, which is something different.[1] Indeed, in practice, the parties often leave the question of the law applicable to their contract open

1. The sole arbitrator referred to Lagarde, Revue de l'arbitrage (1990) p. 668, in a note to the decision of the Paris *Cour d'Appel* of 13 July 1989, in the case *Compañía Valenciana de Cementos Portland v. Primary Coal.*

because they are unable to agree on it, thus leaving it up to the courts or the arbitrators, as the case may be, to determine the applicable law.

[13] "Furthermore, the failure of the parties to agree on the law governing the Agreement cannot, in the sole arbitrator's opinion, be interpreted as an implied reference to some vague international legal or trade principles. Such reference must be made expressly and, if not expressly, then in an implied manner which gives reasonable certainty to the arbitrators or the courts, respectively, that the parties indeed agreed to submit their dispute to anational law or international trade principles, particularly considering the fact that such anational laws and principles, if not properly defined, are difficult if not impossible to assess.

[14] "Consequently, the sole arbitrator must determine the proper law by applying the rule of conflict which he deems appropriate, pursuant to Art. 13(3), sentence two, of the Rules. In ICC arbitration practice, different methods are used by arbitrators to determine the proper law of the contract on the basis of Art. 13(3), sentence two. In the present case, the sole arbitrator has decided to apply both the Irish and the French rules of conflict, given that these are the only ones having a direct connection with the parties and the dispute. This method is generally referred to as 'the cumulative application of the different rules of conflict' of the countries having a relation to the dispute.[2]

[15] "According to the French rules of conflict that were applicable at the time Agreement II was entered into, the prevailing doctrine objectively 'locates the contract', i.e., determines the country with which it has the closest relation by considering the various factors characterizing the contractual relationship, the most relevant of which is held to be the place of performance of the substantive obligations of the contract.[3]

[16] "Under the Irish rules of conflict applicable at the time the Agreement was entered into the approach is similar: the proper law of the contract is generally held to be the law which has the closest and most real connection with the contract.[4]

---

2. The sole arbitrator referred to Craig/Park/Paulsson, *International Chamber of Commerce Arbitration* (New York–London–Rome, 1985) Part III S 17.01 p. 290; Y. Derains, "L'application cumulative par l'arbitre des systèmes de conflit de lois intéressés au litige", Revue de l'arbitrage (1972) p. 99 et seq.
3. The sole arbitrator referred to Battifol/Lagarde, *Droit international privé*, 7th ed., vol. II, p. 289 et seq.
4. The sole arbitrator referred to Sandrock, *Handbuch der Internationalen Vertragsgestaltung*, vol. 1, p. 182; and as to the similarity of the approaches: Loussouarn/Bourel, *Droit international privé*, Dalloz, 3rd edition (1988) p. 213.

[17] "The sole arbitrator considers that the country with which Agreement II has the closest connection is Ireland, rather than France. Indeed, the sole arbitrator observes that more factors point to Ireland and not to France, such as the place of performance of the substantive obligations of the Agreement, and also the fact that the form of the Agreement ... and its terminology ... is that followed by the common law system rather than that followed by the French system, and the fact that the Agreement is in the English language. The same considerations apply to Agreement I.

[18] "Furthermore, the sole arbitrator notes that he would have come to the same conclusion had he chosen to apply generally recognized principles of conflict of laws. Under the latter approach, the rules of the Rome Convention on the Choice of Law for Contracts of 19 June 1980 (the Rome Convention) would have been applicable. The Rome Convention went into effect for all ratifying countries, including France, on 1 April 1991. Following the deposit of the instrument of ratification of the Rome Convention by Ireland on 29 October 1991, the Convention entered into force on 1 January 1992 between Ireland and the countries which had already ratified it.[5] More recently, Spain and Portugal have also ratified the Rome Convention.[6] The increasing number of countries ratifying the Rome Convention indicates that the rules contained in it have a wide acceptance. The sole arbitrator therefore considers these rules to reflect generally recognized principles of conflict. As such they could be applied to the case at hand irrespective of the fact that they were not yet in force between France and Ireland when the Agreement was entered into and that they have no retroactive effect.

[19] "An analysis which applies the rules of the Rome Convention (Art. 4(1)) would find that the applicable law in the absence of choice is the law of the country with which the contract is most closely connected. Pursuant to Art. 4(2) of the Rome Convention it is presumed that the contract is most closely connected with the country in which the party who is to carry out the *performance* which is *characteristic* of the contract has its central administration. As applied to the present case, the Rome Convention would therefore designate Irish law as the proper law, since the characteristic performance of the present Agreement is the distribution of the product in Ireland, where defendant as distributor has its offices. Therefore, the application of generally recognized principles of conflict of laws would lead to the same result as the cumulative application of the Irish and French rules of conflict.

[20] "Contrary to claimant's view, the sole arbitrator is not of the opinion that the designation of Irish law as the proper law governing the Agreement

---

5. "Official Journal of the European Communites – OJEC – No. C 24/1 of 31 January 1992".
6. "Communication of the Council 6428/32 of 18 May 1992".

contradicts what the parties had intended when entering into the Agreement. Indeed, as stated above, the sole arbitrator is of the opinion that the parties could simply not agree upon a particular national law. By leaving this issue unresolved, each party assumed the risk, if one wants to refer to it as such, that the sole arbitrator would designate the other party's law as the law applicable to the Agreements.

[21] "Finally, the sole arbitrator observes that he is obliged in any event to take into account the provisions of the contract and the relevant trade usages, pursuant to Art. 13(5) of the Rules."

II. JURISDICTION RELATING TO CLAIMS OF UNFAIR COMPETITION

[22] "... [T]he parties disagree on whether the arbitration clause contained in the applicable law clause of Agreement II confers jurisdiction in respect of the [unfair competition] claims brought by claimant.... On the basis of these claims, claimant is seeking damages due to unfair competition on the basis that defendant has allegedly (i) introduced into the Irish market a product ... which directly competes with claimant's product and (ii) violated claimant's trademarks by writing the word ... which appears on the product in letters which are confusingly similar to those used by claimant....

[23] "Claimant argues ... the unfair competition claims in the Terms of Reference fall within the jurisdiction of the sole arbitrator which is confined to 'disputes relating to the interpretation and the execution and enforcement of the agreement', in accordance with the arbitral clause of Agreement II. Indeed, according to claimant, said claims are based on the abuse of a right which was granted to defendant pursuant to the Agreements, i.e., the right to use letters and labels similar to those normally used by claimant. By using these letters and getup for the sale of the products which are in direct competition with those of claimant while Agreement II was still in existence, defendant has abused those rights granted to it pursuant to the Agreements in order to compete with claimant.

[24] "Defendant's position is as follows: Claimant's claim for damages due to unfair competition is not a claim for damages for infringement of a particular clause in Agreement II. A claim for damages for 'unfair competition' is not a claim which relates to 'the interpretation, the execution or the enforcement' of Agreement II. Specifically, no clause in Agreement II confers on defendant the right to use letters and labels similar to those normally used by claimant. Claimant's allegation that defendant had introduced competing products to the Irish market refers to something that happened long after the contractual relationship between the parties had come to an end. Claimant's claim could

be brought against any third party whether or not that party had ever had any contractual relationship with claimant.

[25] "There is no dispute between the parties as to the fact that the jurisdiction of the sole arbitrator is confined to 'disputes relating to the interpretation and the execution and enforcement of the Agreement' in accordance with the arbitral clause of Agreement II. The sole arbitrator considers the parties' dispute ... as a dispute relating to the execution and possibly to the interpretation of Agreement II. Indeed, in its Request for Arbitration, claimant states that it had 'recently learned' that defendant had introduced competing products to the Irish market. While defendant argues that the alleged competition referred to acts committed after Agreement II had been terminated, claimant contends, in its Additional Submission, that defendant had commenced certain acts of unfair competition while said Agreement was still in force. It is not at this stage of the proceeding that this latter dispute must be decided on its merits. For the purpose of deciding on his own competence, the sole arbitrator must assess only whether the alleged claim falls under the arbitration clause agreed between the parties. Claimant's claim for damages for unfair competition is based on the violation of a contractual right allegedly conferred by claimant to defendant pursuant to Agreement II, while said Agreement was still in force. This is sufficient to conclude that such claim falls within the competence of the sole arbitrator. This conclusion does not taint the question whether such claim is justified on the merits."

III. DECISIONS

[26] "For the reasons set forth above, the sole arbitrator decides that:

1. The proper law by which the Agreements are to be construed and governed is Irish law.
2. The arbitration clause contained in Agreement II confers jurisdiction in respect of the [unfair competition] claims brought by claimant...."

Interim award in case no. 7337 of 1996

Parties:	Claimant: Distributor (Japan) Defendants: (1) Manufacturer (Sweden); (2) New manufacturer as represented by receiver (Sweden)
Place of arbitration:	Düsseldorf, Germany
Published in:	Unpublished
Subject matters:	- jurisdiction - receiver in bankruptcy bound by arbitral clause - successor bound by guarantee obligations including arbitral clause

Facts

Manufacturer and distributor entered into an Exclusive Agency Contract under which manufacturer granted distributor the exclusive right to sell its machinery in Japan. Japanese company X, which had ordered a number of machines prior to the conclusion of the Exclusive Agency Contract, subsequently made a further order for machines and an order regarding modifications.

The guarantee article of the Exclusive Agency Contract provided:

> "Unless the Manufacturer and Distributor have agreed to apply other conditions the Manufacturer assumes the obligations provided for in the articles relating to the guarantee in the 'Conditions 188'."

"Conditions 188" was a reference to the United Nations Economic Commission for Europe "General Conditions No. 188 for the Supply of Plants and Machinery for Export" of March 1953. These Conditions contain an arbitral clause providing that "any dispute arising out of the Contract" shall be settled by ICC arbitration. Further, the Exclusive Agency Contract also contained an arbitral clause providing for ICC arbitration.

Manufacturer terminated the Exclusive Agency Contract prior to its expiration due to various reasons. Distributor refused to accept the termination. In the meantime, the machines ordered by distributor had been delivered to company X and had in part been found to be defective. Distributor alleged to have informed manufacturer of the problems and to have received no answer. Further, distributor alleged that it had not billed company X and had advised not to operate them. However, without informing distributor, manufacturer had sent engineers to company X to recondition the machines and had concluded an agreement with company X confirming that the complaints had been settled. Distributor asserted that the machines were still his property.

Shortly after the termination of the contract, manufacturer was declared bankrupt and a receiver was appointed. Distributor was not notified of the bankruptcy. All of the assets of manufacturer were acquired by "new manufacturer" through its parent company, investment company A, and manufacturer's business was continued under the name of "new manufacturer".

In the preamble of the purchase agreement it was stated:

> "Following negotiations between the official receiver and investment company A, the transfer of the business conducted by manufacturer to investment company A has been agreed, subject to the following conditions."

Assets subject to the transfer were enumerated in the "assets article" which stated that:

> "The agreement also includes leasing agreements relating to machines, inventories and vehicles as specified in the appended catalogues."

At the end of the enumeration the agreement provided:

> "Investment company A shall take over the business conducted by the bankrupt company, together with the responsibility for the results."

The "guarantee article" of the agreement provided regarding the guarantee liability for products supplied by manufacturers:

> "With regard to machines for which the period of guarantee has expired, but which are the subject of claims negotiations, and with regard to machines which have been supplied and for which guarantees remain in force, the parties have concluded an agreement whereby investment company A, on taking over the business, shall indemnify the bankrupt's estate against all guarantee liability relating to these machines."

Distributor initiated arbitration against manufacturer. After the receiver informed the ICC that manufacturer had been declared bankrupt, distributor amended his request nominating "manufacturer as represented by the receiver" as defendant no. 1 and "new manufacturer", the alleged successor in interest of defendant no. 1, as defendant no. 2. Both defendants challenged the jurisdiction of the arbitral tribunal. The sole arbitrator first appointed an expert on Swedish law to give his opinion on questions of Swedish law on which the decision on jurisdiction depended.

The sole arbitrator found that he had jurisdiction over defendant no. 1 with respect to claims relating to breach of the Exclusive Agency Contract. However, any award in favor of claimant would be binding on the bankruptcy estate only as a basis for claimant's share as a creditor in the bankruptcy. The sole arbitrator also found that he had jurisdiction over defendant no. 2 only with respect to the claims regarding the guarantee liability for machines, as he had not succeeded to the liability under the Exclusive Agency Contract.

Excerpt

I. APPLICABLE LAW

[1] "The agreement to arbitrate in the Exclusive Agency Contract, which is de jure an exclusive distributorship contract, was entered into between claimant and manufacturer. The receiver of defendant no. 1 asserts that manufacturer has ceased to exist and that the bankruptcy estate is not a party to the arbitration. In regard to the arbitrator's jurisdiction over defendant no. 1 the first issue that shall have to be addressed is the identity of defendant no. 1 – which may be the debtor or may be the bankruptcy estate and whether defendant no. 1 has the capacity to be party to the arbitration and is bound by the agreement to arbitrate. The legal capacity of a party is determined according to the law at its place of domicile, which in regard to defendant no. 1 is Swedish law."

II. ISSUES

[2] "The issues which have to be addressed in regard to defendant no. 2 are whether defendant no. 2 is bound by the agreement to arbitrate under statutory law or under contract in respect to the claims of claimant relating to the breach of the distributorship contract as well as in respect to the claims relating to the delivery of defective machines. Defendant no. 2 has not signed

the distributorship contract containing the agreement to arbitrate and objects to being brought into the arbitration. The issue of a possible succession of defendant no. 2 into the legal position of manufacturer as party to the agreement to arbitrate is outside the scope of the exclusive distributorship contract made between claimant and manufacturer and its applicable law; it must be determined according to the law applicable to the relationship between defendant no. 1 and defendant no. 2, i.e. Swedish law."

1. Defendant no. 1

a. Identity of defendant no. 1

[3] "Claimant submits that manufacturer has not ceased to exist and retains the capacity of being a party to the present arbitration. Claimant also submits that the arbitrator has jurisdiction to try claimant's claims against manufacturer in bankruptcy, i.e. the bankruptcy estate represented by the receiver. Defendant no. 1 submits that manufacturer does not exist any more because it has been declared bankrupt and that, furthermore, the bankruptcy estate has refused to replace the bankrupt company in the arbitration against manufacturer. A pending lawsuit or arbitration against a bankrupt company is not automatically taken over by the bankruptcy estate. As the bankruptcy estate has refused to substitute for the debtor in the present case, it is not a party to the arbitration. Although a receiver may under Swedish law participate in an arbitration, this requires, pursuant to the Swedish Bankruptcy Act, Chapter 3, Sect. 9, that the bankruptcy estate enter the arbitration against the debtor in progress or that the estate itself is a party in the arbitration.

[4] "The assertion of defendant no. 1 that manufacturer has ceased to exist because the company has been declared bankrupt is erroneous. According to the Swedish Companies Act of 1975, Chapter 13, Sect. 19, a bankrupt company is dissolved only when the bankruptcy proceedings are terminated without any surplus. The bankrupt company, i.e. the debtor, does retain the capacity of being a defendant in a legal proceeding. However at the time of the bankruptcy declaration the debtor loses the right to administer and dispose of his property includable in the estate. Under Swedish law universal succession takes place when a corporation is declared bankrupt. The rights and obligations of the corporation are assumed by the bankruptcy estate.[1] The bankrupt company and the bankruptcy estate are, according to Swedish law, two independent legal entities. An award arising from proceedings against the debtor is not binding against the bankruptcy estate.

1. "*Arbitration in Sweden*, 2nd ed. (1984) p. 36."

[5] "At the time when claimant filed its Request for Arbitration manufacturer had already been declared bankrupt, without claimant's knowledge. As soon as claimant had been informed of this fact it changed the designation of defendant no. 1 in the Request for Arbitration into 'manufacturer, represented by the receiver of manufacturer'. It is not clear and open to interpretation whether the Request for Arbitration was thus directed against the debtor, i.e. the bankrupt company, to be represented by its board, or against the bankruptcy estate, i.e. manufacturer in bankruptcy, represented by the receiver.
[6] "Although an arbitration may be pursued against the debtor, the bankruptcy estate is the proper party to all post-bankruptcy legal proceedings as it has assumed, by universal succession, all rights and obligations of the debtor. In consequence, the designation of defendant no. 1 in the amended Request to Arbitrate, in which claimant added the words 'represented by the receiver of manufacturer' can reasonably only be understood to mean the bankruptcy estate, namely manufacturer in bankruptcy, represented by the receiver. It may be pointed out in this connection that the asset purchase agreement between the bankruptcy estate and investment company A, is signed by the receiver 'for manufacturer in bankruptcy'. In view of the above, the omission of the words 'in bankruptcy' in the designation of defendant no. 1 in the Request for Arbitration does not compellably lead to the conclusion that it was the intention of claimant to institute legal proceedings against the debtor as distinct from the bankruptcy estate. Furthermore, the present case does not concern the situation where legal proceedings have been instituted against the debtor and the bankruptcy estate is given the opportunity to enter into the proceedings, but declines to do so. In the present case the Request for Arbitration was filed after the date of bankruptcy and designated the bankruptcy estate itself as defendant no. 1. The bankruptcy estate represented by the receiver, i.e. manufacturer in bankruptcy is therefore party to the arbitration."

b. Bankruptcy estate bound by the agreement to arbitrate?

[7] "The question remains to be answered however, whether defendant no. 1, the bankruptcy estate, is bound by the agreement to arbitrate in the exclusive distributorship agreement between claimant and manufacturer. Claimant submits, based on Swedish Supreme Court decisions, that arbitration agreements entered into by the debtor prior to bankruptcy are binding on the bankruptcy estate.[2] Defendant no. 1 submits that the bankruptcy estate has no agreement with claimant. Furthermore, even if the claims were justified,

2. "Supreme Court decisions NJA 1913, p. 191, NJA 1931, p. 647, and NJA 1993, p. 641."

claimant would not receive a dividend in bankruptcy because dividends will only be distributed to creditors enjoying priority by law.

[8] "It is a general principle of law that a contract can bind only the parties that have entered into it. There are, however, exceptions. A party may be substituted by universal succession or by singular succession. An agreement to arbitrate is therefore valid between the parties and their legal successors. As has been pointed out, under Swedish law universal succession is deemed to take place when a debtor is declared bankrupt. Thus the bankruptcy estate substitutes by operation of law in all rights and obligations of the debtor pertaining to the property includable in the estate. In the case of manufacturer, a company which manufactured and sold machinery, the contracts with its distributors, such as its contract with claimant, which included the agreement to arbitrate, were part of the property includable in the estate. It would therefore seem appropriate that in a dispute concerning claims based on such a contract, the bankruptcy estate should be bound by the agreement to arbitrate contained therein.

[9] "According to the opinion of the Expert, it is unclear in Swedish law to what extent an agreement to arbitrate in a contract entered into by a debtor prior to his bankruptcy is binding on the bankruptcy estate.... [T]he Expert elaborates on some 'good reasons' why the estate should not be bound which are discussed in Swedish literature. However, he admits that this opinion is not easily reconciled with the Supreme Court precedents cited by claimant, and that 'normally' these precedents are interpreted to hold that a bankruptcy estate is indeed bound by an arbitration agreement in a contract entered into by the debtor prior to bankruptcy. The arbitrator subscribes to the latter opinion prevailing in Swedish jurisprudence and literature which is in conformity with the principle of universal succession.

[10] "However, as the Expert points out, an arbitration based on an agreement to arbitrate entered into by the debtor before his bankruptcy can under Swedish law not result in an award of fulfillment against the bankruptcy estate. If victorious, the claimant can only obtain an award of declaration on an amount, which is binding on the estate as the base on which the dividends are calculated.

[11] "The arbitrator therefore concludes in consideration of the above that the bankruptcy estate is bound by the agreement to arbitrate in the exclusive distributorship contract between claimant and manufacturer. Consequently, he has jurisdiction to try claimant's claims against defendant no. 1, although any award on the merits in favour of claimant would be binding on the bankruptcy estate only as the basis for claimant's dividend as a creditor in bankruptcy."

2. *Defendant No. 2 Bound by the Agreement to Arbitrate?*

a. *Statutory law*

[12] "Claimant is of the opinion that defendant no. 2 has succeeded into the legal position of manufacturer, including as a party to the arbitration agreement, both with respect to the liability for the breach of the exclusive distributorship agreement and the liability for machines. Claimant argues that defendant no. 2 in adopting the bankrupt company's name has given to third parties the impression of having assumed all the bankrupt company's rights and debts, while in the present case the difference of the legal entities is emphasized, and therefore a double standard is applied. Claimant has also argued that the bankruptcy in the present case can be deemed to have been premeditated prior to the transfer of business, and it alleges that there has been an abnormality in the bankruptcy procedure concerning manufacturer, involving the official receiver, defendant no. 2 and 'fraudulent conveyance', which according to claimant's opinion should result in a jurisdiction of the arbitrator superseding that of a transfer of the agreement to arbitrate. Defendant no. 2 asserts that having similar names has no obligating effect.
[13] "The arbitrator understands the argument of claimant that defendant no. 2 is giving the impression of having assumed all rights and debts of manufacturer by using the name of manufacturer to mean that under such circumstances defendant no. 2 should be liable by law for manufacturer's debts. Such a concept exists, for example in German law, where Art. 25(1) of the Commercial Code provides:

> 'One who carries on a business acquired *inter vivos* under the previous firm name, with or without an addition revealing the successor relationship, assumes liability for all obligations of the previous owner arising out of his conduct of the business.'

However if the business is purchased from a bankruptcy estate, this continuity of liability is interrupted, even if the business is continued under the name of the bankrupt company. In such a case the debts are not assumed by the purchaser by statutory assumption of debt, as from the viewpoint of the creditors the sale of the business is part of the liquidation of the company.
[14] "The interruption of the continuity of liability in case of purchase of a business from a bankruptcy estate has led to the practice of 'company

reconstruction by transfer from the bankruptcy estate',[3] a practice which as such is not contrary to law. If in the present case fraudulent actions of even a criminal character were taken in connection with the bankruptcy of manufacturer, as claimant alleges, these would have to be dealt with by the state courts. An arbitral proceeding cannot be the proper forum to adjudicate on such allegations. In respect to the present case it must be concluded that there is no basis in statutory law for a legal succession of defendant no. 2 into the legal position of manufacturer as purchaser of the business of the bankrupt manufacturer who continues the business under the name of new manufacturer."

b. Liability under exclusive distributorship contract

[15] "The issue then is whether the rights and obligations under the exclusive distributorship contract between claimant and manufacturer, with the agreement to arbitrate as its integral part, were assigned to defendant no. 2 under the purchase agreement between the bankruptcy estate and defendant no. 2.

[16] "Claimant submits that the acquisition of assets under the purchase agreement is a singular succession under Swedish law. Claimant is of the opinion that under the agreement, defendant no. 2 took over the ongoing business from the bankrupt and was generally substituted for manufacturer. Defendant no. 2 acquired the rights and obligations under the distributorship contract with the agreement to arbitrate as its integral part together with the assets from the bankruptcy estate. The rights and obligations under the distributorship contract were included because defendant no. 2 had an interest to take over the ongoing business of the bankrupt manufacturer including its relationship with third parties. Although the distributorship contract with claimant is not specifically enumerated in the purchase agreement it is included under the Swedish law doctrine of *naturalia negotii*, because agency and distributorship contracts normally belong to the business conducted by the bankrupt and transferred to defendant no. 2. Claimant furthermore submits that under Swedish law defendant no. 2 is bound by the agreement to arbitrate contained in the distributorship contract assigned to it by the bankruptcy estate in the purchase agreement.

[17] "Defendant no. 2 submits that it has never had a business relationship with claimant and that the assets purchase agreement with the bankruptcy estate, did not confirm any obligations to companies which had established business relationships with manufacturer. The purchase agreement concerns the

3. The arbitrator cited *Methode der übertragenden Sanierung*, Karsten Schmidt, *Handelsrecht* (Commercial Law), 3rd ed. (1987) p. 225.

acquisition of assets of the estate of a bankrupt company, where it does not follow that the purchaser becomes the legal successor. According to Swedish law, the purchaser of such assets cannot become liable for the bankrupt's debts unless the purchaser has come to an agreement with the receiver on becoming liable for these. Defendant no. 2 asserts that the distributorship contract was not affected by the purchase agreement, and consequently there is no agreement to arbitrate between claimant and defendant no. 2.

[18] "For the purpose of the following considerations it is to be assumed that the distributorship contract between claimant and manufacturer was still in effect at the time of the purchase agreement.... Although the acquisition by defendant no. 2 under the purchase agreement does constitute a singular succession and may result in party substitution in the assignment of contracts, this can only be the case in respect to the rights and obligations which are in fact covered by the agreement. The Expert in Swedish law has confirmed that the acquisition of assets of a bankrupt company including its firm name from the bankruptcy estate and the continuation of the business of the bankrupt does not have the effect, as a general principle, that the acquirer succeeds into the rights and obligations under contracts to which the bankrupt was party at the time of bankruptcy.

[19] "It is evident that otherwise it would hardly be possible for the official receiver to sell the business as such in order to obtain the maximum amount of funds for distribution to the creditors in bankruptcy. The sale of assets and rights by the bankrupt company may be accompanied by corresponding obligations, but this is a matter of negotiation. It is therefore necessary to examine and interpret the concrete terms and conditions of the purchase agreement.

[20] "Clearly defendant no. 2 had an interest to take over the ongoing business of the bankrupt, but not comprehensively including all debts to creditors. Consequently it is provided in the preamble of the purchase agreement that the transfer of business has been agreed 'subject to the following conditions'. The assets, rights and obligations taken over by defendant no. 2, such as machinery, inventories, work in progress and finished products, patents, personnel (with which new contracts of employment are to be concluded), are specified in the agreement. It is also specifically stated that the purchase agreement includes 'leasing agreements relating to machines, inventories and vehicles'. However there is no mention of agreements with sales agents and distributors as being included in the agreement.

[21] "The doctrine of *naturalia negotii* may be applicable in general transfers of business by mergers and acquisitions, but it cannot apply without qualification in case of an assets purchase from a bankruptcy estate. The purchaser will normally not want to acquire the debts of the bankrupt by summarily

taking over the existing agreements, which he is not obliged to do. It is more reasonable for him to negotiate, where in his interest, and to conclude, either expressly or tacitly, new agreements individually with the agents and distributors of the bankrupt. If the opinion of claimant were correct that it was intended for defendant no. 2 to take over the complete ongoing business of the bankrupt manufacturer including its relationship with third parties, there would have been no need for a specific guarantee liability provision in the agreement and other detailed terms and conditions of the transfer.

[22] "The provision of the purchase agreement which reads, '... investment company A shall take over the business conducted by the bankrupt company, together with responsibility for results', can in this context only mean that defendant no. 2 took over the business of manufacturer subject to the specific terms and conditions of the purchase agreement together with the liability for the results, not retroactively, but starting from the date of the purchase agreement. Consequently defendant no. 2 did thereby not accept any liability for the acts of manufacturer prior to said date.

[23] "The conclusion must be that since the distributorship contract between claimant and manufacturer was not included in the purchase agreement between the bankruptcy estate and defendant no. 2, the agreement to arbitrate as an integral part of the distributorship contract cannot have become binding on defendant no. 2."

c. *Guarantee liability*

[24] "Claimant is of the opinion that the original Swedish wording of the guarantee article of the purchase agreement clearly sets out that defendant no. 2 was substituted for manufacturer with respect to guarantee liability relating to the machines that were the subject of claims negotiations with customers. Defendant no. 2 has therefore assumed the liability for the guarantee claims with full discharge of the original debtor. Since most of the deliveries on claimant's orders were incomplete, the guarantee period has not started to run in this respect. Claim negotiations regarding the defective deliveries existed between claimant and manufacturer at the time of the purchase agreement between the bankruptcy estate and defendant no. 2, and still have not been concluded. Defendant no. 2 is therefore bound by the agreement to arbitrate for the settlement of the claims made by claimant. Claimant points out that the delivery of machines by manufacturer pursuant to its orders to manufacturer were all subject to the UN General Sales Conditions No. 188. These General Conditions contain an arbitration clause in Paragraph 13, whereby all disputes shall be submitted to arbitration according to the Rules of the ICC.

[25] "Defendant no. 2 concedes that manufacturer supplied all machines pursuant to claimant's orders subject to the General Conditions No. 188. However, defendant no. 2 asserts that the guarantee commitments made by defendant no. 2 in the guarantee article of the purchase agreement do not cover the machines bought by claimant as the guarantee period has expired. Furthermore manufacturer has fulfilled all demands on behalf of the purchaser of the machines as established in the agreement between manufacturer and company X.

[26] "It is not evident from the wording of the guarantee article of the purchase agreement whether the parties intended the purchaser to substitute for the bankruptcy estate in respect to the obligations regarding claims relating to the guarantee liabilities specified therein. The English translation of the second sentence of the guarantee article reads in part that 'Investment company A, on taking over the business shall indemnify the bankrupt's estate against all guarantee liability relating to these machines', and the term 'indemnify' literally means 'to compensate for damages or expenses incurred'.

[27] "In view of this literal meaning, the Expert on Swedish law holds the opinion that the second sentence of the guarantee article does not express a substitution of the parties in the obligations relating to guarantee liability. He points out that a contract shall if possible be interpreted in a way that makes sense in the light of the implied purpose. A substitution of the parties seems to him to make no sense because the obligor is a bankruptcy estate whose obligations are restricted to the distribution of dividends on the claims in bankruptcy, and there is nothing to gain for either the obligor or the obligee if the obligee assumes full responsibility for the obligations by way of substitution. Furthermore, if the obligee were to take full responsibility for the obligations assumed, the bankruptcy estate would have to accept a reduction of the purchase price for the business assets, which would unlawfully favour the creditors of the delegated obligations at the cost of other creditors in bankruptcy.

[28] "However, – starting from the principle of interpretation stated by the Expert, namely that a contract shall be interpreted in a way that makes sense in the light of the implied purpose – the arbitrator finds that a substitution of the parties under the guarantee article of the purchase agreement makes more sense than the interpretation that the purchaser undertook to literally indemnify the bankruptcy estate against guarantee liability claims. If understood to mean substitution, the purchaser, defendant no. 2, would respond directly to the customers and fulfill the guarantee liability as required in the individual cases. Such a procedure is in the interest of defendant no. 2 because it is continuing the business of manufacturer under the name of manufacturer

and must therefore respond to the customers' claims in order to protect the goodwill of manufacturer and to keep up the relation to the customers.

[29] "On the other hand, the creditors in bankruptcy are not put at a disadvantage by such an agreement, because their dividends will increase in amount since less claims in bankruptcy will be filed. There is also no evidence that the assumption of these obligations by defendant no. 2 resulted in a reduction of the purchase price for the business, and this need not be the case as the assumption of the obligations in regard to present and potentially future customers is in the own interest of the purchaser of the business.

[30] "Finally, defendant no. 2 itself has confirmed that in the guarantee article of the purchase agreement the purchaser has assumed the responsibility for the guarantees, and not that it has undertaken to compensate the bankruptcy estate for its damages and expenses in this respect. The arbitrator is therefore of the opinion that the wording of the guarantee article means that the purchaser, defendant no. 2, has assumed the debts of manufacturer with full discharge of the original debtor in respect to the guarantee liabilities regarding all claims relating to defects of machines which are the subject of claims negotiations or for which guarantees remain in force.

[31] "The arbitrator also finds that the guarantee liability taken over in the guarantee article of the purchase agreement is not restricted to the machines specified in a list submitted by defendant no. 2. There is no mention of such list as a supplement in the purchase agreement, and it is not included among the documents under seal delivered by the notary public. There is no evidence that the obligations assumed by the purchaser under the guarantee article of the purchase agreement were to be restricted to specific machines.

[32] "The issue of whether the guarantee period for the machines purchased by claimant has expired is not relevant if the machines were at the time of bankruptcy the subject of claims negotiations. After the machines purchased by claimant and delivered to company X had been found to be defective and non-delivered on inspection, claimant immediately notified manufacturer of the defects in writing. Claims negotiations are initiated when a purchaser notifies the vendor in writing of the defects that have appeared pursuant to Paragraph 9 of the General Conditions No. 188. However, although claimant notified manufacturer repeatedly, it received no answer, and this is the reason why it is still raising its respective claims against defendant no. 2 as legal successor of manufacturer. The claims negotiations between claimant and manufacturer were therefore not concluded at the time manufacturer was declared bankrupt, so that defendant no. 2 has assumed the guarantee liability also in respect of the machines purchased by claimant.

[33] "Defendant no. 2 asserts that the defects have been remedied as follows from the agreement between manufacturer and company X, and that claimant

has no rights over and above those enjoyed by company X. This however is a question of the merits of the claims raised by claimant which is not to be dealt with at this stage. It is a general principle also of Swedish contract law that a debtor cannot validly transfer his obligations to a third party without the consent of the creditor. The consent by claimant as remaining party of the delegation of the liability obligations in regard to the defective machines can be inferred from the fact that claimant raises claims in this respect against defendant no. 2 to be settled by arbitration.

[34] "The arbitrator has concluded that the exclusive distribution contract between claimant and manufacturer and consequently the agreement to arbitrate as its integral part were not transferred to defendant no. 2 under the purchase agreement. However, defendant no. 2 has under the guarantee article of the purchase agreement assumed manufacturer's contractual guarantee liability in respect to machines which were sold subject to the UN General Conditions No. 188. This applies to all machines sold to claimant pursuant to the orders in question.

[35] "Under Paragraph 13(1) of the Conditions No. 188 any dispute in respect to guarantee liability is to be settled in accordance with the Rules of Conciliation and Arbitration of the International Chamber of Commerce. Since manufacturer was bound by this arbitration agreement in respect to guarantee claims relating to its machines, it is appropriate that defendant no. 2, having been substituted for manufacturer with respect to the guarantee liability relating to machines that were the subject of claims negotiations with customers, shall also have succeeded into the arbitration agreement between manufacturers and its customers in this respect. Defendant no. 2 was fully aware of the fact that the guarantee liability was subject to arbitration as it knew that the bankrupt company supplied its products in accordance with the UN General Conditions No. 188. The arbitration clause passes on automatically as incident to the delegated obligation, thus binding the obligee to the arbitration agreement. Defendant no. 2 is therefore bound by said arbitration clause for the settlement of guarantee claims relating [to] the machines delivered on claimant's orders at issue."

III. CONCLUSION

[36] "For the reasons set forth above the arbitrator finds that he has jurisdiction on defendant no. 1 with respect to claimant's claims relating to breach of the exclusive distributorship agreement and jurisdiction on defendant no. 2 with respect to claimant's claims relating to guarantee liability for machines."

Final award in case no. 8486 of 1996

Parties:	Claimant: Manufacturer (Netherlands) Defendant: Buyer (Turkey)
Place of arbitration:	Zurich, Switzerland
Published in:	Journal du droit international (1998, no. 4) pp. 1047-1052. Original in German
Subject matters:	- hardship - application of national law in light of UNIDROIT Principles - application of national law to international relationships - termination of contract - costs influenced by behaviour parties

Facts

A Dutch manufacturer and Turkish buyer contracted by means of an order confirmation for the sale of a plant for manufacturing a certain product for the Turkish market. The agreed price was for the entire installation.

The order confirmation, which was on a form provided by the Dutch manufacturer, was based on the UN/ECE General Conditions for the Supply of Plant and Machinery for Export, to which it explicitly referred both in its introductory and final sentence. The General Conditions contain, inter alia,the following provisions:

> "10. Delay in the Acceptance of the Delivery
> 10.1. If the buyer does not accept the delivery on the contractually agreed date, he shall nonetheless proceed to make the payments on the agreed dates as if the delivery had taken place....
> 10.2. If the delay in the acceptance does not depend on one of the circumstances in Art. 25, the manufacturer can request the buyer in writing to accept the delivery within a given time limit. If for any reason the buyer does not comply with the request within this time limit, the manufacturer can terminate the contract with regard to the part of the

delivery which was not accepted by a simple written communication (without judicial assistance) and claim compensation for the damages caused by the buyer's non-performance. The compensation for damages is limited to the sum indicated in the Annex under A or – if no indication has been made – to the contractual price of the relevant part of the delivery.

11. Payment
(....)
11.7. .... If the buyer does not pay within the time limit indicated in the Annex under C, the manufacturer can terminate the contract by a simple written communication (without judicial assistance) and claim compensation for damages up to the sum mentioned in the Annex under A.

25. Grounds for Relief
25.1. The following circumstances are grounds for relief if they intervene after the conclusion of the contract and hinder its performance: labour disputes and all circumstances independent of the will of the parties, such as fire, mobilization, expropriation, embargo, prohibition to transfer currency, riots, lack of means of transportation, generalized lack of supplies, restrictions on energy.
(....)

26. Limitation of Damages
26.1. If a party owes compensation for damages, this compensation shall not exceed the damage which that party could foresee at the time of concluding the contract."

The order confirmation provided for ICC arbitration and the application of Dutch law. The order further provided that the equipment was to be delivered to the buyer on the condition that the buyer had paid 5% of the sales price one year prior to delivery and had opened an irrevocable letter of credit two months before delivery

Due to financial difficulties, the buyer only paid 3% of the contractual price as advance payment and did not open the letter of credit within the agreed time limit. The manufacturer offered to deliver only half of the installation. The buyer accepted the offer and the manufacturer issued an invoice for half of the original sales price. The buyer made an offer of approximately 60% of the reduced delivery price. The manufacturer refused this offer and reserved its rights under the original agreement concerning the full delivery.

Following unsuccessful negotiations, the manufacturer commenced ICC arbitration as provided for in the contract. The manufacturer claimed an amount in payment for the part of the manufacturing system which could not be sold to other buyers as it had been made expressly for the Turkish buyer, interest and legal fees. The buyer objected that it was discharged of its obligations under the contract because of the dramatic drop in the price of the relevant product on the Turkish market, which amounted to hardship. The buyers also counterclaimed its advance payment.

The sole arbitrator granted the claim for damages of the manufacturer, denied in part its claim for interest and denied the counterclaim filed by the defendant, which sought to recover the advance payment made to the claimant. In particular, the sole arbitrator found that the circumstances for discharge from payment due to unforeseen circumstances were not met. The mandatory provisions of Dutch law on this matter were to be applied with restraint and international contractual and arbitral practice, including the UNIDROIT Principles, were to be taken into consideration.

Excerpt

I. VALID CONTRACT

[1] "The contract between the claimant and the defendant is valid. Contrary to the defendant's opinion, the parties did not provide that the validity of the contract depended on the defendant obtaining the necessary financing. Rather, the parties agreed, [in] the order confirmation, on a manner of payment which is customary in international relations (an advance payment and a guarantee for the manufacturer on the remaining sum by means of an irrevocable letter of credit). Further, the delivery of the equipment depended on the defendant opening a letter of credit before the agreed time.

[2] "The delivery of the equipment presupposes a valid contract. Neither the text nor the construction of the payment clause gives us reason to believe that the parties intended the opening of the letter of credit to be a condition for the validity of the contract. This would also be contradicted by the fact that the defendant made the advance payment and by the behaviour of the parties when concluding the contract. In its correspondence with the claimant..., the defendant only discussed the price requested by the claimant, apparently assuming that the contract was valid. For this reason it made the advance payment. At that time, the defendant also assumed that there was a legally binding agreement on the sales price, as it requested that the claimant 'adjust the price' because of the changed circumstances on the Turkish market.... In

its turn, the claimant started manufacturing the equipment after concluding the contract. From its behaviour too it undoubtedly appears that the contract with the defendant was originally valid."

II. HARDSHIP

[3] "The circumstances alleged by the defendant do not allow the tribunal to discharge the defendant from its obligation to pay on the ground of unforeseen circumstances (*onvoorziene omstandigheden*) in the sense of Art. 6:258 of the Dutch Civil Code (*Burgerlijk Wetboek*, BW).[1]

[4] "The provisions of the Dutch Civil Code, being the law of the manufacturer, apply to the contract by virtue of Art. 13(3) first sentence of the ICC Arbitration Rules[2] together with Clause [28] of the General Conditions. [The application of Dutch law] also ensues from Art. 13(3) second sentence of the ICC Arbitration Rules together with Art. 187(1) second alternative of the Swiss Federal Act on Private International Law (PILA).[3] The Swiss PILA applies to the present arbitration by virtue of its Art. 176(1) because Zurich,

1. Art. 258 of Book 6 of the Dutch Civil Code (BW) reads:

"1. The court may, upon request of one of the parties, modify the effects of an agreement or terminate it in part or in its entirety on the basis of unforeseen circumstances of such nature that the other party may not, according to criteria of reasonableness and fairness (*redelijkheid en billijkheid*), expect the agreement to be maintained in an unmodified form. The modification or termination may be given retroactive effect.
2. The modification or termination may not be pronounced to the extent that these circumstances are to be borne by the party relying upon them, according to the nature of the agreement or commercial common opinion.
3. For the application of this Article, the party to whom a contractual right or obligation has been ceded equals a party to the contract."

2. Art. 13(3) of the 1988 ICC Rules of Conciliation and Arbitration reads:

"The parties shall be free to determine the law to be applied by the arbitrator to the merits of the dispute. In the absence of any indication by the parties as to the applicable law, the arbitrator shall apply the law designated as the proper law by the rule of conflict which he deems appropriate."

3. Art. 187(1) of the Swiss Private International Law Act (PILA) reads:

"The arbitral tribunal shall decide the case according to the rules of law chosen by the parties or, in the absence of such a choice, according to the rules of law with which the case has the closest connection."

Switzerland, was indicated as the seat of the arbitration by the ICC and both parties have their seat outside Switzerland.[4] Further, the claimant, being the manufacturer, performed the characteristic performance of the contract; hence, the dispute has its closest connection with the law of the claimant (see in general Berger, *International Economic Arbitration* (1993) p. 503 et seq.).

[5] "Art. 6:258 applies here even if the parties agreed on specific 'grounds for discharge' in Clause 25 of the General Conditions, as, according to Art. 6:250 BW, the parties may not derogate contractually from [Art. 6:258], which must be applied mandatorily (see Nieuwenhuis/Stolker/Valk, *Burgerlijk Wetboek*, 2nd ed. (1994), Books 3, 5 and 6, Art. 258, note 1).

[6] "However, the conditions of [Art. 6:258] are not met in the present case. We start from the premise that [Art. 6:258] must be applied with the utmost restraint because, among others, it is a special rule with respect to the general possibility, under Art. 6:248(2) together with Art. 3:12 of the Dutch Civil Code, to consider certain contractual provisions inapplicable on grounds of reasonableness and fairness (*redelijkheid en billijkheid*) in certain circumstances (see, on the lex specialis character of Art. 6:258, Nieuwenhuis/Stolker/Valk, op. cit.).[5]

[7] "In Dutch national legal practice, the general provision [of Art. 6:248 BW] is applied with the utmost restraint (see Nieuwenhuis/Stolker/Valk, *Burgerlijk Wetboek*, op. cit., Art. 248, note 4). According to Art. 3:12 BW, 'Dutch common opinion of law' is the determining factor in the first place; it is replaced by the common opinion in international contract law when the provision is applied in an international context. Both are influenced in a

---

4. Art. 176 (1) of the Swiss PILA reads:

> "The provisions of this chapter shall apply to all arbitrations if the seat of the arbitral tribunal is situated in Switzerland and if, at the time when the arbitration agreement was concluded, at least one of the parties had neither its domicile nor its habitual residence in Switzerland."

5. Art. 248(2) of Book 6 BW reads:

> "A contractual provision valid between the parties does not apply to the extent that it would be unacceptable in the given circumstances according to requirements of reasonableness and fairness."

Art. 12 of Book 3 BW reads:

> "In determining the requirements of reasonableness and fairness (*redelijkheid en billijkheid*), generally recognised principles of law, Dutch common opinion of law and the social and personal interests concerned in the given case must be considered."

decisive manner by the principle of contractual good faith (*pacta sunt servanda*) expressed in Art. 1.3 of the UNIDROIT Principles for International Commercial Contracts[6] (see UNIDROIT, ed., *Principles of International Commercial Contracts* (1994) p. 4; see also Fouchard, *L'Arbitrage Commercial International* (1965) p. 442; Paulsson, 'La Lex Mercatoria dans l'Arbitrage CCI', Revue de l'Arbitrage (1990) p. 55, 82 et seq.; ICC Award No. 4972, in Jarvin/Derains/ Arnaldez, eds., *Collection of ICC Arbitral Awards* (1994) p. 380, 383; ICC Award No. 5485, *Yearbook Commercial Arbitration* XIV (1989) p. 156, 168; ICC Award No. 5953, Clunet (1990) p. 1056). This common opinion of law must also be taken into account for the application of national law to international relationships (see Berger, *Formalisierte oder 'schleichende' Kodifizierung des transnationalen Wirtschaftsrechts* (1996) p. 174 et seq.). The necessity and admissibility of the interpretation of national law in the light of the UNIDROIT Principles is also asserted especially for Dutch law (Kuijer, 'Een vergelijking van "hardship" uit de UNIDROIT-regeling met de onvoorziene omstandigheden uit artikel 6:258 van het BW', Ars Aequi (1996) p. 16, 19).

[8] "The same restraint should be exercised, according to the Dutch legislator, when applying the special provision of Art. 6:258 (Nieuwenhuis/ Stolker/Valk, op. cit., Art. 258, note 1, with reference to the travaux préparatoires). This restraint is also in line with international contractual and arbitral practice. It is also to be taken into consideration in the context of Dutch national law (see Kuijer, op. cit., p. 20).

[9] "Hence, the termination of a contract for unforeseen circumstances ('hardship', '*clausula rebus sic stantibus*') should be allowed only in truly exceptional cases (ICC Award No. 1512, in Jarvin/Derains, eds., *Collection of ICC Arbitral Awards* (1990) p. 3, 4). In international commerce one must rather assume in principle that the parties take the risks of performing under and carrying out the contract upon themselves, unless a different allocation of risk is expressly provided for in the contract (ICC Award No. 1512, cited above). Art. 6.2.1 of the UNIDROIT Principles expressly provides that the mere fact that the performance of the contract entails a higher economic burden for one of the parties does not suffice to assume that there is 'hardship' (see UNIDROIT, ed., *Principles of International Commercial Contracts* (1994)

6. Art. 1.3 of the UNIDROIT Principles reads:

> "A contract validly entered into is binding upon the parties. It can only be modified or terminated in accordance with its terms or by agreement or as otherwise provided in these Principles."

p. 145).[7] Also the ICC Principles on 'Force Majeure and Hardship' provide that a party cannot argue that performance is impossible only because the contract happens to have become unprofitable (ICC Publication No. 421, p. 22). Accordingly, a Dutch arbitral tribunal held that a dramatic fall in the price [of a product] as well as currency fluctuations alone are not unforeseen circumstances and thus do not justify the termination of a contract. In the opinion of the arbitral tribunal, these circumstances fall rather within the risk sphere of the party concerned (Ad Hoc [NOFOTA] Award of 10 September 1975, Yearbook II (1977) p. 156, 158; see also ICC Award No. 3099, 3100, Yearbook VII (1982) p. 87, 92; Nassar, *Sanctity of Contract Revisited* (1995) p. 205).

[10] "In the present case, the defendant bases its objections to the validity of its obligation to pay on such circumstances only. This clearly appears in particular from the fax of the defendant to the claimant ..., in which the changes on the Turkish market are described in detail. The defendant referred to this description several times in the course of the correspondence preceding the arbitration as well as in this arbitration. The rising of a private manufacturing sector and the connected fall in the price [of the product] described therein, as well as the general trade situation in Turkey, only concern the economic frame of the Turkish market and thus fall within the risk sphere of the defendant.

[11] "Further, the defendant also indicated that it was aware of these commercial risks in the relevant trade.... Defendant it made clear that it was perfectly aware of the unstable commercial situation in Turkey and that it always had to consider that 'the situation ... can change suddenly'.

[12] "With respect to these unstable circumstances on the Turkish market, which were known to the defendant, it does not seem maintainable that the defendant wants to shift the commercial risks related thereto onto the claimant. Further, the claimant helped the defendant when concluding the contract, in that by [accepting] the financing clause [contained therein] it accepted a significant pre-financing risk, apparently in consideration of the good commercial relations which had existed until then between the parties. Also, during the entire proceedings the claimant has indicated its willingness

7. Art. 6.2.1 of the UNIDROIT Principles reads:

> "Where the performance of a contract becomes more onerous for one of the parties, that party is nevertheless bound to perform its obligations subject to the following provisions on hardship."

to cooperate in an economic solution of the problem which is acceptable for the defendant.

[13] "In the light of the above situation, the circumstances raised by the defendant fall within the economic risk to be borne by the defendant, also according to the interpretation valid in international commercial relations. The arbitral tribunal may not, according to Art. 6:258(2) BW, consider them unforeseen circumstances in the sense of this provision (see also Kuijer, op. cit., p. 20)."

III. TERMINATION OF THE CONTRACT

[14] "The claimant validly terminated the contract with the defendant. We can leave aside the question whether, by its counsel's letter ..., the claimant validly terminated the contract by way of annulment (*vernietiging*) according to Art. 3:39 BW or of dissolution (*ontbinding*) according to Art. 6:267(1) BW. The parties validly derogated from these provisions of Dutch law, which law is in itself applicable (see above under [4], by [referring to] the UN/ECE 'General Conditions for the Supply of Plant and Machinery for Export' (No. 188 A) annexed to the confirmation of order. The General Conditions give the claimant the right to terminate the contract and to claim compensation for damages.

[15] "The General Conditions are validly incorporated in the contract of the parties. Art. 6:234(1)(1) BW together with Art. 6:233(b) BW require that the party drafting [the General Conditions] 'make [the conditions] available, before or at the conclusion of the contract' to the other party, so that the other party has 'the reasonable possibility to take cognizance' of the contents of these provisions. The order confirmation, which was initialled and signed by both parties and thus constitutes the proper text of the contract, contains both in its opening formula and in its concluding sentence an express reference to the General Conditions, which were also attached to the contract.

[16] "According to Clause 10.2 of the General Conditions, the claimant could, if reception of the delivery were delayed, request the defendant in writing to receive [the delivery] within an adequate time limit, and free itself from the contract at the expiry of that time limit by a simple written communication. The claimant complied with these requirements. It indicated several times to the defendant that the equipment was 'at its disposal'. It was in good faith (Art. 3:11 BW) unnecessary to set a time limit, because of the defendant's final refusal to receive the delivery, contained in its fax to the claimant....

[17] "The same consequence would ensue from Clause 11.7 of the General Conditions, because the defendant had failed to make the agreed payments in

due time, so that the claimant also had the right according to that provision to terminate the contract by a simple written notice.

[18] "The termination had future (ex nunc) effect, as the General Conditions provide that damages for non-performance, not the retroactive annulment of the contract, are the legal consequence of the termination. This ensues also from Clause 27.1 of the General Conditions. Hence, the termination of the contract does not entail the loss of the rights of the parties which arose under the contract until the termination thereof."

IV. DAMAGES

[19] "Relying on its valid termination of the contract, the claimant claims damages from the defendant under Clause 10.2 second sentence and Clause 11.7 of the General Conditions. According to these provisions, [a party] may claim compensation of the contractual value of the part of the delivery at issue. Since the claimant, in observance of its general obligation to reduce damage (Clause 26.1 of the General Conditions), has been able to sell the standard parts of the equipment made for the defendant, its claim is limited to a compensation for the parts which are not otherwise sellable because made according to the special requirements of the defendant. According to the statement of witness A, Sales Director of the claimant, in the oral hearings, the parts concerned are especially those parts which met the specific product specifications for the Turkish market ... and thus cannot be sold on another market."

[20] The sole arbitrator found that the value of these parts was equal to the amount claimed by the claimant. He held: "These damages could be foreseen by the defendant because of Clause 26.1 of the General Conditions. Each item of the claim for damages concerns parts or tools which were part of the contract. Since the equipment would also cut the product in the size wished by the defendant, the defendant could undoubtedly foresee at the time of concluding the contract that [the equipment] was especially made [for the defendant] and that, therefore, its parts would be included in a request by the claimant for compensation of damages.

[21] "Further, the claimant claims payment of interest on the original sum until the day on which the sellable parts of the plant were sold by the claimant. From this sum, which was originally owed, we should deduct the advance payment, which the defendant undisputedly paid. The claimant can thus claim interest on the remainder only.

[22] "Interest does not run, as alleged by the claimant, from the conclusion of the contract. It ensues from the payment clause in the contract that the sales price was not yet due at the time of concluding the contract. Nor would it

become due when the letter of credit was opened. In this case, the bank's obligation to pay depended on the suspensive condition of the submission of the necessary documents. Hence, the claimant could actually require payment, and the invoice sum would become due, only at that time. According to the payment clause, the invoice sum would become due only when the transport document were handed over, respectively 6 and 12 months after the date of expedition. However, the exact date of the expedition cannot be determined. The delivery clause in the contract provides that delivery shall take place ... on the condition that the entire advance payment is made and that the letter of credit is opened. Neither has happened. Hence, the claimant's claim for interest is not based on Clause 11.7 first sentence of the General Conditions.

[23] "However, because of the delay in the payment, the claimant has a right to interest at the legal rate according to Art. 6:119 and following together with Art. 6:81 of the Dutch Civil Code. The conditions for delay provided for in Art. 6:81 et seq. BW are met here.[8] The invoice sum was due. The defendant had not opened the letter of credit as agreed. According to Clause 10.1 of the General Conditions, the buyer shall make the agreed payments, 'as if the delivery had been made' even if it does not accept the delivery at the time agreed in the contract. The parties negotiated the further development of the contract and also postponed the contractually agreed time in the sense of this provision.... This applies also to the part of the advanced payment provided for in the contract which was not paid by the defendant. In its fax of ..., the defendant finally refused to accept the entire delivery. The invoice sum was thus due at the latest at this time. At this time there was also delay in the sense of Art. 6:81 BW. The formal notice required by 6:82 BW was superfluous here. According to Art. 6:83(c) BW, such formal request to pay is unnecessary where a communication of the debtor makes it clear to the creditor that the former will not abide by its obligation. This condition is met by the [above-

8. Art. 81 of Book 6 BW reads:

"The debtor is in default for as long as he does not perform when his performance has become due and the requirements of Arts. 82 and 83 are met, unless the delay cannot be imputed to him or performance is already permanently impossible."

Art. 82 of Book 6 BW reads:

"1. Default commences when the debtor is held in default by a written notice granting him a reasonable time to perform, and he does not perform within this time limit.
2. If the debtor's impossibility to perform is temporary or it appears from his behaviour that a notice would be useless, he can be held in default by a written communication from which it appears that he is held responsible for the lack of performance."

mentioned] fax of the defendant. In this fax, the defendant not only made clear that it had not managed to open the letter of credit, so that a further discussion of the affair was useless; it also requested restitution of its advance payment and thus for the first time clearly made the claimant understand that it would no longer meet its obligations under the contract. Hence, interest starts running on the date of the fax."

V. COUNTERCLAIM

[24] "The defendant's counterclaim is unfounded and must be denied. The claimant reduced the main sum, which it first requested, by the advance payment undisputedly paid by the defendant ... during the oral hearings and thereby renounced to the part of its claim corresponding to the advance payment. According to the general principles of arbitration law, the claimant may at any stage in the proceedings totally or partially withdraw its claim by a claim renunciation, saving its corresponding obligation to pay costs vis-à-vis the other party (Reiner, *ICC Schiedsgerichtsbarkeit* (1989) p. 240). Hence, there is no room left for the counterclaim of the defendant, which claims restitution of the advance payment."

VI. COSTS

[25] "According to Art. 20 of the ICC Rules of Arbitration, the arbitral tribunal must, together with its decision on the merits, render a decision on the costs of the arbitration and decide which party must bear these costs. According to general principles, the costs of the arbitration must be borne by the party which loses the arbitration (see Berger, *International Economic Arbitration* (1993) p. 617). In the present case the defendant loses its counterclaim, but the claimant's claim is granted only in part. Further, the claimant must pay the costs related to its partial claim renunciation to the defendant....

[26] "Nonetheless, the costs of the arbitration shall be borne totally by the defendant. According to the general principles of international arbitration law, the arbitral tribunal must take into account for its decision on costs not only the result of the proceedings but also the behaviour of the parties during the proceedings (Reiner, op. cit., p. 283; Berger, op. cit., p. 617). According to good faith, the parties to an international arbitration must in particular facilitate the proceedings and abstain from all delaying tactics (Berger, op. cit., p. 374). The behaviour of the defendant during the entire proceedings did not

comply with these requirements in any way. The defendant made none of the advance payments on costs which are required for the proceedings. Further, not only did it file its counterclaim belatedly, that is, only after the first draft of the terms of reference; it also refused to sign the terms of reference, which had been modified according to its wishes, notwithstanding a detailed explanation by the arbitral tribunal of the terms' meaning and legal consequences, and it did not participate in the oral hearings although it had been given sufficient notice to appear. Further, it also contributed to unnecessary delay and confusion in the proceedings by appointing counsel at the last moment, that is, after the closing of the oral hearings and shortly before the expiry of the latest time limit for a statement concerning the minutes of the hearings; compounded by counsel's renunciation to the mandate only a few days afterward. The proceedings were further complicated by the same counsel again accepting his mandate on the same day, a fact which had not been communicated to the arbitrator. For the above reasons, the defendant shall also reimburse to the claimant the advance payment on costs, which the latter paid for these proceedings.

[27] "The defendant's obligation to pay costs includes, according to Art. 20(2) of the ICC Arbitration Rules, the 'normal legal costs incurred by the parties'. The claimant has claimed ... legal fees for.... This sum comprises counsel's fees as well as expenses and further procedural costs (translations etc.). The normality of the legal costs is defined according to the general principles of the law on the costs of arbitration. It is decisive to this aim whether the legal costs are objectively necessary and adequate with respect to the factual and legal complexity of the case, including the presumable time spent [for the proceedings]. The arbitral tribunal decides this issue at its discretion (Craig/Park/Paulsson, *ICC Arbitration*, 2nd ed. (1990) p. 338; Berger, op. cit., p. 618). The legal costs claimed by the claimant appear necessary and adequate to the tribunal with respect to the legal issues raised in the proceedings and taking into account the development of the proceedings described above; they are also 'normal', therefore, in the sense of Art. 20(2) of the ICC Arbitration Rules. Hence, the defendant must bear them in their entirety."

Final award in case no. 8938 of 1996

Parties:	Claimant: Exclusive agent (Belgium) Defendant: Manufacturer (France)
Place of arbitration:	Luxembourg, Luxembourg
Published in:	Unpublished. Original in French
Subject matters:	- autonomy of arbitral clause - European Convention 1961 - arbitrability of dispute in international arbitration - indemnification for termination of agency contract

Facts

The French manufacturer and the Belgian agent concluded an agency contract whereby the Belgian agent would represent manufacturer's products in Belgium. The contract provided for ICC arbitration and the application of French law.

A dispute arose between the parties when the French manufacturer terminated the contract after less than two years. The agent initiated arbitration, seeking damages and payment of certain outstanding commission fees. The manufacturer objected to the jurisdiction of the arbitrator, relying, inter alia, on Art. 27 of the Belgian Law of 13 April 1995 which prevented a Belgian company from concluding a contract providing for arbitration unless Belgian law applies.

The sole arbitrator found that the arbitration clause between the parties was valid and held, on the merits, that the contract had been validly concluded and that the manufacturer had terminated it "untimeously, without just cause or legal grounds allowed by the law, hence wrongly". The arbitrator calculated the damage incurred by the agent by quantifying the commissions it would have earned on the minimum sales obligation set by the manufacturer over the duration of the contract.

Excerpt

I. JURISDICTION

(....)

[1] "The parties to the dispute are two commercial companies, one French, one Belgian; the former has granted to the latter the distributorship of its products, manufactured in France, in Belgium. It appears from the file of the case and the information submitted that this business relationship implied a cross-frontier movement of goods and money. According to both law and jurisprudence, a contract is international when it implicates international commercial interests, that is, when it causes a two-way movement over borders.[1] The international character of an arbitration can be thus deduced from the nature of the economic operation involved, which implicates international commercial interests, independent of the place of arbitration, the law applicable to the merits or the nationality of the contracting parties, all elements which do not suffice to this aim."[2]

1. *Jurisdiction and Arbitrability*

[2] "The arbitral clause is doubly autonomous: in relation to the arbitral agreement,[3] and in relation to the law of the contract.[4] It has long been recognized, in general, that in international matters the arbitrator has jurisdiction over his own jurisdiction in so far as the arbitrability of the dispute in the light of international public policy.[5] In particular, Art. 8(3) of the ICC Arbitration Rules fully enables the arbitrator to take any decision as to his own jurisdiction.[6] Taking the lex fori into account, the international

---

1. "*Cour d'appel*, Paris, 19 February 1992 (*SABA v. Coopsette*), Recueil Dalloz (1992) IR p. 137."
2. "*Cour d'appel*, Paris, 14 November 1991 (*Legrand v. European Country Hotels Limited*), Recueil Dalloz (1992) IR p. 57."
3. "*Jurisclasseur de Droit International Privé Français*, Arbitrage Commercial International, binder 586-1a, Nature du principe d'autonomie, nos. 7 and 2 et seq., and the numerous quotations and references therein."
4. "Id., Autonomie de la clause d'arbitrage par rapport à toute loi étatique, no. 34 et seq., and numerous quotations therein; J. Robert, *L'Arbitrage*, 6th ed. (Dalloz) no. 267."
5. "*Cour d'appel*, Paris, 29 March 1991 (*Kinsqnhalasi v. Société Nationale des Chemins de fer Tunisiens*), Recueil Dalloz (1991) IR p. 123."
6. Art. 8(3) of the ICC Rules of Conciliation and Arbitration (1988) reads:

   "Should one of the parties raise one or more pleas concerning the existence or validity of the agreement to arbitrate, and should the Court be satisfied of the prima facie existence of such an agreement, the Court may, without prejudice to the admissibility or merits of the plea or

arbitrator sitting in Luxembourg has at this stage no other limitation as to his jurisdiction than the limitations resulting from the international public policy of Luxembourg.

[3] "Luxembourg is a party to both the [European Convention of 1961] and the [Agreement of 1962].[7] At a domestic law level, arbitration is based in Arts. 1003 and following of the Code of Civil Procedure.

[4] "In virtue of the independent rule of international arbitration law, embodied in Art. 8(4) of the Rules,[8] the arbitral clause is autonomous and juridically independent from the main contract in which it is contained either directly or by reference, and its existence and validity are to be ascertained, taking into account the mandatory rules of national law and international public policy, in the light of the common intention of the parties, without necessarily referring to a state law.[9]

[5] "The principle of 'compétence-compétence', which is actually inserted at the end of the article on jurisdiction of the contract at issue, is widely recognized by doctrine and jurisprudence.[10]

[6] "It is beyond doubt here that the present dispute concerns property rights of which the parties may freely dispose, and it can be inferred from the manufacturer's final statement that the manufacturer bases its objection of lack of jurisdiction only on allegations of non-arbitrability in French and Belgian law."

---

pleas, decide that the arbitration shall proceed. In such a case any decision as to the arbitrator's jurisdiction shall be taken by the arbitrator himself."

7. "Law of 26 November 1981, ratifying the Convention and the Protocol."
8. Art. 8(4) of the ICC Rules of Conciliation and Arbitration (1988) reads:

"Unless otherwise provided, the arbitrator shall not cease to have jurisdiction by reason of any claim that the contract is null and void or allegation that it is inexistent provided that he upholds the validity of the agreement to arbitrate. He shall continue to have jurisdiction, even though the contract itself may be inexistent or null and void, to determine the respective rights of the parties and to adjudicate upon their claims and pleas."

9. "*Cour de cassation*, 20 December 1993 (*Comité populaire de la Municipalité de Kons v. Dalico Contractors*), Recueil Dalloz (1994) IR p. 13."
10. "*Jurisclasseur*, Convention d'arbitrage, Effets, nos. 586-5 (Droit International) and 1062 (Procédure Civile) B- Compétence du Tribunal Arbitral pour régler les litiges visés par la convention d'arbitrage, nos. 25-38."

2. *The Grounds Raised by the Parties*

[7] "The parties stipulated in the contract at issue that the International Chamber of Commerce has jurisdiction to decide by arbitration on all disputes arising from the contract or in connection with it. In French law, Art. 48 of the French New Code of Civil Procedure[11] does not enjoin merchants (*commerçants*) from concluding forum selection clauses which derogate directly or indirectly from the rules of territorial competence; also, Art. 48 does not apply to international disputes. An arbitration clause is thus in principle allowed, and its validity is embodied in Art. 1492 of the French New Code of Civil Procedure.[12]

[8] "The manufacturer argues that an agent is not a *commerçant* in French law, and arbitration would thus be precluded. This contention, summarily argued, does not hold against French jurisprudence in the field of private international law. In fact, it has been held that notwithstanding contractual references to French law, to which the parties have explicitly submitted, an agent's mandate, and even a mixed mandate, may be the subject of an arbitration clause concluded by the parties, beyond the domain allowed by French law, since in international arbitration an arbitration agreement is completely autonomous in relation to the juridical act to which it belongs.[13]

[9] "It has also been held that in international matters an arbitration clause is allowed per se in virtue of the general principle of its autonomy, an independent rule which gives efficacy to the arbitration clause independent of the law applicable to the contract and to the parties to the contract, with the sole limitation of international public policy, in particular as to the arbitrability of the dispute. Hence, even the civil or commercial nature of the main contract has no impact on the validity of the arbitration agreement, which must be applied notwithstanding the provision invoked by the French party,

---

11. Art. 48 of the French New Code of Civil Procedure reads:

> "Any clause which derogates, directly or indirectly, from the rules of territorial competence is to be deemed as not written insofar as it has not been agreed among parties who are all merchants, or if it has not been very clearly specified in the undertaking of the party who has included it."

12. Art. 1492 of the French New Code of Civil Procedure reads:

> "An arbitration is international if it implicates international commercial interests."

13. "*Cour d'appel*, Paris, see fn. 1."

based on French domestic law, which provides that an arbitration clause in non-commercial contracts is null.[14]

[10] "The manufacturer also argues that the Belgian Law of 13 August 1995 enjoins the agent from referring to arbitration in the present case. In Belgian law, Art. 1676 of the Judicial Code, which implements the provisions of the European Convention providing a Uniform Law on Arbitration, done at Strasbourg on 20 January 1966, approved by Law of 4 July 1972 and published in the Official Gazette of 8 August 1972, provides that: '1. Any dispute which has arisen or may arise out of a specific legal relationship and in respect of which it is permissible to compromise may be the subject of an arbitration agreement'. In its turn, save for the application of the international conventions to which Belgium is a party, the Belgian Law of 13 April 1995 provides that the activity of an agent having his principal place of business in Belgium falls under Belgian law and the jurisdiction of the Belgian courts. The Belgian legislator did not exclude therewith the referral to arbitration and more specifically to international arbitration at all. Hence, Belgian law, and more particularly the above-mentioned Art. 27 of the Belgian Law of 13 April 1995, do not hinder the referral [of this dispute] to the International Court of Arbitration and to this arbitrator.

[11] "It also appears from the exchange of correspondence at the time of drafting the contract that the parties clearly intended to refer later disputes to arbitration, that the arbitration clause was indeed the clause on which they agreed and that the manufacturer wanted an arbitration clause at least as much as the agent,...

[12] "Last, the EC directive of 18 December 1986, to which counsel for the manufacturer refers without further detail or clarification, was integrated in the French juridical system by Law no. 91-593 of 25 June 1991 and Decree no. 92-506 of 10 June 1992, and in the Belgian legal system by the Law of 13 April 1995. Nor does this directive, which has two goals – the harmonization of national laws and the protection of agents – contain a provision which can interfere with the parties' agreement to refer the disputes arising under their relationship to arbitration.

[13] "Consequently, the arbitrator has jurisdiction to hear the present dispute."

---

14. "*Cour d'appel*, Paris, 14 November 1991 (*Forestier v. PRIFD*), Recueil Dalloz (1992) IR p. 57."

II. THE MERITS

1. *Applicable Law*

[14] "The parties intended their relationship to be governed by French law, as it appears from the article of the contract which concerns the applicable law, and was confirmed to the arbitrator at the hearing. The principle of the autonomy of the parties' will, to which Art. 13(5) of the Arbitration Rules refers,[15] is accepted in both the French and Belgian legal system. In the present case, the parties to the dispute have affirmed and reaffirmed their clear intention not to submit the merits of the present dispute to Belgian law. By so doing, they have applied Art. 13(3) of the ICC Rules of Arbitration, to which they chose to submit, and their choice, which does not violate international public policy, must be recognized as valid notwithstanding all possible contrary provisions of a national law [of a State] on the territory of which the decision is not even sought to be enforced. Consequently, the arbitrator does not see any obstacle to the application of French law to the present dispute, in conformity with the intention expressed by the parties." (....)

2. *No Valid Termination*

[15] After determining that the contract was valid the arbitrator dealt with the question of its termination as follows: "As to the arguments raised by the manufacturer to justify its initiative to terminate, it should be noted first that the parties determined that their relationship would last five years and would be tacitly extended for three years unless a notice of termination would be sent six months before expiry.

[16] "A contract concluded for a given period of time may not be terminated before expiry unless there is a serious breach by one of the parties or force majeure.[16] The manufacturer in this case has acted without waiting for the

15. Art. 13(3) of the ICC Rules of Conciliation and Arbitration (1988) to which the arbitrator was apparently referring reads:

"The parties shall be free to determine the law to be applied by the arbitrator to the merits of the dispute. In the absence of any indication by the parties as to the applicable law, the arbitrator shall apply the law designated as the proper law by the rule of conflict which he deems appropriate."

16. "Commentaries on the Law no. 91-593 of 25 June 1991 on the Relations between Agents and Principals, Actualité législative Dalloz (1992) Conn. p. 131, no. 33."

former or alleging the latter; its recriminations are furthermore either unfounded, contradicted by uncontested documents submitted in the proceedings, or mere conjectures.

[17] "It is worth mentioning here that it appears from the documents in the file, which have been freely discussed, not only that the agent timeously accepted the minimum result obligation required by its co-contractor, which by the way it had already amply reached in the first year, but also that the first results of the second year, unilaterally interrupted by the manufacturer, led to believe that the same would be easily true in that year. The documented results ... show[] a constant progression since the beginning of the relationship.

[18] "Consequently, the manufacturer cannot seriously support without further proof its allegation that it did not believe that in the future the agent would not bring more in than in the past, since the documented results until then were apparently more than satisfactory according to its own criteria.

[19] "For the sake of completeness, the agent is enjoined [by the terms of the contract] from ceding the contract without the previous and explicit agreement of the principal, and the manufacturer reserves its faculty to terminate the contract only in the case in which the agent is bought by or rents out its professional activity to a third party. None of these situations exists or is alleged here.

[20] "Had the above been different, the contract still imposed a trial period of six months on the manufacturer, at the end of which six months the agent was supposed to have obtained a given result.

[21] "The arbitrator considers therefore that it is established that the manufacturer breached the agency contract with the agent untimeously, without just cause or legal grounds, hence wrongly.

[22] "This is a violation of an obligation (not) to do something, and, according to Art. 1142 of the French Civil Code as well as Art. 12 of the French Law of 25 June 1991, it results in an obligation to pay damages and interest indemnifying the damage incurred [by the party], this being the option chosen by the French legislator between the two options in Art. 17 of the European directive, which provides for either the payment of an indemnification corresponding to one year [of commissions] or the indemnification of the damage incurred."[17]

3. *Indemnification*

[23] "In a letter from manufacturer's counsel to the agent's counsel, the former refers to the agent's contractual renunciation of the termination

17. "Op. cit., see fn. 16, no. 35."

indemnity provided for in the EC directive, which renunciation was apparently suggested by the then representative of the agent to offset his desired reduction of the annual minimum result obligation, a condition for territorial exclusivity, by the manufacturer. Manufacturer's counsel already hinted [in that letter] that such a renunciation would risk being set aside for violation of public policy. Art. 16 of the French Law indeed provides that any clause or agreement will be considered as not written which, inter alia, derogates, at the disadvantage of the agent, from the agent's right to an indemnification for the damage incurred at the termination of the contract. In fact, the [present] agency contract does not contain a renunciation of the termination indemnity. The reference to a remuneration appears not to be interpreted in this sense. The agent's claim for an indemnification is thus admissible in principle and justified as to the merits.

[24] "It has been said above that, faced with the alternative offered by the European directive, the French legislator chose the indemnification of the concrete damage rather than a lump sum indemnification. By doing so, it harmonized French law with the pre-existing French jurisprudence, which generally quantified the termination indemnity owed to the agent in two years of commissions, although no law or rule imposes a limit on this point, and the rule that the indemnification must indemnify the damage without exceeding it still prevails.[18] The principles which would have governed the termination of a contract concluded for an undetermined period of time, that is, notices, do not apply to the termination of a contract concluded for a determined period of time."[19]

[25] The arbitrator proceeded to determine the damage concretely incurred by the agent in the present case, and concluded: "[T]he agent may legitimately claim an indemnification corresponding to its loss of commissions until the first expiry date of the contract. On the basis of the results in the first year and the first three months of the second year, it appears that the agent would have reached and even surpassed the minimum result required by the manufacturer without much difficulty. Further considering that the indemnification may not be higher than the damage concretely incurred so as to become a gain, and further considering that certain advantages will directly or indirectly result from the early payment, as an indemnification, of sums corresponding to activities which will not have to take place, the arbitrator evaluates the damage to be indemnified [on this basis]."

---

18. "Op. cit., fn. 16, no. 41; *Cour d'appel*, Paris, 20 January 1995 (*Fenez v. Assistance Réalisation Services en Electronique*), Recueil Dalloz (1997) Sonn. p. 52."
19. "Op. cit., fn. 16, no. 33."

ITALY

ITALIAN ARBITRATION ASSOCIATION

Final award in case no. 66/96 of 16 February 1998*

Arbitrator:	Pierre Fortin
Parties:	Claimant: Company X (Italy) Defendant: Consultant A (Ireland)
Place of arbitration:	Milan, Italy
Published in:	Unpublished
Subject matters:	- management consultancy contract - performance related fee - quantification of savings

Facts

Toward the end of 1994, Company X contacted a number of consulting companies, including, inter alia, Consultant A, with a view to improving its efficiency and productivity. By letter of 27 January 1995, Consultant A proposed to carry out, free of charge, a detailed analysis of the business organization following which it would be in a position to present a working proposal which "if agreed upon, would be structured in various phases with the goal of obtaining: (1) a savings in costs of 20-30%; (2) a significant increase in departmental efficiency; (3) a change in the behavior of the entire work force; (4) a reduction in the cost of inventory; (5) an increase in quality at lower cost". Consultant A further stated in thus letter that "the potential savings in cost or increase in profits which our analysis will have indicated is

* *Note General Editor.* Due to a printing error in Volume XXIII (1998) a portion of the text of this award was omitted. Therefore, it has been reproduced once again in this Volume.

to be considered as a minimum objective and, therefore, there will be guaranteed the achievement of a weekly rate in the improvement of results such that, if projected on an annual basis, will be equal to at least 100% of the fee paid for the intervention" (the so-called "savings commitment" clause).

Following such an analysis by Consultant A, the parties signed a contract on 13 April 1995, for the implementation of the program proposed by Consultant A for a duration of 58 "man weeks" at a total cost of ITL 609,000,000 to be paid on a weekly basis. On 1 September 1995, four weeks before the end of the project, Company X expressed doubts about the achievement of the results guaranteed by Consultant A. Although the parties agreed on a new work program, they did not agree as to the quantification of the results obtained by Consultant A or the correct application of the program which Company X considered had damaged the company.

As the parties were unable to resolve these differences, Company X initiated arbitration, relying on the arbitration clause in the contract which provided for formal arbitration in Milan, under the rules of the Associazione Italiana per l'Arbitrato (Italian Arbitration Association) by a sole arbitrator, deciding ex aequo et bono. Company X sought, inter alia, damages in the amount equal to that paid to Consultant A because the intervention by Consultant A had failed to obtain the agreed-upon objectives.

The sole arbitrator held that since Company X paid almost all the agreed-upon fee and had cooperated in the fulfilment of the contract, it was entitled to invoke the "savings commitment" clause in the contract. Consequently, he awarded Company X damages amounting to the difference between the documented savings and the compensation paid to Consultant A.

Excerpt

(....)

[1] "In respect of the second question [if the Arbitration must limit itself to verifying the force of the provisions of the agreement, with respect to which the dispute has arisen, or also the relation between the parties prior to the agreement], it is to be noted that, in the course of the instruction, it became clear that it would be appropriate to take into account the conduct of the parties before the signing of the agreement, given, among other things, that the signing of the agreement was preceded by, and was arrived at after, an analysis by Consultant A's personnel of Company X's business situation.

[2] "For the sake of clarity, the fourth question [if the agreements reached by the parties after 1 September 1995, with the purpose of realizing a new working program merely amend the agreement or substitute the previous

agreement] is dealt with before the third. In light of the pleadings and briefs of the parties ... as well as of the results of the instruction, it is held that the agreements between the parties after 1 September 1995, are to be considered as integrating and not as substituting the initial agreement.

[3] "The third and fifth questions ... [if the obligations undertaken by the parties have been performed and, if so, to what extent; and if objections made respectively by Consultant A and Company X can be received with respect to the limitation of liability and to the clause of 'exception based upon non-performance'] of the Terms of Reference are herein dealt with together and constitute, as became clear during the instruction, the crux of the matter in the present arbitration proceeding.

[4] "It is first necessary to examine the defendant's arguments.... It is useful at this point to recall the contents of the so-called 'savings commitment' provision at Art. 2 of the agreement which defendant asserts there is no basis for invoking:

> 'If Consultant A did not achieve the weekly improvement specified by the savings commitment in some week at or before the completion of the Phase II project period, Consultant A will provide you with one of the following as determined by Consultant A: A. Consultant A will continue to work on the project at no additional charge to you until such date as weekly improvement reaches the rate of ITL 11,700,000, up to a maximum of three months; or B. Consultant A will refund you the difference between the fee paid and the maximum projected annualized improvements recorded during the project.'

Consultant A sustains that certain of the conditions for the 'savings commitment's' becoming operational, in particular those at Art. 6(A) and (B) (full payment of the consideration on a weekly basis) and (C) (providing Consultant A with a full-time coordinator and full-time cooperation and support in implementing the agreement, including the establishment of mutually acceptable measurement indices for reporting improvements) would not have been respected by Company X resulting in the impossibility of invoking the guarantee provision.

[5] "Defendant's arguments cannot be accepted. As far as the provisions of Art. 6(A) and (B) are concerned, it must be noted that, with the agreement providing for a total consideration of ITL 609,000,000, Company X suspended its payments near the end of the second extension of the project committed to Consultant A after having paid ITL 570,000,000 in accordance with the due-dates set in the agreement. The principle codified in Art. 1460 Civil Code (and not, it is obvious, the rule as such) concerning the exceptio inadempleti

contractus appears to respond to the requirements of equity and can therefore usefully be invoked in these proceedings; in addition, it is also clearly equitable to consider that the payment of almost all of the consideration agreed upon gives plaintiff the right to invoke the guarantee of the 'savings commitment'.

[6] "In so far as the provision of Art. 6(C) is concerned, it must be recalled that the cooperation obligation included – as mentioned above – providing a full-time coordinator and fixing mutually acceptable measurement indices for the reporting of improvements. First of all, it clearly emerges from the 'Progress Reports' prepared by Consultant A as well as from the testimony of Dr. B, Consultant A's 'Project Manager' at the time, that Company X immediately put Mr. Z at Consultant A's disposal and that the same was considered by defendant to be, on the whole, an excellent collaborator.

[7] "In respect of the cooperation for the fixing of 'mutually acceptable' measurement indices for the reporting of improvements, it is first necessary to clarify that this duty of cooperation can in no way be interpreted as being an obligation on Company X to elaborate and propose, autonomously, said measurement indices. In fact, given that these criteria were indices for the measurement of the successful implementation, by Consultant A of the project which had been contractually commissioned, it appears logical and equitable to hold that it was up to Consultant A – and to Consultant A alone – to propose the criteria in discussion. In addition, given that the validity of the guarantee invoked by Company X (the so-called 'savings commitment') depends upon the failure to realize and/or to identify the minimum savings provided for in the agreement, it appears equally logical that it was necessary that Company X itself agree to the measurement indices proposed by Consultant A. And this, in order to protect Company X from the arbitrary and unilateral fixing of criteria by Consultant A. It must, however, also be held that Company X itself had the duty to evaluate in good faith and, therefore, not in a capricious or unmotivated manner, the measurement indices proposed by Consultant A. It is therefore in this light that Company X's conduct must be judged in so far as concerns the coming into play of the guarantee in question.

[8] "We cannot on this point not take into consideration the expert report of Dr. Y who was expressly requested – as indicated above – to establish whether 'the parameters used or proposed by the parties ... can be considered reliable and/or reasonable in light of the specific business context of Company X'. The expert's motivated conclusion is that the only measurement index which can be considered reliable and reasonable is that for 'lead time' (which, according to the expert, results in the identification of savings for a total of ITL 198/203,000,000 taking also into account the 'initiatives program'). This measurement index is, in fact, the only one to which Company X agreed and,

hence, it must be clearly excluded that Company X's conduct, in so far as we are here concerned, was one of capricious, systematic and unmotivated refusal of the measurement indices proposed to it; in short, that Company X acted against the principles of good faith which must be respected even in a proceeding in equity.

[9] "It should finally be added on this subject that it is also true that the determination of a measurement index requires the availability of reliable data concerning the specific business context in question. It has not, however, been proven, apart from a few sporadic and, as such, irrelevant episodes, that Company X did not supply Consultant A with the data necessary for the elaboration of the indices in question.

[10] "In light of the above, it must therefore be held that the conditions for the coming into play of the 'savings commitment' were respected by Company X, and that the clause can, at least in theory, be invoked.

[11] "We must now examine the concrete possibility of invoking of the guarantee. In fact, as indicated above, Art. 2 of the 13 April 1995 agreement provided Consultant A with two alternative obligations in the event of a failure to achieve the global savings promised (equal to ITL 609,000,000). Only one of the alternatives consisted in the payment, to Company X, of the 'difference between the fee paid and the maximum amount of the improvements projected on an annual basis registered in the course of the project'.

[12] "Against Company X's claim for payment of the sum in question, Consultant A argued that [it]'s contractual obligation was not one of results but of means. In other words, Consultant A was not obligated to guarantee the achievement, at the end of the contractual period, of improvements for ITL 609,000,000 in that it could have opted for the first alternative, namely, the continuation of its work for a maximum period of three months 'without any added cost for Company X'.

[13] "The argument in respect of the qualification of Consultant A's obligation might merit the court's attention if it were not for the fact that, in the case at hand, the alternative possibilities were not made available. In fact, from the documents of the case and from the testimony, it emerges clearly that Consultant A never proposed the carrying out of either of the two alternatives above, in that it was always convinced that it had achieved the promised objectives. This conviction, as mentioned above, has been contradicted with motivation by Dr. Y's expert report. Nor can [the] letter of 23 October 1995 be considered as representing an offer to continue work on the project in accordance with the provisions of Art. 2(A) of the 13 April 1995 agreement. In fact, this letter did not offer plaintiff the continuation of work, for a maximum period of three months, 'at no added cost for Company X' (as provided for in Art. 2(A)), but rather a continuation of the work at Company

X's expense for an added twelve 'manweeks', as provided for in the Addendum. It should be recalled that this paid continuation was subject to the condition precedent (not fulfilled) of the achievement, in the contractual period, of the agreed-upon improvements.

(....)

[14] "Consequently, since Consultant A did not offer the 'supplementary' work provided for in Art. 2(A), the alternative obligations of this contractual provision are reduced to one, namely, the obligation for Consultant A to pay Company X the 'difference between the fee paid and the maximum improvements projected on an annual basis, registered in the course of the project'. It is therefore unnecessary to decide on the qualification of the 'savings commitment' as an obligation of means or one of results.

[15] "For the quantification of the savings achieved by Consultant A and the correlative damages which Company X can claim, it is necessary to recall that [the] expert report identifies savings only in the sectors of 'lead time' and 'initiatives program' for ITL 198/203,000,000. It is, however, the arbitrator's conviction that it is impossible not to take into account also the parties' evaluation of such savings contained in the 'weekly savings reports'. These documents were prepared every week and indicated the savings realized and/or identified, projected also on an annual basis. Even if they carried the rubric 'prepared by Z', the coordinator appointed by Company X, the reports were prepared jointly by Mr. Z and by Consultant A's project manager, on the basis of data provided mainly by this latter. These reports were subsequently discussed with Company X's managing director, and with other staff of Company X, in a special weekly meeting.

[16] "The last 'weekly savings report' signed by Dr. B bears the date of 1 September 1995 (when the relationship between the parties could still be qualified as 'peaceful'); the annualized savings indicated therein amount to ITL 388,484,000 and relate to the sectors of 'lead time' and 'initiatives program'. This figure is not totally irreconcilable with the results of Dr. Y's report as indicated above. On the contrary, in so far as the 'lead time' sector is concerned, there is full agreement between the expert report and the 1 September 1995 weekly savings report. The discrepancy in the two documents pertains to the 'initiatives program', which, in any case, was marginal in the context of the entire project proposed by Consultant A. In this regard it should be noted that neither party supplied the expert with the data necessary to identify savings in this area of more than ITL 28,000,000. This means, in other words, that one cannot exclude that the amount of savings could have exceeded this amount.

[17] "In these circumstances, the agreement of opinion between the parties, in a period – we repeat – still 'not suspect', and expressed in the 1 September

1995 'weekly savings report', induces the arbitrator to hold that the savings indicated therein are true and reliable. On the other hand, subsequent to that date – and, in any event, almost at the end of the project when the relationship between the parties had become litigious – there was a frenetic preparation of other 'reports', sometimes on a daily basis, in the attempt (which proved fruitless) to arrive at the identification of other measurement indices.

[18] "The arbitrator considers that he must not take into consideration these reports which, among other things, were not signed by Dr. B. For these reasons, the arbitrator holds – as indicated above – that the amount of the savings realized and/or identified are those indicated in the last 'weekly savings report' signed by the parties, and namely ITL 388,484,000; as a result, the damages suffered by Company X amount to ITL 181,516,000, viz., an amount equal to the difference between the fee paid by Company X to Consultant A (ITL 570,000,000) and the savings achieved. The application of the legal rule corresponds, in this case, to equity.

(....)

[19] "In light of all of the above, the costs of the arbitration are for the account of Consultant A. As for the legal expenses, the arbitrator holds equitable – also in light of Consultant A's partial execution of the agreement – that Consultant A be condemned to pay half of the legal expenses sustained by Company X...."

Final award in case no. 75/97 of 20 July 1998

Arbitrator:	Pierre Fortin
Parties:	Claimant: Italian supplier Defendant: Foreign buyer
Place of arbitration:	Rome, Italy
Published in:	Unpublished. Original in Italian
Subject matters:	– standing of creditor after assignment – liquidated damages (*clausola penale*) – penalty – specific conditions prevail over general conditions

Facts

In 1996, the Italian supplier X and the foreign buyer Y entered into a supply contract. The parties first signed the General Purchasing Conditions (GPC) drafted by Y and subsequently concluded a Purchase Order, both of which were drawn up in English. Art. 16 of the GPC was an arbitration clause referring all disputes to a sole arbitrator under the Rules of the Italian Arbitration Association and providing for the application of Italian law.

Art. 5 of the GPC provided that, in the case of late delivery, Y could either accept the delivery, in which case X would pay a penalty, or terminate the contract, both "without prejudice to Y's right to claim damages". Clause D of the Purchase Order provided for liquidated damages in the case of late delivery.

A dispute arose between the parties when X's delivery to Y was delayed. X alleged that the delay was due partly to the fact that Y only supplied X with certain actuators four months after the agreed date and partly to a national strike. It also offered to pay the maximum liquidated damages provided for in Clause D of the Purchase Order. Y refused, maintaining that it had incurred higher damages.

X commenced arbitration according to the arbitration clause in the contract, claiming payment of its delivery to Y. Y filed a counterclaim for damages exceeding the amount of the liquidated damages.

The sole arbitrator granted X's claim for payment of the delivery minus the liquidated damages and dismissed Y's counterclaim for higher damages. He found that Clause D of the Purchase Order prevailed as contractual lex specialis over the general provisions of the GPC, and in particular over Art. 5, which provided for penalties "without prejudice to Y's right to claim damages". He equated the liquidated damages clause to a *clausola penale* in Italian law, which is regulated by Art. 1382 of the Italian Civil Code (CC). According to this article, no damages may be claimed other than the liquidated damages unless the parties have expressly agreed thereon; the arbitrator found that there was no agreement on the possibility to claim further damages.

Excerpt

[1] "[X maintains that] Clause D of the Purchase Order is inspired by a common law rule and must be interpreted in the light of this rule in order to determine the intention of the parties, although the contract is governed by Italian law. Common law distinguishes between 'penalties' and 'liquidated damages'. The parties only agreed on the latter, and Art. 5 of the GPC is superfluous. In any case, X has not accepted the GPC in writing, so that this provision is invalid. (....)

[2] "[Defendant Y maintains that:] (a) X may not be the claimant in these proceedings, because it has assigned its credit to [a bank]....; the fact that Y has not accepted this assignment does not affect its validity between the parties, since the lack of acceptance is only relevant vis-à-vis the assigned debtor; (b) the GPC, Art. 5 included, were expressly accepted in writing by X by letter of 17 November 1995 ('Acceptance of Order') and are thus binding on X; (c) the contract must be interpreted according to Italian law, which is the law governing the relationship, not according to the laws or practices of common law countries; (d) Art. 5 of the GPC must be read, together with Clause D of the Purchase Order, as a '*clausola penale*' in the sense of Art. 1382 CC, which provides for the possibility to claim further damage...."

I. CAPACITY OF CLAIMANT

[3] The arbitrator first dealt with the issue of X's capacity to be a claimant in the proceedings: "The arbitrator holds that X may be the claimant in these proceedings. The contract provided that X could not transfer its credit with respect to Y; hence, we must take into consideration Art. 1260(2) CC, according to which:

> 'The parties can provide that a credit may not be assigned; however, their agreement may not be opposed to the assignee, if it is not proven that the assignee knew of it at the time of the assignment.'

This provision clearly aims in the first place at protecting the debtor's interest – for whatever reason – not to see its creditor change. However, it also sets this interest against the interest of the assignee of the credit, which latter interest prevails only when the assignee did not know (the authors add: without his fault) of the contractual prohibition to assign [the credit]. It is surprising that Y, the assigned debtor, which agreed on the prohibition (and not the assignee, the bank) relies on the assignment, thereby twisting the contents and the rationale of the provision.

[4] "Also, we cannot forget that Y, upon receiving notification from the bank on 15 January 1997 of the assignment, promptly responded to the bank and to the assignor X on 23 January 1997, that it 'cannot agree to the assignment' because of the [contractual] prohibition to assign. This circumstance is worthy of notice. According to the prevailing interpretation, a contractual prohibition to assign [a credit] means that the assignment has no effect unless the assigned debtor agrees thereto. In other words, the agreement of the debtor is a *condicio sine qua non* for the credit to be transferred to the third party. Hence, where this agreement is lacking, the third party has no *locus standi* in court; he even lacks title to the credit which is the subject of the invalid transferral. According to a different, minority interpretation, the lack of acceptance by the debtor does not lead to the invalidity of the assignment, only to its inefficacy toward the assigned debtor. The assignment is valid between the parties but cannot be opposed to the debtor. Hence, it is still the assignor who can act with respect to the credit, on behalf of the assignee. In both hypotheses, it is the assignor who may act with respect to the credit.

[5] "Y unequivocally denies the validity of the assignment from X to the bank; it is irrelevant whether this denial concerns the assignment of the credit or only [X's] capability to act in court. The behaviour of the bank is also unequivocal; it never acted in respect of the credit and even expressly recognized, by a letter dated 27 March 1998, that the assignment was invalid because the bank knew of the prohibition at the time of the assignment, and that therefore the bank lacked the capability to act against Y – although it cannot be denied that such statement appears to have been made on purpose.

[6] "There are two arguments, therefore, against the alleged lack of X's capability to be a claimant: first, the rationale of Art. 1260(2) CC, which limits the effect of the prohibition to assign [a credit] vis-à-vis the third party, as long as the third party was unaware [of the prohibition] without its fault, and which does not allow the assigned debtor to rely on the assignment (in the

light of Y's letter of 23 January 1997, this would be an inadmissible *venire contra factum proprium*) when the third party acknowledges the existence of such prohibition, leaving aside whether [the third party] knew or could have known of it. Second, even if we take into consideration the atypical allegation of the validity of the assignment, Y's letter of 23 January 1997, the subsequent behaviour of the bank and, lastly, the bank's letter of 27 March 1998 allow us to conclude that the bank knew of the prohibition to assign [the credit] at the time of the assignment. Hence, the assignment is at least incapable of transferring to the bank the right to act with respect to the credit at issue; that right is still X's."

II. DELAY IN DELIVERY

[7] "Art. 5 of the GPC provides that

> 'the delivery date indicated in the Purchase Order is definitive and essential. In all cases of delay ascribable to the Supplier in which Y accepts delayed delivery, penalties according to the Purchase Order shall be automatically charged to the Supplier. If delayed delivery is not accepted, Y shall be entitled to cancel the Purchase Order by means of written notice to the Supplier who shall not be entitled to any compensation. In both the above cases, without prejudice to Y's right to claim damages.'

This clause is part of the contract at issue and is thus binding on X. X's Acceptance of Order – even if we consider the document dated 25 June 1996, which differs from the Acceptance of 17 November 1995 – contains in any case the explicit acceptance of Art. 5. It reads: 'We confirm our full acceptance of all conditions and requirements therein contained with the exceptions stated hereinunder'. However, no exceptions can be found in the document, which also reads: 'In particular we accept...'.

[8] "Clause D of the Purchase Order provides that the liquidated damages for late delivery will be

> '0,5% for each week of delay in delivery, up to a maximum of 5% for each lot in delivery, with a grace period of 15 days, starting from the above delivery date. The percentage will be applied on the total amount of each lot.'

This clause provides for the sole case of late performance. Moreover, it starts from the assumption that the delay is not relied upon to terminate the contract; on the contrary, that it is accepted by the buyer. In other words, the acceptance of a late performance qualifies X's behaviour as a performance. Hence, as mentioned above, Clause D exclusively concerns the compensation of damages incurred for late delivery, not the compensation of damages incurred in the case of termination of the contract for breach of contract.

[9] "This said, we must first qualify the clause at issue in the light of [Italian] law. The clauses's aim is evidently to predetermine the damages to be paid in the case of delay, when delivery is nonetheless accepted. Hence, the clause falls under the provision of Art. 1382 CC (on the '*clausola penale*'), which reads in relevant part:

> 'The effect of the clause by which it is agreed that in the case of ... delay in the performance, one party shall provide a given performance, is to limit compensation to the agreed performance, unless the possibility to claim further damages has been agreed upon'.

The legislator adds that *penale* and performance can be requested together only where the former is agreed on for the case of delay, not for the case of lack of performance, as is the case here.[1]

[10] "The interpretation given by X, which alleges that [Clause D] is not a *clausola penale* but a clause aimed at limiting liability (which would mean proving both the *an* and the *quantum* of the damage), must be dismissed. Moreover, this issue loses all relevance because X subtracted on its own initiative the maximum sum provided for in Clause D from the sum it claimed [from Y].

[11] "This said, we must examine the compatibility of Clause D and Art. 5 of the GPC, which has been examined above. It is sufficiently clear, from a mere reading of the provisions at issue, that they contain provisions which, at least in part, formally diverge. While Clause D concerns 'liquidated damages', Art. 5 concerns, inter alia, 'penalties'. More specifically, as mentioned above, Art. 5 provides, in the case of delay in the performance – the same case regulated in Clause D – that 'penalties according to the Purchase Order shall be automatically charged to the Supplier'. We have noted more than once that

1. Art. 1383 of the Italian Code of Civil Procedure reads:

> "A creditor may not request both performance and *penale*, unless the latter was agreed upon only for the case of delay."

the Purchase Order does not contain provisions concerning 'penalties'; it contains a clause concerning 'liquidated damages'.
[12] "This conflict appears to be incurable. Penalties may not be equated to a *penale* in Italian law; leaving aside all other considerations, penalties do not provide for a prior liquidation of damages, which is the object of liquidated damages. Because of their mostly punitive nature (punitive obviously not having here the meaning which some Italian authors give to Art. 1382 CC and the absence of a need to prove the damage), penalties do not affect the compensation of damages, which are to be assessed autonomously. Art. 5 itself confirms this, since, after providing for the automatic application of penalties in the case of delay, it states that this does not affect the possibility to claim damages ('... without prejudice to Y's right to claim damages').
[13] "Differently, a clause for liquidated damages means that, if the parties have agreed that further damage may be compensated, any sum paid as liquidated damages is subtracted from the proven damage. In the light of the above, the generic provision in Art. 5 concerning the right 'to claim damages' perfectly agrees with an agreement on penalties and not with an agreement on the reimbursement of further damage.
[14] "It is true – and the parties have confirmed it at the hearing of 6 March 1998 – that their contract is regulated by and must be interpreted according to Italian law. It is also true, however, that we have here a contract form drawn by Y in English, and we may not disregard the legal terminology used by the drafting party completely.
[15] "However, even if we disregard the texts – though meaningful – and we manipulate their meaning to hold that, since penalty is limited in Italian law (see for instance the interests following an official request to pay a debt), a penalty is a '*penale*' in the sense of Art. 1382 CC, our conclusion does not change. We may not disregard the relationship which exists – by definition and, in casu, according to an express and actually superfluous agreement – between general and particular conditions of contract, as well as the latter's prevalence or, in other words, the latter's complementary nature with respect to the former, and if necessary that it derogates from the former. Even if we disregard the fact that the generic formulation 'to claim damages' is hard to interpret as a provision for the compensation of further damage, the clause in the Purchase Order does not leave any doubt as to the fact that further damage may not be compensated. In this clause, the damage which Y may claim in the case of late performance is liquidated beforehand and there is no hint of the possibility to claim further damages. This suffices to hold that the lex specialis of the contract includes the damage which can be claimed for delay in the sum indicated in [Clause D].

[16] "This conflict is not unusual. What we have here – as is normally the rule – is a contract consisting of general and particular conditions. It is well known that the former, for evident reasons of efficiency, aim at setting uniform rules for an indeterminate number of future contracts which the drafting party may stipulate. The latter are the lex specialis of the concrete relationship. Thus it can happen – and not infrequently it does happen – that the general conditions and the particular conditions contain conflicting provisions, which must be solved in favour of the latter.

[17] "Furthermore, a possible conflict is expressly provided for and solved in the above manner in the premise to the GPC, where it is provided that 'if the present General Purchasing Conditions do not comply with the Purchase Order, the Supplier shall consider valid the conditions stated in the Purchase Order itself'.

[18] "The argument in support of a different interpretation which only deserves a mention – leaving aside its scarcely juridical character – that the a *penale* of ITL 50,000,000 maximum is hard, if not impossible, to understand as [the price of] the delivery amounted to approximately ITL 1 billion. Briefly, whichever the interpretation of Art. 5, it is in any case valid and binding – and it also ensues from the general principles of Art. 1453 et seq. CC – that in the case of a substantial delay affecting the balance of the contract, Y could choose to terminate the contract, thus opening the way for a compensation of the (whole) damage allegedly incurred."

[19] The arbitrator then examined and dismissed Y's counterclaim. "Since the conflict between Clause D of the Purchase Order and Art. 5 of the GPC, as said, is incurable and must be solved in favour of the prevalence of the former provision, it is only to Clause D that we must turn for determining whether Y's counterclaim should be granted. If we keep in mind the contents of Clause D, quoted above, and its qualification as a *penale* ex Art. 1382 CC, the further damage claimed by Y with respect to the amount of the *penale* could be granted only if the parties had agreed that it could be reimbursed. Nothing is provided for on this point in Clause D, nor can we find such an agreement in the generic formulation of Art. 5 GPC, as already discussed in detail above. The counterclaim must be denied."

CHAMBER OF NATIONAL AND INTERNATIONAL ARBITRATION OF MILAN

Final award in case no. 1795 of 1 December 1996

Parties:	Claimant: Company X (US) Defendant: Company Y (Italy)
Place of arbitration:	Milan, Italy
Published in:	Unpublished. Original in Italian
Subject matters:	- termination of contract - UNIDROIT Principles

Facts

In 1983, the Italian company Y and the US company X entered into a joint venture which lasted until 1987, when Mr. Z, general manager of the US company, became the export director of the Italian company by a consultancy and brokerage contract concluded between the Italian company with the US company. The contract was entered into for two years and was tacitly renewable for the same period.

The contract was renewed twice and would have come up for a third renewal in the spring of 1994. In September 1993, however, the Italian company and Mr. Z negotiated an exclusive agency contract which was signed on 1 January 1994. The contract provided that Mr. Z would be based in Perth, Australia, as the Italian company's exclusive agent in the Far East.

The agency contract was concluded for a period of three years and was to be tacitly renewed unless notice of non-renewal was given six months before expiry (Clause 3). Clause 18 of the contract provided:

> "Each party may terminate this agreement before its expiry or renewal if the other party shall find that this agreement has been violated by the other party and the violation has not been cured. In case of termination by one of the parties, all the conditions of this contract shall be terminated as of the date of the notice, with the following exceptions: a) the

> agent shall leave all advertising and sales materials supplied by the principal at the principal's disposal on the agent's premises; b) the principal shall pay to the agent all commission fees for orders received, independent of when the orders have been accepted or confirmed or when delivery takes place or the invoices are issued by the principal."

The contract also contained a clause referring all disputes to the Chamber of National and International Arbitration in Milan.

On 23 January 1995, the Italian company Y, alleging unsatisfactory sales results, terminated the contract as of 1 January 1995 by a fax to Mr. Z personally. On 9 March 1995, the Italian company confirmed the termination by a letter to the US company X.

The sole arbitrator deciding ex aequo et bono and applying the UNIDROIT Principles of International Commercial Contracts, held that the unilateral termination of the agency contract was invalid as it was in violation of the terms of the contract and the UNIDROIT Principles. The arbitrator awarded the commission fees due to the agent at the contractually agreed rate of 15% as well as compensation for loss of profit.

Excerpt

I. DATE OF TERMINATION

[1] "On 23 January 1995, Mr. W, managing director of the Italian principal, sent a fax to Mr. Z, reading as follows:

> 'Dear Z, we have examined the results of your first year of activity as our agent in the Far East and we unfortunately have to conclude that they have not improved in your area in comparison to the time you were here.... We have received no new order from any Far East country, although that is a fast-growing area. Hence, as you have not met even half of your budget, please consider this letter as terminating our agency contract as of 1 January 1995. As to the licenses, on the contrary, we are open to further discussions if the contractual clauses are complied with and payment guarantees are given.'

On 9 March 1995, [Mr. W] wrote the following letter to the US company:

> 'We hereby confirm what we wrote on 24 January 1995 and, in so far as necessary, terminate the contract which we concluded with you on 1

> January 1994 because of your serious non-performance, since you have not met the sales target provided for in ... the said contract'.
> (....)

[2] "Clearly, the first issue is whether the agreement of 1 January 1994 was terminated on 23 January 1995 or on 9 March 1995. The arbitral tribunal finds that the date of 23 January 1995 prevails, considering: (a) that the fax of that date unambiguously expresses the Italian company's intention to terminate the contract of 1 January 1994 as of 1 January 1995; (b) that [Mr. W], who wrote both letters, declared to the arbitral tribunal:

> 'On 9 March I sent a formal termination of contract letter to the US company.... That letter was a mere formality, it was only a repetition of the letter of 23 January which this time I sent to the exact address, therefore I did not give further explanations. As far as I was concerned, the contract was terminated on 23 January';

(c) that during the arbitral proceedings the Italian company has always maintained that the decision was taken on 23 January 1995 and that the contract of 1 January 1994 was terminated as of that date. Hence, the fact that in its last statement the Italian company maintains for the first time that 'the Italian company did not in reality terminate the contract by its letter of 2[3] January 1995 but only suggested a modification of the contract, in the sense that the termination of the contract would have meant the end of all its effects, whereas the letter, leaving aside its wording, suggested a different relation to the US company, the 'continuation of the contract with reference to the licenses', is not consistent with the facts and the statements of the legal representative of the Italian company.

[3] "The date of 23 January 1995 is thus confirmed in law as being the date of termination of the contract of 1 January 1994. According to the interpretation rule in Art. 4.1 of the *UNIDROIT Principles of International Commercial Contracts* (UNIDROIT Principles), which also applies to the interpretation of unilateral acts such as a notice of termination of contract (see [the publication] *UNIDROIT Principles of International Commercial Contracts* [UNIDROIT] (Rome 1995), ad 1 p. 97), a contract must be interpreted: '(1) ... according to the common intention of the parties' and '(2) ... according to the meaning that reasonable persons of the same kind as the parties would give to it in the same circumstances'.

[4] "As this is a unilateral act, the sole 'intention' to be considered is that of Mr. W, the author of the notice of termination. As evidenced by Mr. W's above-mentioned statement, the fax of 23 January 1995 aimed at terminating

the contract of 1 January 1994. As far as the second alternative in Art. 4.1 UNIDROIT Principles is concerned, the fax of 23 January 1995 contained the words 'consider this letter as terminating our agency contract as of 1 January 1995'. It appears to the tribunal that the 'meaning' of these words does not leave any doubt as to the contents and impact of the Italian company's decision."

II. NO VALID TERMINATION

[5] "The termination of 23 January 1995 was prompted by the US company not having met 'even half of [the] budget'. The confirmation of said termination on 9 March 1995 (exclusively) referred to 'your serious non-performance, since you have not met the sales targets provided for in ... the said contract'. The Italian company maintained in the arbitration that the termination of the agency contract was due to 'repeated serious non-performances by the US company', that is, serious failure to meet the sales target provided for in the contract; illegal cashing of US$ 75,000 paid by a customer; modifications of the sales conditions for old customers of the Italian company, which had not been authorized by the Italian company, aimed at increasing [Z's] commissions; failure to communicate with the Italian company for a long time.

[6] "The tribunal shall examine the various grounds invoked by the Italian company to justify the termination of 23 January 1995, although it is established that the Italian company was motivated by the sole failure to meet the contractual sales target."

1. *Failure to Reach the Contractual Sales Target*

[7] ".... As to the facts: According to the Italian company, the 1994 sales in the countries exclusively covered by the US company were ITL 1,746,489,224 (on a target of 2 billion) for product A and ITL 50,207,226 (on a target of 800 million) for product B, the total being ITL 1,769,696,450. This sum is accepted by the US company. The tribunal notes that the failure to meet the contractual target for product A was moderate; not so for product B. A termination of the contract of 1 January 1994 because of a 'fundamental' non-performance could thus only concern product B.

[8] "As to the law: It must be mentioned in the first place that according to Art. 1.3 of the UNIDROIT Principles, the basic principle of contract law, that of '*pacta sunt servanda*' requires that

> 'a contract may be modified or terminated whenever the parties so agree. Modification or termination without agreement are on the contrary the exception and can therefore be admitted only when in conformity with the terms of the contract or when expressly provided for in the Principles'

(UNIDROIT pp. 9-10)."

2. *Was the Termination Allowed under the Contract?*

[9] ".... If no distribution or sales contracts were concluded, 'it will be decided by agreement if there will be a renegotiation as to the area and/or the agent's commissions'. Also, each party could terminate the agreement before its expiry 'if the other party shall find that this agreement has been violated by the other party and the violation has not been cured' (Clause 15 of the contract).

[10] "It clearly appears from the above that the parties to the contract explicitly intended that in case the sales target were not met (up to the point of not having concluded contracts or sales), the parties were to decide by agreement whether to renegotiate the area and/or the commission fees. Hence, the termination of the contract on this ground was excluded by the parties.

[11] "Further, Clause 18 of the contract, which concerns the possibility to terminate the contract before expiry, apparently should be interpreted, notwithstanding its meandering wording, in the sense that non-performance under the contract should be communicated to the non-performing party so that it could, if possible, remedy such non-performance. The Italian company does not contest that no oral or written warning preceded the termination of 23 January 1995. Hence, the termination was in any case not in agreement with the stipulations of the parties in the contract of 1 January 1994.

[12] "The same result is reached by applying the UNIDROIT Principles on termination. According to Art. 7.3.1 of the Principles, 'A party may terminate the contract where the failure of the other party to perform an obligation under the contract amounts to a fundamental non-performance'. In order to ascertain whether the non-performance, respectively the obligation which the non-performance concerns, is fundamental, we must again consider the intention of the parties. It seems impossible to deem fundamental for the termination a situation which was explicitly and expressly provided for by the parties to the contract as being renegotiable, by an agreement of the parties, as to the area or the commission fees.

[13] "The conclusion to be drawn from this analysis of the facts, the contract and the law applicable to the dispute is that the termination of the contract of

1 January 1994 on 23 January 1995 was unfounded. Hence, it is unnecessary to ascertain whether, as maintained by the US company and contested by the Italian company, the failure to meet the sales target was imputable to the Italian company, in particular in [certain cases]. If the failure to meet the contractual target did not as such allow the Italian company to terminate the contract, this is irrelevant for reaching a decision in this arbitration."

[14] The tribunal also rejected the Italian company's further allegations mentioned under [5].

III. EFFECT OF THE TERMINATION

[15] "Art. 7.3.5 of the UNIDROIT Principles provides: 'Termination of the contract releases both parties from their obligation to effect and to receive future performance'. Hence, both parties are freed of their obligations and may no longer rely on their rights under the contract of 1 January 1994. In particular, the US company may not, since 23 January 1995, use the name of the Italian company, either on its own or together with other words. It should be said that the US company has not objected to this legitimate request of the Italian company.

[16] "However, it must be stressed that, according to the explicit intention of the parties to the contract of 1 January 1994 (Clause 18), the termination of the contract entails that

> 'all the conditions of this contract shall be terminated as of the date of the notice, with the following exceptions: a) the agent shall leave all advertising and sales materials supplied by the principal at the principal's disposal on the agent's premises; b) the principal shall pay to the agent all commissions fees for orders received, independent of when the orders have been accepted or confirmed or when delivery takes place or the invoices are issued by the principal.'

[17] "A contractual obligation ex Clause 18 exists here. Indeed, Art. 7.3.5(3) of the UNIDROIT Principles provides that: 'Termination does not affect any provision in the contract for the settlement of disputes or any other term of the contract which is to operate even after termination'."

IV. DAMAGES

[18] "As the termination of the contract of 1 January 1994 was not in agreement with the contract and was not 'excused' under the UNIDROIT Principles (Art. 7.4.1),[1] the agent is entitled to the commission fees under the contract and also to compensation of the damages caused by the termination of 23 January 1995, which damages, according to Art. 7.4.2. of the UNIDROIT Principles, include 'both any loss which it suffered and any gain of which it was deprived, taking into account any gain to the aggrieved party resulting from its avoidance of cost or harm'."

1. *Loss suffered*

[19] ".... [T]he agent maintains that 'the Australian choice' was thought of and agreed upon in order to give effect to the agency contract stipulated with the Italian company, since nothing could have prevented the agent and the US company from requesting the continuation of the preexisting relationship in Italy, as [that relationship] was not terminated timeously by the Italian company. Hence, the US company claims the costs incurred by its managing director Mr. Z for settling down with his family in Australia, being ITL 198,227,000.

[20] "According to the comment to Art. 7.4.3 of the UNIDROIT Principles (UNIDROIT, ad 3 p. 218), harm must be certain and must be a direct consequence of the non-performance. It appears here that the expenses listed by the US company relate to the performance of the contract of 1 January 1994 and have not been caused by the termination thereof on 23 January 1995. This would not apply to the fact that Mr. Z had to sell his house because the [agency] contract was terminated before expiry. However, according to Art. 7.4.4 of the UNIDROIT Principles,

> 'The non-performing party is liable only for harm which it foresaw or could reasonably have foreseen at the time of the conclusion of the contract as being likely to result from its non-performance.'

---

1. Art. 7.4.1 of the UNIDROIT Principles of International Commercial Contracts (UNIDROIT Principles) reads:

   "Any non-performance gives the aggrieved party a right to damages either exclusively or in conjunction with any other remedies except where the non-performance is excused under these Principles."

The purchase of a house by the agent does not fall under the above definition of damage.

[21] "We can add that it is doubtful that the US company, as a party to the contract of 1 January 1994, is the creditor for the expenses incurred by the family of Mr. Z. The arbitral tribunal holds that the US company may not claim a credit of another party, in casu the family of Mr. Z, in the arbitration. For the above reasons, the claim of the US company for a compensation of the expenses incurred by the family of Mr. Z for settling in Australia may not be granted.

[22] "The US company also claims as set-up costs 50% of the expenses for furnishing its office,... being ITL 21,759,105. The US company itself stresses that 'these costs would certainly not have been incurred if the Italian company had not stipulated ... the agency contract at issue'. The Italian company maintains that these expenses concern goods and services relating to the US company's activity. The contract provided that the US company would pay the costs relating to its activity as an agent, and that the Italian company would only pay commission fees. Hence, there is again no causal link between the termination of the contract of 1 January 1994 and the costs claimed by the US company according to Art. 7.4.4 of the UNIDROIT Principles discussed above.

[23] "Further, refunding the costs incurred for setting up the office would be contrary to Art. 7.4.2 of the UNIDROIT Principles, according to which 'the aggrieved party must not be enriched by damages for non-performance' (UNIDROIT ad 3 p. 215).

[24] "It should be noted that according to ... the contract, the agent was entitled to a compensation of 'legal costs', that is, apparently, of the legal costs incurred in the performance of its contractual obligations. However, the US company does not claim 'legal and commercial costs' under this heading and the sole invoice concerning legal costs submitted by the US company concerns Mr. Z's [taking up] domicile [in Australia] and is addressed to him and not to the US company. For the above reasons, the US company's claim for compensation of set-up costs may not be granted."

[25] The arbitral tribunal also rejected the US company's claim for certain costs incurred in the performance of the contract (travel, secretarial assistance, rent of the office, etc.) on the same grounds.

2. *Interest*

[26] The arbitral tribunal calculated the commission fees due to the agent and then discussed the issue of interest thereon. "The US company also claims interest at the contractually agreed rate of 15% on [certain invoices]....

According to Clause 14 of the contract, the commission fees 'shall be due and paid to the agent within 20 days from the date in which the Italian company received payment' and 'the late payment of commission fees due to a fault of the Italian company will entail payment of interest at a rate of 15% on all fees become due'.

[27] "First, this contractual clause is in conformity with the UNIDROIT Principles as to both the moment on which interest starts running (Art. 7.4.9)[2] and the agreed rate (Art. 7.4.13).[3] Second, although the US company clearly requested interest on the commission fees which had become due in its statement of 15 September 1996, the Italian company did not object thereto, although it knew of the invoices at issue, and thus of their dates of expiry, since 15 May 1996. Hence, interest at a rate of 15% shall be paid on the fees to which the above invoices refer, as confirmed by the tribunal in the present award, since their date of expiry and until final payment.

(....)

[28] "The US company also claims interest on late payment of invoices.... The Italian company does not contest the US company's claim. Taking into account the dates of expiry of the [invoices],... the interest due according to Clause 14 of the contract at the rate of 15% is the following: .... The US company claims that this interest should also run until final payment. In the absence of any specific provision in the applicable UNIDROIT Principles (Art.

---

2. Art. 7.4.9 of the UNIDROIT Principles reads:

"(1) If a party does not pay a sum of money when it falls due the aggrieved party is entitled to interest upon that sum from the time when payment is due to the time of payment whether or not the non-payment is excused.

(2) The rate of interest shall be the average short-term bank lending rate to prime borrowers prevailing for the currency of payment, or where no such rate exists at that place, then the same rate in the State of the currency of payment. In the absence of such a rate at either place the rate of interest shall be the appropriate rate fixed by the law of the State of the currency of payment.

(3) The aggrieved party is entitled to additional damages if the non-payment caused it greater harm."

3. Art. 7.4.13 of the UNIDROIT Principles reads:

"(1) Where the contract provides that a party who does not perform is to pay a specified sum to the aggrieved party for such non-performance, the aggrieved party is entitled to that sum irrespective of its actual harm.

(2) However, notwithstanding any agreement to the contrary the specified sum may be reduced to a reasonable amount where it is grossly excessive in relation to the harm resulting from the non-performance and to the other circumstances."

7.4.9), the tribunal applies Italian law as the law applicable to the currency of payment (see UNIDROIT, ad 2 p. 228) and establishes the interest rate at 10% (Art. 1284 Italian Civil Code) from the date of the request in court (Art. 1283 Italian Civil Code) ... until final payment."

(....)

3. Loss of Profit

[29] ".... According to the above-mentioned Art. 7.4.2 of the UNIDROIT Principles, 'The loss of profit or, as it is sometimes called, consequential loss, is the benefit which would normally have accrued to the aggrieved party if the contract had been properly performed' (UNIDROIT, ad 2 p. 214). The contract of 1 January 1994 was concluded for three years and could be renewed tacitly for a further three years unless notice of non-renewal was sent six months before expiry. The letter of 23 January 1995, which could not validly terminate the contract, must be considered a notice of non-renewal according to Clause 3 of the contract.

[30] "According to Art. 7.4.2 of the Principles, the US company is entitled to find itself in the same situation in which it would have found itself if the contract of 1 January 1994 had been normally executed until its first expiry, that is, until 31 December 1996, always taking into account 'any gain to the aggrieved party resulting from its avoidance of cost or harm' (Art. 7.4.2.1 of the Principles)."

[31] The arbitral tribunal quantified the US company's loss of gain and concluded: "The US company suggests that the sum due for loss of gain be reduced by 20-25% in consideration of the costs which the US company would have incurred in the performance of the contract in the years 1995 and 1996. Art. 7.4.2.1 does indeed provide for such a reduction. The arbitral tribunal, deciding ex aequo et bono, establishes this reduction at 20%....

[32] "The US company also claims compensation of non-material damages caused by the allegedly 'extremely harmful' behaviour of the Italian company. The Italian company objects that the US company is not entitled to a compensation of non-material damages caused not the company but to its managing director. The tribunal notes on this point that the US company may not claim damages for harm done to Mr. Z, and that that harm, according to the UNIDROIT Principles and various legal systems, among which the Italian legal system, only concerns physical persons. Hence the terminology of 'loss of certain amenities of life' and 'aesthetic prejudice' (UNIDROIT, ad 5 p. 216) or 'health', 'aesthetic' or 'biological' prejudice (Cian/Trabucchi, *Commentario Breve al Codice Civile* (Milan 1994), ad Art. 2059 pp. 2131 et seq.). The US

company, being a company, cannot claim such damages; the US company's claim for moral damages cannot be granted by the tribunal."

V. COSTS

[33] "Considering that all the objections of the Italian company, as well as its request that the US company's claim be denied, are denied, and considering also the particular circumstances of the case and the long relationship between the US company and the Italian company before the termination of the contract, the tribunal directs the Italian company to pay all the costs of the arbitration as well as the costs incurred by the US company for its defence..., with interest thereon at the rate of 10% since the date of notification of the award until final payment.

[34] "These conclusions, which are reached in law, are not to be modified or mitigated in equity, the application of which the parties wished to moderate possible excesses of the law. The application of the law appears to lead to a satisfying balance of interests, so that the conclusions reached in law do not need to be mitigated in equity, also taking into account the agent's alternative work opportunities."

JAPAN

TOKYO MARITIME ARBITRATION COMMISSION OF THE JAPAN SHIPPING EXCHANGE

Final award of 18 March 1997

Arbitrators:	Shigeto Yunoki; Tsutomu Kishida; Jozo Yajima
Parties:	Claimants: (1) First Buyer (Panama); (2) Second Buyer (Panama) Respondent: Shipbuilder (Rep. of China)
Published in:	38 The Bulletin of the Japan Shipping Exchange (March 1999) pp. 14-21
Subject matter:	– valid settlement agreement precludes arbitration

Facts

First claimant and respondent entered into a shipbuilding contract on 1 October 1993 (Contract I) for the construction of a general cargo vessel (Vessel I). The original contractual delivery date of 30 October 1994 was revised to 30 October 1995. According to first claimant, on 30 October 1995, respondent demanded an increase in the contract price of Vessel I, asserting that if first claimant did not accept this increase, it would not deliver the vessel. First claimant rejected this demand and the vessel was delivered 1 November 1995.

First claimant and respondent entered into a second shipbuilding contract also dated 1 October 1993 (Contract II). Although the delivery date provided in Contract II was 30 January 1995, Vessel II was delivered on 10 May 1996.

Second claimant, a sister company of first claimant, and respondent entered into a third shipbuilding contract dated 29 January 1994 (Contract III) for Vessel III. Respondent, however, gave second claimant notice of cancellation of Contract III on 5 October 1994 and did not start construction work.

All of the contracts provided for arbitration by The Japan Shipping Exchange, Inc.

Disputes arose regarding the contracts and first and second claimants initiated arbitration. Respondent replied by filing a Preliminary Protocol of Delivery, dated 10 May 1996 and signed by both parties on delivery of Vessel II. Respondent contended that the parties had mutually agreed by this Protocol to terminate the arbitration proceedings.

The three arbitration proceedings were consolidated into one, since first and second claimants (jointly "claimant") were deemed subsidiaries of the same company and these companies all had the same President.

The arbitral tribunal rejected claimant's contention that it had signed the Protocol under duress and dismissed the application for arbitration.

Excerpt

[1] "Claimant applied for arbitration in accordance with the arbitration clause of each contract and respondent [submitted] its counterclaims. Then on 20 June 1996, respondent filed the Preliminary Protocol of Delivery signed by both parties on delivery of Vessel II, dated 10 May 1996, and contended that both parties had mutually agreed to terminate the arbitration proceedings as was stipulated therein. Claimant argued, to the contrary, that the Protocol had been signed by duress from the respondent and that it was therefore void under Art. 74 of the Civil Code of the Republic of China.

[2] "We now consider the validity of the Protocol. As for the governing law, Art. XX.1 of Contract II provided:

> 'The parties hereto agree that the validity and interpretation of this Contract and of each Article and part thereof shall be interpreted under the laws of the country where the vessel is built.'

[3] "The Civil Code of the Republic of China (hereinafter Code) provides in Art. 74:

> 'A juristic act that takes advantage of the difficulties, indiscretion or inexperience of another in exchange for pecuniary gain or the promise of pecuniary gain, which is patently unfair under the applicable circumstances, may be cancelled (or the gain resulting therefrom may be reduced) by the court upon application of the injured party.'

[4] "Claimant referred to a published judgment interpreting Art. 74 of the Code.[1] This case dealt with the situation where a contractor who was completing a construction project incurred numerous debts during the project that were to be paid off with the construction price to be paid by the owner. The owner learned of the contractor's plight and took advantage of the contractor's urgent need for the construction money by delaying payment until the contractor was forced to accept a much lower price than originally agreed upon. The court found that the owner's ploy was patently unfair at the time and justified the invalidation of the new price.

[5] "It is clear beyond doubt, in our judgment, that the Protocol was properly signed by the presidents of both parties without any defect. We now consider whether claimant was forced to sign the Protocol under duress by the respondent in view of Art. 74 of the Code and the said Supreme Court judgment. There is no such evidence nor witness as to persuade us that claimant was forced under duress by the respondent to sign the Protocol on delivery of Vessel II.

[6] "On 25 April 1996, respondent faxed a draft of the protocol which included item 8

> 'The Owner and Builder mutually agree that Owner will terminate the conciliation proceeding of Arbitration [sic] and all costs of the Arbitration including lawyer's fees and potential cost shall be for the account of first claimant.'

It was then returned by facsimile to respondent on 6 May 1996, with some handwritten words, i.e., 'We would like to amend item 8 as follows. [Please] give me your comments.' and '8 ... cost shall be paid by both parties at own expense' instead of the words '8 ... cost shall be for the account of first claimant...'.

[7] "We hold that the Protocol was made after negotiation between the parties as stated above and that if they did not agree to terminate the instant arbitration, claimant should have insisted on continuing the arbitration proceedings in that fax. As there is no evidence showing that claimant could not protest against the respondent's proposal in that fax, the expressions without any reference to the continuation of arbitration proceedings should be understood that claimant acceded to terminate them without reserve. Even assuming that there was a situation where claimant hastened to take delivery of Vessel II, it would be difficult to say that claimant could not carry on negotiations with respondent and had no choice but to sign the Protocol.

1. ROC Supreme Court judgment, 50th Year (1961), Tai Shang Tze No. 707.

[8] "In conclusion, we cannot help saying that claimant decided to terminate the arbitration proceedings after deliberate consideration, and following their business judgment. As we could not find any reasonable ground for the claimant's argument on the invalidity of the Protocol, this application for arbitration must be dismissed in accordance with the Protocol.
[9] "The matter of the costs of arbitration shall be decided by the Arbitrators in accordance with Sect. 33 of the TOMAC Rules,[2] notwithstanding any agreement thereon between the parties. We deem it appropriate that the costs of arbitration shall be Yen 4,758,600 which shall be equally shared between claimant and respondent."
(....)

2. Art. 33, presently Art. 39, of the Tokyo Maritime Arbitration Commission Rules, reads:

> "The costs of arbitration shall be paid from the Arbitration Fee paid to the Secretariat under the preceding Section and the ratio in which they shall be borne shall be decided by the Tribunal."

NORTH AMERICAN FREE TRADE AGREEMENT

UNCITRAL

Decision of 28 November 1997 and Award of 24 June 1998

Arbitrators:	Karl-Heinz Böckstiegel (Germany) (Chairman); Charles N. Brower (US); Marc Lalonde (Canada)
Parties:	Claimant: Ethyl Corporation (USA) Respondent: The Government of Canada
Place of arbitration:	Toronto, Canada
Published in:	Unpublished
Subject matters:	- place of arbitration determined according to the circumstances (Art. 16(1) UNCITRAL Rules) - investor - scope of treaty - requirement to attempt settlement - timely application

Facts

Ethyl Corporation (Ethyl), a US corporation is the sole shareholder of Ethyl Canada, Inc. Ethyl manufactures and distributes, inter alia, methylcyclopentadienyl manganese tricarbonyl (MMT), a fuel additive used at the refinery level to provide octane enhancement for unleaded gasoline.

Ethyl alleged that the Canadian Manganese-based Fuel Additives Act, 1997, S.C. 1997 c. 11 (MMT Act) which came into force on 24 June 1997 deprived it of business as of that date.

Sect. 4 of the Act provides:

> "No person shall engage in interprovincial trade in or import for commercial purpose a controlled substance except under an authorization referred to in section 5."

The only "controlled substances" listed in the schedule to the Act was MMT. Sect. 5 of the MMT Act expressly precluded any authorization for additions to unleaded gasoline. Ethyl alleged that prior to the Act, its MMT was blended into more than 95 percent by volume of unleaded gasoline sold in Canada.

On 14 April 1997, Ethyl gave Notice of Arbitration under Art. 1120(1)(c) of the North American Free Trade Agreement Treaty, choosing among the alternatives provided for the arbitration of investment disputes in Art. 1120[1] to arbitrate under the UNCITRAL Arbitration Rules as modified by Sect. B of Chapter 11 NAFTA.

Canada asserted that Ethyl's claim was outside the scope of Chapter 11, and that in any event, Ethyl had failed to fulfill certain requirements of Sect. B of Chapter 11 so that the Tribunal was without jurisdiction over Ethyl's claim.

The parties disagreed on the place of arbitration, Ethyl urging that it should be New York City and Canada requesting that the place should be Ottawa, or alternatively, Toronto. On 28 November 1997, the arbitral tribunal issued a reasoned decision regarding the place of arbitration which was determined to be Toronto, Canada (see below [1]-[24]).

On 24 June 1998, the arbitral tribunal issued an Award on Jurisdiction in which it rejected a number of Canada's objections to jurisdiction and joined the remainder to the merits. The parties settled the case in July 1998.

Excerpt

Decision Regarding the Place of Arbitration, 28 November 1997

[1] "Our decision on this point, Ethyl suggests ... has 'importance ... not only for this arbitration but is a persuasive precedent for future NAFTA investor-state arbitrations held under the auspices of the UNCITRAL Arbitration Rules.' Doubtless this view arises from the fact, as the Tribunal is informed, that the present arbitration is the first NAFTA dispute between Canada and an alien investor.

1. NAFTA Art. 1120 provides three alternatives for the arbitration of investment disputes: ICSID arbitration pursuant to the 1965 Washington Convention; the ICSID Additional Facility Rules or the UNCITRAL Arbitration Rules.

[2] "Our decision is governed by NAFTA Art. 1130(b), which provides that absent 'the disputing parties agree[ing] otherwise, a Tribunal shall hold an arbitration in the territory of a Party [to NAFTA] that is a party to the New York Convention, selected in accordance with ... the UNCITRAL Arbitration Rules if the arbitration is under those Rules.' All three NAFTA Parties, i.e., Canada, Mexico and the United States, are parties to the New York Convention. Therefore our selection is to be made from among sites in those three countries.

[3] "The UNCITRAL Rules themselves provide only, in Art. 16(1), that 'the place where the arbitration is to be held ... shall be determined by the arbitral tribunal, *having regard to the circumstances of the arbitration*.' (Emphasis added)

[4] "The Tribunal also has been referred by both parties to UNCITRAL's Notes on Organizing Arbitral Proceedings. These Notes, which are not binding,[2] state (in para. 22):

> 'Various factual and legal factors influence the choice of the place of arbitration, and their relative importance varies from case to case. Among the more prominent factors are: (a) suitability of the law on arbitral procedure of the place of arbitration; (b) whether there is a multilateral or bilateral treaty on enforcement of arbitral awards between the State where the arbitration takes place and the State or States where the award may have to be enforced; (c) convenience of the parties and the arbitrators, including the travel distances; (d) availability and cost of support services needed; and (e) location of the subject-matter in dispute and proximity of evidence.'[3] [4]

[5] "Canada makes two threshold arguments that must be addressed at the outset. It urges, ... first, that Art. 16(1) of the UNCITRAL Rules 'permits the

---

2. "See Introduction to the Notes, para. 2:

   'No legal requirement binding on the arbitrators or the parties is imposed by the Notes. The arbitral tribunal remains free to use the Notes as it sees fit and is not required to give reasons for disregarding them.'"

3. "Consideration (b) would appear not to be relevant here, given that all potential places of arbitration are in States Parties to the New York Convention."

4. "Canada correctly points out that a sixth consideration, namely, 'perception of a place as being neutral', was eliminated from an earlier draft of the Notes as being 'unclear, potentially confusing' although something that a tribunal 'might wish to discuss ... with the parties'. Report of the United Nations Commission on International Trade Law on the work at its twenty-eighth session (Vienna, 2-26 May 1995), U.N. Doc. A/50/17, para. 337, reprinted in Vol. XXVI UNCITRAL Yearbook (1995)."

Tribunal to take into account certain general, universally applied considerations which usually are found in the doctrine of forum conveniens', which 'provides that the forum in which to try a matter should be the jurisdiction that has the closest connection with the action and the parties'. Canada then proceeds ... to list factors 'which most directly connect [this arbitration] to Ottawa'. Leaving aside the issue as to whether that municipal law doctrine has a place in international arbitration, the Tribunal is constrained to say that in its view its decision regarding the place of arbitration in this case must be made, as Art. 16(1) prescribes, 'having regard to the circumstances of the arbitration', meaning all such circumstances, including those elements offered for consideration in para. 22 of the Notes, and without any individual circumstance being accorded paramount weight irrespective of its comparative merits. In the end, Canada appears to agree, having stated ... that it cited the doctrine 'only to demonstrate that the criteria which provide guidance in determining the appropriate forum appear to be practically the same criteria which are cited in the UNCITRAL Notes....'

[6] 'Canada then argues, second, that since under NAFTA Chap. 20 (Rule 22 of the Model Rules of Procedure for NAFTA) the place of arbitration of a State-to-State NAFTA arbitration is the capital of the respondent State, '[a] fortiori, where a private commercial party brings a complaint under Chapter 11, it should follow that the circumstances of the case lend themselves to the government of a sovereign country responding in its own capital.' The Tribunal does not share this view. The fact that the respondent State's capital has been expressly designated by rule adopted pursuant to Chap. 20 would suggest, to the contrary, that the omission to do so in connection with Chap. 11 was, if anything, deliberate. In any event, NAFTA's Chap. 11 clearly contemplates the possibility of disputes under it against any NAFTA Party being arbitrated in Washington, DC, since Art. 1120 allows a disputing investor to choose arbitration (if and when it becomes available)[5] under the ICSID Convention, Art. 62 of which provides that in the absence of agreement of the arbitrating parties 'arbitration proceedings shall be held at the seat of the Centre' i.e., Washington, DC.[6]

5. "To date neither Canada nor Mexico is a party to the ICSID Convention. Thus although the United States is a party to that Convention no present prospect of such an arbitration exists. Under Arts. 20 and 21 of the ICSID Additional Facility Arbitration Rules, to which Art. 1120 also allows resort, 'the place of arbitration shall be determined by the Arbitral Tribunal after consultation with the parties and the Secretariat' and must be in a State Party to the New York Convention."

6. "ICSID Convention Art. 2 fixes the seat of the Centre at 'the principal office' of the World Bank, i.e., Washington, DC. While it is true, as Canada has noted ..., that Washington, DC is not thereby the 'place of arbitration', that concept itself is not relevant to the self-contained

[7] "Having disposed of these threshold issues, the Tribunal now turns its attention to the four factors relevant under the UNCITRAL Notes, considering each of them in relation to the respective proposed places of arbitration: Ottawa (or, alternatively, Toronto) and New York City.[7]

[8] "As to criterion (a) of the Notes – 'suitability of the law on arbitral procedure' – the Tribunal concludes that all proposed fora are equally suitable. It appears undisputed that Canada's Commercial Arbitration Act is based on the UNCITRAL Model Law on International Commercial Arbitration and by its terms would apply to this arbitration under NAFTA Chap. 11. It appears to be equally undisputed that the relevant laws of the United States, and, to the extent relevant, the State of New York, are no less suitable. The fact that the laws applicable to this arbitration, were it situated in New York City, have been in place longer than Canada's Commercial Arbitration Act, and therefore are judicially more elaborated, does not, in the view of the Tribunal, significantly affect their comparative suitability.

[9] "Criterion (c) of the Notes[8] – 'the convenience of the parties and the arbitrators, including the travel distances' – likewise seems not to be significantly better served by one proposed alternative as opposed to any other. As to the Tribunal, the President, who normally is resident in Cologne, Germany, can travel with more or less equal ease to New York City, Ottawa and Toronto. Mr. Lalonde, a resident of Montreal, can travel to Ottawa or Toronto just as well as Judge Brower can from his Washington, DC residence to New York City. By the same token, Judge Brower would be no more and no less inconvenienced by travel to Ottawa or Toronto than would Mr. Lalonde be by the need to appear in New York City. (footnote omitted)

[10] "The situation of the parties is substantially similar. Canada has noted ... that:

ICSID system."

7. "The Tribunal, as previously noted, has the power, under NAFTA Art. 1130(b), to select as the place of arbitration any situs in Canada, Mexico or the United States. The Tribunal notes that Ethyl ... has 'submitted that if this Tribunal finds that it is inappropriate to have the place of arbitration in either Canada or the United States, the claimant suggests that the place of arbitration be in Mexico'. The Tribunal limits itself in this case, however, to the sites recommended by the parties. In doing so it emphasizes that it is in no way precluded by the parties' respective proposals from considering other locations. It proceeds as it does because it believes the parties objectively have searched out those places that are most likely in fact to be most appropriate, 'having regard to the circumstances of the arbitration'."

8. "The Tribunal already has determined that criterion (b) – 'whether there is a multilateral or bilateral treaty on enforcement of arbitral awards between the State where the arbitration takes place and the State or States where the award may have to be enforced' – is not 'relevant here'. See note 3, *supra*."

> 'The investment which Ethyl Corporation alleges has been damaged is the wholly owned subsidiary, Ethyl Canada, which has its head office in Mississauga, adjoining the City of Toronto, in the Province of Ontario. Its blending facility, where it processes MMT, is in Corunna, in the Province of Ontario.'

[11] "In response to this Ethyl simply contends that it has 'its head office in [the Commonwealth of] Virginia' and that the 'location of subsidiary offices is not a relevant factor for this arbitration'. For purposes of criterion (c) alone this may well be correct. If it is, there is no significant difference in the convenience factor between Canada having to travel to New York City and Ethyl having to be present in Ottawa or Toronto. If it is not, then a degree of preference would be indicated for a Canadian venue.

[12] "Canada has introduced as a consideration the location of counsel to the parties, emphasizing that Ethyl's counsel has an office in Toronto as well as in New York City. Ethyl disputes the relevance of counsel's convenience, while nonetheless pointing out that 'The Government of Canada also maintains a large consulate in New York City as well as a Permanent Mission to the United Nations which can support the needs of the Government of Canada's legal team....' Canada terms this latter assertion 'incorrect', as '[t]hese are diplomatic offices and are not set up to act as alternative legal offices, such as [claimant's counsel] apparently has available to him'.[9]

[13] "The Tribunal is inclined to the view that the convenience of counsel is a relevant consideration, subsumed under the 'convenience of the parties'. Certainly the convenience of attorneys appointed by the parties, which translates into cost factors, affects their clients. The Tribunal also believes that the availability for temporary use by government lawyers of facilities at a consular post or diplomatic mission is not comparable to a dedicated office of counsel. Accordingly, the Tribunal concludes that it is relevant to consider that fixing the place of arbitration in either Ottawa or Toronto will serve the convenience of counsel collectively better than New York City.

[14] "We now turn to criterion (d), 'availability and cost of support services needed'. It is clear that all necessary support services for this arbitration are available in all three of the cities that have been proposed. The Tribunal believes it appropriate to take judicial notice of the fact that such services inevitably will be more costly in New York City than in either Ottawa or Toronto. This includes transportation, hotels, meal service, hearing rooms and counsel rooms, and certified stenographic reporting services. Therefore

9. "As regards Ethyl's counsel this point would appear to apply equally to New York City and Toronto."

application of criterion (d) favors Ottawa or Toronto over New York City, but does not discriminate between them.

[15] "The Tribunal does not, however, take into consideration in this regard, as Canada has proposed, the presence and availability in Ottawa of NAFTA Secretariat facilities. As Canada itself records ..., 'The NAFTA Secretariat operates in all three NAFTA countries, *each of which funds the local office*'. (Emphasis added.) While the Tribunal accepts fully, as Canada itself has stressed, that 'those offices operate independently of their host country and are viewed by the NAFTA Parties as neutral centers', the Tribunal nonetheless is concerned that to avail itself of such facilities could be viewed as inconsistent with at least the spirit of the requirement of the UNCITRAL Rules (Arts. 9-10)[10] that it act so as to leave no doubt whatsoever as to its complete independence of any party. This is all the more so where, as here, Ethyl has registered its objection ... that the use of such facilities 'would be inappropriate'.

[16] "The last criterion of the Notes – '(e) location of the subject-matter in dispute and proximity of evidence' – finally turns the Tribunal definitely to selection of a place of arbitration in Canada. Clearly the subject-matter in dispute is fixed in Canada. Ethyl charges ... that certain legislative and other acts of Canada 'remov[ing] MMT [methylcyclopentadienyl manganese tricarbonyl] from Canadian gasoline' have resulted in breaches by Canada of Arts. 1102, 1106 and 1110 of NAFTA, thereby 'harm[ing] Ethyl Corporation and the value of its Canadian investment, Ethyl Canada'. The 'location of the subject-matter in dispute' is not subject to serious debate.

[17] "The parties have little to say as regards 'the proximity of evidence'. Perhaps the nature of the case and the early stage in which it now is make it difficult to be explicit on this subject. For its part, Canada has said ... only that 'virtually the whole of the cause of action in this case relates to Canadian laws, the Canadian law-making process, the actions of the Canadian Parliament and certain ministers', and that it 'should be evident ... that the witnesses to this process of law-making and policy-making are for the most part located in Ottawa'.[11]

---

10. Arts. 9 and 10 of the UNCITRAL Rules stipulate, respectively, the requirement of disclosure for a prospective arbitrator and the grounds for challenge.

11. "Canada argues ... also that certain 'related proceedings' are 'additional factors that point to Canada as the appropriate place of arbitration...' Those proceedings are (1) a suit by Ethyl's Canadian subsidiary seeking 'a declaration ... that [the relevant legislation] is of no legal force and effect' as well as injunctive relief, and (2) a formal complaint by the Province of Alberta against Canada which will be subject to dispute resolution proceedings. The Tribunal does not believe that the pendency of those proceedings has any bearing on its determination of the place of arbitration."

[18] "In response Ethyl effectively asserts ... that no such witnesses will be required, as it 'intends to provide proof of statements made by Canadian officials through the introduction of authoritative writings, such as Hansard', which the Tribunal understands to be the official record of debates in the Canadian Parliament.

[19] "In reply, Canada argues ... that 'it is potentially the whole process of law making and parliamentary procedure and practice which is to be examined through the evidence of witnesses'. In affirmative support of New York City as the place of arbitration Ethyl states only that, '[a]s an example, all important documents on the issue of damages are located in Richmond, Virginia', where its headquarters are situated. Thus the Tribunal is afforded little insight into just how any considerations of the proximity of evidence should affect its decision.

[20] "Traditionally arbitrating parties, desiring both the reality and the appearance of a neutral forum, incline to agree on a place of arbitration outside their respective national jurisdictions. This is especially the case where a sovereign party is involved. Where an arbitral institution or a tribunal must make the selection, this tendency is, if anything, even greater, and for the same reasons. Art. 16(1) of the UNCITRAL Rules easily accommodates this consideration as one of the 'circumstances of the arbitration'.

[21] "Here, however, NAFTA Art. 1130(b) circumscribes our powers, limiting possible places of arbitration to either of the two States here involved or Mexico. A Mexican venue surely would represent neutrality in this case, and in all such cases. The Tribunal concludes, however, that had the NAFTA Parties felt that every arbitration under Chapter 11 of NAFTA must be sited in the NAFTA Party not involved in the dispute they would have said so and would not have remitted us to Art. 16(1) of the UNCITRAL Rules. The Tribunal has readily concluded that a Mexican venue would not serve other important 'circumstances' of this arbitration.[12]

[22] "The Tribunal concludes on the basis of all of the foregoing that, on balance, the place of arbitration should be in Canada. Although as to a number of the 'circumstances of the arbitration', notably the respective suitability of the law on arbitral procedure and the convenience of the arbitrators, all three cities in contention are equally appropriate, other circumstances weigh in favor of Canada and none point toward New York City. Most significantly, Canada

12. "The fact that the UNCITRAL Notes omitted (see note 4, supra) 'perception of a place as being neutral' from its list of criteria for selection of a place of arbitration because it was 'unclear, potentially confusing' does not mean that such criterion cannot be considered. UNCITRAL, in taking this step, itself indicated 'that the arbitral tribunal, before deciding on the place of arbitration, might wish to discuss that with the parties'."

indisputably is the location of the subject-matter in dispute. In addition, a Canadian venue offers less costly support services and overall would better suit the convenience of counsel for the parties. It is far less certain, but likely, that Canada overall is more convenient for the parties themselves and as regards the proximity of evidence. In the end, therefore, the Tribunal finds a Canadian venue more appropriate as the place of arbitration in this case than New York City.

[23] "Once the Tribunal has determined to select a Canadian venue, none of the specific factors considered weighs strongly in favor of Toronto, Canada's alternative proposal, rather than Ottawa. The Tribunal has some reluctance, however, to choose Ottawa. This is due to the fact that it is the capital of Canada.

[24] "The Tribunal therefore has determined to designate Toronto as the place of arbitration, for the reason that while it is no more, and no less, appropriate than Ottawa when measured by the other applicable criteria, it is likely to be perceived as a more 'neutral' forum."

Award on Jurisdiction, 24 June 1998

(....)

I. GENERAL CONSIDERATION FOR THE INTERPRETATION OF THE RELEVANT NAFTA PROVISIONS

1. *Applicable Law*

[25] "The Tribunal finds it useful to set out here the rules it is required to apply in interpreting and applying NAFTA. Art. 1131 of NAFTA is the first guide:

> "Art. 1131: Governing Law
> 1. A Tribunal established under this Section shall decide the issues in dispute in accordance with this Agreement and applicable rules of international law.
> 2. An interpretation by the Commission of a provision of this Agreement shall be binding on a Tribunal established under this Section."

No Party has argued, and the Tribunal is not otherwise informed, that the NAFTA Commission has provided any interpretation here relevant. The Tribunal therefore looks to NAFTA itself and 'applicable rules of international law'.

[26] "The applicable rules of international law include the Vienna Convention on the Law of Treaties (Vienna Convention), done at Vienna, 23 May 1969, entered into force 27 January 1980 ... in particular Arts. 31 and 32....[13]
[27] "Canada is a party to the Vienna Convention, having acceded to it on 14 October 1970, and the United States accepts it as a correct statement of customary international law.[14] Moreover, given that 84 States are parties to the Vienna Convention (as of 15 April 1998), and that Arts. 31 and 32 'were adopted without a dissenting vote', these Articles clearly 'may be considered as declaratory of existing law.'[15]

---

13. Arts. 31 and 32 of the Vienna Convention read:

"*Article 31. General rule of interpretation*
1. A treaty shall be interpreted in good faith in accordance with the ordinary meaning to be given to the terms of the treaty in their context and in the light of its object and purpose.
2. The context for the purpose of the interpretation of a treaty shall comprise, in addition to the text, including its preamble and annexes:
(a) any agreement relating to the treaty which was made between all the parties in connexion with the conclusion of the treaty;
(b) any instrument which was made by one or more parties in connexion with the conclusion of the treaty and accepted by the other parties as an instrument related to the treaty.
3. There shall be taken into account, together with the context:
(a) any subsequent agreement between the parties regarding the interpretation of the treaty or the application of its provisions;
(b) any subsequent practice in the application of the treaty which establishes the agreement of the parties regarding its interpretation;
(c) any relevant rules of international law applicable in the relations between the parties.
4. A special meaning shall be given to a term if it is established that the parties so intended."

Article 32. Supplementary means of interpretation
"Recourse may be had to supplementary means of interpretation, including the preparatory work of the treaty and the circumstances of its conclusion, in order to confirm the meaning resulting from the application of article 31, or to determine the meaning when the interpretation according to article 31:
(a) leaves the meaning ambiguous or obscure; or
(b) leads to a result which is manifestly absurd or unreasonable."

14. "See *The Islamic Republic of Iran v. The United States of America*. Dec. No. 32-A18-FT (6 April 1984), reprinted in 5 Iran-U.S. Cl. Trib. Rep. 251, 259 (1984). U.S. courts look to the Convention when interpreting the text of a treaty. See, e.g., *Kreimerman v. Casa Veerkamp, A.S. de C.V.*, 22 F.3d 634, 638 (5th Cir. 1994), cert. den'd, 115 S.Ct. 577 S.Ct. 577 (1994); *Day v. Trans World Airlines, Inc.* 528 F.2d 31, 33 (2d Cir. 1975), cert. den'd, 429 U.S. 890 (1976)."

15. "De Aréchaga, *International Law in the Past Third of a Century*, 159 Recueil des Cours 1, 42 (1978) ('Legal rules concerning the interpretation of treaties constitute one of the Sections of the Vienna Convention which were adopted without a dissenting vote at the Conference and consequently may be considered as declaratory of existing law')."

[28] "On the procedural level, Art. 1120(2) of NAFTA provides that:

> 'The applicable arbitration rules [here the UNCITRAL Arbitration Rules] shall govern the arbitration except to the extent modified by this Section [B].'"

2. *Determination of Jurisdiction as a Preliminary Question*

[29] "Art. 21(4) of the UNCITRAL Arbitration Rules, which is not modified by any provision of Section B, provides:

> 'In general, the arbitral tribunal should rule on a plea concerning its jurisdiction as a preliminary question. However, the arbitral tribunal may proceed with the arbitration and rule on such a plea in their final award.'

The present jurisdictional phase takes place in adherence to Art. 21(4)."

3. *Particular Considerations Relevant to the Determination of Jurisdiction*

[30] "The Tribunal considers it appropriate first to dispense with any notion that Sect. B of Chap. 11 is to be construed 'strictly'. (footnote omitted) The erstwhile notion that 'in case of doubt a limitation of sovereignty must be construed restrictively'[16] has long since been displaced by Arts. 31 and 32 of the Vienna Convention.[17] As was so aptly stated by the Tribunal in *Amco Asia Corporation v. Indonesia (Jurisdiction)*, ICSID Case No. ARB/81/1 (Award of 25 September 1983), reprinted in 23 I.L.M. 351, 359 (1983) and 1 ICSID Rep. 389 (1993):

> '[L]ike any other conventions, a convention to arbitrate is not to be construed *restrictively*, nor, as a matter of fact, *broadly* or *liberally*. It is to be construed in a way which leads to find out and to respect the common will of the parties; such a method of interpretation is but the application of the fundamental principle *pacta sunt servanda*, a principle

---

16. "*Free Zones of Upper Savoy and the District of Gex* (Fr. v. Switz.), 1932 P.C.I.J., ser. A/B, No. 46 at 167 (Judgment of 7 June)."
17. "'The Vienna Convention resolved past debates concerning the wisdom of pronouncements by international tribunals that limitations of sovereignty must be strictly construed.'

    United States-Iran, Case A17, Decision No. DEC 37-A17-FT (13 May 1985) (Brower, J., concurring), reprinted in 8 Iran-U.S. Cl. Trib. Rep. 189, 207 (1989)."

common, indeed, to all systems of internal law and to international law.' (Emphasis in original)

[31] "Given the relevance under Art. 31(1) of the Vienna Convention of NAFTA's 'object and purpose', it is necessary to take note of NAFTA Art. 102, particularly its (1)(c) and (e)....[18]

[32] "The Tribunal reads Art. 102(2) as specifying that the 'object and purpose' of NAFTA within the meaning of those terms in Art. 31(1) of the Vienna Convention are to be found by the Tribunal in Art. 102(1), and confirming the applicability of Arts. 31 and 32 of the Vienna Convention."

II. THE DISTINCTION BETWEEN JURISDICTIONAL PROVISIONS AND PROCEDURAL RULES

[33] "It is important to distinguish between jurisdictional provisions, i.e., the limits set to the authority of this Tribunal to act at all on the merits of the dispute, and procedural rules that must be satisfied by claimant, but the failure to satisfy which results not in an absence of jurisdiction ab initio, but rather in a possible delay of proceedings followed ultimately, should such non-compliance persist, by dismissal of the claim. Canada argues that all of its objections fall into the first category, whereas Ethyl is of the view that such objections as may have been valid at one point fall into the second category and have since been obviated.

[34] "The sole basis of jurisdiction under NAFTA Chapter 11 in an arbitration under the UNCITRAL Arbitration Rules is the consent of the Parties. Unlike ICSID and its Additional Facility Rules, there exist under the

18. Art. 102 NAFTA reads in relevant part:

"1. The objectives of this Agreement, as elaborated more specifically through its principles and rules, including national treatment, most-favored-nation treatment and transparency, are to:

...

(c) increase substantially investment opportunities in the territories of the Parties;

...

(e) create effective procedures for the implementation and application of this Agreement, for its joint administration and for the resolution of disputes;

(....)

2. The Parties shall interpret and apply the provisions of this Agreement in the light of its objectives set out in paragraph 1 and in accordance with applicable rules of international law."

UNCITRAL Rules no other jurisdictional criteria.[19] It is clear that Ethyl has consented to this arbitration by the very act of commencing it. Normally such act is taken as consent to the arbitration thereby initiated.[20]

[35] "The fundamental jurisdictional issue here, therefore, is whether Canada has consented to this arbitration. It has two aspects, as the jurisdictional proceedings have underscored. One aspect is that of scope: Is Ethyl's claim within the types of claims that Canada has consented in Chapter 11 to arbitrate? The other aspect is that of conditions to consent: To what extent, if any, is Canada's consent to arbitration in Chapter 11 conditioned absolutely on the fulfillment of specified procedural requirements at a given time?"

III. DOES ETHYL CLAIM A BREACH UNDER CHAPTER 11?

1. *Claim for Breach of Section A*

[36] "On the face of the Notice of Arbitration and the Statement of Claim, Ethyl states claims for alleged breaches by Canada of its obligations under Art. 1102 (National Treatment), Art. 1106 (Performance Requirements) and Art. 1110 (Expropriation and Compensation). The claimant indisputably is an 'investor of a Party', namely the United States, and alleges that it has 'incurred loss or damage by reason of, or arising out of' such breaches, all as required by Art. 1116(1). It likewise is beyond doubt that claimant has acted within three years of the time when it 'first acquired, or should have first acquired, knowledge of the alleged breach and knowledge that [it] incurred loss or damage' as stipulated in Art. 1116(2). Claimant's Statement of Claim satisfies prima facie the requirements of Art. 1116 to established the jurisdiction of this Tribunal. As was stated in Administrative Decision No. II (1922), Decisions and Opinions, Mixed Claims Commission, United States and Germany (1925) 6-7, quoted in K.S. Carlston, *The Process of International Arbitration* 77 (1946): 'when the allegations in a petition ... bring a claim within the terms of the Treaty, the jurisdiction of the Commission attaches'. See also *Ambatielos Case*

19. "For a discussion of ICSID's objective criteria see *Vacuum Salt Products Limited v. The Government of the Republic of Ghana*, ICSID Case No. ARB/92/1 (Award of 16 February 1994), reprinted in 9 ICSID Rev.-F.I.L.J. 72 (1994)."

20. "See., e.g., Christoph Schreuer, Commentary on the ICSID Convention, 11 ICSID Rev.-F.I.L.J. 318, para. 277 (1996) (In the context of ICSID, jurisdiction may be established by virtue of an offer to arbitrate by a host State contained in its legislation or in a treaty, which may be accepted by an investor. The time of mutual consent is determined by the investor's acceptance of the offer. This offer may be accepted through bringing a request for arbitration to the Centre.)"

(Greece v. United Kingdom), merits: obligation to arbitrate, 1953 I.C.J. Rep. 10, 11-12 (Judgment of 19 May) ('[T]he words "claims ... based on the provisions of the Treaty of 1886" ... can only mean claims depending for support on the provisions of the Treaty of 1886.... The fact that a claim purporting to be based on the Treaty may eventually be found by the Commission of Arbitration to be unsupportable under the Treaty, does not of itself remove the claim from the category of claims which, for the purpose of arbitration, should be regarded as falling within the terms of the Declaration of 1926.'); and *United States of America ex rel. Albert Flegenheimer v. The Italian Republic*, Case No. 20, Decision No. 182, 5 Decisions Italian-United States Conciliation Commission 18-19 (20 Sept. 1958)."

2. *Relation to Investment or Trade in Goods*

[37] "Canada asserts that since the MMT Act excludes MMT from importation into Canada, and prohibits inter-provincial trade in MMT, it should be viewed as affecting trade in goods and therefore falling within NAFTA Chapter 3, which covers 'National Treatment and Market Access for Goods' within a broader Part 2 on 'Trade In Goods' (which embraces Chapters 3-8). The argument made is that issues of trade in goods under Chapter 3 give rise to government-to-government dispute settlement procedures under Sect. B of Chapter 20, and, it is contended, thereby necessarily exclude the possibility of investor-State arbitration under Chapter 11.

[38] "Canada cites no authority, and does not elaborate any argument, however, as to why the two necessarily are incompatible. Canada confines itself in this regard to a reference to Art. 1112, which simply requires that 'In the event of any inconsistency between this Chapter [11] and another Chapter [e.g., 3], the other Chapter shall prevail to the extent of the inconsistency.'

[39] "As Ethyl has pointed out, Canada indicated at the Hearing on jurisdiction that this was not 'an issue that was absolutely critical to be disposed of at [that] hearing'. In the circumstances, further treatment of this issue, if any, must abide another day. The Tribunal cannot presently exclude Ethyl's claim on this basis."

3. *Requirement of a "Measure"*

[40] "The bulk of the written and oral proceedings have been devoted to what constitutes a 'measure' within the meaning of Art. 1101, which stipulates that Chapter 11 (including, therefore, Arts. 1102, 1106 and 1110, all of which Ethyl claims Canada has breached) 'applies to measures adopted or maintained

by a Party'. ('Measure' appears also several times in Art. 1106,[21] and Art. 1110 addresses specifically 'a measure tantamount to nationalization or expropriation'.) Succinctly, Canada has argued that no legislative action short of a statute that has passed both the House of Commons and the Senate and has received Royal Assent constitutes a 'measure' subject to arbitration under Chapter 11. Since at the time Ethyl's claim was 'submitted to arbitration', i.e., 14 April 1997, by delivery of its Notice of Arbitration (see Art. 1137(1)(c)),[22] the MMT Act had not yet received Royal Assent (which was forthcoming eleven days later), Canada argues that jurisdiction fails.

[41] "In addressing what constitutes a measure the Tribunal notes that Canada's *Statement on Implementation of the North American Free Trade Agreement*, Can. Gaz. Part IC(1), January 1994 (hereinafter *Canadian Statement on Implementation of NAFTA*) (at 80) states that:

> 'The term "measure" is a non-exhaustive definition of the ways in which governments impose discipline in their respective jurisdictions.'

This is borne out by Art. 201(1), which provides that:

---

21. "Specifically, Art. 1106(2) and (6):

> '2. A measure that requires an investment to use a technology to meet generally applicable health, safety or environmental requirements shall not be construed to be inconsistent with paragraph 1(f). For greater certainty, Arts. 1102 and 1103 apply to the measure.
> ...
> 6. Provided that such measures are not applied in an arbitrary or unjustifiable manner, or do not constitute a disguised restriction on international trade or investment, nothing in paragraph 1(b) or (c) or 3(a) or (b) shall be construed to prevent any Party from adopting or maintaining measures, including environmental measures:
> (a) necessary to secure compliance with laws and regulations that are not inconsistent with the provisions of this Agreement;
> (b) necessary to protect human, animal or plant life or health; or
> (c) necessary for the conservation of living or non-living exhaustible natural resources."

22. Article 1137(1)(c) reads:

> "Time when a Claim is submitted to Arbitration
> 1. A claim is submitted to arbitration under this Section when:
> ...
> (c) the notice of arbitration given under the UNCITRAL Arbitration Rules is received by the disputing Party."

> 'measure includes any law, regulation, procedure, requirement or practice.'

Clearly something other than a 'law', even something in the nature of a 'practice', which may not even amount to a legal stricture, may qualify.

[42] "Nonetheless, Canada argues, not without effect, that an unenacted legislative proposal, which is unlikely to have resulted even in a 'practice', cannot constitute a measure. It is reinforced in this connection by the fact that Art. 1803(1) and (2) employ the term 'proposed or actual measure':

> '1. To the maximum extent possible, each Party shall notify any other Party with an interest in the matter of any proposed or actual measure that the Party considers might materially affect the operation of this Agreement or otherwise substantially affect that other Party's interests under this Agreement.
> 2. On request of another Party, a Party shall promptly provide information and respond to questions pertaining to any actual or proposed measure, whether or not that other Party has been previously notified of that measure."

Canada draws further strength from the reference to 'an actual or proposed measure' in Art. 2004, which provides 'Recourse to Dispute Settlement Procedures' by the three NAFTA Parties themselves. The implication is that whereas any of these may complain of a 'proposed measure', an investor cannot.

[43] "In the end, however, the MMT Act did come into force 24 June 1997, after having received Royal Assent on 25 April 1997, just eleven days following claimant's delivery of its Notice of Arbitration. The MMT Act is, Canada concedes, a measure within the meaning of Art. 1101(1). (footnote omitted) Canada's objection, then, is that Ethyl 'jumped the gun', and, having done so, should be required to commence an entirely new arbitration, which, it is conceded, it can (subject to any scope limitations).

[44] "The Tribunal notes that the MMT Act, according to the allegations of claimant's Notice of Intent, Notice of Arbitration, and Statement of Claim, was the realization of a legislative program of the Canadian Government, sustained over a period of time. As of the date on which claimant delivered its Notice of Intent pursuant to Art. 1119, on 10 September 1996, Bill C-94, the original proposal that resulted in the MMT Act and that had died after it had had a second reading (and been reported back by committee without amendment) due to the prorogation of Parliament, had been reinstated as Bill C-29 and deemed to have been read the second time, reported out of

committee without amendment and subject to third reading. In other words, the new Parliament was persuaded by the Government to pick up where the previous one had left off. Within the 90-day minimum period Ethyl was then required by Art. 1119 to wait before commencing arbitration, C-29 had passed the House of Commons and been introduced in the Senate, which, the Tribunal understands from Canada's legislative expert witnesses, generally concurs in House action. (footnote omitted) As already noted, by the time claimant's Notice of Arbitration was delivered on 14 April 1997, Bill C-29 had in fact passed the Senate, five days earlier on 9 April 1997, and only awaited Royal Assent, which, the Tribunal is given to understand, is granted as a matter of course once the Government has requested it.[23]

[45] "In any event, the MMT Act is, as of 24 June 1997, a reality, and therefore the Tribunal is now presented with a claim based on a 'measure' which has been 'adopted or maintained' within the meaning of Art. 1101."

4. *Limitation of Claims to the Territory of Canada*

[46] "Canada asserts that 'Ethyl's claim in respect of expropriation of its intellectual property, reputation, and goodwill throughout the world is not within the scope of NAFTA,' since Art. 1110(1)(b) applies Chapter 11 only to 'investments of investors of another [NAFTA] Party *in the territory of* the Party',[24] and Art. 1110, one of the three provisions alleged to have been breached by Canada, likewise addresses nationalizations or expropriations by a NAFTA Party of 'an investment of an investor of another Party *in its territory*'. (Emphasis added)

[47] "A distinction must be made, however, between the locus of the claimant's breach and that of the damages suffered. It is beyond doubt that the MMT Act was adopted, and purports to have, and in fact has, legal force only in Canada. It bans MMT from importation into Canada and prevents its movement between provinces. Ethyl's claim is premised on the legal force the MMT Act has in relation to its investment in Canada, i.e., Ethyl Canada.

[48] "Ethyl has argued, however, that the damages resulting to it in consequence of the MMT Act include losses suffered outside of Canada. As Ethyl itself succinctly notes..., 'the Investor [Ethyl] claims that an expropriation

23. "Canada concedes that a Bill becomes a 'measure' upon the giving of Royal Assent, even though the Act may not come into force in accordance with its terms for some time, e.g., 60 days as in the case of the MMT Act."

24. "Art. 1101(c) applies Art. 1106 specifically to 'all investments *in the territory* of the Party'. (Emphasis added)"

occurred inside Canada, but the Investor's resulting losses were suffered both inside and outside Canada'.

[49] "Determination of the extent to which the damages claimed by Ethyl are in fact compensable under Chapter 11 is an issue that can be considered by the Tribunal only in the context of the merits....

[50] "The Tribunal therefore decides that it cannot at this time exclude any portion of the claim due to considerations of territoriality. (footnote omitted)"

IV. PROCEDURAL REQUIREMENTS

[51] "It remains to determine whether our jurisdiction fails due to lack of fulfillment by Ethyl of any of the several procedural requirements to which Canada points.

[52] "There is no doubt that Chapter 11 embodies certain requirements that an arbitrating investor must meet before a Tribunal can proceed to consider its claim. The question rather is whether the NAFTA Parties intended that any of these conditions must be fulfilled prior to or simultaneously with delivery of a Notice of Arbitration in order for a Tribunal's jurisdiction to attach.

[53] "Canada argues that such is the case. Ethyl, noting that by now all of the requirements cited by Canada have been fulfilled, urges the contrary. In effect, it takes the view that their fulfillment was a prerequisite to its claim being admissible, and thus impliedly accepts that a prolonged absence of compliance with them would have justified dismissal of the claim. It contends, however, that our jurisdiction ab initio cannot be denied. Ethyl adds the quite practical points that Canada has in no way been prejudiced, that Canada concedes Ethyl could now commence a new arbitration addressed to the MMT Act with all conditions fulfilled, and hence that the sole result of a dismissal for lack of jurisdiction on these grounds would be the inefficiency, and, as Ethyl sees it, the injustice, of having to 'start all over again'."

1. *The Requirement of Consultation or Negotiation*

[54] "While Canada does not raise the point directly, it could be understood as implying that Ethyl failed to heed Art. 1118, styled 'Settlement of a Claim through Consultation and Negotiation':

> 'The disputing parties should first attempt to settle a claim through consultation or negotiation.'

[55] "It is difficult to credit the possibility, however, that Canada would through consultation or negotiation desist from a course which, according to claimant's allegations, was determined on and persisted in by the Canadian Government through two Parliaments as a matter of important national policy. Certainly, Canada has given no indication that it would have relented and the Tribunal discerns none.

[56] "In any event, claimant's undisputed proof in this phase of the arbitration is that it in fact approached Canada as urged by Art. 1118 and was rebuffed. Through a witness affidavit of Mr. Jeffrey Paul Smith, Vice President, Public Affairs, and Deputy General Manager, Marketing, of the Ottawa office of Hill and Knowlton Canada, sworn to 28 January 1998, Ethyl details attempts at high levels to achieve a mutually satisfactory solution, beginning with the introduction of Bill C-94. In particular, Mr. Smith confirms that a meeting held with Canadian Government officials on 12 November 1996, two months following delivery of Ethyl's Notice of Intent, '[n]one ... claimed to have authority to consult or negotiate'. He specifically identified 'Mr. [John] Gero, the senior representative from the International Trade Branch', with whom counsel of Ethyl had exchanged three letters dated 5 and 8 (two) November 1996 in his capacity as Director General, Trade Policy Bureau II, Department of Foreign Affairs and International Trade. It is noteworthy that on 12 November 1996, apparently just moments prior to that meeting, counsel for Ethyl received a telefaxed message from Mr. Steve Brereton, Investment Trade Policy Division, stating that 'apparently it needs to be clarified that, in our view, today's meeting is not a consultation'."[25]

2. *Notice of Intent to Arbitrate and The Six-Month Rule of Article 1120*

[57] "Claimant's Notice of Intent to Submit a Claim to Arbitration pursuant to Art. 1119 was delivered 10 September 1996. More than seven months elapsed from then until 14 April 1997, when claimant delivered its Notice of Arbitration and thereby submitted its claim to arbitrate pursuant to Art. 1137(1)(c). Thus the former was delivered 'at least 90 days before' the latter as required by Art. 1119.

[58] "Canada's only objection as regards Art. 1119 is that it appears to question the effectiveness of the Notice of Intent when, in its view, neither at the date of its delivery, nor at the time of the subsequent delivery of the Notice of Arbitration, could Canada have 'breached an obligation' under

25. "It is possible that the Canadian officials feared that admitting a 'consultation' might compromise the position that Bill C-94, then pending third reading in the House of Commons, was not a 'measure'."

Section A of Chapter 11, which is the basis of its consent to arbitration in Art. 1116, because no 'measure' was in effect as required by Art. 1101.

[59] "Similarly, Canada argues forcefully that claimant failed to comply with the requirement of Art. 1120 that it is only 'provided that six months have elapsed since the events giving rise to a claim [that] a disputing investor may submit the claim to arbitration.'

[60] "A claim is 'submitted to arbitration' under the UNCITRAL Arbitration Rules, according to Art. 1137(1)(c), when 'the Notice of Arbitration ... is received by the disputing Party'. Claimant's Notice of Arbitration was received 14 April 1997. Therefore, according to Canada, as of six months earlier, namely 14 October 1996, 'events giving rise to a claim' must have existed. Canada maintains that since as of 14 October 1996 Bill C-29 was still awaiting third reading in the House of Commons, hence had not even been introduced in the Senate, and Royal Assent lay more than six months in the future, no 'measure' existed to be breached and hence no 'events giving rise to a claim' existed.

[61] "Initially, there is an issue as to whether the phrase 'events giving rise to a claim' is intended to include all events (or elements) required to constitute a claim, or instead some, at least, of the events leading to crystallization of a claim. The argument is made that the object and purpose of NAFTA, set forth in its Art. 102(1)(c) and (e), to 'increase substantially investment opportunities' and at the same time to 'create effective procedures ... for the resolution of disputes' would not be best served by a rule absolutely mandating a six-month respite following the final effectiveness of a measure until the investor may proceed to arbitration. Had the NAFTA Parties desired such rigidity, it is contended, they explicitly could have required passage of six months 'since the adoption or maintenance of a measure giving rise to a claim'. It nonetheless remains debatable, we are told, whether as of 14 October 1996 the status of Bill C-29 was sufficient to constitute 'events giving rise to a claim'.

[62] "There also is an issue as to whether a six-month 'cooling off period' should be applicable at all in this case, given the events discussed above. The Tribunal has been given no reason to believe that any 'consultation or negotiation' pursuant to Art. 1118, which Canada confirms the six-month provision in Art. 1120 was designed to encourage, (footnote omitted) was even possible. It is argued, therefore, that no purpose would be served by any further suspension of claimant's right to proceed. This rule is analogized to the international law requirement of exhaustion of remedies, which is disregarded

when it is demonstrated that in fact no remedy was available and any attempt at exhaustion would have been futile.[26]

[63] "The Tribunal finds no need to address these arguments as to Arts. 1119 and 1120 since the fact is that in any event six months and more have passed following Royal Assent to Bill C-29 and the coming into force of the MMT Act. It is not doubted that today claimant could resubmit the very claim advanced here (subject to any scope limitations). No disposition is evident on the part of Canada to repeal the MMT Act or amend it. Indeed, it could hardly be expected. Clearly a dismissal of the claim at this juncture would disserve, rather than serve, the object and purpose of NAFTA.

[64] "In the specific circumstances of this case the Tribunal decides that neither Art. 1119 nor Art. 1120 should be interpreted to deprive this Tribunal of jurisdiction.[27]

[65] "The Tribunal notes, however, that claimant could have avoided controversy over these issues by first awaiting Royal Assent to Bill C-29 on 25 April 1997 before delivering its Notice of Intent to Submit to Arbitration, and then allowing another six months to pass, i.e., until 25 October 1997, before commencing arbitration. It thus would have lost just over six months' delay in proceeding, and thus would be six months further away from a resolution of the dispute.

[66] "The claimant may have 'jumped the gun' for tactical reasons relating to the legislative process. The Tribunal notes that the House of Commons debate on Bill C-29 on third reading commenced 25 September 1996, and claimant may have decided to file its Notice of Intent on 10 September 1996 for the purpose of affecting that debate. This is inferentially confirmed by the witness affidavit of Mr. Smith of Hill and Knowlton, which states (Paragraph 17) that:

> 'On 5 February 1997 [after Bill C-29 had passed the House of Commons], representatives from Ethyl Corporation appeared before the

26. "*Finnish Ships Arbitration* (Finland v. U.K.), (Award of 9 May 1934) (Bagge, sole arb.), reprinted in 3 R.I.A.A. 1479 (1934) (Finland's failure to appeal to the Court of Appeal did not mean that it had not exhausted local remedies. Such an appeal would have been 'obviously futile' because the Court of Appeal could not have reversed the Boards' finding of fact); *Panevezys-Saldutiskis Railway Case* (Estonia v. Lithuania), P.C.I.J. Rep. Ser. A/B, No. 76, p. 18 (1939) ('There can be no need to resort to the municipal court if ... the result must be a repetition of a decision already given.')."

27. "Specifically, the Tribunal concludes that this results from interpreting those Articles in good faith in accordance with the ordinary meaning to be given to the terms thereof in their context and in the light of the object and purpose of NAFTA, as prescribed by Art. 31 of the Vienna Convention, and that, considering particularly the circumstances of NAFTA's conclusion, any different interpretation would lead to a result which manifestly absurd or unreasonable within the meaning of Art. 32 of the Vienna Convention."

> Senate Standing Committee on Energy, the Environment and Natural Resources [and] proposed as a means to resolve the dispute that Ethyl Corporation would not proceed with its pending NAFTA claim if the Government of Canada would not pass Bill C-29.'

Certainly the Notice of Arbitration was delivered right on the heels of Senate passage of Bill C-29, i.e., five days later.

[67] "Had Ethyl first awaited Royal Assent to Bill C-29, and then bided its time another six months, the Tribunal would not have been required to deal with this issue. The Tribunal deems it appropriate to decide, therefore, that claimant shall bear the costs of the proceedings on jurisdiction insofar as these issues are involved."

3. Consent and Waivers under Article 1121

[68] "Canada argues that jurisdiction here is absent because the written consent of Ethyl to arbitration, and the written waivers by Ethyl and also Ethyl Canada of any rights to certain other dispute settlement procedures, which were required by Art. 1121 (according to its title) as 'Conditions Precedent to Submission of a Claim to Arbitration', were provided only with the Statement of Claim, delivered 2 October 1997, and not with the Notice of Arbitration, delivered 14 April 1997, which, according to Art. 1137(1)(c), is when the 'claim [was] submitted to arbitration' under Section B. The sufficiency of the consent and waivers thus provided is not otherwise questioned.

[69] "The Tribunal has not gained any insight into the reasons for the formalities prescribed by Art. 1121, which on their face seem designed to memorialize *expressis verbis* what normally is the case in any event, namely, that the initiation of arbitration constitutes consent to arbitration by the initiator, whereby access to any court or other dispute settlement mechanism is precluded (except as allowed ancillary to or in support of the arbitration). The Tribunal likewise is uninformed as to any reasons for Ethyl's not having provided the required documentation with the Notice of Arbitration, and equally is unaware of any resulting prejudice to Canada.

[70] "The Tribunal has little trouble deciding that claimant's unexplained delay in complying with Art. 1121 is not of significance for jurisdiction in this case. While Art. 1121's title characterizes its requirements as 'Conditions Precedent', it does not say to what they are precedent. Canada's contention that they are a precondition to jurisdiction, as opposed to a prerequisite to admissibility, is not borne out by the text of Art. 1121, which must govern. Art. 1121(3), instead of saying 'shall be included in the submission of a claim

to arbitration' – in itself a broadly encompassing concept – could have said 'shall be included with the Notice of Arbitration' if the drastically preclusive effect for which Canada argues truly were intended. The Tribunal therefore concludes that jurisdiction here is not absent due to claimant's having provided the consent and waivers necessary under Art. 1121 with its Statement of Claim rather than with its Notice of Arbitration.

[71] "Here, too, however, the Tribunal deems it appropriate that claimant be responsible for the costs of the jurisdictional proceedings insofar as they have related to the issues arising in connection with Art. 1121. No reason appears why the consent and waivers were not furnished with the Notice of Arbitration, which would have been the better practice. Had they been, a certain part of these proceedings would have been obviated."

4. *Has a 'New Claim' Been Asserted?*

[72] "The Tribunal finally deals with Canada's contention that reliance in the Statement of Claim on the MMT Act, which was enacted some six months following delivery of the Notice of Arbitration, which Notice was directed at Bill C-29 (which became the MMT Act), and specific reference in the Statement of Claim for the first time to the product Greenburn,[28] constitute the assertion of 'new claims' which the Tribunal is prohibited from considering.

[73] "The revised and expanded terminology in the Statement of Claim is not intrinsically of such great significance. This is particularly so, bearing in mind that Art. 3 of the UNCITRAL Arbitration Rules, which in this regard remains unmodified by anything in Part B, and which prescribes the form of a notice of arbitration, requires (in (3)(e)) simply that such notice include 'The general nature of the claim and an indication of the amount involved, if any'. By contrast, Art. 18 of those Rules, likewise unmodified by Part B, requires (at (1)(b) and (c)) that a statement of claim set forth a 'statement of the facts supporting the claim' and the 'points in issue'. Thus a greater elaboration of detail in the Statement of Claim is permissible, if not, indeed, required.

28. The Tribunal referred to note 2 reading:

> "Ethyl also produces a second product, known as 'Greenburn', a fuel additive which contains MMT but is designed for use in products other than unleaded gasoline, such as home heating, commercial boiler, and various diesel fuels. Ethyl asserts in its Statement of Claim that it was dissuaded from implementing earlier plans to market this product in Canada starting in 1996 by the introduction of the draft legislation that became the MMT Act."

[74] "The nub of the matter, however, is that the specific inclusion of references to the MMT Act and the product Greenburn in the Statement of Claim is not, as the Tribunal sees it, to be viewed as adding 'new claims', but rather, if anything, as amending the claim previously described in the Notice of Arbitration. Art. 20 of the UNCITRAL Arbitration Rules, which Part B does not modify, provides that claimant 'may' so amend 'unless the arbitral tribunal considers it inappropriate to allow such amendment having regard to the delay in making it or prejudice to the other party or any other circumstances'. An amendment of Ethyl's claim, if one there has been, made as early as in the Statement of Claim hardly can be regarded as involving any 'delay'.[29] No prejudice or any other circumstances are cited by Canada which would tend to rebut Art. 20's presumption of amendability[30] and the Tribunal apprehends none. Therefore, to the extent, if any, that the Statement of Claim amends the claim of Ethyl, the Tribunal accepts such amendment."

V. AWARD

[75] "For the reasons set forth above the Tribunal awards as follows:

29. "Normally it is a statement of claim that is itself amended at a later stage. The issue of a possible amendment made by a statement of claim to a notice of arbitration arises in the NAFTA context, however, because of the procedural strictures discussed above."

30. "As pointed out by Baker & Davis, *The UNCITRAL Arbitration Rules in Practice: The Experience of the Iran-United States Claims Tribunal* (Kluwer 1992) pp. 91-92:

'Article 20 of the UNCITRAL Rules gives parties the right to amend or supplement their claims or defenses during the course of the arbitration. A tribunal may deny an amendment, but only if it is "inappropriate" because of "delay in making" the amendment, prejudice to the other party or "any other circumstances". The amendment must be rejected if it would cause the claim to fall outside the tribunal's jurisdiction under the arbitration clause or agreement.

As originally proposed, Article 20 would have required a claimant to secure the permission of the arbitrators before he could supplement or amend his claim. The drafting committee chose to omit the clause "with the permission of the arbitrators" in order to "mak[e] it clear that, in principle, the parties were entitled to amend". Indeed, despite the seemingly broad authority to disapprove amendments in "any other circumstances", the *travaux* clearly show that the tribunal's authority is not meant to discourage legitimate amendments to claims and defenses, but rather to prevent frivolous or vexatious amendments.'

(Footnotes omitted.) See also Pellonpää & Caron, *The UNCITRAL Arbitration Rules as Interpreted and Applied* (Finnish Lawyers' Publishing 1994) pp. 388-410."

1. The Tribunal rejects Canada's objections to jurisdiction based on Arts. 1101 (except for 1101(b) addressed in 2 below), 1116, 1119, 1120 and 1121 of NAFTA.
2. The Tribunal joins to the merits Canada's objections to jurisdiction based on Arts. 1110(1) and 1101(b) (as referred to in Paragraphs [46]-[49], supra), and on Arts. 1112(1) and Chapter 3 of NAFTA (as referred to in Paragraphs [37]-[39], supra).
3. The costs of the Government of Canada and of the Tribunal attributable to the jurisdictional proceedings insofar as they have related to issues raised under NAFTA Arts. 1119, 1120 and 1121 shall be borne by the claimant, and will be set forth in the Final Award."

RUSSIAN FEDERATION

INTERNATIONAL COMMERCIAL ARBITRATION COURT AT THE CHAMBER OF COMMERCE AND INDUSTRY OF THE RUSSIAN FEDERATION

Final award in case no. 31/1998 of 20 October 1998

Arbitrators:	S.N. Lebedev (Chairman); V.V. Dozortsev; K.L. Razumov
Parties:	Claimant: Seller (Russian Fed.) Defendant: Trading company (UK)
Place of arbitration:	Moscow, Russian Federation
Published in:	Unpublished. Original in Russian
Subject matters:	– succession of arbitral institution – applicable law to period of limitation

Facts

Claimant contracted to supply a quantity of metal to defendant. The goods were only paid for in part, the last payment being on 24 November 1994.

The standard conditions of the contract provided for arbitration at the Arbitration Court for Foreign Trade at the Chamber of Commerce and Industry of the Russian Federation, Moscow. A dispute arose regarding the payment for the goods and claimant initiated arbitration at the International Commercial Arbitration Court (ICAC) on 3 February 1998 by a claim dated 14 January 1998. The trading company requested a postponement of the hearings because it required extra time to prepare its case. However, its preliminary view showed that the period of limitation had expired, and also a Frame Agreement between the parties provided for arbitration at a second arbitral institution. Defendant subsequently requested another postponement because the second arbitral institution had accepted the case.

Claimant relied on the New York Convention on the Limitation Period in International Sale of Goods of 14 June 1974, which provides a limitation period of four years, arguing that the period should be calculated from 25 November 1994 until the date of the claim, 14 January 1998.

The arbitral tribunal first held that it had jurisdiction because the Court of Arbitration at the CCI RF was renamed as the International Commercial Arbitration Court. Moreover, the contract for the supply of goods was independent from the Frame Agreement and was not affected by the reference in the Frame Agreement to the second arbitral institution. Finally, as the Russian Federation had not succeeded to the 1974 New York Convention on Limitation, Russian law which provides a limitation period of three years applied. Therefore, claimant was out of time in its application.

Excerpt

I. JURISDICTION

[1] "In relation to its jurisdiction to settle the dispute, the International Court of Arbitration at the Chamber of Commerce and Industry of the Russian Federation (CCI RF) concludes that its jurisdiction is based on Art. 1 of the standard conditions of the Contract which states that any disputes that may arise in connection with the contract should be settled by the Court of Arbitration for Foreign Trade at the CCI RF, Moscow, according to the rules of this court. By the Decree of the Supreme Soviet of the Russian Federation dated 7 July 1993, 'On making effective the law of the Russian Federation "On International Commercial Arbitration"', the Court of Arbitration at the CCI RF was renamed to the International Commercial Arbitration Court at the CCI RF.

[2] "The claimant's reference to provision for arbitration at another arbitral institution, mentioned in a so-called Frame Agreement signed between claimant and a number of foreign legal entities providing for their long-term co-operation in no way affects the validity of the provision referring to arbitration in Moscow contained in the independent contract for supply of goods between claimant and defendant. The Frame Agreement was signed on 23 April 1993 and the contract between claimant and defendant was signed on 11 May 1993. This means that the parties had every opportunity to choose the same provision as in the Frame Agreement, but since they preferred the provision for arbitration in Moscow, it is fully binding on them. Considering

the above, the International Commercial Arbitration Court finds that it has jurisdiction to settle this dispute."

II. APPLICABLE LAW TO LIMITATION

[3] "In relation to the question of the applicable law, the arbitrators acknowledged the applicability of Russian civil law (Civil Code of the Russian Federation 1964) as the law of the country of the seller on the basis of Art. 166 of the Fundamentals of Civil Legislation of the USSR and Soviet Republics, in effect in the territory of the Russian Federation since 3 August 1992, taking into account the fact that this article is still effective.

[4] "In relation to the issue of limitation which, according to defendant, was not observed by claimant, the Arbitration Court states that in accordance with Art. 78 of the Civil Code of the Russian Federation of 1964, the limitation period for the contracts in dispute is three years, and in accordance with Art. 83,[1] is tolled from the day when a person learns or should have learned that his right was violated. The claimant's reference to provisions of the New York Convention on the Limitation Period in the International Sale of Goods of 1974 is not valid since the Convention, although signed by the USSR, has not yet been ratified by Russia. Thus, for the question of limitation, we must apply Russian law.

[5] "Claimant's reference to the letter from the Ministry of Foreign Relations dated 15 December 1995 stating that claimant did not receive all of the currency earnings cannot be considered as influencing the beginning of the limitation period. Claimant, himself, in his explanations mentioned 25 November 1994, as the date of the beginning of the limitation period.

---

1. Arts. 78 and 83 of the [1964] Civil Code of the Russian Federation read:

Article 78
"The general period within which a person whose rights have been violated may bring an action to defend those rights (period of limitation of actions) is three years, and for actions brought by state organizations, collective farms and other cooperative and public organizations against each other, one year."

Article 83
"A period of limitation of actions begins to run on the day upon which the right to bring an action arises; the right to bring an action arises on the day upon which a person knows or should know of the violation of his rights. Exceptions to this rule, as well as grounds for the interruption or suspension of the running of a period of limitation are established by legislation of the USSR and by this Code."

Claimant did not present any other evidence about any other date of the beginning of the limitation period.

[6] "The defendant's letter dated 13 January 1995 may be considered as an acknowledgement of the debt, interrupting the limitation period, and according to claimant's statement, claimant received this letter only this year from the other arbitral institution. But this statement by claimant does not seem conclusive, since the case materials show that the letter was sent to the claimant's address by telex, and a copy was sent by [courier] to the Moscow office of claimant. In the letter itself defendant confirms that out of 10,000 tons of metal, only 1,3 were supplied; this is exactly what claimant says. But even if their letter may be considered as a reason for interrupting the limitation period (Art. 80 Civil Code),[2] it has to be admitted that the three year period was missed by the claimant, because the envelope containing the claim is stamped on 21 January 1998.

[7] "The claimant's request to reestablish the limitation period on the basis of Art. 87 (Civil Code)[3] cannot be granted, since claimant had given no valid reasons to reestablish the limitation period. Replacement of management, poor accounting and other similar matters mentioned by claimant cannot be accepted as valid reasons.

[8] "Considering the above and in pursuance of Arts. 38, 39 and 40 of its Rules, the International Commercial Arbitration Court at the CCI RF holds: The claim is rejected."

---

2. Art. 80 of the [1964] Civil Code of the Russian Federation reads:

"A change by agreement of the parties of a period of limitation of actions or of the manner in which such period is calculated is not permitted."

3. Art. 87 of the [1964] Civil Code of the Russian Federation reads:

"Expiration of a period of limitation of actions prior to the bringing of an action is a basis for rejection of the actio.

If the court, *arbitrazh* or private arbitrators find a valid reason for extending the period of limitation, the violated right may be enforced by an action."

Final award in case no. 17/1998 of 8 February 1999

Arbitrators:	V.V. Vitryansky (Chairman); V.V. Dozortsev; I.A. Filatov
Parties:	Claimant: Manufacturer (Russian Fed.) Defendants: (1) Trading company (UK); (2) Trading company (Cyprus)
Place of arbitration:	Moscow, Russian Federation
Published in:	Unpublished. Original in Russian
Subject matters:	– succession of arbitral institution – period of limitation

Facts

A contract was concluded on 10 May 1993 between manufacturer and the UK trading company whereby manufacturer was to supply a quantity of metal to the UK trading company. The metal was supplied but not paid for.

On 13 March 1993, manufacturer and the Cypriot trading company signed a contract for the supply of medical equipment by the Cypriot trading company. The medical equipment was not supplied and was not paid for.

On 2 July 1993, manufacturer, the UK trading company and the Cypriot trading company signed an agreement whereby manufacturer was to supply a quantity of metal in accordance with the contract of 10 May 1993 in exchange for medical equipment supplied by the Cypriot trading company to manufacturer in accordance with the contract of 13 March 1993. The medical equipment was not supplied.

The contracts of 10 May 1993 and of 13 March 1993 provided for arbitration at the Court of Arbitration for Foreign Trade at the Chamber of Trade and Industry of the Russian Federation, Moscow, and the Court of Arbitration at the Chamber of Trade and Industry of the Russian Federation, Moscow, respectively.

The manufacturer initiated arbitration against both trading companies. The Cypriot trading company replied that since it had not received any prepayment from manufacturer, it had no contractual obligations to manufacturer.

Prior to the first hearing, the manufacturer requested to postpone the case to allow it more time to prepare the case and await the award in an arbitration pending at a second arbitral institution between the UK trading company and the manufacturer.

Neither the representative of the manufacturer (claimant) nor the representative of Cypriot trading company (co-defendant) appeared at the arbitration hearing.

The arbitral tribunal first found that it had jurisdiction as the Court of Arbitration at the Chamber of Commerce and Industry of the Russian Federation (CCI RF) had been renamed as the International Commercial Arbitration Court (ICAC) at CCI RF. Moreover, the manufacturer's claim was not within the period of limitation established by the Civil Code of the Russian Federation.

Excerpt

I. JURISDICTION

[1] "ICAC's jurisdiction to settle the dispute arises from the arbitration clauses in Art. 1 of the Standard Conditions of Contract in the contract of 10 May 1993 signed between claimant and defendant and Art. 9 on Arbitration in the contract of 13 March 1993 signed by claimant and co-defendant. The arbitration clauses provide in case of a dispute the parties address, respectively, the Court of Arbitration for Foreign Trade at the Chamber of Trade and Industry of the Russian Federation, Moscow, and the Court of Arbitration at the Chamber of Trade and Industry of the Russian Federation, Moscow.

[2] "Since the parties incorrectly named the arbitration institution in the arbitration clauses, the arbitral tribunal, in considering this matter, based their opinion on the fact that by the date when the above-mentioned contracts were signed, the arbitration structure at the CCI RF, having jurisdiction to settle disputes emerging from contracts relating to foreign trade activity was the Court of Arbitration at the CCI RF, later renamed the International Commercial Arbitration Court at the CCI RF in accordance with Art. 2 of the Decree of the Supreme Soviet of the Russian Federation of 7 July 1993, 'On making effective the law of the Russian Federation "On International Commercial Arbitration"'.[1] Therefore, there is every reason to conclude that the parties

1. Art. 2 of the Decree of the Supreme Soviet of the Russian Federation of 7 July 1993, 'On making effective the law of the Russian Federation "On International Commercial Arbitration"' reads in relevant part:

when signing the arbitration agreement, intended to settle all possible disputes by the arbitral institution having jurisdiction to settle such disputes, and the International Commercial Arbitration Court (ICAC) at the CCI RF is exactly this institution.

[3] "ICAC's jurisdiction to settle the parties' dispute is substantiated by the fact that the claimant submitted his claim to the ICAC, defendant confirmed the jurisdiction of this court at the arbitration hearing, and co-defendant, in submitting his response to the claim to ICAC, made no objections to ICAC's jurisdiction to settle the dispute.

[4] "Considering the above and according to Arts. 7 and 16 of the Russian Federation Law of 7 July 1993 'On Commercial Arbitration'[2] and Art. 1(5) of the Rules,[3] the arbitral tribunal acknowledged that it has jurisdiction to settle the dispute.

[5] "Examining the possibility of hearing the case in the absence of the claimant and the co-defendant, the arbitral tribunal found that the claimant and co-defendant were properly informed about the time and place of the arbitration.... Thus, the arbitral tribunal concluded that claimant and co-defendant received the procedural documents in keeping with the existing procedure as stipulated by the Russian Federation Law of 7 July 1993 'On Commercial Arbitration', Art. 3(1).[4]

"For the purposes of the present Law:
– 'arbitration' means any arbitration (third party tribunal) whether conducted by a tribunal set up specifically for a given case or administered by a permanent arbitral institution, in particular the Court of International Commercial Arbitration or the Maritime Arbitration Commission at the Chamber of Commerce and Industry of the Russian Federation...."

2. Arts. 7 and 16 of the Russian Federation Law of 7 July 1993 on International Commercial Arbitration regulate, respectively, the arbitration agreement and the jurisdiction of the arbitral tribunal to determine its own jurisdiction.
3. Art. 1(5) of the Rules of the International Commercial Arbitration Court (ICAC Rules) reads in relevant part:

   "The question of the ICAC jurisdiction in a given case shall be decided by the arbitral tribunal considering the case...."

4. Art. 3(1) Russian Federation Law of 7 July 1993 on International Commercial Arbitration reads:

   "Unless otherwise agreed by the parties:
   – any written communication is deemed to have been received if it is delivered to the addressee personally or if it is delivered at his place of business, permanent residence or mailing address; if none of these can be found after making a reasonable inquiry, a written communication is deemed to have been received if it is sent to the addressee's last-known place

[6] "The claimant's motion of 1 December 1998, to postpone the case hearing for 45 days cannot be granted, since the reasons referred to by claimant in support of his request to postpone the hearing are not found to be reasonable by the arbitral tribunal. It is the arbitral tribunal's opinion that claimant had sufficient time to establish its arguments and to clarify all circumstances related to the issue in dispute. The arbitral tribunal also rejected the claimant's motion of 8 December 1998 to postpone the case hearing for indefinite time, since the arbitral tribunal found no causal relation between the award of the second arbitral institution and the settlement of the dispute in question by the arbitral tribunal.

[7] "On the basis of the above, and considering the fact that in the course of the arbitration hearing, defendant requested not to postpone the hearing, the arbitral tribunal, guided by Art. 28(2) of the Rules[5] found that it could hear the case in the absence of the representative of the claimant and co-defendant."

II. APPLICABLE LAW

[8] "As to the issue of applicable law, the arbitral tribunal proceeded from the assumption that claimant in his statement of claim, supported his claims by reference to the norms of Russian law. At the same time, defendant, responding to the claim, agreed to the applicability of such norms and co-defendant did not object to the applicability of the law of the Russian Federation. On the basis of the above, the arbitral tribunal decided to follow the norms of the Russian law in relation to the dispute in question."

III. CONTRACTS

[9] "... Claimant based his claims on the contract on 10 May 1993, signed by claimant and defendant, on the contact signed by claimant and co-defendant

of business, permanent residence or mailing address by registered letter or any other means which provides a record of the attempt to deliver it;
– the communication is deemed to have been received on the day it is so delivered."

5. Art. 28(2) of the ICAC Rules reads:

"Failure to appear by a party who has been duly notified of the time and place of the hearing shall not prevent the case from being examined and the award from being made, unless the defaulting party has requested in writing to adjourn the proceedings for good reasons."

on 13 March 1993, and on the trilateral mutual settlements agreement signed by claimant, defendant and co-defendant on 2 July 1993. Analyzing the agreement of 2 July 1993, which provided for the supply by claimant to defendant of a quantity of metal according to the terms of the contract of 10 May 1993 in exchange for medical equipment supplied to claimant by co-defendant according to the terms of the contract of 13 March 1993, the arbitral tribunal came to the conclusion that the clauses of the contract did not change any of the essential terms of the above contracts. Thus, it is the arbitral tribunal's opinion that there are many reasons to qualify the trilateral agreement of 2 July 1993, as an alleged deal made without the intention to create corresponding legal consequences.

[10] "According to Art. 170(1) of the Civil Code of the Russian Federation,[6] such deals are considered negligible, that is, void. Considering the above, the arbitral tribunal assumes that claimant states its claims to defendant on the basis of the contract of 10 May 1993, and to co-defendant on the basis of the contract of 13 March 1993. Besides, the arbitral tribunal finds no connection between the above contracts and thus considers it right to consider the claims against defendant and co-defendant separately from each other."

IV. PERIOD OF LIMITATION

[11] "Since defendant raised the expiry of the period of limitation, the arbitral tribunal in considering the claims against the defendant, started by analyzing the issue of limitation and established the following:

[12] "In accordance with the contract of 10 May 1993, claimant shipped a quantity of metal to defendant which is corroborated by the invoice of 19 September 1993. The date of this invoice is mentioned by claimant in his claim and is not disputed by defendant. According to Art. 8 of the same contract, payment should be made within 10 banking days after the date of the invoice. Thus, the arbitral tribunal established that the defendant was to pay for the supplied goods, that is, to fulfill its contractual obligations before 30 September

6. Art. 170(1) of the Civil Code of the Russian Federation reads:

> "A fictitious transaction, that is, a transaction concluded only for form, without the intention to create legal consequences corresponding to it, shall be void."

> *Note General Editor.* The English translations of the Civil Code of the Russian Federation are from W.L. Butler, *Civil Code of the Russian Federation Parts One and Two*, Second Edition (Simmonds & Hill Publishers, Ltd.).

1993 and the period of limitation started on that date (Art. 200(2) of the Civil Code of the Russian Federation).[7]

[13] "It is also clear that claimant stated its claim to the ICAC on 27 January 1998.... Thus, the arbitral tribunal concludes that more than four years have passed since the beginning of the limitation period (30 September 1993) and until the date of the statement of claim (27 January 1998). Since claimant did not present any evidence of suspension and/or interruption in the limitation period, that may have occurred before the claim date, the arbitral tribunal concluded that claimant missed the total limitation period of three years, stipulated by Art. 196 of the Civil Code of the Russian Federation.[8]

[14] "According to Art. 199(2) of the Civil Code of the Russian Federation,[9] expiry of the period of limitation in relation to the disputable issue constitutes a reason for rejecting the claim. On the basis of the above and in accordance with Art. 199(2) of the Civil Code of the Russian Federation, the arbitral tribunal decided to reject the claim to recover from defendant the debt....

[15] "It has been made clear by the arbitral tribunal above that claimant made its claim to co-defendant on the basis of the contract of 13 March 1993 between claimant and co-defendant. In accordance with the above contract co-defendant undertook the obligation to supply medical equipment to claimant and claimant undertook to make an advance payment of 100% of the contract sum by wire transfer to the account of the co-defendant.

[16] "In the file there are no documents proving that claimant made the advance payment for the equipment, supplied in accordance with the contract. Moreover, in the statement of claim, claimant acknowledged that he did not make those payments. Thus, since claimant did not fulfill its contractual obligations, the arbitral tribunal assumes that co-defendant has no liabilities to claimant and, consequently, claimant has no grounds to make claims to co-defendant in relation to the contract.

---

7. Art. 200(2) of the Civil Code of the Russian Federation reads:

"With regard to obligations with a specified period of performance, the running of the limitations shall commence upon the end of the period of performance."

8. Art. 196 of the Civil Code of the Russian Federation reads:

"The general period of limitations shall be established as three years."

9. Art. 199(2) of the Civil Code of the Russian Federation reads:

"Limitations shall be applied by a court only upon the application of the party to the dispute which was made before the rendering of the decision by the court."

[17] "On the basis of the above, the arbitral tribunal finds no legal grounds to consider the claims against co-defendant related to the contract of 13 March 1993 and decides not to deal with the claims.

(....)

[18] "On the basis of the above and following Art. 39 of the Rules the [arbitral tribunal] holds that the claim of claimant ... is rejected [and] the claims of co-defendant are not considered."

Index of Arbitral Awards

INTRODUCTION

When using this Index, the reader should note that only the **first principal mention** of a subject matter in a given award has been recorded. For indexing purposes, dissenting opinions are treated as separate awards. Thus, when the same subject matter is discussed in the award and in the dissenting opinion, there will be two entries in the Subject Index. Apart from this exception, subsequent discussions of the subject are not included in the Subject Index. **After having examined the first principal mention of the subject matter, the reader is advised to examine the remainder of the award or dissenting opinion for additional information.**

The Subject Index of Arbitral Awards covers the arbitral awards published in Part II – A of this Volume XXIVa of the Yearbook. Earlier Subject Indexes are as follows:

- Index of Arbitral Awards Volumes I (1975) – XV (1990) published in *Yearbook Key 1990*
- Index of Arbitral Awards Volumes XVI (1991) – XX (1995) published in Volume XX (1995)
- Index of Arbitral Awards Volume XXI published in Volume XXI (1996)
- Index of Arbitral Awards Volume XXII published in Volume XXII (1997)
- Index of Arbitral Awards Volume XXIII published in Volume XXIII (1998).

This Volume of the Yearbook also contains on pp. 354-358 a cumulative *Index of Articles* of the UNCITRAL Model Law Reported in CLOUT, as reproduced in Part II – C of the Yearbook Volume XIX (1994) through Volume XXIV (1999).

Finally, a systematic *Index of Cases on the New York Convention of 1958 reported in Volume XXIV (1999)*, linked to the Consolidated Commentary on the New York Convention of 1958 by Prof. Albert Jan van den Berg, will be published along with the Consolidated Commentary in Yearbook Commercial Arbitration Volume XXIVb.

Index of Arbitral Awards

Part II

B. Court Decisions on Arbitration

Note General Editor. This Part of the Yearbook reports on selected leading cases in the field of international commercial arbitration. Court decisions applying the major multilateral arbitration conventions are reported in the various divisions of Part V. These Parts are as follows:

- Part V – A. Court Decisions on the New York Convention 1958
- Part V – B. Court Decisions on the European Convention 1961
- Part V – C. Court Decisions on the Washington Convention 1965
- Part V – D. Court Decisions on the Panama Convention 1975.

Part V – D on the Panama Convention was introduced for the first time in Volume XXII of the Yearbook.

We would like to express our gratitude to our correspondents who provided the texts or assisted with the translations included in this Part:

Court of Justice of the European Communities: V.V. Veeder, QC
France: Emmanuel Gaillard and Dominique Hascher
Germany: Franz Hubert Timmermann
India: H.C. Johari and Fali Nariman
Sweden: James Carter, Sigvard Jarvin and Michael Marks Cohen
USA: Michael Marks Cohen and Christopher Paparella

EGYPT

Cairo Court of Appeal, 5 December 1995

Parties:	Claimant: Ministry of Defense of the Republic of Egypt Respondent: Chromalloy Aeroservices Inc. (US)
Published in:	Revue de l'arbitrage (1998, no. 4) pp. 723-728 (in French, original in Arabic) with note by Ph. Leboulanger, pp. 728-732
Subject matters:	– administrative contract – failure to apply law chosen by parties

Facts

The Facts in this case are also reported in Yearbook XXII (1997) pp. 691-692 and 1001-1002. On 16 June 1998, Chromalloy Aeroservices Inc. (Chromalloy) and the Ministry of Defense of the Arab Republic of Egypt (Egypt) entered into a contract where Chromalloy agreed to provide parts, maintenance and repair for helicopters belonging to the Egyptian Air Force. The contract provided for penalties for late delivery which could be imposed as soon as a delay occurred, without notification or other official procedure, nor recourse to a judicial procedure. In certain cases of non-performance due to force majeure, the government had the right to cancel the contract by notifying the supplier by registered letter or telex, without giving formal notice or other judicial or formal procedures.

In December 1991, Egypt terminated the contract. Chromalloy notified Egypt that it rejected the cancellation of the contract and commenced arbitration on the basis of the arbitration clause contained in the contract. On 24 August 1994, an award was made against Egypt.

On 28 October 1994, Chromalloy sought enforcement of the award in the United States District Court, District of Columbia. On 13 November 1994, Egypt appealed to the Egyptian Court of Appeal seeking annulment of the award. Egypt subsequently requested the United States District Court on 1 March 1995 to adjourn Chromalloy's petition to enforce the award. On 4

April 1995, the Egyptian Court of Appeal suspended the award and Egypt, on 5 May 1995, requested the US District Court to dismiss the petition to enforce the award. On 5 December 1995, the Egyptian Court of Appeal at Cairo, in the decision reported here, annulled the award, finding that the contract was an administrative contract and that the arbitral panel had failed to apply the applicable Egyptian administrative law.

On 31 July 1996, the US District Court found the award to be valid under US law and granted enforcement. This decision is reported in Yearbook XXII (1997) pp. 1001-1012, as US no. 230.

In the meantime, Chromalloy had also sought to enforce the award in France, where it was granted exequatur on 4 May 1995 by the Paris Court of First Instance. Egypt appealed against this decision and on 14 January 1997, the Court of Appeal of Paris upheld the decision of the court below, finding that although the award had been annulled in Egypt, it remained in existence and its enforcement in France would not be in violation of international public policy. This decision is reported in Yearbook XXII (1997) pp. 691-695, as France no. 26.

Excerpt

(....)

[1] "Claimant criticizes the arbitral award for having deviated from the law applicable to the dispute, contending that the dispute concerned an administrative contract for the supply of materials and services for the benefit of the Armaments Administration of the Egyptian Air Force of the Egyptian Ministry of Defense, which results in the application of Egyptian administrative law, including Law No. 9 of 1983 relating to adjudication, and not Egyptian Civil Law as was decided in the award.

[2] "Arbitration is an exceptional method, in comparison with ordinary judicial means for settlement of disputes before tribunals. Thus arbitration is limited to the matters which the parties agree to submit to it, and the Egyptian legislator provided in Art. 39, paras. 1, 2 and 3 of Law No. 27 of 1994 Promulgating the Law Concerning Arbitration in Civil and Commercial Matters, the legal rules applicable by the arbitral tribunal.

[3] "This article provides that 1) the arbitral panel applies the rules agreed upon by the parties to the substance of the dispute. If they have chosen to apply the law of a given State, only the substantive rules of this law will be applied, not the conflict of laws rules, unless otherwise agreed by the parties; 2) if the two parties have not agreed upon the applicable law to the substance, the arbitral panel applies the substantive rules of the law which it considers

most closely connected to the dispute; 3) the arbitral panel shall, when it decides on the merits, decide in accordance with the terms of the contract in dispute and the usages of the trade applicable to this type of transaction.

[4] "The legislator has allowed the parties to the arbitration to have recourse against an arbitral award in the cases enumerated in Art. 53 of the above-mentioned Law No. 27 of 1994, the first paragraph of which states: 'An arbitral award may be annulled only: ... d) if the arbitral award failed to apply the law agreed upon by the parties to govern the subject matter in dispute....'

[5] "In view of the above, it was agreed between the parties that Egyptian law was applicable to the dispute, and it is incontestable that the contract which is the subject of the dispute was concluded between the Armaments Administration of the Egyptian Air Force, which operates under the Egyptian Ministry of Defense and the defendant company, an American private sector company, and that the object of the contract was the supply of spare parts for the helicopter fleet indicated in the contract, as well as the maintenance and the organization of the warehousing of the spare parts.

[6] "Egyptian law does not define administrative contracts and does not delineate the specific characteristics which distinguish them from other contracts because they contain clauses which remove them from the jurisdiction of the ordinary courts.

[7] "Contracts concluded by the administration with private law persons are not considered as administrative contracts unless they concern the carrying out or the organization of a public service and if the administration expressed its intention to apply the rules of administrative law by including non-private law clauses in the contract.

[8] "In view of the above, it has been proven to this Court that the contract which is the subject of the dispute is an administrative contract concluded with a public service for the purpose of supplying materials and services connected to its task and organization.

[9] "In the contract – as has been indicated in the submissions of both parties – the administration intended to apply the rules of public law and protected its rights by means of direct execution; it also has the right to impose monetary penalties in certain cases, and the power to cancel the contract unilaterally simply by giving notice by means of a registered letter, which derogates from private law.

[10] "The provision in the contract that the applicable law is Egyptian law, means that Egyptian administrative law applies.

[11] "Whereas the arbitral award applied Egyptian civil law and not Egyptian administrative law, it thus deviated from the parties' contractual choice of law, which constitutes a ground for annulment of the arbitral award, according to the above-cited Art. 53(1) of Law No. 27 of 1994.

[12] "Thus, the ground for annulment of the arbitral award that it deviated from the parties' choice of law is grounded in fact and in law, and it shall be granted without examining the other grounds raised by the claimant."
(....)

COURT OF JUSTICE OF THE EUROPEAN COMMUNITIES

Court of Justice of the European Communities, 17 November 1998, Case C-391/95

Parties:	Claimant: Van Uden Maritime BV trading as Van Uden Africa Line (Netherlands) Defendant: Kommanditgesellschaft in Firma Deco-Line and Another (Germany)
Published in:	English version not yet published
Subject matter:	– jurisdiction under the Brussels Convention to order interim measures in aid of arbitration

Facts

In March 1993, Van Uden Maritime BV trading as Van Uden Africa Line (Van Uden) and Kommanditgesellschaft in Firma Deco-Line and Another (Deco-Line) concluded a "slot/space charter agreement" under which Van Uden undertook to make available to Deco-Line cargo space on board vessels operated by Van Uden. In return Deco-Line was to pay charter hire. Disputes arose between the parties regarding the failure by Deco-Line to pay certain invoices and Van Uden instituted arbitration proceedings in The Netherlands.

Van Uden also applied to the President of the Court of First Instance in Rotterdam (*Rechtbank*) for interim relief on the grounds that Deco-Line was not displaying the necessary diligence in the appointment of arbitrators and that non-payment of its invoices was disturbing its cash flow. In its application, it sought an order against Deco-Line for payment of DM 837,919.13 to cover four debts due under the agreement. The President dismissed Deco-Line's objection that the Netherlands court had no jurisdiction and that it could only be sued in Germany on the ground that an order sought as interim relief must be regarded as a provision measure within the meaning of Art. 24 of the Brussels Convention.[1]

Referring to Art. 126(3) of the Code of Civil Procedure (CCP),[2] the President decided that, as court of the plaintiff's domicile, he had jurisdiction to entertain an application made by a plaintiff residing in The Netherlands against a defendant with no known domicile or recognised place of residence there. He further concluded that the case had the requisite minimum connection with Netherlands law, for two reasons: (i) Deco-Line was engaged in international trade and would thus become a creditor in The Netherlands, so that any judgment against it could be enforced there, and (ii) such a judgment could also be enforced in Germany. Finally, the President of the *Rechtbank* took the view that his jurisdiction was in no way affected by the fact that the parties had agreed to have their dispute determined by arbitration in The Netherlands since, under Art. 1022(2) CCP, an arbitration clause cannot preclude a party's right to seek interim relief.[3] By provisionally enforceable judgment of 21 June 1994, the President of the *Rechtbank*, Rotterdam, therefore ordered Deco-Line to pay Van Uden the sum of DM 377,625.35, together with interest at the statutory rate.

---

1. Art. 24 of the Brussels Convention on Jurisdiction and the Enforcement of Judgments in Civil and Commercial Matters reads:

   "Application may be made to the courts of a Contracting State for such provisional, including protective, measures as may be available under the law of that State, even if, under this Convention, the courts of another Contracting State have jurisdiction as to the substance of the matter."

2. Art. 126 of The Netherlands Code of Civil Procedure reads in relevant part:

   "1. The defendant shall be sued in the court of his domicile.
   (....)
   3. If he has no fixed address in The Netherlands, [he shall be sued] in the court of the claimant's domicile.
   (....)"

3. Art. 1022(2) of The Netherlands Code of Civil Procedure reads:

   "2. An arbitration agreement shall not preclude a party from requesting a court to grant interim measures of protection, or from applying to the President of the District Court for a decision in summary proceedings in accordance with the provisions of article 289. In the latter case the President shall decide the case in accordance with the provisions of article 1051."

On appeal by Deco-Line, the Court of Appeal of The Hague (*Gerechtshof*) reversed. In its view, the fact that the case had to have a sufficient connection with Netherlands law meant, in the context of the Brussels Convention, that it must be possible for the interim order applied for to be enforced in The Netherlands. The mere fact that Deco-Line could acquire assets there in the future was, it considered, insufficient for that purpose.

On appeal to the Supreme Court of the Netherlands (*Hoge Raad*), the Supreme Court stayed the proceedings and requested a preliminary ruling by the European Court of Justice (ECJ) regarding the jurisdiction question. The eight questions put to the ECJ are reproduced at [1] below. In its preliminary ruling the ECJ found that where parties have referred a dispute to arbitration, and the debtor resides in another Contracting State, provisional measures may not be ordered on the basis of Art. 5(1) of the Brussels Convention.[4] However, the fact that the substance of the dispute is submitted to arbitration does not prevent parties from relying on the exorbitant jurisdiction provided for in Art. 24 to request provisional measures since provisional measures are not ancillary to arbitration, but are ordered in parallel to arbitration and are intended as measures of support. The granting of provisional measures is conditional on the existence of a real connecting link between the subject-matter of the measures sought and the territorial jurisdiction of the Contracting State of the court before which the measures are sought. Furthermore, where the interim measure sought consists of an interim payment of a contractual consideration, in casu the full sum of the debt, there are two further conditions: security must be given for the sum awarded and the measure must relate only to assets located or to be located within the jurisdiction.

Excerpt

[1] The Supreme Court of the Netherlands requested a preliminary ruling by the Court on the following questions:

> '(1) Where an obligation to pay a sum or sums due under a contract must be performed in a Contracting State – so that, under Art. 5, point

4. Art. 5(1) of the Brussels Convention reads in relevant part:

> "A person domiciled in a Contracting State may, in another Contracting State, be sued:
> 1. in matters relating to a contract, in the courts for the place of performance of the obligation in question;..."

1, of the Brussels Convention, the creditor is entitled to sue his defaulting debtor in the courts of that State with a view to obtaining performance, even though the debtor is domiciled in another Contracting State – do the courts of the first-mentioned State (for that same reason) have jurisdiction also to hear and determine a claim brought by the creditor against his debtor in interim [*kort geding*] proceedings for an order requiring the debtor, by provisionally enforceable judgment, to pay a sum which, in the view of the court hearing the interim application, is very probably due to the creditor, or do additional conditions apply in relation to the jurisdiction of the court hearing the interim application, for example the condition that the relief sought from that court must take effect (or be capable of taking effect) in the Contracting State concerned?
(2) Does it make any difference to the answer to Question 1 whether the contract between the parties contains an arbitration clause and, if so, what the place of arbitration is according to that clause?
(3) If the answer to Question 1 is that, in order for the court hearing the interim application to have jurisdiction, the relief sought from it must also take effect (or be capable of taking effect) in the Contracting State concerned, does that mean that the order applied for must be capable of enforcement in that State, and is it then necessary for this condition to be fulfilled when the interim application is made, or is it sufficient that it can be reasonably expected to be fulfilled in the future?
(4) Does the possibility, provided for in Art. 289 et seq. of the Netherlands Code of Civil Procedure, of applying on grounds of pressing urgency to the President of the *Arrondissementsrechtbank* for a provisionally enforceable judgment constitute a "provisional" or "protective" measure within the meaning of Art. 24 of the Brussels Convention?
(5) Does it make any difference to the answer to Question 4 whether substantive proceedings on the main issue are, or may become, pending and, if so, is it material that arbitration proceedings had started in the same case?
(6) Does it make any difference to the answer to Question 4 that the interim relief sought is an order requiring performance of an obligation of payment, as referred to in Question 1?
(7) If Question 4 must be answered in the affirmative, and "the courts of another Contracting State have jurisdiction as to the substance of the matter", must Art. 24, and in particular the reference therein to "such provisional ... measures as may be available under the law of [a Contracting] State", be interpreted as meaning that the court hearing the application for interim measures has (for that same reason) jurisdiction

if it has jurisdiction under provisions of its national law, even where those provisions are referred to in the second paragraph of Art. 3 of the Brussels Convention,[5] or is its jurisdiction in the latter case conditional on the fulfilment of additional conditions, for example that the interim relief sought from that court must take effect, or be capable of taking effect, in the Contracting State concerned?
(8) If the answer to Question 7 must be that, in order for the court hearing the application for interim relief to have jurisdiction, it is also required that the relief sought from it must take effect (or be capable of taking effect) in the Contracting State concerned, does that mean that the order applied for must be capable of enforcement in that State, and is it then necessary for this condition to be fulfilled when the application for interim relief is made, or is it sufficient that it can reasonably be expected to be fulfilled in the future?'

[2] "The questions raised relate to the jurisdiction, under the Convention, of a court hearing applications for interim relief. The national court wishes to know both whether such jurisdiction could be established on the basis of Art. 5, point 1, of the Convention (Questions 1 to 3) and whether it could be established on the basis of Art. 24 (Questions 4 to 8). In both cases, the national court's questions relate to

- first, the relevance of the fact that the dispute in question is subject, under the terms of the contract, to arbitration,
- next, whether the jurisdiction of the court hearing the application for interim relief is subject to the condition that the measure sought must take effect or be capable of taking effect in the State of that court, in particular that it must be enforceable there, and whether it is necessary that such a condition should be met at the time when the application is made, and
- finally, the relevance of the fact that the case relates to a claim for interim payment of a contractual consideration.

5. Art. 3(2) of the Brussels Convention reads in relevant part:

"Persons domiciled in a Contracting State may be sued in the courts of another contracting State only by virtue of the rules set out in Sects. 2 to 6 of this Title:

In particular the following provisions shall not be applicable as against them:

(....)

- In the Netherlands: Articles 126(3) and 127 of the code of civil procedure (*Wetboek van Burgerlijke Rechtsvordering*),

(....)"

[3] "The first point to be made, as regards the jurisdiction of a court hearing an application for interim relief, is that it is accepted that a court having jurisdiction as to the substance of a case in accordance with Arts. 2 and 5 to 18 of the Convention also has jurisdiction to order any provisional or protective measures which may prove necessary. In addition, Art. 24, in Sect. 9 of the Convention, adds a rule of jurisdiction falling outside the system set out in Arts. 2 and 5 to 18, whereby a court may order provisional or protective measures even if it does not have jurisdiction as to the substance of the case. Under that provision, the measures available are those provided for by the law of the State of the court to which application is made. Art. 5, point 1, of the Convention provides that in matters relating to a contract a defendant may be sued, in a Contracting State other than that in which he is domiciled, in the courts for the place of performance of the obligation in question. Thus, the court having jurisdiction as to the substance of a case under one of the heads of jurisdiction laid down in the Convention also has jurisdiction to order provisional or protective measures, without that jurisdiction being subject to any further conditions, such as that mentioned in the national court's third question.

[4] "However, in the present case, the contract signed between Van Uden and Deco-Line contains an arbitration clause. Where the parties have validly excluded the jurisdiction of the courts in a dispute arising under a contract and have referred that dispute to arbitration, there are no courts of any State that have jurisdiction as to the substance of the case for the purposes of the Convention. Consequently, a party to such a contract is not in a position to make an application for provisional or protective measures to a court that would have jurisdiction under the Convention as to the substance of the case. In such a case, it is only under Art. 24 that a court may be empowered under the Convention to order provisional or protective measures.

[5] "In that connection, Deco-Line and the German and United Kingdom Governments agreed that, since the parties have agreed to submit their dispute to arbitration, interim proceedings also fall outside the scope of the Convention. The German Government argues in particular that measures sought in interim proceedings, when they are intrinsically bound up with the subject-matter of an arbitration procedure, fall outside the scope of the Convention. In the United Kingdom Government's view, the measures sought in the present case may be regarded as ancillary to the arbitration procedure and are thus excluded from the scope of the Convention.

[6] "Van Uden and the Commission, however, contend that the existence of an arbitration clause does not have the effect of excluding an application for interim measures from the scope of the Convention. The Commission points out that the subject-matter of the dispute is decisive and that the issue

underlying the interim proceedings concerns the performance of a contractual obligation – a matter which falls within the scope of the Convention.

[7] "It must first be borne in mind here that Art. 24 of the Convention applies even if a court of another Contracting State has jurisdiction as to the substance of the case, provided that the subject-matter of the dispute falls within the scope ratione materiae of the Convention, which covers civil and commercial matters. Thus the mere fact that proceedings have been, or may be, commenced on the substance of the case before a court of a Contracting State does not deprive a court of another Contracting State of its jurisdiction under Art. 24 of the Convention.

[8] "However, Art. 24 cannot be relied on to bring within the scope of the Convention provisional or protective measures relating to matters which are excluded from it (Case 143/78 *De Cavel v. De Cavel* [1979] ECR 1055, paragraph 9). Under Art. 1, second paragraph, point 4, of the Convention, arbitration is excluded from its scope. By that provision, the Contracting Parties intended to exclude arbitration in its entirety, including proceedings brought before national courts (Case C-190/89 *Rich v. Società Italiana Impianti* [1991] ECR I-3855, paragraph 18).[6]

[9] "The experts' report drawn up on the accession of the Kingdom of Denmark, Ireland and the United Kingdom of Great Britain and Northern Ireland to the Convention (OJ 1979 C 59, p. 71, at pp. 92-93) specifies that the Convention does not apply to judgments determining whether an arbitration agreement is valid or not or, because it is invalid, ordering the parties not to continue the arbitration proceedings, or to proceedings and decisions concerning applications for the revocation, amendment, recognition and enforcement of arbitration awards. Also excluded from the scope of the Convention are proceedings ancillary to arbitration proceedings, such as the appointment or dismissal of arbitrators, the fixing of the place of arbitration or the extension of the time-limit for making awards.

[10] "However, it must be noted in that regard that provisional measures are not in principle ancillary to arbitration proceedings but are ordered in parallel to such proceedings and are intended as measures of support. They concern not arbitration as such but the protection of a wide variety of rights. Their place in the scope of the Convention is thus determined not by their own nature but by the nature of the rights which they serve to protect (see Case C-261/90 *Reichert and Kockler v. Dresdner Bank* [1992] ECR I-2149, paragraph 32).

[11] "It must therefore be concluded that where, as in the case in the main proceedings, the subject-matter of an application for provisional measures

6. Reported in Yearbook XVII (1992) pp. 233-240.

relates to a question falling within the scope ratione materiae of the Convention, the Convention is applicable and Art. 24 thereof may confer jurisdiction on the court hearing that application even where proceedings have already been, or may be, commenced on the substance of the case and even where those proceedings are to be conducted before arbitrators.

[12] "Next, as regards the conditions set out in the Convention for the grant of an application under Art. 24, Van Uden submits that no further condition need be fulfilled for the court hearing such an application to have jurisdiction provided that it has jurisdiction under provisions of its national law even where those provisions are among those listed in the second paragraph of Art. 3 of the Convention. Deco-Line, however, maintains that the imposition of stricter conditions is clearly justified and that, in any event, the fact that Art. 24 refers to national rules on jurisdiction implies that the court in question is free to hold that its jurisdiction is subject to such conditions.

[13] "In the German Government's view, Art. 24 does not authorise a court acting on the basis of one of the rules of jurisdiction listed in the second paragraph of Art. 3 of the Convention to order provisional measures unless the rule of jurisdiction in question is subject to the urgency of the decision or based upon that reasoning and unless the provisional measure, at the time when it is ordered, has a sufficient connecting link with the State of that court. The latter condition is satisfied when the provisional measure can be enforced in that State. In that regard, it must be remembered that the expression 'provisional, including protective, measures' within the meaning of Art. 24 of the Convention is to be understood as referring to measures which, in matters within the scope of the Convention, are intended to preserve a factual or legal situation so as to safeguard rights the recognition of which is otherwise sought from the court having jurisdiction as to the substance of the case (*Reichert and Kockler*, cited above, paragraph 34).

[14] "The granting of this type of measure requires particular care on the part of the court in question and detailed knowledge of the actual circumstances in which the measures sought are to take effect. Depending on each case and commercial practices in particular, the court must be able to place a time-limit on its order or, as regards the nature of the assets or goods subject to the measures contemplated, require bank guarantees or nominate a sequestrator and generally make its authorization subject to all conditions guaranteeing the provisional or protective character of the measure ordered (Case 125/79 *Denilauler v. Couchet Frères* [1980] ECR 1553, paragraph 15).

[15] "In that regard, the Court held at paragraph 16 of *Denilauler* that the courts of the place – or, in any event, of the Contracting State – where the assets subject to the measures sought are located are those best able to assess the circumstances which may lead to the grant or refusal of the measures

sought or to the laying down of procedures and conditions which the plaintiff must observe in order to guarantee the provisional and protective character of the measures authorised.

[16] "It follows that the granting of provisional or protective measures on the basis of Art. 24 is conditional on, inter alia, the existence of a real connecting link between the subject-matter of the measures sought and the territorial jurisdiction of the Contracting State of the court before which those measures are sought. It further follows that a court ordering measures on the basis of Art. 24 must take into consideration the need to impose conditions or stipulations such as to guarantee their provisional or protective character.

[17] "With regard more particularly to the fact that the national court has in this instance based its jurisdiction on one of the national provisions listed in the second paragraph of Art. 3 of the Convention, it must be borne in mind that, in accordance with the first paragraph of that article, persons domiciled in a Contracting State may be sued in the courts of another Contracting State only by virtue of the rules set out in Sects. 2 to 6 of Title II, that is to say Arts. 5 to 18, of the Convention. Consequently, the prohibition in Art. 3 of reliance on rules of exorbitant jurisdiction does not apply to the special regime provided for by Art. 24.

[18] "Finally, with regard to the question whether an interim order requiring payment of a contractual consideration may be classified as a provisional measure within the meaning of Art. 24 of the Convention, Deco-Line and the Government of the United Kingdom argue that it cannot. The German Government considers that the main proceedings appear to fall outside the definition of provisional or protective measures.

[19] "Van Uden and the Commission do not share that view. In the Commission's view, provisional measures must be taken to mean those whose validity lapses when the main issue is determined or on the expiry of a specified period. They may comprise positive measures, that is to say an order to perform some act such as the handing-over of property or the payment of a sum of money.

[20] "Here, it must be noted that it is not possible to rule out in advance, in a general and abstract manner, that interim payment of a contractual consideration, even in an amount corresponding to that sought as principal relief, may be necessary in order to ensure the practical effect of the decision on the substance of the case and may, in certain cases, appear justified with regard to the interests involved (see, in the context of Community law, Case C-393/96 P(R) *Antonissen v. Council and Commission* [1997] ECR I-441, paragraph 37).

[21] "However, an order for interim payment of a sum of money is, by its very nature, such that it may preempt the decision on the substance of the case. If, moreover, the plaintiff were entitled to secure interim payment of a

contractual consideration before the courts of the place where he is himself domiciled, where those courts have no jurisdiction over the substance of the case under Arts. 2 to 18 of the Convention, and thereafter to have the order in question recognised and enforced in the defendant's State, the rules of jurisdiction laid down by the Convention could be circumvented.

[22] "Consequently, interim payment of a contractual consideration does not constitute a provisional measure within the meaning of Art. 24 unless, first, repayment to the defendant of the sum awarded is guaranteed if the plaintiff is unsuccessful as regards the substance of his claim and, second, the measure sought relates only to specific assets of the defendant located or to be located within the confines of the territorial jurisdiction of the court to which application is made.

[23] "In the light of the foregoing considerations, the answer to the first and second questions must be that

- on a proper construction of Art. 5, point 1, of the Convention, the court which has jurisdiction by virtue of that provision also has jurisdiction to order provisional or protective measures, without that jurisdiction being subject to any further conditions, and
- where the parties have validly excluded the jurisdiction of the courts in a dispute arising under a contract and have referred that dispute to arbitration, no provisional or protective measures may be ordered on the basis of Art. 5, point 1, of the Convention.

The answer to the fifth question must be that

- where the subject-matter of an application for provisional measures relates to a question falling within the scope ratione materiae of the Convention, the Convention is applicable and Art. 24 thereof may confer jurisdiction on the court hearing that application even where proceedings have already been, or may be, commenced on the substance of the case and even where those proceedings are to be conducted before arbitrators.

Finally, the answer to the fourth, sixth, seventh and eighth questions must be that

- on a proper construction, the granting of provisional or protective measures on the basis of Art. 24 of the Convention is conditional on, inter alia, the existence of a real connecting link between the subject-matter of the measures sought and the territorial jurisdiction of the Contracting State of the court before which those measures are sought, and

- interim payment of a contractual consideration does not constitute a provisional measure within the meaning of Art. 24 of the Convention unless, first, repayment to the defendant of the sum awarded is guaranteed if the plaintiff is unsuccessful as regards the substance of his claim and, second, the measure sought relates only to specific assets of the defendant located or to be located within the confines of the territorial jurisdiction of the court to which application is made.

(....)

[24] "On those grounds, the Court, in answer to the questions referred to it by the *Hoge Raad der Nederlanden* by judgment of 8 December 1995, hereby rules:

1. On a proper construction of Art. 5, point 1, of the Convention of 27 September 1968 on Jurisdiction and the Enforcement of Judgments in Civil and Commercial Matters, as amended by the Convention of 9 October 1978 on the accession of the Kingdom of Denmark, Ireland and the United Kingdom of Great Britain and Northern Ireland, and by the Convention of 25 October 1982 on the accession of the Hellenic Republic, the court which has jurisdiction by virtue of that provision also has jurisdiction to order provisional or protective measures, without that jurisdiction being subject to any further conditions.
2. Where the parties have validly excluded the jurisdiction of the courts in a dispute arising under a contract and have referred that dispute to arbitration, no provisional or protective measures may be ordered on the basis of Art. 5, point 1, of the Convention of 27 September 1968.
3. Where the subject-matter of an application for provisional measures relates to a question falling within the scope ratione materiae of the Convention of 27 September 1968, that Convention is applicable and Art. 24 thereof may confer jurisdiction on the court hearing that application even where proceedings have already been, or may be, commenced on the substance of the case and even where those proceedings are to be conducted before arbitrators.
4. On a proper construction, the granting of provisional or protective measures on the basis of Art. 24 of the Convention of 27 September 1968 is conditional on, inter alia, the existence of a real connecting link between the subject-matter of the measures sought and the territorial jurisdiction of the Contracting State of the court before which those measures are sought.
5. Interim payment of a contractual consideration does not constitute a provisional measure within the meaning of Art. 24 of the Convention of 27 September 1968 unless, first, repayment to the defendant of the sum awar-

ded is guaranteed if the plaintiff is unsuccessful as regards the substance of his claim and, second, the measure sought relates only to specific assets of the defendant located or to be located within the confines of the territorial jurisdiction of the court to which application is made."

FRANCE

Cour d'Appel [Court of Appeal], Paris, 1 July 1997

Parties:	Claimant: Agence Transcongolaise des Communications – Chemin de fer Congo Océan (ATC-CFCO) (Congo) Defendant: Compagnie Minière de l'Ogooue – Comilog S.A. (Gabon)
Published in:	Revue de l'arbitrage (1998, no. 1) pp. 131-136 with note D. Hascher, pp. 136-142
Subject matters:	– international arbitration – truncated arbitral tribunal

Facts

By a contract of 27 March 1957, the Congolese authorities granted Compagnie Minière de l'Ogooue Comilog S.A. (Comilog) the right to transport manganese from a Gabon mine through the Congo by the public railway Congo Océan (CFCO). This agreement was to be completed by further agreements concerning specific shipments. The present case concerns one of these specific agreements (a traction agreement), which was concluded on 3 June 1991. The traction agreement provided that disputes which could not be amicably settled were to be referred to arbitration according to the arbitration clause in the 1957 contract.

On 5 September 1991, a train composed of a Comilog engine driven by a Comilog employee and of wagons owned by the Agence Transcongolaise des Communications – Chemin de fer Congo Océan (ATC-CFCO) collided with a Congolese passenger train.

The parties did not find an amicable solution to the dispute concerning the assessment of their respective responsibilities and commenced arbitration in Paris. ATC-CFCO and Comilog appointed their respective arbitrators; the president of the French Railways (SNCF) appointed the chairman of the arbitral tribunal as provided for in the 1957 contract.

On 15 September 1995, upon receiving the draft award from the chairman of the tribunal, the arbitrator appointed by ATC-CFCO resigned. In his letter to the chairman, the arbitrator affirmed that his resignation was in protest against the intervention of a SNCF legal staff representative in the arbitral deliberations. In its turn, ATC-CFCO expressed its intention to commence summary proceedings on the issue before the president of the Paris Court of First Instance and to challenge the two remaining arbitrators, affirming that the arbitral tribunal should be reconstituted entirely, and appointing a new arbitrator.

On 25 September 1995, the tribunal rendered an award by which it found that ATC-CFCO was to bear responsibility for 90% of the accident. The award was not signed by ATC-CFCO's arbitrator, who had been "notified but was absent".

ATC-CFCO sought annulment of the award for violation of due process, irregularity in the composition of the arbitral tribunal, violation of international public policy and of the right to defense.

The Court of Appeal held that the arbitral tribunal was no longer duly constituted at the time of rendering the award and annulled the award without considering ATC-CFCO's further grounds for setting aside.

Excerpt

I. JURISDICTION OF THE COURT OF APPEAL

[1] "Comilog relies on Art. 1493 of the New Code of Civil Procedure (NCCP)[1] to allege that the Paris Court of Appeal in Paris has no jurisdiction. Art. 1493 concerns difficulties in the constitution of the arbitral tribunal; it is irrelevant for solving the present problem, which must be solved exclusively under Art. 1502 et seq. NCCP.

1. Art. 1493 of the French New Code of Civil Procedure (NCCP) reads:

> "The arbitration agreement may, directly or by reference to a set of arbitration rules, appoint one or more arbitrators or provide the manner for their appointment.
>
> If any difficulty arises in the constitution of the arbitral tribunal with respect to an arbitration taking place in France, or to one for which the parties have agreed that French procedural law should apply, either party may, in the absence of a clause to the contrary, apply to the President of the Court of First Instance in Paris in the manner set forth in Art. 1457."

[2] "An arbitral award rendered in France in international arbitration may, according to Art. 1504 NCCP, be the object of an action for setting aside in the cases provided for in Art. 1502.[2] The action shall be filed with the Court of Appeal in the district of which the award was rendered."

II. INTERNATIONAL ARBITRATION

[3] "Comilog alleges that the Paris Court of Appeal lacks jurisdiction over the validity of a purely domestic arbitration, the seat of which was in Pointe Noire in the Congo.

[4] "The domestic or international character of an arbitration is to be inferred exclusively from the economic nature of the economic transaction which gave rise to the arbitration, independent of the arbitration's seat, of the law applicable to the merits or of the nationality of the parties. In application of this principle, an arbitration is international which concerns an economic operation implying a movement of goods, services or a payment across borders and thus implicating international commercial interests. In the present case, the railway accident of 5 September 1991 happened in the Congo. It concerned a train of Congolese wagons pulled by an engine owned by the Gabonese company Comilog and driven by an employee of the latter. It travelled in the Congo in the context of agreements between the Congo and Gabon which allowed the latter to ship its manganese under the best possible conditions against payment of a toll fee. Contrary to Comilog's opinion, the operation underlying the arbitration does imply a movement of services and payments across the borders of Gabon and the Congo, and therefore concerns international commerce. Hence, the arbitration is an international arbitration governed by the above-mentioned provisions.

[5] "Although clause 7 of the traction agreement of 3 June 1991 provides that the seat of a possible arbitration is Pointe Noire, in the Congo, the parties

---

2. Art. 1502 NCCP reads:

> "An appeal against a decision granting recognition or enforcement may be brought only in the following cases:
> 1. If the arbitrator decided in the absence of an arbitration agreement or on the basis of a void or expired agreement;
> 2. If the arbitral tribunal was irregularly composed or the sole arbitrator irregularly appointed;
> 3. If the arbitrator decided in a manner incompatible with the mission conferred upon him;
> 4. Whenever due process has not been respected;
> 5. If the recognition or enforcement is contrary to international public policy (*ordre public*)."

expressly agreed during the first arbitration hearing (minutes of 23 July 1993) that, in derogation from this general stipulation, the seat of the arbitration in this case would be Paris, where the award has been rendered."

III. SETTING ASIDE

[6] "According to Arts. 1502(2) and 1504 NCCP, the arbitral award is annulled if the arbitral tribunal was irregularly constituted, and ATC-CFCO indeed alleges that the arbitral tribunal, with an arbitrator who had resigned and two challenged arbitrators (a decision on the challenge was to be taken in a hearing on 27 September 1995), was no longer regularly constituted when it rendered its award on 25 September 1995.
[7] "The parties tried unsuccessfully to settle their dispute amicably according to clause 7 of the traction agreement of 3 June 1991, and then commenced arbitration as provided for in clause 27 of the same agreement, which provides that

> 'where the conclusions are not accepted by either party, [the dispute] shall be settled by arbitration as provided for in clause 21 of the contract of 27 March 1957.'

Clause 21 provides that

> 'if a dispute arises between the parties concerning the application of this agreement ... it shall be decided by arbitration ... the arbitral tribunal shall be composed of three arbitrators; the party commencing arbitration shall appoint an arbitrator ... within thirty days of this notification the other party shall appoint an arbitrator ... within thirty days of this notification the two arbitrators shall appoint a third arbitrator ... if the two arbitrators do not agree on the appointment of the third arbitrator either party may request the president of the SNCF to appoint the arbitrator'.

In application of these provisions, Comilog and ATC-CFCO respectively appointed Mr. René Schlemmer, an expert registered with the *Cour de cassation*, and Jean Petro, a lawyer in Pointe Noire, as arbitrators on 21 and 26 June 1992. The president of SNCF appointed Georges Dobias as the third arbitrator and the latter accepted his mandate on 2 January 1993.
[8] "After several hearings, exchange of statements, hearing of witnesses and an expert report, the case was pleaded on 20 June 1995. After having partici-

pated in the deliberation on 13 September 1995 and having received the draft award from the chairman, Jean Petro informed the latter of his resignation by letter of 15 September sent the following day by fax.

[9] "Notwithstanding this difficulty, Mr. Dobias, who had acknowledged the resignation of Jean Petro on 19 September and who knew of the procedure commenced by ATC-CFCO before the president of the Paris Court of First Instance on the basis of Art. 1457 NCCP,[3] informed the parties that he would nevertheless render the award on 25 September 1995, and he did so, mentioning that Mr. Petro had been notified but was absent.

[10] "Comilog essentially alleges, in order to oppose the action for setting aside commenced by ATC-CFCO against the award rendered under these circumstances:

> '(1) that the resignation of Jean Petro, made for false reasons, is a dilatory tactic just like the [court] proceedings subsequently commenced and aims at avoiding the rendition of an award which does not satisfy the Congolese party; (2) that [this resignation] is "inoperative", since Art. 1462 NCCP requires the arbitrator to continue his mission until it is completed,[4] Art. 1465 NCCP provides that the arbitration is interrupted only for the reasons listed in Arts. 369-376, and Art. 371 provides that there is no interruption if the event takes place after the opening of the debate, which is the case here; and (3) that the award, which was rendered by majority of votes, according to the agreement of the parties,

---

3. Art. 1457 NCCP reads:

> "In the cases covered by Arts. 1444, 1454, 1456 and 1463, the president of the court, seized as in urgent proceedings (*référé*) by a party or the arbitral tribunal, shall decide by non appealable order.
>
> Nevertheless, such order may be appealed if the president declares that no appointment is to be made for one of the reasons defined in Art. 1444(3). The appeal is to be filed, examined and decided in the same manner as with respect to jurisdictional disputes.
>
> The president having jurisdiction is the president of the court designated by the arbitration agreement or, in the absence of such an agreement, the president of the court within the district where said agreement localized the arbitral proceedings. If the agreement is silent, the president having jurisdiction is the president of the court of the defendant's residence or of one of the defendants or, if the defendant does not reside in France, the president of the court in the place of the plaintiff's residence."

4. Art. 1462 NCCP reads:

> "Arbitrators are to continue their mission until it is completed.
>
> An arbitrator may not be dismissed except by the parties' unanimous consent."

> and after deliberation by the arbitral tribunal, the absent arbitrator having been duly notified, is formally and substantively valid.'

[11] "First, the possible dilatory and abusive character of the resignation of Jean Petro is irrelevant in so far as the present dispute, which is limited to the question whether the award was rendered by a regularly constituted tribunal, is concerned. Second, we must note that, independent of his possible obligations and of his responsibility thereunder to be determined in other proceedings, Jean Petro did not complete his mandate. This fact, which does not concern the parties, but the tribunal and its enduring jurisdiction, which is exclusively based on the agreement to arbitrate and moreover dependent on a perfect correspondence with the requirements therein, does not constitute a ground for interruption of the arbitration as provided for in the provisions referred to by Comilog, which do not apply here. Last, it is undisputed that Jean Petro resigned during the deliberation of the award, so that at the moment of rendering [the award] the arbitral tribunal was constituted only by the arbitrator appointed by Comilog and by the chairman Dobias.

[12] "It ensues from the above that, contrary to the hypothesis advanced by Comilog, according to which the award remains valid because it is rendered by the tribunal chosen by the parties even if one of the arbitrators does not participate in the deliberation or refuses to sign the award, since by continuing to accept his mission he still may exercise his prerogatives, the award at issue has been rendered by an arbitral tribunal lacking one of its members and the composition of which no longer conformed to the agreement on which its jurisdictional power was based.

[13] "The award rendered under these circumstances, when, moreover, the president of the Court of First Instance had been seized of the issue and ATC-CFCO had already appointed a new arbitrator, must be annulled on this ground alone. It is therefore useless to examine the further grounds for setting aside raised by the claimant."

Cour d'Appel [Court of Appeal], Paris, 15 September 1998

Parties:	Appellant: Cubic Defense Systems, Inc. (US) Appellee: International Chamber of Commerce (France)
Published in:	Revue de l'arbitrage (1999, no. 1) pp. 103-113 with note P. Lalive, pp. 113-120
Subject matters:	- prescription of action - contract with arbitral institution - ICC arbitration - scrutiny of draft award - European Convention on Human Rights, Art. 6 - liability of arbitral institution

Facts

On 23 October 1977, Cubic Defense Systems, Inc. (Cubic) and the Ministry of War for the Armament of the Government of Iran concluded a sale contract and a services contract. Both contracts contained an arbitration clause reading:

> "all dispute, controversy or claim arising under the present contract or related to it or any violation of this contract shall be settled by arbitration in Zurich, Switzerland, according to the laws of Iran as in force at the date of the present contract".

Performance under the contracts was interrupted at the beginning of 1979 as a consequence of the revolution in Iran. On 19 January 1982, Iran filed a claim against Cubic with the Iran-US Claims Tribunal at the Hague. On 28 April 1987, the Iran-US Claims Tribunal issued an Order stating that it lacked jurisdiction to hear the matter.

On 25 September 1991, the Ministry of Defense and Support to the Armed Forces of the Islamic Republic of Iran (the Ministry) filed a request for arbitration against Cubic with the International Chamber of Commerce. The Secretariat of the ICC Court of International Arbitration (CIA) informed Cubic of the request for arbitration by a letter of 3 October 1991; the Secretariat enclosed the ICC Rules and appendixes and also informed Cubic that it had thirty days to respond. An US law firm replied by fax to the

Secretariat on behalf of Cubic, confirming a telephone conversation of 10 October 1991 in which it had indicated one of its partners as Cubic's legal representative, and requesting a postponement of 45 days to file a statement in reply. The Terms of Reference were eventually signed on 14 July 1993.

On 6 April 1995, the arbitral tribunal issued interim procedural order no. 6 on the issue of prescription of the Ministry's claim. By a letter to the CIA of 17 April 1995, Cubic objected to the order, affirming that "the decision of the arbitral tribunal makes this arbitration, as well as the time and money Cubic had to spend in order to defend itself against a fifteen year old request which has lapsed, ridiculous. It is not too much for Cubic to say that the order of 6 April, which is objectively insufficient, unreasoned and ultra petita, may seriously jeopardize the ICC Court's credibility with the business and legal community in the United States." Cubic also requested that the arbitrator appointed by the Ministry and the chairman of the tribunal, who had been appointed by the ICC, be substituted. On 17 May 1995, the CIA denied Cubic's request.

On 15 January 1997 – before the arbitrators issued their final award, on 5 May 1997, directing Cubic to pay the Ministry US$ 2,808,519 –[1] Cubic commenced court proceedings against the ICC before the Court of First Instance in Paris, seeking annulment of its contract with the ICC, restitution of US$ 185,000 paid by Cubic as arbitration fees and payment of US$ 1,815,975 in damages. On 21 May 1997, the Court of First Instance denied the request on all points.

The Court of Appeal found that, contrary to the lower court's opinion, Cubic's action to annul the arbitration contract had been brought after the five-year period prescribed by French law had lapsed, but affirmed the lower decision in holding that Cubic had not proven any failure by the ICC to perform under its contractual obligations. In particular, the scrutiny of the award by the Court of International Arbitration did not constitute an interference in the arbitrator's task or a modification of the award. Nor was it proven by Cubic that its case had not been heard within a reasonable time in violation of Art. 6 of the European Convention on Human Rights. Moreover, this Convention bound States, not the ICC Court of International Arbitration which is an institution, not a jurisdiction. Also it had not been found that there was any provision in the ICC Rules which would entitle the Court of International Arbitration to reclassify a procedural order as an award.

1. The decision of the United States District Court for the Southern District of California of 7 December 1998 granting enforcement of the award is reported in this volume as US no. 282, pp. 875-881.

Excerpt

(....)
[1] "The parties agree that French law applies in these appellate proceedings."

I. PRESCRIPTION

[2] "According to Art. 1304 Civil Code, an action for the annulment or termination of a contract [may be brought within] five years unless a shorter time is provided by a specific law.[2] The Court of First Instance did not apply this provision, the application of which was requested by the ICC, holding that a nullity for lack of consideration in the contract, which ensues from the absence of an essential condition for balancing the mutual obligations of the parties, is an absolute nullity which falls under the thirty year prescription of Art. 2262 of the Civil Code[3] rather than under Art. 1304 of the same Code.
[3] "However, only Cubic's property rights would be affected by the alleged lack of consideration under the contract at issue. Hence, the prescription of the action for the annulment of that contract is governed by [Art. 1304 Civil Code]. Since the contract for arbitration was concluded on 20 December 1991, the action for annulment filed by Cubic on 9 January 1997 has lapsed."

---

2. Art. 1304 of the French Civil Code reads:

"Unless it is limited by a specific law to a shorter time, an action for the annulment or termination of a contract may be brought within five years.

In the case of violence, this period runs from the day [violence] ceased; in the case of mistake or fraud, from the day on which they were discovered.

With respect to acts done by a minor, this period runs from the day on which he comes of age or is emancipated; with respect to acts done by a minor under guardianship, from the day on which he became aware of such acts and could validly re-do them. It only runs against the heirs of an incapacitated person from the day of death unless it started running before."

3. Art. 2262 of the French Civil Code reads:

"The prescription for all actions, both in rem and in personam, is thirty years; a party relying on this prescription does not need to justify [this prescription], nor can an objection of bad faith be opposed to it."

II. INVALIDITY OF THE ARBITRATION CONTRACT

[4] "The examination of this ground for appeal first requires an analysis of the nature of the relations between Cubic and ICC. By filing its statement in reply and counterclaim, Cubic, which had received the [ICC Rules] on 3 October 1991, agreed that the arbitration be administered by the ICC. Art. 7 of the [ICC] Rules informed Cubic that if it did not reply within thirty days or if it refused [to take part in] the arbitration, the Ministry would be informed that the arbitration could not take place.

[5] "By accepting the arbitration, Cubic accepted the ICC Rules, which require it, in particular: 1) to pay the fees; and 2) to respect the time limits and formalities (number of examples of each statement) for filing a statement in reply and a counterclaim. The same Rules require the CIA: 1) to appoint or confirm the arbitrators (Art. 2.1); 2) to appoint the third arbitrator (Art. 2.4); 3) to decide whether a challenge is admissible and founded (Art. 2.9); 4) to replace an arbitrator (Art. 2.11); 5) to obtain a decision from the arbitrator within six months unless this time limit is extended (Art. 18); 6) to scrutinize the form of the draft final award of the arbitrator; and 7) to notify the award.

[6] "According to its Rules (Art. 1), the CIA is an international arbitration body whose members are appointed by the Council of the ICC and whose task is to provide for the settlement by arbitration of business disputes. Unlike the ICC, the CIA has no legal personality; it is a service of the latter with a specific aim, the arbitral settlement of disputes; its independence ensues from its statute.

[7] "The obligations of the CIA thus juridically bind the ICC. The ICC does not settle disputes through the CIA. This is excluded by Art. 2 of the Rules and is the specific task of the arbitrator or of the arbitral tribunal. Rather, it provides a structure allowing for arbitration proceedings which are efficient, that is, expected to be speedy; in accordance with the Rules; and enforceable.

[8] "Cubic maintains that the arbitration contract is invalid because it violates the distinction between the jurisdictional and the administrative function in an arbitration.

[9] "If it is important that the final award reflect the exact opinion of the arbitrator, the process of reaching such an award must essentially correspond to the common intention of the parties, which are master of their rights and of the manner in which they are exercised. In the present case, this common intention has clearly been to refer to the ICC Rules. Consequently, the parties cannot criticize the delimitation of the jurisdictional function of the arbitral tribunal under these Rules, nor [can they criticize] the role they agreed to assign to the CIA.

[10] "Although the CIA must be prudent under all circumstances and operate equitably to attain its goal, it is not proven that it has breached this obligation. Further, the communication of the draft award to the CIA is motivated by the parties' wish for efficiency and a desire to provide them with an enforceable award. There is no interference in the arbitrator's task or modification of the award, only an advice on the drafting [of the award].

[11] "Cubic alleges that the arbitration contract violates Art. 6 of the European Convention on Human Rights.[4] However, Cubic does not prove that its case was not heard within a reasonable time, taking into consideration the complexity of the case, by an impartial and independent tribunal. Moreover, the above-mentioned Convention of 4 November 1950, which has been signed by the governments of the members of the Council of Europe, binds the Contracting States, not an institution which is not a jurisdiction. Under these circumstances, the Court of First Instance correctly held that the arbitration contract was valid."

III. BREACH OF CONTRACT

[12] "A party to an agreement, be it also an arbitral institution, is liable if it fails [to perform] under its contractual obligations. In the present case, the ICC does not rely on an exclusion of liability clause such as the one included in its new Rules,[5] which were issued after the conclusion of the contract at issue; this exclusion, if valid, does not apply to the present dispute.

[13] "Cubic accuses the ICC of not having been diligent as to the duration of the arbitration, which lasted more than five years; of not having verified the nature of order no. 6; and of having refused to replace the arbitrators.

[14] "On the first ground, Cubic's complaint that the arbitration, which should have lasted six months, lasted five years does not suffice to make the ICC liable. Cubic has the burden of proving that the CIA of the ICC breached its contractual obligations by granting a particular extension as provided for in the Rules. Cubic does not formulate any specific critique on this issue; hence, this ground must fail. Moreover, it appears from the documents filed

---

4. Art. 6 of the 1950 Rome Convention on the Protection of Human Rights and Fundamental Freedoms reads in relevant part:

"In the determination of his civil rights and obligations or any criminal charge against him, everyone is entitled to a fair and public hearing within a reasonable time by an independent and impartial tribunal established by law...."

5. See Art. 34 of the 1998 ICC Rules.

at the hearings that the extensions, some of them granted at the request of Cubic, were justified by the complexity of the case and the need to guarantee a fair debate.

[15] "On the second ground, the qualification of order no. 6, Cubic does not indicate which provision would give the CIA the power to qualify an order rendered by the arbitrators. Neither Art. 21 of the Rules nor Art. 17 of the internal rules[6] authorize the CIA to substitute its opinion for that of the arbitral tribunal. Thus, the CIA could only ask the arbitrators, as it did on 19 June 1995, to verify whether the order was an award under the applicable law.

[16] "On the third ground, it is undisputed that the CIA refused to replace the arbitrators. Cubic does not prove in which way this refusal of the CIA was incorrect, when the common intention of the parties to the arbitration, expressed by accepting the ICC Rules, was that the CIA decide on such request, as it did on 17 May 1995, on the written applications of the parties to the arbitration, finally (Art. 2.13) and without giving reasons."

IV. EXTRA-CONTRACTUAL LIABILITY

[17] "Cubic maintains that it had no experience of ICC arbitration and that it was 'strongly urged to accept the ICC Rules under incorrect circumstances', that the ICC played on its reputation and took good care not to inform Cubic of the freedom it had to refuse the proposed [arbitration] contract or of the peculiarities of the Rules.

[18] "Even if Cubic were not accustomed to arbitration, which is doubtful considering its activity, we note that from the beginning it received the Rules and appendixes, a complete text which is sufficiently short and clear to be

6. Art. 21 of the 1988 Rules of Arbitration and Art. 17 of the 1988 Internal Rules read:

Article 21

"Before signing an award, whether partial or definitive, the arbitrator shall submit it in draft form to the Court. The Court may lay down modifications as to the form of the award and, without affecting the arbitrator's liberty of decision, may also draw his attention to points of substance. No award shall be signed until it has been approved by the Court as to its form."

Article 17

"When it scrutinizes draft arbitral awards in accordance with Article 21 of the ICC Rules of Arbitration, the Court of Arbitration pays particular attention to the respect of the formal requirements laid down by the law applicable to the proceedings and, where relevant, by the mandatory rules of the place of arbitration, notably with regard to the reasons for awards, their signature and the admissibility of dissenting opinions."

understood by any entrepreneur. From this text it appeared that Cubic could choose not to reply, which would result in the ICC not being seized. Moreover, Cubic's acceptance of an arbitration administered by the CIA was made through legal specialists, the law firm Arent Fox Mc Garrahan and Heard.

[19] "Cubic, which does not invoke [the ICC's] intention to deceive, does not prove that the ICC breached its obligation to inform. Its appeal based on extra-contractual liability must be denied."

Cour d'Appel [Court of Appeal], Paris, 19 June 1998

Parties:	Appellant: UNESCO – United Nations Educational, Scientific and Cultural Organisation, in the person of its legal representatives (France) Appellee: Max-Henri Boulois (France)
Published in:	Revue de l'arbitrage (1999, no. 2) pp. 343-345 with note Ch. Jarrosson, pp. 345-349
Subject matters:	– immunity from jurisdiction – *pacta sunt servanda* – European Convention on Human Rights (Art. 6)

Facts

On 21 June 1996, UNESCO and Mr. Boulois entered into a contract containing an arbitration clause.

On 20 October 1997, alleging the existence of a dispute relating to the performance of the contract, Mr. Boulois obtained an order in summary proceedings (*ordonnance de référé*) from the President of the Paris Court of First Instance directing UNESCO to appoint an arbitrator within fifteen days.

UNESCO appealed, maintaining that there was no dispute between the parties and relying on its immunity from jurisdiction based on Art. 12 of the France-UNESCO Agreement of 2 July 1954; it also argued that the President of the *Tribunal de Grande Instance* wrongly inferred a waiver of immunity from the existence of an arbitration clause in the contract with Mr. Boulois.

The Court of Appeal affirmed the decision of the President, reasoning that immunity from jurisdiction should not be a means to escape from the principle of *pacta sunt servanda*.

Excerpt

I. IMMUNITY FROM JURISDICTION

[1] "The immunity from jurisdiction on which UNESCO relies cannot allow it to escape from the principle of *pacta sunt servanda* by refusing to appoint an arbitrator according to the arbitration clause in the contract with

Max-Henri Boulois on the ground, which falls squarely under the sole appreciation of the arbitrators, that there is no dispute as to the performance of the said contract.

[2] "Further, granting appellant's request against Mr. Boulois would inevitably lead to preventing [Mr. Boulois] from bringing his case to a court. This situation would be contrary to public policy as it constitutes a denial of justice and a violation of the provisions of Art. 6(1) of the European Convention for the Protection of Human Rights and Fundamental Liberties; thus, the state court – which furthermore intervenes in the present case only as a supporting court (*juge d'appui*) – should grant the appellee's request.

[3] "For these reasons and the reasons given by the lower court, which this Court takes as its own, the attacked order shall be fully affirmed on this point."

II. INADMISSIBILITY OF THE APPEAL

[4] "In opposition to the order rendered by the President of the Paris Court of First Instance based on Art. 1444(1) of the New Code of Civil Procedure,[1] the appeal filed by UNESCO does not allege that the arbitration clause in ... the contract signed by the parties on 21 June 1996 is manifestly null or insufficient to allow for the constitution of the arbitral tribunal, and the appeal must be declared inadmissible according to Art. 1457(1) of the same Code."[2]

1. Art. 1444(1) of the French New Code of Civil Procedure reads:

"If, after the dispute has arisen, the constitution of the arbitral tribunal encounters a difficulty due to the acts of one of the parties or with respect to the functioning of the method of appointment, the President of the *Tribunal de Grande Instance* shall appoint the arbitrator or arbitrators."

2. Art. 1457(1) of the French New Code of Civil Procedure reads:

"In the cases covered by Arts. 1444, 1454, 1456 and 1463, the President of the court, seized as in urgent proceedings (*référé*) by a party or the arbitral tribunal, shall decide by non-appealable order."

Cour d'Appel [Court of Appeal], 1 July 1999

Parties:	Petitioner: Braspetro Oil Services Company – Brasoil (Cayman Islands) Respondent: The Management and Implementation Authority of the Great Man-Made River Project (Libya)
Published in:	14 Mealey's International Arbitration Report (1999, no. 8) pp. G-1 – G-7. Original in French
Subject matters:	– request to review partial award – qualification of award – scrutiny of award by ICC – due process – fraud

Facts

By a contract of 6 July 1986, Braspetro Oil Services Company (Brasoil) agreed to drill a number of wells in the Libyan desert for The Management and Implementation Authority of the Great Man-Made River Project (GMRA), a Libyan public entity. The contract was governed by Libyan administrative law and contained an ICC arbitration clause.

In 1990, the water was found to contain an excessive amount of sand and it was discovered that the walls of some wells had collapsed. Alleging that the wall containment structure was inadequate, GMRA terminated the contract, whereupon Brasoil commenced ICC arbitration.

By a partial award of 9 March 1995, the arbitral tribunal held that inadequate wall containment was the cause of the poor quality of the water and that Brasoil was consequently responsible for the malfunctioning of the wells. The tribunal postponed the quantification of the damages to a final award to be rendered after a second evidence-taking phase of the arbitration.

On 29 May 1997, during the second phase of the proceedings concerning the damages, GMRA submitted certain documents in the arbitration. Alleging that these documents had been fraudulently withheld and that they would have led the arbitrators to reach a different conclusion on liability, Brasoil requested the arbitrators to review (*recours en révision*) the partial award.

On 14 May 1998, the arbitral tribunal denied Brasoil's request by an "order" in which it held: (1) that a request for a review is governed by French law; (2) that according to French law the only reason for reviewing an award rendered in an international arbitration in France is fraud; (3) Brasoil would have to prove the existence of fraud for the request for review to be admissible; (4) that Brasoil did not prove that there had been fraud.

Brasoil sought to have this decision set aside. The Court of Appeal granted Brasoil's request, holding that, although it was qualified as an "order", the decision of the arbitrators was in fact an award and that the arbitrators had violated the applicable ICC Rules by not submitting the award to the scrutiny of the Court of Arbitration. The Court of Appeal also found that the arbitrators violated due process by allowing a misunderstanding on the contents of the oral hearing on the admissibility of the review and thereby depriving Brasoil of its right to present its case on the issue of the alleged fraud.

Excerpt

I. QUALIFICATION OF THE DECISION

[1] "The qualification of [a decision as an] award does not depend on the terms used by the arbitrators or by the parties. On 15 October 1997, Brasoil requested the arbitrators to review the partial award of 5 March 1995, alleging that GMRA had fraudulently withheld essential documents which it already had in its possession at the beginning of the arbitration and which could have affected the decision on who was responsible for the malfunctioning [of the wells], and that in any case these documents revealed an essential fact of which Brasoil was unaware through no fault of its own. GMRA maintained that the request was inadmissible and unfounded. The parties exchanged statements on this issue and were heard at the hearing of 19 December 1997 together with their 'respective experts'.

[2] "In the light of all these elements and after a five-month deliberation, the arbitral tribunal rendered the 'order' of 14 May 1998, by which, after a lengthy examination of the parties' positions, it declared that the request could not be granted because Brasoil had not proven that there had been fraud as alleged. This reasoned decision – by which the arbitrators considered the contradictory theories of the parties and examined in detail whether they were founded, and solved, in a final manner, the dispute between the parties concerning the admissibility of Brasoil's request for a review, by denying it and thereby ending the dispute submitted to them – appears to be an exercise of its jurisdictional power by the arbitral tribunal.

[3] "GMRA's objection that the 'order' at issue refuses to open an appellate instance and thus amounts to 'decisions on the administration of the proceedings' made by arbitral institutions to refuse commencement of an arbitration or joinder of a third party, is unfounded. Even if the similarity were perfect, the main reason for which the decisions of the ICC, whatever the nature of the problems they solve and the procedure followed, are not awards, is that they are not rendered by an arbitral tribunal, which clearly is not the case here.

[4] "Contrary to GMRA's opinion and notwithstanding its qualification as an 'order', the decision of 14 May 1998, which did not concern the evidence-taking in the arbitration, is thus indeed an award. Hence, Brasoil's request [to the Court of Appeal] is admissible."

II. SETTING ASIDE

[5] "Arts. 1504 and 1502 of the New Code of Civil Procedure provide that an arbitral award can be set aside if '3. the arbitrator has rendered his decision in accordance with the mandate conferred upon him' and '4. whenever due process has not been respected'. Brasoil maintains, inter alia, that the decision of 14 May 1998 should be set aside precisely on these two grounds. First, Brasoil maintains that since the decision was an award and not merely a procedural order, the arbitrators were bound under Arts. 21 and 23 of the ICC Arbitration Rules to submit it for a scrutiny by the International Court of Arbitration of the ICC before signing it and notifying it to the parties. By failing to comply with this prerequisite, the arbitral tribunal failed to comply with its mandate to render an award in conformity with the Arbitration Rules chosen by the parties. Second, Brasoil maintains that the arbitrators violated the fundamental right to defend oneself and the principle of contradictory proceedings [*principe de la contradiction*] as well as Art. 11 of the Arbitration Rules they were bound to apply, on the one hand by dismissing Brasoil's request for a review on the ground that GMRA's fraud was not proven while this issue had not been discussed in a contradictory debate and while Brasoil was not given the opportunity to prove it notwithstanding its requests and protests, and on the other hand, by dealing, though 'prima facie', with the merits of the dispute in violation of the agenda for the hearing, which they had agreed would be limited to the mere admissibility of the request [for a review]."

1. Failure to Comply with Mandate

[6] "As to the first ground, according to Art. 21 of the [1988] ICC Rules, to which the parties agreed to refer,

> 'Before signing an award, whether partial or definitive, the arbitrator shall submit it in draft form to the Court. The Court may lay down modifications as to the form of the award and, without affecting the arbitrator's liberty of decision, may also draw his attention to points of substance. No award shall be signed until it has been approved by the Court as to its form.'

According to Art. 23, the ICC Secretariat then notifies the award made under the above conditions to the parties. It is undisputed that in the present case the arbitrators did not submit their draft 'order' to the International Court of Arbitration and that the decision was notified to the parties without this scrutiny. Hence, an essential and characteristic requirement of the ICC Rules, which aims at guaranteeing to the parties, which refer thereto, the award's compliance with minimum formal and substantial requirements, and at ensuring that the parties obtain a decision in conformity with those Rules, has not been complied with and the arbitrators did not comply with their mandate.

[7] "GMRA maintains that Brasoil waived its right to rely on the irregularity it now invokes since it did not object immediately thereto, waited six months before filing a request for setting aside and refused the regularisation which it had suggested itself. However, a waiver can only be opposed to a party which knew of an irregularity of the arbitration during the arbitration itself and voluntarily did not raise an objection, leaving the proceedings to continue until the end. In the present case, Brasoil only knew of the arbitrators' mistake when the decision was rendered and notified to the parties, when its request for review had been denied and the arbitrators were no longer seized of the dispute they had decided. Thus, Brasoil cannot have waived a right to rely on an irregularity of which it was not aware before the decision. Also, no regularisation was possible once the 'order' had been rendered, as recognized even by the president of the arbitral tribunal in its letter of 29 January 1999 to the lawyers of the parties. Hence, GMRA may not maintain that Brasoil has no right to invoke the arbitrators' failure to comply with the Arbitration Rules. The fact of waiting before filing an action [for setting aside] does not prove an intention to waive the right thereto.

[8] "Hence, the decision of 14 May 1998 must be set aside on this first ground."

2. *Lack of Due Process*

[9] "As to the second ground, the arbitrators must respect the equality of parties and the principle of contradictory proceedings. They must allow each party to present its case on issues of fact and law, to know the case of its adversary and to discuss it.

[10] "On 15 October 1997, Brasoil requested the arbitral tribunal to review the partial award of 9 March 1995, stating:

> 'To sum up: it is undoubted that an international arbitral tribunal, including an ICC tribunal, has the intrinsic power to review its decision if new facts of fundamental importance are discovered before the tribunal becomes functus officio, on the condition that the party could not reasonably obtain that evidence in time. The fraud, including the withholding of documents or other evidence, is a "new fact" in the sense of a review. A new fact is "decisive" if, "when added to the other, previously examined facts of the case it seriously tips the scales and consequently modifies the conclusions reached by the tribunal". Since this power to review is inherent to the power of the tribunal to determine its own procedures, it has not been expressly mentioned in the terms of reference or in the constitution of the tribunal. The power to review has long been recognized as confirming rather than contradicting the principle of finality.'

[11] "In two accompanying letters of the same day, Brasoil requested the arbitral tribunal to admit its request and 'that the question of a review be debated in a hearing on the merits ...'. GMRA was given time until 31 October to comment 'as to the admissibility and as to the merits' (letter of the arbitral tribunal of 17 October) and requested a postponement until 14 November 1997 because it needed 'to oppose an appropriate defense to the request'. GMRA obtained this postponement but it was only on 18 November 1997 that it finally submitted a statement in reply of more than 500 pages, in which it maintained in particular that proof of fraud was necessary for the admissibility of the review request and that in casu that proof had not been supplied. On 19 November, Brasoil objected to the admissibility of this statement and replied to it by a note of two pages essentially addressing the issue of admissibility and the issue of whether admissibility implied the proof of the alleged fraud or whether it was sufficient that the claimant establish 'prima facie that the discovery of new decisive facts is founded'. The note also repeated Brasoil's request for a hearing to 'decide on the admissibility of its request for a review', and, in case the request be admitted, 'to determine the procedure to be subse-

quently followed'. By an order of 20 November 1997, the arbitral tribunal decided to allow GMRA's statement in reply, although it had been submitted late, and granted Brasoil a time limit until 21 November 1997 to reply thereto. It also announced that no further statement would be accepted after that date. On 21 November, GMRA [rectius Brasoil] replied succinctly on the issue of admissibility. Last, on 27 November 1997, the arbitral tribunal fixed the date for the hearing on the review request on 1 December and stated:

> 'This hearing will be limited to the admissibility in principle of the request of the Claimant, including the power of the Tribunal to decide on that request in the light of Art. 1491 of the New Code of Civil Procedure or otherwise'.[1]

[12] "During the hearing, which was eventually held on 19 December 1997, the president of the arbitral tribunal informed the parties that they were to discuss the existence or non-existence of fraud as a condition for admissibility. GMRA, which had explained its position on this issue in its statement of 18 November referred thereto, whereas Brasoil protested, alleging that it had been misled as to the meaning of admissibility, and requested immediately, as well as later by a pleading note of 9 January 1998, that the discussion be re-opened to allow it to make a statement on the proof of fraud and to reply on this point to the long statement submitted by GMRA only three days before the closing of the evidence-taking phase. However, considering that the two parties had had 'the occasion to present their case on the issue of admissibility, both in their written statements and at the hearing of December 1997', and that 'the principle of contradictory proceedings has been complied with', the arbitral tribunal decided to render a decision as the case stood (order of 17 March 1998). It is under these conditions that it declared the request for review inadmissible because Brasoil had failed to prove the alleged fraud.

[13] "It ensues from the above that, although GMRA was invited to make a statement 'on the merits' and the arbitral tribunal never clearly excluded the proof of the alleged fraud from the agenda of the review hearing, the tribunal allowed to say the least an ambiguity to exist. The tribunal announced on 27 November 1997 that the hearing would be limited to the 'admissibility in

1. Art. 1491 NCCP reads:

> "A motion to revise the arbitral award may be brought in the same cases and under the same conditions as those that apply to court judgments.
>
> Such a motion is to be brought before the Court of Appeal which would have had jurisdiction with respect to the other means of recourse against the award."

principle' of the request for a review, that the pleadings would be limited to one hour each and that the decision would be handed down the same day, from which it could legitimately be inferred, in the absence of a clarification, that the hearing, as requested by Brasoil, would exclusively aim at defining the juridical framework of the means of recourse and the rules applicable to it, which still had to be determined, in particular as to the scope of the proof of fraud, on which scope the parties fundamentally disagreed. [However], the tribunal eventually chose to pass onto the next step by discussing the existence of the alleged fraud.

[14] "Although Brasoil had discussed this issue in its initial request, it had not further developed its position on this point and had not endeavoured to supply proof of its allegations. Since the hearing was to be limited, as indicated by the arbitral tribunal itself, 'to the admissibility in principle' of its request, Brasoil also had not deemed it necessary to reply to the very long statement submitted on the issue by GMRA only three days before expiry nor did it try to obtain a further postponement to do so.

[15] "The arbitrators did not dispel this evident misunderstanding by clearly stating to the parties what they meant by 'admissibility in principle'. [By so doing] and by deciding under these conditions without even ordering a re-opening of the discussion the arbitrators violated the principle of contradictory proceedings and due process.

[16] "GMRA again objects that by not immediately objecting to the order of 17 March 1998 Brasoil waived its right to rely on this irregularity. However, it is precisely because Brasoil protested against what it believed was a violation of its fundamental rights that the order of 17 March 1998 was rendered, and it is hard to imagine what Brasoil could have done other than commencing an action for setting aside before the Court of Appeal as it has done.

[17] "It ensues that also the second ground for setting aside is founded and that the 'decision' of 14 May 1998 must be set aside on this ground as well."

GERMANY

Oberlandesgericht [Court of Appeal], Düsseldorf, 18 July 1997

Parties:	Claimant: Not indicated Defendants/appellees: Not indicated
Published in:	Rechtsprechung Kaufmännischer Schiedsgerichte, Vol. 6 (in preparation), A 1 no. 96; Recht der internationalen Wirtschaft (1998) p. 967
Subject matters:	- effect of foreign "administration order" - applicable law inadmissible - existence of arbitration agreement - no review on merits in enforcement under Brussels Convention 1968

Facts

The parties were involved in court proceedings in Germany concerning the sale of shares. The party which had prevailed in the German proceedings sought enforcement of the German court decision in its favour in England. The German decision had denied the defendants' request to refer the dispute to arbitration, finding that the arbitration agreement between the parties was invalid.

The present proceedings concern the claimant's request to the German court to determine that the defendants may not rely on the arbitration agreement in the English enforcement proceedings.

The Court of Appeal held that under the Brussels Convention the decision on an alleged ground for refusal of enforcement belongs to the enforcement court, in casu the English High Court, and that "[i]t would be an unacceptable intrusion in these proceedings if a German court decided by a binding decision on the merits of a means of defence raised" in the enforcement proceedings. The Court also noted that it was unlikely that the defendants' objection would be granted as according to Art. 34(3) of the Brussels Convention the enforcement court may not review the merits of the foreign judgment.

In the first part of the decision, the Court of Appeal held that it could proceed against one of the defendants although an administration order had been issued in England against that defendant's assets. The Court held that an administration order is not a bankruptcy in the sense of German law and that in any case foreign bankruptcy proceedings, unlike German proceedings, do not suspend proceedings before a German court.

Excerpt

I. FOREIGN BANKRUPTCY PROCEEDINGS

[1] "These appellate proceedings ... against the first defendant are admissible. Although an 'administration order' has been issued against [the first defendant's] assets in England, this does not lead to a suspension of the proceedings [in Germany] according to Sect. 240 ZPO.[1] The Supreme Court has held that German proceedings against a foreigner (passive participation [in court proceedings]) whose assets are the object of bankruptcy proceedings abroad are not to be suspended (BGH NJW 1988, 3096; see also ZIP 1988, 247; in agreement: Hartmann, BLAH, ZPO, 55th ed., Sect. 240 note 2 and references therein).

[2] "Even if we did not follow this opinion and applied Sect. 240 ZPO in the presence of foreign bankruptcy proceedings (see Zöller-Greger, ZPO, 20th ed., Sect. 240 note 1 and references therein; in the case of an active participation in the proceedings: OLG Düsseldorf, OLGR 1994, 305 and references therein), still the proceedings against defendant would not be suspended, since the recognition of a foreign bankruptcy in Germany presupposes that the foreign insolvency proceedings are bankruptcy proceedings according to domestic criteria (BGHZ 95, 256, 270). This is not the case of the English 'administration order', a proceedings which solves liquidity difficulties by paying [creditors] proportionally and enables the enterprise to continue its activity. In that it is essentially different from German bankruptcy proceedings, which aims at a forced liquidation of the assets of the debtor (see Summ, *Anerkennung ausländischer Konkurse in der BDR*, pp. 31-32 and 114-115)."

(....)

---

1. Sect. 240 of the German Code of Civil Procedure (ZPO) reads:

   "If bankruptcy proceedings are commenced against the assets of a party, the action shall be suspended, if it concerns the estate of the bankrupt, until it can be resumed according to the provisions applicable to bankruptcy or until the bankruptcy proceedings are terminated."

II. APPLICABILITY OF GERMAN LAW

[3] "The claimant requests [the court] to find that only German law applies to the legal relationship between the parties, which concerns a speculation in shares. The Court of First Instance rightly denied the admissibility of this request.

[4] "A request for a determination according to Sect. 256 ZPO[2] can only concern the determination of a legal relationship, not the determination of preliminary questions or elements of a legal relationship (BGH NJW-RR 1992, 252; OLG Munich NJW-RR 1995, 485; Hartmann, BLAH, ZPO, 55th ed., Sect. 256 note 6). The determination requested by the claimant concerns a preliminary question of law. It does not matter that the claimant maintains that this is an interim request for determination according to Sect. 256(2) ZPO. Such request too can only concern the determination of a legal relationship, not the settlement of preliminary questions relating thereto (see BGH NJW 1982, 1879 and references therein). The determination of which legal system applies, requested [by the claimant], does not aim at determining the legal relationship of the parties but at answering the preliminary question of which legal provisions apply to their legal relationship."

III. OBJECTION BASED ON THE EXISTENCE OF AN ARBITRATION AGREEMENT

[5] "The claimant requests [the Court] to hold that the first and second defendant may not rely on the arbitration agreement concluded [by the parties]. It is not quite clear from the wording of its claim whether the claimant requests [the Court] to find that the first and second defendant may not in principle raise the objection based on the arbitration agreement or that

2. Sect. 256 ZPO reads:

"(1) An action for the determination of the (non)existence of a legal relationship or for the recognition of a document or the determination that it is false may be brought if the claimant has a legitimate interest in the judicial determination of the legal relationship or of the authenticity or falsity of the document.
(2) Before the end of the oral hearing at which judgment is rendered, [both] the claimant, by amending its statement of claim, and the defendant, by raising a counterclaim, may request that a legal relationship which became the subject of a dispute during the proceedings, and upon the (non)existence of which the decision wholly or partly depends, be determined judicially."

they cannot do so successfully because the objection is unfounded. In both cases the request cannot be granted.

[6] "The finding that an objection based on an arbitration agreement, raised in English enforcement proceedings, is unfounded on the merits is a preliminary question to be answered in the English proceedings according to Art. 31 et seq. of the EC Convention on Jurisdiction and the Enforcement of Judgments in Civil and Commercial Matters [EEX]. As held above, a preliminary question may not be the subject matter of a request for determination. Apart from that, the decision on the objection must be left to the competent English court of enforcement (the High Court of Justice, according to Art. 32 EEX), which must conduct the proceedings according to Art. 31 et seq. EEX at the request of the claimant and order the registration of the judgment which is necessary for enforcement according to Art. 31(2) EEX.[3] It would be an unacceptable intrusion in these proceedings if a German court decided by a binding decision on the merits of a means of defence raised therein.

[7] "In any case, we do not see how an objection based on the existence of an arbitration agreement, raised in enforcement proceedings under Art. 31 et seq. EEX, could hinder the registration of the judgment, as the English court seized [of the dispute] must take into account the provision of Art. 34(3) EEX, according to which a foreign judgment may in no case be reviewed on the merits.[4] This also applies to the case where an objection based on an arbitration agreement was not granted in the foreign judgment to be enforced (see Geimer, Geimer-Schütze, *Internationale Urteilsanerkennung*, I, pp. 47-49).

[8] "Hence, the English court does not need to ascertain whether the objection based on the arbitration agreement ought to have hindered the passing of the judgment in Germany. Under the circumstances it cannot be feared that the English court will deny registration of the judgment on the ground that the arbitration agreement, contrary to the opinion of the German courts, is valid. This would be different if there were known cases in which the English courts, in violation of Art. 34(3) EEX, had denied [registration to]

3. Art. 31 EEX reads in relevant part:

"A judgment given in a Contracting State and enforceable in that State shall be enforced in another Contracting State when, on the application of any interested party, it has been declared enforceable there.
(....)"

4. Art. 34(3) EEX reads:

"Under no circumstances may the foreign judgment be reviewed as to its substance."

a foreign judgment on the ground that there was a valid arbitration agreement and, therefore, the judgment could not be enforced as it was based on a defective basis. Such a case has apparently not occurred until now. The defendants maintain ... that the High Court recognized in parallel proceedings [the existence of] the arbitration agreement at issue. This, however, is not the same, because at the time there was not yet a binding decision of a German court, on whose registration [the English court] had to decide according to Arts. 31 and 34(3) EEX. As long as this does not happen, we must start from the premise that the English courts will not, in proceedings according to Art. 31 EEX, override the provision of Art. 34(3) EEX and will order the registration required for enforcement.

[9] "The claimant requests [the Court] to find that the first and second defendant may not raise the objection based on the arbitration agreement in the English enforcement proceedings. On the grounds mentioned above, this request cannot be granted. If the validity of the arbitration agreement is irrelevant in the English enforcement proceedings in the light of Art. 34(3) EEX, then the claimant does not have a legal interest in preventing the first and second defendant from raising an objection based thereon.

[10] "Apart from that, in order to find that the first and second defendant may not raise an objection based on an arbitration agreement in the English enforcement proceedings we should presuppose that the claimant has a right to exclude this objection, which right it does not have. A party in civil proceedings does not have, in principle, the right to exclude submissions in defence made by the other party. Whether the facts on which these submissions are based are true or relevant, it is up to the court seized [of the dispute] to decide. A different opinion would mean an inadmissible intervention in other proceedings.

[11] "There is generally no interest in such right [of exclusion] (see BGH ZIP 1987, 1081, 1083; BGH VersR 1991, 435, 436; VersR 1992, 443; Palandt-Thomas, BGB, 56th ed., Sect. 823 note 21). This is also true for a request to exclude submissions in future proceedings (see BGH NJW 1977, 1681, 1682; VersR 1992, 443, 444). The first and second defendant cannot simply be prohibited from submitting a certain means of defence in enforcement proceedings to be conducted in England. It is true that the claimant affirms that it does not wish to deny the defendants their common procedural rights. Yet, a determination that the first and second defendant may not rely on the objection based on the arbitration agreement would in fact lead to that.

[12] "The claimant could at best request that the objection based on the arbitration agreement be disregarded if raising it would violate public policy

(Sect. 1004 Civil Code together with Sect. 826 Civil Code).[5] However, we cannot assume that. The first and second defendant would only, by their arbitration objection, repeat the opinion they already expressed in the [German] proceedings, which cannot be denied to them. The mere fact that [the objection] aims at avoiding or delaying enforcement by the claimant does not make raising it a violation of public policy.

[13] "Further, we must take into account that the English courts apparently hold the arbitration agreement to be valid. It cannot be deemed to be a violation of public policy that the first and second defendant share this favourable opinion and rely on it in the English enforcement proceedings, though, in the light of Art. 34(3) EEX, with no apparent hope of success."

---

5. Sect. 1004 of the German Civil Code reads:

"(1) If ownership is interfered with otherwise than by dispossession or withholding, the owner may demand from the disturber that the interference be removed. If further interference is expected, the owner may request an injunction.
(2) This claim is excluded where the owner is obliged to tolerate the interference."

Sect. 826 of the German Civil Code reads:

"A person who intentionally causes damage to another in violation of public policy shall compensate the other for the damage."

INDIA

Supreme Court of India, 13 January 1999, Civil Appeal Nos. 141-143 of 1999

Parties:	Appellant: Sundaram Finance Ltd. (nationality not indicated) Respondent: NEPC India Ltd. (nationality not indicated)
Published in:	Arbitration Law Reporter (1999, no. 1) pp. 305-314
Subject matter:	– availability of interim measures before commencement of arbitration

Facts

NEPC India Ltd. (NEPC) entered into a hire-purchase agreement with Sundaram Finance Ltd. (Sundaram) for the supply of two wind-turbine generators. The agreement provided for payment by instalments and contained an arbitration clause. After making a number of payments, NEPC defaulted on the payments and Sundaram filed an application under Sect. 9 of the Indian Arbitration and Conciliation Act, 1996, before the City Trial Court, Chennai, seeking the appointment of an Advocate Commissioner to take custody of the generators and to return them to it. This request was granted by the court.

NEPC appealed under Art. 227 of the Constitution to the High Court at Madras where it argued that an action for interim relief was not maintainable as there was no arbitration proceeding pending, nor had an arbitrator been appointed. On 22 June 1998, the High Court allowed the appeal. In its judgment, after referring to Sect. 41 of the Arbitration Act, 1940 and the relevant provisions of the 1996 Act, the High Court observed:

> "Second Schedule to the 1940 Act is the powers of the Court and item No. 4 is 'interim injunction or the appointment of a receiver'. Therefore, there is no virtual difference between Sect. 41 read with Schedule 2 and present Sect. 9 of the Arbitration Act. Moreover, if an interpretation such as the one contended by the Learned Counsel for the appellant is

> to be given to Sect. 9 the very object of the Act would be defeated. Any party, who has an agreement for arbitration with another can rush to Civil Court and straight away get an order under Sect. 9 and thereafter keep quiet without referring the matter to Arbitration. That will have a very serious consequence on the provisions of the Act. It could not have been the intention of the legislature in enacting the present Arbitration Act. Further, the very fact that Sect. 9 comes after Sect. 8 which deals with the reference of disputes to Arbitration, the only interpretation that could be given to Sect. 9 is that it could be availed of when an arbitration proceeding is pending before the Arbitral Tribunal or is at the reference stage before the Court or after the Arbitral award has been made."

On appeal by special leave, the Supreme Court of India, per Sujata V. Manohar and B.N. Kirpal, JJ, held that the court has jurisdiction to entertain an application for interim measures under Sect. 9 of the Arbitration and Conciliation Act 1996 either before or during arbitral proceedings, or after the making of the award.

Excerpt

[1] "Under the provisions of the Arbitration Act, 1940, the powers of the Court to pass interim orders were derived from Sect. 41(b) read with 2nd Schedule to the Arbitration Act, 1940. Mr. Gopal Subramaniam, learned senior counsel appearing for the respondent, places reliance on *Sant Ram & Co. v. State of Rajasthan and others*,[1] wherein at page 150, it was observed that 'The initiation of pendency of any proceedings in the Court in relation to the arbitration proceedings would, therefore, be a precondition for the exercise of the power by the Civil Court under the Second Schedule of the Act'. Even if this be the position under the 1940 Act we still have to examine whether there has been any change in the law with the promulgation of the Arbitration and Conciliation Act, 1996.

[2] "Prior to the promulgation of the 1996 Act the law on arbitration in India was substantially contained in three enactments, namely: The Arbitration Act, 1940, the Arbitration (Protocol and Convention) Act, 1937 and the Foreign Awards (Recognition and Enforcement Act, 1961. In the Statement of Objects and Reasons appended to the Bill it was stated that the 1940 Act, which contained the general law of arbitration, had become outdated. The said

---

1. "(1997) 1 SCC 147 = 1997(1) Arb. LR 209."

objects and reasons noticed that the United Nations Commission on International Trade Law [UNCITRAL] adopted in 1985 the Model Law on International Commercial Arbitration.... '... The present Bill seeks to consolidate and amend the law relating to domestic arbitration, international commercial arbitration, enforcement of foreign arbitral awards and to define the law relating to conciliation taking into account the said UNCITRAL Model Law and Rules.'

[3] "The 1996 Act is very different from the Arbitration Act, 1940. The provisions of this Act have, therefore to be interpreted and construed independently and in fact reference to the 1940 Act may actually lead to misconduction. In other words the provisions of the 1996 Act have to be interpreted as being uninfluenced by the principles underlying the 1940 Act. In order to get help in construing these provisions it is more relevant to refer to the UNCITRAL Model Law rather than the 1940 Act.

[4] "Some of the provisions of the 1996 Act which are relevant in the present case are Sects. 2(*d*), 9, 17 and Sect. 21. Sect. 2(*d*) defines an Arbitral Tribunal to mean a sole arbitrator or a panel of arbitrators. Sect. 9 of the 1996 Act, which gives power to the Court to pass interim orders, and with the interpretation of which we are concerned in the present case, reads thus:

> **'9. Interim measures by a Court**
> A party may, before or during arbitral proceedings or at any time after the making of the arbitral award but before it is enforced in accordance with Section 36, apply to a court: –
> ...;
> (ii) for an interim measure of protection in respect of any of the following matters, namely: –
>
> (a) the preservation, interim custody or sale of any goods which are the subject-matter of the arbitration agreement;
> (b) securing the amount in dispute in the arbitration;
> (c) the detention, preservation or inspection of any property or thing which is the subject-matter of the dispute in arbitration, or as to which any question may arise therein and authorising for any of the aforesaid purposes any person to enter upon any land or building in the possession of any party, or authorising any samples to be taken or any observation to be made, or experiment to be tried, which may be necessary or expedient for the purpose of obtaining full information or evidence;
> (d) interim injunction or the appointment of a receiver;

(e) such other interim measure of protection as may appear to the court to be just and convenient,

and the Court shall have the same power for making orders as it has for the purpose of, and in relation to, any proceedings before it.'

[5] "As this section refers to 'Arbitral Tribunal' the same has to be read along with Sect. 21 which relates to the commencement of the arbitral proceedings....[2] The Arbitral Tribunal has also been given jurisdiction to pass interim orders by Sect. 17 of the said Act....[3]

[6] "The reading of Sect. 21 clearly shows that the arbitral proceedings commence on the date on which a request for a dispute to be referred to arbitration is received by the respondent. It is in this context that we have to examine and interpret the expression 'before or during arbitral proceedings' occurring in Sect. 9 of the 1996 Act. We may here observe that though Sect. 17 gives the arbitral tribunal the power to pass orders the same cannot be enforced as orders of a Court. It is for this reason that Sect. 9 admittedly gives the Court power to pass interim orders during the arbitration proceedings.

[7] "The position under the Arbitration Act, 1940 was that a party could commence proceedings in Court by moving an application under Sect. 20 for appointment of an arbitrator[4] and simultaneously it could move an application

---

2. Sect. 21 of the Arbitration and Conciliation Act 1996 reads:

"Unless otherwise agreed by the parties, the arbitral proceedings in respect of a particular dispute commence on the date on which a request for that dispute to be referred to arbitration is received by the respondent."

3. Sect. 17 of the Arbitration and Conciliation Act, 1996 reads:

"(*1*) Unless otherwise agreed by the parties, the arbitral tribunal may, at the request of a party, order a party to take any interim measure of protection as the arbitral tribunal may consider necessary in respect of the subject-matter of the dispute.
(*2*) The arbitral tribunal may require a party to provide appropriate security in connection with a measure ordered under sub-section (*1*)."

4. Sect. 20 of the Arbitration Act, 1940 read in relevant part:

"(1) Where any persons have entered into an arbitration agreement before the institution of any suit with respect to the subject-matter of the agreement or any part of it, and where a difference has arisen to which the agreement applies, they or any of them, instead of proceeding under Chapter II, may apply to a Court having jurisdiction in the matter to which the agreement relates, that the agreement be filed in Court.
(....)

for interim relief under the Second Schedule read with Sect. 41(*b*) of the 1940 Act.[5] The 1996 Act does not contain a provision similar to Sect. 20 of the 1940 Act. Nor is Sect. 9 or Sect. 17 similar to Sect. 41(*b*) and the Second Schedule to the 1940 Act. Sect. 8 of the new Act[6] is not in pari materia with Sect. 20 of the 1940 Act. It is only if in an action which is pending before the Court that a party applies that the matter is the subject of an arbitration agreement does the Court get jurisdiction to refer the parties to arbitration. The said provision does not contemplate, unlike Sect. 20 of the 1940 Act, a party applying to a Court for appointing an arbitrator when no matter is pending before the Court. Under the 1996 Act appointment of arbitrator(s) is made as per the provision of Sect. 11 which does not require the Court to pass a judicial order appointing arbitrator(s). The High Court was, therefore wrong in referring to these provisions of the 1940 Act while interpreting Sect. 9 of the new Act.

[8] "Under the 1996 Act the Court can pass interim orders under Sect. 9. Arbitral proceedings, as we have seen, commence only when the request to refer the dispute is received by the respondent as per Sect. 21 of the Act. The material words occurring in Sect. 9 are 'before or during the arbitral proceedings'. This clearly contemplates two stages when the Court can pass [an] interim order, i.e., during the arbitral proceedings or before the arbitral proceedings. There is no reason as to why Sect. 9 of the 1996 Act should not be literally construed. Meaning has to be given to the word 'before' occurring

---

(4) Where no sufficient cause is shown, the Court shall order the agreement to be filed, and shall make an order of reference to the arbitrator appointed by the parties whether in the agreement or otherwise, or, where the parties cannot agree upon an arbitrator, to an arbitrator appointed by the Court.
(....)"

5. Sect. 41(*b*) of the Arbitration Act, 1940 read:

"the Court shall have, for the purpose of, and in relation to, arbitration proceedings, the same power of making orders in respect of any of the matters set out in the Second Schedule as it has for the purpose of, and in relation to, any proceedings before the Court;"

The Second Schedule defines the powers of the Court, inter alia, with respect to the taking of interim measures.

6. Sect. 8 of the Arbitration and Conciliation Act, 1996 reads in relevant part:

"(1) A judicial authority before which an action is brought in a matter which is the subject of an arbitration agreement shall, if a party so applies not later than when submitting his first statement on the substance of the dispute, refer the parties to arbitration.
(....)"

in the said section. The only interpretation that can be given is that the Court can pass interim orders before the commencement of arbitral proceedings. Any other interpretation, like the one given by the High Court, will have the effect of rendering the word 'before' in Sect. 9 as redundant. This is clearly not permissible. Not only does the language warrant such an interpretation but it was necessary to have such a provision in the interest of justice. But for such a provision no party would have a right to apply for interim measure before notice under Sect. 21 is received by the respondent. It is not unknown when it becomes difficult to serve the respondents. It was, therefore, necessary that provision was made in the Act which could enable a party to get interim relief urgently in order to protect its interest. Reading the section as a whole it appears to us that the court has jurisdiction to entertain an application under Sect. 9 either before arbitral proceedings or during arbitral proceedings or after the making of the arbitral award but before it is enforced in accordance with Sect. 36 of the Act.

[9] "Sect. 9 of the said Act corresponds to Art. 9 of the UNCITRAL Model Law which is as follows:

> 'It is not incompatible with an arbitration agreement for a party to request, before or during arbitral proceedings, from a court an interim measure of protection and for a court to grant such measure.'

This article recognises, just like Sect. 9 of the 1996 Act, a request being made before a Court for an interim measure of protection before arbitral proceedings. It is possible that in some countries if a party went to the Court seeking interim measures of protection that might be construed under the local law as meaning that the said party had waived its right to take recourse to arbitration. Art. 9 of the UNCITRAL Model Law seeks to clarify that merely because a party to an arbitration agreement requests the court for an interim measure 'before or during arbitral proceedings' such recourse would not be regarded as being incompatible with an arbitration agreement. To put it differently the arbitration proceedings can commence and continue notwithstanding a party to the arbitration agreement having approached the Court for an order for interim protection. The language of Sect. 9 of the 1996 Act is not identical to Art. 9 of the UNCITRAL Model Law and the expression 'before or during arbitral proceedings' used in Sect. 9 of the 1996 Act seems to have been inserted with a view to give it the same meaning as those words have in Art. 9 of the UNCITRAL Model Law. It is clear, therefore, that a party to an arbitration agreement can approach the Court for interim relief not only during the arbitral proceedings but even before the arbitral proceedings.

To that extent Sect. 9 of the 1996 Act is similar to Art. 9 of the UNCITRAL Model Law."

[10] The court referred to Sect. 44 of the English Arbitration Act 1996 and the case of *The Channel Tunnel Group Ltd. and France Manche S.A. v. Balfour Beatty Construction Ltd. and others*[7] as being in conformity with the view that the court is allowed to grant interim relief before the commencement of arbitral proceedings. It then continued:

[11] "It was submitted by Mr. Subramaniam that even if the Court can exercise jurisdiction under Sect. 9 before the arbitral proceedings have commenced the party seeking to invoke Sect. 9 must express a manifest intention to arbitrate. The learned counsel submitted that this intention can take the following forms:

> (a) In an application under Sect. 9, the party would have to state that it unequivocally relies on the arbitration agreement and makes an averment that it would invoke the arbitration clause;
> (b) At the time when the Court passes an interim order under Sect. 9, an express undertaking is given by the party before the Court that it would invoke the arbitration clause forthwith and within a fixed period; and
> (c) A notice invoking [the] arbitration clause should have been issued to the opposite party. It was contended that mere filing of an application under Sect. 9 was not sufficient to establish manifest intention to this extent.

[12] "When a party applies under Sect. 9 of the 1996 Act it is implicit that it accepts that there is a final and binding arbitration agreement in existence. It is also implicit hat a dispute must have arisen which is referable to the arbitral tribunal. Sect. 9 further contemplates arbitration proceedings taking place between the parties. Mr. Subramaniam is, therefore, right in submitting that when an application under Sect. 9 is filed before the commencement of the arbitral proceedings there has to be manifest intention on the part of the applicant to take recourse to the arbitral proceedings if, at the time when the application under Sect. 9 is filed, the proceedings have not commenced under Sect. 21 of the 1996 Act. In order to give full effect to the words 'before or during arbitral proceedings' occurring in Sect. 9 it would not be necessary that a notice invoking the arbitration clause must be issued to the opposite party before an application under Sect. 9 can be filed. The issuance of a notice may, in a given case, be sufficient to establish the manifest intention to have the dispute referred to [an] arbitral tribunal, but a situation may so demand that

7. "1992(2) Lloyd's Law Reports."

a party may choose to apply under Sect. 9 for an interim measure even before issuing a notice contemplated by Sect. 21 of the said Act. If an application is so made the Court will first have to be satisfied that there exists a valid arbitration agreement and the applicant intends to take the dispute to arbitration. Once it is so satisfied the Court will have the jurisdiction to pass orders under Sect. 9 giving such interim protection as the facts and circumstances warrant. While passing such an order and in order to ensure that effective steps are taken to commence the arbitral proceedings, the Court while exercising jurisdiction under Sect. 9 can pass [a] conditional order to put the applicant to such terms as it may deem fit with a view to see that effective steps are taken by the applicant for commencing the arbitral proceedings. What is apparent, however, is that the Court is not debarred from dealing with an application under Sect. 9 merely because no notice has been issued under Sect. 21 of the 1996 Act.

(....)

[13] "In view of the aforesaid discussions it follows that the High Court erred in coming to the conclusion that the Trial Court had no jurisdiction in entertaining the application under Sect. 9 because arbitration proceedings had not been initiated by the appellant."

[14] The Court further recommended that the High Court exercise its power to make rules to deal with the procedure to be followed by the Courts when exercising jurisdiction under Sect. 9 of the Act.

SWEDEN

Swedish Supreme Court, 15 October 1997, Case no. Ö 3174/95

Parties:	Claimant: *MS "EMJA"* Braack Schiffahrts KG (Germany) Defendant: Wärtsilä Diesel Aktiebolag (Sweden)
Published in:	Nytt Juridiskt Arkiv (1997) p. 866 et seq.
Subject matter:	– assignment of arbitration clause

Facts

The Dutch shipyard, Scheepswerf Ferus Smit BV (Ferus), contracted on 22 February 1989 with Sand Firden BV, also a Dutch company, for the construction of a ship which would ultimately be named the *MS EMJA*. On 30 January 1990, the German shipping company Emja, purchased the ship during the course of its construction, acquiring Firden's rights and obligations under the shipbuilding contract.

Ferus sub-contracted with another shipyard, Scheepswerf Bijlsma BV (Bijlsma), for the construction of the ship. Bijlsma contracted on 8 February 1990 with Wärtsilä Diesel Aktiebolag (Wärtsilä) for the delivery of the Emja's diesel engines. This contract referred to the ECE 188 standard conditions and to the Marine Equipment Addendum 1987, and for services of technical personnel, to the General Conditions TP 73 E, both of which contain an arbitration clause. Both clauses provide for the application of Swedish law.

After delivery of the ship in 1991, problems arose with the diesel engine. In order to enable Emja to bring a claim against Wärtsilä, both Ferus and Bijlsma assigned to Emja all rights which they had with respect to Wärtsilä regarding the engine. The assignment was embodied in a written document entitled "Deed of Transfer of Assignment", dated 1 and 16 December 1993.

Relying on the Deed of Transfer of Assignment, Emja instituted proceedings against Wärtsilä at the Court of First Instance of Trollhättan regarding the defects in the engine. The Trollhätten court and the Court of Appeal for Western Sweden both ruled that they lacked jurisdiction and that the dispute should be referred to arbitration.

On appeal the Swedish Supreme Court examined the question of the assignment of the arbitration agreement, holding in general that the "remaining party" should be bound by the arbitration agreement, unless there were "particular reasons" why it should not be. In casu, there were no such reasons and Emja was bound by the arbitration agreement.

Excerpt

[1] "The question at issue, whether and to what extent an arbitration clause binds a third party, is a very controverted question. It must generally be accepted that where a change in parties has taken place by a universal assignment, the universal successor is bound by the arbitration clause, except regarding questions relating to real property rights (cf. Håstad in *Process och exekution*, Vänbok till Robert Boman, p. 177 et seq.)

[2] "Here, however, it is a question of a singular assignment. The law is not very clear on this question (Report of the Governmental Expert Committee on Arbitration relative to the new law on arbitration procedure. SOU 1994:81, p. 91 et seq.). There are no statutes and the doctrine is divided.

[3] "The debate has focussed primarily on the question of whether the assignee is bound by the arbitral clause. It appears, according to the prevailing doctrine, that that is the case, provided the assignee knew, or should have known of the arbitral clause (Cf. Dillén, Bidrag till läran om skiljeavtalet (1933) p. 245 et seq.; Edlund, Svensk Juristtidning (1993) p. 905 et seq.; Hassler-Cars, 'Skiljeförfarande', 2nd edition (1989) p. 45 et seq.; Hobér, Swedish and International Arbitration (1983) p. 43 et seq.; Håstad, see the reference above; and Welamson, Lindskog and Nowotny in the arbitral award of 5 March 1997 reported in Mealey's International Arbitration Report (March 1997) p. 3;[1] compare however, Heuman, *Festskrift för Sveriges Advokatsamfund* (1987) p. 229; Heuman, *Current Issues in Swedish Arbitration* (1990) p. 41 et seq. as well as Vahlén, Avtal och tolkning, 1960, p. 153 et seq.). However, in The Netherlands and Germany, the prevailing interpretation seems to be that the new party is bound by the arbitral clause. (For an international overview, see Girsberger and Hausmaninger, Arbitration International, 1992, p. 121 et seq.)

[4] "In support of the fact that the new party should be bound, it was argued that, if the opposite were true, the remaining party would be in a much less favorable position. It should be assumed that he, like the original party,

1. *Note General Editor.* See the excerpt of the decision of the Svea Court of Appeal of 31 March 1999, published in this Yearbook on pp. 321-328, concerning the reference by the Supreme Court to the arbitral award of 5 March 1997.

wished to have disputes between them settled by arbitration. It should not be accepted that the original party [the assignor] be unilaterally released from the arbitral clause by the assignment. If the assignee does not agree to the arbitral clause, he can always refuse to acquire the rights from the assignor.

[5] "Wärtsilä raised similar points before the Supreme Court. In particular, Wärtsilä relied on the fact that the sales contracts incorporated the general conditions which are at issue in this case. There are important reasons why Wärtsilä, in its commercial relations, wished to have possible future disputes settled by means of arbitration. One of these is that the disputes which arise often relate to complicated technical questions and arbitration offers more of an opportunity than litigation in court, to appoint an arbitrator with specialized knowledge. Another of these reasons is the fact that in the area of trade, and particularly in the domain within which Wärsilä operates, there is very fierce competition, particularly on the technical level. Experience has shown that the disputes often concern questions of manufacture and construction and it is in that area that Wärtsilä has a clear interest in being protected against any indiscretion. Arbitration provides a greater possibility for confidentiality than court proceedings.

[6] "It must be accepted that it would entail a serious weakening of Wärtsilä's position if the consequence of the assignment of rights relating to the delivery contract to Emja would be that disputes would be settled in the courts. Moreover, Wärtsilä was powerless to oppose the assignment. Wärtsilä's arguments are very strong because the arbitral clauses which were inserted in the delivery contract at issue in this case should not only apply in a dispute between the original contracting parties, but should also bind Emja, who assumed the rights according to the contract.

[7] "It is also a basic legal principle that when a contractual right is assigned, the new creditor cannot have more rights that the assignor (cf. Sect. 27 Statute on Debts). The principle relates in the first place to civil law exceptions such as, for example, nullity, but there is also good reason for it to include agreements to arbitrate concluded by the assignor.

[8] "In support of its application, Emja argued that if the arbitral clauses could be invoked against it, there could be a risk of a miscarriage of justice. What would happen if Emja's suit was not admissible in state courts, and consequently it were to have recourse to arbitration? Could Wärtsilä, in order to profit from the situation, object that the arbitration clauses only existed between the original parties so that the request for arbitration would be denied?

[9] "With regard to the remaining party being bound by the arbitral clause, doctrine has relied on the possibility that the clause may arise from a strong personal relationship between the original parties. Here, this goes against the

fact that the remaining party must be bound by the clause vis-à-vis the party who acquires a right under the contract. Such a personal bond is, however, rather unusual in commercial relations, and in any case, did not exist between Wärtsilä, on one side, and Ferus and Bijlsma on the other.

[10] "However, above all, it is the risk that the assignee will not be able to pay the costs of arbitration and the possibility that the original party may escape from being responsible for such costs by an assignment which gives cause for concern to many legal authors. The existence of this risk leads to the recommendation that the remaining party have the right to choose between litigation and arbitration. Such a rickety bond whereby the assignee, but not the remaining party, is bound by the arbitration agreement, also gives rise to objections, because it would give the remaining party the opportunity to speculate on the choice of the forum of the dispute. This speaks for the view that the remaining party is bound by the arbitral clause, unless there are particular circumstances. No such circumstances have been advanced in this case. It follows that there is no reason to consider that Emja would suffer a miscarriage of justice. On the basis of the above, Emja is held to be bound by the arbitral clauses and the appeal is denied."

Svea Court of Appeal, Dept. 16, 30 March 1999

Parties:	Appellant: A.I. Trade Finance Inc. (USA) Respondent: Bulgarian Foreign Trade Bank Ltd.
Published in:	14 Mealey's International Arbitration Report (1999, no. 4) pp. A-1 – A-3[1]
Subject matters:	– confidentiality of arbitral award – confidentiality of arbitral proceedings

Facts

On 26 August 1983, a loan contract was concluded between Bulgarian Foreign Trade Bank Ltd. (Bulbank) and Girozentrale und Bank der Österreichischen Sparkassen Aktiengesellschaft (GiroCredit), making a credit of 250 million Austrian Schillings (later 350 million AS) available to Bulbank. On 11 March 1994, GiroCredit transferred the right to payment of some of Bulbank's loans to A.I. Trade Finance, Inc. (AIT).

A dispute arose regarding the risk transfer. The loan contract between GiroCredit and Bulbank contained an arbitral clause providing for arbitration under the Arbitration Rules of the United Nations Economic Commission for Europe (ECE Rules) in Stockholm. AIT, which had not received any payment from Bulbank for the loan debts transferred by GiroCredit, initiated arbitration proceedings on 15 March 1996 in Stockholm. Bulbank claimed that the arbitration agreement between it and GiroCredit was not binding on Bulbank in relation to AIT. The three-man arbitral tribunal, chaired by Lars Welamson, former Justice of the Swedish Supreme Court, issued an award on jurisdiction on 5 March 1997, holding that it had jurisdiction to deal with the dispute and that the arbitration agreement was valid.

As described by the Stockholm City Court, which later had to decide on a challenge to the validity of the award:

> "The decision was referred to, in the Spring of 1997, in the periodical Mealey's International Arbitration Report, which is published in the USA. AIT has acknowledged that the decision was made available to the

1. The translation from Swedish used in this excerpt is largely based on that in Mealey's International Arbitration Report, with minor revisions.

> periodical through the representatives of a party in the USA. Claes Broman, Attorney, received in March or April, per telefax from AIT's American Counsel a copy of that published in Mealey's. He later sent this on to Lars Welamson."

Shortly thereafter, the Swedish Supreme Court, in a judgment of 15 October 1997, dealing with the issue of whether an arbitration clause that is incorporated into a contract for supply binds a party who acquires rights under the contract, mentioned the award, referring to the citation in Mealey's.[2]

In the next stage of the arbitral proceedings, Bulbank claimed that the arbitration agreement had been cancelled, alleging that AIT had committed a gross breach of contract by allowing the Tribunal's decision to be made public and by releasing it to a third party. Bulbank also claimed that Lars Welamson was disqualified and requested that the proceedings be concluded. On 12 November 1997, the arbitral tribunal issued a decision rejecting these claims. A final award was issued on 22 December 1997.

Bulbank applied to the Stockholm City Court requesting that the award be declared invalid or, alternatively, set aside. In its decision, the Stockholm City Court found, contrary to Bulbank's contention, that there was a valid arbitration agreement between Bulbank and AIT.

Bulbank had further argued that the publication of the arbitral tribunal's decision had breached the requirement of confidentiality applicable during arbitration proceedings and that AIT had thereby committed a breach of contract against the arbitration agreement. The City Court agreed, finding that there was a fundamental breach of contract constituting grounds for Bulbank to avoid the contract. AIT had done so on 11 November 1997 and as of that date, there was no valid arbitration agreement.

The Stockholm City Court summarised its holding on this issue as follows:

> "Arbitration proceedings are, as an element of the private sector of community life, linked with a rule about the observance of confidentiality. The absence of any express rule on whether confidentiality applies in arbitration proceedings – laid down by law or contractual – and that the issue has been passed over in silence by learned writers cannot thus be used to support the opposite position. Instead, the City Court conclude[s] that confidentiality under Swedish law applies in and for the arbitration proceedings unless otherwise agreed between the parties and that an interpretation of the ECE Rules tend[s] to indicate

2. *Note General Editor.* An excerpt of the Supreme Court of 15 October 1997 is published in this Yearbook on pp. 317-320.

that these rules imply a system of regulations corresponding to that in Swedish law.

When GiroCredit and Bulbank concluded the arbitration agreement they have thus, in the opinion of the City Court, when nothing else was agreed, at the same time undertaken that the arbitration proceedings would be concluded with the observance of confidentiality. The City Court finds that AIT by co-operating in making the dispute known, as regards its existence and partially as regards its content, thereby breached the arbitration agreement.

Bulbank has claimed that this breach of contract was fundamental and therefore comprised grounds for avoidance. Confidentiality comprises a basic and fundamental rule in arbitration proceedings. Set against this background alone, the City Court finds that (a breach of confidentiality, as a main rule must be regarded as a fundamental breach of the arbitration agreement. The City Court do[es] not consider that it is of any material importance what has become known concerning the arbitration proceedings or in which manner it took place. The decisive factor is instead *that* something became known and that this occurred through the co-operation of a party. This particularly applies if the publication takes place in such a manner that everybody is entitled to pass it on further, which involves a possibility of wide dissemination. Unless every such publication were a fundamental breach of contract, the confidentiality rule would be difficult to maintain in practice. Thus, in the view of the City Court, where the publication was made or the extent of the dissemination is not significant. It is possible that some exception should exist concerning the main rule stated by the City Court – that breach of confidentiality is viewed as a fundamental breach of the arbitration agreement – but the City Court does not consider that the situation here calls for a deviation from such a main rule.

The breach of contract, which was thereby fundamental, constituted valid grounds for Bulbank to avoid the contract."

On appeal the Svea Court of Appeal upheld the decision of the Stockholm City Court on the question of the existence of a valid arbitration agreement, but reversed the setting aside, finding that the publication of the partial award of 5 March 1997 did not constitute sufficient grounds to avoid the contract. Although the Court of Appeal agreed with the City Court that Swedish legislation does not deal with the matter of a duty of confidentiality in arbitration proceedings, it found, in contrast to the City Court, that the ECE Rules do not expressly govern the issue of duty of confidentiality as regards the written procedure and making of arbitral awards and decisions. The making public of information in arbitration proceedings could be viewed "as a breach of the duty of good faith imposed on the parties in relation to each other". Whether such a breach occurred depends on the circumstances of the publication, e.g., the nature of the information and the reason for publication, the extent of damage to the other party and whether there was intent to cause harm. The sanction for such disclosure normally comprises compensation for loss proven. The right to avoid the arbitration agreement is very limited and considering the circumstances of the publication and the nature of the information disclosed in the award, Bulbank did not show any cause that could afford a right to avoid the arbitration agreement.

Excerpt

I. FINAL JUDGMENT OF THE COURT OF APPEAL

[1] "Revoking the judgment of the City Court, the Court of Appeal rejects Bulgarian Foreign Trade Bank Ltd's (Bulbank) action and also orders Bulbank to indemnify the litigation costs of A.I. Trade Finance Inc. (AIT) in the city Court of one hundred and fifty seven thousand, nine hundred and sixteen kronor, of which 95,000 kronor comprises representative's fees, together with interest in accordance with Sect. 6 of the Interest Act (1975:635) from 10 September 1998 until payment is made. The Court of Appeal orders Bulbank to indemnify the litigation costs of AIT in the Court of Appeal of four hundred and fifty two thousand, six hundred and sixty kronor, of which 200,000 kronor comprises representative's fees, together with interest in accordance with Sect. 6 of the Interest Act (1975:635) from this date until payment is made."
(....)

II. THE REASONS OF THE COURT OF APPEAL

(....)

1. *Was It Possible to Avoid the Arbitration Agreement on the Grounds of Breach of Contract Prior to the Arbitral Award Being Made?*

[2] "As a result of the objection of AIT described above, the Court of Appeal first wishes to state the following. According to the Arbitration Act, if an arbitral award is made without an arbitration agreement existing there is either an invalidity or a ground of appeal, depending on whether the inade-

quacy is original or the arbitration agreement ceased to exist later (see inter alia, Hassler-Cars, *Skiljeförfarande*, [Arbitration Proceedings], second edition, p. 132 et seq.). The Court must therefore, in cases concerning appeals against arbitral awards, be considered competent to consider the allegations of a party in both these situations. The Court could hardly fulfil its duty otherwise. In the view of the Court of Appeal, the fact that the arbitration panel – for example in accordance with Art. 18 of the ECE Rules – has been afforded power to decide itself on its jurisdiction, and about the existence or validity of an arbitration agreement that is questioned, does not give cause to make another assessment.

[3] "Bulbank has claimed that AIT by publicising the interim award of 5 March 1997 committed a disloyal, and for Bulbank injurious, act and also that this, in combination with the general duty of secrecy[3] in arbitration proceedings, constituted sufficient grounds to avoid the contract. Like the City Court, the Court of Appeal must therefore settle the issue of whether, and to what extent, a duty of confidentiality applies to a party under the ECE Rules and according to Swedish law.

[4] "First, as regards the ECE Rules, there is only one provision that governs the issue of secrecy, namely Art. 29. The provision is found under the heading 'the hearing' (in French *L'audience*) and states that 'the proceedings shall be held in camera' unless the parties request 'that they be held in public'. The placing of the provision under a heading that normally could not probably relate to anything else other than a session for oral processing means that the provision must be considered to relate to insularity for this and not prescribe any duty of confidentiality in the arbitration proceedings generally. The wording and the special use of the expression 'in camera', which is aimed at negotiations or discussions behind closed doors, also supports this standpoint.

[5] "That the word 'proceedings' (in French here *la procédure*) in Art. 26, which governs the matter of translation of documents and interpretation, is used in a broader sense does not alter what is stated here. Nor is there any secrecy rule in conjunction with the provisions of Art. 41 concerning the recording of arbitral awards. The Court of Appeal thus comes to the conclusion, in contrast to the City Court, that the ECE Rules do not expressly govern the issue of duty of confidentiality as regards the written procedure and making of arbitral awards and decisions. Obviously, this does not imply that the arbitrators and parties should consider that they are free to neglect the application of discretion on matters concerning the arbitration proceedings, but this requirement has another basis.

3. "Translator's note: Literally translated, though 'confidentiality' may be a more appropriate term."

[6] "As stated by the City Court, Swedish legislation does not deal with the matter of a duty of confidentiality in arbitration proceedings (c.f. however, the provision on duty of confidentiality for witnesses under Chapter 8, Sect. 17 of the Swedish Secrecy Act (1980:100), which enters into force on 1 April 1999). It is also clear that secrecy, in the form of insularity in negotiations and discretion concerning the matter of the proceedings generally, nonetheless constitutes a fundamental element of arbitration proceedings and is one of the most important reasons for arbitration proceedings often being chosen. It is fundamental for the arbitration proceedings that they, as a civil law procedural instrument, are removed from the public right of access to information applicable to both judicial proceedings as well as other official activity. The implication of this is that a third party cannot claim a right of insight into the proceedings, rather than that a party in arbitration proceedings is subjected to any duty of confidentiality (see, inter alia, Official Government Report – SOU 1995:65, p. 186). However, the advantages involved for the parties in having access to arbitration proceedings pre-suppose that the parties apply discretion to preserve the value of the proceedings.

[7] "Even if the confidentiality of parties in arbitration proceedings has not been governed statutorily nor can hardly – as it seems to be in certain other countries – be generally regarded as being incorporated as a silent and implied contractual obligation when concluding arbitration agreements, it is likely in many cases that the making public of information in arbitration proceedings could be viewed as a breach of the duty of good faith [lit. loyalty] imposed on the parties in relation to each other. In this assessment, great importance should be attached to what kind of information is made public. Thus it is, for example, likely that information touching on the operations of one of the parties or its explanation of the action in the arbitration dispute may normally be regarded as more worthy of protection than information that an arbitration dispute between the parties is in progress or information that concerns purely procedural issues of a general nature. Furthermore, it should be taken into account, inter alia, whether there was an acceptable reason for the publicising, to what extent the other party has been caused damage by this and, should it occur, whether the information was given with the purpose of harming the opposing party.

[8] "In those cases touched upon here, the sanction against a party who without permission discloses information about the arbitration proceedings most likely normally comprises compensation payable to the other party for loss proven. In order to avoid an arbitration agreement it is required – as with the avoidance of other civil law contracts – that a party committed a fundamental breach of contract. Having regard to the far-reaching consequences

that avoidance of an arbitration agreement may involve, the scope afforded for a right to avoid must be very limited.

[9] "It is undisputed in this case that AIT allowed the publicising of the decision of the arbitrators of 5 March 1997 in the American Journal Mealey's. The more detailed circumstances concerning the publicising and also the reasons for this have not been established in the case. The first page (approx.) of the decision contains under the heading 'Introduction' brief information about the parties, the credit contract, the risk distribution contract and the transfer of certain debts to AIT and also that arbitration proceedings were in progress between AIT and Bulbank. The decision contains on the other nine pages, subject to a minor exception, the argumentation of the parties and the deliberation of the arbitrators on the purely legal issue concerning whether the arbitration agreement had accompanied the transfer of certain debts to AIT. The great majority of that publicised thus relates to deliberations on legal principles concerning a purely procedural issue of general interest. The Court of Appeal considers, having regard to this and referring to that previously stated, that Bulbank has not shown any cause that could afford a right to avoid the arbitration agreement. The arbitration agreement was thus valid on the date that arbitral award was made. Therefore, nor should Bulbank's action be granted on the subsidiary ground referred to."

2. *Was Lars Welamson, Chairman of the Arbitration Panel, Disqualified?*

[10] "It is indicated by the investigation that Lars Welamson in the course of pending arbitration proceedings, knowing that a decision was publicised in Mealey's, without obtaining Bulbank's consent, both discussed the decision of 5 March 1997 with a Member of the Supreme Court and also handed over a copy of the decision to the Court. Bulbank has claimed that Lars Welamson, irrespective of whether AIT's publication of the decision in Mealey's was allowable or not, has acted against the interests of Bulbank and also that he thereby gave Bulbank cause to question his impartiality. Bulbank has in that connection stated that Lars Welamson's actions have meant that AIT's standpoint on the procedural issue, which was accepted by the arbitration panel, was introduced into the deliberation of the Supreme Court on a corresponding issue in a case pending at the Court, and furthermore that this action was in practice advantageous to AIT and detrimental to Bulbank. Furthermore, Bulbank has stated that it would never, had it been asked, have consented to the Supreme Court being informed about the decision in the way that it was.

[11] "In accordance with Sect. 5, first paragraph, item 4 of the Arbitration Act (1929:145), an arbitrator is disqualified if special circumstances exist that

are likely to reduce confidence in his integrity or impartiality. Lars Welamson has stated that he, after he learnt that the full text of the decision had already been publicised and become available to everybody, did not reflect upon there possibly being any impediment to mentioning it to a former colleague who said that he had to adopt a position on the same problematical issue. He has added that the practice in arbitrator circles is that one does not reveal any information that is not otherwise known, for which reason the matter would have been dealt with differently if the decision had not already been publicised.

[12] "Lars Welamson's act has obviously been caused exclusively by an interest in participating in legal developments in the field in question. Nor, in the view of the Court of Appeal, has any justified reason been found for Bulbank to question Lars Welamson's impartial handling of the arbitration dispute, even if it as such may appear to have been appropriate to inform Bulbank about the transfer of the decision to the Supreme Court. Thus, the Court of Appeal considers that which occurred on the part of Lars Welamson was not likely to reduce confidence for his integrity or impartiality. Therefore, nor should the arbitral award be avoided on that ground."

(....)

UNITED KINGDOM

Court of Appeal, Civil Division, 30 January 1998

Parties:	Appellant: Sion Soleimany (United Kingdom) Respondent: Abner Soleimany (United Kingdom)
Published in:	[1998] 3 Weekly Law Reports pp. 811-832
Subject matters:	– enforcement of illegal contract – violation of public policy

Facts

Sion Soleimany and his son, Abner Soleimany were engaged in the export of Persian carpets from Iran. Between 1980 and 1983, Abner Soleimany arranged for the export of the carpets from Iran in contravention of Iranian Revenue laws and export controls. The carpets were sold by Sion Soleimany in England or elsewhere outside Iran.

Disputes arose between Mr. Soleimany and his son relating mainly to whether Abner Soleimany had received what he claimed was due to him from the proceeds of the sale of the carpets that he alleged to have arranged to export from Iran.

Mr. Soleimany and his son, agreed to submit the dispute to arbitration by the Jewish Beth Din, the court of the Chief Rabbi. According to a leaflet provided by the Beth Din, the system of law to be applied by the Beth Din is Jewish law, albeit "sometimes other systems of law may also be relevant ... by way of the doctrine of incorporation ..." but the decision as to which law to apply "is that of the Dayanim...".

In the award made by the Beth Din on 23 March 1993, it was noted that "Abner purchased quantities of carpets and exported them illegally out of Iran." The award further recognised that the activities in Iran were illegal, stating, e.g., that "By the very nature of the illicit enterprise, few records were kept.... In assessing profits the award disallows the full sum claimed by Abner on the basis inter alia that no allowance has been made for 'smugglers' fees'." After assessing Abner's share of the profits, the Dayan awarded him UK£ 576,574 and his costs.

Abner Soleimany applied to register the award as a judgment under Sect. 26 of the Arbitration Act 1950 as his father had failed to comply with it. On 4 May 1993, Master Gowers granted leave to enforce the award. Sion Soleimany applied to set aside the leave for enforcement on the ground that the illegality which was at the root of the enterprise rendered the claim void or unenforceable in an English court, and that it would be contrary to public policy for an award founded on an illegal agreement or transaction to be enforced as a judgment.

Sion Soleimany also sought leave to appeal the award in several instances, but was unsuccessful in this respect. However he was successful regarding the application to set aside the leave for enforcement of the award. The Court of Appeal, per Morritt, LJ, Waller, LJ and Sir Christopher Staughton, held that the award, which purported to enforce an illegal contract, was not enforceable in England and Wales.

Excerpt

I. WHAT IS THE LAW RELATING TO ILLEGALITY?

[1] "What is the law relating to illegality so far as the English court is concerned? That point has been recently summarised in the judgment of Stuart-Smith LJ in a decision of the Court of Appeal in *Royal Boskalis NV v. Mountain* [1997] 2 All ER 929 at 946:

> 'What is the law so far as the English court is concerned? In *St. John Shipping Corp. v. Joseph Rank Ltd.* [1956] 3 All ER 683 at 687, [1957] 1 QB 267 at 283, Devlin J stated the law in relation to illegal contracts as follows:
>
> "There are two general principles. The first is that a contract which is entered into with the object of committing an illegal act is unenforceable. The application of this principle depends on proof of the intent, at the time the contract was made, to break the law; if the intent is mutual the contract is not enforceable at all, and, if unilateral, it is unenforceable at the suit of the party who is proved to have it."

[2] "'And in *Archbolds (Freightage) Ltd. v. S. Spanglett Ltd. (Randall, third party)* [1961] 1 All ER 417 at 424, [1961] 1 QB 374 at 388 Devlin LJ said:

> "The effect of illegality on a contract may be threefold. If at the time of making the contract there is an intent to perform it in an unlawful way, the contract, although it remains alive, is [un]enforceable at the suit of the party having that intent; if the intent is held in common, it is not enforceable at all. Another effect of illegality is to prevent a plaintiff from recovering under a contract if in order to prove his rights under it he has to rely on his own illegal act; he may not do that even though he can show that at the time of making the contract he had no intent to break the law and that at the time of performance he did not know that what he was doing was illegal. The third effect of illegality is to avoid the contract ab initio, and that arises if the making of the contract is expressly or impliedly prohibited by statute or is otherwise contrary to public policy."'
> (....)

[3] "There is a distinction, which may not be unimportant in the context of this case, to be drawn between a 'joint venture' agreement with an object of committing illegal acts in a foreign and friendly state which will be totally unenforceable, and a contract which does not have that objective. In the latter case, the question may arise whether the plaintiff, in order to establish his rights, has to rely on his own illegal act."

II. TYPE OF CONTRACT

[4] "Is it apparent from *the award itself* what type of contract the arbitrator was dealing with? We pose the question in this way because it seems to us important to emphasise that we are dealing with a case where it is apparent from the face of the award that: (1) the arbitrator rejected Abner's case that he had exported carpets purchased by himself which had then been sold by his father on his behalf; and (2) the arbitrator was dealing with what he termed an illicit enterprise under which it was the joint intention that carpets would be smuggled out of Iran illegally. This was the view of Judge Langan as we understand it, and we did not understand Mr. Serota to quarrel with that view. It must follow that Dayan Berkovits was right in the affidavit he has sworn for the purposes of these proceedings that the arbitrator did not take the same view as an English court would have taken, but considered the illegality to be of no relevance 'since he was applying Jewish law, under which, any purported illegality would have no effect on the rights of the parties.'"

III. ATTITUDE ENGLISH COURT

[5] "What attitude would the English court take if a foreign court had decided as a matter of fact that there was a contract entered into with the object of committing an illegal act in a foreign and friendly state, but by the law of the foreign court, either illegality of that sort had no effect on the rights of the parties, or the foreign court was empowered to award compensation, and had awarded compensation? Mr. Serota drew our attention to Lord Goff's reference to New Zealand Legislation in his speech in *Tinsley v. Milligan* [1994] 1 AC 340 at 364, which gives the New Zealand courts a very broad discretion to award compensation even though the illegal contract by the same legislation is recognised to have 'no effect'. He suggested that the English court should be prepared to recognise a system of law that showed a more relaxed approach to illegality than that shown by the English courts heretofore.

[6] "There are of course Conventions covering the enforceability of judgments which have been brought into effect in England by statute. There are in the result express statutory provisions which exclude from registration in England a judgment 'which was in respect of a cause of action which for reasons of public policy ... could not be entertained by the registering court' (the Administration of Justice Act 1920); or which provide that registration may be set aside if 'the enforcement of the judgment would be contrary to public policy in the country of the registering court' (the Foreign Judgments (Reciprocal Enforcement) Act 1933). The distinction between those two provisions may be important, the 1933 Act being concerned with recognition of the *judgment*, and the 1920 Act with the original cause of action. Dicey & Morris (*The Conflict of Laws* 12th Edn. Rule 44 p. 511) suggests that the rule at common law is that a judgment is impeachable 'on the ground that its enforcement or as the case may be, its recognition, would be contrary to public policy'.

[7] "It seems that there are very few cases in which foreign judgments in personam have been denied enforcement or recognition for reasons of public policy. Those relevant were examined by Colman J in *Westacre Investments Inc. v. Judoimport-SDPR Holding Co. Ltd.*, unreported, 19 December 1997.[1] They included a decision of Astbury J in *In Re Macartney* [1921] 1 Ch 522; *Israel Discount Bank of New York v. Hadjipateras* [1984] 1 WLR 137; and *Vervaeke v. Smith* [1983] AC 145. In *Macartney*, Astbury J concluded that the principle

1. The High Court decision is reported in Yearbook XXIII (1998) pp. 836-879 (UK no. 51). The Court of Appeal judgment in this case is reported in Part V-A of this Volume as UK no. 54, pp. 753-776.

that the English court would not enforce a contract against the public policy of this country wherever it was made, applied as 'directly to the enforceability of foreign judgments founded on contracts contrary to public policy or rights of that character'.

[8] "In relation to *Vervaeke v. Smith* we gratefully adopt Colman J's synopsis and comments. It was a case

> 'in which a petitioner for a decree of nullity of an English marriage in the English courts on the grounds of lack of consent to the marriage, having failed to obtain such decree, obtained a declaration from the Belgian court that the English marriage was void ab initio on the ground that the marriage was merely a device to obtain a British passport so that she could work as a prostitute without being deported and that the parties had no intention of living together. That was substantially the ground on which she had relied in the English courts. She then applied for a declaration in the English court that the Belgian decree was entitled to be recognised in England under the Foreign Judgments (Reciprocal Enforcement) Act 1933 and the bilateral convention between the UK and Belgium. She lost at first instance and in the Court of Appeal. The House of Lords dismissed the appeal on two grounds. All members of the House concluded that the earlier English judgment gave rise to an estoppel *per rem judicatam* which precluded reliance on the Belgian decree. Secondly, Lord Hailsham LC and Lord Simon, with whom Lord Brandon agreed, held that recognition of the Belgian decree should be refused on grounds of public policy. Lord Simon observed at p. 164 that:
>
> "There is little authority for refusing, on the ground of public policy, to recognise an otherwise conclusive foreign judgment – no doubt because the conclusiveness of a judgment of a foreign court of competent jurisdiction is itself buttressed by the rule of public policy, *interest reipublicae ut sit finis litium*, the 'commonwealth' in conflict of laws extending to the whole international community."

[9] "'Although an English court would decline recognition of a foreign judgment "with extreme reserve", the instant case called for that course. This was firstly because English public policy treated "sham" marriages as valid in conflict with Belgian law. Secondly, since the marriage took place in England, English public policy should be preferred to Belgian law. The appellant first invoked the jurisdiction of the English courts before going to the Belgian courts. The marriage had its most real and substantial connection with England and by it the appellant took

advantage of English public law. The underlying reasons for the course adopted by the appellant was her attempt to succeed to property in England which she could only do if she were not married to Smith and validly married to the deceased owner of the property.

[10] "'This conclusion is founded on the primary consideration that recognition of the validity of "sham" marriages in England was a matter of English public policy and that, since the Belgian decree was, as appeared from the judgment, founded on an inconsistent principle of Belgian law, the appellant was claiming relief which was equally inconsistent with English public policy. An analogous claim would be one to enforce a foreign judgment which on the face of it, held to be enforceable a contract governed by English law which was illegal at common law. The enforcement of such a judgment would seem to be contrary to public policy. However, Lord Simon's conclusion is not based solely on the substance of the Belgian decree being contrary to English public policy but upon other considerations, such as the place of the marriage ceremony, as factors to be weighed in the balance in relation to recognition.'

[11] "It may be that legislation of the New Zealand type would provide different arguments for the party trying to enforce a judgment because it could be said, first, that the judgment is not enforcing an illegal contract but awarding compensation pursuant to a perfectly valid statute; and thus, second, there is no reason in public policy not to recognise the judgment. However, it would seem to us that if what the foreign court did was to recognise by its judgment that a contract had been entered into with the object of committing an illegal act in a state which England recognised as a foreign and friendly state, and to enforce the rights of the parties under it, then there would be no room for recognising the more relaxed approach of a different jurisdiction. That, as it would seem to us, is the very type of judgment which the English court would not recognise on the grounds of public policy.

[12] "We stress that we are dealing with a judgment which *finds as a fact* that it was the common intention to commit an illegal act, but enforces the contract. Different considerations may apply where there is a finding by the foreign court to the contrary or simply no such finding, and one party now seeks such a finding from the enforcing court. Thus our conclusion would be that if the award were a judgment of a foreign court, the English court would not enforce it"

IV. ENFORCEMENT OF ARBITRATION AWARD

[13] "Does it make any difference that the question of enforcement relates to an arbitration award? There are material distinctions between awards and foreign judgments. First, an award can only be valid if the arbitrator had jurisdiction founded on a contract between the parties. If that contract is itself invalid the award will be unenforceable. In this case we were referred to the cases relating to the separability of an arbitration clause. It was sought to demonstrate that the rather broad statement of Denning LJ in *Taylor v. Barnet* [1953] 1 WLR 562 that 'an arbitrator has no jurisdiction or authority to award damages on an illegal contract' must be read in the context of the facts with which that case was concerned. The most important case in this area is *Harbour v. Kansa* [1993] 1 QB 701[2] where the Court of Appeal held that the arbitration clause in an insurance contract was separate from the main contract with the effect that (a) invalidity of the main contract did not deprive the arbitrator of jurisdiction, and (b) the arbitrator had jurisdiction to decide the question of illegality of the main contract.

[14] "But, the fact that in a contract alleged to be illegal the arbitration clause may not itself be infected by the illegality, does not means that it is always so, and does not mean that an arbitration agreement that is separate may not be void for illegality. There may be illegal or immoral dealings which are from an English law perspective incapable of being arbitrated because an agreement to arbitrate them would itself be illegal or contrary to public policy under English law. The English court would not recognise an agreement between the highwaymen to arbitrate their differences any more than it would recognise the original agreement to split the proceeds. Ralph Gibson LJ in *Harbour* when dealing at 712F with a case concerned with betting and an arbitration provision collateral to that contract, *Joe Lee Ltd. v. Lord Dalmeny* [1927] 1 Ch 300, recognised the possibility of an agreement containing an arbitration clause of such a nature that the arbitration clause itself was invalid. It must also follow that an arbitration agreement made separately in relation to an illegal or immoral dispute would not be recognised.

[15] "At one stage it seemed to us that Mr. Serota was conceding that what Abner and Sion sought to have arbitrated was how to split the proceeds of a joint venture that had as its object the commission of offences in Iran. If that were so, we would incline to the view that the arbitration clause was invalid, so that there was no award to enforce. But, on reflection, and having analyzed the way the matter was put before the arbitrator, it seems to us that it is not fair to characterise the matter in that way. Disputes between Abner and Sion

2. Reported in Yearbook XX (1995) pp. 771-790 (UK no. 39).

arising out of a claim by Abner for an account of the proceeds of sale, was what was referred to the arbitrator. It was during the arbitration that the arbitrator took the view that he was dealing with a joint venture with the objects we have already indicated. Accordingly it seems to us that the original arbitration agreement was a valid agreement, and that it was within the jurisdiction of the arbitrator to consider questions of illegality insofar as they might affect the rights of the parties.

[16] "That brings us to the second possible distinction between a judgment and an award. In enforcing an award, whether by action or by registration under Sect. 26 of the Arbitration Act, the plaintiff is enforcing a promise either implied into the reference to arbitration, or, as in this case, expressed in the reference to arbitration. If the reference to arbitration is valid, it can be argued, and is argued by Mr. Serota, that since at the enforcement stage the court is only concerned with enforcement of that promise, the court should not examine what underlies the award any further. Thus, he argues, all that he has to establish is a valid arbitration agreement, an award, and a failure to meet the award. The crucial question is whether that submission is right and we now address that issue.

[17] "In *London Export Corporation v. Jubilee Coffee Roasting Co. Ltd.* (1958) 1 WLR 271 at 277 Diplock J said:

> 'When the arbitration agreement has been construed and no breach of the agreed procedure found there may nevertheless arise a second and quite separate question: that is, whether, as a matter of public policy, a particular award, made pursuant to that agreed procedure, ought not to be enforced and ought, therefore, to be set aside; for an arbitrator's award, unless set aside, entitles the beneficiary to call upon the executive power of the State to enforce it, and it is the function of the court to see that that executive power is not abused.'

This passage was endorsed by McNair J in *James Laing Son & Co. Ltd. v. Eastcheap Dried Fruit Company* (1962) 1 LLR 285 at 290.

[18] "An English court exercises control over the enforcement of arbitral awards as part of the lex fori, whatever the proper law of the arbitration agreement or the place where the arbitration is conducted. If a claimant wishes to invoke the executive power in this country to enforce an award in his favour, he can only do so subject to our law. For the purposes of the present dispute, that means Sect. 26 of the Arbitration Act 1950. There was no express provision in that section that an award would not be enforced if enforcement was contrary to public policy; but there was such a provision in relation to foreign awards in Sect. 37(1), and it is hard to suppose that a more liberal

regime applied to English awards. (It is now expressly provided in Sect. 68(2) of the Arbitration Act 1996 that an award may be challenged on the ground that it is contrary to public policy, and Sect. 2(2)(b) of that Act in effect provides that the enforcement of awards shall be governed by English law even if that is not otherwise the law applicable to the arbitration). It follows that an award, whether domestic or foreign, will not be enforced by an English court if enforcement would be contrary to the public policy of this country.

[19] "It is clear that it is contrary to public policy for an English award (i.e., an award following an arbitration conducted in accordance with English law) to be enforced if it is based on an English contract which was illegal when made. That follows from the decision of this court in *David Taylor & Sons Ltd. v. Barnet Trading Company* [1953] 1 WLR 562, where the award was based on a contract for the sale of Irish stewed steak at two shillings and four pence per pound, whereas the maximum price allowed under the Defence (General) Regulations was two shillings and three farthings per pound.

[20] "There was for some time a dispute as to whether that decision was based on the theory that an arbitrator had no jurisdiction to make an award on an illegal contract, or that it was misconduct for an arbitrator to do so. That dispute has been concluded, so far as this court is concerned, in the case of *Harbour Assurance Co. (UK) Ltd. v. Kansa General International Insurance Co. Ltd.* [1993] QB 701. That was an action brought for a declaration that some reinsurance policies were void for illegality, and that the plaintiffs were not liable under them. The illegality alleged was that the defendants were not registered or approved to carry on insurance or reinsurance business under the Insurance Companies Acts. The illegality was denied. This court granted a stay of the action in favour of arbitration, on the ground that the illegality pleaded did not affect the validity of the arbitration clause. All three members of the Court of Appeal held that the *David Taylor* decision was not based on jurisdiction but on misconduct by the arbitrator. It was also held that the arbitration clause in the *Harbour Assurance* contracts was wide enough to enable an arbitrator to decide on the illegality there alleged.

[21] "The *Harbour Assurance* case was not concerned with enforcement of an award, but with whether there should be a stay of legal proceedings in favour of arbitration. The illegality was at that stage contested, and at least in view of Hoffmann LJ (at p. 224) it was open to question whether there was illegality such that the contracts were void ab initio. By contrast it may be that in the case of *palpable illegality* (to use the expression adopted by Colman J in *Westacre Investments Inc. v. Judoimport – SDPR Holding Co. Ltd.* 19 December 1997 unreported),[3] an English court would declare that there was no arbitrable

3. See fn. 1.

dispute, or refuse to grant a stay in favour of arbitration, on the ground that an arbitrator could not lawfully enforce the contract. As already indicated, there may be classes of contract – trading with the enemy was cited as a plausible example, and the robbers referring their dispute would be another – where the making of the contract will itself be an illegal act, and where the court would be driven *nolen volens* to hold that the arbitration clause was itself void.

[22] "So we turn to the enforcement stage, on the basis (as we have already concluded), that the arbitrators had jurisdiction. Even if we were wrong in the view already expressed that an arbitration agreement between robbers (for example) to arbitrate their disputes would itself be void, it is in our view inconceivable that an English court would enforce an award made on a joint venture agreement between bank robbers, any more than it would enforce an agreement between highwaymen. *Everet v. Williams, Lindley on Partnership* 13th Edn. p. 130 Note 23. Where public policy is involved, the interposition of an arbitration award does not isolate the successful party's claim from the illegality which gave rise to it. If Buxton J expressed a contrary view in *S.R. v. H.H.* 8 December 1994, unreported, we have to say that we do not agree with it. Mr. Serota on this appeal accepted than an English court could go behind the award, at least if the arbitration was governed by English law.

[23] "The reason in our judgment is plain enough. The court declines to enforce an illegal contract, as Lord Mansfield said in *Holman v. Johnson* (1775) 1 Cowp 341 not for the sake of the defendant, nor (if it comes to the point) for the sake of the plaintiff. The court is in our view concerned to preserve the integrity of its process, and to see that it is not abused. The parties cannot override that concern by private agreement. They cannot by procuring an arbitration conceal that they, or rather one of them, is seeking to enforce an illegal contract. Public policy will not allow it. In the present case the parties were, it would seem, entitled to agree to an arbitration before the Beth Din. It may be that they expected that the award, whatever it turned out to be, would be honoured without further argument. It may be that Abner can enforce it in some place outside England and Wales. But enforcement here is governed by the public policy of the lex fori.

[24] "The difficulty arises when arbitrators have entered upon the topic of illegality, and have held that there was none. Or perhaps they have made a non-speaking award, and have not been asked to give reasons. In such a case there is a tension between the public interest that the awards of arbitrators should be respected, so that there be an end to lawsuits, and the public interest that illegal contracts should not be enforced. We do not propound a definitive solution to this problem, for it does not arise in the present case. So far from

finding that the underlying contract was not illegal, the Dayan in the Beth Din found that it was.

[25] "It may, however, also be in the public interest that this court should express some view on a point which has been fully argued and which is likely to arise again. In our view, an enforcement judge, if there is prima facie evidence from one side that the award is based on an illegal contract, should enquire further to some extent. Is there evidence on the other side to the contrary? Has the arbitrator expressly found that the underlying contract was not illegal? Or is it a fair inference that he did reach that conclusion? Is there anything to suggest that the arbitrator was incompetent to conduct such an enquiry? May there have been collusion or bad faith, so as to procure an award despite illegality? Arbitrations are, after all, conducted in a wide variety of situations; not just before high-powered tribunals in international trade but in many other circumstances. We do not for one moment suggest that the judge should conduct a full scale trial of those matters in the first instance. That would create the mischief which the arbitration was designed to avoid. The judge has to decide whether it is proper to give full faith and credit to the arbitrator's award. Only if he decides at the preliminary stage that he should not take that course does he need to embark on a more elaborate enquiry into the issue of illegality.

[26] "The approach is in our view consonant with, and supported by, the recent authorities. In the first place it accords well with the rule that there can be a bona fide compromise of an issue as to whether a contract is illegal. That was decided by this court in *Binder v. Alachouzos* [1972] 2 QB 151, where a contract recited that the parties had been advised by solicitors and counsel that the Moneylenders Acts did not apply to transactions which were the subject of legal proceedings between them, and went on to provide for a compromise....

[27] "There are also cases directly in point. In *Soinco SACI & Anr. v. Novokuznetsk Aluminium Plant & Ors.* 16 December 1997, unreported,[4] the issue was whether NKAP should have an extension of time for applying to set aside an order that a Swiss arbitration award be enforced as a judgment. The facts were that the contract provided for arbitration under the International Arbitration Rules of the Zurich Chamber of Commerce. The arbitrators considered an assertion of illegality by NKAP, and rejected it with reasons. Thereafter a decision of a Russian court, in proceedings at which only NKAP and the public prosecutor were present, held that the contract was illegal. A Swiss court was then asked to have the arbitration award revised and refused

4. Reported in Yearbook XXIII (1998) pp. 795-801 (UK no. 49).

to do so. Waller LJ, (with whom Chadwick and Phillips LJJ agreed) said this at p. 8

> 'I am unpersuaded that it is arguable that under English law enforcement of this award would be contrary to English public policy. The reasons are separate and distinct. *First it is the award with which the English court is concerned and not the underlying contract.* The question of illegality having been raised and dealt with by the Arbitrators, and there being no requirement as a result to perform some act which English law would regard as illegal under English law or contrary to the recognised morals of this country, the public policy is if anything in favour of abiding by the terms of the convention and enforcing the award. Second, in any event if an offence will be committed by NKAP in Russia as a party to the award in paying the same, that is the result of their own failure to obtain the requisite consents, and English public policy would in my view be offended if that relieved that party from its obligation to meet the award.'

Emphasis was placed on the fact that it was an award with which the court was concerned, but at the same time the court did examine the way in which illegality had been dealt with by the arbitrators, and the reasoning of the arbitrators had not led to any anxiety that the question of illegality had not been dealt with properly.

[28] "Another recent and important decision is that Colman J, in the *Westacre* case on 19 December 1997. The underlying contract in that case was a consultancy agreement, under which it was said to be contemplated or intended (or both) that the plaintiffs would bribe Kuwaiti officials in order to obtain contracts for the purchase of military equipment. The contract was governed by Swiss law and provided for arbitration by the International Chamber of Commerce in Geneva. The arbitrators were clearly a highly sophisticated tribunal composed of a German chairman (Dr. Raeschka-Kessler), Prof. François Perret (Swiss, later replaced by Mr. Patry) and Prof. Mitrovic (Yugoslav). They held by a majority that the underlying contract was not, (as it would seem in law and in fact), illegal. A Swiss court upheld the award.

[29] "After a lengthy review of the authorities, Colman J set out six principles which he held to be the law. The first three concerned the question whether an arbitrator has jurisdiction to decide whether the underlying contract is affected by illegality. His conclusion in principle (iii) was that it:

> 'Depends upon whether the nature of the illegality is such that, in the case of statutory illegality the statute has the effect of impeaching that

> agreement as well as the underlying contract, and, in the case of illegality at common law, public policy requires that disputes about the underlying contract should not be referred to arbitration.'

That is not very different from our own view already stated, that there may be cases where an arbitrator has no jurisdiction to make an award when a contract is said to be affected by an issue of illegality.
[30] "In principles (iv) to (vi), [Colman J] deals with the stage of enforcement, although in principle (iv) he returns at the end to jurisdiction. His conclusion, with which we can readily agree, was this –

> 'If the issue before the arbitrators was whether money was due under a contract which was indisputably illegal at common law, an award in favour of the claimant would not be enforced for it would be contrary to public policy that the arbitrator should be entitled to ignore palpable and undisputed illegality.'

It may well be that the same rule applies to illegality by statute. We would not frame it in precisely the same way as Colman J. In our view it is not so much a question of what the arbitration is *entitled* to do; the Dayan was *entitled* to make his award in the present case. But the court will not enforce it.
[31] "In other cases, Colman J holds that prima facie the court would enforce the resulting award; and with that too we agree. But, in an appropriate case it may enquire, as we hold, into an issue of illegality even if an arbitrator had jurisdiction and has found that there was no illegality. We thus differ from Colman J, who limited his sixth proposition to cases where there were relevant facts not put before the arbitrator.
(....)
[32] "Finally, under this head, we should state explicitly what may already have been apparent: when considering illegality of the underlying contract, we do not confine ourselves to English law. An English court will not enforce a contract governed by English law, or to be performed in England, which is illegal by English domestic law. Nor will it enforce a contract governed by the law of a foreign and friendly state, or which requires performance in such a country, if performance is illegal by the law of that country. That is well established as appears from the citations earlier in this judgment. This rule applies as much to the enforcement of an arbitration award as to the direct enforcement of a contract in legal proceedings.
[33] "The award in this case, which purports to enforce an illegal contract, is not enforceable in England and Wales. In reaching that conclusion we are differing from Judge Langan. However, he was not referred to the *Harbour*

Assurance case which threw a different light on the *David Taylor* case; and he did not have the advantage of the recent decisions in *Soinco* and *Westacre*. The judge was impressed by what the Master of the Rolls had said in an earlier stage of the dispute, that there was no prospect of an appeal against the award of the Beth Din succeeding. That may well be right. But it does not affect the question whether the award will be enforced here. As Mr. Serota himself argued at that stage, illegality was matter for consideration in enforcement proceedings and not on an appeal against the award."

(....)

UNITED STATES

Supreme Court of New York, Appellate Division, First Department, 13 August 1998

Parties:	Plaintiffs/appellants: Tony Brower, et al. (US) Defendants/respondents: Gateway 2000, Inc., et al. (nationality not indicated)
Published in:	676 New York Supplement, Second Series, p. 569 et seq.; 1998 N.Y. App. Div. LEXIS 8872
Subject matter:	– ICC arbitration clause unconscionable in consumer contract

Facts

Consumers who purchased Gateway computers or software products through a direct-sales system, by mail or telephone order, received the materials along with a copy of Gateway's "Standard Terms and Conditions Agreement". The Agreement carried a heading that informed the customer that by keeping the computer system beyond 30 days after the date of delivery, they would accept the Terms and Conditions.

Paragraph 10 of the Terms and Conditions contains a dispute resolution provision reading:

> "Any dispute or controversy arising out of or relating to this Agreement or its interpretation shall be settled exclusively and finally by arbitration. The arbitration shall be conducted in accordance with the Rules of Conciliation and Arbitration of the International Chamber of Commerce. The arbitration shall be conducted in Chicago, Illinois, U.S.A. before a sole arbitrator...."

The plaintiffs, dissatisfied with the service provided by Gateway, initiated a court action in the Supreme Court of New York County, against Gateway on behalf of themselves and others similarly situated for compensatory and punitive damages, alleging deceptive sales practices, including breach of warranty, breach of contract, fraud and unfair trade practices, in particular focusing on Gateway's representations and advertising of "service when you need it".

Gateway moved to dismiss the action relying on the arbitration clause in the Agreement. Plaintiffs argued that the arbitration clause was invalid under the Uniform Commercial Code (U.C.C.) Sect. 2-207, unconscionable under U.C.C. Sect. 2-302 and an unenforceable contract of adhesion. Specifically, they claimed that "the provision was obscure; that a customer could not reasonably be expected to appreciate or investigate its meaning and effect; that the International Chamber of Commerce (ICC) was not a forum commonly used for consumer matters; and that because ICC headquarters were in France, it was particularly difficult to locate the organization and its rules."

Moreover, they contended that the cost of ICC arbitration was prohibitive, particularly given the amount of the typical consumer claim involved. For example, a claim of less than $50,000 required advance fees of $4,000 (more than the cost of most Gateway products), of which the $2000 registration fee was nonrefundable even if the consumer prevailed at the arbitration. Consumers would also incur travel expenses disproportionate to the damages sought, which appellants' counsel estimated would not exceed $1,000 per customer in this action, as well as bear the cost of Gateway's legal fees if the consumer did not prevail at the arbitration; in this respect, the ICC Rules follow the "loser pays" rule used in England. Also, although Chicago was designated as the site of the actual arbitration, all correspondence must be sent to ICC headquarters in France.

The Supreme Court (the IAS Court), per Shainswit, J, dismissed the complaint on 21 October 1997. On appeal, the Appellate Division, per Milonas, JP, Nardelli, Mazzarelli and Saxe, JJ, modified the decision, vacating the portion of the arbitration agreement that required ICC arbitration. The court found that the designation of a financially prohibitive forum effectively barred consumers from the forum, and gave leave to the parties to seek appointment of an arbitrator pursuant to the Federal Arbitration Act.

Excerpt

[1] The Appellate Division first confirmed the lower court's holding that the arbitration clause was not invalid under Sect. 2-207 U.C.C. as the arbitration

clause was not a material alteration of the agreement.[1] The contract was formed and manifested when the merchandise had been retained for more than thirty days. The court then continued:

[2] "Finally, we turn to appellants' argument that the IAS court should have declared the contract unenforceable, pursuant to U.C.C. Sect. 2-302, on the ground that the arbitration clause is unconscionable due to the unduly burdensome procedure and cost for the individual consumer.[2] The IAS court found that while a class-action lawsuit, such as the one herein, may be a less costly alternative to the arbitration (which is generally less costly than litigation), that does not alter the binding effect of the valid arbitration clause contained in the agreement (see, *Harris v. Shearson Hayden Stone*, 82 A.D.2d 87, 92-93, 441 N.Y.S.2d 70, aff'd 56 N.Y.2d 627, 450 N.Y.S.2d 482, 435 N.E.2d 1097 for reasons stated below; see also, *Matter of Ball*, 236 A.D.2d 158, 665 N.Y.S.2d 444, appeal dismissed 91 N.Y.2d 921, 669 N.Y.S.2d 262, 692 N.E.2d 131).

---

1. The Uniform Commercial Code (U.C.C.) Sect. 2-207 reads:

"(1) A definite and seasonable expression of acceptance or a written confirmation which is sent within a reasonable time operates as an acceptance even though it states terms additional to or different from those offered or agreed upon, unless acceptance is expressly made conditional on assent to the additional or different terms.

(2) The additional terms are to be construed as proposals for addition to the contract. Between merchants such terms become part of the contract unless:
(a) the offer expressly limits acceptance to the terms of the offer;
(b) they materially alter it; or
(c) notification of objection to them has already been given or is given within a reasonable time after notice of them is received.

(3) Conduct by both parties which recognizes the existence of a contract is sufficient to establish a contract for sale although the writings of the parties do not otherwise establish a contract. In such case the terms of the particular contract consist of those terms on which the writings of the parties agree, together with any supplementary terms incorporated under any other provisions of this Act."

2. U.C.C. Sect. 2-302 reads:

"(1) If the court as a matter of law finds the contract or any clause of the contract to have been unconscionable at the time it was made the court may refuse to enforce the contract, or it may enforce the remainder of the contract without the unconscionable clause, or it may so limit the application of any unconscionable clause as to avoid any unconscionable result.

(2) When it is claimed or appears to the court that the contract or any clause thereof may be unconscionable the parties shall be afforded a reasonable opportunity to present evidence as to its commercial setting, purpose and effect to aid the court in making the determination."

[3] "As a general matter, under New York law, unconscionability requires a showing that a contract is 'both procedurally and substantively unconscionable when made' (*Gillman v. Chase Manhattan Bank*, 73 N.Y.2d 1, 10, 537 N.Y.S.2d 787, 534 N.E.2d 824). That is, there must be 'some showing of "an absence of meaningful choice on the part of one of the parties together with contract terms which are unreasonably favorable to the other party" [citation omitted]' (*Matter of State of New York v. Avco Financial Services*, 50 N.Y.2d 383, 389-390, 429 N.Y.S.2d 181, 406 N.E.2d 1075). The *Avco* court took pains to note, however, that the purpose of this doctrine is not to redress the inequality between the parties but simply to ensure that the more powerful party cannot 'surprise' the other party with some overly oppressive term (id.). (....)

[4] "With respect to the substantive element, which entails an examination of the substance of the agreement in order to determine whether the terms unreasonably favor one party (*Gillman v. Chase Manhattan Bank*, supra, 73 N.Y.2d at 12), we do not find that the possible inconvenience of the chosen site (Chicago) alone rises to the level of unconscionability. We do find, however, that the excessive cost factor that is necessarily entailed in arbitrating before the ICC is unreasonable and surely serves to deter the individual consumer from invoking the process (see, *Matter of Teleserve Systems*, 230 A.D.2d 585, 594, 659 N.Y.S.2d 659, lv. denied __ N.Y.2d __, 1997 N.Y. App. Div. LEXIS 10626). Barred from resorting to the courts by the arbitration clause in the first instance, the designation of a financially prohibitive forum effectively bars consumers from this forum as well; consumers are thus left with no forum at all in which to resolve a dispute. In this regard, we note that this particular claim is not mentioned in the *Hill* decision,[3] which upheld the clause as part of an enforceable contract.

[5] "While it is true that, under New York law, unconscionability is generally predicated on the presence of both the procedural and substantive elements, the substantive element alone may be sufficient to render the terms of the provision at issue unenforceable (see, *Gillman v. Chase Manhattan Bank*, supra, at 12; *Matter of State of New York v. Avco Financial Services*, supra, at 389; *State of New York v. Wolowitz*, 96 A.D.2d 47, 68, 468 N.Y.S.2d 131)). Excessive fees, such as those incurred under the ICC procedure, have been grounds for finding an arbitration provision unenforceable or commercially unreasonable (see, e.g., *Matter of Teleserve Systems*, supra, at 593-594).

---

3. *Hill v. Gateway 2000, Inc.*, 105 F.3d 1147, cert. denied __ U.S. __, 118 S.Ct. 47.

[6] "In the *Filias* case previously mentioned,[4] the Federal District Court stated that it was 'inclined to agree' with the argument that selection of the ICC rendered the clause unconscionable, but concluded that the issue was moot because Gateway had agreed to arbitrate before the American Arbitration Association (AAA) and sought court appointment of the AAA pursuant to Federal Arbitration Act 9 U.S.C. Sect. 5. The court accordingly granted Gateway's motion to compel arbitration and appointed the AAA in lieu of the ICC. Plaintiffs in that action (who are represented by counsel for appellants before us) contend that costs associated with the AAA process are also excessive, given the amount of the individual consumer's damages, and their motion for reconsideration of the court's decision has not yet been decided. While the AAA rules and costs are not part of the record before us, the parties agree that there is a minimum, nonrefundable filing fee of $500, and appellants claim each consumer could spend in excess of $1,000 to arbitrate in this forum.

[7] "Gateway's agreement to the substitution of the AAA is not limited to the *Filias* plaintiffs. Gateway's brief includes the text of a new arbitration agreement that it claims has been extended to all customers, past, present and future (apparently through publication in a quarterly magazine sent to anyone who has ever purchased a Gateway product). The new arbitration agreement provides for the consumer's choice of the AAA or the ICC as the arbitral body and the designation of any location for the arbitration by agreement of the parties, which 'shall not be unreasonably withheld'. It also provides telephone numbers at which the AAA and the ICC may be reached for information regarding the 'organizations and their procedures'.

[8] "As noted, however, appellants complain that the AAA fees are also excessive and thus in no way have they accepted defendant's offer (see, U.C.C. Sect. 2-209); because they make the same claim as to the AAA as they did with respect to the ICC, the issue of unconscionability is not rendered moot, as defendant suggests. We cannot determine on this record whether the AAA process and costs would be so 'egregiously oppressive' that they, too, would be unconscionable (*Avildsen v. Prystay*, 171 A.D.2d 13, 14, 574 N.Y.S.2d 535, appeal dismissed, 79 N.Y.2d 841, 580 N.Y.S.2d 193, 588 N.E.2d 91). Thus, we modify the order on appeal to the extent of finding that portion of the arbitration provision requiring arbitration before the ICC to be unconscionable and remand to Supreme Court so that the parties have the opportunity to seek appropriate substitution of an arbitrator pursuant to the Federal Arbitration Act (9 U.S.C. Sect. 1 et seq.), which provides for such

4. *Filias v. Gateway 2000, Inc.*, "an unreported case that interprets the same Gateway agreement" (No. 97C 2523 [N.D.Ill., 15 January 1998, transferred by 1997 U.S. Dist. LEXIS 7115 [E.D.Mich]).

court designation of an arbitrator upon application of either party, where, for whatever reason, one is not otherwise designated (9 U.S.C. Sect. 5).

[9] "Appellants make the final argument that the arbitration clause does not apply to the cause of action for false advertising (with respect to the promised round-the-clock service) under various sections of the General Business Law on the ground that there is no mention of arbitration in the technical service contract itself. Although they raise this claim for the first time on this appeal, we find the promise of technical support to be within the scope of arbitration as it is clearly a 'dispute or controversy arising out or relating to [the] Agreement or its interpretation'. Put another way, the service contract does not apply to some separate product that could be retained while the computer products – and the accompanying agreement – could be returned.

[10] "Accordingly, the order of Supreme Court, New York County (Beatrice Shainswit, J), entered 21 October 1997, which, to the extent appealed from, granted defendants' motion to dismiss the complaint as to appellants on the ground that there was a valid agreement to arbitrate between the parties, should be modified, on the law and the facts, to the extent of vacating that portion of the arbitration agreement as requires arbitration before the International Chamber of Commerce, with leave to the parties to seek appointment of an arbitrator pursuant to 9 U.S.C. Sect. 5 and remanding the matter for that purpose, and otherwise affirmed, without costs. All concur."

Part II

C. Court Decisions Applying the UNCITRAL Model Law

Note General Editor. The Yearbook commenced its reporting on the UNCITRAL Model Law on International Commercial Arbitration in Volume XVII (1992) when the new Part II – C was created to accommodate court decisions on the Model Law.

Commencing with Volume XIX (1994), the portion of "Case Law on UNCITRAL Texts (CLOUT)" containing extracts of court decisions applying the Model Law has been reproduced in the Yearbook. This is made possible thanks to the willing cooperation of the editors of CLOUT, the UNCITRAL Secretariat.

For the convenience of the reader who wishes to consult how a particular article of the Model Law has been interpreted and applied, a cumulative "Index of Articles of the UNCITRAL Model Law Reported in CLOUT" is included on pp. 354-358. This Index covers CLOUT nos. 1-23 as reproduced in Yearbook, Volume XIX (1994) through Volume XXIV (1999).

The Model Law was adopted by UNCITRAL in 1985. Since then, the following countries have enacted legislation based on the Model Law: Australia; Bahrain; Bermuda; Bulgaria; Canada (federal and provinces); Cyprus; Egypt; Germany; Guatemala; Hong Kong Special Administrative Region; Hungary; India; Iran; Ireland; Kenya; Lithuania; Malta; Mexico; New Zealand; Nigeria; Oman; Peru; Russian Federation; Scotland; Singapore; Sri Lanka; Tunisia; Ukraine; within the United States of America: California, Connecticut, Oregon and Texas; Venezuela and Zimbabwe. With the exception of the individual States within the United States, the texts of the Model Law as enacted in these countries have been published, or will be published in the forthcoming supplement of the companion publication to the Yearbook, ICCA's *International Handbook on Commercial Arbitration*. The Handbook also contains a “Commentary on the UNCITRAL Model Law” by Dr. Aron Broches.

UNITED NATIONS COMMISSION ON INTERNATIONAL TRADE LAW

CASE LAW ON UNCITRAL TEXTS (CLOUT)[1]

INTRODUCTION

This compilation of abstracts forms part of the system for collecting and disseminating information on court decisions and arbitral awards relating to Conventions and Model Laws that emanate from the work of the United Nations Commission on International Trade Law (UNCITRAL). Information about the features of that system and about its use is provided in the User Guide (A/CN.9/SER.C/GUIDE/1).[2] CLOUT documents are available on the website of the UNCITRAL Secretariat on the Internet (http://www.un.or.at/uncitral).

Unless otherwise indicated, the abstracts have been prepared by National Correspondents designated by their Governments. It should be noted that neither the National Correspondents nor anyone else directly or indirectly involved in the operation of the system assumes any responsibility for any error or omission or other deficiency.

---

2. *Note General Editor.* Excerpts from the "User Guide" are reproduced in Yearbook XIX (1994) pp. 251-253.

UNCITRAL MODEL LAW ON INTERNATIONAL COMMERCIAL ARBITRATION 1985

ABSTRACTS OF CASES[3]

A/CN.9/Ser.C/ABSTRACTS/18, 17 August 1998
A/CN.9/Ser.C/ABSTRACTS/19, 4 November 1998
A/CN.9/Ser.C/ABSTRACTS/20, 22 February 1999
A/CN.9/Ser.C/ABSTRACTS/21, 11 March 1999
A/CN.9/Ser.C/ABSTRACTS/22, 24 March 1999 and
A/CN.9/Ser.C/ABSTRACTS/23, 6 July 1999
(*excerpts*)

ZIMBABWE

Case 233: Arts. 35(1) and 36(1)(b)(ii) MAL
Zimbabwe: Harare High Court (Judge Chatikobo); Judgment No. HH-133-97
10 July and 20 August 1997
Durco (Pvt) Ltd. v. Dajen (Pvt) Ltd.
Original in English
Published in English in [1997] 2 Zimbabwe Law Reports 199 (Harare)

Two parties, a grain producer and a miller, had submitted their dispute to a single arbitrator which resulted in an award in favour of the miller. As a third party was involved who had not been a party to the arbitration, it was feared that further proceedings might ensue. Accordingly, it was felt to be in the interests of all concerned to submit to a second arbitration which would be binding on all three parties.

---

3. The materials on the UNCITRAL Model Law contained in A/CN.9/Ser.C/ABSTRACTS/20, 22 February 1999 are reproduced here. The remaining issues of CLOUT published in this reporting period (nos. 18, 19, 21, 22 and 23) do not contain cases on the Model Law.

   An **Index of Articles of the UNCITRAL Model Law reported in CLOUT** as reproduced in Volumes XIX (1994) through XXIV (1999) is included on pp. 354-358 of this Yearbook.

The second arbitration, before a panel of three arbitrators, however, resulted in an award against the miller. The miller refused to comply with the second award and the grain producer applied to the High Court for its recognition and enforcement under Art. 35 MAL. The miller opposed the award on the grounds that it would be contrary to public policy to enforce the award in terms of Art. 36(1)(b)(ii) MAL, contending that since there was already an award it would offend the principle of finality in arbitration to enforce the second award.

The court held that, by agreeing to submit to a second arbitration, the miller had waived its rights to finality of the first award. Accordingly, the miller was now bound by the second award and the court ordered that it should be recognised and enforced. The miller appealed (see CLOUT case no. 234) to the Supreme Court.

Case 234: Arts. 35(1) and 36(1)(b)(ii) MAL
Zimbabwe: Supreme Court of Zimbabwe (Judges of Appeal: Muchechetere, Ebrahim and Sandura); Judgment No. SC 141/98
22 June and 7 September 1998
Dajen (Pvt) Ltd. v. Durco (Pvt) Ltd.
Original in English
Unpublished

The miller, the unsuccessful party in CLOUT case no. 233, appealed to the Supreme Court. In dismissing the appeal, the Supreme Court held that the principle of finality did not destroy or supplant a party's power to waive any right derived from an award and that this is what the miller had done by submitting to the second arbitration.

INDEX OF ARTICLES

(as reproduced in Yearbook Volumes XIX (1994) – XXIV (1999))

Art. 9 MAL
Canada, case 11, YB XIX (1994); case 68, YB XX (1995); case 71, YB XX (1995)
Hong Kong, case 39, YB XIX (1994); case 42, YB XIX (1994); case 77, YB XX (1995)

Art. 10 MAL
Hong Kong, case 20, YB XIX (1994)
India, case 177, YB XXIII (1998)

Art. 11 MAL
Hong Kong, case 20, YB XIX (1994); case 60, YB XX (1995); case 62, YB XX (1995)

Art. 11(3)(a) MAL
Hong Kong, case 101, YB XXI (1996)

Art. 11(4) MAL
Hong Kong, case 40, YB XIX (1994)

Art. 11(4)(a) MAL
Hong Kong, case 59, YB XX (1995)

Art. 16 MAL
Bermuda, case 127, YB XXII (1997)
Canada, case 13, YB XIX (1994); case 18, YB XIX (1994); case 182, YB XXIII (1998)

Art. 16(1) MAL
Argentina, case 27, YB XIX (1994)
Canada, case 114, YB XXI (1996)
Hong Kong, case 20, YB XIX (1994)
Russian Federation, case 147, YB XXII (1997)

Art. 16(2) MAL
Russian Federation, case 148, YB XXII (1997)

Art. 16(3) MAL
Canada, case 182, YB XXIII (1998)
Russian Federation, case 147, YB XXII (1997); case 148, YB XXII (1997)

Art. 36(1)(a)(ii) MAL
Hong Kong, case 88, YB XXI (1996)

Art. 36(1)(a)(iii) MAL
Canada, case 67, YB XX (1995)

Art. 36(1)(a)(iv) MAL
Hong Kong, case 76, YB XX (1995)

Art. 36(1)(b)(ii) MAL
Canada, case 37, YB XIX (1994); case 185, YB XXIII (1998)
Zimbabwe, case 233, YB XXIV (1999); case 234, YB XXIV (1999)

Part III

A. Arbitration Rules

AMERICAN ARBITRATION ASSOCIATION*

CONTENTS

Page

COMMERCIAL MEDIATION RULES

As Amended and Effective on 1 January 1999

M-1. Agreement of Parties
Whenever, by stipulation or in their contract, the parties have provided for mediation or conciliation of existing or future disputes under the auspices of the American Arbitration Association (AAA) or under these rules, they shall be deemed to have made these rules, as amended and in effect as of the date of the submission of the dispute, a part of their agreement.

M-2. Initiation of Mediation
Any party or parties to a dispute may initiate mediation by filing with the AAA a submission to mediation or a written request for mediation pursuant to these rules, together with the appropriate Filing Fee. Where there is no submission to mediation or contract providing for mediation, a party may request the AAA to invite another party to join in a submission to mediation.

---

* The address of the American Arbitration Association is 335 Madison Avenue, New York, NY 10017-4605, USA, tel.: 1 212 716 5800, fax: 1 212 716 5905, Internet: http://www.adr.org.
The AAA International Arbitration Rules, as in effect 1 April 1997, are reproduced in Yearbook XXII (1997) pp. 303-319.

Upon receipt of such a request, the AAA will contact the other parties involved in the dispute and attempt to obtain a submission to mediation.

M-3. Requests for Mediation
A request for mediation shall contain a brief statement of the nature of the dispute and the names, addresses, and telephone numbers of all parties to the dispute and those who will represent them, if any, in the mediation. The initiating party shall simultaneously file two copies of the request with the AAA and one copy with every other party to the dispute.

M-4. Appointment of the Mediator
Upon receipt of a request for mediation, the AAA will appoint a qualified mediator to serve. Normally, a single mediator will be appointed unless the parties agree otherwise or the AAA determines otherwise. If the agreement of the parties names a mediator or specifies a method of appointing a mediator, that designation or method shall be followed.

M-5. Qualifications of the Mediator
No person shall serve as a mediator in any dispute in which that person has any financial or personal interest in the result of the mediation, except by the written consent of all parties. Prior to accepting an appointment, the prospective mediator shall disclose any circumstance likely to create a presumption of bias or prevent a prompt meeting with the parties. Upon receipt of such information, the AAA shall either replace the mediator or immediately communicate the information to the parties for their comments. In the event that the parties disagree as to whether the mediator shall serve, the AAA will appoint another mediator. The AAA is authorized to appoint another mediator if the appointed mediator is unable to serve promptly.

M-6. Vacancies
If any mediator shall become unwilling or unable to serve, the AAA will appoint another mediator, unless the parties agree otherwise.

M-7. Representation
Any party may be represented by persons of the party's choice. The names and addresses of such persons shall be communicated in writing to all parties and to the AAA.

M-8. Date, Time, and Place of Mediation
The mediator shall fix the date and the time of each mediation session. The mediation shall be held at the appropriate regional office of the AAA, or at

any other convenient location agreeable to the mediator and the parties, as the mediator shall determine.

M-9. Identification of Matters in Dispute
At least ten days prior to the first scheduled mediation session, each party shall provide the mediator with a brief memorandum setting forth its position with regard to the issues that need to be resolved. At the discretion of the mediator, such memoranda may be mutually exchanged by the parties.

At the first session, the parties will be expected to produce all information reasonably required for the mediator to understand the issues presented.

The mediator may require any party to supplement such information.

M-10. Authority of the Mediator
The mediator does not have the authority to impose a settlement on the parties but will attempt to help them reach a satisfactory resolution of their dispute. The mediator is authorized to conduct joint and separate meetings with the parties and to make oral and written recommendations for settlement. Whenever necessary, the mediator may also obtain expert advice concerning technical aspects of the dispute, provided that the parties agree and assume the expenses of obtaining such advice. Arrangements for obtaining such advice shall be made by the mediator or the parties, as the mediator shall determine.

The mediator is authorized to end the mediation whenever, in the judgment of the mediator, further efforts at mediation would not contribute to a resolution of the dispute between the parties.

M-11. Privacy
Mediation sessions are private. The parties and their representatives may attend mediation sessions. Other persons may attend only with the permission of the parties and with the consent of the mediator.

M-12. Confidentiality
Confidential information disclosed to a mediator by the parties or by witnesses in the course of the mediation shall not be divulged by the mediator. All records, reports, or other documents received by a mediator while serving in that capacity shall be confidential. The mediator shall not be compelled to divulge such records or to testify in regard to the mediation in any adversary proceeding or judicial forum.

The parties shall maintain the confidentiality of the mediation and shall not rely on, or introduce as evidence in any arbitral, judicial, or other proceeding:

a. views expressed or suggestions made by another party with respect to a possible settlement of the dispute;
b. admissions made by another party in the course of the mediation proceedings;
c. proposals made or views expressed by the mediator; or
d. the fact that another party had or had not indicated willingness to accept a proposal for settlement made by the mediator.

M-13. No Stenographic Record
There shall be no stenographic record of the mediation process.

M-14. Termination of Mediation
The mediation shall be terminated:

a. by the execution of a settlement agreement by the parties;
b. by a written declaration of the mediator to the effect that further efforts at mediation are no longer worthwhile; or
c. by a written declaration of a party or parties to the effect that the mediation proceedings are terminated.

M-15. Exclusion of Liability
Neither the AAA nor any mediator is a necessary party in judicial proceedings relating to the mediation.

Neither the AAA nor any mediator shall be liable to any party for any act or omission in connection with any mediation conducted under these rules.

M-16. Interpretation and Application of Rules
The mediator shall interpret and apply these rules insofar as they relate to the mediator's duties and responsibilities. All other rules shall be interpreted and applied by the AAA.

M-17. Expenses
The expenses of witnesses for either side shall be paid by the party producing such witnesses. All other expenses of the mediation, including required traveling and other expenses of the mediator and representatives of the AAA, and the expenses of any witness and the cost of any proofs or expert advice produced at the direct request of the mediator, shall be borne equally by the parties unless they agree otherwise.

ADMINISTRATIVE FEES

The Filing Fee

The case filing or set-up fee is $150 per party.

Additionally, the parties are charged a fee based on the number of hours of mediator time. The hourly fee is for the compensation of both the mediator and the AAA and varies according to region. Check with your local office for specific availability and rates.

There is no charge to the filing party where the AAA is requested to invite other parties to join in a submission to mediation. However, if a case settles after AAA involvement but prior to dispute resolution, the filing party will be charged a $150 filing fee.

The expenses of the AAA and the mediator, if any, are generally borne equally by the parties. The parties may vary this arrangement by agreement.

Where the parties have attempted mediation under these rules but have failed to reach a settlement, the AAA will apply the administrative fee for the mediation toward subsequent AAA arbitration filed with the AAA within ninety days of the termination of the mediation.

Deposits

Before the commencement of mediation, the parties shall each deposit such portion of the fee covering the cost of mediation as the AAA shall direct and all appropriate additional sums that the AAA deems necessary to defray the expenses of the proceeding. When the mediation has terminated, the AAA shall render an accounting and return any unexpended balance to the parties.

Refunds

Once the parties agree to mediate, no refund of the administrative fee will be made.

COMMERCIAL ARBITRATION RULES

As Amended and Effective on 1 January 1999

*R-1. Agreement of Parties**

The parties shall be deemed to have made these rules a part of their arbitration agreement whenever they have provided for arbitration by the American Arbitration Association (hereinafter AAA) under its Commercial Arbitration Rules or for arbitration by the AAA of a domestic commercial dispute without specifying particular rules. These rules and any amendment of them shall apply in the form in effect at the time the demand for arbitration or submission agreement is received by the AAA. The parties, by written agreement, may vary the procedures set forth in these rules.

R-2. AAA and Delegation of Duties

When parties agree to arbitrate under these rules, or when they provide for arbitration by the AAA and an arbitration is initiated under these rules, they thereby authorize the AAA to administer the arbitration. The authority and duties of the AAA are prescribed in the agreement of the parties and in these rules, and may be carried out through such of the AAA's representatives as it may direct. The AAA may, in its discretion, assign the administration of an arbitration to any of its offices.

R-3. National Panel of Arbitrators

The AAA shall establish and maintain a National Panel of Commercial Arbitrators and shall appoint arbitrators as provided in these rules. The term "arbitrator" in these rules refers to the arbitration panel, whether composed of one or more arbitrators and whether the arbitrators are neutral or party-appointed.

R-4. Initiation under an Arbitration Provision in a Contract

(a) Arbitration under an arbitration provision in a contract shall be initiated in the following manner:

---

* A dispute arising out of an employment relationship will be administered under the AAA's National Rules for the Resolution of Employment Disputes, unless all parties agree otherwise after the commencement of AAA administration.

i. The initiating party (the "claimant") shall, within the time period, if any, specified in the contract(s), give to the other party (the "respondent") written notice of its intention to arbitrate (the "demand"), which demand shall contain a statement setting forth the nature of the dispute, the names and addresses of all other parties, the amount involved, if any, the remedy sought, and the hearing locale requested.
ii. The claimant shall file at any office of the AAA two copies of the demand and two copies of the arbitration provisions of the contract, together with the appropriate filing fee as provided in the schedule included with these rules.
iii. The AAA shall confirm notice of such filing to the parties.

(b) A respondent may file an answering statement in duplicate with the AAA within 15 days after confirmation of notice of filing of the demand is sent by the AAA. The respondent shall, at the time of any such filing, send a copy of the answering statement to the claimant. If a counterclaim is asserted, it shall contain a statement setting forth the nature of the counterclaim, the amount involved, if any, and the remedy sought. If a counterclaim is made, the party making the counterclaim shall forward to the AAA with the answering statement the appropriate fee provided in the schedule included with these rules.

(c) If no answering statement is filed within the stated time, respondent will be deemed to deny the claim. Failure to file an answering statement shall not operate to delay the arbitration.

(d) When filing any statement pursuant to this section, the parties are encouraged to provide descriptions of their claims in sufficient detail to make the circumstances of the dispute clear to the arbitrator.

R-5. Initiation under a Submission

Parties to any existing dispute may commence an arbitration under these rules by filing at any office of the AAA two copies of a written submission to arbitrate under these rules, signed by the parties. It shall contain a statement of the nature of the dispute, the names and addresses of all parties, any claims and counterclaims, the amount involved, if any, the remedy sought, and the hearing locale requested, together with the appropriate filing fee as provided in the schedule included with these rules. Unless the parties state otherwise in the submission, all claims and counterclaims will be deemed to be denied by the other party.

R-6. Changes of Claim

After filing of a claim, if either party desires to make any new or different claim or counterclaim, it shall be made in writing and filed with the AAA. The party asserting such a claim or counterclaim shall provide a copy to the other party, who shall have 15 days from the date of such transmission within which to file an answering statement with the AAA. After the arbitrator is appointed, however, no new or different claim may be submitted except with the arbitrator's consent.

R-7. Applicable Procedures

Unless the parties or the AAA in its discretion determines otherwise, the Expedited Procedures shall be applied in any case where no disclosed claim or counterclaim exceeds $75,000, exclusive of interest and arbitration costs. Parties may also agree to use the Expedited Procedures in cases involving claims in excess of $75,000. The Expedited Procedures shall be applied as described in Sections E-1 through E-10 of these rules, in addition to any other portion of these rules that is not in conflict with the Expedited Procedures. All other cases shall be administered in accordance with Sections R-1 through R-56 of these rules.

R-8. Jurisdiction

(a) The arbitrator shall have the power to rule on his or her own jurisdiction, including any objections with respect to the existence, scope or validity of the arbitration agreement.

(b) The arbitrator shall have the power to determine the existence or validity of a contract of which an arbitration clause forms a part. Such an arbitration clause shall be treated as an agreement independent of the other terms of the contract. A decision by the arbitrator that the contract is null and void shall not for that reason alone render invalid the arbitration clause.

(c) A party must object to the jurisdiction of the arbitrator or to the arbitrability of a claim or counterclaim no later than the filing of the answering statement to the claim or counterclaim that gives rise to the objection. The arbitrator may rule on such objections as a preliminary matter or as part of the final award.

R-9. Mediation

At any stage of the proceedings, the parties may agree to conduct a mediation conference under the Commercial Mediation Rules in order to facilitate settlement. The mediator shall not be an arbitrator appointed to the case. Where the parties to a pending arbitration agree to mediate under the AAA's rules, no additional administrative fee is required to initiate the mediation.

R-10. Administrative Conference

At the request of any party or upon the AAA's own initiative, the AAA may conduct an administrative conference, in person or by telephone, with the parties and/or their representatives. The conference may address such issues as arbitrator selection, potential mediation of the dispute, potential exchange of information, a timetable for hearings and any other administrative matters. There is no administrative fee for this service.

R-11. Fixing of Locale

The parties may mutually agree on the locale where the arbitration is to be held. If any party requests that the hearing be held in a specific locale and the other party files no objection thereto within 15 days after notice of the request has been sent to it by the AAA, the locale shall be the one requested. If a party objects to the locale requested by the other party, the AAA shall have the power to determine the locale, and its decision shall be final and binding.

R-12. Qualifications of an Arbitrator

(a) Any neutral arbitrator appointed pursuant to Section R-13, R-14, R-15, or E-5, or selected by mutual choice of the parties or their appointees, shall be subject to disqualification for the reasons specified in Section R-19. If the parties specifically so agree in writing, the arbitrator shall not be subject to disqualification for those reasons.

(b) Unless the parties agree otherwise, an arbitrator selected unilaterally by one party is a party-appointed arbitrator and is not subject to disqualification pursuant to Section R-19.

R-13. Appointment from Panel

If the parties have not appointed an arbitrator and have not provided any other method of appointment, the arbitrator shall be appointed in the following manner:

(a) Immediately after the filing of the submission or the answering statement or the expiration of the time within which the answering statement is to be filed, the AAA shall send simultaneously to each party to the dispute an identical list of names of persons chosen from the panel. The parties are encouraged to agree to an arbitrator from the submitted list and to advise the AAA of their agreement.

(b) If the parties are unable to agree upon an arbitrator, each party to the dispute shall have 15 days from the transmittal date in which to strike names objected to, number the remaining names in order of preference, and return the list to the AAA. If a party does not return the list within the time specified, all persons named therein shall be deemed acceptable. From among the persons who have been approved on both lists, and in accordance with the designated order of mutual preference, the AAA shall invite the acceptance of an arbitrator to serve. If the parties fail to agree on any of the persons named, or if acceptable arbitrators are unable to act, or if for any other reason the appointment cannot be made from the submitted lists, the AAA shall have the power to make the appointment from among other members of the panel without the submission of additional lists.

(c) Unless the parties have agreed otherwise no later than 15 days after the commencement of an arbitration, if the notice of arbitration names two or more claimants or two or more respondents, the AAA shall appoint all the arbitrators.

R-14. Direct Appointment by a Party

(a) If the agreement of the parties names an arbitrator or specifies a method of appointing an arbitrator, that designation or method shall be followed. The notice of appointment, with the name and address of the arbitrator, shall be filed with the AAA by the appointing party. Upon the request of any appointing party, the AAA shall submit a list of members of the panel from which the party may, if it so desires, make the appointment.

(b) If the agreement specifies a period of time within which an arbitrator shall be appointed and any party fails to make the appointment within that period, the AAA shall make the appointment.

(c) If no period of time is specified in the agreement, the AAA shall notify the party to make the appointment. If within 15 days after such notice has been sent, an arbitrator has not been appointed by a party, the AAA shall make the appointment.

R-15. Appointment of Neutral Arbitrator by Party-Appointed Arbitrators or Parties

(a) If the parties have selected party-appointed arbitrators, or if such arbitrators have been appointed as provided in Section R-14, and the parties have authorized them to appoint a neutral arbitrator within a specified time and no appointment is made within that time or any agreed extension, the AAA may appoint a neutral arbitrator, who shall act as chairperson.

(b) If no period of time is specified for appointment of the neutral arbitrator and the party-appointed arbitrators or the parties do not make the appointment within 15 days from the date of the appointment of the last party-appointed arbitrator, the AAA may appoint the neutral arbitrator, who shall act as chairperson.

(c) If the parties have agreed that their party-appointed arbitrators shall appoint the neutral arbitrator from the panel, the AAA shall furnish to the party-appointed arbitrators, in the manner provided in Section R-13, a list selected from the panel, and the appointment of the neutral arbitrator shall be made as provided in that section.

R-16. Nationality of Arbitrator

Where the parties are nationals or residents of different countries, the AAA, at the request of any party or on its own initiative, may appoint as a neutral arbitrator a national of a country other than that of any of the parties. The request must be made prior to the time set for the appointment of the arbitrator as agreed by the parties or set by these rules.

R-17. Number of Arbitrators

If the arbitration agreement does not specify the number of arbitrators, the dispute shall be heard and determined by one arbitrator, unless the AAA, in its discretion, directs that three arbitrators be appointed. The parties may request three arbitrators in their demand or answer, which request the AAA will consider in exercising its discretion regarding the number of arbitrators appointed to the dispute.

R-18. Notice to Arbitrator of Appointment

Notice of the appointment of the neutral arbitrator, whether appointed mutually by the parties or by the AAA, shall be sent to the arbitrator by the AAA, together with a copy of these rules, and the signed acceptance of the arbitrator shall be filed with the AAA prior to the opening of the first hearing.

R-19. Disclosure and Challenge Procedure

(a) Any person appointed as a neutral arbitrator shall disclose to the AAA any circumstance likely to affect impartiality or independence, including any bias or any financial or personal interest in the result of the arbitration or any past or present relationship with the parties or their representatives. Upon receipt of such information from the arbitrator or another source, the AAA shall communicate the information to the parties and, if it deems it appropriate to do so, to the arbitrator and others.

(b) Upon objection of a party to the continued service of a neutral arbitrator, the AAA shall determine whether the arbitrator should be disqualified and shall inform the parties of its decision, which shall be conclusive.

R-20. Communication with Arbitrator

(a) No party and no one acting on behalf of any party shall communicate unilaterally concerning the arbitration with a neutral arbitrator or a candidate for neutral arbitrator. Unless the parties agree otherwise or the arbitrator so directs, any communication from the parties to a neutral arbitrator shall be sent to the AAA for transmittal to the arbitrator.

(b) The parties or the arbitrators may also agree that once the panel has been constituted, no party and no one acting on behalf of any party shall communicate unilaterally concerning the arbitration with any party-appointed arbitrator.

R-21. Vacancies

(a) If for any reason an arbitrator is unable to perform the duties of the office, the AAA may, on proof satisfactory to it, declare the office vacant. Vacancies shall be filled in accordance with the applicable provisions of these rules.

(b) In the event of a vacancy in a panel of neutral arbitrators after the hearings have commenced, the remaining arbitrator or arbitrators may continue with the hearing and determination of the controversy, unless the parties agree otherwise.

(c) In the event of the appointment of a substitute arbitrator, the panel of arbitrators shall determine in its sole discretion whether it is necessary to repeat all or part of any prior hearings.

R-22. Preliminary Hearing

(a) At the request of any party or at the discretion of the arbitrator or the AAA, the arbitrator may schedule as soon as practicable a preliminary hearing with the parties and/or their representatives. The preliminary hearing may be conducted by telephone at the arbitrator's discretion. There is no administrative fee for the first preliminary hearing.

(b) During the preliminary hearing, the parties and the arbitrator should discuss the future conduct of the case, including clarification of the issues and claims, a schedule for the hearings and any other preliminary matters.

R-23. Exchange of Information

(a) At the request of any party or at the discretion of the arbitrator, consistent with the expedited nature of arbitration, the arbitrator may direct (i) the production of documents and other information, and (ii) the identification of any witnesses to be called.

(b) At least five (5) business days prior to the hearing, the parties shall exchange copies of all exhibits they intend to submit at the hearing.

(c) The arbitrator is authorized to resolve any disputes concerning the exchange of information.

R-24. Date, Time, and Place of Hearing

The arbitrator shall set the date, time, and place for each hearing. The parties shall respond to requests for hearing dates in a timely manner, be cooperative in scheduling the earliest practicable date, and adhere to the established hearing schedule. The AAA shall send a notice of hearing to the parties at least 10 days in advance of the hearing date, unless otherwise agreed by the parties.

R-25. Attendance at Hearings

The arbitrator and the AAA shall maintain the privacy of the hearings unless the law provides to the contrary. Any person having a direct interest in the arbitration is entitled to attend hearings. The arbitrator shall otherwise have the power to require the exclusion of any witness, other than a party or other essential person, during the testimony of any other witness. It shall be discretionary with the arbitrator to determine the propriety of the attendance of any other person other than a party and its representatives.

R-26. Representation

Any party may be represented by counsel or other authorized representative. A party intending to be so represented shall notify the other party and the AAA of the name and address of the representative at least three days prior to the date set for the hearing at which that person is first to appear. When such a representative initiates an arbitration or responds for a party, notice is deemed to have been given.

R-27. Oaths

Before proceeding with the first hearing, each arbitrator may take an oath of office and, if required by law, shall do so. The arbitrator may require witnesses to testify under oath administered by any duly qualified person and, if it is required by law or requested by any party, shall do so.

R-28. Stenographic Record

Any party desiring a stenographic record shall make arrangements directly with a stenographer and shall notify the other parties of these arrangements at least three days in advance of the hearing. The requesting party or parties shall pay the cost of the record. If the transcript is agreed by the parties, or determined by the arbitrator to be the official record of the proceeding, it must be provided to the arbitrator and made available to the other parties for inspection, at a date, time, and place determined by the arbitrator.

R-29. Interpreters
Any party wishing an interpreter shall make all arrangements directly with the interpreter and shall assume the costs of the service.

R-30. Postponements
The arbitrator may postpone any hearing upon agreement of the parties, upon request of a party for good cause shown, or upon the arbitrator's own initiative. A party or parties causing a postponement of a hearing will be charged a postponement fee, as set forth in the administrative fee schedule.

R-31. Arbitration in the Absence of a Party or Representative
Unless the law provides to the contrary, the arbitration may proceed in the absence of any party or representative who, after due notice, fails to be present or fails to obtain a postponement. An award shall not be made solely on the default of a party. The arbitrator shall require the party who is present to submit such evidence as the arbitrator may require for the making of an award.

R-32. Conduct of Proceedings
(a) The claimant shall present evidence to support its claim. The respondent shall then present evidence to support its defense. Witnesses for each party shall also submit to questions from the arbitrator and the adverse party. The arbitrator has the discretion to vary this procedure, provided that the parties are treated with equality and that each party has the right to be heard and is given a fair opportunity to present its case.

(b) The arbitrator, exercising his or her discretion, shall conduct the proceedings with a view to expediting the resolution of the dispute and may direct the order of proof, bifurcate proceedings and direct the parties to focus their presentations on issues the decision of which could dispose of all or part of the case.

(c) The parties may agree to waive oral hearings in any case.

R-33. Evidence
(a) The parties may offer such evidence as is relevant and material to the dispute and shall produce such evidence as the arbitrator may deem necessary to an understanding and determination of the dispute. Conformity to legal rules of evidence shall not be necessary. All evidence shall be taken in the presence of all of the arbitrators and all of the parties, except where any of the parties is absent, in default or has waived the right to be present.

(b) The arbitrator shall determine the admissibility, relevance, and materiality of the evidence offered and may exclude evidence deemed by the arbitrator to be cumulative or irrelevant.

(c) The arbitrator shall take into account applicable principles of legal privilege, such as those involving the confidentiality of communications between a lawyer and client.

(d) An arbitrator or other person authorized by law to subpoena witnesses or documents may do so upon the request of any party or independently.

R-34. Evidence by Affidavit and Posthearing Filing of Documents or Other Evidence

(a) The arbitrator may receive and consider the evidence of witnesses by declaration or affidavit, but shall give it only such weight as the arbitrator deems it entitled to after consideration of any objection made to its admission.

(b) If the parties agree or the arbitrator directs that documents or other evidence be submitted to the arbitrator after the hearing, the documents or other evidence shall be filed with the AAA for transmission to the arbitrator. All parties shall be afforded an opportunity to examine and respond to such documents or other evidence.

R-35. Inspection or Investigation

An arbitrator finding it necessary to make an inspection or investigation in connection with the arbitration shall direct the AAA to so advise the parties. The arbitrator shall set the date and time and the AAA shall notify the parties. Any party who so desires may be present at such an inspection or investigation. In the event that one or all parties are not present at the inspection or investigation, the arbitrator shall make an oral or written report to the parties and afford them an opportunity to comment.

*R-36. Interim Measures***

(a) The arbitrator may take whatever interim measures he or she deems necessary, including injunctive relief and measures for the protection or conservation of property and disposition of perishable goods.

(b) Such interim measures may take the form of an interim award, and the arbitrator may require security for the costs of such measures.

(c) A request for interim measures addressed by a party to a judicial authority shall not be deemed incompatible with the agreement to arbitrate or a waiver of the right to arbitrate.

R-37. Closing of Hearing

The arbitrator shall specifically inquire of all parties whether they have any further proofs to offer or witnesses to be heard. Upon receiving negative

---

** The Optional Rules are reproduced below at pp. 385 388.

replies or if satisfied that the record is complete, the arbitrator shall declare the hearing closed.

If briefs are to be filed, the hearing shall be declared closed as of the final date set by the arbitrator for the receipt of briefs. If documents are to be filed as provided in Section R-34 and the date set for their receipt is later than that set for the receipt of briefs, the later date shall be the closing date of the hearing. The time limit within which the arbitrator is required to make the award shall commence, in the absence of other agreements by the parties, upon the closing of the hearing.

R-38. Reopening of Hearing

The hearing may be reopened on the arbitrator's initiative, or upon application of a party, at any time before the award is made. If reopening the hearing would prevent the making of the award within the specific time agreed on by the parties in the contract(s) out of which the controversy has arisen, the matter may not be reopened unless the parties agree on an extension of time. When no specific date is fixed in the contract, the arbitrator may reopen the hearing and shall have 30 days from the closing of the reopened hearing within which to make an award.

R-39. Waiver of Rules

Any party who proceeds with the arbitration after knowledge that any provision or requirement of these rules has not been complied with and who fails to state an objection in writing shall be deemed to have waived the right to object.

R-40. Extensions of Time

The parties may modify any period of time by mutual agreement. The AAA or the arbitrator may for good cause extend any period of time established by these rules, except the time for making the award. The AAA shall notify the parties of any extension.

R-41. Serving of Notice

(a) Any papers, notices, or process necessary or proper for the initiation or continuation of an arbitration under these rules, for any court action in connection therewith, or for the entry of judgment on any award made under these rules may be served on a party by mail addressed to the party, or its representative at the last known address or by personal service, in or outside the state where the arbitration is to be held, provided that reasonable opportunity to be heard with regard to the dispute is or has been granted to the party.

(b) The AAA, the arbitrator and the parties may also use overnight delivery or electronic facsimile transmission (fax), to give the notices required by these rules. Where all parties and the arbitrator agree, notices may be transmitted by electronic mail (E-mail), or other methods of communication.

(c) Unless otherwise instructed by the AAA or by the arbitrator, any documents submitted by any party to the AAA or to the arbitrator shall simultaneously be provided to the other party or parties to the arbitration.

R-42. Majority Decision

When the panel consists of more than one arbitrator, unless required by law or by the arbitration agreement, a majority of the arbitrators must make all decisions.

R-43. Time of Award

The award shall be made promptly by the arbitrator and, unless otherwise agreed by the parties or specified by law, no later than 30 days from the date of closing the hearing, or, if oral hearings have been waived, from the date of the AAA's transmittal of the final statements and proofs to the arbitrator.

R-44. Form of Award

(a) Any award shall be in writing and signed by a majority of the arbitrators. It shall be executed in the manner required by law.

(b) The arbitrator need not render a reasoned award unless the parties request such an award in writing prior to appointment of the arbitrator or unless the arbitrator determines that a reasoned award is appropriate.

R-45. Scope of Award

(a) The arbitrator may grant any remedy or relief that the arbitrator deems just and equitable and within the scope of the agreement of the parties, including, but not limited to, specific performance of a contract.

(b) In addition to a final award, the arbitrator may make other decisions, including interim, interlocutory, or partial rulings, orders, and awards. In any interim, interlocutory, or partial award, the arbitrator may assess and apportion the fees, expenses, and compensation related to such award as the arbitrator determines is appropriate.

(c) In the final award, the arbitrator shall assess the fees, expenses, and compensation provided in Sections R-51, R-52, and R-53. The arbitrator may apportion such fees, expenses, and compensation among the parties in such amounts as the arbitrator determines is appropriate.

(d) The award of the arbitrator(s) may include: (a) interest at such rate and from such date as the arbitrator(s) may deem appropriate; and (b) an award of attorneys' fees if all parties have requested such an award or it is authorized by law or their arbitration agreement.

R-46. Award upon Settlement
If the parties settle their dispute during the course of the arbitration and if the parties so request, the arbitrator may set forth the terms of the settlement in a "consent award".

R-47. Delivery of Award to Parties
Parties shall accept as notice and delivery of the award the placing of the award or a true copy thereof in the mail addressed to the parties or their representatives at the last known addresses, personal or electronic service of the award, or the filing of the award in any other manner that is permitted by law.

R-48. Modification of Award
Within 20 days after the transmittal of an award, any party, upon notice to the other parties, may request the arbitrator, through the AAA, to correct any clerical, typographical, or computational errors in the award. The arbitrator is not empowered to redetermine the merits of any claim already decided. The other parties shall be given 10 days to respond to the request. The arbitrator shall dispose of the request within 20 days after transmittal by the AAA to the arbitrator of the request and any response thereto.

R-49. Release of Documents for Judicial Proceedings
The AAA shall, upon the written request of a party, furnish to the party, at the party's expense, certified copies of any papers in the AAA's possession that may be required in judicial proceedings relating to the arbitration.

R-50. Applications to Court and Exclusion of Liability
(a) No judicial proceeding by a party relating to the subject matter of the arbitration shall be deemed a waiver of the party's right to arbitrate.

(b) Neither the AAA nor any arbitrator in a proceeding under these rules is a necessary party in judicial proceedings relating to the arbitration.

(c) Parties to an arbitration under these rules shall be deemed to have consented that judgment upon the arbitration award may be entered in any federal or state court having jurisdiction thereof.

(d) Neither the AAA nor any arbitrator shall be liable to any party for any act or omission in connection with any arbitration conducted under these rules.

R-51. Administrative Fees
As a not-for-profit organization, the AAA shall prescribe filing and other administrative fees and service charges to compensate it for the cost of providing administrative services. The fees in effect when the fee or charge is incurred shall be applicable.

The filing fee shall be advanced by the party or parties making a claim or counterclaim, subject to final apportionment by the arbitrator in the award.

The AAA may, in the event of extreme hardship on the part of any party, defer or reduce the administrative fees.

R-52. Expenses
The expenses of witnesses for either side shall be paid by the party producing such witnesses. All other expenses of the arbitration, including required travel and other expenses of the arbitrator, AAA representatives, and any witness and the cost of any proof produced at the direct request of the arbitrator, shall be borne equally by the parties, unless they agree otherwise or unless the arbitrator in the award assesses such expenses or any part thereof against any specified party or parties.

R-53. Neutral Arbitrator's Compensation
(a) Unless the parties agree otherwise, members of the National Panel of Commercial Arbitrators appointed as neutrals on cases administered under the Expedited Procedures with claims not exceeding $10,000, will customarily serve without compensation for the first day of service. Thereafter, arbitrators shall receive compensation as set forth herein.

(b) Arbitrators shall be compensated at a rate consistent with the arbitrator's stated rate of compensation, beginning with the first day of hearing in all cases with claims exceeding $10,000.

(c) If there is disagreement concerning the terms of compensation, an appropriate rate shall be established with the arbitrator by the AAA and confirmed to the parties.

(d) Any arrangement for the compensation of a neutral arbitrator shall be made through the AAA and not directly between the parties and the arbitrator.

R-54. Deposits
The AAA may require the parties to deposit in advance of any hearings such sums of money as it deems necessary to cover the expense of the arbitration, including the arbitrator's fee, if any, and shall render an accounting to the parties and return any unexpended balance at the conclusion of the case.

R-55. Interpretation and Application of Rules
The arbitrator shall interpret and apply these rules insofar as they relate to the arbitrator's powers and duties. When there is more than one arbitrator and a difference arises among them concerning the meaning or application of these rules, it shall be decided by a majority vote. If that is not possible, either an arbitrator or a party may refer the question to the AAA for final decision. All other rules shall be interpreted and applied by the AAA.

R-56. Suspension for Nonpayment
If arbitrator compensation or administrative charges have not been paid in full, the AAA may so inform the parties in order that one of them may advance the required payment. If such payments are not made, the arbitrator may order the suspension or termination of the proceedings. If no arbitrator has yet been appointed, the AAA may suspend the proceedings.

EXPEDITED PROCEDURES

As Amended and Effective on 1 January 1999

E-1. Applicability
Unless the parties or the AAA determines otherwise, these procedures shall apply in any case in which no disclosed claim or counterclaim exceeds $75,000, exclusive of interest and arbitration fees and costs. Parties may also agree to use these procedures in larger cases. Unless the parties agree otherwise, these procedures will not apply in cases in which there is no disclosed monetary claim or in cases involving more than two parties.

E-2. Limitation on Extensions
Except in extraordinary circumstances, the AAA or the arbitrator may grant a party no more than one seven-day extension of time to respond to the demand for arbitration or counterclaim as provided in Section R-4.

E-3. Changes of Claim or Counterclaim
A claim or counterclaim may be increased in amount, or a new or different claim or counterclaim added, upon the agreement of the other party, or the consent of the arbitrator. After the arbitrator is appointed, however, no new or different claim or counterclaim may be submitted except with the arbitrator's consent.

If an increased claim or counterclaim exceeds $75,000, the case will be administered under the regular procedures unless all parties and the arbitrator agree that the case may continue to be processed under the Expedited Procedures.

E-4. Serving of Notices

In addition to notice provided by Section R-41(b), the parties shall also accept notice by telephone. Telephonic notices by the AAA shall subsequently be confirmed in writing to the parties. Should there be a failure to confirm in writing any such oral notice, the proceeding shall nevertheless be valid if notice has, in fact, been given by telephone.

E-5. Appointment and Qualifications of Arbitrator

(a) The AAA shall simultaneously submit to each party an identical list of five proposed arbitrators drawn from its panel from which one arbitrator shall be appointed.

(b) The parties are encouraged to agree to an arbitrator from this list and to advise the AAA of their agreement. If the parties are unable to agree upon an arbitrator, each party may strike two names from the list and return it to the AAA within seven days from the date of the AAA's mailing to the parties. If for any reason the appointment of an arbitrator cannot be made from the list, the AAA may make the appointment from other members of the panel without the submission of additional lists.

(c) The parties will be given notice by the AAA of the appointment of the arbitrator, who shall be subject to disqualification for the reasons specified in Section R-19. The parties shall notify the AAA within seven days of any objection to the arbitrator appointed. Any such objection shall be for cause and shall be confirmed in writing to the AAA with a copy to the other party or parties.

E-6. Exchange of Exhibits

At least two business days prior to the hearing, the parties shall exchange copies of all exhibits they intend to submit at the hearing. The arbitrator shall resolve disputes concerning the exchange of exhibits.

E-7. Proceedings on Documents

Where no party's claim exceeds $10,000, exclusive of interest and arbitration costs, and other cases in which the parties agree, the dispute shall be resolved by submission of documents, unless any party requests an oral hearing, or the arbitrator determines that an oral hearing is necessary. The arbitrator shall establish a fair and equitable procedure for the submission of documents.

E-8. Date, Time, and Place of Hearing
There shall not be an administrative conference. In cases in which a hearing is to be held, the arbitrator shall set the date, time, and place of the hearing, to be scheduled to take place within 30 days of confirmation of the arbitrator's appointment. The AAA will notify the parties in advance of the hearing date.

E-9. The Hearing
(a) Generally, the hearing shall not exceed one day. Each party shall have equal opportunity to submit its proofs and complete its case. The arbitrator shall determine the order of the hearing, and may require further submission of documents within two days after the hearing. For good cause shown, the arbitrator may schedule additional hearings within seven business days after the initial day of hearings.

(b) Generally, there will be no stenographic record. Any party desiring a stenographic record may arrange for one pursuant to the provisions of Section R-28.

E-10. Time of Award
Unless otherwise agreed by the parties, the award shall be rendered not later than fourteen days from the date of the closing of the hearing or, if oral hearings have been waived, from the date of the AAA's transmittal of the final statements and proofs to the arbitrator.

OPTIONAL PROCEDURES FOR LARGE, COMPLEX COMMERCIAL DISPUTES

As Amended and Effective on 1 January 1999

L-1. Applicability
(a) Unless the parties agree otherwise, these Optional Procedures for Large, Complex Commercial Disputes (hereinafter "Procedures") shall apply to all cases administered by the AAA under the Commercial Arbitration Rules in which the disclosed claim or counterclaim of any party is at least $1,000,000 exclusive of claimed interest, arbitration fees and costs, and in which either (1) all parties have elected to have the Procedures apply to the resolution of their dispute; or (2) a court or governmental agency of competent jurisdiction has determined that a dispute should be resolved before the AAA pursuant to the procedures. Parties may also agree to using the Procedures in cases involving

claims or counterclaims under $1,000,000, in non-monetary cases or in cases involving claims of undetermined amount. The Procedures are designed to complement the Regular Commercial Arbitration Rules. To the extent that there is any variance between such rules and these Procedures, the Procedures shall control. Any such cases are herein referred to as Large, Complex Cases.

(b) The parties to any arbitration proceeding that is to be subject to the Procedures may, prior to the appointment of the arbitrator(s) and by consent of all parties, agree to eliminate, modify or alter any of the Procedures, and, in such case, these Procedures as so modified or altered shall apply to that particular case. After appointment of the arbitrator(s), such modifications may be made only with the consent of the arbitrator(s).

L-2. Administrative Conference

Prior to the dissemination of a list of potential arbitrators, the AAA shall, unless it determines same to be unnecessary, conduct an administrative conference with the parties and/or their attorneys or other representatives, either in person or by conference call, at the discretion of the AAA. Such administrative conference shall be conducted for the following purposes and for such additional purposes as the parties or the AAA may deem appropriate:

(a) to obtain additional information about the nature and magnitude of the dispute and the anticipated length of hearing and scheduling;
(b) to discuss the views of the parties about the technical and other qualifications of the arbitrators;
(c) to obtain conflicts statements from the parties; and
(d) to consider, with the parties, whether mediation or other non-adjudicative methods of dispute resolution might be appropriate.

L-3. Arbitrators

(a) Large, Complex Commercial Cases shall be heard and determined by either one or three arbitrators, as may be agreed upon by the parties. If the parties are unable to agree upon the number of arbitrators, then three arbitrator(s) shall hear and determine the case.

(b) The AAA shall appoint arbitrator(s) as agreed by the parties. If they are unable to agree on a method of appointment, the AAA shall appoint arbitrators from the Large, Complex Commercial Case Panel, in the manner provided in the Regular Commercial Arbitration Rules. Absent agreement of the parties, the arbitrator(s) shall not have served as the mediator in the mediation phase of the instant proceeding.

L-4. Preliminary Hearing

As promptly as practicable after the selection of the arbitrator(s), a preliminary hearing shall be held among the parties and/or their attorneys or other representatives and the arbitrator(s). With the consent of the arbitrator(s) and the parties, the preliminary hearing may: (a) be conducted by the Chair of the panel rather than all the arbitrator(s); (b) be conducted by telephone conference call rather than in person; or (c) be omitted.

At the preliminary hearing the matters to be considered shall include, without limitation: (a) service of a detailed statement of claims, damages and defenses, a statement of the issues asserted by each party and positions with respect thereto, and any legal authorities the parties may wish to bring to the attention of the arbitrator(s); (b) stipulations to uncontested facts; (c) the extent to which discovery shall be conducted; (d) exchange and premarking of those documents which each party believes may be offered at the hearing; (e) the identification and availability of witnesses, including experts, and such matters with respect to witnesses including their biographies and expected testimony as may be appropriate; (f) whether, and the extent to which, any sworn statements and/or depositions may be introduced; (g) the extent to which hearings will proceed on consecutive days; (h) whether a stenographic or other official record of the proceedings shall be maintained; and (i) the possibility of utilizing mediation or other non-adjudicative methods of dispute resolution.

L-5. Management of Proceedings

(a) Arbitrators shall take such steps as they may deem necessary or desirable to avoid delay and to achieve a just, speedy and cost-effective resolution of Large, Complex Commercial Cases.

(b) Parties shall cooperate in the exchange of documents, exhibits and information within such party's control if the arbitrator(s) consider such production to be consistent with the goal of achieving a just, speedy and cost-effective resolution of a Large, Complex Commercial Case.

(c) The parties may conduct such document discovery as may be agreed to by all the parties provided, however, that the arbitrator(s) may place such limitations on the conduct of such discovery as the arbitrator(s) shall deem appropriate. If the parties cannot agree on document discovery, the arbitrator(s) for good cause shown and consistent with the expedited nature of arbitration, may establish the extent of same.

(d) The arbitrator(s) upon good cause shown may order the conduct of the deposition of, or the propounding of interrogatories to, such persons who may possess information determined by the arbitrator(s) to be necessary to a determination of a Large, Complex Commercial Case.

(e) Generally hearings will be scheduled on consecutive days or in blocks of consecutive days in order to maximize efficiency and minimize costs.

(f) The arbitrator(s) may direct the recording of the hearings, the cost of which shall be borne equally by the parties.

OPTIONAL RULES FOR EMERGENCY MEASURES OF PROTECTION

As Amended and Effective on 1 January 1999

O-1. Applicability
Where parties by special agreement or in their arbitration clause have adopted these rules for emergency measures of protection, a party in need of emergency relief prior to the constitution of the panel shall notify the AAA and all other parties in writing of the nature of the relief sought and the reasons why such relief is required on an emergency basis. The application shall also set forth the reasons why the party is entitled to such relief. Such notice may be given by facsimile transmission, or other reliable means, but must include a statement certifying that all other parties have been notified or an explanation of the steps taken in good faith to notify other parties.

O-2. Appointment of Emergency Arbitrator
Within one business day of receipt of notice as provided in Section O-1, the AAA shall appoint a single emergency arbitrator from a special AAA panel of emergency arbitrators designated to rule on emergency applications. The emergency arbitrator shall immediately disclose any circumstance likely, on the basis of the facts disclosed in the application, to affect such arbitrator's impartiality or independence. Any challenge to the appointment of the emergency arbitrator must be made within one business day of the communication by the AAA to the parties of the appointment of the emergency arbitrator and the circumstances disclosed.

O-3. Schedule
The emergency arbitrator shall as soon as possible, but in any event within two business days of appointment, establish a schedule for consideration of the application for emergency relief. Such schedule shall provide a reasonable opportunity to all parties to be heard, but may provide for proceeding by telephone conference or on written submissions as alternatives to a formal hearing.

O-4. Interim Award

If after consideration the emergency arbitrator is satisfied that the party seeking the emergency relief has shown that immediate and irreparable loss or damage will result in the absence of emergency relief, and that such party is entitled to such relief, the emergency arbitrator may enter an interim award granting the relief and stating the reasons therefor.

O-5. Constitution of the Panel

Any application to modify an interim award of emergency relief must be based on changed circumstances and may be made to the emergency arbitrator until the panel is constituted; thereafter such a request shall be addressed to the panel. The emergency arbitrator shall have no further power to act after the panel is constituted unless the parties agree that the emergency arbitrator is named as a member of the panel.

O-6. Security

Any interim award of emergency relief may be conditioned on provision by the party seeking such relief of appropriate security.

O-7. Special Master

A request for interim measures addressed by a party to a judicial authority shall not be deemed incompatible with the agreement to arbitrate or a waiver of the right to arbitrate. If the AAA is directed by a judicial authority to nominate a special master to consider and report on an application for emergency relief, the AAA shall proceed as provided in Section O-1 of this article and the references to the emergency arbitrator shall be read to mean the special master, except that the special master shall issue a report rather than an interim award.

O-8. Costs

The costs associated with applications for emergency relief shall initially be apportioned by the emergency arbitrator or special master, subject to the power of the panel to determine finally the apportionment of such costs.

ADMINISTRATIVE FEES

The administrative fees of the AAA are based on the amount of the claim or counterclaim. Arbitrator compensation is not included in this schedule. Unless the parties agree otherwise, arbitrator compensation and administrative fees are subject to allocation by the arbitrator in the award.

FILING FEES

A nonrefundable filing fee is payable in full by a filing party when a claim, counterclaim or additional claim is filed, as provided below.

Amount of Claim	Filing Fee
Up to $ 10,000	$ 500
Above $ 10,000 to $ 50,000	$ 750
Above $ 50,000 to $ 100,000	$1,250
Above $ 100,000 to $ 250,000	$2,000
Above $ 250,000 to $ 500,000	$3,500
Above $ 500,000 to $1,000,000	$5,000
Above $1,000,000 to $5,000,000	$7,000
Above $5,000,000	Negotiated

When no amount can be stated at the time of filing, the minimum fee is $2,000, subject to increase when the claim or counterclaim is disclosed.

When a claim or counterclaim is not for a monetary amount, an appropriate filing fee will be determined by the AAA.

The minimum filing fee for any case having three or more arbitrators is $2,000.

Expedited Procedures are applied in any case where no disclosed claim or counterclaim exceeds $75,000, exclusive of interest and arbitration cost.

HEARING FEES

For each day of hearing held before a single arbitrator, an administrative fee of $150 is payable by each party.

For each day of hearing held before a multi-arbitrator panel, an administrative fee of $250 is payable by each party.

There is no AAA hearing fee for the initial Procedural Hearing.

There is no hearing fee for the initial hearing in cases in which no party's claim exceeds $10,000, administered under the Expedited Procedures.

POSTPONEMENT/CANCELLATION FEES

A fee of $150 is payable by a party causing a postponement/cancellation of any hearing scheduled before a single arbitrator.

A fee of $250 is payable by a party causing a postponement/cancellation of any hearing scheduled before a multi-arbitrator panel.

HEARING ROOM RENTAL

The Hearing Fees described above do not cover the rental of hearing rooms, which are available on a rental basis. Check with the AAA for availability and rates.

CHINA INTERNATIONAL ECONOMIC AND TRADE ARBITRATION COMMISSION*

ARBITRATION RULES[1]

Effective as from 10 May 1998

CHAPTER I. GENERAL PROVISIONS

Section 1 – Jurisdiction

Article 1
These Rules are formulated in accordance with the Arbitration Law of the People's Republic of China and the provisions of the relevant laws and pursuant to the "Decision" of the former Government Administration Council of the Central People's Government and the "Notice" and "Official Reply" of the State Council.

Article 2
China International Economic and Trade Arbitration Commission (originally named Foreign Trade Arbitration Commission of the China Council for the Promotion of International Trade, later renamed as Foreign Economic and Trade Arbitration Commission of the China Council for the Promotion of

* The address of the China International Economic and Trade Arbitration Commission is 6/F Golden Land Building, No. 32 Liang Ma Qiao Road, Beijing 100016, China, tel.: 86 10 6464 6688, fax: 86 10 6464 3500/3520, e-mail: cietac@public.bta.net.cn. The addresses of the Sub-Commissions are: CIETAC Shenzhen Sub-Commission, 19/F, Block B, Zhongyin Building, 5015 Caitian Road, Futian District, Shenzhen 518026, China, tel.: 86 755 350 1700, fax: 86 755 250 0591, e-mail: szcietac@public.szptt.net.cn; Shanghai Sub-Commission, 7/F No 2 Building, 28 West Jin Ling Road, Shanghai 200021, China, tel: 86 21 6587 7878/6387/8686, fax 86 21 6387 7070, e-mail: cietac@sh.col.com.cn.

1. Revised and Adopted by the China Chamber of International Commerce on 6 May 1998.

International Trade, and presently called China International Economic and Trade Arbitration Commission, hereinafter referred to as the Arbitration Commission) independently and impartially resolves, by means of arbitration, disputes arising from economic and trade transactions, contractual or non-contractual.

The disputes stated in the preceding paragraph include:

(1) international or foreign related disputes;
(2) disputes related to the Hong Kong SAR, Macao or Taiwan regions;
(3) disputes between the enterprises with foreign investment and disputes between an enterprise with foreign investment and another Chinese legal person, physical person and/or economic organization;
(4) disputes arising from project financing, invitation for tender, bidding, construction and other activities conducted by Chinese legal persons, physical persons and/or other economic organizations through utilizing the capital, technology or service from foreign counties, international organizations or from the Hong Kong SAR, Macao and Taiwan regions; and
(5) disputes that may be taken cognizance of by the Arbitration Commission in accordance with special provisions of or upon special authorization from the law or administrative regulations of the People's Republic of China.

Article 3

The Arbitration Commission takes cognizance of cases in accordance with an arbitration agreement between the parties concluded before or after the occurrence of the dispute to refer their dispute to the Arbitration Commission for arbitration and upon the written application by one of the parties.

An arbitration agreement means an arbitration clause stipulated by the parties in their contract or a written agreement concluded by the parties in other forms to submit their dispute for arbitration.

Article 4

The Arbitration Commission has the power to decide on the existence and validity of an arbitration agreement and the jurisdiction over an arbitration case. If a party challenges the validity of the arbitration agreement and requests the Arbitration Commission to make a decision thereupon and the other party applies to the People's Court for a ruling, the Court's ruling shall prevail.

Article 5

An arbitration clause contained in a contract shall be regarded as existing independently and separately from the other clauses of the contract, and an arbitration agreement attached to a contract shall be treated as a part of the contract existing independently and separately from the other parts of the contract. The validity of an arbitration clause or an arbitration agreement shall not be affected by the modification, rescission, termination, invalidity, revocation or non-existence of the contract.

Article 6

Any objections to an arbitration agreement and/or jurisdiction over an arbitration case shall be raised before the first hearing conducted by the arbitration tribunal. Where a case is examined on the basis of documents only, the objections to jurisdiction should be raised before submission of the first substantive defense.

Article 7

Once the parties agree to submit their dispute to the Arbitration Commission for arbitration, it shall be deemed that they have agreed to conduct the arbitration under these Rules. In case the parties have agreed otherwise which is also agreed by the Arbitration Commission, the parties' agreement shall prevail.

Section 2 – Organization

Article 8

The Arbitration Commission has one honorary Chairman and several advisers.

Article 9

The Arbitration Commission is composed of one Chairman, several Vice-Chairmen and a number of Commission members. The Chairman performs the functions and duties vested in him by these Rules and the Vice-Chairmen may perform the Chairman's functions and duties with the Chairman's authorization.

The Arbitration Commission has a secretariat to handle its day-to-day work under the leadership of the Secretary-General of the Arbitration Commission.

Article 10

The Arbitration Commission maintains a Panel of Arbitrators. The arbitrators are selected and appointed by the Arbitration Commission from among Chinese and foreign personages with special knowledge and practical experience in the fields of law, economics and trade, science and technology, and other fields.

Article 11
The Arbitration Commission is located in Beijing. The Arbitration Commission has a Shenzhen Sub-Commission in Shenzhen Special Economic Zone and a Shanghai Sub-Commission in Shanghai. The Sub-Commissions are an integral part of the Arbitration Commission.

The Sub-Commissions have their own secretariats to handle their day-to-day work under the leadership of the Secretaries-General of the Sub-Commissions.

These Rules uniformly apply to the Arbitration Commission and its Sub-Commissions. When arbitration proceedings are conducted in the Sub-Commissions, the functions and duties under these Rules to be carried out by the Chairman, the secretariat and the Secretary-General of the Arbitration Commission shall be performed by the Vice-Chairmen authorized by the Chairman, the secretariats and the Secretaries-General of the Sub-Commissions respectively and accordingly.

Article 12
The Parties may agree to have their dispute submitted for arbitration conducted by the Arbitration Commission in Beijing or by its Shenzhen Sub-Commission in Shenzhen or by its Shanghai Sub-Commission in Shanghai.

In the absence of such an agreement, the Claimant may opt to have the arbitration conducted by the Arbitration Commission in Beijing or by its Shenzhen Sub-Commission in Shenzhen or by its Shanghai Sub-Commission in Shanghai.

When exercising such option, the option first made shall prevail. If a dispute arises over the option, it shall be decided by the Arbitration Commission.

CHAPTER II. ARBITRATION PROCEEDINGS

Section 1 – Application for Arbitration, Defense and Counterclaim

Article 13
The arbitration proceedings shall commence from the date on which the Notice of Arbitration is sent out by the Arbitration Commission or its Sub-Commissions.

Article 14
The Claimant shall satisfy the following requirements when submitting his Application for Arbitration:

(1) an Application for Arbitration in writing shall be submitted and the following shall be specified in the Application for Arbitration:

(a) the name and address of the Claimant and those of the Respondent, including the zip code, telephone number, telex number, fax number, cable number or other telecommunications means, if any;
(b) the arbitration agreement relied upon by the Claimant;
(c) the facts of the case and the main points of dispute;
(d) the Claimant's claim and the facts and reasons on which his claim is based.

The Application for Arbitration shall be signed and/or stamped by the Claimant and/or the attorney authorized by the Claimant.
(2) When an Application for Arbitration is submitted to the Arbitration Commission, the relevant documentary evidence on which the Claimant's claim is based shall accompany the Application for Arbitration.
(3) The Claimant shall pay an arbitration fee in advance to the Arbitration Commission according to the Arbitration Fee Schedule of the Arbitration Commission.

Article 15
After receipt of the Application for Arbitration and its attachments and when the secretariat of the Arbitration Commission, after examination, deems that the Claimant has not completed the formalities required for arbitration, the secretariat shall demand the Claimant to complete them, and when the secretariat deems that the Claimant has completed the formalities, the secretariat shall immediately send to the Respondent a Notice of Arbitration together with one copy each of the Claimant's Application for Arbitration and its attachments as well as the Arbitration Rules, the Panel of Arbitrators and the Arbitration Fee Schedule of the Arbitration Commission, and shall simultaneously send to the Claimant one copy each of the Notice of Arbitration, the Arbitration Rules, the Panel of Arbitrators and Arbitration Fee Schedule.

The secretariat of the Arbitration Commission, after sending the Notice of Arbitration to the Claimant and Respondent, shall appoint one of its staff-members to take charge of procedural administration of the case.

Article 16
The Claimant and the Respondent shall, within 20 days as from the date of receipt of the Notice of Arbitration, appoint an arbitrator from among the Panel of Arbitrators of the Arbitration Commission or authorize the Chairman of the Arbitration Commission to make such appointment.

Article 17

The Respondent shall, within 45 days from the date of receipt of the Notice of Arbitration, submit his written defense and relevant documentary evidence to the secretariat of the Arbitration Commission.

Article 18

The Respondent shall, at the latest within 60 days from the date of receipt of the Notice of Arbitration, lodge with the secretariat of the Arbitration Commission his counterclaim in writing, if any. The arbitration tribunal may extend that time limit if it deems that there are justified reasons.

When lodging a counterclaim, the Respondent must state in his written statement of counterclaim his specific claim, the facts and reasons upon which his claim is based, and attach to his written statement of counterclaim the relevant documentary evidence.

When lodging a counterclaim, the Respondent shall pay an arbitration fee in advance according to the Arbitration Fee Schedule of the Arbitration Commission.

Article 19

The Claimant may request to amend his claim and the Respondent may request to amend his counterclaim; but the arbitration tribunal may refuse such an amendment if it considers that it is too late to raise the request and the amendment may affect the arbitration proceedings.

Article 20

When submitting application for arbitration, written defense, statement of counterclaim, documentary evidence and other documents, the party/parties shall submit them in quintuplicate. If the number of the parties exceeds two, additional copies shall be submitted accordingly; if the number of arbitrator[s] of the arbitration tribunal is one, two copies may be reduced.

Article 21

The arbitration proceedings shall not be affected in case the Respondent fails to file his defense in writing or the Claimant fails to submit his written defense against the Respondent's counterclaim.

Article 22

The parties may authorize arbitration agents to deal with the matters relating to arbitration; the authorized attorney must produce a Power of Attorney to the Arbitration Commission.

Chinese and foreign citizens can be authorized to act as arbitration agents.

Article 23

When a party applies for property preservative measures, the Arbitration Commission shall transmit the party's application for a ruling to the people's court in the place where the domicile of the party against whom the property preservative measures are sought is located or in the place where the property of the said party is located.

When a party applies for taking interim measures of protection of evidence, the Arbitration Commission shall transmit the party's application for a ruling to the people's court in the place where the evidence is located.

Section 2 – Formation of Arbitration Tribunal

Article 24

Each of the parties shall appoint one arbitrator from among the Panel of Arbitrators of the Arbitration Commission or entrust the Chairman of the Arbitration Commission to make such appointment. The third arbitrator shall be jointly appointed by the parties or appointed by the Chairman of the Arbitration Commission upon the parties' joint authorization.

In case the parties fail to jointly entrust the Chairman of the Arbitration Commission to appoint the third arbitrator within 20 days from the date on which the Respondent receives the Notice of Arbitration, the third arbitrator shall be appointed by the Chairman of the Arbitration Commission. The third arbitrator shall act as the presiding arbitrator.

The presiding arbitrator and the two appointed arbitrators shall jointly form an arbitration tribunal to jointly hear the case.

Article 25

Both parties may jointly appoint or jointly authorize the Chairman of the Arbitration Commission to appoint a sole arbitrator to form an arbitration tribunal to hear the case alone.

If both parties have agreed on the appointment of a sole arbitrator to hear their case alone but have failed to agree on the choice of such a sole arbitrator within 20 days from the date on which the Respondent receives the Notice of Arbitration, the Chairman of the Arbitration Commission shall make such appointment.

Article 26

If the Claimant or the Respondent fails to appoint or authorize the Chairman of the Arbitration Commission to appoint an arbitrator according to Article 16 of these Rules, the Chairman of the Arbitration Commission shall appoint an arbitrator for the Claimant or the Respondent.

Article 27
When there are two or more Claimants and/or Respondents in an arbitration case, the Claimants' side and/or the Respondents' side each shall, through consultation, appoint or entrust the Chairman of the Arbitration Commission to appoint one arbitrator from among the Panel of Arbitrators of the Arbitration Commission.

If the Claimants' side or the Respondents' side fails to make such appointment or entrustment within 20 days as from the date on which the Respondents' side receives the Notice of Arbitration, the appointment shall be made by the Chairman of the Arbitration Commission.

Article 28
Any appointed arbitrator having a personal interest in the case shall himself disclose such circumstances to the Arbitration Commission and request a withdrawal from his office.

Article 29
A party may make a request in writing to the Arbitration Commission for the removal of an appointed arbitrator from his office, if the party has justified reasons to suspect the impartiality and independence of the appointed arbitrator. In the request, the facts and reasons on which the request is based and evidence thereof must be given.

A challenge against an arbitrator for a removal from his office must be put forward in writing no later than the first oral hearing. If the grounds for the challenge come out or are made known after the first oral hearing, the challenge may be raised after the first hearing but before the end of the last hearing.

Article 30
The Chairman of the Arbitration Commission shall decide on the challenge.

Article 31
If an arbitrator cannot perform his duty owing to withdrawal, demise, removal or other reasons, a substitute arbitrator shall be appointed in accordance with the procedure pursuant to which the original arbitrator was appointed.

After the appointment of the substitute arbitrator, the arbitration tribunal has discretion to decide whether the whole or part of the previous hearings shall be started again.

Section 3 – Hearing

Article 32
The arbitration tribunal shall hold oral hearings when examining a case. At the request of the parties or with their consent, oral hearings may be omitted if the arbitration tribunal also deems that oral hearings are unnecessary, and then the arbitration tribunal may examine the case and make an award on the basis of documents only.

Article 33
The date of the first oral hearing shall be fixed by the arbitration tribunal in consultation with the secretariat of the Arbitration Commission.

The notice of the date of the hearing shall be communicated by the secretariat of the Arbitration Commission to the parties 30 days before the date of the hearing. A party having justified reasons may request a postponement of the date of the hearing. His request must be communicated to the secretariat of the Arbitration Commission 12 days before the date of the hearing and the arbitration tribunal shall decide whether to postpone the hearing or not.

Article 34
The notice of the date of hearing subsequent to the first hearing is not subject to the 30-day time limit.

Article 35
In case the parties have agreed the place of arbitration, the hearing of the case shall be conducted in the place of arbitration. Unless otherwise agreed by the parties, the cases taken cognizance of by the Arbitration Commission shall be heard in Beijing, or in other places with the approval of the Secretary-General of the Arbitration Commission. The cases taken cognizance of by a Sub-Commission of the Arbitration Commission shall be heard in the place where the Sub-Commission is located, or in other places with the approval of the Secretary-General of the Sub-Commission.

Article 36
The arbitration tribunal shall not hear cases in open session. If both parties request a hearing to be held in open session, the arbitration tribunal shall decide whether to hold the hearing in open session or not.

Article 37
When a case is heard in closed session, the parties, their attorneys, witnesses, arbitrators, experts consulted by the arbitration tribunal, appraisers appointed by the arbitration tribunal and the relevant staff-members of the secretariat of the Arbitration Commission shall not disclose to outsiders the substantive or procedural matters of the case.

Article 38
The parties shall produce evidence for the facts on which their claim, defense or counterclaim is based.

The arbitration tribunal may undertake investigations and collect evidence on its own initiative, if it deems it necessary. If the arbitration tribunal investigates and collects evidence on its own initiative, it shall timely inform the parties to be present on the spot if it deems it necessary. Should one party or both parties fail to appear on the spot, the investigation and collection of evidence shall by no means be affected.

Article 39
The arbitration tribunal may consult an expert or appoint an appraiser for the clarification of special questions relating to the case. Such an expert or appraiser can be an organization or a citizen, Chinese or foreign.

The arbitration tribunal has the power to order the parties and the parties are also obliged to submit or produce to the expert or appraiser any materials, documents, properties or goods related to the case for check-up, inspection and/or appraisal.

Article 40
The expert's report and the appraiser's report shall be copied to the parties so that the parties may have the opportunity to give their opinions thereon. At the request of any party to the case and with the approval of the arbitration tribunal, the expert and appraiser may be present at the hearing and give explanations of their reports when the arbitration tribunal deems it necessary and appropriate.

Article 41
The evidence submitted by the parties shall be examined and decided by the arbitration tribunal. The adoption of the expert's report and the appraiser's report shall be determined by the arbitration tribunal.

Article 42
Should one of the parties fail to appear at the hearing, the arbitration tribunal may proceed with the hearing and make an award by default.

Article 43
During the hearing, the arbitration tribunal may make a record in writing and/or by tape-recording. The arbitration tribunal may, when it deems it necessary, make a minute stating the main points of the hearing and ask the parties and/or their attorneys, witnesses and/or other persons involved to sign their names on it and/or affix their seals to it.

The record in writing or by tape-recording is only for the use and reference of the arbitration tribunal.

Article 44
If the parties reach an amicable settlement agreement by themselves, they may either request the arbitration tribunal to make an award in accordance with the contents of their amicable settlement agreement to end the case or request a dismissal of the case.

The Secretary-General of the Arbitration Commission shall decide on the dismissal of an arbitration case if the decision on dismissal is made before the formation of the arbitration tribunal, and the arbitration tribunal shall decide thereon if the decision on dismissal is made after the formation of the arbitration tribunal.

If the party or the parties refer the dismissed case again to the Arbitration Commission for arbitration, the Chairman of the Arbitration Commission shall decide whether to accept the reference or not.

Article 45
If both parties have a desire for conciliation or one party so desires and the other party agrees to it when consulted by the arbitration tribunal, the arbitration tribunal may conciliate the case under its cognizance in the process of arbitration.

Article 46
The arbitration tribunal may conciliate cases in the manner it deems appropriate.

Article 47
The arbitration tribunal shall terminate conciliation and continue the arbitration proceedings when one of the parties requests a termination of conciliation

or when the arbitration tribunal believes that further efforts to conciliate will be futile.

Article 48

If the parties have reached an amicable settlement outside the arbitration tribunal in the course of conciliation conducted by the arbitration tribunal, such settlement shall be deemed as one which has been reached through the arbitration tribunal's conciliation.

Article 49

The parties shall sign a settlement agreement in writing when an amicable settlement is reached through conciliation conducted by the arbitration tribunal, and the arbitration tribunal shall end the case by making an arbitration award in accordance with the contents of the settlement agreement unless otherwise agreed by the parties.

Article 50

Should conciliation fail, any statement, opinion, view or proposal which has been made, raised, put forward, acknowledged, accepted or rejected by either party or by the arbitration tribunal in the process of conciliation shall not be invoked as grounds for any claim, defense and/or counterclaim in the subsequent arbitration proceedings, judicial proceedings or any other proceedings.

Article 51

A party who knows or should have known that any provision or requirement of these Rules has not been complied with and yet proceeds with the arbitration proceedings without explicitly raising in writing his objection to non-compliance in a timely manner shall be deemed to have waived his right to object.

Section 4 – Award

Article 52

The arbitration tribunal shall render an arbitral award within 9 months as from the date on which the arbitration tribunal is formed. The Secretary-General of the Arbitration Commission may extend this time limit at the request of the arbitration tribunal if the Secretary-General of the Arbitration Commission considers that it is really necessary and the reasons for extension are truly justified.

Article 53
The arbitration tribunal shall independently and impartially make its arbitral award on the basis of the facts, in accordance with the law and the terms of the contracts, with reference to international practices and in compliance with the principle of fairness and reasonableness.

Article 54
Where a case is heard by an arbitration tribunal composed of three arbitrators, the arbitral award shall be decided by the majority of the arbitrators and the minority opinion may be written in the record and docketed into the file.

When the arbitration tribunal cannot attain a majority opinion, the arbitral award shall be decided in accordance with the presiding arbitrator's opinion.

Article 55
The arbitration tribunal shall state in the arbitral award the claims, the facts of the dispute, the reasons on which the arbitral award is based, the result of the arbitral award, the allocation of the arbitration costs, the date on which and the place at which the arbitral award is made. The facts of the dispute and the reasons on which the arbitral award is based may not be stated in the arbitral award if the parties have agreed not to state them in the arbitral award, or the arbitral award is made in accordance with the contents of the settlement agreement reached between the parties.

Article 56
Unless the arbitral award is made in accordance with the opinion of the presiding arbitrator or the sole arbitrator, the arbitral award shall be signed by all the arbitrators or the majority arbitrators sitting on the arbitration tribunal. An arbitrator who has a dissenting opinion may sign or not sign his name on the arbitral award.

The arbitrator shall submit his draft arbitral award to the Arbitration Commission before signing the award. The Arbitration Commission may remind the arbitrator of any issue related to the form of the arbitral award on condition that the arbitrator's independence of decision is not affected.

The Arbitration Commission's stamp shall be affixed to the arbitral award.

The date on which the arbitral award is made is the date on which the arbitral award comes into legal effect.

Article 57
The arbitration tribunal may, if it deems it necessary or the parties so request and the arbitration tribunal agrees, make an interlocutory award or partial award on any issue of the case at any time in the course of arbitration before

the final award is made. Either party's failure to perform the interlocutory award does not affect the continuation of the arbitration proceedings and the making of the final award by the arbitration tribunal.

Article 58
The arbitration tribunal has the power to determine in the arbitral award the arbitration fee and other expenses to be eventually paid by the parties to the Arbitration Commission.

Article 59
The arbitration tribunal has the power to decide in the arbitral award that the losing party shall pay the winning party as compensation a proportion of the expenses reasonably incurred by the winning party in dealing with the case. The amount of such compensation shall not in any case exceed 10% of the total amount awarded to the winning party.

Article 60
The arbitral award is final and binding upon both disputing parties. Neither party may bring a suit before a law court or make a request to any other organization for revising the arbitral award.

Article 61
Either party may request in writing that a correction be made to the writing, typing, calculating and similar errors contained in the arbitral award within 30 days from the date of receipt of the arbitral award; if there is really an error in the arbitral award, the arbitration tribunal shall make a correction in writing within 30 days from the date on receipt of the written request for correction, and the arbitration tribunal may by itself make a correction in writing within 30 days from the date on which the arbitral award is issued. The correction in writing forms a part of the arbitral award.

Article 62
If anything that should be awarded has been omitted in the arbitral award, either of the parties may make a request in writing to the arbitration tribunal for an additional award within 30 days from the date on which the arbitral award is received.

If something which should be awarded is really omitted, the arbitration tribunal shall make an additional award within 30 days from the date of receipt of the request in writing for an additional award. The arbitration tribunal may also by itself make an additional award within 30 days from the date on which the arbitral award is issued. The additional award forms a part of the arbitral award which has been previously issued.

Article 63

The parties must automatically execute the arbitral award within the time limit specified in the arbitral award. If no time limit is specified in the arbitral award, the parties shall carry out the arbitral award immediately.

In case one party fails to execute the arbitral award, the other party may apply to the Chinese court for enforcement of the arbitral award pursuant to Chinese law or apply to the competent foreign court for enforcement of the arbitral award according to the 1958 Convention on Recognition and Enforcement of Foreign Arbitral Awards or other international treaties that China has concluded or participated in.

CHAPTER III. SUMMARY PROCEDURE

Article 64

Unless otherwise agreed by the parties, this Summary Procedure shall apply to any case in dispute where the amount of the claim totals not more than RMB 500,000 yuan, and to any case in dispute where the amount of the claim totals more than RMB 500,000 yuan provided that one party applies for arbitration under this Summary Procedure and the other party agrees in writing.

Article 65

When an application for arbitration is submitted to the Arbitration Commission after examination and the Summary Procedure is applicable, the secretariat of the Arbitration Commission shall immediately send a Notice of Arbitration to the parties.

Unless both parties have jointly appointed one sole arbitrator from among the Panel of Arbitrators of the Arbitration Commission, they shall jointly appoint or jointly entrust the Chairman of the Arbitration Commission to appoint one sole arbitrator within 15 days from the date on which the Notice of Arbitration is received by the Respondent. Should the parties fail to make such appointment or entrustment, the Chairman of the Arbitration Commission shall immediately appoint one sole arbitrator to form an arbitration tribunal to hear the case.

Article 66
The Respondent shall, within 30 days from the date of receipt of the Notice of Arbitration, submit his defense and relevant documentary evidence to the secretariat of the Arbitration Commission; a counterclaim, if any, shall be filed with documentary evidence within the said time limit.

Article 67
The arbitration tribunal may hear the case in the way it deems appropriate. The arbitration tribunal has discretion to hear the case only on the basis of the written materials and evidence submitted by the parties or to hold an oral hearing as well.

Article 68
The parties must hand in written materials and evidence needed for the arbitration in compliance with the requirements of the arbitration tribunal within the time limit given by the arbitration tribunal.

Article 69
For a case which needs an oral hearing, the secretariat of the Arbitration Commission shall, after the arbitration tribunal has fixed a date for hearing, inform the parties of the date of the hearing 15 days before the date of the hearing.

Article 70
If the arbitration tribunal decides to hear the case orally, only one oral hearing shall be held. However, the arbitration tribunal may hold two oral hearings if really necessary.

Article 71
Should one of the parties fail to act in compliance with this Summary Procedure during summary proceedings, such failure shall not affect the arbitration tribunal's conduct of the proceedings and the arbitration tribunal's power to render an arbitral award.

Article 72
The conduct of the summary proceedings shall not be affected by any amendment of the claim or by the lodging of a counterclaim, except that the disputed amount of the revised arbitration claim or counterclaim is in conflict with the provision of Article 64.

Article 73
Where a case is heard orally, the arbitration tribunal shall make an arbitral award within 30 days from the date of the oral hearing if one hearing is to be held, or from the date of the second oral hearing if two oral hearings are to be held. Where a case is examined on the basis of documents only, the arbitration tribunal shall render an arbitral award within 90 days from the date on which the arbitration tribunal is formed. The Secretary-General of the Arbitration Commission may extend the said time limit if such extension is necessary and justified.

Article 74
For matters not covered in this Chapter, the relevant provisions in the other Chapters of these Rules shall apply.

CHAPTER IV. SUPPLEMENTARY PROVISIONS

Article 75
The Chinese language is the official language of the Arbitration Commission. If the parties have agreed otherwise, their agreement shall prevail.

At the hearing, if the parties or their attorneys or witnesses require language interpretation, the secretariat of the Arbitration Commission may provide an interpreter for them or the parties may bring with them their own interpreter.

The arbitration tribunal and/or the secretariat of the Arbitration Commission may, if it deems it necessary, request the parties to hand in corresponding translation copies in Chinese language or other languages of the documents and evidential materials submitted by the parties.

Article 76
All the arbitration documents, notices and materials may be sent to the parties and/or their attorneys in person, or by registered letter or express airmail, telefax, telex, cable or by any other means which are deemed proper by the secretariat of the Arbitration Commission.

Article 77
Any written communication to the parties is deemed to have been properly served if it is delivered to the addressee or delivered at his place of business, habitual residence or mailing address; or if none of these can be found after making a reasonable inquiry, a written communication is deemed to have been properly served if it is sent to the addressee's last known place of business, habitual residence or mailing address by registered letter or by any other

means which provides a record of the attempt to deliver it.

Article 78

Apart from charging arbitration fees from the parties according to the Arbitration Fee Schedule of the Arbitration Commission, the Arbitration Commission may collect from the parties other extra, reasonable and actual expenses including arbitrators' special remuneration and their travel and boarding expenses for dealing with the case and the fees and expenses for experts, appraisers and interpreters appointed by the arbitration tribunal, etc.

If a case is withdrawn after the parties have reached between themselves an amicable settlement, the Arbitration Commission may charge a certain amount of fees from the parties in consideration of the quantity of work and the amount of the actual expenses incurred by the Arbitration Commission.

Article 79

Where an arbitration agreement or an arbitration clause contained in the contract provides for arbitration to be conducted by China International Economic and Trade Arbitration Commission or its Sub-Commissions or by the formerly named Foreign Trade Arbitration Commission or Foreign Economic and Trade Arbitration Commission of the China Council for the Promotion of International Trade, it shall be deemed that the parties have unanimously agreed that the arbitration shall be conducted by China International Economic and Trade Arbitration Commission or by its Sub-Commissions.

When an arbitration agreement or an arbitration clause contained in the contract provides for arbitration by China Council for the Promotion of International Trade/China Chamber of International Commerce or by the arbitration commission of China Council for Promotion of International Trade/China Chamber of International Commerce, it shall be deemed that the parties have unanimously agreed that the arbitration shall be conducted by China International Economic and Trade Arbitration Commission.

Article 80

These Rules shall come into force as from May 10, 1998. For cases which have been taken cognizance of by the Arbitration Commission or by its Sub-Commissions before the date on which these Rules become effective, the Rules of Arbitration effective on the date when the cases were taken cognizance of shall apply. However, these Rules shall be applied if the parties so agree.

Article 81

The power to interpret these Rules is vested in the Arbitration Commission.

CHINA INTERNATIONAL ECONOMIC & TRADE ARBITRATION COMMISSION

ARBITRATION FEE SCHEDULE

Effective as from 10 May 1998

Amount of Claim (RMB)	Amount of Fee (RMB)
1,000,000 Yuan or less	4% of the Claimed Amount, minimum 20,000 Yuan
1,000,000 Yuan to 5,000,000 Yuan	40,000 Yuan plus 3% of the excess over 1,000,000 Yuan
5,000,000 Yuan to 10,000,000 Yuan	160,000 Yuan plus 2% of the excess over 5,000,000 Yuan
10,000,000 Yuan to 50,000,000 Yuan	260,000 Yuan plus 1% of the excess over 10,000,000 Yuan
50,000,000 Yuan or more	660,000 Yuan plus 0.5% of the excess over 50,000,000 Yuan

When applying for arbitration, each case shall be charged an additional amount of RMB 10,000 Yuan as a Registration Fee which includes the expenses for examining the application for arbitration, accepting the case, computerizing management and filing the documents.

Where the amount of the claim is not ascertained at the time when application for arbitration is handed in, or there exists special circumstance, the amount of the arbitration fee shall be determined by the secretariat of the Arbitration Commission or the secretariats of the Sub-Commissions of the Arbitration Commission.

If the arbitration fee is charged in foreign currency, an amount of foreign currency equivalent to the corresponding RMB value specified in this schedule shall be paid.

Apart from charging [the] arbitration fee according to this Arbitration Fee Schedule, the Arbitration Commission may collect other extra, reasonable and actual expenses pursuant to the relevant provisions of the Arbitration Rules.

For arbitration cases taken cognizance of by the Arbitration Commission in accordance with Paragraph 2(3), (4) and (5) of Article 2 of the Arbitration Rules, the arbitration fees shall be charged pursuant to The Methods of Charging Fees by the Arbitration Commissions formulated by the General Office of the State Council.

INTERNATIONAL BAR ASSOCIATION*

IBA RULES ON THE TAKING OF EVIDENCE IN INTERNATIONAL COMMERCIAL ARBITRATION

*David W. Rivkin***

On 1 June 1999, the IBA Council adopted new IBA Rules on the Taking of Evidence in International Commercial Arbitration. The Rules provide methods for gathering and presenting evidence in international commercial arbitration. They reflect a blending of common law and civil law procedures, which parties and Arbitral Tribunals should find useful in conducting international arbitrations.

The new IBA Rules of Evidence replace the Supplementary Rules Governing the Presentation and Reception of Evidence in International Commercial Arbitration originally adopted in 1983.[1] As the conduct of international arbitration has progressed over the last decade and a half, the IBA's Committee D decided that it was time to update the Rules to current norms. Moreover, the growth of international arbitration and its use in areas of the world where international arbitration was not previously accepted have led to many new parties being subject to international arbitration proceedings for the first time. The Rules can assist such parties in determining what procedures are appropriate and expected in an international arbitration.

The Rules are designed to fill the void intentionally left in most institutional and ad hoc rules between the submission of initial pleadings and the issuance of the award. Most institutional and ad hoc rules leave the procedures to the discretion of the parties, so long as each party has an opportunity to present its evidence. The IBA Rules of Evidence protect this party autonomy and present one method for conducting the proceedings of an arbitration. Parties and arbitral tribunals may adopt them in whole or in part – at the time of

---

* The address of the International Bar Association is 271 Regent Street, London W1R 7PA, England; website: http://www.ibanet.org.

** Debevoise & Plimpton; Chair, International Bar Association, Committee on Arbitration and ADR (Committee D).

1. Reproduced in Yearbook X (1985) pp. 157-166, with an Introduction by David W. Shenton, pp. 145-151.

drafting the arbitration clause in a contract or once an arbitration commences – or they may use them as guidelines. As the Rules themselves note, "They are not intended to limit the flexibility that is inherent in, and an advantage of, international arbitration, and Arbitral Tribunals and parties are free to adapt them to the particular circumstances of each arbitration."

The Rules are based on the principle that "each party shall be entitled to know, reasonably in advance of any Evidentiary Hearing, the evidence on which the other party intends to rely." They provide a mechanism for the submission of relevant documents, including limited requests for other parties to produce documents – a process that is carefully supervised by the arbitral tribunal; the possibility of Witness Statements exchanged in advance of the hearing, which may serve as each witness's direct testimony; the use of Party-Appointed Experts and Tribunal-Appointed Experts, each of whom must submit written reports and be subject to examination; and the possibility of on-site inspection. The Rules also include provisions for the conduct of the Evidentiary Hearing, which permit the structuring of the hearing by particular issues or the presentation of certain witnesses simultaneously and in confrontation with each other. The Rules set forth certain limitations on the admissibility of evidence, such as legal privileges and "grounds of commercial or technical confidentiality that the Arbitral Tribunal determines to be compelling".

The Rules were drafted by a Working Party led by Giovanni M. Ughi of Italy, who, as then-Chairman of Committee D, led the preparation of the first IBA Rules of Evidence. Other members of the Working Party included Hans Bagner, Sweden; John Beechey, England; Jacques Buhart, France; Peter Caldwell, Hong Kong; Bernardo M. Cremades, Spain; Otto de Witt Wijnen, The Netherlands; Emmanuel Gaillard, France; Paul A. Gélinas, France; Pierre A. Karrer, Switzerland; Wolfgang Kühn, Germany, former Chair of Committee D; Jan Paulsson, France; Hilmar Raeschke-Kessler, Germany; David W. Rivkin, United States and current Chairman of Committee D; Hans van Houtte, Belgium; and Johnny Veeder, England.

IBA Rules on the Taking of Evidence in International Commercial Arbitration

Adopted 1 June 1999

PREAMBLE

1. These IBA Rules on the Taking of Evidence in International Commercial Arbitration (the "IBA Rules of Evidence") are intended to govern in an efficient and economical manner the taking of evidence in international commercial arbitrations, particularly those between Parties from different legal traditions. They are designed to supplement the legal provisions and the institutional or ad hoc rules according to which the Parties are conducting their arbitration.

2. Parties and Arbitral Tribunals may adopt the IBA Rules of Evidence, in whole or in part, to govern arbitration proceedings, or they may vary them or use them as guidelines in developing their own procedures. The Rules are not intended to limit the flexibility that is inherent in, and an advantage of, international arbitration, and Parties and Arbitral Tribunals are free to adapt them to the particular circumstances of each arbitration.

3. Each Arbitral Tribunal is encouraged to identify to the Parties, as soon as it considers it to be appropriate, the issues that it may regard as relevant and material to the outcome of the case, including issues where a preliminary determination may be appropriate.

4. The taking of evidence shall be conducted on the principle that each Party shall be entitled to know, reasonably in advance of any Evidentiary Hearing, the evidence on which the other Parties rely.

Article 1 – Definitions

In the IBA Rules of Evidence:

"*Arbitral Tribunal*" means a sole arbitrator or a panel of arbitrators validly deciding by majority or otherwise;

"*Claimant*" means the Party or Parties who commenced the arbitration and any Party who, through joinder or otherwise, becomes aligned with such Party or Parties;

"*Document*" means a writing of any kind, whether recorded on paper, electronic means, audio or visual recordings or any other mechanical or electronic means of storing or recording information;

"*Evidentiary Hearing*" means any hearing, whether or not held on consecutive days, at which the Arbitral Tribunal receives oral evidence;

"*Expert Report*" means a written statement by a Tribunal-Appointed Expert or a Party-Appointed Expert submitted pursuant to the IBA Rules of Evidence;

"*General Rules*" mean the institutional or ad hoc rules according to which the Parties are conducting their arbitration;

"*Party*" means a party to the arbitration;

"*Party-Appointed Expert*" means an expert witness presented by a Party;

"*Request to Produce*" means a request by a Party for a procedural order by which the Arbitral Tribunal would direct another Party to produce documents;

"*Respondent*" means the Party or Parties against whom the Claimant made its claim, and any Party who, through joinder or otherwise, becomes aligned with such Party or Parties, and includes a Respondent making a counter-claim;

"*Tribunal-Appointed Expert*" means a person or organization appointed by the Arbitral Tribunal in order to report to it on specific issues determined by the Arbitral Tribunal.

Article 2 – Scope of Application

1. Whenever the Parties have agreed or the Arbitral Tribunal has determined to apply the IBA Rules of Evidence, the Rules shall govern the taking of evidence, except to the extent that any specific provision of them may be found to be in conflict with any mandatory provision of law determined to be applicable to the case by the Parties or by the Arbitral Tribunal.

2. In case of conflict between any provisions of the IBA Rules of Evidence and the General Rules, the Arbitral Tribunal shall apply the IBA Rules of Evidence in the manner that it determines best in order to accomplish the purposes of both the General Rules and the IBA Rules of Evidence, unless the Parties agree to the contrary.

3. In the event of any dispute regarding the meaning of the IBA Rules of Evidence, the Arbitral Tribunal shall interpret them according to their purpose and in the manner most appropriate for the particular arbitration.

4. Insofar as the IBA Rules of Evidence and the General Rules are silent on any matter concerning the taking of evidence and the Parties have not agreed otherwise, the Arbitral Tribunal may conduct the taking of evidence as it deems appropriate, in accordance with the general principles of the IBA Rules of Evidence.

Article 3 – Documents

1. Within the time ordered by the Arbitral Tribunal, each Party shall submit to the Arbitral Tribunal and to the other Parties all documents available to it on which it relies, including public documents and those in the public domain, except for any documents that have already been submitted by another Party.

2. Within the time ordered by the Arbitral Tribunal, any Party may submit to the Arbitral Tribunal a Request to Produce.

3. A Request to Produce shall contain:

(a) (*i*) a description of a requested document sufficient to identify it, or (*ii*) a description in sufficient detail (including subject matter) of a narrow and specific requested category of documents that are reasonably believed to exist;
(b) a description of how the documents requested are relevant and material to the outcome of the case; and
(c) a statement that the documents requested are not in the possession, custody or control of the requesting Party, and of the reason why that Party assumes the documents requested to be in the possession, custody or control of the other Party.

4. Within the time ordered by the Arbitral Tribunal, the Party to whom the Request to Produce is addressed shall produce to the Arbitral Tribunal and to the other Parties all the documents requested in its possession, custody or control as to which no objection is made.

5. If the Party to whom the Request to Produce is addressed has objections to some or all of the documents requested, it shall state them in writing to the Arbitral Tribunal within the time ordered by the Arbitral Tribunal. The reasons for such objections shall be any of those set forth in Article 9.2.

6. The Arbitral Tribunal shall, in consultation with the Parties and in timely fashion, consider the Request to Produce and the objections. The Arbitral Tribunal may order the Party to whom such Request is addressed to produce to the Arbitral Tribunal and to the other Parties those requested documents in its possession, custody or control as to which the Arbitral Tribunal determines that (*i*) the issues that the requesting Party wishes to prove are relevant and material to the outcome of the case, and (*ii*) none of the reasons for objection set forth in Article 9.2 apply.

7. In exceptional circumstances, if the propriety of an objection can only be determined by review of the document, the Arbitral Tribunal may determine that it should not review the document. In that event, the Arbitral Tribunal may, after consultation with the Parties, appoint an independent and impartial expert, bound to confidentiality, to review any such document and to report on the objection. To the extent that the objection is upheld by the Arbitral Tribunal, the expert shall not disclose to the Arbitral Tribunal and to the other Parties the contents of the document reviewed.

8. If a Party wishes to obtain the production of documents from a person or organization who is not a Party to the arbitration and from whom the Party cannot obtain the documents on its own, the Party may, within the time

ordered by the Arbitral Tribunal, ask it to take whatever steps are legally available to obtain the requested documents. The Party shall identify the documents in sufficient detail and state why such documents are relevant and material to the outcome of the case. The Arbitral Tribunal shall decide on this request and shall take the necessary steps if in its discretion it determines that the documents would be relevant and material.

9. The Arbitral Tribunal, at any time before the arbitration is concluded, may request a Party to produce to the Arbitral Tribunal and to the other Parties any documents that it believes to be relevant and material to the outcome of the case. A Party may object to such a request based on any of the reasons set forth in Article 9.2. If a Party raises such an objection, the Arbitral Tribunal shall decide whether to order the production of such documents based upon the considerations set forth in Article 3.6 and, if the Arbitral Tribunal considers it appropriate, through the use of the procedures set forth in Article 3.7.

10. Within the time ordered by the Arbitral Tribunal, the Parties may submit to the Arbitral Tribunal and to the other Parties any additional documents which they believe have become relevant and material as a consequence of the issues raised in documents, Witness Statements or Expert Reports submitted or produced by another Party or in other submissions of the Parties.

11. If copies are submitted or produced, they must conform fully to the originals. At the request of the Arbitral Tribunal, any original must be presented for inspection.

12. All documents produced by a Party pursuant to the IBA Rules of Evidence (or by a non-Party pursuant to Article 3.8) shall be kept confidential by the Arbitral Tribunal and by the other Parties, and they shall be used only in connection with the arbitration. The Arbitral Tribunal may issue orders to set forth the terms of this confidentiality. This requirement is without prejudice to all other obligations of confidentiality in arbitration.

Article 4 – Witnesses of Fact

1. Within the time ordered by the Arbitral Tribunal, each Party shall identify the witnesses on whose testimony it relies and the subject matter of that testimony.

2. Any person may present evidence as a witness, including a Party or a Party's officer, employee or other representative.

3. It shall not be improper for a Party, its officers, employees, legal advisors or other representatives to interview its witnesses or potential witnesses.

4. The Arbitral Tribunal may order each Party to submit within a specified time to the Arbitral Tribunal and to the other Parties a written statement by

each witness on whose testimony it relies, except for those witnesses whose testimony is sought pursuant to Article 4.10 (the "Witness Statement"). If Evidentiary Hearings are organized on separate issues (such as liability and damages), the Arbitral Tribunal or the Parties by agreement may schedule the submission of Witness Statements separately for each Evidentiary Hearing.

5. Each Witness Statement shall contain:

(a) the full name and address of the witness, his or her present and past relationship (if any) with any of the Parties, and a description of his or her background, qualifications, training and experience, if such a description may be relevant and material to the dispute or to the contents of the statement;
(b) a full and detailed description of the facts, and the source of the witness's information as to those facts, sufficient to serve as that witness's evidence in the matter in dispute;
(c) an affirmation of the truth of the statement; and
(d) the signature of the witness and its date and place.

6. If Witness Statements are submitted, any Party may, within the time ordered by the Arbitral Tribunal, submit to the Arbitral Tribunal and to the other Parties revised or additional Witness Statements, including statements from persons not previously named as witnesses, so long as any such revisions or additions only respond to matters contained in another Party's Witness Statement or Expert Report and such matters have not been previously presented in the arbitration.

7. Each witness who has submitted a Witness Statement shall appear for testimony at an Evidentiary Hearing, unless the Parties agree otherwise.

8. If a witness who has submitted a Witness Statement does not appear without a valid reason for testimony at an Evidentiary Hearing, except by agreement of the Parties, the Arbitral Tribunal shall disregard that Witness Statement unless, in exceptional circumstances, the Arbitral Tribunal determines otherwise.

9. If the Parties agree that a witness who has submitted a Witness Statement does not need to appear for testimony at an Evidentiary Hearing, such an agreement shall not be considered to reflect an agreement as to the correctness of the content of the Witness Statement.

10. If a Party wishes to present evidence from a person who will not appear voluntarily at its request, the Party may, within the time ordered by the Arbitral Tribunal, ask it to take whatever steps are legally available to obtain the testimony of that person. The Party shall identify the intended witness, shall describe the subjects on which the witness's testimony is sought and shall state why such subjects are relevant and material to the outcome of the case.

The Arbitral Tribunal shall decide on this request and shall take the necessary steps if in its discretion it determines that the testimony of that witness would be relevant and material.

11. The Arbitral Tribunal may, at any time before the arbitration is concluded, order any Party to provide, or to use its best efforts to provide, the appearance for testimony at an Evidentiary Hearing of any person, including one whose testimony has not yet been offered.

Article 5 – Party-Appointed Experts

1. A Party may rely on a Party-Appointed Expert as a means of evidence on specific issues. Within the time ordered by the Arbitral Tribunal, a Party-Appointed Expert shall submit an Expert Report.

2. The Expert Report shall contain:

(a) the full name and address of the Party-Appointed Expert, his or her present and past relationship (if any) with any of the Parties, and a description of his or her background, qualifications, training and experience;
(b) a statement of the facts on which he or she is basing his or her expert opinions and conclusions;
(c) his or her expert opinions and conclusions, including a description of the method, evidence and information used in arriving at the conclusions;
(d) an affirmation of the truth of the Expert Report; and
(e) the signature of the Party-Appointed Expert and its date and place.

3. The Arbitral Tribunal in its discretion may order that any Party-Appointed Experts who have submitted Expert Reports on the same or related issues meet and confer on such issues. At such meeting, the Party-Appointed Experts shall attempt to reach agreement on those issues as to which they had differences of opinion in their Expert Reports, and they shall record in writing any such issues on which they reach agreement.

4. Each Party-Appointed Expert shall appear for testimony at an Evidentiary Hearing, unless the Parties agree otherwise and the Arbitral Tribunal accepts this agreement.

5. If a Party-Appointed Expert does not appear without a valid reason for testimony at an Evidentiary Hearing, except by agreement of the Parties accepted by the Arbitral Tribunal, the Arbitral Tribunal shall disregard his or her Expert Report unless, in exceptional circumstances, the Arbitral Tribunal determines otherwise.

6. If the Parties agree that a Party-Appointed Expert does not need to appear for testimony at an Evidentiary Hearing, such an agreement shall not be

considered to reflect an agreement as to the correctness of the content of the Expert Report.

Article 6 – Tribunal-Appointed Experts

1. The Arbitral Tribunal, after having consulted with the Parties, may appoint one or more independent Tribunal-Appointed Experts to report to it on specific issues designated by the Arbitral Tribunal. The Arbitral Tribunal shall establish the terms of reference for any Tribunal-Appointed Expert report after having consulted with the Parties. A copy of the final terms of reference shall be sent by the Arbitral Tribunal to the Parties.

2. The Tribunal-Appointed Expert shall, before accepting appointment, submit to the Arbitral Tribunal and to the Parties a statement of his or her independence from the Parties and the Arbitral Tribunal. Within the time ordered by the Arbitral Tribunal, the Parties shall inform the Arbitral Tribunal whether they have any objections to the Tribunal-Appointed Expert's independence. The Arbitral Tribunal shall decide promptly whether to accept any such objection.

3. Subject to the provisions of Article 9.2, the Tribunal-Appointed Expert may request a Party to provide any relevant and material information or to provide access to any relevant documents, goods, samples, property or site for inspection. The authority of a Tribunal-Appointed Expert to request such information or access shall be the same as the authority of the Arbitral Tribunal. The Parties and their representatives shall have the right to receive any such information and to attend any such inspection. Any disagreement between a Tribunal-Appointed Expert and a Party as to the relevance, materiality or appropriateness of such a request shall be decided by the Arbitral Tribunal, in the manner provided in Articles 3.5 through 3.7. The Tribunal-Appointed Expert shall record in the report any non-compliance by a Party with an appropriate request or decision by the Arbitral Tribunal and shall describe its effects on the determination of the specific issue.

4. The Tribunal-Appointed Expert shall report in writing to the Arbitral Tribunal. The Tribunal-Appointed Expert shall describe in the report the method, evidence and information used in arriving at the conclusions.

5. The Arbitral Tribunal shall send a copy of such Expert Report to the Parties. The Parties may examine any document that the Tribunal-Appointed Expert has examined and any correspondence between the Arbitral Tribunal and the Tribunal-Appointed Expert. Within the time ordered by the Arbitral Tribunal, any Party shall have the opportunity to respond to the report in a submission by the Party or through an Expert Report by a Party-Appointed Expert. The Arbitral Tribunal shall send the submission or Expert Report to the Tribunal-Appointed Expert and to the other Parties.

6. At the request of a Party or of the Arbitral Tribunal, the Tribunal-Appointed Expert shall be present at an Evidentiary Hearing. The Arbitral Tribunal may question the Tribunal-Appointed Expert, and he or she may be questioned by the Parties or by any Party-Appointed Expert on issues raised in the Parties' submissions or in the Expert Reports made by the Party-Appointed Experts pursuant to Article 6.5.

7. Any Expert Report made by a Tribunal-Appointed Expert and its conclusions shall be assessed by the Arbitral Tribunal with due regard to all circumstances of the case.

8. The fees and expenses of a Tribunal-Appointed Expert, to be funded in a manner determined by the Arbitral Tribunal, shall form part of the costs of the arbitration.

Article 7 – On Site Inspection

Subject to the provisions of Article 9.2, the Arbitral Tribunal may, at the request of a Party or on its own motion, inspect or require the inspection by a Tribunal-Appointed Expert of any site, property, machinery or any other goods or process, or documents, as it deems appropriate. The Arbitral Tribunal shall, in consultation with the Parties, determine the timing and arrangement for the inspection. The Parties and their representatives shall have the right to attend any such inspection.

Article 8 – Evidentiary Hearing

1. The Arbitral Tribunal shall at all times have complete control over the Evidentiary Hearing. The Arbitral Tribunal may limit or exclude any question to, answer by or appearance of a witness (which term includes, for the purposes of this Article, witnesses of fact and any Experts), if it considers such question, answer or appearance to be irrelevant, immaterial, burdensome, duplicative or covered by a reason for objection set forth in Article 9.2. Questions to a witness during direct and re-direct testimony may not be unreasonably leading.

2. The Claimant shall ordinarily first present the testimony of its witnesses, followed by the Respondent presenting testimony of its witnesses, and then by the presentation by Claimant of rebuttal witnesses, if any. Following direct testimony, any other Party may question such witness, in an order to be determined by the Arbitral Tribunal. The Party who initially presented the witness shall subsequently have the opportunity to ask additional questions on the matters raised in the other Parties' questioning. The Arbitral Tribunal, upon request of a Party or on its own motion, may vary this order of proceeding, including the arrangement of testimony by particular issues or in such a manner that witnesses presented by different Parties be questioned at the

same time and in confrontation with each other. The Arbitral Tribunal may ask questions to a witness at any time.

3. Any witness providing testimony shall first affirm, in a manner determined appropriate by the Arbitral Tribunal, that he or she is telling the truth. If the witness has submitted a Witness Statement or an Expert Report, the witness shall confirm it. The Parties may agree or the Arbitral Tribunal may order that the Witness Statement or Expert Report shall serve as that witness's direct testimony.

4. Subject to the provisions of Article 9.2, the Arbitral Tribunal may request any person to give oral or written evidence on any issue that the Arbitral Tribunal considers to be relevant and material. Any witness called and questioned by the Arbitral Tribunal may also be questioned by the Parties.

Article 9 – Admissibility and Assessment of Evidence

1. The Arbitral Tribunal shall determine the admissibility, relevance, materiality and weight of evidence.

2. The Arbitral Tribunal shall, at the request of a Party or on its own motion, exclude from evidence or production any document, statement, oral testimony or inspection for any of the following reasons:

(a) lack of sufficient relevance or materiality;
(b). legal impediment or privilege under the legal or ethical rules determined by the Arbitral Tribunal to be applicable;
(c) unreasonable burden to produce the requested evidence;
(d) loss or destruction of the document that has been reasonably shown to have occurred;
(e) grounds of commercial or technical confidentiality that the Arbitral Tribunal determines to be compelling;
(f) grounds of special political or institutional sensitivity (including evidence that has been classified as secret by a government or a public international institution) that the Arbitral Tribunal determines to be compelling; or
(g) considerations of fairness or equality of the Parties that the Arbitral Tribunal determines to be compelling.

3. The Arbitral Tribunal may, where appropriate, make necessary arrangements to permit evidence to be considered subject to suitable confidentiality protection.

4. If a Party fails without satisfactory explanation to produce any document requested in a Request to Produce to which it has not objected in due time or fails to produce any document ordered to be produced by the Arbitral Tri-

bunal, the Arbitral Tribunal may infer that such document would be adverse to the interests of that Party.

5. If a Party fails without satisfactory explanation to make available any other relevant evidence, including testimony, sought by one Party to which the Party to whom the request was addressed has not objected in due time or fails to make available any evidence, including testimony, ordered by the Arbitral Tribunal to be produced, the Arbitral Tribunal may infer that such evidence would be adverse to the interests of that Party.

STOCKHOLM CHAMBER OF COMMERCE ARBITRATION INSTITUTE*

CONTENTS

ARBITRATION RULES

Adopted and in force as of 1 April 1999

I. ORGANISATION OF THE SCC INSTITUTE

Article 1 – The SCC Institute

The Arbitration Institute of the Stockholm Chamber of Commerce (hereinafter referred to as "the SCC Institute") is a body dealing with matters of dispute resolution. The SCC Institute is part of but independent from the Stockholm Chamber of Commerce. The SCC Institute does not itself settle disputes. Its objectives are:

- to assist in the settlement of domestic and international disputes in accordance with the Rules of the Arbitration Institute of the Stockholm Chamber of Commerce (hereinafter referred to as "the SCC Rules");

* The address of the Arbitration Institute of the Stockholm Chamber of Commerce is Jakobs Torg 3, PO Box 16050, SE-10321 Stockholm, Sweden, tel.: 46 8 555 10050, fax: 46 8 566 31650, e-mail: arbitration@chamber.se, internet: http://www.chamber.se.

- to assist in the settlement of disputes in accordance with other rules which have been adopted by the SCC Institute;[1]
- to assist, as determined by the SCC Institute, in proceedings which are conducted in a manner which differs, either in part or in whole, from that anticipated by the SCC Institute's rules;
- to provide guidelines concerning settlement of disputes under the SCC Institute's rules; and
- to provide information concerning arbitration and mediation matters.

Article 2 – The Board

(1) The SCC Institute shall have a Board composed of six members who shall be appointed for a period of three years by the Board of Directors of the Chamber. The Board of Directors of the Chamber shall appoint a Chairman and a Vice Chairman from among the members of the Board of the SCC Institute. The Chairman and the Vice Chairman shall be lawyers.

(2) The Board of Directors of the Chamber may, if there are extraordinary reasons for doing so, remove a member of the Board of the SCC Institute. If a member resigns or is removed during his term of office, the Board of Directors of the Chamber will appoint a new member for the remainder of his term.

Article 3 – Decisions by the Board

Two members of the Board shall form a quorum. If no majority is attained, the Chairman shall cast the deciding vote. The Chairman or the Vice Chairman shall have the power to take decisions on behalf of the Board in urgent matters. Decisions of the Board are final and cannot be reviewed by the Chamber.

Article 4 – The Secretariat

The SCC Institute shall have a Secretariat under the direction of a Secretary General who shall be a lawyer.

1. The SCC Institute has adopted Rules for Expedited Arbitrations, Insurance Arbitration Rules, Mediation Rules and Procedures and Services under the UNCITRAL Arbitration Rules. The Rules for Expedited Arbitrations and the Mediation Rules are also reproduced in this Volume of the Yearbook.

II. ARBITRATION RULES OF THE SCC INSTITUTE

Initiation of Proceedings

Article 5 – Request for Arbitration
Arbitration is initiated by the Claimant filing with the SCC Institute a Request for Arbitration which shall include:

(i) a statement of the names, addresses, telephone and facsimile numbers and e-mail addresses of the parties and their counsel;
(ii) a summary of the dispute;
(iii) a preliminary statement of the relief sought by the Claimant;
(iv) a copy of the arbitration agreement or clause under which the dispute is to be settled; and
(v) if applicable, a statement identifying the arbitrator appointed by the Claimant, including such arbitrator's address, telephone and facsimile numbers and e-mail address.

Article 6 – Registration Fee
(1) At the same time as the Request for Arbitration is filed, the Claimant shall pay a Registration Fee. The amount of the fee is fixed in accordance with the SCC Institute's Regulations for Arbitration Costs in force on the date of the Request for Arbitration.

(2) If the required Registration Fee is not paid when filing the Request for Arbitration, the SCC Institute will fix a period of time within which the Claimant must pay such fee.

Article 7 – Dismissal
If it is clear that the SCC Institute lacks jurisdiction over the dispute or if the Registration Fee has not been paid in due time, the Claimant's Request for Arbitration shall be dismissed.

Article 8 – Date of Commencement of the Arbitration
The arbitration shall be deemed to have been commenced on the date on which the Request for Arbitration was received by the SCC Institute.

Article 9 – Procedures of the SCC Institute
The SCC Institute shall maintain the confidentiality of the arbitration and shall deal with the arbitration in an impartial, practical and expeditious manner.

Article 10 – The Respondent's Reply

(1) The Request for Arbitration shall be communicated by the SCC Institute to the Respondent. The Respondent shall be asked to submit a Reply to the SCC Institute. The Reply shall be submitted within the period of time determined by the SCC Institute and shall include:

(i) comments regarding the Request for Arbitration by the Claimant; and
(ii) if applicable, a statement identifying the arbitrator appointed by the Respondent, including such arbitrator's address, telephone and facsimile numbers and e-mail address.

(2) If the Respondent wishes to raise any objection concerning the validity or applicability of the arbitration agreement, such objection shall be made in the Reply together with the grounds therefore.

(3) If the Respondent wishes to file a counterclaim or a set-off claim, a statement to that effect should be made in the Reply and should include the nature of the claim and a preliminary statement of the relief sought. The grounds for any counterclaim or set-off claim must be based on the arbitration agreement.

(4) The SCC Institute shall communicate the Respondent's Reply to the Claimant. The Claimant shall be given an opportunity to comment on any objections and pleas advanced by the Respondent.

(5) Failure by the Respondent to submit a Reply shall not prevent the arbitration from proceeding pursuant to these Rules.

Article 11 – Amplification and Periods of Time

(1) The SCC Institute may request a party to expound upon any written comments to the SCC Institute. If the Claimant fails to comply with such a request, the SCC Institute may decide to dismiss the case. If the Respondent fails to comply with a request to expound upon a counterclaim, the counterclaim may be dismissed by the SCC Institute. Failure by the Respondent otherwise to comply with a request to expound upon a written statement shall not prevent the arbitral proceedings from continuing.

(2) If the SCC Institute has requested a party to perform any act within a specified period of time, such period of time may be extended by the SCC Institute.

Article 12 – Notice

(1) Any notice or other communication from the SCC Institute shall be delivered to the last known address of the addressee.

(2) Any notice or other communication shall be delivered by courier or

registered mail, facsimile transmission, e-mail or by any other means of communication that provides a record of the sending thereof.

(3) A notice or communication sent in accordance with paragraph two shall be deemed to have been received, by the addressee, at the latest on the date it would normally have been received given the chosen means of communication.

Article 13 – Appointment of Arbitrators and Place of Arbitration
When the exchange of written submissions pursuant to Articles 5-11 has been concluded, the SCC Institute shall

(i) decide the number of arbitrators, if not agreed by the parties;
(ii) when so required pursuant to Article 16, appoint a sole arbitrator or chairman of the Arbitral Tribunal and, if necessary, a co-arbitrator;
(iii) decide the Place of Arbitration, if not agreed upon by the parties; and
(iv) fix the Advance on Costs pursuant to Article 14.

Article 14 – Advance on Costs
(1) The Advance on Costs shall be equivalent to the estimated amount of the Arbitration Costs pursuant to Article 39.

(2) Each party shall contribute half of the Advance on Costs. The SCC Institute may fix separate amounts for counterclaims and set-off claims. After notification by the Arbitral Tribunal, the SCC Institute may, in the course of the proceedings, decide that additional amounts are to be paid.

(3) If a party fails to make a required payment, the SCC Institute shall afford the other party an opportunity to do so within a specified period of time. If the required payment is not made, the case shall be dismissed either wholly or partly to such extent as is attributable to the missing payment.

(4) The SCC Institute may during or after the proceedings draw on the Advance on Costs to cover the fee(s) of the arbitrator(s) and other arbitration costs.

(5) The SCC Institute may decide that the Advance on Costs may partly consist of a bank guarantee or other form of security.

Article 15 – Referral of a Case to the Arbitral Tribunal
When the Arbitral Tribunal has been appointed and the Advance on Costs has been paid, the SCC Institute shall refer the case to the Arbitral Tribunal.

Composition of Arbitral Tribunals

Article 16 – Number of Arbitrators and Manner of Their Appointment
(1) The parties are free to determine the number of arbitrators. Where the

parties have not agreed on the number of arbitrators, the Arbitral Tribunal shall consist of three arbitrators, unless the SCC Institute, taking into account, inter alia, the complexity of the case, the amount in dispute and other circumstances, decides that the dispute is to be settled by a sole arbitrator.

(2) Where the Arbitral Tribunal shall consist of more than one arbitrator, each party shall appoint an equal number of arbitrators. Where a party fails to appoint an arbitrator within the period of time stipulated by the SCC Institute, the SCC Institute shall make the appointment, unless otherwise agreed by the parties.

(3) Where there are multiple parties on either side and the dispute is to be decided by more than one arbitrator, the multiple Claimants, jointly, and the multiple Respondents, jointly, shall appoint an equal number of arbitrators. If either side fails to make such joint appointment, the SCC Institute shall make the appointment for that side. If the circumstances so warrant the SCC Institute may appoint the entire Arbitral Tribunal, unless otherwise agreed by the parties.

(4) Where the Arbitral Tribunal is to consist of more than one arbitrator, the Chairman shall be appointed by the SCC Institute, unless otherwise agreed by the parties.

(5) Where the dispute is to be decided by a sole arbitrator, the SCC Institute shall make the appointment, unless otherwise agreed by the parties.

(6) Where an arbitrator appointed by a party dies, the party in question shall appoint another arbitrator. Where an arbitrator appointed by the SCC Institute dies, the SCC Institute shall appoint another arbitrator.

(7) Where an arbitrator resigns or is removed, the SCC Institute shall appoint another arbitrator. If the arbitrator had been appointed by a party, the SCC Institute shall solicit the views of the appointing party. Where the Arbitral Tribunal consists of three or more arbitrators, the SCC Institute may decide that the remaining arbitrators shall proceed with the case. Prior to making such a decision, the views of the parties and the arbitrators shall be solicited.

(8) If the parties are of different nationalities the SCC Institute shall appoint a sole arbitrator or a Chairman of the Arbitral Tribunal of a nationality other than of the parties, unless the parties have agreed differently or if otherwise deemed appropriate by the SCC Institute.

Article 17 – Impartiality and Independence and Duty of an Arbitrator to Disclose

(1) An arbitrator must be impartial and independent.

(2) A person asked to accept an appointment as arbitrator must disclose any circumstances likely to give rise to justifiable doubts as to his impartiality and independence. If he is nevertheless appointed, he shall immediately, in a

written statement, make the same disclosure to the parties and the other arbitrators.

(3) An arbitrator who becomes aware of any circumstances which may disqualify him, must immediately, in writing, inform the parties and the other arbitrators thereof.

Article 18 – Challenge of Arbitrator

(1) Where a party wishes to challenge an arbitrator that party shall send a written statement to the SCC Institute setting forth the reasons for the challenge.

(2) Notification of a challenge must be made within 15 days as from the date on which the allegedly disqualifying circumstance became known to the party. Failure by a party to notify the SCC Institute of a challenge within the stipulated period of time will be considered a waiver of the right to initiate such a challenge.

(3) The SCC Institute shall provide the parties and the arbitrators the opportunity to comment on the challenge.

(4) The SCC Institute shall make the final decision on the challenge. If the SCC Institute finds an arbitrator disqualified, it shall remove the arbitrator.

Article 19 – Removal of Arbitrator

(1) Where an arbitrator is prevented from de facto fulfilling his duties or fails to perform his functions in an adequate manner, the SCC Institute shall remove the arbitrator.

(2) Before removing an arbitrator, the SCC Institute shall solicit the views of the parties and the arbitrators.

The Proceedings Before the Arbitral Tribunal

Article 20 – Procedures of the Arbitral Tribunal

(1) The manner of conducting the proceedings is to be determined by the Arbitral Tribunal in compliance with the conditions set down in the arbitration agreement and these Rules, with due account taken to the wishes of the parties.

(2) The Arbitral Tribunal may decide that the Chairman alone may make procedural rulings.

(3) The Arbitral Tribunal shall maintain the confidentiality of the arbitration and conduct each case in an impartial, practical and expeditious manner, giving each party sufficient opportunity to present its case.

(4) The Arbitral Tribunal may, after consultation with the parties, decide to conduct hearings at a location other than the Place of Arbitration.

(5) Article 12 shall apply with respect to communications from the Arbitral Tribunal.

Article 21 – Statement of Claim and Defence
(1) The Claimant shall, within the period of time determined by the Arbitral Tribunal, submit a Statement of Claim which, unless previously provided in the case, shall include:

(i) the specific relief sought;
(ii) the material facts and circumstances on which the Claimant relies; and
(iii) a preliminary statement of the evidence on which the Claimant intends to rely.

(2) The Respondent shall, within the period of time determined by the Arbitral Tribunal, submit a Statement of Defence, which, unless previously provided in the case, shall include:

(i) a statement as to whether and to what extent the Respondent accepts or denies the relief sought by the Claimant;
(ii) the material facts and circumstances on which the Respondent relies;
(iii) any counterclaim or set-off claim and the grounds on which it is based; and
(iv) a preliminary statement of the evidence on which the Respondent intends to rely.

(3) The Arbitral Tribunal may determine that the parties are to submit additional written statements.

Article 22 – Amendments to Claim or Defence
(1) A party may amend his claim or defence in the course of the proceedings if his case, as amended, is still comprised by the arbitration agreement, unless the Arbitral Tribunal considers it inappropriate having regard to the point of time at which the amendments are requested, the prejudice that may be caused to the other party or other circumstances.

(2) The provisions of Article 10 shall not preclude the preceding paragraph from being applied with respect to the right of a party to introduce a counterclaim or a set-off claim.

Article 23 – Language
Unless the parties have agreed in the arbitration agreement on the language or languages to be used in the proceedings, the Arbitral Tribunal shall, after

consultation with the parties, make such decision.

Article 24 – Applicable Law

(1) The Arbitral Tribunal shall decide the merits of the dispute on the basis of the law or rules of law agreed by the parties. In the absence of such an agreement, the Arbitral Tribunal shall apply the law or rules of law which it considers to be most appropriate.

(2) Any designation made by the parties of the law of a given state shall be construed as directly referring to the substantive law of that state and not to its conflict of laws rules.

(3) The Arbitral Tribunal shall decide the dispute ex aequo et bono or as amiable compositeur only if the parties have expressly authorized it to do so.

Article 25 – Oral Hearing

(1) An oral hearing shall be arranged if requested by either party, or if the Arbitral Tribunal considers it appropriate. If a hearing is held, the Arbitral Tribunal, taking into account the wishes of the parties, shall determine the time for the hearing, its duration and how it is to be organised, including the manner in which evidence is to be presented.

(2) If an arbitrator is replaced in the course of the proceedings, the newly composed Arbitral Tribunal shall decide whether and to what extent a previously held oral hearing is to be repeated.

Article 26 – Evidence

(1) At the request of the Arbitral Tribunal, the parties shall state the evidence on which they intend to rely, specifying what they intend to prove with each item of evidence, and present the documentary evidence on which they rely.

(2) The Arbitral Tribunal may refuse to accept evidence submitted to it if it considers such evidence to be irrelevant, non-essential or if proof can be established by other means which it considers more convenient or less expensive.

Article 27 – Experts

(1) Unless otherwise agreed by the parties, the Arbitral Tribunal may appoint one or more experts to report to it on a specific issue.

(2) At the request of a party, the parties shall be given the opportunity to put questions to any such expert.

Article 28 – Failure of a Party to Appear

If any of the parties, without showing valid cause, fails to appear at a hearing or otherwise fails to comply with an order of the Arbitral Tribunal, such failure shall not prevent the Arbitral Tribunal from proceeding with the case nor from rendering an Award.

Article 29 – Failure to Object to Procedural Irregularities
A party, who during the proceedings fails to object within a reasonable time to any deviation from provisions of the arbitration agreement, these Rules or other rules applicable to the proceedings, shall be deemed to have waived his right to invoke such irregularity.

Article 30 – Voting
When a vote is taken, that opinion shall prevail which has received more votes than any other opinion. If such majority is not attained, the opinion of the Chairman shall prevail, unless otherwise agreed by the parties.

Article 31 – Interim Measures
(1) Unless the parties have agreed otherwise, the Arbitral Tribunal may, during the course of the proceedings and at the request of a party, order a specific performance by the opposing party for the purpose of securing the claim which is to be tried by the Arbitral Tribunal. The Arbitral Tribunal may order the requesting party to provide reasonable security for damage which may be inflicted on the opposing party as a result of the specific performance in question.

(2) A request addressed by a party to a judicial authority for interim measures shall not be deemed to be incompatible with the arbitration agreement or these Rules.

The Award

Article 32 – Award
(1) The Award shall be deemed to have been rendered at the Place of Arbitration. It shall state the date on which it was rendered, contain an order or a declaration, as well as the reasons for it, and shall be signed by the arbitrators. In absence of the signature of an arbitrator, an Award may be rendered provided that the Award has been signed by a majority of the arbitrators with a verification to the effect that the arbitrator whose signature is missing participated in deciding the dispute.

(2) If any arbitrator fails without valid cause to participate in the deliberations of the Arbitral Tribunal on an issue, such failure will not preclude a decision being made by the other arbitrators.

(3) The parties may agree that the Chairman alone shall sign the Award.

(4) An arbitrator may attach a dissenting opinion to the Award.

(5) If a settlement is reached, the Arbitral Tribunal may, at the request of the parties, record the settlement in the form of an Award.

(6) The Arbitration Costs, in accordance with Article 39, and its apportionment between the parties shall be fixed in the Award or other order by which the arbitral proceedings are terminated. An Award may be rendered solely for costs.

(7) The Arbitral Tribunal shall immediately send the Award to the parties.

Article 33 – Time for Rendering an Award
An Award shall be rendered not later than six months as from the date when the case was referred to the Arbitral Tribunal. The SCC Institute may extend the period of time for rendering an Award.

Article 34 – Separate Award
(1) At the request of a party, a separate issue or a part of the matter in dispute may be decided in a Separate Award.

(2) Where a party has partially admitted a claim, a Separate Award, based on such admission may be rendered.

Article 35 – Right to an Award
(1) If a party withdraws a claim the Arbitral Tribunal shall dismiss such part of the dispute, unless the other party requests the Arbitral Tribunal to rule on the claim.

(2) If a party, who has not paid an Advance on Costs, requests the Arbitral Tribunal to rule on a withdrawn claim, the SCC Institute may, as a condition for such ruling, order the requesting party to pay an Advance on Costs.

Article 36 – Effect of an Award
When rendered an Award is final and binding for the parties.

Article 37 – Correction and Interpretation of an Award and Additional Award
(1) Any obvious miscalculation or clerical error in an Award or Decision shall be corrected by the Arbitral Tribunal.

(2) Within 30 days of receiving the Award, the Arbitral Tribunal shall, if a party so requests, decide a question which should have been decided in the Award but which was not decided therein.

(3) Within 30 days of receiving the Award, the Arbitral Tribunal may, if a party so requests, provide an interpretation thereof in writing.

(4) Before the Arbitral Tribunal takes any action in accordance with the second and third paragraphs, the views of the parties shall be solicited.

Article 38 – Filing of Awards
An Arbitral Tribunal shall, after the close of the proceedings, submit to the SCC Institute one copy of every Award and written order issued in the case, as well as of all recorded minutes therein. The above mentioned documents shall be kept on file by the SCC Institute.

Costs

Article 39 – Arbitration Costs
(1) The Arbitration Costs consist of:

(i) the arbitrator's fee;
(ii) the Administrative Fee of the SCC Institute;
(iii) compensation due to the arbitrator and the SCC Institute to cover their expenses during the proceedings; and
(iv) the fees and expenses of any expert appointed by the Arbitral Tribunal pursuant to Article 27.

(2) Amounts referred to in sections (i) through (iii) above shall be finally fixed by the SCC Institute in accordance with the Regulations for Arbitration Costs in force at the time of the commencement of the arbitration. The amounts in section (iv) shall be finally fixed by the Arbitral Tribunal.

Article 40 – Payment of Arbitration Costs
(1) The parties are jointly and severally liable for all payments of all costs mentioned in Article 39.

(2) The Arbitral Tribunal decides on the apportionment of the Arbitration Costs as between the parties with regard to the outcome of the case and other circumstances.

Article 41 – Costs Incurred by a Party
Unless the parties have agreed otherwise, the Arbitral Tribunal may, at the request of a party, in an Award or other order by which the arbitral proceedings are terminated, order the losing party to compensate the other party for legal representation and other expenses for presenting its case.

Exclusion of Liability

Article 42 – Exclusion of Liability
The SCC Institute is not liable to any party for any act or omission in connection with the arbitration unless such act or omission is shown to constitute

wilful misconduct or gross negligence by the SCC Institute. An arbitrator is liable only if shown to have caused damage by wilful misconduct or gross negligence.

Effectiveness

These Rules enter into force on 1 April 1999 and will replace the former Rules of the Arbitration Institute of the Stockholm Chamber of Commerce. These Rules will be applied to any arbitration commenced on or after this date, unless otherwise agreed by the parties.

III. APPENDIX

Regulations for Arbitration Costs

I. Registration Fee

The Registration Fee in Article 6 of the Rules of the Arbitration Institute of the Stockholm Chamber of Commerce (hereinafter referred to as "the SCC Rules") is EUR 1,000.

The Registration Fee is non-refundable and shall constitute a part of the Administrative Fee due to the SCC Institute under Section III, Article 2 below and shall be deducted from the Advance on Costs to be paid by the Claimant pursuant to Article 14 of the SCC Rules.

II. Advance on Costs

According to Article 13 of the SCC Rules, the SCC Institute shall fix an amount which, together with the accrued interest, shall constitute an advance on the Arbitration Costs. The amount shall cover the estimated Arbitration Costs pursuant to Article 39 of the SCC Rules and, if required, value added tax. Amounts referred to in the first paragraph, sections (i) through (iii), in Article 39 of the SCC Rules are to be determined pursuant to these Regulations.

III. Arbitration Costs

Article 1 – Arbitrator's Fee

(1) Unless otherwise agreed by the parties, the SCC Institute shall decide the

fees of the arbitrator in accordance with the table below, based on the amount in dispute. If so required by law, value added tax shall be added to such fees.

(2) For the purpose of calculating the amount in dispute, the value of any counterclaim or set-off claim is to be added to the amount of the claim with the exception of interest claims. Where the amount in dispute is not specified, the SCC Institute will fix the fee on the basis of an assessment of the size of the case. Each party must provide the SCC Institute with the information deemed necessary for such assessment.

(3) If a case has required substantially more or less work than is considered normal, the SCC Institute may deviate from the amounts stated in the table.

(4) The fee due to the co-arbitrator is fixed per person to 60 per cent of the total fee paid to the Chairman, unless the SCC Institute decides otherwise in view of any special circumstances of the case.

Article 2 – Administrative Fee of the SCC Institute

(1) The SCC Institute shall decide the Administrative Fee due to it. The decision is based on the amount in dispute in accordance with the table below. If so required by law, value added tax shall be added to the Administrative Fee.

(2) For the purpose of calculating the amount in dispute, the value of any counterclaim or set-off claim is to be added to the amount of the claim, with the exemption of interest claims. Where the amount in dispute is not specified, the SCC Institute will fix the Administrative Fee on the basis of an assessment of the size of the case. Each party must provide the SCC Institute with the information deemed necessary for such assessment.

(3) If a case has required substantially more or less work than is considered normal, the SCC Institute may deviate from the amounts stated in the table.

Article 3 – Expenses

In addition to the fee(s) of the arbitrator(s) and the Administrative Fee of the SCC Institute, the SCC Institute shall fix an amount, to be provided by the parties, to cover reasonable expenses for the arbitrator(s) and to the SCC Institute.

IV. Effectiveness

These Regulations enter into force on 1 April 1999 and will replace the former Regulations. The Regulations will be applied to any arbitration commenced on this date or thereafter.

Arbitrator's Fee

Amount in dispute (EUR)	Chairman of the Tribunal/Sole Arbitrator (EUR) Minimum	Maximum
up to 25 000	2 500	5 000
from 25 001 to 50 000	2 500 + 2% on amount above 25 000	5 000 + 10% on the amount above 25 000
from 50 001 to 100 000	3 000 + 2% on the amount above 50 000	7 500 + 5% on the amount above 50 000
from 100 001 to 500 000	4 000 + 1% on the amount above 100 000	10 000 + 3% on the amount above 100 000
from 500 001 to 1 000 000	8 000 + 0,8% on the amount above 500 000	22 000 + 2,4% on the amount above 500 000
from 1 000 001 to 2 000 000	12 000 + 0,5% on the amount above 1 000 000	34 000 + 2% on the amount above 1 000 000
from 2 000 001 to 5 000 000	17 000 + 0,2% on the amount above 2 000 000	54 000 + 1% on the amount above 2 000 000
from 5 000 001 to 10 000 000	23 000 + 0,1% on the amount above 5 000 000	84 000 + 0,52% on the amount above 5 000 000
from 10 000 001 to 50 000 000	28 000 + 0,03% on the amount above 10 000 000	110 000 + 0,1% on the amount above 10 000 000
from 50 000 001 to 75 000 000	40 000 + 0,02% on the amount above 50 000 000	150 000 + 0,08% on the amount above 50 000 000
from 75 000 001 to 100 000 000	45 000 + 0,012% on the amount above 75 000 000	170 000 + 0,048% on the amount above 75 000 000
from 100 000 001	48 000 + 0,01% on the amount above 100 000 000	182 000 + 0,045% on the amount above 100 000 000

Administrative Fee of the SCC Institute

Amount in dispute (EUR)	Administrative Fee of the SCC Institute (EUR)
up to 25 000	1 000
from 25 001 to 50 000	1 000 + 4% on the amount above 25 000
from 50 001 to 100 000	2 000 + 2% on the amount above 50 000
from 100 001 to 500 000	3 000 + 1% on the amount above 100 000
from 500 001 to 1 000 000	7 000 + 0,8% on the amount above 500 000
from 1 000 001 to 2 000 000	11 000 + 0,3% on the amount above 1 000 000
from 2 000 001 to 5 000 000	14 000 + 0,1% on the amount above 2 000 000
from 5 000 001 to 10 000 000	17 000 + 0,06% on the amount above 5 000 000
from 10 000 001 to 50 000 000	20 000 + 0,02% on the amount above 10 000 000
from 50 000 001 to 75 000 000	28 000 + 0,01% on the amount above 50 000 000
from 75 000 001	30 500 + 0,01% on the amount above 75 000 000 Maximum 60 000

RULES FOR EXPEDITED ARBITRATIONS

In force 1 April 1999

Initiation of Proceedings

Article 1 – Request for Arbitration

Arbitration is initiated by the Claimant filing with the SCC Institute a Request for Arbitration which shall include:

(i) a statement of the names, addresses, telephone and facsimile numbers and e-mail addresses of the parties and their counsel;
(ii) a summary of the dispute;
(iii) a preliminary statement of the relief sought by the Claimant; and
(iv) a copy of the arbitration agreement or clause under which the dispute is to be settled.

Article 2 – Registration Fee

(1) At the same time as the Request for Arbitration is filed, the Claimant shall pay a Registration Fee. The amount of the fee is fixed in accordance with the SCC Institute's Regulations for Arbitration Costs for Expedited Arbitrations in force on the date of the Request for Arbitration.

(2) If the required Registration Fee is not paid when filing the Request for Arbitration, the SCC Institute will fix a period of time within which the Claimant must pay such fee.

Article 3 – Dismissal

If it is clear that the SCC Institute lacks jurisdiction over the dispute or if the Registration Fee has not been paid in due time, the Claimant's Request for Arbitration shall be dismissed.

Article 4 – Date of Commencement of the Arbitration

The arbitration shall be deemed to have been commenced on the date on which the Request for Arbitration was received by the SCC Institute.

Article 5 – Procedures of the SCC Institute

The SCC Institute shall maintain the confidentiality of the arbitration and shall deal with the arbitration in an impartial, practical and expeditious manner.

Article 6 – The Respondent's Reply

(1) The Request for Arbitration shall be communicated by the SCC Institute to the Respondent. The Respondent shall be asked to submit a Reply to the SCC Institute. The Reply shall be submitted within the period of time determined by the SCC Institute and shall include comments regarding the Request for Arbitration by the Claimant.

(2) If the Respondent wishes to raise any objection concerning the validity or applicability of the arbitration agreement, such objection shall be made in the Reply together with the grounds therefore.

(3) If the Respondent wishes to file a counterclaim or a set-off claim, a statement to that effect should be made in the Reply and should include the nature of the claim and a preliminary statement of the relief sought. The grounds for any counterclaim and set-off claim must be based on the arbitration agreement.

(4) The SCC Institute shall communicate the Respondent's Reply to the Claimant. The Claimant shall be given an opportunity to comment on any objections and pleas advanced by the Respondent.

(5) Failure by the Respondent to submit a Reply shall not prevent the

arbitration from proceeding pursuant to these Rules.

Article 7 – Amplification and Periods of Time

(1) The SCC Institute may request a party to expound upon any written comments to the SCC Institute. If the Claimant fails to comply with such a request, the SCC Institute may decide to dismiss the case. If the Respondent fails to comply with a request to expound upon a counterclaim, the counterclaim may be dismissed by the SCC Institute. Failure by the Respondent otherwise to comply with a request to expound upon a written statement shall not prevent the arbitral proceedings from continuing.

(2) If the SCC Institute has requested a party to perform any act within a specific period of time, such period of time may be extended by the SCC Institute.

Article 8 – Notice

(1) Any notice or other communication from the SCC Institute shall be delivered to the last known address of the addressee.

(2) Any notice or other communication shall be delivered by courier or registered mail, facsimile transmission, e-mail or by any other means of communication that provides a record of the sending thereof.

(3) A notice or communication sent in accordance paragraph two shall be deemed to have been received, by the addressee, at the latest on the date it would normally have been received given the chosen means of communication.

Article 9 – Appointment of Arbitrator and Place of Arbitration

When the exchange of written submissions pursuant to Articles 1-7 has been concluded, the SCC Institute shall:

(i) appoint an Arbitrator, if not agreed upon by the parties;
(ii) decide the Place of Arbitration, if not agreed upon by the parties; and
(iii) fix the Advance on Costs pursuant to Article 10.

Article 10 – Advance on Costs

(1) The Advance on Costs shall be equivalent to the estimated amount of the Arbitration Costs pursuant to Article 34.

(2) Each party shall contribute half of the Advance on Costs. The SCC Institute may fix separate amounts for counterclaims and set-off claims. After notification by the Arbitrator, the SCC Institute may, in the course of the proceedings, decide that additional amounts are to be paid.

(3) If a party fails to make a required payment, the SCC Institute shall afford the other party an opportunity to do so within a specified period of

time. If the required payment is not made, the case shall be dismissed either wholly or partly to such extent as is attributable to the missing payment.

(4) The SCC Institute may during or after the proceedings draw on the Advance on Costs to cover the fee of the Arbitrator and other arbitration costs.

(5) The SCC Institute may decide that the Advance on Costs may partly consist of a bank guarantee or other form of security.

Article 11 – Referral of a Case to the Arbitrator

When the Arbitrator has been appointed and the Advance on Costs has been paid, the SCC Institute shall refer the case to the Arbitrator.

The Arbitrator

Article 12 – Appointment of the Arbitrator

(1) The arbitral tribunal shall consist of a sole Arbitrator who shall be appointed by the SCC Institute, unless otherwise agreed by the parties.

(2) If the Arbitrator dies, resigns or is removed, the SCC Institute shall appoint another Arbitrator.

(3) If the parties are of different nationalities the SCC Institute shall appoint an Arbitrator of a nationality other than of the parties, unless the parties have agreed differently or if otherwise deemed appropriate by the SCC Institute.

Article 13 – Impartiality and Independence and Duty of the Arbitrator to Disclose

(1) The Arbitrator must be impartial and independent.

(2) A person asked to accept an appointment as Arbitrator must disclose any circumstances likely to give rise to justifiable doubts as to his impartiality and independence. If he is nevertheless appointed, he shall immediately, in a written statement, make the same disclosure to the parties.

(3) An Arbitrator who becomes aware of any circumstances which may disqualify him, must immediately, in writing, inform the parties thereof.

Article 14 – Challenge of Arbitrator

(1) Where a party wishes to challenge the Arbitrator that party shall send a written statement to the SCC Institute, setting forth the reasons for the challenge.

(2) Notification of a challenge must be made within 15 days as from the date on which the allegedly disqualifying circumstance became known to the party. Failure by a party to notify the SCC Institute of a challenge within the stipulated period of time will be considered a waiver of the right to initiate such a challenge.

(3) The SCC Institute shall provide the parties and the Arbitrator an opportunity to comment on the challenge.

(4) The SCC Institute shall make the final decision on the challenge. If the SCC Institute finds an Arbitrator disqualified, it shall remove the Arbitrator.

Article 15 – Removal of Arbitrator

(1) Where the Arbitrator is prevented from de facto fulfilling his duties or fails to perform his functions in an adequate manner, the SCC Institute shall remove the Arbitrator.

(2) Before removing the Arbitrator, the SCC Institute shall solicit the views of the parties and the Arbitrator.

The Proceedings before the Arbitrator

Article 16 – Procedures of the Arbitrator

(1) The manner of conducting the proceedings is to be determined by the Arbitrator in compliance with the conditions set down in the arbitration agreement and these Rules, with due account taken to the wishes of the parties.

(2) The Arbitrator shall maintain the confidentiality of the arbitration and conduct each case in an impartial, practical and expeditious manner, giving each party sufficient opportunity to present its case. The parties must seek to limit the scope of the case.

(3) The Arbitrator may, after consultation with the parties, decide to conduct hearings at a location other than the Place of Arbitration.

(4) The Arbitrator shall prepare and distribute to the parties a time schedule for the proceedings.

(5) The following shall apply to the proceedings, unless the Arbitrator, for special reasons, decides otherwise.

(i) In addition to the Statement of Claim and the Statement of Defence, the parties each may only submit one written statement, including statements of evidence.
(ii) The statements must be brief.
(iii) The time limits within which the documents shall be submitted may not exceed ten working days.

(6) The Arbitrator may order a party to finally state his claims for relief and the facts relied on as grounds thereof, and the evidence on which the party relies. At the expiration of the time period for such statement, the party may not amend his claim for relief nor adduce additional facts or evidence, unless the Arbitrator, for special reasons, so permits.

(7) Article 8 shall apply with respect to communication from the Arbitrator.

Article 17 – Statement of Claim and Defence

(1) The Claimant shall, within the period of time determined by the Arbitrator, submit a Statement of Claim which, unless previously provided in the case, shall include:

(i) the specific relief sought;
(ii) the material facts and circumstances on which the Claimant relies; and
(iii) a preliminary statement of the evidence on which the Claimant intends to rely.

(2) The Respondent shall, within the period of time determined by the Arbitrator, submit a Statement of Defence, which, unless previously provided in the case, shall include:

(i) a statement as to whether and to what extent the Respondent accepts or denies the relief sought by the Claimant;
(ii) the material facts and circumstances on which the Respondent relies;
(iii) any counterclaim or set-off claim and the grounds on which it is based;
(iv) a preliminary statement of the evidence on which the Respondent intends to rely.

(3) The Arbitrator may determine that the parties are to submit additional written statements.

Article 18 – Amendments to Claim or Defence

(1) A party may amend his claim or defence in the course of the proceedings if his case, as amended, is still comprised by the arbitration agreement, unless the Arbitrator considers it inappropriate having regard to the point of time at which the amendments is requested, the prejudice that may be caused to the other party or other circumstances.

(2) The provisions of Article 6 shall not preclude the preceding paragraph from being applied with respect to the right of a party to introduce a counterclaim or a set-off claim.

Article 19 – Language

Unless the parties have agreed in the arbitration agreement on the language or languages to be used in the proceedings, the Arbitrator shall, after consultation with the parties, make such decision.

Article 20 – Applicable Law

(1) The Arbitrator shall decide the merits of the dispute on the basis of the law or rules of law agreed by the parties. In the absence of such an agreement, the Arbitrator shall apply the law or rules of law which the Arbitrator considers to be most appropriate.

(2) Any designation made by the parties of the law of a given state shall be construed as directly referring to the substantive law of that state and not to its conflict of law rules.

(3) The Arbitrator shall decide the dispute ex aequo et bono or as amiable compositeur only if the parties have expressly authorized the Arbitrator to do so.

Article 21 – Oral Hearing

An oral hearing shall be arranged only if requested by either party and if the Arbitrator deems it necessary. If a hearing is held, the Arbitrator, taking into account the wishes of the parties, shall determine the time for the hearing, its duration and how it is to be organised, including the manner in which evidence is to be presented.

Article 22 – Evidence

(1) At the request of the Arbitrator, the parties shall state the evidence on which they intend to rely, specifying what they intend to prove with each item of evidence, and present the documentary evidence on which they rely.

(2) The Arbitrator may refuse to accept evidence submitted to him if he considers such evidence to be irrelevant, non-essential or if proof can be established by other means which the Arbitrator considers more convenient or less expensive.

Article 23 – Expert

(1) Unless otherwise agreed by the parties, the Arbitrator may appoint one or more experts to report to the Arbitrator on a specific issue.

(2) At the request of a party, the parties shall be given the opportunity to put questions to any such expert.

Article 24 – Failure of a Party to Appear

If any of the parties, without showing valid cause, fails to appear at a hearing or otherwise fails to comply with an order of the Arbitrator, such failure shall not prevent the Arbitrator from proceeding with the case nor from rendering an award.

Article 25 – Failure to Object to Procedural Irregularities
A party, who during the proceedings fails to object within a reasonable time to any deviation from provisions of the arbitration agreement, these Rules or other rules applicable to the proceedings, shall be deemed to have waived his right to invoke such irregularity.

Article 26 – Interim Measures
(1) Unless the parties have agreed otherwise, the Arbitrator may, during the course of the proceedings and at the request of a party, order a specific performance by the opposing party for the purpose of securing the claim which is to be tried by the Arbitrator. The Arbitrator may order the requesting party to provide reasonable security for damage which may be inflicted on the opposing party as a result of the specific performance in question.

(2) A request addressed by a party to a judicial authority for interim measures shall not be deemed to be incompatible with the arbitration agreement or these Rules.

The Award

Article 27 – Award
(1) The Award shall be deemed to have been rendered at the Place of Arbitration. The Award shall be signed by the Arbitrator. It shall state the date on which it was rendered. In addition to information about the parties and the Arbitrator, it shall contain an order or declaration. The Award shall also in brief include the relief claimed by the parties together with supporting statements. A party may request a reasoned Award no later than at the closing statement.

(2) If a settlement is reached, the Arbitrator may, at the request of the parties, record the settlement in the form of an Award.

(3) The Arbitration Costs, in accordance with Article 34, and its apportionment between the parties shall be fixed in the Award or other order by which the arbitral proceedings are terminated. An Award may be rendered solely for costs.

(4) The Arbitrator shall immediately send the Award to the parties.

Article 28 – Time for Rendering an Award
An Award shall be rendered not later than three months as from the dated when the case was referred to the Arbitrator. The SCC Institute may extend the period of time for rendering an Award.

Article 29 – Separate Award
(1) At the request of a party, a separate issue or a part of the matter in dispute may be decided by a Separate Award.

(2) Where a party has partially admitted a claim, a Separate Award, based on such admission may be rendered.

Article 30 – Right to an Award
(1) If a party withdraws a claim the Arbitrator shall dismiss such part of the dispute, unless the other party requests the Arbitrator to rule on the claim.

(2) If a party, who has not paid an Advance on Costs, requests the Arbitrator to rule on a withdrawn claim, the SCC Institute may, as a condition for such ruling, order the requesting party to pay an Advance on Costs.

Article 31 – Effect of an Award
When rendered an Award is final and binding for the parties.

Article 32 – Correction and Interpretation of an Award and Additional Award
(1) Any obvious miscalculation or clerical error in an Award or Decision shall be corrected by the Arbitrator.

(2) Within 30 days of receiving the Award, the Arbitrator shall, if a party so requests, decide a question which should have been decided in the Award but which was not decided therein.

(3) Within 30 days of receiving the Award, the Arbitrator may, if a party so requests, provide an interpretation thereof in writing.

(4) Before the Arbitrator takes any action in accordance with the second and third paragraphs, the views of the parties shall be solicited.

Article 33 – Filing of Awards
An Arbitrator shall, after the close of the proceedings, submit to the SCC Institute one copy of every Award and written order issued in the case, as well as of all the recorded minutes therein. The above mentioned documents shall be kept on file by the SCC Institute.

Costs

Article 34 – Arbitration Costs
(1) The Arbitration Costs consists of:

(i) the Arbitrator's Fee;
(ii) the Administrative Fee to the SCC Institute;
(iii) compensation due to the Arbitrator and the SCC Institute to cover their

expenses during the proceedings; and
(iv) the fees and expenses of any expert appointed by the Arbitrator pursuant to Article 23.

(2) Amounts referred to in sections (i) through (iii) above shall be finally fixed by the SCC Institute in accordance with the Regulations for Arbitration Costs for Expedited Arbitrations in force at the time of the commencement of the arbitration. The amounts in section (iv) shall be finally fixed by the Arbitrator.

Article 35 – Payment of Arbitration Costs
(1) The parties are jointly and severally liable for all payments of all costs mentioned in Article 34.

(2) The Arbitrator decides on the apportionment of the Arbitration Costs as between the parties with regard to the outcome of the case and other circumstances.

Article 36 – Costs Incurred by a Party
Unless the parties have agreed otherwise, the Arbitrator may, at the request of a party, in an Award or other order by which the arbitral proceedings are terminated order the losing party to compensate the other party for legal representation and other expenses for presenting its case.

Exclusion of Liability

Article 37 – Exclusion of Liability
The SCC Institute is not liable to any party for any act or omission in connection with the arbitration unless such act or omission is shown to constitute wilful misconduct or gross negligence by the SCC Institute. The Arbitrator is liable only if shown to have caused damage by wilful misconduct or gross negligence.

Effectiveness

These Rules enter into force on 1 April 1999 and will replace the former Rules for Expedited Arbitrations. These Rules will be applied to any arbitration under the Expedited Rules commenced on or after this date, unless otherwise agreed by the parties.

APPENDIX – REGULATIONS FOR ARBITRATION COSTS FOR EXPEDITED ARBITRATIONS

I. Registration Fee

The Registration Fee in Article 2 of the Rules for Expedited Arbitrations (hereinafter referred to as "the Expedited Rules") is EUR 500.

The Registration Fee is non-refundable and shall constitute a part of the Administrative Fee due to the SCC Institute under Section III, Article 2 below and shall be deducted from the Advance on Costs to be paid by the Claimant pursuant to Article 10 of the Expedited Rules.

II. Advance on Costs

According to Article 9 of the Expedited Rules, the SCC Institute shall fix an amount which, together with the accrued interest, shall constitute an advance on the Arbitration Costs. The amount shall cover the estimated Arbitration Costs pursuant to Article 34 of the Expedited Rules and, if required, value added tax. Amounts referred to in the first paragraph, sections (i) through (iii), in Article 34 of the Expedited Rules are to be determined pursuant to these Regulations.

III. Arbitration Costs

Article 1 – Arbitrator's Fees

(1) Unless otherwise agreed by the parties, the SCC Institute shall decide the fee of the Arbitrator in accordance with the table below, based on the amount in dispute. If so required by law, value added tax shall be added to such fee.

(2) For the purpose of calculating the amount in dispute, the value of any counterclaim or set-off claim is to be added to the amount of the claim with the exception of interest claims. Where the amount in dispute is not specified, the SCC Institute will fix the fee on the basis of an assessment of the size of the case. Each party must provide the SCC Institute with the information deemed necessary for such assessment.

(3) If a case has required substantially more or less work than is considered normal, the SCC Institute may deviate from the amounts stated in the table.

Article 2 – Administrative Fee of the SCC Institute

(1) The SCC Institute shall decide the Administrative Fee due to it. The decision is based on the amount in dispute in accordance with the table below. If so required by law, value added tax shall be added to the Administrative Fee.

(2) For the purpose of calculating the amount in dispute, the value of any counterclaim or set-off claim is to be added to the amount of the claim, with the exemption of interest claims. Where the amount in dispute is not specified, the SCC Institute will fix the Administrative Fee on the basis of an assessment of the size of the case. Each party must provide the SCC Institute with the information deemed necessary to such assessment.

(3) If a case has required substantially more or less work than is considered normal, the SCC Institute may deviate from the amounts stated in table.

Article 3 – Expenses

In addition to the fee to the Arbitrator and the Administrative Fee to the SCC Institute, the SCC Institute shall fix an amount to be provided by the parties, to cover reasonable expenses of the Arbitrator and the SCC Institute.

IV. Effectiveness

These Regulations enter into force on 1 April 1999 and will replace the former Regulations. The Regulations will be applied to any arbitration commenced on this date or thereafter.

Arbitrator's Fee

Amount in dispute (EUR)	Arbitrator's Fee (EUR)
up to 25 000	2 500
from 25 001 to 50 000	2 500 + 2% of the amount above 25 000
from 50 001 to 100 000	3 000 + 2% of the amount above 50 000
from 100 001 to 500 000	4 000 + 1% of the amount above 100 000
from 500 001 to 1 000 000	8 000 + 0,8% of the amount above 500 000
from 1 000 001 to 2 000 000	12 000 + 0,5% of the amount above 1 000 000
from 2 000 001 to 5 000 000	17 000 + 0,2% of the amount above 2 000 000
from 5 000 001 to 10 000 000	23 000 + 0,1% of the amount above 5 000 000
from 10 000 001 to 50 000 000	28 000 + 0,03% of the amount above 10 000 000
from 50 000 001 to 75 000 000	40 000 + 0,02% of the amount above 50 000 000
from 75 000 001	45 000 + 0,012% of the amount above 75 000 000

Administrative Fee of the SCC Institute

Amount in dispute (EUR)	Administrative Fee of the SCC Institute (EUR)
to 25 000	500
from 25 001 to 50 000	500 + 3,2% of the amount above 25 000
from 50 001 to 100 000	1 300 + 1% of the amount above 50 000
from 100 001 to 500 000	1 800 + 0,5% of the amount above 100 000
from 500 001 to 1 000 000	3 800 + 0,5% of the amount above 500 000
from 1 000 001 to 2 000 000	6 300 + 0,2% of the amount above 1 000 000
from 2 000 001 to 5 000 000	8 300 + 0,1% of the amount above 2 000 000
from 5 000 001 to 10 000 000	11 300 + 0,06% of the amount above 5 000 000
from 10 000 001	14 300 + 0,01% of the amount above 10 000 000 Maximum 30 000

STOCKHOLM CHAMBER OF COMMERCE MEDIATION INSTITUTE*

MEDIATION RULES

Adopted and in force as of 1 April 1999

I. MEDIATION RULES OF THE SCC MEDIATION INSTITUTE

The Mediator

Article 1 – Role of the Mediator

(1) A Mediator must be impartial and independent.

(2) A Mediator may not act as arbitrator in any future arbitration relating to the subject matter of the dispute, unless otherwise agreed by the parties.

Article 2 – Duty of the Mediator to Disclose

(1) A person asked to accept appointment as Mediator must disclose any circumstances likely to give rise to justifiable doubts as to his impartiality and independence.

(2) A Mediator who becomes aware of any circumstances referred to in the first paragraph of this article, must immediately, in writing, inform the parties thereof.

Confidentiality

Article 3 – Duty to Respect the Confidentiality of the Mediation

(1) The Mediator, the SCC Mediation Institute, the parties, and any other persons participating in the Mediation, shall respect the confidentiality of the

* The address of the Mediation Institute of the Stockholm Chamber of Commerce is Jakobs Torg 3, PO Box 16050, SE-10321 Stockholm, Sweden, tel.: 46 8 555 10050, fax: 46 8 566 31650, e-mail: arbitration@chamber.se, internet: http://www.chamber.se.

Mediation, unless otherwise agreed by the parties. The need for appropriate confidentiality undertakings should be taken into consideration.

(2) At the request of a party, any submission, document or other materials supplied in the course of the Mediation, shall be returned to the party having provided it, without any copy being retained.

(3) At the request of a party, any notes taken in the course of the Mediation shall be destroyed upon the termination of the Mediation.

(4) A party may not introduce as evidence in any judicial or arbitration proceeding any views expressed or statements made in the course of the Mediation. A party may not involve as witness in any judicial or arbitration proceeding the Mediator or any expert that has participated in the Mediation.

Initiation of Mediation

Article 4 – Request for Mediation

(1) A Request for Mediation shall be submitted to the SCC Mediation Institute by the parties jointly or by one of them. It shall be in writing and include:

(i) a statement of the names, addresses, telephone and facsimile numbers and e-mail addresses of the parties and their counsel;
(ii) a summary of the dispute; and
(iii) a statement wether the parties have agreed to mediate the dispute.

(2) Where a Request for Mediation is submitted by one party only, the SCC Mediation Institute shall communicate the Request to the other party who shall be asked to state whether or not it agrees to participate in the Mediation.

Article 5 – Registration Fee

(1) At the same time as the Request for Mediation is filed a Registration Fee of EUR 400 shall be paid.

(2) If the Registration Fee is not paid when the Request for Mediation is filed, the SCC Mediation Institute shall fix a period of time within which the parties may pay such fee.

Article 6 – Appointment of Mediator

(1) Unless otherwise agreed by the parties, a sole Mediator shall be appointed by the SCC Mediation Institute. Before the appointment, the SCC Mediation Institute shall solicit the views of the parties.

(2) If the parties jointly propose a person to act as Mediator, such person shall be appointed by the SCC Mediation Institute.

(3) In absence of an agreement between the parties to the contrary, where more than one Mediator shall be appointed, each party shall appoint an equal number of Mediators and, in case of an odd number of Mediators, the SCC Mediation Institute shall appoint a Mediator who shall act as Chairman.

Article 7 – Removal of the Mediator
(1) Where the Mediator is prevented from de facto fulfilling his duties or fails to perform his functions in an adequate manner, the SCC Mediation Institute shall remove the Mediator and appoint a new Mediator in accordance with Article 6.

(2) Before removing the Mediator, the SCC Mediation Institute shall solicit the views of the parties and the Mediator.

Article 8 – Advance on Costs
(1) The SCC Mediation Institute shall fix an Advance on Costs which shall be equivalent to the estimated amount of the Mediation Costs pursuant to Article 13.

(2) Each party shall contribute half of the Advance on Costs, unless otherwise agreed by the parties. One party may pay the entire amount.

(3) After notification by the Mediator, the SCC Mediation Institute may, in the course of the Mediation, decide that additional amounts are to be paid.

(4) The SCC Mediation Institute may during or after the Mediation draw on the Advance on Costs to cover the cost of the Mediation.

(5) If a required payment pursuant to paragraph (2) of this Article 8 is not made, the dispute shall be dismissed either wholly or partly to such an extent as is attributable to the missing payment.

Article 9 – Referral of a Dispute to the Mediator
When the Mediator has been appointed and the Advance on Costs has been paid, the SCC Mediation Institute shall refer the dispute to the Mediator.

The Proceedings before the Mediator

Article 10 – Conduct of the Mediation
(1) Giving consideration to the wishes of the parties, the Mediator shall determine the conduct of the Mediation, with a view for reaching an expeditious and efficient resolution of the dispute.

(2) Each party shall be given sufficient opportunity to present its case.

(3) Where the Mediator believes that the dispute between the parties is not likely to be resolved through mediation, the Mediator may propose other means of resolving the dispute, for the consideration of the parties.

Termination of the Mediation

Article 11 – Termination

(1) Unless otherwise agreed by the parties, the Mediation shall be terminated within two months of the date when the dispute was referred to the Mediator pursuant to Article 9. At the request of the Mediator, the SCC Mediation Institute may extend this period of time.

(2) The Mediation shall be terminated:

(i) by a settlement agreement between the parties;
(ii) by a declaration of the Mediator to the parties and the SCC Mediation Institute, to the effect that further efforts of Mediation are unlikely to lead to the resolution of the dispute; or
(iii) by a written request from a party to the Mediator that the Mediation shall be terminated.

(3) Upon the termination of the Mediation, the Mediator shall notify the SCC Mediation Institute.

Article 12 – Confirmation of a Settlement Agreement in an Arbitral Award

Upon reaching a settlement agreement the parties may, subject to the approval of the Mediator, agree to appoint the Mediator as an Arbitrator and request him to confirm the settlement agreement in an arbitral award.

Costs

Article 13 – Mediation Costs

(1) The Mediation Costs consist of:

(i) the Mediator's Fee;
(ii) the Administrative Fee of the SCC Mediation Institute; and
(iii) compensation due to the Mediator and the SCC Mediation Institute to cover their expenses in the course of the Mediation.

(2) The Registration Fee under Article 5 shall be deducted from the amount due to the SCC Mediation Institute pursuant to the previous paragraph.

(3) Amounts referred to in paragraph (1) in this Article 13 shall be finally fixed by the SCC Mediation Institute in accordance with the Regulations for Mediation Costs in force at the date of the Request for Mediation.

Article 14 – Payment of Mediation Costs

(1) The parties are jointly and severally liable for all payments of all costs mentioned in Article 13.

(2) Unless they agree differently, the parties shall, as between themselves, bear the Mediation Costs in equal shares.

II. ORGANISATION OF THE SCC MEDIATION INSTITUTE

Article 15 – The SCC Mediation Institute

The Mediation Institute of the Stockholm Chamber of Commerce is part of the Arbitration Institute of the Stockholm Chamber of Commerce. Its objectives are:

- to assist in the settlement of domestic and international disputes in accordance with the Rules of the Mediation Institute;
- to assist, as determined by the SCC Mediation Institute, in mediations which are conducted in a manner which differs, either in part or in whole, from that anticipated by the SCC Institute Mediation Rules; and
- to provide information on mediation matters.

Article 16 – The Board

(1) The SCC Mediation Institute shall have a Board composed of six members who shall be appointed for a period of three years by the Board of the Arbitration Institute of the Stockholm Chamber of Commerce. The Board of the Arbitration Institute of the Stockholm Chamber of Commerce shall appoint a Chairman and a Vice Chairman from among the members of the Board of the SCC Mediation Institute. The Chairman and the Vice Chairman shall be lawyers.

(2) The Board of the Arbitration Institute of the Stockholm Chamber of Commerce may, if there are extraordinary reasons for doing so, remove a member of the Board of the SCC Mediation Institute. If a member resigns or is removed during his term of office, the Board of the Arbitration Institute of the Stockholm Chamber of Commerce will appoint a new member for the remainder of his term.

Article 17 – Decisions by the Board

Two members of the Board shall form a quorum. If no majority is attained, the Chairman shall cast the deciding vote. The Chairman or the Vice Chairman shall have the power to take decisions on behalf of the Board in urgent matters. Decisions of the Board are final and cannot be reviewed by the Board of the Arbitration Institute of the Stockholm Chamber of Commerce.

Effectiveness

These Rules enter into force on 1 April 1999 and will replace the former Conciliation Rules of the Arbitration Institute of the Stockholm Chamber of Commerce. These Rules will be applied to any Mediation commenced on or after this date, unless otherwise agreed by the parties.

APPENDIX

Regulations for Mediation Costs

Article 1 – Mediator's Fee
(1) Unless otherwise agreed by the parties, the SCC Mediation Institute shall decide the fee of the Mediator in accordance with the table below, based on the amount in dispute. If so required by law, value added tax shall be added to such fee.

(2) Where the amount in dispute is not specified, the SCC Mediation Institute will fix the fee on an assessment of the size of the dispute. Each party must provide the SCC Mediation Institute with the information deemed necessary for such assessment.

(3) If a Mediation has required substantially more or less work than is considered normal, the SCC Mediation Institute may deviate from the amounts stated in the table.

Article 2 – Administrative Fee of the SCC Mediation Institute
(1) The SCC Mediation Institute shall decide the Administrative Fee due to it. The decision is based on the amount in dispute in accordance with the table below. If so required by law, value added tax shall be added to the Administrative Fee.

(2) Where the amount in dispute is not specified, the SCC Mediation Institute will fix the fee on an assessment of the size of the dispute. Each party must provide the SCC Mediation Institute with the information deemed necessary for such assessment.

(3) If a Mediation has required substantially more or less work than is considered normal, the SCC Mediation Institute may deviate from the amounts stated in the table.

Article 3 – Expenses

In addition to the fee of the Mediator and the Administrative Fee of the SCC Mediation Institute, the SCC Mediation Institute shall fix an amount to be provided by the parties, to cover reasonable expenses of the Mediator and the SCC Mediation Institute.

Effectiveness

These Regulations enter into force on 1 April 1999 and will be applied to any Mediation commenced on this date or thereafter.

Amount in Dispute (EUR)	Mediator's Fee (EUR)
to 25 000	1 200
from 25 001 to 50 000	1 200 + 2% of the amount above 25 000
from 50 001 to 100 000	1 700 + 1% of the amount above 50 000
from 100 001 to 500 000	2 200 + 0,5% of the amount above 100 000
from 500 001 to 1 000 000	4 200 + 0,4% of the amount above 500 000
from 1 000 001 to 2 000 000	6 200 + 0,3% of the amount above 1 000 000
from 2 000 001 to 5 000 000	9 200 + 0,1% of the amount above 2 000 000
from 5 000 001 to 10 000 000	12 200 + 0,05% of the amount above 5 000 000
from 10 000 00	114 700 + 0,03% of the amount above 10 000 000

Amount in Dispute (EUR)	Administrative Fee of the SCC Mediation Institute (EUR)
to 25 000	400
from 25 001 to 50 000	400 + 0,8% of the amount above 25 000
from 50 001 to 100 000	600 + 0,6% of the amount above 50 000
from 100 001 to 500 000	900 + 0,3% of the amount above 100 000
from 500 001 to 1 000 000	2 100 + 0,2% of the amount above 500 000
from 1 000 001 to 2 000 000	3 100 + 0,1% of the amount above 1 000 000
from 2 000 001 to 5 000 000	4 100 + 0,06% of the amount above 2 000 000
from 5 000 001 to 10 000 000	5 900 + 0,03% of the amount above 5 000 000
from 10 000 001	7 400 + 0,01% of the amount above 10 000 000 Maximum 15 000

Part III

B. Iran-US Claims Tribunal

INTRODUCTION

This Volume of the Yearbook covers the Tribunal's work during the fourteen-month period from 1 November 1997 through 31 December 1998. This Introduction describes events related to the Tribunal's operations. The section entitled Survey of Awards, Decisions and Orders reviews and analyzes the Tribunal's significant holdings during the reporting period. The Yearbook's treatment of the Tribunal's work concludes with a section excerpting significant Tribunal Awards issued during the reporting period.

1. *Composition*

As of 31 December 1998, the three Chambers of the Tribunal were composed of the following Members:

Chamber One:	Bengt Broms (Chairman), Finland Charles T. Duncan, USA Assadollah Noori, Iran
Chamber Two:	Krzysztof Skubiszewski (Chairman and President of the Tribunal), Poland George H. Aldrich, USA Koorosh H. Ameli, Iran
Chamber Three:	Gaetano Arangio-Ruiz (Chairman), Italy Mohsen Aghahosseini, Iran Richard M. Mosk, USA

There were no changes in the composition of the Chambers during the reporting period. The Full Tribunal Awards issued during the reporting period, however, were signed by Richard C. Allison (the Member of Chamber Three replaced by Richard M. Mosk) pursuant to Art. 13(5) of the Tribunal Rules, which provides:

> "After the effective date of a member's resignation he shall continue to serve as a member of the Tribunal with respect to all cases in which he had participated in a hearing on the merits, and for that purpose shall be

considered a member of the Tribunal instead of the person who replaces him."

2. Agents

Throughout the reporting period, Mohammad H. Zahedin-Labbaf served as the Agent of the Islamic Republic of Iran. Sean D. Murphy served as the Agent of the United States until 30 June 1998, when he was replaced by Allen S. Weiner.

3. Replenishment

In the Algiers Declarations, Iran agreed to maintain a minimum amount of U.S.$ 500 million in the Security Account. In the past, the Security Account has been replenished in part with funds from a separate Interest Account, which holds interest earned by the Security Account itself. Several years ago, the balance in the Security Account fell below U.S.$ 500 million, prompting the United States to file a claim against Iran for replenishment. This claim was designated as Case No. A28, which the Tribunal had not fully resolved by the end of this reporting period. As of 31 December 1998, the balance in the Security Account was approximately U.S.$ 107.6 million, and the balance in the Interest Account was approximately U.S.$ 27.9 million.

4. Full Tribunal Workload

During the reporting period, the Full Tribunal held a hearing in Case No. A11 and issued one Award in Case No. A27, one Partial Award in Cases Nos. A15(IV) and A24, no Decisions, and no Interlocutory Awards.

5. Statistical Summary of Tribunal Work

The Tribunal finalized five claims during the reporting period:

Contested Awards	4
Awards on Agreed Terms	1
	—
Total	5

6. *Tribunal Reports*

The Yearbook publishes extracts of Tribunal Awards, Decisions and Orders that it deems to be of particular interest to its readers and includes a brief survey of the Tribunal's work product during the reporting period.

All Tribunal Awards and Decisions were published in full on a bimonthly basis in *Iranian Assets Litigation Reporter*. This publication was discontinued in 1997. In addition, Grotius Press publishes Tribunal documents in the *Iran-United States Claims Tribunal Reports*. At the end of this reporting period, Grotius Press had published twenty-eight volumes covering Awards through 30 December 1992. Selected Awards are occasionally published in *International Legal Materials*, the *Arbitration Journal*, *World Trade and Arbitration Materials* and *Mealey's International Arbitration Report*. Information about the Tribunal's Awards and Orders is also available on WESTLAW, the computer-assisted legal-research service.

Tribunal Awards are a matter of public record. They may be obtained from the Tribunal Registry (Parkweg 13, 2585 JH The Hague, The Netherlands) at a nominal charge. The Secretary-General of the Tribunal issues detailed indices to the Awards of the Tribunal as an annex to the Tribunal's Annual Report. These indices are also publicly available.

SURVEY OF AWARDS, DECISIONS AND ORDERS

1. *Introduction*

This Survey provides an overview of the Tribunal's recent jurisprudence. During the current reporting period (1 November 1997 to 31 December 1998), the Tribunal addressed various significant substantive, procedural, and jurisdictional issues in its Awards. This Survey provides an overview of certain of the Tribunal's significant rulings.

2. *Jurisdiction*

a. *Claims of dual nationals*

In **Case 457**, *Davidson*, Chamber One held that the Claimant who emigrated to the United States in 1972 at the age of sixteen and became a United States national in March 1980 was a dominant and effective United States national by June 1980 when his claim arose. The Chamber emphasized that since 1972 his "private, professional and public activities ... ha[d] been solely and entirely centered in the United States".

In **Case 953**, *Hakim*, Chamber Two held that the Claimant was a dominant and effective United States national. He was born in Iran but moved to the United States in 1956 to attend high school. He continued to live in the United States from that year until the date his claim arose. During those years, he attended and graduated from college; he married a United States national, with whom he had four children; he conducted a successful real estate business in New York City; and he paid United States taxes since 1964. According to the Claimant, his wife and children never visited Iran, and he visited that country approximately once every two years but for a maximum of two weeks per visit. The Claimant did not submit his original United States certificate of naturalization dated 14 November 1973, but, claiming that he lost it, he did submit several items of evidence relating to his naturalization, including a letter from the United States State Department confirming that the Claimant had been nationalized on 14 November 1973.

b. Ownership

In **Case 953**, *Hakim*, Chamber Two rejected the Claimant's assertion of ownership over real estate in the Vanak district. The Claimant had no title deed to the land but contended that his mother had invested approximately U.S.$ 2.4 million on his behalf in a residential development project operated by the Claimant's uncle. According to the Claimant, his uncle possessed all the documentation evidencing the Claimant's ownership of the land but had been forced to leave it behind when he fled from Iran. Chamber Two noted that, while it had to take care so as not to expose the Respondent to claims not properly evidenced, it recognized that a person making a sudden departure from Iran during the revolution might well leave behind evidence that could prove a claim and that it would be unfair to impose a rigorous standard of proof on a claimant under such circumstances. Chamber Two further held that the fact that the Claimant's interest was not recorded in the relevant land registration files is not on its own sufficient to dismiss the claim; however, Chamber Two, pointing to the "vague and imprecise" affidavits the Claimant submitted, concluded that he had failed to proffer any documentation of adequate probative value to overcome the strong legal presumption against him.

Also in **Case 953**, *Hakim*, Chamber Two rejected the Claimant's assertion of beneficial ownership of more than 20% of the shares in three family-owned companies on the ground that the evidence the Claimant submitted was far short of the "strong evidence" necessary to prove that the Claimant "and not the person registered as the legal owner, was in reality the true owner of the property".

3. Expropriation

In **Case 457**, *Davidson*, Chamber One held that the actions of the Revolutionary Prosecutor in ordering the tenants of Claimant's real property to pay rent only to the Government and stating that the Claimant's family no longer owned the properties effectively deprived the Claimant of his fundamental rights of ownership and therefore constituted a taking.

In **Case 953**, *Hakim*, Chamber Two rejected the Claimant's allegation that Iran had taken measures adversely affecting his property rights in connection with certain Velenjak property. The Claimant based his claim on the 1979 Abolition Act and its Regulations that were aimed at "mawat" and "bayer" undeveloped property. The regulations to the Abolition Act excepted from the Act's reach land on which acceptable development had been made, and it listed nine categories of such acceptable development. The Claimant alleged that he had spent U.S.$ 857,000 to buy the land, to pay taxes on it, and to fund improvements such as brick walls, wells, trees, shrubs, a hothouse, and a small cottage. Pointing to these improvements, Chamber Two held that the Claimant failed to meet his burden of proving that the Velenjak property fell within the scope of the Abolition Act.

In **Case 953**, *Hakim*, Chamber Two also reviewed the evidence concerning the alleged expropriation of a manufacturing company and concluded that while Iran's November 1980 appointment of an "observer" did not rise to the level of an expropriation by 19 January 1981, it did constitute measures affecting the Claimant's property rights. Chamber Two emphasized the fact that Iran gave the observer, along with two employees of the company, the power to sign all financial and obligatory instruments. Although Iran appointed the observer only after receiving repeated requests from the workers of the company to make such an appointment, and the observer issued notices inviting the owners to return, the Tribunal nevertheless concluded that Iran's actions had denied the Claimant and the company's other shareholders of significant rights attached to their ownership interests.

Finally in **Case 953**, *Hakim*, Chamber Two dismissed a claim for expropriation of an urban residence because the Claimant had not submitted adequate proof that the residence was expropriated or that it was subjected to other measures affecting the Claimant's property rights.

4. *Dual Nationals and the A18 Caveat*

In **Case 457**, *Davidson*, Chamber One held that the caveat did not apply because the Claimant acquired the real property at issue before he acquired United States nationality and because the expropriation claim arose less than a year after he acquired United States nationality. The Chamber said that Iranian law (Arts. 988 and 989 of the Civil Code) permits Iranians who obtain foreign nationality to hold their Iranian real property for up to one year before being obliged to sell it.

5. *Procedural Matters*

a. *Late filings*

In **Case 953**, *Hakim*, the Claimant submitted several documents at the hearing. Chamber Two admitted those documents that were publicly available, and it admitted a document that had earlier requested the Respondent to produce. After reviewing the factors listed in *Harris Int'l Communications, Inc.* and *Islamic Republic of Iran, et al.*, Award No. 323-409-1 (2 November 1987), reprinted in 17 Iran-U.S. C.T.R. 31, pertaining to late-filed documents, the Tribunal noted that the prejudice to which *Harris* refers arises only when the non-submitting party is not afforded the opportunity to respond to the substance of late-filed documents. Chamber Two concluded that the Respondent was not prejudiced by the admission of the late-filed documents in *Hakim* because the Respondent had been given ample time to respond and because the document both was publicly available and had always been in the Respondent's possession.

b. Evidence

In **Case 457**, *Davidson*, Chamber One held that the Claimant had failed to prove beneficial ownership of certain alleged percentages of several real properties in Iran. The Chamber pointed to inconsistent statements which it said, as a general rule, should be construed against the party making them, and the Chamber emphasized that official title deeds are "strong" prima facie evidence of title. The Chamber also found the testimony of the agent for the Claimant's father persuasive and corroborative of the testimony by the Claimant's father in showing a deprivation of property attributable to Iran. Finally, the Chamber noted that the consistency of the Claimant's oral testimony at the hearing and affidavits "strengthens their probative value".

6. Valuation

a. Standard of compensation

In **Case 953**, *Hakim*, Chamber Two applied the Treaty of Amity standard of full compensation without deciding whether the Treaty itself is applicable to claims of dual nationals whose dominant and effective nationality was that of the United States.

b. Amount of compensation

In **Case 457**, *Davidson*, Chamber One considered widely varying appraisals of real property submitted by the parties. The Chamber noted that its task was to determine the properties' fair-market value at the time of taking, and it noted the difficulties presented by the fact that in June 1980 no real-estate market existed in Iran in any ordinary sense. In view of the widely divergent estimates by the experts, the Chamber held that it "is bound to make reasonable approximations within the limits of the given appraisals by the experts". The Chamber awarded roughly double the amount indicated by Iran's experts and slightly more than half of the amounts indicated by the Claimant's experts.

In **Case 953**, *Hakim*, Chamber Two noted that the parties had put forward widely divergent but largely unsupported assessments as to the value of the Claimant's interest in a manufacturing company. Chamber Two utilized the dissolution method of valuation because both parties had utilized that method. Noting the paucity of evidence presented by both parties, Chamber Two made an approximation as to the value that is "reasonable and equitable taking into account all the circumstances in this Case" and concluded that the value of the manufacturing company as of 26 November 1980 was 250,000,000 rials, of which the Claimant's 20% share was 50,000,000 rials.

7. *Interest and Costs*

In **Case A27**, the Tribunal awarded simple interest on the amount of the Tribunal's *Avco* Award at an annual rate of 10% from the date the *Avco* Award was issued until the date the United States Court of Appeals refused to enforce the Award. The Tribunal reasoned that, had the United States courts enforced the Award as they should have, they would have granted pre-judgment interest. The Tribunal also noted that, although one of the two Iranian parties to be paid in the *Avco* Award had not requested, and therefore not received, post-award interest in the original Award, an enforcing court in the United States would likely have exercised its discretion to award such interest to both parties. In a separate opinion, an American arbitrator disagreed with this conclusion as speculative, and argued that the Iranian party in question should not have received post-award interest.

The Tribunal awarded post-judgment interest on the total amount due to Iran at an annual rate of 5% from the date the United States court of appeals refused to enforce the Award until payment. Iranian arbitrators filed two separate opinions arguing that the Tribunal should have applied the rate of 10% until payment by the United States.

The Tribunal refused to award Iran compensation for legal expenses incurred in seeking to enforce the *Avco* Award before the United States Court of Appeals after Iran failed to appear at the court of first instance to contest a summary judgment motion. The Tribunal reasoned that Iran would have had to incur the expenses in question even if the court of appeals had enforced the Award, and therefore the expenses were not recoverable as damages. The separate opinions of the Iranian arbitrators disagreed with this conclusion.

8. *Treaty Interpretation*

In **Case A27**, the Tribunal analyzed the obligations of the States Parties to enforce Tribunal Awards under the Algiers Declarations. The Case concerned the failure of the United States courts to enforce the Tribunal's Award in *Avco, Case 261*. The United States district court had granted summary judgement to Avco, denying Iran's claim for enforcement. On appeal, the court of appeals applied defenses available under the New York Convention to deny enforcement on the grounds that the Tribunal had not allowed Avco an opportunity to present its case.

Relying on the requirement in the Claims Settlement Declaration that its Awards are "final and binding", the Tribunal found that the United States was liable for the failure of its courts to enforce the Tribunal Award in the *Avco* case. In reaching this conclusion, the Tribunal relied on its interpretation of the parties' enforcement obligations in *Case A21*, where it had rejected Iran's contention that the Declarations obligated the United States to satisfy any Award rendered by the Tribunal in favor of Iran. The Tribunal had found instead that the States Parties had some latitude in prescribing the means of enforcement of Tribunal Awards. Nevertheless, the Tribunal found that the Claims Settlement Declaration's use of the words "final and binding" imposed an obligation on the States Parties to ensure that awards are treated as valid and enforceable in their jurisdictions and that the Parties would be in violation of their obligations if an award was not enforced or was enforced only after undue delay.

In applying this interpretation to the present dispute, the Tribunal rejected Iran's contention that requiring Iran to pursue enforcement in United States courts constituted "undue delay" or an unreasonable mechanism for enforcement under its decision in *Case A21*. However, United States courts evaluated the Tribunal's *Avco* Award in light of Art. V of the New York Convention, which contains provisions allowing for non-enforcement of awards. The Tribunal found these provisions to be "problematic" in the context of Tribunal Awards and doubted that any of its Awards could fall within the scope of that Article. While the United States was free to adopt the New York Convention to implement Tribunal Awards, the Tribunal found that this choice could not exempt the United States from liability if its courts deny enforcement of an award. The United States courts erred in finding that the Tribunal had failed to provide the Claimant with an opportunity to present its case and, in doing so, had relitigated an issue already decided by the Tribunal. Enforcement proceedings cannot reconsider issues decided on the merits by the Tribunal because the Tribunal's Awards are "final and binding" under the Algiers Declarations and under customary international law.

In Claim A of *Islamic Republic of Iran* and *United States of America*, **Case A15(IV)**, the Tribunal addressed Iran's claim that the United States had violated General Principle B of the General Declarations by failing to terminate all litigation involving claims of United States nationals against Iran that arose before 19 January 1981. General Principle B provides:

> "It is the purpose of both parties, within the framework of and pursuant to the provisions of the two Declarations of the Government of the Democratic and Popular Republic of Algeria, to terminate all litigation as between the government of each party and the nationals of the other, and to bring about the settlement and termination of all such claims through binding arbitration. Through the procedures provided in the Declaration relating to the Claims Settlement Agreement, the United States agrees to terminate all legal proceedings in United States courts involving claims of United States persons and institutions against Iran and its state enterprises, to nullify all attachments and judgments obtained therein, to prohibit all further litigation based on such claims, and to bring about the termination of such claims through binding arbitration."

Through Executive Order 12294, the United States suspended, but did not terminate, all claims which may be presented to the Tribunal. The Executive Order excepted from that suspension, however, counterclaims and set-offs brought by United States nationals in any judicial proceeding pending or subsequently commenced by the Government of Iran as well as suits brought to toll the applicable statute of limitations. The Executive Order provided that the suspension of any claim would terminate upon a determination by the Tribunal that it had no jurisdiction over the claim in question.

The Tribunal began its analysis by holding that General Principle B distinguishes between the United States obligation to terminate "litigation" by United States nationals against Iran in United States courts and its obligation to terminate the "claims" at issue in that litigation. With respect to the latter obligation, the Tribunal interpreted General Principle B as obligating the United States to terminate only those claims that fell within the Tribunal's jurisdiction. As for legal proceedings, the Tribunal held that the Algiers Declarations obligate the United States to terminate legal proceedings initiated by United States nationals against Iran in United States courts involving claims that arguably fall within the Tribunal's jurisdiction.

In evaluating whether the United States suspension of legal proceedings satisfied its obligation to terminate such litigation, the Tribunal noted that there existed a conceptual difference between the two terms: termination implies that the activity being terminated is brought to an end while suspension implies a temporary cessation of activity. However, because the obligations imposed by General Principle B are obligations of result, rather than of conduct or means, this terminological distinction was not sufficient for the Tribunal to conclude that the United States violated the Algiers Declarations. Rather, the Tribunal held that by adopting the suspension mechanism, the United States fulfilled its obligations under the Algiers Declarations if, in effect, the mechanism resulted in a termination of litigation. The Tribunal determined that it would in the second phase of proceedings examine the facts concerning the legal proceedings in which Iran claimed to have been wrongfully compelled to participate, and if the Tribunal concludes that Iran was reasonably compelled in the prudent defense of its interests to make appearances or file documents in United States courts subsequent to 19 July 1981 in any litigation in respect of claims described in Art. II(1) of the Claims Settlement Declaration or in respect of claims filed with the Tribunal until those claims are dismissed by the Tribunal for lack of jurisdiction, then the Tribunal will find the that United States has not complied with its obligations under the Algiers Declarations.

The Algiers Declarations contain no provision setting forth specific deadlines for the United States to terminate legal proceedings in United States courts, so the Tribunal relied on the general treaty interpretation principle of good faith, which led it to conclude that the United States was obligated to terminate litigation within a reasonable period of time. To determine what was reasonable under the circumstances, the Tribunal examined the express time limits the Declarations imposed regarding other related obligations and, in light of these, concluded that it was reasonable to expect the United States to terminate litigation of United States nationals against Iran in United States courts within six months after the signing of the Algiers Declarations.

Finally, in Claim A, the Tribunal addressed the United States authorization of counterclaims against Iran in cases brought by Iran in United States courts. The Tribunal began by noting that claims that would have been within the Tribunal's jurisdiction and were not settled by negotiation were supposed to be presented to the Tribunal, so that if a claimant chose not to present such a claim to the Tribunal, he was not to be permitted thereafter to bring the claim in United States courts. Although the existence of the Security Account ensured that the vast majority of claims deemed meritorious by claimants would be presented to the Tribunal, some claimants did not bring their claims to the Tribunal because they feared that Iran would respond with a meritorious counterclaim. Thus, the Tribunal held, by authorizing United States nationals to bring counterclaims in litigation brought by Iran in United States courts, the United States encouraged such United States claimants not to come to the Tribunal and thereby failed to comply with its Algiers Declarations obligations.

In Claim B of *Islamic Republic of Iran* and *United States of America*, **Case A15(IV)**, the Tribunal addressed Iran's claim that the United States had violated the Algiers Declarations by failing to terminate claims that the Tribunal found to be excluded from its jurisdiction pursuant to Art. II(1) of the Claims Settlement Declaration. Art. II(1) excludes from the Tribunal's jurisdiction "claims arising under a binding contract between the two parties specifically providing that any disputes thereunder shall be within the sole jurisdiction of the competent Iranian courts, in response to the Majlis position". Iran contended that the purpose of the forum-selection-clause exclusion was to preserve the jurisdiction of Iranian courts. The United States defeated that purpose, Iran contended, by allowing United States nationals to take their claims back to United States courts after the Tribunal had dismissed the claims for lack of jurisdiction.

The Tribunal dismissed Iran's claim. It noted that the United States had argued in *Halliburton Company, et al.* and *Doreen/IMCO, et al.*, Interlocutory Award No. ITL 2-51-FT (5 November 1982), reprinted in 1 Iran-U.S. C.T.R. 242, that the word "binding" in the forum-selection-clause exclusion required the Tribunal to determine whether changed circumstances rendered the forum-selection clauses unenforceable. The Tribunal declined that request, holding that it had no jurisdiction to make that determination. In Claim D of *Islamic Republic of Iran* and *United States of America*, **Case A15(IV)**, the Tribunal concluded that to agree with Iran that claims that the Tribunal excluded from its jurisdiction because of the Iranian forum-selection-clause exclusion must be brought in Iranian courts would amount to holding enforceable the Iranian forum-selection clauses in question; that is, it would amount to a holding that would repudiate the Tribunal's conclusion in *Halliburton* that it had no jurisdiction to render such a decision.

In Claim D of *Islamic Republic of Iran* and *United States of America*, **Case A15(IV)**, the Tribunal addressed Iran's contention that the United States violated the Algiers Declarations by allowing its nationals to file suits in United States courts to toll the applicable statutes of limitation after the Algiers Declarations were signed. The United States explained that because General Principle B required it to terminate only those claims that fell within the Tribunal's jurisdiction, it had to devise some mechanism to prevent claims that would later be rejected by the Tribunal on jurisdictional grounds from being barred by the statutes of limitation applicable in United States courts. The mechanism the United States chose was to permit its nationals to initiate suits to toll the limitations period but then to suspend those suits immediately. The Tribunal held that while the Algiers Declarations do not forbid the

United States to utilize certain means of preserving claims in anticipation of the Tribunal's jurisdictional determination, the one means it clearly does forbid is the bringing of suits in United States courts after the date of the Algiers Declarations. Thus, the Tribunal found that the United States did not act consistently with its obligations under General Principle B.

In Claim E of *Islamic Republic of Iran* and *United States of America*, **Case A15(IV)**, the Tribunal rejected Iran's claim that the Algiers Declarations obligate the United States to terminate litigation initiated by United States nationals against Iran in courts outside the United States.

In Claim F of *Islamic Republic of Iran* and *United States of America*, **Case A15(IV)**, the Tribunal rejected Iran's claim that the Algiers Declarations require the United States to nullify attachments made before 14 November 1979, the date the President of the United States froze Iran's assets. The Tribunal held that the United States obligation under General Principle B to nullify "all attachments" must be interpreted in light of General Principle A, which obligates the United States to "restore the financial position of Iran, in so far as possible, to that which existed prior to November 14, 1979". The two provisions together indicate that the United States was obligated to lift the attachments but only to the extent necessary to restore Iran's financial position to that existing before 14 November 1979. To lift attachments made before 14 November 1979 would improve Iran's financial position rather than restore it.

Claim G of *Islamic Republic of Iran* and *United States of America*, **Case A15(IV)**, required the Tribunal to consider (1) whether the United States took a sufficiently active role in fulfilling its obligation to nullify post-14 November 1979 attachments of Iranian assets; and (2) whether the United States succeeded in nullifying those attachments within the period required by the Algiers Declarations. As to the first question, the Tribunal concluded that nothing in the evidence suggested that the United States stopped short of doing everything it could pursuant to the procedures of its legal system to have all post-14 November 1979 attachments lifted. Therefore, the Tribunal determined that the United States had satisfied its good-faith obligation in this respect.

Next, for the same reasons it relied upon when determining the timing of the United States obligation to terminate litigation against Iran in United States courts, the Tribunal held that the United States had six months from the date of the Algiers Declarations to nullify all post-14 November 1979 attachments of Iranian property. The Tribunal held that if there were any post-14 November 1979 attachments still in effect that actually restrained Iranian assets in the United States after that six-month period had expired, thereby limiting the free disposition of those assets by Iran, they constitute a violation of the United States obligation to nullify the attachments in a timely fashion.

In Claim H of *Islamic Republic of Iran* and *United States of America*, **Case A15(IV)**, the Tribunal considered Iran's claim that the United States violated the Algiers Declarations by failing to nullify judgments obtained by United States nationals against Iran in United States courts before the date of the Algiers Declarations. For the same reasons it provided when determining the scope of the United States obligation to terminate claims against Iran, the Tribunal held that the United States is obligated to nullify only judgments that are based on claims that are within the Tribunal's jurisdiction. The Tribunal noted that United States Executive Order 12294, which suspended claims that may be presented to the Tribunal, does not specifically refer to judgments, but because the Algiers Declarations do not contemplate any distinction between a claim and a domestic court judgment entered thereon, the Tribunal concluded that judgments were within the scope of Executive Order 12294 so that the resolution of Claim H tracked that of Claim A. In keeping with Claim A, then, the Tribunal held that if Iran reasonably incurred legal expenses in relation to judgments that remained in existence after 19 July 1981, then the United States breached its obligations under the Algiers Declarations. This question can only be answered on the basis of factual evidence and therefore is one for the subsequent proceedings.

In *Islamic Republic of Iran* and *United States of America*, **Case A24**, the Tribunal considered Iran's claim that the United States allowed a claim against Iran to proceed in United States courts after it had been decided by the Tribunal on the merits in violation of the Algiers Declarations. The Claimants (collectively "Foremost") brought two claims to the Tribunal alleging expropriation of Foremost's 31% interest in Pak Dairy. Foremost also filed suit in a United States District Court to toll the relevant statute of limitations. On 11 April 1986 the Tribunal issued its Award in *Foremost*, wherein it held that Iran's interference with Foremost's rights in Pak Dairy "did not by 19 January 1981 ... amount to an expropriation." On 1 April 1988 Foremost revived its suit in the United States District Court by filing a motion for partial summary judgment. Foremost stated in its motion that it accepted the Tribunal's holding that no expropriation occurred before 19 January 1981, but it asked the District Court to determine whether an expropriation occurred after that date. The case proceeded in the District Court, and on 23 June 1997 the District Court issued a decision, finding that Iran's interference with Foremost's rights had ripened into an expropriation by April 1982.

In **Case A24**, the Tribunal began its analysis by determining that the Statement of Claim Foremost submitted to the Tribunal and the complaint it submitted to the District Court were identical. The Tribunal acknowledged that the Statement of Claim included the allegation that the claims asserted therein were outstanding on 19 January 1981 whereas the complaint contained no such assertion, but the Tribunal determined that because the District Court's jurisdiction was not limited, as was the Tribunal's, the silence in the complaint as to 19 January 1981 was irrelevant to whether or not the two documents were identical. The claim before the Tribunal and the claim before the District Court therefore remained identical until Foremost filed its motion for partial summary judgment in April 1998.

The Tribunal held that by not acting to have the Foremost lawsuit in the District Court dismissed within a reasonable time after the Tribunal issued its Award in April 1986, the United States violated its obligation under the Algiers Declarations to terminate finally litigation in United States courts related to claims resolved by the Tribunal on the merits. Further, the Tribunal held, even if the District Court complaint had been broader than the Statement of Claim, the United States still would have been obligated under the Algiers Declarations to put the District Court on notice, within a reasonable time, after 11 April 1986, that proceedings in the Foremost lawsuit were to be considered terminated to the extent they related to that portion of the claim that had been decided by the Tribunal.

Examining the events occurring after 1 April 1988, the Tribunal held that, although the Foremost litigation as pursued from that date onward relied to a large extent on the same facts as those invoked in the claim before the Tribunal, the cause of action alleged in that lawsuit is materially different from that considered by the Tribunal in *Foremost*: The issue before the Tribunal was whether Iran had expropriated Foremost's property on or before 19 January 1981; the issue before the District Court was whether Iran had expropriated Foremost's property after that date. Indeed, because the Tribunal had no jurisdiction to determine the claim presented to the District Court, the Tribunal held that the Foremost lawsuit, as pursued in the District Court from 1 April 1988 onward, does not fall within the scope of the res judicata of the Tribunal's decision in *Foremost* and, therefore, is not contrary to the Algiers Declarations. The Tribunal turned finally to whether the District Court's 1997 opinion respects the final and binding character of the Tribunal's Award in *Foremost* and, because the District Court gave preclusive effect to all of the Tribunal's findings in *Foremost* concerning matters that were within the Tribunal's jurisdiction, the Tribunal held that it did.

AWARDS OF THE FULL TRIBUNAL

Award in Case No. A15(IV)/A24 (590-A15(IV)/A24-FT) of 28 December 1999

Arbitrators:	Krzysztof Skubiszewski (President), Mohsen Aghahosseini (concurring in part; dissenting in part), George H. Aldrich (concurring in part; dissenting in part), Richard C. Allison (concurring in part; dissenting in part), Koorosh H. Ameli (concurring in part; dissenting in part), Gaetano Arangio-Ruiz, Bengt Broms (dissenting and partly concurring), Charles T. Duncan (concurring in part; dissenting in part), Assadollah Noori (concurring in part; dissenting in part)
Parties:	Claimant: The Islamic Republic of Iran Respondent: The United States of America
Subject matter:	– treaty interpretation

Facts

In Case No. A15(IV) Iran alleged that the United States had failed in a variety of ways to fulfill the obligations it assumed in General Principle B of the General Declaration in relation to the termination of litigation in United States courts by United States nationals against Iran (see I.2 below).

The Tribunal found with respect to Claim A, inter alia, that the United States had satisfied its obligations under the Algiers Declarations if the mechanism it adopted, namely suspension of litigation of legal proceedings involving claims that arose before 19 January 1981 of US nationals against Iran, if, in effect, the mechanism resulted in a termination of litigation and that it was reasonable to have done so within six months after the signing of the Algiers Declarations. The Tribunal would at a later stage determine if Iran had been wrongfully compelled to participate in legal proceedings in the United States courts in the prudent defense of its interests.

Claim B, that the United States had violated the Algiers Declarations by failing to terminate claims that the Tribunal found to be excluded from its jurisdiction, was dismissed, as was Claim D in which Iran contended that the United States had violated the Algiers Declarations by allowing its nationals to file suits in United States courts to toll the applicable statutes of limitation. The Tribunal also rejected Iran's Claim E that the Algiers Declarations obligate the United States to terminate litigation initiated by United States nationals against Iran in courts outside the United States and Claim F that the Algiers Declarations require the United States to nullify attachments made before 14 November 1979, the date the President of the United States froze Iran's assets. The United States was obligated only to lift attachments made after 14 November 1979.

In Claim G the Tribunal determined that the United States had satisfied its good-faith obligations with respect to taking a sufficiently active role in fulfilling its obligation to nullify post-14 November 1979 attachments of Iranian assets provided that they had done so within six months of the date of the Algiers Declarations.

In Claim H, Iran contended that the United States violated the Algiers Declarations by failing to nullify judgments obtained by United States nationals against Iran in United States courts before the date of the Algiers Declarations. In keeping with Claim A, the Tribunal held that if Iran reasonably incurred legal expenses in relation to judgments that remained in existence after 19 July 1981, then the United States breached its obligations under the Algiers Declarations. This factual question would be answered in subsequent proceedings.

In Case No. A24, Iran alleged that the United States allowed the *Foremost* case against Iran to proceed in United States courts after it had been decided by the Tribunal on the merits in violation of the Algiers Declarations. The Tribunal found, inter alia, that the United States District Court's 1997 opinion respects the final and binding character of the Tribunal's Award in *Foremost* and, because the District Court gave preclusive effect to all of the Tribunal's findings in *Foremost* concerning matters that were within the Tribunal's jurisdiction.

Excerpt

I. INTRODUCTION

(....)

2. "In Case No. A15(IV), Iran contends that the Executive Order and certain of the Treasury Regulations that were issued by the United States after 19 January 1981 to implement the United States obligation to terminate litigation violated the United States obligations under the Algiers Declarations, in particular, the United States obligations under General Principle B. Iran asserts eight claims, termed A through H, alleging eight breaches by the United States of General Principle B. Specifically, Iran contends that the United States breached its obligations: (a) by suspending some judicial proceedings in United States courts, instead of terminating all litigation (including counterclaims) of United States nationals against Iran ('Claim A'); (b) by failing to terminate claims in United States courts arising from contracts containing forum selection clauses requiring litigation to be brought before Iranian courts ('Claim B'); (c) by failing to nullify injunctions obtained by United States nationals in United States courts that enjoined United States banks from honoring calls made by Iran on certain standby letters of credit ('Claim C'); (d) by failing to prohibit further litigation in United States courts after the date of the Algiers Declarations ('Claim D'); (e) by failing to forbid United States nationals from engaging in litigation against Iran in courts outside the United States ('Claim E'); (f) by failing to nullify attachments on Iranian assets that were in existence prior to 14 November 1979, the date the President of the United States issued Executive Orders freezing Iranian assets in the United States ('Claim F'); (g) by failing to nullify post-14 November 1979 attachments in a sufficiently prompt fashion ('Claim G'); and (h) by failing to nullify judgments obtained by United States nationals in United States courts ('Claim H').

(....)

4. "In Case No. A24, Iran claims that the United States allowed a case that was decided by the Tribunal, *Foremost Tehran, et al.* and *Islamic Republic of Iran, et al.*, Award No. 220-37/231-1 (11 Apr. 1986), to be revived and to proceed in a United States court as *Foremost-McKesson, Inc. v. Islamic Republic of Iran*, Civ. No. 82-0220-TAF (D.D.C.), and it thereby breached its obligation under the Algiers Declarations to prohibit relitigation of claims already decided by the Tribunal."

(....)

IV. FACTS AND CONTENTIONS (footnote omitted)

a. CASE NO. A15(IV)

1. *Factual Background*

21. "On 14 November 1979, in the aftermath of the seizure of the United States Embassy in Tehran, the President of the United States issued Executive Order No. 12170, which blocked the transfer of Iranian assets subject to the jurisdiction of the United States or in the possession or control of persons subject to the jurisdiction of the United States....

22. "Subsequently, United States nationals filed hundreds of claims against Iran in United States and foreign courts....

23. ".... Iran's conditions for resolving the crisis were formulated by the Majlis, the Iranian Parliament, on 2 November 1980, in a Resolution stating Iran's position concerning the release of the members the United States diplomatic staff detained in the United States Embassy in Tehran.... The Majlis requested the following:

> 'The cancellation and annulment of all economic and fiscal decisions and measures against the Islamic Republic of Iran, the implementation of all requisite administrative and legal measures for the cancellation and annulment of all claims of any sort or kind of the American government and American agencies and companies against Iran, the implementation of all requisite administrative and legal measures to ensure that no new legal, penal, or financial claim of any kind be raised by any official or non-official natural or juridical persons of the American government and/or by American agencies and companies....'

24. "From the outset, the United States made clear that claims could be removed from the United States courts only by the establishment of an alternative arrangement to ensure their settlement.

(....)

27. ".... The provisions of the Declarations that arguably may be relevant to the present claims are the following:

a. "General Principle B of the General Declaration. That Principle, which mirrors the language of Comment 2 of the second American response of 3 December 1980, provides:

> 'It is the purpose of both parties, within the framework of and pursuant to the provisions of the two Declarations of the Government of the Democratic and Popular Republic of Algeria, to terminate all litigation as between the government of each party and the nationals of the other, and to bring about the settlement and termination of all such claims through binding arbitration. Through the procedures provided in the Declaration relating to the Claims Settlement Agreement, the United States agrees to terminate all legal proceedings in United States courts involving claims of United States persons and institutions against Iran and its state enterprises, to nullify all attachments and judgments obtained therein, to prohibit all further litigation based on such claims, and to bring about the termination of such claims through binding arbitration.'

(....)
f. "Article VII, paragraph 2, of the Claims Settlement Declaration, which provides that '[c]laims referred to the arbitration Tribunal shall, as of the date of filing of such claims with the Tribunal, be considered excluded from the jurisdiction of the courts of Iran, or of the United States, or of any other court.'

28. "As part of a series of actions by the United States aimed at implementing its obligations under the Algiers Declarations, on 24 February 1981, the President of the United States issued Executive Order No. 12294 ('Executive Order 12294'), which provides in pertinent part:

> '...
> Section 1. All claims which may be presented to the Iran-United States Claims Tribunal under the terms of Article II of [the Claims Settlement Declaration] and all claims for equitable or other judicial relief in connection with such claims, are hereby suspended, except as they may be presented to the Tribunal. During the period of this suspension, all such claims shall have no legal effect in any action now pending in any court of the United States, including the courts of any state or any locality thereof, the District of Columbia and Puerto Rico, or in any action commenced in any such court after the effective date of this Order. Nothing in this action precludes the commencement of an action after the effective date of this Order for the purpose of tolling the period of limitations for commencement of such action.
> ...

> Section 3. Suspension under this Order of a claim or a portion thereof submitted to the Iran-United States Claims Tribunal for adjudication shall terminate upon a determination by the Tribunal that it does not have jurisdiction over such claim or such portion thereof.
>
> Section 4. A determination by the Iran-United States Claims Tribunal on the merits that a claimant is not entitled to recover on a claim shall operate as a final resolution and discharge of the claim for all purposes. A determination by the Tribunal that a claimant shall have recovery on a claim in a specified amount shall operate as a final resolution and discharge of the claim for all purposes upon payment to the claimant of the full amount of the award, including any interest awarded by the Tribunal.
>
> ...
>
> Section 6. Nothing in this Order shall prohibit the assertion of a counterclaim or set-off by a United States national in any judicial proceeding pending or hereafter commenced by the Government of Iran, any political subdivision of Iran, or any agency, instrumentality, or entity controlled by the Government of Iran or any political subdivision thereof.
>
> ...'

(....)

29. "In the meantime, within days of the signing of the Algiers Declarations, the United States Department of Justice filed Statements of Interest in each case against Iran in United States courts of which it was then aware. The Statements of Interest advised the courts of the conclusion of the Algiers Declarations and notified them that the Declarations and the implementing actions taken by the Executive Branch would 'substantially affect the attachments of Iranian assets and claims by or against the Government of Iran.' The Department of Justice requested that all proceedings in each case be stayed until 26 February 1981.

30. "On or after 26 February 1981, the United States filed a second Statement of Interest in the cases against Iran in United States courts of which it was then aware.... [T]he United States requested that the courts (1) stay litigation of those claims that were arguably within the Tribunal's jurisdiction and (2) vacate the attachments against Iranian assets.

31. ".... On 2 July 1981, the Supreme Court rendered an opinion sustaining the United States President's actions. *See Dames & Moore v. Regan, et al.*, 453 U.S. 654 (1981). Shortly thereafter, the United States filed a further Statement of Interest in lawsuits against Iran, calling the courts' attention to the Supreme

Court's opinion and renewing its request that the courts stay litigation of claims against Iran that might be presented to the Tribunal...."

2. *The Claims*

a. *Claim A*

32. "In this claim, Iran contends that the United States has breached General Principle B by failing to terminate all litigation in United States courts involving claims of United States nationals against Iran that arose before 19 January 1981.... Iran contends that, rather than terminating those legal proceedings, the United States, through Executive Order 12294, has limited itself to suspending some of them. In addition, Iran maintains that the United States has breached General Principle B by permitting cases dismissed by the Tribunal for want of jurisdiction to be revived in United States courts and by allowing United States nationals to assert counterclaims or set-offs in cases brought by Iran in United States courts."

b. *Claim B*

33. "This claim centers on the last clause of Article II, paragraph 1, of the Claims Settlement Declaration, which excludes from the Tribunal's jurisdiction 'claims arising under a binding contract between the parties specifically providing that any disputes thereunder shall be within the sole jurisdiction of the competent Iranian courts, in response to the Majlis position.' Iran contends that the United States has breached its obligations under the Algiers Declarations by failing to terminate litigation against Iran in United States courts involving claims arising from contracts with forum selection clauses referring disputes to the Iranian courts."

c. *Claim D*

34. "This claim arises from Section 1 of Executive Order 12294, which provides that '[n]othing in this action precludes the commencement of an action [in a United States court] after the effective date of this Order for the purpose of tolling the period of limitations for the commencement of such action.' Iran contends that this provision violates General Principle B's requirement that the United States 'prohibit all further litigation' of claims of United States nationals against Iran in United States courts."

d. *Claim E*

35. "In this claim, Iran contends that the United States has breached General Principle B by failing to prohibit litigation initiated by United States nationals against Iran in courts outside the United States."

e. *Claim F*

36. "On 19 January 1981, as part of a series of actions taken to implement the Algiers Declarations, the President of the United States issued Executive Orders which nullified attachments of Iranian assets obtained by United States nationals in United States courts after 14 November 1979, the date on which the President had ordered the freezing of Iranian assets. These Executive Orders left in place attachments obtained by United States nationals prior to 14 November 1979. At issue in this claim is whether the United States was obliged under General Principle B to nullify also such pre-14 November 1979 attachments. Iran argues that it was."

f. *Claim G*

37. "In this claim, Iran contends that the United States has breached the Algiers Declarations by failing to nullify in a sufficiently prompt fashion attachments obtained by United States nationals against Iran in United States courts after 14 November 1979."

g. *Claim H*

38. "In this claim, Iran contends that the United States has violated the Algiers Declarations by failing to nullify judgments that United States nationals obtained against Iran in United States courts before the date of the Algiers Declarations...."

B. *CASE NO. A24*

1. *Factual Background*

39. "On 16 November 1981, Foremost Tehran, Inc., Foremost Shir, Inc., Foremost Iran Corp., Foremost Foods, Inc., and Foremost McKesson, Inc. (collectively 'Foremost') and Overseas Private Investment Company ('OPIC') (footnote omitted) presented a claim to the Tribunal, alleging, *inter alia*, that

Iran, through agencies that it controlled, had expropriated Foremost's 31 percent interest in Sherkat Sahami Labaniat Pasteurize Pak ('Pak Dairy') (....)

41. "On 22 January 1982, Foremost and OPIC filed a complaint against Iran in the United States District Court for the District of Columbia for the purpose of tolling the relevant statute of limitations, in accordance with Section 1 of Executive Order 12294....

42. "On 11 April 1986, the Tribunal issued its Award.... It found that Iran's interference with the substance of Foremost's rights in Pak Dairy 'did not, by 19 January 1981 ... amount to an expropriation.' *Foremost Tehran, et al.* and *Islamic Republic of Iran, et al.*, Award No. 220-37/231-1, at 31, *reprinted in* 10 Iran-U.S. C.T.R. 228, 250.

43. "On 1 April 1988, Foremost (now known as McKesson Corporation) and OPIC filed a Motion for Partial Summary Judgment against Iran before the United States District Court for the District of Columbia, thereby reviving the lawsuit that had been initiated in 1982 for the purpose of tolling the statute of limitations. In their Motion, Foremost and OPIC stated that they were seeking to 'revive the lawsuit and to narrow the issues presented in the [1982] Complaint....' They further stated:

> 'Plaintiffs fully accept, as they must, the conclusion of the majority of the arbitral panel [of the Iran-United States Claims Tribunal] to the effect that there had been no expropriation as of January 19, 1981. Since the Tribunal determined that the expropriation claim had not ripened within the time period submitted to its jurisdiction, it did not purport to rule on the merits of a post-January 19, 1981 expropriation claim. This issue is now suitable for hearing and disposition by this Court...'

(....)

44. "On 13 December 1990, Foremost and OPIC filed a Motion for Leave to Amend their 1982 complaint before the District Court.... The District Court granted Foremost's Motion.

45. "On 23 June 1997, the United States District Court for the District of Columbia issued its decision in the Foremost/OPIC lawsuit, holding that Iran's interference with Plaintiffs' shareholder rights in Pak Dairy had ripened into an expropriation by April 1982. In the Memorandum Opinion ..., the District Court discussed, at the outset, the effect of the Tribunal's decision in *Foremost* on the Foremost/OPIC lawsuit. The District Court, noting that the Algiers Declarations provide that the Tribunal's decisions are 'final and binding,' stated that

> '[u]nder the Accords, then, the Court may not revisit the Claims Tribunal's conclusion that no expropriation occurred as of January 19, 1981, nor may it reconsider the factual basis for the Claims Tribunal's conclusion.... In addition, the Court may not take issue with the legal principles applied by the Tribunal; Article V of the Claims Settlement Declaration states that the Tribunal "shall decide all cases on the basis of respect for law, applying such choice-of-law rules and principles of commercial and international law as *the Tribunal* determines to be applicable, taking into account relevant usages of the trade, contract provisions and changed circumstances."'

46. "The District Court went on to say that it was not bound by the Tribunal's findings concerning events that occurred after 19 January 1981, as those events represented 'matters not consigned to [the Tribunal's] discretion by the arbitration agreement.'... The Court then stated that it was its responsibility to examine the post-cutoff events before it and to determine whether an expropriation of Foremost's equity interest in Pak Dairy had occurred after 19 January 1981; in making that determination, it could consider events occurring before that date, 'as determined by the Tribunal.'

47. ".... It reached the following conclusion:

> 'Given the Claims Tribunal's binding determination that the evidence of an expropriation was "finely balanced" as of January 19, 1981, there is no question in the Court's mind that the interference with McKesson's shareholder rights ripened into an expropriation after that date. The Court finds that the "more or less irreversible deprivation" of McKesson's property, *see* Tribunal Award at 29, constituting an expropriation occurred by April of 1982....'"

2. *The Claim*

48. "In this claim, Iran contends that the United States has breached its obligations under the Algiers Declarations by allowing Foremost and OPIC to file a complaint in the United States District Court for the District of Columbia in 1982 identical to the statement of claim submitted before this Tribunal in Cases Nos. 37 and 231, and by allowing the same lawsuit to be revived in 1988 and to proceed before the District Court."

(....)

VI. MERITS

A. *CASE NO. A15(IV)*

1. *Claim A*

a. *Iran's Position*

50. "Iran contends that the United States has breached its obligations under the Algiers Declarations by failing to terminate all legal proceedings in United States courts involving claims of United States nationals against Iran that arose prior to 19 January 1981. Iran asserts that General Principle B required the United States to terminate all such proceedings. Yet, the United States has, instead, merely suspended some of them through Executive Order 12294. In addition, the United States has permitted cases dismissed by the Tribunal for want of jurisdiction to be revived in United States courts. Iran contends, moreover, that the United States has also breached General Principle B by allowing United States nationals to assert counterclaims or set-offs in judicial proceedings brought by Iran in United States courts.
(....)
53. "Iran states ... that in General Principle B 'all' litigation means 'all,' and not only litigation that falls within the Tribunal's jurisdiction....
54. "According to Iran, claims of United States nationals outstanding on 19 January 1981 that do not fall within the Tribunal's jurisdiction are forever extinguished.
(....)
58. "Finally, concerning the timing of the United States obligation to terminate legal proceedings, Iran argues that this obligation arose immediately upon the conclusion of the Algiers Declarations, although a *de minimis* delay of a few weeks would have been acceptable to Iran...."

b. *The United States Position*

59. ".... The United States contends that General Principle B required it to terminate only the litigation arising from claims that fell within the Tribunal's jurisdiction. Because it could not be known at the outset of the arbitral process which claims would be determined by the Tribunal to be within its jurisdiction, the United States argues that it had to devise some mechanism to prevent the claims that would ultimately be rejected by the Tribunal on jurisdictional grounds from being barred in United States courts by the statutes of

limitation applicable in the United States. The most appropriate mechanism was the suspension of litigation, as set forth in Executive Order 12294....
60. "The United States contends that the plain language of General Principle B explicitly links the United States termination obligation to claims within the Tribunal's jurisdiction.
(....)
69. "The United States concedes that between January and July 1981, some litigation against Iran in the United States continued.... It is clear from the Algiers Declarations, the United States contends, that the Parties estimated that it would take about six months to resolve this litigation.... The United States thus concludes that it had six months within which to terminate litigation against Iran...."

c. *The Tribunal's Decision*

70. "This claim presents three broad issues. First, what is the scope of the United States obligations under the Algiers Declarations with respect to the termination of claims and termination of legal proceedings in United States courts; in other words, what claims and what legal proceedings were to be terminated and when were they to be terminated? Second, did the United States breach its obligations by implementing them through Executive Order 12294; that is, by suspending claims which may be presented to the Tribunal pending their resolution by the Tribunal and by denying them any legal effect in any legal proceeding in United States courts during such period of suspension? Third, did Executive Order 12294 violate the obligations of the United States by allowing counterclaims or set-offs by United States nationals in legal proceedings subsequently commenced by Iran?"

(1) *The Scope of the United States Obligation to Terminate Litigation and Claims*

(a) *The Meaning of General Principle B*

(....)
74. "As an initial matter, the Tribunal agrees with the Parties that General Principle B distinguishes between (i) an obligation of the United States to terminate 'litigation' and 'legal proceedings' by United States nationals against Iran in United States courts and (ii) an obligation of the United States to terminate the 'claims' at issue in those proceedings....
75. "Thus, General Principle B requires the United States to satisfy its termination obligation in two steps: first, through termination of legal

proceedings (or litigation) by United States nationals against Iran in United States courts; and second, through termination of the claims at issue in those legal proceedings 'through binding arbitration' before this Tribunal. The phrase 'through binding arbitration' indicates that a claim will be terminated only after its resolution by the Tribunal on the merits....

76. "Turning to the structure of General Principle B, it should be noted that the first sentence of that Principle states one of the purposes envisaged by the Parties to the Algiers Declarations, namely, the termination of all litigation as between the government of each Party and the nationals of the other and the settlement and termination of all such claims through binding arbitration. This purpose is qualified by the reference to 'the framework' and 'the provisions' both of the General Declaration and the Claims Settlement Declaration. The second sentence of General Principle B, on the other hand, neither confines itself to elaborating on the said purpose nor does it, contrary to the first sentence, concern both States. Rather, it lays out rules of conduct which, in the circumstances, must be distinguished from a mere purpose and which, moreover, are addressed to only one of the two High Contracting Parties, the United States.

77. "Despite these distinguishing features, the two sentences are part and parcel of the same principle. Thus, they must be read as a whole. In particular, the second sentence of General Principle B cannot be divorced from the first sentence because it translates the purpose stated in the first sentence into a concrete obligation, or a series of concrete obligations, of the United States. These obligations, the second sentence provides, are to be performed '[t]hrough the procedures provided in the [Claims Settlement Declaration].'

78. "It is undisputed that ... [c]ertain claims fall outside the Tribunal's jurisdiction by virtue of express exclusions contained in the Declarations.... [B]y agreeing, in General Principle B, to terminate 'all' legal proceedings in United States courts involving claims of United States nationals against Iran, did the United States waive claims that the Parties excluded from the Tribunal's jurisdiction and extinguish them, as argued by Iran?...

79. "... [T]he Tribunal cannot overlook the language in the second sentence of General Principle B, which states that the termination by the United States of 'all' litigation against Iran is to occur '[t]hrough the procedures provided in the [Claims Settlement Declaration].'... [T]his language must be taken into account in interpreting the word 'all.'...

80. "What then are the 'procedures provided in the [Claims Settlement Declaration]' through which the termination of claims and litigation against Iran in United States courts must occur? The Tribunal holds that these procedures are embodied in the following provisions of the Claims Settlement Declaration: (a) Article I, which obliges the two State Parties to promote the

settlement of the claims described in Article II; (b) Article II, which defines the types of claims that shall be resolved by arbitration before this Tribunal; (c) Article IV, paragraph 1, which provides that all decisions and awards of the Tribunal shall be final and binding; and (d) Article VII, paragraph 2, which provides, *inter alia*, that '[c]laims referred to the arbitration Tribunal shall, as of the date of filing of such claims with the Tribunal, be considered excluded from the jurisdiction of the courts of Iran, or of the United States, or of any other court.' All of these provisions relate to the settlement and adjudication of claims that are within the Tribunal's jurisdiction. There are no other provisions in the Claims Settlement Declaration that relate to the 'termination' of claims and litigation."

(b) *Termination of Claims*

81. "Based on the foregoing, the Tribunal concludes that what was referred to by 'procedures provided in the [Claims Settlement Declaration]' in the second sentence of General Principle B was the arbitration mechanism before the Tribunal as set out in that Declaration. It follows that any claims which, under the terms of the Claims Settlement Declaration, cannot be resolved on the merits by the Tribunal are not within the scope of the termination obligation imposed on the United States by General Principle B; this is because those claims cannot possibly be terminated '[t]hrough the procedures provided in the [Claims Settlement Declaration].'

82. "Thus, the United States termination obligation under General Principle B does not cover claims that fall outside the jurisdiction of the Tribunal.... This conclusion implies that the United States obligation to terminate a claim arises only once the claim has been decided on the merits by the Tribunal.

83. "The question remains, however, as to what obligation is imposed on the United States by Article VII, paragraph 2, of the Claims Settlement Declaration, which provides that '[c]laims referred to the arbitration Tribunal shall, as of the date of filing of such claims with the Tribunal, be considered excluded from the jurisdiction of the courts of Iran, or of the United States, or of any other court.'... Article VII, paragraph 2, by requiring that all filed claims be considered excluded from the jurisdiction of courts after they are referred to the Tribunal, implicitly recognizes that such claims may also be pending in other courts while it explicitly obligates the parties to deem them not subject to the jurisdiction of such other courts by ensuring that the claims not proceed unless and until the Tribunal determines that they are outside its jurisdiction. Consequently, until the Tribunal determines its jurisdiction with respect to a filed claim, Article VII, paragraph 2, of the Claims Settlement

Declaration places on the United States an obligation to halt proceedings in its courts with respect to that claim...."

(c) *Waiver*

84. ".... For the following reasons ... the Tribunal holds that, other than the claims referred to in Paragraph 11 of the General Declaration, the United States did not waive any of its nationals' claims against Iran.
85. "Termination of municipal litigation and submission to arbitration as set forth in General Principle B cannot be mistaken for, or identified with, a waiver of any claims. The claims continue to exist, although the nationals no longer have at their disposal any domestic court procedures to pursue their claims....
86. "Nor does the negotiating history of the Algiers Declarations lend any support to the proposition that the United States waived claims of its nationals other than those described in Paragraph 11 of the General Declaration...."

(d) *Termination of Litigation in United States Courts: Suspension*

i) *The United States obligation to terminate litigation*

(....)
89. "The Tribunal holds that the Algiers Declarations oblige the United States to terminate all legal proceedings initiated by United States nationals against Iran in United States courts involving claims that arguably fall within the Tribunal's jurisdiction.... The Tribunal has found that General Principle B requires the United States to terminate only *claims* that fall within the Tribunal's jurisdiction. *See supra*, para. 82. Thus, in conformity with that finding, the United States obligation to terminate *legal proceedings*, as delineated hereabove, ceases with regard to legal proceedings involving claims that have been dismissed by the Tribunal for lack of jurisdiction.
90. "In the history of each claim, whether or not that claim ultimately is found by the Tribunal to be within its jurisdiction, there must always be a period during which there is no litigation related to that claim proceeding in the United States. With respect to claims that the Tribunal finds are outside its jurisdiction, that period ends when the Tribunal renders its jurisdictional decision; those claims can thereafter be litigated in United States courts. By contrast, claims that the Tribunal has decided are within its jurisdiction cannot be revived in domestic courts.
91. "Thus, a timing difficulty becomes apparent: it cannot be known in advance over which claims the Tribunal ultimately will take jurisdiction.

Nevertheless, by acceding to General Principle B, the United States undertook to 'terminate' all legal proceedings against Iran in United States courts...."

ii) *Evaluation of the suspension method against the background of the Algiers Declarations*

92. ".... [T]he United States chose to implement its obligation to terminate all domestic litigation against Iran through the suspension mechanism provided for in Executive Order 12294. The Tribunal will consider whether the choice of this mechanism was consistent with the United States obligations under the Algiers Declarations....

93. ".... It is appropriate to note at the outset that according to their ordinary meaning, the terms 'termination' and 'suspension' imply different rights and obligations and, consequently, different legal effects.

94. ".... Generally, 'termination' implies that the activity being terminated is *brought to an end*. 'Suspension,' on the other hand, implies a temporary cessation of activity. The United States could satisfy its obligations under the Algiers Declarations only by doing what those Declarations said, namely, by 'terminating' all litigation against Iran in United States courts involving claims that arguably fell within the Tribunal's jurisdiction. (footnote omitted) Thus, on its face, 'suspension' could be seen to produce a legal effect different from that produced by 'termination.'

95. "However, the findings made *supra*, in paras. 93-94, do not suffice to conclude that the United States violated its obligation to terminate litigation against Iran in United States courts. The Tribunal must analyze the matter further. Obligations under General Principle B are, generally speaking, obligations of 'result,' rather than of 'conduct' or 'means.' Although it could be said that the United States, by suspending the litigation rather that terminating it, failed to comply with its obligations under the Algiers Declarations, the Tribunal cannot confine itself to a strictly literal or grammatical interpretation of those Declarations but must also test the method chosen by the United States.... The answer to the question whether suspension fulfilled the function of termination depends on practice. Thus, the test is in factual evidence.

96. "Unless otherwise agreed by treaty, general international law permits a state to choose the means by which it implements its international obligations within its domestic jurisdiction. *See Islamic Republic of Iran* and *United States of America*, Decision No. DEC 62-A21-FT, para. 15 (4 May 1987), *reprinted in* 14 Iran-U.S. C.T.R. 324, 331. Nonetheless, a state's freedom with respect to the choice of the means for implementing an international obligation is not absolute. The means chosen must be adequate to satisfy the state's international obligation, and they must be lawful....

97. ".... The Tribunal is aware of, and takes into account, the dilemma faced by the United States: the need to comply with the obligation to terminate litigation without extinguishing claims that did not fall within the Tribunal's jurisdiction.
98. "There is no reason to doubt that the United States acted in good faith when it suspended, rather than terminated, the litigation. By suspending the litigation and declaring that the suspended 'claims shall have no legal effect in any action now pending in any [United States] court,' Section 1 of Executive Order 12294, the United States took a step in the right direction. Whether suspension of litigation, in practice, achieved the same result as termination is another matter.
99. ".... The Tribunal holds that by adopting the suspension mechanism provided for in Executive Order 12294, the United States adhered to its obligations under the Algiers Declarations only if, in effect, the mechanism resulted in a termination of litigation as required by those Declarations....
100. "The Tribunal assumes that the interpretive statements contained in the foregoing paragraphs represent, by themselves, a partial satisfaction to Iran."

iii) *Conclusion*

101. "During the Hearings in this Case, Iran proffered a list of legal proceedings in the United States in which Iran claims to have been wrongfully compelled to participate. The Tribunal will examine these facts in the second phase of the proceedings in this Case. If, as a result of such examination, the Tribunal concludes that Iran was reasonably compelled in the prudent defense of its interests to make appearances or file documents in United States courts subsequent to 19 July 1981 in any litigation in respect of claims described in Article II, paragraph 1, of the Claims Settlement Declaration or in respect of claims filed with the Tribunal until such time as those claims are dismissed by the Tribunal for lack of jurisdiction, then the Tribunal will find that the United States has not complied with its obligations under General Principle B of the General Declaration and under Article I and Article VII, paragraph 2, of the Claims Settlement Declaration. In that event, the United States will be required to compensate Iran for any expenses that Iran was caused to incur as a result of making appearances or filing documents in United States courts after 19 July 1981 in any litigation in respect of claims described hereabove.
102. ".... The Tribunal expects Iran to show in the second phase of these proceedings what expenses it incurred with respect to each specific case and what was the particular justification for the specific sums it spent. Iran will be expected to produce factual evidence of the losses it suffered as a result of its making appearances or filing documents in United States courts subsequent to

19 July 1981 in the prudent defense of its interests with respect to the claims described *supra*, in para. 101. The Tribunal also expects Iran to produce factual evidence of the losses it suffered as a result of the monitoring of the suspended claims and invites both parties to address the question of whether Iran should be compensated for those losses.

103. "The Tribunal will not award any damages related to, or arising from, Iran's participation in United States court litigation during the six-month period following the signing of the Algiers Declarations. *See infra*, para. 110. Nor will it award any damages related to, or arising from, Iran's participation in cases regarding the validity and constitutionality of the Algiers Declarations under United States law."

(e) *Timing of the Termination Obligations of the United States*

(....)

105. "The obligation to terminate claims extends only to those claims found by the Tribunal to fall within its jurisdiction. It is clear, therefore, that this obligation cannot mature until the Tribunal has decided a claim on the merits. The timing of the United States obligations with respect to litigation, however, is different.

106. "Iran argues that the obligation to terminate litigation arose immediately upon the conclusion of the Algiers Declarations, although a *de minimis* delay of a few weeks would have been acceptable to Iran.... The United States argues, in contrast, that it had six months from the date of the Algiers Declarations within which to halt proceedings in United States courts in cases against Iran....

107. "The Algiers Declarations set forth no express deadlines for carrying out the obligations they imposed on the United States with respect to terminating legal proceedings in United States courts.... Thus, in the absence of an express deadline, the Tribunal relies on the general treaty interpretation principle of good faith, which requires the conclusion that the United States was obliged to terminate, within a reasonable period of time, legal proceedings and litigation against Iran in United States courts that were arguably within the jurisdiction of the Tribunal and that consequently should be referred to the Tribunal....

108. "In considering what would be a reasonable time during which the United States was required to fulfil its obligations, it is useful to look to the express time limits that the Declarations imposed regarding other related obligations. Article I of the Claims Settlement Declaration provides for a six to nine-month period during which Iran and the United States would promote the settlement of outstanding claims falling within the Tribunal's jurisdiction

pursuant to Article II of the Claims Settlement Declaration. Article I provides that '[a]ny such claims not settled within [that period] shall be submitted' to the Tribunal. In the Tribunal's view, a similar period logically would constitute a reasonable time frame for terminating the corresponding United States litigation of such outstanding claims.

109. "Similarly, a six-month period is foreseen in Paragraph 6 of the General Declaration as the time that might be required for the return to Iran of Iranian deposits and securities in United States banks.... The Tribunal is persuaded that the six-month delay in the transfer of funds in United States banks was required because many of them were subject to attachments which, like the litigation at issue here, required United States court action to release. Given the separation of powers between the different branches of government in the United States, neither the release of judicial attachments nor the termination of legal proceedings could be accomplished by Executive Order 12294 alone; both required United States court compliance with that Executive Order....

110. "Based on the above indicia in the Algiers Declarations concerning timing, the Tribunal concludes that a six-month period after the signing of the Algiers Declarations was a reasonable time within which the United States was to terminate legal proceedings and litigation of United States nationals against Iran in United States courts...."

(2) *Counterclaims*

111. "The final issue in Claim A is whether the United States violated the Algiers Declarations by allowing United States nationals to bring counterclaims against Iran in United States courts.... Executive Order 12294 allows the assertion of such counterclaims in United States courts, even if they would fall within the Tribunal's jurisdiction.

112. "Iran argues that ... [i]f United States nationals had claims against Iran ... they should have submitted those claims to the Tribunal without waiting to be sued by Iran in the United States.

113. "The United States responds that it would be unfair to allow Iran to present claims against United States nationals in United States courts after the deadline for the filing of claims before the Tribunal, while preventing United States nationals from asserting counterclaims in reply to such claims. The United States argues that the Algiers Declarations relieve Iran of the obligation to defend itself against involuntary litigation in United States courts which falls within the Tribunal's jurisdiction; nothing in the Declarations, however, requires the United States to grant Iran a favored position by precluding the assertion of counterclaims in litigation that Iran itself voluntarily chose to commence in United States courts.

114. "It is clear from General Principle B and from Articles I and II of the Claims Settlement Declaration that claims that would have been within the jurisdiction of the Tribunal and were not settled by negotiation were to be presented to the Tribunal, and that if a claimant chose not to present such a claim to the Tribunal, he was not to be permitted thereafter to raise it in United States courts. Although the existence of the Security Account ensured that the vast majority of claims deemed meritorious by claimants would be presented to the Tribunal, the Tribunal does not doubt that there were some claims not filed with the Tribunal because of concern by the claimants about possible counterclaims by Iran. By including Section 6 in the Executive Order, the United States, in effect, encouraged such claimants not to come to the Tribunal, and thus failed to comply with its obligations under General Principle B and Article I of the Claims Settlement Declaration."
(....)

2. *Claim B*

116. "Iran contends that the United States has breached General Principle B as well as Article II, paragraph 1, and Article VII, paragraph 2, of the Claims Settlement Declaration by suspending, rather than terminating, litigation involving claims arising from contracts with forum selection clauses referring disputes to Iranian courts.
(....)
118. "... [T]he last clause of Article II, paragraph 1, of the Claims Settlement Declaration ... excludes from the Tribunal's jurisdiction 'claims arising under a binding contract between the parties specifically providing that any disputes thereunder shall be within the sole jurisdiction of the competent Iranian courts, in response to the Majlis position.' The question is whether this language means that such claims must be brought in Iranian courts or whether it merely means that such claims may not be heard by the Tribunal."

a. *The Parties' Positions*

119. ".... According to Iran, the purpose of the exclusion contained in Article II, paragraph 1, of the Claims Settlement Declaration was to preserve the jurisdiction of Iranian courts. Thus, if these claims are allowed to return to United States courts after having been dismissed by the Tribunal for lack of jurisdiction, the purpose of excluding them from the Tribunal's jurisdiction to begin with would be defeated.
(....)

121. "The United States ... points out that under General Principle B, it is required to terminate only claims that are within the Tribunal's jurisdiction; it argues that there is no reason to treat claims involving Iranian forum selection clauses differently than any other claims not within the Tribunal's jurisdiction....

122. "The United States asserts that it never expected that United States nationals would be able to take their claims to Iranian courts given the changed circumstances subsequent to the date on which the contracts containing the forum selection clauses had been concluded. As a result, the United States notes, it insisted on inserting the word 'binding' in the exclusion clause in Article II, paragraph 1, of the Claims Settlement Declaration in the hope that the Tribunal would later determine that the changed circumstances rendered the forum selection clauses unenforceable. The United States points out that, although it asked the Tribunal to make that determination, the Tribunal held that the Algiers Declarations did not authorize it to do so, and consequently it did 'not reach the question as to whether changes in Iran may have any impact on the enforceability of forum selection clauses in contracts.' *Halliburton Company, et al.* and *Doreen/IMCO, et al.*, Interlocutory Award No. ITL 2-51-FT, at 7 (5 Nov. 1982), *reprinted in* 1 Iran-U.S. C.T.R. 242, 246 ('*Halliburton*'). In so holding, the Tribunal did not question the right of national courts to determine the enforceability of choice of forum clauses, and the United States asserts that, if the Tribunal is to be consistent with its holdings in the *Halliburton* and other forum clause cases, it cannot now hold such clauses to be, in effect, enforceable by denying all non-Iranian fora the right to examine their enforceability...."

b. *The Tribunal's Decision*

123. "In *Halliburton*, the Tribunal was faced with the question of whether it had jurisdiction to determine the enforceability of forum selection clauses. In that Case, the Tribunal held that

> '[i]t is not generally the task of this Tribunal, or of any arbitral tribunal, to determine the enforceability of choice of forum clauses in contracts. If the parties wished the Tribunal to determine the enforceability of contract clauses specifically providing for the sole jurisdiction of Iranian courts, it would be expected that they would do so clearly and unambiguously. Thus, the Tribunal would be reluctant to assume such a task in the absence of a clear mandate to do so in the Algiers Declaration.'

.... Thus, in *Halliburton* and the other cited forum selection clause cases, the Tribunal held that it has no jurisdiction to decide whether forum selection clauses in the contracts at issue in cases before it are valid and enforceable.
124. "To hold that the purpose of the forum clause exclusion contained in Article II, paragraph 1, of the Claims Settlement Declaration was to protect the sole jurisdiction of the Iranian courts – or, in other words, that claims that the Tribunal excluded from its jurisdiction because of Iranian forum selection clauses must be brought in Iranian courts – would amount to holding that Iranian forum selection clauses in claims excluded from the Tribunal's jurisdiction because of the forum clause exclusion are valid and enforceable. But if the Tribunal were so to hold, it would abjure its 1982 decision in the forum selection clause cases, *see supra*, para. 123, that it has no jurisdiction to determine the enforceability of such clauses....
125. "The Tribunal has no jurisdiction to determine the enforceability of forum selection clauses; that question is for national courts, not the Tribunal, to decide. Consequently the Tribunal is unable to hold that the failure of the United States to terminate litigation with respect to claims that the Tribunal dismissed because of the forum clause exclusion contained in Article II, paragraph 1, of the Claims Settlement Declaration violated any obligation imposed on the United States by the Algiers Declarations. Accordingly, Iran's Claim B is denied."

3. *Claim D*

a. *The Parties' Positions*

126. "Iran contends that the United States has breached General Principle B by permitting its nationals to file suits against Iran ... pursuant to Section 1 of Executive Order 12294, which permits lawsuits to be filed for the sole purpose of tolling the statutes of limitation applicable in the United States while the Tribunal determines whether it has jurisdiction over the underlying claims....
127. "The United States contends that because General Principle B required it to terminate only the claims of its nationals against Iran that fell within the Tribunal's jurisdiction, it had to devise some mechanism to prevent claims rejected by the Tribunal on jurisdictional grounds from being barred by the applicable statutes of limitation. The mechanism the United States chose was to permit its nationals to initiate suits to toll the limitations period but then to suspend these suits immediately; the cases would remain inactive on the courts' dockets but could be revived if the Tribunal found that it lacked jurisdiction over the underlying claims."
(....)

b. *The Tribunal's Decision*

(....)

131. "The Tribunal finds that the mechanism chosen by the United States – allowing the filing of suits to toll the limitations period (footnote omitted) – is not permitted by the first sentence of General Principle B. To allow suits to be filed, even for tolling purposes, conflicts, furthermore, with the letter and spirit of the United States undertaking in the second sentence of that Principle 'to prohibit all further litigation' based on claims by United States nationals against Iran. It is difficult to deny that such suits represent 'further litigation' within the plain meaning of General Principle B. While General Principle B does not forbid that certain means be employed to allow claims outside the Tribunal's jurisdiction to be preserved, the one means it clearly does forbid is the bringing of suits in United States courts after the date of the Algiers Declarations. Tolling the limitations period, by itself, would not conflict with those Declarations; it is the particular method chosen by the United States – the initiation of litigation in the United States after the date of the Declarations – that so conflicts.

132. "Consequently, the Tribunal holds that by allowing the filing of suits after the date of the Algiers Declarations, even for the limited purpose of tolling the applicable statutes of limitation, the United States did not act consistently with its obligations under General Principle B.

133. "The Tribunal shall determine in a subsequent proceeding the nature and the extent of the damages, if any, incurred by Iran as a result of the United States authorizing the filing of tolling suits. Iran will be expected to produce factual evidence of the losses it suffered as a result of its making appearances or filing documents in United States courts subsequent to 19 January 1981 in the prudent defense of its interests with respect to tolling suits filed after 19 January 1981 asserting claims described in Article II, paragraph 1, of the Claims Settlement Declaration or asserting claims filed with the Tribunal until such time as those claims are dismissed by the Tribunal for lack of jurisdiction. The Tribunal also expects Iran to produce factual evidence of the losses it suffered as a result of monitoring the tolling suits and invites both parties to address the question of whether Iran should be compensated for those losses. *See supra*, paras. 101 and 102."

4. *Claim E*

a. *The Parties' Positions*

134. "At issue in this claim is whether the United States was obliged under the Algiers Declarations to terminate litigation initiated by United States nationals against Iran in courts outside the United States.
135. "Iran advances three principal arguments. First, it argues that under the international law principle of espousal of claims, the claims settlement agreement concluded by Iran and the United States extinguished all private claims of their nationals then in existence;...
136. "Second, Iran argues that the clause at the end of the second sentence of General Principle B requiring the United States 'to prohibit all further litigation on such claims' necessarily refers to litigation in courts outside the United States. If not, that passage would be superfluous since the first clause of the second sentence of General Principle B already requires the United States to terminate legal proceedings 'in United States courts.'...
137. "Third, Iran argues that Article VII, paragraph 2, of the Claims Settlement Declaration, which states that claims filed with the Tribunal are considered 'excluded from the jurisdiction of the courts of Iran, or of the United States, or of any other court,' obliges the United States to prevent its nationals from pursuing claims against Iran in 'any other court,' including courts outside the United States.
(....)
139. "The United States contends that the plain language of General Principle B obliges it to terminate only litigation in United States courts.... General Principle B says nothing about proceedings in foreign courts...."

b. *The Tribunal's Decision*

(....)
141. "As an initial matter, the Tribunal dismisses Iran's argument based on the principle of espousal of claims. The Tribunal has held previously that by entering into the Algiers Declarations, Iran and the United States did not espouse the claims of their nationals. *See Islamic Republic of Iran* and *United States of America* (Case No. A21), *supra*, para. 12, 14 Iran-U.S. C.T.R. at 330.
142. "Turning next to the plain language of General Principle B, the Tribunal holds that the term 'such claims' in the penultimate clause of General Principle B refers to the preceding clause, which requires the United States 'to terminate all legal proceedings in United States courts.' Nothing in General Principle B

suggests that 'such claims' refers to litigation in courts outside the United States or that the United States undertook to terminate such litigation.
(....)
145. "The Tribunal concludes that General Principle B does not oblige the United States to terminate litigation involving claims of United States nationals against Iran in courts outside the United States.... Iran's Claim E is dismissed."

5. *Claim F*

a. *The Parties' Positions*

146. "As part of a series of actions to implement the Algiers Declarations, on 19 January 1981 the President of the United States issued Executive Orders Nos. 12277 and 12279-12281, which nullified attachments of Iranian assets obtained by United States nationals in United States courts after 14 November 1979, the date on which the President had ordered the freezing of Iranian assets. *See supra*, para. 21. These Executive Orders left in place attachments obtained by United States nationals before 14 November 1979; (footnote omitted) this, Iran claims, is a breach of the Algiers Declarations.
147. "Iran argues that Paragraphs 4-9 of the General Declaration, as well as General Principle B, require the United States to nullify attachments made before 14 November 1979.
(....)
150. "The United States denies that the Algiers Declarations required it to nullify attachments that United States claimants had obtained, through normal processes and without Executive Branch license, before the President's freeze of Iranian assets on 14 November 1979...."
(....)

b. *The Tribunal's Decision*

158. "The critical provisions for the resolution of this claim are General Principle A, Paragraphs 4-9 of the General Declaration, and General Principle B. In General Principle A, the United States undertook to 'restore the financial position of Iran, in so far as possible, to that which existed prior to November 14, 1979.' General Principle A goes on to provide: 'In this context, the United States commits itself to ensure the mobility and free transfer of all Iranian assets within its jurisdiction, as set forth in Paragraphs 4-9 [of the General Declaration].' (footnote omitted)
159. "In the Tribunal's view, the most logical reading of General Principle A is that the commitment of the United States to ensure the mobility and free

transfer of all Iranian assets within its jurisdiction is expressly tied to, and limited by, the requirement in the same provision that the United States restore Iran's financial position to that existing prior to 14 November 1979.
(....)
161. "The Tribunal holds that the United States obligation, under General Principle B, to nullify 'all attachments' must be interpreted in light of General Principle A, which requires the United States to ensure the free disposition of Iranian assets – and thus, implicitly, to lift the attachments restraining those assets – only to the extent necessary to restore Iran's financial position to that existing before 14 November 1979.... [I]f Iranian assets were restrained by attachments on 14 November 1979, those attachments were a component of Iran's financial position at that date. To lift those attachments would therefore improve Iran's position, rather than merely restore it. Hence, General Principle B should be understood as requiring the United States to nullify only attachments of Iranian property that were obtained by United States nationals in United States courts on or after 14 November 1979.
(....)
164. ".... Iran's Claim F is denied."

6. *Claim G*

a. *The Parties' Positions*

165. "On 19 January 1981, the United States issued Executive Orders to implement the Algiers Declarations. These Orders nullified attachments obtained by United States nationals against Iran in United States courts after 14 November 1979. In this claim, Iran asserts that the United States has violated the Algiers Declarations by failing to take a sufficiently active role in enforcing those Executive Orders so that all attachments were nullified promptly.
166. "Iran alleges that some United States courts allowed attachments to remain in place as a result of the United States passivity in implementing those Executive Orders. For example, rather than intervening before the courts as a party, the United States merely filed Statements of Interest in the various lawsuits. As a result, in several instances Iran was forced to appear in court to obtain the nullification of attachments restraining its property.
(....)
169. "The United States denies Iran's allegations and contends that it acted vigorously and promptly to nullify all attachments made after 14 November 1979 on Iranian property....

170. "The United States contends, further ... [i]n January, February, June, and July of 1981, the Executive Branch filed Statements of Interest in all proceedings pending against Iran in United States courts, including those involving attachments of Iranian assets. In addition, the Executive Branch filed Statements in particular cases where it deemed that those four previous Statements were not sufficient. Moreover, attorneys for the United States appeared at numerous hearings before federal and state courts to explain the terms of the Algiers Declarations and the requirements of the Executive Orders and implementing regulations. The United States maintains that the attachments were lifted as a result of these efforts, regardless of whether Iran took any action in court. "
(....)

b. *The Tribunal's Decision*

173. "This claim raises two questions. The first is whether the United States took a sufficiently active role in fulfilling its obligation under the Algiers Declarations to nullify attachments of Iranian assets made in United States courts after 14 November 1979. The second is whether the United States succeeded in nullifying those attachments within the period required by the Algiers Declarations.
174. "As to the first question, the Algiers Declarations impose on the United States a duty to implement them in good faith and to take steps to ensure their effectiveness. 'This good faith obligation leaves a considerable latitude to the States Parties as to the nature of the procedures and mechanisms' applied to fulfill their treaty obligations. *Islamic Republic of Iran* and *United States of America* (Case No. A21), *supra*, para. 15, 14 Iran-U.S. C.T.R. at 331....
175. "The evidence shows that the United States devoted extensive resources to carrying out this obligation. Nothing in the evidence suggests that the United States stopped short of doing everything it could pursuant to the procedures of its legal system to have all post-freeze attachments lifted. The Tribunal therefore holds that the United States has satisfied its good faith obligation in this respect. Consequently, Iran's claim that the United States has failed to take a sufficiently active role in nullifying attachments made after 14 November 1979 is dismissed.
176. "Concerning the second question, the United States agreed in General Principle B to 'nullify all attachments ... obtained [in United States courts].' The Tribunal has found that this nullification obligation covered only attachments made on or after 14 November 1979. *See supra*, para. 161. The issue here is when the United States obligation to nullify such attachments arose. For the same reasons it relied upon when it determined the timing of

the United States obligation to terminate litigation against Iran in United States courts, *see supra*, paras. 108-10, the Tribunal holds that the United States had six months from the date of the signing of the Algiers Declarations within which to nullify all post-freeze attachments of Iranian property....

177. "If there were any post-freeze attachments that were still in effect and that actually restrained Iranian assets in the United States after that six-month period had expired, thereby limiting the free disposition of those assets by Iran, then they constitute a violation of the United States obligation to nullify post-freeze attachments in a timely fashion. The Tribunal shall determine in a subsequent proceeding whether any such attachments were still in effect at that date and, if so, the nature and the amount of damages, if any, Iran suffered as a result of those attachments. *See supra*, para. 102."

7. *Claim H*

a. *The Parties' Positions*

178. "In this claim Iran contends that the United States has violated the Algiers Declarations by failing to nullify judgments obtained by United States nationals against Iran in United States courts before the date of the Algiers Declarations...."

(....)

b. *The Tribunal's Decision*

184. "As an initial matter, for the same reasons it provided when determining the scope of the United States obligation to terminate claims against Iran, *see supra*, paras. 81-82, the Tribunal holds that the United States is obliged to nullify only judgments that are based on claims that are within the jurisdiction of the Tribunal, as defined in Article II, paragraph 1, of the Claims Settlement Declaration. As to when that obligation accrued, the reasoning behind the Tribunal's decision concerning the timing of the United States obligation to terminate litigation against Iran applies with equal force here. *See supra*, paras. 108-10. Accordingly, the Tribunal holds that the United States had six months from the date of the signing of the Algiers Declarations within which to nullify judgments pursuant to General Principle B.

185. "Executive Order 12294 provides that

> '[a]ll claims which may be presented to the Iran-United States Claims Tribunal under the terms of Article II of the [Claims Settlement Declaration] ... are hereby suspended.... During the period of this sus-

> pension, all such claims shall have no legal effect in any action now pending in any court of the United States....'

Thus, Executive Order 12294 does not specifically refer to 'judgments.' The question therefore arises whether judgments obtained by United States nationals against Iran in United States courts are nevertheless included within the scope of that Order.

186. "In the Tribunal's view, the Algiers Declarations do not contemplate any distinction between a claim and a domestic court judgment entered thereon. A judgment has no status under the Declarations independent of the claim upon which it is based (*see* the conclusion reached by the Tribunal in *Burton Marks, et al.* and *Islamic Republic of Iran*, Interlocutory Award No. ITL 53-458-3 (26 Jun. 1985), *reprinted in* 8 Iran-U.S. C.T.R. 290, 294-95). It should also be noted that there seems to be no dispute that Executive Order 12294 in fact suspended the execution of judgments in cases within the Tribunal's jurisdiction.... The Tribunal therefore concludes that judgments were included within the scope of Executive Order 12294.

187. "The resolution of Claim H, then, is similar to that of Claim A, because the judgments at issue in Claim H have no status independent of the claims at issue in Claim A. Pursuant to the Tribunal's conclusions in Claim A, therefore, the United States is obliged to nullify only those judgments that are based on claims that the Tribunal decides on the merits. As to the United States obligations under Article I and Article VII, paragraph 2, of the Claims Settlement Declaration, the United States chose to implement them through Executive Order 12294 – that is, by suspending the judgments and declaring them to be without legal effect during the period of suspension.

188. "In line with its conclusions in Claim A, the Tribunal holds that, if Iran reasonably incurred legal expenses in relation to judgments that remained in existence after 19 July 1981, then the United States breached its obligations under the Algiers Declarations concerning nullification of judgments against Iran...."

B. *CASE NO. A24*

1. *Iran's Position*

189. "Iran contends that the claim pursued by Foremost and OPIC before the United States District Court for the District of Columbia is the same as the claim that was decided by the Tribunal in *Foremost*. Iran argues that, by allowing the Foremost/OPIC lawsuit to be brought before the District Court,

the United States has breached its obligation under the Algiers Declarations to prohibit all further litigation of claims resolved by the Tribunal....
190. "Iran points out that the Complaint that Foremost and OPIC filed in the United States District Court in January 1982 tracked the Statement of Claim they filed before the Tribunal in Case No. 37....
191. "Moreover, Iran contends that in deciding *Foremost*, the Tribunal considered all the relevant facts, including those that occurred after 19 January 1981 (in particular, events that occurred in October and November 1981). Iran states that the Tribunal 'considered and evaluated developments even after that date to determine whether any' such events could 'shed additional light on the claimed impairment' of Foremost's shareholder rights before 19 January 1981."
(....)

2. *The United States' Position*

194. "The United States contends that it had no obligation to terminate the litigation in the United States District Court because Foremost's and OPIC's claim in that forum is different from the claim decided by the Tribunal in *Foremost*. The latter was for an expropriation alleged to have occurred in 1980, while the former is for an expropriation alleged to have occurred in October 1981.
195. "The United States argues that the claim before the United States District Court is based on a broader set of facts than the claim decided by the Tribunal in *Foremost*. According to the United States, Foremost and OPIC allege new facts before the District Court, including new and intensified expropriatory measures that arose or continued after January 1981....
196. "The United States further argues that, even if Foremost and OPIC had presented no new facts to the District Court, the United States still would not have been obligated to terminate the District Court lawsuit because the Tribunal in its *Foremost* Award did not resolve and could not resolve on the merits the claim now before the District Court. While the Tribunal held that the expropriation claim was not ripe by 19 January 1981, it made no determination as to whether the claim could be considered ripe at a later date. Indeed, the United States continues, the Tribunal had no jurisdiction to determine whether a taking of the property in question occurred at any date after 19 January 1981. Consequently, because the Algiers Declarations do not require the United States to terminate claims that do not fall within the Tribunal's jurisdiction, the United States had no obligation to preclude the Foremost/OPIC lawsuit."
(....)

3. *The Tribunal's Decision*

a. *The Foremost/OPIC lawsuit during the period from 11 April 1986 until 1 April 1988*

198. "The Statement of Claim Foremost submitted to the Tribunal in Case No. 37 on 16 November 1981 and the Complaint it filed on 22 January 1982 before the District Court for the District of Columbia for purposes of tolling the limitations period were identical....

199. "It is true that, while the Statements of Claim before the Tribunal specifically alleged that '[t]he claims asserted [therein] were outstanding on January 19, 1981' [Statement of Claim in Case No. 37, para. 8], the Complaint before the District Court did not specifically state that the claim asserted therein was likewise outstanding at that date. In the Tribunal's view, however, this apparent difference does not mean that the Complaint before the District Court was broader than the Statements of Claim before the Tribunal in that it arguably also included an expropriation claim that arose after 19 January 1981.... Because there was no jurisdictional requirement before the United States District Court that the claim be outstanding at 19 January 1981, silence in the Complaint as to this fact is irrelevant to the issue discussed in the present paragraph.

(....)

202. "The Tribunal's decision in *Foremost* represents both its finding that the claim before it fell within its jurisdiction and its final resolution of that claim. The Tribunal has held that once a claim is found by the Tribunal to fall within its jurisdiction, the United States is required by the Algiers Declarations to terminate finally all litigation related to such claim in United States courts....

203. "The Tribunal holds that, by not acting to have the Foremost/OPIC lawsuit in the District Court dismissed from the District Court's docket within a reasonable time after 11 April 1986, the date the Tribunal issued its award in *Foremost*, the United States has violated its obligation under the Algiers Declarations to terminate finally litigation in United States courts related to claims resolved by the Tribunal on the merits.

204. "Even if the original Complaint Foremost and OPIC filed before the District Court was broader than the Statements of Claim they filed before the Tribunal in *Foremost*, *see supra*, para. 199, the United States still would have been obliged under the Algiers Declarations to put the District Court on notice, within a reasonable time after 11 April 1986, that proceedings in the Foremost/OPIC lawsuit were to be considered terminated to the extent they related to that portion of the claim that had been decided by the Tribunal in

Foremost (*i.e.*, the claim for a pre-19 January 1981 expropriation of Foremost's ownership interest in Pak Dairy).

205. "As a result of the United States omission, Iran is entitled to damages to the extent it was reasonably compelled in the prudent defense of its interests to make appearances or file documents with respect to the Foremost/OPIC lawsuit from 11 April 1986 until 1 April 1988, to the extent those expenses are not already sought by Iran in Case No. A15(IV). *See supra*, paras. 101, *et seq.*"

b. *The Foremost/OPIC lawsuit from 1 April 1988 onward*

(....)

209. "Although the Foremost/OPIC lawsuit, as pursued from 1 April 1988 onward, relies, to a large extent, on the same facts as those invoked in the claim before the Tribunal, the cause of action alleged in that lawsuit is materially different from that considered by the Tribunal in *Foremost*: the issue before the Tribunal was whether Iran had expropriated Foremost's property on or prior to 19 January 1981; the issue before the District Court was whether Iran had expropriated Foremost's property after that date. In the Tribunal's view, extensive reliance on the same facts, without more, does not cause two claims between the same parties that are based on different causes of action to become identical for purposes of precluding a claim. In this connection, it should also be noted that in the Foremost/OPIC lawsuit, the plaintiffs asserted new rights based on facts that they had not relied on before the Tribunal in *Foremost*, namely, Iran's alleged failure to pay stock and cash dividends that were declared and became due only after 19 January 1981....

210. "Although in *Foremost* the Tribunal considered certain events that took place after 19 January 1981, it limited its decision to a determination that no expropriation had occurred on or prior to that date.... The Tribunal did not, and was not competent to, decide whether an expropriation had materialized after that date. (footnote omitted) The consideration by the Tribunal of certain facts that occurred after 19 January 1981 for the purpose of clarifying Iran's relevant behavior on or before that date ... cannot imply any binding determination about whether Iran's behavior after 19 January 1981 amounted to an expropriation. (footnote omitted)

211. "What is important here is that the Tribunal would not have been competent to decide on the merits the claim before the District Court as pursued by Foremost and OPIC from 1 April 1988 onward. This factor is crucial. Consequently, the conclusion is unavoidable that the Foremost/OPIC lawsuit, as pursued from 1 April 1988 onward, does not fall within the scope of the *res judicata* of the Tribunal's decision in *Foremost* and, therefore, is not contrary to the Algiers Declarations.

212. "The Tribunal now turns to the Memorandum Opinion rendered by the United States [District] Court for the District of Columbia on 23 June 1997 in the Foremost/OPIC lawsuit, holding that Iran's interference with Plaintiffs' shareholder rights in Pak Dairy had ripened into an expropriation by April 1982.... As to whether the Opinion respects the final and binding character of the Tribunal's award in *Foremost*, the Tribunal holds that it so does.... [T]he Memorandum Opinion gives preclusive effect to all of the Tribunal's findings in *Foremost* concerning matters that were within the Tribunal's jurisdiction as defined in Article II, paragraph 1, of the Claims Settlement Declaration. It should be beyond dispute that only such findings acquired the force of *res judicata* and are thus covered by the final and binding language of Article IV, paragraph 1, of that Declaration....

213. "For the foregoing reasons, Iran's claim in this Case, to the extent it relates to the period beginning on 1 April 1988, must be dismissed."

Separate Opinion of George H. Aldrich, Richard C. Allison, and Charles T. Duncan Concurring in Part and Dissenting in Part

"We concur in the Award in these two Cases, except for certain findings in Claim D of Case No. A15(IV) and in Case No. A24.

"In Claim A of Case No. A15(IV), the Tribunal correctly holds that '[o]bligations under General Principle B are, generally speaking, obligations of "result," rather than of "conduct" or "means".' Award, para. 95. For this reason, the Tribunal concludes that it need not answer the abstract question of whether the United States breached General Principle B by authorizing the suspension of litigation rather than its termination, but rather holds that the United States breached General Principle B only if, in practice, suspension of litigation proved less effective than termination. Award, paras. 95 and 98. That is, in Claim A the Tribunal concludes that the United States breached General Principle B only if 'Iran was reasonably compelled in the prudent defense of its interests to make appearances or file documents in United States courts subsequent to 19 July 1981 in any litigation in respect of claims described in Article II, paragraph 1, of the Claims Settlement Declaration or in respect of claims filed with the Tribunal until such time as those claims are dismissed by the Tribunal for lack of jurisdiction.' Award, para. 101. We concur in that conclusion.

"Having followed that logical and pragmatic approach in Claim A, the Tribunal proceeds to ignore it in Claim D of Case No. A15(IV) and in Case No. A24. The resolution of Claim D follows directly from the resolution of Claim A, and Case No. A24 is a specific application of the standards set forth in Claim A, yet the Tribunal's resolution of both of these claims is entirely at odds with Claim A. While in those two cases, the Tribunal properly finds the same fact-specific, limited liability of the United States – that is, liability only to the extent, if any, that Iran was reasonably compelled in the prudent defense of its interests to make appearances or file documents in United States courts in any litigation in respect of claims described in paragraph 101 of the Award – the Tribunal nevertheless, in Claim D and Case No. A24, unnecessarily and erroneously divines non-existent obligations and holds the United States in breach thereof.... [W]e believe the Tribunal should have remained consistent with its analysis in Claim A and should have held that the United States was in breach of its obligations in Claim D and in Case No. A24 only if Iran was reasonably compelled in the prudent defense of its interests to make appearances or file documents in any litigation in respect of claims described in paragraph 101 of the Award. We therefore dissent from the Tribunal's conclusion in Claim D that the United States failed to act consistently with General Principle B by authorizing lawsuits in its courts for the limited purpose of tolling the statutes of limitations. Award, para. 132. We also dissent from three of the Tribunal's holdings in Case No. A24: that the claim Foremost filed in the Tribunal was identical with the claim it filed in District Court; that because the claims were identical, the United States breached the Algiers Declarations by failing to have Foremost's case in the District Court dismissed within a reasonable time after the Tribunal issued its award; and, that even if the Foremost's claim in the Tribunal had not been identical with its claim in the District Court, the United States would still have violated the Algiers Declarations by failing to put the District Court on notice of that portion of Foremost's claim that had been decided by the Tribunal. Award, paras. 198, 203 and 204."

Case No. A15(IV) Claim D

(....)

"While recognizing that General Principle B of the General Declaration did not preclude steps intended to preserve claims that fell outside the Tribunal's jurisdiction, the Tribunal nevertheless holds in the context of Iran's Claim D in Case No. A15(IV) that the method selected by the United States to preserve such claims – the tolling suit – violated its General Principle B commitment to terminate the litigation of claims against Iran and to prohibit all further litigation based on such claims. Award, paras. 131-132.

"Simply by posing the question of whether the United States' authorization of tolling suits violated General Principle B, the Tribunal ignores the careful and pragmatic approach it adopted in Claim A. The Tribunal held in Claim

A that the United States could be considered to have violated General Principle B only if Iran was required to file documents or make appearances with respect to the claims described in paragraph 101, and the proper resolution of Claim D follows directly from that holding. Pursuant to Claim A, just as it is irrelevant whether, in the abstract, 'suspension' can be said to equal General Principle B's requirement of 'termination,' it is likewise irrelevant whether, in the abstract, the tolling suit mechanism can be said to be inconsistent with the requirements of General Principle B. Whether a suit had been filed in the United States courts before the signing of the Algiers Declarations or only after by means of a tolling suit, the scope of United States liability is the same: The United States breached General Principle B and must pay damages to the extent, if any, that Iran was compelled in the prudent defense of its interests to file documents or make appearances in United States courts with respect to the claims discussed in paragraph 101. And that liability is unrelated to any conclusion the Tribunal might reach as to the appropriateness of the tolling suit mechanism; that is, the Tribunal's conclusion that the tolling suit mechanism was inconsistent with General Principle B does not subject the United States to any liability if Iran was not compelled to file documents or make appearances in United States courts with respect to such suits. The Tribunal recognizes this in its description of United States liability in paragraph 133. Conversely, the United States could not escape liability had the Tribunal determined that the tolling suit mechanism was consistent with General Principle B if Iran was in fact compelled to file documents or make appearances in United States courts with respect to such suits. The United States' obligation is one of result.

"Regrettably, the Tribunal's conclusion that the tolling suit mechanism violates General Principle B is not only unnecessary and without effect on the liability of the United States; it is also wrong.... [A]s the Award correctly states at paragraph 96, the specific manner of compliance is – unless it is stipulated in the agreement itself – left up to the complying state.... The mechanism must by any objective standard be both reasonable and effective. The tolling suit mechanism was both. Paralyzed and of 'no legal effect' from the moment of its filing, the tolling suit can hardly be deemed 'litigation' in any normal sense. Moreover, any of the other conceivable methods by which the United States might have preserved the claims pending the Tribunal's jurisdictional determination were certain to have raised complex and difficult issues that would have been costly and vexatious to Iran. The tolling suit mechanism raised none of those difficulties; most importantly, it gave Iran exactly what it was entitled to expect under General Principle B – freedom from litigation of claims that were to be decided by the Tribunal."

(....)

Case No. A24

"In Claim A of Case No. A15(IV), the Tribunal set forth with great care and detail the obligations the United States assumed in adhering to General Principle B. The Tribunal held that the United States breached General Principle B if Iran was reasonably compelled in the prudent defense of its interests to make appearances or file documents subsequent to 19 July 1981 in any litigation in respect of claims described in paragraph 101. It went on [to] say that it would, in the second phase of proceedings, apply that standard to the facts of the cases in American courts in which Iran claims a violation. However, one of those cases, Case No. A24, had already been consolidated with Case No. A15(IV) and so provided the Tribunal its first opportunity to apply the standards it established in Claim A to a particular case filed in United States courts.

(....)

"The Tribunal's initial conclusion – that Foremost's Statement of Claim and its District Court complaint were identical – is patently wrong. The Tribunal acknowledges that the Statement of Claim contained the allegation that Foremost's claim for expropriation was outstanding on 19 January 1981 while the complaint contained no such allegation, but the Tribunal concludes that this apparent difference does not mean that the Complaint 'before the District Court was broader than the Statements of Claim before the Tribunal in that it arguably also included an expropriation claim that arose after 19 January 1981.' Award, para. 199.

"Far from being an 'apparent' difference, the fact that the Statements of Claim alleged an expropriation which culminated by 19 January 1981 while the complaint contained no such date restriction is a real and important textual difference which reflects the real and decisive difference between the two claims....

"... [T]he Tribunal erroneously finds that Foremost filed a claim in the District Court that was identical to the claim it filed in the Tribunal; it then reasons from that finding that the United States should have had Foremost's suit in the District Court dismissed within a reasonable time after the Tribunal issued its award in *Foremost* and that by failing to do so, the United States 'violated its obligation under the Algiers Declarations to terminate finally litigation in United States courts related to claims resolved by the Tribunal on the merits.' Award, para. 203. In so holding, the Tribunal creates an obligation that is both wrong on the merits and that flouts the standards the Tribunal so carefully set forth in Claim A.

"The Tribunal assumes in Case No. A24 that, in order to satisfy its obligation to terminate finally cases decided by the Tribunal on the merits, the

United States is obliged to remove cases from the dockets of the relevant United States courts once the Tribunal has issued its awards in those cases on the merits. The holding is wrong because the Algiers Declarations impose on the United States no such obligation. In our opinion, the United States satisfied its obligation to terminate finally claims decided by the Tribunal on the merits by promulgating Section 4 of Executive Order 12294, which provides that '[a] determination by the Iran-United States Claims Tribunal on the merits that a claimant is not entitled to recover on a claim shall operate as a final resolution and discharge of the claim for all purposes.' In Claim A the Tribunal set forth the standards applicable to cases such as Case No. A24, and it notably did not impose on the United States an obligation to remove cases from the dockets of United States courts. The reason the Tribunal imposes no such obligation on the United States in Claim A is that the approach the Tribunal does adopt in Claim A precludes such an imposition. The Tribunal states in Claim A that the United States can be considered to have breached General Principle B only if Iran was reasonably compelled in the prudent defense of its interests to make appearances or file documents in the cases described in paragraph 101. Thus, a dead case which remains in name only on the docket of a United States court after the Tribunal has issued an award on the merits of the case is not a violation of General Principle B. Only if Iran was required to file documents or make appearances in such a case would the United States violate General Principle B.

(...)

"The Tribunal's alternative dictum for imposing liability on the United States in Case No. A24 is equally inappropriate. The Tribunal holds in the alternative that even if it believed that the complaint in the District Court had been broader than the Statement of Claim in the Tribunal, the United States would still have been obliged 'to put the District Court on notice within a reasonable time after 11 April 1986 that proceedings in the Foremost lawsuit were to be considered terminated to the extent that they related to that portion of the claim that the Tribunal had decided.' Award, para. 204. Again, we disagree – here even more vehemently – with the Tribunal's determination that such an obligation exists.... The Algiers Declarations contain no language whatever that can be interpreted as requiring the Executive Branch of the United States government to remind the Judicial Branch – a co-equal branch of the same government – of the obvious: that it must comply with the United States obligations under the Algiers Declarations. The Tribunal likewise errs in not recognizing that even if General Principle B did obligate the Executive Branch to 'put the District Court on notice' that the Foremost proceedings were to be considered terminated to the extent that they related to that portion of the claim the Tribunal had decided, the Executive Branch would have satisfied that obligation by its promulgation of Section 4 of Executive Order 12294. As noted above, Section 4 provides as a matter of United States law that '[a] determination by the Iran-United States Claims Tribunal on the merits that a claimant is not entitled to recover on a claim shall operate as a final resolution and discharge of the claim for all purposes.'...

"But, ultimately, the Tribunal errs, yet again, in reaching a conclusion precluded by the Tribunal's resolution of Claim A. If, as the Tribunal's alternative theory correctly presumes, the claim Foremost filed in the District Court was not identical to the claim it filed in the Tribunal, then pursuant to Claim A, the United States breached the Algiers Declarations only if Iran was compelled in the prudent defense of its interests to file documents or make appearances in the District Court in that portion of the case that had been decided by the Tribunal on the merits. The United States' liability is in no way affected by whether or not the Executive Branch 'put the District Court on notice.' Regardless of any measures the Executive Branch might have taken, the United States remains liable to Iran if and only if Iran had to file documents or make appearances in the District Court in that portion of the case decided by the Tribunal on the merits. In the Tribunal's words in Claim A, 'the test is in factual evidence.' Award, para. 95."

(....)

Dissenting and Partly Concurring Opinion of Bengt Broms

"I am not able to concur with the majority as regards several central issues in the two Cases....

"The first of my concerns relates to the findings with respect to Claim A of Case No. A15. In my opinion, the majority should have been satisfied with the conclusions reached concerning the differences between the terms 'suspension' and 'termination'.... I cannot accept the findings in the subsequent paragraphs 95-100, essentially signalling that suspension may, under certain conditions, be regarded as sufficient to fulfil the obligation to terminate litigation.

"Second,... I disagree with the majority's treatment of the timing of the Respondent's termination obligation *vis-à-vis* litigation. The majority correctly states that in the absence of a clear provision in the Algiers Declarations in this respect, the conclusion is required that the United States was obliged to terminate such litigation within a reasonable period of time. The majority has, nevertheless, found that such a reasonable time is a six-month period, based on the analogous implementation of the time limits mentioned in Article I of the Claims Settlement Declaration and paragraph 6 of the General Declaration. A careful reading of those provisions reveals that those time limits do not relate to the present issue and that the application of an analogy is therefore inappropriate....

"Bearing in mind that Article I of the Claims Settlement Declaration provided a time limit of six to nine months, during which the Parties should promote settlement of the outstanding claims, it would be contrary to the object and purpose of this provision, within the meaning of Article 31 of the Vienna Convention, if litigation would have been allowed to take place concurrently during a six-month period.... For the above-mentioned reasons, I find the Claimant's argument convincing that in the absence of express provisions, the obligation to terminate litigation arose within a few weeks after the conclusion of the Algiers Declarations. Consequently, I am of the opinion that the Respondent's liability for the Claimant's litigation costs ensued after the Algiers Declarations had been in force for one month.

"The other central finding of the majority with which I disagree is its treatment of Claim B. At a very late stage of the deliberations, the majority has taken the *Halliburton* award (footnote omitted) – one of the pilot cases on the forum selection clauses – as a starting point for the findings of the Tribunal.... What the majority overlooks is that the award in *Halliburton* was not a request by either of the Parties to the Algiers Declarations to interpret Article II, paragraph 1, of the Claims Settlement Declaration. It was rather a claim by a private party for compensation. What makes the Tribunal's statement in *Halliburton* even more curious is that it involves a fundamental paradox. The Tribunal is faced with the issue of enforceability of a forum selection clause in every case wherein such a clause is invoked, and it has not avoided considering such clauses. If the Tribunal has proceeded with a case where enforceability is an issue, it undoubtedly will also have determined that the forum selection clause is ineffective to bar proceedings at the Tribunal. My conclusion is that the *Halliburton* award did not attempt to pronounce on the *general question* of whether the Tribunal, in abstract terms, has jurisdiction to determine the enforceability of forum selection clauses....

"Although an argument could be made that the *Halliburton* award in 1982 did not close the doors of any non-Iranian court to a United States claimant whose claim was considered barred in this Tribunal by the wording of Article II, paragraph 1, of the Claims Settlement Declaration, that award could not be relied upon as a basis for initiating subsequent proceedings in the United States.... It is my firm opinion that the Parties have used specific terms to exclude from the Tribunal's jurisdiction 'claims arising under a binding contract between the parties specifically providing that any disputes thereunder shall be within the sole jurisdiction of the competent Iranian courts.' Such claims that the Tribunal consequently has found to be outside its jurisdiction cannot later be revived in United States courts because of the explicit commitment made by the Respondent to exclude such claims from the jurisdiction of this Tribunal in favour of competent Iranian courts....

"Furthermore, I cannot agree with the findings of the majority with respect to the part of the Award dealing with Case No. A24. It is my view that the Respondent's obligation to terminate litigation operates independently from the issue of whether or not the later proceedings in the Foremost/OPIC lawsuit gave appropriate preclusive effect to the *Foremost* award by this Tribunal. Therefore, the Tribunal should have concluded that – from the point of view of the Respondent's international obligation to terminate domestic litigation – it is impertinent to determine whether the domestic lawsuit, as amended, and the subsequent Summary Judgement in June 1997, respect the *res judicata* effect of the Tribunal's award in *Foremost*....

"The only legally defendable solution would have been for the majority to hold that the Foremost/OPIC lawsuit should have been finally terminated well before the proceedings in the United States courts were resumed in 1988. By allowing the Foremost/OPIC lawsuit to be pending with the District Court during the time the case was pending before this Tribunal and also long after 11 April 1986, the date the Tribunal issued its award in *Foremost*, the United States violated its obligation under the Algiers Declaration to terminate claims that have been resolved on the merits by the Tribunal. (footnote omitted) To the extent Iran was reasonably compelled in the prudent defence of its interests to make appearances or file documents in the Foremost/OPIC lawsuit, it should therefore have been compensated for those losses by the Respondent to the extent that those expenses are not sought under Claim D.

"The only parts of the present Award I believe were correctly decided were Claims D, E, and F of Case No. A15. I also concur in the findings with respect to Claims G and H, except as regards the timing of the respective obligations. (footnote omitted)"

Award in Case No. A27 (586-A27-FT) of 5 June 1998*

Arbitrators:	Krzysztof Skubiszewski (President), Mohsen Aghahosseini (separate opinion), George H. Aldrich, Richard C. Allison (separate opinion), Koorosh H. Ameli (concurring), Gaetano Arangio-Ruiz, Bengt Broms, Charles T. Duncan, Assadollah Noori (separate opinion)
Parties:	Claimant: The Islamic Republic of Iran Respondent: The United States of America
Subject matters:	– applicablity of 1958 New York Convention to "international" award – treaty interpretation – interest and costs

Facts

On 18 July 1988 the Tribunal issued Partial Award No. 377-261-3, requiring that Avco Corporation pay Iranian parties on certain counterclaims.[1] The Award rejected part of Avco's claim as based on insufficient evidence, where Avco had submitted an accounting of the underlying invoices at issue, rather than the invoices themselves. One arbitrator issued a separate opinion dissenting on this issue, stating that Avco had been advised at a pre-hearing conference by a previous Chairman of the Chamber to submit an accounting of the invoices in dispute rather than copies of the invoices themselves. The dissenter found that the Tribunal's failure to accept the accounting as sufficient evidence constituted a denial to Avco of the ability to present its case.

Iran sought to enforce the Award in the United States. On 10 December 1991, the District Court for the District of Connecticut declined to enforce the Award. On appeal, the Court of Appeals for the Second Circuit refused enforcement because in its view Avco was "unable to present [its] case within

* This Award is also included in the reporting on the New York Convention in Part V of this Volume. See Part V – A under Iran-United States Claims Tribunal no. 1, pp. 696-697.

1. Reported in Yearbook XIV (1989) pp. 377-382.

the meaning of Art. V(1)(*b*) of the New York Convention.[2] In another case, *Gould Marketing, Inc.*, Award No. 136-49/50-2 (29 June 1984), United States courts affirmed the Tribunal's Award only after significant delays.[3]

Iran's claim in *Case A27* accused the United States of breaching its obligations under the Algiers Declarations concerning the enforcement of Tribunal Awards, as interpreted by the Tribunal in Decision No. DEC 62-A21-FT (4 May 1987), by failing to enforce the *Avco* Award and causing undue delay in enforcement of other Awards. Iran requested that the United States pay Iran the amount awarded in *Avco*, along with expenses incurred in seeking enforcement in the United States and interest. Iran also asked for costs awarded to it in twenty-four other Awards for which Iran had not yet sought enforcement in the United States. Finally, Iran asked for an order requiring the United States to establish a suitable procedure for the enforcement of future Awards in favor of Iran.

The Tribunal approached these issues on the basis of its decision in *Case No. A21*, which interpreted the phrase in the Declarations that the Awards of the Tribunal are "final and binding". That decision held that the Parties were required to provide some mechanism for municipal enforcement of Tribunal Awards, and stated that a Party would violate its obligations under the Declarations if recourse to municipal enforcement procedures resulted in undue delay or failure of enforcement. Applying this standard to the present Case, the Tribunal found that the United States had indeed violated its obligations because its courts failed to enforce the *Avco* Award as they should have.

The Tribunal noted that the enforcement mechanism for Tribunal Awards in the United States is the New York Convention as applied by courts. However, the obligations of the Algiers Declarations are international in character, the Tribunal is "clearly an international tribunal" and by definition international arbitral awards, if final, are binding. It was hard for the Tribunal to believe that any of its Awards could fall within the scope of Art. V of the Convention. Therefore, United States courts cannot rely on defenses available under the New York Convention to readjudicate the merits of Tribunal Awards. By effectively adopting the view of the minority Member that had been rejected by the Tribunal, the United States court reconsidered a specific issue raised and conclusively decided by the Tribunal. In effect the Court of

2. See *Iran Aircraft Industries and Iran Helicopter Support and Renewal Company v. Avco Corporation*, reported in Yearbook XVIII (1993) pp. 596-605 (US no. 143).
3. See US Court of Appeals for the Ninth Circuit, 30 June 1992 *Ministry of Defence of the Islamic Republic of Iran v. Gould Inc., et al.*, reported in Yearbook XVIII (1993) pp. 590-595 (US no. 142).

Appeals repudiated the merits of the Tribunal's Award and failed to treat the Award as "final and binding".

The Tribunal rejected, however, Iran's contention that the procedures available for enforcement cause undue delay, and therefore the Tribunal found no need to address Iran's request for an order requiring the United States to adjust its enforcement procedures.

The Tribunal awarded Iran the amount of the Award in *Avco*, along with simple pre-judgment interest at the annual rate of 10% through the denial of enforcement in the United States. This totaled U.S.$ 5,042,481.65. The Tribunal also awarded simple post-judgment interest at the annual rate of 5%. It rejected Iran's request for legal expenses incurred in pursuing the enforcement of the *Avco* Award before the Court of Appeals, as the expenses would have been incurred even if enforcement had been granted. The Tribunal also rejected Iran's request that it be awarded immediate payment for arbitration costs awarded in twenty-four other Awards, because Iran had not yet made attempts to enforce them.

Excerpt

I. INTRODUCTION

1. "At issue in this Case are the United States obligations under the Algiers Declarations (footnote omitted) concerning the enforcement in the United States of Tribunal awards rendered against United States nationals in favor of Iran....

2. "In Case A21, Iran had requested that the Tribunal hold that the Algiers Declarations obliged the United States to satisfy any award rendered by the Tribunal against United States nationals in favor of Iran. The Tribunal concluded that the Algiers Declarations did not impose on the United States any obligation, either express or implicit, to satisfy any such awards, and it denied Iran's request. In reaching this conclusion, the Tribunal pointed out, however, that '[t]he Parties to the Algiers Declarations are obligated to implement them in such a way that the awards of the Tribunal will be treated as valid and enforceable in their national jurisdictions.' [*Islamic Republic of Iran* and *United States of America*, Decision No. DEC 62-A21-FT (4 May 1987), *reprinted in* 14 Iran-U.S. C.T.R. 324 (hereinaftaer 'Case A21')] at para. 14, 14 Iran-U.S. C.T.R. at 330.

3. "In this Case, Iran contends that the United States has breached its obligations under the Algiers Declarations concerning the enforcement of Tribunal awards, which obligations, Iran asserts, were delineated by the Tri-

bunal in its Decision in Case A21. As a basis for its claim, Iran invokes the refusal by the United States courts to enforce the Tribunal's Partial Award in *Avco Corporation* and *Iran Aircraft Industries, et al.*, Partial Award No. 377-261-3 (18 Jul. 1988), *reprinted in* 19 Iran-U.S. C.T.R. 200 (hereinafter '*Avco*'). Iran also adduces an alleged undue delay by the United States courts in enforcing the Tribunal's Award in *Gould Marketing, Inc.* and *Ministry of Defence of the Islamic Republic of Iran*, Award No. 136-49/50-2 (29 Jun. 1984), *reprinted in* 6 Iran-U.S. C.T.R. 272 (hereinafter '*Gould*')."
(....)

II. FACTS AND CONTENTIONS

A. *FACTUAL BACKGROUND*

(....)
2. *The* Gould *Enforcement Proceedings in the United States*

12. "On 29 June 1984, the Tribunal rendered Award No. 136-49/50-2 in *Gould Marketing, Inc.* and *Ministry of Defence of the Islamic Republic of Iran*.... Gould failed both to pay the award and to make the equipment available to Iran. Thus, in June 1987, Iran sought confirmation and enforcement of the Tribunal's award by petitioning the United States District Court for the Central District of California....
13. "The District Court held that it had jurisdiction to hear Iran's enforcement action because the Tribunal's award in *Gould* satisfied the requirements of the New York Convention.
(....)
16. "On 31 March 1993, Iran and Gould concluded a settlement agreement,..."

3. *The* Avco *Enforcement Proceedings in the United States*

a. *The Tribunal's Award in* Avco

17. "On 14 January 1982, Avco Corporation (hereinafter 'Avco') presented a Statement of Claim against the Islamic Republic of Iran and certain entities controlled by the government of Iran.... Iran asserted certain counterclaims against Avco. On 18 July 1988, the Tribunal issued Award No. 377-261-3, *Avco Corporation* and *Iran Aircraft Industries, et al.*, *see supra*, para. 3, awarding Iran a total of U.S.$ 3,513,086.03, plus interest, on its counterclaims. In the Award,

the Tribunal, *inter alia*, rejected part of Avco's claims for unpaid invoices. To substantiate its invoice claims, Avco had submitted, *inter alia*, a verification of the underlying invoices by an independent accountant, but not the invoices themselves. In rejecting the invoice claims, the Tribunal said that, while the method of evidence chosen by Avco provided the Tribunal 'with adequate evidence of the existence of the invoices listed in Avco's accounts receivable ledgers,' it did not 'include any material allowing the Tribunal to find that the [claimed invoices] were actually payable.' *Id.* at para. 32, 19 Iran-U.S. C.T.R. at 208....

18. "In a Concurring and Dissenting Opinion appended to the *Avco* Award, Judge Charles N. Brower, the United States-appointed Arbitrator participating in the Case, stated with respect to Avco's invoice claims that Avco had been advised to submit the independent invoice verification, and not to submit the copies of the many underlying invoices, by the previous Chairman of Chamber Three at a Pre-Hearing Conference in 1985. In Judge Brower's view, '[s]ince Claimant did exactly what it previously was told to do by the Tribunal the denial in the present Award of any of those invoice claims on the ground that more evidence should have been submitted constitutes a denial to Claimant of the ability to present its case to the Tribunal.'..."

b. *The* Avco *Enforcement Proceedings*

19. "Avco failed to pay the *Avco* award voluntarily. Thus, on 5 June 1991, Iran petitioned the United States District Court for the District of Connecticut for an order confirming the award. Avco responded by filing a motion for summary judgment, requesting that the District Court deny enforcement. Under the applicable rules of procedure, Iran was required to file its response to Avco's motion by 28 November 1991 but failed to do so.... On 10 December 1991, the District Court, 'after careful review and absent objection,' granted Avco's motion for summary judgment and, consequently, denied enforcement of the *Avco* award.

(....)

21. "On 7 February 1992, Iran appealed ... before the United States Court of Appeals for the Second Circuit. In the appellate proceedings, Iran argued that the Tribunal's awards were directly enforceable in United States courts because, pursuant to Article IV, paragraph 1, of the Claims Settlement Declaration, all decisions and awards of the Tribunal 'shall be final and binding.' Iran argued, in the alternative, that the *Avco* award was enforceable in accordance with the New York Convention. Avco ... contended that the District Court had properly denied enforcement of the award pursuant to Article V(1)(*b*) of the 1958 New York Convention. That Article provides for

the nonenforcement of an award when '[t]he party against whom the award is invoked was not given proper notice of the appointment of the arbitrator or of the arbitration proceedings or was otherwise unable to present his case....' In Avco's view, it was unable to present its case to the Tribunal because the Tribunal had misled it as to the proper method to substantiate its invoice claim.

22. "On 24 November 1992, following briefing and oral argument, the Court of Appeals held that the District Court had been right in denying enforcement of the *Avco* award.... In reaching this conclusion, the Court of Appeals ... held that the 'final and binding' language found in the Claims Settlement Declaration did not bar consideration of the defenses to enforcement provided for in the New York Convention....

23. "According to the Court of Appeals, the Tribunal never made Avco aware that 'the Tribunal now required the actual invoices to substantiate Avco's claim. Having thus led Avco to believe it had used a proper method to substantiate its claim, the Tribunal then rejected Avco's claim for lack of proof.'...

> '.... Avco was "unable to present [its] case" within the meaning of Article V(1)(*b*) [of the 1958 New York Convention], and enforcement of the Award was properly denied.'"

(....)

B. *THE PARTIES' CONTENTIONS*

1. *Iran*

26. "Iran contends that the United States has breached its obligations under the Algiers Declarations concerning the enforcement of Tribunal awards rendered in favor of Iran against United States nationals....

27. "With regard to the Tribunal's Decision in Case A21, Iran points in particular to paragraph 15 thereof, which states ...

> 'Certainly, if no enforcement procedure were available in a State Party, or if recourse to such procedure were eventually to result in a refusal to implement Tribunal awards, or unduly delay their enforcement, this would violate the State's obligations under the Algiers Declarations.'

(....)

29. "Iran asserts, moreover, that not only must the United States ensure that all Tribunal awards are enforced, but it also must ensure that they are enforced promptly and at a reasonable cost to Iran....

(....)

32. "... [B]ecause both the Tribunal and its awards are international in character, a Tribunal award would be final and binding even if no express language to that effect were found in the Algiers Declarations.... Iran asserts that principles of customary international law require that awards rendered by an international tribunal be recognized and enforced in domestic courts. Domestic authorities may not review or refuse to enforce such an award; authenticity is the only aspect of the award that they may verify.

33. "Iran maintains that the enforcement mechanism provided by the United States pursuant to the New York Convention does not satisfy the United States['] obligations ... because the New York Convention ... by its own terms, does not apply to international awards; it covers the enforcement of foreign arbitral awards only. The Convention is inadequate, most notably, because, under conditions specified in Article V, it allows for a court to refuse recognition and enforcement of an award.... Because the international nature of the Tribunal's awards mandates that they be enforced in the domestic sphere, Iran urges, Article V of the Convention cannot apply to those awards....

(....)

35. "As damages ... Iran seeks U.S.$ 3,513,086.03, the amount that the Tribunal awarded the Iranian parties in *Avco*, and U.S.$ 48,914, the legal expenses that Iran allegedly incurred in connection with the *Avco* enforcement proceedings in the United States.

36. "In addition, Iran seeks U.S.$ 344,767.80, the total amount of arbitration costs that the Tribunal awarded Iran in twenty-four awards."

(....)

2. *The United States*

39. ".... Iran's arguments, the United States contends, are directed toward the revision of the Tribunal's Decision in Case A21. As recognized by that Decision, the Declarations do not require the United States to step in and pay Tribunal awards rendered against United States nationals in favor of Iran. Rather, they simply require that the United States (1) provide procedures in its domestic law whereby enforcement of Tribunal awards may be obtained; (2) ensure that Iran has access to those procedures; and (3) see that the procedures made available to Iran are at least as favorable as those afforded other parties wishing to enforce foreign arbitral awards. This the United States has done.

(....)
44. "The United States observes that the Declarations do not ... expressly provide for any obligation concerning the enforcement of awards made against nationals of either government....
45. "As to the Tribunal's legal nature, the United States argues that the Tribunal is a hybrid entity. It is clearly a creature of public international law established by treaty; but it is also capable of, and indeed charged with, deciding disputes of a commercial character.
(....)
49. "The United States denies that the enforcement mechanism available in the United States unduly delays enforcement of Tribunal awards, as Iran argues based on the history of the *Gould* enforcement proceedings.... Iran's argument ignores that the *Gould* enforcement action presented a case of first impression, where a United States court for the first time was asked to apply the terms of the New York Convention to the enforcement of Tribunal awards. The United States notes in this connection that the *Avco* enforcement action moved through the courts much faster than *Gould*."
(....)

III. JURISDICTION

55. "The Tribunal's jurisdiction over this Case is undisputed...."

IV. MERITS

A. *THE CLAIM RELATED TO THE NONENFORCEMENT OF THE AWARD IN* AVCO *AND THE ALLEGED UNDUE DELAY*

(....)
58. "The Tribunal was established by an international agreement concluded between Iran and the United States. The States Parties empowered it to decide intergovernmental claims as well as claims by nationals of one State Party against the government of the other State Party. Under contemporary international law, the fact that an individual or a private entity is party to proceedings before a forum created by an international agreement does not deprive that forum and its proceedings of their international legal nature. The Tribunal is 'clearly an international tribunal,' *Islamic Republic of Iran* and *United States of America*, Decision No. DEC 32-A18-FT, at 18 (6 Apr. 1984), *reprinted in* 5 Iran-U.S. C.T.R. 251, 261.... By definition, international arbitral

awards, if final, are binding. Recourse to this Tribunal implies the undertaking to respect its awards.

(....)

62. "In its decision denying enforcement of the *Avco* award, the Second Circuit held that the Algiers Declarations did not bar consideration of the defenses to enforcement provided for in Article V of the New York Convention....

63. "The Tribunal agrees that those provisions are problematic in the context of Tribunal awards, particularly when viewed in the light of the States Parties' obligations under the Algiers Declarations relating to the enforcement of those awards....

64. "Indeed, it is difficult for the Tribunal to believe that any of its awards could fall within the scope of Article V of the New York Convention. In any event, the fact that the mechanism chosen by the United States to enforce this Tribunal's awards is the New York Convention does not exempt the United States from liability if its courts err by denying enforcement of an award that should, by virtue of the Algiers Declarations, have been enforced....

65. "In denying enforcement of the *Avco* award, the Second Circuit held that Avco had been 'unable to present [its] case' before the Tribunal within the meaning of Article V(1)(*b*) of the New York Convention....

66. "This decision by the Second Circuit was erroneous. A careful reading of the Tribunal's award in *Avco* shows that it was based not on the absence of the invoices underlying Avco's claims, but on a lack of proof that those invoices were payable.

(....)

68. "Indeed, the fact that the Second Circuit effectively adopted the dissenting view of the Tribunal Member in the minority illustrates an additional problem with its decision. That Member argued that Avco had been unable to prove its claim solely because the Tribunal supposedly misled it into not submitting its invoices. A majority of Chamber Three of the Tribunal considered this argument and, by not adopting the minority's view, rejected it. The Second Circuit thus reconsidered a specific question raised and conclusively decided by the Tribunal; in effect, the Second Circuit repudiated the merits of the Tribunal's award in *Avco*.

69. "By reconsidering an issue that had been already aired and decided by the Tribunal, the Second Circuit, in violation of Article IV, paragraph 1, of the Claims Settlement Declaration, failed to treat the Tribunal's decision as 'final and binding.' Once an issue has been raised and decided by the Tribunal, no enforcing court may reexamine that same issue – whether under the guise of the New York Convention or by any other means – without violating that

Article's proviso that '[a]ll decisions and awards of the Tribunal shall be final and binding.'
(....)
71. "Based on the foregoing, the Tribunal holds that, through the refusal by the United States Court of Appeals for the Second Circuit to enforce the *Avco* award, the United States has violated its obligation under the Algiers Declarations to ensure that a valid award of the Tribunal be treated as final and binding, valid, and enforceable in the jurisdiction of the United States.
(....)
73. "With respect to the alleged delay of enforcement, the Tribunal finds that the record, as it stands, does not support Iran's contentions that the procedures available in the United States unduly delay enforcement of Tribunal awards and that it is not cost-effective to attempt to enforce Tribunal awards in the United States....
74. "In view of its decision in this Case, the Tribunal need not address Iran's request for an order requiring the United States to establish a suitable procedure for the enforcement of all future Tribunal awards rendered in favor of Iran against United States nationals.
75. ".... In the circumstances, the Tribunal holds that the United States is liable to compensate Iran in the amount of the award in *Avco*, namely U.S.$ 3,513,086.03.
76. "The Tribunal further holds that Iran is entitled to pre-judgment interest on that amount, as the Second Circuit would likely have awarded such interest if its decision had been to grant enforcement of the *Avco* award. (footnote omitted) The Tribunal therefore awards Iran simple pre-judgment interest at the annual rate of 10 percent (footnote omitted) (365-day basis) from 18 July 1988, the date the *Avco* award was issued, until 24 November 1992, the date the Second Circuit rendered its decision denying enforcement of that award.
77. "Iran also seeks reimbursement of the legal expenses it incurred in pursuing the enforcement of the award in *Avco* after the United States District Court for the District of Connecticut denied enforcement of that award on 10 December 1991. These expenses, however, would have been incurred even if the decision of the Second Circuit had been to grant enforcement. Consequently, they are not recoverable as damages.
78. "Consequently, the Tribunal awards Iran a total of U.S.$ 5,042,481.65 on its claim related to the nonenforcement of the Tribunal's award in *Avco*.... The Tribunal further awards simple post-judgment interest on U.S.$ 5,042,481.65 at the annual rate of 5 percent (365-day basis) from 25 November 1992 up to and including the date of payment of this Award."

B. *THE CLAIM RELATED TO THE 24 COST AWARDS*

79. "Iran seeks U.S.$ 344,767.80 – the total amount of arbitration costs that the Tribunal awarded it in twenty-four awards. Iran argues that, having demonstrated that there is no realistic prospect of enforcing Tribunal awards in the United States, it is entitled to seek payment of the cost awards in question directly from the United States....

80. "In its Decision in Case A21, the Tribunal held that the Algiers Declarations did not contain any express or implied obligation of the United States to step in and satisfy Tribunal awards rendered against its nationals in favor of Iran. *See* Case A21, *supra*, paras. 10-13, 14 Iran-U.S. C.T.R. at 328-30. On the evidence before it, the Tribunal is not prepared to assume that, because United States courts denied enforcement of a single award, they will also deny or unduly delay enforcement of the cost awards that are the subject of this claim.

81. "Only after Iran has made timely attempts to enforce those cost awards in United States courts, and only if Iran establishes that those courts have wrongfully refused to implement the awards or have unduly delayed their enforcement, 'would the question arise as to what ... measures, if any, the United States might be required to take in order to ensure the 'effectiveness' of the Algiers Declarations.' *Id.* para. 16, 14 Iran-U.S. C.T.R. at 331....

82. "Consequently, Iran's claim relating to the twenty-four cost awards must be dismissed."

Separate Opinion of Assadollah Noori and Mohsen Aghahosseini

(....)

1. "In line with a long-established precedent of this Tribunal, we would have preferred the application of a 10% rate of interest for the post-violation period....

2. "Innappropriate is also the decision in the Award not to grant to Iran the costs it incurred for its enforcement efforts before the United States Court of Appeals....

"As the Award notes, some twenty-four cost awards rendered so far by this Tribunal in favor of Iran have remained unenforced. Since these are relative small amounts, and since the expenses of resorting to the United States courts for enforcement are relatively high, Iran would have no financially sound reason to incur such expenses unless it is assured that, should the United States once again violate the terms of the Algerian Declarations, Iran's expenses would be compensated by this Tribunal."

(....)

Separate Opinion of Richard C. Allison

(....)

2. "In my view it would have been preferable for the Full Tribunal to have adhered to the Award as Chamber Three rendered it and not to have granted post-award/pre-judgment interest on the amount owed to IHSRC. This would have obviated the need for speculation about how an enforcing United States court might have exercised its discretion whether to grant post-award interest when the award itself declined to do so...."

Concurring Opinion of Koorosh H. Ameli

(....)

"I would have preferred that for the rate of interest for the post-breach period, that is, from 24 November 1992 to the date of payment, 10% be applied in accordance with the long established practice of the Tribunal.... In inter-governmental claims, the Tribunal has consistently applied this rate....

"As to the Claimant's legal expenses concerning the *Avco* proceeding before the United States Court of Appeals for the Second Circuit, I would have preferred the Tribunal to grant them for they clearly constitute 'damages to compensate for a loss resulting from a breach of this Declaration or the Claims Settlement [Declaration]' under paragraph 17 of the General Declaration. In accordance with Article 32, paragraph 2, of the Tribunal Rules, the parties have also undertaken 'to carry out the award without delay.'

"... [T]he legal expenses should be recoverable here, given Article 32, paragraph 2, of the Tribunal Rules and the conduct of Avco in refusing to comply with the award, not seeking its revision before the Tribunal under its practice ... and only contesting it in the U.S. court enforcement proceeding.

"But what is disturbing in the denial of these legal expenses is its effects on the denial of the 24 cost awards for [an] average amount of $ 15,000 each on the ground that Iran has not yet sought their enforcement before U.S. courts against the award debtors and U.S. courts have not refused their enforcement and ... by denial of the legal expenses concerning the Avco proceedings, the Tribunal has also made obviously ineffective its own cost awards, as legal expenses for their even successful enforcement would clearly exceed the amount of every cost award,..."

AWARDS OF THE CHAMBERS

Award in Case No. 457 (585-457-1) of 5 March 1998

Arbitrators:	Bengt Broms (Chairman), Assadollah Noori (dissenting), Charles T. Duncan
Parties:	Claimant: George E. Davidson (Homayounjah) Respondent: The Islamic Republic of Iran
Subject matters:	- dual nationality - *A18* caveat - proof of ownership of real property - expropriation

Facts

The claimant alleged that around 1 June 1980 the respondent expropriated five Tehran properties in which he held interests: the Kamran Building (one-half interest), the Manouchehri Building (one-half interest), the Ahar Building (one-third interest), the Jalleh Building (one-third interest), and the Caravan Hotel (one-third interest). The claimant sought U.S.$ 3.65 million, plus interest and costs. The respondent argued that the claimant had failed to establish his ownership of the properties, their expropriation, or his dominant and effective U.S. nationality at the time the claim allegedly arose.

The Tribunal held that the claimant owned some, but not all, of the claimed property; that the so-called "*A18 caveat*" did not apply; that the property was expropriated in June 1980; and that the expropriated property was worth approximately U.S.$ 278 thousand.

Excerpt

(....)

III. *JURISDICTION*

1. *The Dual Nationality of the Claimant*

24. ".... To determine whether the Claimant has standing, the Tribunal must establish whether he was a national of the United States of America or of the Islamic Republic of Iran, or of both countries during the relevant period, *i.e.*, from the date the Claim arose until 19 January 1981, the date on which the Claims Settlement Declaration entered into force. If the Claimant was a dual national during that time, the Tribunal must determine the Claimant's dominant and effective nationality during that period. *See Case No. A18*.... In this Case the relevant period commences on or about 1 June 1980, *i.e.*, when the Respondent allegedly expropriated the properties for which the Claimant now seeks compensation.

25. "George E. Davidson was born on 10 June 1956 in Tehran, Iran, to Iranian parents. The Claimant acknowledges that these facts suffice to establish his Iranian nationality under Iranian law (Article 976 of the Iranian Civil Code)....

26. "With regard to the Claimant's United States nationality, it is undisputed that he was naturalized as a United States citizen on 5 March 1980.... Accordingly, the Tribunal concludes that during the relevant period the Claimant was a national of both Iran and the United States."

2. *The Dominant and Effective Nationality of the Claimant*

(....)

2.2. *The Tribunal's Findings*

42. "Having found that during the relevant period the Claimant was a citizen of both Iran and the United States, the Tribunal must determine the Claimant's dominant and effective nationality during that period. For that purpose the Tribunal must establish the country with which the Claimant had stronger factual ties....

43. "Looking at the evidence as a whole, in support of the Claimant's dominant and effective Iranian nationality during the relevant period is the fact that he lived his childhood until the age of sixteen in Iran, that he became a United States national only about three months prior to the date his Claim arose and less than eleven months before the entering into force of the Claims Settlement Declaration. He also appears to have some financial interests in

Iran. The Respondent asserts that the Claimant was present in Iran when the duplicate of his Identity Card was issued in 1977. However, since the Respondent failed to substantiate the assertion, there is no evidence that the Claimant returned to Iran after 1972, *e.g.* to live, to work or to continue his family business there.

44. "Turning then to the facts supporting the Claimant's dominant and effective U.S. nationality during the relevant period, the Tribunal finds that even before the Claimant moved to the United States with a green card in 1972, he had spent lengthy periods there during the summers, starting in 1964. His parents, brothers and other close family members have all emigrated to the United States. By obtaining an education, the Claimant laid the basis for an independent life in the United States and this enabled him to start a career in computer technology. During his studies he was elected class president and became active in various extracurricular activities. The Respondent has made reference to *Arakel Khajetoorians*,... and *Ardavan Peter Samrad*,... in which schooling in the United States did not as such indicate attachment by the individual to the country. It should, however, be kept in mind that in those cases the claimants submitted no further evidence in favor of dominant and effective United States nationality.

45. "The Claimant registered with Selective Service for potential conscription into the U.S. military in 1975, long before becoming naturalized, and he applied for U.S. citizenship as soon as he qualified for it. The Claimant has been employed in the United States both during his studies and after his graduation. He also purchased real estate in the United States. The fact that he married a woman with some Iranian roots is only a token of the common human interest in finding a partner with similar background. That he was granted a duplicate of his Iranian identity card in 1977, a new verification of a power of attorney in his Iranian passport in 1982 and a new Iranian passport in 1984, also do not necessarily show that his Iranian nationality was dominant and effective during the relevant period. The record does not show that the Claimant ever used these documents or that he had any intention of moving back to Iran. All these findings support the conclusion that after the Claimant's departure from Iran, his private, professional and public activities, both prior to and after his naturalization, have been solely and entirely centered in the United States.

46. "Therefore, although the period during which the Claimant was a United States national prior to the entering into force of the Algiers Declarations is short, it appears to the Tribunal that during the relevant period the Claimant's ties to the United States outweighed his ties to Iran. Consequently, the Tribunal decides that during the relevant period from the time his Claim arose

until 19 January 1981 the Claimant's dominant and effective nationality was that of the United States."

IV. *MERITS: FACTS AND CONTENTIONS*

1. *Ownership*

1.1. *The Claimant's Contentions*

(....)

55. ".... The Claimant argues that in 1978 and early 1979 his father[, Edward Davidson,] redistributed, on the basis of documents giving him power of attorney to act on behalf of his sons and his wife, the family's ownership interests in the properties at issue, to adapt to a possibly altering situation in Iran. The redistribution increased the Claimant's ownership interests in certain properties and decreased it in others. At the Hearing, Edward Davidson maintained that he left the documents giving him power of attorney and other documents related to the deeds in question in the safe deposit box No. 416 at Bank Sepah and that the Respondent later confiscated the contents of the box. Therefore, he was allegedly prevented from carrying out the necessary formalities at the Notary Public Office in Tehran to effectuate the transfers. Edward Davidson also asserted at the Hearing that after being arrested twice, he tried to register the documents effecting the redistribution, but these efforts were frustrated by the authorities. Therefore, he attempted to execute the transfers himself and deposited the documents in the safe deposit box."

1.2. *The Respondent's Contentions*

(....)

58. "With regard to the Kamran Building, the Respondent points out that the title deed ... indicates that seven individuals, Edward, George, David, Henry, Robert and Jack Homayounjah and Rosalin Sassoon purchased the property for 5,600,000 Rls. The record further shows that the property was mortgaged to Bank Melli for fifteen years in 1973. Thus, the Respondent concludes that the ownership interest of the Claimant amounted to one-seventh of the property. The Respondent refers to the Executive Transfer Deed dated 5/2/1364 (25 April 1985), produced as evidence. It explains that the bank had an executive writ issued in its favor, because the owners failed to pay their debt within the prescribed time limit and that the property was transferred to the bank on 1 May 1985. The Respondent maintains that Bank Melli has acted

in accordance with Iranian laws and regulations as well as terms and conditions included in the mortgage agreement, and that as a result, the Claimant no longer has any ownership interests in the Kamran Building.

59. "As to the Manouchehri Building, the Respondent has submitted a copy of a title deed.... According to this document eight members of the Homayounjah family purchased the property in 1976, including Edward, Kamran, George, Henry, David, Robert and Jack Homayounjah and Rosalin Sassoon. Each transferee acquired one-eighth of the property. The record shows that the property was mortgaged to Bank Melli for fifteen years in 1976. The Respondent contends that Bank Melli lawfully foreclosed on the property because of the owners' failure to perform their contractual obligations. The writs of execution were notified to the debtors on 10/4/1360 (1 July 1981). As the debtors failed to apply within the prescribed time limit for the auction of the mortgaged property, failed to object to the execution process and failed to pay the creditor, the property was assigned to the creditor. An execution transfer deed was registered at the office of Notary Public No. 285 on 21/5/1363 (12 August 1984).

60. "According to the Respondent, the Ahar Building ... was purchased by Rosalin Sassoon in 1959 and was mortgaged to Bank Melli in 1976 by Edward Homayounjah, acting on her behalf.... The Respondent emphasizes that the Claimant never owned the property and thus cannot claim compensation for it.

61. ".... The Respondent does not dispute that the Claimant had an ownership interest in the [Jalleh Building]. The Respondent maintains, however, that in 1978 the property was subject to a transaction in which Rosalin Sassoon sold five of six undivided shares of the property to David, Kamran, Henry, George, Robert and Jack Homayounjah, so that each of the children acquired ownership of one-sixth of the five undivided shares and she retained the remaining one share. Therefore, according to the Respondent, the Claimant's ownership interest amounts to one-sixth of five-sixths of the Jalleh Building.

62. "With regard to the Caravan Hotel Building, the Respondent contends that the documentary evidence concerning the property ... demonstrates that the Claimant never held any ownership interests in the property."

(....)

1.3. *The Tribunal's Findings*

69. "The Tribunal notes that in order to meet his burden of proof the Claimant must establish the following elements: that he had ownership interests or other property rights at issue, and that an expropriation or other

measures amounting to an expropriation affecting his ownership interests or other property rights, attributable to Iran, took place. (footnote omitted)

70. "The Tribunal notes that the Claimant has not provided any official title deeds or other authorized documents showing title to the alleged property. Instead, the Claimant tries to carry his initial burden of proving his ownership through a number of inconsistent statements by himself and his closest relatives. As a general rule, contradictory statements of an interested party should be construed against that party. (footnote omitted)

71. "Moreover, the ownership asserted by the Claimant has changed throughout the proceedings, and at a very late stage the Claimant claims that he has a beneficial ownership in the property because his father had redistributed ownership interests. However, the Claimant provides no official documents of transfer related to the alleged redistribution of ownership. The Tribunal holds that the Respondent has provided sufficient rebuttal evidence on the applicable provisions of Iranian laws and the Tribunal's practice concerning the transactions of properties such as the five buildings in this case. The documentary evidence submitted by the Respondent shows that such properties must be registered to give the transfer of ownership legal validity.

72. "The Claimant has asserted that his father could not register the redistribution of ownership because his father was prevented from carrying out the necessary formalities at Notary Public Office No. 64. However, the Claimant is unsuccessful in corroborating his father's account. The Respondent, on the other hand, has provided evidence in rebuttal, showing that during 1978 and 1979 the Claimant's father carried out a large number of other registration formalities at the same Notary Public Office and at other administrative or judicial offices. The Tribunal concludes that, even if Edward Davidson intended to transfer or redistribute ownership interests in the five properties, it has been proven neither that he gave effect to his intention nor that he did it in the manner required by Iranian law and according to the approved practice of the Tribunal. A mere intent, even if it existed, cannot effectuate a legally valid transfer of real property.

73. "Additionally, the Respondent has presented the title deeds to the five properties. An official title deed is *prima facie* strong evidence indicating that the title to real property has been officially conferred on the person whose name appears on the deed as the owner or transferee. *See Rouhollah Karubian* and *The Government of the Islamic Republic of Iran*, Award No. 569-419-2 (6 Mar. 1996), para. 114, *reprinted in* ___ Iran-U.S. C.T.R. ___. Consequently, the Tribunal concludes that, as reflected in the deeds, the Claimant's ownership interests were one-seventh in the Kamran Building, one-eighth in the Manouchehri Building, none in the Ahar Building, five thirty-sixths in the Jalleh Building and none in the Caravan Hotel. The Tribunal notes that the

Kamran and Manouchehri Buildings were later, in 1985 and 1984, transferred to Bank Melli due to the owners' failure to fulfill their contractual obligations under their mortgage agreements. These transactions were based on executive writs and accordingly registered. The significance of these transfers will be dealt with in the discussion of the alleged expropriation by the Respondent."

2. *The Caveat*

(....)

2.2. *The Tribunal's Findings*

76. "In this case the Tribunal has already decided that the Claimant was a dual national of Iran and the United States from his naturalization in the United States in March 1980 and that during the relevant period the Claimant's dominant and effective nationality was that of the United States. *See*, *supra*, para. 46. The Full Tribunal has stated about the caveat in *Case No. A18* that, 'the other nationality may remain relevant to the merits of the Claim.' *See Case No. A18*, *supra*, at 265-266. The Tribunal also discussed the substance of the caveat in *Saghi*, *supra*, paras. 45-64. The caveat has been applied by the Tribunal as an instrument of equity intended to prevent abuses of right. Therefore, claims by dual nationals for benefits generally limited by relevant Iranian laws to persons who are nationals solely of Iran have been considered barred. Consequently, these persons have been refused an award in their favor.

77. "The Tribunal notes that the Claimant acquired the property in question before he became a national of the United States on 5 March 1980 and possessed this property as a dual national until the alleged expropriation around 1 June 1980. The Tribunal concludes that the ownership of the property remained legal at the time of the alleged expropriation, since Iranian law permitted those Iranians who obtained foreign nationality to hold their Iranian real property up to a year before being obliged to sell it. *See* Civil Code of Iran, Articles 988 and 989. As it has been shown neither that the Claimant enjoyed his property rights by violating municipal law, nor that he would have enjoyed them by abusing his Iranian nationality, the Tribunal holds that the Caveat expressed by the Full Tribunal in *Case No. A18* is not applicable to this Case."

3. *Expropriation*

3.1. *The Claimant's Contentions*

78. "The Claimant asserts that the properties at issue were expropriated in June 1980, when the Government of Iran interfered with his property rights to an extent that rendered them valueless. Until 1979, when he left Iran, the Claimant's father managed the five properties at issue here.
(....)
88. "At the Hearing, the Claimant's witnesses Edward Davidson and Nejat Haim testified that before Edward Davidson left Iran in the summer of 1979 he made arrangements with Mr. Haim to collect rents from the tenants in the five buildings. Mr. Haim said he had an official power of attorney for the Kamran Building and that he acted upon oral instructions from the Davidsons as regards the other buildings. From the rent he collected, Mr. Haim was to pay the mortgage payments, taxes and other expenses relating to the properties, and he was to send the balance to Edward Davidson for distribution to his sons. This arrangement worked until about 20 June 1980 when payments stopped coming from Mr. Haim to Edward Davidson. On or about 20 June 1980, the Revolutionary Prosecutor General's Office told Mr. Haim that the Homayounjah (Davidson) family no longer owned the five properties and that the Revolutionary Court now supervised and owned these properties. Mr. Haim said he was told to send the money that remained from the collected rentals after paying the mortgage, taxes and expenses to the Revolutionary Prosecutor General's Office, and he followed instructions. On or about 25 June 1980 that office told Mr. Haim not to make any mortgage payments to Bank Melli, and he again obeyed orders. Later, after the relevant period, some tenants received letters from the authorities regarding these matters and Mr. Haim informed Edward Davidson that the Prosecutor General's Office had instructed some tenants of these five properties to pay the rents directly to the Revolutionary Government."

3.2 *The Respondent's Contentions*

(....)
99. "At the Hearing, the Respondent's witness Mr. Safari explained that he worked in the Prime Minister's Office from 1979 until he was appointed to the Revolutionary Prosecutor General's Office on 5 October 1980. Mr. Safari met Mr. Haim when Ms. Maki made a complaint about the Caravan Hotel, whose owner was abroad. The Office sent an invitation to the owners' representative, Mr. Haim, and he came to the Office, showing a power of attorney relating

to the Kamran Building. Mr. Safari asserts that Mr. Haim asked him to help make the tenants pay their rents. Later Mr. Safari invited some of these tenants to the Office and told them to pay their rents. Mr. Safari denies collecting rents from Mr. Haim or from the tenants of the Kamran Building. Mr. Safari also denied having received or seen the two letters that Mr. Haim allegedly wrote to the Revolutionary Prosecutor General's Office.

(....)

102. "The Respondent concludes that during the relevant periods it neither interfered in the properties, nor exercised supervision over them. Therefore, the Respondent requests the Tribunal to dismiss the Case for want of jurisdiction."

3.3. *The Tribunal's Findings*

103. "The Tribunal notes that the Parties disagree as to whether the Government of Iran ever formally expropriated the Claimant's ownership interests, *e.g.*, by rendering a judgment. The Claimant asserts that this did not happen until 24 April 1982, when the Islamic Revolutionary Court passed a ruling to this effect. If the Tribunal were to base its findings on that date only, it would have to dismiss the claim for want of jurisdiction, since that date is beyond the jurisdictional cutoff date of the Tribunal. But the Claimant has based its claim not on a formal taking, but rather on the alleged interference with his property rights prior to the jurisdictional cutoff date.

104. "Measures taken by a State can interfere with property rights to such an extent that these rights must be deemed to have been expropriated. Such an expropriation occurs, for example, when the owner is deprived of the effective use, control, and benefits of his property. Thus, an expropriation may take place even though the State does not admit having expropriated and the legal title to the property remains with the original owner. (footnote omitted)

105. "According to Article II, paragraph 1, of the Claims Settlement Declaration, the Tribunal has jurisdiction over claims that were outstanding on 19 January 1981, whether or not filed with any court. Hence, for the Tribunal to have jurisdiction in the present Case, the Claimant must establish that the claims had arisen prior to that date. In the Tribunal's practice it has been established that a claim for the taking of property is outstanding on the day of the taking. Should the alleged expropriation have been carried out by way of a series of interferences in the enjoyment of property, the cause of action is deemed to have arisen on the day when the interference ripened into an irreversible deprivation of property rather than on the date these events began. The point at which interference ripens into a taking depends on the circum-

stances of the case and does not require the transfer of legal title. (footnote omitted)

106. "While a government's assumption of control over property does not automatically and immediately justify a conclusion that the property has been taken by the government, thus requiring compensation under international law, such a conclusion is warranted whenever events demonstrate that the owner has been deprived of fundamental rights of ownership and it appears that this deprivation is not merely ephemeral. In establishing expropriation, less significance is to be attached to the intent of the government and to the form of these measures of control or interference than to the reality of their impact on the owner. (footnote omitted) This does not, however, relieve a claimant asserting expropriation from the obligation to demonstrate the requisite government interference. *See United Painting Company Inc....*

107. "In this Case the title deeds provided by the Respondent establish that the Claimant had ownership interests in three of the five buildings in question, namely one-seventh in the Kamran Building, one-eighth in the Manouchehri Building and five thirty-sixths in the Jalleh Building. These title deeds do not mention any measures amounting to an expropriation. However, the Tribunal notes that the lack of any official written documentary evidence of an expropriation within the relevant period does not exclude the possibility of a taking.

108. "The Tribunal refers to the testimony at the Hearing of Edward Davidson and Nejat Haim as regards their arrangements for managing the family properties. The Tribunal also refers to the testimony of Mr. Haim concerning events of the summer of 1980 (*See*, *supra*, para. 88). The Tribunal finds the testimony of Mr. Haim persuasive and his statement corroborates that of the Claimant's father. The evidence provided by [five affiants,] Mr. Muslavi, Ms. Israel, Mr. Jahanbani, Ms. Foroozan and Mr. Kalimi Isfahani[,] also corroborates the key statements made by Edward Davidson and Mr. Haim. Moreover, [affiant] Mr. Kalimi Isfahani states that in June 1980 Mr. Safari of the Revolutionary Prosecutor General's Office personally told him that the Davidsons no longer owned the property and that it had been taken over by the Revolutionary Government. Mr. Kalimi Isfahani paid the rent to Mr. Haim, who confirmed that he was collecting the rent for the Revolutionary Government.

109. "In conclusion, all oral statements and affidavits of [the Claimant's two Hearing witnesses and five affiants] are consistent, and that consistency strengthens their probative value. Even if the Tribunal evaluates the probative value of this evidence with caution to protect the Respondent against claims not properly founded, it demonstrates that in the summer of 1980 the Iranian Revolutionary authorities ordered the tenants to cease paying their rent to the Davidson family, as the properties in question were under the effective

supervision of the Revolutionary Government. As a result, the Claimant did not receive any rents. Mr. Safari's testimony does not convince the Tribunal of the opposite. First, the Respondent has not submitted contemporaneous evidence to support his assertion that Mr. Haim had asked him to force the tenants to pay their rent. For this reason Mr. Safari's statement fails to convince the Tribunal that he played only a passive role in the collection of rent for the Davidson properties. Second, the Respondent presented Mr. Safari as a witness at the last possible moment, which unfairly prevented the Claimant from doing much more than confirming Mr. Safari's identity.

110. "The actual transfer of the properties to Bank Melli occurred after the alleged taking and subsequent to the relevant period. Thus, their only relevance to this Case is to demonstrate the result of the Respondent's action not to permit mortgage payments.

111. "Therefore, The Tribunal holds that the Respondent permanently deprived the Claimant of his fundamental rights of ownership, because he could not control, use or enjoy the benefits of these properties. Even if legal title was not transferred, the Tribunal concludes that the Respondent's interference with the Claimant's property rights ripened into a taking at the latest on 1 July 1980."

4. *Valuation*

(....)

4.2 *The Tribunal's Findings*

117. "The Tribunal notes that the Parties have presented quite similar figures regarding the mortgages and they have agreed that these mortgage debts should be deducted from the value of the properties. Apart from this, the Parties disagree on their value. The Parties have referred to three valuation reports by experts and the Claimant has also referred to a valuation made by his father. The Tribunal must attempt to determine the properties' fair market value, which has been described by the Expert in *Starrett* as 'the price that a willing buyer would buy given goods at and the price at which a willing seller would sell it at on condition that none of the two parties are under any kind of duress and that both parties have good information about the relevant circumstances involved in the purchase.' *See Starrett Housing Corporation et al.* and *The Government of the Islamic Republic of Iran et al.*, Award No. 314-24-1 (14 Aug. 1987), para. 18, *reprinted in* 16 Iran-U.S. C.T.R. 112.

118. "The difficulty is, however, in determining a fair market value at the time of the alleged taking in the summer of 1980, because at that time no real estate market existed in Iran in an ordinary sense. Due to the revolution the general economic, political and social conditions were exceptional and no fixed

price level existed in the real estate market.... [The] Tribunal is bound to make reasonable approximations within the limits of the given appraisals by the experts. After deducting appreciated mortgage debts, the Tribunal finds that the values of the properties at the time of the expropriation were as follows:

Kamran Building ...	120,000,000 rials
Manouchehri Building ...	7,000,000 rials
Jalleh Building ...	10,000,000 rials

Consequently, as the Claimant's ownership interest is one-seventh in the Kamran Building, one-eighth in the Manouchehri Building and five thirty-sixths in the Jalleh Building, the compensation to the Claimant is as follows:[15]

Kamran Building ...	17,142,857 rials	($245,178)
Manouchehri Building ...	875,000 rials	($12,514)
Jalleh Building ...	1,388,889 rials	($19,864)
Total ...	19,406,746 rials	($277,556)

As a result, the Tribunal decides that the Respondent should pay the Claimant U.S.$ 277,556 with interest, calculated at a rate the Tribunal considers appropriate, from the date on which the Claimant's property is deemed to have been taken, *i.e.*, on 1 July 1980."

V. *INTEREST*

119. "The Tribunal considers it appropriate to award interest to the Claimant at the rate of 7.789% in accordance with the principles outlined in *Sylvania Technical Systems, Inc.* and *The Government of the Islamic Republic of Iran*, Award No. 180-64-1 (27 June 1985), *reprinted in* 8 Iran-U.S. C.T.R. 298, 320-322, from the date of interference with the property rights."
(....)

VII. *AWARD*

121. "For the foregoing reasons, THE TRIBUNAL AWARDS AS FOLLOWS:

15. "The exchange rate applied is the average exchange rate for June 1980 (69.920 rials to one U.S. dollar) as listed by the International Monetary Fund. *See* International Financial Statistics, Supplement on Exchange Rates, Suppl. Ser. No. 9 (1985)."

(a) The Claim for the expropriation of the Claimant's ownership interest in the Ahar Building is dismissed for failure to prove any ownership interest;
(b) The Claim for the expropriation of the Claimant's ownership interest in the Caravan Hotel is dismissed for failure to prove any ownership interest;
(c) The Respondent, THE GOVERNMENT OF THE ISLAMIC REPUBLIC OF IRAN, is ordered to pay the Claimant, GEORGE E. DAVIDSON, the amount of ... U.S.$ 277,556, plus simple interest at the rate of 7.789% per annum (365 day basis) from 1 July 1980 up to and including the day on which the Escrow Agent instructs the Depositary Bank to effect payment to the Claimant out of the Security Account, for its interference with the Claimant's property rights in respect of the Kamran, Manouchehri and Jalleh Buildings in Tehran, Iran.
(d) The Respondent is ordered to pay the Claimant costs of arbitration in the amount of ... U.S.$ 20,000."

Award in Case No. 953 (587-953-2) of 2 July 1998

Arbitrators:	Krzysztof Skubiszewski (Chairman), George H. Aldrich, Koorosh H. Ameli (concurring in part; dissenting in part)
Parties:	Claimant: Kamran Hakim Respondent: The Islamic Republic of Iran
Subject matters:	- late filings - dual nationality - proof of ownership - expropriation - valuation

Facts

The claimant alleged that the respondent expropriated several parcels of land in the Velenjak and Vanak regions and a residence on Pirasteh Street in Tehran. He also claimed that the respondent expropriated his 20% interest in Emerson Electric Company, Pars Union Company, Ranel Frigo Company, and Pars Machine Manufacturing Company. As finally pleaded, the claimant sought U.S.$ 11,958,930 plus interest and costs.

The Tribunal dismissed the claimant's claims concerning the properties in Velenjak, Vanak and on Pirasteh Street. The Tribunal held that the claimant had not adequately proved his ownership of the Vanak parcels and that he had not adequately proved the expropriation of the Pirasteh Street residence. The claimant had contended that the respondent effected its expropriation of the Velenjak properties by means of the Act Concerning Abolition of Ownership of *Mawat* [Undeveloped] Urban Lands and the Method for Development of Such Lands of 1 July 1979 ("Abolition Act"). However, the regulations to the Abolition Act excepted from the Act's reach land on which acceptable development had been made, and in light of the claimant's allegations as to his development of the parcels, the Tribunal held that the claimant failed to meet his burden of proving that the Velenjak property fell within the scope of the Abolition Act.

The Tribunal next dismissed for lack of proof of ownership the claimant's claims with respect to Emerson Electric Company, Pars Union Company, and Ranel Frigo Company. With respect to Pars Machine Manufacturing Company, the Tribunal awarded the claimant U.S.$ 691,611 for his 20% interest in the company, holding that the respondent's appointment of an observer did not rise to the level of an expropriation but did deprive the claimant of the use and control of his property such that the respondent was liable for compensation.

Excerpt

II. LATE FILED DOCUMENTS

(....)

6. "At the commencement of the Hearing, the Claimant submitted a dossier consisting of 33 documents and requested that it be admitted into the record....

7. "The dossier contained numerous documents that the Claimant had submitted to the Tribunal previously and which the Tribunal had previously rejected. Thus, at the Hearing, the Tribunal reiterated its earlier rejection of these documents. The Tribunal went on to admit one document, a judgment of 6 March 1984 by the Islamic Revolutionary Court of Tehran against the Claimant and his siblings. Finally, although noting that it had not received an adequate explanation for the Claimant's delay in presenting the documents, the Tribunal held that it nonetheless would be prepared to admit any of the remaining documents, provided that the Claimant could prove that they were publicly available.

(....)

9. ".... [At issue here are] a letter dated 26 November 1980 from the Iranian Ministry of Industries and Mines to Mr. Morteza Khatibi (the IMIM letter of appointment) and a hand-written document entitled 'Notice of Changes in Pars Machine Manufacturing Co.,' dated 29 November 1980 (the notice of changes). The IMIM letter appointed Mr. Khatibi as a governmental observer of PMMC for a period of three months and specified his functions and powers in that position. *See infra*, para. 56. The notice of changes, signed by Mr. Khatibi and two other PMMC employees described certain changes which assertedly had been made in PMMC's operation and management....

(....)

13. "The Tribunal notes that the IMIM letter of appointment appears on its face to be an internal government communication. Thus, without further information, one might think it not publicly available. However, in its June 1997 response, which has been admitted by the Tribunal, the Respondent annexed an official Ministry of Justice Notice of Appointment, issued by the Bureau for the Registration of Companies and dated 1 December 1980. This

document is an official publication of Mr. Khatibi's appointment as an observer for PMMC, and it refers to the IMIM letter of appointment. That reference shows the public nature of the IMIM letter of appointment. A full understanding of the Ministry of Justice Appointment Notice required an examination of the IMIM letter of appointment, and the Tribunal infers that the Ministry of Justice Appointment Notice would not have referred to the IMIM letter unless it could be so examined. Thus, the Tribunal considers the IMIM letter of appointment to be a document of public nature admissible pursuant to the Order communicated to the Parties at the Hearing.

14. "By contrast, whether or not the notice of changes is a publicly available document is not clear. That document is signed by Mr. Khatibi and two other PMMC employees, and it purports to make certain changes in PMMC, including dissolving PMMC's board of directors and cancelling its contracts. However, the above-mentioned Ministry of Justice Notice of Appointment indicates that the three signatories to the notice of changes exceeded in that notice the powers conferred upon them by the IMIM letter of appointment. Consequently, several decisions purported to have been made in the notice of changes were not approved by the Iranian Bureau for the Registration of Companies and presumably were not made available to the public. However, in light of the Tribunal's decision in paragraph 105, *infra*, a decision on the admissibility of the notice of changes is rendered moot.

(....)

16. "In the present Case there are two reasons why the Respondent is not prejudiced by the admission of the IMIM letter of appointment. First, the Respondent has been given ample opportunity to respond to that document (more than six months). More importantly for the present circumstances, that appointment letter was a publicly available document, *see supra*, para. 13, and has always been in the Respondent's possession."

(....)

IV. FACTS AND CONTENTIONS: PROPERTY AND COMPANY INTERESTS

1) *The Velenjak Property*

28. "In his Statement of Claim, Mr. Hakim sought compensation for four parcels of land in Velenjak, Iran....

29. "The Claimant contends that he made various improvements to the properties, and he submits a letter and an affidavit by Mr. Ralph Sassouni in support of this contention. Mr. Sassouni ... confirms the existence of brick walls, water wells, planted trees and shrubs, a hot house, and a small cottage

on the Claimant's Velenjak property.... The Claimant contends that $857,000 was spent on purchasing the land, on various taxes and on the improvements.
30. "The Claimant maintains that the property was expropriated by the Respondent pursuant to the Act Concerning Abolition of Ownership of *Mawat* [Undeveloped] Urban Lands and the Method for Development of Such Lands of 1 July 1979 (the '1979 Abolition Act') and its implementing Regulations.
31. "The Respondent asserts, by contrast, that the 1979 Abolition Act was not applied and was not applicable to the Velenjak property in light of the Claimant's admission that various improvements had been made to the property."
(....)

3) *The Vanak Property*

40. "The Claimant alleges ownership in five parcels of real estate located in the Vanak district. He submitted no title deeds to the property, however, and asserts that all the relevant documentation proving his ownership of these parcels was in the possession of his maternal uncle, Mr. Yaghoub (Jack) Hay, who was forced to leave it behind when he fled from Iran. At the Hearing, Counsel for the Claimant conceded that the Vanak properties were not registered in the Claimant's name.
(....)
43. "The Respondent denies the Claimant's ownership of the Vanak property...."
(....)

4) *Pars Machine Manufacturing Company ("PMMC")*

47. "[The Claimant contends that he owned 20% of the shares in] Pars Machine Manufacturing Company [which he claims was expropriated.]...
48. ".... Claimant's elder brothers, Masud and Said Hakim, were responsible for its daily management because they were residing in Iran....
49. ".... Said Hakim asserts that he left Iran after the Revolution, returned in September 1979 but left again around the end of November 1979 after he became aware that an order for his arrest was being prepared. He maintains that after leaving Iran he made a number of telephone calls from New York to his office in Tehran. He adds:

> 'During the earlier calls I spoke with my employees, but later representatives of the [workers' committee] picked up the phone. I was told that

> they had taken control and I should only speak with them.... They said I had no right anymore....'

50. ".... [The Claimant's sister, Parvin Hakim,] contends that as time passed, the workers' committee representatives acquired more and more control of the business, and by the time she left Iran in August 1980 'it was clear there was no way to exercise the ownership rights of my brothers any longer.'
(....)
52. "The Respondent denies interfering with the affairs of the company between 1979 and early 1981. It asserts that the Claimant and his family abandoned the company and left Iran because their mismanagement pushed PMMC to the verge of bankruptcy, and that the company could not pay its employees' wages. The Respondent asserts that, consequently, the workers took over the management of the company. In its post-Hearing submission of June 1997, the Respondent maintains that the appointment of Mr. Khatibi on 26 November 1980 as an observer was neither an expropriation nor an interference with the Claimant's property rights.
53. "The late-filed documents admitted into the record by the Tribunal contain, *inter alia*, the letter dated 22 December 1980 from the Office of the Revolutionary Prosecutor addressed to the Bonyad Mostazafan. That letter states:

> 'In view of the report received in connection with Pars Machine, Emerson Electric and affiliated companies belonging to the Hakim family, who are fugitives, it is appropriate to take measures in regard to the supervision and reactivation of these companies and to provide this office with a report of your activities as soon as possible.'

54. "... [T]he Respondent explained that this letter was dispatched by the Revolutionary Prosecutor only after the PMMC workers had repeatedly asked in 1979 and 1980 for government representatives to assume the management of the company due to the absence of PMMC's regular management and its deteriorating situation....
55. "The PMMC workers' letters of appeal to the government were submitted by the Respondent as exhibits to its June 1997 response. The earliest dates from 29 December 1979 and the following is an example of such a letter. Addressed to the Revolutionary Prosecutor, signed by fifty-five workers and dated 5 May 1980, it states in relevant part:

> 'Respectfully, we, the employees of [PMMC], pursuant to our letter No. 7394 dated 29 December 1979 concerning the company's lack of the

management, shareholders and budget for ordering the raw materials as well as non-existence of an authorized and responsible person which has led to insufficiency of production, request you to order the Ministry of Industries and Mines to take appropriate measures for running this manufacturing unit which has been left in uncertain conditions since the victory of the Revolution.'

56. "The exhibits to the Respondent's June 1997 response also show that PMMC workers had made repeated requests to the IMIM to send a representative to assist in the management and operation of the company.... The IMIM appointment letter of 26 November to Mr. Khatibi states:

> 'By virtue of Legal Bills No. 6738 dated [16 June 1979] and No. 8780 dated [7 July 1979] of the Provisional Government of the Islamic Republic of Iran and in accordance with this letter of appointment, you are hereby appointed as observer of Pars Machine Manufacturing Company Co. for a maximum period of three months.
>
> It is appropriate that you fully observe all the affairs of the said entity using the powers conferred on you pursuant to the above-referenced Bills.
>
> Meanwhile, financial and obligatory instruments or documents of the Company will be signed jointly by you, one of the members of the Workers Council namely, Mr. Hassan Palizadar, and the Company's accountant, Mr. Hassan Paryab.'

57. "Mr. Khatibi contends that after his appointment, he basically engaged in studying the records [of PMMC] and publishing notices of invitation of shareholders and directors in pertinent newspapers."
(....)

VI. MERITS

1) *The Velenjak Property*

(....)
76. "Mr. Hakim alleges that his Velenjak property was taken as a result of the 1979 Abolition Act and its Regulations, which he asserts applied to 'mawat' (undeveloped) and 'bayer' (previously developed) urban lands.
77. "In *Rouhollah Karubian* and *Islamic Republic of Iran*, Award No. 569-419-2, para. 111 (6 Mar. 1996) ('*Karubian*'), the Tribunal held that the very

existence and binding force of the 1979 Abolition Act and its Regulations did not by themselves constitute an expropriation of the claimant's real property in Iran. Accordingly, to the extent that Mr. Hakim's claim is for the expropriation of the Velenjak property, it must fail.

78. "Nonetheless, the Tribunal must also examine whether other measures within the meaning of Article II, paragraph 1, of the Claims Settlement Declaration affected the Claimant's property rights. Tribunal precedent has recognized that a claim for expropriation necessarily includes a claim for other measures as provided in Article II. *See Eastman Kodak Company, et al.* and *Government of Iran, et al.*, Award No. 329-227/12384-3 (11 Nov. 1987), *reprinted in* 17 Iran-U.S. C.T.R. 153, 169.

79. "In *Karubian* the Tribunal held that while the cumulative effect of the Iranian land reform legislation at the time of the Revolution and related governmental action did not rise to the level of an expropriation, the interference could be of such a degree as to constitute other measures affecting property rights. *Karubian, supra*, Award No. 569-419-2, at para. 144. In so holding, the Tribunal noted that the 1979 Abolition Act, as amended, along with its implementing Regulations 'made all undeveloped or unutilized properties in both urban and rural areas vulnerable to a determination that they were *mawat*, and as a consequence of that determination, subject to immediate cancellation of their title deeds by Iran.' *Id.*, at para. 143. The Tribunal held in *Jahangir Mohtadi, et al.* and *Islamic Republic of Iran*, Award No. 573-271-3, para. 68 (2 Dec. 1996) ('*Mohtadi*') that lands which were in fact *bayer* might also have been affected by that Act and its Regulations by virtue of the definition of *mawat* land in the Regulations.

80. "In light of the *Karubian* and *Mohtadi* Awards, the Tribunal must determine whether the Velenjak land was affected by the 1979 Abolition Act or its implementing Regulations.

81. "Article 2 of the Regulations to the 1979 Abolition Act appears to exempt from the Act's application land on which 'acceptable development and improvement' has been made, and it sets forth nine categories of such acceptable development and improvement. Land falling within these categories presumably is considered neither *mawat* nor *bayer*.

82. "The language of Article 2 is ambiguous in that it does not indicate whether development or improvement other than what is specifically defined therein is acceptable. In addressing ambiguities contained in other Iranian land legislation, the Tribunal in *Mohtadi* stated that it

> 'normally would view the responsibility for providing a complete and persuasive explanation of Iranian legislation as falling upon the Res-

> pondent. This is because the Respondent is surely better positioned than a claimant to explain the meaning and effect of its own laws....
>
> On the other hand, it falls to the Claimant to demonstrate with clarity the facts that bring his property within the scope of the legislation that allegedly expropriated his property....'

83. "In view of the above, and considering the absence of any evidence that the property was subject to any physical interference by the Respondent, it is the Tribunal's opinion that Mr. Hakim has the burden of proving that his Velenjak property was of the type which fell within the scope of the 1979 Abolition Act and that it was not exempted under the implementing regulations. Because the Claimant has submitted evidence of substantial development of the property and has claimed that substantial funds were spent, in part, on developing the property, the Tribunal is unable to determine whether the Velenjak property was affected by the laws and regulations on which he relies.... Thus, the Claimant has not met his burden of showing that the Velenjak property fell within the scope of that legislation."

(....)

3) *The Vanak Property*

87. "The Claimant admitted at the Hearing that no formal agreement, title deed or other contemporaneous documentary evidence exists to prove his ownership of the Vanak property, and the Respondent's expert witness, Mr. Karimi, testified that he found no entry in the official land registration files to show that the Claimant possessed an ownership interest in the Vanak property.

(....)

89. "Mr. Hay has stated that because he fled Iran, he left behind the documents evidencing the Claimant's ownership of the Vanak property. The Tribunal is mindful that a person making a sudden departure from Iran during the revolutionary events prevailing at the time may have left behind documentation or other material that could prove a claim. It would be unfair to impose a rigorous standard of proof on a claimant in such instances. However, in adopting such an approach, the Tribunal also must be careful not to expose the Respondent to claims not properly evidenced. *See W. Jack Buckamier* and *Islamic Republic of Iran, et al.*, Award No. 528-941-3, para. 67 (6 Mar. 1992), *reprinted in* 28 Iran-U.S. C.T.R. 53, 74-76. There is no precise formula to balance these competing concerns; each case is to be decided with due regard to the particular circumstances which surround it.

90. "It seems clear that the Claimant's alleged interest is not recorded in the relevant land registration files. Although that fact, on its own, may not be sufficient to find against the Claimant, the Claimant has failed to proffer any documentation of adequate probative value to overcome the strong legal presumption against him. It may be true that documentary evidence was left behind in Iran but the affidavits and statements relied on by the Claimant are not sufficient to prove that the Claimant possessed an ownership interest in the Vanak lands. The affidavits submitted in support of the Claimant's ownership of the Vanak property are vague and imprecise....

91. "The Tribunal also notes that where a Claimant alleges a proprietary interest of the magnitude at issue here, it would be reasonable to expect the Claimant to have with him in the United States some documentation, which would have evidenced his ownership interest in that property. The Claimant here has proffered nothing of the kind.

92. "Based on the foregoing, the Tribunal dismisses for lack of proof the portion of the Claim relating to the Vanak property."

4) *Pars Machine Manufacturing Company*

93. ".... [T]he Tribunal now turns to examine whether the appointment of Mr. Khatibi as an observer at PMMC in November 1980 constitutes an expropriation or other measures affecting the Claimant's property rights under Article II, paragraph 1, of the Claims Settlement Declaration for which the Respondent bears responsibility.

94. "Mr. Khatibi was appointed pursuant to Legal Bill No. 6738, the 'Law Concerning the Appointment of Provisional Manager(s) to Supervise Productive, Industrial, Commercial, Agricultural and Services Units in the Private and Public Sectors' ('Law of 16 June 1979'). That same law has been the subject of detailed consideration in previous awards. Indeed, in determining whether an expropriation occurred in prior cases, the Tribunal has examined both the text of the law pursuant to which the appointment was made and the events occurring after the appointment.

95. "In *Thomas Earl Payne* and *Islamic Republic of Iran*, Award No. 245-335-2, para. 20 (8 Aug. 1986), *reprinted in* 12 Iran-U.S. C.T.R. 3, 10 ('*Payne*'), the Tribunal held that the 'effect [of the Law of 16 June 1979] is to strip the original managers of affected companies of all authority and to deny shareholders significant rights attached to their ownership interest.'... Likewise, the Tribunal here notes that the Law of 16 June 1979 provides that once an observer is appointed he will remain in his position, and the shareholders have no rights whatsoever to appoint a person in his place for the period of his

appointment unless it is earlier revoked by the appointing authority. Article 2 of the Law of 16 June 1979.

96. "The mere appointment of an observer under that Law is, however, not conclusive of a finding of expropriation. In addition to examining the powers that were conferred pursuant to the appointment itself, prior cases have generally contained a detailed discussion of the specific actions actually taken by the appointee. For instance, in *Harold Birnbaum* and *Islamic Republic of Iran*, Award No. 549-967-2, para. 30 (6 Jul. 1993) ('*Birnbaum*'), the Tribunal noted that the appointed manager testified that he had 'assumed control over all of AFFA's affairs on the basis that the law ... gave complete authority to conduct the firm's business.' *Id.* He testified further that he 'also felt obligated to exclude the owners of the firm from all management responsibilities.' *Id.* The manager went on to say that 'he did not try to contact AFFA's partners who were outside of Iran because he was not in a position to do so.' *Id.* In *Faith Lita Khosrowshahi, et al.* and *Islamic Republic of Iran et al.*, Award No. 558-178-2 (30 Jun. 1994) ('*Khosrowshahi*'), as in the instant case, the Government of Iran had appointed an observer, as opposed to a manager. There, the Tribunal determined on the evidence before it that once the observer was appointed and assumed his duties, 'he immediately excluded the existing Khosrowshahi management. There is no evidence that [the observer's] appointment was intended to be or in fact was temporary. The subsequent appointment of directors and chairman of the board also shows that the intention of the Government was permanent exclusion of the existing management.' *Id.*, at para. 25.

97. "In the instant case, although Mr. Khatibi was appointed pursuant to the Law of 16 June 1979, the evidence of his actual interference in PMMC falls short of that described in *Birnbaum* and *Khosrowshahi*. In contrast to the latter two cases, the evidence concerning PMMC indicates that the relevant government authorities resisted involvement in PMMC and appointed Mr. Khatibi only at the insistence of PMMC workers.

98. "Mr. Khatibi states in his affidavit that PMMC workers had been managing the company before he arrived and that they continued to do so after he assumed his position. He asserts that he 'basically engaged in studying the records and publishing notices of invitation of shareholders and directors in pertinent papers.'... Thus, in the instant case, the Tribunal has not been presented with the evidence of the exercise of actual control that was present in *Birnbaum* and *Khosrowshahi*, among other cases. Furthermore, the evidence is insufficient to hold that between the appointment of Mr. Khatibi, 26 November 1980, and the end of the relevant period, 19 January 1981, the Respondent's actions had ripened into an outright taking of property....

99. "Therefore, taking into account the particular circumstances of the present case, the Tribunal finds that the appointment of the observer was not an interference of a degree sufficient to justify a conclusion that PMMC was expropriated within the relevant period. But a finding that there was no expropriation does not preclude a determination that the above governmental actions deprived the Claimant of his property rights.

100. ".... Mr. Khatibi was also given significant powers in the company by virtue of the appointment letter and pursuant to the bill under which he was appointed. As noted above, *see supra*, para. 95, the law under which he was appointed stripped the shareholders of their rights to choose others in his place. Moreover, the IMIM appointment letter authorized Mr. Khatibi to 'observe all the affairs of [PMMC] using the powers conferred upon [him] pursuant to the above-referenced Bills.'...

101. "By conferring the power over financial matters on Mr. Khatibi, the Government of Iran prevented the legitimate company officials from signing documents on behalf of the company.... Thus, the effect of the appointment was to impair significantly the rights belonging to PMMC's owners. They lost control over the contracts PMMC would subsequently enter and were deprived of the right to liquidate or sell the company as they saw fit.... Thus, by preventing the shareholders from signing financial documents and from affecting management decisions, the Respondents deprived the shareholders of their right to participate in the operation of the company. The effect was to deny shareholders significant rights attached to their ownership interests....

102. "As discussed above, the Tribunal is mindful that the IMIM appointed Mr. Khatibi because the legitimate managers of PMMC had left Iran and the workers had repeatedly requested a government supervisor. Nevertheless, Tribunal practice dictates that '[t]he intent of the government is less important than the effects of the measures on the owner.' *Tippetts, Abbett, McCarthy, Stratton* and *TAMS-AFFA Consulting Engineers of Iran, et al.*, Award No. 141-7-2, at 11 (29 Jun. 1984), *reprinted in* 6 Iran-U.S. C.T.R. 219, 225-226 (*Tippetts*).

103. ".... The Tribunal is aware of and understands the social circumstances of the appointment. But the reasons for assuming control of a company, however compelling, cannot relieve a government from the obligation to compensate for the loss suffered.... Furthermore, due to the conditions prevailing in Iran, the departure of the Hakims and managers of PMMC at the time was not unjustified....

104. The Tribunal is also aware that the appointment of Mr. Khatibi was deemed to be a temporary one. The terms of his appointment expressly limited his duties to a period of three months, although Mr. Khatibi himself has stated that this period was extended for a second three-month period. Nevertheless, in the practice of the Tribunal, provisional or temporary appointments have

not precluded a finding that a taking occurred. *See Motorola, Inc.* and *Iran National Airlines Corporation et al.*, Award No. 373-481-3, para. 58 (28 Jun. 1988), *reprinted in* 19 Iran-U.S. C.T.R. 73, 85; *Birnbaum*, *supra*, Award No. 549-967-2, at para. 29.... The control established by Iran with regard to PMMC was not simply a temporary interruption of the existing management.

105. "The Tribunal concludes that while the interference created by Mr. Khatibi's appointment did not rise to the level of an expropriation, it did deprive the Claimant of his basic rights as a PMMC shareholder...."

(....)

Part IV

Recent Developments in Arbitration Law and Practice

RECENT DEVELOPMENTS IN ARBITRATION LAW AND PRACTICE

INTRODUCTION

The reporting in Part IV on Recent Developments in Arbitration Law and Practice consists of short announcements on *Belgium*, *Costa Rica*, *Ireland*, *Latvia*, *Macao*, *Sweden*, *Taiwan* and *Venezuela*. For further information, the reader is referred to ICCA's *International Handbook on Commercial Arbitration* where the text of the new legislation will be soon reproduced in full.

New or amended arbitration and mediation rules are reported in Part III – A where the reporting this year includes new rules of the American Arbitration Association, the China International Economic and Trade Commission, the Stockholm Chamber of Commerce and the International Bar Association.

COUNTRIES

BELGIUM: The Belgian law on arbitration has been amended by the "Law of 19 May 1998 Amending the Provisions of the Judicial Code concerning Arbitration" in force 17 August 1998.[1] This is the second amendment of these provisions since 1972 when Belgium adopted the Uniform Law attached to the 1966 European Convention on Arbitration done at Strasbourg (Strasbourg Uniform Law), incorporated as Part 6 of the Judicial Code (Arts. 1676-1723). The first amendment was by the Law of 27 March 1985[2] which added a fourth paragraph to Art. 1717 of the Judicial Code excluding the possibility of an application to set aside an award made in Belgium between two non-Belgian parties. This paragraph has been modified by the Law of 19 May 1998, along with a number of other modifications and additions as briefly described below.

Part Six of the Judicial Code, as amended, will be reproduced in a future

1. Published in the Official Journal on 7 August 1998.
2. Published in the Official Journal on 13 April 1985.

Supplement of the *International Handbook on Commercial Arbitration*, in anticipation of an Updating of the National Report Belgium.

The capacity of legal persons of public law (the State, provinces, municipalities and public establishments) to agree to arbitration, which they previously only could do when authorized by a treaty, has been enlarged in the amended Art. 1676(2). Legal persons of public law may now conclude an arbitration agreement with respect to disputes relating to the "formation or performance" of a contract. They may also conclude arbitration agreements in respect of matters which are determined by law or regarding which a Royal Decree, deliberated in the Council of Ministers, has empowered them to do so. All this remains subject to Art. 1676(3) which is unchanged and provides that the provisions of paragraph 2 are subject to exceptions provided by law.

The grounds for challenging an arbitrator no longer refer to the grounds for challenging judges. In Art. 1690(1) they have been brought in line with the general formulation of Art. 12(2) of the UNCITRAL Model Law, namely, "circumstances giving rise to justifiable doubts regarding their impartiality or independence".

Art. 1700 has extended the freedom of the parties to agree that the arbitrators will decide as *amiables compositeurs*, by removing the prior restriction that they could only do so after the dispute had arisen, adding, however, that legal persons of public law may only stipulate *amiable composition* if this possibility has been provided for in a specific law.

The determination of the place of arbitration is now regulated in more detail in Art. 1693(1) which has added the rule that if the place of arbitration has not been determined by the parties or the arbitral tribunal, the place where the arbitral award is rendered, as stated in the award, shall be deemed to be the place of arbitration. Paragraph 2 confirms that hearings and meetings may be conducted at any other location.

Art. 1696(1) fills a lacuna in the previous regime by adding a specific provision that the arbitral tribunal may order provisional or conservatory measures. Art. 1696(2) inserts the general principle that the arbitral tribunal may decide on the "admissibility of the evidence and on its conclusive force". The new Art. 1696*bis* provides for the intervention and joinder of parties in the arbitral proceedings, subject to the conclusion of an arbitration agreement among all the parties concerned and the unanimous consent of the arbitral tribunal.

Art. 1699, which previously empowered the arbitral tribunal to make one or more final awards, has been amended to allow the arbitral tribunal to make final or interlocutory awards. Art. 1709*bis* gives the arbitrators a new power to order a party to pay a penalty sum. Art. 1702*bis* introduces the possibility for the arbitral tribunal, either at its own initiative or at the request of a party, to correct an award, or at the request of a party to interpret the award.

Art. 1703(2) now regulates the possibility for the parties to agree to allow appeal against the award to a second arbitral tribunal.

As mentioned above, paragraph 4 of Art. 1717, introduced in 1985, has been amended. Instead of excluding by operation of law the possibility of setting aside of awards made in Belgium between non-Belgian parties, the parties may now agree to the exclusion by an explicit declaration, either in the arbitration agreement or concluded thereafter.

COSTA RICA: On 9 December 1997, the President of Costa Rica gave his assent to Law No. 7727 on Alternative Resolution of Disputes and Promotion of Freedom from Social Unrest. As the reference in the title to ADR suggests, the Law included provisions on mediation and conciliation (Arts. 4-17) as well as arbitration (Arts. 18-70), and for the establishment of institutions to administer arbitration and other means of alternative dispute resolution (Arts. 71-73). A number of the provisions demonstrate the influence of the UNCITRAL Model Law.

Parties, including the State, may submit to arbitration present or future disputes on economic matters regarding which they may freely dispose (Art. 18), subject to their having agreed to do so in writing.

Arbitration may be either "at law" or ex aequo et bono (Art. 19) and the number of arbitrators must always be an uneven number (Art. 24). Arbitrators at law must always be lawyers with a minimum of five years of membership in the Costa Rica Bar Association (Art. 25). Arbitrators may be challenged on the same grounds as judges as well as on the general criteria found in Art. 12(2) of the UNCITRAL Model Law, namely, justified doubts as to their impartiality or independence (Art. 31).

The new Law recognizes the principles of competence-competence of the arbitrators and separability of the arbitral clause in Art. 37. The arbitral tribunal's decision on its own jurisdiction may be appealed to the Supreme Court, subject to the arbitral tribunal finding the appeal admissible (Art. 38).

The parties are free to determine the arbitral procedure, provided it respects the principles of due process and the right to defense and contradiction (Art. 39). If the parties do not agree otherwise, the language of the arbitration shall be Spanish (Art. 41) and the hearings will be private (Art. 51). Parties or the arbitral tribunal, on its own behalf or on behalf of a party, may request interim measures of protection from the court (Art. 52). The arbitral tribunal shall apply the substantive law chosen by the parties, failing which they shall apply Costa Rican law, including its conflict of law provisions (Art. 22).

The award shall be made by majority vote and the presiding arbitrator shall have the decisive vote if no majority can be reached (Art. 57). The award in arbitration at law must always be reasoned. A dissenting vote must be expressly noted on the award, with reasons, but failure to do so on the part of the dissenting arbitrator will not nullify the award (Art. 59). The award shall be made public unless the parties have agreed to the contrary (Art. 60). Parties may request that the award be corrected or clarified, or that an addition be made to it, within three days of notification and the appropriate action taken by the arbitrators within ten days (Art. 62).

If the parties wish to resort to conciliation or mediation during the arbitral proceedings, the arbitral tribunal will suspend the proceedings. If the conciliation or mediation results in a settlement, the arbitral tribunal will record it in the form of an award. If the parties fail to reach a settlement, they will have to present the arbitral tribunal with evidence of having attempted to reach a settlement before the arbitral tribunal resumes the proceedings (Art. 63).

The application to set aside the award must be made within fifteen days of notification of the award. The grounds for setting aside are that the award was not made within the prescribed time limit, the award is extra or infra petita, the dispute was not arbitrable, due process was not observed, the award is in violation of public policy or the arbitral tribunal lacked jurisdiction (Art. 67).

Arbitrators are to be compensated according to a percentage of the amount in dispute and this amount shall be borne equally by the parties unless the award provides otherwise.

IRELAND: On 20 May 1998 the Arbitration (International Commercial) Act, 1998 was enacted. This Act brings the UNCITRAL Model Law on International Commercial Arbitration (contained in the Schedule to the Act) into effect in Ireland for international commercial arbitration.

Domestic arbitration in Ireland is still governed by the Arbitration Act 1954 which largely resembles the English Arbitration Act 1950, the latter having been replaced in England by the Arbitration Act 1996 which applies to both domestic and international arbitration.

In Ireland, the Arbitration Act 1954 has been amended by Sect. 17 of the 1998 Act, which now specifically provides in Sect. 34 that the arbitral tribunal may award interest, thus filling a lacuna in the Arbitration Act, 1954. The Arbitration Act 1980 gives effect to the 1958 New York Convention and the 1965 Washington Convention and also regulates the staying of court proceedings when a party invokes an arbitration agreement, whether domestic or international. Sect. 5 of this Act has been amended to include the possibility in respect of small claims of relying on alternative methods provided by the Rules of Court.

The Model Law has been enacted in its entirety, subject to the provisions of the 1998 Act. The *travaux préparatoires* of the Model Law may be considered in interpreting the Model Law (Sect. 5(2) of the 1998 Act). The 1998 Act designates the High Court as the court to by specified by Art. 6 of the Model Law. The powers of the court for the purpose of ordering interim measures (Art. 9 Model Law) or assistance in the taking of evidence (Art. 27 Model Law), are set out in Sect. 7 of the 1998 Act and are without prejudice to the generality of Arts. 9 and 27. They include the preservation, interim custody or sale of any goods which are the subject matter of the arbitral proceedings, securing the amount at issue in the arbitral proceedings, issuing interim injunctions, and ordering the detention, preservation or inspection of property or things which are the subject matter of the arbitration. Security for costs may not be ordered solely on the ground that the party is not a resident or does not have its seat in Ireland (Sect. 7(2)).

Interim measures ordered by the arbitral tribunal under Art. 17 shall be treated as an award unless the parties agree otherwise (Sect. 14(3)) a provision not found in the Model Law.

The court may also assist in the taking of evidence by securing the attendance of witnesses before the arbitral tribunal, examining witnesses under oath or affirmation, issuing a request for the examination of a witness outside of Ireland and ordering discovery of documents (Sect. 7(1)). The arbitral tribunal may also order that witnesses testify under oath or affirmation, unless parties agree otherwise (Sect. 8).

The time limit for requesting the setting aside of an award on the ground that it is in violation of public policy has been changed from the three months allowed in Art. 34(3) of the Model Law to an unlimited period.

The 1998 Act also regulates a number of matters not covered by the Model Law. Sect. 9 allows for voluntary consolidation or the holding of concurrent hearings. Sect. 10 on interest provides, subject to parties agreeing otherwise, that the arbitral tribunal may award pre-award or post-award interest, simple or compounded. Sect. 11 provides an extensive regulation of the recoverable costs of arbitration and recoverable fees and expenses of the arbitral tribunal which may be determined by the arbitral tribunal or the court. Sect. 12 exempts arbitrators, arbitral institutions and their employees and agents from liability with respect to the arbitration unless their acts or omissions have been in bad faith. Witnesses, barristers and solicitors and patent agents are granted the same immunities as before the court.

LATVIA: On 1 March 1999, the new Part D on Arbitration of the Code of Civil Procedure of Latvia (Arts. 486-537) came into effect. A brief summary is given here of some of its distinctive features.

The Code provides for both institutional and ad hoc arbitration, according to institutional rules or the provisions of the Code, respectively. According to Art. 487 CCP, all civil law disputes may be submitted to arbitration with a number of specified exceptions relating to civil status and immovables. Disputes in which one party is the State or a municipal institution are also excluded.

The arbitration agreement shall be in writing in a form which expresses the will of the parties to submit the dispute to arbitration (Art. 492(2)) and provision is made for the separability of the arbitral clause if the contract has terminated or is invalid (Art. 493(3)). The validity of the arbitration agreement is subject to Latvian law, unless the parties have agreed otherwise (Art. 494). Art. 495 provides that the arbitral tribunal has the power to decide on its own jurisdiction.

The arbitrator may be of any nationality (Art. 497(2)) and there must always be an odd number of arbitrators (Art. 498(1)). The arbitrator may be challenged for lack of independence or impartiality, or lack of the agreed-upon qualifications (Art. 501). Unless the parties have otherwise agreed, the challenge will be decided under the applicable institutional rules or, in ad hoc arbitration, by the arbitral tribunal or the sole arbitrator (Art. 502).

The arbitral proceedings may be conducted in accordance with institutional rules, procedures agreed upon by the parties, or failing this, as determined by the arbitrators (Art. 506). The language of the proceedings shall be Latvian, unless the parties have agreed otherwise. Art. 512 provides that the hearings shall be closed and the proceedings confidential. If a party fails promptly to object to a violation or omission by the arbitral tribunal of the agreed upon procedure, it waives its right to do so (Art. 525). If the parties agree to a settlement during the arbitral proceedings, their settlement may be recorded in the form of an award, provided that its provisions are not unlawful (Art. 528). At the request of a party, the award may be supplemented, corrected or interpreted by the arbitral tribunal (Art. 530).

A procedure is provided for the execution of the arbitral award. The application for execution may be refused on grounds similar to those found in Art. V of the 1958 New York Convention or Art. 36 of the UNCITRAL Model Law, unless a party has waived the right to rely on such grounds because it did not object during the arbitral proceedings (Art. 536, see also Art. 525 above). If execution is refused, the dispute may be settled by the court or, if the execution has been refused due to procedural errors, re-submitted to arbitration (Art. 537).

MACAO: The arbitration legislation of the territory of Macao has undergone two recent changes. On 15 September 1996, Decree Law no. 29/96/M of

11 June 1996 entered into force, regulating domestic arbitration. This has been followed by Decree Law no. 55/98/M of 23 November 1998 to govern "foreign" commercial arbitration. In its Preamble, the 1998 Decree recognizes the growing importance of arbitration in the settlement of disputes relating to foreign investment and commercial transactions. In conformity with the goal of the UNCITRAL Model Law to unify arbitration law, the Model Law on International Commercial Arbitration has been adopted with only the minimum changes required to implement the Law in the Macao legal system. Thus, the text of the Model Law is virtually unchanged.

SWEDEN: The Swedish Arbitration Act of 1999 (SFS 1999: 116) came into effect on 1 April 1999.[3] The Act repeats a number of provisions of the Arbitration Act 1929 which it replaces along with replacing the Foreign Arbitration Act 1929. It also incorporates many features of the UNCITRAL Model Law. The text of the Act will be reproduced in a future Supplement of the *International Handbook on Commercial Arbitration* with a new National Report by Ulf Franke. In this brief summary, a number of new or special features will be described. The new Arbitration Rules and Rules for Expedited Arbitrations of the Arbitration Institute, and the new Mediation Rules of the Mediation Institute of the Stockholm Chamber of Commerce are reproduced in Part III - A of this Volume, starting on p. 448.

The scope of the Act is defined in Sect. 46 which provides that the Act applies to arbitrations taking place in Sweden irrespective of whether the dispute has an international connection. All matters which may be the subject of a settlement may be arbitrated and, as already seen in the Draft, the domain of arbitration has been specifically expanded in Sect. 1, para. 1 to include a determination on the existence of a particular fact and decisions ruling on the civil law effects of competition law as between parties. An innovation is the second paragraph of Sect. 1 which provides that arbitrators may fill gaps in contracts. Generally speaking, arbitration agreements relating to consumer transactions are only valid if entered into after the dispute has arisen (Sect. 6, para. 1).

The jurisdiction of the arbitral tribunal is regulated in a number of Sections. The principle of competence-competence is confirmed in Sect. 2, para. 1. This same paragraph also provides that this does not prevent a party, pending the arbitration, from requesting a decision on jurisdiction from the court, a possibility not found, e.g., in the Model Law. A party shall forfeit his right to invoke the arbitration agreement in court proceedings if it has opposed a

3. A brief description of the Draft Arbitration Act, circulated by the Swedish Government in 1994, is published in Yearbook XXI (1996) pp. 382-384.

request to arbitrate, failed to appoint an arbitrator in due time or failed to pay its share of the advance for the arbitrator's fees (Sect. 5). On the other hand, a party does not waive its right to object to the jurisdiction of the arbitral tribunal solely by having appointed an arbitrator (Sect. 34, para. 2). Should the arbitral tribunal find that it does not have jurisdiction, this decision shall take the form of an award (Sect. 27, para. 1). Such an award may be amended, in whole or in part, by the court (Sect. 36, para. 1).

Sect. 48, para. 1 provides that when an arbitration agreement has an international connection, it shall be governed by the law chosen by the parties, or failing this, the law of the place of arbitration. An arbitrator may be challenged if there are circumstances which diminish confidence in his impartiality and Sect. 8 enumerates a non-exclusive list of such circumstances, such as close relations with a party or persons who may benefit from the outcome of the dispute, or having previously taken a position in the dispute as an expert. As foreseen in the Draft, the challenge is to be decided by the arbitral tribunal (Sect. 10, para. 1), with the possibility to appeal a decision rejecting the challenge to the District Court (Sect. 10, para. 3). Parties may also agree that the challenge will be decided conclusively by an arbitral institution (Sect. 11).

Sect. 18 contains a condition not found in the Model Law, whereby the District Court, when requested to appoint an arbitrator, may reject the request if it "is manifest that the arbitration is not legally permissible", e.g., because of the invalidity of the arbitration agreement or the non-arbitrability of the subject matter.

As was the case under the former law, and in the Draft, the Act does not contain any provision on the law to be applied by the arbitrators to the substance of the dispute. However, a new power granted to the arbitral tribunal in Sect. 25, para. 4 is the power to order interim measures of protection, subject to contrary agreement by the parties. Also new is the regulation in Sect. 30, para. 1 of truncated tribunals, whereby if, without valid cause, an arbitrator fails to participate in the determination of an issue, the remaining arbitrators are still allowed to rule on the matter. Also, if a majority cannot be obtained, the opinion of the chairman shall prevail (Sect. 30, para. 2).

An entire chapter of the Act is devoted to the regulation of the costs of arbitration. Two distinctive features of this chapter are, first, the provision that if the arbitrators make an award stating that they lack jurisdiction, the party which did not request the arbitration will not be liable for the compensation of the arbitrators, unless there are special circumstances which require it (Sect. 37, para. 1), and second, that the arbitrators may not withhold the award pending compensation (Sect. 40).

Enforcement of a Swedish award is granted by the execution authority which makes a prima facie determination that the award may be executed. This procedure is regulated by the Enforcement Procedure Code, rather than in the Arbitration Act. The award may be challenged due to absolute or relative invalidity. The award is absolutely invalid (1) if it determines issues which according to Swedish law are not arbitrable; (2) the award or its making were incompatible with the basic principles of the Swedish legal system; or (3) if it does not meet the requirements regarding form and signatures (Sect. 33). It may be held to be invalid if (1) there is no valid arbitration agreement; (2) the arbitrators have exceeded their mandate, which includes exceeding the time limit for making the award; (3) the arbitral proceedings should not have taken place in Sweden; (4) the arbitral tribunal has been improperly constituted; (5) an arbitrator was not capable of being an arbitrator or a ground for challenge existed; or (6) an irregularity in the proceedings occurred which probably influenced the outcome of the case (Sect. 34, para. 1). Setting aside on all or some of these grounds of relative invalidity may be excluded by an express written agreement if both parties to the arbitration are foreign (Sect. 51, para. 1). The grounds for absolute invalidity may not be excluded and there is no time limit for raising them. When such an exclusion has been agreed upon, the award shall be enforced under the regime for foreign awards (Sect. 51, para. 2). Sect. 54 contains the grounds on which enforcement of a foreign award shall be refused; these grounds reproduce the grounds for refusal provided in the New York Convention with the addition that enforcement shall be refused if the parties to the arbitration agreement were not properly represented.

TAIWAN: The new Taiwan Arbitration Act 1998 was promulgated on 24 June 1998 and came into force six months later on 24 December 1998. It contains a number of provisions closely resembling the UNCITRAL Model Law as well as provisions which are specific to Taiwan.

The new law applies to arbitration without being limited to commercial disputes as was the case in the past, and is limited in Art. 1(1) to disputes which can be settled by arbitration according to law. There are specific provisions regarding the persons who may or may not be arbitrators. Arbitrators are required to be judges, district attorneys, prosecutors or persons with relevant professional qualifications (Art. 6) and are subject to a requirement to be trained or attend seminars on arbitration to be organized by the Ministry of Justice (Art. 8). Arbitrators may be challenged if they do not possess the qualifications agreed upon by the parties or if they have been in the employ or an agent of a party or his agent or due to other impediments specified in the Code of Civil Procedure (Arts. 15 and 16). The challenge is to be decided in first instance by the arbitral tribunal and may be appealed to the court. The challenge of a sole arbitrator is to be decided by the court (Art. 17).

If the parties have not agreed on the regulation governing the arbitral proceedings, they are covered by the Act, supplemented by the Code of Civil Procedure and other procedural laws (Art. 20). The service of documents during the arbitral proceedings shall be done according to the relevant provisions in the Code of Civil Procedure (Art. 28).

The arbitral tribunal may decide as *amiables compositeurs* if expressly empowered to do so by the parties (Art. 31), but no conflict rules are provided regarding the applicable law to the substance of the dispute. Art. 36 provides for expedited proceedings either according to the provisions of the Code of Civil Procedure or the rules of an arbitral institution.

Parties may request interim measures of protection from the court (Art. 39) which may also order the parties to commence arbitration (Art. 39). The Act does not contain a provision empowering arbitrators to order interim measures.

Foreign arbitral awards, which are classified as awards made outside of Taiwan or within Taiwan in accordance with foreign law (Art. 47), may be enforced in Taiwan on the basis of reciprocity, subject to requirements similar to those found in the New York Convention and the Model Law (Arts. 48 and 49).

VENEZUELA: A new law on arbitration, the Commercial Arbitration Law, incorporating many features of the UNCITRAL Model Law, came into effect in Venezuela on 7 April 1998. An English translation of the new Law will be published in a coming supplement of the *International Handbook on Commercial Arbitration* in anticipation of a National Report Venezuela. The salient features of the new Law, in particular those deviating from the Model Law, are briefly described below.

The Law applies to both domestic and international commercial arbitration (Art. 1). The domain of arbitration is both defined and limited in Art. 3 which provides that any dispute which may be freely settled by the parties may be arbitrated, but stipulates a number of restrictions including matters which would be in violation of public policy and matters in which the State or legal persons of public law are exercising their *imperium*. Arbitration agreements concluded by companies in which the Republic, a state or municipality, or a public institution has more than a fifty percent interest must be approved by the organ authorized by their statute and by the appropriate Ministry (Art. 4).

The arbitration agreement must be in writing and may be incorporated by reference (Art. 6, para. 1). The arbitration agreement must be in a form which demonstrates the parties' desire to submit to arbitration, without further stipulation in the Law regarding the medium, i.e., telegrams, telexes, telefaxes, etc. In adhesion contracts and standard contracts (*contratos normalizados*), the agreement to submit the contract to arbitration must, however, be "express and independent" (Art. 6, para. 2). Art. 5, para. 2 expressly provides that by agreeing to arbitration, the parties have renounced the possibility of bringing their dispute before the courts.

The law makes provision in Chapters II and III for institutional and ad hoc arbitration respectively. Chapter II sets out the requirements for the creation of arbitral institutions, such as the adoption of rules and a procedure for creating a list of arbitrators. When parties agree to institutional arbitration, the proceedings will be governed by the rules of the institution, including any challenge procedure (Art. 12). Chapter III provides fall-back provisions for constituting the arbitral tribunal when the parties have not submitted their arbitration to the rules of an institution. There shall be an uneven number of arbitrators and the arbitrators must accept their appointment in writing within ten days of notification (Arts. 15-17).

Arbitrators may be challenged on the grounds established in the Code of Civil Procedure for challenge (Art. 35), thus not adopting the general formula of the Model Law, and the challenge must be raised within five days of when a party becomes aware of the ground for challenge. Likewise, the arbitrator must reply within five days (Art. 36). If the remaining two arbitrators cannot agree or a sole arbitrator has been challenged, the court shall decide (Art. 38). If the majority, or all of the arbitrators have been successfully challenged, the mandate of the arbitral tribunal is terminated and the parties are free to bring their dispute before the court or to re-initiate arbitral proceedings (Art. 39).

Chapter IV regulates the arbitral procedure, unless the parties have chosen to arbitrate under the rules of an arbitral institution. Provision is made for the establishment of the arbitrators' fees and deposits by the parties (Arts. 19-21). If the parties have not provided a time limit for making the award, it shall be six months, subject to extension (Art. 22). The arbitral tribunal may decide on its own jurisdiction, and objections to jurisdiction must be raised within five days of the first hearing (Art. 25). The new Law does not contain a conflict rule regarding the law to be applied by the arbitrators to the substance of the dispute, but the arbitrators shall decide according to provisions of law (*disposiciones de derecho*), unless authorized to decide as *amiables compositeurs (equidad)* and must always take account of the provisions of the contract and trade usages (Art. 8). The award may be interpreted, corrected or completed ex officio by the arbitrators or at the request of one of the parties (Art. 32), thus varying from the Model Law which requires the consent of both parties to interpretation (Art. 33(1) Model Law). When the arbitrators have completed their mandate, the chairman of the tribunal will make a final settlement of the fees, deposits, etc. (Art. 34).

Chapter VI imposes various obligations on the arbitrators. Art. 41 requires that an arbitrator who misses two sessions without good cause or four sessions with good cause will be removed and forfeit a portion of his fee as determined by the arbitral tribunal. Art. 42 imposes a duty of confidentiality on the arbitrators.

The action for setting aside must be requested within five days of the notification of the award (Art. 43). The grounds for setting aside closely follow the Model Law with several exceptions. The invalidity of the arbitration agreement is not specifically mentioned as a ground for setting aside, and the ground that the award has been set aside or suspended by the competent authorities has been added (Art. 44).

Enforcement of an award, whether domestic or foreign, may only be refused on essentially the same grounds as those set out in Art. V of the 1958 New York Convention, Art. 5 of the 1975 Panama Convention and Art. 36 of the Model Law.

Part V

A. Court Decisions on the New York Convention 1958

NEW YORK CONVENTION OF 1958

INTRODUCTION

The principal multilateral arbitration conventions are reported on in Part V – A through V – D of the Yearbook. Part V – A contains the reporting on the New York Convention of 1958. Part V – B reports on the European (Geneva) Convention of 1961 and Part V – C reports on the Washington (ICSID) Convention of 1965. Part V – D on the Inter-American (Panama) Convention of 1975 appeared for the first time in Yearbook XXII (1997).

In 1998, the New York Convention celebrated its 40th anniversary. This event was marked by ICCA's International Arbitration Congress held in Paris on 3-6 May. The Congress proceedings have been published as *ICCA's Congress Series no. 9*. This was followed by the celebration organized on 10 June by UNCITRAL at the United Nations headquarters in New York of "New York Convention Day". The proceedings of this Conference, entitled *Enforcing Arbitration Awards under the New York Convention: Experiences and Prospects*, have been published by the United Nations (see Bibliography under I. General, 2. Congresses).

The reporting on the New York Convention in this Volume comprises 42 decisions rendered in 13 countries and two jurisdictions (Court of Justice of the European Communities and the Full Tribunal of the Iran-United States Claims Tribunal), bringing the total to 829 decisions from 44 countries and two jurisdictions. According to the latest figures reported by the Treaty Section of the United Nations, there are, as of 1 October 1999, 121 Contracting States (and 26 extensions) to the New York Convention.

In addition to publishing court decisions and up-to-date lists of Contracting States to these Conventions, the Yearbook also includes regularly updated Commentaries. An updated version of the "Commentary on the European Convention on International Commercial Arbitration" by Mr. Dominique Hascher was published in Volume XX (1995). Yearbook XVIII (1993) contains in Part V – C the contribution by Dr. Aron Broches, "Convention on the Settlement of Investment Disputes Between States and Nationals of Other States of 1965, Explanatory Notes and Survey of its Application".

A Consolidated Commentary on the New York Convention (Volume XX (1995) – Volume XXI (1996)) by the General Editor was published in Yearbook XXI (1996). **The next Consolidated Commentary on the New**

York Convention (Volume XXII (1997) - Volume XXIV (1999)) will be published as Volume XXIVb of the Yearbook.

The reporting of the court decisions in Part V - A includes the heading "Commentary Cases". This heading links the court decisions to the numbered sections of the Consolidated Commentary on the New York Convention, by indicating where portions of the court decision will be discussed in the Commentary. For example, **[1]-[5] = ¶ 101** indicates that paragraphs [1] through [5] of the court decision are discussed in section 101 of the Commentary.

In order to present the widely varied material contained in the Yearbook in a consistent manner, all decisions have been translated into English. The headings in the excerpts in some cases have been slightly modified or headings may have been added or deleted. The paragraphs of the excerpts are numbered to facilitate consultation and reference to the Commentary. In addition, minor editorial changes have been made in the texts which in no way affect the substance of the decision.

The extraordinary number of court decisions on the New York Convention reported in this Volume is largely a result of the willing support and assistance of the many readers who drew our attention to, or sent copies of, new court decisions on the New York Convention. Our thanks go to all of them for their invaluable assistance. Their names are listed below according to the country on which they have informed us.

Australia:	Michael Marks Cohen (New York)
Belgium:	André Faurès (Brussels)
	Bernard Hanotiau (Brussels)
Bermuda:	UNCITRAL (Vienna)
France:	Emmanuel Gaillard (Paris)
Germany:	Franz Hubert Timmermann (Hamburg)
Hong Kong:	Neil Kaplan (Hong Kong)
India:	H.C. Johari (Calcutta)
	Fali Nariman (New Delhi)
Italy:	Mauro Ferrante (Rome)
Luxembourg:	Patrick Kinsch (Luxembourg City)
Netherlands:	Jacomijn van Haersolte-van Hof (Rotterdam)
United Kingdom:	Michael Marks Cohen (New York)
	V.V. Veeder, QC (London)
United States:	American Arbitration Association (New York)
	Barry Garfinkel (New York)
	Michael Marks Cohen (New York)
	Christopher Paparella (New York)

INTRODUCTION

Lucy Reed (New York)
Nancy Turck (London)

The General Editor would like to call upon readers to assist him by sending copies of relevant court decisions, published or unpublished, for reporting in the forthcoming volumes of the Yearbook. Copies can be sent to either of the addresses below.

ICCA Publications
c/o International Bureau of the
Permanent Court of Arbitration
Carnegieplein 2
2517 KJ The Hague, The Netherlands
E-mail: icca@pca-cpa.org

Prof. Dr. Albert Jan van den Berg
c/o Freshfields
Coengebouw, 6th floor
Kabelweg 37
1014 BA Amsterdam
and as of 1 February 2000:
Gebouw Minerva
Appollolaan 151
1077 AR Amsterdam
The Netherlands
E-mail: ajvandenberg@freshfields.com

NEW YORK CONVENTION OF 1958
LIST OF CONTRACTING STATES

(as of 1 October 1999)[1]

State	*Ratification, Accession (a), Succession (s)*	*Reservation*[2]
Algeria	7 Feb. 1989a	1 - 2
American Samoa[3]	*3 Nov. 1970*	*1 - 2*
Antigua and Barbuda	2 Feb. 1989a	1 - 2
Argentina[4]	14 Mar. 1989	1 - 2
Armenia	29 Dec. 1997a	1 - 2
Australia	26 Mar. 1975a	–
Australian Antartic Territory[5]	*26 Mar. 1975a*	–
Austria	2 May 1961a	–
Bahrain	6 Apr. 1988a	1 - 2
Bangladesh	6 May 1992a	–
Barbados	16 Mar. 1993a	1 - 2
Belarus[6]	15 Nov. 1960	1

1. This list is compiled by the Editorial Staff of the *Yearbook Commercial Arbitration*, in consultation with the United Nations Treaty Section and UNCITRAL. Countries that have acceded to the Convention during the course of 1998-1999 are indicated in **boldface type**. Extensions are indicated in *italics*.
2. Two reservations are contained in Art. I(3). The 1st reservation is the so-called "reciprocity reservation" (at present made by 91 States including extensions). On 23 April 1993, Switzerland withdrew its reciprocity reservation. The 2nd is the so-called "commercial reservation" (at present made by 52 States including extensions).
3. Extension made by the United States of America upon acceding to the Convention.
4. Argentina declared that the present Convention should be construed in accordance with the principles and rules of the National Constitution in force or with those resulting from reforms mandated by the Constitution.
5. Extension made by Australia upon acceding to the Convention.
6. With regard to awards made in the territory of non-Contracting States, State will apply the Convention only to the extent to which these States grant reciprocal treatment.

Belgium	18 Aug. 1975	1
Belize[7]	*24 Feb. 1981*	*1*
Benin	16 May 1974a	–
Bermuda[7]	*12 Feb. 1980*	*1*
Bolivia	28 Apr. 1995a	–
Bosnia and Herzegovina[8]	1 Sep. 1993s	1 - 2
Botswana	20 Dec. 1971a	1 - 2
Brunei Darussalam	25 July 1996a	1
Bulgaria[6]	10 Oct. 1961	1
Burkina Faso	23 Mar. 1987a	–
Cambodia	5 Jan. 1960a	–
Cameroon	19 Feb. 1988a	–
Canada[9]	12 May 1986	2
Canton Island[3]	*3 Nov. 1970*	*1 - 2*
Cayman Islands[7]	*24 Feb. 1981*	*1*
Central African Republic	15 Oct. 1962a	1 - 2
Chile	4 Sep. 1975a	–
China, PR[10]	22 Jan. 1987a	1 - 2
Christmas Island[5]	*26 Mar. 1975a*	–
Cocos (Keeling) Island[5]	*26 Mar. 1975a*	–
Colombia[11]	25 Sep. 1979a	–
Comoro Islands[12]	*26 June 1959*	*1*
Costa Rica	26 Oct. 1987	–
Côte d'Ivoire	1 Feb. 1991a	–
Croatia[8]	26 July 1993s	1 - 2
Cuba[6]	30 Dec. 1974a	1 - 2
Cyprus	29 Dec. 1980a	1 - 2

7. Extension made by the United Kingdom on the date indicated in the List.
8. State will apply the Convention only to those arbitral awards which were adopted after the coming of the Convention into effect.
9. The commercial reservation does not apply to the province of Quebec.
10. On 6 June 1997 the Government of China made the following declaration:

    "The Convention will be applied in the Hong Kong Special Administrative Region only to the recognition and enforcement of awards made in the territory of another Contracting State."

11. On 20 November 1990, Law no. 39 of 1990 was promulgated implementing the Convention in Colombia. This law fills a lacunae created by the decision of 6 October 1988, by which the Supreme Court declared the unconstitutionality of the Law no. 37 of 1979, implementing the New York Convention in Colombia.
12. Extension made by France on the date indicated in the List.

Czech Republic[13]	30 Sep.	1993s	1
Denmark	22 Dec.	1972a	1 - 2
Djibouti	14 June	1983s	–
Dominica	28 Oct.	1988a	–
Ecuador	3 Jan.	1962	1 - 2
Egypt	9 Mar.	1959a	–
Enderberry Island[3]	*3 Nov.*	*1970*	*1 - 2*
El Salvador	**26 Feb.**	**1998**	**–**
Estonia	30 Aug.	1993a	–
Faeroe Islands[14]	*10 Feb.*	*1976*	*1 - 2*
Finland	19 Jan.	1962	–
France	26 June	1959	1
French Polynesia[12]	*26 June*	*1959*	*1*
Georgia	2 June	1994a	–
Germany[15]	30 June	1961	1
	(GDR: 20 Feb.	1975a)	
Ghana	9 Apr.	1968a	–
Gibraltar[7]	*24 Sep.*	*1975*	*1*
Greece	16 July	1962a	1 - 2
Greenland[14]	*10 Feb.*	*1976*	*1 - 2*
Guam[3]	*3 Nov.*	*1970*	*1 - 2*
Guatemala	21 Mar.	1984a	1 - 2
Guernsey[7]	*19 Apr.*	*1985*	*1*
Guinea	23 Jan.	1991a	–
Haiti	5 Dec.	1983a	–
Holy See	14 May	1975a	1 - 2
Hong Kong[16]	*21 Apr.*	*1977*	*1*
Hungary	5 Mar.	1962a	1 - 2
India	13 July	1960	1 - 2
Indonesia	7 Oct.	1981a	1 - 2
Ireland	12 May	1981a	1
Isle of Man[7]	*23 May*	*1979*	*1*

13. The Convention was signed by the former *Czechoslovakia* on 3 October 1958 and an instrument of ratification was deposited on 10 July 1959. Czechoslovakia made the 1st reservation and declared that with regard to awards made in the territory of non-contracting States, State will apply the Convention only to the extent to which these States grant reciprocal treatment. On 28 May 1993, *Slovakia* and, on 30 September 1993, the *Czech Republic* deposited instruments of succession.
14. Extension made by Denmark on the date indicated in the List.
15. Extension made by FR Germany to West Berlin, 30 June 1961.
16. Extension made by PR China with effect from 1 July 1997. See fn. 10.

Israel	5 Jan. 1959	–
Italy	31 Jan. 1969a	–
Japan	20 June 1961a	1
Jordan	15 Nov. 1979	–
Kazakstan	20 Nov. 1995	–
Kenya	10 Feb. 1989a	1
Korea	8 Feb. 1973a	1 - 2
Kuwait	28 Apr. 1978a	1
Kyrgyszstan	18 Dec. 1996	–
Laos People's Democratic Republic	**17 June 1998a**	**–**
Latvia	14 Apr. 1992a	–
Lesotho	13 June 1989a	–
Lithuania[6]	14 Mar. 1995a	1 - 2
Luxembourg	9 Sep. 1983	1
Madagascar	16 July 1962a	1 - 2
Malaysia	5 Nov. 1985a	1 - 2
Mali	8 Sep. 1994a	–
Mauritania	30 Jan. 1997	–
Mauritius	19 June 1996	1 - 2
Mexico	14 Apr. 1971a	–
Moldova[8]	**18 Sep. 1998a**	**1**
Monaco	2 June 1982	1 - 2
Mongolia	24 Oct. 1994a	1 - 2
Morocco	12 Feb. 1959a	1
Mozambique[17]	**11 June 1998a**	**–**
Nepal	**4 Mar. 1998a**	**1 - 2**
Netherlands	24 Apr. 1964	1
Netherlands Antilles[18]	*24 Apr. 1964*	*1*
New Caledonia[12]	*26 June 1959*	*1*
New Zealand	6 Jan. 1983a	1
Niger	14 Oct. 1964a	–
Nigeria	17 Mar. 1970a	1 - 2
Norfolk Island[5]	*26 Mar. 1975*	–
Norway[19]	14 Mar. 1961a	1

17. The Republic of Mozambique reserves the right to enforce the Convention on the basis of reciprocity, where the arbitral awards have been pronounced in the territory of another Contracting State.
18. Extension made by The Netherlands on the date indicated in the List.
19. State will not apply the Convention to differences where the subject matter of the proceedings is immovable property situated in the State, or a right in or to such property.

Oman	**25 Feb.**	**1999a**	–
Panama	10 Oct.	1984a	–
Paraguay	5 Oct.	1997a	–
Peru	7 July	1988a	–
Philippines	6 July	1967	1 - 2
Poland[20]	3 Oct.	1961	1 - 2
Portugal	18 Oct.	1994a	1
Puerto Rico[3]	*3 Nov.*	*1970*	*1 - 2*
Romania[6]	13 Sep.	1961a	1 - 2
Russian Federation[6,21]	24 Aug.	1960	1
San Marino	17 May	1979a	–
Saudi Arabia	19 Apr.	1994a	1
Senegal	17 Oct.	1994a	–
Singapore	21 Aug.	1986a	1
Slovak Republic[13]	28 May	1993s	1
Slovenia[8]	6 July	1992s	1 - 2
South Africa	3 May	1976a	–
Spain	12 May	1977a	–
Sri Lanka	9 Apr.	1962	–
St. Pierre et Miquelon[12]	*26 June*	*1959*	*1*
Sweden	28 Jan.	1972	–
Surinam[22]	24 Apr.	1964	1
Switzerland[2]	1 June	1965	–
Syrian Arab Republic	9 Mar.	1959a	–
Tanzania, United Republic of	13 Oct.	1964a	1
Thailand	21 Dec.	1959a	–
The former Yugoslav Republic of Macedonia[8]	10 Mar.	1994s	1 - 2
Trinidad and Tobago	14 Feb.	1966a	1 - 2
Tunisia	17 July	1967a	1 - 2
Turkey	2 July	1992a	1 - 2

20. Poland made both reservations when signing the Convention. However, the Document of Ratification does not repeat the reservation and the Polish Government officially recognizes that Poland is bound by the Convention in its entirety.
21. The Russian Federation continues, as from 24 December 1991, the membership of the former Union of Soviet Socialist Republics (USSR) in the United Nations and maintains, as from that date, full responsibility for all the rights and obligations of the USSR under the Charter of the United Nations and multilateral treaties deposited with the Secretary-General.
22. On 25 November 1975, Surinam became independent. By letter of 29 November 1975, of the then Prime Minister, to the Secretary General of the U.N., Surinam has declared that it will remain bound to the Treaties and Conventions which The Netherlands has made applicable.

Uganda	12 Feb. 1992a	1
Ukraine[6]	10 Oct. 1960	1
United Kingdom	24 Sep. 1975a	1
United States of America	30 Sep. 1970a	1 - 2
Uruguay	30 Mar. 1983a	–
Uzbekistan[6]	7 Feb. 1996a	–
Venezuela	8 Feb. 1995	1 - 2
Vietnam[6]	12 Sep. 1995	1 - 2
Virgin Islands[3]	*3 Nov. 1970*	*1 - 2*
Wake Island[3]	*3 Nov. 1970*	*1 - 2*
Wallis and Futuna Islands[12]	*26 June 1959*	*1*
Yugoslavia[8]	26 Feb. 1982a	1 - 2
Zimbabwe	29 Sep. 1994a	–

AUSTRALIA

Accession: 26 March 1977
No Reservations

15. Supreme Court, New South Wales, Commercial Division, 26 March 1998

Parties:	Appellant: American Diagnostica, Inc. (US) Appellees: (1) Gradipore Ltd. (Australia); (2) Centerchem, Inc. (nationality not indicated)
Published in:	(1998) 44 New South Wales Law Review, pp. 312-342
Articles:	General reference to Convention
Subject matters:	– agreement cannot displace compulsory application of local arbitration law – UNCITRAL Arbitration Rules are exclusion agreement? (no) – arbitration agreement by party from "Convention country" not outside scope of New South Wales Commercial Arbitration Act 1984
Commentary Cases:	[4]-[30] = ¶ 102 (by implication); [8]-[12] = ¶ 216; [31]-[44] = ¶ 202 + ¶ 514 (by implication)

Facts

The facts of this case are recounted in more detail in the decision of the United States District Court, Southern District of New York, of 15 February 1996, reported in Yearbook XXII (1997) pp. 944-947 as US no. 220.

A distribution agreement between American Diagnostica, Inc. and Gradipore for the distribution of a medical diagnostic test, known as Lupo-Test, contained an arbitration agreement requiring disputes to be determined by arbitration in Sidney, Australia. Following the expiry of the agreement,

American Diagnostica developed and marketed its own test product, while Gradipore appointed Centerchem, Inc. as distributor of its products. The products competed in the United States market. Diagnostica instituted court proceedings in the United States District Court, Southern District of New York alleging trade mark and trade dress infringement. Centerchem and Gradipore (referred to below collectively as Gradipore) succeeded in their motion to stay these proceedings and compel arbitration (see US no. 220 mentioned above).

The parties then renegotiated the terms of their arbitration agreement. The original agreement referred to arbitration "pursuant to the rules of the Australian American Arbitration Agreement in effect at that time or if there shall be no such Agreement in effect then in accordance with the Arbitration Act current in New South Wales, Australia". As apparently there was nothing in effect answering the description of the rules of the Australian American Arbitration Agreement, at the suggestion of Gradipore, the parties eventually agreed to the UNCITRAL Arbitration Rules without any further reference to the New South Wales Commercial Arbitration Act 1984 (CAA 1984).

The sole arbitrator was appointed and on 20 November 1997 he issued an interim award in favor of Gradipore. American Diagnostica applied to the Supreme Court of New South Wales for leave to appeal on a question of law pursuant to Sect. 38 CAA 1984. Gradipore argued unsuccessfully that the CAA 1984 did not apply to an arbitration agreement to which a party from a Contracting State to the New York Convention (Convention country) was a party.

The court, per Giles, CJ, further held that although the parties could chose a lex arbitri different from the place of arbitration, they could not exclude the mandatory local procedural rules of the place of arbitration. In selecting the UNCITRAL Arbitration Rules to govern their arbitration the parties had not validly concluded an exclusion agreement to exclude appeal under the CAA 1984. Although the court found that it had jurisdiction to hear the application for leave to appeal under Art. 38 CAA 1984, it rejected the application for leave finding that the requirements of Art. 38 were not fulfilled.

Excerpt

[1] After recounting the details of the revision of the arbitration agreement the court stated: "I do not think it matters whether there was reference to the [CAA 1984 (referred to here as the Act)] in connection with agreement on the UNCITRAL Arbitration Rules. It became quite clear, and was accepted by Gradipore, that whatever passed between the attorneys at the meeting was

subject to referral to their clients, and that what was referred to American Diagnostica and Gradipore and agreed to by them was the 'understandings' recorded in the subsequent letters. There was no agreement between American Diagnostica and Gradipore in the terms that the UNCITRAL Arbitration Rules be used 'rather than the New South Wales Commercial Arbitration Act 1984 as amended, including its rules and procedure'. There was agreement that the UNCITRAL Arbitration Rules be adopted 'as the rules governing the arbitration', and later in these reasons I will come to the significance of that agreement.

(....)

[2] "American Diagnostica applied pursuant to Sect. 38 of the Commercial Arbitration Act 1984....[1] Sect. 40 referred to in 38(4)(b) deals with exclusion agreements whereby the right of appeal in relation to an award may be excluded.... [A]n exclusion agreement must be in writing, in some circumstances a purported agreement will be of no effect, and it is expressly provided that Sect. 38 has effect unless there is an exclusion agreement 'notwithstanding anything in any agreement purporting ... to prohibit or restrict access to the Supreme Court ... [or] to restrict the jurisdiction of the Supreme Court'.

[3] "There can be appeal only on a question or questions of law arising out of the interim award. Since Gradipore did not consent to the appeal, leave is necessary: hence American Diagnostica's application. Leave may not be granted unless Sect. 38(5) is satisfied. The issues in the application included whether the errors on the part of the arbitrator alleged by American Diagnostica gave rise

1. Sect. 38 of the New South Wales Commercial Arbitration Act 1984 reads in relevant part:

"(....)

(2) Subject to subsection (4), an appeal shall lie to the Supreme Court on any question of law arising out of an award.

(....)

(4) An appeal under subsection (2) may be brought by any of the parties to an arbitration agreement –

(a) with the consent of all parties to the arbitration agreement; or

(b) subject to section 40, with the leave of the Supreme Court.

(5) The Supreme Court shall not grant leave under subsection (4)(b) unless it considers that:

(a) having regard to all the circumstances, the determination of the question of law concerned could substantially affect the rights of one or more parties to the arbitration agreement; and

(b) there is:

(i) a manifest error of law on the face of the award; or

(ii) strong evidence that the arbitrator or umpire made an error of law and that the determination of the question may add, or may be likely to add, substantially to the certainty of commercial law.

(....)"

to questions of law arising out of the award and, if they did, whether Sect. 38(5) was satisfied. But Gradipore also contended: (a) that leave to appeal could not be granted because the Act does not apply to the arbitration at all; (b) alternatively that leave to appeal could not be granted because there was an exclusion agreement; (c) alternatively again, that leave to appeal should not be granted (strictly, that the application for leave to appeal should be permanently stayed) on forum non conveniens grounds; (d) that American Diagnostica's application for leave to appeal was out of time."

I. DOES THE ACT APPLY TO THE ARBITRATION?

[4] "By Sect. 3(2)(a) of the Act it applies to '... an arbitration agreement ... and to an arbitration under such an agreement'. The definition of 'arbitration agreement' in Sect. 4(1) is '... an agreement in writing to refer present or future disputes to arbitration'.... Within these general topics are a diverse collection of provisions, many stated to apply subject to the arbitration agreement, unless a contrary intention is expressed in the arbitration agreement, or unless it is otherwise agreed in writing by the parties to the arbitration agreement, but some stated to apply notwithstanding any agreement to the contrary between the parties.... The Act does not set out procedures for the conduct of an arbitration, but provides by Sect. 14 that subject to the Act and to the arbitration agreement the arbitrator 'may conduct proceedings under that agreement in such manner as the arbitrator ... thinks fit'.

[5] "At the heart of the application of the Act is the arbitration agreement. But the Act will not apply to any and every arbitration agreement in the world: an arbitration agreement between two Ruritanian subjects, made in Ruritania concerning a Ruritanian dispute and with the conduct of the arbitration in Ruritania, could hardly be subjected to its provisions. The reach of the Act is as found in its terms, but provided that a sufficient nexus appears between the Act operating as so found and the territory of New South Wales so that there is a valid exercise of the power conferred by Sect. 5 of the Constitution Act 1902 to make laws 'for the peace, welfare and good government of New South Wales': see *Union Steamship Co of Australia Pty Ltd v. King* (1988) 166 CLR 1.

[6] "The arbitration clause in the distribution agreement is an arbitration agreement within the definition in the Act, and as a matter of language the Act applied and applies to it. The evidence did not disclose where the distribution agreement, and so the arbitration agreement, was made. The distribution agreement identifies American Diagnostica as a Connecticut company and Gradipore as a New South Wales company, so sufficient reason can be seen for

the parties' choice of New South Wales law in cl. 19 and the agreement in cl. 18 that any arbitration should take place in Sydney is readily understandable. Even if the default agreement that the referral to arbitration be in accordance with the Arbitration Act current in New South Wales be put aside, the arbitration agreement is not of the Ruritanian kind. It is unnecessary, and unwise, to seek to canvass all criteria by which the reach of the Act might be determined: given the other connections with New South Wales, the fact that the arbitration was to take place in New South Wales and did take place in New South Wales is in my view sufficient to attract the Act's application to the arbitration agreement for the purposes of grant of leave to appeal. Subject to the submissions to which I now come, I did not understand Gradipore to say otherwise.

[7] "Gradipore's contention that leave to appeal could not be granted because the Act does not apply to the arbitration was put in two ways. First, it was submitted that the Act does not apply to the arbitration because the arbitration agreement was international in nature. Secondly, it was submitted that the Act does not apply to the arbitration because of the agreement on the UNCITRAL Arbitration Rules as the rules governing the arbitration in June 1996."

1. An Arbitration Agreement International in Nature

[8] "The submission began by categorising the arbitration agreement as a foreign arbitration. By a foreign arbitration agreement Gradipore meant an arbitration agreement a party to which was domiciled or ordinarily resident in a Convention country, as described in Sect. 7(1)(d) of the International Arbitration Act 1974 (Cth).[2] A Convention country is a country, other than Australia, that is a Contracting State within the meaning of the Convention on the Recognition and Enforcement of Foreign Arbitral Awards adopted in 1958 by the United Nations Conference on International Commercial Arbitration (the Convention) approval to accession to which was given by Sect. 4

2. Sect. 7(1)(d) of the International Arbitration Act 1974 reads:

> "(1) Where:
> (....)
> (d) a party to an arbitration agreement is a person who was, at the time when the agreement was made, domiciled or ordinarily resident in a country that is a Convention country; this section applies to the agreement."

of the International Arbitration Act 1974 (Cth).[3] American Diagnostica was domiciled in Connecticut in the United States of America, and the United States of America is a Contracting State.

[9] "How categorisation as a foreign arbitration agreement then led to the submission's conclusion was unclear. It may have been argued that the Act did not in its own terms apply to a foreign arbitration agreement, but if that was argued I do not accept it. There is nothing to exclude from the application of the Act via Sect. 3(2)(a) and the definition of arbitration agreement - an arbitration agreement a party to which was when the agreement was made, or thereafter, domiciled or ordinarily resident in a Convention country. On the contrary, provisions in the Act reflect an intention that it apply to an arbitration agreement a party to which is domiciled or ordinarily resident outside Australia (see Sects. 11(2), 40(7) and 55(2)),[4] and there is no reason in the terms of the Act to distinguish domicile or residence outside Australia in a Convention country from domicile or residence outside Australia not in a Convention country.

[10] "The submission otherwise seemed to be that because the arbitration was an international arbitration it could not be regarded as a domestic arbitration, and therefore was not subject to the Act. So it was asserted in Gradipore's written submissions that 'Australia does not consider an arbitration under the International Arbitration Act when the parties have opted out of the UNCITRAL Model Law as a domestic arbitration'; that: 'It could never have been the legislative intention that arbitrations, even with their situs in Australia, with an international flavour such as the arbitration in this case, must be regarded as domestic arbitrations under the Commercial Arbitration Acts of the various States and Territories with all of their parochial provisions including applications for leave to appeal against manifest errors of law, (a procedure eschewed by most international arbitral regimes in other jurisdictions), merely because the parties have used Sect. 21 of the International Arbitration Act 1974 (Cth) to opt out of the provisions of the UNCITRAL

---

3. Sect. 4 of the International Arbitration Act 1974 reads:

"Approval is given to accession by Australia to the Convention without any declaration under sub-article 3 of Article I but with a declaration under Article X that the Convention shall extend to all the external Territories other than Papua New Guinea."

4. Sect. 11(2) excludes the application of the provision for replacement of an arbitrator or umpire removed by the court when all parties are not ordinarily resident or domiciled in Australia; Sect. 40(7) defines a "domestic arbitration agreement" for the purposes of an exclusion agreement; and Sect. 55(2) limits the effect of *Scott v. Avery* clauses to arbitration agreements to which all the parties are domiciled or ordinarily resident in Australia.

Model Law'; and that 'The recognition of international awards and any challenge thereto, should be dealt with by legislation concerning such matters and not by legislation dealing with domestic arbitrations'.

[11] "I endeavoured in the course of oral submissions to identify the reasoning to the submission's conclusion. The result was inconsistencies and non sequiturs. I have endeavoured thereafter to reconcile all that was said and understand the reasoning: I have not been able to do so. Assuming an international arbitration, the International Arbitration Act 1974 (Cth) gives the UNCITRAL Model Law the force of law in Australia (Sect. 16(1)), whereby the arbitration may be in accordance with the Model Law. It seemed to be said that it is the intention of the Federal legislature that, in that event, the Act cannot apply to the arbitration. But that the intention takes effect because of inconsistency between the Federal legislation and the State legislation was emphatically eschewed, it was accepted that nothing in the International Arbitration Act 1974 (Cth) in terms so provides, and in the end the argument seemed to be that the Act does not apply to an international arbitration simply because it is an international arbitration (with further reference to the description of a foreign arbitration agreement in Sect. 7(1)(d) of that Act). Even at this point the submission's conclusion is reached by a leap of faith rather than a process of reasoning.

[12] "But the International Arbitration Act 1974 (Cth) provides that the Model Law does not apply in relation to the settlement of a dispute if the parties agree that the dispute is to be settled otherwise than in accordance with the Model Law (Sect. 21). Whatever other agreement is to be found in cl. 18 of the distribution agreement and the subsequent adoption of the UNCITRAL Arbitration Rules, there was clearly agreement that disputes falling within the arbitration clause were to be settled otherwise than in accordance with the Model Law. The arbitration was not to be in accordance with the Model Law, the optional provisions of the International Arbitration Act 1974 (Cth) were not taken up (Sects. 21-23), and the proposition that the Act does not apply to the arbitration because it is an international arbitration is not maintainable. The application of the Act must be found from its terms, properly construed and with regard to the extent of the legislative power of the Parliament of New South Wales, and absent any question of inconsistency with the terms or effect of the International Arbitration Act 1974 (Cth) its application so arrived at is not negated because an arbitration has an international flavour or because an advocate describes the provisions of the Act as parochial."

2. *Agreement on the UNCITRAL Arbitration Rules*

[13] "The submission was put in three ways: that there was a variation to the arbitration clause whereby the UNCITRAL Arbitration Rules applied to the exclusion of the Act; that there was an election by American Diagnostica that the Act would not apply to the arbitration and that there 'was an implied rejection' of the Act. Can the Act, if otherwise applying to the arbitration, be excluded by act of the parties?

[14] "In *Naviera Amazonica Peruana SA v. Compania Internacional de Seguros del Peru* [1988] 1 Lloyd's Rep. 116, Kerr LJ,[5] with whom Russell LJ and Sir Denys Buckley agreed, identified three systems of law potentially relevant to an arbitration with a foreign element, namely the law governing the substantive contract, the law governing the agreement to arbitrate and the performance of that agreement, and the law governing the conduct of the arbitration. As to the law governing the conduct of the arbitration, his Lordship said (at 119):

> 'English law does not recognise the concept of a "de-localised" arbitration ... (see *Dicey & Morris* (at 541, 542)) or of "arbitral procedures floating in the trans national firmament, unconnected with any municipal system of law" (*Bank Mellat v. Helliniki Techniki SA* [1984] QB 291 at 301 (Court of Appeal)). Accordingly, every arbitration must have a "seat" or locus arbitri or forum which subjects its procedural rules to the municipal law which is there in force.'

[15] "The seat of the arbitration is not necessarily where it is held, although where the parties have failed to choose the law governing the conduct of the arbitration it will prima facie be the law of the country in which the arbitration is held because that is the country most closely connected with the proceedings: see *James Miller & Partners Ltd v. Whitworth Street Estates (Manchester) Ltd* [1970] AC 583 at 607, 609, 616; *Black Clawson International Ltd v. Papierwerke Waldhof-Aschaffenburg AG* [1981] 2 Lloyd's Rep. 446 at 453-454; *Bank Mellat v. Helliniki Techniki SA* [1984] GB 291 at 301.

[16] "Although the law governing the conduct of the arbitration (the lex arbitri) is said to be concerned only with procedural matters, it goes beyond, for example, the production of documents or the order of witnesses. The appointment, removal, and replacement of arbitrators, time-limits, interim relief, consolidation of arbitrations, representation before the arbitrator, the form and validity of the award, and the finality of the award, are amongst the

5. Reported in Yearbook XIII (1988) pp. 156-164.

matters which can fall within the lex arbitri. The de-localisation theory, and what it means, have been much debated: see, eg, the series J. Paulsson, 'Arbitration Unbound: Award Detached from the Law of its Country of Origin' (1981) 30 ICLQ 358; W.W. Park, 'The Lex Loci Arbitri and International Commercial Arbitration' (1983) 32 ICLQ 25; J. Paulsson, 'Delocalisation of International Commercial Arbitration: When and Why it Matters' (1983) 32 ICLQ 53. But in principle de-localisation 'is only possible if the local rules permit it': A. Redfern and M. Hunter, *Law and Practice of International Commercial Arbitration*, 2nd ed (1991) Sweet & Maxwell, London at 90. That is, the law of the seat of the arbitration, or of a jurisdiction asserting with a sufficient nexus control over the conduct of the arbitration, may according to its terms apply so as to govern the conduct of the arbitration, and even recognition of the concept of a de-localised arbitration will not necessarily mean freedom from local rules. The Act provides a lex arbitri, and lays down local rules. If the seat of the arbitration is New South Wales, its procedural rules (in the expanded sense above) are subject to the Act (*Naviera Amazonica Peruana SA v. Compania Internacional de Seguros del Peru* [1988] 1 Lloyd's Rep. 116); even if its seat is elsewhere or it can be regarded as de-localised, local rules may apply.

[17] "Gradipore's submission involved that the parties could overcome the application of the local rules by agreement. If there be agreement not to invoke the exercise of a discretionary power available under the lex arbitri, that will be an important consideration in whether the power should be exercised (see *Bank Mellat v. Helliniki Techniki SA* (at 302)), although the lex arbitri will remain as the law governing the conduct of the arbitration. The submission was not that the agreement on the UNCITRAL Arbitration Rules went to this Court's discretion. It could not reasonably have been put in that way, when leave to appeal is in question and by specifically regulating exclusion of the right of appeal in relation to an award (Sect. 40 dealing with exclusion agreements) the Act puts aside as a discretionary factor contrary agreement not constituting an exclusion agreement. Rather, the submission was that there could be agreement that the Act will not apply at all.

[18] "That there can be a lex arbitri different from the law of the country in which the arbitration is held is implicit in what was said in *James Miller & Partners Ltd v. Whitworth Street Estates (Manchester) Ltd*, *Black Clawson International Ltd v. Papierwerke Waldhof-Aschaffenburg AG* and *Bank Mellat v. Helliniki Techniki SA* referred to above. The place where the arbitration is held is not necessarily conclusive of the seat of the arbitration, as is obvious when one considers a peripatetic arbitration, and in *Naviera Amazonica Peruana SA v. Compania Internacional de Seguros del Peru*, Kerr LJ said (at 120):

> 'There is equally no reason in theory which precludes parties to agree that an arbitration shall be held at a place or in country X but subject to the procedural laws of Y. The limits and implications of any such agreement have been much discussed in the literature, but apart from the decision in the instant case there appears to be no reported case where this has happened. This is not surprising when one considers the complexities and inconveniences which such an agreement would involve.'

[19] "Can agreement on a lex arbitri different from the law of the country in which the arbitration is held entirely escape the local rules? The foundation for agreement on a lex arbitri is that all arbitrations are consensual, party autonomy being the cornerstone of modern arbitration, and so Gradipore said that the consensual nature of the arbitration permitted American Diagnostica and Gradipore to agree to exclude the Act if it would otherwise have applied to their arbitration. But there must be a limit to the parties' freedom, because their choice of the place of their arbitration may carry with it application to the arbitration of the law of that place according to its terms so as to govern the conduct of the arbitration. The freedom is to choose the place. So far as the local rules compulsorily apply and are inconsistent with the chosen lex arbitri, they cannot be put aside by agreement that they do not apply.

[20] "Hence in principle it seems to me that the application of the Act so far as it provides for leave to appeal, a compulsory local rule applying to the arbitration, cannot be put aside by agreement that the Act will not apply to the arbitration at all. I think that finds some support in the reasons of Saville J in *Union of India v. McDonnell Douglas Corporation* [1993] 2 Lloyd's Rep. 48.[6] The arbitration agreement provided that the arbitration should be conducted in accordance with the procedure in the Arbitration Act 1940 (India); it also provided that the seat of the arbitration should be London. The arbitration was about to begin in London. His Lordship was asked to determine whether the law governing the arbitration was Indian law or English law. He held in favour of English law, expressing his conclusion (at 51) in the terms that the arbitration and any award would be 'subject to the supervisory jurisdiction' of the English courts. The reasoning included, in the emphasised part of the passage next set out, that the supervisory jurisdiction of the English courts could not be excluded by the agreement.

[21] "His Lordship referred (at 50) to the choices of a law to govern the commercial bargain, a law to govern the arbitration, and a law to govern the procedures in any arbitration. These laws corresponded to those identified in

6. Reported in Yearbook XIX (1994) pp. 223-234.

Naviera Amazonica Peruana SA v. Compania Internacional de Seguros del Peru. He said that in theory, and subject to a proviso to which he would return, the parties could choose a different law for each of these purposes....

[22] "Earlier in *Bank Mellat v. Helliniki Techniki SA*, Goff LJ had said (at 315) that if parties choose to arbitrate in England '... English law will, as the curial law, apply to the conduct of the arbitration; and the parties will, by holding their arbitration here, subject themselves for that purpose to English law ...'. His Lordship was not addressing agreement on a different curial law, but appears not to have doubted the application of English curial law of its own force.

[23] "In M.J. Mustill and S.C. Boyd, *Commercial Arbitration*, 2nd ed (1989) ..., the law governing the conduct of the arbitration is part of the curial law. The authors observe (at 64) that an express choice of curial law different from the law of the country in which the arbitration is to be held is almost unknown, '... no doubt because of the formidable conceptual and practical problems which are likely to arise should it be necessary to invoke the power of a court in relation to the reference'. They say (at 90):

> 'The choice of a foreign curial law does not, we submit, deprive the English court of jurisdiction. It has never, so far as we are aware, been suggested that parties may validly contract out of the power to set aside or remit an award for misconduct; and if an explicit agreement cannot accomplish this, it is hard to see how it could be achieved indirectly by the choice of a foreign curial law. Nevertheless the choice of a foreign curial law is a strong reason for the court refusing leave to serve proceedings abroad or to grant discretionary remedies.'

[24] "This passage was cited with approval by Staughton LJ, with whom Woolf LJ and Neill LJ agreed, in *Channel Tunnel Group Ltd v. Balfour Beatty Construction Ltd* [1992] 1 QB 656 at 675.[7] In that case it was held that the connecting factor for the application of Sect. 12(6)(h) of the Arbitration Act 1950 (UK), dealing with interim injunctions, to a case containing a foreign element was the place the parties had chosen as the seat of the arbitration. If the seat was in England or Wales, the court could grant an injunction, it seems in his Lordship's view even if the parties had agreed on the procedural laws of another country.

[25] "In Collins (ed) *Dicey and Morris, The Conflict of Laws*, 12th ed (1993) ... it is said (at 581-582):

7. Reported in Yearbook XVIII (1993) pp. 446-456 (UK no. 33).

> '... Although most systems of arbitration allow the parties considerable procedural freedom (for example, to stipulate the extent of discovery or the admission of oral evidence) it does not follow that the parties can for all purposes contract out of the mandatory procedural rules of the place where the arbitration is being conducted. Thus where there are rules of English procedure which the parties cannot validly exclude by express agreement, a choice of foreign procedural law would not prevent those English rules being applicable to an arbitration in England....'

[26] "There is thus some judicial and other guidance contrary to Gradipore's submission. In principle, party autonomy does not mean a complete freedom to exclude a system of law, or particular elements of a system of law, from the relationship between the parties. Confining attention to statutory law, if the statute on its proper construction and with regard to the legislative power of the legislature applies to the parties and their conduct of the arbitration, and expressly or by necessarily implication cannot be excluded by agreement, the agreement of the parties to exclude it will count for nothing. If the statute applies to the arbitration, a prohibition against contracting out cannot be avoided by contracting out of the prohibition.

[27] "For these reasons I do not accept the foundation for Gradipore's submission. But in any event I do not think the facts support it. I return to the significance of the agreement that the UNCITRAL Arbitration Rules be adopted as the rules governing the arbitration.

[28] "In my opinion, that agreement did not carry with it agreement that the Act should not apply. In the light of the preceding communications between the parties, the rules governing the arbitration were supplementary to the Act not in substitution for it.... They were what Mr. Haidt had described ... as the rules of arbitration determined by agreement or by the arbitrator, as distinct from the Act as the curial law for the arbitration. While the facts were quite different, there is a degree of similarity with *Union of India v. McDonnell Douglas Corporation*.

[29] "Taking the agreement in context, the UNCITRAL Arbitration Rules as the rules governing the arbitration were to govern the procedures of the arbitration so far as not inconsistent with the Act as the chosen law in accordance with which there had been the referral to arbitration. All this is supported by the fact that, as was presumably well-known to Messrs. Jacobs [counsel for Gradipore] and Haidt [counsel for American Diagnostica], the UNCITRAL Arbitration Rules provided by Art. 1(2) that they should govern the arbitration 'except that where any of these Rules is in conflict with a provision of the law applicable to the arbitration from which the parties cannot derogate, that provision shall prevail'. The Act was such a law and

contained some such provisions, including Sect. 38 from which the parties could derogate only to the extent permitted by Sect. 40. So the Act was left to apply, relevantly so far as it provided for leave to appeal subject to any exclusion agreement.

[30] "Addressing each of the ways Gradipore put its submission, there was not a variation of the arbitration clause whereby the referral to arbitration was not to be accordance with the Act, but at most a variation of the arbitration clause by the addition that the referral to arbitration should be in accordance with the Act and, in its procedures, the UNCITRAL Arbitration Rules, with the Act prevailing in the event of inconsistency...."

II. AN EXCLUSION AGREEMENT?

[31] "Sect. 40 of the Commercial Arbitration Act 1984 provides:

> '(1) Subject to this section and section 41:
> (a) the Supreme Court shall not, under section 38(4)(b), grant leave to appeal with respect to a question of law arising out of an award; and
> (b) no application may be made under section 39(1)(a) with respect to a question of law;
> if there is in force an agreement in writing (in this section and section 41 referred to as an "exclusion agreement") between the parties to the arbitration agreement which excludes the right of appeal under section 38(2) in relation to the award or, in a case falling within paragraph (b), in relation to an award to which the determination of the question of law is material.'
> (....)

[32] ".... As will appear, in the consideration of Sect. 40 regard must be had to Sect. 28 of the Act, which provides:

> 'Unless a contradictory intention is expressed in the arbitration agreement, the award made by the arbitrator or umpire shall, subject to this Act, be final and binding on the parties to the agreement.'

[33] "Gradipore submitted that there was an exclusion agreement because the parties had agreed in writing, in the exchange of letters in June 1996, that the UNCITRAL Arbitration Rules be adopted as the rules governing the arbitration, and had thereby agreed that the award should be final and binding

because Art. 32(2) of the UNCITRAL Arbitration Rules dealing with the form and effect of the award states:

> '2. The award shall be made in writing and shall be final and binding on the parties. The parties undertake to carry out the award without delay.'

[34] "(Gradipore also submitted that there was an exclusion agreement because the entire Act had been rejected, repeating the submission considered in the preceding portion of these reasons. The logical difficulty of excluding the Act entirely but relying on its provisions as to an exclusion agreement need not be explored; for the reasons I have given, there was not the entire rejection.)

[35] "There appears to be little guidance in the cases as to the effect of the parties' agreement. Speaking of the equivalent to Sect. 40 of the Act, Sect. 3 of the Arbitration Act 1979 (UK), M.J. Mustill and S.C. Boyd, *Commercial Arbitration*, 2nd ed (1989) ... suggest (at 635) that there is '... room for uncertainty as to what exactly the Act contemplates by way of an exclusion agreement'. The authors advert to the equivalent to Sect. 40(4) as possibly indicating that a general ouster of a right of appeal is ineffective, but I consider they correctly find this unconvincing on the ground that the subsection is intended to ensure that only a valid exclusion agreement will suffice.

[36] "In *Arab African Energy Corp Ltd v. Olieprodukten Nederland BV* [1983] 2 Lloyd's Rep. 419, the parties agreed that their arbitration should be 'according to ICC Rules'. Art. 24 of the ICC Rules provided:

> '1. The arbitral award shall be final.
> 2. By submitting the dispute to arbitration by the International Chamber of Commerce, the parties shall be deemed to have undertaken to carry out the resulting award without delay and to have waived their right to any form of appeal insofar as such waiver can validly be made.'

[37] "It was held that the parties had entered into an exclusion agreement within Sect. 3 of the Arbitration Act 1979 (UK)....[8]

---

8. Sect. 3 of the Arbitration Act 1979 reads in relevant part:

> "(1) Subject to the following provisions of this section and section 4 below –
> (a) the High Court shall not, under section 1(3)(b) above, grant leave to appeal with respect to a question of law arising out of an award....
> if the parties to the reference in question have entered into an agreement in writing ... which excludes the right of appeal under section 1 above ....

[38] "This decision was accepted as correct by the Court of Appeal in *Marine Contractors Inc v. Shell Petroleum Development Co of Nigeria Ltd* [1984] 2 Lloyd's Rep. 77. Gradipore said that the decision supported its submission because both the ICC Rules and the UNCITRAL Arbitration Rules stated that the award should be final (in the case of the UNCITRAL Arbitration Rules adding that it should be binding) and both the ICC Rules and the UNCITRAL Arbitration Rules provided that the parties undertook to carry out the award without delay. However, the decision was founded not on the statement as to finality or the undertaking to carry the award out but on the deemed waiver of the parties' right to any form of appeal. The waiver is not to be found in the UNCITRAL Arbitration Rules. American Diagnostica did not submit that the exclusion agreement, if there was one, could not be by incorporation by reference of Art. 32(2) of the UNCITRAL Arbitration Rules, and I do not think Gradipore gains any assistance from *Arab African Energy Corporation Ltd v. Olieprodukten Nederland BV* as to the effect of Art. 32(2).

[39] "In *White Constructions (NT) Pty Ltd v. Mutton* (1988) 57 NTR 8, the arbitrator told the parties he would accept nomination 'on the clear understanding that my award as arbitrator will be accepted by both parties as final and binding...'. The parties agreed. The statute was materially in the same terms as the Act. It was held that any exclusion agreement was not in writing, but Martin J considered whether there was an exclusion agreement and held that there was.

[40] "His Honour observed (at 12) that it would not be right to approach the question of an exclusion agreement on the basis that either the arbitrator or the parties to the arbitration were ignorant of the provisions of the Act, and that their agreement could only have meaning if it was directed to excluding the qualified right of appeal in Sect. 38(2). After discussion making it clear that he had in mind both the equivalent to Sect. 28 of the Act and that part of the arbitration clause providing that the arbitrator's award should be final and binding on the parties, Martin J said (at 15):

> 'Although it is undoubtedly preferable that the terms of an exclusion agreement incorporates specific reference to such of Sects. 38(2) and 39(1)(a) as the parties seek to exclude from operation, it is not necessary that they do so. The Act does not expressly require it and such a requirement should not be implied. It is up to the parties as to how they express their agreement and, if an intention to exclude the right of appeal (or to have a preliminary exclusion [sic question] of law determined) can be fairly seen from the words they choose to employ, then it should be made effectual. I consider that if parties agreed that they would both

accept an arbitrator's award as "final and binding"' they thereby exclude the qualified right of appeal under Sect. 38(2).'

[41] "This was a stronger case than the present case. The parties' attention was specifically directed to the status of the award, and they agreed not just that it *would be* final and binding (which was already the case, quite apart from Sect. 28 of the Act, by virtue of the arbitration clause) but that it *would be accepted as* final and binding. That the parties intended by their further agreement more than that the award should be final and binding subject to the statutory right of appeal, and intended to exclude the right of appeal, can be accepted. I do not think that Gradipore really gains support from this decision, and I do not accept Gradipore's argument that the fact that the arbitration in this case has an international flavour suggests that the parties intended to exclude what were called parochial rights of appeal in aid of finality of the arbitral process.

[42] "A decision in the opposite direction is *Corner v. C&C News Pty Ltd* (Yeldham J 28 April 1989, unreported). The arbitration clause included: 'The parties agree that the Award of the Arbitrator shall be final, conclusive and binding upon them.' It was held that the arbitration agreement was a domestic arbitration agreement, and by force of Sect. 40(6) of the Act any exclusion agreement would have been of no effect. His Honour said, however (431-432):

> 'Although, on the face of it, the words "final, conclusive and binding upon them", being words of considerable width, would appear to be sufficient to exclude a right of appeal, the reality is that the expression "final and binding" is to be found in Sect. 28, and in the old Arbitration Act 1902 in the Second Schedule, as well as in Sect. 16 of the Arbitration Act 1950 (UK). Such expression was employed to bring finality, subject to, well recognised methods of challenging awards, to arbitral proceedings. Certainly such expressions (and the word "conclusive" does not alter the situation) do not constitute an attempt to oust the jurisdiction of the court: see *Ford v. Clarkson's Holidays Ltd* [1971] 1 WLR 1412. I think it is correct to submit, as counsel for the plaintiff in the present case did, that the words here employed in cl. 7(e) merely restate what has long been the rule in relation to arbitrations, namely that an award is final and binding in the traditional sense, and such an award creates a res judicata and an issue estoppel, subject to judicial review by the courts.'

(....)

[43] "[I]n my opinion agreement that an award shall be final and binding and an added undertaking to carry out the award without delay (which is the most which can be found in the agreement in relation to the UNCITRAL Arbitration Rules) is insufficient for an agreement which excludes the right of appeal under Sect. 38(2) in relation to the award. In accordance with a long history, reference to an award as final and binding leaves it subject to challenges properly available to a dissatisfied party. Sect. 28 of the Act continues that position; consistently with it, mere repetition that the award is final and binding cannot make an exclusion agreement."

(....)

[44] The Court rejected Gradipore's forum non conveniens submission as well as its submission that the application was out of time. Having found that it had jurisdiction, the Court rejected the application for leave to appeal.

16. Supreme Court of Victoria, Causes Jurisdiction, 16 October 1998

Parties:	Plaintiff: ABI Group Contractors Pty. Ltd. (nationality not indicated) Defendants: (1) Transfield Pty. Limited (nationality not indicated); (2) Obayashi Corporation and others (nationality not indicated)
Published in:	14 Mealey's International Arbitration Report (1999, no. 1) pp. G-1 - G-10
Articles:	II(3) (by implication)
Subject matters:	- can mandatory referral to arbitration be excluded by agreement of the parties? (yes) - mandatory referral to arbitration under the 1958 New York Convention - agreement on non-application of the New York Convention permissible - discretionary referral to arbitration under Victoria Commercial Arbitration Act 1984 - risk of multiple proceedings and contrary results
Commentary Cases:	¶ 218; [13] = ¶ 217; [20]-[23] = ¶ 201; [24]-[36] = ¶ 226 + ¶ 227

Facts

The joint venture Transfield Pty. Limited and Obayashi Corporation (TOJV) were involved as designers, project managers and contractors in the construction of the Melbourne Citylink project. In February 1997, ABI Group Contractors (ABI) entered into a form of sub-contract with TOJV to carry out the Southbank works. A dispute arose between ABI and TOJV and others and ABI initiated court proceedings against eight defendants including TOJV, alleging, inter alia, breaches of the Trade Practices Act 1974.

TOJV objected to the jurisdiction of the court, relying on the arbitration clause contained in the General Conditions of Sub-contract. ABI alleged that there was no formal binding sub-contract and thus no agreement to arbitrate.

In interlocutory proceedings on affidavit, the Court, per Gillard, J, found that although it was unable to decide on the affidavit material presented to it, ABI was precluded by its own pleadings from arguing that there was not a "binding and concluded sub-contract in law containing a dispute resolution clause". The Court held that the proceedings should be stayed under the 1958 New York Convention, but if the case were decided under the Victoria Commercial Arbitration Act, it would not order a stay, pointing to the impracticality of the chance of multiple proceedings.

Excerpt

(....)

I. DOES THE INTERNATIONAL ARBITRATION ACT 1974 APPLY?

[1] "It is common ground between the parties that the conditions of what is described as the Southbank Interchange Design and Construct Sub-contract applied to the sub-contract pleaded by the plaintiff. If there was a binding sub-contract, the invitation to tender dated 24 September 1996 expressly incorporated the 'General Conditions of Sub-contract'.

[2] "TOJV rely upon Sect. 7 of the Commonwealth International Arbitration Act 1974.[1] If certain prerequisites are satisfied then the court is bound to

1. Sect. 7 of the International Commercial Arbitration Act 1974 reads in relevant part:

"(1) Where:

(a) the procedure in relation to arbitration under an arbitration agreement is governed, whether by virtue of the express terms of the agreement or otherwise, by the law of a Convention country;

(b) the procedure in relation to arbitration under an arbitration agreement is governed, whether by virtue of the express terms of the agreement or otherwise, by the law of a country not being Australia or a Convention country, and a party to the agreement is Australia or a State or a person who was, at the time when the agreement was made, domiciled or ordinarily resident in Australia;

(c) a party to an arbitration agreement is the Government of a Convention country or part of a Convention country or the Government of a territory of a Convention country, being a territory to which the Convention extends; or

(d) a party to an arbitration agreement is a person who was, at the time when the agreement was made, domiciled or ordinarily resident in a country that is a Convention country;

this section applies to the agreement.

(2) Subject to this Part, where:

(a) proceedings instituted by a party to an arbitration agreement to which this section applies against another party to the agreement are pending in a court; and stay the proceedings and refer the parties to arbitration. The words of the section are mandatory and once the prerequisites are satisfied then the court is bound to refer the matter to arbitration unless the court finds 'that the arbitration agreement is null and void, inoperative or incapable of being performed'. See Sect. 7(5).

[3] "There was no contest that TOJV had established the necessary statutory requirements and accordingly, prima facie, the section applied. There was no submission made by the plaintiff that the arbitration agreement was null or void, inoperative or incapable of being performed. It sought to rely upon Sect. 87 of the Trade Practices Act to mount an argument that the arbitration agreement may be null and void but for reasons which I have already stated, in my opinion the claim for the relief does not preclude the application of the Act.[2]

[4] "However, Mr. Digby, Q.C. submitted on behalf of the plaintiff that the parties had agreed expressly or impliedly to exclude the application of Sect. 7 of the Commonwealth Act. He submitted that the wording of the conditions of the sub-contract made it clear that the parties intended that any arbitration should be conducted in accordance with the Commercial Arbitration Act 1984 of this State.

[5] "This submission raised two arguments. First, is it open to parties to an agreement to exclude the application of Sect. 7 of the Commonwealth Act and if it is, have the parties under the present sub-contact excluded its operation?"

II. EXCLUSION OF INTERNATIONAL ARBITRATION ACT

[6] "As a general proposition, parties to a contract can exclude the operation of the law in certain circumstances. There are a variety of principles of law which may make their attempts to do so ineffective.

(b) the proceedings involve the determination of a matter that, in pursuance of the agreement, is capable of settlement by arbitration;

on the application of a party to the agreement, the court shall, by order, upon such conditions (if any) as it thinks fit, stay the proceedings or so much of the proceedings as involves the determination of that matter, as the case may be, and refer the parties to arbitration in respect of that matter.

(....)

(5) A court shall not make an order under subsection (2) if the court finds that the arbitration agreement is null and void, inoperative or incapable of being performed."

2. Sect. 87 of the Trade Practices Act gives the court the power to set aside an agreement and to declare it void.

[7] "As Fletcher-Moulton, LJ said in *Perry v. National Provincial Bank of England* (1910) 1 Ch. 464 at 476 –

> 'If the meaning is that it is impossible to make a legal contract which would have certain legal effects we cannot accept such law. ... Moreover it would be quite meaningless. People can contract to do anything.'

Subject to public policy and statute law, parties to a contract can agree to do anything.

[8] "Mr. Digby, Q.C. referred me to the decision of the High Court in *Lieberman v. Morris* (1944) 69 C.L.R. 69. The case was concerned with a testator's family maintenance application under the New South Wales Act. The court held that a person was not precluded from making an application under the Act by reason of having covenanted with the testator not to do so. The legislation provided a statutory right to defined dependants to make a claim on the estate of the deceased for adequate provision out of the estate.

[9] "The question was whether a dependant by contract could exclude himself from claiming a right given by statute. The answer to the question depended upon a consideration of the scope and policy of the Act. Rich, J. at p. 84 stated the principles which guide a court on such an application. He said –

> 'Whenever, a statute creates new rights, public policy in a broad sense is always involved, because the legislature must be assumed to have thought it desirable in the public interest that the right should be brought into existence. But it does not necessarily follow that an agreement to release or abandon rights so conferred should be regarded as opposed to public policy in general or even to the policy of the particular Act. As was pointed out in *Admiralty Commissions v. Valverda (Owners)*. "The problem must be solved on a consideration of the scope and policy of the particular statute."'

The High Court held after considering the provisions of the legislation, that it was the intention of Parliament that a dependant could not covenant not to make an application.

[10] "It is necessary to consider the scope and policy of the Act. Sect. 7 of the Act gives the right to parties to a foreign arbitration agreement to apply to a court to stay any court proceedings. Sect. 7 does not contain any express provision precluding a party to an arbitration agreement agreeing not to apply for a stay. The Act is silent on the issue. What Sect. 7 does is to give the right to an entity who does not reside or is not domiciled in Australia and is party

to an arbitration agreement to apply for a stay of the court proceeding. There is no suggestion that it would be contrary to public policy or that the general law precludes a party to such an agreement from covenanting not to make application pursuant to Sect. 7 of the Act to stay court proceedings. It follows that prima facie the parties can agree not to make an application pursuant to Sect. 7 and a covenant to that effect should be upheld by the court. In other words, an agreement to that effect should be enforced.

[11] "The question is whether there is anything in the Act which shows the intention of Parliament to deny the right to the contracting parties to covenant not to apply for a stay? As has often been said, if the Parliament intended to exclude the right it would have been easy to have said so. It did not do so. The Act is divided into a number of parts and each part deals with a discrete area. The long title to the Act is –

> 'An Act relating to the recognition and enforcement of foreign arbitral awards, and the conduct of international commercial arbitrations, in Australia, and for related purposes.'

[12] "In Part II the Act gives effect to the 1958 New York Convention on the recognition and enforcement of foreign arbitral awards which is set out in Schedule 1 to the Act. The Act provides accession by Australia to the Convention. Part II which contains Sect. 7 is concerned with the provisions of that Convention. Australia is a Convention country. Part II is concerned with enforcement of foreign arbitration agreements; recognition and enforcement of foreign arbitration awards and proof of matters relating to the Convention. A perusal of Part (II) and the Convention reveals that it does not deal with any procedural matters to be applied in the arbitration.

[13] "Part III of the Act gives effect to the United Nations Commission on International Trade Law's Model Law on International Commercial Arbitration. Subject to Part III of the Act, the Model Law has the force of law in Australia. It is reproduced in Schedule 2. The Model Law covers a wider range of topics than the Convention. Again, there is nothing in Part III or the Model Law which precludes a party to a foreign arbitration agreement from excluding the operation of the Act or the Convention or the Model Law. In my opinion there is nothing in the Act which shows an intention by the Commonwealth Parliament to exclude the rights of parties to an arbitration agreement, to agree that the provisions of the Act, Convention or Model Law do not apply to a foreign arbitration. Indeed, Mr. Shaw, Q.C. did not contend otherwise.

[14] "Further, a party to any foreign arbitration agreement must make application to the court in order to stay the proceedings. It must follow that

if no application is made then the section would not apply. It follows that in my opinion the parties to a foreign arbitration agreement within the meaning of the Act can, by agreement, exclude the operation of the Act. The conclusion I have reached does not defeat the object of the Act."

III. HAS THE OPERATION OF THE COMMONWEALTH ACT BEEN EXCLUDED BY THE PARTIES?

[15] "The plaintiff submits that the parties have by their agreement excluded the operation of the Commonwealth International Arbitration Act 1974. The general conditions of sub-contract which the plaintiff has pleaded form part of the sub-contract between the parties sets out in some detail, provisions concerning dispute resolution. Clause 13 sets out a procedure that is to be followed in relation to a dispute under the sub-contract. The procedure goes through negotiation, followed by mediation, and then clause 13.5(a) provides –

> '(a) Any dispute not resolved by mediation or expert determination, other than a dispute under or in respect of any of the matters the subject of any of clauses 12.1 to 12.9 inclusive, must be resolved by arbitration.'

[16] "The plaintiff relies upon clause 13.5(d) which provides –

> '(d) The arbitration must [be] conducted in accordance with the following rules and procedures:
> (i) the place of arbitration must be in Melbourne, Victoria;
> ...
> (iv) the cost of the reference to arbitration and award are at the discretion of the arbitrator, but the arbitrator does not have the power to tax any award of costs made under Section 34 of the Commercial Arbitration Act of Victoria;
> ...
> (vi) the Commercial Arbitration Act of Victoria applies to the arbitration except to the extent it is inconsistent with the preceding provisions of this clause.'

[17] "Mr. Digby, Q.C. submitted that the paragraph excluded the provisions of Sect. 7 of the Act. He drew attention to para. (iv) and para. (vi) and submitted that the reference to the Commercial Arbitration Act of Victoria made it clear that the International Arbitration Act 1974 of the Com-

monwealth had been excluded and the applicable Act was the Commercial Arbitration Act of Victoria.

[18] "It is noted that the paragraph is concerned with the conduct of the arbitration. This is made clear by the opening words of the paragraph. In my opinion the paragraph does not exclude Sect. 7 of the Commonwealth Act and there is nothing in the clause which is inconsistent with that conclusion. In my opinion, Sect. 7 does apply but that is not to say that the procedures set out in the Commercial Arbitration Act of Victoria do not apply to the conduct of the arbitration.

[19] "In addition, Mr. Digby, Q.C. relied upon clause 17.2(a) which provides –

> '(a) The proper law of the sub-contract and of the dispute resolution procedures is the law of Victoria.'

In my opinion this sub-clause does not exclude the operation of the Commonwealth Act. The Commonwealth Act is part of the law of Victoria. Further, the sub-clause does not address the question of whether or not a court can stay the court proceeding pursuant to Sect. 7. The law of Victoria concerning dispute resolution procedures applies but this does not exclude the right of a party to apply for a stay. I therefore find that the parties have not excluded the operation of Sect. 7 of the Act."

IV. IS TOJV ENTITLED TO A STAY?

[20] "TOJV, having established the various elements required by Sect. 7(1) and (2) of the Act, is entitled to a stay of the court proceedings. There was no dispute between the parties that the plaintiff's court proceeding involves the determination of a matter that is capable of settlement by the arbitration agreement between the parties. Clause 1 of the sub-contract defines dispute as 'a dispute, difference, claim or any unresolved issue arising between the parties relating to the interpretation of the sub-contract or any matter arising under, or relating to, the sub-contract or the sub-contract works.' The definition is indeed extremely wide and clause 13.5 provides that any dispute must be resolved by arbitration.

[21] "Sect. 7(2) empowers the court to stay so much of the proceeding as involves the determination of a matter that is capable of settlement by arbitration. Clearly the wide definition of 'dispute' covers all the claims made by the plaintiff against the TOJV defendants which concern the pre-contract negotiations and the alleged breaches of sub-contract. The claims made

pursuant to the Trade Practices Act would also be included – see *Francis Travel Marketing Pty. Ltd. v. Virgin Atlantic Airways* (1966) 39 N.S.W.L.R. 160. The only question is whether the quantum meruit claims ... are covered.

[22] "The question is not without controversy. In two recent decisions in New South Wales, single judges have held that a quantum meruit claim fell within the sub-clause in the agreement in question. In both cases the dispute clause was extremely wide and covered a dispute concerning the contract 'or in connection therewith'. That phrase is not found in the dispute definition in the present sub-contract. The New South Wales decisions are *O'Conner v. Leaw Pty. Ltd.* (1997) 43 N.S.W.L.R. 285 and *Elkateb v. Lawindi* (1997) 42 N.S.W.L.R. 396.

[23] "The question is whether the phrase 'or relating to the sub-contract or the sub-contract works' is wide enough to cover a true quantum meruit claim. The parties did not make submissions in relation to this question and accordingly I am not prepared to conclude as presently advised that the quantum meruit claims ... are covered by the arbitration agreement. However, nothing would be gained from a practical point to stay all the causes of action between the plaintiff and the first and second defendants and leave the quantum meruit claims to proceed in the court. I encourage the parties to enter into an agreement to ensure that the quantum meruit claims can also be heard in the arbitration."

V. COMMERCIAL ARBITRATION ACT 1984 (VICTORIA)

[24] "If Sect. 7 of the Commonwealth Act does not apply, then TOJV rely upon Sect. 53 of the Victorian Commercial Arbitration Act 1984.[3] Unlike the

---

3. Sect. 53 of the Victoria Commercial Arbitration Act 1984 reads:

"(1) If a party to an arbitration agreement commences proceedings in a court against another party to the arbitration agreement in respect of a matter agreed to be referred to arbitration by the agreement, that other party may, subject to subsection (2), apply to that court to stay the proceedings and that court, if satisfied –
(a) that there is no sufficient reason why the matter should not be referred to arbitration in accordance with the agreement; and
(b) that the applicant was at the time when the proceedings were commenced and still remains ready and willing to do all things necessary for the proper conduct of the arbitration –
may make an order staying the proceedings and may further give such directions with respect to the future conduct of the arbitration as it thinks fit.
(2) An application under sub-section (1) shall not, except with the leave of the court in which the proceedings have been commenced, be made after the applicant has delivered pleadings or taken any other step in the proceedings other than the entry of an appearance.

Commonwealth Act, an application under Sect. 53 involves the exercise of a discretion by the court. In other words, it is a matter of discretion whether the court will stay the proceeding. The authorities establish a general practice in favour of staying court proceedings where parties have agreed to refer their disputes to arbitration.

[25] "It was submitted on behalf of the plaintiff that the court should not stay the court proceeding because the plaintiff has brought proceedings against six other defendants. I accept as a general proposition that it's desirable that all issues in dispute between parties be determined in the one proceeding by the same tribunal. Whilst that is a general rule and one of the rationales for it is the avoidance of multiplicity of proceedings and possible inconsistent findings, nevertheless, there may be circumstances where it is clear that the risk of such results is small.

(....)

[26] "Sect. 53(2) of the Commercial Arbitration Act 1984 provides that a court may stay a proceeding if satisfied, inter alia, 'that there is no sufficient reason why the matter should not be referred to arbitration'. The question is, is there a sufficient reason why the matter should not be referred to arbitration?

[27] "The plaintiff submitted that the claim under the Trade Practices Act against TOJV is outside the scope of the arbitration agreement. The dispute which is referred to the arbitrator is a 'dispute, difference, claim or any unresolved issue arising between the parties relating to the interpretation of the sub-contract *or any matter* arising under, *or relating to, the sub-contract* or the sub-contract works'. (My emphasis) In my opinion the words emphasised show the intention of the parties to invest the arbitrator with a wide authority to decide disputes between them and in my opinion, the authority is wide enough to embrace a claim under Sect. 52 of the Trade Practices Act. Further, contrary to the submission put by the plaintiff, in my opinion the arbitrator would be clothed with the power to grant remedies pursuant to that Act. See *Francis Travel Marketing Pty. Ltd. v. Virgin Atlantic Airways* (1996) 39 N.S.W.L.R. 160 at p. 167.

[28] "The plaintiff also submits that it is not open to the arbitrator to consider the cause of action pleaded based on a breach of a collateral warranty.

---

(3) Notwithstanding any rule of law to the contrary, a party to an arbitration agreement shall not be entitled to recover damages in any court from another party to the agreement by reason that that other party takes proceedings in a court in respect of the matter agreed to be referred to arbitration by the arbitration agreement."

In my opinion, for the same reasons, the arbitrator does have authority to determine that dispute.

[29] "In my view, the real issue comes down to whether the causes of action involving the plaintiff and eight defendants are so intertwined that there is a real prospect of multiplicity of proceedings, with increase in legal costs and the prospect of inconsistent findings and maybe results. Any stay that is granted is only in relation to the causes of action against the first and second defendants, TOJV. The proceedings will continue against the other defendants. (....)

[30] "The real dispute involves four separate parties in respect of the pre-contract events. The four parties are –

(i) the plaintiff as builder;
(ii) TOJV as the proprietor;
(iii) the design consultants;
(iv) the geotechnical consultants.

Prior to the sub-contract, certain investigation works were performed by the design consultants and the geotechnical consultants which ultimately led to the preparation of a number of designs in relation to a number of works. In a nutshell, the complaint is that the two consultants negligently performed their works with the consequences that their results were wrong, their designs were defective and could not be relied upon. It is asserted that TOJV knew that the design created by the two consultants were erroneous, incorrect and defective but nevertheless incorporated them in the works to be performed pursuant to the sub-contact.

[31] "The plaintiff states that TOJV and both consultants each owed a duty of care to the plaintiff as a future tenderer. It is stated that the three entities made misrepresentations to the plaintiff in the tender stage. The plaintiff pleads that it entered into the sub-contract in reliance of the representations that were made and the designs prepared. As a result it pleads the following causes of action against TOJV, the design consultants and the geotechnical consultants –

(i) common law negligence;
(ii) negligent pre-contract misrepresentations;
(iii) breach of Sect. 52 of the Trade Practices Act.

In addition the plaintiff asserts a breach of a collateral warranty against TOJV arising out of the same circumstances.

[32] "I have considered the statement of claim. In my opinion the issues concerning the four parties are inextricably bound up. The result would be

that there would be two pieces of litigation being conducted involving much the same issues with parties present before the particular forum seeking to blame parties who may not be present. There is the ever present risk of inconsistent findings and/or results. This would reflect upon the administration of justice. Further, there will be a substantial increase in the overall legal costs involved. It is clear that the one tribunal should hear causes of action based on the pre-contract events. In addition, if the court stayed the court proceeding against the first and second defendant and the plaintiff exercised its right to continue against the other defendants, the other defendants would seek contribution from TOJV. This would involve TOJV in the court proceeding at a time when the claims brought against it by the plaintiff are stayed.

[33] "All these factors lead to the conclusion that the one forum would hear all the plaintiff's claims against the defendants named in the proceeding. I am not satisfied that there is no sufficient reason why the matter should not be referred to arbitration and accordingly, if the application has to be decided under Sect. 53 of the Commercial Arbitration Act 1984, I would not stay the court proceeding."

VI. PRACTICAL COURSE

[34] "Although I have found that the court is bound to stay the court proceeding by the plaintiff against the first and second defendants under the International Arbitration Act 1974 (Commonwealth) I think the result is unpractical, is likely to lead to multiplicity of proceedings with attendant increases in legal costs and the real risk of inconsistent findings. Further, there is the possibility that the plaintiff and TOJV will be fighting two cases at the same time if some defendants file notices of contribution against the TOJV defendants.

[35] "I think that the parties should give thought to not proceeding with the arbitration but leave the disputes to be litigated in the court proceeding. There is another practical solution and that is that the court proceedings be referred to arbitration pursuant to Rule 50.08(1) of the Rules of Court. It is noted that all parties to the litigation should have to consent to that course.

[36] "It is said that one of the advantages of going to arbitration is that the matters in dispute can be resolved earlier than in a court proceeding. One of the objects of the Building List is to court manage cases and I have no doubt the court can mould suitable directions which would ensure that the court proceeding would be ready for trial within a short period. I accept that the court could not hear the proceeding earlier than if it was arbitrated, but the

cost would be substantially less. In the end, it is a matter for the parties. I encourage the parties to consider the comments I have made...."

BELGIUM

Accession: 18 August 1975
1st Reservation

11. Cour de Cassation [Supreme Court], 5 June 1998

Parties:	Petitioner: Inter-Arab Investment Guarantee Corporation (Kuwait) Respondent: Banque Arabe et Internationale d'Investissements (France)
Published in:	Journal des Tribunaux (1998) pp. 701-702
Articles:	III; V(1)(*c*); V(1)(*e*)
Subject matter:	– "binding" nature of award
Commentary Cases:	[3]-[10] + [16]-[20] = ¶ 514; [12]-[13] + [21] = ¶ 301; [23]-[26] = ¶ 512

Facts

The facts of this case are also reported in Yearbook XXII (1997) pp. 643-668 and Yearbook XXI (1996) pp. 13-39.

The Inter-Arab Investment Guarantee Corporation (IAIGC), an international organization with its seat in Kuwait, was established in 1975 by the Convention Establishing the Inter-Arab Investment Guarantee Corporation (the 1975 Convention). Its aim is to provide insurance coverage to Arab investors by entering into insurance and other contracts with eligible parties, as defined in Art. 17 of the 1975 Convention.[1]

1. Art. 17(1) and (2) of the 1975 Convention reads:

Article 17(1)
"(i) To be accepted as a party to an insurance contract, the investor must be either a natural

On 17 November 1984, Banque Arabe et Internationale d'Investissements (BAII) extended a credit facility of US$ 20 million to the Baghdad Sewage Board (BSB), Iraq, under a Loan Agreement. Repayment of the loan by BSB was guaranteed by the Rafidain Bank (Rafidain). BAII subsequently concluded an agreement with five banks, which undertook jointly to fund 65% of the BSB loan.

On 29 November 1984, BAII also entered into a Guarantee Contract with IAIGC, whereby IAIGC agreed to indemnify BAII against part of the losses which BAII might sustain under the Loan Agreement with BSB. The General Conditions annexed to the Guarantee Contract contained an arbitral clause.

When BSB failed to pay according to the repayment schedule, BAII concluded a Deferment Agreement with Rafidain in September 1988, providing for deferral of payment of the entire loan. However, Rafidain and BSB also failed to meet the deferred payment schedule.

BAII notified IAIGC of all defaults by Rafidain and BSB as they occurred, both under the original agreements and the Deferment Agreement. By an exchange of letters in November 1988, BAII and IAIGC entered into an Extension Agreement, by which they extended the period of the Guarantee, established a new payment schedule and certain new contractual provisions. Starting in January 1989, when the Extension Agreement entered into force, IAIGC regularly satisfied BAII's calls for indemnity.

On 7 July 1990, Banque Nationale de Paris became the majority shareholder of BAII, and BAII ceased to fulfil the Arab nationality requirement under the 1975 Convention. IAIGC suspended payment of the remaining compensation and, on 16 February 1991, terminated the Guarantee Contract.

---

person, who is a national of a contracting country, or a juridical person whose stocks or shares are substantially owned by one or more of the contracting countries or by their nationals, and whose main seat is located in one of these countries.
(ii) Nevertheless, a juridical person may, by a resolution of the Council, be accepted as a party to an insurance contract, even if his seat is located in a non-contracting country, provided that such juridical person is owned by not less than fifty percent to one or more of the contracting countries or to their nationals or to the juridical persons who are, under the above paragraph, acceptable as party to the insurance contract. In no event shall such an investor be a national of the host country."

Article 17(2)
"All insurance contracts shall embody a term enabling the Corporation to amend or rescind the Contract or to take any other measures in cases where, after the conclusion of the relevant contract, any of the conditions set forth in the preceding paragraph ceases to obtain. Such conditions must also be satisfied at the time any claim is made by an investor for compensation due in respect of an insured loss."

BAII initiated arbitration as provided in the General Conditions attached to the Guarantee Contract. The seat of arbitration was Amman, Jordan, and the UNCITRAL Arbitration Rules supplemented the arbitration provisions in the Guarantee Contract.

By an award rendered on 17 November 1994, the arbitrators directed IAIGC to pay BAII the remaining indemnities provided for in the Guarantee Contract. A supplement to the award was issued on 21 January 1995, and the arbitrators issued two corrections on 21 January and 28 February 1995. The award is published in Yearbook XXI (1996) pp. 13-39.

BAII sought enforcement of the award in Belgium. On 28 July 1995, the President of the Court of First Instance in Brussels granted BAII's ex parte request and apposed the enforcement formula to the award. IAIGC appealed to the Court of First Instance in Brussels against the ex parte order. Among other grounds, IAIGC alleged that the award was not binding on the parties as under Jordanian law an award is binding only if it has been confirmed by a competent court.

On 25 January 1996, the Court of First Instance in Brussels affirmed the enforcement of the Jordanian award. It held that the award was binding on the parties, as the arbitration clause in the General Conditions attached to the Guarantee Contract provided that the award "shall be final and binding immediately after it has been rendered". It reasoned that Jordanian law did not apply to this issue, as the history of Art. V(1)(*e*) shows that the reference to the law of the country of rendition in that Article refers to the second part of the Article, that is, to the hypothesis of the award having been set aside.

IAIGC appealed to the Court of Appeal in Brussels. On 24 January 1997, the Court of Appeal rejected the appeal and affirmed the lower court's decision on all points. The decisions of the Brussels Court of First Instance and Court of Appeal are published in Yearbook XXII (1997) pp. 643-668.

IAIGC took recourse to the Supreme Court, which rejected the appeal. The Supreme Court held that the award was binding on the parties as the arbitration clause between the parties, and not Jordanian law, applied to the issue of the award's binding nature.

Excerpt

I. IAIGC'S FIRST GROUND FOR APPEAL

[1] "[IAIGC's] first ground for appeal alleges the violation of Arts. III, V, and in particular V(1)(*e*) of the [1958 New York Convention], Arts. 1719 and

1723 of the Judicial Code,[2] and Arts. 12(1) and (2), 15, 16, 17 and 18 of the Jordanian Law on Arbitration, no. 18 of 29 December 1953."[3]

---

2. Art. 1719 of the Belgian Judicial Code provides that the President of the Court of First Instance has jurisdiction over a request for enforcement of a foreign award; it also contains procedural details concerning the enforcement request.
   Art. 1723 of the Belgian Judicial Code reads:

   "Except when a treaty between Belgium and the country where the award has been rendered is applicable, the President refuses to grant exequatur:
   1. if the arbitral award is still open to appeal before the arbitrators and if the arbitrators have not ordered provisional enforcement notwithstanding appeal;
   2. if the award or its enforcement is contrary to *ordre public*, or if the dispute is not capable of settlement by arbitration;
   3. if there exists a ground for setting aside as provided in Art. 1704."

3. Arts. 12(1) and (2), 15, 16, 17 and 18 of the Jordanian Law on Arbitration, no. 18 of 29 December 1953 read:

   Article 12(1) and (2)
   "1. In all cases where disputes are referred to arbitration, the court may remit to the arbitrators or the umpire the questions which were subject to the arbitration, for a review of all or part thereof.
   2. In case of such a remittal, the arbitrators or umpire must make their award within three months following the making of the award, unless the decision for remittal provides otherwise.
   (....)"

   Article 15
   "When a request for the enforcement of an award is made, this is immediately notified to the defendant. This notification states that he is entitled to object thereto within seven days following the date thereof and that, if he refrains from objecting, the court can make a decision approving the award upon request of the other party following an 'ex parte' hearing."

   Article 16
   "After expiry of the above-mentioned time-limit, the court may approve the award if it is established that the defendant received the notification and made no objection within the time fixed."

   Article 17
   "After the court has confirmed the award, it may be enforced just like any other court judgment or decision."

   Article 18
   "1. Any request presented to the court under the provisions of this law must be made in compliance with the rules of the Code of Civil Procedure.
   2. The requests for the removal of an arbitrator or an umpire as well as for extension of the time for making the award, granting leave to enforce the award or setting it aside are

1. *Alleged Violation of Article V(1)(e)*

[2] The Supreme Court illustrated at the outset the first part of IAIGC's first ground for appeal, based on the alleged violation of Art. V(1)(*e*) of the Convention, and the relevant part of the Court of Appeal decision.

a. *The Court of Appeal decision*

[3] "The arbitral award in dispute was rendered 'in Amman, Jordan'. [IAIGC] maintained [before the Court of Appeal] that the binding nature of an arbitral award in the sense of Art. V(1)(*e*) of the New York Convention 'must be determined by reference to the law of the country of origin of the award, in this case, by reference to Jordanian law, pursuant to which an award becomes binding only after having being confirmed by the courts'. The decision [of the Court of Appeal] rejected this ground and affirmed the [Court of First Instance]'s dismissal of [IAIGC]'s objection against the order that, at the request of [BAII], had granted exequatur to the arbitral award.
[4] "The [Court of Appeal's] decision was based, on the one hand, on the consideration that from a reading of the New York Convention

> 'it clearly appears that the Convention considers the will of the parties to be fundamental to the arbitration proceedings. Read as a whole, these provisions indicate that the award must be binding "on the parties".... Both letters *a* and *d* refer to the law of the country where the award is rendered only where an indication, of a law or agreement, by the parties is lacking. The alternative of letter *e* follows the same logic. The interpretation given on this point by the lower court ... is relevant, and this Court refers to it. The agreement of the parties provides that the award of the arbitral tribunal shall be final and binding, and thus immediately enforceable upon being rendered. It does not provide for an appeal. According to the agreement of the parties, the award has become binding upon being rendered. In fact, the arbitral award states that it "is effective

---

examined by the court to which they are referred.
3. The decisions of the justices of the peace, Courts of First Instance and Courts of Appeal approving, setting aside or remitting the award to the arbitrators or umpire are subject to appeal and 'cassation' in compliance with the rules provided for appeal and 'cassation' for other judgments.
4. When the court considers a request for approval or the setting aside of the award, the claimant must present to the court a certified copy of the award sent by the arbitrators or the umpire."

> as of the date hereof". Further, the award has been neither annulled nor suspended by a competent authority of Jordan or of a country under the law of which it was made.'

Further, [the Court of Appeal reasoned that '[IAIGC] does not prove that the application of Jordanian law is justified in law'.

[5] "On the other hand, [the decision of the Court of Appeal was also founded] on the consideration in the reasons set forth [under paras. [53]-[57], Yearbook XXII (1997) pp. 660-661], which are included here by reference, that, pursuant to the Jordanian Law on Arbitration, the confirmation of the arbitral award by the courts has no effect on the binding nature of the arbitrators' award on the parties, but 'appears ... to be an exequatur proceeding, which is superfluous for the enforcement of the arbitral award in Belgium'."

b. IAIGC's allegations

[6] "According to the first part [of IAIGC's first ground for appeal], Art. V(1)(*e*) of the New York Convention provides that

> 'recognition and enforcement of the award may be refused, at the request of the party against whom it is invoked, only if that party furnishes to the competent authority where the recognition and enforcement is sought, proof that:
>
> ...
>
> (*e*) the award has not yet become binding on the parties, or has been set aside or suspended by a competent authority of the country in which, or under the law of which, that award was made'.

According to the opinion most in accord with the intention of the drafters of the New York Convention and with the understanding of the role of the seat of the arbitration at the time the Convention was negotiated and signed, the arbitral award can be considered, for the application of this provision, to be binding on the parties only if it is binding pursuant to the law of the country in which it has been rendered. This law is usually competent for conferring a binding nature on the award, under the conditions and according to the modalities that it sets.

[7] "As the decision [of the Court of Appeal] acknowledges that the arbitral award at issue was rendered 'in Amman, Jordan', Jordanian law is in principle applicable to determine whether said award has 'become binding upon being rendered', as provided, according to the findings of the lower court, in the agreement between the parties.

[8] "Pursuant to Arts. 12, 15, 17 and 18 of the Jordanian Law on Arbitration, and their interpretation by the Jordanian Supreme Court, an arbitral award rendered in Jordan becomes final only after having been confirmed by a court which, when hearing the request for confirmation, 'can refer ... the issues that were the subject matter of the arbitration back to the arbitrators, to be re-examined entirely or in part'. Under Jordanian law, the confirmation of the award is not only an element or a stage in the exequatur proceeding; it also aims at conferring the authority of res judicata on the award and at terminating the mission of the arbitrators.

[9] "Pursuant to the same provisions of the Jordanian Law on Arbitration, the parties to an arbitration agreement cannot validly agree that the award that will be rendered will be final without being confirmed by a competent court. Consequently, an arbitral award rendered in Jordan can be considered, under Jordanian law, to be binding on the parties in the sense of Art. V(1)(*e*) of the New York Convention only after its confirmation by a competent court.

[10] "Hence, the [Court of Appeal], by considering on the one hand that in order to determine whether the arbitral award in question had 'become binding on the parties', it suffices to refer to the arbitration agreement binding [BAII] and [IAIGC], without regard to Jordanian law, and by also considering, on the other hand, that in any case, according to Jordanian law, the binding nature of an arbitral award on the parties does not depend on the award's confirmation by a competent court, did not give sufficient reasons for its holding that 'the ground for appeal based on the violation of Art. V(1)(*e*) of the New York Convention is unfounded', nor for its rejection of [IAIGC]'s objection to the exequatur order (violation of all the legal provisions referred to in that ground, with the exception of Art. III of the [New York Convention])."

2. *Alleged Violation of Article III*

[11] The Supreme Court then summarized the second part of IAIGC's first ground for appeal, based on the alleged violation of Art. III of the Convention.

[12] "Art. III of the New York Convention obliges the Contracting States not to impose 'substantially more onerous conditions or higher fees on the recognition or enforcement of arbitral awards to which the Convention applies than are imposed on the recognition or enforcement of domestic arbitral awards'. This provision means that a Contracting State cannot subordinate the recognition or enforcement of a Convention award in its territory to substantially more onerous conditions and substantially more onerous proceedings than those imposed for the recognition and enforcement of a domestic arbitral award. It does not mean that the courts of the Contracting State in the

territory of which the Convention award is invoked should not, in order to determine whether the award 'has become binding on the parties' in the sense of Art. V(1)(*e*) of the Convention, have recourse to the law of the Contracting State in which the award has been rendered.

[13] "Consequently, to the extent that, after having noted 'that the arbitral award and the judgment are treated equally in Belgium before, as far as the former is concerned, the enforcement formula is apposed upon request', the [Court of Appeal] held that 'the demand of [IAIGC] that the award be preliminarily granted exequatur according to Jordanian law' must be denied as 'it appears to be more onerous than the local – Belgian – law on the enforcement of domestic arbitral awards, as it requires the exequatur of the award before considering it tantamount to a court decision', the Court of Appeal's decision gives Art. III of the New York Convention a scope which is not its own. Hence, it does not give sufficient reasons in law for either its denial of the ground raised by [IAIGC] regarding the violation of Art. V(1)(*e*) of this Convention or, consequently, its rejection of [IAIGC]'s objection to the exequatur order (violation of all the legal provisions referred to in that ground)."

II. THE DECISION

1. *The First Ground for Appeal*

a. *Articles 1719 and 1723 Judicial Code*

[14] "[We deal first with] the objection raised by [BAII] against the ground for appeal where it alleges the violation of Arts. 1719 and 1723 of the Judicial Code. [BAII] concludes that the ground does not specify in which manner these provisions would have been violated.

[15] "The ground for appeal does not specify the substance of the violation of Arts. 1719 and 1723 of the Judicial Code on which it relies. The objection is founded."

b. *Article V(1)(e)*

[16] "The [New York Convention] provides that the recognition and enforcement of an award may be refused, at the request of the party against whom it is invoked, only if that party furnishes to the competent authority where the recognition and enforcement is sought, proof that the award has not yet become binding on the parties or has been set aside or suspended by a

competent authority of the country in which, or under the law of which, that award was rendered. Pursuant to this provision, the competent authority of the country in which, or under the law of which, the award was made has jurisdiction on the setting aside and the suspension of the award. It does not follow from [Art. V(1)(*e*)] that the binding nature of the award can only be ascertained in accordance with the law of the country in which the award was rendered.

[17] "By requiring only that the award become binding on the parties, Art. V(1)(*e*) of the New York Convention intended to avoid that the party requesting the recognition and enforcement of the award first be required to seek an exequatur in the State of origin [of the award], which would amount to imposing the condition that the award be final, as previously stipulated by the Geneva Convention of 26 September 1927. It appears from the set-up of Art. V(1)(*e*) of the New York Convention that the award is binding on the parties, within the meaning of this provision, when it is no longer open to recourse on the merits. The question whether the award is open to such recourse is to be solved by referring, successively and one in the absence of the other, to the arbitration agreement, the law that it designates for such purpose, and, last, the law of the country in which the award was rendered.

[18] "Both in its own reasons and in those of the Court of First Instance, which it adopted, the appealed decision found that the arbitration agreement stipulated that the award was binding on the parties immediately after having been rendered and that it was not subject to appeal. The [Court of Appeal] thereby justified in law its decision not to deny recognition and enforcement of the award.

[19] "The considerations by which the [Court of Appeal] held that, if Jordanian law were applicable, the award would nevertheless be binding pursuant to the provisions of that law, are therefore superfluous.

[20] "To the extent that it invokes the violation of Art. V(1)(*e*) of the New York Convention, [IAIGC's] ground for appeal is unfounded. To the extent that it invokes the violation of the mentioned provisions of the Jordanian Law on Arbitration no. 18 of 29 December 1953, the ground for appeal is moot and therefore inadmissible."

c. *Article III*

[21] "Since the [appealed] decision is justified in law by the reasons it gives, which were unsuccessfully challenged in the first part of this ground for appeal, the second part of this ground for appeal, which only challenges superfluous considerations of the decision, is, as pointed out by [BAII], moot and therefore inadmissible."

2. *The Second Ground for Appeal (Article V(1)(c))*

[22] "[IAIGC's] second ground for appeal is based on the violation of Art. V, and in particular V(1)(*c*), of the [New York Convention], Arts. 1719 and 1723 of the Judicial Code, and Arts. 1319, 1320 and 1322 of the Civil Code.[4]
[23] "Having noted that '[a]s described above, the arbitrators qualified the Extension Agreement as one of the "other contracts", so that the nationality condition does not apply', the [Court of Appeal] rejected the ground raised by [IAIGC] with regard to Art. V(1)(*c*) of the New York Convention. It concluded that in deciding that the Extension Agreement fell into a category of agreements other than the insurance contracts which could be concluded by [IAIGC]'s Director General, the arbitrators '[had] placed [said contract] outside the scope of application of the arbitration agreement, as defined by Art. 36 of the Convention establishing IAIGC (petitioner)'. Hence, the decision affirmed the decision [of the Court of First Instance], which rejected the objection to the exequatur order reasoning as follows:

> '... Arts. 36 and 37 of the [1975 Convention] do not mean what the appellant wants them to mean. Art. 36 of the [1975 Convention] provides that the insurance contracts provide for the settlement of the disputes which may arise between [IAIGC] and the insured investors; Art. 37 concerns disputes with third parties and provides that, with the exception of the disputes provided for in the preceding Articles, all disputes between [IAIGC] and third parties fall under the jurisdiction of the competent judicial authorities in the Contracting States. [BAII] is no

---

4. Arts. 1319, 1320 and 1322 of the Civil Code read:

Article 1319
"An authentic instrument is an instrument which is drawn up in a legal form in the presence of a public official who is competent in the place where it is drawn up."

Article 1320
"The instrument, whether authentic or private provides evidence as between the parties, even of matters which are only included by reference therein, provided the reference is directly connected with the subject of the document. References which are not connected only serve as prima facie evidence."

Article 1322
"A private instrument which is acknowledged by the person to whom it is opposed, or which is legally acknowledged, has the same value as evidence between the signatories of the instrument and between their heirs and beneficiaries."

> "third party" here; it is an "insured investor" in a dispute arisen between [IAIGC] and itself. According to the law of the parties, the arbitration agreement covers the whole of the dispute settled by the arbitrators. The re-qualification of the Deferment Agreement and the Extension Agreement does not affect [BAII]'s status of insured investor, since the correspondence leading to these Agreements was exchanged following the insurance contract. In the narrow sense, and as a whole, this is a dispute provided for in Art. 36 of the [1975 Convention]. In fact, the arbitral tribunal, which had jurisdiction under Art. 36 [read: 57] of the [1975 Convention], finds that the right to indemnities had already been acquired, as the indemnities had become due. These indemnities have been the object of a new contract, a *dation en paiement*, whose entry into force or validity has not been contested by any of the parties. It is not so much the (re)-qualification which is an essential element of the arbitrators' decision; rather, it is the fact that the indemnities became due and the obligations of the appellant under the Guarantee Contract became unconditional.'

Consequently, '[t]he ground based on the lack of jurisdiction of the arbitrators is unfounded'.

[24] "Art. 36 of the Convention establishing the Inter-Arab Investment Guarantee Corporation, inserted in Chapter IX on the settlement of disputes, provides under the title 'Disputes related to insurance contracts', that '[t]he insurance contracts shall determine the dispute resolution mechanism for the disputes which may arise between the corporation and the insured investors'; the dispute resolution mechanism can consist in the submission of the dispute to arbitrators. According to Art. 12 of the same Convention, the duties of the Director General of [IAIGC] particularly include entering into 'insurance contracts with investors as well as other agreements pertaining to the activities of [IAIGC]'. This provision is the basis of the distinction made by the arbitrators between insurance contracts and 'other contracts', in which category they have placed the Extension Agreement entered into by [IAIGC] and [BAII].

[25] "According to [IAIGC], when they decided that the Extension Agreement fell into the category of 'other contracts', the arbitrators should have found that they had no jurisdiction over the dispute between [IAIGC] and [BAII], as Art. 36 of the IAIGC Convention allows only those disputes related to insurance contracts to be referred to arbitration. [IAIGC alleges that], in holding that, although 'the arbitrators qualified the Extension Agreement as one of the "other contracts"', the dispute decided by the arbitrators, '[i]n the narrow sense, and as a whole, ... is ... provided for in Art. 36 of the [1975

Convention]', the Court of Appeal gave this provision, which refers only to the insurance contracts, an interpretation that is irreconcilable with its terms (violation of Arts. 1319, 1320 and 1322 of the Civil Code) and, consequently, did not justify in law its rejection of the ground for appeal raised by [IAIGC] regarding the violation by the arbitral award at issue of Art. V(1)(*c*) of the New York Convention (violation of all the legal provisions referred to in the ground).

[26] "This ground for appeal, without any reference to the arbitration agreement, maintains that the decision [of the Court of Appeal] violated Art. 36 of the [IAIGC] Convention. However, it does not specify in which manner such violation would result in the arbitral award not being within the scope of the arbitration agreement. Even if it were founded, this ground would not lead to reversing [the lower court's decision] and is thus inadmissible."

BERMUDA

Accession: 12 February 1980
(extension by the United Kingdom)
1st Reservation

4. Supreme Court of Bermuda, Civil Jurisdiction 1993, 21 January 1994, No. 381

Parties: Plaintiffs: (1) Skandia International Insurance Company (nationality not indicated);
(2) Mercantile and General Reinsurance Company (nationality not indicated);
(3) Gerling-Konzern Globale Rueckversicherungs-Gesellschaft (nationality not indicated);
(4) Union Rueckversicherungs-Gesellschaft (nationality not indicated);
(5) Assicurazioni Generali SpA (nationality not indicated);
(6) Hannover Rueckversicherungs-Aktiengesellschaft (nationality not indicated);
(7) Muenchener Rueckversicherungs-Gesellschaft (nationality not indicated)
Defendant: Al Amana Insurance and Reinsurance Company Limited (Bermuda)

Published in: Excerpt in CLOUT (Case Law on UNCITRAL Texts) A/CN.9/SER.C/ABSTRACTS/9, 7 June 1996, reproduced in Yearbook XXII (1997) pp. 290-291; no further publication information available

Articles: II(2); II(3)

Subject matters: – power of court to restrain foreign court proceedings in breach of arbitration agreement
– concurrent application Art. II(2) New York Convention and Art. 7 UNCITRAL Model Law

– incorporation of arbitration clause by reference

Commentary Cases: ¶ 217; [21]-[26] + [33]-[41] = ¶ 209; [32] = ¶ 219

Facts

Skandia International Insurance Company (Skandia) and the other plaintiffs were reinsurers of Al Amana, in respect of real and personal property located in Kuwait and belonging to Alghanim Industries and its associated companies. Alghanim sustained extensive property damage in Kuwait during and consequential to the Iraqi invasion of Kuwait in August 1990. Disputes arose as to whether Alghanim's losses were excluded by virtue of a War Risks Exclusion Clause contained in the reinsurance agreements between Al Amana and Skandia and the other plaintiffs.

Alghanim initiated court proceedings in Kuwait against Al Amana which joined Skandia and the other reinsurers as third parties. Skandia and other reinsurers invoked the arbitration clauses in the reinsurance agreements (referred to below as the "Proportional Treaty" and the "Facultative Reinsurance") with Al Amana, arguing that the Kuwaiti court lacked jurisdiction over them with respect to this dispute. Skandia and the other reinsurers initiated arbitration proceedings as well as court proceedings in the Supreme Court of Bermuda, requesting the court to issue an injunction restraining Al Amana from continuing legal proceedings against them in Kuwait on the ground that the there existed an arbitration agreement providing that their disputes be arbitrated at the seat of the defendant party, i.e., Bermuda.

The court, per Vincent W. Meerabux, held that it had jurisdiction to grant the injunction requested by Skandia and the other reinsurers, albeit that it must exercise caution in doing so. Finding the Kuwaiti proceedings to be vexatious and oppressive conduct by Al Amana and that the parties had clearly agreed to arbitration, the court issued the requested injunction.

Excerpt

I. SUPREME COURT'S JURISDICTION

[1] "I think that it is undisputed by counsel for the parties that this Court has jurisdiction to restrain foreign legal proceedings brought in breach of an arbitration agreement, both under its inherent jurisdiction and by virtue of Sect. 19(c) of Bermuda's Supreme Court Act 1905 (Title 8 Item 1) the relevant

portion of which provides that '... an injunction may be granted ... by an interlocutory order of the court in all cases in which it appears to the Court to be just or convenient that such order should be made; and any such order may be made either unconditionally or upon such terms and conditions as the Court thinks just....'

[2] "It is to be observed that Sect. 19(c) of the Supreme Court Act 1905 corresponds to Sect. 37(1) of the Supreme Court Act 1981 of the United Kingdom,...

(....)

[3] "[R]ecent judicial support for the proposition that the Court has jurisdiction to grant injunctive relief generally in support of an arbitration (whether within or without the jurisdiction) is to be found in the highly persuasive decision of the House of Lords in *Channel Tunnel Group Ltd. v. Balfour Beatty Ltd.* [1993] 1 All E.R. 664.[1] At 684 and 685 Lord Mustill said:

> 'Although the words of Sect. 37(1) and its forebears are very wide it is firmly established by a long history of judicial self-denial that they are not to be taken at their face value and that their application is subject to severe constraints.... [I]t is sufficient for present purposes to quote from the speech of Lord Brandon of Oakbrook in the *South Carolina* case [1986] 3 All E.R. 487 at 495-496, [1987] A.C. 24 at 39-40:
>
> "The first basic principle is that the power of the High Court to grant injunctions is a statutory power conferred on it by Sect. 37(1) of the Supreme Court Act 1981,... The second basic principle is that, although the terms of Sect. 37(1) of the 1981 Act and its predecessors are very wide, the power conferred by them has been circumscribed by judicial authority dating back many years.... The third basic principle is that among the forms of injunction which the High Court has power to grant is an injunction granted to one party to an action to restrain the other party to it from beginning, or if he has begun from continuing, proceedings against the former in a foreign court. Such jurisdiction is, however, to be exercised with caution because it involves direct interference with the process of the foreign court concerned."'"

1. Reported in Yearbook XIX (1994) pp. 736-747 (UK no. 37).

II. EXERCISE OF THE COURT'S POWER TO RESTRAIN

[4] "Both sides accept that the Court's discretionary power to restrain a party from commencing or pursuing legal proceedings in a foreign court is stated authoritatively in *Dicey and Morris Conflict of Laws* (Twelfth ed. 1993) at pages 408-419 and in *Castanho v. Brown & Root* [1981] A.C. 557 (*Castanho*) at 572f-575c, *British Airways Board v. Laker* [1985] A.C. 58 (*BAB*) at 81e-g to 95a-b, *South Carolina Insurance Co. v. Assurantie Maatschappij 'de Zeven Provincien', NV* [1987] A.C. 24 (*South Carolina*) 40d to e and *Société Nationale Industrielle Aerospatiale v. Lee* [1987] 1 A.C. 871 (*Aerospatiale*) at 892A-897A, a decision of the Privy Council which is binding. Certain basic principles emerge on which the Court may exercise its power to the cases set out hereunder.

[5] "The Court can exercise its power where it is appropriate to avoid injustice.

(....)

[6] "The Court may exercise such power where a party has sought to institute or pursue proceedings in a foreign court in breach of an arbitration agreement.

(....)

[7] "No doubt the jurisdiction is to be exercised with caution.... The jurisdiction which is to be exercised with caution also applies to a case where the ground relied on for seeking such an injunction is that the foreign proceedings have been instituted in breach of a 'clause giving exclusive jurisdiction to the Court of this country' or in breach of an arbitration agreement...."

III. KUWAITI COURT PROCEEDINGS

[8] "It appears that in ancillary legal proceedings commenced on 3 May 1992 in the Kuwaiti Courts, the defendant claimed against the plaintiffs as its reinsurers. From the outset the plaintiffs challenged the competence of the Kuwaiti Courts under the 1958 New York Arbitration Convention (to which Kuwait is a party). ... Defendant disputed the plaintiffs' challenge to the competence of the Kuwaiti Courts. Mr. Beloff for the defendant submitted that the injunction sought should not be granted on the ground that –

(a) the Kuwaiti Court was the natural forum in which the plaintiffs ought to seek a stay of the proceedings therein the basis relied on namely that Al

Amana had agreed to have disputes as to the plaintiffs' liability to them qua retrocessionaires resolved by arbitration;

(b) the plaintiffs had in fact raised the issue of the arbitration clauses before the Kuwaiti Court;

(c) it was contrary to principle for a court to grant an injunction restraining foreign proceedings where an application was already pending to stay those proceedings. Lloyd J. in *World Pride Shipping Ltd. v. Daiichi Chuo Kisen Kaisha* [1984] 2 LLR 489 p. 498;

(d) it was wrong as a matter of principle for a party to seek a ruling from a court in one jurisdiction and simultaneously to seek to obtain an injunction restraining the continuation of those foreign proceedings; such a course of conduct amounted to abuse of process;

(e) the effect of the grant of an injunction by the Bermuda court would be to pre-empt the consideration of the stay application by the Kuwaiti Court and that it would be contrary to principles of comity for this court to seek to pre-empt a foreign court in circumstances where the foreign court was already seised of the issue.

[9] "Mr. Veeder for the plaintiffs contended that the Kuwaiti Court was not a competent jurisdiction and should be disregarded as a natural forum, that the plaintiffs by challenging the jurisdiction of the Kuwaiti Court did not submit to its jurisdiction and that there was no evidence that the plaintiffs submitted to the jurisdiction of [the] Kuwaiti Court as borne out by the affirmation of Al Sarraf of 20 December 1993.

(....)

[10] "I think that it can be inferred from that affirmation that the plaintiffs have challenged the jurisdiction of the Kuwaiti Court, have raised the issues of the arbitration clauses before the Kuwaiti Court, have applied to the Kuwaiti Court to stay the proceedings as against the defendant, are seeking to rely on the arbitration clauses to stay the Kuwaiti proceedings. Moreover, it seems that the plaintiffs' application to stay the Kuwaiti proceedings are pending before the Kuwait Court. Furthermore it is undisputed that Kuwait is a signatory to the [1958 New York Convention]...."

[11] After citing Art. II(3) of the New York Convention the court continued "The Convention is given effect in Kuwait in Law No. 10 of 1978, dated 26 March 1978....

[12] "Since the plaintiffs have made an application to the Kuwaiti Court to stay the Kuwaiti proceedings as against the defendant would it not be better on ground of judicial comity not to restrain the defendant in prosecuting his claim against the plaintiffs in the Kuwaiti Court until the Kuwaiti Court had decided whether or not it had jurisdiction?

[13] "In *World Pride Shipping Ltd. v. Daiichi Chuo Kisen Kaisha* [1984] 2 LLR 489 proceedings had been commenced in the US courts concurrently with the initiation of arbitration procedures and actions were brought in the US for a stay and in England for an injunction. Lloyd J. refused the injunction. At 498 Lloyd J. said:

> 'The jurisdiction of the Court to grant an injunction to restrain a party from proceeding in a foreign Court has recently been re-affirmed by the Court of Appeal in *Tracomin S.A. v. Sudan Oil Seeds Co. Ltd.* [1983] 2 Lloyd's Rep. 384; [1983] 1 W.L.R. 1026. In an even recent decision, *British Airways Board v. Laker Airways Ltd.* [1983] 3 W.L.R. 544, the Court of Appeal has granted relief in mandatory form. In both cases it was emphasised that the jurisdiction is one which should be exercised with extreme caution. The question I ask myself, therefore, is whether justice in this case now demands that I should grant the mandatory injunction for which World Pride asks. I have come to the conclusion that I should not.
>
> [14] "'The crucial difference between the present case and *Tracomin* [is that] the Swiss Court had already refused a stay pursuant to the arbitration clause. Accordingly there was no way in which the English court could seek to compel the buyers to honour the arbitration agreement except by granting an injunction. In the present case, by contrast, the American court has not yet ruled on the joint motion for continuance. The matter is still open. It seems to me that in those circumstances it would be much better that the District Court should itself rule on the motion for continuance and, if it thinks fit, stay all further proceedings on World Pride's cross-claim, in the light of the judgment I have given upholding the validity of Mr. Eckersley's appointment as arbitrator, rather than that I should seek to pre-empt, and perhaps even seem to dictate the decision of a foreign Court.'
>
> (....)

[15] "But account should be taken of Lord Goff's statement in *Aerospatiale* [1987] 1 A.C. 871 when delivering the opinion of the Privy Council which is binding on this Court. He stated that jurisdiction to stay foreign proceedings was to be exercised with caution and normally confined to cases where the foreign proceedings were either vexatious or oppressive.... Are the Kuwaiti proceedings vexatious or oppressive?

[16] "In *Continental Bank N.A. and Aeakos Compania Naviera S.A. and others T.L.R.*, 26 November 1993 (C.A.) the central question was whether the Continental Bank was entitled by virtue of an exclusive jurisdiction agreement to

an injunction restraining a group of borrowers and guarantors from bringing legal proceedings against the Bank in Greece. The agreement under the European Community's Brussels Convention on Jurisdiction and Judgments conferred exclusive jurisdiction on the English Courts.

[17] "The Court granted an injunction restraining the party concerned from pursuing the Greek proceedings even though the Greek Court was also bound to apply the Brussels Convention. The Court found that the party concerned was in breach of an exclusive jurisdiction agreement and that the continuance of the Greek proceedings amounted to vexatious and oppressive conduct and that a claim for damages for breach of contract would be a relatively ineffective remedy.

(....)

[18] "In the *Continental Bank* case there are certain similarities as in the present case. The issue in that case concerned the breach of an exclusive jurisdiction agreement – the issue in this case is the breach of an arbitration agreement which is an exclusive jurisdiction agreement. The Greek Court was bound to apply the Brussels Convention as is the Kuwaiti Court bound to apply the New York Convention. The matter is first brought before the Greek Court – in the present case the matter is first brought before the Kuwaiti Court. The Greek Court was to decide whether or not it had jurisdiction and likewise the Kuwaiti Court is to decide.

[19] "The question concerning the indirect interference with the workings of a Community Court if an injunction were granted was raised before the Court, the question of proceeding with great caution before granting an injunction was put before the Court, as well as the granting of an injunction only if the ends of justice required it and the granting of an injunction if the pursuit of a remedy in a foreign court would be vexatious and oppressive – like [the] questions are before this Court.

[20] "Thus, on the assumption that the defendant breached the arbitration agreement, which is an exclusive jurisdiction agreement, by the prosecution of the continuance of Kuwaiti proceedings that I think amounts to vexatious and oppressive conduct on the part of the defendant. But are there arbitration agreements and if so are they breached by the defendant?"

IV. ARBITRATION AGREEMENTS

[21] "Next to consider is whether there are arbitration agreements between the parties. It appears from the evidence that there are two forms of written arbitration agreements between the parties – Art. 10 of the Proportional Treaty and General Condition 4 of the Facultative Reinsurance.

[22] "Art. 10 of the Proportional Treaty reads as follows:

'(1) Disputes arising out of this Agreement or differences concerning the validity of this Agreement shall be submitted to the decision of a court of arbitration, consisting of three members, which shall meet at the seat of the defendant party.'
(....)

[23] "General Condition 4 of the Facultative Reinsurance reads as follows:

'ARBITRATION. If any difference arises as to the amount of any loss or damage, such differences shall independently of all other questions be referred to the decision of an arbitrator, to be appointed in writing by each of the parties within two calendar months after having been required so to do in writing by the other party.'
(....)

[24] "As to form it appears that both insurance agreements satisfy the conditions of Sect. 2 of the 1993 Act and Art. 7(1) of the Model Law as set out in Schedule 2 to that Act[2] and Art. II(2) of the New York Arbitration Convention as set out in Schedule 3 to that Act.

[25] "In August 1993 the seven plaintiffs commenced two separate arbitrations in Bermuda under Art. 10 and General Condition 4 respectively of the Treaty Arbitration and the Facultative Arbitration. Both arbitrations were commenced after the operative date of the 1993 Act, that is 29 June 1993 and by virtue of Sect. 38 of the 1993 Act, that Act applies to the two arbitrations notwithstanding that the arbitration agreements were made before the commencement of the 1993 Act.
(....)

---

2. Sect. 2 of the 1993 Bermuda International Conciliation and Arbitration Act reads in relevant part:

"(....)
'arbitration agreement' has the same meaning as Art. 7(1) of the Model Law;...."

Art. 7(1) of the UNCITRAL Model Law on International Commercial Arbitration reads:

"'Arbitration agreement' is an agreement by the parties to submit to arbitration all or certain disputes which have arisen or which may arise between them in respect of a defined legal relationship, whether contractual or not. An arbitration agreement may be in the form of an arbitration clause in a contract or in the form of a separate agreement."

[26] "I think that from a prima assessment of the evidence it can be inferred that there exists arbitration agreements."

V. THE NATURAL FORUM

[27] "Mr. Beloff for the defendant submitted that the Kuwaiti Court was the natural forum in which the plaintiffs ought to seek a stay of the proceedings therein on the basis relied on namely that the defendant had agreed to have disputes as to the plaintiffs' liability to them qua retrocessionaires resolved by arbitration. He also submitted that Kuwait was the defendant's commercial seat. Mr. Veeder for the plaintiffs argues that Bermuda, being the defendant's seat, was identified by Art. 10(1) as the agreed place of the Treaty Arbitration under Art. 20(1) of the Model Law and in respect of the Facultative Re-insurance, Bermuda was the natural forum for the defendant, being its seat and the domicile of the sole arbitrator, being a Bermuda resident in Bermuda with the same consequence, subject to any further decision of the sole arbitrator under Art. 20(1) of the Model Law.[3]

[28] "From the evidence it appears that the defendant is a company incorporated in Bermuda under the Companies Act 1981 and it is also registered as an insurer under the Insurance Act 1978. Its business is regulated under both Acts by the Registrar of Companies. The defendant must comply with the provisions of both legislation. As an insurance company it must have a principal representative resident in Bermuda who is either a registered insurance manager or a person otherwise approved by the Minister of Finance upon certain events relating to the financial position of the company. As a creature of Bermuda legislation it is subject to such legislation and in conse-quence it has a substantial legal connection to Bermuda.... On the other hand the defendant is not authorised to conduct insurance or reinsurance or any other kind of business in or from Kuwait nor can the defendant lawfully maintain any office or employees in Kuwait. The plaintiffs are all European companies. They are not incorporated in Kuwait and have no presence in Kuwait.

[29] "In light of the above I am of view that the defendant's seat lies in Bermuda, the place of its incorporation, registration and regulation. Hence

3. Art. 20(1) of the Model Law reads:

"The parties are free to agree on the place of arbitration. Failing such agreement, the place of arbitration shall be determined by the arbitral tribunal having regard to the circumstances of the case, including the convenience of the parties."

Bermuda being the defendant's seat was identified by Art. 10(1) of the Proportional Treaty as the agreed place of that Treaty Arbitration under Art. 20(1) of the Model Law as set out in Schedule 2 to the 1993 Act. As regards the Facultative Reinsurance I agree with the argument of Mr. Veeder and hold that Bermuda is the natural forum for the defendant."

VI. PLAINTIFFS' CHALLENGE TO JURISDICTION OF KUWAITI COURT

[30] "The plaintiffs have from the outset challenged the competence of the Kuwaiti Courts under the 1958 New York Convention. Mr. Veeder for the plaintiffs denied that by doing so they submitted to the jurisdiction of the Kuwaiti Court. I think that such a position taken by the plaintiffs finds support in *Marc Rich & Co. A.G. v. Società Italiana Impianti P.A.* (No. 2) [1992] 1 LLR 624. Neil L.J. said at 633:

> 'I turn therefore to the question whether Marc Rich submitted to the jurisdiction of the Italian Courts at a time and in a manner which prevents them relying on Sect. 32 because of the non-fulfilment of condition (c). In my judgment it is important that Sect. 33 should not be construed too narrowly. It may well be that it was not necessary for Marc Rich to lodge an alternative defence on the merits in October, 1988, but they made it abundantly clear in the pleading that the primary purpose of the document was to challenge the jurisdiction of the Genoa Court. I am prepared to assume that the first defence did not amount to a submission. As I understand that paragraph, coupled with the answer which was given formally on p. 1689 in para. 2, the Court is there saying that provided the defendant makes it clear in his first defence rather than in some subsequent defence that he is contesting the jurisdiction, that will not amount to a submission even though there is some additional material which constitutes a plea to the merits of the case. That seems to be an additional reason for interpreting Sect. 33 in a broad sense.'
> (....)

[31] "I do not think that the fact that the plaintiffs' raising of the issue of the arbitration clauses in their first defence before the Kuwaiti Court in any [way] indicated that the plaintiffs had submitted to the Court's jurisdiction."

VII. ARBITRABLE DISPUTE

[32] The Court examined the question of whether there was an arbitrable dispute in light of the width and scope of the words "disputes" or "differences" as they were considered in *Hayter v. Nelson* [1990] 2 LLR 265[4] and found that there were "arbitrable disputes under both the Treaty and Facultative Reinsurance".

VIII. FACULTATIVE REINSURANCE – INCORPORATION BY REFERENCE

[33] "The defendant has accepted that by Art. 7(2) of the Model Law it was possible to incorporate an arbitration clause by reference to another document provided that 'the reference is such as to make that clause part of the contract'. The defendant submitted that as a matter of construction of the document relied upon there was no effective incorporation of the arbitration clause contained in the primary insurance policy. Reliance was placed in a telex from MASCO dated 23 January 1990 setting out the details of reinsurance. The relevant part provides –

> 'Cover: all risks of physical loss or damage and LOP therefrom as per wording attached.'

The first and third plaintiffs submitted that the above reference to 'Cover' was sufficient to incorporate the entirety of the primary insurance policy including the general conditions set out therein.

[34] "The defendant submitted that the above reference simply incorporated the description of the risks in respect of which reinsurance was effected for as a matter of plain construction of the words it did not incorporate the entirety of the policy and the description 'Cover' was wholly inadequate to incorporate the arbitration clause contained in another document.

[35] "I think that a scanning of Art. 7(2) of the Model Law is necessary and desirable. The relevant portion of that article provides:

> '.... The reference in a contract to a document containing an arbitration clause constitutes an arbitration agreement provided that the contract is in writing and the reference is such as to make that clause part of the contract.'

4. Reported in Yearbook XIX (1994) pp. 717-724 (UK no. 34).

[36] "By virtue of Sect. 24 of the 1993 Act for the purpose of interpreting the Model Law reference may be made of the *travaux préparatoires*. The *travaux préparatoires* of the Model Law show that it is not necessary for an explicit reference to be made in the contractual documents to the arbitration clause and that general words of incorporation suffice under Art. 7 of the Model Law. (....)

[37] "In Holtzmann & Neuhaus, *Guide to the UNCITRAL Model Law* (1989) at pp. 263 and 264 it is stated:

> '(....)
> The meaning of the requirement that "the reference [be] such as to make [the arbitration] clause a part of the contract" may raise questions. The Working Group made clear that it did not mean the contract had to make explicit reference to the arbitration clause itself. The requirement was adopted as a middle ground between two positions: one view was that the text of the arbitration agreement had to "be before both parties" in order to bind them; another view was that only a "reference" in the contract to general conditions or other documents containing the arbitration clause was enough. The language adopted appears to mean that the general conditions, prior contract or other document must have been intended to be incorporated into the contract, and not merely referred to in, for example, a "whereas" clause or as background to the agreement'

[38] "At page 285 is stated:

> 'FIFTH WORKING GROUP REPORT A/CN.9/246 (6 MARCH 1984)
> (....)
> 19. The Working Group was agreed that the last part of the last sentence of paragraph (2) should not be understood as requiring an explicit reference to the arbitration clause contained in a document referred to.'

[39] "In Berger, *International Economic Arbitration* (1993) at pages 152 and 153 is stated:

> 'The wording of the ML is misleading in that Art. 7(2) 3rd sentence requires a reference which makes "that clause" part of the contract. This does not mean, however, that the ML always requires a specific reference to the arbitration clause contained in some other document. Such a view would not conform with modern commercial practice where parties to

commercial contracts usually refer to other legal texts *as such* rather than to individual clauses like arbitration agreements contained therein in order to avoid loss of time and unnecessary double references. The formula employed in the ML has to be viewed against the proper function of the formal validity rule. The reference to the document containing the arbitration agreement has to be of a kind which ensures that the parties are aware of the fact that they oust the jurisdiction of the competent courts. To meet these requirements, the almost unanimous international doctrine requires that the other party is already in possession of the contract conditions or that the other party is put in a position to check the reference, for example where the conditions are set out on the reverse side of the contract or attached to it or, alternatively, that dispute settlement through arbitration is customary in that particular business.'

[40] "Nevertheless it appears that by Art. 16 of the Model Law, the arbitration tribunal, and not the Court, is the first to decide matters of jurisdiction, including any dispute about the existence, validity and scope of the arbitration agreement invoked by the claimant. Furthermore, it seems that the role of the local court in determining disputes as to the arbitrators' jurisdiction is by virtue of Art. 16(3) of the Model Law strictly confined to intervention by way of appeal from the arbitration tribunal's determination in favour of its jurisdiction.
(....)
[41] "I think in light of the foregoing[5] the construction of the words of the document cannot be on the 'literal rule' basis. It has to take into account the *travaux préparatoires* that shed light on Art. 7 of the Model Law. Thus I do not think that the 'plain construction of words' approach is applicable. Hence I do not accept Mr. Beloff's submissions. In any case in my view the matters raised by the defendant in his submissions are matters that relate to the existence, validity and scope of an arbitration agreement and are matters for the arbitral tribunal first."

---

5. The Court cited *Fung Sang Trading Ltd. v. Kai Sun Sea Products and Food Co. Ltd.* [1992] 1 H.K.L.R. 40 at 51 and 52 [reported in Yearbook XVIII (1992) pp. 289-304] and the Report by E. Gaillard, "Law and Court Decisions in Civil Law Countries" on the topic of "Efforts by a party to seek intervention by a national court for the purpose of delaying or disrupting the arbitration" published in A.J. van den Berg, Gen. Ed., *I. Preventing delay and disruption of arbitration/II. Effective proceedings in construction cases*, ICCA Congress series no. 5 (1990) pp 163-164.

IX. CONCLUSION

[42] "It follows that I grant the relief sought by the plaintiffs. In my judgment there is a clear bargain between the parties that any dispute should be determined in one way only – namely, by reference to arbitration being a condition precedent to any liability of either party and the prosecution of the Kuwaiti proceedings amounts to vexatious and oppressive conduct by the defendant."

COURT OF JUSTICE OF THE EUROPEAN COMMUNITIES

1. Court of Justice of the European Communities, 1 June 1999, C-126/97

Parties:	Appellant/counter-appellee: Eco Swiss China Time Ltd. (Hong Kong) Appellee/counter-appellant:[1] Benetton International N.V. (Netherlands)
Published in:	Publication information not yet available
Articles:	V(2)(*b*)
Subject matters:	- competition law - violation of Art. 81 EC (ex Art. 85) is contrary to public policy - violation of competition law not raised in arbitral proceedings - preliminary ruling open to courts determining validity of arbitral awards - partial award is res judicata with respect to final award
Commentary Cases:	[14]-[17] = ¶ 524 + ¶ 703

Facts

The facts of this case are also reported in Yearbook XXIII (1998) pp. 180-181.

By a contract concluded on 1 July 1986, Benetton International N.V. (Benetton), Eco Swiss China Time Ltd. (Eco Swiss) and Bulova Watch Com-

1. The denomination of the parties as Appellant/counter-appellee and Appellee/counter-appellant refers to their procedural position in the appeal before the Supreme Court of The Netherlands.

pany Inc. (Bulova), a United States company, entered into a license agreement for eight years. Art. 26.A of the agreement provided for the arbitration of all disputes according to Dutch law under the Rules of the Netherlands Arbitration Institute (NAI).

On 24 June 1991, Benetton gave notice of termination of the agreement with effect from 24 September 1991, three years before the end of the period originally provided for. An arbitration ensued between the parties concerning Benetton's unilateral termination of the agreement.

In a Partial Award (PFA) of 4 February 1993, deposited at the registry of the Court of First Instance in The Hague (Rechtbank) on the same date, the NAI arbitrators held that the license agreement continued in full force: they also held that Benetton should compensate Eco Swiss for damages caused by the unilateral termination of the agreement.

In a Final Award (FAA) of 23 June 1995, deposited at the registry of the Court of First Instance in The Hague on 26 June 1995, the arbitrators directed Benetton to pay Eco Swiss US$ 23,750,000 and US$ 2,800,000 to Bulova in compensation for the damage occasioned by Benetton's breach of contract. By order of the President of the Court of First Instance in The Hague of 17 July 1995, leave was given to enforce the FAA.

Three days earlier, on 14 July 1995, Benetton commenced court proceedings in the Court of First Instance in The Hague seeking setting aside of the PFA and FAA (the setting aside proceedings). On 2 October 1996, the Court of First Instance dismissed the application whereupon Benetton appealed to the Court of Appeal, The Hague (Gerechtshof).

On 24 July 1995, Benetton commenced proceedings in the same Court of First Instance, seeking a stay of enforcement of the FAA and, alternatively, that Eco Swiss and Bulova be required to give security (the suspension proceedings). The Court of First Instance in the Hague denied a stay of enforcement of the FAA and granted Benetton's alternative request that Eco Swiss and Bulova post security.

On 28 March 1996, the Court of Appeal in The Hague reversed, granting a stay of enforcement of the FAA and denying Benetton's request for security.

In both the suspension and setting aside proceedings, Benetton had claimed that the PFA and the FAA were invalid because the license agreement violated Art. 85 (now Art. 81) of the EC Treaty. In cassation proceedings against the suspension, the Supreme Court (Hoge Raad) adjourned its decision in order to pose five questions to the EC Court of Justice (see below at [8]). The decisions of the Court of Appeal, The Hague of 28 March 1996, and the Supreme Court of 21 March 1997 are reported in Yearbook XXIII (1998) pp. 180-195.

In its answer to the preliminary questions submitted to it, the European Court of Justice ruled:

> "1. A national court to which application is made for annulment of an arbitration award must grant that application if it considers that the award in question is in fact contrary to Art. 81 EC (ex Art. 85), where its domestic rules of procedure require it to grant an application for annulment founded on failure to observe national rules of public policy.
> 2. Community law does not require a national court to refrain from applying domestic rules of procedure according to which an interim arbitration award which is in the nature of a final award and in respect of which no application for annulment has been made within the prescribed time-limit acquires the force of res judicata and may no longer be called in question by a subsequent arbitration award, even if this is necessary in order to examine, in proceedings for annulment of a subsequent arbitration award, whether an agreement which the interim award held to be valid in law is nevertheless void under Art. 81 EC (ex Art. 85)."

Thus, in essence the ruling stated that a violation of Art. 81 EC would be a violation of public policy to be applied in setting aside proceedings. However, the setting aside of the PFA had not been requested within the three month time limit and it was res judicata with respect to the FAA.

Excerpt

I. DECISION OF THE COURT OF APPEAL, THE HAGUE (GERECHTSHOF) OF 28 MARCH 1996

[1] The European Court of Justice summarized the proceedings in The Netherlands as follows: "The Gerechtshof took the view that Art. 81 EC (ex Art. 85) is a provision of public policy within the meaning of Art. 1065(1)(*e*) of the Code of Civil Procedure,[2] infringement of which may result in annul-

2. Art. 1065 of The Netherlands Code of Civil Procedure (CCP) reads in relevant part:

"1. Setting aside of the award can take place only on one or more of the following grounds:
(....)
(*c*) the arbitral tribunal has not complied with its mandate;
(....)
(*e*) the award, or the manner in which it was made, violates public policy or good morals.
(....)
4. The ground mentioned in paragraph (1)(*c*) above shall not constitute a ground for setting aside if the party who invokes this ground has participated in the arbitral proceedings without invoking such ground, although it was known to him that the arbitral tribunal did not

ment of an arbitration award. However, the Gerechtshof considered that, in the proceedings before it for stay of enforcement, it was unable to examine whether a partial final award such as the PFA was in conformity with Art. 1065(1)(*e*) of the Code of Civil Procedure, since Benetton had not lodged an application for annulment within three months after the lodging of that award at the registry of the Rechtbank, as required by Art. 1064(3) of the Code of Civil Procedure.[3]

[2] "Nevertheless, the Gerechtshof took the view that it was able to examine the FAA in relation to Art. 1065(1)(*e*), particularly as regards the effect of Art. 81(1) and (2) EC (ex Art. 85(1) and (2))[4] on the assessment of damage, since to award compensation for damage flowing from the wrongful termination of the licensing agreement would amount to enforcing that agreement, whereas it was, at least in part, void under Art. 81(1) and (2) EC (ex Art. 85(1) and (2)). The agreement in question enabled the parties to operate a market-sharing

---

comply with its mandate.
(....)"

3. Art. 1064(3) of The Netherlands CCP reads:

"An application for setting aside may be made as soon as the award has acquired the force of res judicata. The right to make an application shall be extinguished three months after the date of deposit of the award with the Registry of the District Court. However, if the award together with leave for enforcement is officially served on the other party, that party may make an application for setting aside within three months after the said service, irrespective of whether the period of three months mentioned in the preceding sentence has lapsed."

4. Art. 81 EC (ex Art. 85) reads in relevant part:

"1. The following shall be prohibited as incompatible with the common market: all agreements between undertakings, decisions by associations of undertakings and concerted practices which may affect trade between Member States and which have as their object or effect the prevention, restriction or distortion of competition within the common market, and in particular those which:
(a) directly or indirectly fix purchase or selling prices or any other trading conditions;
(b) limit or control production, markets, technical development, or investment;
(c) share markets or sources of supply;
(d) apply dissimilar conditions to equivalent transactions with other trading parties, thereby placing them at a competitive disadvantage;
(e) make the conclusion of contracts subject to acceptance by the other parties of supplementary obligations which, by their nature or according to commercial usage, have no connection with the subject of such contracts.
2. Any agreements or decisions prohibited pursuant to this Article shall be automatically void.
(....)"

arrangement, since Eco Swiss could no longer sell watches and clocks in Italy and Bulova could no longer do so in the other countries which were then Member States of the Community. As Benetton and Eco Swiss acknowledge, the licensing agreement was not notified to the Commission and is not covered by a block exemption. The Gerechtshof considered that, in the procedure for annulment, the FAA could be held to be contrary to public policy, and therefore decided to grant the application for a stay in so far as it related to the FAA.

[3] "Eco Swiss brought proceedings in cassation before the Hoge Raad against the decision of the Gerechtshof and Benetton lodged a cross-appeal. The Hoge Raad observes that an arbitration award is contrary to public policy within the meaning of Art. 1065(1)(*e*) of the Code of Civil Procedure only if its terms or enforcement conflict with a mandatory rule so fundamental that no restrictions of a procedural nature should prevent its application. It states that, in Netherlands law, the mere fact that, because of the terms or enforcement of an arbitration award, a prohibition laid down in competition law is not applied is not generally regarded as being contrary to public policy.

[4] "However, referring to the judgment in Joined Cases C-430/93 and C-431/93 *Van Schijndel and Van Veen v. SPF* [1995] ECR I-4705, the Hoge Raad wonders whether the position is the same where, as in the case now before it, the provision in question is a rule of Community law. The Hoge Raad infers from that judgment that Art. 81 EC (ex Art. 85) is not to be regarded as a mandatory rule which is so fundamental that no restrictions of a procedural nature should prevent it from being observed.

[5] "Moreover, since it is not disputed that the question whether the licensing agreement might be void under Art. 81 EC (ex Art. 85) was not raised in the course of the arbitration proceedings, the Hoge Raad considers that the arbitrators would have gone beyond the ambit of the dispute if they had inquired into and ruled on that question. In such a case, their award would have been open to annulment pursuant to Art. 1065(1)(*c*) of the Code of Civil Procedure,[5] because they would have failed to comply with their terms of reference. Furthermore, according to the Hoge Raad, the parties themselves could not have raised the question of the possible nullity of the licensing agreement for the first time in the context of the proceedings for annulment.

[6] "The Hoge Raad states that such rules of procedure are justified by the general interest in having an effectively functioning arbitration procedure and that they are no less favourable to application of rules of Community law than to application of rules of national law. However, the Hoge Raad is uncertain whether the principles laid down by the Court in *Van Schijndel and Van Veen*,

5. For the text of Art. 1065(1)(*c*) of the CCP of The Netherlands, see fn. 2.

cited above, also apply to arbitrators, particularly since, according to the judgment in Case 102/81 *Nordsee v. Reederei Mond* [1982] ECR 1095,[6] an arbitration tribunal constituted pursuant to an agreement under private law, without State intervention, is not to be regarded as a court or tribunal for the purposes of Art. 234 EC (ex Art. 177)[7] and cannot therefore make references for a preliminary ruling under that article.

[7] "The Hoge Raad explains that, under Netherlands procedural law, where arbitrators have settled part of a dispute by an interim award which is in the nature of a final award, that award has the force of res judicata and, if annulment of that interim award has not been sought in proper time, the possibility of applying for annulment of a subsequent arbitration award proceeding upon the interim award is restricted by the principle of res judicata. However, the Hoge Raad is uncertain whether Community law precludes the Gerechtshof from applying such a procedural rule where, as in the present case, the subsequent arbitration award, the annulment of which has been applied for in proper time, proceeds upon an earlier arbitration award."

II. QUESTIONS REFERRED FOR A PRELIMINARY RULING

[8] "In those circumstances, the Hoge Raad der Nederlanden decided to stay proceedings and to refer the following questions to the Court for a preliminary ruling:

> '(1) To what extent is the ruling of the Court of Justice in Joined Cases C-430/93 and C-431/93 *Van Schijndel and Van Veen v. SPF* [1995] ECR I-4705 applicable by analogy if, in a dispute concerning a private law

---

6. Reported in Yearbook VIII (1983) pp. 183-191.
7. Art. 234 EC (ex Art. 177) reads:

> "The Court of Justice shall have jurisdiction to give preliminary rulings concerning:
> (a) the interpretation of this Treaty;
> (b) the validity and interpretation of acts of the institutions of the Community;
> (c) the interpretation of the statutes of bodies established by an act of the Council, where those statutes so provide.
>
> Where such a question is raised before any court or tribunal of a Member State, that court or tribunal may, if it considers that a decision on the question is necessary to enable it to give judgment, request the Court of Justice to give a ruling thereon.
>
> Where any such question is raised in a case pending before a court or tribunal of a Member State, against whose decisions there is no judicial remedy under national law, that court or tribunal shall bring the matter before the Court of Justice."

agreement brought before arbitrators and not before the national courts, the parties make no reference to Art. 85 of the EC Treaty and, according to the rules of national procedural law applicable to them, the arbitrators are not at liberty to apply those provisions of their own motion?
(2) If the court considers that an arbitration award is in fact contrary to Art. 85 of the EC Treaty, must it, on that ground and notwithstanding the rules of Netherlands procedural law ... [according to which a party may claim annulment of an arbitration award only on a limited number of grounds, one ground being that an award is contrary to public policy, which generally does not cover the mere fact that through the terms or enforcement of an arbitration award no effect is given to a prohibition laid down by competition law], allow a claim for annulment of that award if the claim otherwise complies with statutory requirements?
(3) Notwithstanding the rules of Netherlands procedural law ... [according to which arbitrators must not go outside the ambit of disputes and must keep to their terms of reference], is the court also required to allow such a claim if the question of the applicability of Art. 85 of the EC Treaty remained outside the ambit of the dispute in the arbitration proceedings and the arbitrators therefore made no determination in that regard?
(4) Does Community law require the rules of Netherlands procedural law ... [according to which an interim arbitration award that is in the nature of a final award acquires the force of res judicata and is open to appeal only within a period of three months following lodgement of the award at the registry of the Rechtbank] to be disapplied if this is necessary in order to examine, in proceedings for annulment of a subsequent arbitration award, whether an agreement which an interim arbitration award having the force of res judicata has held to be valid may nevertheless be void because it conflicts with Art. 85 of the EC Treaty?
(5) Or, in a case such as that described in Question 4, is it necessary to refrain from applying the rule that, in so far as an interim arbitration award is in the nature of a final award, annulment of that award may not be sought simultaneously with that of the subsequent arbitration award?'"

III. EXAMINATION OF THE QUESTIONS

1. *The Second Question*

[9] "By its second question, which is best examined first, the referring court is asking essentially whether a national court to which application is made for annulment of an arbitration award must grant such an application where, in its view, that award is in fact contrary to Art. 81 EC (ex Art. 85) although, under domestic procedural rules, it may grant such an application only on a limited number of grounds, one of them being inconsistency with public policy, which, according to the applicable national law, is not generally to be invoked on the sole ground that, because of the terms or the enforcement of an arbitration award, effect will not be given to a prohibition laid down by domestic competition law.

[10] "It is to be noted, first of all, that, where questions of Community law are raised in an arbitration resorted to by agreement, the ordinary courts may have to examine those questions, in particular during review of the arbitration award, which may be more or less extensive depending on the circumstances and which they are obliged to carry out in the event of an appeal, for setting aside, for leave to enforce an award or upon any other form of action or review available under the relevant national legislation (*Nordsee*, cited above, paragraph 14).

[11] "In paragraph 15 of the judgment in *Nordsee*, the Court went on to explain that it is for those national courts and tribunals to ascertain whether it is necessary for them to make a reference to the Court under Art. 234 EC (ex Art. 177) in order to obtain an interpretation or assessment of the validity of provisions of Community law which they may need to apply when reviewing an arbitration award.

[12] "In this regard, the Court had held, in paragraphs 10 to 12 of that judgment, that an arbitration tribunal constituted pursuant to an agreement between the parties is not a 'court or tribunal of a Member State' within the meaning of Art. 234 EC (ex Art. 177) since the parties are under no obligation, in law or in fact, to refer their disputes to arbitration and the public authorities of the Member State concerned are not involved in the decision to opt for arbitration nor required to intervene of their own accord in the proceedings before the arbitrator.

[13] "Next, it is in the interest of efficient arbitration proceedings that review of arbitration awards should be limited in scope and that annulment of or refusal to recognise an award should be possible only in exceptional circumstances.

[14] "However, according to Art. 3(g) of the EC Treaty (now, after amendment, Art. 3(1)(g) EC), Art. 81 EC (ex Art. 85) constitutes a fundamental provision which is essential for the accomplishment of the tasks entrusted to the Community and, in particular, for the functioning of the internal market. The importance of such a provision led the framers of the Treaty to provide expressly, in Art. 81(2) EC (ex Art. 85(2)), that any agreements or decisions prohibited pursuant to that article are to be automatically void.
[15] "It follows that where its domestic rules of procedure require a national court to grant an application for annulment of an arbitration award where such an application is founded on failure to observe national rules of public policy, it must also grant such an application where it is founded on failure to comply with the prohibition laid down in Art. 81(1) EC (ex Art. 85(1)).
[16] "That conclusion is not affected by the fact that the New York Convention of 10 June 1958 on the Recognition and Enforcement of Foreign Arbitral Awards, which has been ratified by all the Member States, provides that recognition and enforcement of an arbitration award may be refused only on certain specific grounds, namely where the award does not fall within the terms of the submission to arbitration or goes beyond its scope, where the award is not binding on the parties or where recognition or enforcement of the award would be contrary to the public policy of the country where such recognition and enforcement are sought (Art. V(1)(*c*) and (*e*) and 2(*b*) of the New York Convention).
[17] "For the reasons stated in paragraph [14] above, the provisions of Art. 81 EC (ex Art. 85) may be regarded as a matter of public policy within the meaning of the New York Convention.
[18] "Lastly, it should be recalled that, as explained in paragraph [12] above, arbitrators, unlike national courts and tribunals, are not in a position to request this Court to give a preliminary ruling on questions of interpretation of Community law. However, it is manifestly in the interest of the Community legal order that, in order to forestall differences of interpretation, every Community provision should be given a uniform interpretation, irrespective of the circumstances in which it is to be applied (Case C-88/91 *Federconsorzi* [1992] ECR I-4035, paragraph 7). It follows that, in the circumstances of the present case, unlike *Van Schijndel and Van Veen*, Community law requires that questions concerning the interpretation of the prohibition laid down in Art. 81(1) EC (ex Art. 85(1)) should be open to examination by national courts when asked to determine the validity of an arbitration award and that it should be possible for those questions to be referred, if necessary, to the Court of Justice for a preliminary ruling.
[19] "The answer to be given to the second question must therefore be that a national court to which application is made for annulment of an arbitration

award must grant that application if it considers that the award in question is in fact contrary to Art. 81 EC (ex Art. 85), where its domestic rules of procedure require it to grant an application for annulment founded on failure to observe national rules of public policy."

2. *The First and Third Questions*

[20] "In view of the reply given to the second question, there is no need to answer the first and third questions."

3. *The Fourth and Fifth Questions*

[21] "By its fourth and fifth questions, which can be examined together, the referring court is asking essentially whether Community law requires a national court to refrain from applying domestic rules of procedure according to which an interim arbitration award which is in the nature of a final award and in respect of which no application for annulment has been made within the prescribed time-limit acquires the force of res judicata and may no longer be called in question by a subsequent arbitration award, even if this is necessary in order to examine, in proceedings for annulment of the subsequent award, whether an agreement which the interim award held to be valid in law is nevertheless void under Art. 81 EC (ex Art. 85).

[22] "According to the relevant domestic rules of procedure, application for annulment of an interim arbitration award which is in the nature of a final award may be made within a period of three months following the lodging of that award at the registry of the court having jurisdiction in the matter. Such a period, which does not seem excessively short compared with those prescribed in the legal systems of the other Member States, does not render excessively difficult or virtually impossible the exercise of rights conferred by Community law.

[23] "Moreover, domestic procedural rules which, upon the expiry of that period, restrict the possibility of applying for annulment of a subsequent arbitration award proceeding upon an interim arbitration award which is in the nature of a final award, because it has become res judicata, are justified by the basic principles of the national judicial system, such as the principle of legal certainty and acceptance of res judicata, which is an expression of that principle.

[24] "In those circumstances, Community law does not require a national court to refrain from applying such rules, even if this is necessary in order to examine, in proceedings for annulment of a subsequent arbitration award,

whether an agreement which the interim award held to be valid in law is nevertheless void under Art. 81 EC (ex Art. 85).

[25] "The answer to be given to the fourth and fifth questions must therefore be that Community law does not require a national court to refrain from applying domestic rules of procedure according to which an interim arbitration award which is in the nature of a final award and in respect of which no application for annulment has been made within the prescribed time-limit acquires the force of res judicata and may no longer be called in question by a subsequent arbitration award, even if this is necessary in order to examine, in proceedings for annulment of a subsequent arbitration award, whether an agreement which the interim award held to be valid in law is nevertheless void under Art. 81 EC (ex Art. 85)."

4. Costs

[26] "The costs incurred by the Netherlands, French, Italian and United Kingdom Governments and by the Commission, which have submitted observations to the Court, are not recoverable. Since these proceedings are, for the parties to the main proceedings, a step in the action pending before the national court, the decision on costs is a matter for that court."

IV. CONCLUSION

[27] "On those grounds, the Court, in answer to the questions referred to it by the Hoge Raad der Nederlanden by order of 21 March 1997, hereby rules:

> 1. A national court to which application is made for annulment of an arbitration award must grant that application if it considers that the award in question is in fact contrary to Art. 81 EC (ex Art. 85), where its domestic rules of procedure require it to grant an application for annulment founded on failure to observe national rules of public policy.
> 2. Community law does not require a national court to refrain from applying domestic rules of procedure according to which an interim arbitration award which is in the nature of a final award and in respect of which no application for annulment has been made within the prescribed time-limit acquires the force of res judicata and may no longer be called in question by a subsequent arbitration award, even if this is necessary in order to examine, in proceedings for annulment of a subsequent arbitration award, whether an agreement which the interim award held to be valid in law is nevertheless void under Art. 81 EC (ex Art. 85)."

FRANCE

Accession: 26 June 1959
1st Reservation

29. Cour d'Appel [Court of Appeal], Paris, 22 September 1995 (two decisions)

Parties:	Appellant: Dubois & Vanderwalle (France) Appellee: Boots Frites BV (Netherlands)
Published in:	Revue de l'arbitrage (1996, no. 1) with note E. Gaillard, pp. 100-109; Rivista dell'Arbitrato (1998, no. 1) pp. 67-69 with note A. Bandini, pp. 70-78
Articles:	V(2)(*b*) (by implication)
Subject matters:	– time limit to render award – violation of international public policy – no setting aside of foreign award
Commentary Cases:	[1]-[5] = ¶ 523; [6]-[7] = ¶ 104 + ¶ 516

Facts

By a contract of 27 May 1985, Dubois & Vanderwalle (Dubois) became the exclusive distributor in France of the products manufactured by Boots Frites B.V. (Boots). The contract contained an arbitration clause providing that the arbitral tribunal render its award within three months of its constitution.

When a dispute arose, Boots commenced arbitration proceedings. The arbitral tribunal was constituted on 25 August 1992. The award, which directed Dubois to pay Boots NLG 301,069.26, was signed by the three arbitrators separately: on 23 December 1992 and 5 January 1993, in The Netherlands, by the arbitrator appointed by Boots and the chairman respec-tively; on 7 January 1993 in Versailles by the arbitrator appointed by Dubois.

The Court of First Instance in Bobigny granted enforcement to the award. The Court of Appeal reversed, finding that the failure to comply with the three-months time limit was a violation of international public policy (first decision).

Dubois also sought annulment of the award, maintaining that as the award had been signed in Versailles by its arbitrator, it was a French award and could be challenged in France. The Court of Appeal rejected this contention (second decision).

Excerpt

First Decision

[1] "According to Art. 13(5) of the exclusive distributorship contract of 21 May 1985, 'The arbitral tribunal shall render the award within three months of the day in which it is constituted'. The award, dated 23 December 1992, 5 and 7 January 1993, was rendered more than three months after the oral hearing held in Breda on 25 August 1992.

[2] "Boots Frites replies that Art. 13 only contains an instruction to the arbitrators and does not provide for a sanction in case of non-compliance with the time limit of three months; that Dutch law, which governs the arbitration, explicitly gives the arbitrators the right to determine the time when the award shall be made (Art. 1048 Dutch Code of Civil Procedure (CCP));[1] and that none of the provisions of the [1958 New York Convention] allows for the refusal of recognition and enforcement of the award at issue.

[3] "However, the principle that the time limit set by the parties, as in the present case, for the arbitrators to accomplish their task may not be extended by the arbitrators, reflects a need which pertains to public policy, both domestic and international, in that it is inherent to the contractual character of arbitration.

[4] "Hence, the violation of this principle is a ground for refusal of enforcement under Art. 1502(5) French New Code of Civil Procedure (NCCP), which gives the court control over substantive and procedural public

1. Art. 1048 of the Dutch CCP reads:

"The arbitral tribunal is free to determine the time when the award shall be made."

policy.[2] In taking a power which they did not have, the arbitrators violated international public policy.

[5] "We reverse the order [of the Court of First Instance] and deny enforcement of the award rendered in The Netherlands in the dispute between Boots Frites B.V. and Dubois & Vanderwalle."

Second Decision

[6] "Dubois cannot seriously contest that the arbitration is international under Art. 1492 French NCCP,[3] since the economic activity concerned implicated a transnational movement of goods and payments. It ensues that, by application of Art. 1504 NCCP,[4] the award may be the object of an action for setting aside only if it is rendered in France.

[7] "There is a presumption that the arbitral award is rendered in the country of the seat of the arbitration, that is, in the present case, The Netherlands, since in case of disagreement the third arbitrator was to be appointed by a Dutch organization (the VAVI in The Hague), the hearing was held in Breda and the arbitrators deposited their award with the Registry of the court of first instance of that city. Under these circumstances, the fact invoked by Dubois (signature of the award by its arbitrator in Versailles) is by itself irrelevant. The request for setting aside is inadmissible."

---

2. Art. 1502 of the French NCCP reads in relevant part:

 "Appeal of a court decision granting recognition or enforcement is only available on the following grounds:
 (....)
 5. if recognition or enforcement is contrary to international public policy."

3. Art. 1492 of the French NCCP reads:

 "An arbitration is international if it implicates international commercial interests."

4. Art. 1504 of the French NCCP reads:

 "The action for setting aside is available against arbitral awards rendered in France in international arbitrations, on the grounds of Art. 1502.

 No recourse is available against court orders granting exequatur of such awards. However, the setting aside procedure, within the limits of the case before the court, entails *ipso jure* recourse against the order of the enforcement court or termination of the action before it."

30. Cour de Cassation [Supreme Court], 24 March 1998

Parties:	Petitioner: Excelsior Film TV, srl (Italy) Respondent: UGC-PH (France)
Published in:	Revue de l'arbitrage (1999, no. 2) pp. 255-256 with note Ph. Fouchard, pp. 257-259
Articles:	V(2)(*b*)
Subject matter:	– lack of impartiality of an arbitrator
Commentary Cases:	¶ 521

Facts

An arbitrator had been appointed by the same party in parallel arbitrations one taking place in France and the other in Rome, Italy. The arbitrator allegedly conveyed erroneous information to the Roman arbitral panel which influenced the tribunal's decision on jurisdiction. Excelsior Film TV, srl (Excelsior) sought to enforce the arbitral award rendered in Rome against UGC-PH. On 24 June 1994, the Court of Appeal in Paris refused enforcement on grounds of public policy for lack of impartiality of the arbitrator.

Excelsior appealed to the Supreme Court, which denied the appeal and affirmed the lower court's decision.

Excerpt

(....)

[1] "The Italian company Excelsior Film TV takes issue with the lower judgment (Paris, 24 June 1994) for denying enforcement of an arbitral award rendered in Rome in the dispute between [Excelsior] and the French company UGC-PH for violation of international public policy due to the lack of impartiality of an arbitrator. It argues that the Court of Appeal – apart from having misconstrued the terms of the dispute, misunderstood the nature of the foreign award and failed to address certain submissions – by failing to apply it also violated the [New York Convention], whose provisions, which prevail over domestic law, only provide for a refusal of enforcement based on public

policy when the violation of public policy concerns the recognition or enforcement of the award, and not, as in the present case, the decision-making process.

[2] "However, the provisions of Art. V(2)(*b*) of the [New York Convention] are substantially identical to those of Art. 1502(5) of the new Code of Civil Procedure, which the Court of Appeal applied, in that they allow an arbitral award rendered abroad to be denied enforcement where it violates the public policy of the country of enforcement in respect of both procedure and merits. The Court of Appeal, without misconstruing the object of the dispute or the nature of the arbitral award at issue, held in its discretion that one of the arbitrators, sitting on both the French and Italian arbitral panels, conveyed to the latter erroneous information of such nature as to influence that tribunal's decision on jurisdiction. The Court drew the conclusion that this disloyalty of an arbitrator, who was connected to one of the parties – as revealed in the award, so that it cannot be inferred from UGC-PH's failure to challenge this arbitrator that it waived its right to rely on this irregularity – created an imbalance between the parties, amounting to a violation of due process, so that the award rendered in Italy under such conditions violates French public policy in the sense of both Articles mentioned above.

[3] "The lower judgment, which did not have to address an inoperative argumentation on the jurisdiction of the arbitral tribunal constituted in Italy, thus legally justified its decision."

GERMANY

Accession: 30 June 1961
1st Reservation

48. Bayerisches Oberstes Landesgericht [Court of Appeal of Bavaria], 17 September 1998

Parties:	Petitioner: Not indicated Respondent: Not indicated
Published in:	Recht der internationalen Wirtschaft (1998) p. 965 et seq.; Rechtsprechung Kaufmännischer Schiedsgerichte, Vol. 6 (in preparation), A 1 No. 95, A 4 a No. 41 and A 4 b No. 18
Articles:	II(2); V(1)(*a*); V(2)(*b*)
Subject matter:	– arbitration agreement in writing
Commentary Cases:	[1] = ¶ 702; [2] = ¶ 506; [3] = ¶ 524 (alleged violation by arbitrator of German law)

Facts

The parties concluded a contract for the sale of a Jaguar XJ 220. The front page of the contract, which was signed by both parties, referred to the general conditions of sale on the reverse side as being an integral part of the contract. The general conditions contained a clause for arbitration of all disputes by a sole arbitrator to be appointed by the President of the Law Society in London if the parties failed to agree.

A dispute arose between the parties. The sole arbitrator, appointed by the President of the Law Society, rendered an award before 1 January 1998, the date on which the German Arbitration Law entered into force. The party which had prevailed in the arbitration sought enforcement of the English award in Germany after 1 January 1998.

The Court of Appeal of Bavaria granted enforcement. It held that the new German Arbitration Law applies to enforcement proceedings commenced after 1 January 1998, and dismissed the defendant's objections that the arbitration clause in the contract was not "in writing" according to Art. II(2) of the Convention, that the appointment of the arbitrator was invalid and that the award violated German public policy because the arbitrator did not apply the *clausula rebus sic stantibus*.

Excerpt

[1] "The transitional provision of Art. 4, Sect. 1(3) of the Act on Arbitral Proceedings makes the commencement of the proceedings the dividing moment for the application of the old and of the new law.[1] This appears to be (legally) correct, since it does not result in retroactivity proper, that is, it does not affect facts which have already happened and belong to the past but only influences the future of present, not yet concluded business and legal relations (the so-called improper, retrospective retroactivity ...). The new law concerns but does not affect the result of an arbitration which took place before [1 January 1998] and only affects subsequent, future proceedings. Also, the new law does not make the enforcement of foreign awards more onerous in comparison to the old law, and in fact it does not alter the conditions therefor (see Court of Appeal of Bavaria, NJW 1988 p. 2178).

[2] "The defendant cannot rely on Sect. 1061(1) first sentence ZPO[2] and Art. V(1)(*a*) second alternative of the New York Convention to oppose enforcement, since the arbitration agreement is not invalid according to English law, on which the parties agreed. According to Sect. 5(2) of the English Arbitration Act 1996, there is a written agreement as required in para. 1 if the agreement is made in writing, independent of whether the parties signed it. According to para. 3, an agreement made otherwise than in writing which refers to terms which are in writing is also sufficient.

1. Art. 4, Sect. 1(3) of the Act on Arbitral Proceedings reads:

"Court proceedings pending upon the entry into force of this Act remain subject to the law previously in force."

2. Sect. 1061(1) of the German Code of Civil Procedure (ZPO) reads in relevant part:

"Recognition and enforcement of foreign arbitral awards shall be granted in accordance with the [New York Convention]."

[3] "The violation by the English arbitrator of an essential principle of German law on the intervening lack of privity of contract, alleged by the defendant, is not at odds with German public policy (Art. V(2)(*b*) New York Convention). We can leave aside whether this principle, developed by German jurisprudence, is a general principle of law ... and pertains to the fundamental principles of the German legal system. In so far as the defendant relies on the collapse of the market for luxury cars (the sale concerned a Jaguar XJ 220), it is only its expectations as to that market's development which were not fulfilled. If a hoped for, merely speculative increase in value does not materialize, this is not a case for the application of the *clausula rebus sic stantibus*."

HONG KONG

*Accession: 24 September 1975**
1st Reservation

14. High Court of the Hong Kong Special Administrative Region, Court of First Instance, 30 November 1998, 1998 No. MP 4765

Parties:	Plaintiff: T.K. Bulkhandling GmbH (nationality not indicated) Defendant: Meridan Success International Limited (nationality not indicated)
Published in:	No publication information available
Articles:	III
Subject matters:	– no security for costs by award creditor in enforcement proceedings – more onerous conditions
Commentary Cases:	¶ 301

Facts

Following an arbitration in London with Meridan Success International Limited (Meridan), T.K. Bulkhandling GmbH (Bulkhandling) applied on 15 September 1998 for leave to enforce the award in Hong Kong. The application was made ex parte on affidavit to Mr. Justice Findlay in Chambers. Leave was granted the following day and Meridan was informed that it could apply to set aside the order, which it did on 26 September. On 22 October 1998, Meridan issued a summons seeking security for costs under Order 23 on the ground

* Accession by PR China on 22 January 1987 and extended to Hong Kong with the 1st Reservation, to replace the previous extension by the United Kingdom.

that Bulkhandling was resident outside the jurisdiction. Justice Findlay held that Order 23 did not apply to enforcement procedures provided for in Order 73 and dismissed the application, ordering Meridan to pay Bulkhandling's costs of the application.

Excerpt

[1] "I have before me a summons issued by the 'defendant' on 22 October 1998 under Order 23 for an order that the 'plaintiff' provide security for the 'defendant's' costs on the ground that the 'plaintiff' is resident outside the jurisdiction. I place the descriptions of the parties in parenthesis because, although this is the description in the title of the case, the 'plaintiff' is more correctly the 'creditor' and the 'defendant' more correctly the 'debtor'; the titles used in the applicable Order 73. This, in my view, is not just a matter of nomenclature, but a recognition by Order 73 that the person against whom an award has been made is in a position similar to that of a judgment debtor, and not to a party to an action.

[2] "On 15 September 1998, the creditor applied to me for an order that it be at liberty to enforce an arbitration award made in London. This was an award falling within the New York Convention. This application was made under Sect. 2GG of the Arbitration Ordinance (Cap. 341)[1] and Order 73.

[3] "Sect. 42 of Chap. 341 says that a Convention award is enforceable either by action or in the same manner as a domestic award. The creditor here chose to seek to enforce the award, not by action, but under Sect. 2GG and Order 73.

[4] "Under Order 73, rule 10, the process by which a person seeks leave to enforce an arbitral award is by 'application', although the court hearing the application may direct that an originating summons be issued. Order 73 and the Arbitration Ordinance (Cap. 341) provide the same procedure for enforcing both domestic arbitral awards and foreign arbitral awards enforceable under the New York Convention. Order 73 provides its own code for enforcing

1. Sect 2GG of the Hong Kong Arbitration Ordinance reads:

"An award, order or direction made or given in or in relation to arbitration proceedings by an arbitral tribunal is enforceable in the same way as a judgment, order or direction of the Court that has the same effect, but only with the leave of the Court or a judge of the Court. If that leave is given, the Court or judge may enter judgment in terms of the award, order or direction."

awards under Sect. 2GG, and includes, in rule 10A, a special provision for ordering security by a debtor seeking to set aside an order.[2]

(....)

[5] "On 22 October 1998, the debtor issued a summons seeking security. This is the summons now before me. The summons prays for an order to 'give security for the defendant's costs *in this action*'. The italics are mine. There is, of course, no action here, and nothing in the nature of an action.

[6] "Order 23 provides for the ordering of security for costs 'on the application of a defendant to an action or other proceedings'. Sub-rule (3) makes it clear that 'defendant' refers to a party who is in the position of a defendant. It is also clear that the Order does not cover proceedings that are interlocutory in nature because these are not in the nature of an action.

[7] "Order 5 provides that civil proceedings are begun by writ, originating summons, originating motion or petition. The ex parte application on affidavit before me does not fall under any of these classes.

[8] "I am satisfied that Order 23 does not apply to the enforcement procedures provided for in Order 73.These procedures are not in the nature of an action, and the debtor is not a defendant. If it were envisaged that a debtor involved in the Order 73 procedure should be permitted to apply for security for costs, that would have been provided for in Order 73, and that order has provided for security to be provided by the debtor.

[9] "And I do not believe that this result is accidental. Where an award is made under a domestic arbitration agreement, there is, by definition, no foreign party. The New York Convention provides, in Art. III, that 'There shall not be imposed substantially more onerous conditions or higher fees or charges on the recognition or enforcement of arbitral awards to which this Convention applies than are imposed on the recognition or enforcement of domestic arbitral awards.' If it were so that a creditor seeking to enforce a Convention award might have to provide security for the debtor's costs, this would be a more onerous condition than that facing a creditor seeking to enforce a domestic award, who would have no such liability. In my judgment, the rules have been drafted to avoid that consequence.

[10] "Even if I am wrong in this conclusion, and it is possible to make such an order as sought by a debtor facing enforcement of a Convention award, I

---

2. Rule 10 of Order 73 reads:

"Where a debtor has applied to set aside an order made under rule 10, the Court may, either of its own motion or on an application made by the creditor, and if, having regard to all the circumstances of the case it thinks it just to do so, impose such terms, as to giving security or otherwise, as a condition of the further conduct of the application, as it thinks fit."

believe that this power should be exercised only in the most unusual circumstances. Miss Cheng, with her usual frankness, said that she was conscious that her application might appear unusual given 'the spirit and intent of the New York Convention', and she suggested that I should devise some special safeguards for this type of case; perhaps imposing some 'high standard' on the debtor.

[11] "Well, frankly, I cannot think of the kind of case where it would be appropriate, given the factors I have mentioned, to order a creditor to provide security, so I am unable to suggest such safeguards or high standard. All I am able to say is that I am satisfied that this case is not at all extreme or unusual, and not the sort of case in which, if the jurisdiction existed, it would be appropriate to order security. In the result the debtors application is dismissed...."

15. Court of Final Appeal of the Hong Kong Special Administrative Region, 9 February 1999, FACV No. 10 of 1998

Parties:	Appellant: Hebei Import & Export Corporation (PR China) Respondent: Polytek Engineering Company Limited (Hong Kong)
Published in:	14 Mealey's International Arbitration Report (1999, no. 2) pp. G-1 – G-15
Articles:	V; V(1)(*e*); V(2)(*b*); VI
Subject matters:	– estoppel – grounds not raised or rejected in setting aside proceedings – violation of (international) public policy – validity of award primarily matter for setting aside jurisdiction – residual discretion to grant enforcement despite ground for refusal – scope of review on appeal from leave for enforcement – no proof of actual bias
Commentary Cases:	[12] = ¶ 101; [40]-[55] + [75] = ¶ 303 + ¶ 500; [42]-[45] + [64]-[67] = ¶ 104 + ¶ 516; [44]-[46] = ¶ 524 (public policy of forum); [56] = ¶ 508; [57]-[60], [67], [81] + [83]-[87] = ¶ 518; [60]-[63], [68]-[72] + [82]-[89] = ¶ 518 + ¶ 524 (inspection of factory in the absence of respondent); [88]-[89] = ¶ 521

Facts

The facts of this case are also reported in Yearbook XXIII (1998) pp. 666-684 as Hong Kong no. 12 and pp. 1103-1108 (US no. 268). Polytek Engineering Company Limited (Polytek) contracted with Hebei Import & Export Corporation (Hebei) to sell Hebei equipment for the production of rubber powder. Hebei obtained the equipment from the US manufacturer Jacobson and it was delivered to Hebei's end user factory in China. A dispute arose regarding the equipment and the parties initiated arbitration at the China International Economic and Trade Arbitration Commission (CIETAC). The arbitral tribunal appointed three experts to inspect the equipment at the factory. The Chief Arbitrator was present at the inspection. Two of Hebei's technicians were also present during the inspection. Polytek was not informed of the inspection and was not present.

An award was made on 29 March 1996 which, inter alia, ordered Polytek to refund the purchase price of the equipment.

Hebei requested the enforcement of the award in Hong Kong. On 23 July 1996, Leonard, J, granted ex parte leave for enforcement and entered judgment on the same date. Polytek applied for leave to set aside the leave for enforcement. These proceedings were adjourned at Polytek's request pending setting aside proceedings at the Beijing No. 2 Intermediate Court. Polytek's attempt to set aside the award failed and proceedings in Hong Kong were resumed. On 15 May 1997, Findlay, J, refused to set aside the leave and judgment. On appeal, the Court of Appeal allowed an appeal from the orders made by Findlay, J, and set aside the grant of leave for enforcement and the judgment, finding, inter alia, that the award was in violation of the public policy of Hong Kong as there was a serious breach of natural justice and a strong case of apparent bias. Furthermore, Polytek did not have a proper opportunity to present its case to the arbitral tribunal after the inspection and the compilation of the experts' report.

On 3 April 1996, Polytek had initiated CIETAC arbitral proceedings against its supplier, Jacobson. Polytek sought enforcement of the award which it had obtained in its favour in the US which was granted by the United States District Court, District of Minnesota, on 12 December 1997 (see US no. 268).

In Hong Kong, the Court of Final Appeal unanimously overturned the decision of the Court of Appeal and restored the order of Findlay, J. Justices Li and Ching agreed without further comment with the judgment of Justice Mason, NPJ, which is excerpted in [1] to [63]. The judgments of Mr. Justice Litton, PJ and Mr. Justice Bokhary, PJ, are excerpted after that of Justice Mason, in [64] to [76] and [77] to [90] respectively.

Excerpt

Judgment of Mason NPJ

I. THE ARBITRATION

(....)
[1] "According to the defence, Jacobson was responsible for the failure to resolve problems that arose during the testing and commissioning of the equipment. The defence contained a request that Jacobson be joined as a respondent in the arbitration. The respondent nevertheless denied that there was a *fundamental* breach of contract and claimed that the equipment was not worthless and could be modified to achieve the stipulated production capacity. Accordingly, the respondent requested the Tribunal to appoint 'the relevant authoritative organization' to assess the equipment, to confirm its quality and performance and to propose a 'reasonable modification plan'. The defence asserted that the compensation claimed by the appellant exceeded the loss it suffered from the breach of contract. It is important to note that the respondent was not, in its defence, putting forward a modification plan proposed by itself or Jacobson. It intended that the organization to be appointed would come forward with such a plan.
[2] "At the oral hearing which took place on 10 October 1995, the Tribunal agreed, at the request and at the expense of the respondent, to appoint experts to examine the equipment and to make a report. The Tribunal appointed experts from VETAC (Vision Economic Technology and Consulting Company). When the experts went to the end user's factory for that purpose, the inspection lasted a whole day. Two technicians, described in the Court of Appeal's judgment as 'the plaintiff's technicians', were present to demonstrate the installation and operation of the equipment. I leave for later consideration the character of the technicians, what happened at the inspection and whether there was any communication by the technicians to the Chief Arbitrator.
[3] "The experts' report was delivered in November 1995, but the respondent did not receive a copy until 15 December. Contrary to the respondent's hopes, if not expectations, the report found that the equipment could not be modified so as to achieve the production capacity stipulated by the contract.
[4] "After receiving the experts' report, the Tribunal invited supplemental submissions from the parties. Thereafter the respondent made a further submission on 29 December 1995 and two supplemental submissions on 20 January 1996 and 14 February 1996. The last two submissions were made after the respondent had received from the Tribunal a letter dated 4 January 1996 in which the Tribunal gave an account of the inspection. The respondent

claims that the letter constitutes evidence that there were improper communications between the technicians and the Chief Arbitrator in the absence of the respondent giving rise to a case of apparent bias. Yet the respondent did not raise this point until the matter reached the Court of Appeal. It was not a ground advanced in the application to the Beijing Court or, for that matter, before Findlay J.

[5] "The respondent's submission of 20 January 1996 has significance for the outcome of this appeal. The submission stated

> 'the Respondent, as a trading company, is unable to understand the technological and functional aspects of the equipment as a professional. Therefore, once the arbitration process was started, the Respondent pointed out that it was absolutely necessary to request the American Company to take part in the hearing (whether the American Company was willing to do so is a separate matter) for the purpose of clarifying the facts.... Even if the American Company was unable to act as a respondent ... it was still necessary to ask [it] to serve as a principal witness.'

[6] "In the submission, the respondent requested the Tribunal to require Jacobson, 'to serve as the principal witness' and also requested the Tribunal in the arbitration to hear the observations of Jacobson on the assessment made by the experts and to postpone the making of an award until these steps had been taken and the Tribunal was in position to review the defence of Jacobson to the claim which the respondent was to make against it. Otherwise the submission did not challenge any particular part of the report; nor did it seek a hearing so that the respondent could question the experts, call witnesses or present evidence.

[7] "The Tribunal responded to the submission by refusing a second hearing, stating that it could not compel or call the American company to give evidence. The Tribunal sought the respondent's comments on the experts' report before 16 February 1996.

[8] "In its last submission of 14 February 1996, the respondent sought a postponement of the making of an award for two months to enable the comments of Jacobson on the experts' report to be procured and sent to the Tribunal. It seems that the respondent had not previously taken steps to obtain such comments. The Tribunal refused a postponement on the ground that the case had already taken too long."

II. THE AWARD

[9] "The Award,... set out the substance of the experts' report and their conclusion that the modification proposals put forward by Jacobson were 'completely unacceptable'.
[10] "The Award stated

> 'It would be good if partial replacement and modification of the existing equipment will satisfy the required performance, product quality and the quantity stipulated in the Contract and will also minimise the loss of both parties.'

The Award went on to find that the equipment was not capable of modification in a way that would meet the requirements of the contract in relation to production and that

> 'It should be regarded as reasonable for the [appellant] not to have accepted such modification plan which will cause a long-term loss to the factory.'

In reaching its conclusions the Tribunal placed reliance on the experts' report, the contents of which were set out in some detail.
[11] "It is clear that the experts' findings were based very largely on technical assessments made by experts which took place sometime after the inspection of the equipment at the factory. Chinese experts with relevant experience were invited to study the technical aspects of the equipment and its performance. Comparative analyses with similar equipment in China and other countries were made. Defects in the equipment and the causes of those defects were identified. The possibility of modification was considered and rejected by the experts...."

III. THE COURT OF APPEAL

[12] "The Court of Appeal accepted, and it is not disputed in this Court, that the Award is a Convention award to which Part IV of the Arbitration Ordinance, Cap. 341, (the Ordinance) applies. Sect. 2(1) of the Ordinance defines 'Convention award' to mean

> 'an award to which Part IV applies, namely, an award made in pursuance of an arbitration agreement in a State cr territory, other than Hong Kong, which is a party to the New York Convention.'

I do no more than refer to the discussion of this matter in the judgment of the Court of Appeal.[1]

[13] "The Court of Appeal also concluded that, even accepting that the inspection was not conducted for the purpose of determining whether the equipment was defective, an inspection was material in deciding whether the equipment could be modified and what type of award should be made. It was necessary to determine whether the purchase price should be refunded, whether compensation should be paid and, if so, how much. So the condition of the equipment on inspection was relevant to the outcome of the arbitration and was part of it.

[14] "The Court of Appeal held that there were private communications from the appellant's technicians to the Chief Arbitrator, evidenced by the experts' report and the letter dated 4 January 1996 from the Tribunal, and that the inspection might have affected the quantum of compensation if not also the respondent's liability.

[15] "Having dealt with the facts in this way, their Lordships concluded that, in accordance with Sect. 44(3) of the Ordinance, it would be contrary to public policy in Hong Kong to enforce the Award. This conclusion was based on the perceived departure from natural justice and apparent bias on the part of the Tribunal, which arose from the communications made by the appellant's technicians to the Chief Arbitrator and the experts, and on the view that the respondent was denied a proper opportunity to present its case by reason of the Tribunal's failure to hold a further hearing in relation to the matters which had arisen from the inspection and the experts' report. The Court of Appeal dealt with these matters as policy considerations under Sect. 44(3). The appellant's argument that the Court should exercise a residual discretion to order enforcement, even in a case where enforcement would be contrary to public policy, was rejected."

IV. ISSUES OF FACT

[16] "Before turning to the issues of law which arise in this appeal, it is necessary to determine the contested issues of fact. Miss Eu SC for the appellant submits that the Court of Appeal was in error in stating that the

1. Reported in Yearbook XXIII (1998) p. 666 at pp. 667-669 (Hong Kong no. 12).

inspection took place at the *appellant's* factory and that the reports made to the experts at the inspection were made by the *appellant's* technicians. That the inspection took place at the end user's factory is clearly established by the evidence. It is also clear that the technicians were not members of the appellant's staff.

[17] "It is, however, necessary to take account of the relationship between the appellant and the end user Chenggong Rubber. In the contract, to which that company's representative is a signatory, the end user's factory is described as 'Buyer's Factory'. The seller's guarantee was included in the contract at the request of those controlling Chenggong Rubber, according to the appellant's reply to the respondent's defence in the arbitration. And the appellant's claim to compensation is little more than a reflection of the loss claimed to have been sustained by Chenggong Rubber. In this situation, the inference is irresistible that, in the arbitration, there was a close identity of interest between the two companies. Accordingly, it is of little or no significance that the Court of Appeal may have misdescribed the factory as the appellant's factory.

[18] "It seems that much, if not all, of the appellant's evidence relating to the installation, testing, commissioning and performance of the equipment came from the factory. Mr. Zhang Shan, the Deputy-President and General Manager of Chenggong Rubber, made the principal affirmation in support of the appellant's case in answer to the respondent's application to set aside the judgment entered by Leonard, J.

[19] "On a fair reading of that affirmation, it is reasonable to infer that the two technicians, stated by Mr. Zhang to be present at the inspection, though not officers of the appellant, were technicians who had been present at the installation and testing of the equipment by Jacobson and contributed their knowledge and experience to the appellant's case that the equipment was defective and that the Jacobson modifications tested in December 1994 did not work satisfactorily. Once this fact is appreciated, it is scarcely to the point to say that the technicians were not employees of the appellant.

[20] "Then there is the question whether there was any communication to the Chief Arbitrator. Miss Eu SC for the appellant submits that, on the evidence, the Chief Arbitrator attended the factory on the day of the inspection for the sole purpose of ensuring the impartiality and independence of the experts' examination. The letter dated 4 January 1996 from the Tribunal to the respondent's lawyers, after referring to the appointment of the experts, stated:

> 'For the examination at the spot, the ... Tribunal selected the Chief Arbitrator, and invited the officers of the Secretarial Office to participate. To ensure the impartiality and the independence of the experts'

examination, working conditions were set for the expert people, they were able not to have any unilateral communication with the staff of either party, and refused to accept any treatment of hospitality, meals, gifts ... etc. Upon listening at the spot to the seminars of the technicians who participated in the installation and testing, they only made records of the same, and did not give any comments....

[21] "'According to Article 38 of the Arbitration Rules, the ... Tribunal shall have the right to arrange for independent expert investigation, and does not necessary (sic) be required to inform both parties to be present. Since the equipment in this case could not meet the conditions of the test running, the ... Tribunal considered that it was not necessary to inform both parties to be present.'

[22] "The letter went on to say:

> 'As far as the seminars, discussions, compilation printing etc. of the contents of the expert examination report were concerned, the ... Tribunal and the staff of both disputing parties had not [been] invited to participate.'

[23] "The import of the last sentence is by no means clear. It appears, however, to be directed to 'seminars' or discussions between experts (rather than a presentation or explanation of installation and testing by the technicians) and to other matters going to the preparation and printing of the report. I do not read the sentence or, for that matter, any other part of the letter as denying that the Chief Arbitrator attended the inspection and heard what the technicians had to say.

[24] "The significance of the reference in the letter to Art. 38 – Art. 39, not Art. 38 was mentioned in the Award – is that it authorizes the Tribunal to undertake investigations and collect evidence on its own initiative. The article would, it seems, enable the Chief Arbitrator on behalf of the Tribunal to collect evidence and listen to statements made by the technicians at the inspection, in the absence of the parties or their representatives. It seems also that, under Art. 38, the attendance of the parties at the inspection was required only if the Tribunal deemed it necessary.

[25] "The Award itself stated that the experts

> 'conducted a detailed inspection of various aspects of the equipment's original design, including technical performance ... installation, and testing and commissioning'

and

> 'listened to reports made by those technicians who had taken part in the installation and testing of the equipment.'

[26] "Neither the letter, nor the Award, nor the affirmation of Mr. Zhang, asserted that the Chief Arbitrator absented himself from the actual inspection or the presentation and the reports made by the technicians. On these facts, it would be reasonable to infer that the Chief Arbitrator participated in the inspection and heard what the technicians had to say.

[27] "Whether the Tribunal indicated, on 10 October 1995, that inspection would be conducted in the presence of the representatives of both parties is an issue that I am unable to resolve. The affirmations filed by the parties are in conflict. It does not appear that attendance by the parties at the inspection formed a part of the order or decision made by the Tribunal appointing the experts; nor was attendance by the parties mentioned in the respondent's defence in which such an appointment was sought."

V. APPLICATION OF THE CIETAC ARBITRATION RULES AND THE PRC ARBITRATION LAW

[28] "It is common ground between the parties that the CIETAC Arbitration Rules and PRC Arbitration Law governed the arbitration. The Court of Appeal found that there was no breach of these provisions, except for Art. 32 of the Rules[2] and Art. 45 of the Law. I am unable to accept the finding that there was a violation of these two articles. Although Art. 32 requires an oral hearing, there was an oral hearing on 10 October 1995, and there is no evidence that what happened subsequently amounted to a breach of Art. 32.

[29] "Art. 45 of the Law provides

> 'The evidence should be demonstrated only at the tribunal session, and the parties have the right to question the evidence.'

---

2. Art. 32 of the CIETAC Arbitration Rules reads:

> "The arbitration tribunal shall hold oral hearings when examining a case. At the request of the parties or with their consent, oral hearings may be omitted if the arbitration tribunal also deems that oral hearings are unnecessary, and then the arbitration tribunal may examine the case and make an award on the basis of documents only."

Again there is no evidence that what happened amounted to a breach of this provision. Nor, apart from the belated attempt by the respondent, in its submission of 14 February 1996, to obtain the comments of Jacobson on the report, did the respondent seek to exercise a right to question the report.
[30] "The judgment of the Beijing Court records the relevant grounds advanced by the respondent on which the Award should be set aside and rejected them. The Court concluded:

> '[n]o circumstances existed which would require the setting aside of the ... Award in accordance with the provisions under the law, and the arbitration procedures were in compliance with the Arbitration Rules.'

[31] "This conclusion entails that there was no violation of Art. 53 of the Rules which required the Tribunal to make its award

> 'in accordance with the facts of the case, the law and the terms of the contracts, international practices and the principle of fairness and reasonableness.'

[32] "There is, accordingly, no basis on which we could decline to accept the conclusion reached by the Beijing Court that there was compliance with the relevant provisions of Chinese law.
[33] "There is no evidence that it was open to the respondent to take action under Chinese law to require the Chief Arbitrator to withdraw or to enforce his withdrawal on the ground of misconduct. In the absence of evidence, we would be justified in presuming that Chinese Law on the topic is the same as that of Hong Kong. The matter is dealt with in Arts. 34 to 37 of the Rules, in which provision is made for removal for misconduct. But there is no evidence as to the precise operation of these Rules.
[34] "Art. 45 of the Rules provides that a party who knows or should have known that a provision of the Rules has not been complied with yet proceeds without raising his objection in a timely manner shall be deemed to have waived his right to object. Art. 45 gives effect to an important principle, not confined to Chinese law, namely that a party to an arbitration who wishes to rely on a non-compliance with the rules governing an arbitration shall do so promptly and shall not proceed with the arbitration as if there had been no non-compliance, keeping the point up his sleeve for later use after an award is made, should that course prove to be expedient.
[35] "PRC law makes provision for the setting aside and the non-enforcement of foreign-related arbitration awards in various circumstances (Arbitration Law,

Arts. 70, 71 and Civil Procedure Law, Art. 260).[3] The grounds for non-enforcement are similar to those stated in Sect. 44 of the Ordinance. They include the grounds that the party resisting enforcement 'was unable to present his case due to causes for which he is not responsible', that the composition of the tribunal was not in conformity with the rules of arbitration and that enforcement is contrary to 'the social and public interest of the country' (Art. 260(2), (3) and (4)).

[36] "The importance of the Rules and the Arbitration Law is that the parties entered into the arbitration knowing that it was governed by the provisions of the Rules and the Law. Thus, the appointment of experts and the inspection were necessarily governed by Arts. 38 and 39 of the Rules. As already mentioned, Art. 38 appears to contemplate that the Tribunal may collect evidence otherwise than in the presence of the parties; further, it appears to contemplate that the Tribunal *may* thereafter appoint a time and place at which the parties can deal with the evidence so collected."

VI. QUESTIONS OF LAW IN THIS APPEAL

[37] "On facts as I have stated them, the questions of law which arise this appeal are:

(1) whether, in the light of the Beijing proceedings and the failure to raise in those proceedings the ground that enforcement would be contrary to

---

3. Art. 260 of the Chinese Civil Procedure Law reads:

> "The people's court shall issue an order to refuse the enforcement of the award made by the foreign-related arbitration institution of the People's Republic of China if the party against whom the enforcement is sought has furnished the following proof to the people's court and the people's court has examined and verified through its collegial panel the proof that
> (1) the parties do not have an arbitration clause in their contract and have not subsequently concluded an arbitration agreement in writing; or
> (2) the party against whom the enforcement is sought was not given due notice as to the appointment of arbitrators or the conduct of the arbitration proceedings, or was unable to present his case for reasons for which he is not responsible; or
> (3) the formation of the arbitral tribunal or the arbitral procedure was not in conformity with the arbitration rules; or
> (4) the matters dealt with by the award fall outside the scope of the arbitration agreement or outside the power of the arbitration tribunal.
> Enforcement of an arbitral award shall be disallowed if the enforcement of it goes against social and public interest."

public policy by reason of the communications to the Chief Arbitrator, it was open to the respondent to raise the grounds relied upon, more particularly the ground just mentioned;

(2) whether, in the light of the respondent's conduct in the arbitration, it was open to the respondent to resist the enforcement of the Award on a ground arising out of the communications to the Chief Arbitrator;

(3) whether the respondent has established a ground based on Sect. 44(2)(c) of the Ordinance for not being able to present its case; and whether the respondent made out the public policy ground under Sect. 44(3) of the Ordinance by establishing that enforcement of the Award would violate the most basic notions of justice and morality in Hong Kong;

(4) whether, in any event, the Court should exercise a discretion to enforce the Award."

VII. THE HONG KONG STATUTORY PROVISIONS

[38] "Sect. 2AA of the Ordinance provides:

'(1) The object of this Ordinance is to facilitate the fair and speedy resolution of disputes by arbitration without unnecessary expense.
(2) This Ordinance is based on the principles that –
(a) subject to the observance of such safeguards as are necessary in the public interest, the parties to a dispute should be free to agree how the dispute should be resolved; and
(b) the Court should interfere in the arbitration of a dispute only as expressly provided by this Ordinance.'

[39] "Sect. 44, so far as it is material, provides

'(1) Enforcement of a Convention award shall not be refused except in the cases mentioned in this section.
(2) Enforcement of a Convention award may be refused if the person against whom it is invoked proves –
...
(c) that he was not given proper notice of the appointment of the arbitrator or of the arbitration proceedings or was otherwise unable to present his case; ...

> (3) Enforcement of a Convention award may also be refused if the award is in respect of a matter which is not capable of settlement by arbitration, or if it would be contrary to public policy to enforce the award.
>
> ....
>
> (5) Where an application for the setting aside or suspension of a Convention award has been made to ... a competent authority ..., the court before which enforcement of the award is sought may, if it thinks fit, adjourn the proceedings and may, on the application of the party seeking to enforce the award, order the other party to give security.'"

[40] With respect to the first question of law, it was opined: "In the Court of Appeal and in argument before this Court, reference was made to the possible application of the doctrine of issue estoppel arising from the decision and the proceedings in the Beijing Court and the similarity of the grounds on which an arbitration award can be set aside under PRC law and the grounds on which enforcement of an award can be resisted under the Ordinance. I have difficulty with the notion that the questions here are to be resolved by issue estoppel. The application of the doctrine would require a precise comparison to be made of the relevant provisions of PRC law and the law of Hong Kong with a view to ascertaining whether the respective laws give rise to identical or similar issues. In the absence of evidence of the effect of PRC law, the Court cannot undertake such an exercise. Nor is the difficulty lessened by the suggestion that the doctrine of issue estoppel should be applied flexibly, whatever that suggestion may be intended to mean.

[41] "On the other hand, it is appropriate that the courts should have regard to the principles of finality and comity to the extent to which they are consistent with the provisions of the Ordinance and the Convention. Both the Ordinance and the Convention give effect to the principles of finality and comity by prohibiting refusal of enforcement of a Convention award except in the cases for which they provide (Ordinance, Sect. 2AA(2)(b), Sect. 44(1); Convention, Art. VI). But both provide for exceptions to that prohibition by stating the grounds on which enforcement *may* be refused.

[42] "Under the Ordinance and the Convention, the primary supervisory function in respect of arbitrations rests with the court of supervisory jurisdiction as distinct from the enforcement court (see Ordinance, Sect. 44(5); Convention, Art. VI; *Westacre Investments Inc. v. Judoimport-SPDR Holding Co. Ltd.* [1998] 3 WLR 770 at 808).[4] But this does not mean that the enforcement court will necessarily defer to the court of supervisory jurisdiction.

4. Reported in Yearbook XXIII (1998) pp. 836-859 (UK no. 51).

[43] "The Convention distinguishes between proceedings to set aside an award in the court of supervisory jurisdiction (Arts. V(1)(*e*) and VI) and proceedings in the court of enforcement (Art. V(1)). Proceedings to set aside are governed by the law under which the award was made or the law of the place where it was made, while proceedings in the court of enforcement are governed by the law of that forum. The Convention, in providing that enforcement of an award may be resisted on certain specified grounds, recognises that, although an award may be valid by the law of the place where it is made, its making may be attended by such a grave departure from basic concepts of justice as applied by the court of enforcement that the award should not be enforced.

[44] "It follows, in my view, that it would be inconsistent with the principles on which the Convention is based to hold that the refusal by a court of supervisory jurisdiction to set aside an award debars an unsuccessful applicant from resisting enforcement of the award in the court of enforcement. See *Firm P v. Firm F* (*Yearbook Commercial Arbitration* II (1977) p. 241 [(F.R. Germ. no. 10)] where a German Court of Appeal refused to enforce an award which had been declared to be enforceable by a United States District Court). Even if the proposition stated above should be subject to some limitations, it must apply to a case where the party resisting enforcement is doing so on the ground of public policy. That is because the ground is expressed in the Convention (Art. V(2)(*b*)) as 'contrary to the public policy of the country', that is, the country in which enforcement is sought. In the court of supervisory jurisdiction, the public policy to be applied would be a different public policy, namely that of the supervisory jurisdiction.

[45] "In *Paklito Investment Ltd. v. Klockner East Asia Ltd.* [1993] 2 HKLR 39[5] Kaplan J expressed (at 48-49) the view that a party faced with a Convention award against him has two options. He can apply to the court of supervisory jurisdiction to set aside the award or he can wait to establish a Convention ground of opposition. In my view, such a party is not bound to elect between the two remedies, at any rate when, in the court of enforcement, he seeks to rely on the public policy ground, as the respondent did here.

[46] "It follows also that a failure to raise the public policy ground in proceedings to set aside an award cannot operate to preclude a party from resisting on that ground the enforcement of the award in the enforcing court in another jurisdiction. That is because each jurisdiction has its own public policy.

[47] "What I have said does not exclude the possibility that a party may be precluded by his failure to raise a point before the court of supervisory jurisdiction from raising that point before the court of enforcement. Failure

5. Reported in Yearbook XIX (1994) pp. 664-674 (Hong Kong no. 6).

to raise such a point may amount to an estoppel or a want of bona fides such as to justify the court of enforcement in enforcing an award (see *Chrome Resources S.A. v. Leopold Lazarus* (*Yearbook Commercial Arbitration* XI (1986) pp. 538-542)). Obviously an injustice may arise if an award remains on foot but cannot be enforced on a ground which, if taken, would have resulted in the award being set aside."

[48] With respect to the second question of law, it was opined: "The appellant submits that the respondent's objection to the communications to the Chief Arbitrator should have been advanced, if it was to be advanced at all, in the arbitration itself under the CIETAC Rules and under the Arbitration Law. Once the respondent received the Tribunal's letter of 4 January 1996, it had notice that the Chief Arbitrator accompanied the experts and was present at the factory when the inspection took place. The information in that letter is the foundation of the respondent's case. The later information that the inspection lasted a whole day, which was contained in Mr. Zhang's affirmation, simply reinforced what was in the letter.

[49] "Instead of raising the question on receipt of the letter, the respondent continued to participate in the arbitration. By pursuing this course, the respondent precluded an ascertainment in the arbitration of the extent of the Chief Arbitrator's participation in the inspection and of the nature of any communications made to him by the technicians. Moreover, had the question been raised, it is possible that action may have been taken by the Tribunal to remedy the situation, assuming that such action was necessary or desirable. Also precluded was an investigation of what happened at the inspection and the part that it played in the report and the Tribunal's decision. The respondent's failure to raise the objection in the Beijing Court and before Findlay J, though not directly relevant to the question now under consideration, had a similar effect.

[50] "The respondent's conduct amounted to a breach of the principle that a party to an arbitration who wishes to rely on a non-compliance with the rules governing an arbitration shall do so promptly and shall not proceed with the arbitration as if there had been no compliance, keeping the point up his sleeve for later use (see *China Nanhai Oil Joint Service Corp. Shenzhen Branch v. Gee Tai Holdings Co. Ltd.* [1994] 3 HKC 375 at 387).[6]

[51] "There has been some debate as to the legal basis for declining to refuse enforcement of an award in these circumstances. In the context of absence of the formalities required by Art. II(2) of the Convention, Dr. van den Berg considers that it is a 'question of estoppel as a fundamental principle of good faith'. According to Dr. van den Berg,

6. Reported in Yearbook XX (1995) pp. 671-680 (Hong Kong no. 8).

> '[t]he principle of good faith may be deemed enshrined in the Convention's provisions.'

See A.J. van den Berg, *The New York Arbitration Convention of 1958* (Kluwer, 1981) at p. 182. That approach gives effect to the objects of the Ordinance as stated in Sect. 2AA.

[52] "The approach was adopted by Kaplan J in the *China Nanhai Oil Case* [1994] at 384-387, a case concerning the constitution of a CIETAC arbitration tribunal. His Lordship held that the Ordinance and the Convention conferred a residual discretion on the court of enforcement to decline to refuse enforcement, even if a ground for refusal might otherwise be made out. I agree with his Lordship that the use of the word 'may' in Sect. 44 and Art. V of the Convention enables the enforcing court to enforce an award, notwithstanding that a Sect. 44 ground might otherwise be established. Whether a court would so act in such a case would depend in very large measure on the particular circumstances. It is difficult to imagine that a court would do so, if enforcement were contrary to public policy, but there is no reason why a court could not do so where, as here, the factual foundation for the public policy ground arises from an alleged non-compliance with the rules governing the arbitration to which the party complaining failed to make a prompt objection, keeping the point up its sleeve, at least when the irregularity might be cured.

[53] "Whether one describes the respondent's conduct as giving rise to an estoppel, a breach of the bona fide principle or simply as a breach of the principle that a matter of non-compliance with the governing rules shall be raised promptly in the arbitration is beside the point in this case. On any one of these bases, the respondent's conduct in failing to raise in the arbitration its objection arising from the communications to the Chief Arbitrator was such as to justify the court of enforcement in enforcing the Award.

[54] "Having reached this conclusion, I do not need to deal with the separate question whether failure to raise the point before the Beijing Court was an additional ground for reaching the same conclusion. Without going into that question, I should indicate that I would be disposed to answer it in the affirmative.

[55] "In bringing the appellant's argument based on estoppel within the enforcing court's discretion under Sect. 44 (Art. V) I have answered question (4).

[56] "It has become fashionable to raise the specific grounds in Sect. 44(2) (Art. V(1)(*b*)), which are directed to procedural irregularities, as public policy grounds (Art. V(2)(*b*)). There is no reason why this course cannot be followed. The principal difference between Sect. 44(2) and Sect. 44(3), it is suggested, is that, under Sect. 44(3), the court of enforcement can take the point of its own

motion (A.J. van den Berg, *The New York Arbitration Convention of 1958*, p. 299). If, what the respondent seeks to do is to raise a specific ground under Sect. 44(2) under the guise of public policy, then it is only right that it should bear the onus of establishing that ground.

[57] "In some decisions, notably of courts in civil law jurisdictions, public policy has been equated to international public policy. As already mentioned, Art. V(2)(*b*) specifically refers to the public policy of the forum. No doubt, in many instances, the relevant public policy of the forum coincides with the public policy of so many other countries that the relevant public policy is accurately described as international public policy. Even in such a case, if the ground is made out, it is because the enforcement of the award is contrary to the public policy of the forum (A.J. van den Berg, *The New York Arbitration Convention of 1958*, p. 298).

[58] "However, the object of the Convention was to encourage the recognition and enforcement of commercial arbitration agreements in international contracts and to unify the standards by which agreements to arbitrate are observed and arbitral awards are enforced (*Scherk v. Alberto Culver Co.* (1974) 417 U.S. 506;[7] *Imperial Ethiopian Government v. Baruch-Foster Corp.* (1976) 535 F.2d 334 at 335).[8] In order to ensure the attainment of that object without excessive intervention on the part of courts of enforcement, the provisions of Art. V, notably Art. V(2)(*b*) relating to public policy, have been given a narrow construction. It has been generally accepted that the expression 'contrary to the public policy of that country' in Art. V(2)(*b*) means 'contrary to the fundamental conceptions of morality and justice' of the forum. *Parsons and Whittemore Overseas Co. Inc. v. Société Générale de l'Industrie du Papier (Rakta)* (1974) 508 F.2d 969 at 974[9] (where the Convention expression was equated to 'the forum's most basic notions of morality and justice'); see A.J. van den Berg, *The New York Arbitration Convention of 1958*, p. 376; also *Renusagar Power Co. Ltd. v. General Electric Co.* (*Yearbook Commercial Arbitration* XX (1995) p. 681 at pp. 697-702)).

[59] "The question then is whether the two matters of which the respondent complains, namely the alleged refusal of a hearing and the communications to the Chief Arbitrator were contrary to the fundamental conceptions of morality and justice of Hong Kong. In this respect, the opportunity of a party to present his case and a determination by an impartial and independent tribunal which is not influenced, or seen to be influenced, by private communications are basic to the notions of justice and morality in Hong Kong.

7. Reported in Yearbook I (1976) pp. 203-204 (US no. 4).
8. Reported in Yearbook II (1977) p. 252 (US no. 10).
9. Reported in Yearbook I (1976) p. 205 (US no. 7).

[60] "The critical question, however, is whether what happened in this case was contrary to these basic notions. In approaching this question, it is relevant to take account of the fact that the parties agreed to an arbitration which was to be governed by the CIETAC Arbitration Rules and the PRC Arbitration Law. The fact that the parties agreed to procedures which differ from those which would ordinarily apply in Hong Kong is a circumstance of which we must take account (see Ordinance Sect. 2AA(2)(a)).

[61] "With respect to the argument that the respondent was unable to present its case, the following matters all go to show that the argument is without substance. The respondent was given a copy of the experts' report and an opportunity to deal with it. At no stage did the respondent indicate that it wished to contest any part of the report, to call people from Jacobson or any other experts as witnesses, to question the experts or to present a case that the equipment was capable of appropriate modification. Indeed, the request in the respondent's defence appeared to suggest that its intention was to ask the experts to be appointed to investigate and *determine* whether modification was possible. Instead of taking the steps mentioned above, the respondent requested the Tribunal to call Jacobson as a witness, a course which the Tribunal rightly rejected, and made a belated attempt to seek comments from Jacobson, despite the respondent's declared intention to sue Jacobson.

[62] "The Tribunal was quite entitled to regard the respondent as engaging in dilatory tactics, to refuse an extension of time and to deliver the Award. The facts do not support the claim that the respondent was unable to present its case. They support the view that the respondent had no relevant case to present.

[63] "With respect to the argument arising from the communications to the Chief Arbitrator, the holding of the inspection at the end user's factory and the presentation by the technicians *in the absence of the respondent* were procedures which in Hong Kong might be considered unacceptable. But once the respondent received the report and the letter of 4 January 1996, it was in a position to explore the significance of what had happened. It failed to do so. It did not apply for a re-inspection in the presence of its representatives. It did not apply for removal of the Chief Arbitrator. It simply proceeded with the arbitration as if nothing untoward had happened. In these circumstances, the respondent has not established that the communications to the Chief Arbitrator gave rise to a case falling within Sect. 44(3) of the Ordinance (Art. V(2)(*b*) of the Convention)."

(....)

Judgment of Justice Litton PJ

(....)

VIII. PUBLIC POLICY DEFENCE

[64] "Sect. 44(3) gives effect to Art. V(2)(*b*) of the New York Convention. In considering the *public policy* ground for refusing enforcement, it is important to view the structure of Sect. 44 as a whole. Subsection (1) gives recognition to mutual recognition of awards by saying: 'Enforcement of a Convention award shall not be refused except in the cases mentioned in this section.'

[65] "Subsection (2) then lists the circumstances, in six paragraphs – (a) to (f) – under which enforcement may be refused, the onus of proof being on the person against whom the Convention award is invoked to prove those circumstances. Para. (f) is particularly noteworthy. The court is empowered under this paragraph to refuse enforcement if the award '*has been set aside or suspended by a competent authority of the country in which, or under the law of which, it was made*'. This gives recognition to the principle that the legal validity of an award is, primarily, a matter for the court of the supervisory jurisdiction to decide. We then come to subsection (3) which says:

> '(3) Enforcement of a Convention award may *also* be refused if the award is in respect of a matter which is not capable of settlement by arbitration, or if it would be contrary to public policy to enforce the award.' [Emphasis added].

[66] "As can be seen, refusal of enforcement on public policy grounds in subsection (3) is a residual remedy. It would be an unusual case where the 'competent authority' in subsection 2(f) has ruled in favour of the validity of the award, yet the court in the enforcement jurisdiction nevertheless concludes that enforcement should be denied for public policy reasons. The practical result, as counsel for the appellant Ms. Audrey Eu SC points out, can be extremely unjust: The claimant cannot *enforce* the award because the award has, in effect, been nullified in the eyes of the enforcement court, yet it cannot ask for the arbitration to be instituted afresh in the supervisory jurisdiction because the court in that jurisdiction has *upheld* its validity.

[67] "The expression *public policy* as it appears in Sect. 44(3) is a multi-facetted concept. Woven into this concept is the principle that courts should recognise the validity of decisions of foreign arbitral tribunals as a matter of comity, and give effect to them, unless to do so would violate the most basic notions of morality and justice. It would take a very strong case before such a conclusion can be properly reached, when the facts giving rise to the allegation have been

made the subject of challenge in proceedings in the supervisory jurisdiction, and such challenge has failed."

IX. THE FACTS

[68] "It is an admitted fact that the seller received a copy of the experts' report in mid-December 1995. Sir Anthony Mason NPJ has in his judgment referred to the letter of 4 January 1996 from the tribunal to the seller, where the Chief Arbitrator's presence at the inspection was disclosed. There were further submissions thereafter from the seller, in the course of which the seller asked that the American manufacturer of the equipment Jacobson Inc. be made a party to the arbitration proceedings or be called as a witness to explain the defects in the equipment. Not surprisingly this was declined by the tribunal. In its reply dated 25 January 1996 the tribunal went on to say:

> 'If you have any opinion on the contents of the expert assessment report, please submit the same in writing to the Tribunal before 16 February 1996'

[69] "The seller responded on 14 February 1996 with lengthy submissions and ended up by saying:

> 'The equipment has up to now failed to attain the targets prescribed in the Agreement. Although this was not caused by the deliberate act of ... the seller, and [the seller] was in fact a victim, [the seller] is willing to assume its own responsibility of compensation if the equipment is repairable....'

[70] "There was then an admission of liability to the tune of US$ 55,994.38 and RMB 77,309.39. This was followed by a request that the tribunal should postpone making an award for two months. Not surprisingly, this was not accepted by the tribunal which then published its detailed award on 29 March 1996.

[71] "On the facts I conclude that the seller comes nowhere near establishing a case for intervention by the court on public policy grounds. As I read the Court of Appeal's judgment, it was led astray by the notion that, at the inspection at the end-user's factory, there was some process of assessment of the state of the equipment by the Chief Arbitrator in the presence of the experts, but in the absence of the other two arbitrators, and of the seller.

Whether such a process, had it occurred, might have brought the case within Sect. 44(3) is beside the point. There is no evidence that this had occurred....

[72] "The Court of Appeal, in my judgment, made far too much of the so-called briefing by the technicians on the history of the equipment, when the experts attended at the end-user's factory, accompanied by the Chief Arbitrator. On the evidence, this was the first view of the equipment by the experts. They had been appointed by the tribunal at the seller's request, and their initial task was to see whether, as the seller contended, the equipment might be modified so as to perform to the contract specification. That was the focus of the 'briefing'. On these facts, it was not open to the Court of Appeal to conclude that the seller, being absent at the inspection, had been prevented from presenting its side of the case. The inspection at the factory was not a 'hearing' nor was it an occasion for either party to present its case."

X. ARTICLE 32 OF THE CIETAC ARBITRATION RULES AND ARTICLE 45 OF THE ARBITRATION LAW OF THE PRC

[73] "The Court of Appeal found as a fact that there had been breaches of Arts. 32 and 45. The Court of Appeal made its findings despite the conclusion of the Beijing Court that there had been *no* breaches of the arbitration rules. The Court of Appeal's findings cannot stand. The 'rules' which apply in this jurisdiction are those set out in Sect. 44(2) of the Ordinance. Before Findlay J the seller invoked Sect. 44(2)(c) and failed. It did not appeal against that finding but, in the Court of Appeal, invoked a *different* provision, Sect. 44(3), on the basis that *public policy* was a common-law concept which had no equivalence in PRC law. As put by the Court of Appeal:

> 'In the present case, the defendant's main contention is that it would be contrary to public policy to enforce the award under Sect. 44(3) of the Ordinance. We doubt whether the defendant would have been able to rely on this ground when it applied to set aside the award before the Beijing Court. The nearest equivalent in the statutory provisions of the PRC is the second paragraph of Art. 260 which refers to the "social and public interest of the country". The concept of public policy in Hong Kong is something which is generally part of the common law and it is difficult to see how it could be the same as that relating to the "social and public interest" of the PRC.'

[74] "There was no evidence before the Court of Appeal as to the circumstances under which enforcement of a Convention award might be refused

under the second paragraph of Art. 260, on the ground that enforcement would be against the 'social and public interest of the country'. The Court of Appeal simply assumed that the grounds under that rubric must necessarily be very different from those comprised in the *public policy* defence in Sect. 44(3) of the Hong Kong Ordinance, and therefore concluded that, despite having taken proceedings in the Beijing Court to contest the award, it was open to the seller to resist enforcement in Hong Kong. I have already explained earlier why that conclusion is, in my judgment, erroneous. Whether that view be right or wrong there was no warrant in my judgment for the Court of Appeal to embark upon a collateral issue, to enquire into alleged breaches of Arts. 32 and 45 of the Mainland rules concerning arbitration. Its jurisdiction was confined to entertaining an appeal against Findlay J's finding that the rule in Sect. 44(2)(c) of the Hong Kong Ordinance governing the arbitral proceedings had not been breached. And if there was no appeal against that, the matter should have ended there."

XI. ESTOPPEL

[75] "Estoppel, a term developed in the English law of equity, does not lie comfortably in the context of enforcing a Convention award. It is not a legal concept of universal currency among the contracting states to the New York Convention. If what is suggested by *estoppel* is no more than this, that a party invoking Sect. 44(3) must act in *good faith*; that he must not string the claimant along by taking procedural points in contesting the award, and then, when all else has failed, attempts to resist enforcement by taking a *public policy* point for the first time, then this is no more than expressing another facet of public policy, as expressed in Sect. 44(3). In my view *estoppel* as such cannot be an answer to the seller's application to refuse enforcement in this case, and it is fruitless to inquire whether the 'issues' now raised are the same as, or similar to, the ones put before the Beijing Court. Rather, the point should be put on a broader basis. Having regard to the seller's conduct, a court in Hong Kong should be slow to entertain its application to refuse enforcement of the award."

XII. CONCLUSION LITTON PJ

[76] "In my judgment, on the facts of this case, the seller has come nowhere near proving a case for refusing enforcement based on public policy grounds. I would allow the buyer's appeal and make the orders as Sir Anthony Mason NPJ has proposed."

Judgment of Justice Bokhary PJ

XIII. FACTS

[77] "This appeal is concerned with the enforcement in Hong Kong of a Convention award i.e. an award made in pursuance of an arbitration agreement in a State or territory, other than Hong Kong, which is a party to the New York Convention. The full facts are set out in the judgment of Sir Anthony Mason NPJ. I respectfully agree with him, and wish only to emphasise the following matters.

[78] "In the Court of Appeal's judgment delivered by the Chief Judge, two crucial statements as to the facts are made. The first is that 'the award ... was apparently based on the condition of the equipment as assessed by the experts and the Chief Arbitrator during the inspection'. And the second one, immediately following the first, is that: 'How far they were influenced by the briefing of the [appellant buyer's] staff in the absence of the [respondent seller] is unknown'. The implication is that the experts and the Chief Arbitrator were – and therefore the award itself was – so influenced to *some* extent.

[79] "If I had felt able wholly to share the Court of Appeal's view of the facts, I might have been disposed to affirm the result which it reached, which was to refuse enforcement of the award. It might be mentioned that if the facts were indeed as the Court of Appeal saw them, the seller may, for all we know, have succeeded in its application to the court in the supervisory jurisdiction, the Beijing No. 2 Intermediate Court, for the setting aside of the award....

[80] "What the evidence suggests is as follows. Two technicians, who were in the end-user's employ but acted as agents for the buyer, assisted the experts to the extent necessary for them to carry out the inspection. (It was of course the seller itself which had wanted an inspection done.) Probably the technicians did tell the experts, in the Chief Arbitrator's hearing, what had gone wrong in the past. But that would have been of limited importance since the experts were not there to consider what the equipment had failed to do. They were concerned to discover what the equipment could be made to do through modification."

XIV. INABILITY TO PRESENT CASE?

[81] "True it is that the seller did not attend the inspection because it had not been notified of it. And I think that this lack of notice did provide the seller with some cause for complaint. But in all the circumstances, including the seller's inaction after discovering the existence of this cause for complaint, I do

not think that the complaint can legitimately be taken so far as to say that the seller had been unable to present its case."
(....)

XV. CONTRARY TO PUBLIC POLICY?

[82] "What remains is the seller's second submission. This is the submission that enforcement of the award in question should be refused under Sect. 44(3) of the Arbitration Ordinance which provides that enforcement of a Convention award may also be refused if it would be contrary to public policy to enforce the award. Here the seller's argument runs thus. The Chief Arbitrator had, in the seller's absence, been in contact with the buyer's employees or agents. This involved justice not being seen to be done. And it gave the appearance of bias. Accordingly, the argument concludes, it is contrary to public policy to permit enforcement of the award in Hong Kong.
[83] "In my view, there must be compelling reasons before enforcement of a Convention award can be refused on public policy grounds. This is not to say that the reasons must be so extreme that the award falls to be cursed by bell, book and candle. But the reasons must go beyond the minimum which would justify setting aside a domestic judgment or award. A point to similar effect was made in a comparable context by the United States Supreme Court in *Mitsubishi Motors Corp. v. Soler Chrysler-Plymouth Inc.* 473 U.S. 614 (1985).[10] There the question was whether an antitrust claim was to be referred to arbitration outside the United States. In holding that it was, the majority said this (at p. 629):

> '... concerns of international comity, respect for the capacities of foreign and transnational tribunals, and sensitivity to the need of the international commercial system for predictability in the resolution of disputes require that we enforce the parties' agreement, even assuming that a contrary result would be forthcoming in a domestic context'.

The considerable strength of this demand for comity is apparent from what it was able to overcome, namely the advantages of dealing with antitrust claims by way of litigation in the United States rather than by way of arbitration elsewhere. These advantages are detailed in the dissenting judgment of the minority.

10. Reported in Yearbook XI (1986) pp. 555-566 (US no. 59).

[84] "When a number of States enter into a treaty to enforce each other's arbitral awards, it stands to reason that they would do so in the realisation that they, or some of them, will very likely have very different outlooks in regard to internal matters. And they would hardly intend, when entering into the treaty or later when incorporating it into their domestic law, that these differences should be allowed to operate so as to undermine the broad uniformity which must be the obvious aim of such a treaty and the domestic laws incorporating it.

[85] "In regard to the refusal of enforcement of Convention awards on public policy grounds, there are references in the cases and texts to what has been called 'international public policy'. Does this mean some standard common to all civilized nations? Or does it mean those elements of a State's own public policy which are so fundamental to its notions of justice that its courts feel obliged to apply the same not only to purely internal matters but even to matters with a foreign element by which other States are affected? I think that it should be taken to mean the latter. If it were the former, it would become so difficult of ascertainment that a court may well feel obliged – as the Supreme Court of India did in *Renusagar Power Co. Ltd. v. General Electric Co. Yearbook Commercial Arbitration* XX (1995) p. 681 at p. 700 – to abandon the search for it.

[86] "None of this is to say that the proper approach is insular. It is eclectic for this reason. When deciding, under this approach, whether to enforce a Convention award made in circumstances where a domestic judgment or award would have to be set aside, it is appropriate to examine how far the courts of other Convention jurisdictions have been prepared to go in enforcing Convention awards made in circumstances which do not meet their domestic standards. Thus many Convention courts' decisions were cited in this appeal. These decisions include that of the Italian Court of Appeal in *Bobbie Brooks Inc. v. Lanificio Walter Banci s.a.s. Yearbook Commercial Arbitration* IV (1979) p. 289 at p. 292. That court permitted enforcement of a Convention award made in the United States even though the award contained no reasons while the giving of reasons for decisions was a principle of the Italian Constitution.

[87] "In my judgment, the position is as follows. Before a Convention jurisdiction can, in keeping with its being a party to the Convention, refuse enforcement of a Convention award on public policy grounds, the award must be so fundamentally offensive to that jurisdiction's notions of justice that, despite its being a party to the Convention, it cannot reasonably be expected to overlook the objection.

(....)

[88] "In the present context, I think that a distinction can and should be made between the effect of actual bias and that of apparent bias. (When I say 'bias'

I mean a lack of the impartiality required of judges and arbitrators.) Actual bias would be more than our courts could overlook even where the award concerned is a Convention award. But short of actual bias, I do not think that the Hong Kong courts would be justified in refusing enforcement of a Convention award on public policy grounds as soon as appearances fall short of what we insist upon in regard to impartiality where domestic cases or arbitrations are concerned. Our stance must be that something more serious even than that is required for refusing such enforcement. In adopting such a stance, we would be proceeding in conformity with the stance generally adopted in regard to Convention award enforcement by the commercial jurisdictions whose decisions from around the globe have been cited to us by leading counsel for the buyer.

(....)

[89] "There is no attack on the good faith of the Chief Arbitrator or any of the other arbitrators. That being so, once the seller's argument that it had been unable to present its case breaks down, there remains in the circumstances of this case simply no warrant for saying that it would be contrary to public policy to enforce the Convention award in question. It is unnecessary, therefore, to consider the pleas of waiver and estoppel raised by the buyer against the seller."

XVI. CONCLUSION OF BOKHARY PJ

[90] "Despite the able arguments advanced by leading counsel for the seller, I am of the view that the buyer is entitled to succeed...."

INDIA

Ratification: 13 July 1960
1st and 2nd Reservations

28. Supreme Court, 4 December 1997

Parties:	Appellant: Sumitomo Heavy Industries Ltd. (nationality not indicated) Respondent: ONGC Ltd. (India) and another (nationality not indicated)
Published in:	Arbitration Law Reporter (1998, no. 1) pp. 10-18
Articles:	I(1) (by implication)
Subject matters:	– filing of award outside the place of arbitration – law applicable to arbitration
Commentary Cases:	¶ 104

Facts

On 7 September 1983, ONGC Ltd. (ONGC), the Oil & Natural Gas Commission of India, entered into a contract with Sumitomo Heavy Industries Ltd. (Sumitomo) for the turnkey installation of an oil platform at Bombay High, approximately 100 miles north-west of Bombay. Clause 17.1 of the contract provided that "All questions, disputes or difference arising under, out of or in connection with this Contract shall be subject to the laws of India"; Clause 17.2 provided for ICC arbitration in London by two arbitrators and an umpire.

A dispute arose between the parties, whereupon Sumitomo initiated ICC arbitration as provided for in the contract. Each party appointed an arbitrator and the two arbitrators appointed an umpire.

When ONGC failed to file its statement in defence in the arbitration, Sumitomo petitioned the High Court (Commercial Court) in London for an order under Sect. 5 of the English Arbitration Act, 1979.[1] Potter, J granted Sumitomo's request. The order was later set aside by the High Court.[2]

The two party-appointed arbitrators did not reach an agreement and, on 27 June 1995, the umpire rendered an award in favour of Sumitomo.

On 26 July 1995, ONGC summoned Sumitomo and the umpire in the High Court in Bombay, seeking an order directing the umpire to file the London award in Bombay under Sect. 14(2) of the Indian Arbitration Act, 1940,[3] as a prerequisite for a request to set aside the award. The Court granted ONGC's petition on 25 October 1996.

The Supreme Court affirmed the lower court's decision. It found that the procedural law governing the arbitration, in casu, English law, ceases to have effect with the making of the award. Hence, the filing of the award in court is not part of the arbitration proceedings; rather, it pertains to the subsequent (enforcement or annulment) proceedings, which are governed by the law governing the arbitration agreement. In casu, the law governing the arbitration agreement was undisputedly Indian law and, more in particular, the Indian Arbitration Act, 1940, which allows a court to direct an arbitrator to file his award in court. The Supreme Court found that the Foreign Awards (Recogni-

1. Sect. 5 of the English Arbitration Act, 1979, reads in relevant part:

"*Interlocutory orders.*
(1) If any party to a reference under an arbitration agreement fails within the time specified in the order or, if no time is so specified, within a reasonable time to comply with an order made by the arbitrator or umpire in the course of the reference, then, on the application of the arbitrator or umpire or of any party to the reference, the High Court may make an order extending the powers of the arbitrator or umpire as mentioned in subsection (2) below.
(2) If an order is made by the High Court under this section, the arbitrator or umpire shall have power, to the extent and subject to any conditions specified in that order, to continue with the reference in default of appearance or of any other act by one of the parties in like manner as a judge of the High Court might continue with proceedings in that court where a party fails to comply with an order of that court or a requirement of rules of court.
(....)"

2. [1994] 1 Lloyd's Rep. 45.

3. Sect. 14 of the Indian Arbitration Act, 1940, reads in relevant part:

"(2) The arbitrators or umpire shall, at the request of any party to the arbitration agreement or any person claiming under such party or if so directed by the Court and upon payment of the fees and charges due in respect of the arbitration and award and of the costs and charges of filing the award, cause the award or a signed copy of it, together with any depositions and documents which may have been taken and proved before them, to be filed in Court, and the Court shall thereupon give notice to the parties of the filing of the award.
(....)"

tion and Enforcement) Act, 1961 did not apply as the award was made on the basis of an arbitration agreement governed by the law of India.

Excerpt

[1] "The decision rendered by Potter, J in the Commercial Court is of some importance because the jurisdiction of the English courts was discussed. The learned Judge said:

> 'Before stating my reasons for that conclusion and then turning to the "frustration" argument, and because questions have arisen as to whether English law or Indian law is appropriate to be applied at various stages of this application, I propose briefly to advert to the various laws potentially applicable to the various aspects of the arbitral relationship which may fall for consideration in cases of this kind:
> (1) The proper law of the underlying contract, i.e., the law governing the contract which creates the substantive rights and obligations of the parties out of which the dispute has arisen.
> (2) The proper law of the arbitration agreement, i.e., the law governing rights and obligations of the parties arising from their agreement to arbitrate and, in particular, their obligations to submit their disputes to arbitration and to honour an award. This includes inter alia questions as to the validity of the arbitration agreement, the validity of the notice of arbitration, the constitution of the tribunal and the question whether an award lies within the jurisdiction of the arbitrator.
> (3) The proper law of the reference, i.e., the law governing the contract which regulates the individual reference to arbitration. This is an agreement subsidiary to but separate from the arbitration agreement itself, coming into effect by the giving of a notice of arbitration from which point a new set of mutual obligations in relation to the conduct of the reference arise upon lines canvassed in the *Bremer Vulkan Schiffbau- und Maschinenfabrik v. South Indian Shipping Corporation*,[4] and developed by Mr. Justice Mustill (as he then was) in *Black Clawson International Ltd. v. Papierwerk Waldhof-Aschaffenburg A.G.*,[5] that law governs the question of whether by reason of subsequent circumstance the parties have been discharged (whether by repudiation or frustration) from their obligation to continue with the reference of the individual

4. "[1981] 1 Lloyd's Rep. 253."
5. "[1981] 2 Lloyd's Rep. 446."

dispute, while leaving intact the continuous agreement to refer future disputes pursuant to the arbitration agreement.
(4) The curial law, i.e., the law governing the arbitration proceedings themselves, the manner in which the reference is to be conducted. It governs the procedural powers and duties of the arbitrators, questions of evidence and the determination of the proper law of the contract.

In respect of many arbitrations, the applicable law will be the same in all four cases. (1) will usually be decisive as to (2), in the absence of an express contrary choice; (2) and (3) will very rarely differ. However, as to (4), it is not uncommon to encounter the incidence of a different curial law in cases where the parties have made an express choice for arbitration (frequently in London) in a jurisdiction divorced from the jurisdiction with which the contract in (1) has most real connection.

In this case, as to (1), the parties have made an express choice of Indian law as the proper law of the contract. As to (2), it seems to me likely (although it is not necessary finally to decide) that the proper law of the arbitration agreement is similarly Indian law, since the arbitration agreement is part of the substance of the underlying contract and the terms of Clause 17.1 are clear in that respect. As to (3), it matters not for the purposes of this application whether the governing law is English or Indian law, because [counsel for ONGC] has conceded before me that there is no material difference between the two so far as applicable to the doctrine of frustration upon which he relies....

As to (4), the curial law, it seems to me plain that it is the law of England. There is, it is true, no express choice of curial law. However, there is a clear requirement that the arbitration proceedings be held in London. In the absence of express agreement there is a strong prima facie presumption that the parties intend the curial law to be the law of the "seat" of the arbitrator, i.e., the place at which the arbitration is to be conducted, on the ground that [it] is the country most closely connected with the proceedings – see Mustill and Boyd, 2nd ed., p. 64.'

[2] "Neither of the parties having filed an appeal from the judgment of Potter, J, its findings bind them. Based upon these findings, it was contended by [counsel for Sumitomo] that the petition filed by [ONGC] in the High Court at Bombay fell outside the jurisdiction of that Court for a direction to the [arbitrator] to file his award in Court could be given only by the Courts administering the curial law, that is to say the Courts in England. The answer of [counsel for ONGC] is that the award having been made, the procedural or curial law had ceased to have effect and, accordingly, the Courts administering

the curial law had no jurisdiction to issue to the [arbitrator] a direction to file his award therein.

[3] "This, then, is the central issue in the appeal: what is the area of operation of the curial law. In *Bank Mellat v. Helliniki Techniki S.A.*,[6] the Court of Appeal said that the fundamental principle was that in the absence of any contractual provision to the contrary, '*the procedural or curial law governing* arbitrations' was that of the forum of the arbitration, since this was the system of law with which the agreement to arbitrate in the particular forum would have its closest connection. Parties to international arbitrations might well choose London as a convenient neutral forum and '*English law will, as the curial law, apply to the conduct of the arbitration; and* the parties will by holding their arbitration there, subject themselves for that purpose to English law....' (Emphasis supplied).

[4] "In *Naviera Amazonica Peruana S.A. v. Compañía Internacional De Seguros del Peru*,[7] Lord Justice Kerr summarised the state of the relevant jurisprudence thus:

> 'A. All contracts which provide for arbitration and contain a foreign element may involve three potentially relevant systems of law. (1) The law governing the substantive contract. (2) The law governing the agreement to arbitrate and the performance of that agreement. (3) *The law governing the conduct of the arbitration*. In the majority of cases all three will be the same. But (1) will often be different from (2) and (3). And occasionally, but rarely, (2) may also differ from (3).'

He said, 'Prima facie, i.e., in the absence of some express and clear provision to the contrary, it must follow that an agreement that *the curial or procedural law of an arbitration* is to be the law of X has the consequence that X is also to be the "seat" of the arbitration. The lex fori is then the law of X, and accordingly X is the agreed forum of the arbitration. A further consequence is then that the *Courts which are competent to control or assist the arbitration* are the Courts exercising jurisdiction at X.' The learned judge observed that there was no reason in theory which precluded 'parties to agree that an arbitration shall be held at a place or in Country X but subject to the *procedural laws* of Y'. (Emphasis supplied)

[5] "In *The Law and Practice of Commercial Arbitration in England*, Second Edition, by Mustill and Boyd, there is a chapter on 'The applicable law and

6. "WB (1984, no. 1) p. 291."

7. "[1988] 1 Lloyd's Rep. 116."

the jurisdiction of the court'. Under the sub-title, 'Laws Governing the Arbitration', it is said,

> 'An agreed reference to arbitration involves two groups of obligations. The first concerns the mutual obligations of the parties to submit future disputes, or an existing dispute to arbitration, and to abide by the award of a tribunal constituted in accordance with the agreement. It is now firmly established that the arbitration agreement which creates these obligations is a separate contract, distinct from the substantive agreement in which it is usually embedded, capable of surviving the termination of the substantive agreement and susceptible of premature termination by express or implied consent, or by repudiation or frustration, in much the same manner as in more ordinary forms of contract. Since this agreement has a distinct life of its own, it may in principle be governed by a proper law of its own, which need not be the same as the law governing the substantive contract.
>
> *The second group of obligations, consisting of what is generally referred to as the "curial law" of the arbitration concerns the manner in which the parties and the arbitrator are required to conduct the reference of a particular dispute.* According to the English theory of arbitration, these rules are to be ascertained by reference to the express or implied terms of the agreement to arbitrate. This being so, [it] will be found in the great majority of cases that the *curial law, i.e., the law governing the conduct of the reference*, is the same as the law governing the obligation to arbitrate. It is, however, open to the parties to submit, expressly or by implication, the conduct of the reference to a different law from the one governing the underlying arbitration agreement. *In such a case, the court looks first at the arbitration agreement to see whether the dispute is one which should be arbitrated, and which has validly been made the subject of the reference, it then looks to the curial law to see how that reference should be conducted, and then, returns to the first law in order to give effect to the resulting award.* (....)
>
> It may therefore be seen that problems arising out of an arbitration may, at least in theory, call for the application of any one or more of the following laws:
>
> (1) The proper law of the contract, i.e., the law governing the contract which creates the substantive rights of the parties, in respect of which the dispute has arisen.
>
> (2) The proper law of the arbitration agreement, i.e., the law governing the obligation of the parties to submit the disputes to arbitration, and to honour an award.

(3) *The curial law, i.e., the law governing the conduct of the individual reference.* (....)
(1) *The proper law of the arbitration agreement governs the validity* of the arbitration agreement, the question whether a dispute lies within the scope of the arbitration agreement; the validity of the notice of arbitration; the constitution of the tribunal; the question whether an award lies within the jurisdiction of the arbitrator; the formal validity of the award; the question whether the parties have been discharged from any obligation to arbitrate future disputes.
(2) *The curial law governs: the manner in which the reference is to be conducted; the procedural powers and duties of the arbitrator; questions of evidence; the determination of the proper law of the contract.*
(3) The proper law of the reference governs: the question whether the parties have been discharged from their obligation to continue with the reference of the individual dispute. (....)
In the absence of an express agreement, there is a strong prima facie presumption that the parties intend the curial law to be the law of the "seat" of the arbitration, i.e., the place at which the arbitration is to be conducted, on the ground that [it] is the country most closely connected with the proceedings. So in order to determine the curial law in the absence of an express choice by the parties it is first necessary to determine the seat of the arbitration, by construing the agreement to arbitrate.' (Emphasis supplied)

[6] "The conclusion that we reach is that the curial law operates during the continuance of the proceedings before the arbitrator to govern the procedure and conduct thereof. The Courts administering the curial law have the authority to entertain applications by parties to arbitrations being conducted within their jurisdiction for the purpose of ensuring that the procedure that is adopted in the proceedings before the arbitrator conforms to the requirements of the curial law and for reliefs incidental thereto. Such authority of the Courts administering the curial law ceases when the proceedings before the arbitrator are concluded.

[7] "The proceedings before the arbitrator commence when he enters upon the reference and conclude with the making of the award. As the work by Mustill and Boyd aforementioned puts it, with the making of a valid award the arbitrator's authority, powers and duties in the reference come to an end and he is '*functus officio*' (para. 404). The arbitrator is not obliged by law to file his award in Court but he may be asked by the party seeking to enforce the award to do so. The need to file an award in Court arises only if it is required to be enforced, and the need to challenge it arises if it is being enforced. The

enforcement process is subsequent to and independent of the proceedings before the arbitrator. It is not governed by the curial or procedural law that governed the procedure that the arbitrator followed in the conduct of the arbitration.

[8] "[Counsel for Sumitomo] relied upon observations in Dicey and Morris on *The Conflict of Laws, 12th Edition*. The first Rule under the heading 'Arbitration' in the Chapter on 'Arbitration and Foreign Awards' reads thus:

> 'Rule 57-(1). The validity, effect and interpretation of an arbitration agreement are governed by its applicable law.
> (2) The law governing arbitration proceedings is the law chosen by the parties, or in the absence of agreement, the law of the country in which the arbitration is held.'

In discussing Clause (2) of the Rule aforementioned, this is stated:

> 'The procedural law of the arbitration will determine how the arbitrators are to be appointed, in so far as this is regulated in the arbitration agreement, the effect of one party's failure to appoint an arbitrator, e.g., whether an arbitrator may be appointed by a Court, or whether the arbitration can proceed before the sole arbitrator appointed by the other party, and whether the authority of an arbitrator can be revoked. That law will also determine what law the arbitrators are to apply, and whether they are expected or allowed to decide ex aequo et bono *or* as amiables compositeurs, and if not, whether the parties can give them this power or impose on them this duty. That law will also determine the procedural powers and duties of the arbitrators, e.g., whether they must hear oral evidence (but not their jurisdiction to decide the dispute, which is governed by the arbitration agreement and the law applicable to it) or whether the arbitrators have been guilty of misconduct. *It will also determine what judicial remedies are available to a party* who wishes to apply for security for costs or for discovery or *who wishes to challenge the award once it has been rendered and before it is sought to enforce it abroad*, and the circumstances in which judicial remedies may be excluded.' (Emphasis supplied)

[9] "[Counsel for Sumitomo] submitted, relying upon the proposition that the procedural law would determine what judicial remedies were available to a party 'who wishes to challenge the award once it has been rendered and before it is sought to enforce it abroad', that the court that administered the curial law of the arbitration had the jurisdiction to entertain a challenge to the

award and, therefore, the jurisdiction to receive it. The footnote relative to the above proposition (at p. 583) reads thus: '*Whitworth Street Estates (Manchester) Ltd. v. James Miller & Partners Ltd.* (remedies not available in Scots arbitration)'.[8]

[10] "[Counsel for ONGC] submitted, and it seems to us correctly, that the case of *James Miller & Partners v. Whitworth Street Estates*, does not bear out the proposition. The facts of the case, shortly put, were these: A contract was entered into between an English company, Whitworth, and a Scottish company, James Miller. The Scottish company was to carry out work at the English company's premises in Scotland. The contract did not provide for the place of arbitration or its procedure. Disputes arose between the parties and were referred to arbitration. The arbitration was held in Scotland, in accordance with Scottish law. The English company asked the arbitrator to state his award in the form of a special case for the decision of the English Courts. The arbitrator refused to do so on the ground that the arbitration was a Scottish arbitration, and he issued his final award. The issue was whether the arbitrator should be requested to state his award in the form of a special case. The case was, therefore, concerned with the question of which law governed the proceedings before the arbitrator and not with the question of which law governed proceedings to set aside an award.

[11] "We think that our conclusion that the curial law does not apply to the filing of award in court must, accordingly, hold good. We find support for the conclusion in the extracts from Mustill and Boyd which we have quoted earlier. Where the law governing the conduct of the reference is different from the law governing the underlying arbitration agreement, the Court looks to the arbitration agreement to see if the dispute is arbitrable, then to the curial law to see how the reference should be conducted, 'and then return to the first law in order to give effect to the resulting award'.

[12] "The law which would apply to the filing of the award, to its enforcement and to its setting aside would be the law governing the agreement to arbitrate and the performance of that agreement. Having regard to the clear terms of Clause 17 of the contract between [Sumitomo] and [ONGC], we are in no doubt that the law governing the contract and the law governing the rights and obligations of the parties arising from their agreement to arbitrate, and, in particular, their obligation to submit disputes to arbitration and to honour the award, are governed by the law of India, nor is there any dispute in this behalf.

[13] "Sect. 47 of the Indian Arbitration Act, 1940, reads thus:

---

8. "[1970] A.C. 583."

'*47. Act to apply to all arbitrations.* Subject to the provisions of Section 46, and save in so far as is otherwise provided by any law for the time being in force, the provisions of this Act shall apply to all arbitrations and to all proceedings thereunder:

Provided that an arbitration award otherwise obtained may with the consent of all the parties interested be taken into consideration as a compromise or adjustment of a suit by any Court before which the suit is pending.'

[14] "The only other statute which is required to be considered in the context of the provisions of Sect. 47 of the 1940 Act is the Foreign Awards (Recognition and Enforcement) Act, 1961. For the purposes of determining whether the provisions of the 1940 Act are subject to the provisions of the 1961 Act, Sect. 9 is relevant. It reads thus:

'9. *Saving* – Nothing in this Act shall:
(a) Prejudice any rights which any person would have had of enforcing in India any award or of availing himself in India of any award if this Act had not been passed, or
(b) apply to any award made on an arbitration agreement governed by the law of India.'

[15] "By reason of Sect. 9(b), the 1961 Act does not apply to any award made on an arbitration agreement governed by the law of India. The 1961 Act, therefore, does not apply to the arbitration agreement between [Sumitomo] and [ONGC]. The 1940 Act, applies to it and, by reason of Sect. 14(2) thereof, the courts in India are entitled to receive the award made by the [arbitrator]. We must add in the interests of completeness that it is not the case of [Sumitomo] that the High Court at Bombay lacked the territorial jurisdiction to do so.

[16] "In the result, the appeal must fail, and it is dismissed with costs."

29. Delhi High Court, 19 February 1999

Parties:	Petitioner: Fuerst Day Lawson Ltd. (nationality not indicated) Respondent: Jindal Exports Ltd. (nationality not indicated)
Published in:	Arbitration Law Reporter (1999, no. 1) pp. 571-589
Articles:	III; IV; V
Subject matters:	– change in implementing legislation – enforcement versus execution
Commentary Cases:	¶ 113, ¶ 301 + ¶ 401

Facts

Fuerst Day Lawson Ltd. (FDL) and Jindal Exports Ltd. (Jindal) entered into a contract on 1 August 1994 whereby Jindal was to supply certain goods to FDL. Disputes arose between the parties and FDL initiated arbitration before the International General Produce Association. The request for arbitration was received by Jindal on 20 November 1995, FDL filed claims with arbitrators on 18 December 1995 and the arbitral tribunal was constituted on 24 January 1996. An award was made on 13 August 1996 which allowed FDL's claim and awarded US$ 408,600.

FDL filed an execution application for the execution of the foreign award. The application was treated as an execution petition and in the purported exercise of powers vested under Order 21 of the Code of Civil Procedure, warrants of attachment were issued against property belonging to Jindal. Jindal filed an application raising a preliminary objection to the maintainability of the execution petition and sought for dismissal of the execution petition on the ground that the petition was not maintainable. In order to allow Jindal to continue its business, the court accepted Jindal's offer to deposit bond certificates in court as security.

Jindal argued that the execution proceedings instituted by FDL were premature as it was first necessary for the court to be satisfied that the award was enforceable.

The court, per Dr. M.K. Sharma, J, held that the Foreign Awards (Recognition and Enforcement) Act, 1961, rather than the Arbitration and Conciliation Act 1996 applied, but in either case it was necessary for the other party to be given an opportunity to present his objections before enforcement or execution of a foreign award. No execution proceeding could be instituted without first filing a suit, obtaining an order for filing the award and making the award a rule of the court.

Excerpt

[1] The Court first compared the provisions of the Foreign Awards (Recognition and Enforcement) Act, 1961, (FARE Act) Sects. 2-7 and the Arbitration and Conciliation Act, 1996, Chapter 1, New York Convention Awards, Sect. 44-49. It then continued: "A particular and specified mode and manner is provided for and prescribed for enforcement of a foreign award in India both under the Foreign Awards (Recognition and Enforcement) Act, 1961 as also the Arbitration and Conciliation Act, 1996. With the coming into force of the Arbitration and Conciliation Act, 1996 the provisions of the FARE Act, 1961 stood repealed subject to the saving clause.

[2] "The new provisions which have been enacted for enforcing an award in India would indicate that before the said foreign award could be enforced there is a necessity for a party to obtain a foreign award which is defined under the provisions of Sect. 44 of the Arbitration and Conciliation Act, 1996.[1] After a foreign award is made the same could be enforced in India when the court is satisfied that the foreign award is enforceable. The said satisfaction is arrived at when the party in whose favour the award is made appl[ies] for its enforcement. Thus a party has to apply for under Sects. 46 and 47 of the Arbitration Act seeking for enforcement of the foreign award. A foreign award

1. Sect. 44 of the Arbitration and Conciliation Act, 1996 reads:

"*Definition* – In this Chapter, unless the context otherwise requires 'foreign award' means an award on differences between persons arising out of legal relationships, whether contractual or not, considered as commercial under the law in force in India, made on or after the 11th day of October 1960:
(a) in pursuance of an agreement in writing for arbitration to which the Convention set forth in the Schedule applies, and
(b) in one of such territories as the Central Government, being satisfied that reciprocal provisions have been made may by Notification in the Official Gazette, declare to be territories to which the said Convention applies."

becomes binding between the persons as against whom the same is made for all practical purposes when the same is enforceable under the provisions of Sects. 46 to 49 of the Arbitration and Conciliation Act. Sect. 47 provides that a person seeking for enforcement of a foreign award has to apply for the said relief before the court enclosing therewith the documents as mentioned specifically in Sect. 47 of the Act.

[3] "A right is given to the party as against whom the foreign award is sought to be enforced, to raise objections as against the aforesaid enforcement of a foreign award on any of the grounds as mentioned in the provisions of Sect. 48. Sect. 49 on the other hand provides that it is only when the court is satisfied that the foreign award is enforceable under Chap. I of Part II, the award could be deemed to be a decree of the particular court.

[4] "Counsel for the petitioner submitted that the words 'enforcement' and 'execution' are synonymous and therefore, a party in whose favour a foreign award is made is entitled to treat the award as a decree itself and file an execution petition immediately seeking for enforcement/execution of the decree. According to him upon the making of an application under Sect. 47 of the Act the award is deemed enforceable as if it were a decree by virtue of a legal fiction in Sect. 49 but the enforceable process is set in motion by a party against whom the award is enforced by moving an appropriate application under Sect. 48. Counsel submitted that at the initial stage requirement of notice upon filing of the execution application is excluded by the express repeal of the provisions of Sect. 5 for the FARE Act, 1961 and the modification of Sect. 6 with the repeal of Sect. 6(2) thereof. In support of his submission the learned Counsel sought to rely upon the Statement of Objects and Reasons of the Arbitration and Conciliation Act, and certain passages from the commentary on the said new Act by Shri S.K. Chawla and Dr. P.C. Rao. Counsel also relied upon certain passages from the Interpretation of Statutes by Maxwell and also the decisions of the Supreme Court in *State of Punjab v. Amar Singh*,[2] *Renusagar Power Company Ltd. v. General Electric Company*,[3] and *Director of Enforcement v. Deepak Mahajan*.[4]

[5] "The aforesaid submission of the learned Counsel for the petitioner was refuted by the learned Counsel appearing for the respondent contending inter alia that when the language of the provisions is clear and unambiguous, no external aid is to be supplied. He further submitted that the interpretation sought to be given by the petitioner to the scheme of the Act is fallacious as

---

2. "1974(2) SCC 70."
3. "AIR 1985 SC 1156=1984 Arb. LR 240 [Reported in Yearbook X (1985) pp. 431-449 (India no. 10)]."
4. "1994(3) SCC 440."

while interpreting a Statute its plain meaning must be given effect to irrespective of the consequences. Inasmuch as where the language of a Statute is clear and unambiguous its plain words are to be interpreted on its own terms and no other mode of interpretation is permitted.

[6] "It is settled law that Statement of Objects and Reasons accompanying the legislation when introduced in the Parliament cannot be used as the only determining factor of the true meaning of the intent and substance of the Statute. However, as was held by the Supreme Court in *Chern Toong Shang v. Commander S.D. Baijal*,[5] the Objects and Reasons of the Act could be taken into consideration in interpreting the provisions of the Statute in case of doubt. Such statement of objects and reasons seeks only to explain what reason induced the mover to introduce the Bill in the House, what object is sought to be achieved and what objects and reasons are not voted upon by Members.

[7] "The Bill, if it is introduced in the House, and during the course of its discussion and during the process till it is approved by the House and becomes an Act may undergo radical changes during its passage through the House or Houses and there is no guarantee that the reasons which led to its introduction and the Objects thereby sought to be achieved have remained the same throughout till the Bill emerges from the House as an Act of the Legislature.... In other words the Statement of Objects and Reasons may be the evidence of surrounding circumstances. At the same time it is also settled law that where the language of the Act is clear and explicit, the court must give effect to it whatever may be the consequences, for in that case the words of the Statute speak the intention of the Legislature.

[8] "A comparative reading of the provisions of the FARE Act and the new provisions of [the] Arbitration and Conciliation Act, so far [as] enforcement of a foreign award is concerned indicate that the provisions of the two Acts are almost *pari materia* except for the provisions of Sect. 5 of the FARE Act[6] which stood deleted and substantial change in Sect. 6 of FARE Act in the new Arbitration and Conciliation Act, 1996. Under the FARE Act a procedure was

---

5. "AIR 1985 SC 603."
6. Sect. 5 of the Foreign Awards (Recognition and Enforcement) Act 1961 reads:

"(1) Any person interested in a foreign award may apply to any court having jurisdiction over the subject matter of the award that the award be filed in court.
(2) The application shall be in writing and shall be numbered and registered as a suit between the applicant as plaintiff and the other parties as defendants.
(3) The court shall direct notice to be given to the parties to the arbitration, other than the applicant, requiring them to show cause, within a time specified why the award should not be filed."

laid down for filing of foreign award in Court and making the same a rule of Court, which has since been done away with under the provisions of the new Act. Except for that change there is no other material change in the new provisions enacted for enforcement of a foreign award. That was probably because of the fact that both the FARE Act of 1961 and the Arbitration and Conciliation Act, 1996 are founded on the New York Convention. According to Sect. 46 a foreign award, in order to be treated as binding, has to be enforceable, for which a specific mode is provided for enjoining the party to apply for such enforcement of a foreign award by issuing an application and along with the application some documents are to be enclosed therewith.

[9] "Sect. 48 lays down the conditions for enforcement of foreign awards and if a party can prove to the satisfaction of the court that any of the conditions mentioned therein is attracted, enforcement of the foreign award would be refused. Sect. 48 contains two types of objections which could be used to oppose enforcement of an award:

> (a) those that can be raised by a party against whom the award is sought to be enforced under Sect. 48(1);
> (b) those which the court must suo motu itself under Sect. 48(2).

[10] "In this regard the observation of the Supreme Court in *Renusagar Power Company Ltd. v. General Electric Company* (supra), is relevant and material and I quote

> 'under the New York Convention the party against whom the award is sought to be enforced can object to recognition and enforcement of foreign award on grounds set out in sub-clauses (a) to (e) of Clause (1) of Article V(1)(*d*) and the Court can, on its own motion, refuse recognition and enforcement of a foreign award for two additional reasons set out in Sub-clauses (a) and (b) of Clause (2) of Article V.'

The same provisions exist both under FARE Act and the Arbitration and Conciliation Act, 1996. Thus there is no change at all in the aforesaid provisions.

[11] "The satisfaction of the court as contemplated under Sect. 49 can be arrived at only after the court is satisfied that none of the grounds as mentioned in Sect. 48(2) of the Act exists and that if an objection is filed as contemplated under Sect. 48(1) of the Act by the party is dismissed. It is only after that satisfaction which was required to be arrived at by the court under Sect. 48 that the foreign award is enforceable is reached and recorded then only the award becomes a deemed decree of the court.

[12] "The foresaid provisions postulate and/or pre-suppose that in order to arrive at the aforesaid satisfaction the court itself has the responsibility to scrutinise the award even in absence of an objection by a party to come to a satisfaction that the award does not suffer from any of the vices as mentioned in Sect. 48(2) of the Act. When it is found that none of the conditions as mentioned in the said provisions is attracted the court would explicitly record its satisfaction that the award is enforceable and then and then only and thereupon the award becomes deemed decree of that court. The execution petition could be filed in an appropriate court only when there is a decree.... Thus, in order to arrive at and to express the explicit satisfaction by the Court the parties are to be heard even on the issue of Sect. 48(2) and also on objections if any filed by the aggrieved party seeking for refusing enforcement. It is only when the parties are heard then only the court could arrive at a reasonable and sound satisfaction.

[13] "It is not necessary that requirement of the principles of natural justice is required to be specified in all the provisions of the Statute. It could at times be implied in the provisions and procedure prescribed by law. It is settled law that the principles of natural justice such as opportunity of hearing is implicit in the exercise of power conferred by the provisions in spite of the fact that there is no express requirement in that regard in the statutory provisions. Under Sect. 48(2) of the Act the court has to be satisfied and also come to a definite conclusion that the enforcement of the award would not be contrary to the public policy of India. In *Central Inland Water Transport Corporation Ltd. v. Brojo Nath Ganguly*,[7] it was held that the principles governing public policy must be and are capable, on proper occasions, of expansion and modification. In a matter like that and to come to such a conclusion the court must have the assistance of both the parties and should give an opportunity of hearing to both the parties.

[14] "The same issue could also be looked into from another angle. Under [Sect. 48(1)] of the Act, the Court has been empowered to refuse enforcement of a foreign award if the party against whom the foreign award is sought to be enforced is able to prove and establish that any of the grounds mentioned therein is satisfied. Such steps could be taken by the party concerned only when it receives a notice from the court, to the effect that the said award is sought to be enforced against him in that particular court. Otherwise there could also be the possibility of institution of proceedings in different courts for cause of action for the proceedings could also arise in parts in two different courts having territorial jurisdiction. For if cause of action arises in two different courts a proceeding for enforcement might be filed in one court

---

7. "AIR 1986 SC 1571."

whereas objections against the award could be filed in a different court which also may have territorial jurisdiction to try the proceedings and thus leading to complications.

[15] "Accordingly, in my considered opinion, rules and principles of natural justice are embodied in the aforesaid provisions and, therefore, when a party applies seeking for enforcement of a award notice has to go to the other party at least to the extent of intimating him that such an application has been filed in the court seeking for enforcement of the award. On service of notice the court shall proceed to hear the parties in order to determine and record its satisfaction and at that stage the court would examine existence or otherwise of the two conditions as found in Sect. 48(2) of the Act as also the objection if filed by the party under Sect. 48(1) of the Act is disposed of by recording satisfaction as envisaged under Sect. 49 of the Act. Any contrary argument and decision to the effect that no notice is required to be given to the parties at that stage, in my considered opinion, is fallacious and without merit. Once the award is held to be enforceable by the court then the same becomes binding on all the parties connected with the said award and thus the said award becomes deemed decree in accordance with the provisions of the Act, which would be and could be executed through the process of the court.

[16] "The petitioner has in the present case straightaway filed an execution petition construing as if the award has already become a decree. A bare perusal of the application filed would show that the same was filed in the format ... for an application for execution of a decree.... The provisions for enforcement of a foreign award however, specifically state that only when the court is satisfied and holds that the award is enforceable then and then only the award would be deemed to be a decree of that court. Therefore, so long the process for recording the satisfaction that the award is enforceable is not complete, the same does not become a decree and therefore, cannot be executed as if it was a decree. The said foreign award per se cannot be said to be final and binding so long as it is not held as enforceable and does not become a deemed decree by virtue of the provisions of Sect. 49 of the Act."

[17] Although the court examined the situation under the new Arbitration Act of 1996, it rejected the allegation that the new Act applied, finding that the arbitration had commenced before its coming into force. The application of the Rules of Arbitration and Appeal of The International General Produce Association did not constitute an agreement to opt into the new regime. Consequently the FARE Act 1961 applied to the enforcement of the award. The court continued:

[18] "In terms of the ... provisions [of the FARE Act] the person who is interested in a foreign award has to apply to the court having jurisdiction over the subject matter of the award that the award be filed in court and on filing

of such a petition a regular suit has to be registered and the court has to direct notice to the parties to the arbitration requiring them to show cause why the award should not be filed. There is a total non-compliance with the provisions of Sect. 5 in the present case. There is no application by the petitioner in terms of Sect. 5 seeking for filing of the award in this court, and for making the award Rule of the court. In my considered opinion, the present petition could not be converted to a petition for filing of the award and making the award a Rule of the court. If a particular act is required to be done in a particular manner, the same should be done in that manner alone.... The proceeding initiated by the petitioner is not maintainable in its present form and is therefore, liable to be dismissed.... Since it is held that this petition is not maintainable the securities furnished ... stands released."

IRAN-UNITED STATES CLAIMS TRIBUNAL

1. Award in Case No. A27 (Award No. 586-A27-FT) of 5 June 1998

Arbitrators:	Krzysztof Skubiszewski (President), Mohsen Aghahosseini (separate opinion), George H. Aldrich, Richard C. Allison (separate opinion), Koorosh H. Ameli (concurring), Gaetano Arangio-Ruiz, Bengt Broms, Charles T. Duncan, Assadollah Noori (separate opinion)
Parties:	Claimant: The Islamic Republic of Iran Respondent: The United States of America
Published in:	To be published in Iran-United States Claims Tribunal Reports
Articles:	I (by implication); III (by implication); V(1)(*b*)
Subject matters:	– applicability of 1958 New York Convention to "international" award – final and binding award – no review on the merits
Commentary Cases:	¶ 114; [21]-[23] + [62]-71] = ¶ 511; [69] = ¶ 514; [73]-[74] = ¶ 301; [76] = ¶ 307

Note General Editor

An excerpt of this Award is reported in Part III – B on the Iran-United States Claims Tribunal, pp. 512-523. It is mentioned here in Part V – A in the reporting on the court decisions applying and interpreting the New York Convention as it represents a decision of an international tribunal on the enforceability of its awards under the New York Convention. It is also incorporated in the Consolidated Commentary Cases Reported in Volumes XXII (1997) - XXIV (1999).

For a history of the Iran-United States Claims Tribunal, and its constitutive instruments, see Yearbook Volume VII (1982) pp. 253-267 as well as Part III - B of all ensuing Volumes for a Survey of Orders, Decisions and Awards and excerpts of awards.

ITALY

Accession: 31 January 1969
No Reservations

150. Corte di Cassazione [Supreme Court], 20 September 1995, no. 9980[1]

Parties:	Appellant/respondent: srl Campomarzio Impianti (Italy) Appellee/petitioner: Lampart Vegypary Gepgyar (Hungary)
Published in:	Rivista dell'Arbitrato (1996, no. 1) pp. 78-79
Articles:	IV
Subject matters:	– failure to submit original award and arbitration "at the time of application" agreement cannot be cured by later submission – failure does not prevent party from filing a new request for enforcement
Commentary Cases:	[1]-[10]= ¶ 405; [3] = ¶ 401

Facts

Lampart Vegypary Gepgyar (Lampart) granted srl Campomarzio Impianti (Campomarzio) the exclusive distributorship for its industrial machinery in Italy. The contract contained an arbitration clause.

1. *Note General Editor.* In conformity with the Italian practice of publishing court decisions, the date of the decision is that on which the decision is filed with the *Cancelleria* of the court, and not on which the decision was actually made.

On 17 June 1988, Lampart commenced arbitration in Budapest, claiming US$ 182,514 from Campomarzio for unpaid deliveries. This amount was reduced to US$ 109,647 after a partial payment.

The arbitrators issued a partial award, directing Campomarzio to pay US$ 86,849 to Lampart, and a final award, denying Campomarzio's counterclaims and directing it to pay a further US$ 44,809.

Lampart sought enforcement of the Hungarian awards before the Court of Appeal in Rome. By a decision rendered on 22 January/7 June 1991, the Court of Appeal held that the request for enforcement was inadmissible because Lampart had not submitted the original or duly authenticated copy of the arbitration agreement and the awards, as provided for in Art. IV(1) of the New York Convention, at the time of filing the request for enforcement. This defect could not be cured by a later submission.

The Court of Appeal also held that a timeous submission of the documents indicated in Art. IV is a prerequisite for commencing the enforcement proceedings (*presupposto processuale*), not a condition on which the merits of the request depend (*condizione per l'azione*); the enforcement proceedings were thus held not to have been commenced. Consequently, the Court's decision was not a decision on the merits, capable of becoming res judicata and preventing a new request for enforcement. Campomarzio appealed to the Supreme Court, objecting that, on the contrary, the submission of the arbitration agreement and awards is a condition on which the merits of the action depend; hence, the decision of the Court of Appeal was a decision on the merits.

The Supreme Court denied the appeal. It examined the two opposite tendencies in the Court's jurisprudence on the issue of the nature of the submission under Art. IV, and concluded that such submission is a prerequisite for commencing the enforcement proceedings. It is thus possible to file a new request for enforcement when the first request has been declared inadmissible for lack of compliance with Art. IV of the Convention.

Excerpt

[1] "By its sole ground for appeal, Campomarzio alleges the violation and erroneous application of Art. IV of the [1958 New York Convention]. It argues that the Court of Appeal held that the failure to submit the original awards or a duly authenticated copy thereof led to the inadmissibility of the request for enforcement, whereas, on the contrary, this requirement concerns the evidence in support of the request, and, according to Art. IV of the Convention, the documents must be submitted at the time of filing the

request. Hence, the request [for enforcement] should have been denied on the merits.

[2] "[First], we must answer the preliminary question of the inadmissibility of the appeal for lack of interest, alleged in [Lampart's] counterclaim and in the oral statements of the Public Prosecutor. This objection must be dismissed. If the requirement in Art. IV of the Convention is qualified as a condition on which the merits of the action depend, rather than a prerequisite for commencing the proceedings, as was held in the impugned decision, the failure to meet it leads to a decision on the merits, and there is res judicata on the request for recognition. Hence, the party opposing recognition has an evident legal interest in obtaining a decision which precludes a new request [for enforcement] in further proceedings.

[3] "The Court does not agree with Campomarzio's thesis [in the ground for appeal]. The jurisprudence of the Supreme Court on this issue has not been univocal. There is a majority tendency, followed by this First Chamber in [several] decisions,[2] that the submission of the original of the award and the arbitration agreement (or an authenticated copy thereof) is a prerequisite for the proceedings and thus concerns the very possibility of commencing the enforcement proceedings. As such it must exist at the time of commencing the proceedings. Its lack, which can be raised ex officio, leads to a declaration that the request is inadmissible....

[4] "In the [*Jassica*] decision, [the First Chamber of the Supreme Court held] that this conclusion follows from the special discipline of the enforcement proceedings which can be inferred from a joint reading of Arts. IV and V of the Convention. While the former only provides that the party seeking recognition and enforcement of the foreign arbitral award shall submit the original award and arbitration agreement, or an authenticated copy thereof, 'at the time of the application', Art. V provides for the cases, other than the failure to comply with the above obligation, in which 'recognition and enforcement' may be 'refused'.

[5] "A different theory was followed by this First Chamber in its decision of 19 December 1991.[3] Here the issue was solved on the basis of the general rules on the recognition of foreign court decisions contained in Art. 797 Italian

---

2. The First Chamber of the Supreme Court referred to its decisions of 26 May 1981, no. 3456 (*Vicerè Livio v. Prodexport*), reported in Yearbook VII (1982) pp. 345-346 (Italy no. 47); 12 February 1987, no. 1526 (*Jassica SA v. Ditta Gioacchino Polojaz*), reported in Yearbook XVII (1992) pp. 525-528 (Italy no. 109); and 12 November 1992, no. 12187 (*srl Ditta Michele Tavella v. Palmco Oil Mill L.D.N. B.M.D.*) in reported Yearbook XIX (1994) pp. 692-693 (Italy no. 127).

3. *Corte di Cassazione*, 19 December 1991, no. 13665 (*Israel Portland Cement Works (Nesher) Ltd v. Moccia Irme SpA*), reported in Yearbook XVIII (1993) pp. 419-421 (Italy no. 120).

Code of Civil Procedure (CCP).[4] Since Art. 797(1) provides that the jurisdiction of the foreign court is a condition for obtaining enforcement and a condition on which the merits of the action depend, as are all conditions listed in this Article, and not a prerequisite for commencing the proceedings, the requirement in Art. IV of the New York Convention would aim at proving that the arbitrators had jurisdiction and would thus concern the merits of the request.

[6] "The Court holds that this second theory is not to be followed. The principles in Art. 796 et seq. CCP are derogated from by the provisions of international conventions, in casu, the [New York Convention]. The system of the Convention is indeed incompatible with several provisions in Arts. 797 and 800 CCP.

[7] "Hence, we must refer to the special discipline of the Convention in order to answer the question whether the requirement in Art. IV is a prerequisite for commencing the proceedings or a condition for the action, and, consequently, whether the failure to meet this requirement leads to a declaration that the request for enforcement is inadmissible or to the request's dismissal on the merits.

[8] "The problem of the qualification of certain facts or situations as a prerequisite for commencing proceedings or a condition on which the action depends may not be solved on the basis of abstract criteria. The authors have constantly held, in particular, that the prerequisites for the proceedings may be of a general (e.g., jurisdiction and competence) or special nature, for certain given procedures.

[9] "As far as the special procedure provided for in the New York Convention is concerned, we have held above that the obligation to submit the award and the arbitration agreement is contained in a specific provision, which treats it as a formal requirement for the enforcement request, while another provision (Art. V), which contains an exhaustive list of cases in which the court may 'refuse' recognition and enforcement, defines the limits of the examination of whether the request is founded.

---

4. Art. 797 of the Italian Code of Civil Procedure lists the conditions for enforcing a foreign court decision in Italy. In particular, Art. 797(1) reads:

"The Court of Appeal renders a judgment enforcing the foreign decision in the [Italian] Republic where it ascertains:
1. that the court of the State in which the decision was rendered could hear the case according to the jurisdictional principles of the Italian legal system;
(....)"

[10] "It ensues herefrom that the obligation in Art. IV is a prerequisite for commencing the proceedings or, more precisely, a prerequisite for rendering a decision on the merits. Hence, the decision which finds that there is such defect does not prevent a subsequent request to enforce the same award.

[11] "The appeal must be denied. The complexity of the issue justifies the compensation of the costs [between the parties]."

151. Corte di Appello [Court of Appeal], Bologna, 27 May 1996

Parties:	Petitioner: Bastogi SpA (Italy) Respondent: Kone Italia SpA (Italy)
Published in:	Rivista dell'Arbitrato (1997, no. 2) pp. 345-346 with note E. Zucconi Galli Fonseca, pp. 347-370
Articles:	III
Subject matters:	- more onerous conditions for enforcement - enforcement decree not provisionally enforceable
Commentary Cases:	¶ 301

Facts

On 26 January 1995, an arbitral award was rendered in Paris in a dispute between Bastogi SpA (Bastogi) and Kone Italia SpA (Kone).

Bastogi sought enforcement of the award before the President of the Court of Appeal in Bologna under the procedural system for enforcement introduced by the Italian arbitration law reform of 1994. This procedure consists of a decree of the President of the Court of Appeal, rendered ex parte (Art. 839 Italian Code of Civil Procedure (CCP)).[1] The decree may be opposed by the

1. Art. 839 of the Italian CCP reads:

"The party wishing to enforce a foreign award in the Republic shall file a petition with the President of the Court of Appeal of the district in which the other party has its domicile; if that party has no domicile in Italy, the Court of Appeal of Rome shall have jurisdiction.

The petitioner shall supply the original award or a certified copy thereof, together with the original arbitration agreement or an equivalent document, or a certified copy thereof.

If the documents specified in the second paragraph are not written in Italian, the petitioner shall in addition produce a certified translation thereof.

The President of the Court of Appeal after having ascertained the formal regularity of the award, shall declare by decree the enforceability of the foreign award in the Republic unless:
1) the subject matter is not capable of settlement by arbitration under Italian law;
2) the award contains provisions contrary to public policy."

party against whom the award is relied upon in opposition proceedings before the full Court of Appeal (Art. 840 CCP).[2]

The President granted enforcement to the French award. While the time limit (thirty days) for Kone to commence opposition proceedings was still pending, Bastogi sought provisional enforcement of the award before the Court

2. Art. 840 of the Italian CCP, which was also introduced by the Italian arbitration law reform of 1994, reads:

"An opposition may be filed against the decree granting or denying enforcement of the foreign award by filing a writ of summons with the Court of Appeal within thirty days of communication of the decree denying enforcement or notification of the decree granting enforcement.

After the filing of the opposition, the proceedings shall be held in accordance with Arts. 645 and following, in so far as they are applicable. The Court of Appeal decides in a judgment subject to recourse before the Supreme Court.

The Court of Appeal shall refuse the recognition or the enforcement of the foreign award if in the opposition proceedings the party against which the award is invoked proves the existence of one of the following circumstances:
1) the parties to the arbitration agreement were, under the law applicable to them, under some incapacity, or the arbitration agreement is not valid under the law to which the parties have subjected it or, failing any indication thereon, under the law of the State where the award was made;
2) the party against which the award is invoked was not informed of the appointment of the arbitrator or of the arbitration proceedings or was otherwise unable to present its case in the proceedings;
3) the award decided upon a dispute not contemplated in the submission to arbitration or in the arbitration clause, or exceeded the limits of the submission to arbitration or of the arbitration clause; nevertheless, if the decisions in the award which concern questions submitted to arbitration can be separated from those concerning questions not so submitted, the first can be recognized and enforced;
4) the composition of the arbitration tribunal or the arbitration proceedings was not in accordance with the agreement of the parties or, failing such an agreement, with the law of the place where the arbitration took place;
5) the award has not yet become binding on the parties or has been set aside or suspended by a competent authority of the State in which, or under the law of which, it was made.

If an application for the setting aside or suspension of the effects of the award has been made to the competent authority indicated at number 5) of the third paragraph, the Court of Appeal may adjourn the decision on the recognition or enforcement of the award; on the request of the party seeking enforcement it may, in the case of suspension, order the other party to give suitable security.

Recognition or enforcement of a foreign award shall be refused also where the Court of Appeal shall ascertain that:
1) the subject matter is not capable of settlement by arbitration under Italian law;
2) the award contains provisions contrary to public policy.

In all cases, the provisions of international treaties shall be applicable."

of Appeal in Bologna. The Court denied the request, finding that the Italian Code of Civil Procedure provides for a "consistent system which implicitly excludes the direct enforceability of the President's decree while the time limit to file an opposition is still pending". On the allegation that, in compliance with Art. III of the 1958 New York Convention, the President's decree should be directly enforceable as is the exequatur granted by the *Pretore* to domestic awards, the Court of Appeal held that a decree ex parte, rendered in a simplified procedure, meets the requirement not to impose substantially more onerous conditions for the enforcement of foreign awards, even if such decree is not directly enforceable.

Excerpt

[1] "Bastogi argues that the decree by which, according to Art. 839 CCP, the President of the Court of Appeal enforces a foreign award in Italy is directly enforceable for the following reasons: (1) notwithstanding the lack of an express provision on this point in Chapter VII [Foreign Awards] of Title VIII [Arbitration] of the [Fourth] Book [of the Code of Civil Procedure], it would make no sense to postpone the possibility to execute the award to a moment subsequent to the President's decree which, according to Art. III of the New York Convention, should be the instrument for recognizing a foreign arbitral award and for *enforcing it*; (2) According to Art. III [second sentence] of the New York Convention, the recognition or *enforcement* of foreign or international awards should not be subject to stricter conditions than are imposed on the recognition or enforcement of domestic arbitral awards; hence, the President's decree should have the same direct efficacy of the exequatur granted by the Magistrate's Court [*Pretore*] according to Art. 825 CCP;[3] (3) The system

3. Art. 825 of the Italian CCP reads:

"The arbitrators shall prepare the award in as many original copies as there are parties and shall serve notice thereof upon each party by delivery of an original copy, or by sending it by registered mail, within ten days from the date of the last signature.

The party intending to have the award enforced in the territory of the Republic shall file an original copy of the award or a certified copy thereof, together with the submission to arbitration or the document containing the arbitration clause or an equivalent document in original or in certified copy, with the Registry (*cancelleria*) of the Magistrate's Court (*pretura*) of the district in which the arbitration has its seat.

The Magistrate (*Pretore*), after ascertaining that the award meets all formal requirements, enforces it by decree. The award which has been declared enforceable shall be registered in all cases where a judgment of the same content would be subject to registration.

of the Brussels Convention of 1968 may not be relied upon as it does not apply to arbitration in virtue of its Art. 1(4);[4] (4) The authors reach conclusions in the above sense, with one 'irrelevant and unsupported' exception.

[2] "The provisions on the recognition of foreign arbitral awards do not include a provision allowing the opposition court (Art. 840 CCP) to suspend the alleged direct enforceability of the President's decree. The doctrine referred to by Bastogi fills this gap by suggesting the application by analogy of Art. 649 CCP,[5] concerning a decree which has been declared provisionally enforceable according to Art. 642 CCP.

[3] "All the above argumentations point to the objective existence of consistent system which implicitly excludes the direct enforceability of the President's decree while the time limit to file an opposition is still pending.

[4] "This system consists of the following provisions: (a) Art. 839 CCP provides that the President of the Court [of Appeal] 'shall declare ... the enforceability of the foreign award in the Republic'. Notwithstanding the title of the Article (Recognition and enforcement of foreign arbitral awards), such wording allows for a restrictive interpretation of the effects of the decree, in the sense of a mere control of the existence of the minimum requirements for the validity of the award in the domestic legal system; (b) Art. 840 CCP on the opposition proceedings provides in its fourth paragraph that if an application for the setting aside or suspension of the effects of the award has been

---

The Registry (*cancelleria*) shall notify the parties of the filing and of the Magistrate's decree provided for in Article 133, paragraph 2.

A recourse against the decree denying enforcement of the award may be filed by petition with the Court (*tribunale*) within thirty days of notification; the Court (*tribunale*), meeting in chambers and after having heard the parties, shall issue an order against which there shall be no recourse."

4. Art. 1 of the EC Convention on Jurisdiction and the Enforcement of Judgments in Civil and Commercial Matters, done at Brussels on 27 September 1968, reads in relevant part:

"The Convention shall not apply to:
(....)
(4) arbitration."

5. Art. 649 of the Italian CCP reads:

"Upon request of the opposing party, the judge [*giudice istruttore*] may, when there are serious reasons therefor, suspend the provisional execution of the decree, granted according to Article 642, by an order against which there shall be no appeal."

Art. 642 of the Italian CCP provides for the cases in which provisional execution may be granted to a court's decree.

made to the competent authority of the State in which, or under the law of which, the award has been rendered, the *tool* to avoid contradictory effects in the national system is the *mere suspension of the opposition proceedings*, which *necessarily postulates* that the award *has not yet acquired* direct efficacy by virtue of the President's decree. This interpretation is supported by the consideration that the guarantees provided for later in that Article protect the party seeking recognition, not the party against whom enforcement is sought; (c) In such a legal mechanism, the absence of a provision allowing the opposition court to suspend the alleged direct enforceability of the President's decree is perfectly consistent.

[5] "As far as compliance with Art. III of the New York Convention is concerned, we should note that this same Convention provides for proceedings for the enforcement of foreign awards (Arts. V and VI). The system of these proceedings (which the Italian legislator almost literally mirrored in the system of opposition proceedings to the President's decree) is the paradigm of the minimum jurisdictional guarantees on which the Contracting States agreed to harmonize their domestic systems.

[6] "Even if Art. III went beyond the limit provided for in the system of the Convention, a President's decree rendered *inaudita altera parte* suffices to meet the requirement not to impose *substantially* stricter *conditions* for the recognition or enforcement of foreign awards, even if such decree is not directly enforceable. Taking into account the difference, in function, latitude of the review and importance of the effects, between the exequatur granted by the Magistrate for domestic awards and the President's decree ex Art. 839 CCP, a simplified procedure, *inaudita altera parte*, which can lead to a prompt execution if no opposition is filed, suffices.

[7] "Lastly, we must note that, although there is no provision allowing the opposition court to grant provisional enforcement of the President's decree and no system analogous to the system provided for in Art. 39 of the Brussels Convention,[6] the party seeking recognition enjoys interim protection as reference

6. Art. 39 of the EC Convention on Jurisdiction and the Enforcement of Judgments in Civil and Commercial Matters, done at Brussels on 27 September 1968, reads:

"During the time specified for an appeal pursuant to Article 36 and until any such appeal has been determined, no measures of enforcement may be taken other than protective measures taken against the property of the party against whom enforcement is sought.

The decision authorizing enforcement shall carry with it the power to proceed to any such protective measures."

can be made to the procedures of Arts. 669-*ter* and 669-*quater* of the Code of Civil Procedure,[7] as is maintained by the most authoritative doctrine."

7. Art. 669-*ter* and Art. 669-*quater* of the Italian CCP provide for interim measures of protection in court proceedings.

152. Corte di Cassazione [Supreme Court], 23 April 1997, no. 10229

Parties:	Petitioner: Dalmine S.p.A. (Italy) Respondent: M. & M. Sheet Metal Forming Machinery A.G. (Switzerland)
Published in:	Rivista dell'Arbitrato (1998, no. 4) pp. 41-44 with note F. Pietrangeli, pp. 45-55
Articles:	V(1)(*a*); V(1)(*b*)
Subject matters:	- capacity to enter into arbitration agreement - due process (no examination of witness) - burden of proof
Commentary Cases:	[1] = ¶ 505 + ¶ 506; [2] + [9] = ¶ 503; [3]-[7] = ¶ 505; [8]-[11] = ¶ 511

Facts

On 24 June 1990, M. & M. Sheet Metal Forming Machinery A.G. (M. & M.) obtained an award in its favour in its dispute with Dalmine S.p.A. (Dalmine). The award was rendered in Lugano.

On 10 January 1995, the Court of Appeal in Milan granted enforcement of the Swiss award in Italy.

The Supreme Court affirmed the enforcement. It held that, although the alleged lack of power by Dalmine's representatives to sign the arbitration clause was a matter of capacity to be examined under the law applicable to them, rather than a case of invalidity of the clause, which the Court of Appeal had examined under Swiss law, the Dalmine managers had the power to enter into the arbitration clause under Italian law. It also affirmed the Court of Appeal's finding that the failure by the arbitrators to grant a further postponement for hearing a Dalmine witness was not a violation of due process.

Excerpt

[1] In the proceedings before the Court of Appeal, Dalmine maintained that enforcement of the award should be denied on the basis of the first part of

Art. V(1)(*a*), because the two managers who had signed the contract with M. & M. lacked the power, under the law applicable to them, i.e., Italian law, to bind Dalmine to an arbitration clause. Differently, the Court of Appeal applied Swiss law to this issue, thereby indicating that it considered Dalmine's objection to be a case of alleged invalidity of the arbitration clause (second part of Art. V(1)(*a*)). By its first ground for appeal, Dalmine maintained that the Court of Appeal should have applied Italian law. The Supreme Court held that this ground for appeal "is basically correct, but the alleged violation has no important consequences, since in its final statement the Court of Appeal referred, in respect of [this] objection, to the law which [Dalmine] believes to be applicable, although it drew a different conclusion from [this law].

[2] "According to Art. V(1)(*a*) of the New York Convention, it is the party against which enforcement is sought in the proceedings for the enforcement of a foreign arbitral award which has the burden to prove that the parties who entered into the arbitration clause were 'under the law applicable to them, under some incapacity' or that the agreement 'is not valid under the law to which the parties have subjected it or, failing any indication thereon, under the law of the country where the award was made'.

[3] "The disagreement of the parties as to whether the present case falls under the first or second hypothesis [of Art. V(1)(*a*)] is to be solved in favour of [Dalmine]. Although 'capacity' in Art. 17 of the Preliminary Dispositions to the Civil Code[1] refers to the capacity of physical persons – as is made clear by the inclusion in this provision of personal status and capacity and family relations – the 'incapacity' of the parties to the arbitration 'agreement' in [Art. V(1)(*a*)], which generally concerns entities engaged in international commercial relations, has a broader meaning. In the New York Convention provision at issue, capacity means not only the capacity of a physical person to perform an act, but any capacity, both a legal capacity to perform an act – with an eye to the so-called special legal incapacities – and the capacity of physical and legal persons; in the latter case, special attention is given to representation by the organs [of an entity] and their representation powers, including legitimation [*legittimazione*]. The scope of the applicable norm is thus defined. Since the New York Convention – as [M. & M.] maintains for a different reason – provides for a complete and self-sufficient system of both substantial and

1. Art. 17 of the Preliminary Dispositions to the Civil Code, which has been abrogated by the Italian private international law reform of 1995, read in relevant part:

"The status and capacity of persons and family relations are governed by the law of the State to which they belong.
(....)"

procedural requirements for the enforcement of a foreign award by the Contracting States,[2] Italian law [should be applied] to the issue whether Dalmine was 'under some incapacity' to enter into the arbitration clause.

[4] "On this point, the additional reason in the challenged decision, mentioned above, reads as follows:

> 'In any case, such power, which is explicitly provided for by Law no. 25/1994 (which, when redrafting Art. 808 of the Italian Code of Civil Procedure (CCP), established that "the capacity to enter into the contract includes the capacity to agree to the arbitration clause"), was in any case implied, according to the Italian law then in force, in the broad wording of the power given by the Board of Directors of Dalmine S.p.A. to the General Manager (under the conditions mentioned in the relevant decision ...) to conclude contracts concerning movable goods in the name and on behalf of the company'.

[5] "This statement is challenged with the first ground for appeal. Art. 807(3) CCP,[3] when providing that the provisions on the validity of the contracts exceeding the ordinary administration apply to the arbitration agreement (and, because of its autonomy, to the arbitration clause), does not imply that the General Manager (together with another officer, in casu, the Central Manager) automatically lacked the power to enter into arbitration clauses relating to contracts that he was explicitly allowed to conclude. In a case relating to an *amministratore*,[4] this Court already held on this point that the distinguishing criterion between ordinary and extraordinary administration in enterprises cannot be the 'conservative' character of the act (although this is a valid criterion in the administration of the estate of the incapacitated), since an entrepreneurial activity necessarily presupposes that goods are disposed of. Rather, this distinction must depend on the relation between the act and the

2. *Corte di Cassazione*, 7 June 1995, no. 6426 (*WTB – Walter Thosti Boswau Bauaktiengesellschaft v. Costruire Coop. srl*), reported in Yearbook XXII (1997) pp. 727-733 (Italy no. 144).

3. Art. 807 of the Italian CCP reads in relevant part:

   "(....)
   The submission to arbitration is subject to the provisions governing the validity of contracts which go beyond administration in the ordinary course of business."

4. *Translator's Note.* The board of directors of a company is its *amministratore*, i.e., the organ entrusted with its management and responsible for its acts. The *amministratore* may delegate some of its tasks to an officer, e.g., as in the present case, a general manager (*direttore generale*). As mentioned below by the Court in this same paragraph [5], the curator of the estate of an incapacitated is also called the *amministratore* of that estate.

'normal' (and thus 'ordinary') administration of an enterprise of that dimension (Supreme Court decision no. 4856 of 1995. Hence, while acts modifying the economic-administrative structure of an enterprise are to be considered 'extraordinary' administration, the conclusion of an arbitration clause cannot be numbered among the acts 'exceeding' ordinary administration, with the consequence that also an administrator, whose powers are limited to ordinary administration, is fully able to conclude said clause.

[6] "The same applies, on certain conditions, to the General Manager (in the present case, together [with the Central Manager], as already explained). Although he is a corporate employee who assists the Board of Directors in its tasks, he carries out [the Board's] decisions and has his own broad or limited powers of decision and representation, thereby 'integrating' the work of the board. Art. 2396 of the Italian Civil Code (CC),[5] which provides that a General Manager has the same responsibility as an *amministratore*, allows us to conclude that General Managers appointed by the shareholders' meeting or the statute of incorporation may bind the company in external relations only if they have been specifically entrusted with this power or if such power is inherent to the nature of their tasks (Supreme Court decision no. 2667 of 1970). In the present case it is not contested that [the General Manager and Central Manager] were duly appointed and there is no doubt as to their power to conclude the contracts underlying the dispute decided by the arbitral tribunal. Hence, we must find, in application of the principle indicated above with respect to the *amministratore* – the [Board of Directors] who appointed the General Manager and Central Manager as provided for in the statute of incorporation – that the power to agree, with respect to those contracts, to an arbitration clause, was no 'extraordinary' administration in the sense of Art. 807 CCP and was inherent to the nature of [the above managers'] tasks.

[7] "Although it did so in its secondary reasons – which therefore become the only relevant ones, with the above clarifications – the Court of Appeal abided by these principles. Hence, its decision is free from the alleged defect of violation of law. Also, its reference to the Law no. 25 of 1994 only points out a development, that is, the innovative character of the new Art. 808 CCP, which does not apply to arbitration agreements and arbitration clauses con-

---

5. Art. 2396 of the Italian CC reads:

> "The provisions regulating the responsibility of the *amministratore* also apply to the managers appointed by the shareholders' meeting or the statute of incorporation, in respect of the tasks entrusted to them."

cluded before the entry into force of the Law (Supreme Court decision no. 4856 of 1995, above).

[8] "Nor is there a further violation of the law, as maintained by the second ground for appeal, being a lack of proper reasoning with respect to Art. V(1)(*b*) of the New York Convention, which was allegedly violated by the failure to hear a [decisive] witness who could not appear [on time].

[9] "The said provision, when placing the burden to prove that 'it was not given proper notice of the appointment of the arbitrator or of the arbitration proceedings or was otherwise unable to present his case' on the party against whom the foreign arbitral award is invoked, refers to facts which negatively affect the possibility to be timeously informed of the arbitral proceedings or the essential moments of its development;[6] this implies a strict proof of the 'otherwise' reason which allegedly hindered [the party's] defence. The Court of Appeal reasoned thus:

> 'This ground is unfounded. Defendant had the burden to prove the existence of grounds for refusal of enforcement of the award, and, in particular, the alleged impossibility to defend itself.[7] Defendant did not prove its allegation (since, independent of any consideration as to the relevance of the fact alleged to be a violation of due process, no sufficient proof has been supplied as to the impossibility of the witness ... to appear before the arbitral tribunal). Claimant, on the contrary, has proven, by producing the minutes, that counsel for defendant was granted two hearings (10 October 1988 and 17 February 1989) to hear the said witness.'

[10] "The Court of Appeal correctly held that [Dalmine] did not prove that it was unable to defend itself, as it was granted two postponements for hearing [the witness], who eventually was not heard, and found that it was not proven that the witness was still unable to appear.

[11] "[Also], an allegation that the telegram by which the witness requested a further postponement is a relevant document for the decision – whereas it is only proof of an alleged impediment – is not a sufficient basis for a ground for appeal. The Court of Appeal did not ignore [the telegram]; it correctly found that it could not be a proof of 'the impossibility of the witness' to appear."

---

6. *Corte di Cassazione*, 22 February 1992, no. 2183 (*Trans World Film S.p.A. v. Film Polski Import and Export of Films*), reported in Yearbook XVIII (1993) pp. 433-436 (Italy no. 123).
7. See fn. 6.

LUXEMBOURG

Ratification: 9 September 1983
1st Reservation

2. Cour d'Appel [Court of Appeal], 28 January 1999

Parties:	Appellant: Sovereign Participations International S.A. (Luxembourg) Appellee: Chadmore Developments Ltd. (Ireland)
Published in:	No publication information available
Articles:	IV; V; V(1)(*b*); V(1)(*e*); V(2)(*b*); VI; VII(1)
Subject matters:	– grounds for refusal are exhaustive – due process – no review of merits – award infra petita not ground for refusal under the Convention – "binding" – discretion not to suspend enforcement pending action for setting aside – more-favourable-right provision
Commentary Cases:	[1]-[5] = ¶ 301; [6] = ¶ 101; [7] = ¶ 503; [8] + [13] = ¶ 518; [9] = ¶ 401; [10]-[16] = ¶ 511; [7], [12] + [27] = ¶ 501; [16] = ¶ 502; [17] = ¶ 512; [19]-[27] = ¶ 517 + ¶ 601; [22] = ¶ 514; [25]-[26] = ¶ 702

Facts

In 1992, a group headed by Mr. Manuel De Prado, a resident of Switzerland, negotiated the sale of two hotels and a golf course located in Spain to the Credicom group, headed by Mr. Clément Vaturi, a resident of France. The Credicom group consisted of Credicom Crédit Commercial International S.A.

(Credicom Crédit), Credicom Exploitation S.A., two Belgian companies; and Sovereign Participations International S.A. (SPI), a Luxembourg company. Mr. De Prado was the General Manager of Gratinis Investments Corp. N.V., a company incorporated in the Netherlands Antilles; Corndean Inc., a company incorporated in the British Virgin Islands; and Trebol International S.A., a Spanish company. The De Prado group also included Colombine B.V., the owner of the hotels, and Chadmore Developments Ltd. (Chadmore).

On 19 December 1992, Mr. De Prado and Mr. Vaturi reached a final agreement concerning the sale of the hotels; Mr. De Prado guaranteed minimum profits and undertook to make up for any shortfall over the following five years. The sale was finalized by a contract concluded on 8 January 1993, by which Gratinis Investment Corp. N.V. (Gratinis) sold its shares in Colombine B.V., owner of the hotels, to the Credicom group for BF 1,848,000,000. On the same day, Chadmore bought 314,760 shares of Credicom Crédit at BF 5,000 per share. SPI undertook to buy the shares from Chadmore upon request.

On 18 November 1994, Chadmore informed SPI that it wished to sell the Credicom shares in its possession, whereupon SPI argued that the request had been made untimeously regarding 29,160 shares. A dispute also arose between the Credicom group and Mr. De Prado, when the former alleged that the hotels had lost approximately BF 50,000,000 in 1993 and sought compensation from Mr. De Prado, who in turn alleged mismanagement of the hotels.

The two groups commenced court proceedings in several countries before deciding to solve the dispute amicably. By an agreement concluded on 24 February 1995, the parties agreed to terminate all court proceedings and commence arbitration under the Rules of the Chamber of Commerce of Geneva. SPI also bought back 285,600 Credicom shares from Chadmore; the remaining 29,160 shares were set aside as a guarantee for the compensation by the De Prado group of the shortfalls in the hotels' profits, if ordered by the arbitrators.

According to the agreement of 24 February 1995, the terms of reference for the arbitrators were: (1) to decide whether Chadmore had validly requested SPI to buy back 29,160 Credicom shares, and if so, which price should be paid; (2) to decide on the claims by Credicom Crédit concerning the alleged profit shortfalls; (3) to decide on the claim by Mr. De Prado, Gratinis, Chadmore and Corndean Inc. against the Credicom group for US$ 3,800,000; (4) to decide on all disputes related to the sale of the two hotels by the De Prado group to the Credicom group.

By an award made on 26 January 1998, the arbitrators directed SPI to pay BF 145,000,000 to Chadmore for the 29,160 Credicom shares; they also directed Mr. De Prado, Gratinis and Trebol International S.A. to pay Credicom

Crédit several amounts, with a set-off of US$ 3,500,000 owed by Credicom Crédit to Corndean Inc. The part of the award in favour of Chadmore was based on SPI's obligation to buy back the Credicom shares; the part of the award in favour of Credicom Crédit was based on Mr. De Prado's obligation to make up for any shortfall in the hotels' profits.

On 3 July 1998, Chadmore obtained enforcement of the award in Luxembourg against SPI. SPI took recourse to the Court of Appeal, arguing that the arbitrators had omitted to decide on the issues submitted to them by the parties. SPI also requested the Court of Appeal to suspend the enforcement proceedings pending a request for review (*révision*) of the part of the award against it before the Swiss Supreme Court.

The Court of Appeal denied the appeal and affirmed the enforcement, holding that no review on the merits, under the cover of public policy, was allowed. The requirement of a fair hearing had been met and there was thus no violation of international public policy. The court also did not find grounds for suspending enforcement of the award pending the request for review which had been filed in Switzerland.

Excerpt

I. ADMISSIBILITY OF THE APPEAL

[1] Chadmore objected that SPI's appeal was inadmissible because SPI had accepted the arbitral award and because SPI could not rely on the review proceedings in Switzerland, which only concerned the issue of the profits guarantee between Mr. De Prado and Credicom Crédit.

[2] The Court reasoned: "Chadmore has neither defined nor developed its objection that SPI accepted the arbitral award 'in the context of an agreement between the parties to set-off the debts and credits in the award'. This objection must, therefore, be rejected.

[3] "As to the alleged lack of direct and personal interest of SPI, even if we do not consider that the different issues of the dispute referred to the arbitrators concerned two groups of companies so closely interconnected that the debts and credits of the companies of the two groups could be set off, so that one necessarily affects the others, SPI challenges here an order enforcing in Luxembourg an arbitral award directing it to pay Chadmore BF 145,000,000 for certain shares. The order may thus affect SPI and SPI has a direct and personal interest to challenge it as provided by Art. 546(6) of the [Luxembourg] Code of Civil Procedure (CCP)."

II. APPLICABLE LAW

[4] "SPI relies on both the Luxembourg [CCP] (Art. 1023 et seq.) and the [New York Convention]. Before examining whether the grounds for appeal are founded, we must thus determine the 'nationality' of the award and the rules applicable to the opposition to the enforcement order.

[5] "Whereas 'Luxembourg' awards are enforced by an order of the President of the Court of Appeal and can be challenged by an opposition before the Court of Appeal on twelve grounds exhaustively listed in Arts. 1020-1028 CCP, 'foreign' arbitral awards are enforced at the request [of a party] by the President of the Court of Appeal according to the rules applicable to the enforcement of foreign judgments given in accordance with a convention on the recognition and enforcement of such judgments (Art. 1028-1 CCP).[1] An appeal from such order can be made to the Supreme Court on the grounds provided for by Art. 1028-2,[2] which refers in part to the grounds for setting

1. Art. 1028-1 of the Luxembourg CCP reads in relevant part:

> "(....)
> In addition, there shall be observed the rules applicable to the enforcement of foreign judgments given in accordance with a convention on the recognition and enforcement of such judgments (Grand Ducal Regulation of 8 December 1981)."

2. Art. 1028-2 of the Luxembourg CCP reads:

> "Subject to the provisions of international conventions, the judge shall refuse to grant an order for enforcement (exequatur):
> 1. if the award may still be attacked before the arbitrators and the arbitrators have not ordered provisional enforcement notwithstanding appeal;
> 2. if the award or its enforcement is contrary to public policy or if the dispute was not susceptible of settlement by arbitration;
> 3. if it is established that there exist grounds for annulment envisaged in Article 1023 nos. 3 to 12 (Grand Ducal Regulation of 8 December 1981)."

aside in Art. 1023 nos. 3 to 12,[3] though 'subject to the provisions of international conventions', in casu the New York Convention."

III. REFUSAL OF ENFORCEMENT

1. *Article 1023 of the Code of Civil Procedure*

[6] "The [New York Convention], which binds both Luxembourg (Law of 20 May 1983) and Switzerland for the enforcement of arbitral awards, applies thus to the enforcement. The provisions in Arts. 1023 and 1028 are only supplementary and limited to the enforcement of awards rendered in a non-Contracting State to the Convention.

[7] "Luxembourg undertook by this Convention to recognize arbitration agreements and not to refuse enforcement of arbitral awards rendered on the basis of an arbitration agreement unless on the grounds exhaustively listed in Art. V of the Convention. For the enforcement court to deny enforcement on one of these grounds, the party against whom enforcement is sought shall prove the existence of [one] such ground (Art. V(1)). Hence, the party seeking

---

3. Art. 1023 of the Luxembourg CCP reads:

"An arbitral award may be contested before a District Court only by way of an action for annulment.

Annulment may be declared only in the following cases:

1. if the award is contrary to public policy;
2. if the dispute was not susceptible of settlement by arbitration;
3. if there was no valid agreement as to arbitration;
4. if the arbitral tribunal exceeded its terms of reference or powers;
5. if the arbitral tribunal failed to rule on one or more matters in dispute and if the matters omitted cannot be dissociated from the matters on which a ruling was given;
6. if the award was made by an irregularly constituted arbitral tribunal;
7. if there was any failure to observe the right to a fair hearing;
8. if the award does not state the reasons on which it is based, unless the parties released the arbitrators from that requirement;
9. if the award contains contradictory provisions;
10. if the award was obtained by fraud;
11. if the award is based on evidence which is declared false by an irrevocable judicial decision or on evidence admitted to be false;
12. if after the award is made a document or other item of evidence is discovered which would have had a decisive influence on the award and was held back by action of the opposite party.

The cases mentioned in paragraphs 3, 4 and 6 shall not be treated as grounds for annulment where the party seeking to rely on them had notice of them during the arbitral procedure and did not raise them at that time (Grand Ducal Regulation of 8 December 1981)."

enforcement does not have to prove anything. The court may refuse enforcement ex officio only if the award violates [Luxembourg's] public policy or where the subject matter of the dispute cannot be settled by arbitration according to the law applicable to it (Art. V(2)).

[8] "Hence, we must deny the grounds raised by SPI in its appeal in so far as they are based on Art. 1023 CCP, to the exception of those concerning the violation of international public policy, which shall be dealt with herebelow."

2. *Article V(1)(b) and V(2) of the New York Convention*

[9] "We must first note that Chadmore has supplied the documents required by Art. IV of the Convention together with the request, that is, a duly authenticated copy of the original award of 28 January 1998 and the original of the agreement of 24 February 1995 containing the arbitration clause.

[10] "The control by the [enforcement] court essentially concerns the question whether the award has been rendered in proceedings which respected due process and, further, whether the law applied to the merits of the award is compatible with [the court's] international public policy, as defined herebelow, although due to the general similarity of the laws of the two Contracting States there is little risk that the Swiss law applied by the arbitrators violate the principles of public policy of the [enforcement] court.

[11] "The introduction, under the cover of public policy, of supplementary grounds for refusal of recognition and enforcement, which would result either in a review of the merits of the case or in establishing grounds for setting aside, which are provided for in Art. 1023 CCP, must be rejected in any case. The case here concerns the effect in Luxembourg of rights acquired abroad; hence, public policy intervenes only in its attenuated form and is less stringent than if the case concerned the acquisition of the same rights in Luxembourg.

[12] "The grounds exhaustively listed in Art. V of the Convention, which must be invoked by the party opposing the recognition or enforcement, are, beyond those concerning the setting aside or suspension of the award in the country of origin (Art. V(1)(*e*)), the invalidity of the arbitration agreement (Art. V(1)(*a*)), the violation of due process (Art. V(1)(*b*)), the excess by the arbitrator of his authority (Art. V(1)(*c*)), as well as the irregularities affecting the composition of the arbitral tribunal or the arbitral procedure as agreed, to which we must add those grounds which can even be raised ex officio, i.e., the non-arbitrability of the dispute (Art. V(2)(*a*)) and the violation by the award of international public policy (Art. V(2)(*b*)).

[13] "The Court holds on the basis of the documents in the file that Chadmore acquired its rights in Switzerland as a result of an arbitration freely agreed upon by the parties according to clause 4 of their agreement of 24

February 1995. The award to be enforced was rendered after the parties were given ample opportunity to present their case by filing statements, statements in reply and documents in support of their respective claims, according to a procedural order rendered on 23 August 1995 by the arbitrators, who had heard the parties on this subject matter, so that one of the necessary principles of due process, that is, adversarial proceedings (*contradictoire*), has been scrupulously respected (Art. V(1)(*b*)). Neither the impartiality nor the independence of the arbitrators have been criticized by SPI, so that the requirement of a fair hearing has been met. Hence, this foreign award does not from this point of view violate international public policy, which violation could have been raised even ex officio in the country of enforcement.

[14] "SPI alleges in particular that the arbitrators violated due process because SPI could not present its counterclaim – an allegation which it also makes in support of its claim to review the award and to justify its request for suspension. When requested by Chadmore to take back 29,160 shares and pay for them, the Credicom group (and consequently also SPI) filed a counterclaim for the payment of five years of the profits guarantee (1993-1997) given by Mr. De Prado. When the arbitrators requested the counterclaimants to submit all accounting documents proving the alleged losses, the counterclaimants only managed to submit to the arbitrators the accounts concerning the first two years (1993 and 1994), since they had sold the hotels one year before the commencement of the arbitration to a third company which refused to deliver the said documents for the years 1995-1997. Considering the [counterclaimants'] impossibility to submit the relevant documents, the arbitrators concluded – wrongly, according to SPI which alleges that it reserved all its rights – that the counterclaim had been withdrawn, and rejected it by their award of 28 January 1998. In July 1998, the Credicom group bought back the hotels and can now submit all accounting documents for the three years at issue, on which documents it bases its action to review the award.

[15] "We must first consider that it appears from a reading of the award that the arbitrators did acknowledge that the Credicom group intended to reserve its rights against Mr. De Prado for the three years at issue. However, they amply motivated in fact and in law, with the support of Swiss doctrine and jurisprudence, the considerations which led them to conclude that there was 'an attitude of the claimants (towards) a tacit consent to a partial withdrawal of the claim', and to deny their [counter]claim.... SPI's ground for appeal reproaches the arbitrators that they wrongly decided on a part of SPI's [counter]claim, rather than that they omitted to decide on that part or that they prevented 'the counterclaimants from presenting their case', respectively, that they violated due process by preventing [the counterclaimants] from freely

presenting their point of view and 'from subsequently submitting documents, by deciding ex officio that SPI had withdrawn part of its [counter]claim'.

[16] "However, the Convention does not allow the enforcement court in any case to review the manner in which the arbitrators decided on the merits, with the sole exception of the compliance with international public policy. Even if the arbitral tribunal makes a gross mistake of fact or law, this is not a ground for refusing enforcement of the award. This is the case, in particular, of the accusation that the arbitrators wrongly evaluated certain documents, respectively, did not consider them at all, starting from the assumption that they were indeed submitted, and applies a fortiori to the case in which the counterclaimants could not even submit the documents.

[17] "In so far as this ground for appeal reproaches the arbitrators for not deciding on all issues of the dispute, this ground, even if proven, could not prevent the recognition of the award, as the case of 'infra petita', which is, on the contrary, a ground for setting aside under Art. 1023 CCP, is not provided for in the Convention."

3. *Article V(1)(e) of the New York Convention*

[18] "The ground for appeal which argues that the arbitral award has no res judicata effect because of the request for review before the Swiss Supreme Court will be examined below together with the request for suspension."

IV. SUSPENSION

[19] "According to Art. V(1)(*e*) of the Convention, recognition and enforcement shall be refused if 'the award has not yet become binding on the parties, or has been ... suspended by a competent authority of the country in which ... that award was made'. According to Art. VI of the Convention, the authority before which the award is sought to be relied upon may, 'if it considers it proper', adjourn the decision on the enforcement of the award if the award's annulment or suspension is sought before the competent authority referred to in Art. V(1)(*e*), that is, that of the country where the award has been rendered.

[20] "SPI relies in this respect on its request for review filed with the Swiss Supreme Court on 18 September 1998, which, it alleges, has as a consequence that the arbitral award rendered on 28 January 1998 is not yet res judicata, so that the Court must at least suspend its decision while awaiting the final decision on the request for review.

[21] "We must note first that by order of 14 December 1998, the President of the First Civil Chamber of the Swiss Supreme Court rejected [SPI's] request

for suspensive effect, filed on 9 December 1998, on the ground that 'the requesting party did not make in this respect any point which could be taken into consideration'.

[22] "We must also consider that the parties agreed that 'the arbitral award shall not be open to appeal' (see ... the arbitration agreement of 24 February 1995), so that the award is final and can no longer be attacked before the arbitrators as far as the arbitral procedure is concerned, the parties themselves having decided implicitly, by requesting the arbitrators to decide 'without appeal', and thus finally, that their award must be considered binding in the sense of the Convention.

[23] "In fact, apart from its reference to its appeal before the Swiss Supreme Court, SPI does not raise any ground (see Art. V(1) first paragraph of the Convention) against the binding effect of the arbitral award on the parties. The order rendered on 14 December 1998 by the President of the First Civil Chamber of the Swiss Supreme Court confirms, if necessary, that filing such a request does not have a suspensive effect in Swiss law.

[24] "SPI alleges that the Court should then at least suspend its decision, as it would be 'absurd to maintain that the court of enforcement could enforce an award which the court of the country of origin has annulled or could annul.... In this case the Luxembourg court would enforce an award which does not exist any longer or which could later be annulled in its country of origin.'

[25] "We must recall that Art. VI of the Convention does not mandate a suspension of the decision, but only gives the court a faculty to do so, if it 'considers it proper'. Art. VI must from this point of view be seen together with Art. VII(1), which provides that 'the provisions of the present Convention shall not ... deprive any interested party of any right he may have to avail himself of an arbitral award in the manner and to the extent allowed by the law or the treaties of the country where such award is sought to be relied upon'. Thus, the principle of *favor arbitrandum* which permeates the Convention led its drafters to promote enforcement as much as possible.

[26] "The above provision in Art. VII(1) is a 'more-favourable-right' provision aimed at making the enforcement of foreign awards possible in the highest number of cases, to such point that the possibilities of refusal listed in Art. V(1) of the Convention are only a minimum for the recognition of awards, leaving each State free to decide whether it should be more liberal.[4] Art. VII can thus lead to seemingly unexpected – absurd, according to SPI – situations, in that the possible setting aside in Switzerland of the award at issue does not

4. The Court of Appeal referred to "Clunet", Journal du droit international (1998) p. 645 et seq., no. 27.

prevent its enforcement in Luxembourg by virtue of Art. 1028(2) CCP, which does not include among the grounds for refusal of recognition and enforcement of a foreign award its setting aside in its country of origin, as provided for in Art. V(1)(*e*) of the Convention.[5]

[27] "Hence, since according to the Convention the Luxembourg court can only deny enforcement on one of the grounds provided for in its national law and since Art. 1028(2) (Grand Ducal Regulation of 8 December 1981) CCP does not include among these grounds the case that the award is being challenged abroad, it does not appear appropriate under these circumstances to suspend the decision."

5. The Court of Appeal referred to *Cour de Cassation*, 9 October 1984 (*Pabalk Ticaret Ltd. Sirketi v. Norsolor SA*), reported in Yearbook XI (1986) pp. 484-491 (France no. 7), and 23 March 1994 (*Hilmarton Ltd. v. Omnium de Traitement et de Valorisation - OTV*), reported in Yearbook XX (1995) pp. 663-665 (France no. 23). It also referred to *Tribunal de Première Instance*, Brussels, 25 January 1996 (*Inter-Arab Investment Guarantee Corp. v. Banque Arabe et Internationale d'Investissements*), reported in Yearbook XXII (1997) pp. 643-668 (Belgium no. 10).

NETHERLANDS

Accession: 24 April 1964
1st Reservation

25. Arrondissementsrechtbank [Court of First Instance], Zutphen, 11 November 1998

Parties:	Claimant: China Packaging Design Corporation (China) Defendant: SCA Recycling Reukema Trading B.V. (Netherlands)
Published in:	Unpublished
Articles:	IV(2); V(2)(*b*)
Subject matters:	- translation of arbitration agreement - due process - CIETAC as successor to FETAC
Commentary Cases:	[1] = ¶ 101; [2] = ¶ 502; [3]-[5] = ¶ 406; [5] = ¶ 106; [6] = ¶ 202 + ¶ 507; [6]-[7] = ¶ 303 + ¶ 500; [7]-[8] = ¶ 511

Facts

China Packaging Design Corporation (China Packaging) sought enforcement in The Netherlands of a Chin International Economic and Trade Arbitration Commission (CIETAC) award rendered on 8 March 1996 against SCA Recycling Reukema Trading B.V. (Reukema).

The Court of First Instance in Zutphen granted enforcement finding that the failure to submit a translation into Dutch of the arbitration agreement and the appointment of an arbitrator on behalf of Reukema did not constitute grounds for refusal. The succession of the Foreign Economic and Trade Arbitration Commission (FETAC) by CIETAC was insufficient to infer that the parties no longer intended to submit possible disputes to arbitration, especially since Reukema did not object to this change at the commencement of the arbitration. Furthermore, the award and the way in which it was made did not violate Dutch public policy.

Excerpt

[1] "The arbitral award at issue is in principle enforceable in The Netherlands under the [New York Convention] as both China and The Netherlands are party to the Convention, which is in force in both States.

[2] "We must first note that, according to Art. 985 of the Code of Civil Procedure,[1] a dispute which has been the subject matter of an arbitration may not be reviewed in the context of the present inquiry. Reukema's attempt to re-discuss the decision rendered on the merits by CIETAC must be left aside.

[3] "Reukema's defence is essentially the following: the [arbitration] agreement has not been supplied in Dutch as required by the Convention; also, the arbitral award was rendered between China Packing Design Corporation and Reukema instead of between China Packaging Design Corporation and Reukema; the parties agreed that their disputes would be decided by the 'Foreign Economic and Trade Arbitration Commission of the China Council for the Promotion of International Trade' (FETAC), whereas the award was rendered by CIETAC, which cannot be deemed to be the same as FETAC; there has been a violation of due process as [Reukema's] arbitrator was appointed by CIETAC, not by [Reukema]. Further, Reukema was not given the opportunity to react on the written submission by which China Packaging initiated the proceedings, since its request for adjournment was not granted; this resulted in a violation of the principle of contradictory proceedings. Hence, recognition or enforcement of the award against Reukema would violate the Convention and public policy.

[4] "The fact that the agreement has not been supplied in Dutch is immaterial as the agreement is written in an understandable language.

---

1. Art. 985 of the Netherlands Code of Civil Procedure reads in relevant part:

"When a decision rendered by a court of a foreign State is enforceable in the Netherlands under a convention or by force of law, it is enforced only after obtaining a leave thereto from a court. The merits shall not be re-examined...."

[5] "The fact that the award writes 'Packing' instead of 'Packaging' appears to be a typographical error, the more so as it is unclear whether the mistake was made by CIETAC or in the translation.

[6] "Reukema's objection that the award was rendered by CIETAC, which cannot be considered the same as FETAC, must be denied. The parties intended to have their disputes solved by arbitration. The mere fact that CIETAC succeeded FETAC is insufficient to conclude that the parties no longer intended to submit possible disputes to arbitration, the more so as neither is it proven nor does it appear that Reukema objected to this change at the beginning of the arbitration.

[7] "It appears from a letter dated 14 June 1995, submitted by Reukema, that the president of the arbitral tribunal appointed Ms. Jia Junlan as the arbitrator for Reukema according to Art. 26 of the CIETAC Rules.[2] This does not mean that Reukema was not duly informed of the appointment of the arbitrator. Further, Reukema could have objected to the appointment of the arbitrator and failed to do so.

[8] "Reukema knew already in June 1995 that China Packaging would request the arbitral tribunal to render an award. The final hearing was held on 27 November 1995, so that it cannot be said that the principle of contradictory proceedings was violated, as Reukema had sufficient time to select a lawyer and prepare its case as well as to file written submissions. That Reukema allegedly could not properly do so depends on circumstances pertaining to [Reukema's] risk sphere.

[9] "Consequently, we must conclude that neither the arbitral award nor the way in which it came to be rendered appear to violate Dutch public policy, the only ground, in so far as relevant, which could lead to deny the request [for enforcement]."

---

2. Art. 26 of the Arbitration Rules of the China International Economic and Trade Arbitration Commission (CIETAC) reads:

"If the Respondent fails to appoint or authorize the Chairman of the Arbitration Commission to appoint an arbitrator according to Article 16 of these Rules, the Chairman of the Arbitration Commission shall appoint an arbitrator for the Respondent."

SWITZERLAND

Ratification: 1 June 1965
No Reservations

32. Bundesgerichtshof [Supreme Court], 19 December 1997

Parties:	Petitioners: (1) Compañía Minera Condesa SA (Peru); (2) Compañía de Minas Buenaventura SA (Peru) Respondents: (1) BRGM-Pérou SAS (formerly La-Source, Compagnie Minière SAS) (France); (2) ICC Arbitral Tribunal
Published in:	13 Mealey's International Arbitration Report (1998, no. 9) pp. C-1 – C-7
Articles:	II(3)
Subject matter:	– litispendence between arbitral tribunal and court
Commentary Cases:	¶ 227; [5] = ¶ 216; [6] = ¶ 219

Facts

Compañía de Minas Buenaventura SA (Buenaventura) and the French state agency Bureau de Recherches Géologiques et Minières (BRGM) negotiated in 1984 the participation of the Buenaventura group in Cedimin SA, a Peruvian daughter company of BRGM owned by Société d'Études de Recherches et d'Exploitations Minières, presently called BRGM-Pérou SAS (BRGM-Pérou). Buenaventura, BRGM-Pérou and Cedimin SA signed an agreement on 2 February 1985 and also agreed that the statutes of Cedimin SA would be modified to include a pre-emption right for the shareholding companies. Both the agreement and the modified statutes contained an ICC arbitration clause.

In 1996, BRGM sold a substantial part of its shares in BRGM-Pérou to Normandy Mining Ltd. (Normandy), an Australian company. Alleging a violation of their pre-emption right, Buenaventura and Compañía Minera

Condesa SA (Condesa) commenced court proceedings in Lima, Peru, against BRGM and BRGM-Pérou on 6 February 1995. On 16 December 1996, the Court of Appeal in Lima denied BRGM-Pérou's objection that the dispute should be referred to arbitration.

On 30 May 1995, BRGM-Pérou had commenced ICC arbitration in Switzerland against Condesa and Buenaventura. By an interim award of 19 November 1996, the arbitral tribunal found that it had jurisdiction over the dispute.

Condesa and Buenaventura sought annulment of the award. The Supreme Court denied the request, finding that the Peruvian court had no jurisdiction over the dispute, which should have been referred to arbitration.

Excerpt

[1] "The petitioners maintain that the arbitral tribunal should have stayed the arbitration according to Art. 9(1) of the Private International Law Act (PILA) as the dispute was already pending before the Peruvian courts at the time of commencing the arbitration and, when the Peruvian decision became final, should have dismissed the claim according to Art. 9(3) PILA. In its turn, the arbitral tribunal argues that [the principle of] litispendence only regulates the relationship between two equally competent state courts; where there is an arbitration agreement, the jurisdiction of the state courts is excluded.

[2] "According to Art. 9(1) PILA, a Swiss court stays the proceedings if a claim on the same matter between the same parties has already been filed abroad and where it is to be expected that the foreign court will render, within a reasonable of time, a judgment which can be recognized in Switzerland. It is disputed whether the principle of litispendence also applies to the relationship between a state court and an arbitral tribunal. Some stress the need to avoid contrasting decisions and thus request the arbitral tribunal to stay the proceedings until there is a decision by the state court on the question of jurisdiction (Rüede/Hadenfeldt, *Schweizerisches Schiedsgerichtsrecht*, 2nd ed. (Zurich 1993) p. 231). Others find that the arbitral tribunal must be able to continue with the proceedings in any case, regardless of an existing litispendence, if the state court has not yet decided on its jurisdiction (Martin L. Müller, *Die Zuständigkeit des Schiedsgerichts* (dissertation Zurich 1977) p. 112).

[3] "The question whether the arbitral tribunal should have stayed the arbitration pending court proceedings may remain open if the judgment of the Lima Court of Appeal, which affirmed the jurisdiction of the Peruvian courts, proves not to be recognizable in Switzerland.

[4] "Even if Art. 9(1) PILA also covered the relationship between courts and arbitral tribunals, court proceedings pending on a dispute before a foreign court could result in the exclusion from the outset of arbitral proceedings in Switzerland – as ensues from the letter of [Art. 9(1)] – only if the foreign judgment were recognizable (Lalive/Poudret/Reymond, *Le droit de l'arbitrage interne et internationale en Suisse* (Lausanne 1989) p. 288; Werner Wenger, in *Kommentar zum schweizerischen Privatrecht* (Basel 1996) [*Kommentar*] note 9 to Art. 186 PILA; Martina Wittibschlager, *Rechtshängigkeit in internationalen Verhältnissen* (dissertation Basel 1992) p. 123 et seq.). The consideration of a pre-existing foreign litispendence is a 'necessary consequence of the recognition of the decision' (Georg Leuch, *Die Zivilprozessordnung für den Kanton Bern* (Bern 1956) note 4 to Art. 160 Bern ZPO; see also BGE 105 II 229 E. 1a p. 232; Pierre Karrer, in *Kommentar*, note 28 to Art. 187 PILA; Oskar Vogel, SJZ 86/1990 p. 80 et seq.). Similarly, a judgment already rendered by a foreign court only prevents a decision on the same dispute by a national arbitral tribunal when the foreign judgment may be recognized in Switzerland according to Art. 25 PILA (Lalive/Poudret/Reymond, op. cit., p. 386; Rüde/Hadenfeldt, op. cit., p. 232; Werner Wenger, op. cit., note 8 to Art. 186 PILA, and in Andreas Kellerhals, ed., *Schiedsgerichtsbarkeit* (Zurich 1997) p. 242 et seq.).[1] No different conclusion can be drawn from BGE 121 III 495, which the

1. Arts. 25 and 27 of the Swiss PILA reads:

Article 25
"A foreign decision is recognized in Switzerland:
(a) if jurisdiction lay with the judicial or administrative authorities of the country in which the decision was rendered;
(b) if no ordinary judicial remedy can any longer be brought against the decision or if the decision is final; and
(c) if no ground for non-recognition under Article 27 exists."

Article 27
"1. A foreign decision is not recognized in Switzerland if its recognition would be clearly incompatible with Swiss public policy.
2. A foreign decision is also not recognized if a party proves:
(a) that neither according to the law of its domicile nor according to the law of its habitual residence was the party properly served with process, unless the party entered an unconditional appearance in the proceedings;
(b) that the judgment was rendered in violation of essential principles of Swiss procedural law, especially, the party was denied the right to be heard;
(c) that a lawsuit between the same parties concerning the same case was first commenced or decided in Switzerland, or was first decided in a third country, provided that the prerequisites for the recognition of that decision are met.
3. In no other respects may the foreign decision be reviewed on the merits."

petitioners mention on this point. In an obiter dictum in that decision, the Supreme Court determined that conflicts of jurisdiction between state courts and arbitral tribunals are to be solved in the light of the rule of litispendence, the dispute at issue and in particular the recognition and enforcement of the foreign decision according to Art. 25 et seq. PILA (BGE 121 III 495 E 6c p. 502). Hence, we must ascertain whether the judgment of the Court of Appeal in Lima is enforceable in Switzerland.

[5] "The conditions for the recognition of a foreign judgment in Switzerland are laid down in Art. 25 PILA, unless conventional provisions take precedence (Art. 1(2) PILA). According to Art. 25(a) PILA, it is necessary for the recognition of a foreign judgment, inter alia, that the jurisdiction of the court or authority of the State concerned was founded. Jurisdiction ensues from Art. 26 PILA or from pertinent treaty provisions (Berti/Schnyder, *Kommentar*, note 14 to Art. 26 PILA; Wittibschlager, op. cit., p. 125). In the field of international arbitration the [1958 New York Convention] is to be considered in particular. Both Switzerland (as of 30 August 1965) and Peru (as of 5 October 1988) are party to this Convention.

[6] "According to Art. II(3) of the Convention, which corresponds to Art. 7(b) PILA (BBl 1983 I 303; Lalive/Poudret/Reymond, op. cit., p. 287), the court of a Contracting State, when seized of an action in a matter in respect of which the parties have made an arbitration agreement, shall, at the request of one of the parties, refer the parties to arbitration unless it finds that the said agreement is null and void, inoperative or incapable of being performed. Hence, according to the Convention, if a party relies on the arbitration agreement before a state court, the jurisdiction of the state court to decide on the dispute is derogated from, on the conditions of Art. II(3), independent of whether the arbitration has already commenced (Albert Jan van den Berg, *The New York Arbitration Convention of 1958* (Deventer 1981) p. 131 et seq.; Peter Schlosser, *Das Recht der internationalen privaten Schiedsgerichtsbarkeit*, 2nd ed. (Tubingen 1989) note 400, p. 302 et seq.). A foreign state court which, notwithstanding the presence of the conditions of Art. II of the Convention, does not refer the parties to arbitration but takes the dispute into its own hands lacks thus indirect jurisdiction in the sense of Art. 25(a) PILA, and its decision cannot be recognized in Switzerland, unless the lack of jurisdiction of the arbitral tribunal is determined by the tribunal itself or in the context of a review by a state court.

[7] "The Lima Court of Appeal, in its decision of 16 December 1996, rejected the objection based on the arbitration agreement essentially because Normandy and Cedimin, to which the arbitration clause could not be opposed, would participate in the proceedings – with Buenaventura on the side of the claimants; with BRGM on the side of the defendants. However, a

decision in this dispute would affect all parties, so that they must have the possibility to participate in the arbitration. Also, [the Lima Court] failed to recognize that the parties which were not subject to the arbitration agreement could be referred to proceedings before the state courts. The mere danger of contrasting decisions rendered in different proceedings does not, according to the Convention, make the arbitration clause inoperative or incapable of being performed or exclude the jurisdiction of the arbitral tribunal (Albert Jan van den Berg, op. cit., p. 167 with references to jurisprudence).

[8] "The Court of Appeal in Lima did not establish other grounds on which the arbitration clause would not meet the conditions of Art. II(3) of the Convention, nor were such grounds proven by the petitioners. Under these circumstances the parties should have been referred to arbitration. In the absence of indirect jurisdiction, the judgment of the Peruvian court is not recognizable in Switzerland, unless in the future it appears from a review of the disputed decision that the arbitral tribunal incorrectly found it had jurisdiction."

UNITED KINGDOM

Accession: 24 September 1975
1st Reservation

52. High Court, Queen's Bench Division (Commercial Court), 20 January 1997

Parties:	Plaintiffs: China Agribusiness Development Corporation (China) Defendants: Balli Trading (UK)
Published in:	[1998] 2 Lloyd's Law Reports, Part I, pp. 76-80
Articles:	V; V(1)(*d*)
Subject matters:	– application of current arbitration rules – discretion to refuse enforcement
Commentary Cases:	[1] = ¶ 101; [1]-[13] = ¶ 202, ¶ 507 + ¶ 513; [14]-[18] = ¶ 303 + ¶ 500

Facts

On 15 June 1994, China Agribusiness Development Corporation (CADC) contracted to buy a quantity of hot rolled steel coils from Balli Trading (Balli). The contract contained an arbitration clause providing for arbitration at the Foreign Economic and Trade Arbitration Commission (FETAC) of the China Council for the Promotion of International Trade in accordance with its Rules. When disputes arose between the parties and CADC sought in October 1994 to initiate arbitration in accordance with the clause, it came to light that the FETAC had changed its name to the China International Economic and Trade Arbitration Commission (CIETAC). The FETAC Rules to which the arbitral clause referred had ceased to have effect on 1 July 1989. The rules that then come into effect had been succeeded by a subsequent set of rules which had come into force on 1 June 1994.

CIETAC accepted the request for arbitration and sent a copy of the current rules to Balli which did not respond. An award was made in CADC's favour. CADC sought to enforce the award in England. Master Trench gave ex parte leave on 24 June 1996 and on 6 November 1996 refused to set aside the ex parte leave.

On appeal, Longmore, J, held that the award must remain enforceable. The parties had agreed that the Rules of FETAC or any successor body should apply and that the rules would be the rules current at the time the arbitration was held. Further, under the terms of the Arbitration Act 1975, refusal to enforce a Convention award was matter of discretion of the court.

Excerpt

(....)

[1] "Although various points were argued before Master Trench it is now accepted that the award is one to which the New York Convention applies, and that therefore enforcement must take place as of right unless the defendant can show that one of the grounds set out in Sect. 5(2) of the Arbitration Act, 1975 exists. What is said by Balli is that they agreed to arbitrate under the provisional rules of FETAC. They accept that FETAC and CIETAC are the same entity, but they submit that they expressly agreed to arbitration under the old provisional rules and not to arbitration under the current rules.

[2] "Since it is common ground that CIETAC made their award pursuant to rules current at the time when the dispute arose and arbitration was invoked, Balli submit that they have proved within the terms of Sect. 5(2)(e) of the 1975 Arbitration Act that 'the arbitral procedure was not in accordance with the agreement of the parties'. The arbitration agreement is no doubt governed by Chinese law, but I have no evidence that for this purpose it is any different from English law. As a matter of English law it is clear that if an arbitration agreement requires an arbitration to be held according to the rules of a particular institution that agreement prima facie refers to the rules current at the time when the arbitration is begun. (See *Offshore International S.A. v. Banco Central S.A.*, [1976] 2 Lloyd's Rep. 402, *Bunge S.A. v. Kruse*, [1979] 1 Lloyd's Rep. 279 and *Mertens & Co. P.V.B.A. v. Veevoeder Import Export Vimex B.V.*, [1979] 2 Lloyd's Rep. 372).

(....)

[3] "For Balli, Mr. Freedman submits:

1. That the express words of the contract must here yield a different interpretation because it was expressly agreed that the arbitration was to be held under the provisional rules.

2. That it made no difference if, which is here disputed on the evidence, the arbitral body would refuse to apply the provisional rules. The agreement for arbitration was, says Mr. Freedman, conditional on that arbitration being held under the provisional rules. If that agreement could not be performed there was no arbitration agreement and it followed that if the plaintiffs wished to assert their legal rights they had to sue Balli in court, presumably in England. He relied on a passage in *Offshore International v. Banco* where Mr. Justice Ackner said at p. 408:

> 'If the parties had wanted to provide for the 1955 rules to be the rules that were applicable to any arbitration that took place between them, they could have so provided. There can be no doubt that as from 1 June 1975, the 1975 rules were the only rules of the ICC then in force under which arbitrations could be held.'

3. That Balli's stance was entirely rational and comprehensible since the provisional rules allowed the arbitrators to charge a maximum fee of 1 per cent. of the amount at stake, whereas the current rules permitted charging according to a sliding scale which resulted in this case in a charge being levied of 2.7 per cent. of the amount at stake.

[4] "Mr. Landau, for the plaintiffs, submits:

1. That the arbitration clause is or was a standard FETAC arbitration clause which merely identified the relevant rules; agreement on that clause did not amount to an express agreement for an earlier version of the rules as in the example given by Mr. Justice Ackner.

2. That the evidence was clear that CIETAC would refuse to arbitrate under an old, let alone a doubly old, set of rules. There was thus a stark choice between arbitration under the current rules and or no arbitration at all. The clause should be construed in such a way as to permit arbitration as the agreed manner of resolving the dispute, even if that was to vary the agreement of the parties that arbitration should be conducted pursuant to earlier provisional rules.

3. The relevantly full wording of Sect. 5(2)(e) of the Act is: 'Enforcement of a Convention award *may* be refused ...'. I emphasize the word 'may':

> '... if the person against whom it is invoked proves: (e) that the composition of the arbitral authority or arbitral procedure was not in accordance with the agreement of the parties.'

[5] "Mr. Landau emphasizes the word 'may' and submits that the Court has a discretion, not an obligation, to refuse to enforce an award made pursuant

to an arbitral procedure which did not accord with the agreement of the parties. That discretion should not be exercised, he submitted, in a case where (a) the current rules had been sent to Balli who had expressed no objection at the time but had merely taken no part in the arbitration and (b) the differences in fee charging, being the main respect in which Balli allege prejudice, amounted to no more than £ 1500."

I. CONSTRUCTION

[6] "I agree with Mr. Landau that the correct construction of this contract is that the parties agreed that the rules of FETAC, or any successor body, should apply and that the rules would be the rules current at the time the arbitration was begun. He referred me to a standard Chinese text book called 'China Trade Documents' published in 1985 in which a clause in almost identical words is set out at p. 97 by way of a sample arbitration clause. I understand that FETAC never had any rules other than the provisional rules and I conclude that the word 'provisional' is no more than a word of identification, not a word of differentiation intended to indicate an earlier version of rules by which, and by which alone, the parties were to be bound.

[7] "In this context it is relevant to consider whether CIETAC, as FETAC became, would have been prepared to accept the reference to arbitration under the old provisional rules. Although Balli have obtained evidence from a Chinese lawyer (Mr. Peter Jiang), that they would, that lawyer does not address himself to the critical clauses of the current rules or the question of charging. The plaintiffs' Chinese lawyers, the Jung Hee Law Office, have asked the staff of CIETAC themselves who have said that the latest rules always applied to any dispute. The lawyers conclude that it was impossible for CIETAC to apply the provisional rules. Mr. Landau can also claim support from Arts. 7 and 80 of the current Rules[1] and from the only literary work

1. Arts. 7 and 80 of the 1994 CIETAC Rules read:

Article 7
"Once the parties agree to submit their dispute to the Arbitration Commission for arbitration, it shall be deemed that they have agreed to conduct the arbitration under these Rules."

Article 80
"These Rules shall come into force as from June 1, 1994. For cases taken cognizance of by the Arbitration Commission or its Sub-Commissions before the date on which these Rules become effective, the Rules of the Arbitration Commission which came into force as from January 1, 1989 shall still apply. However, these Rules shall be applied if the parties so agree."

which has considered the question. (See Kaplan Spruce and Moser, *Hong Kong and China Arbitration Cases and Materials*, p. 322.)

[8] "In the result I ... conclude that CIETAC would not have accepted the reference to arbitration if the parties had asked them to conduct the arbitration under the old provisional rules. It seems therefore that if the agreement were to be construed as an agreement to arbitrate only under the provisional rules, the parties would have agreed to do something impossible. Of course, parties to a contract are free to agree something which is in the event impossible and the courts will have to determine the legal consequence, but a court will try to avoid imputing to the parties an intention to do something which cannot be done.

[9] "The question here is whether the parties have agreed that there shall be arbitration and that it shall take place in China, or whether they have gone further and agreed that if any arbitration is to take place it will only take place in China under provisional and out of date rules, and if that cannot be done there is to be no arbitration at all. I have no hesitation in rejecting the latter construction and saying that the parties intended to and did agree that there was to be arbitration in China under the appropriate rules of the relevant arbitral institution.

[10] ".... A similar point to the present case arose in *Chen Jen Nan Dar Industrial and Trade United Co. Ltd. v. F. M. International Ltd.*, [1992] 1 H.K. Cases 328. The argument run in that case does not seem to be precisely the same argument as that addressed to me by Mr. Freedman, viz. that the parties had agreed the provisional rules and no other. The argument was rather that if one compared the two versions of the rules the new rules were not merely in different terms but in terms more prejudicial to the respondents.

[11] "Mr. Justice Kaplan held that the new rules were more 'liberal' than those they replaced and then said ...

> 'In my judgment there is nothing in this point. The fact that the arbitral institution chosen by the parties has improved its rules between contract and arbitration is not sufficient to justify refusing enforcement. Such a complaint does not come within the grounds set out in figure [5](2)E.'

I substitute the figure 5 for the relevant section of the Hong Kong Ordinance.

[12] "Mr. Freedman criticized this passage since he submitted that the new rules, at any rate as to charging, were not an 'improvement' if one looked at the matter from the point of view of the ultimately paying party. He also submitted that the critical question for the purpose of Sect. 5(2)(e) of the 1975 Act was 'what arbitral procedure had the parties agreed'. The question whether the arbitration had been conducted under 'better' or 'worse' or more or less

'liberal' rules was beside the point. There is, as it seems to me, some limited force in Mr. Freedman's submissions. It must, however, be remembered that Mr. Justice Kaplan was dealing with the argument put to him which asserted that prejudice had been caused to the respondents in the arbitration by the use of the new rules.

[13] "For my own part, as a matter of construction I conclude that the parties in the present case agreed that there would be arbitration if required in China, and that such arbitration would be held under the rules of the relevant institution at the time when arbitration was invoked. In other words the parties have not used clear enough words to contract out of the prima facie construction of such clauses as laid down by the English cases to which I have referred."

II. DISCRETION

[14] "Mr. Freedman acknowledged the presence of the word 'may' in Sect. 5(2)(e) of the 1975 Act. He submitted, however, that the statute in this respect was merely following the terms of the New York Convention which was concerned to make clear that a Contracting State which permitted enforcement to be refused in certain limited circumstances was not in breach of the Convention. No doubt that is the sense of the Convention. But the terms in which the English legislature has in fact enacted the power to refuse enforcement must remain relevant for an English Judge. It is clear from the terms of the statute that refusal to enforce a Convention award is a matter for the discretion of the court. In that context it must be relevant to assess the degree of prejudice to Balli by the arbitration being conducted under the current, rather than the provisional, rules. Mr Justice Kaplan so decided in the *Chen Jen* case and I gratefully follow his lead. (See [1992] 1 H.K. Cases 328 at p. 336.)

[15] "In order to show prejudice Mr. Freedman relied mainly on the enhanced power to assess the fees of the arbitration contained in the new rules. He also sought to submit that a record of the arbitration proceedings was not available to Balli as of right under the current rules while it would have been under the provisional rules. I am not satisfied that it was in fact so available under the provisional rules and I pay no further attention to that consideration.

[16] "Mr. Landau submitted that the change in fee structure was so insubstantial (the extra bill was no more than £ 1500 overall) that there was not sufficient prejudice to justify refusal to enforce what is a Convention award. I agree with that contention, and if I had jurisdiction to refuse to enforce this award, in the sense that I was satisfied that this was a case coming

within the Sect. 5(2)(e) of the 1975 Act, I would not be prepared to exercise that jurisdiction in this case.

[17] "It is also relevant to observe that the argument that the arbitration could only proceed under the provisional rules has been raised at a very late stage. When the plaintiffs invoked arbitration the new CIETAC Rules were sent to Balli. Balli did not at that stage say that they had only agreed arbitration under the FETAC provisional rules. They never gave any reason for refusing to participate in the arbitration. They waited until the award had been made and proceedings were brought to enforce that award. The plaintiffs were never given any opportunity to consider what action, e.g. an ad hoc arbitration or litigation in England, might be appropriate in the light of an argument that any arbitration had to take place under the old FETAC provisional rules and in no other way.

[18] "It is a matter of record that Balli and their lawyers appear to have been unaware of the content of the provisional rules when they first applied to set aside the order of Master Trench. The provisional rules first surfaced in an affidavit of Mr. Evans on 2 October 1996. A party who, only at the door of the enforcing court, dreams up a reason for suggesting that a Convention award should not be enforced is unlikely to have the court's sympathy exercised in his favour, and for this reason also I would not on the facts of this case be prepared to refuse enforcement of the award."

(....)

53. Queen's Bench Division (Commercial Court), 20 January 1999

Parties:	Plaintiff: Minmetals Germany GmbH (Germany) Defendant: Ferco Steel Ltd. (UK)
Published in:	[1999] 1 All ER (Comm) p. 315 et seq.
Articles:	V(1)(*b*); V(1)(*c*); V(1)(*d*); V(2)(*b*)
Subject matters:	– inability to present case – reliance by arbitrators on undisclosed award – remittal of award by setting aside court – failure to use opportunity to present case – burden of proof of inarbitrability and violation of public policy on party seeking enforcement – waiver of right to invoke procedural irregularity – "substantial injustice" (no) – public policy to respect decision of setting aside court (supervisory jurisdiction)
Commentary Cases:	[1] = ¶ 101, ¶ 501 + ¶ 503; [2] = ¶ 512; [4]-[12] = ¶ 511; [13]-[17] = ¶ 513; [16]-[17] = ¶ 303 + ¶ 500; [18]-[31] = ¶ 524 ("substantial injustice" and failure to disclose award); [24]-[26] = ¶ 104 + ¶ 516

Facts

By contract of 3 March 1993, Ferco Steel Ltd. (Ferco) agreed to sell to Minmetals a quantity of steel channels. The contract provided for arbitration by the Foreign Trade Arbitration Commission of the China Council for the Promotion of International Trade in accordance with its Rules. On 4 March 1993, Minmetals entered into a sub-sale contract under which they agreed to sell steel channels of the same quality, quantity and description to China Resources Metals and Minerals Co. (China Resources).

Disputes arose between Ferco and Minmetals regarding the quality of the steel and on 27 December 1993 Minmetals referred its claim against Ferco to arbitration by the China International Economic and Trade Arbitration Commission (CIETAC). In their award of 29 September 1995, the arbitrators apparently calculated the compensation resulting from Ferco's breach of contract according to an arbitration award, made by the same arbitrators a day earlier, between Minmetals and China Resources (the sub-sale award). The sub-sale award had never been referred to or put in evidence in the arbitration between Ferco and Minmetals.

On 24 January 1996, Ferco applied to the Beijing Intermediate People's Court for revocation of the award. Ferco argued the award was in breach of Art. 53 of the CIETAC Arbitration Rules[1] in that it had not had any opportunity to consider the sub-sale award and to make submissions on it. The Beijing court agreed and on 8 October 1996 the Court directed that the award be remitted to CIETAC "for a resumed arbitration", because "for reasons for which it was not responsible" the respondent was not able to state its views.

On 10 October 1996, the arbitral tribunal issued to the parties a notice giving directions as to the resumed arbitration and requiring Ferco to provide no later than 20 October a copy of its application to the Beijing court with supporting reasons for revocation of the award. Ferco's Beijing attorney, Mr. Jiang, declined to do so for various reasons. In response to the arbitral tribunal's invitation to submit "supplementary opinions" prior to an oral hearing scheduled for 30 January 1997, Mr. Jiang submitted two points relating to the actual fate of the steel channels in dispute and whether the contract required the steel to be marked with quality marks. The submissions contained no specific mention of the arbitrators' having relied upon the sub-sale award, which had never been shown to Ferco, in order to quantify the loss sustained by Minmetals. The submissions also did not contain any explanation of the basis on which Ferco applied to the Beijing court for revocation of the award. Ferco also did not invite the arbitrators to disclose the sub-sale award. In his skeleton argument for the resumed hearing dated 27 January 1997, Mr. Jiang did not mention the arbitrators' reliance on the evidence of their own award in the sub-sale arbitration or the fact that the award had never been provided to Ferco.

On 20 March 1997, the arbitrators issued their award in the resumed arbitration, maintaining the award of 29 September 1995. The second award contained no consideration of the propriety of the arbitrators' reliance on the sub-sale award or of whether, without it, the buyers had proven their loss.

---

1. Art. 53 of the CIETAC Arbitration Rules reads:

"The arbitration tribunal shall independently and impartially make its arbitral award in accordance with the facts of the case, the law and the terms of the contracts, international practices and the principle of fairness and reasonableness."

Ferco applied on 4 April 1997 to the Beijing court to revoke the second award, arguing that the arbitrators had wrongly continued to rely on the sub-sale award despite the fact that it had never been disclosed to Ferco and Ferco had never been permitted to make submissions about it. The Beijing court rejected Ferco's application. The court took the view that the arbitrators had in the course of the first arbitration infringed the CIETAC procedural rules of arbitration but that, by giving Ferco the opportunity to comment on the sub-sale award in the course of the resumed arbitration, the arbitrators had cured the original defect. Ferco applied for a retrial in the Beijing court the outcome of which was not known at the time of the judgment in casu.

On 12 January 1998, Cresswell, J made an order under Sect. 101 of the Arbitration Act 1996[2] giving leave to Minmetals to enforce the award of 29 September 1995 in the initial arbitration and the award of 20 March 1997 in the resumed arbitration. Ferco applied for the leave to enforce to be adjourned pending determination of the application to the Beijing court for retrial and possible revocation of the award. The High Court, per Colman, J, ordered the adjournment of the application against security representing 80% of the claim. Ferco failed to provide the security and in the ensuing proceedings the court found that there were no grounds for setting aside the leave to enforce. In particular the court found that Ferco's failure to refer to the sub-sale award in the resumed arbitration constituted a waiver of the right to rely on the arbitrators' failure to reveal it to them. Moreover, "the countervailing policy considerations in favour of enforcement of awards are so strong that they displace the policy consideration of non-enforcement in the face of procedural defects going to a breach of natural justice."

Excerpt

[1] "It is common ground that the awards were New York Convention awards. Nor is it disputed by Ferco that unless it can persuade the Beijing court to order a retrial of the application to revoke and, as a result of that retrial, the Beijing court orders revocation, the awards are, as they stand, final and enforceable under Chinese law. Sect. 103(1) and (2) of the 1996 Act

2. Sect. 101 of the Arbitration Act 1996 reads in relevant part:

"(1) A New York Convention award shall be recognised as binding on the persons as between whom it was made, and may accordingly be relied on by those persons by way of defence, set-off or otherwise in any legal proceedings in England and Wales or Northern Ireland. (....)"

expressly provides that such awards must be enforced unless the party against whom enforcement is sought proves that the case falls within one of the exceptions in sub-Sect. (2).[3] With regard to the court's power under Sect. 103(3) to decline to enforce or recognise an award on grounds of inarbitrability of the subject matter or of enforcement being contrary to public policy, whereas it is always open to the court to take an illegality point of its own volition, if a respondent to enforcement wishes to rely on matters within this subsection, the burden of making good the objection to enforcement, in my judgment, clearly rests on that party.

[2] "Before dealing with the issues of real substance on this application, one of the matters raised on behalf of Ferco can be dealt with quite briefly. That is the submission that the awards contain decisions on matters beyond the scope of the submission to arbitration within Sect. 103(2)(d). The function of this exception is to exclude from enforcement awards made on issues falling outside those which were referred for decision to the arbitrators. The vice of the awards upon which Ferco rely is the arbitrators' reliance on evidence derived from their own investigations and not previously provided to Ferco. That evidence, however, went to a central issue within the overall dispute referred to arbitration, namely what loss had been caused to Minmetals by Ferco's breaches of contract. Whether in relying upon that evidence or in omitting to disclose it to Ferco the tribunal acted in accordance with the CIETAC rules or with any other procedural requirements of Chinese law is entirely irrelevant to the question whether the tribunal's decision was inside or outside 'the scope of the submission'. That scope falls to be defined by reference to the issues to be resolved by the arbitrators and not by reference to the procedure to be adopted for that purpose. This is clear beyond doubt from the wording of Sect. 103(2)(c) which expressly covers deviation of the actual procedure from the agreed procedure. This head of objection to enforcement must therefore be rejected.

[3] "I now turn to the three remaining issues to which I refer as: the inability to present a case issue; the Sect. 103(2)(e) issue; and the public policy issue."

I. THE INABILITY TO PRESENT A CASE ISSUE

[4] "Although many of those States who are parties to the New York Convention are civil law jurisdictions or are those which like China derive the

3. Sect. 103(2)(a)-(f) repeats the grounds of Art. V(1) of the New York Convention for refusal of enforcement of a Convention award.

whole or part of their procedural rules from the civil law and therefore have essentially an inquisitorial system, Art. V of the Convention protects the requirements of natural justice reflected in the *audi alteram partem* rule. Therefore, where the tribunal is procedurally entitled to conduct its own investigations into the facts, the effect of this provision will be to avoid enforcement of an award based on findings of fact derived from such investigations if the enforcee has not been given any reasonable opportunity to present its case in relation to the results of such investigations. Art. 26 of the CIETAC Rules by reference to which the parties had agreed to arbitrate provided:

> 'The parties shall give evidence for the facts on which their claim or defence is based. The arbitration tribunal may, if it deems it necessary, make investigations and collect evidence on its own initiative.'

[5] "That, however, was not treated by the Beijing court as permitting the tribunal to reach its conclusions and make an award without first disclosing to both parties the materials which it had derived from its own investigations. That quite distinctly appears from the grounds of the court's decision – that Ferco was, for reasons for which it was not responsible, unable 'to state its view'. Those reasons could only have been its lack of prior access to the sub-sale award and the evidence which underlay it. I conclude that it was to give Ferco's lawyer an opportunity to refute this material that the Beijing court ordered a 'resumed' arbitration.

[6] "It is to be observed that when CIETAC issued a new set of rules effective from 1 October 1995 it expanded Art. 26, renumbered as Art. 38, to introduce a provision requiring that where the tribunal carried out its own investigations and collected evidence on its own initiative it should 'timely inform the parties to be present at the place where the arbitration deems it necessary'. By Art. 40, where the tribunal consults an expert or appraiser, his report is to be copied to the parties 'so that they may have the opportunity to give their opinions thereon'.

[7] "The concept of a resumed hearing in Chinese law is said by Minmetals' solicitor, Yvonne Percival, on the information and advice of its Chinese lawyer and of the vice-chairman of CIETAC, to have been introduced as part of a concerted effort to modernise Chinese arbitration law and is specifically based on the United Nations Commission on International Trade Law (UNCITRAL) Model Law, of which Art. 34(4) provides:

> 'The court, when asked to set aside an award, may, where appropriate and so requested by a party, suspend the setting aside proceedings for a

> period of time determined by it in order to give the arbitral tribunal an opportunity to resume the arbitral proceedings or to take such other action as in the arbitral tribunal's opinion will eliminate the grounds for setting aside.'

This is clearly an extremely useful and flexible procedural device which may avoid the wholesale setting aside of an award following a procedural defect in the conduct of an arbitration.

[8] "The position, therefore, following the court's order for a resumed arbitration, was therefore that it was open to Ferco's counsel to ask to see the sub-sale award and the evidence on which it was based and then to make further submissions and indeed, if so advised, to adduce further evidence to persuade the tribunal that it should not base the recoverable loss on the liability of Minmetals to China Resources. If Ferco had any case to present, that was it.

[9] "However, Mr. Jiang, Ferco's counsel, apart from raising a number of procedural and jurisdictional issues relating to the resumed arbitration apparently proceeded on the assumption that, by reason of the court's order, he could ignore the arbitrator's reliance on the sub-sale award and evidence and make submissions as if such reliance was no longer open to the arbitrators. That, however, was neither the effect nor purpose of the order for a resumed hearing.

[10] "In the event, when the arbitrators came to prepare their second award, they had before them the further submissions by Mr. Jiang which did not specifically address or challenge the underlying evidence upon which their first award was based. In confirming their first award they took the view that nothing that Mr. Jiang had submitted displaced their earlier factual conclusion. In these circumstances, I have no doubt whatever that Ferco had not been unable to present its case. On the contrary, it had been given every opportunity to do so. What had gone wrong was that its counsel had simply failed to take that opportunity.

[11] "Mr. Swainston, on behalf of Ferco, submitted that there was in effect a continuing inability to present its case because the arbitrators continued to fail to disclose the sub-sale award and the underlying evidence prior to making their second award. That submission has to be considered against the facts that Ferco's counsel not only refused to inform the tribunal of why the application had been made to the court to revoke their first award but failed to ask them for a copy of the sub-sale award so that he could advance a case as to why it should be the factual foundation for the arbitrator's quantification of Minmetals' loss.

[12] "In my judgment, the inability to present a case to arbitrators within Sect. 103(2)(c) contemplates at least that the enforcee has been prevented from presenting his case by matters outside his control. This will normally cover the case where the procedure adopted has been operated in a manner contrary to the rules of natural justice. Where, however, the enforcee has, due to matters within his control, not provided himself with the means of taking advantage of an opportunity given to him to present his case, he does not in my judgment bring himself within that exception to enforcement under the Convention. In the present case that is what has happened. I therefore reject the submissions of Ferco that it was unable to present its case."

II. THE SECTION 103(2)(e) ISSUE

[13] "It is submitted that the awards were arrived at by an arbitral procedure not in accordance with the agreement of the parties. By the arbitration clause the parties agreed to the CIETAC Rules. In addition to Art. 53, which I have already set out, those Rules provided:

> *Article 14*
> 'The Claimant shall satisfy the following requirements when submitting his Application for Arbitration: (i) an Application for Arbitration in writing shall be submitted and the following shall be specified in the Application for Arbitration (d) the Claimant's claim and the facts and evidence on which his claim is based[....]'
>
> *Article 20*
> 'When submitting the Application for Arbitration relevant documentary evidence and other documents, apart from supplying a copy of the secretariat of the Arbitration Commission, the party/parties shall provide duplicate copies in the same number as the number of other party/parties and the arbitrators composing the arbitration tribunal.'

It is argued that the tribunal acted in breach of these Rules, as well as of Art. 53.

[14] "There is, in my judgment, no basis for that submission with regard to Arts. 14 and 20 in relation to either arbitration award. Both Articles are concerned with the procedure to be adopted by the parties as distinct from that to be adopted by the tribunal. Art. 53, however, is clearly and expressly applicable to the conduct of the arbitrators in making their award. I am in no doubt that, as regards the first award, they did not act in accordance with

'international practices and the principle of fairness and reasonableness'. Their omission to give Ferco a prior opportunity to deal with the sub-sale award was not in compliance with these requirements. However, the position following the Beijing court's order for a resumed hearing was that the evidence relied on by the arbitrators was open to challenge by means of a request for sight of the award and of the evidence on which it was based. As I have held, no such challenge was advanced.

[15] "Art. 45 of the CIETAC Rules provides as follows:

> 'A party knows or should have known that any provision or requirement of these Rules has not been complied with and yet proceeds with the arbitration proceedings without explicitly raising in writing his objection to non-compliance in a timely manner shall be deemed to have waived his right to object.'

[16] "There can be no doubt that Ferco's representatives were fully aware of the arbitrators' failure to act in accordance with the rules when they embarked upon their application to the court to revoke the award and when they participated in the resumed hearing. However, they proceeded without explicitly raising with the arbitrators their objection as to such non-compliance. By Art. 45 they therefore waived their right to object to the continuing omission of the arbitrators to disclose the award. Indeed, it is difficult to envisage a more glaringly obvious waiver of procedural irregularity than that found in this case. I therefore accept the submission on behalf of Minmetals that it is no longer open to Ferco to rely on non-compliance with the rules for the purposes of resisting enforcement of the award.

[17] "I would only add that the concept of express or implied waiver of procedural objection is well established in the context of international arbitration law. It is now reflected in Sect. 73 of the 1996 Act."[4]

---

4. Sect. 73(1) of the Arbitration Act 1996 reads:

> "(1) If a party to arbitral proceedings takes part, or continues to take part, in the proceedings without making, either forthwith or within such time as is allowed by the arbitration agreement or the tribunal or by any provision of this Part, any objection –
> (a) that the tribunal lacks substantive jurisdiction,
> (b) that the proceedings have been improperly conducted,
> (c) that there has been a failure to comply with the arbitration agreement or with any provision of this Part, or
> (d) that there has been any other irregularity affecting the tribunal or the proceedings,
> he may not raise that objection later, before the tribunal or the court, unless he shows that, at the time he took part or continued to take part in the proceedings, he did not know and could not with reasonable diligence have discovered the grounds for the objection."

III. THE PUBLIC POLICY ISSUE

[18] "It is accepted that, if Ferco is to rely on this exception, it must establish that the awards now sought to be enforced were arrived at by means which were contrary to the requirements of substantial justice contained in English law as explained in *Adams v. Cape Industries plc* [1991] 1 All ER 929, [1990] Ch 433. Mr. Swainston relied on that decision as exemplifying English public policy as to the enforcement of foreign judgments. He referred in particular to the statement of principle:

> 'The notion of substantial justice must be governed in a particular case by the nature of the proceedings under consideration. The purpose of an in personam monetary judgment is that the power of the state through the process of execution will take the defendant's assets in payment of the judgment. In cases of debt and in many cases of contract the amount due will have been fixed by the acts of the parties and in such cases a default judgment will not be defective for want of judicial assessment. When the claim is for unliquidated damages for a tortious wrong, such as personal injury, both our system and the federal system of the United States require, if there is no agreement between the parties, judicial assessment. That means that the extent of the defendant's obligation is to be assessed objectively by the independent judge upon proof by the plaintiff of the relevant facts. Our notions of substantial justice include, in our judgment, the requirement that in such a case the amount of compensation should not be fixed subjectively by or on behalf of the plaintiff.' (See [1991] 1 All ER 929 at 1049-1050, [1990] Ch 433 at 566-567.)

[19] "It was then argued that a similar approach should apply in this case where there had been a continuing failure to provide Ferco with the evidence on which the arbitrators relied. That, it was submitted, was a continuing breach of natural justice and therefore the awards were made in circumstances contrary to the requirements of substantial justice in English law. Mr. Swainston emphasised that in *Adams v. Cape Industries plc* [1991] 1 All ER 929 at 1053, [1990] Ch 433 at 570-571, as is clear from the judgment, the defendants could have attended the plaintiff's default judgment application and thereby informed themselves of the usual means of quantification of damages which was adopted by the American judge, and could have taken steps to challenge such damages by applying to set aside the judgment, but failed to do so, yet the English court still held enforcement of the default judgment to be contrary to public policy.

[20] "*Adams v. Cape Industries plc* involved quite exceptional facts. It is clear that the Court of Appeal regarded it as relevant to the public policy issue to consider both the availability of remedial steps in the local jurisdiction and the reasonableness of the defendant's conduct in omitting to take them. This is clear from the following passage:

> 'Since the ultimate question is whether there has been proof of substantial injustice caused by the proceedings, it would, in our opinion, be unrealistic in fact and incorrect in principle to ignore entirely the possibility of the correction of error within the procedure of a foreign court which itself provides fair procedural rules and a fair opportunity for remedy. The court must, in our judgment, have regard to the availability of a remedy in deciding whether in the circumstances of any particular case substantial injustice has been proved. However, the relevance of the existence of the remedy and the weight to be attached to it must depend upon factors which include the nature of the procedural defect itself, the point in the proceedings at which it occurred and the knowledge and means of knowledge of the defendants of the defect and the reasonableness in the circumstances of requiring or expecting that they made use of the remedy in all the particular circumstances.' (See [1991] 1 All ER 929 at 1052-1053, [1990] Ch 433 at 570.)

[21] "Amongst the considerations which, as appears from the passages of the judgment, weighed in favour of the court's conclusion that there had been substantial injustice was the lack of knowledge by the defendants of facts which could have led them to anticipate injustice or which might suggest to them that injustice had occurred in the course of the default hearing (see [1991] 1 All ER 929 at 1053-1054, [1990] Ch 433 at 571). That lack of knowledge made their omission to avail themselves of local remedies not unreasonable.

[22] "Although that case was concerned with public policy in relation to the enforcement of foreign judgments and not of foreign arbitration awards, it illustrates the principle that, in the sphere of enforcement, considerations of public policy involve investigation not only of the core procedural defect relied upon by way of objection to enforcement but of all those other surrounding circumstances which are material to the English court's decision whether, as a matter of policy, enforcement should be refused. Such circumstances may give rise to policy considerations which so strongly favour enforcement as to outweigh policy considerations to the contrary.

[23] "An example in the rather different environment of the public policy against enforcement of arbitration awards in respect of contracts contra bonos mores is to be found in the recent decision of this court in *Westacre Invest-*

ments Inc. v. Jugoimport-SPDR Holding Co. Ltd. [1998] 4 All ER 570, [1998] 3 WLR 770.[5] In that case the issue was whether the enforcement of a New York Convention award should be refused on the grounds of public policy in a case where it was alleged that the commission contract containing the arbitration agreement envisaged the corrupt purchase of personal influence from Kuwait government officials but where the issue had already been raised in an International Chamber of Commerce arbitration and it had been determined that the contract was not illegal under its proper law. In concluding that the award should be enforced in the face of the allegation of illegality it was necessary to have regard not only to the public policy of discouraging international commercial corruption, but to the countervailing policy of giving effect as far as possible to the finality of international arbitration awards and to discouraging the relitigation of issues already determined by the arbitrators by adducing evidence not shown to have been unavailable before the arbitrators.

[24] "In the present case, the public policy issue arises in the context of a New York Convention award made pursuant to a Chinese arbitration clause by the agreed Chinese arbitral authority. In international commerce a party who contracts into an agreement to arbitrate in a foreign jurisdiction is bound not only by the local arbitration procedure but also by the supervisory jurisdiction of the courts of the seat of the arbitration. If the award is defective or the arbitration is defectively conducted the party who complains of the defect must in the first instance pursue such remedies as exist under that supervisory jurisdiction. That is because by his agreement to the place in question as the seat of the arbitration he has agreed not only to refer all disputes to arbitration but that the conduct of the arbitration should be subject to that particular supervisory jurisdiction. Adherence to that part of the agreement must, in my judgment, be a cardinal policy consideration by an English court considering enforcement of a foreign award.

[25] "In a case where a remedy for an alleged defect is applied for from the supervisory court, but is refused, leaving a final award undisturbed, it will therefore normally be a very strong policy consideration before the English courts that it has been conclusively determined by the courts of the agreed supervisory jurisdiction that the award should stand. Just as great weight must be attached to the policy of sustaining the finality of international awards, so also must great weight be attached to the policy of sustaining the finality of the determination of properly referred procedural issues by the courts of the supervisory jurisdiction. I use the word 'normally' because there may be exceptional cases where the powers of the supervisory court are so limited that

5. Reported in Yearbook XXIII (1998) pp. 836-879 (UK no. 51). See Court of Appeal's decision of 19 May 1999 reported in this Yearbook as UK no. 54, pp. 753-776.

they cannot intervene even where there has been an obvious and serious disregard for basic principles of justice by the arbitrators or where for unjust reasons, such as corruption, they decline to do so. However, outside such exceptional cases, any suggestion that under the guise of allegations of substantial injustice procedural defects in the conduct of an arbitration which have already been considered by the supervisory court should be reinvestigated by the English courts on an enforcement application is to be most strongly deprecated.

[26] "In summary, therefore, in a case where an enforcee alleges that a New York Convention award should not be enforced on the grounds that such enforcement would lead to substantial injustice and therefore be contrary to English public policy the following must normally be included amongst the relevant considerations: (i) the nature of the procedural injustice; (ii) whether the enforcee has invoked the supervisory jurisdiction of the seat of the arbitration; (iii) whether a remedy was available under that jurisdiction; (iv) whether the courts of that jurisdiction have conclusively determined the enforcee's complaint in favour of upholding the award; and (v) if the enforcee has failed to invoke that remedial jurisdiction, for what reason, and in particular whether he was acting unreasonably in failing to do so.

[27] "In the present case, following the initial award and the first order of the Beijing court, Ferco's counsel did not in the course of the resumed hearing take the opportunity to inform the tribunal of the reasons for the hearing or to obtain the sub-sale award or, having done so, to challenge its evidential basis or the arbitrators' reliance on it. He appears to have regarded the order for a resumed arbitration as made without jurisdiction and have failed to understand its purpose. I am not persuaded that in so doing he was acting reasonably. That the sub-sale award remained undisclosed was due to his failure to take advantage of the remedy provided by the supervisory court. Further, as I have held, under Art. 45 of the CIETAC Rules there was a contractual waiver of the right to object to the defects.

[28] "In these circumstances the application to the Beijing court to revoke the second award appears to have been bound to fail. It may be that the court was left by the CIETAC minute of the resumed hearing with the impression that Mr. Jiang had made little in the way of submission, but it is clear beyond doubt that it must have been aware from the contents of the second award that he had never sought to obtain the sub-sale award or to raise with the arbitrators the one objection to the first award on the basis of which the court had ordered the resumed hearing.

[29] "In these circumstances, does the enforcement of these awards lead to substantial injustice? In my view, it does not. The unreasonable conduct of Ferco in the manner of its subsequent conduct of the arbitration which has,

in effect, deprived it of its local remedies has left it in exactly the same position in substance as if it had wholly ignored the availability of such remedies. Moreover, although the arbitrators acted wrongly in failing to disclose the sub-sale award, they had heard and investigated the evidence in the sub-sale arbitration and had reached their conclusions on the issue of loss to the sub-purchasers of the steel. They then transposed their conclusions on that evidence to the issue of Minmetals' recoverable losses in the main arbitration. Because of the way in which Ferco has conducted itself in relation to that arbitration it is not in the position to invite the inference that even if the award had been disclosed to it the arbitrators would probably have been persuaded to arrive at a conclusion of fact more favourable to Ferco. The highest it can be put is that they might have done so.

[30] "In the circumstances, even if one takes account of a continuing feature of injustice in the failure to disclose the sub-sale award prior to the second award and of the possibility that the arbitrators would have arrived at a conclusion more favourable to Ferco if disclosure had been made, the countervailing policy considerations in favour of enforcement of the awards are, in my judgment, so strong that they displace the policy consideration of non-enforcement in the face of procedural defects going to a breach of natural justice.

[31] "In the course of argument Mr. Swainston referred me to a decision of the Hong Kong Court of Appeal in *Apex Tech Investment Ltd. v. Chuang's Development (China) Ltd.* [1996] 2 HKC 293, where, following the hearing, CIETAC arbitrators had investigated the facts and produced an award based on their findings without first informing the parties of the results of their investigation. The hearing before the Court of Appeal proceeded on the basis that the facts were within the New York Convention exception of inability to present the enforcee's case and the only question was whether the judge had properly exercised his discretion in ordering enforcement on the basis that disclosure of the investigation would not have affected the ultimate result. The judgment was reversed on the ground that on the facts the result might have been affected. That authority is, however, of no direct assistance on the issues which I have had to consider. I have not decided to uphold enforcement on the basis of a residual discretion but on the basis that Ferco have failed to bring themselves within any of the Sect. 103 exceptions to enforcement. Had I concluded that Ferco had brought themselves within any of the exceptions to enforcement upon which they relied I would not have thought it appropriate in this case to exercise my discretion in favour of enforcement."

IV. CONCLUSION

[32] "In the event the order of Cresswell J giving leave to enforce the awards as a judgment will be upheld.

[33] "There is, however, an outstanding point on which the parties may wish to address further argument. Ferco has applied to the Beijing court for a retrial of its application for revocation of the second award. That application has yet to be heard. Although the prospects of success appear to be distinctly slender it is not impossible that such application will succeed and that, if it does, that the second award will be revoked. If that were to happen and the award had already been satisfied by Ferco, Minmetals would be under a duty to reimburse the amount paid. In these circumstances, in view of the fact that the application for retrial does not fall within Sect. 103(5) of the Act, the question arises whether there should be a stay of execution pending the decision on the retrial application. This matter should be dealt with when this judgment is formally pronounced."

54. Court of Appeal (Civil Division), 12 May 1999

Parties:	Plaintiff/respondent: Westacre Investments, Inc. (Panama) Defendant/appellant: Jugoimport - SDPR Holding (F.R. Yugoslavia)[1]
Published in:	No publication information available
Articles:	V(2)(*b*)
Subject matters:	- bribery - finality versus illegality - no review on the merits
Commentary Cases:	¶ 524 (bribery)

Facts

The facts of this case are also reported in Yearbook XXIII (1998) pp. 836-839. Westacre Investments, Inc. (Westacre) entered into an agreement dated 12 April 1988 with Udruzena Beogradska Banka (the Bank) and the Federal Directorate of Supply and Procurement of the Socialist Federal Republic of Yugoslavia (the Directorate) whereby the Directorate appointed Westacre its consultant for the sale of military equipment in Kuwait. Westacre was to receive a substantial percentage of the value of the contracts entered into by the Directorate. The Bank guaranteed the payment of fees due to Westacre under the agreement.

In July 1989, the Directorate, after it had secured a contract with the Kuwaiti Ministry of Defence dated 29 May 1989 for US$ 500,546,000 and UK£ 440,329, repudiated the Agreement, alleging it was in violation of mandatory law of Kuwait as set out in a Ministry of Defence Circular (MOD Circular). The MOD Circular prohibited the use of agents or intermediaries in the making of contracts with the Kuwait Ministry of Defence.

Westacre commenced ICC arbitration in Geneva under the arbitration clause in the contract. In the ensuing award, the arbitrators, applying Swiss law as provided in the Agreement, awarded Westacre approximately US$ 50,000,000

1. In the decision of the High Court, 19 December 1997 (UK no. 51) reported in Yearbook XXIII (pp. 836-869), the name of the defendant is spelled Judoimport-SDPR Holding.

plus interest. The arbitrators held that there was no violation of bona mores and thus the consultancy agreement was valid. Furthermore, it had not been established that the MOD Circular was part of the mandatory law of Kuwait, as distinct from a term of the M-84 tanks contract, or that it belonged to international public policy. They also held that the defendants had failed to establish that the consultancy agreement was a nullity on the grounds that the parties to it had intended, when they made the agreement, to procure a contract with the Kuwaiti Government by illicit means such as bribery. Accordingly, the consultancy agreement did not violate international public policy. In the arbitral tribunal's view, lobbying by private enterprises to obtain public contracts was not as such an illegal activity and contracts to carry out such activities were not illegal.

The Directorate and the Bank appealed against the award to the Swiss Federal Tribunal. By order dated 6 January the Swiss Federal Court rejected the appeal (reported in Yearbook XXI (1996) pp. 172-180)) holding, inter alia, that the arbitral tribunal had not violated public policy in finding the consultancy agreement to be in conformity with the law.

On 15 August 1995, Westacre obtained an ex parte order in the United Kingdom from Buxton, J granting leave to enforce the award. The Directorate and the Bank sought to set aside that order. On 19 April 1996, Waller, J ordered that the proceedings to enforce the award should be continued as if begun by writ and that provision be made for the enforcement question to be fully pleaded.

On 23 April 1996, Westacre commenced proceedings by writ whereby they brought an action on the award itself, as distinct from applying for leave to enforce it. At that time the Federal Directorate of Supply and Procurement of the Federal Republic of Yugoslavia (successor to the above-mentioned Directorate) and Beogradska Banka DD (successor to the above-mentioned Bank) were joined in the proceedings as defendants. The defendant's application was supported by an affidavit sworn by legal counsel to the Directorate, Miodrag Milosavljevic (M.M.). On 21 March 1997, Tuckey, J ordered that there should be a trial of a preliminary issue:

> "That on the basis that the facts ... in the Affidavit of M.M. are correct and in light of the award dated 28 February 1994 and the decision of the Swiss Court dated 30 December 1994 and the provisions of Swiss law and the legal status of the defendants herein the defendants' pleaded case discloses no defence to enforcement of the Award."

The effect of the preliminary issue was that both the primary facts and the inferences of fact drawn by M.M. in the affidavit were assumed to be proved.

The High Court, per Colman, J concluded that on the facts of the case, the public policy of sustaining international arbitration awards outweighs the public policy of discouraging international commercial corruption. This decision is reported in Yearbook XXIII (1998) pp. 836-879.

The present successors, Jugoimport – SDPR Holding (F.R. Yugoslavia) and Beogradska Banka DD appealed this decision. Mantell, LJ and Sir David Hirst formed the majority and dismissed the appeal, finding that the arbitrator's finding of fact in the bribery issue could not be challenged in the enforcement proceedings. Waller, LJ whose summary of the facts and reasoning is reproduced first below, dissented, opining that the public policy against enforcing a corrupt bargain of the nature of the agreement should prevail and that the appellants were entitled to prove the facts set out in the affidavit.

Excerpt

Dissenting Opinion of Lord Justice Waller

I. THE MIODRAG MILOSAVLJEVIC AFFIDAVIT

[1] "On 15 August 1995 Buxton J (as he then was) granted an ex parte order that Westacre be at liberty to enforce the Award in the United Kingdom. That led to the defendants serving on Westacre a summons dated 15 November 1995 to set that order aside. That application was ultimately supported by an affidavit sworn by Miodrag Milosavljevic [(M.M.)] dated 13 December 1995. The affidavit was of considerable length but the judge's summary of it is as follows: –

[2] "'(i) The consultancy agreement was entered into in the wider context of the negotiation between Yugoslavia and Kuwait of a so-called debt-swapping agreement or memorandum of understanding under which the outstanding debts of Yugoslavia to Kuwait would be reduced by the supply of goods and services to Kuwait. In the course of the negotiation of that agreement the Secretary General of the Council of Ministers of Kuwait, Mr. Al-Otaibi, attended apparently in his private capacity a meeting in Yugoslavia with the Yugoslav Minister of Finance and the then General Manager of the old Directorate. In the course of a visit to Kuwait by an official Yugoslav delegation in early March 1988 there was agreement in principle to a debt-swapping arrangement but it was made clear by certain high-placed Kuwaiti officials that no contracts for

military equipment would be placed unless a consultancy agreement with a nominated consultant was first entered into.

[3] "'(ii) The plaintiffs, as the old Directorate's exclusive consultant, were to receive a commission of 15 per cent of the value of all contracts entered into during the term of the agreement (three years renewable) for military products and for related training services (whether actually provided or not) and a commission of 20 per cent on all contracts for the supply of spare parts for 20 years from the date of the first supply of military equipment.

[4] "'(iii) [In] the affidavit M.M. stated:

"Memorandum of Understanding and the consultancy contract with Westacre formed part of a scheme engineered by Mr. Al-Otaibi and his associates by which he was able to ensure (a) that Yugoslav military equipment would be chosen in preference to that of other suppliers; and (b) that Westacre, and those who stood behind it, would receive substantial sums."

[5] "'(iv) In the course of 1989, while negotiations were taking place in respect of the supply of the M-84 tanks, Yugoslav negotiators encountered Mr. Al-Otaibi who was passing on information obtained from inside Kuwaiti Ministry of Defence and giving advice generally, including advice to ignore the prohibition of consultants in relation to armaments contracts in Kuwait.

[6] "'(v) Following the signature of the M-84 contract on 29 May 1989, under which the agreed price for 214 tanks was over US$ 500 million and £ 11,440,329.29, there were meetings in Cairo between General Nikodin Jovanavic, then general manager of the old Directorate, and Mr. Al-Otaibi relating to the expressed concern of the Yugoslavs as to the terms of the armaments contract under which in accordance with Kuwait decree No. 4A/88 the old Directorate warranted that it had not promised any person at any place "any commissions, doles, expenses, disbursements, bonuses (or) gifts" and that prices had been fixed "exclusive of any hidden additions to meet commissions of agents or expenses" and undertook to cancel any such pre-existing arrangements on pain of very substantial monetary penalties. A document known as the MOD-Circular was also provided to the old Directorate prior to the conclusion of the M-84 contract. It prohibited the use of agents or intermediaries in the making of contracts with the Kuwait Ministry of Defence. The MOD-Circular provided:

"Since it is imperative that the deals which the Ministry of Defence may conclude with you regarding: arms, ammunition and spare parts, should be accorded the utmost secrecy, it is requested that any such future deals be concluded directly between the Ministry of Defence and your goodselves without the interference of any agent or intermediary. The Ministry insists on this as an essential provision of the contract, the breach of which will result in considering you to have committed a serious breach of the contract, in addition to all legal consequences including the annulment of the contract. The Ministry also emphasise that it does not acknowledge any commission you may pay to an agent or intermediary and that it will deduct any such commission from the price apart from considering such an action as a breach of the aforesaid essential provision."

At the meeting in Cairo Mr. Al-Otaibi expressed concern at the old Directorate's having raised questions about these provisions and explained that his "group" had succeeded in procuring the armaments contract against the opposition and were very powerful.

[7] "'(vi) Subsequently, by its letter of 5 July 1989 the old Directorate cancelled the consultancy agreement without having paid the consultancy fees attributable to the armaments contract.

[8] "'(vii) In describing the arbitration M.M. refers [] to the issue as to who owned the plaintiff company. One of the two witnesses who claimed to be the controllers and only shareholders, Mr. Al-Wazzan, was the son-in-law of Mr. Al-Otaibi. He expresses the opinion that "Westacre was a company behind which Mr. Al-Otaibi and his associates sheltered in order to maintain their anonymity". [He later] states:

"In my respectful submission, it was obvious, both from my own researches and from the evidence given at the arbitration, that the contract with Westacre was a contract to buy influence in government circles in Kuwait. It must, in my respectful submission, have been contemplated that the large commission to be earned by Westacre would be applied to 'reward' those who influenced or made the decision to buy tanks and other military equipment from Yugoslavia. Of course, quite how it was applied was not a concern of the old Directorate; but in my respectful submission, it must have been contemplated by those who made the contract that promises of 'largesse' would be made to individuals within the Kuwaiti Government who had power to influence the decision from whom to buy military equipment."

[9] "'(viii) [M.M. further] states:

> "Not every agency or consultancy agreement to promote the sales of military equipment is of this character. Sometimes all that the consultant is required to do is to put the supplier of military equipment into contact with the relevant individuals in government who have the job of determining which weapons etc., a particular state will buy. Sometimes the consultant will undertake lobbying of government officials, or will assist with arranging demonstrations. But the rate of commission in this case, 15%-20%, is, in my experience, unusually high. I draw the inference that it must have been appreciated by those involved in the making of the contract that some of the money at least would be applied to 'illegitimate' purposes."'

[10] ".... Mr. Gaisman [counsel for defendant/appellant] in summary submits very much as his clients did to the Swiss Federal Court that if the facts set out in M.M.'s affidavit are correct, they establish (perhaps not something fully emphasised by the judge's summary)

(i) that the Agreement was a contract to pay Mr. Al-Otaibi a bribe through a vehicle, Westacre, and intended to be such by one or both parties to the Agreement from the outset; and
(ii) that the evidence put forward by Westacre at the arbitration portraying Mr. Al-Wazzam and Mr. Al-Ghanim as playing central and important roles was false and put forward deliberately to conceal Mr. Al-Otaibi's role."

II. THE PRELIMINARY ISSUE

[11] "Mr. Hollander's [counsel for the plaintiff/respondent] submission, again in summary, is that this is a totally different stance from that taken before the arbitration tribunal; that there are matters asserted contrary to findings by the arbitrators; that there is nothing now produced which could not have been produced to the arbitrators and no reason why if this was or is the Directorate's case it should not have been made at the arbitration.
[12] "It was in the context of M.M.'s affidavit that on 19 April 1996, when sitting in the Commercial Court, I gave directions for pleadings and granted a stay of execution in the meanwhile. On 23 April 1996 Westacre commenced a second action on the Award and on 8 May 1996 served points of claim in accordance with my directions. Nothing turns on the fact that there are two

actions. Defences were served in both actions raising the facts set out in the affidavit of Miodrag Milosavljevic.

[13] "It was in that context that on 11 March 1997 Tuckey J (as he then was) ordered, by consent, that the following preliminary questions be tried: –

> 'That on the basis that the facts set out in paragraphs 5-82 of the affidavit of Miodrag Milosavljevic sworn herein on 13 December 1995 are correct and in the light of the award dated 28 February 1994 (The Award) and the decision of the Swiss Court dated 30 December 1994 and the provisions of Swiss law and the legal status of the defendants herein the defendants pleaded case discloses no defence to enforcement of the award.'

[14] "The judge in his judgment described the effect of the preliminary issue in the following terms: –

> 'The effect of that preliminary issue is that both the primary facts and the inferences of fact drawn by M.M. in that affidavit are to be assumed to be proved. Accordingly, the primary issue is essentially whether, if both the plaintiffs and the old Directorate intended that in order to obtain the armaments contract the plaintiffs should exercise personal influence over the officials of the government of Kuwait and contemplated that for that purpose such officials would be bribed, the enforcement of the award would be contrary to English public policy. The defendants argue that at Common Law public policy would be a good defence to an action on the award and that in any event the order for enforcement of the award should be set aside by reason of Sect. 5(3) of the Arbitration Act 1975 which provides:
>
> "Enforcement of a Convention award may also be refused if the award is in respect of a matter which is not capable of settlement by arbitration, or if it would be contrary to public policy to enforce the award."'

[15] "One of the matters which has given the court and counsel some cause for concern is the way in which the preliminary issue has been framed. Mr. Gaisman submits that one must assume in deciding the preliminary issue that his clients have established the correctness of the affidavit of M.M. He supports the way the judge framed the question posed in the passage just quoted, which appears to assume that the facts have been established. When pressed on the subject Mr. Veeder QC [counsel for Westacre] suggested that if the judge's formulation was to be interpreted as an acceptance that the facts were true

before considering whether to enforce the award, then it was not a proper formulation. He said that if he was forced to accept, or in effect admit for the preliminary issue purposes that the contract was one for bribes, he really had no argument that the award should be enforced....

[16] "I have not found the interpretation of the wording of the preliminary issue easy, but it would not be to the advantage of either party to allow the wording to dictate the answer to what is on any view a difficult problem. Mr. Gaisman accepted that at any full trial there would be two questions: should the appellants be allowed now to assert the facts as set out in M.M.'s affidavit in the light of the fact that the bribery issue was an issue before the arbitrators? If so, on the assumption that those facts are correct, should the English court enforce the award? In my view, whatever the proper interpretation of the wording of the preliminary issue the court ought to address those issues.

[17] "As already indicated, as I understand Mr. Veeder's position, he would actually accept that if the appellants are entitled to establish the facts they now allege, and if one assumes those facts to be correct, then he would accept that enforcement of the award should be refused. That is because (a) he accepts the correctness of the decision in this court in *Soleimany v. Soleimany* [1998] 3 W.L.R. 811[2] and indeed the judge's view that 'where public policy is involved, the interposition of an arbitration award does not isolate the successful party's claim from the illegality that gave rise to it' (823H); (b) because he accepts that a contract to pay a bribe, and thus an award that enforces a contract to pay a bribe would be unenforceable under English law as contrary to public policy; and (c) because he accepts that the English court may refuse to enforce an award under the New York Convention 'if it would be contrary to public policy to enforce the award' (Sect. 5(3) of the Arbitration Act 1975).

[18] "The key issue accordingly is whether the appellants should, in these enforcement proceedings, be entitled to prove the facts as set out in the affidavit of M.M. It is this issue which the judge took first and it is this issue which the parties argued first. I however think it would be more satisfactory to deal with the two other issues which arise on the appeal before turning to the key issue, and I do so because it seems to me that logically if on the first of those issues 'the Lemenda point', the appellants are right in submitting that the award would be unenforceable without going beyond the facts that appear in the award and its reasons, then what is undoubtedly the more difficult point would not arise, and because in relation to the second of those issues 'the fraud amendment point' it seems to me there is some interaction with what I am describing as the key issue."

---

2. Reported in this Yearbook, pp. 329-342.

III. THE *LEMENDA* POINT

[19] "For this point the appellants rely on a decision of Phillips J in *Lemenda Trading Co. Ltd. v. African Middle East Petroleum Co. Ltd.* [1988] 1 Q.B. 448. It is important as a starting point to see what that case decided. The case was concerned with a contract under which an intermediary was obliged to use personal influence so as to obtain a contract in Qatar. The judge refused to enforce that contract on the grounds that it was contrary to English public policy founded on general principles of morality, and because it contravened a similar public policy in the country of performance. He held: –

> 'The principles underlying the public policy in the present case are essentially principles of morality of general application. The practice of exacting payment for the use of personal influence, particularly where the person to be influenced is likely to be unaware of the pecuniary motive in involved, is unattractive whatever the context. Yet it is questionable whether the moral principles involved are so weighty as to lead an English court to refuse to enforce an agreement regardless of the country of performance and regardless of the attitude of that country to such a practice. The later English decisions were influenced, at least in part, by the effect of the practice in question upon good government in England. It is at this stage that, in my judgment, it becomes relevant to consider the law of Qatar. The significant fact in *Kaufman v. Gerson* was that the contractual adventure was not contrary to French law and the contract was valid and enforceable in France. In the present case Qatar, the country in which the agreement was to be performed and with which, in my view, the agreement had the closest connection, has the same public policy as that which prevails in England. Because of that policy, the courts of Qatar would not enforce the agreement.
>
> In my judgment, the English courts should not enforce an English law contract which falls to be performed abroad where: (i) it relates to an adventure which is contrary to a head of English public policy which is founded on general principles of morality, and (ii) the same public policy applies to the country of performance so that the agreement would not be enforceable under the laws of that country.'

[20] "In the instant case if the appellants were not to be allowed to go behind the award and were not to be allowed to establish facts inconsistent with the findings of the majority arbitrators, they assert that in any event the arbitrators' findings amounted to holding that the agreement was a contract for the

purchase of personal influence similar in almost every detail to the contract being considered by Phillips J in *Lemenda*.

[21] "It was and is however accepted that it is not solely on the findings of the arbitrators that the appellants can rely. They accept that it was an important aspect of Phillips J's finding that the English court should not enforce the contract in *Lemenda* that the contract was also contrary to the public policy of the place of performance and its proper law, in that case Qatar. They accept that in the instant case there was no finding on Kuwait public policy by the arbitrators because the point was not raised by the appellants at the arbitration. They seek to excuse not raising the point at the arbitration on the basis that there would have been no point in doing so because under the proper law of the agreement and under the curial law of the arbitration, Swiss law (a) a contract for the purchase of personal influence short of bribery would not be contrary to the public policy of Switzerland; and (b) because it would not be contrary to public policy in Switzerland to enforce a contract that involved the commission of acts contrary to the public policy of Kuwait or any other foreign and friendly state as opposed to being 'illegal' by the law of that state.

[22] "The appellants accordingly sought to establish at the hearing before Colman J by expert evidence (a) that by the law of Kuwait the agreement involved a performance that was contrary to the public policy of that country; and (b) to make good their point that there was no purpose in calling that evidence during the arbitration, that as a matter of Swiss law (the proper law of the agreement and the curial law of the arbitration) the agreement was not contrary to public policy, and would have been enforced despite the public policy of Kuwait.

[23] "The appellants' argument is then that apart from the necessity to call the evidence on Kuwait law the case is on all fours with *Soleimany* where because the illegality of the agreement being enforced by the arbitration award was clear on the face of the award this court held that the English court should not enforce the award.

[24] "In *Soleimany v. Soleimany* the court was concerned with an award made by the Beth Din under Jewish law, which on its face purported to enforce an illicit enterprise for the smuggling of carpets out of Iran. This court took the view as previously indicated that the interposition of an arbitration award did not isolate the successful party's claim from the illegality that gave rise to it. It took the view that at the enforcement stage it was the function of the court to see that its executive power was not abused, and it refused to enforce the award.

[25] "When the judge ruled on this aspect of the case, *Soleimany* had not been decided by the Court of Appeal. However, his reasoning received, save in one

respect of relevance in the key issue to which I have yet to turn, broad approval. It is however right to stress that there are clear distinctions between the facts and the award in this case, and the facts and the award being considered in *Soleimany*. It was plain on the face of the award in *Soleimany* that the award was enforcing an enterprise unlawful by the place of performance. So far as the award in this case is concerned the reasons expressly state that performance would not be illegal by the laws of Kuwait, and there is nothing in the reasons to suggest that public policy in Kuwait would be offended by performance of the same. Furthermore there is every suggestion that Swiss public policy has been considered at least on the bribery issue, and accordingly the English court looking at the award and its reasons would contemplate, as indeed turns out to be correct, that so far as Swiss law is concerned the agreement is not either illegal by that law or considered contrary to Swiss public policy.

[26] "These distinctions are apparent from the judge's consideration of the *Lemenda* point. His ruling on that point can I think be summarised as follows:

1. He thought that it was difficult to see why outside the field of such universally condemned activities such as terrorism, drug trafficking, prostitution, paedophilia, anything short of corruption or fraud in international commerce should invite the attention of English public policy in relation to contracts which are not performed within the jurisdiction of the English courts. It was, he thought, thus international comity (i.e. because performance in *Lemenda* was against public policy in the place of performance as well as in England), that led the English court not to enforce the contract;
2. He thought that in this instance the fact that the court was concerned with enforcement of the award valid by its curial law, and by the proper law of the contract, as opposed to the underlying contract, was material;
3. He thought it was material that the illegality did not appear on the face of the award, and that it was necessary to have the evidence relating to Kuwait; and
4. He further thought that if one carried out a balancing exercise as between the public policy of enforcing awards and the public policy of not enforcing illegal contracts that since the offensiveness of the illegality alleged in this instance was not at the highest level, the balance was in favour of upholding the award.

[27] "It is right to add that the judge did accept the evidence of Prof. Ballantyne called by the appellants, that the agreement in this case would have been unenforceable in Kuwait as contrary to public policy there. His understanding of that evidence was: –

> 'I did not find that Mr. Al Awadhi's evidence was supported by any source material as compelling as that of Prof. Ballantyne. In this connection, my understanding of the substance of the latter's evidence was that any commission contract under which an intermediary is paid to lobby a government official and which may involve the persuasion of that official to reach a decision with regard to any consideration other than the best interests of good government is treated as void as contrary to public policy, even if it does not involve corruption.'

He also accepted that under Swiss law a contract to lobby a government minister was not contrary to public policy. Bribery and corruption made the difference.

[28] "The respondents have put in a respondents' notice challenging those findings, but so far as Kuwait law was concerned all that Mr. Hollander's submissions came to was to emphasise that albeit an intermediary would not be able to enforce a contract for his remuneration in Kuwait, that was because that was 'high policy', and 'high policy' because of the secrecy that should have been accorded to sales to the MOD of Kuwait, and because of the increase the payment of commissions to intermediaries was likely to make to the price.

[29] "As regards Swiss law the point was not much pressed but it was pointed out that the experts on Swiss law had some difficulty in discerning any major distinction between the English court's attitude to contracts so far as public policy was concerned, but were of the view that a contract to lobby was not contrary to public policy in Switzerland.

[30] "I accept that, as Mr. Gaisman submitted, there were many similarities between the contract in *Lemenda* and the agreement as found by the Arbitrators to be the subject of this case. Mr. Hollander sought to suggest that one distinction on the findings of the arbitrators in this case related to the openness with which the 'intermediary' conducted his negotiations. In *Lemenda* Phillips J held: –

> 'Mr. Silber for the plaintiffs submitted that the nature of the agreement between the parties must have been quite apparent to Mr. Jaida. The evidence does not support that submission. Mr. Yassin did not tell Mr. Jaida that he was to be paid for his services, let alone that he was to be paid on a commission basis. He told Mr. Jaida that Mr. Abdelnour was a friend of his and urged him to support a fellow Arab. Mr. Yassin agreed, when cross-examined, that Mr. Jaida must have known of the policy of the Qatar Government and would not have wished to be involved in an activity of which the government or the minister would

disapprove. If Mr. Jaida was loyal to Q.G.P.C., and there was no suggestion that he was not, it was plainly important that he should not be aware of the nature of the agreement between Mr. Yassin and Mr. Abdelnour. I find that he had no knowledge of this.'

[31] "Mr. Hollander points to the finding of the arbitrators in the following terms: –

> 'To the majority of the Arbitral Tribunal, these and other statements of Mr. Al-Wazzan and Mr. Al-Ghanim, which might imply secret activities, do not seen illegal. The statements must be considered in their context. Mr. Al-Ghanim also said he had acted "on behalf of the company", that is, he openly represented the Claimant. The majority of the Arbitral Tribunal qualifies the answers of Mr. Al-Wazzan and Mr. Al-Ghanim as not suggesting secret activities but as trying not to disclose their professional know how to third persons. This is neither illicit nor illegal.'

Furthermore it really does not seem very likely that anyone acting on behalf of the Kuwait MOD would not appreciate that Mr. Al-Wazzan and Mr. Al-Ghanim were not representatives of the Directorate but were intermediaries. But be all that as it may, the openness factor does not appear to have been the critical issue so far as Phillips J was concerned having regard to the language he used ... already quoted.

[32] "What in my view *Lemenda* decided was (1) there are some rules of public policy which if infringed will lead to non-enforcement by the English court whatever their proper law and wherever their place of performance but others are based on considerations which are purely domestic; (2) contracts for the purchase of influence are not of the former category; thus (3) contracts for the purchase of personal influence if to be performed in England would not be enforced as contrary to English domestic public policy; and (4) where such a contract is to be performed abroad, it is only if performance would be contrary to the domestic public policy of that country also that the English court would not enforce it. There is also an implied recognition as it seems to me that if all that can be said of a contract is that performance in a foreign country will be contrary to the domestic public policy of that state, enforcement will only be refused if performance would be contrary to the domestic public policy in England. If that was not so, consideration of English public policy would not in fact have been necessary or relevant.

[33] "It must also follow, as it seems to me, that an English court would take notice of the fact that different courts and different tribunals might have

different views as to the enforceability of contracts for the purchase of personal influence depending on the proper law of the contracts and where they were to be performed. It would be for example legitimate for a foreign tribunal to take the view (indeed consistent with the English court's own view if I am right on the above implication), that albeit performance was contrary to domestic public policy in its place of performance, since it was not contrary to the domestic public policy either of the country of the proper law and/or the curial law, enforcement should be allowed.

[34] "It is in this context, in my view, that albeit the award is not isolated from the underlying contract, it is relevant that the English court is considering the enforcement of an award, and not the underlying contract. The English court takes cognisance of the fact that the underlying contract, on the facts as they appear from the award and its reasons, does not infringe one of those rules of public policy where the English court would not enforce it whatever its proper law or place of performance. It is entitled to take the view that such domestic public policy considerations as there may be, have been considered by the Arbitral Tribunal. It is legitimate to conclude that there is nothing which offends English public policy if an Arbitral Tribunal enforces a contract which does not offend the domestic public policy under either the proper law of the contract or its curial law, even if English domestic public policy might have taken a different view.

[35] "On the *Lemenda* point accordingly I would hold that the judge was right, and that thus unless the appellants are entitled to go behind the facts as found by the arbitrators there is no public policy answer to the enforcement of the award."

IV. FRAUD AMENDMENT

[36] "The appellants seek leave to amend their defence to allege that Westacre, through its witnesses, gave perjured evidence at the arbitration. ... [T]he thrust of the amendment is to seek to allege that Westacre dishonestly put forward the case at the arbitration that the agreement was a genuine consultancy agreement with Mr. Al-Wazzam and Mr. Al-Ghanim playing significant roles, whereas the truth was that the agreement was a vehicle providing bribes particularly to Mr. Al-Otaibi. It will be seen that there is a close interaction between what the appellants would seek to assert under this amendment and the key issue, but at this stage I am going to leave on one side the factor that if the appellants were allowed leave to amend it might enable them to establish their public policy defence in relation to bribery. In other words I will consider the point as if it were alleged following any foreign arbitration award

simply that the party seeking to enforce the award had given perjured evidence at the arbitration.

[37] "It is also right to emphasise that it was no part of the judge's decision that leave to amend should be refused as a matter of discretion. His decision on the amendment was that it should not be allowed because it raised no arguable point.

[38] "As the judge pointed out if it is open to a party to seek to get an enforcing court to retry issues of fact which the arbitrators had before them, and which they had to and did determine, it would appear to present an open invitation to disappointed litigants to relitigate their disputes by alleging perjury, and a major inroad would be made into the finality of Convention awards. However Mr. Gaisman submits that much the same could be said of the rule that relates to foreign judgments, and yet that rule exemplified by *Abouloff v. Oppenheimer & Co* (1882) 10 Q.B.D. 295 does allow a person against whom a foreign judgment has been given to resist enforcement simply on the basis that the foreign judgment was obtained by the perjury of witnesses, notwithstanding that the truth of that evidence was an issue before the foreign court.

[39] "Dicey & Morris, *Conflict of Laws*, 12th Edition (1993) at pp. 505-506 points up the distinction between the attitude of the English court to its own judgments as compared with that to foreign judgments. As regards domestic judgments a second action can be brought to set aside the judgment on the basis that it was obtained by fraud, but it will be summarily dismissed 'unless the plaintiff can produce evidence newly discovered since the trial, which evidence could not have been produced at the trial with reasonable diligence, and which is so material that its production at the trial would probably have effected the result, and (when the fraud consists of perjury) so strong that it would reasonably be expected to be decisive at the rehearing and if unanswered must have that result.' That test bears some similarity to, but is if anything more stringent than, the test by reference to which fresh evidence may be introduced in the Court of Appeal as laid down in *Ladd v. Marshall* [1954] 1 W.L.R. 1489 at 1491: –

> 'To justify the reception of fresh evidence or a new trial, three conditions must be fulfilled: first, it must be shown that the evidence could not have been obtained with reasonable diligence for use at the trial; secondly, the evidence must be such that, if given, it would probably have an important influence on the result of the case, though it need not be decisive; thirdly, the evidence must be such as is presumably to be believed, or in other words, it must be apparently credible, though it need not be incontrovertible.'

(....)
[40] "It also bears a similarity to the test supported by *Mustill & Boyd 2nd Edition* and by Hirst J in *The Vimeira* [1985] 2 Lloyd's Rep. 377 at 400 in relation to the situation in which remission of an award of arbitrators might have been ordered prior to the Arbitration Act 1996 coming into force i.e. the evidence would have had a substantial effect or an important influence on the result, and it must have been unavailable to the party at the time of the hearing of the arbitration. I have not considered fully what the position is now that the 1996 Act is in force, but in this context it is difficult to think that if under Sect. 68(2)(g) it was suggested an award had been obtained by fraud and that relief under Sect. 68(3)[3] should be granted, the court would not insist on the same condition i.e. unavailability of the evidence produced as at the time of the arbitration, and that such evidence would have had an important influence on the result.
[41] "It does seem anomalous that enforcement of a foreign judgment can be attacked without any requirement that the evidence must be evidence not available at the trial, and apparently without regard to the question whether the impact of that evidence would be likely to be decisive. As the cases referred to by the judge show albeit the House of Lords felt unable to overrule *Abouloff* in *Owens Bank Limited v. Bracco* [1992] 2 A.C. 443, it is a decision which has been distinguished, and its application weakened wherever possible....
[42] "In *Interdesco S.A. v. Nullifire Ltd.* [1992] 1 Lloyd's Rep. 180 Phillips J concluded that in a case where the judgment being enforced in England was being so enforced under the Convention on Jurisdiction and Enforcement of Judgments in Civil and Commercial Matters which has the force of law pursuant to Sect. 2 of The Civil Jurisdiction and Judgments Act 1982, the rule

---

3. Sect. 68(2)(g) and (3) of the Arbitration Act 1996 reads (in relevant part):

"(2) Serious irregularity means an irregularity of one or more of the following kinds which the court considers has caused or will cause substantial injustice to the applicant –

...

(g) the award being obtained by fraud or the award or the way in which it was procured being contrary to public policy;

...

(3) If there is shown to be serious irregularity affecting the tribunal, the proceedings or the award, the court may –
(a) remit the award to the tribunal, in whole or in part, for reconsideration,
(b) set the award aside in whole or in part, or
(c) declare the award to be of no effect, in whole or in part.
(....)"

in *Abouloff* had no application at least as he put it in its 'most extreme formulation' because under that Convention the English court was not entitled to review the findings of another Convention court where the very points had been in issue before it.

(....)

[43] "The judge in his judgment did not extend the principle in *Abouloff* to the enforcement of an award under the New York Convention. He appears to have done so suggesting first that the foundation for the *Abouloff* principle was that public policy should prevent a party from benefiting from his own fraud, and recognising that that public policy was present as much in domestic judgments as in foreign judgments and thus logically it also should apply to the sphere of arbitration. But he concluded that under the New York Convention a party should only be entitled to pursue the allegation that an award has been obtained by fraud on certain conditions which he put this way: –

> 'Where a party to a foreign New York Convention arbitration award alleges at the enforcement stage that it has been obtained by perjured evidence that party will not normally be permitted to adduce in the English courts additional evidence to make good that allegation unless it is established that: (i) the evidence sought to be adduced is of sufficient cogency and weight to be likely to have materially influenced the arbitrators' conclusion had it been advanced at the hearing; and (ii) the evidence was not available or reasonably obtainable either (a) at the time of the hearing of the arbitration; or (b) at such time as would have enabled the party concerned to have adduced it in the court of supervisory jurisdiction to support an application to reverse the arbitrators' award if such procedure were available. Where the additional evidence has already been deployed before the court of supervisory jurisdiction for the purpose of an application for the setting aside or remission of the award but the application has failed, the public policy of finality would normally require that the English courts should not permit that further evidence to be adduced at the stage of enforcement.
>
> The defendants have not established that they could justify the introduction of the evidence in M.M.'s affidavit either on the basis that such evidence could not reasonably have been obtained at the time of the arbitration or subsequently in time to engage Swiss court procedures for challenging the award on the basis that the plaintiffs had adduced perjured evidence. The procedure available under Swiss law for "revision" of an award on the grounds that it has been obtained by perjured evidence must be invoked within a time limit of 90 days from the discovery of the dishonest evidence, according to a letter of advice

> provided to the plaintiffs by a Swiss lawyer, M Andre Gillioz. This was clearly not done. That being so, I have no doubt that, notwithstanding the apparent strength of the evidence of M.M. on which they would rely, the defendants should not be permitted to reopen under the public policy exception to enforcement under Sect. 5(3) of the Act of 1975 the issues of fact already determined by the arbitrators. Accordingly, the defendants' application for leave further to re-amend their points of defence must be refused.'

[44] "I agree with the judge that the principle in *Abouloff* in its extreme formulation should not be extended to arbitration awards but would put the matter a little differently but only in degree. I would suggest that the reason why the *Abouloff* principle should not be extended to foreign arbitration awards is first that an arbitration award is an award from the tribunal chosen by the parties to decide their dispute; that will very often not be the case either when a domestic or a foreign judgment has been obtained. Second, there is thus a logic in placing foreign arbitration awards into the same category as domestic arbitration awards and not into the same category as foreign judgments. I am not for my part much influenced by the fact that the award is a New York Convention award, because I do not see that the provisions of that Convention can in any way be equated with those of the Brussels Convention relied on by Phillips J in *Interdesco*.

[45] "But I would thus agree with the judge that normally the conditions to be fulfilled will be (a) that the evidence to establish the fraud was not available to the party alleging the fraud at the time of the hearing before the arbitrators; and (b) where perjury is the fraud alleged i.e. where the very issue before the arbitrators was whether the witness or witnesses were lying, the evidence must be so strong that it would reasonably be expected to be decisive at a hearing, and if unanswered must have that result. I would prefer not to express a concluded view as to whether if under the curial law the local court had the power to review or remit an award, it should always be a pre-condition that the fresh evidence should not have been available prior to the expiry of the period for making the application to the local court. I am anxious about making that aspect too inflexible a condition, since it is clear that if an application to the local court is made and fails, the result may be an estoppel as per *House of Spring Gardens v. White* [[1991] 1 Q.B. 241]. However, I agree with the judge that in the instant case, no good reason has been shown as to why the appellants should not have applied to the Swiss court within the period of 90 days, raising the allegation that the award had been obtained by perjured evidence, and that is an added factor against granting the appellants leave to amend to raise the issue in this jurisdiction. Thus, unless the bribery

element provides a factor which makes for an exception, I agree with the judge that the amendment should be refused."

V. CAN THE FACTS BE RE-OPENED?

[46] "I return thus to the key issue. Should this court allow the facts as found by the arbitrators to be re-opened? Both parties accept for present purposes what was said in *Soleimany* including the view expressed obiter as to the approach of the court to enforcement when the arbitrators have entered upon the topic of illegality and held there was none. What we said in *Soleimany v. Soleimany* was as follows: –

> 'The difficulty arises when arbitrators have entered upon the topic of illegality, and have held that there was none. Or perhaps they have made a non-speaking award, and have not been asked to give reasons. In such a case there is a tension between the public interest that the awards of arbitrators should be respected, so that there be an end to lawsuits, and the public interest that illegal contracts should not be enforced. We do not propound a definitive solution to this problem, for it does not arise in the present case. So far from finding that the underlying contract was not illegal, the Dayan in the Beth Din found that it was.
>
> It may, however, also be in the public interest that this court should express some view on a point which has been fully argued and which is likely to arise again. In our view, an enforcement judge, if there is prima facie evidence from one side that the award is based on an illegal contract, should inquire further to some extent.... We do not for one moment suggest that the judge should conduct a full-scale trial of those matters in the first instance. That would create the mischief which the arbitration was designed to avoid. The judge has to decide whether it is proper to give full faith and credit to the arbitrator's award. Only if he decided at the preliminary stage that he should not take that course does he need to embark on a more elaborate inquiry into the issue of illegality.'

[47] "We furthermore expressed our disagreement with Colman J on one aspect, when we said that although we agreed that where the arbitrator had jurisdiction to decide the issue of illegality, and decided there was none, prima facie the court would enforce the award. We continued: –

> 'But, in an appropriate case it [the court] may inquire ... into an issue of illegality even if an arbitrator had jurisdiction and has found there was no illegality....'

[48] "It is in fact of interest that as we read Colman J's formulation in his sixth proposition even he was not taking what one might term a full *Ladd v. Marshall* approach. His sixth proposition contemplates a balancing exercise simply on the basis that certain facts were not placed before the arbitrator without a requirement that those facts should not have been available to the party resisting enforcement at the time of the hearing. The reason for not taking a strict *Ladd v. Marshall* approach, and indeed for taking the approach we advocated which went a little further, is that when questions of illegality could be in issue, cases may be fought by the parties either in a way that disguises illegality from the tribunal, or at the least from one party's point of view seeks to shine the best light on their own conduct.

[49] "What I believe we, and indeed Colman J, were recognising was that although normally at the enforcement stage a party who brings an action on the award will be estopped from attempting to re-argue the points on which he has lost the arbitration (see *Mustill & Boyd* p. 419 and the cases cited at note 17), there are exceptional circumstances where the court will not allow reliance on an estoppel....[4]

[50] "There are authorities which in my view support the proposition that where illegality is raised and at least where the evidence of illegality is so strong that if not answered it would be decisive of the case, the court would not allow reliance on issue estoppel, or on the principle in *Henderson v. Henderson* to prevent the point being ventilated. In other words illegality can if raised provide the special circumstances in which an estoppel will not provide a defence.[5]

(....)

[51] "That case [*Man v. Haryanto*] in my judgment is important. It demonstrates that even if a party had obtained a declaration from the English court as to the validity of a contract in a situation in which the defendant had not raised a public policy issue in relation, for example, to the fact that the contract was for the importation of drugs, the English court would not allow the plaintiff to rely on an issue estoppel to prevent 'argument on principles of public policy which are of the greatest importance'. The position may be different if the public policy issue relates to a rule of Indonesian domestic law.

4. Walter LJ referred to *Arnold v. Natwest Bank Plc* [1990] 1 Ch 573.
5. Walter LJ referred to *Kok Hoong v. Leong Cheong Kweng Mines Ltd.* [1964] A.C. 993 and *E.D. & F. Man (Sugar) LTD v. Yani Haryanto (No. 2)* [1991] 1 Lloyd's Rep. 429.

[52] "It thus supports the view that was being expressed obiter in *Soleimany* that there will be circumstances in which, despite the prima facie position of an award preventing a party re-opening matters either decided by the arbitrators or which the party had every opportunity of raising before the arbitrators, the English court will allow a re-opening. The court is in this instance performing a balancing exercise between the competing public policies of finality and illegality; between the finality that should prima facie exist particularly for those that agree to have their disputes arbitrated, against the policy of ensuring that the executive power of the English court is not abused. It is for those reasons that the nature of the illegality is a factor, the strength of case that there was illegality also is a factor, and the extent to which it can be seen that the asserted illegality was addressed by the arbitral tribunal is a factor.

[53] "The judge performed the balancing exercise and narrowly came down on the side of upholding the finality of the award. It would seem that if the case had concerned a drug trafficking contract he might well have taken a different view but he placed 'commercial corruption' at a different level of opprobrium from drug trafficking.

[54] "I have reached a different conclusion to that of the judge. I disagree with him as to the appropriate level of opprobrium at which to place commercial corruption. It seems to me that the principle against enforcing a corrupt bargain of the nature of this agreement, if the facts in M.M.'s affidavit are correct, is within that bracket recognised by Phillips J in *Lemenda* and by Neill LJ in *Man v. Haryanto* as being based on public policy of the greatest importance and almost certainly recognised in most jurisdictions throughout the world. I believe it important that the English court is not seen to be turning a blind eye to corruption on this scale. I believe that if unanswered the case at present made on M.M.'s affidavit would be conclusive against Westacre being entitled to enforce the agreement and thus the award as a matter of English public policy. I also believe that the judge did not sufficiently consider the extent to which the case now presented on bribery was examined by the Arbitration Tribunal. When one examines the circumstances of this case one can see that in truth the bribery issue has not been ventilated properly before the Swiss Arbitral Tribunal. Mr. Gaisman would suggest that that is because Westacre put forward a dishonest case if the facts of M.M.'s affidavit are to be taken as correct. It is by no means as simple as that. Mr. Gaisman's clients chose not to run the case as it is now being run. He submits that that was inadvertence or incompetence. The alternative explanation is that the claimants did not want to accept what they now put forward as their case that they or employees of theirs were involved and intended the agreement to constitute the vehicle by which a bribe was to be paid. There was not collusion which

we suggested in *Soleimany* might lead the court to look carefully at the question of enforcement, but the effect is the same, and both parties, if the facts in M.M.'s affidavit are correct, bear responsibility for the fact that the matter was not properly considered.

[55] "The fact is that the arbitrators simply did not have an opportunity of considering the case as now made, and whatever their suspicions, the majority did not feel it in their place to make inquiries. I draw attention to the quotation from the reasons of the majority at the commencement of this judgment, where they say, if the defendant does not present the facts 'an Arbitral Tribunal does not have to investigate', and to the fact that they asserted to the Swiss court that the allegation that the appellants were themselves involved in the bribery was not part of the case before the arbitrators.

[56] "What of course gives one cause for concern is the way the matter can be put so powerfully in relation to finality. The appellants chose not to run the point they now run before the arbitrators, and on the bribery issue they raised they lost; they took the matter to the Swiss Federal Court and lost; the point, if it is successful, prevents at least in this jurisdiction enforcement so as to require payment of that part of the price paid under the main arms contract which would otherwise have gone to Westacre.

[57] "The answer is that so far as public policy is concerned it is always unattractive for one party to be able to take the point, but the English court is concerned with the integrity of its own system, and concerned that its executive power is not abused. If the agreement represented a contract to pay a bribe, Westacre should not be entitled to enforce the agreement before an English court and should not be entitled to enforce an award based on it. In addition, it may be possible to give some opportunity to the Ministry of Defence in Kuwait to make whatever claim they might have against either party if the appellants were to succeed in establishing the facts in M.M.'s affidavit.

[58] "If the court were concerned with a domestic arbitration and citizens of this country, I would have thought that if a party were to come before the English court and seek to prove that an agreement was unenforceable because it was in fact an agreement to pay a bribe, in addition to the contract not being enforced by the English court, the papers would be sent to the Director of Public Prosecutions. There is no such sanction available in relation to an agreement between foreign citizens. However, I would suggest that it would be appropriate to draw the attention of the Ministry of Defence to the allegations being made so that they could consider what remedies might be available to them."

Opinion of Lord Justice Mantell

[59] "I gratefully adopt the summary of facts provided by Waller LJ. I respectfully agree with the reasoning by which he rejects what he has called 'the Lemenda point' and 'the fraud amendment point'. I also agree that the preliminary issue raises two separate questions; is it open to the appellants in the enforcement proceedings to challenge the arbitrators' findings of fact on the bribery issue and secondly, if so and if successful in proving the assertions set out in the affidavit of Miodrag Milosavljevic, should the English court enforce the award. Clearly the questions have to be addressed in that order and the key question is the first. On that key question I regret to say that I am unable to agree with Waller LJ. I hope I shall be forgiven for stating my reasons shortly.

[60] "It is of crucial importance to evaluate both the majority decision in the arbitration and the ruling of the Swiss Federal Court. Swiss law being both the proper law of the contract and the curial law of the arbitration and Switzerland, like the United Kingdom, being a party to the 1958 New York Convention. From the award itself it is clear that bribery was a central issue. The allegation was made, entertained and rejected. Had it not been rejected the claim would have failed, Swiss and English public policy being indistinguishable in this respect. Authority apart, in those circumstances and without fresh evidence I would have thought that there could be no justification for refusing to enforce the award.

[61] "However, in the obiter passage cited by Waller LJ from the judgment in *Soleimany* it seems to have been suggested that some kind of preliminary inquiry short of a full scale trial should be embarked upon whenever 'there is prima facie evidence from one side that the award is based on an illegal contract'. For my part I have some difficulty with the concept and even greater concerns about its application in practice, but, for the moment and uncritically accepting the guidelines offered, it seems to me that any such preliminary inquiry in the circumstances of the present case must inevitably lead to the same conclusion, namely, that the attempt to re-open the facts should be rebuffed. I so conclude by reference to the criteria given by way of example in *Soleimany* itself. First, there was evidence before the Tribunal that this was a straightforward, commercial contract. Secondly, the arbitrators specifically found that the underlying contract was not illegal. Thirdly, there is nothing to suggest incompetence on the part of the arbitrators. Finally, there is no reason to suspect collusion or bad faith in the obtaining of the award. The seriousness of the alleged illegality to which Waller LJ gives weight is not, in my judgment, a factor to be considered at the stage of deciding whether or not to mount a full scale inquiry. It is something to be taken into account as

part of the balancing exercise between the competing public policy considerations of finality and illegality which can only be performed in response to the second question, if it arises, namely, should the award be enforced. Accordingly I would dismiss the appeal."

Opinion of Sir David Hirst

[62] "I also would dismiss this appeal for the reasons given by Mantell LJ, with which I entirely agree. I would only add that, had the second question arisen, I would have answered it in favour of the respondent for the same reasons as those given by Colman J at [1998] 3 WLR 770 at pp. 798B to 800C. Here, in my judgment, Colman J struck the correct balance, and, in doing so (contrary to Waller LJ's view) gave ample weight to the opprobrium attaching to commercial corruption (see especially the passage at pp. 798F to 799G)."

55. High Court of Justice, Queen's Bench Division (Commercial Court), 24 May 1999

Parties:	Applicant/respondent in the arbitration: Omnium de Traitement et de Valorisation S.A. (France) Respondent/claimant in the arbitration: Hilmarton (UK)
Published in:	14 Mealey's International Arbitration Report (1999, no. 6) pp. A-1 – A-5
Articles:	V(1)(*b*); V(1)(*d*); V(2)(*b*)
Subject matters:	– bribery – public policy – commencing second arbitration
Commentary Cases:	[1]-[15] = ¶ 524 (bribery); [16] = ¶ 511; [17]-[18] = ¶ 513; [19]-[20] = ¶ 301

Facts

The facts of this case are also reported in Yearbook XXII (1997) pp. 696-697. Hilmarton contracted with Omnium de Traitement et de Valorisation S.A. (OTV) to be the legal and tax consultant and deal with the administration of the different parties involved in the design and completion of a project in Algeria. After OTV obtained the contract, a dispute arose between the parties regarding payment of the remaining 50% of the contractually agreed consultancy fee. Hilmarton instituted an ICC arbitration in Switzerland in which it requested the remainder of its fee. The sole arbitrator found that, as the real object of the contract was traffic in influence, it violated Algerian law and Swiss public policy. In his award, rendered in Geneva on 19 August 1988 (first award), Hilmarton's request was rejected.

This award was annulled by the Geneva Court of Appeal on 17 November 1989, whose decision was confirmed by the Swiss Supreme Court (*Tribunal Fédéral*) on 17 April 1990 (both reported in Yearbook XIX (1994) at pp. 214-222). However, the first award was granted exequatur in France by the Court of Appeal of Paris on 19 December 1991 (reported in Yearbook XIX (1994) at pp. 655-657 (France no. 18)). This decision became final on 23 March 1994 when the French Supreme Court (*Cour de Cassation*) rejected the appeal brought by Hilmarton against it (reported in Yearbook XX (1995) at pp. 663-665 (France no. 23)).

In the interval, a second arbitral tribunal was constituted in Switzerland and on 10 April 1992, a second award was rendered granting Hilmarton's claim.

Hilmarton sought exequatur of the second award in France. This was granted by the Court of First Instance of Nanterre on 25 February 1993 (reported in Yearbook XX (1995) at pp. 194-197). Hilmarton also sought enforcement of the decision of the Swiss Supreme Court annulling the first award, which was granted by the Court of First Instance of Nanterre on 22 September 1993. OTV appealed against both these decisions and on 29 June 1995 the Versailles Court of Appeal rendered two decisions (reported in Yearbook XXI (1996) at pp. 524-525 (France no. 24)):

- *decision no. 315* in which it upheld the enforcement of the Swiss Supreme Court decision setting aside the first award; and
- *decision no. 316* in which it upheld the enforcement of the second award.

OTV appealed against the decisions of the Versailles Court of Appeal to the French Supreme Court. Hilmarton lodged a third party incidental appeal (*pourvoi provoqué éventuel*) against both decisions. On 10 June 1997, the Supreme Court overturned the two decisions, finding that a final French decision bearing on the same subject between the same parties creates an obstacle to any recognition in France of court decisions or arbitral awards rendered abroad which are incompatible with it (reported in Yearbook XXII (1997) pp. 696-698 (France no. 27)).

Hilmarton sought enforcement in England of the second award. Granting its application Tuckey, J, made an ex parte order on 3 September 1998 giving effect to the award in England. OTV applied to set aside this order under Sect. 103 of the Arbitration Act 1996.

The court, per Walker, J, rejected the application finding that there were no public policy grounds on which the enforcement of the award could be refused. Absent a finding of fact of corrupt practices, the fact that English law might have arrived at a different result was not to the point. That the result under Swiss law, the law chosen by the parties, was different led, as a result of the policy of upholding international arbitral awards, to enforcing the award. Nor was there any indication that OTV had been unable to present its case nor that the procedure was not in accordance with the parties' agreement.

Excerpt

[1] "It is OTV's principal case that the Award should not be enforced in England because such enforcement would be contrary to public policy. That can of course only be English public policy. As Waller LJ said in *Soleimany v. Soleimany* [1998] 3 W.L.R. 811 at 824 C[1] '... enforcement here is governed by the public policy of the lex fori'. I must also have in mind the precise scope of the duty of the English court to enforce New York Convention awards. Under Sect. 103 of the Arbitration Act 1996[2] (which is in identical terms to its predecessor Sect. 5 of the Arbitration Act 1975) enforcement of a Convention award 'shall not be refused' except in certain limited cases, and enforcement 'may also be refused' if it would be contrary to public policy to enforce the award.

[2] "The public policy point invoked by OTV is that the agreement was unlawful in its place of performance. It is however in my judgment necessary for OTV to go further, and establish that this infects the Award as well.

[3] "The first step is to evaluate the Award itself – see the approach of the Court of Appeal in *Westacre Investments Inc. v. Jugoimport*[3] per Mantell LJ at [60], with whom Sir David Hirst agreed. Under the agreement the subject of the arbitration, OTV appointed Hilmarton 'to be the legal and tax consultant and deal with the administration and coordination of the different parties involved in the design and completion of the various stages of the Drainage

1. Reported in this Yearbook, pp. 329-342.
2. Sect. 103 of the English Arbitration Act 1996 reads in relevant part:

"(1) Recognition or enforcement of a New York Convention award shall not be refused except in the following cases.
(2) Recognition or enforcement of the award may be refused if the person against whom it is invoked proves –
...
(c) that he was not given proper notice of the appointment of the arbitrator or of the arbitration proceedings or was otherwise unable to present his case;
...
(e) that the composition of the arbitral tribunal or the arbitral procedure was not in accordance with the agreement of the parties or, failing such agreement, with the law of the country in which the arbitration took place;
...
(3) Recognition or enforcement of the award may also be refused if the award is in respect of a matter which is not capable of settlement by arbitration, or if it would be contrary to public policy to recognise or enforce the award.
(....)"

3. Reported in this Yearbook, pp. 753-776 as UK no. 54.

Project for the town of Algiers'.... OTV was to pay Hilmarton fees, the condition for the payment of which was the awarding of the Public Contract to OTV by the City of Algiers. This condition was met. OTV only paid Hilmarton half the agreed fees.

[4] "Under the relevant arbitration clause, the parties unequivocally chose Swiss law as the proper law of the contract ('this agreement is wholly governed by the laws of Switzerland'), chose ICC Arbitration, and chose the curial law of the Canton of Geneva, the seat of the arbitration. Hilmarton therefore brought ICC arbitration proceedings to recover the unpaid balance, some 2.5 million French Francs. The Request for Arbitration was filed on 25 April 1986, and it was not until 10 April 1992 that the Award at issue in this case was published.

[5] "It is a lengthy document. The sole arbitrator went into all the matters raised with great care. Its length is partly accounted for by the setting out in the Award of the litigation history, including appeals to the Court of Justice of Geneva and the Supreme Court of Switzerland, together with an account of the proceedings before the original sole arbitrator who had heard the oral evidence, but who resigned subsequent to the reversal of his decision by the Swiss Courts. The new sole arbitrator directed himself, entirely correctly as a matter of Swiss law, that he was bound by the opinions expressed by the Court of Justice and the Supreme Court.

[6] "The only matters relevant for present purposes are the findings of the (second) sole arbitrator on OTV's contention that Hilmarton's claim should be dismissed because it was 'contrary to a mandatory law of the place of performance of the contract'. In summary, the arbitrator held: –

(1) the work performed by Hilmarton, with OTV's agreement, consisted of approaching public servants and Algerian Government officials in order to obtain the public contract. Such activity 'wittingly' breached an Algerian statute which prohibits the intervention of a middleman in connection with any Public Contract or agreement within the ambit of foreign trade....

But (2) this activity did not involve any bribery or other similar corrupt activity. Thus

> 'No bribe was foreseen. It has not been established that the claimant would have paid bribes, carried out "lobbyist" or "insider" acts intended to divert Public Servants or Ministers from their duties, or indulged in the trading of favours.'

....

It would of course be quite wrong for this Court to entertain any attempt to go behind this explicit and vital finding of fact. Nor was one made.
(3) as a matter of Swiss law (the law chosen by the parties) the agreement, albeit that it breached Algerian law, was not unlawful 'from the point of view of Swiss law'. It was not contra bonae mores, in the absence of bribes and other dubious activities or illicit practices.... The Algerian statute in question constituted a prohibited measure of a protectionist nature, to ensure that Algeria maintains a state monopoly on foreign trade; thus ethically speaking, it could not take priority over the parties' freedom of contract....

[7] "Therefore Swiss law made its own evaluation of the foreign statute, and in the light of the finding of fact that no corrupt activity was involved, refused to admit any illegality or public policy defence to the claim. Indeed, the Court of Justice regarded it as 'absolutely shocking' that OTV, which had regularly paid the amounts due until the Public Contract was awarded, then refused to comply fully with its contractual obligations.

[8] "Thus the very point which OTV now puts forward as a reason for refusal of enforcement in England was (1) ruled upon on the face of the Award, and (2) rejected by the application of the law chosen by the parties, (3) on the basis of a finding of fact that no corrupt practices were involved.

[9] "It may well be that an English arbitral tribunal, chosen by the parties, and applying English law as chosen by the parties, would have reached a different result. It may well be that such a tribunal would have dismissed Hilmarton's claim, applying the full rigour of the principle stated by Viscount Simonds in *Regazzoni v. Sethia* [1958] AC 301 at p. 317 thus: –

> '... whether or not the proper law of the contract is English law, an English court will not enforce a contract, or award damages for its breach if its performance will involve the doing of an act in a foreign and friendly State which violates the law of that State.'

I should add that in applying this principle it is immaterial whether the contract itself is governed by English or foreign law.

[10] "But I am not adjudicating upon the underlying contract. I am deciding whether or not an arbitration award should be enforced in England. In this context it seems to me that (absent a finding of fact of corrupt practices which would give rise to obvious public policy considerations) the fact that English law would or might have arrived at a different result is nothing to the point. Indeed, the reason for the different result is that Swiss law is different from English law, and the parties chose Swiss law and Swiss arbitration. If anything, this consideration dictates (as a matter of policy of the upholding of international arbitral awards) that the Award should be enforced.

[11] "In *Westacre Investments v. Jugoimport* (op. cit.) Waller LJ in the Court of Appeal, when dealing with the '*Lemenda*' point, made some observations which in my judgment are directly relevant and applicable to the present case. His reasoning on this point was that of all three members of the Court of Appeal. He said this (at [33]-[34]): –

> 'It must also follow, as it seems to me, that an English court would take notice of the fact that different courts and different tribunals might have different views as to the enforceability of contracts for the purchase of personal influence depending on the proper law of the contracts and where they were to be performed. It would be for example legitimate for a foreign tribunal to take the view (indeed consistent with the English court's own view if I am right on the above implication), that albeit performance was contrary to domestic public policy in its place of performance, since it was not contrary to the domestic public policy either of the country of the proper law and/or the curial law, enforcement should be allowed.
>
> It is in this context, in my view, that albeit the award is not isolated from the underlying contract, it is relevant that the English court is considering the enforcement of an award, and not the underlying contract. The English court takes cognisance of the fact that the underlying contract, on the facts as they appear from the award and its reasons, does not infringe one of those rules of public policy where the English court would not enforce it whatever its proper law or place of performance. It is entitled to take the view that such domestic public policy considerations as there may be, have been considered by the Arbitral Tribunal. It is legitimate to conclude that there is nothing which offends English public policy if an Arbitral Tribunal enforces a contract which does not offend the domestic public policy under either the proper law of the contract or its curial law, even if English domestic public policy might have taken a different view.'

[12] "The sentences which I have emphasised are just this case; I respectfully agree with them. Further, in the same case at first instance (reported at [1998] 3 W.L.R. 770 at p. 801H-802B) Colman J said: –

> '... if one assumes that in this case the consultancy agreement did not involve any corrupt practice, but merely the use of personal influence with Kuwaiti government officials and that had the contract been sued upon in Kuwait it would have been unenforceable as contrary to Kuwaiti public policy, one must go on to ask whether if the English

courts were not to enforce this Swiss award, that would offend international comity. To this question, in my judgment, the answer must be "No". This is not a case of direct enforcement of the underlying contract, but of enforcement of the award which is a valid award in accordance with the curial law – Swiss law – chosen by the parties and one made by arbitrators having jurisdiction and in respect of a contract governed by Swiss law.'

Again that is just this case.

[13] "Mr. Dunning in his opening on behalf of OTV said the *Westacre* case was not relevant because in that case the party resisting enforcement did not have the findings it needed on the face of the award, where in this case it does. This was of course the point on which the Court of Appeal disagreed in *Westacre*. But the relevant observations of Lord Justice Waller I have just cited relate to an entirely different part of the case. In his reply however Mr. Dunning said that Waller LJ's observations were not in point, because there is a distinction to be made between performance being illegal and performance being contrary to public policy. I entirely disagree. They are but two strands of the same principle. Further I note that in *Westacre* in the Court of Appeal (at [26]) not only did Waller LJ not differentiate between performance being illegal by the law of Kuwait and performance being contrary to public policy in Kuwait, but he appeared to equate the two concepts (see also Colman J at [1998] 3 W.L.R. at p. 802E-F where the same apparent equation is made).

[14] "Finally, OTV's reliance on *Soleimany v. Soleimany* [1998] 3 W.L.R. 811, where in a judgment delivered by Waller LJ just over a year before his *Westacre* judgment, the Court of Appeal declined to permit enforcement of an arbitral award, was in my view misplaced. In that case it was apparent from the face of the award that the arbitrator was dealing with an illicit enterprise for smuggling carpets out of Iran. It was quite simply a smuggling contract. The case thus clearly fell into the category of cases where as a matter of public policy no award would be enforced by an English court, and the whole of the judgment of the Court of Appeal has to be read in that context. The element of corruption or illicit practice was present which, on the arbitrator's unchallengeable finding of fact in this case, was not present here.

[15] "In my judgment there are no public policy grounds on which the enforcement of this Award could be refused. Thus the case never gets within Sect. 103(3) of the Arbitration Act 1996. It would be artificial to go further and say that in any event on these facts I would have exercised my discretion in favour of the enforcement of this Award.

[16] "The other two grounds put forward by Mr. Dunning under Sect. 103 seem to me to be entirely hopeless. As to the suggestion that OTV was

'otherwise unable to present [its] case' within Sect. 103(2)(c), the thrust of this complaint is that the (second) arbitrator refused to hear oral evidence and only held a short hearing to take closing submissions from both sides. As is often the case with complaints of this kind, it is answered simply by a careful reading of the Award itself. What happened was that the (first) arbitrator heard all the witnesses both sides wished to call on two separate days. He took notes of the evidence. After the second arbitrator was appointed 'neither of the Parties requested supplemental evidence, nor have they alleged new facts in relation to the substance of the case'. Further, the arbitrator made two further findings that bear repeating in full: –

> 'In the case in question the facts of the main issue have already been examined in detail by the first arbitrator, then by the Court of Justice of Geneva and the Swiss Supreme Court. Before the undersigned arbitrator, the Parties waived their right to submit new evidence. The procedure on the main issue is therefore so advanced that from the point of view of procedural economy and the efficiency rule that characterises the arbitration process, postponement of the decision on the merits to a later stage cannot be justified.'

and

> 'In a Procedural Order of 28 October 1991, the Arbitrator considered that he had sufficient knowledge of the decisive facts and rejected the Defendant's request for the re-hearing of the whole matter. The Parties having not required the taking of new evidence, it therefore clearly appeared that, because of the nature of the issues to be determined as they resulted from the Parties['] written pleadings and exhibits and Minutes filed in this matter, starting the hearing of the case afresh would have been a pointless measure and contrary to the Arbitrator's duty to proceed with diligence and to settle disputes referred to him.'

I entirely agree. For good measure, the arbitrator added at the end of the passage I have just quoted 'This procedural decision issued by the Arbitrator has not moreover been challenged by the parties'. There is thus nothing in the suggestion that OTV was unable to present its case.

[17] "As to the contention that the arbitral procedure was not in accordance with the agreement between the parties within Sect. 103(2)(e), this is a complaint that the ICC Rules were not complied with. The quality of the points made can be judged by the fact that the first one taken in Mr. Dunning's written skeleton argument was that there should have been a second

Request for Arbitration, when of course there already was one in existence in relation to the original arbitration. Complaint is also made that no new Terms of Reference were produced; in this context Mr. Dunning makes the strange submission that the ICC Court was in breach of its own Rules, in that it failed to chase up OTV after OTV had itself refused to sign the new draft Terms of Reference. What actually happened was that in the light of this refusal by OTV to sign the new Terms of Reference (as to the absence of which OTV now seeks to complain), the Court of Arbitration simply took note of the original Terms of Reference as countersigned by the (new) arbitrator. The new arbitrator said in the Award on this point 'One does not see why such a procedure would be irregular'. Nor do I.

[18] "In fact, all these procedural points were taken before the arbitrator and failed (see paragraph stating 'Consequently the defendants' arguments intended to prove the arbitrator's lack of jurisdiction are groundless. The sole Arbitrator has been validly appointed in accordance with all relevant legal and regulatory provisions').

[19] "Finally, Mr. Dunning asserts non-disclosure by Hilmarton in obtaining the original ex parte order from Tuckey J. The thrust of the complaint here is that the affidavit did not specifically bring to the attention of the Court the finding in the Award that this was a contract which the arbitrator had held was illegal in the place of performance. It is of course basis principle that it is insufficient, if there is a point which should be drawn to the Judge's attention, simply to leave it buried in an exhibit (see for example *ABCI v. BFT* [1996] 1 Lloyds Rep. 485 at p. 491 column 2 per Waller J as he then was and *Sumitomo v. ONGC* [1994] 1 Lloyds Rep. 45 at p. 62 column 2 per Potter J as he then was).

[20] "I do not accept Hilmarton's contention that when an application is being made ex parte for leave to enforce an award in the same manner as a judgment, the duty of disclosure is somehow different, because the order does not take effect until the defendant has had an opportunity to set it aside. The effect of the granting of the order is to leave the defendant worse off, because it then has an order against it. However, the short answer to the non-disclosure point here seems to me to be that even if the finding as to illegality by the place of performance had been elevated into prime position in the affidavit, it would not have made the slightest difference to the order Tuckey J made.

[21] "In the result the arbitration application fails on all points and is dismissed."

UNITED STATES

Accession: 30 September 1970
1st and 2nd Reservations

270. United States District Court, Southern District of New York, 15 June 1995, No. 90 Civ. 3792; United States Court of Appeals for the Second Circuit, 22 March 1996, No. 95-7722

Parties:	Plaintiff/appellant: Montauk Oil Transportation Corporation (nationality not indicated) Defendant/appellee: Steamship Mutual Underwriting Association (Bermuda) Limited (Bermuda)
Published in:	District Court: no publication information Court of Appeals: 79 Federal Reporter, Third Series, p. 295 et seq.; 1996 U.S. App. LEXIS 5214; 1996 American Maritime Cases, p. 1379 et seq.
Articles:	II(2); V(1)(*a*) (by implication)
Subject matter:	– relationship between consent to be sued in New York ("New York Suable Clause") and arbitration agreement
Commentary Cases:	¶ 202, ¶ 209, ¶ 305 + ¶ 507

Facts

The facts of this case are also reported in Yearbook XVIII (1993) pp. 463-464 (US no. 124). Montauk Oil Transportation Corporation (Montauk) contracted with the Steamship Mutual Underwriting Association (Bermuda) Limited (Steamship) to cover its vessels for protection and indemnity risks. On 15 December 1989, the Cibro Philadelphia spilled oil in New York Harbor, causing Montauk to incur cleanup costs in excess of US$ 1,500,000. After differences arose between Montauk and Steamship regarding the coverage of

Montauk's loss, Montauk commenced an action in the District Court for the Southern District of New York for indemnity against Steamship, relying on the "New York Suable Clause" in the contract. Steamship moved to stay the suit, relying on the arbitration clause in the Club Rules which applied to the contract. The district court suspended the action and referred the parties to arbitration, holding that the New York Suable Clause did not eliminate the obligation to proceed to arbitration (US no. 124 reported in Yearbook XVIII (1993) pp. 463-465).

On 16 November 1994, Steamship obtained an award in London denying coverage and ordering Montauk to pay the arbitrator's fee of UK£ 24,750. Steamship sought confirmation of the award in the United States District Court, Southern District of New York. The district court, per Edelstein, DJ, confirmed the award, noting that all formal requirements had been complied with and none of the grounds stated in Art. V had been proven.

Montauk appealed from the confirmation, arguing that the district court had erred when it had ruled that the arbitration clause was not superseded by the compulsory appearance clause (the New York Suable Clause) in the insurance contract. The Court of Appeal rejected this argument, holding that the New York Suable Clause is intended to resolve the issue of personal jurisdiction over a foreign association "since an arbitration award cannot be enforced without access to the courts". Both the decision of the district court and the court of appeals are reproduced below.

Excerpt

District Court, 15 June 1995

[1] "Currently before this Court is defendant's motion for an order, pursuant to the Convention on the Recognition and Enforcement of Foreign Arbitral Awards (the Convention) as implemented by 9 U.S.C. Sects. 201-208, confirming the arbitration award and entering judgment in favor of defendant.

[2] "9 U.S.C. Sect. 207 provides:

> 'Within three years after an arbitral award falling under the Convention is made, any party to the arbitration may apply to any court having jurisdiction under this chapter for an order confirming the award as against any other party to the arbitration. The court shall confirm the award unless it finds one of the grounds for refusal or deferral of recognition or enforcement of the award specified in the said Convention.'

The Convention requires that the party applying for recognition and enforcement shall submit to the Court a duly certified copy of the award, Convention Art. IV(1)(*a*), a duly certified copy of the agreement to arbitrate, Convention Art. IV(1)(*b*) and Art. II.

[3] "Confirmation of a foreign arbitration award is proper under 9 U.S.C. Sect. 207 if (1) the party moving for confirmation of the arbitration award has complied with the requirements of the Convention; and (2) the party opposing the motion has failed to show the existence of any of the grounds stated in Art. V of the Convention that would bar confirmation of the arbitration award. See *Geotech Lizenz AG v. Evergreen Systems, Inc.*, 697 F. Supp. 1248, 1252 (E.D.N.Y. 1988).[1]

[4] "Defendant has included, as exhibits to its motion papers, a certified copy of the arbitration award and a certified copy of the agreement to arbitrate contained in the contract of insurance. In its response papers, plaintiff has advised this Court that 'Montauk will not oppose confirmation' of the arbitration award. Plaintiff has not asserted any ground upon which the arbitration should not be confirmed. Defendant has complied with all requirements for its motion pursuant to 9 U.S.C. Sect. 207, and plaintiff does not oppose the motion. Accordingly, the motion is granted and the arbitration is confirmed."

Court of Appeals, 22 March 1996

[5] "Steamship Mutual is a Bermuda-based mutual association of shipowners providing marine protection and indemnity insurance to its members. When a member enters the Association to obtain insurance, the member is subject to the standard terms of entry set forth in the Rule Book of the Association (the Club Rules). The Association also issues a 'slip' to each member that confirms the terms of coverage and sets forth any special provisions not stipulated in the Club Rules that are applicable to that member.

(....)

[6] "Rule 36 of the Club Rules provides a mandatory procedure for the settlement of disputes. It states in pertinent part that:

> 'If any difference or dispute shall arise between a Member of the Club concerning the construction of these Rules or of the Rules applicable to any Class in the Club or of any Bye-Law passed thereunder, or the insurance afforded by the Club under these Rules, or any amount due

1. Reported in Yearbook XV (1990) pp. 562-568 (US no. 92).

from the Club to a Member, such difference or dispute shall in the first instance be referred to and adjudicated by the Directors.

If the Member does not accept the decision of the Directors the difference or dispute shall be referred to the arbitration of two arbitrators, one to be appointed by each of the parties, in London, and the submission to arbitration and all the proceedings therein shall be subject to the provisions of the English Arbitration Act....

No Member shall be entitled to maintain any action, suit or other legal proceedings against the Club upon any such difference or dispute unless and until the same has been submitted to the Directors and they shall have given their decision thereon ... and, if such decision be not accepted by the Member ..., *unless and until the difference or dispute shall have been referred to arbitration* in the manner provided in this Rule....' (Emphasis added)

[7] "A typewritten 'NEW YORK SUABLE CLAUSE' was attached to the slip, and states in pertinent part that:

'[T]he Association hereby undertakes to appear in any civil action which the Member may bring against the Association in the United States District Court for the Southern District of New York to recover for any loss or claim payable or alleged to be payable by the Association under the contract of insurance described in this Certificate.... Except as to jurisdiction over the person of the Association, the foregoing provision[] shall not effect [sic] any defence to which the Association would otherwise be entitled and *shall not change the contractual or other substantive rights and obligations of the Association or of the Member*, which shall all be determined in accordance with English Law.' (Emphasis added)

(....)

[8] "Montauk ... brought this suit on 4 June 1990, seeking, inter alia, a declaratory judgment that Steamship Mutual was liable under the insurance contract and money damages for expenses and liabilities arising from the oil spill. In August 1990, Steamship Mutual moved to stay the suit pending arbitration in London. The district court granted Steamship Mutual's motion and ordered that the case be placed on its suspense docket, stating that:

'This exact issue regarding the interpretation of the exact same two clauses has been recently decided by this Court in the course of another dispute between the same two parties. It was recently held that "the

> [New York suable] clause does not eliminate the obligation to proceed with arbitration'. *Montauk Oil Transportation Corporation v. Steamship Mutual Underwriting Association*, No. 90 Civ. 3801 (JFK), [1991 WL 18149, at *2 (S.D.N.Y. 5 February 1991)]; [s]ee also *Neca Ins. Ltd. v. National Union Fire Ins. Co.*, 595 F. Supp. 95(5), 957-958 (S.D.N.Y. 1984). As a result, there is no question but that these two clauses indicate that the parties agreed to arbitrate disputes as provided by Rule 36. *Montauk Oil v. Steamship Mutual*, supra.'

Montauk Oil Transp. Corp. v. Steamship Mut. Underwriting Ass'n (Berm.) Ltd., No. 90 Civ. 3792 (DNE), slip op. at 2 (S.D.N.Y. 20 March 1991).[2]

[9] "Pursuant to Club Rule 36, the dispute was referred to the directors of the Association, who denied Montauk coverage on the basis that it had failed to disclose, prior to renewal, a fact material to the risk borne by the Association under the contract. Montauk then sought arbitration of the dispute. The London arbitrators also ruled in favor of Steamship Mutual on 16 November 1994.

[10] "On 4 January 1995, Steamship Mutual moved for confirmation of the London award pursuant to 9 U.S.C. Sect. 207. (footnote omitted) The district court confirmed the award on 15 June 1995, see *Montauk Oil Transp. Corp. v. Steamship Mut. Underwriting Ass'n (Berm.) Ltd.*, No. 90 Civ. 3792 (DNE), slip op. (S.D.N.Y. 15 June 1995), and entered a final judgment on 3 July 1995 [reproduced above]. This appeal followed.

[11] "On appeal, Montauk argues that the 'New York Suable Clause' in the slip conflicts with, and supersedes, the compulsory arbitration clause contained in Rule 36. This argument is without merit. Club Rule 36 provides a mandatory procedure for the settlement of disputes that requires referral of disputes to the Association's directors, and arbitration in any case in which a member of the Association does not accept the decision of the directors. Under the Federal Arbitration Act, '[a] written provision in any maritime transaction ... to settle by arbitration a controversy thereafter arising out of such ... transaction ... shall be valid, irrevocable, and enforceable, save upon such grounds as exist at law or in equity for the revocation of any contract.' 9 U.S.C. Sect. 2; see also *Morewitz v. West of Eng. Ship Owners Mut. Protection & Indem. Ass'n (Lux.)*, 62 F.3d 1356, 1364 (11th Cir. 1995), cert. denied, 116 S.Ct. 915 (1996). Thus, Steamship Mutual has an affirmative right to arbitrate this dispute. See *Local 1814, Int'l Longshoremen's Ass'n v. New York Shipping Ass'n, Inc.*, 965 F.2d 1224, 1232 (2d Cir. 1992) ('Arbitration is a contractual

2. Reported in Yearbook XVIII (1993) pp. 463-465 (US no. 124).

right....'), cert. denied, 506 U.S. 953 (1992); cf. *Morewitz*, 62 F.3d at 1364 ('Arbitration is clearly an affirmative defense....').

[12] "The New York Suable Clause does not vitiate this contractual right, given its clear statement that it 'shall not change the contractual or other substantive rights and obligations of the Association or of the Member'. See *Hart v. Orion Ins. Co.*, 453 F.2d 1358, 1361 (10th Cir. 1971) ('The assent of the insurer to jurisdiction does not prevent it from raising [an arbitration] defense based on policy terms.'); *West Shore Pipe Line Co. v. Associated Elec. & Gas Ins. Servs. Ltd.*, 791 F. Supp. 200, 204 (N.D.Ill. 1992) ('The ... service of suit clause can therefore reasonably be interpreted to facilitate litigation following arbitration, concerning the validity of enforcement of any arbitration ruling, without curtailing the mandatory arbitration provision in any manner.'); see also *China Union Lines Ltd. v. American Marine Underwriters, Inc.*, 458 F. Supp. 132, 134 n. 5 & 136 n. 13 (S.D.N.Y. 1978) (following *Hart*, 453 F.2d at 1360-1361).

[13] "The principal effect of the New York Suable Clause is to resolve the issue of personal jurisdiction over a foreign association, since 'an arbitration award cannot be enforced without access to the courts'. *Neca*, 595 F. Supp. at 958; see also *Montauk Oil*, 1991 WL 18149 at *2. Montauk argues that this interpretation of the clause is commercially unreasonable because Steamship Mutual has no assets in New York and would be unaffected by judicial enforcement of an award there. However, a contractual provision is not rendered superfluous or ineffective simply because it may not apply to a particular case. The New York Suable Clause was not specially crafted by Montauk and Steamship Mutual for this insurance contract. Rather, it is a standard compulsory appearance provision commonly incorporated into such contracts to enable parties to enforce an arbitral award, see *Neca*, 595 F. Supp. at 958, or to compel arbitration, see *Hart*, 453 F.2d at 1361. The judgment of the district court is affirmed."

271. United States District Court, Western District of Tennessee, Western Division, 14 February 1996, No. 95-2464-M1/V

Parties:	Plaintiff: Indocomex Fibres Pte., Ltd. (nationality not indicated) Defendant: Cotton Company International, Inc. (US)
Published in:	916 Federal Supplement (W.D.Tenn. 1996) pp. 721-729
Articles:	V; V(2)(*b*)
Subject matter:	– jurisdiction of enforcement court not precluded by contract language – no review on the merits – fraud (no) – violation of public policy (no) – ground for setting aside foreign award (no)
Commentary Cases:	[1]-[9] = ¶ 202, ¶ 305 + ¶ 507; [10]-[21] = ¶ 524 (fraud); [11] = ¶ 503; [14] = ¶ 501; [15] = ¶ 518; [19] = ¶ 502

Facts

Indocomex Fibres, Pte., Ltd. (Indocomex) entered into a number of contracts with Cotton Company International, Inc. (CCI) for the purchase of raw cotton. The contracts subjected the parties to the By-Laws and Rules of the Liverpool Cotton Association Limited, United Kingdom (the Association) and provided for arbitration by the Association.

Disputes arose between the parties regarding deficiencies in the quantity delivered and Indocomex submitted the dispute to arbitration. On 15 May 1995, the arbitrators rendered an award in favor of Indocomex. On 13 June 1995, Indocomex brought a suit in the District Court, seeking the enforcement of the award. CCI contested the jurisdiction of the court over the enforcement and argued that the award should be set aside as a result of fraudulent acts committed by Indocomex.

The district court, per McCalla, DJ, granted enforcement of the award holding that the provisions on remedies and enforcement of the Association's

Rules and By-Laws invoked by CCI did not limit the enforcement jurisdiction to the English High Court. The court further held that the allegations of fraud involved the merits of the dispute which the court would not reconsider.

Excerpt

I. THE UNITED STATES DISTRICT COURT'S JURISDICTION

(....)

[1] "Defendant Cotton Company argues that Liverpool Cotton Association Rules and By-Laws prohibit enforcement of the Association's arbitration award by courts of the United States. Plaintiff counters that the Rules and By-Laws do not limit enforcement of arbitration agreements to the High Court of Justice in England, but rather, simply allow that forum as an option, to be weighed by the parties, against other potential forums, such as the courts of the United States. The specific rules in dispute are By-Law 200, Rule 300, Rule 305 and Rule 342(2).

[2] "Association By-Law 200 provides,

> 'Every contract made subject to the By-Laws and/or Rules of the Association, or subject to Liverpool Arbitration, or containing words to a similar effect, is to be construed and take effect as a contract made in England and in accordance with the laws of England and is to be deemed in all respects save as provided by By-Law 202, to be subject to these By-Laws and Rules, and parties to the contract shall be considered to have submitted to the jurisdiction of the High Court of Justice in England, for the purpose of giving effect to the provisions of the By-Laws and Rules.'

Association By-Law 200. (footnote omitted) Defendant argues that By-Law 200 establishes the jurisdictional issue in this case.

[3] "By submitting to the Association for arbitration and agreeing to the Association's Rules, the contract was essentially converted into an English contract, and the High Court thereby obtained jurisdiction over the arbitration decision. Defendant argues that By-Law 200 settles the jurisdictional issue in this case, barring any enforcement proceeding in any court other than the High Court. However, By-Law 200 extends only to the arbitration proceeding and to the terms of the decision, which are to be interpreted by the High Court in accordance with the Association's Rules and By-Laws. By-Law 200 does not extend to the subsequent enforcement of the arbitration award.

[4] "Rule 300 explains how contract disputes, submitted to arbitration, obtain access to the High Court. Rule 300 provides in pertinent part,

> '(1) Whenever any difference touches or arises out of any transaction or contract which is subject to the By-Laws and Rules of the Association or subject to Liverpool Arbitration, or contains words to a similar effect, such differences shall be referred to arbitration in accordance with the By-Laws and Rules.
> (2) It is hereby expressly declared that, in all cases provided for by paragraph (1) hereof the holding of such an arbitration as aforesaid in the obtaining of an Award thereunder shall be a condition precedent to the right of any party to a contract to commence legal proceedings against the other party in respect of any such differences as aforesaid and neither party shall have any right of action against the other touching or arising out of any such matter or contract except to enforce the award in any such arbitration.'

Association Rule 300.
[5] "In submitting to English law, and specifically, to the Association Rules and By-Laws, the parties obtained access to the High Court only post-arbitration award, the first such opportunity being an appeal of the arbitration decision. It does not follow, however, as defendant argues, that simply because the parties only have access to the High Court after the arbitration award has been rendered, that the High Court is the mandated forum for enforcement of the award.
[6] "Defendant contends that mandatory jurisdictional authority for the enforcement of arbitration decisions is most clearly set forth in Rule 342, which provides in pertinent part:

> '(2) Every arbitration conducted in accordance with the By-Laws and Rules of the Association shall have its seat in Liverpool, be governed by English law, shall be conducted in accordance with English law and procedure and shall be subject to the supervisory and appeal jurisdiction (so far as appropriate) of the English Courts and no other courts.'

Association Rule 342(2). However, Rule 342 addresses the supervisory and appeal jurisdiction of the award, it does not address the enforcement of awards.
[7] "In this case, defendants were notified by the arbitrator that they had to submit a notice of appeal by 12 June 1995. There is no evidence that defendant filed an appeal within the relevant time period. Had it appealed the decision in the requisite time, exclusive jurisdiction over the appeal would have be-

longed to the High Court, as authorized by Rule 342. However, an appeal is distinct from an enforcement of an award, and as Rule 342 does not address enforcement of arbitration awards, it does not apply to the issue presently before the Court.

[8] "Rule 305 directly addresses the enforcement of arbitration awards. The language of Rule 305 is permissive rather than mandatory. Rule 305 states,

> 'Any award made under the By-laws and Rules may (without prejudice to the other rights and remedies of the parties under the Rules) be enforced in the manner in the Arbitration Act of 1950 or any statutory modification thereof for the time being enforced.'

Association Rule 305. The Arbitration Act states,

> 'An award on an arbitration agreement may, by leave of the High Court or a judge thereof, be enforced in the same manner as a judgment or order to the same effect, and where leave is so given, judgment may be entered in terms of the award.'

Arbitration Act 1950, Sect. 26(1).

[9] "In combination, the Arbitration Act and Rule 305 authorize the enforcement of arbitration awards in the High Court. However, they do not limit such enforcement to the High Court. In the absence of mandatory forum selection language in the contracts between plaintiff and defendant, Rule 305 does nothing more than confirm that a range of forums, including the High Court, are available to plaintiff for the enforcement of the Association's arbitration award. (footnote omitted)"

II. ENFORCEMENT OF THE ARBITRATION AWARD

[10] "The [1958 New York Convention], implemented by federal law, 9 U.S.C. Sect. 201 et seq., supports not only the United States District Court's jurisdiction over the enforcement of the Association's arbitration awards, but also supports this Court's enforcement of the arbitration award presently before the Court.[1] 'The goal of the Convention, and the principal purpose underlying American adoption and implementation of it, was to encourage the

1. "The Convention is a United Nations treaty to which the United States became a party in December 1970. Legislation implementing the Convention is codified in Chapter 2 of Title 9 of the United States Code."

recognition and enforcement of commercial arbitration agreements in international contracts and to unify the standards by which agreements to arbitrate awards are enforced.' *Imperial Ethiopian Government v. Baruch-Foster Corp.*, 535 F.2d 334, 335 (5th Cir. 1976);[2] *Scherk v. Alberto-Culver Co.*, 417 U.S. 506, 94 S.Ct. 2449, 41 L.Ed.2d 270 (1974).[3] In its memorandum, defendant concedes that '9 U.S.C. Sect. 207 allows parties to enforce foreign arbitration awards in federal district court.'[4]

(....)

[11] "Under 9 U.S.C. Sect. 207, the burden of proof of every element of a defense is on the party defending against enforcement. *Imperial*, 535 F.2d at 336. Public policy favors recognizing and enforcing international arbitration agreements because the consequent reliability of the contracts promotes export by United States merchants of United States goods. *Scherk*, 417 U.S. 506, 94 S.Ct. 2449; *Island Territory of Curaçao v. Solitron Devices, Inc.*, 489 F.2d 1313 (2d Cir. 1973),[5] cert. denied 416 U.S. 986, 94 S.Ct. 2389, 40 L.Ed.2d 763 (1974); *Fotochrome, Inc. v. Copal Co.*, 517 F.2d 512 (2d Cir. 1975).[6]

[12] "9 U.S.C. Sect. 203 grants the United States district courts jurisdiction over arbitration award proceedings. It provides,

> 'An action or proceeding following under the Convention shall be deemed to arise under the laws and treaties of the United States. The district courts of the United States ... shall have original jurisdiction over such an action or proceeding, regardless of the amount in controversy.'

[13] "9 U.S.C. Sect. 207 requires the United States district courts to enforce arbitration awards. Sect. 207 states,

> 'Within 3 years after an arbitral award following under the Convention is made, any party to the arbitration may apply to any court having jurisdiction under this chapter for an order confirming the award as against any other party to the arbitration.'

---

2. Reported in Yearbook II (1977) p. 252 (US no. 10).
3. Reported in Yearbook I (1976) pp. 203-204 (US no. 4).
4. "A party seeking recognition and enforcement of an award must supply with its application the original award and original agreement between the parties, or certified copies of those documents. Convention, Art. IV. Defendant makes no allegation that plaintiff has failed to supply the above documents to the Court."
5. Reported in Yearbook I (1976) p. 201 (US no. 1).
6. Reported in Yearbook I (1976) pp. 202-203 (US no. 3).

[14] "Art. V of the Convention, 9 U.S.C. Sect. 207 mandates that 'the court shall confirm the award unless it finds one of the grounds for refusal or deferral of recognition or enforcement of the award specified in the said Convention.' Because the public policy favoring international arbitration is strong, it has been held that the terms of the Convention are to be construed broadly, and circumstances warranting a denial of enforcement are narrowly drawn. *Geotech Lizenz AG v. Evergreen Systems*, 697 F. Supp. 1248, 1252 (E.D.N.Y. 1988),[7] citing *Bergesen v. Joseph Muller Corp.*, 710 F.2d 928, 932 (2d Cir. 1983).[8] 9 U.S.C. Sect. 207 sets forth seven exceptions to the general mandate to district courts to enforce arbitration awards. Only when one or more of these is met can a district court refuse or defer enforcement; otherwise the Court must confirm the award. (footnote omitted) *Fertilizer Corp. of India v. IDI Management Inc.*, 517 F. Supp. 948, 951 (S.D.Ohio 1981).[9]

[15] "Defendant alleges only the following ground under 9 U.S.C. Sect. 207 as cause for this Court to vacate the Association's arbitration award: (footnote omitted)

> 'Recognition and enforcement of an arbitral award may also be refused if the competent authority in the country where recognition and enforcement is sought finds that
>
> ...
>
> (*b*) The recognition or enforcement of the award would be contrary to the public policy of that country.'

9 U.S.C. Sect. 207, Part 2(*b*) of Art. V. The public policy limitation on the Convention is to be construed narrowly, and should be applied only where enforcement would violate the forum state's most basic notions of morality and justice. *Fotochrome*, 517 F.2d at 516.

[16] "Defendant contends that plaintiff committed fraud by failing to provide a letter of credit in a timely manner. (footnote omitted) It argues that such fraud offends the public policy of the United States, and thus, Part 2(*b*) of Art. V applies to the present matter.

[17] "Similarly, defendant argues that the presence of fraud operates to authorize a court to vacate the arbitration award, pursuant to 9 U.S.C. Sect. 10(a). Sect. 10(a) applies to enforcement actions brought under the Convention, 9 U.S.C. Sect. 207. 9 U.S.C. Sect. 208 states in pertinent part,

---

7. Reported in Yearbook XV (1990) pp. 562-568 (US no. 92).
8. Reported in Yearbook IX (1984) pp. 487-494 (US no. 54).
9. Reported in Yearbook VII (1982) pp. 282-292 (US no. 39).

> 'Chapter 1 [9 U.S.C. Sect. 1 et seq.] applies to actions and proceedings brought under this chapter [9 U.S.C. Sect. 201 et seq.] to the extent that chapter is not in conflict with this chapter or the Convention as ratified by the United States.'

Thus, 9 U.S.C. Sect. 10(a), which falls in Chapter 1, applies to enforcement actions brought pursuant to the Convention. That section provides that a district court 'may make an order vacating the award upon the application of any party to the arbitration ... where the award was procured by corruption, fraud, or undue means ...' 9 U.S.C. Sect. 10(a).

[18] "The Tennessee Cotton Arbitration Act, T.C.A. Sect. 29-5-201 et seq.[10] authorizes a district court's enforcement of a foreign arbitration award. However, defendant argues that fraud is also a basis under state law for vacating the arbitration award,[11] and thus, state law cannot support this Court's enforcement of plaintiff's award. Tennessee law provides that arbitration awards may be vacated where the award was 'procured by corruption, fraud or other undue means'. T.C.A. Sects. 29-5-213(a)(1) and T.C.A. Sects. 29-5-313(a)(1).

[19] "It is unnecessary for the Court to detail defendant's specific allegations of fraud committed by plaintiff because defendant's allegations involve the merits of the contractual dispute and as such are issues not properly before this Court. A court will not reconsider the merits of the breach of contract dispute which is subject to arbitration.

(....)

[20] "Fraud, as covered by 9 U.S.C. Sect. 10(a), requires a showing of bad faith during the arbitration proceedings, such as bribery, undisclosed bias of the arbitrator, or willfully destroying evidence, and further requires that such

10. "The Tennessee Cotton Arbitration Act provides,

> 'Notwithstanding any other provision of law to the contrary, the Court shall not confirm an award under Section 29-5-212 or enter judgment or decree in conformity therewith under Section 29-5-215 where the arbitration hearing or award was made outside of the United States and its territories and the foreign state wherein the award was made does not grant reciprocity in recognition and enforcement of arbitration awards made in the United States or its territories.' T.C.A. Sect. 29-5-220(a)."

11. "Before applying Tennessee law, the Court must determine that it has subject matter jurisdiction. Subject matter jurisdiction exists pursuant to 9 U.S.C. Sect. 203 and pursuant to 28 U.S.C. Sect. 1332, which covers cases where the matter in controversy exceeds $ 50,000 exclusive of interests and costs, and is between a citizen of the State of Tennessee and the subject of a foreign state. T.C.A. Sect. 29-5-212, -215, -312, and -315 provide for the entry of a judgment based upon the arbitration award."

evidence of fraud was unavailable to the arbitrator during the course of the proceeding.

(....)

[21] "In the present matter, defendant does not allege that plaintiff concealed information from the arbitrator, or that the arbitrator was not privy to relevant information. Nor does defendant allege that the proceedings were suspect in any manner, or that evidence of fraud was only discovered after the arbitration proceedings. Defendant simply contends that the arbitrator's decision was faulty. Such an objection cannot constitute fraud under 9 U.S.C. Sect. 10(a), 9 U.S.C. Sect. 207, T.C.A. Sect. 29-5-213(a)(1), or T.C.A. Sect. 29-5-313(a)(1); if it did so constitute, any unsuccessful party would have recourse to contest arbitration claims under those sections.

[22] "For the above reasons, the Court hereby enforces plaintiff's arbitration award."

(....)

272. United States District Court, Central District of California, 1 May 1997, CV 95-2775 RAP (JGX)

Parties:	Plaintiff: Walker & Zanger (West Coast) Ltd. (US) Defendant: Stone Design S.A. (France)
Published in:	4 Federal Supplement, Second Series (C.D.Cal. 1997) pp. 931-940
Articles:	II
Subject matters:	– default court judgment – untimely request for referral to arbitration
Commentary Cases:	¶ 217; [4] = ¶ 216

Facts

From 1988 to 1994, Walker & Zanger (West Coast) Ltd. (Walker Zanger) purchased limestone products from Stone Design S.A. A dispute arose about the quality of certain deliveries and Walker Zanger brought suit in the United States District Court, C.D. California to recoup losses for ten shipments of allegedly unmerchantable limestone for which Stone Design did not accept Walker Zanger's debit memo.

Stone Design were served with the complaint on or about 23 June 1995 and the proof of service was filed with the Court on 2 August 1995. Stone Design did not appear in the action and the clerk of the Court entered default on 8 August 1995. On 30 November 1995, Walker Zanger filed an application for default judgment. The Court granted Walker Zanger's application and a default judgment was entered. On 22 January 1997, the Court granted Walker Zanger's request to appoint a private process-server to serve the writ of execution on Stone Design.

According to Stone Design, Walker Zanger attempted to satisfy a portion of the judgment with the assistance of another corporation which ordered approximately US$ 75,000 worth of limestone from Stone Design and then refused to pay, stating that it had an assignment from Walker Zanger for a portion of the judgment.

Stone Design moved for "Relief from Void Judgment" pursuant to Fed.R.Civ.P. 60(b). Stone Design contended that the judgment was void for lack of subject-matter jurisdiction because (1) pursuant to the parties' arbitration agreement, the dispute had to be arbitrated in France; (2) France's Civil Code gives French courts exclusive jurisdiction over this action because the defendant is a French national; and (3) the Court lacked personal jurisdiction over Stone Design.

The district court, per Paez, DJ, denied relief from void judgment. Regarding the arbitration agreement, the court stated that it did not confer a right to compel arbitration of any dispute at any time. A request brought well over a year after default did not merit reopening the matter.

Excerpt

I. LEGAL STANDARD

[1] "As a general rule a judgment is 'void' if the party against whom default was entered was never properly served or received no actual notice of the action before the answer was due; if the court lacked jurisdiction over the parties; or if the court lacked subject-matter jurisdiction.... Federal Rule of Civil Procedure 60(b)(4) provides, in pertinent part:

> '[o]n motion and upon such terms as are just, the court may relieve a party or a party's legal representative from a final judgment, order, or proceeding for the following reasons ... (4) the judgment is void[.]'

(....)

[2] "Under Fed.R.Civ.P. 55(b)(2) plaintiff need only serve the defendant with notice of the application for default if the defendant has appeared in the action.... Stone Design never appeared before the Court or expressed its intention to defend the lawsuit. Accordingly, defendant was not entitled to notice of the default application."

II. ARBITRATION AGREEMENT DOES NOT MAKE JUDGMENT VOID

[3] The court continued with respect to the arbitration agreement as follows: "Stone Design argues that the judgment is void because the sale contract included an arbitration provision. That provision states:

> 'ARBITRATION: All disputes arising in connection with the present Conditions of Sale will be finally settled under the rules of arbitration of the Court of Commerce of Paris FRANCE.'

At the heart of Stone Design's position is the presumption that the arbitration agreement divests the Court of jurisdiction. As plaintiff points out, international arbitration clauses are governed by the [1958 New York Convention], codified at 9 U.S.C. Sect. 201, to which both France and the United States are signatories. The Federal Arbitration Act is based in part on the Convention, and Sect. 203 provides that district courts shall have original jurisdiction over actions arising under the Convention."

[4] After citing Art. II of the Convention, the court continued: "Commercial legal relationships governed by the Convention include 'a contract evidencing a transaction involving commerce'. *Prograph International, Inc. v. Barhydt*, 928 F. Supp. 983, 988 (N.D.Cal. 1996)[1] (quoting 9 U.S.C. Sect. 2). 'Sect. 2 applies to all contracts that Congress could regulate under the full sweep of its Commerce Clause powers.' Id. (citing *Allied-Bruce Terminix Cos. v. Dobson*, 513 U.S. 265, 115 S.Ct. 834, 839-840, 130 L.Ed.2d 753 (1995)). Consequently, the contracts at issue here fall within the purview of the Convention

[5] "Art. II(3) of the Convention 'imposes a mandatory duty on the courts of a Contracting State to recognize and enforce an agreement to arbitrate....' Id. (quoting *Riley v. Kingsley Underwriting Agencies, Ltd.*, 969 F.2d 953, 959 (10th Cir. 1992)).[2] When a party asks the Court to enforce an agreement under the Convention, 'the Court performs a "very limited inquiry" to decide the following four questions'[]:

(1) Is there an agreement in writing to arbitrate the subject of the dispute?
(2) Does the agreement provide for arbitration in the territory of the signatory of the Convention?
(3) Does the agreement arise out of a legal relationship, whether contractual or not, which is considered as commercial?
(4) Is a party to the agreement not an American citizen, or does the commercial relationship have some reasonable relation with one or more foreign states?

Id. If the Court answers these questions in the affirmative, it is required to order arbitration unless the agreement is void, inoperative or incapable of being performed. Id. (footnote omitted)

1. Reported Yearbook XXIII (1998) pp. 901-909 (US no. 242).
2. Reported in Yearbook XIX (1994) pp. 775-780 (US no. 147).

[6] "Here, all four requirements are clearly satisfied. The contracts provide for arbitration; the arbitration clause is intended to require arbitration in France (plaintiff's protestations to the contrary seem hollow at best); the agreement arises out of commercial transactions between the parties; and Stone Design is not a citizen of the United States. Thus, were the Court faced with a motion to compel arbitration under the Convention, the Court would be required to grant it. However, this case is currently before the Court in a radically different posture.

[7] "Defendant correctly points out that the Supreme Court has articulated a policy favoring international arbitration. See *Mitsubishi Motors Corp. v. Soler Chrysler-Plymouth, Inc.*, 473 U.S. 614, 629, 105 S.Ct. 3346, 87 L.Ed.2d 444 (1985)[3] ('[C]oncerns of international comity, respect for the capacities of foreign and transnational tribunals, and sensitivity to the need of the international commerce system for predictability in the resolution of disputes require that we enforce the parties' agreement [for foreign arbitration], even assuming that a contrary result would be forthcoming in a domestic context').

> 'A parochial refusal by the courts of one country to enforce an international arbitration agreement would not only frustrate these purposes, but would invite unseemly and mutually destructive jockeying by the parties to secure tactical advantages.... [It would] damage the fabric of international commerce and trade, and imperil the willingness and ability of businessmen [and women] to enter into international commercial agreements.'

Id. 473 U.S. at 631. More recently, the Supreme Court, construing the Carriage of Goods by Sea Act (COGSA), stated:

> 'If the United States is to be able to gain the benefits of international accords and have a role as a trusted partner in multilateral endeavors, its courts should be most cautious before interpreting its domestic legislation in such manner as to violate international agreements. That concern counsels against construing COGSA to nullify foreign arbitration clauses because of inconvenience to the plaintiff or insular distrust of the ability of foreign arbitrators to apply the law.'

Vimar Seguros y Reaseguros, S.A. v. M/V Sky Reefer, 515 U.S. 528, 115 S.Ct. 2322, 2329, 132 L.Ed.2d 462 (1995).[4]

3. Reported in Yearbook XI (1986) pp. 555-566 (US no. 59).
4. Reported in Yearbook XX (1995) pp. 974-987 (US no. 186).

[8] "Nonetheless, the Ninth Circuit has made it clear that the policy of the Federal Arbitration Act 'does not confer a right to compel arbitration of any dispute at any time; it confers only the right to obtain an order directing that arbitration proceed in the matter provided for in the parties' agreement.' *Britton v. Co-op Banking Group*, 916 F.2d 1405, 1413 (9th Cir. 1990); see also *Arbitration Between Standard Tallow Corp. and Kil-Management*, 901 F. Supp. 147, 151 (S.D.N.Y. 1995) (holding parties agreement to arbitrate in London valid, but refusing to provide relief where respondents had not filed petition to compel arbitration).

[9] "Likewise, nothing in the Convention suggests the court is required or empowered to sua sponte enforce an arbitration agreement. Rather, the language of the Convention requires a court to refer the parties to arbitration 'at the request of one of the parties'. Defendants provide no authority to suggest that a request brought well over a year after default was entered requires the Court to reopen the matter under Rule 60(b) and refer the parties to arbitration. Consequently, defendant's argument that the Court lacked subject-matter jurisdiction because the parties were required to resolve the dispute pursuant to the terms of the arbitration clause fails.

[10] "Embedded in defendant's argument concerning the arbitration provision is an argument that plaintiff committed fraud upon the court. This argument fails because regardless of whether plaintiff provided the court with copies of the sales contracts that included the arbitration provision, the outcome would have been the same."

III. FRENCH COURTS DO NO HAVE EXCLUSIVE JURISDICTION

[11] "With respect to its arbitration argument, defendant concedes that this court is bound by the Convention. Sect. 203 of the Convention provides that an action falling under the Convention shall be deemed to arise under the laws and treaties of the United States, such that the district courts shall have original jurisdiction regardless of the amount in controversy. 9 U.S.C. Sect. 203. Moreover, diversity jurisdiction was available pursuant to 42 U.S.C. Sect. 1332(a)(2) because the action was one between a citizen of a state and a citizen of a foreign state. Consequently, under the laws of the United States, which this court is bound to follow, the court had subject-matter jurisdiction over plaintiff's action. Thus, even if defendant were correct that the French Code provides for exclusive jurisdiction over all actions against French nationals, the laws of the United States govern this Court's jurisdiction, and the Court could not conclude it lacked jurisdiction.

(....)

[12] "This court did not lack subject-matter jurisdiction over this action at the time the default was entered, and the judgment is not void." The court further found that it had properly asserted personal jurisdiction and denied the motion for relief.

273. United States District Court, District of Colorado, 17 June 1997, Civil Action No. 96-WY-1290-WD

Parties:	Plaintiff: Mangistaumunaigaz Oil Production Association (Kazakhstan) Defendant: United World Trade, Inc. (USA)
Published in:	No publication information available
Articles:	IV(1)(*b*); V; V(1)(*b*); V(2)(*b*)
Subject matters:	– no basis for counterclaim under Convention – no requirement of full hearing on motion to confirm (enforce) award – expense of arbitration does not constitute "unable to present case" – failure to provide original arbitration agreement no defense – failure to make third party a party to the arbitration – international public policy – possibility of sanctions against defendant and its counsel
Commentary Cases:	[1]-[2] = ¶ 304; [3]-[6] = ¶ 301; [7] = ¶ 503; [8]-[9] = ¶ 511; [10] = ¶ 403; [11]-[13] = ¶ 226 + ¶ 524 (failure to make third party a party to the arbitration); [13] = ¶ 518; [14] = ¶ 301

Facts

Mangistaumunaigaz Oil Production Association (MOP), a state organization wholly owned by the Republic of Kazakhstan, and United World Trade, Inc. (UWT) entered into a contract for the sale of crude oil by MOP to UWT. Disputes arose between the parties regarding payment for certain shipments, including an allegation that the bill of lading for two shipments was stolen from a Kazakhstan Commerce Foreign Economic Association (KCFEA) representative.

On 28 September 1992, UWT filed suit against MOP in the United States District Court for the District of Colorado, asserting various claims arising out of the alleged violation of a 17 December 1991 Preliminary Agreement between UWT and MOP. On 16 February 1993, pursuant to Clause 15 of the 23 January 1992 contract which provided, inter alia, "Arbitration, if any, by ICC Rules in London", MOP filed a request for arbitration with the ICC. UWT declined to appoint an arbitrator or to pay its share of the ICC's advance on costs, claiming that the contract did not contain a binding arbitration agreement. UWT further asserted that the arbitration proceedings should be stayed pending the resolution of its suit in the District of Colorado. On 21 May 1993, the district court granted MOP's motion to dismiss the suit for lack of subject matter jurisdiction. UWT appealed to the Tenth Circuit Court of Appeals which on 29 August 1994 affirmed the decision of the district court.[1] The United States Supreme Court refused certiorari on 17 January 1995.

MOP filed an action in the Commercial Court of the High Court in London, England, seeking a determination on the validity of the arbitration agreement. On 21 February 1995, Potter, J held that there was a valid, effective and binding agreement to arbitrate and ordered UWT to pay costs, noting that "the motivation for [UWT's] resistance to arbitration was ... simply an effort to ward off the evil day...."[2]

UWT refused to sign the ICC Terms of Reference and declined to attend the hearing held in London on 15 January 1996. Through its counsel, Dufford & Brown, UWT submitted its objections by written correspondence to the arbitral tribunal. An award for the amount of US$ 7,333,195.68 plus UK£ 83,860 plus interest was made in favor of MOP on 4 April 1996.

MOP sought to enforce the award in the district court. UWT asserted three defenses: (1) absence of the original agreement to arbitrate; (2) the award was contrary to public policy of the United States; and (3) UWT had not been permitted to participate fully in the arbitration proceedings due to the excessive cost. The court found all of MOP's defenses without merit, noting, in particular, that it could not accept the argument that where litigation is expensive a party has established that it was "unable to present its case".

1. Published in 33 F.3d 1232 (10th Cir. 1994).
2. Published in [1995] 1 Lloyd's Rep. 617-622.

Excerpt

I. UWT'S COUNTERCLAIM

[1] "In its answer to plaintiff's Motion to Confirm, defendant has asserted four counterclaims: (1) breach of contract (the 17 December 1991 Preliminary Agreement); (2) anticipatory repudiation of the contract; (3) fraud and misrepresentation; and (4) consequential damages. In response to defendant's Counterclaims plaintiff moved to strike asserting that the New York Convention does not provide for the assertion or determination in a confirmation proceeding. This Court agrees.

[2] "Pursuant to 9 U.S.C. Sect. 207:

> 'Within three years after an arbitral award falling under the Convention is made, any party to the arbitration may apply to any court having jurisdiction under this chapter for an order confirming the award as against any other party to the arbitration. *The court shall confirm the award unless it finds one of the grounds for refusal or deferral of recognition or enforcement of the award specified in the said Convention.*'

Id. (emphasis added). The plain language of Sect. 207 requires that this court may only refuse to confirm the award on one of those bases, set forth in the Convention, for refusal, deferral or enforcement exists. The Convention does not provide any basis for the assertion of counterclaims. See *Evergreen Systems, Inc. v. Geotech Lizenz AG*, 697 F. Supp. 1254, 1257 (E.D.N.Y. 1988)[3] (the right to assert counterclaims in the context of enforcement proceedings appears nowhere in the Convention); *Hewlett-Packard, Inc. v. Berg*, 867 F. Supp. 1126, 1132 (D.Mass. 1994)[4] (Convention only allows for specific and limited attacks on validity of the claim in confirmation proceedings and may not adjudicate a counterclaim); *Fertilizer Corporation of India v. IDI Management, Inc.*, 517 F. Supp. 948, 963 (S.D.Ohio 1981)[5] (holding that counterclaim in confirmation proceedings is inappropriate). Given the narrow nature of the proceedings is inappropriate). Given the narrow nature of the proceedings before the Court, defendant's assertion of counterclaims are clearly inappropriate under the case law and Convention. Accordingly, plaintiff's Motion to Strike must be granted."

---

3. Reported in Yearbook XV (1990) pp. 562-568 (US no. 92).
4. Summarized in Yearbook XXI (1996) pp. 808-814 at p. 809 (US no. 204).
5. Reported in Yearbook VII (1982) pp. 282-292 (US no. 39).

II. UWT'S DEFENSES

[3] "UWT requested and this Court, by minute order dated 15 May 1997, summarily granted it an evidentiary hearing on its defenses to the confirmation of the arbitral award. Plaintiff objected to this hearing, asserting it was unnecessary. This hearing was set for 10 June 1997. On 4 June 1997, counsel for UWT filed a motion to continue the 10 June 1997 evidentiary hearing on the basis that 'counsel for UWT has been unable to reach their clients, despite repeated attempts to do so.' Plaintiff opposed the continuance asserting that no good cause has been shown for continuance and no evidentiary hearing was necessary. This Court denied UWT's motion for a continuance and issued a scheduling order for the 10 June 1997 hearing wherein this Court stated that it expected defendants to be present for the 10 June 1997 hearing.

[4] "At 7:56 a.m. on 9 June 1997, this Court received a facsimile from counsel for UWT in response to the Court's scheduling order. Counsel for UWT stated that on 2 June 1997, it had attempted to contact its client by phone, at which time it learned that UWT's telephone had been disconnected. However, UWT's counsel noted that all of its correspondence sent to UWT had never been returned. Counsel for UWT further stated that he 'attempted to hand-deliver letters to the client's last known addresses, one of which had been bulldozed and the other which has no office building – it is a vacant lot.' Despite this and other efforts counsel was apparently unable to locate its client, UWT.

[5] "Upon receipt of Defense Counsel's facsimile this Court held a telephonic status conference with counsel for both the plaintiff and defendant at 5:00 p.m. on 9 June 1997. At this time counsel for defendant informed the Court that he had been contacted by his client, but that the individual he intended to testify at the hearing was in Salt Lake City, Utah and the other principal for UWT was in Las Vegas, Nevada. Neither could appear in person for the 10 June 1997 hearing, although they could appear by phone. This Court declined to accept unsworn testimony by phone and vacated the evidentiary hearing.

[6] "Based upon the case law and defendant's indifference to its opportunity for 'its day in court' this Court finds that an evidentiary hearing is not required to resolve the defenses assorted by defendant. See *Legion Ins. Co. v. Insurance General Agency, Inc.*, 822 F.2d 541, 543 (5th Cir. 1987) (affirming district court's disposition of motion to confirm an arbitration award on the pleadings); *Booth v. Hume Publishing, Inc.*, 902 F.2d 925, 932 (11th Cir. 1990) (under Federal Arbitration Act district court need not conduct a full hearing on motion to vacate or confirm – such motions may be decided on the papers without oral testimony); *Allen Group, Inc. v. Allen Deutschland GMBH*, 877 F.

Supp. 395, 398 (W.D.Mich. 1994) (same). As set forth below, the legal nature of the defenses raised do not require this Court to hold an evidentiary hearing. Moreover, defendant's conduct and failure to make itself available for the hearing further reveals the hollow nature of defendant's claim for the need of an evidentiary hearing.

[7] "As a preliminary matter this Court notes that public policy favors recognizing and enforcing international arbitration agreements. See *Indocomex Fibres PTE, Ltd. v. Cotton Company International, Inc.*, 916 F. Supp. 721, 726 (W.D.Tenn. 1996).[6] Under 9 U.S.C. Sect. 207, the burden of proof as to every element of a defense is on the party resisting confirmation of the award. Id. citing with approval *Imperial Ethiopian Government v. Baruch-Foster Corp.*, 535 F.2d 334, 336 (5th Cir. 1976).[7]"

1. UWT Was Unable to Present Its Case

[8] "Defendant's first defense to the confirmation of the award is that it in accordance with Art. V(1)(*b*) UWT 'was unable to present its case at the arbitration'. Defense counsel ... asserts that one of the principals for UWT would testify 'that the cost of filing UWT's counterclaims in the International Chamber of Commerce (ICC) arbitration would have exceeded several hundred thousand dollars and was prohibitively expensive.'

[9] "This Court finds defendant's assertion incredulous, especially given the extensive litigation expenses that UWT has clearly expended in attempting to keep this litigation in its home court. Moreover, if this Court was to accept the argument, that where litigation is expensive a party has established that it was 'unable to present his case', it would be difficult to imagine when this defense would not exist. Finally, given the 'stakes of the game', UWT's assertion that the cost was prohibitively expensive is an empty argument – as empty as the vacant lot it used for its address. As set forth in ... the Arbitral Award, UWT refused to participate in the proceedings, but instead chose to plead its case through letters and correspondence to the arbitral tribunal. UWT does not and cannot argue it failed to receive notice of the proceedings or appointment of the arbitrator. Accordingly, this Court finds that UWT was unable to present its case, but chose not to."

6. Reported in this Yearbook as US no. 271, pp. 792-799.
7. Reported in Yearbook II (1977) p. 252 (US no. 10).

2. *Failure to Provide Original Agreement or a Duly Certified Copy in Accordance with Article IV(1)(b)*

[10] "This argument is at best disingenuous. While UWT coyly asserts that MOP failed to provide the original agreement or a duly certified copy thereof, nowhere does UWT suggest that the 23 January 1992 contract which was the subject of the arbitration, is not or was not the agreement entered into by the parties. Absent some proof or claim that the copy of the contract the arbitral tribunal based its decision upon was not the contract entered into between the parties, the Court does not believe this failure to adhere to a technical requirement is a defense to this enforcement action. Accordingly, this Court finds defendant's argument wholly without merit."

3. *Enforcement Is Contrary to Public Policy*

[11] "Defendant further asserts that it would be against public policy to enforce this award based upon the fact that KCFEA was not made a party to the arbitration process. Defendant contends that because KCFEA was not made a party to the process complete relief would not have been afforded by the arbitration process. This argument was addressed by the arbitral tribunal in ... its Award wherein it noted that no claims were made against KCFEA and the arbitrators found they lacked the discretion to add parties which were not identified as the claimants or respondents in the request for arbitration. It should also be noted that while in one breath UWT asserts that it was precluded from asserting counterclaims against KCFEA, in the other breath it asserts 'that the cost of filing UWT's counterclaim in the ... ICC would have exceeded several hundred thousand dollars and was prohibitively expensive.'
[12] "More importantly, UWT does not contend that as a result of the arbitration it is precluded or estopped from pursuing in some forum its alleged claims against KCFEA.
[13] "This Court must, narrowly construe the public policy limitation and as stated in *Indocomex*

> '[t]he public policy limitation on the Convention is to be construed narrowly, and should be applied only where enforcement would violate the forum state's most basic notions of morality and justice.'

supra, at 727 (citations omitted). UWT has failed to present any cogent argument that would support this Court in finding that enforcement of this award would violate the basic notions of morality and justice. To the contrary, based upon the facts and circumstances to refuse to enforce this award would violate the basic principles of fairness and finality. This Court will not serve as a conduit for UWT's continued effort to 'ward off the evil day'. Accordingly, this Court finds UWT's defenses wholly without legal or factual merit.

[14] "This Court finds defendant's Defenses are wholly without legal or factual merit. Moreover, based upon the conduct of defendant and the meritless defenses asserted in response to plaintiff's motion for confirmation of the Arbitral Award, this Court believes that defendant's counterclaims and request for evidentiary hearing may have been done solely for the purpose of causing unnecessary delay in violation of Rule 11(b)(1) and (2), Fed.R.Civ.P.[8] Accordingly, a separate Order to Show Cause will be issued by this Court upon defendant UWT and defendant's counsel to show cause why its conduct should not be sanctioned."

[15] The court granted MOP's motion for confirmation of the award and its motion to strike UWT's counterclaims.

---

8. Rule 11 of the Federal Rules of Civil Procedure reads in relevant part:

"(b) Representations to the Court
By presenting to the court (whether by signing, filing, submitting, or later advocating) a pleading, written motion, or other paper, an attorney or unrepresented party is certifying that to the best of the person's knowledge, information, and belief, formed after an inquiry reasonable under the circumstances, –
(1) it is not being presented for any improper purpose, such as to harass or to cause unnecessary delay or needless increase in the cost of litigation;
(2) the claims, defenses, and other legal contentions therein are warranted by existing law or by a nonfrivolous argument of the extension, modification, or reversal of existing law or the establishment of new law
(....)

(c) Sanctions
If, after notice and a reasonable opportunity to respond, the court determines that subdivision (b) has been violated, the court may ... impose an appropriate sanction upon the attorneys, law firms, or parties that have violated subdivision (b) or are responsible for the violation".

274. United States Court of Appeals, Second Circuit, 23 March 1998, No. 97-9075

Parties:	Petitioner/appellee: AAOT Foreign Economic Association (VO) Technostroyexport (nationality not indicated) Respondent/appellant: International Development and Trade Services, Inc. (nationality not indicated)
Published in:	139 Federal Reporter, Third Series (2nd Cir. 1998) pp. 980-982
Articles:	V(2)(*b*)
Subject matter:	– waiver of right to object to corruption of arbitral tribunal
Commentary Cases:	¶ 524 (bribery of arbitral tribunal); [5]-[7] = ¶ 303

Facts

In 1991 and 1992, International Development and Trade Services, Inc. (IDTS) entered into contracts for the purchase of non-ferrous metals from AAOT Foreign Economic Association (VO) Technostroyexport (Techno). The contracts contained arbitration clauses providing for arbitration at the International Court of Commercial Arbitration of the Chamber of Commerce and Industry of the Russian Federation in Moscow. Disputes arose under the contracts and in the ensuing arbitration, two awards were made in favor of Techno of approximately US$ 200 million. Techno sought enforcement of the awards. IDTS opposed the enforcement arguing that the Arbitration Court was corrupt, as it had "tested" their integrity and found them willing to take bribes. The District Court for the Southern District of New York granted the motion for an order to confirm the awards.

IDTS appealed, but the Court of Appeals, per William W. Schwarzer, SDJ, affirmed the order of the court below, finding that IDTS had knowledge of concrete facts possibly indicating the corruption of the Arbitration Court, but despite this knowledge had remained silent. It had thus waived whatever objections it had to the tribunal.

Excerpt

[1] "Techno filed a petition in the district court to confirm the awards under the [1958 New York Convention] as implemented by 9 U.S.C. Sects. 201-208. IDTS opposed enforcement of the awards under Art. V(2)(*b*) of the Convention as 'contrary to the public policy' of the United States.[1]

[2] ".... Following the initiation of the arbitration proceedings, IDTS sent an interpreter – Tamara Sicular – to Moscow to file papers, clarify the status of the cases and gain an understanding of the procedures that would be followed. On 14 July 1993, Sicular met with Sergey Orlov, the Secretary of the Arbitration Court, and his superior at the Chamber of Commerce. According to IDTS, Sicular, on her own initiative and to test the integrity of the court, asked Orlov whether the court could be 'bought'. Orlov responded affirmatively and offered to 'fix' the cases for IDTS in exchange for a substantial payment. His superior later that day told Sicular he would personally assist IDTS 'sort out' the arbitration. On the next day, Orlov presented Sicular with his plan which called for a payment of US$ 1 million for which he would rig the tribunal.

[3] "There followed a series of communications with Orlov over the next two months in which Sicular ostensibly sought to gather further evidence and establish that the Arbitration Court and its officials were corrupt. They ended inconclusively in September 1993, without any payment being made. Sicular passed all of this information on to IDTS president Edith Reich prior to the commencement of any arbitration hearings. The Arbitration Court held hearings beginning in December 1994 and ending in September 1995. IDTS, represented by several attorneys, participated actively. The final awards in favor of Techno were rendered in March 1996.

[4] "In November 1996, Techno filed its petition to confirm the awards in the district court. In its opposition to the petition, IDTS for the first time disclosed the offer to bribe the Arbitration Court – the sting, as IDTS describes it – in support of its contention that enforcement of an award rendered by a corrupt tribunal would be contrary to the public policy of the United States. The district court determined that IDTS's allegations failed to establish

---

1. "(....)

On appeal, IDTS also argues that it was denied due process, relying on Art. V(1)(*b*) which provides that recognition and enforcement may be denied when a party 'was otherwise unable to present its case.' Although IDTS did raise a due process concern to the district court in a sur-reply memorandum, it did so only as part of the response to Techno's waiver argument and did not squarely present to the district court the argument it now presents to this Court. Therefore, IDTS did not properly raise this point in the district court; in any event, we do not reach it."

that the Arbitration Court was not impartial in these cases;[2] that the use of the public policy exception is not appropriate where one party to an arbitration has initiated the situation itself prior to the commencement of the arbitration hearing, participated thereafter fully in the arbitration, received an unfavorable award, and then alleges that the arbitral proceeding was corrupt as a means of avoiding an unfavorable result; and that IDTS waived its right to assert the public policy exception where it had knowledge of the facts but remained silent until an adverse award was rendered. Because we agree with the court's third ground, it is unnecessary for us to considered whether application of the public policy exception would be appropriate in this case. We also need not address whether IDTS is estopped from arguing that the Arbitration Court was corrupt because it initiated the bribe. Consequently, we do not reach the issue of whether IDTS authorized Sicular to offer the bribe.

[5] "The settled law of this circuit precludes attacks on the qualifications of arbitrators on grounds previously known but not raised until after an award has been rendered. 'Where a party has knowledge of facts possibly indicating bias or partiality on the part of an arbitrator he cannot remain silent and later object to the award of the arbitrators on that ground. His silence constitutes a waiver of the objection.' *Ilios Shipping & Trading Corp., S.A. v. American Anthracite & Bituminous Coal Corp.*, 148 F. Supp. 698, 700 (S.D.N.Y.), aff'd 245 F.2d 873 (2d Cir. 1957) (per curiam); see also *Cook Industries, Inc. v. Itoh & Co. (America) Inc.*, 449 F.2d 106, 107-108 (2d Cir. 1971) ('Appellant cannot remain silent, raising no objection during the course of the arbitration proceeding, and when an award adverse to him has been handed down complain of a situation of which he had knowledge from the first.'); *Swift Indep. Packing Co. v. District Union Local One, United Food & Commercial Workers Int'l Union*, 575 F. Supp. 912, 916 (N.D.N.Y. 1983) (applying waiver doctrine where facts discovered after close of hearing but not disclosed until after rendering of award).

[6] "This law of waiver controls the outcome of this appeal. It is undisputed that IDTS had knowledge of concrete facts possibly indicating the corruption of the Arbitration Court – namely, the apparent willingness of some members of the Arbitration Court to take bribes. Despite this knowledge, IDTS remained silent. Accordingly, it cannot now object to the award based on these facts.

2. "IDTS contends that the district court ignored its corruption challenge and instead addressed partiality, an issue not raised. It argues that a tribunal may be found to be corrupt without regard to whether it is shown to be partial. Our disposition of this appeal makes it unnecessary to address this point."

[7] "IDTS contends that it cannot be charged with waiver because it did not voluntarily and intentionally waive its right to a corruption-free tribunal. It argues that any attempt to seek relief would have been fútile: from the tribunal because it was corrupt, from the Arbitration Court because its officials were corrupt and because its rule precluded it, and from the Russian courts because the applicable law did not permit it. We express no view on the validity of these contentions. But even if they are valid, it was incumbent on IDTS to notify opposing counsel. It is no answer, as IDTS claims, that it was unlikely that Techno would agree to the charge of corruption of the tribunal or to surrender any perceived resulting advantage. Had Techno insisted in the face of IDTS's charges on proceeding with the arbitration as arranged, IDTS would have preserved its objections and been free to raise them in any later confirmation proceeding. Instead IDTS tried to put the case in a posture in which, as the district judge aptly characterized it, 'Heads I win, tails you lose.'

[8] "We therefore conclude that IDTS waived whatever objections it had to the tribunal and affirm."

275. United States District Court, Southern District of New York, 20 May 1998, No. 98 Civil 1057 (BDP)

Parties:	Petitioner: NAR S.p.A. - Industria Nastri Adesivi (Italy) Defendant: I.R. Industries, Inc. (US)
Published in:	5 Federal Supplement, Second Series, p. 203 et seq.; 1998 U.S. Dist. LEXIS 7644
Articles:	IV; V
Subject matter:	- unopposed request for confirmation
Commentary Cases:	¶ 401; ¶ 503

Facts

Pursuant to an arbitration clause in an agreement dated 14 April 1988 between NAR S.p.A. - Industria Nastri Adesivi (NAR) and I.R. Industries, Inc., NAR commenced ICC arbitration in Milan, Italy. An award was made in favor of NAR which moved to have confirmed in the district court. Its motion for confirmation was unopposed and after determining that NAR had complied with the formal requirements for enforcement under the 1958 New York Convention and that there was no ground for refusal which had been invoked by the defendant, the award was confirmed.

Excerpt

[1] "Congress has provided federal district courts with the authority to confirm foreign arbitral awards. 9 U.S.C. Sect. 207; see also *Yusuf Ahmed Alghanim & Sons, W.L.L. v. Toys "R" Us, Inc.*, 126 F.3d 15, 19 (2d Cir. 1997).[1] To obtain enforcement of the arbitral award, a party may apply to federal district court, attaching copies of the arbitral award and the agreement to arbitrate. See Convention, Art. IV (reprinted following 9 U.S.C. Sect. 201). NAR has complied with these requirements. Once the requirements are

1. Reported in Yearbook XXIII (1998) pp. 1058-1067 (US no. 261).

complied with, the district court's role in reviewing a foreign arbitral award is limited: 'The court shall confirm the award unless it finds one of the grounds for refusal or deferral of recognition specified in the said Convention.' 9 U.S.C. Sect. 207. These grounds for refusal must be invoked and proved by the party opposing confirmation of the award, and are not applicable here where the motion is unopposed. See Convention, Art. V. Petitioner's motion to confirm the arbitral award is granted."

276. United States Court of Appeals, Eleventh Circuit, 22 May 1998, Nos. 94-2982, 94-2530

Parties:	Defendants/third-party-plaintiffs/appellants: (1) Industrial Risk Insurers (US); (2) Barnard & Burk Group, Inc. (US); (3) Barnard and Burk Engineers and Constructors, Inc. (US) et al. Third-Party-Defendant/appellee/cross-appellant: M.A.N. Gutehoffnungshütte GmbH (Germany)
Published in:	141 Federal Reporter, Third Series (11th Cir. 1998) pp. 1434-1451
Articles:	I(1); V; V(1)(*d*); V(2)(*b*)
Subject matters:	- award not considered as domestic - violation of procedural rules (no) - "side switching" of expert witness - grounds for refusal of enforcement under Convention are exclusive - no application of domestic grounds for vacating (setting aside) of award to refusal of enforcement - post-award prejudgment interest
Commentary Cases:	[1]-[7] = ¶ 102; [8] = ¶ 503; [12]-[14] = ¶ 513; [15]-[19] = ¶ 524 ("side switching" by expert witness); [20]-[22] = ¶ 501 + ¶ 524 (award "arbitrary and capricious"); [23]-[25] = ¶ 307

Facts

Barnard & Burk Group, Inc. (Barnard & Burk) contracted with Nitram to provide and install a "tail gas expander" in Nitram's nitric acid manufacturing plant in Florida. Barnard & Burk then contracted with the German turbine manufacturer, M.A.N. Maschinenfabrik Augsburg-Nürnberg AG GmbH, for the purchase of the tail gas expander. M.A.N. Gutehoffnungshütte GmbH (MAN GHH) is a spin-off corporation and the successor in interest to M.A.N. Maschinenfabrik Augsburg-Nürnberg AG GmbH.

Serious problems arose following the installation of the tail gas expander causing the machine to be wrecked twice and involving millions of dollars in damage. Disputes arose between Nitram and its business risk insurer Industrial Risk Insurers (IRI) when the latter refused to pay Nitram for certain losses causes by the first wreck. Nitram sued both IRI and Barnard & Burk arguing that one of them had to pay for the remaining losses. Barnard & Burk filed a third-party claim against MAN GHH. Nitram settled its claims with IRI which was subrogated in Nitram's claims against Barnard & Burk.

MAN GHH moved to compel arbitration of Barnard & Burk's third-party claim against it, relying on the arbitration clause in their contract which provided for AAA arbitration in Tampa, Florida. Nitram then stated claims directly against MAN GHH and IRI, as Nitram's subrogee, added a cross-claim against MAN GHH. MAN GHH successfully moved for arbitration of these claims as well. Barnard & Burk settled with Nitram and with IRI, leaving the arbitrators to determine:

(1) Barnard & Burk's third party complaint against MAN GHH;
(2) Nitram's complaint against MAN GHH; and
(3) IRI's cross-claim against MAN GHH as Nitram's subrogee.

All these claims turned on the question whether the wrecks were caused by MAN GHH's expander or Barnard & Burk's design and installation. The arbitrators held that the latter's design and piping had caused the two wrecks and also awarded MAN GHH costs and conversion rate compensation.

Barnard & Burk sought to vacate the awards. On 24 March 1994, the United States District Court for the Middle District of Florida denied the motion and confirmed the awards (published in 848 F. Supp. 162). On appeal, The Court of Appeals, per Tjoflat, CJ, sua sponte examined the source of its jurisdiction and held that the district court had erred in concluding that the case was controlled by Chapter 1 of the Federal Arbitration Act (FAA) which covers domestic arbitral proceedings. The Court of Appeals for the Eleventh Circuit, followed the First, Second, Seventh and Ninth Circuits in holding that an arbitral award made in the United States, under American law, falls within the purview of the New York Convention, and thus Chapter 2 of the FAA, when one of the parties to the arbitration is domiciled or has its principal place of business outside of the United States. On the merits of the appeal, the Court declined to vacate the award, holding, inter alia, that the grounds for vacating the award were exclusively the grounds for refusal of enforcement under the New York Convention and therefore the non-statutory defense against a domestic award that the award is "arbitrary and capricious" could therefore not be invoked against the award.

Excerpt

I. JURISDICTION

[1] "As a threshold matter, we must determine the source of our jurisdiction. We must inquire sua sponte into the source of our jurisdiction whenever it might be in question. See *Miscott Corp. v. Zaremba Walden Co.*, 848 F.2d 1190, 1192 (11th Cir. 1988). The district court proceeded in the belief that its jurisdiction was grounded in diversity, and that its treatment of the arbitral proceedings was therefore controlled by Chapter 1 of the Federal Arbitration Act (FAA), 9 U.S.C. Sects. 1-16 (1994), which covers domestic arbitral proceedings. We conclude that the district court was in error, and hold that the case is controlled by Chapter 2 of the FAA, 9 U.S.C. Sects. 201-208, which covers international arbitral proceedings.

[2] "The instant case presents and issue of first impression in this court: Do the [1958 New York Convention], and thus the provisions of Chapter 2 of the FAA, govern an arbitral award granted to a foreign corporation by an arbitral panel sitting in the United States and applying American federal or state law? We hold that they do.

[3] "The New York Convention was drafted in 1958 under the auspices of the United Nations.... The United States acceded to the treaty in 1970, and Chapter 2 of the FAA was passed that same year. The purpose of the New York Convention, and of the United States' accession to the Convention, is to 'encourage the recognition and enforcement of international arbitral awards', *Bergesen v. Joseph Muller Corp.*, 710 F.2d 928, 932 (2d Cir. 1983),[1] to 'relieve congestion in the courts and to provide parties with an alternative method for dispute resolution that [is] speedier and less costly than litigation'. *Ultra-cashmere House, Ltd. v. Meyer*, 664 F.2d 1176, 1179 (11th Cir. 1981). See also generally Leonard V. Quigley, 'Accession by the United States to the United Nations Convention on the Recognition and Enforcement of Foreign Arbitral Awards', 70 Yale L.J. 1049 (1961) (recounting the deliberations of the New York Convention and describing accession's benefits for the US). The Convention, and American enforcement of it through the FAA, 'provide[] businesses with a widely used system through which to obtain domestic enforcement of international commercial arbitration awards resolving contract and other transactional disputes, subject only to minimal standards of domestic judicial review for basic fairness and consistency with national public policy.' G. Richard Shell, 'Trade Legalism and International Relations Theory: An Analysis of the World Trade Organization', 44 Duke L.J. 829, 888 (1995).

1. Reported in Yearbook IX (1984) pp. 487-494 (US no. 54).

[4] "The New York Convention is incorporated into federal law by the FAA, which governs the enforcement of arbitration agreements, and of arbitral awards made pursuant to such agreements, in federal and state courts. See *Allied-Bruce Terminix Cos. Inc. v. Dobson*, 513 U.S. 265, 269-273, 115 S.Ct. 834, 837-839, 130 L.Ed.2d 753 (1995). Chapter 2 of the Act, 9 U.S.C. Sects. 201-208, mandates the enforcement of the New York Convention in United States courts. See 9 U.S.C. Sect. 201.[2] Chapter 2 generally establishes a strong presumption in favor of arbitration of international commercial disputes, see *Mitsubishi Motors Corp. v. Soler Chrysler-Plymouth, Inc.*, 473 U.S. 614, 638-640, 105 S.Ct. 3346, 3359-3361, 87 L.Ed.2d 444 (1985),[3] and creates original federal subject-matter jurisdiction over any action arising under the Convention. See 9 U.S.C. Sect. 203;[4] H.R. Rep. No. 91-1181, at 2 (1970), reprinted in 1970 U.S.C.C.A.N. 3601, 3602 ('Section 203 gives original jurisdiction over any action or proceeding falling under the Convention to the district court of the United States regardless of the amount in controversy.'). As an exercise of the Congress' treaty power and as federal law, '[t]he Convention must be enforced according to its terms over all prior inconsistent rules of law.' *Sedco, Inc. v. Petroleos Mexicanos Mexican Nat'l Oil Co. (Pemex)*, 767 F.2d 1140, 1145 (5th Cir. 1985).[5]

[5] "The Convention by its terms applies to only two sorts of arbitral awards: 1) awards made in a country other than that in which enforcement of the award is sought, and 2) awards 'not considered as domestic awards in' the country where enforcement of the award is sought. It is apparent that the arbitral award at issue in the instant case does not fall within the first category. We hold, however, that it does fall within the second category. Sect. 202 of the FAA provides that all arbitral awards arising out of commercial relationships fall under the Convention, except for those awards that 'aris[e] out of ... a [commercial] relationship which is entirely between citizens of the United

---

2. 9 U.S.C. Sect. 201 reads:

> "The Convention on the Recognition and Enforcement of Foreign Arbitral Awards of June 10, 1958, shall be enforced in United States courts in accordance with this chapter."

3. Reported in Yearbook XI (1986) pp. 555-566 (US no. 59).
4. 9 U.S.C. Sect. 203 reads in relevant part:

> "An action or proceeding falling under the Convention shall be deemed to arise under the laws and treaties of the United States. The district courts of the United States ... shall have original jurisdiction over such an action or proceeding, regardless of the amount in controversy."

5. Reported in Yearbook XII (1987) pp. 539-546 (US no. 70).

States....' 9 U.S.C. Sect. 202.[6] We read this provision to define all arbitral awards not 'entirely between citizens of the United States' as 'non-domestic' for purposes of Art. I of the Convention.

[6] "We join the First, Second, Seventh, and Ninth Circuits in holding that arbitration agreements and awards 'not considered as domestic' in the United States are those agreements and awards

> 'which are subject to the Convention not because [they were] made abroad, but because [they were] made within the legal framework of another country, e.g., pronounced in accordance with foreign law *or involving parties domiciled or having their principal place of business outside the enforcing jurisdiction*. We prefer this broad[] construction because it is more in line with the intended purpose of the treaty, which was entered into to encourage the recognition and enforcement of international arbitration awards.'

Bergesen, 710 F.2d at 932 (emphasis added) (internal citation omitted); see also *Yusuf Ahmed Alghanim & Sons, W.L.L. v. Toys "R" Us, Inc.*, 126 F.3d 15, 18-19 (2d Cir. 1997);[7] *Jain v. de Mere*, 51 F.3d 686, 689 (7th Cir. 1995)[8] (stating that the New York Convention and Sect. 202 'mandate[] that any commercial arbitral agreement, unless it is between two United States citizens, involves property located in the United States, and has no reasonable relationship with one or more foreign states, falls within the Convention'); *Ministry of Defense of the Islamic Republic of Iran v. Gould Inc.*, 887 F.2d 1357, 1362 (9th Cir. 1989)[9] (holding that New York Convention applies when arbitral 'award (1) ... arise[s] out of a legal relationship (2) which is commercial in nature and (3)

---

6. "The entire section reads:

> 'An arbitration agreement or arbitral award arising out of a legal relationship, whether contractual or not, which is considered as commercial, including a transaction, contract, or agreement described in section 2 of this title, falls under the Convention. An agreement or award arising out of such a relationship which is entirely between citizens of the United States shall be deemed not to fall under the Convention unless that relationship involves property located abroad, envisages performance or enforcement abroad, or has some other reasonable relation with one or more foreign states. For the purpose of this section a corporation is a citizen of the United States if it is incorporated or has its principal place of business in the United States.'
>
> 9 U.S.C. Sect. 202."

7. Reported in Yearbook XXIII (1998) pp. 1058-1067 (US no. 261).
8. Reported in Yearbook XXI (1996) pp. 759-766 (US no. 198).
9. Reported in Yearbook XV (1990) pp. 605-611 (US no. 100).

which is not entirely domestic in scope', and that the award at issue was 'obviously not domestic in nature because Iran [was] one of the parties to the agreement'); *Ledee v. Ceramiche Ragno*, 684 F.2d 184, 186-187 (1st Cir. 1982)[10] (stating that Chapter 2 mandates enforcement of a written commercial arbitral agreement when one of the parties to the agreement is not an American citizen). Specifically for purposes of the case sub judice, we hold that an arbitral award made in the United States, under American law, falls within the purview of the New York Convention – and is thus governed by Chapter 2 of the FAA – when one of the parties to the arbitration is domiciled or has its principal place of business outside of the United States.

[7] "MAN GHH is a German corporation. The arbitral award granted to it by the Tampa panel is therefore non-domestic within the meaning of Sect. 202 of the FAA and Art. I of the New York Convention.[11] We therefore hold federal subject-matter jurisdiction over this appeal."

II. MERITS

[8] "Having established the source of our jurisdiction, we move to address the appeal on the merits. The Tampa panel's arbitral award must be confirmed unless appellants can successfully assert one of the seven defenses against enforcement of the award enumerated in Art. V of the New York Convention. (footnote omitted) See *Imperial Ethiopian Gov't v. Baruch-Foster Corp.*, 535 F.2d 334, 335-336 (5th Cir. 1976);[12] see also *National Oil Corp. v. Libyan Sun Oil Co.*, 733 F. Supp. 800, 813 (D.Del. 1990).[13] The appellants bear the burden of proving that any of these seven defenses is applicable. See *Imperial Ethiopian Gov't*, 535 F.2d at 336.

[9] "Only two of the seven enumerated defenses might apply to the instant case. The first is that found in Art. V(1)(*d*), which provides that a court may refuse to confirm an international arbitral award if 'the arbitral procedure was not in accordance with the agreement of the parties.' The second is that found in Art. V(2)(*b*), which provides that a court may refuse to enforce an arbitral award if 'the recognition or enforcement of the award would be contrary to the public policy of' the country where enforcement is sought.

---

10. Reported in Yearbook IX (1984) pp. 471-474 (US no. 50).
11. "The appellants argue that the award at issue does not fall under the Convention because MAN GHH's American subsidiary was also a party to the arbitration. The presence of the subsidiary does not, however, take the award out of the purview of the Convention, so long as the foreign parent was a party to the proceeding."
12. Reported in Yearbook II (1977) p. 252 (US no. 10).
13. Reported in Yearbook XVI (1991) pp. 651-663 (US no. 110).

[10] "The appellants argue that the procedures of the Tampa panel were not in accordance with the parties' arbitration agreement,[14] and that the award therefore should not have confirmed. They argue that the panel should not have considered the contents of a technical report on the wrecks provided by the German technical institute Rheinisch-Westfälischer Technischer Überwachung Verein (the TÜV report), because that report was provided to the appellants at a relatively late date, very shortly before the proceedings began. In considering that report, the appellants argue, the arbitration panel violated the rules of the American Arbitration Association, which were the agreed-upon rules of procedure for the arbitration. The appellants also assert that the panel should not have heard the testimony of Donald Hansen, a piping expert who had previously been retained by respondent IRI to inspect the tail gas expander onsite at the Tampa plant after the first wreck and who was directly involved in the redesign of the expander before the second wreck. Allowing this testimony, the appellants argue, violated 'the well-established public policy protecting ... fundamental principles of fairness and professional conduct'. The appellants also assert a defense that is not enumerated by the New York Convention: that the arbitral award should be vacated on the ground that it is 'arbitrary and capricious'.

[11] "We review de novo the district court's determinations that the procedures observed by the arbitrators were in accordance with the agreement of the parties, that the admission of Hansen's testimony was not violative of public policy, and that the award was not 'arbitrary and capricious'. See *First Options of Chicago, Inc. v. Kaplan*, 514 U.S. 938, 947-949, 115 S.Ct. 1920, 1926, 131 L.Ed.2d 985 (1995)[15] (requiring de novo review of questions of law involved in a district court's refusal to vacate an arbitral award). We hold that the admission of the TÜV report was in accordance with the AAA Rules and therefore with the agreement of the parties. We also hold that the admission of Hansen's testimony was not a violation of public policy of the sort required

14. "The appellants make this assertion in support of their argument that the arbitration proceedings did not conform to the requirements of Chapter 1 of the FAA. The nonconformity of arbitral procedures to the agreement of the parties 'is a defense under both the [FAA] and the New York Convention. The wording is slightly different but there is no reason to think the meaning different.' *Lander Co. v. MMP Invs., Inc.*, 107 F.3d 476, 481 (7th Cir. 1997) (internal citation omitted) [reported in Yearbook XXII (1997) pp. 1049-1059 (US no. 238)]. We therefore treat the appellants' argument that the nonconformity of the arbitral procedures to the agreement of the parties violated Chapter 1 of the FAA as an argument that that nonconformity was a violation of the New York Convention and Chapter 2. Likewise, we treat the appellants' argument that the admission of Hansen's testimony was a violation of public policy warranting vacatur of the award under Chapter 1 as an argument for vacatur under Chapter 2."

15. Reported in Yearbook XXII (1997) pp. 278-286.

to sustain a defense under the New York Convention. We further hold that no defense against enforcement of an international arbitral award under Chapter 2 of the FAA is available on the ground that the award is 'arbitrary and capricious', or on any other grounds not specified by the Convention."

1. Procedure in Accordance with AAA Rules

[12] "Rule 3 of the AAA's Supplementary Procedures for International Commercial Arbitration provides that

> '[a]t the request of any party, the AAA will make arrangements for the exchange of documentary evidence or lists of witnesses between the parties. In international cases, it is important that parties be able to anticipate what will transpire at the hearing. By cooperating in an exchange of relevant information, the parties can avoid unnecessary delays.'

The TÜV report was provided to the appellants on 8 January 1993 – the Friday before the Monday when the arbitration proceedings began – and was not admitted into evidence by the arbitrators until 26 March 1993. The appellants objected to its admission at the time and were allowed to cross-examine Hansen about the institute's report and about his conclusions based on it. The appellants also rebutted Hansen's testimony with testimony from experts of their own.

[13] "MAN GHH did produce the TÜV report very shortly before the commencement of the arbitration proceedings. But arbitration proceedings 'need not follow all the "niceties" of the federal courts; [they] need provide only a fundamentally fair hearing.'[16] *Grovner v. Georgia-Pacific*, 625 F.2d

16. "The appellants rely on this language from [*Grovner v. Georgia-Pacific*, 625 F.2d 1289, 1290 (5th Cir. Unit B 1980)] as an independent ground for their argument that the arbitral award should not be enforced; they argue that, because the TÜV report was admitted into the arbitral proceedings on such short notice, and because Hansen's testimony was admitted, the proceedings were fundamentally unfair, and the awards arising from that proceeding should be vacated. As a threshold matter, we note that this argument assumes that a defense against enforcement of an international arbitral award is available on the ground that the arbitral proceeding is 'fundamentally unfair'. This is an open question.... We need not decide this question, however, because it is apparent that the admission of Hansen's testimony and the relatively late provision of the TÜV report did not render the proceedings fundamentally unfair. The appellants had ample opportunity to rebut the report and Hansen's testimony, and in fact did so with expert witnesses of their own. Any undue prejudice caused by the admission of Hansen's testimony and of the TÜV report was therefore cured sufficiently to ensure that the proceedings were not rendered fundamentally unfair by the admission of these materials."

1289, 1290 (5th Cir. Unit B 1980). (footnote omitted) 'An arbitrator enjoys wide latitude in conducting an arbitration hearing. Arbitration proceedings are not constrained by formal rules of procedure or evidence.' *Robbins v. Day*, 954 F.2d 679, 685 (11th Cir. 1992), overruled on other grounds, *Kaplan*, 514 U.S. 938, 115 S.Ct. 1920, 131 L.Ed.2d 985. Arbitration rules, such as those of the AAA, are intentionally written loosely, in order to allow arbitrators to resolve disputes without the many procedural requirements of litigation.

[14] "The AAA's Rule 3 is a prime example. It does not require parties to provide all documents by any certain deadline; rather, it notes the importance of predictability in the proceedings and of the efficient exchange of relevant information, and provides only that 'the AAA will make arrangements for the exchange of documentary evidence'. There is thus no notice requirement in Rule 3 that MAN GHH could have violated; instead, arbitrators are left wide discretion to require the exchange of evidence, and to admit or exclude evidence, how and when they see fit. This is the rule to which the parties agreed, and we therefore cannot say that the relatively late provision of the TÜV report, and its admission by the panel, constituted a failure of the panel to adhere to the parties' agreement. (footnote omitted)"

2. *Improper Testimony*

[15] "The appellants also argue that the award should be vacated on the ground that the arbitration panel improperly heard testimony from Hansen, a piping expert who was retained by appellant IRI to inspect the tail gas expander casing onsite at the Tampa plant after the first wreck and who was directly involved in the redesign of the expander casing before the second wreck. The arbitration panel called Hansen to testify sua sponte, after the appellants objected to MAN GHH's attempt to call him.

[16] "The appellants assert that '[f]ederal and Florida cases uniformly prohibit "side-switching"', that is, testimony against a party's interest by an expert witness formerly retained by that party. (footnote omitted) Such testimony, they argue, violates 'the well-established public policy protecting ... fundamental principles of fairness and professional conduct'. The appellants cite no rule of procedure or of evidence, and not a single case, establishing the purported 'rule against side-switching'. Rather, the appellants cite cases prohibiting attorneys from, or disqualifying attorneys for, contacting counterparties' experts in violation of: 1) Fed.R.Civ.P. 26,[17] see *Durflinger v. Artiles*, 727 F.2d 88 (10th

17. "Rule 26(b)(4)(B) provides:

'A party may, through interrogatories or by deposition, discover facts known or opinions

Cir. 1984); 2) attorney-client privilege, see *Rentclub, Inc. v. Transamerica Rental Fin. Corp.*, 811 F. Supp. 651 (M.D.Fla. 1992); 3) the confidentially of work product or litigation strategy, see *MMR/Wallace Power & Indus. Inc. v. Thames Assocs.*, 764 F. Supp. 712 (D.Conn. 1991); *Geralnes B.V. v. City of Greenwood Village*, 609 F. Supp. 191 (D.Colo. 1985). The effect of these rules, taken together, is that parties will rarely be able to avail themselves of the services of the other side's expert witnesses – but that is merely the effect of these rules and not a rule unto itself. In the absence of any precedent, we decline to recognize any blanket rule or policy against 'side-switching'.

[17] "Moreover, none of the concerns in the cases cited by respondents are implicated by the arbitration panel's admission of Hansen's testimony. Rule 26 does not independently apply to arbitration proceedings, and attorney-client privilege is not a concern because there is no allegation that Hansen divulged any information properly protected by the privilege. Concerns about the confidentiality of work product and litigation strategy are not implicated because Hansen was called by the panel, not by MAN GHH, and because his testimony before the panel neither relied upon any confidential work product of IRI's attorneys nor included any information about the respondents' litigation strategy.

[18] "Finally, even if such concerns were implicated by the admission of Hansen's testimony, we could not consider vacatur of the district court's order confirming the award unless that admission fell within one of the New York Convention's seven grounds for refusal to enforce an award. See *M & C Corp. v. Erwin Behr GmbH & Co., KG*, 87 F.3d 844, 851 (6th Cir. 1996)[18] ('[T]he Convention lists the exclusive grounds justifying refusal to recognize an [international] arbitral award.'). Even if the purported 'rule against side-switching' did exist, for instance, it would not control arbitration proceedings unless the parties agreed to be controlled by it. See *Szuts v. Dean Witter Reynolds, Inc.*, 931 F.2d 830, 831 (11th Cir. 1991) (noting that power and authority of arbitrator at arbitration proceeding is dependent upon the provision of the arbitration agreement under which he was appointed).

[19] "Nor have the appellants established that the admission of Hansen's testimony was a violation of public policy of the sort required to sustain a defense under Art. V(2)(*b*) of the New York Convention. We have held that

---

held by an expert who has been retained or specially employed by another party in anticipation of litigation or preparation for trial and who is not expected to be called as a witness at trial, only as provided in Rule 35(b) or upon a showing of exceptional circumstances under which it is impracticable for the party seeking discovery to obtain facts or opinions on the same subject by other means.'"

18. Reported in Yearbook XXII (1997) pp. 993-1000 (US no. 229).

domestic arbitral awards are unenforceable on grounds that they are violative of public policy only when the award violates some 'explicit public policy' that the 'well-defined and dominant ... [and is] ascertained "by reference to the laws and legal precedents and not from general consideration of supposed public interests."' *Drummond Coal Co. v. United Mine Workers, District 20*, 748 F.2d 1495, 1499 (11th Cir. 1984) (quoting *W.R. Grace & Co. v. Local Union 759, Int'l Union of the United Rubber, Cork, Linoleum & Plastic Workers*, 461 U.S. 757, 766, 103 S.Ct. 2177, 2183, 76 L.Ed.2d 298 (1983)). We believe that rule applies with equal force in the context of international arbitral awards. See *Parsons & Whittemore Overseas Co. Inc. v. Société Générale de L'Industrie du Papier (RAKTA)*, 508 F.2d 969, 974 (2d Cir. 1974)[19] (holding that 'the Convention's public policy defense should be construed narrowly'). The appellants cite no laws or precedents in support of their invocation of 'the well-established public policy protecting ... fundamental principles of fairness and professional conduct'. We therefore hold that the appellants have not established a violation of public policy sufficiently to sustain a defense under Art. V(2)(*b*) of the New York Convention."

3. Award "Arbitrary and Capricious"

[20] "Finally, the appellants also argue that the arbitral award should be vacated on the ground that it is 'arbitrary and capricious'. See, e.g., *Ainsworth v. Skurnick*, 960 F.2d 939, 941 (11th Cir. 1992), cert. denied, 507 U.S. 915, 113 S.Ct. 1269, 122 L.Ed.2d 665 (1993). We reject this argument as well. Under the law of this circuit, domestic arbitral awards may be vacated for six different reasons; four are enumerated by the FAA and two are non-statutory defenses against enforcement, derived by the courts from the statutory list. See *Raiford v. Merrill Lynch, Pierce, Fenner & Smith, Inc.*, 903 F.2d 1410, 1412 (11th Cir. 1990). The two non-statutory defenses against enforcement of a domestic award are 1) that the award is 'arbitrary and capricious'[20] and 2) that enforcement of the award would be contrary to public policy. See *Montes v. Shearson Lehman Bros., Inc.*, 128 F.3d 1456, 1458 (11th Cir. 1997).

[21] "As discussed supra, the seven defenses against enforcement of an international arbitral award that are enumerated in the New York Convention include a public policy defense. The Convention does not, however, include

19. Reported in Yearbook I (1976) p. 205 (US no. 7).

20. "A domestic arbitral award may be vacated as 'arbitrary and capricious' if it 'exhibits a wholesale departure from the law [or] if the reasoning is so palpably faulty that no judge, or group of judges, could ever conceivably have made such a ruling'. *Brown v. Rauscher Pierce Refsnes, Inc.* 944 F.2d 775, 781 (11th Cir. 1993)."

a defense against enforcement of an award on the ground that the award is 'arbitrary and capricious'. The omission is decisive. Sect. 207 of Chapter 2 of the FAA explicitly requires that a federal court 'shall confirm [an international arbitral] award unless it finds one of the grounds for refusal or deferral of ... enforcement of the award specified in the [New York] Convention'. 9 U.S.C. Sect. 207 (1997 supp.). The Convention itself provides that 'enforcement of [an] award may be refused, at the request of the party against whom it is invoked, *only if* that party furnishes ... proof that' one of the enumerated defenses is applicable.... In short, the Convention's enumeration of defenses is exclusive. See *Yusuf Ahmed Alghanim & Sons*, 126 F.3d at 20 (holding that 'the grounds for relief enumerated in Art. V of the Convention are the only grounds available for setting aside an arbitral award'); *M & C Corp. v. Erwin Behr*, 87 F.3d 844, 851 (6th Cir. 1996).

[22] "We therefore hold that no defense against enforcement of an international arbitral award under Chapter 2 of the FAA is available on the ground that the award is 'arbitrary and capricious', or on any other ground not specified by the Convention. The appellants' attempt to invoke such a defense thus fails. We therefore decline to vacate the arbitral award granted to MAN GHH by the Tampa panel. Because we affirm the award, we also decline to vacate the derivative awards of costs and conversion rate compen-sation."

III. POST-ARBITRAL AWARD PREJUDGMENT INTEREST

[23] "On cross-appeal, MAN GHH complains of the district court's refusal to award to MAN GHH post-arbitral-award, prejudgment interest. MAN GHH moved the court to enter judgment on the arbitral award and to grant prejudgment interest from the date the last arbitral award was made through the date of the court's entry of the amended final judgment. The court entered judgment on the award but declined to award such interest. The court held that its jurisdiction was grounded in diversity, and that state law therefore would control the award of prejudgment interest. The court then concluded that Florida law does not authorize the granting of post-arbitral-award, prejudgment interest. Because we hold that the district court held federal question jurisdiction over the case pursuant to Chapter 2 of the FAA, ... and that federal law allows awards of post-arbitral-award, prejudgment interest, we remand for a determination whether, in the court's discretion, the circumstances of the instant case warrant such an award.

[24] "Unlike most other countries, the United States has no federal statute governing awards of prejudgment interest on international arbitral awards. See John Y. Gotanda, 'Awarding Interest in International Arbitration', 90 Am. J.

Int'l L. 40, 45 (1996). Instead, awards of prejudgment interest are equitable remedies, to be awarded or not awarded in the district court's sound discretion. See *Osterneck v. E.T. Barwick Ind., Inc.*, 825 F.2d 1521, 1536 (11th Cir. 1987); *Waterside Ocean Navigation Co. v. International Navigation Ltd.*, 737 F.2d 150, 153 (2d Cir. 1984).[21] Under the law of this circuit, '[p]re-judgment interest is not a penalty, but compensation to the plaintiff for the use of funds that were rightfully his', see *Insurance Co. of N. Am. v. M/V Ocean Lynx*, 901 F.2d 934, 942 (11th Cir. 1990), and absent any reason to the contrary, it should normally be awarded when damages have been liquidated by an international arbitral award. See *Waterside Ocean Navigation*, 737 F.2d at 153-154 ('Absent persuasive reasons to the contrary, we do not see why pre-judgment interest should not be available in actions brought under the [New York] Convention.'); see also *Fort Hill Builders, Inc. v. National Grange Mut. Ins. Co.*, 866 F.2d 11, 14 (1st Cir. 1989) (holding that, under either federal or Rhode Island law, post-award, prejudgment interest should be awarded on domestic arbitral award); *Sun Ship, Inc. v. Matson Navigation Co.*, 785 F.2d 59 (3d Cir. 1986) (holding that confirmed domestic arbitral award bears interest from date of award, not from date of judgment confirming award).[22]

[25] "In the absence of a controlling statute, federal courts' choice of a rate at which to determine the amount of prejudgment interest to be awarded is also a matter for their discretion. That choice is usually guided by principles of reasonableness and fairness, by relevant state law, and by the relevant fifty-two week United States Treasury bond rate, which is the rate that federal courts must use in awarding *post*-judgment interest. See 28 U.S.C. Sect. 1961; Gotanda, supra, at 45 and n. 63 (citing cases)."

(....)

IV. CONCLUSION

[26] "For the foregoing reasons, we affirm the district court's denial of the motion to vacate the arbitral award, but vacate the district court's denial of prejudgment interest and remand the case for resolution of that issue. We also reverse the district court's imposition of Rule 11 sanctions against MAN GHH's counsel."

---

21. Reported in Yearbook XI (1986) pp. 568-572 (US no. 61).
22. "We note that international arbitrators often award post-arbitral-award interest. See, e.g., *Bergesen v. Joseph Muller Corp.*, 548 F. Supp. 650, 651 (S.D.N.Y. 1982); *Laminoirs-Trefileries-Cableries De Lens, S.A. v. Southwire Co.*, 484 F. Supp. 1063, 1069 (N.D.Ga. 1980) [reported in Yearbook VI (1981) pp. 247-248 (US no. 32).]"

277. United States District Court, Southern District of Florida, Miami Division, 13 July 1998, No. 97-3833-CIV-MOORE

Parties:	Plaintiffs: Cavalier Construction Company, Ltd. (Bahamas), et al. (Bahamas) Defendants: The Bay Hotel and Resort, Ltd., et al. (Turks and Caicos Islands)
Published in:	Summary in ADR Currents (December 1998) p. 24
Articles:	I(1); I(3)
Subject matters:	– award not considered as domestic – reciprocity reservation
Commentary Cases:	¶ 102 + ¶ 103

Facts

In August 1993, Cavalier Construction Company, Ltd. (Bahamas) (Cavalier Bahamas) and The Bay Hotel and Resort, Ltd. (The Bay) concluded a contract for the construction of a hotel in the Turks and Caicos Islands. The contract contained an arbitration clause providing for arbitration according to the Construction Industry Arbitration Rules of the American Arbitration Association. Disputes arose during the course of the construction and Cavalier Bahamas initiated arbitration in Miami, Florida. An award was issued in favor of Cavalier Bahamas and Cavalier Construction Company, Ltd. (Turks and Caicos Islands) (Cavalier T & C), the latter having been joined in the arbitration. The arbitral tribunal applied the substantive law of the Turks and Caicos Islands to the merits of the dispute.

Cavalier Bahamas and Cavalier T & C moved for the District Court for the Southern District of Florida, Miami Division, to confirm the award which had been issued in the arbitration.

The district court found that the award did not fall within the New York Convention because although the Convention could apply to a non-domestic award rendered in the United States, the reciprocity requirement that the award be made in the territory of another signatory nation was not fulfilled.

Excerpt

[1] "Before turning to the relief requested, the Court must make a threshold inquiry and determine whether it has subject matter jurisdiction to entertain this action. In light of the foreign citizenship of all the parties to this case, the only possible basis for the Court's jurisdiction is the [1958 New York Convention], 9. U.S.C. Sect. 201 et seq. Cf. *Lander Company, Inc. v. MMP Investments, Inc.*, 107 F.3d 476, 479, cert. denied, 118 S.Ct. 55 (1997)[1] (noting that the court therein had jurisdiction under the Federal Arbitration Act because of the diverse citizenship of the parties as well as under the Convention).

[2] "The Convention gives individuals and companies involved in international trade a dispute resolution mechanism by providing for the recognition and enforcement of foreign arbitration awards in signatory countries. Art. I(3) of the Convention, however, gives a signatory country the option of declaring that it will only apply the Convention to awards made in the territory of another signatory to the Convention – that is, on the basis of reciprocity. The United States, in its 1970 declaration of accession to the Convention, opted to apply the Convention on the basis of reciprocity. See Historical and Statutory Notes to 9 U.S.C. Sect. 201.

[3] "The principle of reciprocity is critical to the Court's resolution of the jurisdictional inquiry because the substantive law of a non-signatory nation was applied by the Florida panel in arbitrating the dispute between citizens of non-signatory nations.[2] In other words, the Court must decide whether the Convention applies to an award rendered in the United States under these circumstances. If the Court determines that the Convention does not apply under the factors set forth above, it lacks subject matter jurisdiction over this action and must dismiss the case.

[4] "Other courts have addressed similar jurisdictional issues arising under the Convention. Most recently, in *Lander*, the Seventh Circuit held that the Convention applies to arbitration awards rendered in the United States and resolving a dispute between two United States nationals arising out of contract performance in a foreign country. Id. at 482. In *Bergesen v. Joseph Muller Corporation*, 710 F.2d 928, 933-934 (2d Cir. 1983),[3] the Second Circuit held that the Convention applies to non-domestic awards rendered in the United

1. Reported in Yearbook XXII (1997) pp. 1049-1059 (US no. 238).
2. "A review of the list of signatory nations reveals that neither the Bahamas nor the Turks and Caicos are parties to the Convention. See Historical and Statutory Notes to 9 U.S.C. Sect. 201."
3. Reported in Yearbook IX (1984) pp. 487-494 (US no. 54).

States and arising from a dispute between foreign citizens of signatory nations. Neither case, however, squarely addresses the jurisdictional issue presented to the Court. In fact, the parties have not cited and the Court's independent research has not located a case discussing the precise issue raised herein."

[5] After citing Art. I(1) of the Convention, the Court continued: "The Court finds, and the parties agree, that the arbitration award in question does not meet the territorial criterion found in the first sentence of Art. I(1) because the award was made in Florida and enforcement is sought in the United States. See id. at 932. Therefore, the Convention can only apply if, pursuant to the second sentence of Art. I(1), the arbitration award in question is not considered domestic. On this point, the Court turns to the Second Circuit's decision in *Bergesen*, the case most analogous to the present action.

[6] "In *Bergesen*, the Second Circuit held that 'awards "not considered as domestic" denotes awards which are subject to the Convention not because made abroad, but because made within the legal framework of another country, e.g., pronounced in accordance with foreign law or involving parties domiciled or having their principal place of business outside the enforcing jurisdiction'. Id. Under the *Bergesen* court's definition of awards 'not considered as domestic', the award before the Court which was rendered pursuant to the substantive law of the Turks and Caicos Islands, falls within the purview of the second sentence of Art. I(1).

[7] "The Court's inquiry is not complete, however, until it considers the effect of the Art. I(3) reciprocity requirement under which the United States acceded to the Convention.[4] As noted above, the United States declared that it would only apply the Convention on the basis of reciprocity – that is, to award made in the territory of another signatory nation. See Historical and Statutory Notes to 9 U.S.C. Sect. 201. The Court has already concluded that the award at issue in this action must be considered a non-domestic Turks and Caicos Islands award in order to fall within the scope of the Convention. The Court has also noted that the Turks and Caicos are not signatories to the Convention. The United States' decision to invoke the Convention's reciprocity option would be rendered meaningless if the Court were to find that the Convention, as adopted by the United States, applies to a non-domestic Turks and Caicos award. Accordingly, the Court concludes that the award in ques-

4. "On this point, *Bergesen* does not provide the Court with assistance because the Second Circuit, in arriving at its decision, did not specifically address the question of reciprocity."

tion does not fall within the Convention but, instead, is ultimately excluded by the reciprocity requirement.[5]

[8] "In arriving at its decision, the Court did not fail to note that the United States has little or no interest in enforcing arbitration awards which solely concern citizens of non-signatory nations and the law of a non-signatory State, particularly when the non-signatory State would not reciprocate the United States' efforts."

5. "Cavalier Bahamas and Cavalier T & C attempt to avoid the Court's ruling by arguing that the award, although non-domestic under the second sentence of Art. I(1), should be considered 'made' in the United States for purposes of any reciprocity analysis. This argument amounts to circular reasoning. If the award is 'made' in the United States, it is specifically excluded from the Convention by the first sentence of Art. I(1). If the award is excluded by the first sentence, the Convention can only apply if the award is considered non-domestic within the meaning of the second sentence of Art. I(1)."

278. Court of Appeals of the State of Washington, 27 July 1998, No. 40801

Parties:	Appellants/plaintiffs: (1) Kamaya Co., Ltd. (Japan); (2) Pacific Business Investment, Inc. (US); (3) FT Limited Co. (Japan) et al. Appellees/defendants: (1) American Property Consultants, Ltd. (Japan); (2) APC, Inc. (US) et al.; (3) Grancorp, Inc. (US) et al.
Published in:	91 Wash. App. 703; 959 P.2d 1140; 1998 Wash. App. LEXIS 1114
Articles:	II(3)
Subject matters:	– arbitrability of fraud-in-the-inducement claims – effect of contractual choice-of-law clause on arbitrability
Commentary Cases:	[1]-[16] = ¶ 201 + ¶ 223; [4] = ¶ 219; [5] = ¶ 216; [6]-[7] + [12]-[16] = ¶ 221; [17] = ¶ 226

Facts

APC and Grancorp, among others, formed Inter Co-op No. 2 (IC-2), a Japanese partnership (or *kumiai*) to purchase, own and operate a parcel of Seattle real estate. Kamaya Co., Ltd., Pacific Business Investment, Inc., F.T Limited and several individuals – a mostly Japanese group of passive investors – purchased shares in IC-2. The partnership agreement executed by each investor contained an arbitral clause and a general Japanese choice-of-law provision.

A dispute arose concerning the partnership and the passive investors filed suit against the APC defendants and the Grancorp defendants, among others, alleging violations of the Washington Securities Act, RCW 21.20, including fraud-in-the-inducement of the partnership agreement as a whole. The APC defendants asked the court to stay the proceedings and refer the dispute to arbitration in Japan. The Grancorp defendants filed a Memorandum in Support of the APC defendants' motion to compel. The trial court granted the APC defendants' motion, staying the proceedings against all the defendants, but only compelling arbitration between the plaintiffs and the APC defendants.

On appeal, the court, per Kennedy, CJ, held that the trial court had properly ordered the plaintiffs to arbitrate their fraud-in-the-inducement claims with the APC defendants despite plaintiffs' argument that under Japanese law, general arbitration clauses do not cover such claims. The Federal Arbitration Act (FAA) governs whether the parties agreed to arbitrate a particular contractual dispute. However, the contract's choice-of-law clause was a pertinent factor to be considered in applying the FAA. Moreover, the trial court should have ordered the Grancorp defendants to proceed to arbitration as well.

Excerpt

I. ARBITRABILITY OF PLAINTIFFS' FRAUD-IN-THE-INDUCEMENT CLAIMS

[1] "Plaintiffs contend that Japanese law governs the arbitrability of their fraud-in-the-inducement of the partnership agreement claims, because the partnership agreement contains a general Japanese choice-of-law provision. The APC defendants, on the other hand, contend that the Federal Arbitration Act, 9 U.S.C.A. Sects. 1-307 (FAA), governs the arbitrability of plaintiffs' fraud-in-the-inducement claims, notwithstanding the agreement's Japanese choice-of-law provision, because the partnership agreement is a contract affecting commerce. See 9 U.S.C.A. Sect. 2.[1] We reject both of these 'all-or-nothing' approaches to resolving the issue of which law governs the arbitrability of plaintiffs' fraud-in-the-inducement claims. Although the FAA governs whether the parties agreed to arbitrate a particular contractual dispute, the contract's choice-of-law provision is a pertinent factor that courts must consider in applying the FAA."

1. 9 U.S.C. Sect. 2 reads:

"A written provision in any maritime transaction or a contract evidencing a transaction involving commerce to settle by arbitration a controversy thereafter arising out of such contract or transaction, or the refusal to perform the whole or any part thereof, or an agreement in writing to submit to arbitration an existing controversy arising out of such a contract, transaction, or refusal, shall be valid, irrevocable, and enforceable, save upon such grounds as exist at law or in equity for the revocation of any contract."

1. *Applicability of the Federal Arbitration Act*

[2] "In 1925, Congress enacted Chapter 1 of the FAA to abolish 'the long-standing judicial hostility to arbitration agreements that had existed at English common law and had been adopted by American courts, and to place arbitration agreements upon the same footing as other contracts'. *Gilmer v. Interstate/ Johnson Lane Corp.*, 500 U.S. 20, 24, 111 S.Ct. 1647, 1651, 114 L.Ed.2d 26 (1991). Chapter 1 of the FAA applies in both state and federal courts, and covers all contracts within Congress's power to regulate under the Commerce Clause. See *Allied-Bruce Terminix Cos. v. Dobson*, 513 U.S. 265, 272, 277, 115 S.Ct. 834, 130 L.Ed.2d 753 (1995); see also 9 U.S.C.A. Sect. 2.

[3] "In 1970, Congress enacted Chapter 2 of the FAA, which ratified the [1958 New York Convention]. See 9 U.S.C.A. Sects. 201-208. Chapter 2 expanded the FAA's coverage 'into the field of international commerce, providing for the enforcement of arbitration clauses in commercial transactions in countries that are parties to the Convention'. *Quasem Group, Ltd. v. W.D. Mask Cotton Co.*, 967 F. Supp. 288, 290 n. 1 (W.D.Tenn. 1997)[2] (citing 9 U.S.C.A. Sect. 202). 'The goal of the Convention, and the principal purpose underlying American adoption and implementation of it, was to encourage the recognition and enforcement of commercial arbitration agreements in international contracts and to unify the standards by which agreements to arbitrate are observed and arbitral awards are enforced in the signatory countries.' *Scherk v. Alberto-Culver Co.*, 417 U.S. 506, 520 n. 15, 94 S.Ct. 2449, 41 L.Ed.2d 270 (1974).[3]

[4] "Chapter 2 mandates that both state and federal courts of the United States enforce the Convention. See 9 U.S.C.A. Sects. 201, 205.[4] 'Art. II of the

2. Reported in Yearbook XXIII (1998) pp. 977-983 (US no. 253).
3. Reported in Yearbook I (1976) pp. 203-204 (US no. 4).
4. 9 U.S.C. Sects. 201 and 205 read:

Section 201

"An arbitration agreement or arbitral award arising out of a legal relationship, whether contractual or not, which is considered as commercial, including a transaction, contract, or agreement described in section 2 of this title, falls under the Convention. An agreement or award arising out of such a relationship which is entirely between citizens of the United States shall be deemed not to fall under the Convention unless that relationship involves property located abroad, envisages performance or enforcement abroad, or has some other reasonable relation with one or more foreign states. For the purpose of this section a corporation is a citizen of the United States if it is incorporated or has its principal place of business in the United States."

Section 205

Convention imposes a mandatory duty on the courts of a Contracting State to recognize, and enforce an agreement to arbitrate unless the agreement is "null and void, inoperative or incapable of being performed".' *Riley v. Kingsley Underwriting Agencies, Ltd.*, 969 F.2d 953, 959 (10th Cir. 1992)[5] (citing 9 U.S.C.A. Sect. 201 note). All actions and proceedings falling under the Convention are 'deemed to arise under the laws and treaties of the United States'. 9 U.S.C.A. Sect. 203. But Chapter 1 of the FAA applies to cases brought under Chapter 2 only to the extent that Chapter 1 'is not in conflict with [Chapter 2] or the Convention as ratified by the United States.' 9 U.S.C.A. Sect. 208.

[5] "Plaintiffs do not dispute that the IC-2 partnership agreement – which was marketed and promoted in Japan to elicit investors in Seattle real estate – is a commercial transaction affecting international commerce. And all possibly interested nations – the United States, Japan, and Sweden[6] – are Contracting States to the Convention. See 9 U.S.C.A. Sect. 201 note. Therefore, Chapter 2 of the FAA and the Convention – and Chapter 1 of the FAA to the extent it does not conflict – govern the arbitrability of plaintiffs' fraud-in-the-inducement claims. See *McDermott Int'l, Inc. v. Lloyds Underwriters*, 944 F.2d 1199, 1208 (5th Cir. 1991)[7] ('The parties recognize that this suit concerns an arbitration agreement and is not entirely between United States citizens, so [Chapter 2] governs this case.').

[6] "For example, in *Becker Autoradio U.S.A., Inc. v. Becker Autoradiowerk GmbH*, 585 F.2d 39, 43 (3d Cir. 1978),[8] the court was asked to decide whether a West German corporation and a Pennsylvania corporation should be required to arbitrate their contractual dispute. The court held, notwithstanding ordinary choice-of-law analysis, that the federal substantive law of arbitrability governed whether the parties agreed to arbitrate their dispute:

"Where the subject matter of an action or proceeding pending in a State court relates to an arbitration agreement or award falling under the Convention, the defendant or the defendants may, at any time before the trial thereof, remove such action or proceeding to the district court of the United States for the district and division embracing the place where the action or proceeding is pending. The procedure for removal of causes otherwise provided by law shall apply, except that the ground for removal provided in the this section need not appear on the face of the complaint but may be shown in the petition for removal. For the purposes of Chapter 1 of this title any action or proceeding removed under this section shall be deemed to have been brought in the district court to which it is removed."

5. Reported in Yearbook XIX (1994) pp. 775-780 (US no. 147).
6. "At oral argument, counsel for the Grancorp defendants indicated to this court that Grancorp, Inc. is controlled by Swedish nationals."
7. Reported in Yearbook XVIII (1993) pp. 472-486 (US no. 126).
8. Reported in Yearbook V (1980) pp. 272-274 (US no. 26).

> 'There has been much discussion by the parties concerning the applicability of German law or Pennsylvania law in the resolution of this dispute. It may well be that the question of which law is to be applied will have to be answered in deciding the merits of the underlying controversy. However the case before us presents only the issue of the arbitrability of that controversy. When a contract involves "commerce", as this one does, whether a "suit or proceeding is referable to arbitration ... under an agreement [to arbitrate]" pursuant to the federal Arbitration Act, 9 U.S.C. Sect. 3, or to the Convention on [the] Recognition and Enforcement of Foreign Arbitral Awards, Art. II(3) and 9 U.S.C. Sect. 206, is clearly a matter of federal substantive law. Thus, the question of whether, in contracts involving commerce, there is an agreement to arbitrate an issue or dispute upon which suit has been brought is governed by federal law. Concomitantly, questions of interpretation and construction of such arbitration agreements are similarly to be determined by reference to federal law. As the court in *Coenen v. R.W. Pressprich & Co.*, 453 F.2d 1209, 1211 (2d Cir. 1972), stated "[o]nce a dispute is covered by the [federal Arbitration] Act, federal law applies to all questions of [the arbitration agreement's] interpretation, construction, validity, revocability, and enforceability".
>
> It is true that, if the parties agree that certain disputes will be submitted to arbitration and that the law of a particular jurisdiction will govern the resolution of those disputes, federal courts must effectuate that agreement. However, whether a particular dispute is within the class of those disputes governed by the arbitration and choice of law clause is a matter of federal law.'

Id. at 43 (citations and footnotes omitted) (alterations in original). In other words, the 'first task of a court asked to compel arbitration of a dispute is to determine whether the parties agreed to arbitrate that dispute. The court is to make this determination by applying the "federal substantive law of arbitrability, applicable to any arbitration agreement within the coverage of the [FAA]".' *Mitsubishi Motors Corp. v. Soler Chrysler-Plymouth, Inc.*, 473 U.S. 614, 626, 105 S.Ct. 3346, 87 L.Ed.2d 444 (1985)[9] (quoting *Moses H. Cone Mem'l Hosp. v. Mercury Constr. Corp.*, 460 U.S. 1, 24, 103 S.Ct. 927, 74 L.Ed.2d 765 (1983)).

[7] "As plaintiffs correctly point out, whether the FAA or Japanese arbitration law governs the arbitrability of their fraud-in-the-inducement claims is not a question of federal preemption: 'The Supremacy [C]lause applies to states

9. Reported in Yearbook XI (1986) pp. 555-566 (US no. 59).

and is inapplicable to considerations of federal law versus foreign law.' *Al-Kurdi v. United States*, 25 Cl.Ct. 599, 601 n. 3 (1992); cf. *Southland Corp. v. Keating*, 465 U.S. 1, 16, 104 S.Ct. 852, 79 L.Ed.2d 1 (1984) (holding that the FAA preempts contrary state arbitration law under the Supremacy Clause). And contractual choice-of-law provisions are ordinarily valid under the FAA. See generally *Ford v. NYLCare Health Plans, Inc.*, 141 F.3d 243, 248 n. 6 (5th Cir. 1998) (rejecting argument that, notwithstanding agreement's choice-of-law provision, 'substantive federal law governs the scope of arbitration clause whenever the agreement involves commerce'). But it is axiomatic that courts must have some law to apply when initially determining whether the parties agreed to arbitrate a particular dispute. The FAA provides courts with this necessary analytical framework. Indeed, plaintiffs themselves argue that the partnership agreement's Japanese choice-of-law provision evidences the parties' intent to exclude fraud-in-the-inducement claims from arbitration by citing to FAA cases. Therefore, we hold that although the FAA does not preempt the partnership agreement's Japanese choice-of-law provision, 'whether a particular dispute is within the class of those disputes governed by the arbitration and choice of law clause is a matter of federal law'. *Becker*, 585 F.2d at 43."[10]

2. *Application of the Federal Arbitration Act*

[8] "Questions of arbitrability, like all questions of law, are reviewed de novo. *First Options, Inc. v. Kaplan*, 514 U.S. 938, 943, 115 S.Ct. 1920, 1924, 131 L.Ed.2d 985 (1995);[11] *ACF Property Management, Inc. v. Chaussee*, 69 Wn. App. 913, 919, 850 P.2d 1387 (1993). Courts must consider four guiding principles when determining if two parties agreed to submit a particular dispute to arbitration:

10. "Our holding is consistent with the U.S. Supreme Court's pronouncement on the importance of enforcing foreign choice-of-law provisions in the context of international transactions:

'The expansion of American business and industry will hardly be encouraged if, notwithstanding solemn contracts, we insist on a parochial concept that all disputes must be resolved under our laws and in our courts[.] We cannot have trade and commerce in world markets and international waters exclusively on our terms, governed by our laws, and resolved in our courts.'

Mitsubishi, 473 U.S. at 629 (internal quotation marks and citation omitted). That is, our holding requires courts to consider foreign choice-of-law provisions in determining the arbitrability of a particular dispute, and permits an arbitrator or court – absent a conflicts-of-law impediment – to apply the foreign nation's law to the underlying dispute."

11. Reported in Yearbook XXII (1997) pp. 278-286.

> '(1) the duty to submit a matter to arbitration arises from the contract itself; (2) the question of whether parties have agreed to arbitrate a dispute is a judicial one unless the parties clearly provide otherwise; (3) a court should not determine the underlying merits of a dispute in determining *the arbitrability* of an issue; and (4) arbitration of disputes is favored by the courts.'

W.A. Botling Plumbing & Heating Co. v. Constructors-Pamco, 47 Wn. App. 681, 683, 736 P.2d 1100 (1987) (citing *AT & T Techs., Inc. v. Communications Workers*, 475 U.S. 643, 648, 106 S.Ct. 1415, 1418, 89 L.Ed.2d (1986)). 'The federal policy favoring arbitration is even stronger in the context of international transactions.' *Deloitte Noraudit A/S v. Deloitte Haskins & Sells, U.S.*, 9 F.3d 1060, 1063 (2d Cir. 1993).

[9] "In general, although the intentions of the parties as expressed in the agreement control, 'those intentions are generously construed as to issues of arbitrability'. *ML Park Place Corp. v. Hedreen*, 71 Wn. App. 727, 739, 862 P.2d 602 (1993). In other words, 'any doubts concerning the scope of arbitrable issues should be resolved in favor of arbitration, whether the problem at hand is the construction of the contract language itself or an allegation of waiver, delay, or a like defense to arbitrability.' *Moses H. Cone*, 460 U.S. at 24-25. Therefore, a contractual dispute is arbitrable unless it can be said 'with positive assurance' that the arbitration clause is not susceptible of an interpretation that covers the asserted dispute'. *ML Park*, 71 Wn. App. at 739 (quoting *United Steelworkers v. Warrior & Gulf Navigation Co.*, 363 U.S. 574, 582-583, 80 S.Ct. 1347, 4 L.Ed.2d 1409 (1980)).

[10] "In this case, the IC-2 partnership agreement contains a broad and inclusive internal dispute provision that ultimately requires arbitration of all unresolved disputes and differences between partners, in Tokyo, Japan:

> '1. Any question concerning the interpretation of this Partnership Agreement or any dispute or difference arising from time to time among the partners of this partnership pertaining to the operation of this partnership or any right or obligation with respect to this partnership shall first be presented to the Board of Directors, and the Board of Directors shall render a decision and notify the partners of the partnership in writing.
>
> (....)
>
> 3. Any dispute or differences in opinions which is not resolved within 90 days after a decision is rendered by the Board of Directors and

> notified to pertinent parties may[12] be referred to one arbitrator in Tokyo, Japan, and such arbitration shall definitively resolve such dispute or difference in accordance with the then effective rules of the International Commercial Arbitration Association.'

And plaintiffs do not dispute that under the FAA, general arbitration clauses ordinarily cover claims of fraud-in-the-inducement of a contract as a whole. See *Prima Paint Corp. v. Flood & Conklin Mfg. Co.*, 388 U.S. 395, 403-404, 87 S.Ct. 1801, 18 L.Ed.2d 1270 (1967); but see *Berger v. Cantor Fitzgerald Sec.*, 942 F. Supp. 963, 965 (S.D.N.Y. 1996) (questioning the continued vitality of *Prima Paint* after the Court's decision in *First Options*, 514 U.S. 938); *Northcom, Ltd. v. James*, 694 So.2d 1329, 1332 n. 1 (Ala. 1997) (same). Therefore, absent the partnership agreement's Japanese choice-of-law provision, plaintiffs' fraud-in-the-inducement claims clearly would be arbitrable.

[11] "The U.S. Supreme Court has held that because arbitration 'is a matter of consent, not coercion, and parties are generally free to structure their arbitration agreements as they see fit[,] [parties] may specify by contract the rules under which that arbitration will be conducted'. *Volt Info. Sciences, Inc. v. Board of Trustees*, 489 U.S. 468, 479, 109 S.Ct. 1248, 103 L.Ed.2d 488 (1989).[13] 'It follows, then, that if the parties may select rules of arbitration through the use of choice-of-law provisions, so too may they specify the law governing interpretation of the scope of the arbitration clause.' *Ford*, 141 F.3d at 248.

[12] "Relying on this line of reasoning, plaintiffs contend that the partnership agreement evidences the parties' intent to exclude fraud-in-the-inducement claims from the agreement's general arbitration clause, because the agreement contains a general Japanese choice-of-law provision:

> 'Excluding the provisions contained in Article 6 hereof, the partners of this partnership hereby agree that this Partnership Agreement shall take effect under and shall be construed in accordance with Japanese law and that the rights and obligations of the partners of this partnership shall be governed by Japanese law.'

And – according to plaintiffs – under Japanese law, general arbitration clauses do not cover fraud-in-the-inducement claims.

12. "Although the agreement employs the Japanese translation of the word 'may', the parties agree that the arbitration clause is mandatory if the dispute falls within the purview of the internal dispute resolution provision."
13. Reported in Yearbook XV (1990) pp. 131-141.

[13] "The US Supreme Court, however, rejected a very similar argument in *Mastrobuono v. Shearson Lehman Hutton, Inc.*, 514 U.S. 52, 115 S.Ct. 1212, 131 L.Ed.2d 76 (1995).[14] In that case, the contract contained a general arbitration clause and a New York choice-of-law provision that governed 'the entire agreement'. Id. at 58-59. 'New York law allows courts but not arbitrators, to award punitive damages.' Id at 53. Nonetheless, the arbitrators awarded the Mastrobuonos $ 400,000 in punitive damages. Id. at 54. On appeal, Shearson Lehman argued that 'the [New York] choice-of-law provision in their contract evidence[d] the parties' express agreement that punitive damages should not be awarded in the arbitration of any dispute arising under their contract.' Id. at 56. But the US Supreme Court interpreted the contract's New York choice-of-law provision as having two reasonable interpretations and not as an 'unequivocal exclusion of punitive damages claims' from the contract's general arbitration clause:

> 'Even if the reference to "the laws of the State of New York" is more than a substitute for ordinary conflict-of-laws analysis and, as respondents urge, includes the caveat, 'detached from otherwise-applicable federal law", the provision might not preclude the award of punitive damages because New York allows its courts, though not its arbitrators, to enter such awards. In other words, the provision might include only New York's substantive rights and obligations, and not the State's allocation of power alternative tribunals.'

Id. at 59-60 (citation and footnotes omitted). Therefore, the Court concluded that US policy favoring arbitration dictated that the ambiguity created by the choice-of-law provision be resolved in favor [of] arbitration. Id. at 62. Accordingly, the Court affirmed the arbitrators' award of punitive damages. Id. at 64.

(....)

[14] "On review, the Sixth Circuit Court of Appeals [in *Ferro Corp. v. Garrison Indus., Inc.*, 142 F.3d 926, 927-928 (6th Cir. 1998)] held that '[u]nder the Supreme Court's interpretation of the FAA, the issue of fraudulent inducement of the entire contract is an issue to be resolved by the arbitration process, in the absence of evidence that the contracting parties intended to withhold the issue from arbitration.' Id. (citing *Prima Paint*, 388 U.S. at 403). And under the Supreme Court's reasoning in *Mastrobuono*, 514 U.S. 52, the contract's general Ohio choice-of-law provision did not unequivocally exclude Ferro's fraud-in-the-inducement claims from the contract's standard arbitration

14. Reported in Yearbook XXI (1996) 181-191.

clause. Id. at 937. In other words, the court reasoned that 'if Ferro had intended to either exclude the issue of fraudulent inducement from arbitration, or only allow for arbitration to the extent allowed under Ohio law, it could have written this provision into the [arbitration] clause.' Id. at 936. Therefore, the Court of Appeals reversed the District Court and ordered the parties to arbitrate Ferro's fraud-in-the-inducement claims. Id. 939.

[15] "Likewise, the IC-2 partnership agreement's general Japanese choice-of-law provision neither unequivocally excludes fraud-in-the-inducement claims from its general arbitration provision nor unequivocally invokes Japanese arbitration law. That is, the Japanese choice-of-law provision can reasonably be read as merely specifying that Japanese substantive law be applied to the underlying disputes related to the partnership agreement: '[T]he partners of this partnership hereby agree that this Partnership Agreement shall take effect under and shall be construed in accordance with Japanese law and that the rights and obligations of the partners of this partnership shall be governed by Japanese law.' Therefore, following the Court's reasoning in *Mastrobuono*, 514 U.S. 52, the IC-2 partnership agreement's general Japanese choice-of-law provision does not unequivocally exclude plaintiffs' fraud-in-the-inducement claims from the agreement's general arbitration clause. And it cannot be said 'with positive assurance that the arbitration clause is not susceptible of an interpretation that covers the asserted dispute'. *ML Park*, 71 Wn. App. at 739 (quoting *United Steelworkers*, 363 U.S. at 582-583).

[16] "Unlike *Mastrobuono*, however, this conclusion does not construe the ambiguous language against its presumed drafters, i.e., IC-2's corporate promoters. See *Berg v. Hudesman*, 115 Wn.2d 657, 677, 801 P.2d 222 (1990) (noting that courts ordinarily construe ambiguities in a document against its drafters). But the *Mastrobuono* Court merely cited 'the common-law rule of contract interpretation that a court should construe ambiguous language against the interest of the party that drafted it' as further support for its conclusion that the punitive damages award was arbitrable. *Mastrobuono*, 514 U.S. at 62-63. Therefore, this consideration alone does not render a conclusion of arbitrability inconsistent with the Court's decision in *Mastrobuono*. Accordingly, even assuming that general arbitration clauses do not cover fraud-in-the-inducement claims under Japanese law, the strong federal policy favoring arbitration – especially in the context of international commercial transactions – dictates that plaintiffs' fraud-in-the-inducement claims be submitted to arbitration in Tokyo, Japan."

II. ARBITRABILITY OF PLAINTIFFS' CLAIMS AGAINST GRANCORP DEFENDANTS

(....)

[17] "[O]nce a party moves to compel arbitration of a particular dispute and the court determines that the parties have agreed to arbitrate that dispute, the court must order the parties to proceed to arbitration 'save upon such grounds as exist at law or in equity for the revocation of any contract'. *Dean Witter Reynolds, Inc. v. Byrd*, 470 U.S. 213, 217-218, 105 S.Ct. 1238, 84 L.Ed.2d 158 (1985) (quoting 9 U.S.C.A. Sect. 2). This is especially true when the arbitration agreement falls under the Convention;

> 'The court of a Contracting State, when seized of an action in a matter in respect of which the parties have made an agreement within the meaning of this article, shall, at the request of one of the parties, refer the parties to arbitration, unless it finds that the said agreement is null and void, inoperative or incapable of being performed.'

9 U.S.C.A. Sect. 201 note ([1958 New York Convention] Art. II(3)); accord *Ledee v. Ceramiche Ragno*, 684 F.2d 184, 187 (1st Cir. 1982).[15] The Grancorp defendants have not asserted any legal or equitable grounds for revoking the partnership agreement as a whole or the arbitration clause in particular. Therefore, because the trial court properly found that the partnership agreement required arbitration of plaintiffs' fraud-in-the-inducement claims, the trial court abused its discretion by not compelling arbitration between plaintiffs and the Grancorp defendants."

15. Reported in Yearbook IX (1984) pp. 471-474 (US no. 50).

279. United States District Court, Southern District of New York, 5 August 1998 and 29 September 1998, No. 96 Civ. 0936 (WCC)

Parties:	Petitioner: US Titan, Inc. (US) Respondent: Guangzhou Zhen Hua Shipping Co., Ltd. (PR China)
Published in:	182 F.R.D. 97; 1998 U.S. Dist. LEXIS 15524; 1999 American Maritime Cases p. 863 et seq.
Articles:	I; II (by implication)
Subject matters:	– jurisdiction of court over foreign sovereign – formation of charter party
Commentary Cases:	[1]-[15] = ¶ 105; [19]-[29] = ¶ 220 + ¶ 223; [25] = ¶ 207; [26] = ¶ 212

Facts

In August of 1995, US Titan, Inc. (Titan), located in Pelham, New York, and Guangzhou Zhen Hua Shipping Co., Ltd. (Guangzhou), a Chinese state-owned corporation, began negotiating through their respective brokers, Seabrokers and Seagos, both located in Stanford, Connecticut, a time charter of the *BIN HE*, a tanker owned by Guangzhou. The charter contained three "subjects" or conditions: (1) Titan's satisfactory inspection of the *BIN HE*; (2) the release of the vessel from its previous charterer; and (3) the approval of the charter party by Titan's board of directors within three days of their receipt of the final inspection report. The parties negotiated different periods and rates, as well as several other terms and ultimately, on 26 September 1995, Guangzhou responded with a "firm counter offer" with respect to time and rates. Titan notified its broker, Seabrokers, that agreement had been reached and the same day the broker sent Titan a fixture telex "recap[ping] Owners and Charterers' Agreement". The agreement was based on the "Shelltime 4 Time Charter", a standard time charter. It contained the above conditions as well as an arbitration clause providing for arbitration in London.

Following some initial concern about the vessel's seaworthiness, on receipt of the full inspection report, on 25 October, Titan lifted its inspection "subject". On 26 October, Seabrokers informed Titan that the *BIN HE* had been withdrawn from the previous charters and on 27 October, Titan notified Seabrokers that its board of directors had approved the charter.

Guangzhou's version of the facts was that on 24 October, Titan had rejected the vessel and that the conditions had not been fulfilled. Moreover, according to Guangzhou, on 25 October, "Titan reversed its position and attempted to assert that the vessel had not failed the inspection". Guangzhou claimed that it then terminated all negotiation with Titan.

On 1 November, Seagos faxed Titan suggesting arbitration to resolve the dispute. Later the same day, Titan proposed that the parties submit the dispute to three arbitrators in New York to determine whether the parties had entered into a binding agreement on 26 September subject to the conditions that were subsequently fulfilled. Seabrokers replied, however, that the "Shell Time 4 Camaro proforma is very clear on the simplified arbitration which has been agreed by ... Titan.... There is no need for [an] agreement at all." The parties exchanged several faxes apparently confirming the London arbitration. After parties failed to agree on an arbitrator, on 7 February 1996, Titan faxed Seagos that it would not agree to arbitration outside of the binding Titan/Guangzhou charter. Guangzhou faxed Titan stating that it was not allowed to be in breach of the ad hoc arbitration clause which was "actually running".

Titan initiated proceedings in the district court seeking a summary determination of the making of a binding charter party between Titan and Guangzhou as well as seeking to compel arbitration. Guangzhou objected to the jurisdiction of the court, relying on its sovereign immunity. In order to determine this question, the court, per Conner, Senior DJ, first found that it had the jurisdiction to determine its own jurisdiction. The question of Guangzhou's objection was resolved by finding that although the ad hoc arbitration had "not come to fruition", there was, however, a valid arbitration agreement contained in the charter party which had been formed, and consequently Guangzhou had waived its sovereign immunity.

Excerpt

I. JURISDICTION

[1] "Titan claims that there exists subject matter jurisdiction under Sect. 9 of the FAA. Guangzhou, on the other hand, argues that it is immune from suit under the Foreign Sovereign Immunities Act (FSIA). The Court concludes that it has subject matter jurisdiction under 28 U.S.C. Sect. 1330(a), because Guangzhou waived its immunity under the FSIA."

1. *Subject Matter Jurisdiction Under the FSIA*

[2] "The FSIA provides that 'a foreign state shall be immune from the jurisdiction of the courts of the United States and of the States except as provided in sections 1605 to 1607 of this chapter'. 28 U.S.C. Sect. 1604. A defendant corporation that is owned entirely by a foreign state is also immune from the jurisdiction of the Court. See id. Sects. 1603(a), 1603(b)(2), 1604.[1] If the immunity provisions of the FSIA are applicable, the Court is divested of subject matter jurisdiction over an action. *NYSA-ILA Pension Trust Fund v. Garuda Indonesia*, 7 F.3d 35, 38 (2d Cir. 1993).

[3] "It is undisputed that defendant Guangzhou is wholly owned by the People's Republic of China. Therefore, in order for the Court to have jurisdiction over Titan's motion, there must be an applicable exception to foreign sovereign immunity under the FSIA. See *Verlinden B.V. v. Central Bank of Nigeria*, 461 U.S. 480, 498 (1983). The burden is on Titan 'to go forward with evidence showing that, under the exceptions to the FSIA, immunity should not be granted, although the ultimate burden of persuasion remains with the alleged foreign sovereign'. *Cargill Int'l S.A. v. M/T Pavel Dybenko*, 991 F.2d 1012, 1016 (2d Cir. 1993) (internal citations omitted).[2] If an exception applies,

---

1. 28 U.S.C. Sects. 1603 and 1604 read in relevant part:

   Section 1603
   "For the purposes of this Chapter –
   (a) A 'foreign state', except as used in section 1608 of this title, includes a political subdivision of a foreign state or an agency or instrumentality of a foreign state as defined in subsection (b).
   (b) An 'agency or instrumentality of a foreign state' means any entity –
   ...
   (2) which is an organ of a foreign state or political subdivision thereof, or a majority of whose shares or other ownership interest is owned by a foreign state or political subdivision thereof,..."

   Section 1604
   "Subject to existing international agreements to which the United States is a party at the time of enactment of this Act a foreign state shall be immune from the jurisdiction of the courts of the United States and of the states except as provided in Sections 1605 to 1607 of this chapter."

2. Reported in Yearbook XVIII (1993) pp. 517-523 (US no. 132).

the Court has subject matter jurisdiction over Guangzhou under 28 U.S.C. Sect. 1330."[3]

A. *Arbitration exception*

[4] "The Court holds that Guangzhou has waived its immunity under Sect. 1605(a)(6)(B) of the FSIA. (footnote omitted) Sect. 1605(a)(6)(B) provides an exception to immunity in cases where a foreign state or sovereign entity has agreed to arbitrate a dispute and the arbitration agreement is or may be governed by a treaty signed by the United States calling for the recognition and enforcement of arbitral awards, such as the [1958 New York Convention]. 'An arbitration agreement ... arising out of a legal relationship, whether contractual or not, which is considered as commercial, including a transaction, contract, or agreement described in section 2 of this title, falls under the Convention.' 9 U.S.C. Sect. 202. Congress has authorized the district courts to compel arbitration under the Convention in accordance with the agreement, including arbitration at sites outside the US. Id. Sect. 203.[4]

[5] "Here, Titan alleges that it entered into a charter party with Guangzhou that provided for arbitration in London, which is enforceable under the Convention. Guangzhou contends that the charter party was never formed, because Titan never completed the subjects precedent to the agreement. The US and China are both parties to the Convention.

[6] "*Cargill International S.A. v. M/T Pavel Dybenko* is on point. In *Cargill*, the Second Circuit Court of Appeals considered whether a district court had subject matter jurisdiction to determine whether a charter party, which contained an arbitration clause, applied in a particular case between a sovereign-owned company and a plaintiff that was a third party to the charter. The Court held that the district court had 'jurisdiction to determine jurisdiction',

3. 28 U.S.C. Sect. 1330 reads:

   "The district courts shall have original jurisdiction without regard to the amount in controversy of any non-jury civil action against a foreign state as defined in section 1603(a) of this title as to any claim for relief in personam with respect to which the foreign state is not entitled to immunity under sections 1605-1607 of this title."

4. 9 U.S.C. Sect. 203 reads in relevant part:

   "An action or proceeding falling under the Convention shall be deemed to arise under the laws and treaties of the United States. The district courts of the United States ... shall have original jurisdiction over such an action or proceeding, regardless of the amount in controversy."

and directed the court to consider 'whatever evidence has been submitted' by the parties. 991 F.2d at 1019 (citations omitted). The Court reasoned that regardless of whether there existed an agreement to arbitrate that could be enforced by the plaintiff – the alleged beneficiary of the agreement – the Court had jurisdiction to determine whether 'the arbitration agreement in the Charter Party was intended to benefit [the plaintiff]'. Id. Of particular importance to the Court was that 'the Convention should be broadly interpreted', 'when ... read together with the FSIA[]'. Id. at 1018. It is significant that Cargill was not seeking to enforce an arbitral award, but to determine whether it was a beneficiary of the contract and to enforce the arbitration agreement. Compare id. at 1017-1018 with *Seetransport Wiking Trader Schiffarhtsgesellschaft MBH & Co. v. Navimpex Centrala Navala*, 989 F.2d 572, 577-579 (2d Cir. 1993)[5] (enforcing arbitration award while distinguishing cases where plaintiff sought to have award enforced from cases in which there had been no award).

[7] "*Cargill* is applicable here, where the parties have allegedly entered into an agreement to arbitrate which is governed by the Convention and which is enforceable by the Court. See 991 F.2d at 1020 ('if [the plaintiff] is found to be a third party beneficiary to the Charter Party, it may be proper for the district court to enforce the arbitration agreement against [the defendant]'); see also 9 U.S.C. Sect. 206 (allowing court to order arbitration under the FAA). According to *Cargill*, the FSIA must be read with the FAA to give the Convention a broad interpretation. Accordingly, the Court concludes that it has subject matter jurisdiction to determine whether the parties entered into a binding charter party agreement that required arbitration in London."

B. Commercial activities exception

[8] "Alternatively, the Court has subject matter jurisdiction over the action pursuant to Sect. 1605(a)(2) of the FSIA, which provides, in relevant part:

> 'A foreign state shall not be immune from the jurisdiction of courts of the Unite[d] States in any case ... in which the action is based ... upon an act performed in the United States in connection with a commercial activity of the foreign state elsewhere; or upon an act outside the territory of the United States in connection with a commercial activity of the foreign state elsewhere and that act causes a direct effect in the United States.'

5. Reported in Yearbook XVIII (1993) pp. 524-529 (US no. 133).

The Court concludes that Guangzhou's actions, taken in China, caused a 'direct effect' in the US and that those of its broker, Seagos, were taken 'in connection with a commercial activity' of Guangzhou in China.

[9] "In order for an act taken 'in connection with a commercial activity' to provide an exception to foreign sovereign immunity, it must be a 'legally significant act'. See *Hanil Bank v. PT. Bank Negara Indonesia*, — F.3d —, No. 97 Civ. 7961, 1998 WL 334342, at *6 (2d Cir. 24 June 1998); *Antares Aircraft, L.P. v. Federal Republic of Nigeria*, 999 F.2d 33, 36 (2d Cir. 1993); *WMW Machinery, Inc. v. Werkzeugmaschinenhandel GmbH IM Aufbau*, 960 F. Supp. 734, 741 (S.D.N.Y. 1997). '[A]n effect is "direct" if it follows "as an immediate consequence of the defendant's ... activity."' *Republic of Argentina v. Weltover, Inc.*, 504 U.S. 607, 618 (1992) (quoting *Weltover, Inc. v. Republic of Argentina*, 941 F.2d 145, 152 (2d Cir. 1991)).

[10] "Here, Guangzhou negotiated a contract with Titan, a US corporation, by faxes sent to Titan and both parties' brokers in the US. The act of making and directing this correspondence was 'an act [taken] outside the ... United States', 'in connection with a commercial activity ... elsewhere', that caused Titan allegedly to suffer a 'direct effect' – $1 million in damages – in the US. See *Caribbean Trading & Fidelity Corp. v. Nigerian Nat'l Petroleum Co.*, No. 90 Civ. 4169, 1993 WL 541236, at *8 (S.D.N.Y. 1993).

[11] "That Guangzhou was 'transacting business' with Titan in the US and directing negotiations in this country is enough for it to have waived immunity under Sect. 1605(a)(2) with respect to the formation of the charter party at issue here. See *Gibbons v. Udaras na Gaeltachta*, 549 F. Supp. 1094, 1113 (S.D.N.Y. 1982); see also *Supra Med. Corp. v. McGonigle*, 955 F. Supp. 374, 382 (E.D.Pa. 1997) (finding sufficient 'intentional communications with [plaintiff] giv[ing] rise to the underlying suit'). Titan's identity as a US corporation further strengthens this conclusion. See *International Housing Ltd. v. Rafidain Bank Iraq*, 893 F.2d 8, 11 (2d Cir. 1989) (fact that plaintiff is 'a US corporation ... is relevant to whether [its] financial losses ... constituted a "direct effect"'); Note, Effects Jurisdiction Under the FSIA and the Due Process Clause, 55 N.Y.U. L. Rev. 474, 512 (1980). (footnote omitted) Because we find a 'significant, legal connection' with the US giving rise to Titan's claim, which caused a direct effect in the US, we have subject matter under the FSIA with respect to the formation of the charter party. (footnote omitted)"

2. *Personal Jurisdiction*

[12] "For the same reasons, we conclude that the Court has personal jurisdiction over Guangzhou. See *Shapiro v. Republic of Bolivia*, 930 F.2d 1013, 1020 (2d Cir. 1991) (citations omitted); *New York Bay Co. v. State Bank of*

Patiala, No. 93 Civ. 6075, 1994 WL 369406, at *4 (S.D.N.Y. 12 July 1994); see also *Argentine Republic v. Amerada Hess Shipping Corp.*, 488 U.S. 428, 434 n. 3 (1989) ('personal jurisdiction, like subject matter jurisdiction, exists only when one of the exceptions to foreign sovereign immunity ... applies'). This is because under the FSIA, 'subject matter jurisdiction plus service of process equals personal jurisdiction'. *Texas Trading & Milling Corp. v. Federal Republic of Nigeria*, 647 F.2d 300, 308 (2d Cir. 1981). Since the Court has subject matter jurisdiction over the action and there is no dispute that defendant Guangzhou was properly served pursuant to 28 U.S.C. Sect. 1608, the statutory requirements for personal jurisdiction are met.

[13] "The FSIA, however, 'cannot create personal jurisdiction where the Constitution forbids it'. *Texas Trading*, 647 F.2d at 308. Consequently, '[e]ach finding of personal jurisdiction under the FSIA requires, in addition, a due process scrutiny of the court's power to exercise its authority over a particular defendant'. Id.; accord *Seetransport*, 989 F.2d at 580. Due Process requires that the foreign sovereign entity have 'minimum contacts' with the United States 'such that maintenance of the suit does not offend "traditional notions of fair play and substantial justice"'. *International Shoe Co. v. Washington*, 326 U.S. 310, 316 (1945) (citation omitted). In a case brought under the FSIA, a court may consider contacts beyond the forum state. See *Max Daetwyler Corp. v. R. Meyer*, 762 F.2d 290, 293 (3d Cir. 1985) ('the proper inquiry in determining personal jurisdiction in a case involving federal rights is one directed to the totality of a defendant's contacts throughout the United States'; see also Graham C. Lilly, 'Jurisdiction Over Domestic and Alien Defendants', 69 Va. L. Rev. 85, 130 (1983) ('it [is] reasonably clear that national – not state – contacts are decisive'). Moreover, 'actions relevant to the [case] by an agent on [a] defendant[']s behalf' can support personal jurisdiction over a defendant. *Texas Trading*, 647 F.2d at 314. (footnote omitted)

[14] "The Court concludes that it has personal jurisdiction over Guangzhou because Guangzhou hired Seagos, which is located in Connecticut, to broker the *BIN HE*, and which then directed communications at issue to Seabrokers and to Titan to negotiate the charter party. See *Reed Int'l Trading Corp. v. Donau Bank AG*, 866 F. Supp. 750, 755 (S.D.N.Y. 1994) (exercising personal jurisdiction over foreign sovereign defendant where defendant had appointed US bank as 'advising bank' for letters of credit at issue); *Crimson Semiconductor, Inc. v. Electronum*, 629 F. Supp. 903, 905, 908 (S.D.N.Y. 1986) (same, where defendant's representatives negotiated agreement in the US). Moreover, there is evidence in the record to suggest that Guangzhou may have sent some of these communications directly to Seagos by fax from China. See *Sealift Bulkers, Inc. v. Republic of Armenia*, 965 F. Supp. 81, 85 (D.D.C. 1997) (personal jurisdiction where defendant used US telecommunications systems

to correspond with plaintiff); *Hatzlachh Supply Inc. v. Savannah Bank of Nigeria*, 649 F. Supp. 688, 691 (S.D.N.Y. 1986) (same).

[15] "Accordingly, Guangzhou's contacts with the United States are sufficient to establish personal jurisdiction in this action. By appointing a representative in Connecticut to negotiate the charter party at issue in this case, Guangzhou 'purposefully avail[ed] itself of the privilege of conducting activities with the [United States]'. *Weltover*, 504 U.S. at 620 (quoting *Hanson v. Denckla*, 357 U.S. 235, 253 (1958)) (alterations in original). Guangzhou may not avail itself of US clients, by directing communications to the US, without being held responsible for the content of these communications in the US. Accord *Sealift*, 965 F. Supp. at 85-86. Given its conduct, Guangzhou should reasonably have expected that it could be haled into court here, were it to break off negotiations, because it directed the negotiations here, through Seagos, and because Titan, the target of its negotiations, is located here. See *Worldwide Volkswagen Corp. v. Woodson*, 444 U.S. 286, 297 (1980); *Hanil Bank*, 1998 WL 334342, at *8; see also *Supra Medical*, 955 F. Supp. at 382-383 ('[defendant] cannot now ... complain about a suit concerning the effect of negotiations in the jurisdiction in which some of those negotiations occurred'). (footnote omitted)"

II. VENUE

[16] "We also hold that venue is proper in this Court under 28 U.S.C. Sect. 1391(b). Under this section, 'a civil action wherein jurisdiction is not founded solely on the diversity of citizenship ... may, except as otherwise provided by law, be brought only in ... a judicial district in which a substantial part of the events or omissions giving rise to the claim occurred'. Despite its limiting language, courts have routinely held that Sect. 1391(b) allows venue in more than one district. See *Bates v. C & S Adjusters*, 980 F.2d 865, 867 (2d Cir. 1992) ('the admonition against recognizing multiple venues has been disapproved'); *PI, Inc. v. Quality Prods., Inc.*, 907 F. Supp. 752, 757 (S.D.N.Y. 1995) ('Venue is proper in each district that is the situs of a substantial part of the events or omissions giving rise to the claim.').

[17] "Once an objection to venue has been raised, the plaintiff bears the burden of establishing that venue is proper. *D'Anton Jos, S.L. v. Doll Factory, Inc.*, 937 F. Supp. 320, 321 (S.D.N.Y. 1996); *French Transit, Ltd. v. Modern Coupon Systs., Inc.*, 858 F. Supp. 22, 24 (S.D.N.Y. 1994). Titan therefore bears the burden of establishing that a substantial part of the events giving rise to the lawsuit occurred in the Southern District of New York.

[18] "Titan argues that venue is proper here because the writings at issue were negotiated by means of facsimiles and telephone calls between Pelham, New

York and Stamford, Connecticut. We agree. These faxes reflect 'a substantial part of the events' giving rise to the present claim because the action alleges the creation of a binding charter party through these writings. See *Sacody Tech. Inc. v. Avant, Inc.*, 862 F. Supp. 1152, 1157 (S.D.N.Y. 1994) (venue requirements 'may be satisfied by a communication transmitted to or from the district in which the cause of action was filed, given a sufficient relationship between the communication and the cause of action'); see also *Constitution Reins. Corp. v. Stonewall Ins. Co.*, 872 F. Supp. 1247, 1250 (S.D.N.Y. 1995) (venue proper in breach of contract action where contracts were negotiated through telephone calls and faxes between New York and Texas)."

III. SUMMARY DETERMINATION OF THE MAKING OF A CHARTER PARTY

[19] "Now that the Court has determined that jurisdiction and venue are proper, we must determine whether the parties have agreed to arbitrate the formation of the charter party. We hold that they did not. However, the parties did enter into a binding charter party, by which they agreed to arbitrate disputes in London, upon the election of either party. Because Titan has petitioned this Court to order arbitration, we order such arbitration to determine the parties' rights under the charter party, pursuant to Shell Time 4."

1. Ad Hoc Agreement to Arbitrate Existence of Charter Party

[20] "Guangzhou argues that the parties agreed to arbitrate the very existence of the charter party and, accordingly, that Titan's motion must be dismissed. We disagree. Given the evidence, we conclude that the parties did not enter into the 'ad hoc' arbitration agreement advocated by Guangzhou. (footnote omitted)

[21] "Because 'arbitral jurisdiction is rooted in the consent of the parties', *Three Valleys Mun. Water Dist. v. E.F. Hutton & Co.*, 925 F.2d 1136, 1140-1141 (9th Cir. 1991), the existence of an agreement to arbitrate is a threshold question for a court to resolve, absent a clear and unmistakable delegation of that authority to an arbitrator. *First Options of Chicago, Inc. v. Kaplan*, 514 U.S. 938, 943 (1995);[6] *AT&T Tech., Inc. v. Communications Workers of Am.*, 475 U.S. 643, 649 (1986); *National Union Fire Ins. Co. v. Belco Petroleum Corp.*, 88 F.3d 129, 135 (2d Cir. 1996); see also *Maye v. Smith Barney Inc.*, 897 F. Supp. 100, 106 n. 3 (S.D.N.Y. 1995) ('the question of whether the parties ever

6. Reported in Yearbook XXII (1997) pp. 278-286.

made an agreement to arbitrate is ... to be decided by the courts'). While due regard must be given to federal policy favoring arbitration, *Mastrobuono v. Shearson Lehman Hutton, Inc.*, 514 U.S. 52, 62 (1995);[7] *Volt Info. Sciences, Inc. v. Board of Trustees of Leland Stanford Jr. Univ.*, 489 U.S. 468, 475 (1989);[8] *Moses H. Cone Mem'l Hosp. v. Mercury Constr. Corp.*, 460 U.S. 1, 24-25 (1983), where the parties contest the formation of an agreement, 'any silence or ambiguity about whether such a question is arbitrable reverses the usual presumption that issues should be resolved in [arbitration's] favor'. *Abram Landau Real Estate v. Benova*, 123 F.3d 69, 72 (2d Cir. 1997) (citing *First Options*, 514 U.S. at 943). The question of the formation of the charter party, like that of any other contract, is a question of federal common law. See *First Options*, 514 U.S. at 943; *Genesco, Inc. v. T. Kakiuchi & Co.*, 815 F.2d 840, 845 (2d Cir. 1987).

[22] "From the evidence, it is clear that the parties did begin negotiating an 'ad hoc' arbitration agreement that contained terms different than the original charter party. According to the parties, on 1 November Seagos proposed arbitration to 'resolve the dispute' as to whether the parties had made a binding charter. That same day, Titan proposed arbitration before a panel of three arbitrators in New York. However, the evidence also suggests that on 2 November, Guangzhou cut off negotiations on the ad hoc agreement through Seagos, which, in response to Titan, stated that the 'Shell Time 4' 'is very clear on the [form of arbitration] which has been agreed by US Titan. There is no need for a separate arbitration agreement'.

[23] "We find this language controlling; with it, Seagos, on behalf of Guangzhou, definitively ended negotiations on the 'ad hoc agreement'. (footnote omitted) That it was Guangzhou's intent to end these negotiations is clear from its remaining correspondence, which called for London arbitration 'pursuant to the Shell Time 4 clause 41'. Cf. *Northern Tankers Cyprus Ltd. v. Lexmar Corp.*, 781 F. Supp. 289, 290-291 (S.D.N.Y. 1992) ('agreement to arbitrate, separate and distinct from that contained in the charter party', was formed where plaintiff demanded arbitration 'for damages caused by [defendant's] non-performance of the charter', and defendant accepted that demand). Because the parties' negotiations with respect to the 'ad hoc' agreement did not come to fruition, we cannot order arbitration on the issue of whether the charter party was in fact formed."

7. Reported in XXI (1996) pp. 181-191.
8. Reported in Yearbook XV (1990) pp. 141-148.

2. *The Charter Party*

[24] "We do, however, order arbitration with respect to Guangzhou's alleged breach of the charter party, because we conclude that a charter party providing for arbitration was formed. Whether a charter party has been formed is a question of fact. *Sun Int'l Ltd. v. Terrabo Petroleum Co.*, 747 F.2d 108, 110 (2d Cir. 1984). The Court, however, may determine whether a charter party exists, if the underlying material facts are not in dispute. See *Great Circle Lines Ltd. v. Matheson & Co.*, 681 F.2d 121, 124 (2d Cir. 1982). As with any other contract, a charter party is formed when there is a 'meeting of the minds' on its essential terms. *Interocean Shipping Co. v. National Shipping & Trading Corp.*, 462 F.2d 673, 676 (2d Cir. 1972); *A/S Custodia v. Lessin Int'l, Inc.*, 503 F.2d 318, 320 (2d Cir. 1974). It is not necessary that the proposed charter be signed by either party, id., and even an oral charter party is enforceable by a court of law, *Great Circle Lines*, 681 F.2d at 124 ('binding charter engagements have historically been assumed on nothing more formal than a nod of a head').

[25] "In any case, it is undeniable that charter parties can be and more often than not are formed by way of facsimile or telex. See id.; *In re J. Lauritzen A/S*, No. 84 Civ. 8704, 1986 WL 13441, at *2 (S.D.N.Y. 5 June 1986). This is because '[t]he shipping industry is a fast moving ... business, where dealings between the parties are usually conducted ... under severe time restraints'. *Great Circle Lines*, 681 F.2d at 125. To arrange expeditiously what would otherwise be complicated and time consuming, 'brokers [customarily] receive and send telex [or fax] traffic all over the world'. Id.

[26] "On the facts before us, the existence of a binding charter party is clear. The parties negotiated a charter through their respective brokers, which was confirmed by facsimile on 26 September 1995 by Seagos, which 'recap[ped] Owners and Charterers' agreement'. A 'recap' communication, or 'fixture', is recognized throughout the shipping industry as an agreement to a charter party's essential terms. See *Great Circle Lines*, 681 F.2d at 125 & n. 2; *Maritime Ventures Int'l, Inc. v. Caribbean Trading & Fidelity, Ltd.*, 689 F. Supp. 1340, 1345 (S.D.N.Y. 1988); see also *P.E.P. Shipping (Scandinavia) ApS. v. Noramco Shipping Corp.*, No. 96 Civ. 3136, 1997 WL 358118, at *2 n. 1 (E.D.La. 24 June 1997) ('[a] fixture presupposes a final contract with main terms set and final details to be resolved') (citing *Great Circle Lines*, 681 F.2d at 125 n. 2); *In re Herlofson Mgmt. A/S*, 765 F. Supp. 78, 81 n. 3 (S.D.N.Y. 1991) ('[a] "recap telex" recapitulates the terms of [a] fixture that have been agreed upon'). (footnote omitted) Thus, the 'recap' fax represented an agreement as to the charter party's main terms, which were in accordance with the Shell Time 4, a standard form charter. Accordingly, the parties had entered into a binding agreement as of 26 September 1995, which incorporated each of the Shell Time

4's terms. Cf. *Samsun*, 926 F. Supp. at 441 ('[t]he legal effect of adopting [form charter] is inescapable'); *Keystone Shipping Co. v. Compagnie Marocaine de Navigation*, No. 89 Civ. 1028, 1990 WL 104029, at *4 (S.D.N.Y. 19 July 1990) (fixture incorporating form charter is binding where it 'embodi[ed]' form).

[27] "Moreover, we do not agree with defendant that the charter did not come into effect because of the alleged failure of one of its 'subjects', the approval of the charter by Titan's board of directors upon receiving the final inspection report of the *BIN HE*. First, this argument directly contradicts the weight of the evidence, which suggests that the Board did approve the *BIN HE* within the agreed time period. Second, even had this 'subject' failed, it did not vitiate the charter that had already been formed. It is well established that a 'subject detail' does not create a condition subsequent to a charter party. See *Great Circle Lines*, 681 F.2d at 126; *In re Pollux Marine Agencies, Inc.*, 455 F. Supp. 211, 223 (S.D.N.Y. 1978). In our opinion, there existed a binding charter party between Titan and Guangzhou, in the form of 'Shell Time 4', beginning 26 September 1995. Cf. *E.A.S.T., Inc. of Stamford v. M/V Alaia*, 673 F. Supp. 796, 800 (E.D.La. 1987) (charter not conditioned on plaintiff's acceptance of vessel because charter formed upon agreement of main terms), aff'd, 876 F.2d 1168 (5th Cir. 1989).[9]

[28] "Because there exists a charter between the parties, Titan must arbitrate its dispute in London, according to the Shell Time 4. Cf. *Interocean*, 523 F.2d at 531 (form charter's arbitration clause bound parties where fixture telex adopted 'Mobiltime form charter'); *Keystone*, 1990 WL 104029, at *4 (compelling arbitration where fixture provided that voyage be governed 'per terms and conditions of the North American Grain charter party (pro forma 1982)', which contained arbitration clause); *In re Pollux*, 455 F. Supp. at 213-214 (same, where defendant confirmed 'having fixed the foil ... subject details of Eldece Time', and aforesaid form charter had arbitration clause). The parties agreed to this form charter, as well as to the inclusion of an arbitration clause, until well after this dispute arose. As both parties were familiar to its form, it controls. See *P.E.P. Shipping*, 1997 WL 358118, at *3.

[29] "Moreover, even in the absence of a binding charter party, we would order arbitration in London under the Shell Time 4, because the parties agreed to arbitration in that forum by referencing that form charter while negotiating their own charter's terms. See *Samsun*, 926 F. Supp. at 441 ('A reference to a familiar charter party form which provides for arbitration ... binds the parties to arbitrate any disputes [in the forum provided] ... even though the formal charter party is not executed until later (or not at all)'). Respondent 'was placed on notice, one way or the other', that disputes as to the charter party

9. Reported in Yearbook XV (1989) pp. 555-562 (US no. 91).

– including formation – could be arbitrated in London. Id. Thus, by ordering arbitration in London, the Court gives Guangzhou the benefit of its bargain."

280. United States Court of Appeals, Second Circuit, 2 September 1998, No. 97-7224

Parties:	Plaintiff/appellee: Europcar Italia, S.p.A. (Italy) Defendant/appellant: Maiellano Tours, Inc. (US)
Published in:	156 Federal Reporter, Third Series, p. 310 et seq.; 1998 U.S. App. LEXIS 21484
Articles:	V; V(1)(*e*); V(2)(*b*); VI
Subject matters:	– enforcement of decision made in *arbitrato irrituale* – discretion to adjourn enforcement proceedings
Commentary Cases:	[1] = ¶ 501; [2] = ¶ 503; [4]-[9] = ¶ 108; [8] = ¶ 502; [9] = ¶ 514; [10]-[13] = ¶ 524 (forged contract); [10] = ¶ 518; [11] = ¶ 222; [12] = ¶ 303 + ¶ 500; [13] = ¶ 502; [14]-[22] = ¶ 601; [21 sub 6] = ¶ 515

Facts

In October 1988, Maiellano Tours, Inc. (Maiellano) and Europcar Italia S.p.A. (Europcar) entered into an agreement whereby Europcar agreed to provide rental car services in Italy to customers sent to it by the American travel agency, Maiellano. This agreement contained an arbitration clause providing that the agreement would be governed by Italian law and that

> "[a]ny dispute arising from or in connection with this agreement, included [sic] those related to its validity, performance or termination will be submitted to and finally resolved by a sole arbitrator appointed by the legal counsels selected by the parties. The sole arbitrator shall decide under the rules known in the Italian legal system as '*arbitrato irrituale in equità*' (informal proceedings)."

A dispute arose in 1991 and as the parties were unable to agree on a sole arbitrator as required by the 1988 agreement, they entered into a supplemental arbitration agreement, which provided in relevant part:

> "[t]he agreement between Maiellano Tours, Inc. and Europcar Italia S.p.A. is regulated by Italian law. In the event that any dispute shall arise with respect to the application of this agreement, including its validity, execution or resolution, it shall be settled by a final arbitration by an Arbitration Panel of three arbitrators, as amicable adjusters,... The Panel will decide the controversy pursuant to the rules set forth in the Italian legal system for the '*Arbitrato Irrituale in Equità (procedimento informale)*', (Informal arbitration on equitable grounds)."

An award was made by the panel of three arbitrators in favor of Europcar in June 1992.

In July 1992, Europcar commenced an action in the Italian courts to enforce the arbitration award. Maiellano countered by commencing a collateral action to have the award set aside on the ground of fraud, alleging that the arbitrator's decision was based on a 20 February 1979 agreement that contained a forged Maiellano signature. The Tribunal of Rome consolidated the actions and on 30 March 1996, ruled in favor of Europcar, rejecting all of Maiellano's claims. The tribunal found that Maiellano had not raised the issue of forgery to the arbitrators and that the arbitrators' decision was based principally on the parties' ten-year business relationship rather than on any particular written agreement. Maiellano appealed against the enforcement of the arbitral award to the Rome Court of Appeal.

On 4 August 1994, Europcar had filed an action in the Eastern District of New York seeking recognition and enforcement of the arbitral award. Maiellano opposed enforcement, arguing, inter alia, that the district court lacked subject matter jurisdiction because *arbitrato irrituale* is not covered by the 1958 New York Convention and, in the alternative, that the district court should defer its decision pending the outcome of the trial of the Tribunal of Rome in accordance with *Spier v. Calzaturificio Tecnica S.p.A.*, 663 F. Supp. 871 (S.D.N.Y. 1987).[1]

Europcar moved for summary judgment in October 1994, and the district court referred the motion to Magistrate Judge Gold. Judge Gold rejected Maiellano's arguments and recommended that Europcar's motion for summary judgment be granted. The district court, per Carol Bagley Amon, J, adopted Judge Gold's Report and Recommendation in its entirety, apart from one modification, and entered judgment for Europcar in the amount of US$ 1,102,283 with interest and costs.

On appeal by Maiellano, the Court of Appeals, per Oakes, CJ, Walker, CJ and Brieant, DJ vacated the decision of the district court and remanded for

1. Reported in Yearbook XIII (1988) pp. 602-609 (US no. 79).

reconsideration of the decision not to adjourn the enforcement proceedings pending the outcome of the Italian appeal. Consequently, it was not necessary at this stage to decide the issue of whether awards made in *arbitrato irrituale* were enforceable under the Convention.

Excerpt

[1] "The [1958 New York] Convention provides for the enforcement of arbitration agreements and the confirmation of foreign arbitral awards. Convention, Arts. II, III. District courts have been given original jurisdiction over actions or proceedings falling under the Convention, 9 U.S.C. Sect. 203, and any party to a foreign arbitration may seek confirmation in a district court of an arbitral award within three years after the award is made, 9 U.S.C. Sect. 207. 'The court shall confirm the award unless it finds one of the grounds for refusal or deferral of recognition or enforcement of the award specified in the ... Convention.' Id. The grounds for refusing to enforce an award are limited to the specific defenses enumerated in Art. V of the Convention...."

[2] After quoting Art. V(1)(*e*) and V(2)(*b*), the court continued: "The party opposing enforcement has the burden of proving the existence of one of these enumerated defenses. See *Fotochrome, Inc. v. Copal Co.*, 517 F.2d 512, 518 (2d Cir. 1975);[2] *Parsons & Whittemore Overseas Co. v. Société Générale de L'Industrie du Papier (RAKTA)*, 508 F.2d 969, 973 (2d Cir. 1974).[3]

[3] "On appeal, Maiellano argues, inter alia, that (1) the district court did not have jurisdiction under the Convention to confirm an award granted under *arbitrato irrituale*; (2) the award should not have been enforced because the parties did not intend to be bound by the arbitration award; (3) the district court should have refused to enforce the award because it was based on a forged contract and, therefore, is contrary to United States public policy; and, in any event, (4) the district court should have suspended its decision to await the outcome of the pending Italian litigation."

I. ENFORCEABILITY OF *ARBITRATO IRRITUALE* AWARD

[4] "Maiellano contends that awards granted under the Italian rules known as *arbitrato irrituale* do not give rise to a binding arbitral award of the sort entitled to enforcement under the Convention because *arbitrato irrituale* is an

2. Reported in Yearbook I (1976) pp. 202-203 (US no. 3).
3. Reported in Yearbook I (1976) p. 205 (US no. 7).

informal, extralegal process that lacks procedural safeguards. Moreover, confirmation of the award here would give it greater legal status than it would be accorded in Italy because under Italian law such arbitral awards are considered to be contractual agreements that are not automatically enforceable, but rather are subject to de novo review by an Italian court. Therefore, Maiellano contends, it would be inappropriate to confirm such awards through the summary proceeding and deferential enforcement envisioned by the Convention.

[5] "Maiellano supports these arguments with a decision by Germany's highest court, the *Bundesgerichtshof*, that held that awards rendered under *arbitrato irrituale* were not enforceable under the Convention, see *Compania Italiana di Assicurazioni v. Schwarzmeer und Ostsee Versicherungsaktiengesellschaft*, BGHZ, 8 October 1981 (III ZR 42/80), reprinted in [1982] CEC (CCH) 516,[4] as well as opinions of academicians, including one of the draftsmen of the Convention, that state that the Convention was not meant to apply to *arbitrato irrituale*, see, e.g., Decl. of Hans Smit, 12 November 1996, J.A. at 456; *Spier*, 663 F. Supp. at 874 (quoting declaration of Pieter Sanders, a draftsman of the Convention); Pieter Sanders and Dr. Albert Jan van den Berg, Consolidated Commentary, IV Yearbook Commercial Arbitration 231, 232-233 (1979).

[6] "Europcar, on the other hand, points to four decisions of the Italian Supreme Court, the *Corte de Cassazione*, that have expressly held that *arbitrato irrituale* does fall under the Convention. See *Agracommerz A.G. v. Privilegiata Fabbrica Maraschino Excelsior Girolamo Luxardo S.p.A.*, Cass., 15 January 1992, n. 405;[5] *Federal Commerce and Navigation Ltd. v. Rocco Giuseppe e Figli s.n.c.*, Cass., sez. un., 15 December 1982, n. 6915, Foro. It. 1983, I, 2200;[6] *Carey Hirsch Lumber Co. v. Colella Legnami S.p.A.*, Cass., sez. un., 6 July 1982, n. 4039, Foro It. 1983, I, 736-740;[7] *Butera v. Pagnan*, Cass., sez. un., 18 September 1978, n. 4167.[8] The *Corte di Cassazione* recognized that such awards would be treated differently under the Convention than under Italian law. Nevertheless, it held that in order to be enforceable under the Convention, awards must only be binding on the parties, not necessarily judicially binding in the originating country, and that although awards under *arbitrato irrituale* are merely contractual, and therefore are not immediately enforceable in Italy, they are nevertheless binding on the parties. See, e.g., *Butera*, n. 4167; *Colella Legnami S.p.A.*, n. 4039. See also Giorgio Bernini, *Domestic and International*

4. Reported in Yearbook VIII (1983) pp. 366-370 (FR Germany no. 25).
5. Reported in Yearbook XVIII (1993) pp. 427-432 (Italy no. 122).
6. Reported in Yearbook X (1985) pp. 464-466 (Italy no. 72).
7. Reported in Yearbook IX (1984) pp. 429-431 (Italy no. 62).
8. Reported in Yearbook IV (1979) pp. 296-300 (Italy no. 33).

Arbitration in Italy after the Legislative Reform, 5 Pace L. Rev. 543, 544 (1985) ('[t]he arbitral award stemming from an *arbitrato irrituale* is binding upon the parties but has no executory force') [Hereinafter Bernini, *Italian Arbitration*]; Susan Choi, Note, *Judicial Enforcement of Arbitration Awards under the ICSID and New York Conventions*, 28 N.Y.U. J. Int'l L. & Pol. 175, 195-196 (Fall 1995 – Winter 1996) (discussing *arbitrato irrituale* and noting that, according to Italian case law and authorities, awards are 'binding' within meaning of Convention) [hereinafter Choi, *Judicial Enforcement*]. The *Corte di Cassazione* concluded that in light of the differences in arbitration among the signatory countries, the Convention should be read broadly to cover both formal and informal arbitration. See, e.g., *Colella Legnami*, n. 4039; *Butera*, n. 4167.

[7] "Whether or not the Convention applies to *arbitrato irrituale* is, as far as we can tell, a matter of first impression for any United States federal court. Indeed, apart from the above-cited cases in Germany and Italy, the matter apparently has yet to be ruled on by the Permanent Court of International Justice at the Hague or the courts of any other signatory countries. The only other federal court to be presented with the issue declined to resolve the matter and instead adjourned the proceedings to await the outcome of parallel proceedings in Italy. See *Spier*, 663 F. Supp. at 876. The district court below found the Italian cases persuasive and held that awards under *arbitrato irrituale* are enforceable under the Convention. As the district court observed in *Spier*, the issue of whether or not *arbitrato irrituale* is enforceable under the Convention presents a close question and there are compelling arguments on both sides. Because resolution of this issue is not necessary to the disposition of this case, however, we leave decision on the matter for another day."

II. PARTIES' INTENT TO BE BOUND

[8] "Maiellano next argues that the parties did not intend to be legally bound by the arbitral award, but only to have it serve as a 'contractual advisory'. The district court properly rejected this argument. As the district court noted, both arbitration agreements stated unambiguously that the arbitration was to finally resolve the dispute and the arbitrators found that the parties intended to be bound by their award. Absent extraordinary circumstances, a confirming court is not to reconsider the arbitrator's findings. See *Fotochrome*, 517 F.2d at 516-518; *Halley Optical Corp. v. Jagar Int'l Mktg. Corp.*, 752 F. Supp. 638, 640 (S.D.N.Y. 1990); *International Standard Elec. Corp. v. Bridas Sociedad Anonima Petrolera, Industrial y Comercial*, 745 F. Supp. 172, 181 (S.D.N.Y. 1990).[9]

---

9. Reported in Yearbook XVII (1992) pp. 639-652 (US no. 115).

[9] "Moreover, as discussed above, awards under *arbitrato irrituale* are contractually binding on the parties even if they are not automatically enforceable. See, e.g., *Butera*, n. 4167; *Colella Legnami S.p.A.*, n. 4039. See also Bernini, *Italian Arbitration*, supra, at 544; Choi, *Judicial Enforcement*, supra, at 195-196; cf. Michael H. Strub, Jr., Note, *Resisting Enforcement of Foreign Arbitral Awards Under Article V(1)(E) and Article VI of the New York Convention: A Proposal for Effective Guidelines*, 68 Tex. L. Rev. 1031, 1058 (April 1990) (arguing that parties should state explicitly their intention not to be bound and that words such as 'final' in arbitration agreement indicate intent to be bound) [hereinafter Strub, *Resisting Enforcement*]. Accordingly, the district court did not err in determining that the arbitration award at issue was binding upon the parties under the Convention."

III. ALLEGED FORGERY OF AGREEMENT

[10] "Maiellano also argues that the award was based on the allegedly forged 1979 agreement and therefore enforcement would be contrary to United States public policy. The Convention provides that a federal court 'shall confirm the award unless it finds one of the grounds for refusal or deferral of recognition or enforcement of the award specified in the said Convention.' 9 U.S.C. Sect. 207. Art. V(2)(*b*) of the Convention allows a court to refuse enforcement where to do so would violate the public policy of the enforcing state. However, this public policy exception is to be construed very narrowly and should be applied 'only where enforcement would violate our "most basic notions of morality and justice."' *Waterside Ocean Navigation Co. v. International Navigation Ltd.*, 737 F.2d 150, 152 (2d Cir. 1984)[10] (quoting *Fotochrome*, 517 F.2d at 516); see also *Parsons & Whittemore*, 508 F.2d at 974. No such public policy concerns are implicated in this case.

[11] "Maiellano has apparently confused the issue of a fraudulently obtained arbitration agreement or award, which might violate public policy and therefore preclude enforcement, see *Waterside Ocean*, 737 F.2d at 153; *Tahan v. Hodgson*, 662 F.2d 862, 864 (D.C. Cir. 1981), with the issue of whether the underlying contract that is the subject of the arbitrated dispute was forged or fraudulently induced – a matter to be determined exclusively by the arbitrators. See *Prima Paint Corp. v. Flood & Conklin Mfg. Co.*, 388 U.S. 395, 403-404 (1967); *Riley v. Kingsley Underwriting Agencies, Ltd.*, 969 F.2d 953, 960 (10th Cir. 1992);[11] *Island Territory of Curaçao v. Solitron Devices, Inc.*, 489

10. Reported in Yearbook XI (1986) pp. 568-572 (US no. 61).
11. Reported in Yearbook XIX (1994) pp. 775-780 (US no. 147).

F.2d 1313, 1316 n. 2, 1319 (2d Cir. 1973);[12] *Meadows Indem. Co. v. Baccala & Shoop Ins. Servs., Inc.*, 760 F. Supp. 1036, 1041 (E.D.N.Y. 1991).[13] Indeed, the supplemental arbitration agreement at issue here, whose validity Maiellano does not dispute, incorporates this rule of law by expressly providing that 'any dispute [arising] with respect to the application of [the 1988] agreement, *including its validity*, execution or resolution,... shall be settled by a final arbitration by an Arbitration Panel.' (emphasis added).

[12] "Thus, if Maiellano failed to raise the issue of the forged 1979 agreement to the arbitrators, the issue is forfeited. See *National Wrecking Co. v. International Bhd. of Teamsters, Local 731*, 990 F.2d 957, 960 (7th Cir. 1993) (issues not raised before arbitrator are waived in enforcement proceeding). And if Maiellano did raise the issue to the arbitrators, it cannot seek to relitigate the matter here. See *Barbier v. Shearson Lehman Hutton Inc.*, 948 F.2d 117, 120-121 (2d Cir. 1991); *Fotochrome*, 517 F.2d at 512, 517-518; *Halley Optical*, 752 F. Supp. at 640; *Bridas Sociedad*, 745 F. Supp. at 181. It is also significant that the Italian Tribunal, in confirming the arbitration award, determined that the arbitrators had based their decision primarily on the ten-year business relationship that had existed between the parties, and that the allegedly forged 1979 agreement had only a minor influence on their decision.

[13] "Furthermore, even if the arbitrators erroneously determined that the 1979 agreement was valid, an arbitration award cannot be avoided solely on the ground that the arbitrator may have made an error of law or fact. See *National Wrecking*, 990 F.2d at 960; *Hewlett-Packard, Inc. v. Berg*, 867 F. Supp. 1126, 1130-1132 (D. Mass. 1994) (same rule for foreign arbitration awards under the Convention), vacated and remanded on other grounds, 61 F.3d 101 (1st Cir. 1995).[14] Thus, we agree with the district court that enforcement of the arbitration award would not violate public policy."

IV. DISTRICT COURT'S DECISION NOT TO ADJOURN PROCEEDINGS

[14] "A court has discretion to adjourn enforcement proceedings where an application has been made in the originating country to have the arbitral award set aside or suspended."

[15] After quoting Art. VI of the Convention the court continued: "Maiellano urges that proceedings in the district court should have been adjourned or suspended until his appeal in Italy was decided. The district court denied

12. Reported in Yearbook I (1976) p. 201 (US no. 1).
13. Reported in Yearbook XVII (1992) pp. 686-695 (US no. 121).
14. Reported in Yearbook XXI (1996) pp. 808-814 (US no. 204).

Maiellano's application to adjourn the enforcement proceedings, finding that the confirmed award was immediately enforceable under Italian law notwithstanding the pending appeal and that the defendant had not sought a stay of enforcement in the Italian courts, and concluding that adjournment would thwart arbitration's twin goals of 'settling disputes efficiently and avoiding long and expensive litigation'. See *Folkways Music Publishers, Inc. v. Weiss*, 989 F.2d 108, 111 (2d Cir. 1993). The circumstances under which a district court should adjourn enforcement proceedings to await the outcome of parallel proceedings in the originating forum have received little attention from circuit courts. See *Spier*, 663 F. Supp. at 874; Strub, *Resisting Enforcement*, supra, at 1053.

[16] "As a preliminary matter, no circuit court has enunciated the standard for reviewing a district court's refusal to adjourn. Only one appellate case appears to have addressed the issue. See *Hewlett-Packard Co., Inc. v. Berg*, 61 F.3d 101 (1st Cir. 1995). In *Berg*, the district court had held that it lacked the power to adjourn proceedings pending a second arbitration. On appeal, the First Circuit determined that the Convention did not curtail the ordinary rule that a district court retains discretion to stay proceedings due to the pendency of a related proceeding in another tribunal. Id. at 105. The court then remanded for reconsideration, noting that '[w]hether confirmation ... should be partially deferred pending the resolution of the [second] arbitration is a matter for the district court to determine in the first instance'. Id. at 106.

[17] "Several district courts have interpreted the Convention to grant a district court 'unfettered discretion' to decide whether or not to adjourn the proceedings. *Ukrvneshprom State Foreign Econ. Enter. v. Tradeway, Inc.*, No. 95 Civ. 10278, 1996 WL 107285, at *6 (S.D.N.Y. 12 March 1996);[15] see *Spier*, 663 F. Supp. at 874-875; *Fertilizer Corp. of India v. IDI Management, Inc.*, 517 F. Supp. 948, 961 (S.D.Ohio 1981).[16] We agree with *Berg*, 61 F.3d at 106, that adjournment should be decided by the district court in the first instance. We also conclude that in light of the permissive language of Art. VI of the Convention and a district court's general discretion in managing its own caseload and suspense docket, see *Clinton v. Jones*, 117 S.Ct. 1636, 1650 (1997) ('[T]he District Court has broad discretion to stay proceedings as an incident to its power to control its own docket.'); see also *Berg*, 61 F.3d at 105, the proper standard for reviewing a district court's decision whether to adjourn is for abuse of discretion.

[18] "The issue of whether or not to adjourn under Art. VI of the Convention is a relatively undeveloped area of the law. Few courts of appeals have

15. Reported in Yearbook XXII (1997) pp. 958-966 (US no. 223).

16. Reported in Yearbook VIII (1983) pp. 419-420 (US no. 41).

spoken on the issue, and district courts have resolved it in divergent ways. See, e.g., *Berg*, 61 F.3d at 104-106; *Ukrvneshprom*, 1996 WL 107285, at *6-*8; *Spier*, 663 F. Supp. at 874-875; *Fertilizer Corp.*, 517 F. Supp. at 961-962. Guidance as to when it is appropriate to stay enforcement of an award under the Convention is virtually non-existent. See generally Strub, *Resisting Enforcement*, supra, at 1053 (discussing absence of standards for when district courts should stay proceedings).

[19] "It is plain to us, however, that a district court faced with a decision whether to adjourn arbitral enforcement proceedings to await the outcome of foreign proceedings must take into account the inherent tension between competing concerns. On the one hand, the adjournment of enforcement proceedings impedes the goals of arbitration – the expeditious resolution of disputes and the avoidance of protracted and expensive litigation. Under the law of many countries, an arbitration award is final, binding, and enforceable even if subject to further appeal in court. See *Fertilizer Corp.*, 517 F. Supp. at 955-958, 961-964 (reviewing cases). A stay of confirmation should not be lightly granted lest it encourage abusive tactics by the party that lost in arbitration. See *Berg*, 61 F.3d at 106; *Fertilizer Corp.*, 517 F. Supp. at 961-962.

[20] "On the other hand, certain considerations favor granting a stay. One of the grounds for refusing to enforce an award under Art. V(1)(*e*) is if the award 'has been set aside or suspended by a competent authority of the country in which ... the award was made'. Thus, where a parallel proceeding is ongoing in the originating country and there is a possibility that the award will be set aside, a district court may be acting improvidently by enforcing the award prior to the completion of the foreign proceedings. Moreover, where, as here, it is the plaintiff who first sought to enforce his award in the originating country, the argument for enforcement by the plaintiff in the district court loses force because the possibility of conflicting results and the consequent offense to international comity can be laid at the plaintiff's door. See also *Fertilizer Corp.*, 517 F. Supp. at 962; cf. *Sumitomo Corp. v. Parakopi Compañía Marítima, S.A.*, 477 F. Supp. 737, 741-742 (S.D.N.Y. 1979)[17] (finding that comity concerns did not require stay of action to compel arbitration under the Convention where court in related proceeding in Greece had not yet taken action on the merits), aff'd, 620 F.2d 286 (2d Cir. 1989).

[21] "The limited scope of review allowed under the Convention also favors deference to proceedings in the originating country that involve less deferential standards of review on the premise that, under these circumstances, a foreign court well-versed in its own law is better suited to determine the validity of the award. Cf. *Ottley v. Schwartzberg*, 819 F.2d 373, 377 (2d Cir. 1987)

17. Reported in Yearbook VI (1981) pp. 245-247 (US no. 31).

("'[C]onfirmation of an arbitration award is a summary proceeding that merely makes what is already a final arbitration award a judgment of the court."' (quoting *Florasynth, Inc. v. Pickholz*, 750 F.2d 171, 176 (2d Cir. 1984))); *Barbier v. Shearson Lehman Hutton, Inc.*, 752 F. Supp. 151, 159 (S.D.N.Y. 1990). In the instant case, it is plain that the district court's decision not to adjourn was based on the general objectives underlying the arbitration of disputes. However, it does not appear to us that the district court adequately considered the competing concerns just outlined. We think that a proper balancing of these concerns should lead a district court to consider several factors, including

> (1) the general objectives of arbitration – the expeditious resolution of disputes and the avoidance of protracted and expensive litigation;
> (2) the status of the foreign proceedings and the estimated time for those proceedings to be resolved;
> (3) whether the award sought to be enforced will receive greater scrutiny in the foreign proceedings under a less deferential standard of review;
> (4) the characteristics of the foreign proceedings including (i) whether they were brought to enforce an award (which would tend to weigh in favor of a stay) or to set the award aside (which would tend to weigh in favor of enforcement); (ii) whether they were initiated before the underlying enforcement proceeding so as to raise concerns of international comity; (iii) whether they were initiated by the party now seeking to enforce the award in federal court; and (iv) whether they were initiated under circumstances indicating an intent to hinder or delay resolution of the dispute;
> (5) a balance of the possible hardships to each of the parties, keeping in mind that if enforcement is postponed under Art. VI of the Convention, the party seeking enforcement may receive 'suitable security' and that, under Art. V of the Convention, an award should not be enforced if it is set aside or suspended in the originating country, see also *Berg*, 61 F.3d at 105 (noting that insolvency of one party may play role in determining relative hardships); and
> (6) any other circumstances that could tend to shift the balance in favor of or against adjournment. For example, in the instant case the controversy surrounding the enforceability of *arbitrato irrituale* may tend to favor adjournment because an Italian judgment confirming the award could itself be recognized and enforced in the district court. See, e.g., *Ackerman v. Levine*, 788 F.2d 830, 837, 841-842 & n. 12 (2d Cir. 1986) (discussing recognition and enforcement of foreign judgments); N.Y. C.P.L.R. Sect. 5301 et seq. (New York version of Uniform Foreign Judgments Recognition Act).

[22] "While this is not an exhaustive list, we think it adequately represents the various concerns that come into play when a district court is asked to adjourn enforcement proceedings to await the outcome of parallel foreign proceedings. Because the primary goal of the Convention is to facilitate the recognition and enforcement of arbitral awards, the first and second factors on the list should weigh more heavily in the district court's determination. In the instant case, however, we think the district court should reconsider its decision not to adjourn enforcement of the arbitral award in light of the foregoing considerations. Of course, by so doing, we do not intend in any way to influence the district court's decision."
(....)

281. United States Court of Appeals, Ninth Circuit, 4 September 1998, No. 97-15395[1]

Parties:	Plaintiff/appellant: Randall R. Melton (nationality not indicated) Defendant/appellee: Oy Nautor A.b. (Finland)
Published in:	1998 U.S. App. LEXIS 22100
Articles:	In general
Subject matter:	– forum non conveniens
Commentary Cases:	¶ 301

Facts

Randall R. Melton purchased a yacht from the Finnish manufacturer Oy Nautor A.b. through a sales agent in California. The purchase was financed by a limited liability company which Melton formed on the British Isle of Guernsey. A dispute arose and following arbitration in Finland, Melton obtained an award for US$ 400,000 in his favor.

Melton sought to enforce the award in California under the 1958 New York Convention. The United States District Court for the Northern Division of California dismissed the action for forum non conveniens.

On appeal, the Court of Appeals, per Brunetti, CJ and Graber, CJ affirmed the decision of the court below. It found that as the argument that the New York Convention precluded application of forum non conveniens had not been raised in the court below, it had been waived. Tashima, CJ dissented, opining that since the issue of waiver was subject of the discretion of the court, the applicability of forum non conveniens under the New York Convention should have been considered and if he were to reach the merits of this issue, he would reverse.

1. "This disposition is not appropriate for publication and may not be cited to or by the courts of this circuit except as provided by 9th Cir. R. 36-3."

Excerpt

[1] "Appellant argues for the first time on appeal that the venue provision of the Convention precludes application of forum non conveniens. As this argument was not raised below, it is waived. See, e.g., *Crawford v. Lungren*, 96 F.3d 380, 389 n. 6 (9th Cir. 1996). Our decision is limited to the application of the doctrine of forum non conveniens to the specific facts of this case. We express no opinion as to interpretation of the [1958 New York Convention].

[2] "Under the doctrine of forum non conveniens, the court may grant dismissal if (1) an adequate alternative forum exists, and (2) the balance of relevant private and public interest factors favors dismissal. *Creative Tech. Ltd. v. Aztech System PTE, Ltd.*, 61 F.3d 696, 699 (9th Cir. 1995). In this case, Oy Nautor A.b. and Melton are subject to, or have submitted to, jurisdiction in Finland. An adequate alternative forum exists.

[3] "The private interest factors concern the logistics of assembling a case. They are:

> 'relative ease of access to sources of proof; availability of compulsory process for attendance of unwilling, and the cost of obtaining attendance of willing, witnesses; possibility of view of premises, if view would be appropriate to the action; and all other practical problems that make trial of a case easy, expeditious and inexpensive.'

Gulf Oil Co. v. Gilbert, 330 U.S. 501, 508 (1947). Public interest factors include: judicial administrative difficulties; the burden of jury duty on the community; the local interest in adjudicating the matter; and avoidance of unnecessary conflict of law problems by having a forum apply law foreign to itself. Id. at 509. The fact that the law in the current forum is more favorable to the plaintiff than the law in other forums should not preclude dismissal. *Piper Aircraft Co. v. Reyno*, 454 U.S. 257, 261 (1981).

[4] "The district court addressed the evidence presented and weighed the relevant private and public factors. The district court did not abuse its discretion in concluding that the balance of private and public interests pointed toward dismissal."

Tashima, CJ, Dissenting

[5] "The majority refuses to consider appellant's argument that the venue provision of the statute implementing the [1958 New York Convention], 9

U.S.C. Sect. 204,[2] precludes application of forum non conveniens to cases arising under the Convention, because it is raised for the first time on appeal. The doctrine that a litigant who has not raised an issue below has waived it is one of discretion. See *Self-Realization Fellowship Church v. Ananda Church of Self-Realization*, 59 F. 3d 902, 912 (9th Cir. 1995). We may consider a newly-raised issue if it is one of law. Id. The issue tendered by appellant is such an issue.

[6] "Here, the circumstances counsel in favor of considering the issue, which is one of first impression. It seems to me unwise to apply forum non conveniens to an action to enforce a foreign arbitration award under the Convention, in the absence of any law that forum non conveniens applies to cases arising under the Convention. I would, thus, first decide the underlying legal issue before applying a non-existent rule to this case.

[7] "If I were to reach the merits of the forum non conveniens issue, I cannot agree with the majority's analysis and would, therefore, reverse on that issue. First, the majority concludes that '[a]n adequate forum exists', but the record is bare of any showing as to the adequacy of Finland as a forum; all that the record shows is that a forum does exist there, and nothing more. It is the moving party's burden to make a showing of this factor and Oy Nautor A.b. simply has not done so. I would, thus, hold that the first factor required by the caselaw, see, e.g., *Creative Tech., Ltd. v. Aztech Sys. PTE, Ltd.*, 61 F.3d 696, 699 (9th Cir. 1995), is not present.

[8] "On the balancing of the private and public interest factors, the majority, like the district court, mistakenly relies on factors inapplicable to this case to conclude that those factors support dismissal for forum non conveniens. For example, all of the *Gulf Oil Co. v. Gilbert*, 330 U.S. 501, 508 (1947), factors discussed by the majority are factors that are 'practical problems that make *trial* of a case easy, expeditious and inexpensive'. Id. (emphasis added). In this case, however, we are not dealing with a potential trial, but with a summary proceeding to confirm an arbitration award.[3] See, e.g., *Taylor v. Nelson*, 788 F.2d 220, 225 (4th Cir. 1986). Thus, the proof and logistics factors attendant

---

2. 9 U.S.C. Sect. 204 reads:

"An action or proceeding over which the district courts have jurisdiction pursuant to section 203 of this title may be brought in any such court in which save for the arbitration agreement an action or proceeding with respect to the controversy between the parties could be brought, or in such court for the district and division which embraces the place designated in the agreement as the place of arbitration if such place is within the United States."

3. "In most cases, petitions to confirm arbitration awards are routinely handled as motions on the motions calendar."

to trial are non-existent. The *Gulf Oil* analysis simply does not apply to proceedings to enforce an arbitration award. I would thus find these private interest factors to weigh against defendant.

[9] "The same is largely true of the public interest factors. In a proceeding to enforce a foreign arbitration award, most of them weigh against invoking forum non conveniens – they (e.g., the 'burden of jury duty on the community') simply are inapplicable. The only public interest factor weighing in favor of defendant is any potential problem in applying foreign law. Federal district courts, however, apply foreign law routinely and our procedures are adequate for the purpose. See Fed.R.Civ.P. 44.1.[4] In a case such as this, where the Convention contemplates an enforcement action in this country, we should not let this single factor, in the absence of all other factors, control the application of forum non conveniens.

[10] "For all of these reasons, were I to reach the merits of the forum non conveniens issue, I would reverse the district court's invocation of the doctrine. I, therefore, respectfully dissent."

4. Rule 44.1 of the Federal Rule of Civil Procedure reads:

"A party who intends to raise an issue concerning the law of a foreign country, shall give notice by pleadings or other reasonable notice. The court, in determining foreign law, may consider any relevant material or source, including testimony, whether or not submitted by a party or admissible under the Federal Rules of Evidence. The court's determination shall be treated as a ruling on a question of law."

282. United States District Court, Southern District of California, 7 December 1998, Civ. No. 98-1165-B

Parties:	Petitioner: The Ministry of Defense and Support for the Armed Forces of The Islamic Republic of Iran Respondent: Cubic Defense Systems, Inc. (US)
Published in:	29 Federal Supplement, Second Series (S.D.Cal. 1998) pp. 1168-1174
Articles:	V(1)(*a*); V(1)(*b*); V(1)(*c*)
Subject matters:	- Convention grounds for refusal are exhaustive - scope of Terms of Reference - award based on legal theories different from pleadings
Commentary Cases:	[1] = ¶ 500; [2]-[3] = ¶ 501; [4]-[9] = ¶ 512; [10]-[11] = ¶ 507; [12] = ¶ 511

Facts

The Ministry of Defense and Support for the Armed Forces of The Islamic Republic of Iran (Iran) and Cubic Defense Systems, Inc. (Cubic) entered into two contracts for the sale and service of an Air Combat Maneuvering Range for use by the Iranian Air Force. In late 1978 and early 1979, political unrest and revolution developed in Iran. Dispute arose regarding the performance of the contacts and on 19 January 1982, Iran filed a claim against Cubic with the Iran-US Claims Tribunal at the Hague. On 28 April 1987 the Iran-US Claims Tribunal issued an Order stating that it lacked jurisdiction to hear the matter.

Both contracts contained an arbitration clause providing for arbitration of disputes by ICC arbitration in Zurich, Switzerland, in accordance with Iranian law in effect as of the date of the contracts. On 24 September 1991, Iran initiated arbitration before the ICC. On 11 August, 1993, the arbitral tribunal ordered bifurcation of the dispute, deferring the issue of quantification of the claim and the counterclaim. On 6 April 1995, the arbitral tribunal issued an Order finding that Iran's claim for reimbursement and Cubic's counterclaim were not time-barred by the Iranian statute of limitations and that the bifurcation of the proceedings was no longer applicable. On 5 May 1997, the arbitral tribunal issued its final award in favor of Iran.

On 15 January 1997 before the arbitrators issued their final award, Cubic commenced court proceedings against the ICC before the Court of First Instance in Paris seeking, inter alia, annulment of its contract with the ICC. On 21 May 1997, the Paris Court denied Cubic's request. On appeal, the Paris Court of Appeal held on 15 September 1998 that Cubic's action to annul the arbitration contract was brought after the five-year prescription period, but affirmed the Court of First Instance's decision in holding that Cubic had not proven any failure by the ICC to perform under its contractual obligations. This decision is reported in this Volume of the Yearbook, Part II – B, at pp. 287-293.

Iran petitioned the district court for the confirmation of the award and Cubic cross-motioned for an order vacating the award. The court, per Brewster, SDJ, denied the cross-motion to set aside and ordered the confirmation of the award finding, inter alia, that the use by the arbitral tribunal of legal theories not presented by the parties was acceptable under the Terms of Reference.

Excerpt

I. STANDARD OF LAW

[1] "The Court is asked to confirm the ICC Award pursuant to the [1958 New York Convention]. The United States became a party to the Convention in 1970, and Congress soon after enacted legislation implementing the provisions of the Convention into domestic law, codified as Chapter II of the Federal Arbitration Act (FAA) ... (codified at 9 U.S.C. Sects. 201-208). A district court's 'review of a foreign arbitration award is quite circumscribed'. *Ministry of Defense of the Islamic Republic of Iran v. Gould, Inc.*, 969 F.2d 764, 770 (9th Cir. 1992).[1] There is a general pro-enforcement bias under the Convention. See Id.; see also *Scherk v. Alberto-Culver Co.*, 417 U.S. 506, 519-520 & n. 15, 94 S.Ct. 2449, 41 L.Ed.2d 270 (1974).[2] Upon application for an order confirming the award, the 'district court has little discretion: "The court shall confirm the award unless it finds one of the grounds for refusal or deferral of recognition or enforcement of the award specified in the said Convention."' *Ministry of Defense*, 969 F.2d at 770 (citing 9 U.S.C. Sect. 207)."

1. Reported in Yearbook XVIII (1993) pp. 590-595 (US no. 142).
2. Reported in Yearbook I (1976) pp. 203-204 (US no. 4).

[2] The court cited Arts. V(1)(*a*), (*b*) and (*c*) of the New York Convention and continued: "In particular, courts should narrowly construe Art. V(1)(*c*) in accordance with the Convention's general pro-enforcement bias. See *Ministry of Defense*, 969 F.2d at 770.

[3] "Sect. 10 of the FAA and case law addressing domestic arbitration set forth grounds upon which a court may refuse to confirm an arbitration award. These grounds, however, are not applicable to confirmation under the Convention. The statute implementing the Convention states that a 'court shall confirm the award unless it finds one of the grounds for refusal ... specified in the said Convention'. 9 U.S.C. Sect. 207. Thus, other provisions regarding arbitration are not applicable to petitions requesting confirmation of an arbitration award under the Convention. See *Ministry of Defense*, 969 F.2d at 770 (limiting discretion of district court to grounds to refusal specified in the Convention); *Management & Technical Consultants S.A. v. Parsons-Jurden Int'l Corp.*, 820 F.2d 1531, 1533-1534 (9th Cir. 1987)[3] ('Under the Convention, an arbiter's award can be vacated only on the grounds specified in the Convention'.); see also *Industrial Risk Insurers v. M.A.N. Gutehoffnungshutte GmbH*, 141 F.3d 1434, 1446 (11th Cir. 1998)[4] (finding that 'the Convention's enumeration of defenses is exclusive'); *Yusuf Ahmed Alghanim & Sons, W.L.L. v. Toys "R" Us, Inc.*, 126 F.3d 15, 20 (2d Cir. 1997)[5] ('[T]he grounds for relief enumerated in Art. V of the Convention are the only grounds available for setting aside an arbitral award'.); *M & C Corp. v. Erwin Behr GmbH & Co.*, 87 F.3d 844, 851 (6th Cir. 1996)[6] ('Art. V of the Convention lists the exclusive grounds justifying refusal to recognize an arbitral award.')."

II. CONFIRMATION OF AWARD

1. *Article V(1)(c)*

[4] "Cubic first contends that the ICC Award violates Art. V(1)(*c*) of the Convention because it 'deals with a difference not contemplated by or not falling within the terms of the submission to arbitration' and it 'contains decisions on matters beyond the scope of the submission to arbitration.'[7]

3. Reported in Yearbook XIII (1988) pp. 611-616 (US no. 81).
4. Reported in this Yearbook as US no. 276, pp. 819-831.
5. Reported in Yearbook XXIII (1998) pp. 1058-1067 (US no. 261).
6. Reported in Yearbook XXII (1997) pp. 993-1000 (US no. 229).
7. "Cubic also contends that the Award violated 9 U.S.C. Sect. 10 of the FAA. As explained by this Court, Sect. 10 of the FAA does not apply to claims brought under the Convention."

Cubic also alleges that the award violates Art. V(1)(*c*) because it ignores the terms of the parties' Contracts. Thus, Cubic argues that the 'Terms of Reference constitute the jurisdictional mandate of an arbitral panel, and any decision which exceeds the scope of that jurisdictional reference is improper.'

[5] "Specifically, Cubic argues that the Tribunal decided issues not submitted by the parties and issued a ruling based upon legal theories not contemplated by and/or asserted by the parties. The legal theories and conclusions Cubic takes issue with are: (1) the 'conclusion that the parties agreed in 1979 to discontinue the Contracts at least for the time being, i.e., until the results of Cubic's attempt to resell the System would be known'; (2) the conclusion that there was 'an implicit agreement for the postponement of the maturity date of any such claims until Cubic had resold the equipment or declared its inability to resell'; (3) the conclusion that there was 'a factual termination of the Contracts at the request of Iran'; and, (4) the finding that it can be implied from the Termination for Convenience Clause that 'Cubic shall credit Iran with ... products manufactured for Iran prior to the termination of the Contracts.'

[6] "Cubic's objections are misguided. First, the Terms of Reference allow the Arbitrators leeway in resolving the conflict that the parties presented to them. Cubic cites specific questions framed by the Terms of Reference and claims that the ICC Award's deviations from those particular questions constitutes a deviation from the Terms. However, as Iran points out, the questions posed for the Arbitrators were presented in the following manner in the Terms of Reference:

> 'The issues to be determined shall be those resulting from the parties' submissions and which are relevant to the adjudication of the parties' respective claims and defenses. In particular, *the Arbitral Tribunal may have to consider the following issues (but not necessarily all of these or only these*, and not necessarily in the following order)....'

(Terms of Reference Sect. 4) (emphasis added). The Terms of Reference then proceed to list twelve issues that *may* be considered in the adjudication of the parties' claims and defenses. The Arbitrators were not, however, explicitly required to consider all of these issues in resolving this contractual dispute. The Arbitrators were also not limited to the issues listed, but could consider additional issues in resolving this dispute. Furthermore, the Award is within the parameters of those twelve issues, even if the legal theories applied are different from those presented in the parties' pleadings. Thus, based only on an evaluation of the Terms of Reference, the use of legal theories not presented by the parties is acceptable under the Terms of Reference.

[7] "Second, Cubic's claim that the use of legal theories not presented by the parties precluded confirmation of the Award was rejected by the Ninth Circuit. See *Ministry of Defense*, 969 F.2d at 771. Under the Convention, a court is to determine 'whether the award exceeds the scope of the [arbitration agreement], not whether the award exceeds the scope of the parties' pleadings'. Id. Respondents in *Ministry of Defense* objected to confirmation of that award 'because the award [was] not based on the same legal theory as that stated in the pleadings'. The court found that the subject matter of respondent's claim was 'obvious[ly]' the contracts between the parties and to the extent the 'award resolves the claims and counterclaims connected with the two contracts it ... does not exceed the scope of the submission to arbitration'. Id. Comparing *Ministry of Defense* to this case, the Court finds that the subject matter of this dispute is the Service and Sales Contracts between Cubic and Iran. The ICC Award resolves the parties' claims arising from these Contracts and the fact that the Award is not based on the same legal theories as stated in the pleadings cannot be a basis for refusing to confirm it.

[8] "Cubic also disputes the Tribunal's reference to the Principles of International Commercial Contracts published in 1994 by the Unidroit Institute (UNIDROIT Principles) and the Tribunal's references to principles of fairness such as good faith and fair dealing. Cubic claims that references to such international and equitable principles also violates Art. V(1)(*c*) because this law exceeds the scope of the Terms of Reference. The reference to the UNIDROIT Principles does not exceed the scope of the Terms of Reference. One of the issues presented to the Tribunal was whether general principles of international law apply to this dispute. That Cubic disagrees with the Tribunal's response to the question posed by the parties is not a reason to find that the Tribunal addressed issues beyond the scope of the Terms of Reference. The same is true for Cubic's assertions with regard to the Tribunal's references to equitable principles of contract law.[8]

[9] "As stated earlier, this Court's discretion in reviewing a foreign arbitration award is quite circumscribed. See *Ministry of Defense*, 969 F.2d at 770. The Tribunal's reference to and application of the UNIDROIT Principles and principles such as good faith and fair dealing do not violate Art. V(1)(*c*). The Tribunal applied these principles to differences contemplated by and falling

8. "Cubic relies on *Beacon Journal Publ'g v. Akron Newspaper Guild*, 114 F.3d 596, 600 (6th Cir. 1997), for its contention that arbitration awards based on fairness and equity instead of the terms of the agreement should be overturned. Even if this case were binding on this Court, the case resolves a domestic arbitration dispute arising from a collective bargaining agreement and is therefore not applicable to the confirmation of arbitral awards under the Convention. See *Ministry of Defense*, 969 F.2d at 770; see also *M & C Corp.*, 87 F.3d at 851 (6th Cir. 1996)."

within the terms of the submission to arbitration and therefore the Award does not violate Art. V(1)(*c*)."

2. *Article V(1)(a)*

[10] "Art. V(1)(*a*) provides that a court may refuse to confirm an arbitral award if an agreement in writing, including an arbitral clause in a contract or an arbitration agreement, is not valid under the law to which the parties have subjected it. Cubic appears to be arguing that the four theories of the Tribunal that Cubic contests constitute oral amendments to the Contracts' arbitration clauses and the Terms of Reference. Cubic contends that these oral amendments violate the Convention's requirement that the agreements be in writing. Cubic's construction of the Award and the Convention is strained.

[11] "The arbitration clause in the Contracts and the Terms of Reference validly present the Tribunal with the task of resolving the dispute over the Contracts between Iran and Cubic resulting from the unusual circumstances surrounding the 1979 Iranian Revolution. This Court cannot refuse to confirm the Award simply because the legal theories and conclusions presented in the Award differ from those contemplated by the parties in their pleadings. Legal theories used by adjudicators to resolve contract disputes are not considered oral amendments to the contract to the arbitration agreement. Art. V(1)(*a*) of the Convention does not present this Court with grounds for refusing to confirm the Award."

3. *Article V(1)(b)*

[12] "Art. V(1)(*b*) allows a court to refuse confirmation of an arbitral award if the 'party against whom the award is invoked was not given proper notice of the appointment of the arbitrator or of the arbitration proceedings or was otherwise unable to present [his or her] case'. Cubic contends that it was 'denied a meaningful opportunity to present its case' because: (1) Iran shifted its factual and legal theories throughout the proceedings; (2) the Tribunal issued interim decisions regarding bifurcation of the proceedings; and (3) the legal theories and remedies articulated in the Award were not previously presented. Even if these allegations were true, these claims do not rise to the level required by Art. V(1)(*b*) to justify a refusal by this Court to confirm the Award. Cubic's active participation in the entire process demonstrates notification of the proceedings, therefore Cubic presumably relies on the latter part of Art. V(1)(*b*) to justify its claim. However, Cubic was also 'otherwise able to present [its] case'. Two hearings were held. Cubic also had several opportunities for briefing. Cubic had its 'day in court' and had ample

opportunity to present its interpretation of the facts and its legal theories to the Tribunal. Therefore, the Award does not violate Art. V(1)(*b*)."

283. United States Court of Appeals, Fifth Circuit, 8 December 1998, No. 97-20695

Parties:	Appellant: China National Machinery Import and Export Corporation (China) Appellee: Trans Chemical Limited (Pakistan)
Published in:	161 Federal Reporter, Third Series (5th Cir. 1998) pp. 315-319
Articles:	I(1); I(3)
Subject matters:	- jurisdiction under Foreign Sovereign Immunities Act - applicability of "nondomestic" clause of Art. I(1) to awards rendered in the United States - "foreign commerce" as understood in Federal Arbitration Act - no lack of due process in arbitral proceedings
Commentary Cases:	¶ 102, ¶ 105, ¶ 301 + ¶ 523

Facts

The facts of this case are reported in more detail in Yearbook XXIII (1998) pp. 995-997. Dr. Shardar Khan and Dr. Mohammed Halipoto, both United States citizens, formed Trans Chemical Limited (TCL), a wholly owned subsidiary of United International, an American corporation owned by Dr. Khan and Dr. Halipoto. TCL contracted with China National Machinery Import and Export Corporation (CMC) for the purchase of a complete hydrogen peroxide plant to be built in Pakistan. Disputes arose between the parties which were submitted to AAA arbitration in Houston, Texas. TCL sought to enforce the award made in its favor and CMC sought to vacate it.

On 7 July 1997, the District Court for the Southern District of Texas, Houston Division, confirmed the award (reported as US no. 255 in Yearbook XXIII (1998) pp. 995-1019), holding that CMC was an "agency or instrumentality" of the Chinese government as defined under the Foreign Sovereign Immunities Act (FSIA). The "nondomestic" clause of Art. I(1) of the New York Convention applied to the award rendered in the United States and therefore the award fell within the scope of the Convention. Subject matter jurisdiction under the FSIA exception for actions to confirm arbitration awards was established. Furthermore, the motion to vacate the award was rejected as the award had not been procured by fraud or undue means nor had the arbitrators engaged in conduct that prejudiced CMC's rights to a fundamentally fair hearing. For the same reasons, enforcement of the award under the New York Convention could not be refused and prejudgment interest of 10% compounded annually was awarded.

On appeal, the Court of Appeals, per King, Jolly and Jones, CJJ, affirmed the decision of the district court, agreeing with its analysis of the issues and adopting Parts I-V of its "careful and comprehensive" opinion.

Excerpt

[1] "On appeal, CMC raises four issues: (1) Is CMC, a Chinese corporation, an 'agent or instrumentality of a foreign state' under the Foreign Sovereign Immunities Act, 28 U.S.C. Sect. 1603, such that the district court had subject matter jurisdiction to confirm the arbitral award rendered against CMC, 28 U.S.C. Sect. 1330? (2) Was the arbitral award 'not considered as domestic ... in the State where [its] recognition and enforcement are sought' such that the district court could enforce it pursuant to the [1958 New York Convention], 21 U.S.T. 2517 (1970), reprinted in 9 U.S.C. Sect. 201? (3) Did the contract between CMC and TCL involve 'commerce' such that the district court could enforce the arbitration award pursuant to the Federal Arbitration Act, 9. U.S.C. Sect. 2? (4) Did the district court err in refusing to vacate the award under the Federal Arbitration Act, 9 U.S.C. Sect. 10(a)(1)?

[2] "We agree with the district court's analysis of these issues and therefore adopt Parts I-V [reported as *Facts* and [1]-[45] in US no. 255] of its careful and comprehensive opinion....[1] The judgment of the district court is affirmed."

1. "We do not, of course, imply that the other portions of the opinion are in any way erroneous."

284. United States Court of Appeals, Second Circuit, 26 January 1999, No. 98-7468

Parties:	Appellants: (1) National Broadcasting Company, Inc. (US); (2) NBC Europe, Inc. (nationality not indicated) Appellees: TV Azteca S.A. de C.V. (Mexico) et al.
Published in:	165 Federal Reporter, Third Series, p. 184 et seq.; 1999 U.S. App. LEXIS 933
Articles:	General reference
Subject matter:	– availability of discovery to foreign arbitral tribunal under 28 U.S.C. Sect. 1782
Commentary Cases:	¶ 229

Facts

In 1994, NBC and Azteca, a then-privately-held Mexican television broadcasting company, entered into an agreement under which NBC would provide Azteca with programming and other services. In exchange, NBC's compensation included the option to purchase up to 10% of Azteca's shares. The agreement also contained an arbitration clause providing for arbitration under the Arbitration Rules of the ICC, under Mexican law. Purporting to act under the agreements, NBC on 3 April 1997, sought to purchase 1% of Azteca's shares. On 28 April 1997, Azteca, alleging that NBC had failed to perform under the agreement, initiated arbitration against NBC in Mexico pursuant to the 1994 agreement. NBC counterclaimed that Azteca improperly induced NBC to forgo exercising its option for the full 10% of Azteca's shares by leading NBC to believe, among other things, that (i) Azteca had no plans to conduct an initial public offering of securities (IPO), and (ii) Azteca's estimate of the value of the company's shares was not significantly above the contractually agreed exercise price. Azteca denied these allegations.

In anticipation of the ICC arbitration proceeding in Mexico but prior to the appointment of the arbitration panel, NBC applied ex parte, pursuant to 28 U.S.C. Sect. 1782, to the United States District Court for the Southern District of New York (Deborah A. Batts, Judge) for authorization to serve document subpoenas on the six third-party financial institutions engaged by Azteca with regard to its IPO plans. On 1 August 1997, Judge Batts granted the application, and NBC later served the subpoenas, which demanded the production of documents bearing on the timing of Azteca's IPO plans and the valuation of Azteca shares. Within a month, Azteca and five of the third-party financial institutions (appellees in this instance) moved to quash the subpoenas; NBC cross-moved to compel compliance with them.

On 16 January 1998, Judge Sweet granted the motion to quash the subpoenas and denied NBC's cross-motion, concluding that the term "foreign or international tribunal" in 28 U.S.C. Sect. 1782, a statute authorizing district courts to assist discovery efforts in connection with proceedings before such tribunals, does not encompass private international commercial arbitration. Azteca et al. appealed. The court, per José A. Cabranes, CJ, based on a de novo review of the text of legislative history of Sect. 1782, as well as policy considerations, affirmed the motion quashing the subpoenas and denied the motion to enforce.

Excerpt

[1] "We review the district court's interpretation of 28 U.S.C. Sect. 1782 de novo.... Ordinarily, because commercial arbitration is a creature of contract, only the parties to the arbitration contract are bound to participate. See, e.g., *AT&T Technologies, Inc. v. Communications Workers of Am.*, 475 U.S. 643, 648 (1986) ('[A]rbitration is a matter of contract and a party cannot be required to submit to arbitration any dispute which he has not agreed so to submit.') (internal quotation marks and citation omitted); *Thomson-CSF, S.A. v. American Arbitration Ass'n*, 64 F.3d 773, 776 (2d Cir. 1995). If discovery were to be obtained from the Third Parties – none of which was a party to the arbitration agreement at issue here – the authority to compel their participation would have to be found in a source other than the parties' arbitration agreement. That source, NBC claims, is Sect. 1782.

[2] "Appellees first argue that Sect. 1782, regardless of its meaning, is not available to NBC because the Federal Arbitration Act (FAA), 9 U.S.C. Sect. 1 et seq., which provides a role for the federal courts in arbitration, is the exclusive means for obtaining evidence from non-parties in connection with private arbitration proceedings.

[3] "The FAA applies to private commercial arbitration conducted in this country; and it applies also to arbitrations in certain foreign countries by virtue of legislation implementing the [1958 New York Convention] (implemented at 9 U.S.C. Sects. 201-208), and the Inter-American Convention on

International Commercial Arbitration, 30 January 1975, (implemented at 9 U.S.C. Sects. 301-307) (the IAC). The statute principally provides for the enforcement of agreements to arbitrate, supplying judicial assistance to facilitate arbitration, and providing for confirmation, vacation, or modification of the arbitrators' resulting decisions. Sect. 7 of the FAA provides statutory authority for invoking the powers of a federal district court to assist arbitrators in obtaining evidence. Under this provision, arbitrators may subpoena witnesses and direct those witnesses to bring material documentary evidence to an arbitral hearing; if witnesses fail to comply, the district court for the district in which the arbitrators are sitting may compel compliance with such subpoenas. See 9 U.S.C. Sect. 7.

[4] "The methods for obtaining evidence under Sect. 7 are more limited than those under Sect. 1782 in two, and possibly three, ways. First, Sect. 7 explicitly confers authority only upon *arbitrators*; by necessary implication, the *parties* to an arbitration may not employ this provision to subpoena documents or witnesses. See 9 U.S.C. Sect. 7; see also *Burton v. Bush*, 614 F.2d 389, 390 (4th Cir. 1980) ('While an arbitration panel may subpoena documents or witnesses, the litigating parties have no comparable privilege.') (citations omitted), cited with approval in *St. Mary's Med. Ctr. of Evansville, Inc. v. Disco Aluminum Prods. Co.*, 969 F.2d 585, 591 (7th Cir. 1992); Beth H. Friedman, 'The Preclusive Effect of Arbitral Determinations in Subsequent Federal Securities Litigation', 55 Fordham L. Rev. 655, 672 & n. 126 (1987) ('While an arbitration panel has the power to subpoena documents or witnesses, the parties to the arbitration lack the advantage of discovery.') (footnotes omitted).

[5] "Second, Sect. 7 explicitly confers enforcement authority only upon the 'district court for the district in which such arbitrators, or a majority of them, are sitting'.

[6] "Third, the express language of Sect. 7 refers only to testimony before the arbitrators and to material physical evidence, such as books and documents, brought before them by a witness; open questions remain as to whether Sect. 7 may be invoked as authority for compelling pre-hearing depositions and pre-hearing document discovery, especially where such evidence is sought from non-parties. Compare *Integrity Ins. Co. v. American Centennial Ins. Co.*, 885 F. Supp. 69, 72-73 (S.D.N.Y. 1995) (arbitrator may not rely on Sect. 7 to obtain pre-hearing depositions from non-parties), with *Stanton v. Paine Webber Jackson & Curtis, Inc.*, 685 F. Supp. 1241, 1242-1243 (S.D.Fla. 1988) (Sect. 7 permits pre-hearing document production from non-parties), and *Meadows Indem. Co. v. Nutmeg Ins. Co.*, 157 F.R.D. 42, 45 (M.D.Tenn. 1994) (Sect. 7 power to compel document production from third parties at hearing encompasses lesser power to compel production prior to hearing).

[7] "If the broader evidence-gathering mechanisms provided for in Sect. 1782 were applicable to proceedings before non-governmental tribunals such as private arbitral panels, we would need to decide whether 9 U.S.C. Sect. 7 is exclusive, in which case the two statutes would conflict. Because we conclude instead that Sect. 1782 does not apply to proceedings before private arbitral panels, we need not reach this issue.

[8] "Subsect. 1782(a), which contains the disputed term, reads in relevant part as follows:

> 'The district court of the district in which a person resides or is found may order him to give his testimony or statement or to produce a document or other thing for use in a proceeding in a foreign or international tribunal, including criminal investigations conducted before formal accusation. The order may be made pursuant to a letter rogatory issued, or request made, by a foreign or international tribunal or upon the application of any interested person and may direct that the testimony or statement be given, or the document or other thing be produced, before a person appointed by the court.'

28 U.S.C. Sect. 1782(a). Our inquiry begins with the language of the statute itself, and particularly the phrase 'foreign or international tribunal', which is not otherwise defined in the statute. Because the term 'foreign or international tribunal' is undefined, it is to be given its ordinary or natural meaning. See *FDIC v. Meyer*, 510 U.S. 471, 476 (1994).

[9] "In support of its position, NBC cites numerous references to private arbitration panels as 'tribunals' or 'arbitral tribunals' in court cases, international treaties, congressional statements, academic writings, and even the *Commentaries* of Blackstone and Story. This authority amply demonstrates that the term 'foreign or international tribunals' does not unambiguously *exclude* private arbitration panels. On the other hand, the fact that the term 'foreign or international tribunals' is broad enough to include both state-sponsored and private tribunals fails to mandate a conclusion that the term, as used in Sect. 1782, does include both. See *Robinson v. Shell Oil Co.*, 117 S.Ct. 843, 846-848 (1997) (although term 'employees' was broad enough to include former employees and Congress did not expressly specify 'current employees', use of term in statute was ambiguous). In our view, the term 'foreign or international tribunal' is sufficiently ambiguous that it does not necessarily include or exclude the arbitral panel at issue here.

[10] "Accordingly, we look to legislative history and purpose to determine the meaning of the term in the statute. See *Castellano v. City of New York*, 142 F.3d 58, 67 (2d Cir. 1998) ('Where the language is ambiguous, we focus upon

the broader context and primary purpose of the statute.') (internal quotation marks and citation omitted); *Motor Vehicle Mfrs. Ass'n v. New York State Dep't of Envtl. Conservation*, 17 F.3d 521, 531 (2d Cir. 1994) ('[W]here ambiguity resides in a statute, legislative history and other tools of interpretation may be employed to determine legislative purpose more perfectly.').

[11] "The current version of Sect. 1782 was enacted in 1964 as part of legislation to implement recommendations of the Commission on International Rules of Judicial Procedure (the 'Commission'), a body created by Congress in 1958 to 'study existing practices of judicial assistance and cooperation between the United States and foreign countries with a view to achieving improvements'. Pub. L. No. 85-906, Sect. 2, 72 Stat. 1743 (1958); see also S. Rep. No. 85-2392 (1958), reprinted in 1958 U.S.C.C.A.N. 5201, 5201, 5203. The Commission recommended a series of changes in domestic civil procedure to accommodate international proceedings, in the hopes that foreign countries would be encouraged to reciprocate with procedural improvements of their own. See H.R. Doc. No. 88-88, at 20 (1963).

[12] "The Sect. 1782 that emerged from Congress in 1964 replaced the old Sect. 1782, which had provided limited evidence-gathering assistance to a 'judicial proceeding in any *court* in a foreign country' (emphasis added), and 22 U.S.C. Sects. 270-270g, which conferred certain powers on commissioners or members of 'international tribunals'. With respect to the revisions to the old Sect. 1782, the House and Senate committee reports stated that '[t]he word "tribunal" is used to make it clear that assistance is not confined to proceedings before conventional courts', to which the predecessor statute had been expressly limited. H.R. Rep. No. 88-1052, at 9 (1963) (House Report); S. Rep. No. 88-1580 (1964), reprinted in 1964 U.S.C.C.A.N. 3782, 3788 (Senate Report). Nonetheless, it is apparent in context that the authors of these reports had in mind only governmental entities, such as administrative or investigative courts, acting as state instrumentalities or with the authority of the state. The House and Senate committee reports, in explaining the choice of the word 'tribunal', state that, '[f]or example, it is intended that the court have discretion to grant assistance when proceedings are pending before investigating magistrates in foreign countries'. House Report at 9; Senate Report at 3788. The new Sect. 1782 would facilitate the collection of evidence for use 'before a foreign administrative tribunal or quasi-judicial agency'. Id. The absence of any reference to private dispute resolution proceedings such as arbitration strongly suggests that Congress did not consider them in drafting the statute.

[13] "The legislative history behind the replacement of Sects. 270-270g is even more compelling than that behind the revisions to the old Sect. 1782. The term 'international tribunal' derives directly from Sects. 270-270g, which authorized commissioners or members of international tribunals to administer oaths, to

subpoena witnesses or records, and to charge contempt. There is no question that the statute applied only to intergovernmental tribunals. Congress had enacted Sects. 270-270c in 1930 in direct response to problems that arose in an arbitration proceeding between the United States and Canada, and it added Sects. 270d-270g in 1933 explicitly to accommodate proceedings before the United States-German Mixed Claims Commission. See Hans Smit, 'Assistance Rendered by the United States in Proceedings Before International Tribunals', 62 Colum. L. Rev. 1264, 1264 (1962) ('Assistance Rendered by the United States'). It bears underscoring that those international arbitrations were intergovernmental, not private, arbitrations. More importantly, the old statute applied only to international tribunals 'established pursuant to an agreement between the United States and any foreign government or governments'. Id. at 1269.

[14] "It is clear that the 1964 legislation was intended to broaden the scope of the repealed 22 U.S.C. Sects. 270-270g by extending the reach of the surviving statute to intergovernmental tribunals not involving the United States. Significantly, however, there is no indication that Congress intended for the new provisions to reach private international tribunals, which lay far beyond the realm of the earlier statute. The House and Senate reports stated that the new Sect. 1782 'eliminates the undesirable limitations[] of the assistance extended by sections 270 through 270g'. House Report at 9; Senate Report at 3788-3789. The 'undesirable limitations' were identified earlier in the reports. First, Sects. 270-270c

> 'provided assistance only to a tribunal established by a treaty to which the United States was a party and then only in proceedings involving a claim in which the United States or one of its nationals was interested. This limitation is undesirable. The availability of assistance to international tribunals should not depend on whether the United States has been a party to their establishment or on whether it is involved in proceedings before them.'

Id. at 3784. Further, Sects. 270d-270g were said to 'improperly limit the availability of assistance to the U.S. agent before an international tribunal.... Clearly, the interest of the United States in peaceful settlement of international disputes is not limited to controversies to which it is a formal party.' Id. at 3785.

[15] "Contemporaneous academic literature reinforces our conclusion that the 'international tribunals' that were encompassed by the repealed Sects. 270-270g, and which were the subject of the 1964 legislative reforms, were those created by intergovernmental agreement. The Senate Report, in referring to the

undesirable limitations of Sects. 270-270g, see Senate Report at 3784-3785, 3788-3789, relied on a 1962 article by Professor Hans Smit, director of a project at the Columbia University School of Law that aided the Commission on International Rules of Judicial Procedure in drafting the bill that included the amended Sect. 1782. In that article, Professor Smit asserted that 'an international tribunal owes both its existence and its powers to an international agreement'. 'Assistance Rendered by the United States' at 1267.

[16] "In sum, the legislative history reveals that when Congress in 1964 enacted the modern version of Sect. 1782, it intended to cover governmental or intergovernmental arbitral tribunals and conventional courts and other state-sponsored adjudicatory bodies.

[17] "The legislative history's silence with respect to private tribunals is especially telling because we are confident that a significant congressional expansion of American judicial assistance to international arbitral panels created exclusively by private parties would not have been lightly undertaken by Congress without at least a mention of this legislative intention.

[18] "The popularity of arbitration rests in considerable part on its asserted efficiency and cost-effectiveness – characteristics said to be at odds with full-scale litigation in the courts, and especially at odds with the broad-ranging discovery made possible by the Federal Rules of Civil Procedure. See *Allied-Bruce Terminix Cos. v. Dobson*, 513 U.S. 265, 280 (1995) (advantages of arbitration are that it is 'usually cheaper and faster than litigation;... can have simpler procedural and evidentiary rules;... normally minimizes hostility and is less disruptive of ongoing and future business dealings among the parties') (quoting H.R.Rep. No. 97-542, at 13 (1982)). Few, if any, non-American tribunals of any kind, including arbitration panels created by private parties, provide for the kind of discovery that is commonplace in our federal courts and in most, if not all, state courts. If the parties to a private international arbitration make no provision for some degree of consensual discovery inter se in their agreement to arbitrate, the arbitrators control discovery, and neither party is deprived of its bargained-for efficient process by the other party's tactical use of discovery devices.

[19] "The limitations in Sect. 7 of the FAA, described above, are consistent with these traditional discovery limits, which would be overridden by the application of Sect. 1782 to proceedings before private arbitral panels. Opening the door to the type of discovery sought by NBC in this case likely would undermine one of the significant advantages of arbitration, and thus arguably conflict with the strong federal policy favoring arbitration as an alternative means of dispute resolution. See *Gilmer v. Interstate/Johnson Lane Corp.*, 500 U.S. 20, 25-26 (1991); *Oldroyd v. Elmira Sav. Bank, FSB*, 134 F.3d 72, 76 (2d Cir. 1998). Furthermore, such broad discovery in proceedings before 'foreign

or international' private arbitrators would stand in stark contrast to the limited evidence gathering provided in 9 U.S.C. Sect. 7 for proceedings before domestic arbitration panels. Such an inconsistency not only would be devoid of principle, but also would create an entirely new category of disputes concerning the appointment of arbitrators and the characterization of arbitral panels as domestic, foreign, or international. As noted above, therefore, it is our view that Congress intended not this broad result, but rather only the limited expansion described in the House and Senate reports.

[20] "In sum, policy considerations of some magnitude reinforce our conclusion, based upon an analysis of the text and legislative history of Sect. 1782, that Congress did not intend for that statute to apply to an arbitral body established by private parties.

[21] "The order of the district court quashing – and denying the motion to enforce – the subpoenas served on the Third Parties is affirmed."

285. United States District Court, Southern District of New York, 3 February 1999, No. 98 Civ. 9185 (LAP)

Parties:	Petitioner: Gerling Global Reinsurance Corporation, U.S. Branch (US) Respondent: The Yasuda Fire & Marine Insurance Co., Ltd. (nationality not indicated)
Published in:	1999 U.S. Dist. LEXIS 11480
Articles:	V(1)(*e*); VI
Subject matters:	– competent authority to order posting of security – requirement to post security under New York State insurance law
Commentary Cases:	¶ 301 + ¶ 601

Facts

Gerling Global Reinsurance Corporation, U.S. Branch (Gerling) petitioned to enforce an arbitral award made in its favor against The Yasuda Fire & Marine Insurance Co., Ltd. (Yasuda). Gerling requested a conference with the Court in respect of what it contended was Yasuda's procedurally flawed cross petition and motion in opposition to Gerling's petition to enforce. Parties appeared by telephone.

Although Yasuda characterized its cross petition as an affirmative moving on its part to confirm the award, the district court, per Loretta A. Preska, DJ, found, "off the record" that the import of the pleading was to delay the payment of the award and to decrease the payment. Accordingly, under New York insurance law, which provides for the posting of security before a foreign or alien insurer files any pleading in any proceeding against it, Yasuda could only present its interpretation of the award if it posted security. On 28 July 1999, the award was confirmed by the district court.

Excerpt

[1] "Counsel have brought to my attention Sect. 1213(c) of the New York State insurance law, which states,

> 'Before any unauthorized foreign or alien insurer files any pleading in any proceeding against it, it shall either (A) deposit with the Clerk of the Court in which the proceeding is pending cash or securities or file with the Clerk a bond with good and sufficient sureties to be approved by the Court in an amount to be fixed by the Court sufficient to secure payment of any final judgment which may be rendered in the proceeding ... or (B) procure a license to do an insurance business in the state.'

Clearly (B) is not relevant here.
[2] "As Judge Wood found in *Skandia America Reinsurance Corporation v. Caja Nacional de Ahorro y Seguro*, 1997 U.S. Dist. Lexis 7221 (S.D.N.Y. 1997),[1] 'Pursuant to this provision, if a foreign insurer fails to post security as required, a court can grant the movant party's motion by default. The purpose of this law is to ensure that foreign insurers can meet their insurance obligations.' (Citations omitted).
[3] "As Judge Wood also finds in her opinion in *Caja*, 'The United States acceded to the [1958 New York Convention] on 30 September 1970.' She goes on to find that 'The purpose of the New York Convention was to effectuate arbitration proceedings and their enforcement between companies of different nationalities.' Id. at *14.
[4] "Judge Wood goes on to find, 'Because part of the purpose of the New York Convention was to encourage the enforcement of arbitral awards, the New York Convention allows for the posting of prejudgment security. Specifically, Art. VI of the New York Convention provides that,

> "If an application for the setting aside or suspension of the award has been made to a competent authority referred to in Article V(1)(*e*), the authority before which the award is sought to be relied upon may, if it considers it proper, adjourn the decision on the enforcement of the award and may also, on the application of the party claiming enforcement of the award, order the other party to give suitable security."'

[5] "Judge Wood goes on to state that she notes that 'Under Art. V(1)(*e*), [a competent authority is] "a competent authority of the country in which or

1. Reported in Yearbook XXIII (1998) pp. 956-962 (US no. 250).

under the law of which, the award was made".... Therefore, this court would constitute a competent authority and could, on application of the petitioner, order the respondent to post adequate security.' Id. at *15-16.

[6] "I note Yasuda's argument that its filing of its cross petition to confirm the arbitral award is not a pleading. I decline to so find. Indeed, it certainly appears to be a pleading and, in addition, it appears to be, to some extent, an application for the setting aside or suspension of the award in that it seeks delay in paying the award and, in addition, seeks to decrease the amount of the award as claimed by Gerling."

[7] Counsel for Yasuda explained that the cross petition was not done in an action against Yasuda. Rather, it was an affirmative moving on Yasuda's party to confirm it as written. The court continued: "I understand that that is what it says. However, ... it is clear that the import of the pleading is to delay the payment of the arbitral award and, in addition, to decrease the amount of the arbitral award as calculated by Gerling. Neither one of those positions can fairly be found in substance to be a whole-hearted embrace of the arbitral award. Accordingly, I decline to be bound by the title put on the cross petition and, rather, look to the substance of the cross petition and the discussions thereof by counsel over the last few days. Accordingly, then, under Sect. 1213(c) of the New York insurance law, Yasuda may only present its interpretation of the award and its methods of calculating the amounts due if it first posts the security required by Sect. 1213."

[8] Counsel for Yasuda explained that "[t]he express provision of the award rendered by the arbitral panel directs Gerling to recalculate the principal and interest consistent with the directions of the panel". During certain underwriting years, participations had been reduced and that there were other issues such as the recision of the contracts that were at issue in the arbitration. All Yasuda was trying to do was to have those calculations completed, not to have the award suspended.

[9] The court found: ".... There is never going to be a number that is undisputed and, again, I refuse to be bound by the title placed on the cross petition. It is apparent to me from the conversations of counsel at the conferences we have had over the last few days ... that it is Yasuda's intention here both to delay and to minimize the amounts paid. Not surprisingly, but that is its position. On the other hand, the New York insurance law makes it very clear that an insurance company litigant may not put forth its interpretation of an award in such a matter without posting security. Accordingly, I order that unless security in the amount of US$ 9 million is posted as provided for in Sect. 1213(c) within ten business days of today, Yasuda's cross petition will be stricken."

286. United States Court of Appeals, Second Circuit, 17 March 1999, No. 98-7823(L), 98-7893 (XAP)

Parties:	Plaintiff/appellant/cross-appellee: American Bureau of Shipping (Italy/USA) Defendant/appellee/cross-appellant: Tencara Shipyard S.p.A. (Italy) Defendants/appellees: Société Jet Flint, S.A. et al. (nationality not indicated)
Published in:	170 Federal Reporter, Third Series, p. 349 et seq.; 1999 U.S. App. LEXIS 4254; 1999 American Maritime Cases, p. 1858 et seq.
Articles:	General reference
Subject matter:	– non-signatories bound by arbitration agreement
Commentary Cases:	[1] = ¶ 216; [2]-[7] = ¶ 226; [3] = ¶ 205

Facts

In 1992, Titouan Lamazou and a group of investors (the Owners) entered into a construction contract with the Italian shipyard, Tencara, for the construction of a racing yacht which could "circumnavigate the globe in less than 80 days". The construction contract provided, inter alia, that the ship would be "classed" according "[t]o the quality standards and norms permitting approval of ... the American Bureau of Shipping, Genoa Office"'. In March 1992, in order to obtain an ABS classification for the yacht, which had been named the "Tag Heuer", Tencara entered into a Request for Class Agreement with the American Bureau of Shipping (ABS). This agreement specified that all disputes arising thereunder were to be arbitrated in New York. The Owners received a copy of the Request for Class Agreement from Tencara in May 1992. The coverage that the Owners obtained on the "Tag Heuer" from a variety of insurers (the Underwriters) was premised on the existence of a valid classification.

In February 1993, the yacht was completed and delivered to the Owners. At that time, ABS delivered an Interim Certificate of Classification (ICC) to Tencara pursuant to the Request for Class Agreement. Tencara, in turn gave the ICC to the Owners. The ICC explicitly incorporated by reference the "terms and conditions" of the Request for Class Agreement, including the arbitration clause.

Several months later, the "Tag Heuer" suffered serious hull damage during a cruise. A survey indicated that the craft's damage had been the product of a defective design and of poor construction. The Underwriters indemnified the Owners pursuant to the insurance policies. Tencara subsequently sued ABS in Italy, while the Owners and the Underwriters each filed independent claims against ABS in France. ABS initiated the instant action seeking to compel Tencara, the Owners and the Underwriters to arbitrate their claims pursuant to the Request for Class Agreement, both in itself and as incorporated in the ICC. The District Court for the Southern District of New York, per Harold Baer Jr., J, held on 26 May 1998 held that Tencara was required to arbitrate with ABS because Tencara was acting on its own behalf in signing the Request for Class Agreement, rather than as an agent of a disclosed principal, the Owners. The court rejected ABS's argument that the Owners and the Underwriters were bound to arbitrate with ABS due to the Owners' acceptance of the ICC from ABS. Specifically, the district court held (1) that acceptance of the ICC did not give rise to a contract between the Owners and ABS, and (2) that the Owners were not estopped from denying the obligations of the ICC, as any benefits that they had received from the ICC were only "indirect". Because, in the court's view, the Underwriters' obligations depended on the existence of Owner obligations, this holding also freed the Underwriters from any duty to arbitrate.

The Court of Appeals, per Newman, Walker and Calabaresi, CJs, first found that it had jurisdiction based on admiralty, rather than the New York Convention as the district court had done. It affirmed in part holding that Tencara was obligated to arbitrate. However it reversed in part holding that the Owners and Underwriters were bound to arbitrate since the Owners received several direct benefits from the ICC and the Underwriters were subrogated in the claim. The case was remanded for further proceedings consistent with the holdings.

Excerpt

[1] "Subject-matter jurisdiction in this suit is grounded in admiralty. See 28 U.S.C. 1333 (1994)." In a footnote, the court added: "The district court found jurisdiction on the basis of the Convention on the Recognition and Enforcement of Foreign Arbitral Awards, see 9 U.S.C. 201, 203, since '[t]he defendants all reside in Italy, France or Great Britain', all signatories to the Convention. In view of the presence in the suit of various Lloyd's of London syndicates,

and assuming arguendo that residence in a signatory state is necessary for jurisdiction to lie, that basis of jurisdiction may be problematic as to some defendants. Cf. *E.R. Squibb and Sons, Inc. v. Accident & Cas. Ins. Co.*, 160 F.3d 925, 928-929 (2d Cir. 1998) (describing the structure of Lloyd's and pointing out that syndicates are comprised of thousands of individual underwriters whose identity (and residence) is not disclosed). But since jurisdiction was also claimed, and undoubtedly exists, in admiralty as to all the parties, we need not consider further the perplexities engendered by the presence of the Lloyd's syndicates. See *Advani Enter., Inc., v. Underwriters at Lloyds*, 140 F.3d 157, 161 (2d Cir. 1998) (permitting suit to proceed in admiralty where unknown citizenships of the Lloyd's Underwriters placed diversity jurisdiction in doubt)."

[2] The court then continued: "We review the district court's conclusion as to the existence of an arbitration agreement for clear error. See *Genesco, Inc. v. T. Kakiuchi & Co.*, 815 F.2d 840, 845 (2d Cir. 1987)[1] (stating that the district court's determination that there was an arbitration agreement is a factual finding and citing Fed.R.Civ.P. 52(a), which enunciates the 'clear error' standard of review for factual findings, though legal rulings concerning which entities are bound are reviewed de novo).

[3] "Our first task is to determine whether the Owners of the 'Tag Heuer' can be bound to arbitrate with ABS even though they never signed the arbitration agreement. We have stated that non-signatories may be bound by arbitration agreements entered into by others. See *Thomson-CSF, S.A. v. American Arbitration Ass'n*, 64 F.3d 773, 776 (2d Cir. 1995). This can occur pursuant to five different theories: (1) incorporation by reference; (2) assumption; (3) agency; (4) veil-piercing/alter ego; and (5) estoppel. See id. Because it proves to be sufficient, we focus exclusively on the estoppel theory. (footnote omitted)

[4] "As an initial matter, the Owners assert that – since they were never in privity with ABS – we lack personal jurisdiction over them and cannot consider ABS's estoppel argument. This contention is without merit. It is well-settled that federal courts applying New York law have personal jurisdiction over parties that agree to arbitrate their disputes in New York. See e.g., *Merrill Lynch, Pierce, Fenner & Smith, Inc. v. Lecopulos*, 553 F.2d 842, 844 (2d Cir. 1977). The Owners construe this to mean that personal jurisdiction exists only when there is an express arbitration agreement between the parties. But if the Owners are estopped from denying their obligations under the arbitration agreement between Tencara and ABS, it follows that they are also estopped from asserting a lack of personal jurisdiction based on that agreement. There is no good reason to read the equitable theory of estoppel to allow the defense of 'no personal jurisdiction' while barring the defense of 'no duty to arbitrate'.

1. Reported in Yearbook XIII (1988) pp. 567-588 (US no. 76).

With the Owners estopped from denying personal jurisdiction, the law regards such jurisdiction as established in litigation between these parties.

[5] "We therefore turn to the merits of ABS's estoppel argument. A party is estopped from denying its obligation to arbitrate when it receives a 'direct benefit' from a contract containing an arbitration clause. See *Thomson-CSF*, 64 F.3d at 778-779. ABS argues that the Owners received several direct benefits from the ICC, which incorporated the Request for Class Agreement's arbitration clause by reference. We agree with ABS that the Owners received such benefits, including (1) significantly lower insurance rates on the 'Tag Heuer', and (2) the ability to sail under the French flag. In reaching the conclusion that the Owners had only received an indirect benefit from the ICC, the district court relied heavily on the erroneous assumption that it was Tencara's rather than the Owners' responsibility to register the vessel under the French flag. Whatever the situation might have been under the district court's incorrect assumption, it is patent that on the actual facts the Owners received direct benefits from the ICC. Without the ICC, registration would have been practically impossible. The Owners are hence required to arbitrate their claims against ABS.

[6] "We next confront the issue of whether the yacht's Underwriters can also be compelled to arbitrate with ABS. It is clearly established that 'an insurer-subrogee stands in the shoes of its insured'. See *Gibbs v. Hawaiian Eugenia Corp.*, 966 F.2d 101, 106 (2d Cir. 1992). Accordingly, ABS's motion to compel arbitration against the insured Owners is equally valid against the insurer Underwriters, and we therefore hold that the Underwriters of the 'Tag Heuer' must also submit to arbitration with ABS.[2]

[7] "Finally, we address the cross-appeal of Tencara. Tencara's position is that it was acting solely as the Owners' agent when it signed the Request for Class Agreement, and that, as the agent of a disclosed principal, it cannot be bound by that agreement's arbitration clause. See Restatement (Second) of Agency 320 (1958). We review a determination of an agency relationship de novo. See *Karavos Compania Naviera S.A. v. Atlantica Export Corp.*, 588 F.2d 1, 7-9 (2d Cir. 1978). There is no merit in Tencara's argument, which is based on the mistaken notion that a party must be either solely a principal or solely an agent. See Restatement (Second) of Agency 328 cmt. b ('In many cases the

2. "The Underwriters counter that the French court hearing their suit against ABS will not recognize the arbitration of the Underwriters' claims because '[u]nder French law, Underwriters are entitled to pursue these claims whether or not they have obtained a subrogation agreement from the Owners'. We express no view as to the possible effect under French law of this judgment or of a subsequent arbitration award. Under American law, the Underwriters are clearly required to arbitrate, and that is the only issue before us today."

agent is a party to the contract made by him on behalf of a disclosed principal and, as such, is responsible for its performance.') The shipyard clearly acted, at least in part, on its own behalf when it contracted with ABS for classification services. It itself derived the benefit of fulfilling its ship construction contract with the Owners by hiring ABS in the Request for Class Agreement. And the record shows no exercise of control by the Owners over Tencara sufficient to negate Tencara's role as, at least, one of the principals. As a result, we affirm the district court's conclusion that Tencara must arbitrate its claims with ABS."

287. United States Court of Appeals, Second Circuit, 29 July 1999, No. 97-9436

Parties:	Plaintiff/appellee: Kahn Lucas Lancaster, Inc. (US) Defendant/appellant: Lark International Ltd. (Hong Kong)
Published in:	14 Mealey's International Arbitration Report (1999, no. 8) pp. C-1 – C-6
Articles:	II(1); II(2); XVI(1)
Subject matters:	– principles of treaty interpretation – agreement in writing – contract containing arbitral clause must be signed by parties
Commentary Cases:	[1] = ¶ 216; [6]-[9] = ¶ 001; [10]-[18] = ¶ 205 + ¶ 208

Facts

The facts of this case are also reported in Yearbook XXIII (1998) pp. 1029-1037. Kahn Lucas Lancaster, Inc. (Kahn Lucas) and Lark International Ltd. (Lark) had a business relationship whereby Lark assisted Kahn Lucas in arranging for overseas manufacturers to make garments ordered by Kahn Lucas. As part of this relationship, Lark processed Kahn Lucas's purchase orders and invoices. Pursuant to the terms of the purchase orders, as well as the parties' standing practice, the manufacturers would issue Kahn Lucas a seller's invoice for payment once the ordered garments were completed. Lark would then issue a separate invoice to Kahn Lucas for its commission. Kahn Lucas paid both of these invoices through drawdowns on an existing letter of credit on which Lark was the named beneficiary. Lark would then remit payment to the manufacturer.

Kahn Lucas issued two Purchase Orders, dated 25 January and 1 February 1995 respectively for finished fleece garments to be imported from the Philippines and sold to Sears Roebuck, Inc. The Purchase Orders stated that the garments were "ordered from" Lark, listed "Lark International (Agent)" as seller, and were signed by Kahn Lucas. They were not signed by Lark. The

Purchase Orders specifically called attention to the arbitration clause providing for arbitration in New York, printed on the reverse side. Lark accepted the Purchase Orders without objection.

In July 1995, the manufacturers issued final invoices relating to the ordered garments, and Lark issued its commission invoice. But citing defective garments and failed deliveries, Kahn Lucas refused to release funds to Lark to pay either the seller's invoices or Lark's commission invoice. Kahn Lucas sued Lark in the United States District Court for the Southern District of New York. The district court held that it did not have personal jurisdiction over Lark to adjudicate the then pending claims, but also held that, given the arbitration clauses, it would have personal jurisdiction over Lark if Kahn Lucas were to seek to compel arbitration.

Kahn Lucas converted its complaint to a motion to compel Lark to arbitrate, and also filed a demand for arbitration with the American Arbitration Association. Lark argued that it was not bound by the provisions of the Purchase Orders because they were directed towards the sellers of the garments, namely the manufacturers, and that the arbitration clauses were not enforceable under the 1958 New York Convention because it had not signed the Purchase Orders.

In an Opinion and Order dated 6 August 1997 (reported in Yearbook XXIII (1998) pp. 1029-1037 as US no. 257) the district court held that the arbitration clauses in the Purchase Orders sent by Kahn Lucas to Lark were enforceable under the Convention and bound Lark, despite the fact that Lark had not signed the purchase orders.

The Court of Appeals, per Parker, CJ, reversed. Both the construction of the original languages of the Convention and its drafting history showed that Art. II of the Convention required that the contract containing the arbitral clause be signed.

Excerpt

I. SUMMARY OF DISTRICT COURT HOLDING

[1] "In an Opinion and Order dated 6 August 1997, the district court granted Kahn Lucas's motion to compel arbitration. *Kahn Lucas Lancaster, Inc. v. Lark Int'l Ltd.*, No. 95 CIV. 10506, 1997 WL 458785 at *8 (S.D.N.Y. 11 August 1997) (*Kahn Lucas II*).[1] The district court first noted that subject matter jurisdiction could only be properly based on Sect. 203 of the implementing

1. Reported in Yearbook XXIII (1998) pp. 1029-1037 (US no. 257).

statutes of the Convention, 9 U.S.C. Sect. 203, which provides an independent basis for subject matter jurisdiction; it could not be based on diversity. Id. at *3 (citing *Matimak Trading Co. v. Khalily*, 118 F.3d 76 (2d Cir. 1997) (holding that Hong Kong corporations are not citizens of a foreign state for purposes of diversity jurisdiction)). Sect. 203 states that '[a]n action or proceeding falling under the Convention shall be deemed to arise under the laws and treaties of the United States'. 9 U.S.C. Sect. 203.

[2] "The court next focused on whether the Arbitration Clauses were enforceable under the Convention so as to vest the court with jurisdiction under Sect. 203. The Convention provides that '[e]ach Contracting State shall recognize an agreement in writing under which the parties undertake to submit to arbitration all or any differences which have arisen or which may arise between them ... concerning a subject matter capable of settlement by arbitration.' New York Convention Art. II(1). The Convention goes on to define 'agreement in writing' to include 'an arbitral clause in a contract or an arbitration agreement, signed by the parties or contained in an exchange of letters or telegrams.' New York Convention Art. II(2). Although Lark had not signed the Purchase Orders, the district court held that the Purchase Orders represented an 'arbitral clause in a contract', and therefore an 'agreement in writing' to arbitrate sufficient to bring the dispute within the Convention. In holding that an arbitral clause in a contract need not be signed by the parties to be enforceable under the Convention, the district court relied on the only appellate case interpreting this section of the Convention, *Sphere Drake Ins. PLC v. Marine Towing, Inc.*, 16 F.3d 666, 669 (5th Cir. 1994)[2] (outlining, without much analysis, Art. II(1) of the Convention as including '(1) an arbitral clause in a contract or (2) an arbitration agreement, (a) signed by the parties or (b) contained in an exchange of letters or telegrams'), and declined to follow *Sen Mar, Inc. v. Tiger Petroleum Corp.*, 774 F. Supp. 879, 882 (S.D.N.Y. 1991)[3] ('An arbitration clause is enforceable only if it is found in a signed writing or an exchange of letters.').

[3] "The district court then turned to Lark's argument that it should not be bound by the Arbitration Clauses because it was not the seller of the garments. The district court held that the Purchase Orders embodied 'an agreement between Kahn Lucas and Lark for the sale of goods, as opposed to an agreement between Kahn Lucas and the manufacturers.' *Kahn Lucas II*, 1997 WL 458785 at *5. The district court relied on the fact that Kahn Lucas and Lark were the only parties mentioned on the Purchase Orders, and on the fact that Kahn Lucas was to pay Lark directly for the garments ultimately delivered

2. Reported in Yearbook XX (1995) pp. 937-942 (US no. 181).
3. Reported in Yearbook XVIII (1993) pp. 493-498 (US no. 128).

under the Purchase Orders. See id. Finally, the district court found that Lark was bound to the terms of the Purchase Orders despite the fact it did not sign them because it manifested assent to the Purchase Orders by performing under them, and that the subject of the dispute was therefore within the scope of the Arbitration Clauses. See id. at *6."

(....)

II. ANALYSIS BY THE COURT OF APPEALS

[4] "On appeal, Lark advances largely the same arguments that it did below. First, it argues that in order to be enforceable under the terms of the Convention, any agreement to arbitrate, be it an 'arbitral clause in a contract' or an 'arbitration agreement', must be signed by the parties or contained in an exchange of letters or telegrams. Because the Purchase Orders were not signed by both parties, the argument continues, they are not 'agreements in writing' enforceable under the Convention. Second, Lark argues that the district court erred in finding that it was bound by the terms of the Purchase Orders, including the Arbitration Clauses, because it was not the seller of the garments.

[5] "For the reasons that follow, we hold that the definition of 'agreement in writing' in the Convention requires that such an agreement, whether it be an arbitration agreement or an arbitral clause in a contract, be signed by the parties or contained in a series of letters or telegrams. Therefore, the Arbitration Clauses are not enforceable under the Convention, and both the district court and this Court lack subject matter jurisdiction over the dispute. Because of this holding, we need not consider Lark's second argument, and we accordingly reverse the judgment of the district court and dismiss Kahn Lucas's motion to compel arbitration for lack of subject matter jurisdiction."

1. Applicable Principles of Construction

[6] "Treaties are construed in much the same manner as statutes. See *United States v. Alvarez-Machain*, 504 U.S. 655, 663 (1992); see also *Sale v. Haitian Ctrs. Council, Inc.*, 509 U.S. 155, 177-183 (1993). The district court's construction of the Convention, like the construction of any statute, is a matter of law which we review de novo. See *Stuart v. United States*, 813 F.2d 243, 246 (9th Cir. 1987), rev'd on other grounds, 489 U.S. 353 (1989); see also *Koreag, Controle et Revision S.A. v. Refco F/X Assocs., Inc.*, 961 F.2d 341, 347-348 (2d Cir. 1992). Statutory construction is a 'holistic endeavor' and must account for the statute's 'full text, language as well as punctuation, structure and subject matter'. *United States Nat'l Bank v. Independent Ins. Agents of Am., Inc.*, 508

U.S. 439, 455 (1993) (internal quotations omitted). Thus, the obvious starting point in construing a treaty is its text. See *Eastern Airlines, Inc. v. Floyd*, 499 U.S. 530, 534 (1991). And the plain meaning of a text 'will typically heed the commands of its punctuation'. *United States Nat'l Bank*, 508 U.S. at 454; see also *United States v. Ron Pair Enters.*, Inc., 489 U.S. 235, 241-242 (1989) (holding that the 'grammatical structure of the statute', specifically the placement of commas, mandated a specific construction).

[7] "Among the rules of punctuation applied in construing statues is this: When a modifier is set off from a series of antecedents by a comma, the modifier should be read to apply to each of those antecedents. See *Bingham, Ltd. v. United States*, 724 F.2d 921, 925-926 n. 3 (11th Cir. 1984); see also *Elliott Coal Mining Co. v. Director, Office of Workers' Comp. Programs*, 17 F.3d 616, 630 (3d Cir. 1994) (noting that the 'use of a comma to set off a modifying phrase from other clauses indicates that the qualifying language is to be applied to all of the previous phrases and not merely the immediately preceding phrase'). As stated by the Eleventh Circuit, this rule is a 'supplementary "rule of punctuation"', to the 'doctrine of the last antecedent', which states that a modifier generally applies only to the nearest, or last, antecedent.[4] See *Bingham*, 724 F.2d at 925-926 n. 3 (citing *Quindlen v. Prudential Ins. Co. of Am.*, 482 F.2d 876, 878 (5th Cir. 1973)). Of course, 'these doctrines are not absolute rules', id. at 926 n. 3, and in applying them we are mindful of the Supreme Court's admonition that 'a purported plain-meaning analysis based only on punctuation is necessarily incomplete and runs the risk of distorting a statute's true meaning'. *United States Nat'l Bank*, 508 U.S. at 454.

[8] "In addition to utilizing rules of punctuation, we are aided in our plain-meaning analysis by the fact that the Convention exists in five official languages – French, Spanish, English, Chinese, and Russian – of equal authenticity. See New York Convention Art. XVI(1). Because one purpose of the Convention is to unify the standards under which international agreements to arbitrate are observed, *Scherk v. Alberto-Culver Co.*, 417 U.S. 506, 520 n. 15 (1973),[5] we should, if possible, adhere to an interpretation consistent with all of the official languages. That said, some of the official languages provide more insight into the drafters' intent than others: Of the five official languages, English, French, and Spanish were the working languages of the United

4. "These rules are illustrated by the following examples. Consider a sentence containing two antecedents – 'A' and 'B' – and one modifying phrase – 'with C'. The doctrine of the last antecedent suggests that if the sentence were structured 'A or B with C', the phrase 'with C' should be read to modify only 'B'. However, the 'supplementary rule' of Bingham suggests that if the sentence were structured 'A or B, with C', the phrase 'with C' should be read to modify both 'A' and 'B'."

5. Reported in Yearbook I (1976) pp. 203-204 (US no. 4).

Nations Conference on International Commercial Arbitration, which drafted the Convention. See Rules of Procedure, U.N. Conference on Int'l Commercial Arbitration, Rule 32, E/Conf.26/5/Rev.1 (1958) (hereinafter 'Rules of Procedure'); see also *Eastern Airlines*, 499 U.S. at 536 (considering language employed by drafters to gain insight into intent of parties). All records of Conference meetings were kept in these working languages. Rules of Procedure at Rule 36.

[9] "Finally, to the extent the drafters' intent is unclear from the text of the multiple versions of the Convention, we may turn to the Convention's legislative history for guidance. *Eastern Airlines*, 499 U.S. at 535 (treaty history and negotiations may be consulted in construing difficult or ambiguous treaty passages)."

2. *Construction of the New York Convention*

[10] "As noted above, Art. II(1) of the Convention provides that each contracting state (including the United States, China, the United Kingdom, and Hong Kong) 'shall recognize' an 'agreement in writing' to arbitrate a given dispute. Art. II(2) in turn, defines the term 'agreement in writing' to include 'an arbitral clause in a contract or an arbitration agreement, signed by the parties or contained in an exchange of letters or telegrams.' Lark contends that the modifying clause 'signed by the parties or contained in an exchange of letters or telegrams', modifies both: (1) 'an arbitral clause in a contract' and (2) 'an arbitration agreement' and, as a result, the dispute between the parties is not arbitrable due to the absence of Lark's signature on the Purchase Orders. Kahn Lucas contends, and the district court held, that 'signed by the parties' modifies only the clause immediately preceding it, 'an arbitration agreement', and not the previous clause. Thus, in Kahn Lucas's view, the unsigned Purchase Orders constitute an 'agreement in writing' to arbitrate enforceable under the Convention.

[11] "As an initial matter, we must determine the meaning of the two elements in the series, namely 'an arbitral clause in a contract' and 'an arbitration agreement'. We find the meaning of 'an arbitral clause in a contract' to be self-evident. We also find that the phrase 'an arbitration agreement', because it is used in conjunction with the phrase 'an arbitral clause in a contract', refers to any agreement to arbitrate which is not a clause in a larger agreement, whether that agreement is part of a larger contractual relationship or is an entirely distinct agreement which relates to a non-contractual dispute. The parties agree that the Arbitration Clauses each constitute 'an arbitral clause in a contract' and not 'an arbitration agreement' under the Convention.

[12] "We turn, then, to the plain meaning of the English-language version of the Convention. Taking its lead from the Fifth Circuit's analysis in *Sphere Drake*, 16 F.3d at 669-670, Kahn Lucas argues that the grammatical structure of Sect. 2 compels the conclusion that its dispute with Lark falls within the Convention. We disagree. Sect. 2 takes the structure 'A or B, with C'. This structure is exactly that to which the 'supplementary rule of punctuation' expressed in *Bingham* applies. Grammatically, the comma immediately following 'an arbitration agreement' serves to separate the series ('an arbitral clause in a contract or an arbitration agreement') from the modifying phrase ('signed by the parties or contained in an exchange of letters or telegrams'), and suggests that the modifying phrase is meant to apply to both elements in the series. Indeed, this comma can serve no other grammatical purpose. As a result, Kahn Lucas's reading of the statute would render the comma mere surplusage, a construction frowned upon. Cf. *Trichilo v. Secretary of Health & Human Servs.*, 823 F.2d 702, 706 (2d Cir. 1987) ('we will not interpret a statute so that some of its terms are rendered a nullity').

[13] "Although the grammatical structure of the English-language version of the Convention suggests that the parties' dispute is not arbitrable, we are hesitant to use punctuation as the sole guide to the meaning of the text. See *United States Nat'l Bank*, 508 U.S. at 454-455. But in this case, other available interpretive tools strongly support the conclusion the punctuation suggests.

[14] "First, the plain language of the other working-language versions of the Convention compels the conclusion that, in order to be enforceable under the Convention, both an arbitral clause in a contract and an arbitration agreement must be signed by the parties or contained in an exchange of letters or telegrams. In the French- and Spanish-language versions, the word for 'signed' appears in the plural form, '*signes*' and '*firmados*' respectively. New York Convention, 21 U.S.T. 2524, 2538. Because each of the two antecedents is couched in the singular, the modifier unambiguously applies to both of them. If, as Kahn Lucas argues, only an arbitration agreement need be signed by the parties, the French-language version would utilize the verb '*signe*' and the Spanish '*firmado*'.

[15] "The non-working official-language versions of the Convention do not offer similarly clear-cut support for this interpretation, but do not weigh strongly against it either. The Chinese-language version, like the English-language version, cannot utilize a uniquely plural form of the verb for 'signed'. Nor does it contain punctuation helpful to our task. However, in the Chinese-language version, the modifier 'signed' precedes, rather than follows, the objects it modifies. New York Convention, 21 U.S.T. 2529. Therefore, if the modifier were construed to apply only to one of the objects, it would apply to 'arbitral clause in a contract', rather than 'arbitration agreement', offering

no comfort to Kahn Lucas in this case. The Russian-language version uses the singular form of the verb 'signed' (transliterated as 'PODPECANOYE'), suggesting that it modifies only 'arbitration agreement'. New York Convention, 21 U.S.T. 2533. But because the plain meaning of the French- and Spanish-language versions of the Convention unambiguously supports the conclusion that the modifier applies to both antecedents, the structure of the English-language version suggests such an interpretation, and the Chinese-language version is susceptible of such an interpretation, we are reluctant to allow the seemingly contradictory Russian-language version to dictate a different result. See *Eastern Airlines*, 499 U.S. at 536 (giving controlling weight to meaning of language in which treaty was drafted). This is particularly so in light of the stated purposes of the Convention, one of which is to 'unify the standards by which agreements to arbitrate are observed and arbitral awards are enforced in the signatory countries'. *Scherk*, 417 U.S. at 520 n. 15 (citing the Convention).

[16] "Finally, to the extent the plain meanings of the non-English language versions of the Convention do not resolve any ambiguity that exists in the English-language version, the legislative history of Art. II puts the matter to rest. The text of Art. II, as reported by the Conference's Working Group, and subject only to modification by the Drafting Committee for form, not substance, Summary of the 23d Meeting, U.N. Conference on Int'l Commercial Arbitration, U.N. ESCOR, E/Conf.26/SR.23 at 4, 7 (12 September 1958), reverses the terms 'arbitration agreement' and 'arbitration clause in a contract'. The Working Group text thus reads:

> 'The expression "agreement in writing" shall mean an arbitration agreement or an arbitration clause in a contract signed by the parties, or an exchange of letters or telegrams between those parties.'[6]

Consideration of the Draft New York Convention on the Recognition and Enforcement of Foreign Arbitral Awards, U.N. Conference on Int'l Commercial Arbitration, U.N. ESCOR, E/Conf.26/L.59, Agenda Item 4, ¶ 2 (6 June 1958). Therefore, unless the modifier 'signed' in the Convention applies to both antecedents, the Drafting Committee's editorial changes would amount to an unintended, and unauthorized, substantive amendment to Art. II(2).

[17] "Accordingly, although we are cognizant that the Convention 'should be interpreted broadly to effectuate its recognition and enforcement purposes',

6. "The fact that the Working Group text does not contain a comma between 'arbitral clause in a contract' and 'signed by the parties' offers no refuge for Kahn Lucas. Even when construed according to the doctrine of the last antecedent, the Working Group text requires that an arbitral clause be signed by the parties."

Bergesen v. Joseph Muller Corp., 710 F.2d 928, 933 (2d Cir. 1983),[7] the rules governing our construction do not allow us to follow the Fifth Circuit's interpretation of Art. II(2) as expressed in *Sphere Drake*. Upon review of the Convention's text, punctuation and subject matter, as well as an examination of the Convention's legislative history, we hold that the modifying phrase 'signed by the parties or contained in an exchange of letters or telegrams' applies to both 'an arbitral clause in a contract' and 'an arbitration agreement'.

[18] "Having determined that the Convention requires that 'an arbitral clause in a contract' be 'signed by the parties or contained in an exchange of letters or telegrams', we turn to the application of the Convention to the facts of this case. As noted above, the Arbitration Clauses were contained in the Purchase Orders which were signed only by Kahn Lucas, and not by Lark. There is therefore no 'arbitral clause in a contract ... signed by the parties'. Further, Kahn Lucas does not contend that the Purchase Orders, even together with Lark's Confirmation of Order forms, represent 'an arbitral clause in a contract ... contained in an exchange of letters or telegrams'. As a result, there is no 'agreement in writing' sufficient to bring this dispute within the scope of the Convention.

[19] "Because the dispute in question does not fall within the Convention, subject matter jurisdiction cannot properly be premised on 9 U.S.C. Sect. 203. The district court and this Court thus lack subject matter jurisdiction over this dispute. The judgment of the district court is reversed, and Kahn Lucas's motion to compel arbitration is dismissed with prejudice."

(....)

7. Reported in Yearbook IX (1984) pp. 487-494 (US no. 54).

288. United States Court of Appeals, Second Circuit, 12 August 1999, Nos. 97-9615, 97-9617

Parties:	Petitioner/appellant: Baker Marine (Nig.) Limited (Nigeria) Respondents/appellees: (1) Chevron (Nig.) Limited (Nigeria); (2) Chevron Corp., Inc. (nationality not indicated) Petitioner/appellant: Baker Marine (Nig.) Limited (Nigeria) Respondent/appellee: Danos and Curole Marine Contractors, Inc. (nationality not indicated)
Published in:	14 Mealey's International Arbitration Report (1999, no. 8) pp. D-1 – D-2
Articles:	I(1); V; V(1)(*e*); VII(1)
Subject matters:	– residual dicretion to enforce arbitral award (no) – recognition foreign judgment setting aside arbitral award (no) – enforcement of award set aside in country of origin
Commentary Cases:	[1] = ¶ 101; [3] = ¶ 501; [3]-[8] = ¶ 516; [4]-[6] = ¶ 500 + ¶ 702

Facts

Baker Marine (Nig.) Limited (Baker Marine) and Danos and Curole Marine Contractors, Inc. (Danos) jointly contracted with Chevron (Nig.) Limited and Chevron Corp., Inc. (Chevron) in 1992 to provide barge services, in relation to Chevron's activities in the oil industry in Nigeria. The contract provided for ad hoc arbitration under the UNCITRAL Rules. The contracts also specified that the arbitration "procedure (insofar as not governed by said UNCITRAL Rules ...) shall be governed by the substantive laws of Nigeria" and that the contracts shall be interpreted in accordance with the "laws of the Federal Republic of Nigeria". The contracts also provided that "judgment upon the award of the arbitrators may be entered in any court having jurisdiction thereof", and further that the contract and awards under it "shall be governed by the [1958 New York Convention]".

Disputes arose and the parties initiated arbitrations in Lagos, Nigeria. In one award, the arbitral tribunal condemned Danos to pay US$ 2.23 million and a second arbitral tribunal condemned Chevron to pay US$ 750,000 to Baker Marine.

Baker Marine sought enforcement of both awards in the Nigerian Federal High Court. Danos and Chevron applied for the setting aside of the awards. In decisions of November 1996 and May 1997, the Nigerian court set aside the two awards. The Chevron award was set aside on the grounds that the arbitrators had, inter alia, improperly awarded punitive damages, gone beyond the scope of the submissions, incorrectly admitted parole evidence and made inconsistent awards. The Danos award was set aside on the ground that it was unsupported by the evidence.

In August 1997, Baker Marine sought to enforce the awards in the Northern District of New York under the New York Convention. The district court, per Thomas J. McAvoy, DJ, denied the petitions concluding that under the Convention and the principles of comity, it would not be proper to enforce an award set aside in Nigeria.

On appeal by Baker Marine, the Court of Appeals, per Leval, CJ, upheld the decision of the district court, holding that US arbitration law could not be invoked as the parties had agreed that their dispute would be arbitrated under Nigerian law. Nor had it been contended that the Nigerian courts had acted contrary to Nigerian law. Baker Marine's further argument that Art. V(1)(*e*) gives the courts a discretionary power was rejected as it had not shown adequate reason for refusing to recognize the judgments of the Nigerian courts.

Excerpt

(....)

[1] "The United States and Nigeria are parties to the Convention,... 9 U.S.C. Sect. 201 note.

(....)

[2] "In August 1997, Baker Marine brought these actions in the Northern District of New York seeking confirmation of the awards under the United States law implementing the Convention, chapter 2 of the Federal Arbitration

Act (FAA), 9 U.S.C. Sects. 201-209.[1] The district court denied Baker Marine's petitions to enforce the arbitral awards, concluding that under the Convention and principles of comity, 'it would not be proper to enforce a foreign arbitral award under the Convention when such an award has been set aside by the Nigerian courts.' Baker Marine appeals.

[3] "This dispute falls under the Convention because Baker Marine is seeking enforcement of arbitration awards in a nation other than the nation where the awards were made. See Convention, Art. I.... Under American law, when a party brings an action to confirm an arbitration award falling under the Convention, a court 'shall confirm the award unless it finds one of the grounds for refusal or deferral of recognition or enforcement of the award specified in the said Convention.' 9 U.S.C. Sect. 207. Art. V of the Convention provides that a court may refuse to enforce an arbitration award 'only' upon proof of the conditions specified therein. Convention, Art. V; see also *Yusuf Ahmed Alghanim & Sons v. Toys "R" Us, Inc.*, 126 F.3d 15, 20 (2d Cir. 1997)[2] (Art. V provides exclusive grounds for setting aside an arbitral award), cert. denied, 118 S.Ct. 1042 (1998). Art. V(1)(*e*) provides that a court may refuse enforcement of an award that 'has been set aside or suspended by a competent authority of the country in which, or under the law of which, the award was made.' Convention, Art. V(1)(*e*). Baker Marine does not contest that the Nigerian High Court is a competent authority in the country in which, and under the law of which, the award was made. The district court relied on the decision of the Nigerian court and Art. V(1)(*e*) in declining to enforce the award.

[4] "Baker Marine argues that the district court's ruling failed to give effect to Art. VII of the Convention, which provides that the Convention shall not 'deprive any interested party of any right he may have to avail himself of an arbitral award in the manner and to the extent allowed by the law or the treaties of the count[r]y where such award is sought to be relied upon.' Art. VII(1). Baker Marine contends that the awards were set aside by the Nigerian courts for reasons that would not be recognized under US law as valid grounds for vacating an arbitration award, and that under Art. VII, it may invoke this country's national arbitration law, notwithstanding the action of the Nigerian court.

1. "Chapter 2 provides that within three years of an arbitration award under the Convention, 'any party to the arbitration may apply to any court having jurisdiction ... for an order confirming the award as against any other party to the arbitration.' 9 U.S.C. Sect. 207. United States district courts have original jurisdiction over actions falling under the Convention. See 9 U.S.C. Sect. 203."

2. Reported in Yearbook XXIII (1998) pp. 1058-1067 (US no. 261).

[5] "We reject Baker Marine's argument. It is sufficient answer that the parties contracted in Nigeria that their disputes would be arbitrated under the laws of Nigeria. The governing agreements make no reference whatever to United States law. Nothing suggests that the parties intended United States domestic arbitral law to govern their disputes.[3] The 'primary purpose' of the FAA is 'ensuring that private agreements to arbitrate are enforced according to their terms.' *Volt Information Sciences, Inc. v. Board of Trustees*, 489 U.S. 468, 479 (1989);[4] see also *Prima Paint Corp. v. Flood & Conklin Mfg. Co.*, 388 U.S. 395, 404 n. 12 (1967) (the FAA aimed 'to make arbitration agreements as enforceable as other contracts, but not more so'). Furthermore Baker Marine has made no contention that the Nigerian courts acted contrary to Nigerian law.

[6] "See *Yusuf*, 126 F.3d at 21 ('[A] court in the country under whose law the arbitration was conducted [may] apply domestic arbitral law ... to a motion to set aside or vacate that arbitral award.').

[7] "Baker Marine makes a further argument premised on the language of Art. V(1)(*e*) of the Convention. Art. V(1)(*e*) provides that when a party seeks confirmation of an award, '[r]ecognition and enforcement of the award *may* be refused' if the award has been set aside by a competent authority of the country in which the award was made. Baker Marine argues that this use of the permissive 'may,' rather than a mandatory term, implies that the court might have enforced the awards, notwithstanding the Nigerian judgments vacating them. It is sufficient answer that Baker Marine has shown no adequate reason for refusing to recognize the judgments of the Nigerian court.[5]

---

3. "Furthermore, as a practical matter, mechanical application of domestic arbitral law to foreign awards under the Convention would seriously undermine finality and regularly produce conflicting judgments. If a party whose arbitration award has been vacated at the site of the award can automatically obtain enforcement of the awards under the domestic laws of other nations, a losing party will have every reason to pursue its adversary 'with enforcement actions from country to country until a court is found, if any, which grants the enforcement.' Albert Jan van den Berg, *The New York Arbitration Convention of 1958: Towards a Uniform Judicial Interpretation* (1981) p. 355."

4. Reported in Yearbook XV (1990) pp. 141-148.

5. "This case is unlike *In re Chromalloy*, 939 F. Supp. 907 (D.D.C. 1996) [reported in Yearbook XXII (1997) pp. 1001-1012 (US no. 230)], on which Baker Marine relies. In that case, the government of Egypt had entered a contract with an American company agreeing that disputes would be submitted to arbitration and that the decision of the arbitrator could not 'be made subject to any appeal or other recourse'. Id. at 912. After the arbitrator entered an award in favor of the American company, the American company applied to the United States courts for confirmation of the award, and the Egyptian government appealed to its own courts, which set aside the award. The district court concluded that Egypt was seeking 'to repudiate its solemn promise to abide by the results of the arbitration', and that recognizing the Egyptian judgment would be contrary to the United States policy favoring arbitration. See

[8] "Baker Marine also contends that the district court improperly imposed sanctions on it for failing to reveal in its petitions for enforcement of the awards that they had been vacated by the court of Nigeria. The contention is moot. It is true the court expressed its intention at oral argument to impose sanctions under Rule 11(b), Fed.R.Civ.P., requiring the payment of expenses (not including attorneys fees). However, the judgment ultimately rendered awarded only statutory costs to be taxed by the Clerk, and made no mention of sanctions or of expenses. Accordingly, we have no reason to consider whether the court might properly have imposed sanctions.

[9] "The judgments of the district court declining to enforce the arbitration awards are affirmed. The applications for sanctions are denied."

---

id. at 912, 913.

Unlike the petitioner in *Chromalloy*, Baker Marine is not a United States citizen, and it did not initially seek confirmation of the award in the United States. Furthermore, Chevron and Danos did not violate any promise in appealing the arbitration award within Nigeria. Recognition of the Nigerian judgment in this case does not conflict with United States public policy."

Part V

B. Court Decisions on the European Convention 1961

Note General Editor. Part V – B of the Yearbook reports on the European Convention of 1961. In this Volume XXIV, the reporting consists of the current "List of Contracting States".

Volume XX (1995) of the Yearbook contains an updated "Commentary on the European Convention on International Commercial Arbitration" by Mr. Dominique Hascher (pp. 1006-1041) along with a "List of European Convention Court Decisions and Arbitral Awards" (pp. 1042-1050). Subsequent to the compilation of this List, several further decisions on the European Convention 1961 have been published in the Yearbook both in this Part V – B and in Part V – A when the decision referred predominantly to the 1958 New York Convention. They are as follows:

- Germany no. E11, Hanseatisches Oberlandesgericht, Hamburg, 15 September 1995, Yearbook XXI (1996) pp. 845-849;
- Germany no. E13 (NYC44), Oberlandesgericht, Cologne, 16 December 1992, Yearbook XXI (1996) pp. 535-541;
- Spain no. E12 (NYC30), Tribunal Supremo, 18 February 1993, Yearbook XXII (1997) pp. 785-788.

The reporting in this Volume consists of:

- Austria no. E3, Oberster Gerichtshof, 20 October 1993 and 23 February 1998;
- Germany no. E14, Bundesgerichtshof, 23 April 1998.

We would like to express our gratitude to our correspondents DDr. Werner Melis (Austria) and Prof. Klaus Peter Berger (Germany) for providing texts and assisting with translations.

References to arbitral awards referring to the European Convention which have been published in the twenty-three volumes of the Yearbook are indexed in the subject indices of arbitral awards as follows:

- Index of Arbitral Awards Volumes I (1975) – XV (1990) published in *Yearbook Key 1990*
- Index of Arbitral Awards Volumes XVI (1991) – XX (1995) published in Volume XX (1995)
- Index of Arbitral Awards Volume XXI published in Volume XXI (1996)
- Index of Arbitral Awards Volume XXII published in Volume XXII (1997)
- Index of Arbitral Awards Volume XXIII published in Volume XXIII (1998)
- Index of Arbitral Awards Volume XXIV, published in this Volume of the Yearbook, pp. 249-262.

The Yearbook also reports on the New York Convention 1958 in Part V – A, the Washington Convention 1965 in Part V – C and on the Panama Convention 1975 in the recently created Part V – D which in this Volume reports two decisions.

The General Editor would like to call upon the readers to assist him by sending copies of relevant court decisions, published or unpublished, for reporting in the forthcoming volumes of the Yearbook. Copies can be sent to either address below.

ICCA Publications
c/o International Bureau of the
Permanent Court of Arbitration
Carnegieplein 2
2517 KJ The Hague, The Netherlands
E-mail: icca@pca-cpa.org

Prof. Dr. Albert Jan van den Berg
c/o Freshfields
Coengebouw, 6th floor
Kabelweg 37
1014 BA Amsterdam
and as of 1 February 2000:
Gebouw Minerva
Appollolaan 151
1077 AR Amsterdam
The Netherlands
E-mail: ajvandenberg@freshfields.com

EUROPEAN CONVENTION OF 1961*
LIST OF CONTRACTING STATES AND SIGNATORIES

*(as of 1 October 1999)***

State	*Signature*	*Ratification, Accession (a), succession (s)*
Austria	21 Apr. 1961	6 Mar. 1964
Belarus	21 Apr. 1961	14 Oct. 1963
Belgium[1]	21 Apr. 1961	9 Oct. 1975
Bosnia and Herzegovina		1 Sep. 1993s
Bulgaria	21 Apr. 1961	13 May 1964
Burkina Faso		26 Jan. 1965a
Croatia		26 July 1993s

* This information, compiled by the Editorial Staff of the *Yearbook Commercial Arbitration*, is based on material provided by the United Nations Treaty Section.

The Convention entered into force on 7 January 1964, in accordance with Art. X(8), with the exception of Art. IV(3)-(7) which entered into force on 18 October 1965, in accordance with para. 4 of the Annex to the Convention.

The text of the Convention is reproduced in Volume XX (1995) of the Yearbook in the Commentary on reported cases by Mr. Dominique Hascher, pp. 1006-1041. See also the Protocol to the Convention, the Agreement Relating to Application of the European Convention on International Commercial Arbitration, done at Paris, 17 December 1962, published in United Nations, *Treaty Series*, Vol. 523, p. 94. Contracting States to the Agreement are Austria, Belgium, Denmark, France, F.R. Germany, Italy and Luxembourg.

** Countries that have signed or ratified the Convention in the course of 1998-1999 are indicated in **boldface type**.

1. Upon ratification of the Convention, on 9 October 1975, Belgium made the following declaration:

"In accordance with article II, paragraph 2, of the Convention, the Belgian Government declares that in Belgium only the State has, in the cases referred to in article I, paragraph 1, the faculty to conclude arbitration agreements."

Cuba		1 Sep. 1965a
Czech Republic[2]		30 Sep. 1993s
Denmark[3]	21 Apr. 1961	22 Dec. 1972
Finland	21 Dec. 1961	
France	21 Apr. 1961	16 Dec. 1966
Germany, Federal Republic of	21 Apr. 1961	27 Oct. 1964
(GDR)		20 Feb. 1975a
Hungary	21 Apr. 1961	9 Oct. 1963
Italy	21 Apr. 1961	3 Aug. 1970
Kazakstan		20 Nov. 1995a
Luxembourg[4]		26 Mar. 1982a
Moldova, Republic of		**5 Mar. 1998a**
Poland	21 Apr. 1961	15 Sep. 1964
Romania	21 Apr. 1961	16 Aug. 1963
Russian Federation	21 Apr. 1961	27 Jun. 1962
Slovakia[2]		28 May 1993s
Slovenia		6 July 1992s
Spain	14 Dec. 1961	12 May 1975
The former Yugoslav Republic of Macedonia[5]		10 Mar. 1994s
Turkey	21 Apr. 1961	24 Jan. 1992
Ukraine[6]	21 Apr. 1961	18 Mar. 1963
Yugoslavia	21 Apr. 1961	25 Sep. 1963

2. Czechoslovakia had signed and ratified the Convention on 21 April 1961 and 13 November 1963, respectively.
3. The instrument of ratification contained a declaration to the effect that the Convention for the time being would not extend to the Faröe Islands and Greenland. In a communication received on 12 November 1975, the Government of Denmark declared that it had withdrawn the above-mentioned reservation, the decision to take effect on 1 January 1976.
4. Upon accession to the Convention, on 26 March 1982, Luxembourg made the following declaration:

   "Except where otherwise expressly provided for in the arbitration agreement, the presiding judges of the local courts shall assume the functions entrusted to the presidents of the chambers of commerce under article IV of the Convention. The presiding judges shall hear the disputes in chambers."

5. The succession is effective from 17 September 1991. The former Yugoslav Republic of Macedonia has made the same declaration upon succession as that made by Yugoslavia upon accession.
6. The Ukraine has communicated to the Secretary-General of the United Nations that the Chamber of Commerce and Industry of the Ukraine will exercise the functions conferred by virtue of Art. IV of the Convention.

AUSTRIA

Accession: 6 March 1964

E3. Oberster Gerichtshof [Supreme Court], 20 October 1993 and 23 February 1998

Parties:	Appellant: Kajo-Erzeugnisse Essenzen GmbH (Austria) Appellee: DO Zdravilisce Radenska (Slovenia)
Published in:	Österreichische Juristenzeitung (1994) p. 513 No. 105; French translation of the 1993 decision in Revue de l'arbitrage (1998, no. 2) pp. 419-421 with note P. Lastenouse and P. Senković, pp. 421-430; French translation of the 1998 decision in Revue de l'arbitrage (1999, no. 2) pp. 385-387 with note P. Lastenouse and P. Senković, pp. 387-391
Articles:	IX(1); IX(1)(c); IX(1)(d); IX(2); X
Subject matters:	- derogation of bilateral treaty to 1961 European Convention - setting aside on grounds of public policy no ground for refusal of enforcement - public policy - European competition law - choice of law - alternative arbitral fora

Facts

By a contract concluded on 24 November 1970, Kajo-Erzeugnisse Essenzen GmbH (Kajo) granted DO Zdravilisce Radenska (Radenska) the exclusive licence to produce and distribute a low-calorie drink in Yugoslavia. The contract provided that Radenska should buy the original ingredients to manufacture the drink exclusively from Kajo. The contract also contained a clause providing for arbitration in the country of the defendant and application of the law of the seat.

Starting in 1980, Radenska bought increasingly less ingredients from Kajo while still manufacturing the drink and, on 31 December 1983, it unilaterally terminated the contract. Kajo commenced arbitration before the Foreign Trade Arbitration Court at the Yugoslav Chamber of Commerce in Belgrade.

By an award rendered on 7 July 1988, a panel of three arbitrators directed Radenska to pay Kajo ÖS 30,070,000 in damages for breach of contract. The arbitrators applied Yugoslav law to the merits of the dispute.

Radenska sought annulment of the award while Kajo sought its enforcement. In the annulment proceedings, the Court of First Instance in Murska Sobota, Slovenia, denied Radenska's request to set aside the award on 13 April 1989; this decision was affirmed on 18 November 1991 by the Court of Appeal in Maribor. On 3 July 1992, however, the Supreme Court of Slovenia reversed and set aside the award, finding that the contract between Kajo and Radenska created, if not a monopoly, at least a privileged situation for Kajo, and thus violated the public policy of Slovenia.

In the meantime, Kajo sought to have the award enforced in Austria. On 17 March 1989, the Court of First Instance in Vienna granted leave to enforce the award, whereupon Kajo sought actual enforcement before the District Court in Bad Radkersburg. The District Court denied Radenska's opposition based on the annulment of the award in Slovenia and granted enforcement on 25 November 1992. This decision was reversed on 30 April 1993 by the Court of Appeal in Graz.

By the first of the two decisions reported here, rendered on 20 October 1993, the Austrian Supreme Court reversed the appellate decision and reinstated the decision of the District Court in Bad Radkersburg. The Supreme Court found that the setting aside of an award for violating the public policy of its country of origin is not a ground for refusing enforcement under the European Convention of 1961.

In parallel proceedings, Radenska sought to have the decision of the Court of First Instance in Vienna, granting leave to enforce, annulled. The Vienna Court of First Instance denied the request on 1 December 1994; the Vienna Court of Appeal denied Radenska's appeal on 10 July 1995.

By its second decision, on 23 February 1998, the Austrian Supreme Court affirmed the lower courts' decisions and denied the appeal. The Court reaffirmed its finding in the 1993 decision that the setting aside of an arbitral award in its country of origin on grounds of public policy is not a ground for refusing enforcement under the European Convention, and denied Radenska's allegation that the award violated Austrian public policy and EU competition law.

Excerpt

Decision of 20 October 1993

[1] "Two international agreements are relevant for the present decision: the Treaty of 18 March 1960 between Austria and Yugoslavia on the Mutual Recognition and Enforcement of Arbitral Awards in Commercial Matters ... (the 'Enforcement Treaty') and [the European Convention of 1961]. Like Austria, Yugoslavia was a Contracting State to this Convention.... The Enforcement Treaty applies between Austria and Slovenia 'pragmatically' (Tichy in Österreichisches Zeitschrift für öffentliches Recht und Völkerrecht (1992), p. 134 et seq.; Regierungsvorlage 734, Beilagen zu den stenographischen Protokollen des Nationalrats, 18. Gesetzgebungsperiode p. 12; compare with the decision concerning the comparable situation with Croatia in Recht der Wirtschaft, p. 149 as well as, presently, with the Treaty on the Exchange of Notes between Austria and Slovenia on the continued application of certain Austrian-Yugoslav treaties, ... entered into force on 1 November 1993).

[2] "Since this [pragmatical] solution does not apply to multilateral agreements (Tichy, op. cit., p. 125) and since no declaration by Slovenia confirming that it considers itself bound by the European Convention ('continuation statement') has been published in the Official Gazette, the Supreme Court ... has sought the advice of the Ministry of Justice. The Ministry of Justice has informed [the Supreme Court] that, on 6 July 1992, Slovenia deposited a continuation statement for the European Convention with the Secretary-General of the United Nations, valid as of 25 June 1991.... This statement has not yet been published in the Official Gazette ... but is an official announcement."

[3] The Supreme Court noted that the rule that a convention enters into force on the day of its publication in the Official Gazette applies only to the conventions mentioned in the Austrian Constitution, and that although a declaration of accession has no constitutive effect, by ratifying the European Convention Austria has accepted that any State meeting the requirements of Art. X of the Convention may accede thereto. The Court concluded: "Slovenia is thus a Contracting State of the European Convention, and this applies also to the time in which the decision of the Supreme Court of Slovenia was rendered, due to the retroactive effect of the [continuation] statement.

[4] "Hence, also Art. IX of this Convention, which provides that recognition and enforcement of an arbitral award be refused if the award has been set aside in a Contracting State, is applicable in Austria. Contrary to Radenska's opinion, the application of this provision is not excluded because Art. 2 of the Enforcement Treaty also contains a provision concerning the conditions on

which the recognition and enforcement of an arbitral award must be refused. According to Art. 8 of the Enforcement Treaty, the Treaty does not affect the provisions of other international agreements concerning the recognition and enforcement of arbitral awards. This means that the two international agreements exist side by side (see Neuteufel in Österreichische Juristenzeitung (1967) p. 231). [Radenska] can oppose enforcement only if there exists a ground for refusal according to either agreement (Hoyer/Loewe in Heller/Berger/Stix, p. 784 fn. 45).

[5] "The argument made by [Radenska] in its appeal, that Art. 8 of the Enforcement Treaty should not be taken into consideration because the European Convention is not 'an agreement concerning the recognition and enforcement of arbitral awards' is unconvincing. It is not the title of the Convention but its contents which are decisive, and it is sufficient that only one or some provisions concern the recognition and enforcement of arbitral awards. Furthermore, it is irrelevant in this context that Art. 3 of the Enforcement Treaty provides that enforcement can be suspended if a party can prove the likely existence of a ground for setting aside the award. This provision does not change the rule of Art. 8 of the Enforcement Treaty, according to which the Treaty does not affect the provisions of other international agreements on the recognition and enforcement of arbitral awards. Further, contrary to the opinion of the Court of Appeal, it is irrelevant to ascertain whether the Enforcement Treaty is a lex specialis vis-à-vis the European Convention.

[6] "Where an arbitral award governed by the European Convention – as is the case here – has been set aside in a Contracting State, the setting aside, according to Art. IX of the Convention, can be a ground for refusing recognition or enforcement only if it has been granted in the State in which or under the law of which the award was rendered, and if it is based on one of the grounds specified therein (Art. IX(1)).

[7] "In the present case, it is doubtful that the award was set aside in the State in which or under the law of which it was rendered, as in both cases this State was Yugoslavia and Slovenia is not the successor State to Yugoslavia.

[8] "However, it is unnecessary to decide on this point as a plain reading of Art. IX shows that the setting aside of an arbitral award for violation of the public policy of the Contracting State where it was rendered does not appear among the grounds exhaustively listed in Art. IX(1) of the European Convention as justifying a refusal of recognition or enforcement of an arbitral award. In particular, contrary to the opinion of the Court of Appeal, [public policy] does not underlie letter (c) of Art. IX(1), which provides that enforcement or recognition shall be refused if the award deals with a difference not contemplated by or not falling within the terms of the submission to

arbitration, or it contains decisions on matters beyond the scope of the submission to arbitration. Violation of public policy has nothing to do with the arbitration agreement or arbitration clause. While these latter are the conditions for the admissibility of the arbitration proceedings, a violation of public policy concerns the contents of the arbitral award.

[9] "Furthermore, Klein (Zeitschrift für Zivilprozeß (1963) p. 351 et seq.), taking into account the origin of the European Convention, persuasively demonstrated that a violation of public policy in the country of origin is not one of the grounds to be considered (in this sense also Schlosser, Stein/Jonas, ZPO, Sect. 1044, no. 134). He rightly noticed that this explains the insertion of the second paragraph of Art. IX of the European Convention, which provides that this limitation binds also the States which are parties to both the European Convention and the [New York Convention]. For this reason, it is irrelevant that the New York Convention applies to Austria as well as to Slovenia due to Slovenia's continuation statement ..., and that in this Convention the grounds for refusal of recognition or enforcement of arbitral awards are broader than in the European Convention. According to Art. IX(2) of the European Convention, the effect of paragraph 1 of Art. IX is to limit the application of Art. V(1)(*e*) of the New York Convention, which provides that the setting aside of the arbitral award is a ground for refusal without limitation, to the cases of setting aside set out in Art. IX(1) of the European Convention. The violation of public policy in the country of origin is not one of these grounds.

[10] "Hence, according to Art. IX of the European Convention, the setting aside of the arbitral award ... is not a ground for refusal of enforcement. In the light of the above, it would be irrelevant if [the setting aside would be a ground for refusal] under the Enforcement Treaty; Radenska's arguments on this point do not need to be examined.

[11] "It ensues from the above that the circumstances invoked by Radenska do not constitute a ground for refusal of enforcement. The first court rightly denied Radenska's request for refusal; its decision must be reinstated."

Decision of 23 February 1998

(....)

[12] "The allegation on which this appeal is based is unfounded. In so far as Radenska argues that the setting aside of the arbitral award by the Supreme Court of Slovenia prevents the award's enforcement, respectively justifies an opposition thereto, the Supreme Court already held in its decision [of 20 October 1993] in the enforcement proceedings that a defendant can only

oppose enforcement where there is a ground for refusal according to one of the two relevant international conventions (Heller/Berger/Stix, 14th ed., p. 784). This is not the case where the arbitral award has been set aside by the Supreme Court of Slovenia for violation of Yugoslav public policy. According to Art. IX(1) of the European Convention, the setting aside of an arbitral award for violation of the public policy of the Contracting State in which it has been rendered is not one of the grounds for refusal exhaustively listed in the Convention. Hence, the setting aside of the arbitral award at issue ... is not, according to Art. IX of the European Convention, a ground for refusing its enforcement. The broad arguments made by Radenska concerning the 'escape clauses' in the contract and the democratic principles of Slovenia do not change this situation. The non-accordance of an arbitral award with the public policy of the State in which it has been set aside is not included in the list of Art. IX of the European Convention. This means that an arbitral award which has been set aside in its country of origin for violation of domestic public policy can remain effective in the other Contracting States, the public policy of which it does not violate (Regierungsvorlage 187, Beilagen zu den stenographischen Protokollen des Nationalrats, 18. Gesetzgebungsperiode; Heller/Berger/Stix, op. cit., p. 788).

[13] "The contents of the arbitral clause between the parties add nothing in favour of Radenska's arguments. As mentioned above, the parties agreed by clause 15 of their contract that disputes arising out of that contract would be decided by an arbitral tribunal to the exclusion of the courts. All claims by Kajo would be decided by the arbitral court of the Yugoslav Chamber of Commerce; all claims by Radenska would be decided by the arbitral court of the Austrian Chamber of Commerce and Industry. The law of the country of the seat of the arbitral tribunal would apply to the dispute. Radenska argues that the choice of the law to be applied by the arbitral tribunal depended on 'chance'; the decision was thus insufficiently predictable and such agreement violates public policy.

[14] "We cannot agree with these objections. Not 'chance', but the dispute settlement provisions agreed upon by the parties in clause 15 of their contract decided which law was to be applied in the specific case. Austrian private international law allows choices of law in the field of obligations. Within the context of the admissibility of a choice of law the parties have a freedom of choice in any sense. Any legal system can be chosen. Actually it is irrelevant whether the choice is for a compulsory or chosen legal system. The parties may combine [systems] in any manner. Several legal systems may be applied alternatively or cumulatively to the same issue or situation, also in the sense that the substantive law of the tribunal seized will apply. Such clauses are valid beyond any doubt (Martiny, *Münchner Kommentar*, 2nd ed., no. 14 *ad* Art. 27

Brussels Convention of 1968 and further reference in fns. 29 and 30; von Hoffmann, Soergel, 12th ed., no. 7 *ad* Art. 27 Brussels Convention of 1968). Even a choice for several laws would be admissible (Schwimann, Juristische Blätter (1981) p. 617 et seq.; Schwimann, Rummel, *Allgemeines Bürgerliches Gesetzbuch*, 2nd ed., no. 4 *ad* Sect. 11 of the Private International Law Act).

[15] "The element of chance which troubles Radenska, that is, which party would seize the arbitral tribunal, fades at a closer look. The division of the roles of the parties in the contract made it clear from the start which type of breach of contract by a contracting party would be seen as a ground for commencing arbitration by the other contracting party. The dependence of the admissibility of such an agreement, according to Radenska, on the 'similarity' of the legal systems alternatively agreed upon (see also Neue Juristische Wochenschrift (1969) p. 978), would cause noticeably more uncertainty vis-à-vis the rule chosen by the parties and especially would not do justice to the agreed intentions of the contracting parties. The arbitral clause providing for an alternative choice of law is not contrary to public policy.

[16] "The alleged deficiency of the arbitral award in the sense of Art. IX(1)(c), respectively [the alleged deficiency] of the arbitration agreement in the sense of Art. IX(1)(d) of the European Convention do not help Radenska's position. They would be relevant for the refusal of recognition or enforcement only if the setting aside of the arbitral award were based thereon (Art. IX(1) of the European Convention). However, as also Radenska eventually conceded, the setting aside was not based on such grounds. Radenska maintains that it raised these objections (with no success) in its request for setting aside, and that it was (again) a mere 'chance' that these grounds were not taken into account by the Supreme Court of Slovenia; we have nothing to add.

[17] "It is correct, on the contrary, that the fact that the arbitral award was set aside for violation of the Yugoslav public policy does not mean that it violated domestic public policy (Schlosser, *Das Recht der internationalen privaten Schiedsgerichtsbarkeit*, 2nd ed., no. 665 [rectius: 792]; Klein, Zeitschrift für Zivilprozeß (1963) p. 342 [rectius: 352]. Radenska sees such a violation in the 'substantial distortion of competition' of the contract of 24 November 1970.

[18] "As to the review of public policy, which is embodied in the above-mentioned international conventions and, in particular, in Sect. 81(3) of the Execution Ordinance and Sect. 6 of the Private International Law Act, the lower courts correctly held that it must be applied where the enforcement of the foreign [award] fully disagrees with the domestic legal system. This disagreement must be evident. In no case may the foreign [award] be reviewed from a factual or legal point of view. Certainly, a public policy review may not lack completely; however, it must be used with maximum restraint (among

others, Heller/Berger/Stix, op. cit., p. 782; Herz, Juristische Blätter (1954) p. 213; Scheucher, Zeitschrift für Rechtsvergleichung (1960) p. 15; Roth, *Der Vorbehalt des ordre public gegenüber fremden gerichtlichen Entscheidungen*, p. 139 et seq.; see also Czernich/Tiefenthaler, *Die Übereinkommen von Lugano und Brüssel*, nos. 4 and 6 *ad* Art. 27; Lechner/Mayr, *Das Übereinkommen von Lugano*, p. 116; Kropholler, *Europäisches Zivilprozeßrecht*, 4th ed., no. 1 et seq. *ad* Art. 27; Schwimann, Rummel, *Allgemeines Bürgerliches Gesetzbuch*, no. 1 et seq. *ad* Sect. 6 of the Private International Law Act; Evidenzblatt (1961) p. 27; Evidenzblatt (1983) p. 84; Recht der Wirtschaft (1986) p. 114; Entscheidungen des österreichisches Oberster Gerichtshof in Zivilsachen no. 59 p. 128; Österreichisches Bankarchiv (1990) p. 244).

[19] "The aim of licence provisions in a bottling contract is undoubtedly to grant the bottler the right to manufacture a trade-mark drink according to strict instructions and directions and to make the trade-mark available to the bottler. Consequently, the provisions in such contracts aiming at guaranteeing the constant quality of the product, such as for instance the bottler's obligation to buy the ingredients from the licensor, do not have as a rule the character of a restriction of competition, the more so as the consumer expects products of a constant quality (Österreichische Blätter für gewerblichen Rechtschutz und Urheberrecht (1978) p. 78). The arbitral tribunal held in this sense ... in the arbitral award, that the contract between the parties was a bottling contract and that Radenska should necessarily purchase the raw and basic materials from Kajo. [According to the arbitral tribunal], only in this manner could the quality of the product ... be maintained; just like Coca-Cola is only the drink manufactured from the Coca-Cola syrup, it was necessary, in order to guarantee the quality of [the product], that the raw and basic materials be purchased from Kajo.

[20] "Radenska, which maintained in the first instance that this was a bottling contract ..., now for the first time in these proceedings relies on facts which would prove that this was not a bottling contract 'in the technical sense'. Its argument contravenes the prohibition to rely on new elements (*Neuerungsverbot*) which applies in review proceedings (Sect. 504(2) ZPO); Heller/Berger/Stix, op. cit., p. 888; Evidenzblatt (1962) p. 216).

[21] "Radenska itself concedes that certain restrictions of competition can be justified in several types of contracts (contracts of know-how, licence, trade-mark licence, patent licence, franchising) and are thus admissible. It also acknowledges that it appears from the system of the exceptions made for associations in Art. 85 of the Treaty Establishing the European Community, that the more restrictions of competition are tolerated, the more worthy of protection is the contracting party that grants the other party the exercise of a right. Nonetheless, Radenska raises the objection, which it does not further

specify in these proceedings, that the agreement of the parties evidently violated the principles of 'western European competition rules', and that its enforcement would thus violate public policy. This objection is unfounded.

[22] "Radenska apparently intends to refer with its objection to Art. 85 of the EU Treaty, which, together with Art. 86, is the cornerstone of the rules and basic principles of the Common Market. The priority of community law over national law means that in the Member States of the European Union, among them Austria, Arts. 85 and 86 of the EU Treaty, cornerstones of the rules and basic principles of the Common Market, are part of public policy. An arbitral award which violates Arts. 85 and 86 of the EU Treaty may thus not be enforced in Austria (Gleiss/Hirsch, *Kommentar zum EG-Kartellrecht*, 4th ed., no. 24 et seq.; Neue Juristische Wochenschrift (1969) p. 978). However, there has been in the present case no such violation of public policy; according to the above general considerations, this violation should be evident as the [award] may not be reviewed.

[23] "If the parties to a combined know-how and trade-mark licence contract (concerning beer) agree that the licensee may buy the necessary raw material (yeast) only from the licensor, this is not a forbidden restriction of competition, if only the know-how and raw material together guarantee that the final products (beer) manufactured by the parties and sold under that trade-mark correspond (Gleis/Hirsch, op. cit., no. 367). The European Commission held in this sense, in its decision of 23 March 1990 in *Moosehead v. Whitbread*, between a Canadian and a British brewery, that Art. 85(1) of the EU Treaty did not apply (Amtsblatt no. L 100 of 20 April 1990 pp. 0032-0037 = CELEX doc. no. 390D0186). As far as the present, similar case is concerned, it ensues that there is no violation of public policy which violates the basic fundamental values of the Austrian legal system and community law."

GERMANY

Ratification: 27 October 1964

E14. Bundesgerichtshof [Supreme Court], 23 April 1998

Parties:	Appellant: Buyer (nationality not indicated) Appellee: Seller (Croatia)
Published in:	Neue Juristische Wochenschrift (1998) p. 2452 et seq.
Articles:	VI(2)
Subject matters:	– capacity to enter into arbitration agreement – foreign trade authorization (Yugoslav law) – application of the new German Arbitration Law (no)

Facts

The buyer and the seller were business partners since 1984. As the then Yugoslav seller lacked the state authorization to conclude foreign trade contracts, the contracts between the buyer and the seller were always formally concluded through a third Yugoslav company which possessed a foreign trade authorization. At the time of concluding two new contracts for the sale of steel hatchcovers on 26 October 1988 and 5 January 1989, the seller's representative, C, allegedly informed the buyer that the seller could now enter into foreign trade contracts, whereupon the parties concluded the two contracts directly. The contracts contained an arbitration clause providing for arbitration in Bremen "subject to FRG law regulations".

When the seller failed to meet some of the contractually agreed delivery dates, the buyer commenced arbitration in Bremen seeking damages for late delivery. On 15 April 1993, an arbitral tribunal awarded approximately DM 1,300,000 in damages to the buyer.

On 16 September 1994, the Court of First Instance in Bremen granted enforcement of the award. On 30 May 1996, the Court of Appeal in Bremen reversed, finding that the seller lacked the capacity to enter into foreign trade relations.

The Supreme Court affirmed the decision of the Court of Appeal on the same grounds.

Excerpt

[1] "The appellate court denied the request for enforcement because the [seller] lacked the capacity to enter into foreign trade contracts and related arbitration clauses. The court denied that the buyer was entitled to good faith protection ex Art. 12 first sentence of the Application Law of the Civil Code (EGBGB),[1] because it clearly appears from the letter of this provision that [Art. 12] only concerns physical persons and thus, contrary to a common doctrinal opinion, may not be applied to legal persons. In fact, even if Art. 12 first sentence EGBGB applied, it would be of no help to the buyer, as it should not have relied on the legal capacity of the seller after having used the second, authorized Yugoslav company as intermediary in its earlier business relations with the seller. The buyer could not rely only on the alleged declaration of C, representative of the seller, that the seller could now contract directly.

[2] "The above decision must be affirmed. The request to enforce the arbitral award is unfounded because there is a ground for refusal ex Sect. 1041(1)(1) German Code of Civil Procedure (ZPO) *old*, which according to Sect. 1042(2) ZPO *old* justifies the dismissal of the request, as the arbitral award is not based on a valid arbitration agreement.[2] According to the Yugoslav respectively

---

1. Art. 12 of the Introductory Provisions to the German Code of Civil Procedure (EGBGB) reads in relevant part:

"*Protection of the co-contracting party*. Where a contract is concluded between persons in the same State, a physical person who has legal capacity to act according to the law of that State may rely on his legal incapacity to act under the law of another State only where the co-contracting party knew or could know of this legal incapacity to act at the conclusion of the contract. This does not apply to family or succession law acts and to the disposal of immovable goods located in another State."

2. Sect. 1041(1)(1) of the German Code of Civil Procedure (ZPO) read before the 1998 reform:

"1. Action to set aside the award may be brought:
(1) if the award does not arise out of a valid arbitration agreement or depends in some other manner on an inadmissible procedure".

Croatian law then in force, the seller lacked a foreign trade authorization and consequently was legally incapable of concluding arbitration agreements with a foreign business partner.

[3] "The [German] law in force before the entry into force of the Arbitration Law Reform of 22 December 1997 ..., that is, 1 January 1998, applies according to that Law's Art. 4 Sect. 1(3) and Art. 5(1) to proceedings which, as the present one, were already pending before the court.

[4] "The validity of the arbitration agreement must be ascertained according to German law. The clause providing that the seat of the arbitration was Bremen, 'subject to FRG law regulations' explicitly concerns the arbitral proceedings only. However, if the parties determine the law applicable to the arbitration, the arbitration agreement as a rule follows (Zöller/Geimer, ZPO, 20th ed., Sect. 1025 note 79). According to the applicable German law, a legal person can bind itself contractually only in so far as it has the legal capacity to do so.

[5] "The opinion of the appellate court that the seller had no legal capacity to conclude foreign trade contracts is to be shared.

[6] "According to Art. VI(2) first sentence of the [1961 European Convention], concluded between Germany and the former Socialist Federal Republic of Yugoslavia and applicable to its successor state Croatia, and according to general German conflict of laws, the legal capacity of the seller is to be ascertained according to its personal law, thus according to the law of the federal state Croatia of the former Socialist Federal Republic of Yugoslavia, which consists of transformed federal law of the former Socialist Federal Republic Yugoslavia (hereinafter, Yugoslav law) and national law of the federal republic Croatia.

[7] "The Supreme Court is bound in its review by the determination of the appellate court that the seller lacked the legal capacity to conclude foreign trade contracts under its national law. The appellate court relied for its determination that the seller was not legally capable to conclude foreign trade contracts under Yugoslav law on an expert report of the scientific head of the Institute for East [European] Law, P, who affirmed that, according to Yugoslav law, the legal capacity of a legal person is limited by its statute as registered in the Court Register, which corresponds to the German *Handelsregister*; Yugoslav law thus accepts the English *ultra vires* doctrine; not all enterprises are

---

Sect. 1042(2) ZPO read before the 1998 reform:

"2. An application for an order for enforcement shall be rejected, subject to the setting aside of the award, if one of the reasons for setting aside the award mentioned in Sect. 1041 exists."

authorized to foreign trade business; a registration in the Court Register is required therefor; since the seller was not registered for foreign trade business, the conclusion of the contracts at issue was outside its registered scope of activity. Consequently, the seller was not legally capable with respect to the conclusion of foreign trade contracts.

[8] "The [appellate] court made this expert opinion its own, thereby correctly determining and applying foreign law. The application of the foreign law thus determined may not be reviewed (Zöller/Gümmer, Sect. 548 note 9 and references therein).

[9] "The question discussed at the oral hearing before the Supreme Court, whether the Yugoslav foreign trade provisions which resulted in the seller lacking legal capacity to conclude foreign trade contracts are internationally mandatory norms (*Eingriffsnormen*) and as such should not be considered by the German courts (see on this point Fischer, IPRax (1996) p. 332 at p. 333 and BGHZ 31, p. 367 at p. 371 et seq.; BGHZ 64, p. 183 at p. 188 et seq.; BGHZ 128, p. 41 at p. 52), must be answered in the negative. *Eingriffsnormen* are, in the jurisprudence of the Supreme Court, provisions of foreign economic law which according to their scope – mostly a prohibition to alienate or a limitation of the possibility to dispose – have an effect on domestic contracts. Here, on the contrary, we have foreign provisions of personal status which apply according to German conflict of laws. The fact that these provisions were also meant to support the Yugoslav foreign trade monopoly does not lead to a different conclusion.

[10] "German public policy is not violated. A legal provision of another State is not to be applied when its application leads to a result which violates fundamental principles of German law (Art. 6(1) EGBGB).[3] A premise for the application of [Art. 6(1) EGBGB] is that the application of the foreign law would lead in the concrete case to a result which affects the core of the German legal system.... This is not the case here, where the foreign law regulates the capacity to conclude foreign trade contracts.

[11] "The appellate court correctly denied the buyer the protection of good faith. However, the appeal correctly blames the appellate court for having ignored, when holding that Art. 12 first sentence EGBGB, which protects the good faith of a contractual party as to the legal capacity of the other party,

3. Art. 6(1) EGBGB reads:

"*Ordre public*. A legal provision of another State shall not be applied where its application would lead to a result which clearly conflicts with fundamental principles of German law. In particular it shall not apply where the application thereof conflicts with the Constitution."

does not apply, that this provision is located in the second part of the Law, which only concerns physical persons, and that the legislator of German private international law consciously refrained from laying down a conflict of law provision on legal persons and left the development thereof to jurisprudence and doctrine, so that an application by analogy of Art. 12 first sentence EGBGB to legal persons can in general be considered (see only Palandt/Heidrich, BGB, 57th ed., annex to EGBGB 12 (PIL) note 1). However, the Supreme Court does not need to answer the question whether such analogy is required (see on the various opinions Palandt/Heidrich, op. cit., note 7), since in any case the reasons given by the appellate court to find that the buyer was not in good faith may not be reviewed.

[12] "Art. 12 EGBGB does not offer protection to the party which knew or could know the legal capacity of its contractual partner at the conclusion of the contract. Thus, the good faith of the buyer must be denied if its belief that the seller was authorized to foreign trade was tainted by even a light negligence (Palandt/Heinrich, op. cit., note 3; Fischer, *Verkehrschutz im internationalen Vetragsrecht*, p. 363). The appellate court found, without any error in law, that this was the case and thereby did not stretch the buyer's duty of diligence excessively. The appellate court considered the circumstance that the parties had always used a second, foreign trade authorized Yugoslav company in their previous relations to be determining. It did not consider the alleged declaration of representative C of the seller that this [intermediary] was no longer necessary to be sufficient, also in the light of the economical and political changes in Yugoslavia in 1988, relied upon by the buyer, vis-à-vis the significance of the previous business relations between the parties. This evaluation may not be reviewed by the Supreme Court.

[13] "The appeal claims unsuccessfully that the appellate court did not consider the buyer's assertion that it could not take the time to check the foreign trade capacity of the seller because the order was urgent. This is not sufficient, considering that there were several immediately available and swift ways to obtain information, such as for instance a telephone query to the Federal Ministry for Economy, the Yugoslav Embassy in Germany, the German Embassy in Yugoslavia or the Croatian Chamber of Commerce and Industry, to conclude that it was impossible to check the declaration of witness C and thereby exclude negligence.

[14] "The seller's reliance on the invalidity of the arbitration agreement does not violate good faith since the seller executed most of the main contract, though with partial delay. The prohibition of contradictory behaviour together with the performance under the main contract does not compel the seller to submit to a legally invalid arbitration clause and thereby waive its right to recourse to a court.

[15] "Hence, the appellate decision which denied the request for enforcement of the arbitral award must be affirmed because of the seller's lack of legal capacity to conclude foreign trade contracts and the resulting invalidity of the arbitration clause. According to Sect. 1042(2) ZPO, the binding annulment of the arbitral award must be pronounced together with the refusal of the request for enforcement."

Part V

C. Court Decisions on the Washington Convention 1965

Note General Editor. Part V – C contains a current List of Contracting States and Signatories to the Washington Convention 1965 as of 4 October 1999. Two ICSID cases, *Fedax N.V. v. Republic of Venezuela* and *Ceskoslovenska Obchodni Banka, A.S. v. The Slovak Republic*, are reported in Part II – A. No new court decisions applying this Convention are reported.

Volume XVIII (1993) of the Yearbook contained a contribution by Dr. Aron Broches entitled "Convention on the Settlement of Investment Disputes between States and Nationals of Other States of 1965. Explanatory Notes and Survey of its Application". References to arbitral awards referring to the ICSID arbitral awards and decisions which have been published in the Yearbook are indexed in the subject indices of arbitral awards as follows:

- Index of Arbitral Awards Volumes I (1975) – XV (1990) published in *Yearbook Key 1990*
- Index of Arbitral Awards Volumes XVI (1991) – XX (1995) published in Volume XX (1995)
- Index of Arbitral Awards Volume XXI published in Volume XXI (1996)
- Index of Arbitral Awards Volume XXII published in Volume XXII (1997)
- Index of Arbitral Awards Volume XXIII published in Volume XXIII (1998)
- Index of Arbitral Awards Volume XXIV, published in this Volume of the Yearbook, pp. 249-262.

The Yearbook also reports on the New York Convention 1958 in Part V – A, the European Convention 1961 in Part V – B and on the Panama Convention 1975 in the recently created Part V – D.

WASHINGTON CONVENTION OF 1965

LIST OF CONTRACTING STATES AND SIGNATORIES

(as of 4 October 1999)[1]

State	*Signature*	*Deposit of Ratification*	*Entry into Force*
Afghanistan	30 Sep. 1966	25 June 1968	25 July 1968
Albania	15 Oct. 1991	15 Oct. 1991	14 Nov. 1991
Algeria	17 Apr. 1995	21 Feb. 1996	22 Mar. 1996
Argentina	21 May 1991	19 Oct. 1994	18 Nov. 1994
Armenia	16 Sep. 1992	16 Sep. 1992	16 Oct. 1992
Australia	24 Mar. 1975	2 May 1991	1 June 1991
Austria	17 May 1966	25 May 1971	24 June 1971
Azerbaijan	18 Sep. 1992	18 Sep. 1992	18 Oct. 1992
Bahamas	19 Oct. 1995	19 Oct. 1995	18 Nov. 1995
Bahrain	22 Sep. 1995	14 Feb. 1996	15 Mar. 1996
Bangladesh	20 Nov. 1979	27 Mar. 1980	26 Apr. 1980
Barbados	13 May 1981	1 Nov. 1983	1 Dec. 1983
Belarus	10 July 1992	10 July 1992	9 Aug. 1992
Belgium	15 Dec. 1965	27 Aug. 1970	26 Sep. 1970
Belize	19 Dec. 1986		
Benin, People's Republic of	10 Sep. 1965	6 Sep. 1966	14 Oct. 1966
Bolivia	3 May 1991	23 June 1995	23 July 1995
Bosnia and Herzegovina	25 Apr. 1997	14 May 1997	13 June 1997
Botswana	15 Jan. 1970	15 Jan. 1970	14 Feb. 1970
Burkina Faso	16 Sep. 1965	29 Aug. 1966	14 Oct. 1966

1. This information reported by the Editorial Staff of the Yearbook is provided by the International Centre for Settlement of Investment Disputes. Countries that have signed or ratified the Convention in the course of 1998-1999 are indicated in **boldface type**.

Burundi	17 Feb. 1967	5 Nov. 1969	5 Dec. 1969
Cambodia	5 Nov. 1993		
Cameroon	23 Sep. 1965	3 Jan. 1967	2 Feb. 1967
Central African Republic	26 Aug. 1965	23 Feb. 1966	14 Oct. 1966
Chad	12 May 1966	29 Aug. 1966	14 Oct. 1966
Chile	25 Jan. 1991	24 Sep. 1991	24 Oct. 1991
China, People's Republic of	9 Feb. 1990[2]	7 Jan. 1993	6 Feb. 1993
Colombia	18 May 1993	15 July 1997	14 Aug. 1997
Comoros	26 Sep. 1978	7 Nov. 1978	7 Dec. 1978
Congo, Democratic Republic of	27 Dec. 1965	23 June 1966	14 Oct. 1966
Costa Rica	29 Sep. 1981	27 Apr. 1993	27 May 1993
Côte d'Ivoire	30 June 1965	16 Feb. 1966	14 Oct. 1966
Croatia	16 June 1997	**22 Sep. 1998**	**22 Oct. 1998**
Cyprus	9 Mar. 1966	25 Nov. 1966	25 Dec. 1966
Czech Republic	23 Mar. 1993	23 Mar. 1993	23 Apr. 1993
Denmark	11 Oct. 1965	24 Apr. 1968	24 May 1968[3]
Ecuador	15 Jan. 1986	15 Jan. 1986	14 Feb. 1986
Egypt, Arab Republic of	11 Feb. 1972	3 May 1972	2 June 1972
El Salvador	9 June 1982	6 Mar. 1984	5 Apr. 1984
Estonia	23 June 1992	23 June 1992	23 July 1992
Ethiopia	21 Sep. 1965		
Fiji	1 July 1977	11 Aug. 1977	10 Sep. 1977
Finland	14 July 1967	9 Jan. 1969	8 Feb. 1969
France	22 Dec. 1965	21 Aug. 1967	20 Sep. 1967

2. The Convention was signed on behalf of the Republic of China on 13 January 1966 and ratified on 10 December 1968. At its fourteenth Annual Meeting on 2 October 1980, the Administrative Council considered a communication received from the People's Republic of China, decided that the Republic of China be removed from the list of Contracting States and noted that, pending study by the Government of the People's Republic of the possibility of becoming a party to the Convention, China was not a Contracting State. The People's Republic of China signed the Convention on 9 February 1990.

   On ratifying the Convention, China notified ICSID "that, pursuant to Article 25(4) of the Convention, the Chinese Government would only consider submitting to the jurisdiction of the International Centre for Settlement of Investment Disputes disputes [about] compensation resulting from expropriation and nationalization."
3. Denmark excluded, by a notification received on 15 May 1968, the Faröe Islands; by a notification received on 30 October 1968, Denmark extended the application of the Convention to the Faröe Islands as of 1 January 1969.

Gabon	21 Sep. 1965	4 Apr. 1966	14 Oct. 1966
Gambia, The	1 Oct. 1974	27 Dec. 1974	26 Jan. 1975
Georgia	7 Aug. 1992	7 Aug. 1992	6 Sep. 1992
Germany	27 Jan. 1966	18 Apr. 1969	18 May 1969[4]
Ghana	26 Nov. 1965	13 July 1966	14 Oct. 1966
Greece	16 Mar. 1966	21 Apr. 1969	21 May 1969
Grenada	24 May 1991	24 May 1991	23 June 1991
Guatemala	9 Nov. 1995		
Guinea	27 Aug. 1968	4 Nov. 1968	4 Dec. 1968
Guinea-Bissau	4 Sep. 1991		
Guyana	3 July 1969	11 July 1969	10 Aug. 1969
Haiti	30 Jan. 1985		
Honduras	28 May 1986	14 Feb. 1989	16 Mar. 1989
Hungary	1 Oct. 1986	4 Feb. 1987	6 Mar. 1987
Iceland	25 July 1966	25 July 1966	14 Oct. 1966
Indonesia	16 Feb. 1968	28 Sep. 1968	28 Oct. 1968
Ireland	30 Aug. 1966	7 Apr. 1981	7 May 1981
Israel	16 June 1980	22 June 1983	22 July 1983
Italy	18 Nov. 1965	29 Mar. 1971	28 Apr. 1971
Jamaica	23 June 1965	9 Sep. 1966	14 Oct. 1966
Japan	23 Sep. 1965	17 Aug. 1967	16 Sep. 1967
Jordan	14 July 1972	30 Oct. 1972	29 Nov. 1972
Kazakhstan	23 July 1992		
Kenya	24 May 1966	3 Jan. 1967	2 Feb. 1967
Korea, Republic of	18 Apr. 1966	21 Feb. 1967	23 Mar. 1967
Kyrgyz, Republic of	9 June 1995		
Kuwait	9 Feb. 1978	2 Feb. 1979	1 Mar. 1979
Latvia	8 Aug. 1997	8 Aug. 1997	7 Sep. 1997
Lesotho	19 Sep. 1968	8 July 1969	7 Aug. 1969
Liberia	3 Sep. 1965	16 June 1970	16 July 1970
Lithuania	6 July 1992	6 July 1992	5 Aug. 1992

4. On 3 October 1990, Germany notified the Centre "that, through the accession of the German Democratic Republic to the Federal Republic of Germany with effect from 3 October 1990, the two German States have unified to form one sovereign State, which as a single member of the International Centre for Settlement of Investment Disputes remains bound by the provisions of the Convention on the Settlement of Investment Disputes between States and Nationals of Other States. As from the date of unification, the Federal Republic of Germany will act in the International Centre for Settlement of Investment Disputes under the designation of 'Germany'."

Luxembourg	28 Sep. 1965	30 July 1970	29 Aug. 1970
Madagascar	1 June 1966	6 Sep. 1966	14 Oct. 1966
Malawi	9 June 1966	23 Aug. 1966	14 Oct. 1966
Malaysia	22 Oct. 1965	8 Aug. 1966	14 Oct. 1966
Mali	9 Apr. 1976	3 Jan. 1978	2 Feb. 1978
Mauritania	30 July 1965	11 Jan. 1966	14 Oct. 1966
Mauritius	2 June 1969	2 June 1969	2 July 1969[5]
Micronesia	24 June 1993	24 June 1993	24 July 1993
Moldova	12 Aug. 1992		
Mongolia	14 June 1991	14 June 1991	14 July 1991
Morocco	11 Oct. 1965	11 May 1967	10 June 1967
Mozambique	4 Apr. 1995	7 June 1995	7 July 1995
Namibia	**26 Oct. 1998**		
Nepal	28 Sep. 1965	7 Jan. 1969	6 Feb. 1969
Netherlands	25 May 1966	14 Sep. 1966	14 Oct. 1966[6]
New Zealand	2 Sep. 1970	2 Apr. 1980	2 May 1980[7]
Nicaragua	4 Feb. 1994	20 Mar. 1995	19 Apr. 1995
Niger	23 Aug. 1965	14 Nov. 1966	14 Dec. 1966
Nigeria	13 July 1965	23 Aug. 1965	14 Oct. 1966
Norway	24 June 1966	16 Aug. 1967	15 Sep. 1967
Oman	5 May 1995	24 July 1995	23 Aug. 1995
Pakistan	6 July 1965	15 Sep. 1966	15 Oct. 1966
Panama	22 Nov. 1995	8 Apr. 1996	6 May 1996
Papua New Guinea	20 Oct. 1978	20 Oct. 1978	19 Nov. 1978
Paraguay	27 July 1981	7 Jan. 1983	6 Feb. 1983
Peru	4 Sep. 1991	9 Aug. 1993	8 Sep. 1993
Philippines	26 Sep. 1978	17 Nov. 1978	17 Dec. 1978
Portugal	4 Aug. 1983	2 July 1984	1 Aug. 1984
Romania	6 Sep. 1974	12 Sep. 1975	12 Oct. 1975
Russian Federation	16 June 1992		

5. Until Mauritius attained its independence on 12 March 1968, it was covered by ratification of the United Kingdom.
6. On depositing its instrument of ratification, The Netherlands restricted the application of the Convention to the Kingdom in Europe; by a notification received on 22 May 1970, The Netherlands withdrew that restriction and thus extended the application of the Convention to Surinam and the Netherlands Antilles; Surinam having attained independence on 25 November 1975, the Convention ceased to be applicable to Surinam as of that date. (*Note General Editor.* Compare with n. 22 at p. 572).
7. On depositing its instrument of ratification, New Zealand, pursuant to Art. 70 of the Convention, excluded from its coverage the Cook Islands, Niue and Tokelau.

Rwanda	21 Apr. 1978	15 Oct. 1979	14 Nov. 1979
Samoa	3 Feb. 1978	25 Apr. 1978	25 May 1978
São Tome and Príncipe	**1 Oct. 1999**		
Saudi Arabia	28 Sep. 1979	8 May 1980	7 June 1980
Senegal	26 Sep. 1966	21 Apr. 1967	21 May 1967
Seychelles	16 Feb. 1978	20 Mar. 1978	19 Apr. 1978
Sierra Leone	27 Sep. 1965	2 Aug. 1966	14 Oct. 1966
Singapore	2 Feb. 1968	14 Oct. 1968	13 Nov. 1968
Slovak Republic	27 Sep. 1993	27 May 1994	26 June 1994
Slovenia	7 Mar. 1994	7 Mar. 1994	6 Apr. 1994
Solomon Islands	12 Nov. 1979	8 Sep. 1981	8 Oct. 1981
Somalia	27 Sep. 1965	29 Feb. 1968	30 Mar. 1968
Spain	21 Mar. 1994	18 Aug. 1994	17 Sep. 1994
Sri Lanka	30 Aug. 1967	12 Oct. 1967	11 Nov. 1967
St. Kitts & Nevis	14 Oct. 1994	4 Aug. 1995	3 Sep. 1995
St. Lucia	4 June 1984	4 June 1984	4 July 1984[8]
Sudan	15 Mar. 1967	9 Apr. 1973	9 May 1973
Swaziland	3 Nov. 1970	14 June 1971	14 July 1971[9]
Sweden	25 Sep. 1965	29 Dec. 1966	28 Jan. 1967
Switzerland	22 Sep. 1967	15 May 1968	14 June 1968
Tanzania	10 Jan. 1992	18 May 1992	17 June 1992
Thailand	6 Dec. 1985		
Togo	24 Jan. 1966	11 Aug. 1967	10 Sep. 1967
Tonga	1 May 1989	21 Mar. 1990	20 Apr. 1990
Trinidad and Tobago	5 Oct. 1966	3 Jan. 1967	2 Feb. 1967
Tunisia	5 May 1965	22 June 1966	14 Oct. 1966
Turkey	24 June 1987	3 Mar. 1989	2 Apr. 1989[10]
Turkmenistan	26 Sep. 1992	26 Sep. 1992	26 Oct. 1992

8. Until St. Lucia attained its independence on 22 February 1979, it was covered by the ratification of the United Kingdom.
9. Until Swaziland attained its independence on 6 September 1968, it was covered by the ratification of the United Kingdom.
10. On ratifying the Convention, Turkey declared that:

"With respect to Article 64 of the Convention, the Government of Turkey is of the opinion that the disputes which may arise from the interpretation and application of the Convention can be solved through meaningful negotiations between the parties to the dispute, without the need of having recourse to third party settlement."

Uganda	7 June 1966	7 June 1966	14 Oct. 1966
Ukraine	**3 Apr. 1998**		
United Arab Emirates	23 Dec. 1981	23 Dec. 1981	22 Jan. 1982
United Kingdom of Great Britain and Northern Ireland	26 May 1965	19 Dec. 1966	18 Jan. 1967[11]
United States of America	27 Aug. 1965	10 June 1966	14 Oct. 1966
Uruguay	28 May 1992		
Uzbekistan	17 Mar. 1994	26 July 1995	25 Aug. 1995
Venezuela	18 Aug. 1993	2 May 1995	1 June 1995
Yemen, Republic of	28 Oct. 1997		
Yugoslavia	21 Mar. 1967	21 Mar. 1967	20 Apr. 1967
Zambia	17 June 1970	17 June 1970	17 July 1970
Zimbabwe	25 Mar. 1991	20 May 1994	19 June 1994

11. The United Kingdom, pursuant to Art. 70 of the Convention, excluded from its coverage the following territories for whose international relations it is responsible: Jersey, Isle of Man, British Indian Ocean Territory, Pitcairn Islands, British Antarctic Territory, Sovereign Base Areas of Cyprus. By notifications received on 27 June 1979, and 17 November 1983, respectively, the United Kingdom extended the application of the Convention to Jersey as of 1 July 1979, and to the Isle of Man as of 1 November 1983.

Part V

D. Court Decisions on the Panama Convention 1975

Note General Editor. Yearbook XXII (1997) marked the introduction of a new Part V – D reporting on court decisions applying and interpreting the Inter-American Convention on International Commercial Arbitration of 1975 adopted at Panama City, Panama on 30 January 1975 (the Panama Convention 1975).

Part V – A reports on the New York Convention 1958, Part V – B reports on the European Convention 1961 and Part V – C reports on the Washington Convention 1965.

The reporting on the Panama Convention 1975 in this Volume consists solely of the List of Contracting States.

A General Introduction to Inter-American Commercial Arbitration by Charles Robert Norberg, Director-General of the Inter-American Arbitration Commission, is published in the companion publication to the Yearbook, ICCA's *International Handbook on Commercial Arbitration*, along with the texts of the Panama Convention 1975 and the Rules of Procedure of the Inter-American Commercial Arbitration Commission.

The General Editor would like to call upon the readers to assist him by sending copies of relevant court decisions, published or unpublished, for reporting in the forthcoming volumes of the Yearbook. Copies can be sent to either address below.

☞

ICCA Publications
c/o International Bureau of the
Permanent Court of Arbitration
Carnegieplein 2
2517 KJ The Hague, The Netherlands
E-mail: icca@pca-cpa.org

Prof. Dr. Albert Jan van den Berg
c/o Freshfields
Coengebouw, 6th floor
Kabelweg 37
1014 BA Amsterdam
and as of 1 February 2000:
Gebouw Minerva
Appollolaan 151
1077 AR Amsterdam
The Netherlands
E-mail: ajvandenberg@freshfields.com

PANAMA CONVENTION OF 1975
LIST OF CONTRACTING STATES

(as of 1 October 1999)[1]

State	*Signature*	*Ratification*	*Deposit*
Argentina	15 Mar. 1991	3 Nov. 1994	5 Jan. 1995
Bolivia	8 Feb. 1983	**8 Oct. 1998**	**29 Apr. 1999**
Brazil	30 Jan. 1975	31 Aug. 1995	27 Nov. 1995
Chile	30 Jan. 1975	8 Apr. 1976	17 May 1976
Colombia	30 Jan. 1975	18 Nov. 1986	29 Dec. 1986
Costa Rica	30 Jan. 1975	2 Jan. 1978	20 Jan. 1978
Dominican Republic	18 Apr. 1977		
Ecuador	30 Jan. 1975	6 Aug. 1991	23 Oct. 1991
El Salvador	30 Jan. 1975	27 June 1980	11 Aug. 1980
Guatemala	30 Jan. 1975	7 July 1986	20 Aug. 1986
Honduras	30 Jan. 1975	8 Jan. 1979	22 Mar. 1979
Mexico	27 Oct. 1977[2]	15 Feb. 1978	27 Mar. 1978
Nicaragua	30 Jan. 1975		
Panama	30 Jan. 1975	11 Nov. 1975	17 Dec. 1975
Paraguay	26 Aug. 1975[2]	2 Dec. 1976	15 Dec. 1976
Peru	21 Apr. 1988	2 May 1989	22 May 1989
United States	9 June 1978	10 Nov. 1986[3]	27 Sep. 1990

1. This information has been compiled by the Editorial Staff of the *Yearbook Commercial Arbitration* on the basis of information provided by the Organization of American States (OAS). Countries that have ratified the Convention during the course of 1998-1999 are indicated in **boldface type**.
2. Signed ad referendum.
3. At the time of ratification the United States made the following reservation:

"1. Unless there is an express agreement among the parties to an arbitration agreement to the contrary, where the requirements for the application of both the Inter-American Convention on International Commercial Arbitration and the Convention on the Recognition and Enforcement of Foreign Arbitral Awards are met, if a majority of such parties are citizens of a state or states that have ratified or acceded to the Inter-American Convention and are

Uruguay	30 Jan. 1975	29 Mar. 1977	25 Apr. 1977
Venezuela	30 Jan. 1975	22 Mar. 1985	16 May 1985

---

member states of the Organization of American States, the Inter-American Convention shall apply. In all other cases, the Convention on the Recognition and Enforcement of Foreign Arbitral Awards shall apply.

2. The United States of America will apply the rules of procedure of the Inter-American Commercial Arbitration Commission which are in effect on the date that the United States of America deposits its instrument of ratification, unless the United States of America makes a later official determination to adopt and apply subsequent amendments to such rules.

3. The United States of America will apply the Convention, on the basis of reciprocity, to the recognition and enforcement of only those awards made in the territory of another Contracting State."

UNITED STATES

Ratification: 27 September 1990

P4. United States District Court, District of Delaware, 29 October 1998, No. Civ. A. 98-401-RRM

Parties:	Plaintiff: American Life Insurance Company (US) Defendants: (1) Carlos D. Parra (Argentina); (2) ASIAT, S.A. (Uruguay); (3) The Parkway Corporation (Uruguay)
Published in:	25 Federal Supplement, Second Series (D.Del. 1998) pp. 467-480
Articles:	1; 3
Subject matters:	– jurisdiction to determine arbitrability in international arbitration – scope of forum selection clause

Facts

Subsequent to earlier business dealings, Carlos D. Parra (Parra) and American Life Insurance Company (ALICO) entered into a Master General Agent's Agreement. Pursuant to the Agreement, ALICO appointed ASIAT, S.A., represented by Parra, master general agent. ASIAT was to sell and contract with agents and brokers to sell International Dollar Business policies. On 1 November 1991, Parra and ALICO entered into a Supervising Master General Agent's Agreement, pursuant to which ALICO appointed Parra supervising master general agent. Parra was to sell, and to contract directly with agents and brokers to sell, International Dollar Business policies. The parties agreed Parra was an independent contractor and that either party could terminate the Agreement without cause upon ninety days written notice. The Agreement contained an arbitration clause covering "[a]ny controversy or claim arising out of or relating to this Agreement".

On 2 August 1993, ALICO terminated the Supervising Master General Agent's Agreement without cause. On 1 October 1994 ALICO, Parra and "ASIAT/Parkway" entered into a General Release Agreement. The Release Agreement contained a forum selection clause providing that "any interpretation or adjudication related to this Agreement shall occur in accordance with Delaware law in a court located in the State of Delaware, United States of America".

On 31 July 1996, Parra and ASIAT initiated arbitration pursuant to Art. 3 of the Arbitration Rules of the Inter-American Commercial Arbitration Commission, alleging, inter alia, that ALICO had breached the Supervising Master General Agent's Agreement and intentionally interfered with Parra's agency network and prospective business opportunities by terminating the Agreement without cause. An arbitral tribunal was constituted in September 1997. Parra and ASIAT requested the arbitral tribunal to consider the scope and validity of the General Release Agreement which they alleged had been fraudulently induced. On 6 May 1998, the arbitral tribunal informed the parties that the General Release Agreement's forum selection clause precluded the arbitral tribunal from arbitrating disputes arising out of the agreement, unless ALICO had waived its right to object to arbitration of such disputes and requested the parties to brief the waiver issue. On 29 June 1998, the arbitral tribunal announced it would arbitrate issues related to the General Release Agreement because ALICO had failed to raise timely objections to the arbitral tribunal's jurisdiction.

On 27 July 1998, Parra and ASIAT submitted an amended Statement of Claim alleging that ALICO fraudulently induced Parra to sign the General Release Agreement in order to destroy his agency network, and adding claims for damages arising from a heart attack Parra suffered in January 1997 which they claimed was "a direct and proximate result of ALICO's tortious actions".

On 9 July 1998, ALICO filed an action in the district court seeking to enjoin Parra, ASIAT and Parkway from arbitrating disputes related to the General Release Agreement.

The court, per McKelvie, DJ, first found that under the Panama Convention it had jurisdiction to determine whether the parties agreed to arbitrate disputes arising out of the General Release Agreement, as the parties had not specified in their arbitration agreement that this question was to be determined by the arbitral tribunal. By the terms of the forum selection clause in the General Release Agreement, the parties did not agree to arbitrate disputes arising out of the Agreement. As the further requirements for the issuing of a preliminary injunction had been met, ALICO was entitled to the requested preliminary injunctive relief.

Excerpt

I. PRELIMINARY INJUNCTION

[1] "The purpose of a preliminary injunction 'is to preserve the status quo, not to decide the issues on their merits'. *Anderson v. Davila*, 125 F.3d 148, 156 (3d Cir. 1997). When deciding a motion for a preliminary injunction, the court must evaluate the following four factors: (1) the likelihood that the plaintiff will prevail on the merits at the final hearing; (2) the extent to which the plaintiff is being irreparably harmed by the conduct complained of; (3) the extent to which the defendant will suffer irreparable harm if the preliminary injunction is issued; and (4) the public interest. *New Jersey Hosp. Ass'n v. Waldman*, 73 F.3d 509, 512 (3d Cir. 1995). The court shall issue an injunction 'only if the plaintiff produces evidence sufficient to convince the district court that all four factors favor preliminary relief'. Id."

II. CAN THE DISTRICT COURT DECIDE ARBITRABILITY IN ARBITRATION UNDER THE INTER-AMERICAN (PANAMA) CONVENTION?

[2] "This court must first resolve if, as a threshold matter, it can decide whether the parties are bound to arbitrate disputes related to the General Release Agreement. Plaintiff contends that the court, and not the arbitral panel, should decide whether disputes relating to the General Release Agreement are arbitrable because the parties did not agree the panel could determine the scope of its own jurisdiction. Defendants contend that under the Inter-American Convention, arbitrators, and not courts, decide whether disputes fall within the scope of the parties' agreement to arbitrate disputes.

[3] "The district courts of the United States have original jurisdiction over actions or proceedings falling under the Inter-American Convention regardless of the amount in controversy, pursuant to 9 U.S.C. Sect. 203. See 9 U.S.C. Sect. 203....[1] In actions to enforce arbitration proceedings in courts of law under Chapter 1 of the FAA, the Supreme Court has held courts decide whether a party is bound to arbitrate a matter, unless the parties have agreed

1. 9 U.S.C. Sect. 203 reads in relevant part:

"An action or proceeding falling under the Convention shall be deemed to arise under the laws and treaties of the United States. The district courts of the United States ... shall have original jurisdiction over such an action or proceeding, regardless of the amount in controversy."

to submit arbitrability disputes for arbitration. *First Options of Chicago, Inc. v. Kaplan*, 514 U.S. 938, 943, 115 S.Ct. 1920, 131 L.Ed.2d 985 (1995);[2] *United Steelworkers of America v. Lukens Steel Co.*, 969 F.2d 1468, 1473-1474 (3d Cir. 1992). According to the Third Circuit, 'whether or not [a party is] bound to arbitrate, as well as what issues it must arbitrate, is a matter to be determined by the Court on the basis of the contract entered into by the parties.' *PaineWebber Inc. v. Hofmann*, 984 F.2d 1372, 1376-1377 (3d Cir. 1993). This is because arbitration is a matter of agreement; parties are bound to arbitrate only what they have agreed to arbitrate. See *AT&T Technologies, Inc. v. Communications Workers of America*, 475 U.S. 643, 649, 106 S.Ct. 1415, 89 L.Ed.2d 648 (1986).

[4] "According to the Supreme Court in *First Options of Chicago, Inc. v. Kaplan*, '[c]ourts should not assume that the parties agreed to arbitrate arbitrability unless there is "clea[r] and unmistakabl[e]" evidence that they did so.' *First Options of Chicago, Inc.*, 514 U.S. at 944, 115 S.Ct. 1920. If there is no clear and unmistakable evidence, a court of law should resolve disputes pertaining to agreements to arbitrate. See id.

[5] "Parra and ASIAT commenced arbitration pursuant to an arbitration clause in the Supervising General Master Agent's Agreement. This clause reads:

> 'Any controversy or claim arising out of or relating to this Agreement, or the breach thereof, shall be settled by arbitration.... The arbitrators and the umpire are not to be bound by any strict rules of legal procedure or evidence. They shall decide in accordance with prevailing practices in the Company and with what they think is the fair and right thing to be done between the parties from a business point of view....'

There is no provision in the Supervising Master General Agent's Agreement to submit arbitrability disputes for arbitration. Furthermore, the General Release Agreement contains no arbitration provision whatsoever. Because '[c]ourts should not assume that the parties agreed to arbitrate arbitrability unless there is "clear and unmistakabl[e]" evidence that they did so[,]' id, this court finds the parties did not agreed to submit arbitrability disputes for arbitration.

[6] "Defendants urge the court to distinguish international arbitration proceedings from domestic arbitration proceedings, because a strong presumption exists in favor of arbitrating, as opposed to litigating, disputes arising out of international commercial transactions. Defendants cite *Moses H. Cone Memorial Hospital v. Mercury Construction Corp.*, 460 U.S. 1, 103 S.Ct. 927, 74 L.Ed.2d

---

2. Reported in Yearbook XXII (1997) pp. 278-286.

765 (1983) to establish this presumption. Here the Supreme Court recognized a general presumption in favor of arbitrating disputes. See *Moses H. Cone Memorial Hospital v. Mercury Construction Corp.*, 460 U.S. 1, 22 n. 27, 24-25, 103 S.Ct. 927, 74 L.Ed.2d 765 (1983). The Court has held, however, this presumption goes the other way when courts decide whether they should resolve arbitrability disputes. *First Options of Chicago, Inc.*, 514 U.S. at 944, 115 S.Ct. 1920. Defendants have cited no cases which find a presumption in favor of granting international arbitral panels jurisdiction over disputes pertaining to the arbitrability of matters before the panel.

[7] "Defendants also urge the court to distinguish Inter-American Convention arbitration proceedings from domestic arbitration proceedings because the former are enforced under the FAA's Chapter 3, while the latter are enforced under the FAA's Chapter 1. The Inter-American Convention and IACAC recognize arbitration is a matter of agreement; parties are bound to arbitrate only what they have agreed to arbitrate. See *AT&T Technologies, Inc.*, 475 U.S. at 649, 106 S.Ct. 1415. Art. 1 of the Inter-American Convention states that the Convention enforces agreements to arbitrate disputes relating to commercial transactions.... Art. 1(1) of IACAC's rules limits its jurisdiction to '[w]here the parties to a contract have agreed in writing that disputes in relation to that contract shall be referred to arbitration under the IACAC Rules of Procedure....' .... According to Art. 3(3)(c) of IACAC's rules, a party seeking to initiate arbitration must set out a reference to the arbitration clause or the separate arbitration agreement that is invoked.... IACAC recommends parties who have not agreed in writing to submit disputes for arbitration do so before initiating arbitration under its rules. Id. at 2.

[8] "According to the Supreme Court, the rule 'which follows inexorably' from the principle that arbitration is a matter of contract 'is that the question of arbitrability ... is undeniably an issue for judicial determination'. *AT&T Technologies, Inc.* 475 U.S. at 649, 106 S.Ct. 1415. This court finds no reason to treat international arbitration proceedings differently from domestic arbitration proceedings in this respect. Therefore, this court finds equally applicable the principle that '[u]nless the parties clearly and unmistakably provide otherwise, the question of whether the parties agreed to arbitrate is to be decided by the court, not the arbitrator'. Id. at 649, 106 S.Ct. 1415.

[9] "Defendants present an argument over several steps that Art. 21 of IACAC's rules, authorizing arbitrators to resolve arbitrability disputes, derogates the principle that courts determine whether parties agreed to arbitrate a matter. Defendants argue the Inter-American Convention's Art. 3 incorporates IACAC's Rules of Procedure. See Inter-American Convention on International Commercial Arbitration, Art. 3 ('In the absence of an express agreement between the parties, the arbitration shall be conducted in accordance with the

rules of procedure of [IACAC].'). Pursuant to 9 U.S.C. Sect. 307, defendants argue, the Convention's provisions supersede conflicting provisions of the FAA's Chapter 1. 9 U.S.C. Sect. 307 ('Chapter 1 [of the FAA] applies to actions and proceedings brought under this chapter to the extent Chapter 1 is not in conflict with this chapter or the Inter-American Convention as ratified by the United States.'). Because the Convention incorporates IACAC's rules, defendants argue, IACAC's rules supersede conflicting provisions of the FAA's Chapter 1. Defendants argue Sect. 307 extends to principles of law recognized by courts enforcing arbitration proceedings under the FAA's Chapter 1.

[10] "Art. 21 of IACAC's rules vests arbitral panels with decision-making power over arbitrability disputes.... ('The arbitral tribunal shall have the power to rule on objections that it has no jurisdiction including ... the existence or validity of the arbitration clause....'). Defendants argue Art. 21(1) is in conflict with case law holding that courts, not arbitrators, determine whether the parties agreed to submit disputes for arbitration. Defendants argue, therefore, Art. 21(1) supersedes this case law and, accordingly, arbitrators should settle disputes concerning the arbitrability of matters before them.

[11] "As noted previously, principles recognized by the Supreme Court and the Third Circuit in actions to enforce arbitration proceedings under FAA's Chapter 1 apply with equal force to arbitration proceedings under the Inter-American Convention. Therefore, this court finds case law on arbitrability is not 'in conflict' with the Inter-American Convention and therefore, is not superseded.

[12] "Furthermore, Art. 1(2) of IACAC's rules contains a self correcting measure that preserves conflicting principles of law that cannot be derogated. See IACAC, Rules of Procedure, Art. 1(2) (stating that the rules 'shall govern except that where any of these Rules is in conflict with a provision of the law applicable to the arbitration from which these parties cannot derogate, that provision shall prevail.').

[13] "The Third Circuit instructs 'a statute should not be considered in derogation of the common law unless it expressly so states or the result is imperatively required from the nature of the enactment'. *Bauers v. Heisel*, 361 F.2d 581, 587 (3d Cir. 1966) (en banc); see also *Hernandez v. Kalinowski*, 146 F.3d 196, 200 (3d Cir. 1998) ('Congress must clearly express its intent to change a well-established common law construction.'). Nothing in the Articles of the Inter-American Convention leads this court to find IACAC's rules derogate conflicting common law principles. Accordingly, the principle that courts decide whether parties to a dispute are bound to submit to arbitration should 'prevail' over Art. 21(1) of IACAC's rules.

[14] "Defendants suggest that ALICO agreed to submit arbitrability disputes to the arbitral panel by participating in a proceeding governed by IACAC's

rules. Defendants cite a commentator who notes that 'international arbitration rules normally provide explicitly that the arbitrators have the power to determine their own jurisdiction', which falls into 'the agreement of the parties exception of [*First Options of Chicago, Inc. v. Kaplan*]'. Ian R. MacNeil et al., IV *Federal Arbitration Law: Agreements, Awards And Remedies Under the Federal Arbitration Act* Sect. 44.15.1 (Supp. 1996). ALICO and Parra, however, did not expressly agree to arbitrate disputes according to IACAC's rules. This court, therefore, declines to adopt the suggestion that the parties agreed to submit arbitrability disputes to the arbitral panel by submitting to an arbitration proceeding governed by the IACAC's rules.

[15] "ALICO and Parra agreed to resolve any disputes arising under the General Release Agreement in a Delaware court. As a result, the arbitral panel never had jurisdiction over disputes arising under the General Release Agreement. Because the arbitral panel did not have jurisdiction over the agreement, it never should have reached the waiver issue. Because this court finds that the parties did not agree that the arbitral panel could determine its own jurisdiction, this court concludes it has jurisdiction to decide whether the parties agreed to arbitrate disputes arising under the General Release Agreement."

III. IS ALICO LIKELY TO PREVAIL ON THE MERITS?

[16] "Having concluded the court has jurisdiction, the court now turns to the merits of ALICO's motion for preliminary injunction...."

1. *General Release Agreement*

[17] "According to the Supreme Court, '[w]hen deciding whether the parties agreed to arbitrate a certain matter ... courts generally ... should apply ordinary state-law principles that govern the formation of contracts.' *First Options of Chicago, Inc.*, 514 U.S. at 944, 115 S.Ct. 1920. ALICO and Parra agreed Delaware law would apply to disputes arising under the General Release Agreement. Delaware law requires a court to read a contract as a whole and to give its provisions their ordinary meaning. *Citadel Holding Corp. v. Roven*, 603 A.2d 818, 822 (Del. 1992). See, e.g., *Myers v. Myers*, 408 A.2d 279, 280 (Del. 1979) ('In the absence of ambiguity, there is no room for interpretation or a search for the intent of the parties.'). Courts should give the greatest weight to the express language of the contract itself. See, e.g., *United States v. Armour & Co.*, 402 U.S. 673, 678, 91 S.Ct. 1752, 29 L.Ed.2d 256 (1971).

[18] "In the General Release Agreement, Parra and ALICO agreed 'any interpretation or adjudication' of the agreement would take place in a Delaware

court. This clause clearly expresses the parties' intent to resolve all disputes arising under the General Release Agreement in a Delaware court, which precludes arbitrating disputes. Consequently, this court finds that the parties did not agree to arbitrate disputes arising under the General Release Agreement.

[19] "Defendants argue the Third Circuit has held that previously granted arbitration rights can be waived only by express language. *Patten Securities Corp., Inc. v. Diamond Greyhound & Genetics, Inc.*, 819 F.2d 400 (3d Cir. 1987). The General Release Agreement contains no express arbitration waiver. Defendants argue, under *Patten Securities*, Parra and ALICO did not waive the agreement in the Supervising Master General Agreement to arbitrate disputes relating to the four master general agents when they entered into the General Release Agreement.

[20] "The forum selection clause in *Patten Securities* states that the defendant 'consents and will submit to the jurisdiction of the courts in the State of New Jersey....' *Patten Securities Corp., Inc.*, 819 F.2d at 407. While the defendant in *Patten Securities* agreed to submit to a New Jersey court's jurisdiction, the defendant did not agree to exclude all other forums.

[21] "The General Release Agreement's forum selection clause accomplishes a different purpose from the clause interpreted by the Third Circuit in *Patten Securities*. The General Release agreement states 'any interpretation of adjudication' related to the agreement is to take place 'in a court located in the State of Delaware United States of America.' This clause prevents a party from seeking to resolve disputes arising under the agreement in any forum other than a Delaware court. While *Patten Securities* involved an agreement to submit to a forum's jurisdiction, the present dispute involves an agreement to bind the parties to one exclusive forum. Accordingly, this court finds *Patten Securities* does not apply to the present case. This court finds the General Release Agreement waived Parra and ASIAT's right to arbitrate any disputes related to the four master general agents."

2. *Timely Objection to Jurisdiction*

[22] "Defendants argue the arbitral panel properly found ALICO waived objections to the panel's jurisdiction over disputes arising under the General Release Agreement because ALICO failed to raise timely objections. Defendants argue ALICO had notice that Parra and ASIAT sought to arbitrate disputes related to the General Release Agreement at latest in November, 1996 when Parra and ASIAT sought the production of records pertaining to the business activities of 'members of the Parra organization'. Because ALICO did not raise objections to arbitrating claims related to the General Release

Agreement until 10 March 1998, Parra and ASIAT argue, ALICO waived a lack of jurisdiction defense pursuant to Art. 21(3) of IACAC's rules.

[23] "ALICO had no reason to expect the arbitral proceeding would encompass claims arising out of the General Release Agreement. Parra and ASIAT did not expressly mention the agreement or specific claims released within it until March, 1998. The agreement's purpose was to waive claims and ALICO paid Parra to release the claims in the agreement. The agreement contained a clause requiring all adjudication and interpretation take place in a Delaware court. ALICO raised objections to the panel's jurisdiction over disputes relating to the agreement immediately upon receiving notice in March, 1998 that Parra and ASIAT sought to arbitrate related disputes. Consequently, the court finds that ALICO is likely to prevail in its argument that it raised timely objections to the arbitral panel's jurisdiction over disputes arising under the General Release Agreement."

3. *Validity General Release Agreement*

[24] The court declined to rule on defendants' assertion that the General Release Agreement was invalid because ALICO used economic duress and coercion to force Parra to sign the agreement because the defendants had not yet provided sufficient evidence to evaluate the merits of the defense. Furthermore, as the defendants had not alleged that the forum selection clause in the General Release Agreement was obtained through fraud or duress, the court did not reach this issue.

4. *Arbitrability of Damages Related to Parra's Heart Attack*

[25] "ALICO contends that references in Parra and ASIAT's third amended Statement of Claim to a heart attack suffered by Parra constitute 'personal injury claims' which lie outside the scope of the arbitration provision in the Supervising Master General Agency Agreement. ALICO argues, consequently, Parra and ASIAT should be enjoined from introducing the heart attack in the arbitration proceedings. The Supreme Court has held the FAA 'establishes that, as a matter of federal law, any doubts concerning the scope of arbitrable issues should be resolved in favor of arbitration....' *Moses H. Cone Memorial Hosp.*, 460 U.S. at 24-25, 103 S.Ct. 927. This court will not enjoin Parra and ASIAT to the extent they claim Parra's heart attack is related to disputes arising under the Supervising Master General Agent's Agreement. Parra and ASIAT's claims will be subject to injunction, however, to the extent they claim Parra's heart attack is related to disputes involving the General Release Agreement."

IV. IRREPARABLE HARM IF FORCED TO ARBITRATE GENERAL RELEASE AGREEMENT?

[26] "The Third Circuit recognizes a party is irreparably harmed as a matter of law if forced to arbitrate a matter that it has not agreed to arbitrate. *PaineWeber Inc. v. Hartmann*, 921 F.2d 507, 515 (3d Cir. 1990) ('the harm to a party would be per se irreparable if a court were to abdicate its responsibility to determine the scope of an arbitrator's jurisdiction and, instead were to compel the party, who has not agreed to do so, to submit to an arbitrator's own determination of his authority.'). Accordingly, this court finds that ALICO would be irreparably harmed if forced to arbitrate claims arising out of the General Release Agreement."

V. HARM IF PRELIMINARILY ENJOINED FROM ARBITRATING DISPUTES RELATED TO THE GENERAL RELEASE AGREEMENT?

[27] "This court finds that defendants will not be harmed if temporarily enjoined from arbitrating disputes related to the General Release Agreement. Enjoining the arbitration of disputes arising out of the General Release Agreement will prevent defendants only from arbitrating disputes related to the four master general agents listed in the General Release Agreement. A temporary injunction will not prevent defendants from arbitrating other disputes arising under the Supervising Master General Agent's Agreement, including disputes relating to Parra's other agents and brokers. Defendants may still pursue their claim in a Delaware Court that the General Release Agreement is invalid."

VI. ARBITRATION OF DISPUTES ARISING UNDER GENERAL RELEASE AGREEMENT AGAINST PUBLIC INTEREST?

[28] "The Third Circuit recognizes '[i]f a court determines that a valid arbitration agreement does not exist or that the matter at issue clearly falls outside of the substantive scope of the agreement, it is obliged to enjoin arbitration.' Id. at 511. Allowing arbitrators to decide whether the parties agreed to submit a dispute to arbitration absent express agreement by the parties to this effect goes against 'the principle that a party can be forced to arbitrate only those issues it specifically has agreed to submit to arbitration....' *First Options of Chicago, Inc.*, 514 U.S. at 945, 115 S.Ct. 1920. Accordingly, the court finds it is in the public interest to issue a preliminary injunction pre-

venting the defendants from arbitrating disputes arising under the General Release Agreement."
(....)

P5. United States District Court, Western District of Wisconsin, 5 January 1999, 98-C-0521-C

Parties:	Petitioner: Employers Insurance of Wausau, A Mutual Company (US) Respondent: Banco Seguros Del Estado (Uruguay)
Published in:	34 Federal Supplement, Second Series (E.D.Wis. 1999) pp. 1115-1122
Articles:	5
Subject matters:	- relationship Chap. 1 (domestic arbitration) and Chaps. 2 (New York Convention) and 3 (Inter-American Convention) - proper notice of arbitration - jurisdiction under Foreign Sovereign Immunities Act - relationship Inter-American Convention and New York Convention

Facts

Between 1966 and 1973, Employers Insurance of Wausau Company (US) entered into a series of excess retrocessional insurance "treaties" with underwriters (Retrocessionaires) at Lloyd's of London. The Retrocessionaires were a group comprising more than one hundred individuals and firms, including Banco Seguros Del Estado, the state bank of the Republic of Uruguay (Banco). The underwriter accepting the greatest portion of the risk, the lead underwriter, was the Merrett Syndicate. It is customary that the lead underwriter assumes responsibility for servicing claims on behalf of all the underwriters.

Each of the treaties contained the same arbitration clause as well as a Service of Suit Clause which provided in part:

> "It is agreed that in the event of the failure of [the Retrocessionaires] to pay any amount claimed to be due hereunder, [the Retrocessionaires], at the request of [petitioner], will submit to the jurisdiction of any Court of competent jurisdiction within the United States....

> It is further agreed that service of process in such suit may be made upon Messrs. Mendes & Mount,... New York,...
>
> The above-named are authorised and directed to accept service of process on behalf of [Retrocessionaires] in any such suit and/or upon the request of [petitioner] to give a written undertaking to [petitioner] that [Mendes & Mount] will enter a general appearance upon [the Retrocessionaires'] behalf in the event such a suit shall be instituted."

Beginning in 1984, Wausau sought reimbursement for asbestos-related claims and submitted proofs to Leslie & Godwin, the intermediary through whom communications and transactions were transmitted by the parties. The Merrett Syndicate retained the law firm of Lord, Bissell & Brook to audit Wausau's payment of such claims. When by 1991 the Retrocessionaires still had not reimbursed Wausau for its asbestos-related losses, Wausau initiated arbitration by sending a demand for arbitration to Lord, Bissell & Brook. Lord, Bissell & Brook forwarded the demand to Leslie & Godwin, which responded to Wausau in June 1991, that it had "already advised the leading underwriter" and that it was "now proceeding to notify the remaining market". Leslie & Godwin told Wausau that "[a]s soon as we have contacted the full market, we will confirm this to you".

Leslie & Godwin communicated the arbitration demand to Banco in its usual way via an Argentinean insurance brokerage, Argenhall, S.A.

In August 1991, Wausau instituted a suit in Wisconsin state court asking the court to compel the Retrocessionaires to proceed with arbitration. Banco was named a respondent in the proceeding and was notified by serving notice upon the firm of Mendes & Mount, pursuant to the Service of Suit clause in the treaties.

The arbitral tribunal issued its award on 18 September 1995, determining that Wausau was entitled to a total of US$ 7,783,324. Of this amount, Banco's share was US$ 181,319. Additionally, interest compounded annually at 7.5% would be due if the award was not paid within 45 days and the Retrocessionaires were held jointly and severally liable for attorney's fees and costs of US$ 930,730.

Banco did not appear or participate in the arbitration or related judicial proceedings. Banco asserted that it was not a client of Lord, Bissell & Brook and that it did not participate in the audit performed on behalf of the Retrocessionaires. It also denied that it received the letter of 27 June 1991 or the follow-up facsimile Leslie & Godwin sent to Argenhall, and that its files contain any evidence that it received actual notice of the arbitration.

Wausau sought to confirm the award against Banco pursuant to the Panama Convention. Banco sought to vacate the award, contending that it was invalid because it had not received proper notice of the arbitration.

The court, per Barbara B. Crabb, DJ, denied the motion to vacate and ordered the confirmation of the award. The court reasoned that it had jurisdiction under the Foreign Sovereign Immunities Act and that this Act's notice requirements had been satisfied. Furthermore, the notice requirements for the arbitration had been satisfied by means of the notification to Banco's designated agent. Although both parties were citizens of signatories of the Inter-American Convention, if the New York Convention applied, the result would be the same.

Excerpt

I. EVIDENTIARY HEARING

[1] "The facts are taken from three sources: the allegations of petitioner's petition to confirm the arbitration award, respondent's answer to the petition, and the affidavits and exhibits the parties filed in support of their cross-motions. These materials are properly considered without an evidentiary hearing. The Inter-American Convention incorporates non-conflicting components of the Federal Arbitration Act, 9 U.S.C. Sects. 1-16. See 9 U.S.C. Sects. 208 and 305.[1] One such non-conflicting component is Sect. 6, which provides that applications concerning arbitration awards 'shall be made and heard in the manner provided by law for the making and hearing of motions'. This section affords courts discretion to devise their own procedures for deciding arbitration-related motions, including the power to decide motions

---

1. *Note General Editor*. The court was apparently referring to Sect. 307. The text of Sect. 305 is reproduced below at fn. 11.
9 U.S.C. Sects. 208 and 307 read:

Section 208
"Chapter 1 applies to actions and proceedings brought under this chapter to the extent that chapter is not in conflict with this chapter or the Convention as ratified by the United States."

Section 307
"Chapter 1 applies to actions and proceedings brought under this chapter to the extent chapter 1 is not in conflict with this chapter or the Inter-American Convention as ratified by the United States."

related to arbitral awards without a hearing. See *Legion Insurance Co. v. Insurance General Agency, Inc.*, 822 F.2d 541, 541-543 (5th Cir. 1987) (district court properly declined to consider evidence beyond that presented in documents filed to support and oppose motion to confirm arbitration award); see also *Imperial Ethiopian Government v. Baruch-Foster Corp.*, 535 F.2d 334, 337 n. 10 (5th Cir. 1976)[2] (district court not required to hold evidentiary hearing in order to decide issue under [1958 New York Convention])."

II. FOREIGN SOVEREIGN IMMUNITIES ACT

[2] "The Foreign Sovereign Immunities Act governs subject matter and personal jurisdiction in actions involving foreign states. Concerning subject matter jurisdiction, the Act is drafted in the negative. Federal district courts have subject matter jurisdiction provided the foreign state is *not* entitled to immunity under the Act. See 28 U.S.C. Sect. 1330(a).[3] Also, federal courts may exercise personal jurisdiction over foreign states insofar as they have been given notice in accordance with the Act. See Sect. 1330(b).[4]

[3] "In this action, subject matter jurisdiction exists because the arbitration clause within the retrocessional treaties states that any arbitration 'shall take place in Wausau, Wisconsin'. Under the Foreign Sovereign Immunities Act, a foreign state has no immunity from a proceeding to confirm an arbitral award where the arbitration 'is intended to take place in the United States'. See Sect. 1605(a)(6)(A).[5] Alternatively, subject matter jurisdiction exists because con-

---

2. Reported in Yearbook II (1977) p. 252 (US no. 10).
3. 28 U.S.C. Sect. 1330(a) reads:

"The district courts hall have original jurisdiction without regard to amount in controversy of any nonjury civil action against a foreign state as defined in section 1603(a) of this title as to any claim for relief in personam with respect to which the foreign state is not entitled to immunity either under sections 1605-1607 of this title or under any applicable international agreement."

4. 28 U.S.C. Sect. 1330(b) reads:

"Personal jurisdiction over a foreign state shall exist as to every claim for relief over which the district courts have jurisdiction under subsection (a) where service has been made under section 1608 of this title."

5. 28 U.S.C. Sect. 1605(a)(6)(A) and (B) reads:

"(a) A foreign state shall not be immune from the jurisdiction of courts of the United States or of the States in any case –

firmation of the award is sought under the Inter-American Convention. A foreign state has no immunity from a proceeding to confirm an award that 'may be governed by a treaty ... calling for the recognition and enforcement of arbitral awards'. Sect. 1605(a)(6)(B).

[4] "Moreover, because the Foreign Sovereign Immunities Act's notice requirements have been satisfied, this court may exercise personal jurisdiction over respondent. The parties agree that respondent is an 'agency or instrumentality of a foreign state' under Sect. 1603(b). Under the Act, an agency or instrumentality of a foreign state has sufficient notice of a suit when the summons and complaint are delivered 'in accordance with any special arrangement for service'. See Sect. 1608(b)(1). Respondent was notified of petitioner's intention to confirm the arbitral award pursuant to the Notice of Suit provision of the treaties: petitioner served a summons upon the Retrocessionaires' designated agent, Mendes & Mount."

III. INTER-AMERICAN CONVENTION ON INTERNATIONAL COMMERCIAL ARBITRATION

[5] "The centerpiece of respondent's contention that the award must be vacated rests on Art. 5 on the Inter-American Convention, which provides in pertinent part:

> '1. The recognition and execution of the decision may be refused, at the request of the party against which it is made, only if such party is able to prove to the competent authority of the State in which recognition and execution are requested:
> (....)
> b. That the party against which the arbitral decision has been made was not *duly notified of the appointment of the arbitrator* or of the arbitration

(....)
(6) in which the action is brought, either to enforce an agreement made by the foreign state with or for the benefit of a private party to submit to arbitration all or any differences which have arisen or which may arise between the parties with respect to a defined legal relationship, whether contractual or not, concerning a subject matter capable of settlement by arbitration under the laws of the United States, or to confirm an award made pursuant to such an agreement to arbitrate, if (A) the arbitration takes place or is intended to take place in the United States, (B) the agreement or award is or may be governed by a treaty or other international agreement in force for the United States calling for the recognition and enforcement of arbitral awards,...."

procedure to be followed, or was unable, for any other reason, to present his defense;'

(....)

[6] "There is little case law interpreting the Inter-American Convention. But respondent garnishes its presentation with case law interpreting the related [1958 New York Convention]. It is a good choice because the New York Convention contains a notice provision similar to that of the Inter-American Convention. Art. V(1)(*b*) of the New York Convention provides that a court may decline to confirm an award if the party resisting confirmation was not given 'proper notice'. See also *Productos Mercantiles E Industriales, S.A. v. Faberge USA, Inc.*, 23 F.3d 41, 45 (2d Cir. 1994)[6] ('Congress intended the Inter-American Convention to reach the same results as those reached under the New York Convention.').

[7] "Turning to the meat, respondent first argues that notice of the arbitration, like notice of this lawsuit, should be evaluated under the notice provisions of the Foreign Sovereign Immunities Act. Respondent explains that petitioner's reliance on the lead Retrocessionaire to notify respondent of the arbitration was not part of a 'special arrangement for service'. See 28 U.S.C. Sect. 1608(b)(1). Thus, because petitioner did not meet the alternative methods of service under the Act, such as registered mail sent directly to the agency or instrumentality, see Sect. 1608(b)(3)(B), respondent did not receive adequate notice of the arbitration as a matter of law. In support of the contention that the Foreign Sovereign Immunities Act sets for the standard for service of process in arbitration proceedings, respondent cites *Matter of the Arbitration Between Trans Chem. Ltd. and China Nat'l Mach. Import & Export Corp.*, 978 F. Supp. 266 (S.D.Tex. 1997),[7] aff'd 161 F.3d 314 (5th Cir. 1998).[8]

[8] "This offering is indigestible. Respondent cannot find support in *Trans Chemical Limited* for its contention that the Foreign Sovereign Immunities Act sets forth a standard applicable to arbitration agreements. In *Trans Chemical Limited*, a privately-held Pakistani firm moved to confirm a Texas arbitral award against a state-owned Chinese firm. The Chinese firm argued that the district court lacked jurisdiction to confirm the award because the motion to confirm had not been served in accordance with the Foreign Sovereign Immunities Act. See *Trans Chemical Limited*, 978 F. Supp. at 297. The court disagreed, noting that the agreement between the firms incorporated the Procedures of the American Arbitration Association and that the procedures

6. Reported in Yearbook XX (1995) pp. 955-961 (US no. 184).
7. Reported in Yearbook XXIII (1998) pp. 995 (US no. 255).
8. Reported in this Yearbook as US no. 283, pp. 882-883.

provided for service by mail to the last known address of notice of judicial proceedings to confirm an arbitral award. Thus, the court concluded, the parties' agreement incorporated a 'special arrangement for service' under 28 U.S.C. Sect. 1608(b)(1). See *Trans Chemical Limited*, 978 F. Supp. at 298-299.

[9] "Respondent is correct that the court held that 'since the arbitration agreement entered into by the parties adopted the AAA rules,... this constituted "special arrangement for service under the FSIA"',... but the issue in *Trans Chemical Limited* was whether notice was sufficient for jurisdiction to exist *in the proceeding to confirm the award.* Contrary to respondent's claim, the court was not addressing the separate issue whether the award could be vacated because the Chinese firm did not have adequate notice *of the arbitration.*

[10] "Respondent tries another argument. It cites *Parsons & Whitmore Overseas Co. v. Société Générale de L'Industrie du Papier*, 508 F.2d 969, 975 (2d Cir. 1974),[9] which holds that under the New York Convention, the adequacy of the arbitration notification should be measured in light of the forum state's standards of due process. Respondent cites *Dillon v. Dillon*, 46 Wis.2d 659, 176 N.W.2d 362 (1970), which sets forth the requirements of 'jurisdictional due process' in Wisconsin:

> 'The first requirement is that the manner of service employed must be reasonably calculated to give actual notice. "But when notice is a person's due, process which is a mere gesture is not due process. The means employed must be such as one desirous of actually informing the absentee might reasonably adopt to accomplish it. The reasonableness and hence the constitutional validity of any chosen method may be defended on the ground that it is in itself *reasonably certain to inform those affected.*"'

Id. at 665-666, 176 N.W.2d at 365 (quoting *Mullane v. Central Hanover Bank & Trust Co.*, 339 U.S. 306, 315, 70 S.Ct. 652,94 L.Ed. 865 (1950)). Respondent submits that petitioner's manner of notification was not reasonably calculated to inform respondent of its arbitration demand. Petitioner should have notified it directly, according to respondent; it was improper for petitioner to rely on Leslie & Godwin and the lead Retrocessionaire to act as intermediaries.

[11] "Respondent forgets that there were many Retrocessionaires and only one petitioner. In such circumstances, it is customary at Lloyd's for the party in petitioner's shoes to deal with only one lead underwriter. Respondent expects too much if it believes that petitioner should have searched the globe

9. Reported in Yearbook I (1976) p. 205 (US no. 7).

to confirm that every Retrocessionaire had notice of the arbitration. Indeed, it is unsurprising that custom grants petitioner this advantage when one considers that the arbitration clause favors petitioner in another important respect: petitioner has the option of arbitrating in its home forum.

[12] "Perhaps one could argue that respondent's absence once the arbitration began should have alerted petitioner to the possibility that respondent had not been notified, but that argument has no force when one considers that petitioner had served notice upon Mendes & Mount when it brought the action in Wisconsin state court to compel the arbitration. After that time, petitioner had more reason to believe that respondent had *chosen* not to participate. See *In the Matter of Robin A.G. Jackson*, 964 F.2d 706, 711 (7th Cir. 1992)[10] (observing that respondent had refused to answer the petition to compel arbitration that was filed in state court or join the petition of other Retrocessionaires to remove state proceedings to federal court). Moreover, respondent's stake in the outcome was low. Respondent's share of the risk translated to liability of roughly US$ 181,000, or 2.3% of the total award. If petitioner assumed that respondent had elected to let the other Retrocessionaires represent its interests, it made a reasonable assumption.

[13] "Although it is disputed whether respondent had actual notice of the arbitration, this disputed fact has no effect. At the bottom line, 1) respondent bound itself to treaties containing an arbitration clause drafted in favor of petitioner; 2) custom holds that petitioner need only inform the lead Retrocessionaire of matters relating to the operation of the treaties; and 3) respondent effectively received notice of the arbitration when its designated agent was given notice that respondent was being sued in state court to compel such arbitration. Respondent cannot complain to petitioner that the other Retrocessionaires or its designated agent failed to notify it of the arbitration. Petitioner's notification efforts were reasonable."

IV. CONFIRMATION OF AWARD

(....)

[14] "With respect to the interest sanction, respondent contends that it should be entitled to the forty-five day grace period because its 'failure to make timely payment was solely due to Wausau's failure to properly serve and give notice to Banco'. This contention presupposes that petitioner breached its duty to give notice of the arbitration. It is clear that petitioner met its obligation.

10. Reported in Yearbook XVIII (1993) pp. 560-565 (US no. 137).

[15] "Second, respondent complains that it should not have to pay attorney fees amounting to more than five times its share of actual damages. But respondent has provided no factual support for the proposition that its fellow Retrocessionaires have failed to pay the US$ 930,730 and that this award actually remains unsatisfied. Indeed, even if respondent will be forced to pay the full amount, it has a remedy: respondent may file suit against the other Retrocessionaires to collect the amount unfairly apportioned to it.
[16] "Last, respondent complains that petitioner has not explained to this court the need for the letter of credit. Clearly, the necessity for the letter of credit was a matter addressed at arbitration. Having failed to participate, respondent cannot question the conclusions of the panel."

V. APPLICATION OF INTER-AMERICAN CONVENTION

[17] "I have applied the Inter-American Convention in this matter because the parties agree that it is applicable. However, one reservation to the United States' adoption of the treaty recognized that parties to an international arbitration agreement may be citizens of nations that are signatories of both the Inter-American Convention and the New York Convention. In such circumstances, unless the arbitration agreement states which treaty applies, the reservation holds that [the] Inter-American Convention should be applied only if a *majority* of the parties are citizens of nations that are signatories of the Inter-American Convention. See 9 U.S.C. Sect. 305.[11]
[18] "Although the United States and Uruguay are signatories of both treaties, petitioner and respondent have not provided information concerning the citizenship of the remaining Retrocessionaires. Hence, it is possible that the New York Convention is applicable in this matter. (The parties do not explain why they agree that the Inter-American Convention is applicable.) Nonethe-

11. 9 U.S.C. Sect. 305 reads:

> "When the requirements for application of both the Inter-American Convention and the Convention on the Recognition and Enforcement of Foreign Arbitral Awards of June 10, 1958, are met, determination as to which Convention applies shall, unless otherwise expressly agreed, be made as follows:
> (1) If a majority of the parties to the arbitration agreement are citizens of a State or States that have ratified or acceded to the Inter-American Convention and are member States of the Organization of American States, the Inter-American Convention shall apply.
> (2) In all other cases the Convention on the Recognition and Enforcement of Foreign Arbitral Awards of June 10, 1958, shall apply."

less, the point appears to be technical. Because the two treaties are similar, applying the New York Convention instead of the Inter-American Convention would be unlikely to affect the outcome."

Part VI
Articles on Arbitration

In view of the considerable amount of material in other Parts of this Volume XXIV, the limited space did not allow for articles to be published in this volume.

Part VII
Bibliography

BIBLIOGRAPHY

I. GENERAL

1. REGISTER OF TEXTS

See also under II. Countries: Germany, Michael Bühler, *The German Arbitration Act 1997: Text and Notes*; and Italy, Piero Bernardini, *The Italian Law on Arbitration: Text and Notes*. Many of the books announced elsewhere in the Bibliography also contain an extensive selection of texts in their annexes; see as mentioned in the individual entries.

German Maritime Arbitration Association

SCHIEDSGERICHTSORDNUNG/ARBITRATION RULES, MITGLIEDERVERZEICHNIS/MEMBERSHIP LIST, 4th ed. (1998) loose-leaf, non-sequential pagination, free of charge upon request

German Maritime Arbitration Association, Koelner Strasse 34, D-28327 Bremen, Germany

- This loose-leaf edition contains the current Arbitration Rules of the German Maritime Arbitration Association, adopted 18 November 1998, in both German and English. It is supplemented by a commentary by Rolf Herber, in German. An English translation of the commentary is anticipated in a future update. The loose-leaf also contains a list of the names and addresses of the members of the Association.
  In German and English as indicated.

P. Hamilton, H.C. Requena, L. van Scheltinga, B. Shifman, editors

THE PERMANENT COURT OF ARBITRATION: INTERNATIONAL ARBITRATION AND DISPUTE RESOLUTION: SUMMARIES OF AWARDS, SETTLEMENT AGREEMENTS AND REPORTS (1999) ISBN 90-411-1233-2, xvii + 318 p., NLG 225, US$ 135, UK£ 78.75

Kluwer Law International, PO Box 85889, 2508 CN The Hague, The Netherlands

- This centenary publication of the Permanent Court of Arbitration contains summaries of all Awards, Decisions and Reports rendered with the International Bureau's assistance since the establishment of the Court in 1899. Also included is expert analysis and commentary by J.G. Merrills on the contributions of the Permanent Court of Arbitration to international law and dispute resolution, as well as analyses and commentaries by tribunal members, G.H. Aldrich and K.H. Ameli, on the nearly two decades of experience of the Iran-US Claims Tribunal. With a Foreword by Judge Shi Jiuyong, International Court of Justice and an Introduction by P.J.H. Jonkman, former Secretary-General of the Permanent Court of Arbitration.
  In English.

The Secretary-General and the International Bureau of the Permanent Court of Arbitration, editors

PERMANENT COURT OF ARBITRATION – BASIC DOCUMENTS: CONVENTIONS, RULES, MODEL CLAUSES AND GUIDELINES (1998) xiii + 274 p., and COUR PERMANENTE D'ARBITRAGE – DOCUMENTS DE BASE: CONVENTIONS, RÈGLEMENTS, CLAUSES TYPES ET DIRECTIVES (1998) xiii + 272 p., NLG 25

International Bureau of the Permanent Court of Arbitration, Peace Palace, Carnegieplein 2, 2517 KJ The Hague, The Netherlands

- This collection of documents, with a Foreword by Kofi A. Annan, Secretary-General of the United Nations, contains the texts of the 1899 and 1907 constitutive Conventions of the Permanent Court of Arbitration (PCA) and six sets of optional procedural rules for international dispute resolution, all adopted in the period from 1992 to 1997. The optional rules provide procedures for dispute settlement via arbitration, conciliation or fact-finding, between States as well as between States and non-States, States and International Organizations, and International Organizations and Private Parties.
  Also included are model clauses, guidelines for requesting the Secretary-General of the PCA to designate an Appointing Authority under the UNCITRAL Rules, PCA procedures for cases under the UNCITRAL Rules and the text of the UNCITRAL Arbitration Rules.
  English and French editions.

2. CONGRESSES

See also under II. Countries: Asia, Fabien Gélinas and Desmond Donnelly, ICC Bulletin, *International Commercial Arbitration in Asia*; Central and Eastern Europe, Karl-Heinz Böckstiegel, *Recht und Praxis der Internationalen Scheidsgerichtsbarkeit in Staaten Zentral- und Ost-Europas* and David W. Rivkin and Charles Platto, *Litigation and Arbitration in Central and Eastern Europe*; Germany, DIS, *Alternative Dispute Resolution (ADR), DIS-Materialien V*; Italy, Associazione Italiana fra gli Studiosi del Processo Amministrativo, *Arbitrato e Pubblica Amministrazione*; and Latin America, Bernardo M. Cremades, *Enforcement of Arbitration Agreements in Latin America.*

Two important conferences were organized to celebrate the fortieth anniversary of the *1958 New York Convention*. The ensuing publications are announced below:

Albert Jan van den Berg, general editor

IMPROVING THE EFFICIENCY OF ARBITRATION AGREEMENTS AND AWARDS: 40 YEARS OF APPLICATION OF THE NEW YORK CONVENTION, International Council for Commercial Arbitration Congress Series no. 9, XIVth International Arbitration Congress, Paris, 3-6 May 1998 (1999) ISBN 90-411-1274-X, xii + 732 p., NLG 305, US$ 162, UK£ 101

Kluwer Law International, PO Box 85889, 2508 CN The Hague, The Netherlands

- This ICCA Congress, hosted by the *Comité Français de l'arbitrage*, marked the fortieth anniversary of the 1958 New York Convention. Three Working Groups examined the basic elements of the arbitral process – the arbitration clause, the arbitration procedure and the arbitration award – all in light of forty years of application of the New York Convention. ICCA Congress Series no. 9 encompasses the papers emanating from this Congress.

  The Working Group Reports and Comments are preceded by Keynote Addresses on the New York Convention presented at the Plenary Session by Pieter Sanders, Gerold Herrmann and Albert Jan van den Berg along with an Introduction by Yves Derains. The volume concludes with the address to the Plenary Session by Philippe Fouchard, "Suggestions to Improve the International Efficacy of Arbitral Awards". The 44 Reports and Comments presented to the three Working Groups and the Chairmen's summaries are too numerous to be mentioned individually in this brief announcement.

The text, in English and French, of the New York Convention is annexed and a List of Participants is also included. The text is completed by a subject index.

In English, except as indicated.

United Nations, editor

ENFORCING ARBITRATION AWARDS UNDER THE NEW YORK CONVENTION: EXPERIENCE AND PROSPECTS (1999) ISBN 92-1-133609-0, 51 p., US$ 15

United Nations, New York, New York, USA, Publication Sales No. E.99.V.2

- A special meeting of the United Nations Commission on International Trade Law (UNCITRAL) was held at the United Nations Headquarters to mark the fortieth anniversary of the signing of the 1958 New York Convention. The papers presented at that time are compiled in this volume. The topics and authors are as follows:

The birth: forty years ago: consisting of the Opening Address by the Secretary-General of the United Nations Kofi Annan, and addresses by drafting veterans Pieter Sanders and Ottoarndt Glossner
The value: three assessments: consisting of addresses by Robert Briner, Fali S. Nariman and Emilio J. Cárdenas
The effect: enforceability of arbitration agreements and arbitral decisions: consisting of addresses by Neil Kaplan, Jean-Louis Delvolvé, V.V. Veeder, Sergei N. Lebedev and Jan Paulsson
The bench: judicial application of the Convention: a panel chaired by Howard Holtzmann and responses by Judges M.I.M. Aboul-Enein, Michael Goldie, Supradit Hutasingh, Jon Newman and Ana Piaggi de Vanossi
The future: what needs to be done: consisting of addresses by Gerold Herrmann, José María Abascal Zamora, Albert Jan van den Berg, Werner Melis and Gavan Griffith

In English.

Benjamin G. Davis, editor

IMPROVING INTERNATIONAL ARBITRATION: THE NEED FOR SPEED AND TRUST, Liber Amicorum Michel Gaudet, ICC Publication No. 598 (1998) ISBN 92-842-1255-3, 225 p., FF 168

ICC Publishing S.A., 38, Cours Albert 1[er], 75008 Paris, France

– The Liber Amicorum for Michel Gaudet, Honorary Chairman of the ICC International Court of Arbitration, emanates from the presentations given at the ICC Seminar, "The Need for Speed and Trust", held in May 1998 in his honor.

The topics covered, with contributing authors, are as follows:

"Fast-track arbitration and beyond: is there emerging a new need for speed in international commercial arbitration?", with contributions by Emmanuel Gaillard, Louise Barrington, Bernardo Cremades and Eric A. Schwarz
"Electronic means for dispute resolution: extending the use of modern information technologies", with contributions by Paul-A. Gélinas, Richard Hill, Nabil N. Antaki, Richard A. Horning and Michael E. Schneider
"Accelerating the procedure: the parties", with contributions by Jacques Werner, Dana H. Freyer, Stephen R. Bond and Yves Derains
"Homages to Michel Gaudet", with contributions by Sigvard Jarvin, Fali S. Nariman, Howard M. Holtzmann and Michel Gaudet's response
"Accelerating the procedure: the arbitrator", with contributions by Pierre A. Karrer, Serge Lazareff, Peter S. Caldwell and Mauro Rubino-Sammartano
"National courts and speedier international arbitration", with contributions by Antonias Dimolitsa, Roland Amoussou-Guénou, Alain Prujiner, Wang Sheng Chang and Richard H. Kreindler
"The way ahead", with contributions by Horacio Grigera Naón, Arthur L. Marriott, Samir Saleh and Benjamin G. Davis

In English and French.

Wybo P. Heere, editor

INTERNATIONAL LAW AND THE HAGUE'S 750TH ANNIVERSARY (1999) ISBN 90-6704-109-2, xi + 466 p., NLG 250

T.M.C. Asser Press, R.J. Schimmelpennincklaan 20-22, PO Box 30461, 2500 GL The Hague, The Netherlands

- This volume is the result of a Conference organized to celebrate the 750th Anniversary of the City of The Hague and to highlight the importance of The Hague as a center for international law. From among the many themes of the Conference, the materials on international commercial arbitration may be of interest to readers of the Yearbook. They are as follows:

P.A. Wackie Eysten, "Alternative Dispute Resolution in Commercial Disputes: Introduction"
A.J.A.J. Eijsbouts, "ADR and Arbitration: Advantages and Disadvantages in Commercial Disputes"
H.T. van Staveren, "Why Does Sport Need its Own Jurisdiction?"
M. Reeb, "The Role of the Court of Arbitration for Sport"
J.A.R. Nafziger, "The Court of Arbitration for Sport and the General Process of International Sports Law"
K. Skubiszewski, "The Iran-United States Claims Tribunal and the UNCITRAL Arbitration Rules: Introduction"
H.M. Holtzmann, "The Impact of the UNCITRAL Arbitration Rules on Drafting the Rules of the Iran-United States Claims Tribunal"
K.H. Ameli, "The Application of the Rules of the Iran-United States Claims Tribunal"
J.L.W. Sillevis Smitt, "The Hague as a Venue for Commercial Arbitration – Venue and Interim Measures: A Dutch Perspective"
P.J.H. Jonkman, "The Permanent Court of Arbitration, The Legal Capital of the World, and the UNCITRAL Arbitration Rules"

In English, with a subject index.

International Bar Association

INTERNATIONAL BUSINESS LAWYER: DISPUTE RESOLUTION IN INTERNATIONAL LONG-TERM CONSTRUCTION AND INFRASTRUCTURE PROJECTS, Vol. 27, No. 5 (May 1999) ISSN 0130-97676, pp. 193-240, US$ 32, UK£ 19

International Bar Association, 271 Regent Street, London W1R 7PA, UK

- This issue of the International Business Lawyer has been devoted to reproducing a selection from the speeches delivered on the occasion of the Second IBA International Arbitration Day held on 13 November 1998. Five papers were chosen that illustrate typical problems related to disputes in international long-term projects:

Karl-Heinz Böckstiegel, "Practical Problems in Resolving Disputes in an International Construction and Infrastructure Project"
John Kendall, "Role of the Expert/Adjudicator in Support of Arbitration in International Long-Term Contracts"
Michael E. Davis, "Dispute Resolution in International Long-Term Construction and Infrastructure Projects: the Private Finance Initiative"
Fritz Nicklisch, "Infrastructure Projects: Interlinked Contracts and Interlinked Arbitration?"
Emmanuel Gaillard, "Use of General Principles of International Law in International Long-Term Contracts"
Bernardo M. Cremades, "The Need for Conservatory and Preliminary Measures"

In English.

3. BIBLIOGRAPHIES AND DICTIONARIES

See also under 1. Register of Texts: German Maritime Arbitration Association, *Schiedsgerichtsordnung/Arbitration Rules, Mitgliederverzeichnis/Membership List*.

Eric Dolling, publisher, and Mandy Waller, production editor

MARTINDALE-HUBBELL INTERNATIONAL ARBITRATION AND DISPUTE RESOLUTION DIRECTORY 1999 (1999) ISBN 185739-203-5, xviii + 1390 p., UK£ 135

Martindale-Hubbell International, International Editorial Centre, East Grinstead House, Windsor Court, East Grinstead, West Sussex RH19 1XA, UK

- The fourth edition of "the Martindale-Hubbell" continues to expand its coverage of relevant institutions, texts and information on persons involved in international arbitration and dispute resolution. This edition contains a Foreword by the Director of the WIPO Arbitration and Mediation Center, Francis Gurry, a Dispute Resolution Overview by Paul Mitchard and a survey of Developments in Arbitration from Around the World during 1998 by the White and Case International Dispute Resolution Group.

An innovation in this edition is the division of the listings of persons and firms into two categories, a Geographic roster which contains by country all entries included within the directory, and a more detailed section of

Professional Biographies of multinational firms and "enhanced entries" of individuals and firms. Four additional indexes list the names of individuals and firms according to the services provided, areas of practice, languages spoken, and strictly alphabetically.

The publishers include a disclaimer stating that individuals providing information about themselves and their practices are responsible for its accuracy.

In English.

Pierre A. Karrer, editor

PROFILES OF ASA MEMBERS 1998-2000, Association Suisse de l'Arbitrage/Swiss Arbitration Association, ASA Special Series No. 10 (1998) 361 p., available free of charge

Association Suisse de l'Arbitrage, ASA Secretariat, c/o Dr. Rainer Füeg, St. Alban-Graben 8, PO Box 1548, CH-4001 Basel, Switzerland

- The most recent edition of these Profiles contains brief bibliographical notes on approximately 350 Members of the Swiss Arbitration Association, a significant number of whom reside outside of Switzerland. The information has been provided by the Members on the basis of a questionnaire and under the admonition that their answers should be "true and fair".

  In English.

London Court of International Arbitration

DIRECTORY OF LCIA MEMBERS 1999, at 1 April 1999 (1999) x + 50 p.

London Court of International Arbitration, Hulton House, 161-166 Fleet Street, London EC4A 2DY, UK

- The LCIA Directory lists the name, address, nationality, languages spoken, and specialisations of each of its members from over 70 countries and jurisdictions. The LCIA adds the caveat that the list is not a listing of arbitrators nor an endorsement of the persons or firms listed.

  In English.

4. BOOKS

Klaus Peter Berger

THE CREEPING CODIFICATION OF THE LEX MERCATORIA (1999) ISBN 90-411-1094-1, xxviii + 376 p., NLG 200, US$ 108, UK£ 68

Kluwer Law International, PO Box 85889, 2508 CN The Hague, The Netherlands

– In this study the author reviews approaches to the codification of transnational commercial law and introduces a framework for understanding what he terms the "creeping codification" of transnational commercial law. He first examines the traditional methods used in overcoming deficiencies in the application of domestic law in transnational commercial contexts which, in his view, fail to transcend national boundaries of domestic doctrine and theory. The author then examines the theoretical foundations of the lex mercatoria doctrine and concludes that the application of the lex mercatoria by international arbitrators does not lead to a "*contrat sans loi*".

This is followed by a review of a number of projects that have been undertaken to codify transnational contract law where the author distinguishes between the method of "creeping codification" of transnational law and the more or less formalized codification procedure as exemplified by the UNIDROIT Principles of International Commercial Contracts. The former method consists of drafting lists of rules and principles of the lex mercatoria which have been accepted in international arbitral and contract practice. In the annex, the author provides such a list with references to their sources, consisting of 78 principles, rules and standards.

Further annexes contain the UNIDROIT Principles of International Commercial Contracts and The Principles of European Contract Law. (See also II. Countries: Panama, Gilberto Boutin I., *Del Reconocimiento de la Lex Mercatoria en la Jurisprudencia Panameña* [The Recognition of Lex Mercatoria in Panamanian Jurisprudence].)

The text is completed by an extensive Bibliography and a subject index. In English.

Dennis Campbell, general editor, and Suzanne Rodriguez, editor

INTERNATIONAL EXECUTION AGAINST JUDGMENT DEBTORS, Center for International Legal Studies, Salzburg, Austria (1998) ISBN 0-379-01253-7, loose-leaf, US$ 325

Oceana Publications, Inc., 75 Main Street, Dobbs Ferry, New York 10522-1601, USA

- Prepared under the auspices of the Center for International Legal Studies, this two volume publication consists of a series of reports on the laws and treaties regulating recognition and enforcement of foreign judgments in jurisdictions in Africa, Asia and the Pacific, Europe and North and South America (59 countries or jurisdictions per release 98-1). The reports are written by local practitioners and are directed at both practicing lawyers and academics. Many of the reports also include basic information on the regime for the enforcement of foreign arbitral awards.

  A final chapter summarizes enforcement in the European Union under the Brussels Convention and the texts of the Brussels-San Sebastian and Lugano Conventions are appended.

  In English.

Emmanuel Gaillard and John Savage, editors

FOUCHARD, GAILLARD, GOLDMAN ON INTERNATIONAL COMMERCIAL ARBITRATION (1999) ISBN 90-411-1025-9, xxxiiv + 1280 p., NLG 500, US$ 300

Kluwer Law International, PO Box 85889, 2508 CN The Hague, The Netherlands

- Based on the original *Traité de l'arbitrage commercial international*, published in 1996 by Litec, Paris (announced in Yearbook XXI (1996) pp. 875-876), this volume provides not only an English version of that text, but also it acts as a second and revised edition. Developments such as new arbitration statutes, rules and important decisions and awards of the past three years, along with expanded references, have been incorporated in this volume.

  The text commences with an analysis of the definition of "international commercial arbitration" including a survey of the application of the definition of "international" by the French courts. In the chapter on the sources of international commercial arbitration, the French arbitration regime is examined alongside a number of other national systems. This is followed by a survey of the major international conventions and arbitration rules. Sections on the arbitration agreement, the arbitral tribunal, the status of the arbitrators, the arbitral procedure, the law applicable to the merits of the dispute and court review of the award follow, based on French and other national legislation, international conventions and international practice.

Annexes include French and Swiss arbitration laws; the UNCITRAL Model Law; the 1958 New York, 1961 European and 1975 Panama Conventions; the AAA International Arbitration Rules, the ICC Rules of Arbitration, LCIA Rules and UNCITRAL Arbitration Rules; a comprehensive Bibliography; and extensive tables of arbitration awards, arbitration rules, international instruments, judicial decisions, and legislation cited in the volume. There is also a subject index.

In English.

Mark Huleatt-James and Nicholas Gould

INTERNATIONAL COMMERCIAL ARBITRATION: A HANDBOOK, Dispute Resolution Guides, 2nd ed. (1999) ISBN 1-85978-882-3, xx + 145 p., UK£ 60, US$ 102

LLP Reference Publishing, 69-77 Paul Street, London EC2A 4LQ, UK

– This volume examines the legal and practical dimensions of each stage of an arbitration. As mentioned in the announcement of the first edition of this work in Yearbook XXI (1996) pp. 876-877, the authors have, in their own words, written "a slim volume providing an overview of the subject". It consists of a basic guide to international commercial arbitration, highlighting its principle elements and their interrelationship. The authors have focused on the process in general, rather than the arbitration legislation of a given country, although frequent reference is made to the rules of major arbitral institutions. In particular, this second edition takes into account the recent changes made by the AAA, CIETAC, ICC and LCIA in their rules.

The appendices contain, inter alia, model arbitration clauses and a comparative table of international arbitration rules. The text is completed by a subject index.

In English.

Vesna Lazić

INSOLVENCY PROCEEDINGS AND COMMERCIAL ARBITRATION, International Arbitration Law Library Series (1998) ISBN 90-411-1115-8, 394 p., NLG 175, US$ 95, UK£ 60

Kluwer Law International, PO Box 85889, 2508 CN The Hague, The Netherlands

- Starting from the premise that insolvency and arbitration each has a distinct purpose and field of application, the author sets out to examine the points of interaction of these two very different legal procedures. She begins with an overview of commercial arbitration, insolvency law and the posture of national courts vis-à-vis arbitration. The focus then shifts to the use and effectiveness of arbitration agreements in insolvency proceedings, especially the validity and enforcement of agreements. Relevant provisions of arbitration and insolvency laws in England, France, Germany, The Netherlands and the United States are examined.

  The text is completed with a Bibliography, table of cases and subject index.

  In English.

Konstadinos Massuras

DOGMATISCHE STRUKTUREN DER MEHRPARTEIENSCHIEDSGERICHTSBARKEIT [Dogmatic Structures of Multiparty Arbitration], Europäische Hochschulschriften [European Academical Essays], Series II, Law; Vol. 2419 (1998) ISBN 3-631-33496-6, xxvii + 608 p., SF 135

Peter Lang AG, Jupiterstrasse 15, PO Box 277, CH-3000 Bern 15, Switzerland

- In this doctoral thesis, written at the University of Hannover, the author examines the main issues arising out of multiparty arbitration on the basis of the German law including the draft of the new Arbitration Law (not yet in force when the text was completed) and the most important international instruments and rules regulating arbitration.

  Rather than examining the questions within the narrow confines of the distinction between the contractual and procedural aspects, the author assumes the perspective of the wider concept of multi-participant arbitration. Particular attention is given to the scope of the arbitration clause and procedures for the appointment of arbitrators as well as the usefulness of the possibilities offered by the German Code of Civil Procedure for multiparty proceedings and third party participation.

  The text is supplemented by an extensive Bibliography and a subject index.

  In German.

Jan Paulsson, Nigel Rawding, Lucy Reed and Eric Schwartz

THE FRESHFIELDS GUIDE TO ARBITRATION AND ADR: CLAUSES IN INTERNATIONAL CONTRACTS, 2nd revised ed. (1999) ISBN 90-411-1226-X, xv + 175 p., NLG 75, US$ 45

Kluwer Law International, PO Box 85889, 2508 CN The Hague, The Netherlands

– A book geared for practitioners, this guide, the first edition of which was announced in Yearbook XVIII (1993) p. 733, provides insights into the drafting of the dispute resolution clause. Included is advice on choosing the dispute resolution method, applicable law, the place and language of arbitration, applicable rules, arbitrators, and mechanisms for dealing with particular situations. The guide describes how to put all these elements together in drafting the clause. The advantages and pitfalls of ADR are also examined, along with a check list for drafting ADR clauses for institutional and ad hoc arbitration and various forms of ADR.

Appendices include model clauses for institutional and ad hoc arbitration and various forms of ADR as recommended by a number of major institutions and organizations. The model clauses are supplemented by the authors' annotations containing suggested modifications. Further annexes contain addresses of arbitral institutions and organizations referred to in the text and the UNCITRAL Notes on Organising Arbitral Proceedings.

In English.

Pieter Sanders

QUO VADIS ARBITRATION? SIXTY YEARS OF ARBITRATION PRACTICE (1999) ISBN 90-411-12359, xix + 451 p., NLG 235, US$ 141

Kluwer Law International, PO Box 85889, 2508 CN The Hague, The Netherlands

– Looking back over sixty years of arbitration practice, the author discerns two trends: one towards harmonization of arbitration legislation and the other, a more recent trend, towards the increased use of conciliation.

A broad comparative study of arbitration laws worldwide illustrates the diminishing significance of the differences between civil law and common law systems and of regional features, a development stimulated by the 1958 New York Convention and the UNCITRAL Model Law. A survey of modifications to the Model Law and the additions to the text made by the many states and jurisdictions which have adopted it serves as the basis for suggestions regarding possible future revision of the Model Law.

The author also provides a systematic review of fifteen specific topics ranging from the arbitration agreement to setting aside and expresses his opinion on the desirability of various options and developments, based, as stated in the title, on sixty years of arbitration practice.

The chapter on "Conciliation" surveys the new phenomenon of including statutory provisions on conciliation in arbitration legislation based on the Model Law. These provisions are compared with comparable provisions in the UNCITRAL Arbitration Rules. The concluding chapter, "A Look into the Future" contains suggestions as to the possible contents of a Model Law on Conciliation.

The text is supplemented by a Selected Bibliography and subject index.

In English.

Irineu Strenger

ARBITRAGEM COMERCIAL INTERNACIONAL [International Commercial Arbitration] (1996) ISBN 85-7322-134-8, 655 p.

Editora LTR, Ltd., São Paulo, Rua Apa, 165, CEP 01201-904, São Paulo, SP, Brazil

- This comparative general survey of the theory and practice of international commercial arbitration covers the entire process of arbitration from the arbitration agreement to recourse against and enforcement of the award. Extensive reference is made to standard works on arbitration and a variety of arbitration laws and international instruments. Although the new Brazilian Arbitration Act has not been dealt with in this text, it is anticipated that the author will publish in the near future an article-by-article survey of the new law, the text of which is included in a supplementary annex.

  The remaining annexes (290 p.) contain the texts of international conventions, rules of various international organizations and arbitral institutions and arbitral legislation.

  In Portuguese with annexes in English, Italian, Spanish, French and Portuguese.

5. PERIODICALS

See also I. General, 2. Congresses: International Bar Association, *International Business Lawyer: Dispute Resolution in International Long-Term Construction and Infrastructure Projects*; and II. Countries: Sweden, *Stockholm Arbitration Report*.

ASIAN DISPUTE REVIEW, Quarterly, available upon request, free of charge

Butterworth's Asia, 19/F Commercial Tower, 8 Sun Yip Street, Chai Wan, Hong Kong

- The newly launched Asian Dispute Review covers Hong Kong and international news on dispute resolution as well as upcoming events. The journal also contains reports and commentary on international arbitration and procedure, as well as case reports and articles concerning mediation and other dispute settlement procedures.
  In English.

6. ELECTRONIC PUBLICATIONS

Kluwer Law International, editor

ARBITRATION CD-ROM. RESOURCES ON INTERNATIONAL COMMERCIAL ARBITRATION (1998) ISSN 90-411-1072-0, price single user per annum NLG 3000, UK£ 1625, US$ 1020

Kluwer Law International, PO Box 85889, 2508 CN The Hague, The Netherlands

- The extensive materials found on this CR-Rom include all published volumes of ICCA's *Yearbook Commercial Arbitration* and *International Handbook on Commercial Arbitration* as well as the periodicals, *Arbitration International* (1990-1998), *Journal of International Arbitration* (1990-1998) and *Revue de l'arbitrage* (1996-1998). Back volumes of the periodicals and new issues will be added in subsequent updates. In addition, the Bibliography compiled and regularly updated by the Chamber of National and International Arbitration of Milan is included.

The material (including more than 2,300 cases and statutes from over 70 countries), which has been classified under the main categories of Conventions, Legislation, Rules, Cases and Commentary, is fully searchable. Additional links provide case histories and direct access to commentary on decisions, as well as information on numerous countries regarding ratifications, arbitration legislation and institutions. Particular emphasis has been given to the reporting on the 1958 New York Convention in the *Yearbook* where links have been provided from each case to the relevant portions of the Commentary on the 1958 New York Convention by Profs. Pieter Sanders and Albert Jan van den Berg, as published in the *Yearbook*.

In English and French, according to original source.

II. COUNTRIES

See also under I. General, 3. Bibliographies and Dictionaries: Pierre A. Karrer, *Profiles of ASA Members 1998-2000.*

Arab Countries

Abdul Hamid El-Ahdab

ARBITRATION WITH THE ARAB COUNTRIES, 2nd ed. (1999) ISBN 90-411-1097-6, xxxviii + 985 p., NLG 250, US$ 150, UK£ 88

Kluwer Law International, PO Box 85889, 2508 CN The Hague, The Netherlands

– This work is the second edition of *Arbitration with the Arab Countries* announced in Yearbook XV (1990) p. 701. The book charts the evolution of arbitration in Arab countries. In the ten years since the first edition, the author notes, many Arab countries have modified their laws on arbitration, usually in one of four directions, the New York Convention, the UNCITRAL Model Law, the 1981 French Arbitration Act, or a modern interpretation of the Shari'a.

This second edition is organized in twenty parts as follows: Part One on the Moslem Arbitration Law; Part Two through Eighteen, seventeen Parts containing updated surveys of arbitration law and practice in Algeria, Bahrain, Egypt, Iraq, the Hashemite Kingdom of Jordan, Kuwait, Lebanon, Libya, Morocco, Oman, Qatar, Saudi Arabia, Sudan, Syria, Tunisia, the United Arab Emirates, and Yemen; Part Nineteen on the Amman Arab Convention on Commercial Arbitration (1987); and Part Twenty on the Riyadh Arab Convention on Judicial Cooperation. There are extensive annexes covering statutory provisions on arbitration in the countries reported on.

In English.

Asia

Fabien Gélinas, editor and Desmond Donnelly, special editor

THE ICC INTERNATIONAL COURT OF ARBITRATION BULLETIN SPECIAL SUPPLEMENT: INTERNATIONAL COMMERCIAL ARBITRATION IN ASIA (1998) ICC Publication Number 609, ISBN 92-842-1262-6, 94 p., FF 106

ICC Publishing S.A., 38, Cours Albert 1er, 75008 Paris, France

- ICC Asia, in cooperation with the Hong Kong International Arbitration Centre, the Chartered Institute of Arbitrators Hong Kong Branch, and the Hong Kong Institute of Arbitrators, sponsored a Conference in November 1997 to focus both on the new ICC Rules of Arbitration and recent developments in Asian jurisdictions. The resulting commentary includes reports from China and Hong Kong, Indonesia, Malaysia, Singapore, Taiwan, and Korea as well as Laos and Thailand, and an overview, "Arbitration in Asia", by Michael J. Moser.

  In English.

Canada

Nabil N. Antaki

LE RÈGLEMENT AMIABLE DES LITIGES [The Peaceful Settlement of Disputes] (1998) ISBN 2-89451-284-8, xix + 471 p., Cdn$ 65

Les Éditions Yvon Blais Inc., PO Box 180, Cowansville (Quebec), Canada

- This study consists of an in-depth examination of non-judicial means of dispute resolution, focusing on Canada, and more particularly Quebec, but relying also on sources from the United States and elsewhere. The author commences with an overview of the origins of such methods and cites numerous surveys documenting their increasing acceptance. This is followed by a categorization of the various methods, divided principally between methods controlled by the parties and methods controlled by a third party who may or may not have jurisdictional power.

  At this point, the study focuses specifically on mediation. Both the practical aspects of mediation, such as the choice of mediation rules or a mediator, and the law of mediation are examined. With respect to the latter, the author gives particular attention to the contractual relationships found in mediation, both between the parties and between the parties and the mediator, examining the various obligations arising from these contracts in light of the chosen rules and legal regulations. Among the specific issues examined are the nature of the obligations to negotiate, to respect the settlement and to protect confidentiality.

The author concludes with a list of "myths" regarding mediation which in his view do not hold up under analysis, such as, e.g., "mediation is a voluntary and informal process", or "mediation is a non-judicial method which permits a win-win situation".

Annexed are, inter alia, the texts of the mediation or conciliation rules of UNCITRAL, the Quebec Centre of National and International Commercial Arbitration, the Commercial Arbitration and Mediation Center for the Americas, and the World Intellectual Property Organization.

In French, with a Bibliography, tables of cases and legislation, and a subject index.

Central and Eastern Europe

Karl-Heinz Böckstiegel, editor

RECHT UND PRAXIS DER INTERNATIONALEN SCHIEDS-GERICHTSBARKEIT IN STAATEN ZENTRAL- UND OST-EUROPAS [Law and Practice of International Arbitration in Central and Eastern European Countries], Schriftenreihe der Deutschen Institution für Schiedsgerichtsbarkeit [German Institution of Arbitration Series], Vol. 13 (1998) ISBN 3-452-23776-1, viii + 585 p., DM 312, ÖS 2,278, SF 312

Carl Heymanns Verlag KG, Luxemburger Straße 449, 50939 Cologne, Germany

– This collection of national reports along with texts of legislation and arbitration rules originates from a colloquium organized in Bremen, Germany in June 1996 by the German Foundation for International Legal Cooperation and the German Institution of Arbitration. The colloquium examined the effects of the major changes in the political and economic systems of the countries in Central and Eastern Europe on the regulation of international commercial arbitration.

The volume consists of national reports on Belarus, Bulgaria, Croatia, Czechoslovakia, Estonia, Hungary, Lithuania, Poland, Russian Federation, the Slovak Republic, Slovenia and the Ukraine, accompanied by the relevant legislation and arbitration rules. Relevant texts from Latvia and Romania are also included. In addition there is an Introduction by Peter Schlosser and a Summary of the Discussion by Hubertus W. Labes, along with a list of participants in the colloquium.

In German, with the text of some legislation and rules in English.

David W. Rivkin and Charles Platto, editors

LITIGATION AND ARBITRATION IN CENTRAL AND EASTERN EUROPE, International Bar Association (1998) ISBN 90-411-0583-2, v + 388 p., NLG 230, UK£ 78, US$ 124

Kluwer Law International, PO Box 85889, 2508 CN The Hague, The Netherlands

- Litigation and arbitration procedures in Central and Eastern European countries are explained in reports presented to the 26th Annual Meeting of the International Bar Association in Berlin in October 1996. The reports are written on the basis of a standard questionnaire by experts on a variety of Central and Eastern European countries. The reports which include information on arbitration and their authors are as follows:

Vladimír Zeithaml, Czech Republic
Peter Nogradi, Hungary
Raimonds Bluķis, Latvia
Tomasz Wardyński, Dariusz Oleszczuk and Rafal M. Sarbiński, Poland
Andrey M. Gorodissky, Russian Federation

Among the extensive annexes (267 p.) are included the Statute and Rules of the Stock Exchange Court of Arbitration of the Prague Stock Exchange, The Rules of Proceedings of the Court of Arbitration attached to the Hungarian Chamber of Commerce and Industry and the new Hungarian Arbitration Act LXXI of 1994, the Rules of the Court of Arbitration of the Polish Chamber of Commerce, the Russian Law on International Commercial Arbitration of 7 July 1993 and the Rules of the International Commercial Arbitration Court at the Chamber of Commerce and Industry of the Russian Federation.

In English.

Germany

See also I. General, 1. Register of Texts: German Maritime Arbitration Association, *Schiedsgerichtsordnung/Arbitration Rules, Mitglieder-verzichnis/Membership List.*

Michael Bühler, editor

THE GERMAN ARBITRATION ACT 1997: TEXT AND NOTES, Arbitration Legislation: Text and Notes, Vol. 2 (1998) ISBN 90-411-1041-0, vii + 132 p., NLG 95, US$ 51.50, UK£ 32.50

Kluwer Law International, PO Box 85889, 2508 CN The Hague, The Netherlands

– This volume presents the 1998 German Arbitration Act in three languages, the original German text, along with French and English translations. In each case, the text of the Act is preceded by a brief introduction highlighting the features of the new Act. The Introduction and the provisions of the text are accompanied by 115 footnotes indicating the relationships among the provisions of the Act, changes from the previous regime and their similarity with or deviation from the UNCITRAL Model Law on International Commercial Arbitration, on which the new Act is largely based.

In English, French, and German.

Deutsche Institution für Schiedsgerichtsbarkeit [German Institution of Arbitration], editor

THE NEW GERMAN ARBITRATION ACT 1998, DIS-Materialien III [DIS Materials III] (1998) 99 p., DM 53.50

NEUES DEUTSCHES SCHIEDSVERFAHRENSRECHT/NEUE DIS-SCHIEDSGERICHTSORDNUNG [The New German Arbitration Act/ The New DIS Arbitration Rules], DIS-Materialien IV [DIS Materials IV] (1998) 163 p., DM 42.80

ALTERNATIVE DISPUTE RESOLUTION (ADR), DIS-Materialien V [DIS Materials V] (1999) 113 p., DM 42.80

Deutsche Institution für Schiedsgerichtsbarkeit e.V., Schedestrasse 13, 53113 Bonn, Germany

- The first of these publications, *DIS-Materialien III*, contains a number of English language articles on the new German Arbitration Act of 1998. Following a Preface and Introduction by Karl-Heinz Böckstiegel, Jens Bredow, Klaus Schumacher and Fabian von Schlabrendorff give their views on the new Act. The text of the Act in English is appended.

  DIS-Materialien IV consists of the German language version of the materials contained in DIS-Materialien III by Böckstiegel, Bredow and von Schlabrendorff, along with additional articles by Peter Schlosser on Arbitrability, Rolf Schütze on Interim Measures and Hilmar Raeschke-Kessler on the relationship of courts and arbitration under the new Act. The new DIS Arbitration Rules are described by Jens Bredow and the German texts of the new Act and new Rules are appended.

  DIS-Materialien V covers various aspects of alternative dispute resolution as presented at the conference on this subject organized by the DIS on 11 November 1998. The contents are as follows:

Karl-Heinz Böckstiegel, "Alternative Dispute Resolution (ADR) – Relevanz und Kriterien Einführende Bemerkungen" [Relevance and Critical Introductory Remarks]
Klaus Günther, "Mediation – Ein Vorverfahren zur Streitbeilegung?" [A Preliminary Proceeding for Dispute Settlement?]
Christian Duve, "ADR – Alternative zur Schiedsgerichtsbarkeit?" [ADR – Alternative to Arbitration?]
Reiner Ponschab, "Wirtschaftsmediation" [Business Mediation]
Christian Borris, "Mini-Trial"
Fritz Nicklisch, "Schiedsgerichtsverfahren mit integrierter Schlichtung – Positive Erfahrungen bei Langzeitverträgen und Großprojekten" [Arbitration with Integrated Conciliation – Positive Experiences with Longterm Contracts and Large Projects]
Johannes Trappe, "Schlichtung im deutsch-chinesischen Wirtschaftsverkehr" [Conciliation in German-Chinese Business Relations]
Jürgen Möllering, "Schlichtungsverfahren – eine Aufgabe für die IHK'n?" [Conciliation – A Task for the Chambers of Commerce and Industry?].

Rolf A. Schütze

RECHTSVERFOLGUNG IM AUSLAND: PROZEßFÜHRUNG VOR AUSLÄNDISCHEN GERICHTEN UND SCHIEDSGERICHTEN [Foreign Legal Proceedings: Proceedings before Foreign Courts and Arbitral Tribunals], Schriftenreihe Recht der Internationalen Wirtschaft [International Commercial Law Series], Vol. 27, 2nd ed. (1998) ISBN 3-8005-1194-0, 376 p., DM 198

Verlag Recht und Wirtschaft GmbH, PO Box 105960, 69049 Heidelberg, Germany

– Taking two parallel tracks, the author provides information on foreign legal proceedings and international arbitration, both as seen from the point of view of German procedure. He commences with a Bibliography covering more than fifty countries, followed by a survey of the principle relevant international conventions. The author then proceeds to deal with the specific topics of State immunity, international jurisdiction, forum shopping, concurrent jurisdiction, choice of forum clauses, representation in proceedings, the provision of security, the taking of evidence, the effect of foreign court decisions and litis pendens. This is followed by a chapter focusing specifically on international arbitration, surveying the major arbitral institutions. The volume concludes with a series of ten national reports on important industrialized countries, giving specific information on the above-mentioned topics.

Annexed are, inter alia, the texts of the 1968 Brussels Convention, the 1958 New York Convention and the 1961 European Convention. A subject index is included.

In German.

India

G.K. Kwatra

THE NEW ARBITRATION & CONCILIATION LAW OF INDIA: A COMPARATIVE STUDY OF OLD AND NEW LAW, The Indian Council of Arbitration (1996) xiii + 238 p., Rs 250, UK£ 25, US$ 40

The Indian Council of Arbitration, Federation House, Tansen Marg, New Delhi, 110001, India

– This volume focuses primarily on the new Indian Arbitration and Conciliation Law 1996. The new Act governs both domestic and international arbitration as well as conciliation; all aspects are covered in a systematic comparison with the prior regime. Information on the Indian Council of Arbitration, other international arbitration institutions as well as UNCITRAL is included.

Among the texts reproduced in this volume are the 1996 Act and its Schedules, along with the IBA Rules of Ethics for International Arbitrators, a List of Arbitral Organizations in India, various Specimen Letters, numerous service agreements between the Indian Council of Arbitration and other institutions, the UNCITRAL Notes on Organising Arbitral Proceedings, and Model Clauses.

In English.

Italy

Associazione Italiana fra gli Studiosi del Processo Amministrativo [Italian Association for the Study of Administrative Procedure], editor

ARBITRATO E PUBBLICA AMMINISTRAZIONE [Arbitration and Public Administration] (1999) ISBN 88-14-07573-5, 171 p., ITL 22,000

Dott. A. Giuffrè Editore S.p.A., Via Busto Arsizio, 40, 20151 Milan, Italy

- At a Conference organized in Milan on 20 March 1998, the Italian Association for the Study of Administrative Procedure examined various questions relating to the possibility in Italy of arbitrating disputes with public authorities, especially in the field of public construction contracts where arbitration is the semi-compulsory means of settling disputes. Special attention is given to the relationship between arbitration and administrative procedures and to the arbitrators' code of ethics. The volume contains addresses by Giuseppe Mirabelli, Giuseppe Caia, Bruno Cavallone, Vittorio Domenichelli, Franco Bassi and Francesco Pugliese, Interventions by Francesco Benatti, Giovanni Panzarini, Claudio Consolo and Guido Greco and Concluding Remarks by Riccardo Villata.

  In Italian.

Piero Bernardini, editor

THE ITALIAN LAW ON ARBITRATION: TEXT AND NOTES, Arbitration Legislation: Text and Notes, Vol. 3 (1998) ISBN 90-411-1030-5, xiii + 123 p., NLG 100, US$ 54, UK£ 34

Kluwer Law International, PO Box 85889, 2508 CN The Hague, The Netherlands

- This volume provides analysis of the Italian law on arbitration, including dispute settlement, transnational litigation, conflict of laws, civil law and procedural law. It consists of the text of Arts. 806-840 of the Italian Code of Civil Procedure, found in Book Four, Title VIII on Arbitration, as most recently amended in 1994. The text is provided in an English, French, and German translation, along with the Italian original. The author has provided 82 footnotes to the text, containing information on the historical background of the provisions, links with other provisions of Italian law, current judicial interpretation, and, where relevant, the relationship with international practice.

  In English, French, German and Italian.

Sergio La China

L'ARBITRATO. IL SISTEMA E L'ESPERIENZA [Arbitration. The System and Practice], Ristampa con Aggiornamento [Updated edition] (1999) ISBN 88-14-07519-0, xvi + 245 p., ITL 30,000

Dott. A. Guiffrè Editore S.p.A., Via Busto Arsizio, 40, 20151 Milan, Italy

- Following a brief introduction on the nature of arbitration, the author sets out in simple and practical terms, the regulation of arbitration in Italy, as amended in 1994, from the arbitration agreement to the award and challenges to it. Two final chapters deal with international arbitration in Italy and foreign awards. An updated appendix covers new legislation affecting arbitration such as recent regulations on consumer protection. A subject index completes the work.

  In Italian.

Latin America

Bernardo M. Cremades, editor

ENFORCEMENT OF ARBITRATION AGREEMENTS IN LATIN AMERICA: Papers presented at the 1998 Vancouver IBA Conference (1999) ISBN 90-411-1190-5, ix + 120 p., UK£ 35

Kluwer Law International, PO Box 85889, 2508 CN The Hague, The Netherlands

- The reports (published in association with the International Bar Association) presented at its 1998 Vancouver Conference by local arbitration practitioners provide analyses of arbitration practice in Latin American countries including information on the ratification of international conventions, relevant legislation, and judicial activity. They have been compiled in this volume as follows:

  Bernardo M. Cremades, "Current Status of International Commercial Arbitration in Latin America"
  Osvaldo J. Marzorati, "Enforcement of Arbitration Agreements in Latin America: Argentina"
  Alberto de Orleans e Bragança, "Enforcement of Arbitration Agreements in Latin America: Brazil"
  Arturo Alessandri, "The Arbitration Agreement in Chile"
  Luis A. Andrade, "Arbitration in Ecuadorian Legislation"
  Claus von Wobeser, "Enforcement of Arbitration Agreements in Latin America"
  Rogelio de la Guardia, "The Arbitration Agreement in Panama"
  Ulises Montoya, "Enforcement of Arbitration Agreements in Latin America: Peru"
  Daniel M. Ferrere, "Enforcement of Arbitration Agreements in Uruguay"
  Francisco M. Castillo-Garcia, "Enforcement of Arbitration Agreements in Latin America: Venezuela"
  Horacio A. Grigera Naón, "Recent Trends Regarding Commercial Arbitration in Latin America"

  The two annexes include a discussion of the performance of foreign arbitral awards in Latin American countries and an inventory of Latin American arbitration institutions, both by Alberto de Orleans e Bragança.
  In English, with a subject index.

Panama

Gilberto Boutin I.

DEL RECONOCIMIENTO DE LA LEX MERCATORIA EN LA JURISPRUDENCIA PANAMEÑA [The Recognition of Lex Mercatoria in Panamanian Jurisprudence], 125 p.

Éditions Étude Maitre Boutin, PO Box 55-2715, Paitilla, Panama

– The author takes as his point of departure the recent decision of the Panama Supreme Court in *Banco Exterior de los Andes v. Banco Cafetero de Panamá*. This decision referred to the tri-dimensional character of law which comprises domestic and international law as well as anational norms which are applicable to an international transaction, as a demonstration that the lex mercatoria can be applied in international commercial relationships. The author examines the sources of the lex mercatoria which can be found, inter alia, in Art. 5 of the Panama Commercial Code, which allows for the application of trade usages.

The author identifies a number of universal principles which are also reflected in provisions of Panamanian law, and also examines the history and evolution of these principles in conventions and in the UNIDROIT Principles of International Commercial Contracts (see also I. General, 4. Books: Klaus Peter Berger, *The Creeping Codification of the Lex Mercatoria*).

Annexed are the UNIDROIT Principles and the above-mentioned Supreme Court Decision.

In Spanish.

Poland

Beata Pankowska-Lier

SCHIEDSGERICHTSBARKEIT IN POLEN [Arbitration in Poland], Schriften zur Schiedsgerichtsbarkeit [Essays on Arbitration], Vol. 4 (1998) ISBN 3-8005-1200-9, 270 p., DM 140, ÖS 1022, SF 125

Verlag Recht und Wirtschaft GmbH, PO Box 105960, 69049 Heidelberg, Germany

- In this study the author surveys the past, current and possible future regime for institutional and ad hoc arbitration in Poland. After reviewing the sources of law for both national and international arbitration in Poland, including the transition from the regime of the 1972 Moscow Convention, the organization of arbitral proceedings at the Court of Arbitration at the Polish Chamber of Commerce is set out. Attention is also given to ad hoc arbitration in the international context. This is followed by a description of the newly evolving practice of domestic arbitration. In her conclusion, the author looks forward to the adoption by Poland of the UNCITRAL Model Law in the not-to-distant future.

  Annexed are the texts of the Rules of the Court of Arbitration at the Polish Chamber of Commerce, as well as their Rules for ad hoc arbitration, excerpts from the Private International Law Act and the Code of Civil Procedure, including the provisions regulating arbitral proceedings, and a list of arbitral institutions.

  The text is completed by a Bibliography and a subject index.

  In German.

Slovene Republic

Lojze Ude and Dragica Wedam-Lukić

SCHIEDSGERICHTSBARKEIT IN DER REPUBLIK SLOWENIEN [Arbitration in the Slovene Republic], Schriften zur Schiedsgerichtsbarkeit [Essays on Arbitration], Vol. 6 (1998) ISBN 3-8005-1202-5, 162 p., DM 95, ÖS 694, SF 86.50

Verlag Recht und Wirtschaft GmbH, PO Box 105960, 69049 Heidelberg, Germany

- The arbitration regime in the Slovene Republic following the dissolution of the Yugoslav Federation is set out in this volume. Attention is also given to transitional problems arising from the dissolution and the effects of privatization. The major part of the study is devoted to arbitral proceedings in international cases at the Permanent Court of Arbitration at the Chamber of Economy of the Slovene Republic under its new Rules.

  Annexed are the relevant provisions of the Code of Civil Procedure, the Rules of Procedure of the Permanent Court of Arbitration and the Conflict of Laws Act of 1982.

  The text is completed by a Bibliography and subject index.

In German.

Sweden

Sigvard Jarvin, general editor

STOCKHOLM ARBITRATION REPORT 1999-1, Arbitration Institute of the Stockholm Chamber of Commerce, Bi-annual, ISSN 1404-1715, 152 p., annual subscription EUR 100, single issue EUR 60

Arbitration Institute of the Stockholm Chamber of Commerce, PO Box 16050, SE-10321 Stockholm, Sweden

- This new journal is a continuation of the *Yearbook of the Stockholm Chamber of Commerce* (SCC) in a new format. The change is in response to the increasing resort to arbitration in Stockholm by non-Swedish parties, and the adoption of a new Arbitration Act and new Arbitration Rules at the Arbitration Institute of the SCC. The Report will appear twice a year and contain articles on topical issues (spring issue) and excepts from arbitral awards and court decisions (fall issue). The articles in the first issue are as follows:

Ulf Franke, "A New Arbitration Regime in Sweden"
Jan Ramberg, "The Arbitration Agreement"
Allan Philip, "The Arbitrators"
Sigvard Jarvin, "The Arbitral Proceedings"
Gustaf Möller, "The Arbitral Award"
Kaj Hobér, "Enforcement of Arbitral Awards"

The issue further contains the text of the Swedish Arbitration Act 1999 and the Rules of the Arbitration Institute of the SCC in both English and Swedish.

In English and Swedish as indicated.

Ukraine

Valentina Sourjikova-Giebner

SCHIEDSGERICHTSBARKEIT IN DER UKRAINE [Arbitration in the Ukraine], Schriften zur Schiedsgerichtsbarkeit [Essays on Arbitration], Vol. 5 (1998) ISBN 3-8005-1201-7, 146 p., DM 70, ÖS 511, SF 63.50

Verlag Recht und Wirtschaft GmbH, PO Box 105960, 69049 Heidelberg, Germany

– In 1994 the Ukraine adopted a slightly modified version of the UNCITRAL Model Law for international arbitration. New arbitral institutions have also been established at the Chamber of Commerce and Industry of Ukraine: the Court of International Commercial Arbitration (CICA) and the Maritime Arbitration Commission (MAC), both of which have established new Rules. These developments are described by the author in this account of the current arbitration regime in the Ukraine.

Annexed are the texts of the 1994 Law on International Commercial Arbitration, the Arbitration Rules of the CICA and the MAC, as well as the List of Arbitrators of the CICA. Also included are provisions from the Code of Civil Procedure, including Art. 349, which provides that awards made under the auspices of the CICA and the MAC are directly enforceable like court judgments.

A Bibliography and subject index are also included.

In German.

United Kingdom

See also I. General, 3. Bibliographies and Dictionaries: London Court of International Arbitration, *Directory of LCIA Members*.

Peter L. d'Ambrumenil

WHAT IS DISPUTE RESOLUTION? Dispute Resolution Guides (1998) ISBN 1-85978-834-3, xiv + 208 p., UK£ 45, US$ 77

LLP Reference Publishing, 69-77 Paul Street, London EC2A 4LQ, UK

– The author has produced this work for lay persons interested in dispute resolution. It is aimed, generally, at assisting parties to a dispute in understanding their legal advisor's actions, or in pursuing small claims without the assistance of a professional legal advisor. The book offers an overview of litigation, mediation and arbitration, and gives concrete examples of procedures typical to each of these methods. A chapter on enforcement sets out the Orders which may be issued by the Country Court to realise enforcement.

Annexed are sample letters to debtors, the English Arbitration Act 1996 and the UNCITRAL Arbitration Rules. The text is completed by a subject index.

In English.

D. Mark Cato

SO YOU REALLY WANT TO BE AN ARBITRATOR? Dispute Resolution Guides (1999) ISBN 1-85978-879-3, xvii + 227 p., UK£ 55, US$ 77

LLP Reference Publishing, 69-77 Paul Street, London EC2A 4LQ, UK

– This volume provides the novice with a comprehensive view of the arbitration process. Readers familiar with the author's earlier two volume edition, *The Sanctuary House Case* (announced in Yearbook XXII (1997) pp. 1120-1121), will recognize the characters in this compact guide to arbitration. The book is presented as a series of conversations between the author in the guise of a seasoned arbitrator and his inquiring goddaughter, Thomasina, a young professional interested in learning about arbitration. The text, written in narrative style principally from the point of view of the arbitrator, covers the entire arbitration process from the appointment of the arbitrator through the post-award phase, including many sample check lists and forms as well as illustrations of the reasoning behind the arbitrator's decisions. The author concludes with a brief discussion of other forms of dispute resolution including adjudication, a procedure provided for in the Construction Act 1996.

The text, in English, is completed with a subject index.

Harold Crowter

INTRODUCTION TO ARBITRATION, Dispute Resolution Guides (1998) ISBN 1-85978-883-1, xxvii + 305 p., UK£ 52, US$ 88

LLP Reference Publishing, 69-77 Paul Street, London EC2A 4LQ, UK

- This volume provides a practical, general guide to all aspects of the arbitration process as governed by the Arbitration Act 1996. It is written in plain language, specifically for those "with little or no knowledge of the subject".
  Within the context of this broad survey, the author gives particular attention to the organization of a preliminary meeting, providing a sample agenda containing 40 points, along with annotations to these points. The UNCITRAL Notes on Organizing Arbitral Proceedings are included in the Appendices. The author also focuses on the effect of settlement offers on the costs of arbitration.
  Appended are, inter alia, the Arbitration Act 1996 and the Rules of the Supreme Court (Amendment) 1996. A subject index is also provided.
  In English.

Robert Merkin

ARBITRATION LAW, Lloyd's Commercial Law Library, loose-leaf (most recent update 7 April 1999) ISBN 1-85044-367-X, main work: UK£ 325, US$ 553; updating service: UK and Europe UK£ 195, rest of the World UK£ 205, North America and SE Asia US$ 365

LLP Reference Publishing, Ltd., 69-77 Paul Street, London EC2A 4LQ, UK

- This two volume loose-leaf comprises an extensive survey of past and current English arbitration law and practice. The main treatise consists of five chapters – arbitration agreements, arbitrators, arbitration proceedings, the award, and judicial control – thus covering the full scope of the arbitration process. In addition, the author provides a separate chapter on the Arbitration Act 1996, containing an article-by-article commentary.
  The appendices contain the relevant statutes and statutory instruments including the texts of the 1950, 1979 and 1996 Arbitration Acts, as well as background documents to the new Act issued by the Department Advisory Committee on Arbitration Law; Rules of the Supreme Court and Practice Directions; international conventions; and a large collection of international and national arbitration rules.
  Also included are a subject index and tables of cases, legislation, rules and reports.
  In English.

III. JOURNALS ON ARBITRATION

Australia

THE ARBITRATOR, published by The Institute of Arbitrators & Mediators Australia, Level 1, 22 William Street, Melbourne, Victoria 3000. National Headquarters E-mail: instarb@werple.net.au; Web site: http://www.instarb.com.au. ISSN 0729-7904. Tri-annual. In English. Annual subscription: Aus$ 80.

Bahrain

GCC COMMERCIAL ARBITRATION BULLETIN, published by the Commercial Arbitration Centre, Bahrain, PO Box 2338, Manama; E-mail: arbit395@batelco.com.bh. Reports on activities of the Centre and international developments. Quarterly. In English and Arabic. Free of charge.

Belgium

CEPANI/CEPINA NEWSLETTER, published by the Belgian Centre for Arbitration and Mediation, Rue des Sols 8, 1000 Brussels; E-mail: info@cepani.be; Web site: http://www.cepani.be. Reports on activities of the Centre and developments in arbitration in Belgium and elsewhere. Available on Web site.

Canada

CANADIAN ARBITRATION AND MEDIATION JOURNAL, published by the Arbitration and Mediation Institute of Canada Inc., 329 March Road, Suite 232, Box 11, Kanata, Ontario K2K 2E1; E-mail: amic@lgs.net; Web site: http://www.amic.org. Bi-annual. In English and French. Annual subscription: Canada, Cdn$ 8; elsewhere, Cdn$ 10.

Cyprus

MEDITERRANEAN AND MIDDLE EAST ARBITRATION QUARTERLY, published by the Mediterranean and Middle East Institute of Arbitration, 29 Stasikrates Street, Suite 101, 1st Floor, PO Box 2119, Nicosia. Reports on arbitration awards and court decisions relating to arbitration. In English.

France

EUROPEAN ARBITRATION, published by Michael Chapman, E-mail: mchapman.ca@interarb.com. ISSN 1286-4528. An electronic newsletter providing talking points and an up-to-date Diary of Events on arbitration. Monthly. In English. To subscribe: send an e-mail to subs.ca@interarb.com. Free of charge.

INTERNATIONAL ARBITRATION GAZETTE, published under the auspices of the Young Lawyers' International Association (AIJA), International Arbitration Commission, c/o Thierry Bernard, 3 rue La Boétie, 75008 Paris. Bi-annual. In English and French. Subscription: members of the AIJA, BF 1,500; non-members of the AIJA, BF 2,000.

REVUE DE L'ARBITRAGE, published by Librairies Techniques (Litec) under the auspices of the Comité français de l'arbitrage, subscription address: 6 rue Victor-Cousin, 75005 Paris. Articles, court decisions, arbitral awards and texts. Quarterly. In French. Subscription: in France, FF 750; elsewhere, FF 825.

Germany

RECHT UND PRAXIS DER SCHIEDSGERICHTSBARKEIT, edited by the Deutsche Institution für Schiedsgerichtsbarkeit e.V. (DIS) [The German Institution of Arbitration], published as a bi-annual annex to Betriebs-Berater, Zeitschrift für Recht und Wirtschaft by Verlag Recht und Wirtschaft GmbH, PO Box 105960, 69049 Heidelberg. Commenced 1992. In German. Individual copies available from Verlag Recht und Wirtschaft GmbH, DM 11 per copy.

Hong Kong

ASIAN DISPUTE REVIEW, published by the Hong Kong International Arbitration Centre, Hong Kong Institute of Arbitrators, Chartered Institute of Arbitrators and Hong Kong Mediation Council. Distributed by Butterworths, Asia, 19/F, Eight Commercial Tower, 8 Sun Yip Street, Chai Wan, Hong Kong; Web site: http://www.butterworths-asia.com. In English. Appears several times per year. Free of charge.

ICC

THE ICC INTERNATIONAL COURT OF ARBITRATION BULLETIN/BULLETIN DE LA COUR INTERNATIONALE D'ARBITRAGE DE LA CCI, published by the International Court of Arbitration of the International Chamber of Commerce, 38 Cours Albert 1er, 75008 Paris, France; E-mail: pub@iccwbo.org; Web site: http://www.iccwbo.org. ISSN 1017-284X (English); ISSN 1017-2831 (French). Commenced 1990. Bi-annual. In French and English. Annual subscription: English or French version in France, FF 600.

ICSID

ICSID REVIEW – FOREIGN INVESTMENT LAW JOURNAL, published by the International Centre for Settlement of Investment Disputes, 1818 H Street, NW, Washington, DC 20433, USA. Subscription address: Journals Publishing Division, The Johns Hopkins University Press, 2715 North Charles Street,

Baltimore, MD 21218-4363, USA. ISSN 0258-3690. Contains current material on the law and practice relating to foreign investments. Bi-annual. In English. Subscription: in the US, US$ 65; Canada and Mexico, US$ 70.60; all others, US$ 74; non-OECD countries, US$ 32.50

NEWS FROM ICSID, published by the International Centre for Settlement of Investment Disputes, 1818 H Street, NW, Washington, DC 20433, USA; Web site: http://www.worldbank.org/icsid. Newsletter. Bi-annual. In English. Free of charge and available on Web site.

India

ICA ARBITRATION QUARTERLY, published by YP Singh for the Indian Council of Arbitration, Federation House, Tansen Marg, New Delhi - 110 001. Quarterly. In English. Subscription: Rs 50, US$ 8.

Indonesia

BULLETIN, BADAN ARBITRASE NASIONAL INDONESIA (BANI), published by the Indonesian National Board of Arbitration (BANI), c/o KADIN, 20 Jalan M.H. Thamrin, Gedung Chandra, 5th Floor, Jakarta Pusat. Appears several times per year. In Bahasa Indonesia (documents are reproduced in the original language).

Italy

RIVISTA DELL'ARBITRATO, published by the Associazione Italiana per l'Arbitrato, Via XX Settembre 5, 00187 Rome. Subscription administration: Dott. A. Giuffrè Editore S.p.A., Via Busto Arsizio, 40, 20151 Milan; E-mail: vendite @giuffre.it; Web site: http://www.giuffre.it. ISSN 1122-0147. Tri-annual. In Italian. Subscription: in Italy, LIT 120,000; elsewhere, LIT 180,000.

Japan

THE BULLETIN OF THE JAPAN SHIPPING EXCHANGE, INC., published by the Japan Shipping Exchange, Inc., Wajun Bldg., Koishikawa 2-22-2, Bunkyo-ku, Tokyo 112-0002; Web site: http://www.jseinc.org. ISSN 0448-8741. Publishes typical examples of awards rendered by the JSE, as well as contract forms, and other relevant materials. Bi-annual. In English. Free of charge and articles from past issues available on Web site.

JCA JOURNAL, published by The Japan Commercial Arbitration Association, Taishoseimei Hibiya Bldg. 4th Floor, 9-1, Yurakucho 1-chome, Chiyoda-ku, Tokyo 100-0006; E-mail: jcaa@ta2.so-net.or.jp; Web site: http://www.jcaa.or.jp. Monthly. In Japanese. Annual subscription: JP¥ 10,200.

JCA NEWSLETTER (formerly Japan Commercial Arbitration Quarterly), published by The Japan Commercial Arbitration Association, Taishoseimei Hibiya Bldg. 4th Floor, 9-1, Yurakucho 1-chome, Chiyoda-ku, Tokyo 100-0006; E-mail: jcaa@ta2.so-net.or.jp; Web site: http://www.jcaa.or.jp. Annual. In English. Free of charge.

MARITIME LAW REVIEW, published by the Japan Shipping Exchange, Inc., Wajun Bldg., Koishikawa 2-22-2, Bunkyo-ku, Tokyo 112-0002; Web site: http://www.jseinc.org. Bi-monthly. In Japanese. Annual subscription: JP¥ 7,200.

Korea

ARBITRATION JOURNAL, published by the Korean Commercial Arbitration Board (KCAB), 43rd Floor, Korea World Trade Center, 159-1, Samsung-dong, Kangnam-ku, Seoul 135-729; Web site: http://www.kcab.or.kr. ISSN 1229-4195. Quarterly. In Korean. Free of charge.

Netherlands

JOURNAL OF INTERNATIONAL ARBITRATION, published by Kluwer Law International. Subscription address: Order Department, Distribution Centre, Kluwer Law International, PO Box 322, 3300 AH Dordrecht; E-mail: sales@kli.wkap.nl. ISSN 0255-8106. Contains primarily full-length articles, as well as reports and news, notes and comments on recent awards, court cases and national legislation. Quarterly. In English. Annual subscription: NLG 625, US$ 312.50, UK£ 195.

TIJDSCHRIFT VOOR ARBITRAGE, published by Kluwer Juridische Uitgevers, under the auspices of Stichting Tijdschrift voor Arbitrage, Secretariat: PO Box 202, 3000 AE Rotterdam, attn: F.D. von Hombracht-Brinkman; E-mail: fvonhombracht@nai-nl.org. Subscription address: Kluwer Juridische Uitgevers, PO Box 23, 7400 GA Deventer. ISSN 0167-1359. Quarterly. In Dutch. Annual subscription: NLG 145 (including binder).

TIJDSCHRIFT VOOR MEDIATION, published by Law & Practice Publishers B.V., PO Box 384, 7400 AJ Deventer. Quarterly. In Dutch. Annual subscription: NLG 179 (including binder).

WORLD TRADE AND ARBITRATION MATERIALS (formerly Arbitration Materials), published by Kluwer Law International. Subscription address: Order Department, Distribution Centre, Kluwer Law International, PO Box 322, 3300 AH Dordrecht; E-mail: sales@kli.wkap.nl. ISSN 1022-6583. Contains, inter alia, full texts of arbitral awards, court decisions, statutes, arbitration rules and profiles of arbitrators. Bi-monthly. In English. Annual subscription: NLG 597, US$ 298.50, UK£ 186.50.

New Zealand

NEWSLETTER, published by the Arbitrators' and Mediators' Institute of New Zealand Inc., 16 Palmer Street, PO Box 1477, Wellington. Quarterly. In English. Costs covered by member subscriptions.

Permanent Court of Arbitration

PERMANENT COURT OF ARBITRATION ANNUAL REPORT, published by the International Bureau of the Permanent Court of Arbitration, Peace Palace, Carnegieplein 2, 2517 KJ The Hague, The Netherlands; Web site: http://www.pca-cpa.org. Report on the activities and functioning of the Court. Annual. In English and French. Available on request.

Russian Federation

COLLECTION OF INFORMATION MATERIALS, Chamber of Commerce and Industry of the Russian Federation, Section of Law, 6 Kuibyshev Street, 103684 Moscow. Commenced 1954. The publication deals, inter alia, with the practice of the Foreign Trade Arbitration Commission. In Russian. Free of charge.

MERCHANT SHIPPING AND MARITIME LAW, COLLECTION OF ARTICLES AND MATERIALS, Chamber of Commerce and Industry of the Russian Federation, Section of Merchant Shipping and Maritime Law, 6 Kuibyshev Street, 103684 Moscow. Commenced 1963. The publication deals, inter alia, with the practice of the Maritime Arbitration Commission. In Russian.

Singapore

SINGAPORE ARBITRATOR, published by the Singapore International Arbitration Centre (SIAC), 1 Coleman Street #05-08, The Adelphi, Singapore; Web site: http://siac.tdb.gor.sg. Contains information on the activities of SIAC, conferences as well as brief articles and case briefs. Quarterly. In English. Free of charge. Available in printed form or on the Web site.

Spain

REVISTA DE LA CORTE ESPAÑOLA DE ARBITRAJE, published by the Consejo Superior de Cámaras de Comercio, Industria y Navegación de España, C/. Velázquez, 157 - 1°, 28002 Madrid; Web site: http://www.cscamaras.es/consejo/cortes. Distributed by Editorial Civitas, Grucer 3 (Parque Grucer), 28017 Madrid. Contains articles and reports of court decisions relating to national and international arbitration, as well as documents and texts. Annual. In Spanish. Subscription: SPT 3000.

BULLETÍ OF THE TRIBUNAL ARBITRAL DE BARCELONA, published by the Tribunal under the auspices of the Catalan Association for Arbitration, Casa Llotja de Mar, Passeig d'Isabel II, no. 1, 08003 Barcelona. Contains information about the Tribunal, articles, reports of awards of the Tribunal and relevant court decisions. Annual. In Spanish. Free of charge.

Sweden

STOCKHOLM ARBITRATION REPORT, replacing Yearbook of the Arbitration Institute of the Stockholm Chamber of Commerce, published by the Arbitration Institute of the Stockholm Chamber of Commerce, PO Box 16050, S-10321 Stockholm; E-mail: arbitration@chamber.se; Web site: http://www.chamber.se. Contains articles and summaries of awards and court decisions. Bi-annual. In English with some material in German and French. Subscription: EUR 100.

Switzerland

BULLETIN, published by the Swiss Arbitration Association, St. Alban-Graben 8, CH-4001 Basel; Web site: http:/www.arbitration-ch.org. Quarterly. Articles in French, German, Italian and English. Annual subscription: SF 100.

United Kingdom

ARBITRATION, The Journal of the Chartered Institute of Arbitrators, International Arbitration Centre, 24 Angel Gate, City Road, London EC1V 2RS; E-mail: 71411.2735@compuserve.com; Web site: http://www.arbitrators.org. ISSN 0003-78-77. Quarterly. In English. This is the journal of the Chartered Institute and is sent free to members. Annual subscription non-members: UK£ 115.

ARBITRATION INTERNATIONAL, published by Kluwer Law International, on behalf of the LCIA. Subscription address: Order Department, Distribution Centre, Kluwer Law International, PO Box 322, 3300 AH Dordrecht, The Netherlands; E-mail: sales@kli.wkap.nl. ISSN 0957-0411. Contains articles on academic and practical topics by authorities in the field of international arbitration. Quarterly. In English. Annual subscription: NLG 570, US$ 285 UK£ 178.50.

THE ARBITRATION AND DISPUTE RESOLUTION LAW JOURNAL, published by Lloyd's of London Press Ltd. Subscription address: 69-77 Paul Street, London

EC2A 4LQ; Web site: http://www.llplimited.com. ISSN 0965-7053. Commenced March 1992. Contains practical information in the form of articles and case reports on legal aspects of arbitration and dispute resolution. Quarterly. In English. Annual subscription (including bound volume and postage): in the UK, UK£ 235; North America and SE Asia US$ 420; rest of the world, UK£ 245.

CHARTERED INSTITUTE OF ARBITRATORS NEWSLETTER, published by the Chartered Institute of Arbitrators, International Arbitration Centre, 24 Angel Gate, City Road, London EC1V 2RS; E-mail: 71411.2735@compuserve.com; Web site: http://www.arbitrators.org. Contains information on Chartered Institute activities and recent developments on arbitration. Quarterly. Enclosure with Arbitration, see above.

INTERNATIONAL ARBITRATION LAW REVIEW, published by Sweet & Maxwell Ltd., Cheriton House, North Way, Andover, Hampshire SP10 5BE; Web site: http://www.smlawpub.co.uk. ISBN 1-367-8272. Contains opinion, articles, news items, procedure tips, summaries of court decisions, book reviews, and diary of events. Commenced 1997. Six issues per year. In English. Annual subscription: UK and Europe, UK£ 175; rest of the world, UK£ 186.

LCIA ARBITRATION INTERNATIONAL NEWSLETTER, published by LCIA Arbitration International, Hulton House, 6th Floor, 161-166 Fleet Street, London EC4A 2DY; E-mail: lcia@lcia-arbitration.com; Web site: http://www.lcia-arbitration.com/lcia; sponsored by Kluwer Law International. Appears several times per year. In English.

ARBITRATION AND ADR. NEWSLETTER OF COMMITTEE D (ARBITRATION AND ADR) OF THE INTERNATIONAL BAR ASSOCIATION SECTION ON BUSINESS LAW, published by *Committee D* (Arbitration and ADR) of the International Bar Association Section on Business Law and distributed to members. For membership details contact: International Bar Association, 271 Regent Street, London W1R 7PA; Web site: http://www.ibanet.org. Bi-annual. In English.

United Nations Commission on International Trade Law

CASE LAW ON UNCITRAL TEXTS (CLOUT), A/CN.9/Ser. C/ABSTRACTS/1 etc., published by the United Nations Commission on International Trade Law, UNCITRAL Secretariat, Vienna International Centre, PO Box 500, A-1400 Vienna, Austria; Web site: http://www.un.org.at/uncitral. Published in all six official UN languages at irregular intervals when sufficient material has been accumulated. Materials from CLOUT on the UNCITRAL Model Law are reproduced in Part II – C of this Volume. Available on Web site.

United States of America

ADR CURRENTS, published by the American Arbitration Association, 335 Madison Ave., New York, NY 10017-4605; E-mail: usadrpub@arb.com; Web site: http://www.adr.org. Subscription address: American Arbitration Association, PO Box 21658, St. Paul, MN 55121. Offers articles, a news update, and reports of court cases. Incorporates the former Lawyers' Arbitration Letter. Quarterly. In English. Annual subscription: US, US$ 70; Canada, US$ 77; all other countries, US$ 85.

THE ALTERNATIVE NEWSLETTER, published by Mistofoles, James B. Boskey, Seton Hall Law School, 1 Newark Center, Newark, NJ 07102-5210; E-mail: Tan@mediate.com; Web site: http://www.mediate.com/tan. Includes list of events, book review and opinion page. In English. Available on Web site.

AMERICAN REVIEW OF INTERNATIONAL ARBITRATION, published under the auspices of the Parker School of Foreign and Comparative Law, Columbia University, by Juris Publishing, Inc., Executive Park, One Odell Plaza, Yonkers, NY 10701; Web site http://www.arbitrationlaw.com. Quarterly. In English. Annual subscription: US$ 252.

THE ARBITRATOR, published by the Society of Maritime Arbitrators, Inc., 14 Wall Street, Suite 8A15, New York, NY 10005-2101; E-mail: info@smany.org; Web site: http://www.smany.org. Quarterly. In English. Free of charge and available on Web site.

AWARD SERVICE, published by the Society of Maritime Arbitrators, 14 Wall Street, Suite 8A15, New York, NY 10005-2101; Web site: http://www.smany.org. Each issue contains approximately 20-25 individual full-length arbitration awards. A consolidated Index and Digest has been published every 4-5 years. Quarterly. In English. Annual subscription: US$ 495.

DISPUTE RESOLUTION JOURNAL (as of December 1993; formerly Arbitration Journal), published by the American Arbitration Association, 335 Madison Ave., New York, NY 10017-4605; E-mail: usadrpub@arb.com; Web site: http://www.adr.org. ISSN 1074-8105. Quarterly. In English. Annual subscription non-members: in the US, US$ 125; Canada, US$ 130; foreign, US$ 150; for educational institutions, US$ 85.

DISPUTE RESOLUTION TIMES (as of December 1993, formerly Arbitration Times), published by the American Arbitration Association, 335 Madison Ave., New York, NY 10017-4605; E-mail: usadrpub@arb.com; Web site: http://www.adr.org. Newspaper format reporting on current matters in arbitration. Quarterly in four sector editions. In English. Annual subscription: US, US$ 25; Canada, US$ 27.50; other non-US, US$ 40.

INTERNATIONAL CENTER REPORTER, published by the American Arbitration Association, 335 Madison Ave., New York, NY 10017-4605; E-mail: usadrpub@arb.com; Web site: http://www.adr.org. Reports on developments in international dispute resolution. Bi-annual. In English. Free to AAA members.

INTERNATIONAL DISPUTE RESOLUTION, published by White & Case LLP, 1155 Avenue of the Americas, New York, NY 10036; Web site: http://www.whitecase.com. Reports on firm news and recent developments in international arbitration. In English. Free of charge.

INTERNATIONAL FEDERATION OF COMMERCIAL ARBITRATION INSTITUTIONS NEWSLETTER, published by IFCAI, 335 Madison Ave., New York, NY 10017-4605. Annual. In English. Free for members.

MEALEY'S INTERNATIONAL ARBITRATION REPORT, published by Mealey Publications, Inc., PO Box 62090, King of Prussia, PA 19406-0230; E-mail: news@mealeys.com; Web site: http://www.mealeys.com. ISSN 1089-2397. Contains materials on international commercial arbitration. Monthly. In English. Subscription: US$ 695 per six months; US$ 1190 per year.

NEWS AND NOTES FROM THE INSTITUTE FOR TRANSNATIONAL ARBITRATION, published for the Institute for Transnational Arbitration by The Southwestern Methodist University School of Law. Subscription address: ITA Director, The Southwestern Legal Foundation, PO Box 830707, Richardson, TX 75083-0707; E-mail: marksmith@swlegal.org. Contains a scoreboard of adherence to transnational arbitration treaties including the New York Convention, the ICSID Convention, the Convention Establishing the Multilateral Investment Guarantee Agency of 1985, the Inter-American Convention on International Commercial Arbitration of 1975, US Bilateral Investment Treaties, and the Agreement supporting programs of US Overseas Private Investment Corporation. Quarterly. In English. Annual subscription: US$ 20.

THE PUNCH LIST, published by the American Arbitration Association, 335 Madison Ave., New York, NY 10017-4605; E-mail: usadrpub@arb.com; Web site: http://www.adr.org. Contains articles on alternative dispute resolution. Quarterly. In English. Annual subscription: US, US$ 30; Canada, US$ 33; other non-US, US$ 45.

WORLD ARBITRATION AND MEDIATION REPORT, published by Juris Publishing, Inc., Executive Park, One Odell Plaza, Yonkers, NY 10701; Web site http://www.arbitrationlaw.com. ISSN 0960-0949. Commenced 1990. Newsletter with information on all forms of dispute resolution. Monthly. In English. Annual subscription: US and Canada, US$ 535 including binder; US$ 595 elsewhere.

Zimbabwe

COMMERCIAL DISPUTE RESOLUTION BULLETIN, published by the Commercial Arbitration Centre in Harare, PO Box 2901, Harare; E-mail: iando@durolink.gaia.co.zw. Commenced in 1995. Newsletter containing information on arbitration in Zimbabwe, arbitration cases, articles on arbitration topics, as well as training workshops and seminars. Quarterly. In English. Subscription: US$ 25.

INTERNATIONAL COUNCIL FOR COMMERCIAL ARBITRATION (ICCA)

Correspondence address:
Mr. Ulf Franke
Secretary General ICCA
c/o Arbitration Institute of the
Stockholm Chamber of Commerce
Jakobs Torg 3
PO Box 16050, S-10321 Stockholm
Sweden
Phone: (46-8) 55510050
Telefax: (46-8) 56631650
E-mail: arbitration@chamber.se

LIST OF OFFICERS AND MEMBERS

October 1999

OFFICERS

Honorary Presidents

PROF. PIETER SANDERS (Schiedam, The Netherlands)
Honorary President, Netherlands Arbitration Institute; Professor Emeritus, Faculty of Law, Erasmus University of Rotterdam

PROF. GIORGIO BERNINI (Bologna, Italy)
Professor, University of Bologna, Chair of Arbitration and International Commercial Law; President, Association for the Teaching and Study of Arbitration (AISA); Member, Executive Committee, Italian Arbitration Association; Advocate, Studio Bernini & Associati, Bologna-Rome

President

MR. FALI S. NARIMAN (New Delhi, India)
President, Bar Association of India; Honorary Member, International Commission of Jurists; Past President, Law Association for Asia and the Pacific (LAWASIA); Member, LCIA; Vice Chairman, International Court of Arbitration of the International Chamber of Commerce (ICC); Member, Human Rights Institute of the International Bar Association (IBA); Senior Advocate, Supreme Court of India

Honorary Vice Presidents

JUDGE HOWARD M. HOLTZMANN (New York, USA)
Chairman, International Arbitration Committee and Honorary Chairman of the Board, American Arbitration Association (AAA); Former Judge, Iran-United States Claims Tribunal, The Hague

PROF. SERGEI LEBEDEV (Moscow, Russian Federation)
President, Maritime Arbitration Commission; Member of the Presidium, International Commercial Arbitration Court of the Russian Federation Chamber of Commerce and Industry; Head of the Chair of Private International and Civil Law Department, Moscow Institute of International Relations

Vice Presidents

MR. MICHAEL HOELLERING (New York, USA)
General Counsel, American Arbitration Association (AAA); President, International Federation of Commercial Arbitration Institutions

DDR. WERNER MELIS (Vienna, Austria)
Chairman, International Arbitral Centre of the Austrian Federal Economic Chamber, Vienna; Vice President, LCIA

MS. TINUADE OYEKUNLE (Lagos, Nigeria)
Member, Association of Arbitrators of Nigeria; Fellow, The Chartered Institute of Arbitrators; Member, Arbitration Committee of the Lagos Chamber of Commerce; Correspondent Member, The Chartered Institute of Arbitrators, London; Chairman, Steering Committee of the Nigerian Branch of the Chartered Institute of Arbitrators; Barrister and Solicitor of the Supreme Court of Nigeria, Arbitrator and Notary Public

Secretary General

MR. ULF FRANKE (Stockholm, Sweden)
Secretary General, Arbitration Institute of the Stockholm Chamber of Commerce

MEMBERS

MR. GUILLERMO AGUILAR ALVAREZ (Mexico D.F., Mexico)
Past General Counsel, International Court of Arbitration of the International Chamber of Commerce (ICC); Partner, Serra & Associates International

DR. HUSSAIN M. AL-BAHARNA (Manama, Bahrain)
Former Minister of State for Legal Affairs, Bahrain; Member, Arbitration Board of the Bahrain Centre for International Commercial Arbitration; Member of the UN International Law Commission, Geneva; Practising Advocate, Court of Cassation, Bahrain; Barrister-at-law of Lincoln's Inn, London

PROF. DR. ALBERT JAN VAN DEN BERG (Amsterdam, The Netherlands)
General Editor, ICCA (*Yearbook Commercial Arbitration* and *ICCA Congress Series*); Vice President, Netherlands Arbitration Institute; Vice President, LCIA; Professor of Arbitration Law, Rotterdam; Attorney, Amsterdam

DR. PIERO BERNARDINI (Rome, Italy)
Professor of Arbitration Law, LUISS University, Rome; Director, Italian Arbitration Association; Vice Chairman, International Court of Arbitration of the International Chamber of Commerce (ICC)

DR. ROBERT BRINER (Geneva, Switzerland)
Chairman, International Court of Arbitration of the International Chamber of Commerce (ICC); Past President, Iran-United States Claims Tribunal, The Hague

PROF. DR. KARL-HEINZ BÖCKSTIEGEL (Bergisch-Gladbach, Germany)
Chair of International Business Law, University of Cologne; Chairman, German Institution of Arbitration (DIS); Past President, LCIA; Past President, Iran-United States Claims Tribunal, The Hague

PROF. BERNARDO M. CREMADES (Madrid, Spain)
Professor, Faculty of Law, Madrid University; Lawyer

M[E] YVES DERAINS (Paris, France)
Past Secretary General, International Court of Arbitration of the International Chamber of Commerce (ICC); Member of the Paris Bar

MR. DONALD FRANCIS DONOVAN (New York, USA)
Co-Chair, International Arbitration Committee, American Branch of the International Law Association; Member, Advisory Board, Institute for Transnational Arbitration; Attorney-at-law

PROF. AHMED S. EL-KOSHERI (Cairo, Egypt)
Professor of International Economic Law and Vice President, International University for African Development (Alexandria); Member, *l'Institut de Droit International*; Partner, Kosheri, Rashed & Riad Law Firm

DR.DR. OTTOARNDT GLOSSNER (Kronberg, Germany)
Honorary President, German Institution of Arbitration (DIS); Past President, International Chamber of Commerce (ICC) Commission on International Arbitration; Vice Chairman, International Court of Arbitration ICC; Attorney-at-law

PROF. DR. GEROLD HERRMANN (Vienna, Austria)
Secretary, United Nations Commission on International Trade Law (UNCITRAL); Member, Presiding Council of the International Arbitral Centre of the Austrian Federal Economic Chamber, Vienna; Honorary Professor, University of Vienna; Member, LCIA; Fellow and Director, International Entry Course, The Chartered Institute of Arbitrators

PROF. J. MARTIN H. HUNTER (London, United Kingdom)
Sweet & Maxwell Professor of International Dispute Resolution, Nottingham Law School; Vice President, UK Government Committee on Arbitration Law; Member, LCIA; Honorary Dean of Postgraduate Studies, T.M.C. Asser Instituut, The Hague; Barrister

MR. MICHAEL HWANG (Singapore)
Fellow, The Chartered Institute of Arbitrators; Fellow, Singapore Institute of Arbitrators; Member, Advisory Council, Singapore International Arbitration Centre; Member, Permanent Court of Arbitration, The Hague; Former Acting High Court Judge, Singapore; Advocate and Solicitor, Singapore

MR. NEIL KAPLAN, QC (Hong Kong)
Former Judge, High Court, Hong Kong; Chairman, Hong Kong International Arbitration Centre; Former Visiting Professor, City University of Hong Kong; Vice President, The Chartered Institute of Arbitrators

MS. GABRIELLE KAUFMAN-KOHLER (Geneva, Switzerland)
Professor of International and European Civil Procedure and Private International Law, Geneva University Law School; Practicing Attorney, Partner, Brunschwig Wittmer

PROF. ALEXANDER S. KOMAROV (Moscow, Russian Federation)
Professor, Russian Academy of Foreign Trade; President, International Commercial Arbitration Court at the Russian Federation Chamber of Commerce and Industry

PROF. DR. PIERRE LALIVE (Geneva, Switzerland)
Honorary President, Swiss Arbitration Association (ASA); Professor Emeritus, Geneva University; Honorary Chairman, Institute of International Business Law and Practice (ICC); Member (Former President), *l'Institut de Droit International*; Member, LCIA; Attorney-at-law, Lalive & Partners, Geneva

THE HON. MARC LALONDE (Montreal, Canada)
Former Justice and Attorney General; Former Minister of Energy, Mines and Resources; Former Minister of Finance; Senior Partner, Stikeman, Elliott

MR. ARTHUR MARRIOTT, QC (London, United Kingdom)
Board Member, LCIA; Director, City Dispute Panel; Board Member, Hong Kong International Arbitration Centre; Solicitor

JUDGE KÉBA MBAYE (Lausanne, Switzerland)
Former Vice President, International Court of Justice; Former Vice Chairman, International Court of Arbitration of the International Chamber of Commerce (ICC)

MS. DELIA REVOREDO MARSANO DE MUR (Lima, Peru)
Senior Professor of Civil Law and Private International Law, Pontificia Universidad Católica del Perú; Professor of Private International Law, Universidad de Lima; Honorary Professor

M[E] CARLOS NEHRING NETTO (São Paulo, Brazil)
Former Member, International Court of Arbitration of the International Chamber of Commerce (ICC)

DR. JAN PAULSSON (Paris, France)
General Editor, ICCA (*International Handbook on Commercial Arbitration*); Vice President, LCIA; General Editor, *Arbitration International*

DR. ALAIN PLANTEY (Paris, France)
Former Member of the *Conseil d'État de France*; Former President, *Institut de France*; Member and Former President, Academy of Moral and Political Sciences (*Institut de France*); Former Ambassador of France; Former Professor of Law, University of Paris I; Honorary President, International Court of Arbitration of the International Chamber of Commerce (ICC)

MR. ANDREW JOHN ROGERS, QC (Sydney, Australia)
Former Chief Judge, Commercial Division, Supreme Court of New South Wales; Chairman, National Dispute Centre Sydney

MR. IBRAHIM F.I. SHIHATA (Washington, USA)
Senior Vice President, International Bank for Reconstruction and Development; Secretary General, International Centre for Settlement of Investment Disputes (ICSID)

PROF. DR. HEINZ STROHBACH (Berlin, Germany)
Board Member, German Institution of Arbitration (DIS), Bonn/Berlin; Vice President, Federation on the Promotion of Arbitration, Berlin; President, Berlin Court of Arbitration

PROF. DR. IVÁN SZÁSZ (Budapest, Hungary)
Professor of Law, University of Economic Sciences, Budapest; Member, Presidential Council of the Arbitration Court and Honorary President, Legal Commission at the Hungarian Chamber of Commerce; Past Ambassador of Hungary to the European Communities; Member, Institute of International Business Law and Practice (ICC); Attorney-at-law

PROF. HOUZHI TANG (Beijing, People's Republic of China)
Vice Chairman, China International Economic and Trade Arbitration Commission; Vice Chairman, Beijing Conciliation Centre; Professor, Law School of the People's University of China; Visiting Professor, Amoy University School of Law; Arbitration Adviser, UN International Trade Centre; Fellow, The Chartered Institute of Arbitrators; Member, LCIA; Honorary Professor, Hong Kong University School of Law

PROF. YASUHEI TANIGUCHI (Kyoto, Japan)
Professor Emeritus, Kyoto University; Past President, Japan Association for Civil Procedure; Chairman, Rule Making Committee of the Japan Commercial Arbitration Association (JCAA)

THE HON. S. AMOS WAKO (Nairobi, Kenya)
Attorney General, Republic of Kenya; Former Chairman, Arbitration Tribunal, Kenya Chamber of Commerce and Industry; Vice President, LCIA – Africa Region; Arbitrator, Vienna Convention on Law of Treaties, Centre for Settlement of International Disputes; Former Chairman, Law Society of Kenya; Member, International Advisory Committee of WIPO; Former Member, International Commission of Jurists; Former Deputy Secretary-General, International Bar Association

Advisory Members

MR. ROBERT COULSON (Connecticut, USA)
Past President, American Arbitration Association (AAA)

PROF. DR. RADOMIR DJUROVIĆ (Belgrade, Yugoslavia)
Past President, Court of Arbitration at the Yugoslav Chamber of Economy; Professor of International Commercial Law, Belgrade University

DR. MAURO FERRANTE (Rome, Italy)
Secretary General, Italian Arbitration Association

M^E MICHEL GAUDET (Paris, France)
Former Member of the *Conseil d'État de France*; Honorary President, International Court of Arbitration of the International Chamber of Commerce (ICC); Honorary Member, Institute of International Business Law and Practice (ICC); Former Director, General Legal Service of the European Commission

DR. SVETOZAR HANÁK (Prague, Czech Republic)
Honorary President, Arbitration Court attached to the Economic and Agricultural Chambers of the Czech Republic; Co-President, Arbitration Court for Marine and Inland Navigation; Attorney-at-law

MR. MARK LITTMAN, QC (London, United Kingdom)
Barrister

JUDGE NILS MANGÅRD (Stockholm, Sweden)
Judge of Appeal (ret.); Former President of Chamber, Iran-United States Claims Tribunal, The Hague

PROF. TUDOR R. POPESCU (Bucharest, Romania)
Professor of International Commercial Law; President (ad hoc), Court of International Commercial Arbitration; Member of Academy; Member (ad hoc), Governing Council for Unification of Law (UNIDROIT), Rome

PROF. DR. JOSÉ LUIS SIQUEIROS (Mexico City, Mexico)
Past President, Mexican Academy of International Commercial Arbitration; Past President, Inter-American Bar Association; Past Chairman, Inter-American Juridical Committee (OAS)

MR. DONALD B. STRAUS (New York, USA)
President, Research Institute of the American Arbitration Association (AAA)

DR. HABIL. TADEUSZ SZURSKI (Warsaw, Poland)
Past President, Court of Arbitration at the Polish Chamber of Commerce; Vice President, Polish Arbitration Association; Vice President, International Federation of Commercial Arbitration Institutions; Member, Polish Bar Society; Lecturer on arbitration, Warsaw University; Legal Consultant